AFRICAN
HIGHER
EDUCATION

AFRICAN
HIGHER
EDUCATION

AN INTERNATIONAL REFERENCE HANDBOOK

EDITED BY

Damtew Teferra   Philip G. Altbach

INDIANA University Press
Bloomington & Indianapolis

BLOOMINGTON & INDIANAPOLIS

This book is a publication of

Indiana University Press
601 North Morton Street
Bloomington, IN 47404-3797 USA

http://iupress.indiana.edu

Telephone orders   800-842-6796
Fax orders   812-855-7931
Orders by e-mail   iuporder@indiana.edu

Library of Congress Cataloging-in-Publication Data

African higher education : an international reference handbook / edited by Damtew Teferra and Philip G. Altbach.
  p. cm.
Includes bibliographical references and index.
ISBN 0-253-34186-8 (cloth : alk. paper)
1. Education, Higher—Africa—Handbooks, manuals, etc. I. Teferra, Damtew, date II. Altbach, Philip G.
LA1503 .A39 2003
378.6—dc21
2002014598

1 2 3 4 5 08 07 06 05 04 03

CONTENTS

Part 3. Higher Education Resources

Preface

This book is a complex undertaking that requires some explanation of its purpose, method, and focus. *African Higher Education: An International Reference Handbook* is a benchmark—it is the first comprehensive volume to provide extended analysis of higher education in Africa. It includes analytic essays on all of Africa's fifty-four countries as well as several key topics relating to African higher education. We also include a comprehensive bibliography of books, reports, and articles and a listing of theses and dissertations dealing with African higher education. Our aim is simple—to extend knowledge and analysis on this important topic with the goal of contributing to policymaking and to a research base.

To this end, we searched for the best possible researchers to contribute essays to this volume. We provided each author with a set of guidelines, but purposely left authors with sufficient leeway to deal with their topics as they thought best. The chapters in this book are independent analyses by talented researchers. Each chapter provides both data and analysis, but each is also an individual contribution. In some cases, data on some aspects of higher education did not exist, and thus there may not be full compatibility among all of the chapters in terms of common data presentation.

Locating authors for this book was not an easy task. Even though we have succeeded in covering all the countries in the continent, we feel that a few topics of importance are missing. The reason for this is simple—authors commissioned to write did not deliver their contributions. While we found a replacement for those who dropped out earlier, time did not permit us to seek an alternative for a few others.

All of our authors have relevant expertise on their topics—we made serious effort to find authors working in Africa, and in most cases we succeeded; but there are a number of authors, Africans and non-Africans, working outside Africa who have contributed excellent chapters to this book.

The lack of a higher education research community in Africa made developing this book more difficult. Outside of South Africa, there is no significant research center focusing on higher education. Few, if any, governments collect detailed analysis and data about higher education. There are few higher education experts working for international or regional agencies, governments, or academic institutions in Africa. There are no opportunities in Africa to train senior academic leaders and administrators. The Association of African Universities is beginning to fill some of these gaps. We are convinced that expertise about higher education is necessary if Africa's growing academic systems are to effectively develop and mature.

Language is a perennial problem for African research and higher education. This volume is in English. We are unable to provide a French edition at this time, although we hope that a translation may become possible. Several of the chapters were written in French for this book, and we translated them into English. We recognize and regret the lack of a French edition of this book.

This volume has been more than two years in the making. It is the result of a massive amount of networking on four continents. We were able to make use of the Internet extensively for our work and have experienced its potential for the development of the field of higher education studies as well as for communicating knowledge and analysis about higher education. The comprehensiveness and the magnitude of this book is such that it will be a key reference book for those interested in both higher education in Africa and in development issues relating to Africa.

Damtew Teferra and Philip G. Altbach
Chestnut Hill, Massachusetts, United States
December 2002

Acknowledgments

A volume as diverse and comprehensive as this one would not have been possible without the support, encouragement, and involvement of many individuals and institutions. We would like to extend our gratitude to all those who helped us.

We are especially indebted to the Ford Foundation, which provided the funding for this book, for their support; we particularly thank Jorge Balan. It is no exaggeration to say that this volume, unprecedented in its scope and coverage, was a challenge to put together. It was made all the more difficult because of the limited size and scope of the higher education research community in Africa. Not only is this community small, but its members are burdened with many responsibilities. We are deeply indebted to our authors, all of whom are accomplished researchers committed to higher education in Africa.

Our advisory committee, consisting of Narciso Matos, then secretary-general of the Association of African Universities and now with the Carnegie Corporation of New York (New York, United States), David Court of the World Bank (Washington D.C., United States), and Juma Shabani, higher education expert at UNESCO (Dakar, Senegal), were of great help to us in identifying authors and assisting with some of the contributions. Many colleagues were helpful to us as we sought to find experts to write on countries and topics.

This volume is part of the research program of the Center for International Higher Education at Boston College. Several colleagues at the university assisted us with this book. Salina Kopellas, the Center's secretary, provided administrative and secretarial support. Hassan Ez-zaïm assisted us with the translation of several essays from French into English. Yoshikazu Ogawa, Alma Maldonado-Maldonado, Laura Rumbly, and Jef Davis assisted in the preparation of the comprehensive bibliography and dissertation listing. Anthony Arnove edited most of the chapters. Francesca Purcell helped in proofreading the chapters. Roberta Bassett has also assisted in editing some of the chapters. Alma Maldonado-Maldonado helped in preparing the index. Our colleagues at Indiana University Press, especially Dee Mortensen, provided friendly and professional publishing expertise.

With the cooperation of Indiana University Press and with funding from the Ford Foundation, this book is being distributed without cost to African research institutions, libraries, and higher education leaders.

DAMTEW TEFERRA AND PHILIP G. ALTBACH
Chestnut Hill, Massachusetts, United States
December 2002

PART 1

Themes

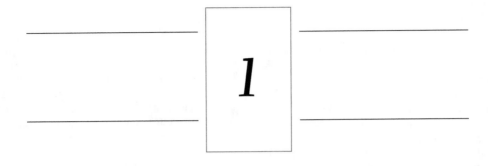

1

Trends and Perspectives in African Higher Education

Damtew Teferra and Philip G. Altbach

INTRODUCTION

African higher education, at the beginning of the new millennium, faces unprecedented challenges. Not only is the demand for access unstoppable, especially in the context of Africa's traditionally low postsecondary attendance levels, but higher education is recognized as a key force for modernization and development. Africa's academic institutions face obstacles in providing the education, research, and service needed if the continent is to advance. The dawning of the twenty-first century is being recognized as a knowledge era, and higher education must play a central role. In this chapter, we reflect on some of the key challenges facing African higher education.

Generalizing about a continent as large and diverse as Africa is difficult. Yet there are some common elements—and there are certainly some common challenges.[1] In our discussion, we are not generally optimistic either in analyzing the current reality in much of Africa or in pointing to future prospects. The fact is that African universities currently function in very difficult circumstances, and the road to future success will not be an easy one.

If Africa is to succeed economically, culturally, and politically, it must have a strong postsecondary sector; academic institutions are central to the future. After being shunted to the side by national governments and international agencies alike for almost two decades, higher education is again recognized as a key sector in African development.

Africa, a continent with fifty-four countries, has no more than 300 institutions that fit the definition of a university. By international standards, Africa is the least developed region in terms of higher education institutions and enrollments. While a few countries on the continent can claim comprehensive academic systems, most have just a few academic institutions and have not yet established the differentiated postsecondary systems required for the information age (Task Force on Higher Education and Society 2000). Nigeria, Sudan, South Africa, and Egypt each has forty-five, twenty-six, twenty-one, and seventeen universities, respectively, and each country has many additional postsecondary institutions as well. A few countries, including Cape Verde, Djibouti, Gambia, Guinea-Bissau, Seychelles, and São Tomé and Principe have no universities; but even in these countries, preparations have been underway to create one or more major postsecondary institutions. Others, including Somalia, Angola, and the Democratic Republic of Congo (DRC), have lost university-level institutions as the result of political turmoil and are trying to rebuild a postsecondary sector.

Generalization is difficult because of the tremendous diversity evident in Africa. There are exceptions to almost every rule. For example, we sometimes underestimate the extent of postsecondary education by ignoring the nonuniversity sector. Zambia has only two universities, but it also has fifty or so colleges for "further education." Our distinction between universities and colleges is based on how they are considered at the local level, irrespective of their size and the program of studies. Diversity in function, quality, orientation, financial support, and other factors are evident in Africa; national circumstances and realities vary significantly. Nonetheless, generalizations can be made, and it is important to understand the broader themes that shape African higher education realities at the beginning of the twenty-first century.

The overall reality of inadequate financial resources combined with unprecedented demand for access, the legacy of colonialism, long-standing economic and social crises in many countries, the challenges of HIV/AIDS in parts of the continent, and other significant issues present a particularly difficult reality. It is our purpose here to provide a broad portrait of African higher education realities as a backdrop for further analysis and future change.

AFRICAN HIGHER EDUCATION
IN HISTORICAL PERSPECTIVE

Higher education in Africa is as old as the pyramids of Egypt, the obelisks of Ethiopia, and the Kingdom of Timbuktu. The oldest university still existing in the world is Egypt's Al-Azhar, founded as and still the major seat of Islamic learning. Indeed, Al-Azhar is currently the only major academic institution in the world that is organized according to its original Islamic model. All other universities in Africa, and, indeed, the rest of the world have adopted the Western model of academic organization. While Africa can claim an ancient academic tradition, the fact is that traditional centers of higher learning in Africa have all but disappeared or were destroyed by colonialism. Today, the continent is dominated by academic institutions shaped by colonialism and organized according to the European model. As is the case in the developing world, higher education in Africa is an artifact of colonial policies (Altbach and Selvaratnam 1989; Lulat 2002).

A multitude of European colonizers—including Belgium, Britain, France, Germany, the Netherlands, Italy, Portugal, and Spain—have shaped Africa's route of development. These colonial legacies affect contemporary African higher education. The most important of the colonial powers in Africa, Britain and France, have left by far the greatest lasting impact, not only in terms of the organization of academe and the continuing links to the metropole but in the language of instruction and communication.

Colonial higher education policy had some common elements. Among these are:

- *Limited access.* Colonial authorities feared widespread access to higher education. They were interested in training limited numbers of African nationals to assist in administering the colonies. Some colonial powers, notably the Belgians, forbade higher education in their colonies. Others, such as the Spanish and the Portuguese, kept enrollments very small. The French preferred to send small numbers of students from its colonies to study in France. Throughout all of Africa, the size of the academic system was very small at the time of independence. A World Bank (1991) study reports that at independence less than one-quarter of all professional civil service posts were held by Africans; most trade and industry throughout the continent was foreign-owned; and only 3 percent of high school–age students received a secondary education. With all its copper wealth, Zambia had only 100 university graduates and 1,000 secondary school graduates. In 1961, the University of East Africa (serving Kenya, Tanzania, and Uganda) turned out a total of only 99 graduates for a combined population area of 23 million. Zaire (now Democratic Republic of Congo), for example, reached independence without a single national engineer, lawyer, or doctor. Between 1952 and 1963, French-speaking Africa produced a mere four graduates in the field of agriculture, while English-speaking Africa turned out 150 (Eisemon 1982).
- *Language.* The language of instruction in every case was the language of the colonizer. In some countries, existing forms of local languages used in "higher forms of education" were replaced by the language of the colonizers.
- *Limited freedom.* Limits on academic freedom and on the autonomy of academic institutions were the norm.
- *Limited curriculum.* The curricula of universities in Africa at the time of independence was dramatically restricted. The colonizers tended to support disciplines such as law and related fields that would assist colonial administration and that were not costly to implement. Scientific subjects were rarely offered.

The legacy of colonialism remains a central factor in African higher education. Independence has been the national reality for most of Africa for less than four decades, and the ties to the former colonizers have, in general, remained strong. The fact that no African country has changed the language of instruction from the colonial language is significant and illustrative. The impact of the colonial past and of the continuing impact of the former colonial powers remains crucial in any analysis of African higher education.

ACCESS

In virtually all African countries, demand for access to higher education is growing, straining the resources of higher education institutions. Students have had to be admitted into institutions and dormitories that were originally designed for fewer students and enrollments have escalated, but financial resources have not kept pace. In many countries, resources have actually declined due to inflation, devaluation of the currency exchange rate, economic and political turmoil, and structural adjustment programs, further stressing the financial stability of institutions and systems.

We estimate that between 4 and 5 million students are currently enrolled in the continent's postsecondary institutions. An older count by the Task Force on Higher Education and Society (2000) puts this figure at 3,489,000 students. Over 150,000 faculty work in Africa's postsecondary institutions. Egypt has the highest enrollment figures in Africa, with over 1.5 million (including about a quarter of a million part-time) students. It also has the largest number of members of the academic profession at about 31,000. The enrollment ratio for the 18–22 age group is approximately 22 percent.

Nigeria is second with close to 900,000 students enrolled in its postsecondary institutions. It has forty-five universities, sixty-three colleges of education, and forty-five polytechnics—the largest number in Africa. Of the total student population, 35 percent go to universities and 55 percent to colleges of education. However, the gross enrollment ratio for ages 18 to 25 is only about 5 percent.

South Africa, with more than half a million students in its twenty-one universities and fifteen technikons (postsecondary vocational colleges), is third in the number of enrolled students on the continent. Of these, 55 percent go to universities. Tunisia and Libya have enrollments of close to 210,000 and over 140,000, respectively.

With a population of 32 million, the enrollment in Tanzanian higher education institutions for the year 2000 was under 21,000. With a population of about 65 million, Ethiopia has no more than 50,000 students in its postsecondary institutions. Today Guinea counts 14,000 students from the population of 7.66 million, Senegal has 25,000 students for 7.97 million inhabitants, and Côte d'Ivoire has 60,000 for its population of 13.7 million.

It should be noted that the number of institutions and student figures are not always directly correlated. Sudan, with its twenty-six public universities and twenty-one private universities and colleges, has an enrollment of about 40,000.

Enrollment in Ghana is less than 3 percent of the eligible age group, and in many countries the figure is under 1 percent of the eligible age cohort. For instance, in Malawi and Tanzania, the proportion is 0.5 percent and 0.3 per cent of the eligible age group, respectively. Those who have access to postsecondary education in Africa overall represent less than 3 percent of the eligible age group—the lowest in the world by a significant percentage. This is one of the reasons for the current surging demand for access to education as Africa seeks to catch up with the rest of the world.

Africa faces a significant challenge in providing access to higher education, not only to reach the levels of other developing and middle-income countries but also to satisfy the demand of populations that are eager for opportunities to study and that have achieved a level of secondary education that qualifies them for postsecondary study.

FUNDING AND FINANCING

The central reality for all African higher education systems at the beginning of the twenty-first century is severe financial crisis. Academe everywhere, even in wealthy industrialized nations, faces fiscal problems, but the magnitude of these problems is greater in Africa than anywhere else. The causes are not difficult to discern, and many are discussed in this chapter. They include:

- The pressures of expansion and "massification" that have added large numbers of students to most African academic institutions and systems
- The economic problems facing many African countries that make it difficult, if not impossible, to provide increased funding for higher education
- A changed fiscal climate induced by multilateral lending agencies such as the World Bank and the International Monetary Fund
- The pressure of providing care for those with HIV/AIDS on government budgets
- The inability of students to afford the tuition rates necessary for fiscal stability
- Misallocation of the financial resources that are available, such as the provision of free or highly subsidized accommodations and food for students

Not all of these elements are, of course, present in every African country, and financial circumstances vary, but overall, funding issues loom very large in any analysis of African higher education.

Higher education is a four-to-five-billion-dollar enterprise in Africa.[2] With Africa's largest student population, Egypt's higher education is a US$1.29 billion enterprise. Nigeria, with an estimated half-a-billion-dollar budget, accounts for about a third of the remaining total figure. South Africa, Tunisia, Libya, and Algeria appear to dispense a significant portion of the remaining expenditures when compared to other countries of the continent.

For a continent of more than 700 million people, this is a remarkably small amount. The total yearly expenditure for higher education in Africa as a whole does not even come close to the endowments of some of the richest universities in the United States. The budgets of individual universities in many industrialized countries exceed the entire national budgets for higher education in many African nations. These comparisons clearly illustrate the disparity between the financial situations of higher education institutions in Africa and in industrialized nations.

It comes as no surprise, then, that virtually all African universities suffer from the effects of scarce financial resources. Serious shortages of published materials such as books and journals, the lack of basic resources for teaching, the absence of simple laboratory equipment and supplies (such as chemicals) to do research and teaching, and, in some countries, delays of salary payments for months are just some of the common problems faced by institutions across the continent.

The bulk of funding for higher education is generated from state resources. While small variations in the proportion of resources allotted to higher education by country exist, African governments consistently provide more than 90 to 95 percent of the total operating budgets of higher education. The remaining percentages come from fees for tuition, services, consultancy, renting facilities, and other sources. In addition, there is a growing trend toward funding from external sources. Research, for example, is largely funded by donor agencies, and this naturally has implications for the nature of the research and for its impact on African higher education.

In many countries, governments pay stipends and living allowances to students, and this consumes a substantial proportion of university resources. In Guinea, for instance, scholarship money given to students accounts for as much as 55 percent of the total government allocations to the universities. In most countries, student fees have traditionally not provided more than token support.

There are some rare exceptions. In Lesotho, for instance, much of the money the University of Lesotho takes in comes from student fees, and this is a major source of income for the university. Students in Lesotho also repay student loans as soon as they have completed their studies and have secured jobs. The arrangements for loan payments are also contingent upon where graduates eventually work; that is, in public, private, regional, or international sectors.

The enormous support for the provision of nonacademic activities and facilities is now facing scrutiny in many countries. Such support not only consumes major parts of university budgets; it may also serve as an incentive for students to take longer to complete their studies. In situations where jobs for graduates are not immediately available, students have been reported to delay the completion of their studies, which then blocks the opportunity for potential upcoming students to enroll. Initiatives to curtail such support schemes are often precipitated by declining resources from governments and by multinational pressures on African governments to cut social services.

We can measure the scope of the financial challenges facing African higher education by examining what universities request from their governments and what they actually receive. In Ghana, according to Paul Effah, five universities requested a total of $32 million in 2000. The government only provided $18 million—a mere 56 percent of what they requested; and the pattern is the same for the former polytechnic institutions whose statuses have been upgraded. In 1999–2000, the education sector in Uganda received 33 percent of the total government discretionary recurrent budget, and tertiary education accounted for only 18 percent of this total.

Without exception, African universities are under considerable financial pressure and face serious financial problems. That said, there are a few places where the financial situation appears to be relatively less severe or even improving gradually. In Nigeria—a country that suffered serious social, economic, and political upheavals during a series of military regimes in the past—funds are expected to increase by 252 percent under the current elected government. Botswana, which has a small population and considerable mineral wealth, has provided its higher education sector with adequate funding.

Over the last decade or so, the pressure to expand the revenue base of higher education has been clear. Universities have either taken it upon themselves or have been pressured by governments to expand the financial and resource base as resources have dwindled against mounting enrollments and escalating demand. Various forms of ideas to generate revenue and a variety of programs have been experimented with and implemented in many countries. While governments, sometimes with pressure from external and donor agencies, have been interested in expanding revenues from and the resource base for higher education, there has often been resistance from the public and, especially, from students.

Some universities, such as Uganda's Makerere University, however, have been claimed as models of successful transformation of the ingrained culture of government support as the sole source of income for the university. Nakanyike Musisi reports that in 1992–1993, 5 percent of the students in Makerere paid their way; seven years later, 80 percent were doing so (Musisi 2001). In Tanzania, the new trend is to adopt policies to equitably share costs between the government and those who use the university's services. The government is confining itself to funding the direct costs of education and leaving the remaining costs (such as residence fees, food, and the like) to be met by students, parents, and family members.

The complex dynamics that enabled fiscal reforms to succeed in some countries and to fail in others need careful analysis. The sustainability of such reforms; their perceived, real, and potential benefits and concealed drawbacks and ramifications;

and the significance of external and internal forces are interesting topics for further research.

In virtually all cases, the authors in this volume observe the constant decline of direct and indirect resources allocated for higher education by governments. The impact of this trend and how this over time has eroded the quality of teaching and research, the moral and physical well-being of the academic profession, and the general state of the universities as a whole remain a subject for more discussion and analysis.

GOVERNANCE AND AUTONOMY

Public higher education institutions predominate in Africa, and governmental involvement in university affairs is the norm. The current governance structure in most African universities reflects this legacy. Throughout much of Africa, the head of state holds the ultimate authority as the chancellor or president in appointing vice-chancellors and others down the administrative line; this is especially typical in Anglophone Africa.

Power Structure

In Anglophone countries, the chancellorship is a symbolic position. The vice-chancellor, who is equivalent to an American university president, has the executive power as furnished by the board of directors, who themselves are composed largely of government-appointed members and, in some countries, students. The vice-chancellors have also been known to be appointed by a minister of education with or without the approval of Parliament or even a chancellor. For example, in the Democratic Republic of Congo, under normal circumstances, university presidents are nominated by the members of the academic community; however, it is the president of the republic who makes the final decision on the selection of the vice-chancellor upon the recommendation of the minister of education.

The chain of administrative power starts with the vice-chancellor, then moves to deans/directors, and then department heads. The deans and directors in most cases are appointed either by the vice-chancellor, directly by government officials, or by boards of directors or trustees. In many cases, fellow members elect the department heads. In a few countries, a shortlist of candidates for the highest positions is submitted to the government as a compromise between the university community and the government. In most cases, the professorial authority that is typical in Western industrialized nations is lacking in much of Africa. The academic profession has less power in the African context than it does in the West.

Staff Size

The teaching and research staff in quite a large number of African institutions is smaller than the nonacademic/administrative staff. The administrative bureaucracy in African universities is disproportionately large. A few examples illustrate this disparity:

• At National University of Lesotho, Matora Ntimo-Makara reports, there are twice as many nonacademic support staff as there are academics, and more than 60 percent of the institution's budget goes to staff costs. The financial resources of the university are, therefore, mainly used on nonteaching personnel costs. This imposes limitations on the creation of additional teaching positions to enhance capacity in academic programs.

- In Madagascar, James Stiles reports, the student-to-administrator ratio remains high relative to other countries (with 6 students to each administrator) and high relative to the ratio of students to teachers (47 to 1 in 1993 and 22 to 1 in 1996). This remains true even after the number of administrative staff was reduced in 1997 by 5 percent while the teaching corps increased.
- Togo, Emmanuel Edee reports, has 1,136 administrative and technical staff in higher education, yet the academic staff numbers fewer than 730, of whom only 55 percent are full-time. While the number of nonacademic staff is high, they face several problems, including overstaffing and lack of communication between the different services and the students.

The number of nonacademic personnel and the proportion of resources allocated to this sector are disproportionately high, and the quality and performance of the administrative cadre leaves much to be desired. Bureaucracy and inefficiency are rampant. Training and skills development for the nonacademic staff are rarities.

While the nonacademic staff of African educational institutions is crucial, its disproportionate presence takes away the resources needed for the basic functions of universities: teaching and research. In countries where such resources are very scarce, universities must consider minimizing this significant and unsustainable fiscal burden in order to direct resources to the priority areas. While seldom discussed as a key issue for academic development in Africa, the complex issues surrounding the administrative staff in African universities deserve careful attention.

Management Issues in Universities

Efficient management and administrative systems are of paramount significance to the productivity and effectiveness of any enterprise; academic institutions are no exception. By and large, however, African universities suffer from poor, inefficient, and highly bureaucratic management systems. Poorly trained and poorly qualified personnel; inefficient, ineffective, and out-of-date management and administrative infrastructures; and poorly remunerated staff are the norm throughout the many systems.

Some chapters in this handbook cite anecdotal reports alleging mismanagement and even embezzlement of both internally and externally generated sources, though accounts of serious corruption charges and embezzlement of funds in African universities are not common. Some blame misappropriation of funds and poor prioritization as one of the factors for financial difficulties in the universities. For instance, the fiscal crisis in Kenyan public universities, Charles Ngome observes, is worsened by the misappropriation of the scarce resources. As students continue living and studying under deplorable conditions, the top administrators in the universities are regularly accused by the national auditor general's office of mismanaging funds and having misplaced priorities. During the 1995–1996 financial year, it was reported that Maseno University lost over US$660,000 (Kshs. 50 million), most of it through theft and false allowance payments. Even though the issues of mismanagement tend to be generally similar across nations and systems, it is important to note that the manner in which the university is governed and the leadership is appointed often contributes to the magnitude and scope of the problems.

PRIVATE HIGHER EDUCATION

In many African countries, the provision of higher education by private institutions is a growing phenomenon. When compared to other parts of the world, however, most African countries have been slow to expand the private sector in higher education (Altbach 1999). The trend toward private higher education has been enhanced by a number of factors: a burgeoning demand from students for access, the declining capacity of public universities, the retrenchment of public services, pressure by external agencies to cut public services, a growing emphasis on and need for a highly skilled labor force that targets the local market, and the beginning of interest by foreign providers. In terms of numbers, there are now more private institutions than public ones in some countries, although the private schools are smaller and tend to specialize in specific fields, such as business administration. The following examples showcase the development of private higher education in Africa:

- Kenya has nineteen universities, of which thirteen are private.
- In Sudan, Mohamed Elamin El Tom observes, the number of private higher education institutions increased from one in 1989 to sixteen in 1996 and to twenty-two in 2001. The number of students enrolled in private higher education institutions increased nearly ninefold within four years—from under 3,000 in 1990–1991 to close to 24,000 in 1994–1995.
- In the Democratic Republic of Congo, over 260 private institutions were operating in 1996, of which 28.9 percent were approved by the government, 32.3 percent were authorized to operate, and 38.8 percent were being considered for authorization. Many newly established institutions, unfortunately, do not meet the required higher education standards because of their organization and the conditions within which they operate.
- In Ghana, there has been an upsurge, especially among religious organizations, in the establishment of private higher education institutions. By August 2000, the National Accreditation Board had granted accreditation to eleven private tertiary institutions to offer degree programs. Ghana has five public universities and eight polytechnics whose status has been upgraded.
- In Uganda, over ten private universities are established or being established. Currently, Uganda has two public universities; and the founding of two more public universities was also recently announced by the government.

- Togo—a country that has one major university and four other postsecondary institutions—has encouraged the creation of private institutions of higher education. Today, there are twenty-two private postsecondary institutions, of which eighteen were created between 1998 and 2000.
- Ethiopia, with a very small public academic sector, has seen the establishment of numerous private postsecondary institutions recently.

It is important to point out that most of these institutions are based in the major capital cities and in cities where the student pool is robust and the infrastructure is relatively good. It also should be noted that even though the number of private institutions on the continent has increased dramatically and appears higher in absolute numbers than the number of public institutions, student enrollment in public institutions outnumbers enrollment in private institutions in nearly all countries. For instance, while the enrollment in the six public universities in Madagascar was not more than 9,000, the total enrollment of the sixteen private institutions was less than 2,000, and none of the private institutions had more than 500 students.

Kenya is one of the few countries in Africa that has a well-developed private university system, yet only 20 percent of the 50,000 enrolled students attend the thirteen private universities. In Uganda, the total student population of the ten private institutions amounts to 3,600, while the two public universities enroll 23,000 students.

Private institutions in Africa are secular as well as sectarian. In religious-based private institutions, the funding of the institutions relies heavily on the founding religious organizations—based both locally and abroad—or their affiliates. Most other secular private institutions in Africa depend on student tuition and fees to generate their revenue. As a consequence, the cost of education in these institutions is generally higher in comparison to other educational institutions.

Governments do not give financial support to private institutions in most African countries. In certain cases, however, the private institutions receive direct financial support from governments. In Liberia, for instance, the state provides subsidies to private and church-operated postsecondary institutions. It also provides financial aid to students attending these institutions to cover the cost of tuition and textbooks. In Togo, private institutions that offer short-period technician degrees are subsidized by the state in the same way as other institutions. In Mozambique, some scholarships are also made available to private higher education students to help them pay their tuition fees.

The courses taught in most private higher education institutions are generally similar across the continent and narrow in their program coverage. The most common ones are computer science and technology, accounting and management, banking, finance, marketing, and secretarial science. The courses are generally targeted toward the needs of the local market.

Most private institutions hire faculty from public institutions. Characteristically, most of the faculty continue to hold full-time positions in the public institutions. In some countries, the massive flow of faculty from public institutions to newly established private institutions has seriously constrained certain departments in public universities. For many faculty, however, these private teaching positions have become an important source of extra income.

The general trend, then, has been to moonlight at the newly established institutions while maintaining bases in major public universities. In some cases, lured by highly lucrative salaries and benefits, faculty have been reported to join private institutions full-time by abandoning their public institutions. Unable to control this growing trend, some universities and departments enter into negotiations with faculty whose disciplines tend to have an attractive market value at private teaching institutions and elsewhere.

There still looms a strong public perception across Africa that public institutions are academically better than private institutions—even when a few of the private institutions hire the best faculty and maintain new and up-to-date instruments, equipment, and facilities. It is plausible that this prevalent attitude emanates from the rigorous selection process prior to enrollment and fierce competition for admission in limited, yet "free," public universities. As student enrollment escalates across the continent, the entrance requirements for the limited spaces in public institutions have become increasingly rigorous so that those students that are admitted are clearly the nation's best. In general, private institutions primarily enroll those students who cannot make it to public institutions—for numerous reasons—and that continues to affect the general perceptions of private institutions as secondary to public institutions.

Whereas the emergence of private higher education as a business enterprise is an emerging phenomenon, a number of issues plague its development, including legal status, quality assurance, and cost of service. The status of many private postsecondary institutions in Africa is shady. Many operate without licenses, commensurate resources, or appropriate infrastructure. The quality of service by many is also shoddy, even at a few of the institutions that possess better equipment, newer buildings, and better facilities than the major universities in their country.

The quality of education at many private postsecondary institutions has also been an issue of some concern. Many multinational businesses across the world provide educational services today that are driven by the profit motive. Multinational companies and a few foreign-based universities have established satellite campuses in countries where there is a big market for higher education. These transplanted institutions are often criticized for lack of accountability or social responsibility and for potentially threatening and eroding the cultural fabric of a nation.

Private higher education is a growing trend in much of Africa and is being propelled by a variety of forces. The forces behind this private diversification and expansion are both internal and external. A thorough examination of the process of diversification of private institutions must take into account national as well as international economic, political, and educational realities.

GENDER

Gender imbalance is a common phenomenon in the continent's educational institutions. Cultural, sociological, economical, psychological, historical, and political factors foster these inequalities. While a number of efforts are now underway to rectify gender imbalances, much still remains to be done across all of the educational sectors. The gender imbalance in higher education is acute in virtually all African countries and in most disciplines. Various efforts and initiatives have been made to increase the participation of female students in postsecondary institutions.

- In Ethiopia, according to Habtamu Wondimu, efforts have been made to improve the female enrollment rate—which has been only about 15 percent for the past several years—by lowering the cutoff in the grade point average required for admission. This "affirmative action," he notes, has improved the admission rate of female students. The higher attrition rate among women, however, continues to plague the overall status and numbers of women in Ethiopian higher education.
- In Malawi, where only 25 percent of the student population is female, an affirmative selection policy for women has been implemented.
- In Mozambique, the proportion of female students gradually increased since 1992. The ratio between genders remained high (at the range of between 2.79 and 3.06) between 1990 and 1996 but fell to 2.45 and 2.59 in 1998 and 1999. This improvement was partly due to the opening of private higher education institutions, where, on average, 43 percent of all students enrolled in 1999 were female; only 25 percent of students enrolled were female in the public sector.
- Most Tanzanian institutions have been taking steps to improve the participation of female students, who currently make up between 25 and 30 percent of enrolled students. The Faculty of Arts and Social Sciences at the University of Dar es Salaam was able to register 49 percent females in the 2000–2001 first-year intake. As in Ethiopia, the grade-point-average cutoff point for female candidates has been lowered to enable more females to qualify for admission.
- Uganda's gender disparity is reported to have decreased in the past ten years. Women constituted 27 percent of University of Makerere's total student intake in 1990–1991 but today account for 34 percent of the enrollments. Like institutions in Ethiopia, Malawi, and Tanzania, Ugandan universities are giving preferential treatment to female students. With awarding of additional points, the proportion of female students enrolled has risen to 34 percent.
- In Zimbabwe, university entry qualifications have also been reduced to increase female enrollments.

Significant gender disparities remain, however, in the more competitive faculties and departments and in hard sciences, where female student participation is particularly low. In Kenya, for instance, female students make up about 30 percent of total enrollments in the public universities but only 10 percent of enrollments in engineering and technically based professional programs. The female student population in the natural sciences across African public higher education is consistently lower than that of male students. The pattern appears to be a universal phenomenon around the world, though the proportion of the disparity across countries can and does differ significantly.

There are, however, examples of exceptions where female students outnumber their male compatriots in African coun-

tries. In Mauritius, even though overall enrollment shows a more or less even gender distribution (47 percent female), these enrollments do vary by gender across faculties, with a predominance of male students (76 percent) in the Faculty of Engineering and a predominance of female students (68 percent) in the Faculty of Social Studies and Humanities.

In Lesotho, more females than males are enrolled in education, social sciences, and humanities (arts) programs. Overall, the total number of females represents about 56 percent of all enrolled students in the University of Lesotho. In Uganda, the private universities, Uganda Martyrs and Nkumba, report female student enrollments of over 50 and 56 percent respectively. In Tunisia, female student enrollments went from 21.1 percent in 1987–1988 to 50.4 percent in 1999–2000 and currently stands at 51.9 percent—the first time more women than men were enrolled at the university level.

Female faculty are even smaller in proportion than female students in African institutions. In Guinea, out of 1,000 faculty members only twenty-five—a mere 2.5 percent—are female. Out of 2,228 faculty in Ethiopia, 137—or 6 percent—are female. In Congo, Nigeria, and Zambia, no more than 15 percent of all university faculty is female. In Uganda, female faculty occupy fewer than 20 percent of the established academic posts. In a few countries, the figures are a little better: Morocco, Tunisia, and South Africa have 24, 33, and 36 percent female faculty respectively. The underrepresentation of female faculty in higher ranks and qualification levels and in certain fields of study is particularly severe. For instance, in 1997, men in South Africa constituted 90 percent of professors, 78 percent of associate professors, and 67 percent of senior lecturers, but only about 47 percent of the junior ranks.

Overall, gender disparities are common trends across the continent's higher education institutions. The disparity increases in magnitude as one climbs the educational ladder. The gravity of the disparity is most severe in the faculty ranks with some variations in different fields and disciplines. Gender issues in African higher education are complex and require and deserve further study.

As we discussed above, a variety of initiatives have been implemented to remedy this unhealthy scenario. While a few of these initiatives have been productive, others have yet to achieve any real change. These initiatives continue to be plagued by subtle resistance, implicit and explicit oversight, a lack of serious recognition, and ignorance.

RESEARCH AND PUBLISHING

Long before the world entered into what is being called the knowledge era, research was recognized as a central priority for higher education. Since the founding of the University of Berlin in 1810, research has been a defining element for many academic institutions and systems (Ben-David 1968; Ben-David 1977). In the increasingly global world that is largely being shaped by knowledge and information, establishing a strong research infrastructure has more than ever before become a sine qua non in this highly competitive world.

Universities, as creators and brokers of these products, are situated at the center of the knowledge and information supermarket. For all practical purposes, universities remain the most important institutions in the production and consumption of knowledge and information, particularly in the Third World. This is particularly so in Africa, where only a few such institutions serve as the preeminent and dominant centers of knowledge and information transactions.

By all measures and accounts, research and publishing activities in Africa are in critical condition. The general state of research in Africa is extremely poor, and its research infrastructure is inadequate. Scarcity of laboratory equipment, chemicals, and other scientific paraphernalia; a small number of high-level experts; poor and dilapidated libraries; alarmingly low and declining salaries of faculty and research staff; a massive brain drain out of the academic institutions; the "expansion" of undergraduate education; poor oversight of research applicability; and declining, nonexistent, and unreliable sources of research funds all remain major hurdles to the development of research capacity across the continent.

Most countries in Africa have practically no funds allocated to research in the university budgets. Expenditures on research and development (R&D) in Ghana, for example, show a declining trend from around 0.7 percent of the gross domestic product (GDP) in the mid-1970s to 0.1–0.2 percent of the GDP in 1983–1987. There is little evidence to suggest that this trend has changed. Paul Effah reports that the University of Ghana received only US$1.4 million to fund the operations of its ten research institutes in 2000.

In Uganda, the amount earmarked for research at Makerere University for the financial year 1999–2000 was a mere US$80,000. As a consequence, research in the country has remained underdeveloped and heavily dependent on donor funding. In Malawi, a mere 0.7 percent of the whole University of Malawi budget was allocated to research and publications in 1999.

Tracking frontiers of knowledge is crucial for research and development. Having access to indicators of the knowledge frontiers, such as journals, periodicals, and databases, is a major prerequisite to undertaking viable, sustainable, and meaningful research. In much of Africa, these resources are either lacking or are extremely scarce. The escalating cost of journals and ever-dwindling library and university funds have exacerbated the problem. Many universities in Africa have dropped most of their subscriptions, while others have simply cancelled their subscriptions altogether. Such extreme measures cannot be surprising in light of the fact that some of these universities cannot even pay salaries on a regular basis.

The local publishing infrastructure has also become weak and, generally, unreliable. The issue of local publications is complicated by many competing factors, including the small number of researchers with the energy, time, funds, and support needed to sustain journals; the lack of qualified editors and editorial staff; a shortage of publishable materials; a restrictive environment that inhibits freedom of speech; and a lack of commitment to and appreciation of journal production by university administrators.

It is remarkable that even though the state of research in much of Africa remains precarious, many of the authors in this book report that academic promotion of faculty depends to a large extent on publishing. Even when the environment does not appear to support research, publishing, as a universal tool of measuring productivity, remains a yardstick for academic promotion in Africa. It is a stark contradiction that African academics are expected to publish their work in an academic context that does not even provide them with access to the journals, databases, and other publications that are vital in keeping abreast of international developments in science and scholarship (Teferra 2002).

Many of the research activities that are undertaken in the continent are largely funded—and to a certain extent, managed and directed—by external agencies, such as bilateral and multilateral bodies, nongovernmental organizations (NGOs), foundations, and others. Estimates of the percentage of external support for research in Africa range from 70 percent to as much as 90 percent. The ramifications of this external funding, especially with regard to what is researched, are far-reaching and have become the focus of discussions at numerous national, regional, and international forums.

Academic institutions in many countries are frequently linked by their participation in an international system of knowledge distribution. Universities in the large industrialized nations are the major producers and distributors of scholarly knowledge. Academic institutions in other countries, particularly in developing countries, are largely consumers of scholarly materials and research produced elsewhere.

It will be extremely difficult—perhaps even impossible—for Africa to compete effectively in a world increasingly dominated by knowledge and information unless it consciously, persistently, and vigorously overhauls its potential and its most crucial institutions: its universities. Africa should and must do much more to develop its universities—its only institutions that generate and utilize knowledge and information. The international knowledge system has centers and peripheries in the production and distribution of knowledge. Africa, as a continent, finds itself on the very edge of the knowledge periphery (Altbach 1987) and appears to be increasingly isolated from the center.

Research and publishing must be strengthened. Governments, major donor institutions, NGOs, and bilateral organizations should and must direct their policies toward prioritizing the revitalization of these important areas of African higher education if Africa is to cope effectively with the challenges of the present and the future. The current situation, in which donor agencies and international organizations fund the large proportion of Africa-based research, presents additional challenges. While it is unlikely that major research funding will be available from indigenous sources in the near future, it is important to ensure that the research that is taking place, regardless of the source of funding, meets the needs of African scientists and the broader interest of African societies.

ACADEMIC FREEDOM

Academic freedom makes it possible for new ideas, research, and opinions to emerge; for widely accepted views to be tested and challenged; and for critics to comment on and criticize the status quo. Academic freedom is an ideal that faces challenges all over the world. There is, however, little doubt that academic freedom is crucial in nurturing national academic and scholarly cultures. Ideally, academic freedom ensures that faculty will be able to teach freely, undertake research of their own interest, and communicate findings and ideas openly and without any fear of persecution.

A civil society thrives on tolerance and freedom of expression. A country with robust freedom of expression allows a great variety of perspectives and views to be considered, entertained, and contested. Academic freedom is a crucial element of a civil society, and the development of a civil society is stunted in the absence of freedom of expression and academic freedom.

Most African governments are intolerant of dissent, criticism, nonconformity, and free expression of controversial, new, or unconventional ideas. Aman Attieh notes that since 1992 serious violations of freedom of speech and expression by security forces, opposition groups, and militant groups in Algeria have silenced not only scholars but also the citizens as a whole. In Kenya, Charles Ngome writes, unwarranted government interference and abuses of academic freedom have eroded the autonomy and quality of the higher learning institutions. The summary expulsion of over forty university professors and lecturers from Addis Ababa University, Ethiopia, in the mid-1990s also epitomizes a gross violation of academic freedom and illustrates the intolerance of academic freedom that governments in many African countries have.

In such an environment, the academic community is often careful not to overtly offend those in power. This contributes to the perpetuation of a culture of self-censorship. Those who courageously speak their mind and express their views often find themselves facing dictators capable of using terror, kidnapping, imprisonment, expulsion, torture, and even death to silence dissident voices.

The stability of a culture of academic freedom in a nation is measured by that nation's tolerance of open and frank debates, criticisms, and comments. As African countries slowly move away from one-party authoritarian and autocratic rule to elected democratic governments and leadership, it is hoped that academic freedom will eventually improve in African academic institutions. African universities have a special responsibility to build a culture of academic freedom in teaching, research, and learning, as well as in societal expression. Developing such a culture in the postcolonial context of political instability and dictatorship will prove a daunting task (Altbach 2001).

THE BRAIN DRAIN AND
THE ISSUE OF CAPACITY BUILDING

One of the most serious challenges facing many African countries is the departure of their best scholars and scientists away from universities. The flow away from domestic academe occurs with regard both to internal mobility (locally) and to regional and overseas migration. The term "brain drain" is frequently used to describe the movement of high-level experts from developing countries to industrialized nations. Much of the literature reflects this particular phenomenon—often pointing out its grave immediate and future consequences—within the context of capacity-building issues. In much of the literature on academic mobility, we read about the brain drain of academ-

ics in the context of migration overseas. The classification and the terms we use here reflect that idea of brain drain, and we are aware that the movement of high-level expertise is an area of much discussion and debate.

The internal mobility of scholars can be best described as the flow of high-level expertise from the universities to better-paying government agencies and private institutions and firms that may or may not be able to utilize their expertise and talent effectively. As the state of African universities has deteriorated, academics have sought employment opportunities outside universities, consequently draining institutions of their faculty members. Major public institutions in many countries have lost significant numbers of their key faculty members to emerging private higher education institutions and other commercially oriented institutions, perhaps not only in terms of the physical removal of those who leave but also in terms of the time, commitment, and loyalty of remaining faculty. In many countries, faculty often hold more than one job outside the university to help make ends meet and as a consequence may spread themselves too thin to fulfill their university responsibilities of teaching, research, and service.

Academic staff are also lured away by a variety of government agencies, where salaries are often better and the working environment more comfortable. In many cases, the salaries and benefits in universities are lower than comparative positions in and outside of the civil service. For instance, a comparative salary analysis in Ghana in 1993 revealed that salary levels in sectors such as energy, finance, revenue collection, and the media were all higher than those of the universities.

In many of the emerging private institutions, salaries and benefits are rather handsome when compared to salaries and benefits in academe. In Ethiopia, for instance, a private college is reported to be paying faculty a monthly salary as much as three times what a public university is paying. In Uganda, the migration of senior staff from tertiary institutions, especially from Makerere University, was of paramount concern in the early 1990s. The relative improvement of employment conditions, salaries, the standard of living, and fringe benefits to the faculty, Nakanyike Musisi holds, has worked to halt this exodus and brain drain from Uganda. However, the growing and better-paid private sector and the higher-level civil service continue to lure seasoned academicians away from tertiary institutions. The internal brain drain, though rarely discussed, is nonetheless an issue of great importance to higher education. It is especially important because it is something that African countries can themselves at least partly solve.

Civil strife, political persecutions, and social upheavals instigated the massive exodus of highly trained personnel from countries such as Somalia, Liberia, Ethiopia, Togo, Sierra Leone, and Nigeria. Rwanda and Algeria have also seen systematic killings of academics and intellectuals because of their ethnicity and religious predilections.

Regional migration—academic migration to regional and neighboring countries—has also brought about serious shortages of high-level faculty in some countries. Many academic departments have lost their preeminent faculty to regional universities in other parts of Africa. For instance, several senior scholars from Addis Ababa University, Ethiopia, hold faculty positions at the University of Botswana. Southern African countries such as Zambia have also been complaining about the migration of their graduates and faculty to South Africa and Zimbabwe. Some have observed that expatriate Zambians staff entire departments in some institutions in these countries.

A 1998 study shows that in 1990, nearly 7,000 Kenyans with tertiary-level education migrated to the United States. In the same year, nearly 120 doctors were estimated to have emigrated from Ghana. Between 600 and 700 Ghanaian physicians, a number equal to about 50 percent of the total population of doctors remaining in the country, are known to be practicing in the United States alone (Sethi 2000); and yet, according to Paul Effah, an analysis of existing vacancies in the tertiary institutions in Ghana indicates that about 40 percent of faculty positions in the universities and more than 60 percent of those in the polytechnics are vacant. Munzali Jibril reports that two-thirds of the 36,134 faculty position in Nigeria remain vacant.

Quoting several sources, Habtamu Wondimu describes the large number of Ethiopian academic staff who quit their teaching profession to take other jobs or go abroad for training or other reasons and did not come back. Though the number varies from institution to institution, the estimate of the brain drain from Ethiopian universities might be as much as 50 percent. In Eritrea, one of the critical bottlenecks to the university's development plans, according to Cheryl Sternman Rule, has been the shortage of qualified academic staff and its excessive dependence on expatriate staff.

In Rwanda, as Jolly Mazimhaka and G. F. Daniel report, skilled personnel and professionals have been either killed or have gone into exile, leaving a huge vacuum in the intellectual labor force, a phenomenon that has greatly affected every domestic sector and curbed the process of national development. Even before 1994, when the infamous genocide took place, many sectors of the national economy suffered from a serious shortage of professionals and management staff; the war and genocide have aggravated this situation.

Matora Ntimo-Makara points out that Lesotho's capacity to retain highly trained personnel is low. The South African job market provides better salary packages, and many leave. Lesotho's institutional capacity is eroded as a result. Students from Lesotho who study at and graduate from South African institutions seldom return home upon completion of their studies and instead take positions in South Africa. In Swaziland, according to Margaret Zoller Booth, not only has the flight of schoolteachers created a negative climate for educational progress but the university has also suffered from the exodus of professors seeking better positions in other countries, particularly South Africa. To curb this problem, a review is being considered to improve conditions for the faculty and staff.

Academics and other professionals in Nigeria have migrated to other countries, most notably the United States, South Africa, Botswana, Saudi Arabia, and member countries of the European Union. According to Munzali Jibril, it is estimated that there are at least 10,000 Nigerian academics and 21,000 Nigerian doctors in the United States alone.

Reports indicate that many of the best and most experienced academics from South Africa are migrating to Australia, Britain, Canada, the United States, and other developed countries. It is ironic that while several countries complain about the loss of their highly skilled labor to South Africa, South Africa itself bemoans its loss of talent to other countries. It is useful to understand this "hopping" phenomenon in discerning the effects of brain-drain issues nationally, regionally, and internationally.

The causes of migration—be it regional or international—are a complex phenomenon. The reasons why scholars migrate or decide to stay abroad are products of a complex blend of economic, political, social, cultural, and psychological factors. The impact and chemistry of each factor varies from country to country and individual to individual and fluctuates with time—even for the same individual (Teferra 2000).

While African countries and many major regional, international, and nongovernmental organizations have tried to stem massive movements of African expertise, the results of these efforts are far from satisfactory. Even though various attempts have been made to stem the brain drain, efforts were rare to tap the expertise of immigrant communities at their new places of residence. As communication technology is slowly expanding across Africa and physical distance is becoming a less serious obstacle, an active policy of mobilizing the remotely stationed intellectual capital and vital resource of migrated nationals needs to be given more emphasis (Teferra 2000).

Africa is not alone in seeking to stem the brain drain. Developing countries on other continents and, indeed, many industrialized countries have also sought to minimize the migration of talent in an increasingly globalized labor market. These efforts have largely been unsuccessful. Migration from poorer to wealthier countries is commonplace, as is migration from smaller and less cosmopolitan academic systems to larger and more central systems. At present, there is a small exodus from the United Kingdom to the United States and several other countries because of lower academic salaries in Britain. The international migration of highly educated people is by no means limited to Africa. It is a worldwide and perhaps unprecedented phenomenon.

The challenges to capacity building in African institutions also emanate from health-related problems. Recent studies indicate that the impact of HIV/AIDS has taken its toll on the faculty, and the consequences of this disease on African academic institutions are massive. The levels of sickness and death among faculty members from this disease have added to the teaching, financial, and administrative burdens already facing the rest of the academic community.

Social upheavals, political instabilities, economic uncertainties, real and perceived persecutions, and poor working and living conditions are often the most common variables facing the migratory community. Most African countries are yet unable to rid themselves of these economic, social, and political hurdles that drive away many of their highly qualified and trained experts.

LANGUAGE OF INSTRUCTION

More than half a dozen languages are currently in use in African higher education. These include Afrikaans, Arabic, English, French, Italian, Portuguese, and Spanish. Only Arabic and, arguably, Afrikaans are languages indigenous to Africa.

Overall, Arabic, English, French, and Portuguese remain the major international languages of instruction at African higher learning institutions. At a time when globalization has become such a powerful force, the dominant position of European languages has become even more accentuated and evident. English has become particularly powerful, even dominating over other major European languages. The predominance of English is fueled by, among other things, the Internet and globalization.

In some African countries, languages struggle for dominance in the higher education sector. There is an interesting trend toward a transition in the language used as the instructional medium in Rwanda, for instance, where the core of the leadership in government and power is changing. This is also the case in Sudan, where the political predilections are shifting, and in Equatorial Guinea and, to some extent, Somalia, where perceived socioeconomic benefits appear to be dictating the choice of language for instruction. South Africa is discussing the future of Afrikaans as a language of higher education in a context of English domination. Language remains a volatile social issue in many African countries.

The development of vernacular languages into an instructional medium in higher education will continue to be confronted by numerous issues, including:

- the multiplicity of languages on the continent
- the controversy surrounding the identification and delegation of a particular language as a medium of instruction
- the developmental stages of languages for use in writing and publications
- a paucity of published materials
- poor vocabularies and grammatical conventions of indigenous languages that make it difficult to convey ideas and concepts
- a poor infrastructure for producing, publishing, translating, and developing teaching materials locally
- the pressures of globalization

African universities rely on the knowledge system that has been conceived, developed, and organized based on Western languages. The Western world produces the majority of knowledge conveyed in those languages. African universities do not have the capacity to generate enough knowledge of their own, nor do they have the capacity and infrastructure to process and translate existing ones virtually from the Western world—yet. Most books, journals, databases, and other resources that are used in higher education institutions are imported, and these are communicated in Western languages. In the age of the Internet, globalization, and expanding knowledge systems, which are all driven by a few Western languages, no country can afford to remain shielded in a cocoon of isolation brought about by language limitations. Such isolation would prove both disastrous and, likely, impossible to achieve.

Many in this book have charged that the use of European languages in higher education in Africa has contributed to the decline of African higher education and the alienation of academe from the majority of the population. Others have argued that the use of metropolitan languages has contributed to national unity. Language conflict is by no means limited to Africa. It is a central issue in many developing countries as well as in a number of multilingual industrialized nations. Canada, for example, faced the possibility of the secession of the province of Quebec because of largely linguistic conflicts. Language also remains an issue of tension in Belgium, and it will remain one of the most significant challenges facing African academic development.

STUDENT ACTIVISM

Student activism is prevalent in many African countries. Students have protested alleged social, economic, cultural, political, and personal injustices, and they are vocal in defending their interests and benefits. Student protests about poor student services, delay of stipends, and/or removal of perquisites and benefits are dominant confrontational issues in many African countries today.

As universities have been forced to cut budgets and resource rationalization has become a reality, students have fought fiercely to maintain elements of the status quo. While students have been known to fight vigorously to ensure the continuation of their benefits or resist an increase in tuition and fees, they have not been much concerned about issues of academic quality or the curriculum. Self-interest seems to be the dominant force driving student unrest in Africa today.

University protests have led to government instability and have played different roles in political power shifts. In a few cases, they have even toppled governments. When such protests take place, officials, conscious of their possible consequences, take them seriously—often brutally crushing and subduing them. Hundreds of students have been seriously hurt, imprisoned, persecuted, and even killed during protests in Africa. According to a study by Federici and Caffentzis (2000), there were more than 110 reported student protests in Africa between the years 1990 and 1998. This study demonstrates that government responses to student protests were "inhumane," "brutal," and "excessively cruel."

Student protests are generally perceived as a reflection of the grievances of the wider community. As civil societies are slowly developed and opposition groups become legitimized and tolerated in Africa, it will be interesting to track how these protests are perceived and how they are going to evolve.

CONCLUSION

That African higher education faces severe challenges is unquestionable. This chapter has provided a discussion of some of the key problems evident throughout the continent at the beginning of the twenty-first century. The problems are difficult and may even be getting worse as the pressure for academic and institutional expansion comes into conflict with limited resources. Continuing political instability exacerbates the economic decline seen in many African countries, yet there are signs of progress as well. The emergence of democratic political systems and of a civil society is positive. The revival of academic freedom and the commitment by many in the higher education community to build successful institutions despite difficult circumstances show the viability of academic systems. A recent recognition—by the international community, particularly the leading donor agencies and major lending institutions—that African higher education is a vital area for development is also positive. African higher education is at a turning point. Recognition of the aforementioned problems can lead to positive solutions with proper planning and effective leadership.

NOTES

1. Many of the insights in this chapter come from our book *African Higher Education: An International Reference Handbook* (Teferra and Altbach 2003). See also William Saint's outstanding overview of African higher education issues (Saint 1992).

2. These figures are estimated from analyses in Teferra and Altbach (2003).

REFERENCES

Altbach, P. G. 1987. *The Knowledge Context: Comparative Perspectives on the Distribution of Knowledge*. Albany: State University of New York Press.

———. 2001. "Academic Freedom: International Realities and Challenges." *Higher Education* 41, no. 1–2: 205–219.

Altbach, P. G., ed. 1999. *Private Prometheus: Private Higher Education and Development in the 21st Century*. Westport, Conn.: Greenwood.

Altbach, P. G., and Selvaratnam, V., eds. 1989. *From Dependence to Autonomy: The Development of Asian Universities*. Dordrecht, Netherlands: Kluwer.

Ben-David, J. 1968. *Fundamental Research and the Universities*. Paris: Organization for Economic Cooperation and Development.

———. 1977. *Centers of Learning: Britain, France, Germany, United States*. New York: McGraw-Hill.

Eisemon, T. O. (1982). *The Science Profession in the Third World: Studies from India and Kenya*. New York, N.Y.: Praeger.

Federici, S., and G. Caffentzis. 2000. "Chronology of African University Students' Struggles: 1985–1998." In *A Thousand Flowers: Social Struggles against Structural Adjustment in African Universities*, edited by Silvia Federici, George Caffentzis, and Ousseina Alidou, 115–150. Trenton, N.J.: Africa World Press.

Lulat, Y. G.-M. 2003. "The Development of Higher Education in Africa: A Historical Survey." In Teferra and Altbach, *African Higher Education: An International Reference Handbook* (Bloomington, Ind.: Indiana University Press, 2003).

Musisi, N. B. 2001. "A Reflection on and Taking Stock of Innovations at Makerere University." A paper presented at the Ford Foundation conference on Innovations in African Higher Education, October 1–3, 2001, Nairobi, Kenya.

Saint, W. S. 1992. *Universities in Africa: Strategies for Stabilization and Revitalization*. Washington, D.C.: World Bank.

Sethi, M. 2000. "Return and Reintegration of Qualified African Nationals." In *Brain Drain and Capacity Building in Africa*, edited by Sibry Tapsoba, Sabiou Kassoum, Pascal V. Houenou, Bankole Oni, Meera Sethi, and Joseph Ngu, 38–48. Dakar, Senegal: ECA/IDRC/IOM.

Task Force on Higher Education and Society. 2000. *Higher Education in Developing Countries: Peril and Promise*. Washington, D.C.: World Bank.

Teferra, D. 2000. "Revisiting the Doctrine of Human Capital Mobility in the Information Age." In *Brain Drain and Capacity Building in Africa*, edited by S. Tapsoba, Sabiou Kassoum, Pascal V. Houenou, Bankole Oni, Meera Sethi, and Joseph Ngu, 38–48. Dakar, Senegal: ECA/IDRC/IOM.

———. 2002. "Scientific Communication in African Universities: External Agencies and National Needs." Ph.D. dissertation, Boston College.

Teferra, D., and Altbach, P. G., eds. 2003. *African Higher Education: An International Reference Handbook*. Bloomington: Indiana University Press.

World Bank. 1991. *The African Capacity Building Initiative: Toward Improved Policy Analysis and Development Management*. Washington, D.C.: World Bank.

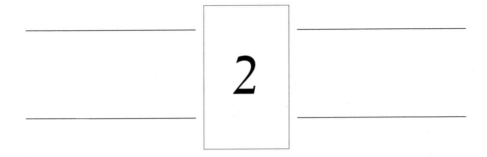

2

The Development of Higher Education in Africa
A Historical Survey

Y. G.-M. LULAT

INTRODUCTION

This chapter is an effort at both a descriptive and an analytical survey of the history of the development of higher education in Africa from antiquity to the present. From the perspective of a single book chapter, this is an ambitious project, for Africa is a huge continent, not only in geographic terms but also in terms of its wide diversity of races, ethnicities, and cultures. In addition, Africa has a complex variety of colonial legacies stemming from colonization by, initially, the Greeks, Romans, and Arabs and later by almost all the European colonial powers, including Belgium, Britain, the Netherlands, France, Portugal, and Spain. No other continent has as many countries within it as does Africa, which has more than fifty (a quarter of all the nations of the United Nations). Therefore, this chapter presents only the broadest of sketches of the history of higher education in Africa and its significance in comprehending the present.

The chapter commences, in part one, with a geographic focus on Arabic Africa. Part two examines the colonial and post-independence development of higher education in Anglophone and Europhone Africa. Part three looks at the development of higher education in countries with special historical circumstances vis-à-vis colonialism (Ethiopia, Eritrea, Liberia, and South Africa), and part four is concerned with specific themes in higher education of current relevance from a historical perspective. The chapter ends with an examination of the legacy of history. The ultimate function of history is that it allows us to understand the present; there is no present without a past, just as there is no future without a present.

The term *colonies* is used in this chapter in a loose sense to cover not only the legally defined colonies but all the territories the European powers ruled: trust territories, protectorates, and so forth. The term *higher education* refers primarily, except where indicated, to education at the university and college level.

PART I: PRECOLONIAL AFRICA

Given the high degree of resemblance between African and Western higher education institutions today, there is often the assumption that higher education in Africa is a Western colonial invention. Consequently, one must begin a historical survey of African higher education by asking whether or not higher education institutions existed in precolonial Africa. Ashby (1966, 147) states that they did, but emphasizes that they are of no relevance to the development of modern higher education in Africa today. Why? Because there is no continuity between precolonial higher education and modern African higher education, which he asserts is an entirely Western invention. Ashby, by and large, is correct about the matter of continuity but is absolutely mistaken about the second assertion.

In any case, whether or not precolonial higher education institutions in Africa have any relevance to the development of modern higher education in Africa, it is still necessary to consider them for two important reasons. First, African history does not begin with the arrival of European colonialism. For the sake of historical accuracy, any survey of the development of higher education in Africa must consider its entire history. Second, consideration of precolonial higher education helps to refute the idea that no progress would have come about in Africa without European colonialism. (Surely the existence of complex civilizations in Africa prior to the arrival of Europeans ought to have long ago put to rest any notion of a "dark" continent, immobilized in time.)

Because precolonial formal higher education was rooted in Northern Africa (much of which today is Arabic Africa), this chapter also surveys the postcolonial development of higher education in Arabic Africa.

The Library at Alexandria

The first institution on the African continent that even approximates a modern higher education institution was the famous museum and library complex at Alexandria established by the Greek rulers of Egypt, the Ptolemies, in the third century B.C. (Ajayi, Goma, and Johnson 1996). The complex, comprised of living quarters for the community of scholars that ran it, a lecture hall, a botanical garden, a zoological park, an astronomical observatory, and the great library, was founded by Ptolemy I Soter just before his death in 283 B.C. His son, Ptolemy II Philadelphus, built on his father's vision and developed the complex.

The library was a truly great monument to human knowledge, built to gather together—either through purchase or systematic copying—every available work known to the librarians. It is thought to have had more than half a million works on rolls of papyri in an age when there was no paper and no printing press. The library's presence helped to sustain a thriving publishing "industry," thereby assisting in the dissemination of the knowledge that the library acquired (and produced). From this perspective, the library was also indirectly responsible for helping to permanently preserve works that would have been lost forever when it underwent periodic and later final destruction at the hands of invaders.

The library and museum attracted scholars from near and far, including the Egyptian, Hellenic, Roman, and Judaic worlds. While the library complex did not undertake systematic teaching and credentialing of bodies of students, even though research and learning took place there, it resembled in many ways a research institute with librarians acting as scholars in residence. In this sense, then, the library was undoubtedly a type of higher education institution.

The library became the source of prodigious and remarkable intellectual scholarship which, many centuries later, through the agency of the Muslims, would help spark the European Renaissance. It boasted among its patrons such famous scholars as Archimedes, Euclid, Herophilus, Eratosthenes, Manetho, and Theophrastus (Canfora 1989; El-Abbadi 1992; and Fraser 1972). Tragically, the library, in time, declined as a result of fire accidents, civil strife, and the withering of the fortunes of the Roman Empire before its final destruction.

The Islamic Mosque Universities

On July 16, A.D. 622, Islam was effectively born with the arrival in Medina from Mecca of four fugitives, the Prophet Muhammed and three companions; yet within only twenty-two years, the Muslims had taken over the areas that today are called Saudi Arabia, Syria, and Egypt and had conquered Alexandria; by 670, they ruled most of North Africa; by 711, they were in Spain; two years later, they had arrived in Portugal, and a year later, in 714, they were in France, to be eventually stopped in their westward expansion in 732 by Charles Martel at the Battle of Poitiers.

That the library at Alexandria would suffer its final destruction at the hands of the Muslims is ironic for two reasons. First, the Muslims would become the custodians of the knowledge

that came out of that library when the lights of learning were reduced to a flicker all over Europe during the so-called Dark Ages. Second, the only known precolonial higher education institutions in Africa were those created by the Ethiopians and four institutions founded by the Muslims: the Ez-Zitouna madrassa in Tunis, founded in 732; the Quaraouiyine mosque university, founded in 859 in Fez by the Idrisids Muslim dynasty; the Al-Azhar mosque university in Cairo founded by the Abbasids Muslim dynasty in 969; and the Sankore mosque university founded by the Askia Muslim dynasty in Timbuktu in present-day Mali sometime in the twelfth century.

Except for one, Sankore, all four institutions have survived to this day, but not without undergoing major Westernizing transformations along the way. As with the later Islamic universities, such as the Nizamiyyah University (established in 1065 in Baghdad) and its successor, the Mustansiriyyah University (founded in 1234), and like the earliest medieval European universities of Bologna, Paris, Oxford, and Cambridge, these early Islamic universities stretch, to some extent, the definition of a university. Two of the critical differences between these older higher education institutions and the modern university are the curriculum the older institutions pursued and their general approach to knowledge: the curriculum was narrow and heavily religious in orientation, and their approach to knowledge lacked the secular method of rationalism and scientific inquiry.

The modern university that was brought to Africa by the colonial powers is as much Western in origin as it is Islamic. The Europeans acquired from the Muslims five elements that would be absolutely central to the foundation of the modern Western university. First, they acquired a huge corpus of knowledge that the Muslims had gathered together over the centuries through a combination of their own investigations and by gathering knowledge from other cultures as well as through translations of classical Greek texts of scholars such as Aristotle. Second, they learned rationalism from the Muslims, combined with, in Burke's words, the secular, investigative approach typical of Arab natural science (1995, 42).

The third critical element was an elaborate and intellectually sophisticated map of knowledge. The Muslims provided the Europeans a body of knowledge that was already divided into a host of academic subjects in a way that was very unfamiliar to the Europeans, including "medicine, astrology, astronomy, pharmacology, psychology, and physiology," among others (Burke 1995, 42).

The fourth was the extrication of the individual from the grip of what de Libera (1997) describes as the "medieval world of social hierarchies, obligations and highly codified social roles," so as to permit the possibility of a civil society, without which no university was possible. A university could only come into being on the basis of a community of scholars who were individuals in their own right.

The fifth was that the West took from the Muslims the institutional seed that would eventually grow into the modern university: the college, an institution that was already common in Islam. It is not surprising, therefore, that the earliest college in the West was most probably modeled on the Islamic college. This was the College des Dix-Huit founded in Paris in 1180 by

John of London who, as Makdisi (1981) observes, had just returned from a pilgrimage to Jerusalem. He most likely came to learn of the idea of the college as he passed through Muslim lands.

Arabic Africa

Colonialism came to Arabic Africa in various ways and at various times. Nearly all the European colonial powers were represented in Arabic Africa in one colonial guise or another: as so-called protectors, as claimants to spheres of influence, or as outright colonizers.

The Portuguese were the first colonial power in the region; they arrived in Morocco by capturing Ceuta in 1415. However, a century and a half later, the Moroccans threw out the Portuguese by dealing them a severe defeat in 1578. Two and a half centuries on (in 1859–1860), the Spanish invaded Morocco and, together with the French, who came in 1904, controlled different portions of it until its independence in 1956. However, full independence did not come to Morocco until 1969, because the Spaniards continued to occupy some territory and a number of cities. Given the differing economic strengths of the French and the Spanish, the predominant influence in the education sector in Morocco has been that of the French. The first modern university to be created (in 1957), the University of Rabat (reconstituted as Mohammed V. Agdal University in 1975), used French as the principal medium of instruction and was patterned on French universities. In addition to the university, the Averroes School of Applied Medicine was founded in Casablanca in 1959. Other higher education institutions present at this time were the Islamic universities of Quaraouiyine in Fez and Ben Youssef University in Marrakech. Following independence, a host of higher education institutions were established, including three created in 1975: Hassan II University (in Casablanca), Sidi Mohammed Ben Abdellah University (in Fez), and Cadi Ayyad University (in Marrakech).

Besides Morocco, the Spanish also ruled Western Sahara. The Spanish approach to colonialism was similar to that of the French in that they saw their colonies as overseas provinces. Local provision for higher education was nonexistent in Western Sahara, and to this day it has no higher education institution of any kind—in part also because of the continuing struggle for independence against Morocco, which annexed the country in 1979. The French had other colonies in Arabic Africa: Algeria, Djibouti, Libya, Mauritania, and Tunisia. Given the large French settler population, the education system in Algeria was, in relative terms, well developed by the time of independence. It boasted one of the earliest modern universities in Arabic Africa: the University of Algiers, founded in 1879.

Djibouti experienced a French colonial presence in the 1850s but did not become an overseas territory of France until 1946. It would be among the last countries in Africa to gain independence (in 1977). The relatively small size of the country has precluded it from opening its own university. Libya was ruled for a time by the Italians, the French, and the English. It gained independence in 1952. The oldest university in Libya is Al Fateh University, which was founded in 1957 as the University of Libya. In 1974, the university split into two separate institutions with the creation of the University of Garyounis in Benghazi. Other major Libyan universities are Sebha University (established in 1983 in Sebha), Al-Arab Medical University (founded in 1984 in Benghazi), and the Bright Star University of Technology (set up in 1981 in Adjabia). France took over Mauritania in 1905 as it expanded its sphere of colonization in French West Africa. The country became independent in 1960. It has only one university, the University of Nouakchott (founded in 1981 in Nouakchott). France invaded Tunisia in 1881. In 1955, after widespread nationalist agitation, Tunisia was granted limited self-rule, to be followed a year later by complete independence. Prior to independence, higher education was provided primarily by the Institut des Hautes Etudes (established in 1945) and the theologically based Ezzitouna Islamic University. Following independence in 1960, these two institutions were absorbed into the newly created University of Tunisia.

British colonialism in Arabic Africa began in Egypt in 1882 when Tawfik Pasha's government asked Britain to help it quell a mutinous army. This "temporary" British sojourn in Egypt lasted until a military coup brought Gamal Abdel Nassar to power in 1953, thus ending British colonial rule. Besides Al-Azhar University, the oldest university in Egypt is Cairo University (known for a brief period, 1940–1953, as Fouad I University). The university, established in 1908, is among the largest in Africa, with a student population today numbering more than 77,000. In 1942, the faculties of arts, law, and engineering separated from the university to form Alexandria University (known as Farouk I University up until 1953). In 1972, Alexandria would also give birth to a new university, Tanta University.

Besides Egypt, Britain also ruled a portion of Somalia that had become a British protectorate in 1887. In time, it passed into the hands of the Italians. After Somalia, the next Arabic African country to be ruled by the British was Sudan. In 1899, Sudan became a colony of Britain that lasted until 1953, when it became a sovereign state. The oldest Sudanese university is the University of Khartoum. The second oldest is the Sudan University for Science and Technology, which was originally founded in 1950 as Khartoum Technical Institute. The institute became a polytechnic in 1967 and achieved university status in 1975. In 1990, it was reconstituted to become the institution it is today. The third oldest is Omdurman Islamic University, which was originally founded as the Islamic Institute in 1912. In 1924, it became a college and in 1965 acquired university status. In 1975, it was reconstituted, assuming its present status.

The Italian presence in Arabic Africa began hesitantly. Beginning its intrusion in the Somali coastal region at the end of the nineteenth century, Italy later took control of Eritrea and Ethiopia. In 1959, the Italians established the University Institute of Somalia from an earlier institution founded in 1954. In 1970, the university was transformed to become the National University of Somalia, and in 1979, it acquired its present status as the Somali National University. The development of education, including higher education, has been set back significantly as Somalia has disintegrated into virtual anarchy–ridden "fiefdoms."

One might assume that the twin combination of the heritage of Islamic higher education and Western colonialism would create fertile conditions for a healthy development of higher education in postcolonial Arabic Africa. To some extent, it did; however, its development has been set back as a result of economic disarray and political instability in many of the countries that belong to this region.

PART II: COLONIAL AND POST-INDEPENDENCE AFRICA

British Colonial Africa

In Africa, Britain's colonial possessions numbered more than twenty, making it the largest colonial power on the continent. The countries ranged from Egypt on the Mediterranean to South Africa on the South Atlantic and from Nigeria on the Atlantic to Kenya on the Indian Ocean.

In British colonial Africa, among the first institutions of higher education to be established were those founded in the nineteenth century, including Fourah Bay College in Freetown (1826), Gordon Memorial College in Khartoum (1898), Lovedale Institution in South Africa (1841), the South African College at Cape Town (1829), the University of the Cape of Good Hope (1873), and Victoria College at Stellenbosch (1829). Until 1948, Fourah Bay College was the first and only higher education institution in all of West Africa. Consequently, in historical terms, Fourah Bay is an important institution, not only for chronological reasons but also because it came to play an important role in the genesis of a West African nationalist elite. Like many other higher education institutions in British colonial Africa, Fourah Bay was founded for the purposes of theological training through the initiative of Christian missionaries, the Church Missionary Society, based in England. Their motives for establishing Fourah Bay were similar to those of other missionaries working in colonial Africa. European Christian missionaries became involved with formal education almost from the moment they arrived in Africa for a number of reasons specific to their proselytizing mission, including the promotion of literacy to facilitate religious instruction and the training of local teachers and pastors to accelerate evangelization (Berman 1975).

In the early years of British colonialism, direct government involvement in the provision of formal education was minimal, restricted by and large to providing subventions to educational institutions founded and run by missionaries. In fact, as Ashby (1966) observes, there was no formal educational policy for the colonies in Africa in the period preceding the First World War. A partial explanation for this situation lies in the general view held in the nineteenth century by Europeans that Africans were uneducable because they were considered intellectually inferior—notwithstanding the protestations of the missionaries to the contrary (Lyons 1970). According to Nwauwa (1996), other factors included resistance from colonial officials in the colonies who did not wish to lose their jobs to educated Africans and British wariness of increasing expenditures in the colonies.

The first official effort, of a kind, to investigate the state of educational provision in the colonies took place, according to Lyons (1970), through the agency of Dr. Richard R. Madden, who was sent to West Africa as the royal commissioner broadly charged with a survey of the political, economic, and other conditions in the settlements of Gambia, Sierra Leone, and the Gold Coast. In the report he submitted in 1841, he preposterously indicated, on the basis of the flimsiest evidence, that while the African exhibited a learning capability in his childhood comparable to that of the European, by the time he or she reached adulthood, this capability had atrophied significantly to the point where the African was now intellectually inferior. (He blamed this development, in consonance with the pseudoscientific thinking of his day, on Africa's tropical climate.) He recommended that the schooling of Africans should be aimed at teaching nonintellectual pursuits, specifically vocational training.

Madden's basic message, that Western education should be adapted to the special circumstances of Africans, was reiterated in different guises and eventually became part of official educational policy for a time. By the early 1920s, not only had Britain committed itself to the colonial project of the post–1884 Berlin Conference era but the missionary presence in the educational field in the African colonies had grown sufficiently to exert pressure on the British government to play a larger role in the provision of education in the colonies. The specific mechanism involved was the publication of the findings of a U.S. missionary–instigated commission, the Phelps-Stokes Commission, on the state of education in British colonial Africa in 1922. This report, coupled with perennial demands for education from Africans themselves (in the 1920s, the call would be taken up by nationalists such as J. E. Casely Hayford, the founder of the National Congress of British West Africa) and the increasingly clear recognition in the corridors of Whitehall that colonial overlordship should gradually be replaced with colonial "trusteeship," prompted the government to establish a permanent advisory committee in 1923.

With the Advisory Committee on Education in the Colonies, the British government became formally and actively involved with the development of education in its colonies. The committee, through its advice to the colonial secretary, set the tone for British colonial policy on education in the African colonies:

- To supplement and not to compete with the existing missionary educational effort
- To extend the benefits of basic literacy to as many people as resources would permit
- To provide training for the development of a cadre of low-level government officials (such as office clerks, interpreters, and messengers)
- To provide vocational educational opportunities
- To permit the development of some level of further education, especially in such areas as teacher, agricultural, veterinary, and paramedical training (Brown 1964)

In sum, the first formally adopted policy on education by the British was largely determined by the educational philosophy enunciated by the Phelps-Stokes Commission, namely, to adapt Western education to the colonial circumstance of the Africans by emphasizing industrial and vocational training at the expense of literary and academic education (Ajayi, Goma, and Johnson 1996).

Initially, official educational policy paid scant attention to the provision of higher education; however, this situation would change by the approach of the Second World War. Through a number of committees and reports, the British moved to establish higher education in a number of its African territories on a firm footing (Ashby 1966). As the Second World War ended, the British colonial secretary, acting in the spirit of the generally accepted view in British ruling circles that independence in its colonies was simply a matter of time, appointed the Asquith Commission. Headed by Justice Cyril Asquith, its mandate was to look into the establishment of university colleges (with affiliation to universities in Britain) in the colonies, in line with the ideas that had been formulated by Currie, De La Warr, Channon, and others. Many recognized that if the colonies were to achieve independence, then indigenization of the government civil service and establishment of more primary and secondary schools would create a demand for trained leadership and human capital resources.

In an impressively short time, on the recommendation of the commission's report, which was published in 1945, a number of higher education institutions (sometimes referred to as the Asquith Colleges) were established through the agency of a remarkable and admirable combination of British government finance (facilitated by the Colonial Development and Welfare Acts of 1940 and 1950) and British university expertise in the form of the Inter-University Council for Higher Education in the Colonies (established in 1946). These institutions, which for the most part were an upgrade of existing ones, were to be residential and provide a university-level education that emphasized liberal arts and the sciences. Their governance involved British universities (principally the University of London) and the Inter-University Council. Graduates of the Asquith Colleges received their degrees from the University of London on the basis of the affiliation of the colleges to the university. While the council was responsible for recruiting staff, the university, in cooperation with the faculty of the colleges, set the curricular and examination standards. Examples of the Asquith Colleges include: University College of Ghana (at Legon, opened in October 1948 with an enrollment of 92 students); University College of Sierra Leone (established by upgrading the existing Fourah Bay College in 1960, with an enrollment of about 350 students); University College at Ibadan (opened in 1947 with 104 students); Khartoum University College (created in 1949 by merging the existing Gordon Memorial College and the Kitchener Medical School, with an enrollment of close to 1,700 by 1961); Makerere College (upgraded in 1949, with an enrollment of some 1,000 by independence); the Royal Technical College at Nairobi (founded in 1951, with approximately 500 students at independence); and the segregated University College of Salisbury (established in 1953, but upgraded two years later to become the University College of Rhodesia and Nyasaland, with affiliation to the University of London and an enrollment in 1961 of about 250 students).

On the eve of independence, some form of higher education at the university level was in place in most of British colonial Africa. Moreover, its rigor and quality was comparable to that in the metropole (Ashby 1966, 256). However, establishment of full-fledged university education in which institutions would grant their own degrees would have to await independence.

The Era of National Universities

The end of colonial rule ushered in a new phase in the history of higher education in Africa: the era of national universities. Country after country, in the wake of independence, founded national universities either by creating completely new institutions or by transforming existing ones. The impetus for the development of this phase grew out of a mixture of nationalistic ambitions (the national university joined such other symbols of sovereignty as the flag, the national anthem, the international airport, the national bank, a national currency, etc.) and genuinely perceived discontent with the university colleges that the colonial powers had established.

The British, understandably, had looked to their own universities for models when creating the Asquith Colleges. At the time the colleges were set up, general African opinion in Anglophone Africa was that the British university model was the best one and that any modification of it would imply a lowering of standards. In Ashby's words, "The debate was overwhelmingly in favor of preserving the British academic heritage" (1966, 236). Most African leadership circles considered an indigenous degree from the newly created colleges to be inferior. Even the idea of adapting the curriculum was initially resisted by Africans for fear that it would mean dilution of quality and standards.

However, despite the initial preferences of the African leadership elite, the British university model was not the most appropriate for the specific circumstances of Africa. In response, some proposed a model that incorporated two key features of the land-grant colleges in the United States: democratic student recruitment and democratic degree structures and curricular outlay (Ajayi, Goma, and Johnson 1996). Perhaps not surprisingly, therefore, the first major higher education commission to advise an independent African country was funded by the United States and U.S. educators (the Ashby Commission).

Elsewhere in former British colonial Africa, the early 1960s saw the attempt to implement a bold experiment in East Africa with the creation of an autonomous, degree-granting, federated university (still supervised to some extent by the Inter-University Council in London), the Federal University of East Africa. The federation included three constituent colleges: the Royal University College (formerly a technical college) in Kenya, Makerere University College in Uganda, and the newly established University College of Dar es Salaam in Tanzania. Among other things, such a university would serve as an important symbol of unification in the new East African Community, but with its collapse, the federated university also fragmented. The three constituent units emerged as independent universities: Makerere University, the University of Nairobi, and the University of Dar es Salaam.

Sir John Lockwood was also responsible for the creation of a university in a country, Zambia, that was once part of yet another failed experiment at political unification of contiguous

British colonies with shared elements of colonial and precolonial history: the partially autonomous Federation of Rhodesia and Nyasaland, located in the upper reaches of Southern Africa. Lockwood chaired the committee that was instrumental in founding the University of Zambia in 1966, an independent institution with an initial enrollment of about 300 students.

The newly created African universities represented a move to a university education that was characterized by structural diversity, flexibility, and curricular relevance without sacrificing high quality and standards. The specific changes that this move entailed included

- The move away from a specialized single-subject honors degree in the arts to a general degree in any number of fields, including professional fields of study
- The broadening of the disciplinary structure to include medicine and applied technology, specifically the various fields of engineering
- The expansion of curricula to include vocational subjects
- The move from a three-year degree to a four-year degree in order to eliminate the sixth-form A-level General Certificate in Education as a university entrance requirement (entrance requirements would be based on the fifth form O-level, thereby broadening the field of student recruitment)
- The dedication of the first year to a general program of study with required courses
- The postponement of specialization to the graduate level
- The broadening of the mission of the university to include community outreach through programs such as agricultural extension services, public health education, extramural evening courses, and long-distance correspondence courses

Independence permitted some African countries to modify the British model to better suit their circumstances by turning to a model of higher education developed in yet another former British colonial possession: the United States.

Belgian Africa

The transformation in 1908 of the Congo Free State from a personal fiefdom of Belgian's King Leopold II to a Belgian colony renamed Belgian Congo after an international outcry against the horrors perpetrated by his agents on the Congolese people created a modicum of support for educational development in the Congo, in cooperation with the missionaries. The educational policy that the Belgians pursued was based on the idea that all administrative posts were to be held by Belgians; therefore, the primary purpose of education was to provide vocational training for the Congolese. The only ones who were to have access to literary education were the select few chosen for priesthood. Following the Second World War, a slight change in policy was made with the implementation of an academic-oriented curriculum at the secondary level and the establishment of the Lovanium University Center in 1949 in Kinshasha. The center became the overseas campus of the Catholic University of Louvain in Belgium in 1954.

Independence came to Belgian Congo on June 30, 1960, quickly and unexpectedly. The Belgians had not planned for it, nor were the Congolese ready for it. Perhaps not surprisingly, the postindependence history of this country has been marked by military dictatorships, kleptocracy, massive violations of human rights, economic chaos, and civil war (Kelly 1993; Nzongola-Ntalaja 1988). Given this awful post-independence history, the development of higher education, like almost every other aspect of civil society, suffered enormous setbacks.

Besides Belgian Congo, the Belgians had also ruled the small but densely populated neighboring territory of Ruanda-Urundi, which they had inherited from the Germans as trust territories. As in the Congo, educational provision in Ruanda-Urundi was left primarily in the hands of Catholic missionaries. Local higher education opportunity for the very select few came only with the creation of the University of the Belgian Congo and Ruanda-Urundi. (Lovanium University would also become available for students from Ruanda-Urundi.) In 1960, however, a truly local institution was established with the founding of the University of Ruanda-Urundi in Usumbura. The university had all of two departments (agronomy and applied science) and an enrollment of thirty. In 1962, this territory became independent and became two countries: Rwanda and Burundi. A year later, the National University of Rwanda was founded in Butare, while Burundi had already established its own university, the University of Burundi in Bujumbura, in 1960.

Because of the presence of centuries-old ethnic rivalries between the minority Nilo-Hamitic—the Tutsi—and the majority Bantu peoples—the Hutu—both countries have experienced genocidal conflagrations of mind-numbing proportions (Gourevitch 1998; Prunier 1995). Given this backdrop, all forms of education, including higher education, would come to periodic standstills in both countries. Although meaningful progress had been achieved in developing the universities in both countries in the 1980s, today the situation in Rwanda is one of retrogression, while Burundi is only slightly better in comparison.

Francophone Africa

In the decades leading up to the eve of the Second World War, the colonial policies of assimilation and association pursued by the French in Africa, based on the absurd claim that its African colonies were provinces of France separated from the mother country only by geography, ensured that, in comparative terms, the development of any form of formal education, let alone higher education, would be weakly developed or almost nonexistent in the African colonies. This was an outcome of several factors. First, the French government, unlike the British, did not usually encourage missionaries to establish educational facilities because it felt that the primary purpose of Western education was to universalize French secular culture, not evangelization (Mumford 1970). Second, it staffed the civil service in the colonies almost exclusively with French personnel at all levels, including even the clerical level; as a result, the demand for trained African clerical personnel was considerably dampened. Third, unlike in the case of French colonies in Indochina, the Africans did not possess an autonomous and indigenous formal educational system that would have required replacement in the interest of political stability in the colonial order. In the areas where Islam was dominant, some formal schooling existed in the form of the Quranic schools, but the French did not see such schooling as an incubator of oppositional culture (Kelly 1984).

As for the almost total absence of higher education, two factors were critical: a poorly developed lower-level educational tributary system and the belief that higher education was best provided in France itself for the few elite Africans (the *evolue*) who qualified (Ajayi, Goma, and Johnson 1996). Ashby (1966, 368) also mentions one social force that initially discouraged the development of higher education in French colonial Africa: the African elite itself. That is, even after the French had become relatively more aggressive in creating a formal educational system at the primary and secondary levels (especially after the Second World War), the African elite was concerned that local institutions would be inferior, either in perception or in reality, to those in France. The allure of education in the metropole meant that African *évolués* were often less interested in the development of local higher education than in ensuring that Africans would continue to receive higher education in France.

Up until the 1950s, therefore, the only higher education institutions in all of French colonial Africa that are worthy of mention are the Tananarive Medical Institute (founded in 1896); a medical college in Dakar created in 1918 (later reconstituted in 1948 as the Medical and Pharmaceutical School); the Insitut Français d'Afrique Noire (founded in Dakar in 1938 for the purpose of research into Arab and African societies); the Ecole Normal William Ponty (established in Goree in 1903 and named after Governor William Ponty), which provided teacher training and rudimentary medical training; the School of Marine Engineering (in Goree); and a school of veterinary medicine and a polytechnic in Bamako.

However, with the commencement of the 1950s, the French became more cognizant of their higher education responsibilities in the colonies, prompted in part by the increasing cost of educating Africans at French universities and in part out of a conscious and unabashed belief that they had to do more to culturally bind the colonies to the metropole in preparation for the eventuality of some form of political autonomy in the colonies.

Consequently, France began to create overseas branches of French universities in the African colonies in the form of institutes of higher education that in time became the basis for national universities. In Madagascar, for instance, besides the school of medicine, institutes for law, science, and education were created by French universities at various times, beginning in 1941. They were eventually gathered together in 1960 to form the University of Tananarive, which was reconstituted in 1973 as the University of Madagascar.

In developing these universities, the French made absolutely sure that they would not be autonomous institutions. Given its assimilationist policy, and considering that the French higher education system is highly bureaucratized, this was, perhaps, to be expected. The French government plays a very intrusive role through administrative decrees in the day-to-day operations of the university. When France established higher education institutions in the colonies, therefore, they were virtually the overseas campuses of French universities. So, for example, when the University of Dakar was established, a decree from the French Ministry of Education named it the eighteenth university in the French higher education system. Initially, Africans themselves

would not have it any other way. Close administrative and curricular alliances with French higher education institutions held the promise, even if not always realized in practice, of fluid transitions between institutions in the former colonies and in the metropole for students and staff as well as the equivalency of educational qualifications in the Francophone world, irrespective of the geographic location of the awarding institutions.

In fact, even after independence, universities in the former French colonies continued to maintain strong administrative links with French universities. At least in the immediate postindependence period, then, one could state without any hesitation that the university in Francophone Africa was a very close copy of the university in France (Ashby 1966, 371). France not only took care of staffing the institutions, but it was even responsible for their financing, at least into the early part of the post-independence period (Ajayi, Goma, and Johnson 1996).

As the first decade of political independence drew to a close and the 1970s began, the close higher education ties that had existed between France and the independent Francophone countries started to loosen. France relinquished its financial responsibility for the higher education institutions in these countries. This occurred in the areas of personnel and the curriculum. That is, hesitant but clearly perceptible Africanization of the universities was now underway. Ratios between African and French teaching staff, for example, began to change favorably in the direction of the Africans. This Africanization took place for three principal reasons: the growth of educators' confidence, arising out of experience and maturity, that they could develop in autonomous directions; an increasing awareness of the obviousness of the necessity for adapting higher education to local needs and circumstances; and the development of resurgent nationalism (Ajayi, Goma, and Johnson 1996).

The 1970s also saw two other important developments regarding higher education in Francophone Africa. First, the smaller countries that had not acquired their own universities at independence were now busy setting up university-centered national higher education systems, many on the basis of higher education centers created in the preceding decade. Second, the pace of enrollment in higher education institutions escalated rapidly; student populations virtually exploded, multiplying in some instances by three to four times the original numbers of the preceding decade (Ajayi, Goma, and Johnson 1996).

Higher education came to French colonial Africa relatively late compared to British colonial Africa, but the French soon made up for the delay. At the same time, universities in former French colonial Africa have benefited greatly in infrastructural terms from their close association with the French—much more so than the universities in former British colonial Africa. However, this close association has also come with a price: the space for experimentation and adaptation has been narrowly confined. Even today, one is struck by how closely universities in Francophone Africa continue to be patterned on the French model.

Lusophone Africa

Portugal's education policy in its African colonies paralleled that of the French. Higher education was reserved only for an elite few (the *assimilado*) and was provided in Portugal to ensure authenticity (Kitchen 1962). Such a policy reflected the interests of the relatively resource-poor Portuguese colonial government, which also had a long history of neglecting the education of its own people in Portugal itself (Samuels 1970). Despite the fact that the Portuguese were in Africa for a far longer period than any other colonial power (from the late fifteenth century), their educational record was absolutely abysmal. In fact, it is thought that the illiteracy rate among Africans in 1958 was close to 100 percent in Angola and Mozambique (Kitchen 1962; Azvedo 1980).

No form of higher education existed in Portuguese colonial Africa until the early 1960s. In 1962, however, Portugal set up two higher education institutions that in 1968 would become the University of Luanda and the University of Lourenco Marques. Both, though, were established to serve primarily the children of the Portuguese settlers. Out of a student population of 540 at the University of Lourenco Marques in 1966, only one student was a Mozambican African (Azvedo 1970, 199).

The Portuguese were forced to leave their colonies in 1975 as a result of wars of liberation fought by African nationalists in the three colonies of Angola, Guinea-Bissau, and Mozambique. In Angola and Mozambique, this forcible exit, however, did not really spell peace. The two countries would descend into chaos of unimaginable proportions, and Angola has yet to see peace (Ciment 1997; Maier 1996; Stockwell 1997).

This postcolonial history has had a very negative impact on educational development. Still, universities now exist in Angola and Mozambique. In Angola, the original University of Luanda became the University of Agostinho Neto in 1985. It has campuses in Huango and Lubango. In Mozambique, the University of Laurenço Marques became the Eduardo Mondlane University Maputo in 1976. Mozambique also boasts two other public higher education institutions: the Higher Institute for International Relations and Pedagogical University.

Portugal's other two former colonies, Guinea-Bissau and São Tomé and Principe, do not have universities. Guinea-Bissau, however, does have a number of teacher training colleges.

PART III: ETHIOPIA, ERITREA, LIBERIA, AND SOUTH AFRICA

These four countries merit separate treatment because of their unique historical circumstances: of the first three, Ethiopia and Liberia did not experience Western colonial rule. As for South Africa, while it was once a colony of Britain, it had long achieved independence from it. However, its uniqueness stems from the fact that independence did not lead to democracy by way of majority rule but instead by minority rule based on severe racism, militarism, and authoritarianism.

Ethiopia

Any discussion of higher education in Ethiopia must begin with a chronological demarcation between the modern and the pre-modern periods. In the pre-modern period, which stretches back hundreds of years to the founding of the Kingdom of Ak-

sum in the first century A.D., higher education was essentially theological. The antecedent of its development was the conversion of the kingdom to Christianity in the early part of the fourth century through the missionary effort of Saint Frumentius (d. A.D. 383). The Ethiopian Church set up a monastic educational system (beginning probably in the twelfth century) that eventually became in practice the preserve of the ruling elite. Its graduates were destined for either secular or religious leadership (or both), depending upon their lineage. The pinnacle of this educational system, which usually took twenty-eight years to reach, according to Wagaw (1990), was occupied by a higher education institution known as Metsahift Bet (or the School of Holy Books). Wagaw states that the Metsahift Bet was "in essence a university where the whole approach to learning, including the qualifications of the professors, methods of teaching and learning, and the popular attitude toward the leadership of the community of scholars, reflected maturity of mind and the ideal of democracy in action" (1979, 21).

However, the failure of the Ethiopian monastic educational system to adapt to changing circumstances—the shortcoming of all theologically based pre-modern educational systems—would eventually render it irrelevant. The modernization of Ethiopia would see the call for wholesale replacement of the monastic system with a secular and modern educational system, complete with a modern university that had no tangible connection with the pre-modern period.

The modern period of higher education commenced with the expulsion of the Italians from Ethiopia. Ethiopia, like Liberia, was never truly a colony of any European power. To be sure, it suffered foreign occupation during the Italian invasion, but it was only for a brief period. The Italian occupation of Ethiopia was marked by the unusual bar against all efforts to develop Western-style education already underway under the aegis of Emperor Haile Selassie. Educational development in Ethiopia had to await Italy's defeat and the end of the Second World War.

Efforts to develop higher education resumed in Ethiopia with the creation of Trinity College in 1949. Initial enrollment at Trinity was twenty-one students, and the language of instruction was English. In July 1950, the college was upgraded and became the University College of Addis Ababa. Unlike other college-level higher education institutions in colonial Africa, the University College did not have a direct affiliation with any overseas university. Instead, the Ethiopians invited educators from different countries to help in the development of higher education—in some cases, individually and in others, through the mechanism of bilateral and multilateral aid agreements. In fact, Trinity College was founded with the assistance of Canadian Jesuits. Tentative efforts were made to affiliate Trinity College to the University of London, but the Ethiopians decided to go it alone because they found that too many strings were attached to the affiliation (Wagaw 1990).

Between 1950 and 1961, the college underwent considerable expansion, adding a variety of university-level fields of study, including biology, law, education, social work, and business administration. In 1961, the college became Haile Selassie I University with the assistance of foreign aid from the United States and other countries. In 1975, with the abolition of the monarchy, the university was renamed Addis Ababa University. Its student population today is approximately 20,000. Ethiopia's other principal higher education institution is the Alemaya University of Agriculture, which was founded in 1985 by incorporating the College of Agriculture that was established in 1954.

Eritrea

In 1952, Eritrea became a federated part of Ethiopia when the Allies dissolved the Italian colonies after the Second World War. During the short period of the federation, a higher education institution was founded in Asmara, Eritrea's capital, in 1958. This institution was the basis of the University of Asmara, founded in 1991, which had an enrollment of about 4,000 in 2000. The language of instruction in the new university, interestingly, is not Italian, but English. After a long armed struggle, Eritrea became independent in 1993.

Liberia

Liberia was founded at Cape Mesurado in 1820 as a coastal settlement for free African Americans who had gained freedom from slavery. The force behind this enterprise was the American Colonization Society, which had managed to settle close to 19,000 African-American settlers in Liberia by the time the U.S. Civil War broke out.

The first higher education institution in Liberia, founded with the help of grants from a Boston-based philanthropy, the Trustees of Donations for Education in Liberia, was Liberia College at Monrovia. It opened in 1862. Missionary educational activity in Liberia by the U.S.-based Protestant Episcopal Church would lead to the establishment of other higher education institutions: the Hoffman Institute, a vocational college, in 1889, and a divinity school in 1897. The institute and the divinity school became the basis of an upgraded institution in 1949 called the Cuttington University College. After a major fire burned Liberia College to the ground, it was rebuilt and reopened as the University of Liberia in 1951. The university also incorporated two other institutions: the College of West Africa (a teacher training college founded in 1838) and the Booker T. Washington Institute (which became the university's School of Agricultural and Mechanical Arts). As would be expected, the general pattern of governance and the curriculum were patterned on U.S. educational institutions. Liberia's formal education and other institutions suffered a severe setback during nearly two decades of violent civil war, starting in the 1980s.

South Africa and Namibia

The development of higher education in South Africa, as in most other parts of British colonial Africa, began with missionary initiatives. Missionary societies such as the Paris Evangelical Mission, the London Missionary Society, and the Scottish Presbyterian Mission all felt the need to establish higher education institutions in the areas of pastoral, teacher, and agriculture training as a logical extension of their evangelical work. Among the better known early missionary-founded higher education in-

stitutions was the Lovedale Institution, established by the Presbyterians in 1841. It was modeled on African-American colleges of the day, including the Hampton Institute and the Tuskegee Institute in the United States. It emphasized industrial and vocational training and for the most part eschewed liberal arts.

Since racial segregation had always been part of South African history from the first day Jan van Ribeeck and his party stepped ashore in 1652, missionary educational activity was not limited to an African clientele. Supported by government subventions, private higher education initiatives led, for example, to the establishment of the South African College in Cape Town in 1829 for the English-speaking Anglo South Africans, and Victoria College for the Afrikaans-speaking Dutch South Africans (Boers) in Stellenbosch. The earliest government foray into higher education, however, was initially limited to the creation of an examining body in 1858, the Board of Public Examinations in Literature and Science, which was responsible for administering exams to graduates of various colleges with the aim of standardizing higher education credentials. The functions of the board were taken over in 1873 by a nonteaching institution, the University of the Cape of Good Hope (today the University of South Africa).

Although Dr. James Stewart of Lovedale called for a government-funded college for Africans in 1902, its fruition would await the formation of the union. The college opened its doors as the Inter-State Native College in 1916 with just two teaching staff and twenty-two students. In time, the college evolved toward the model of the white university colleges and acquired the right to prepare its students for the external degree examinations offered by the University of South Africa. In 1951, it was reconstituted as the University College of Fort Hare and affiliated with Rhodes University in Grahamstown. With the creation of the "homeland" political system after it had become a university in 1969, Fort Hare came under the control of the homeland government of the Ciskei in 1986. Today, with the homeland system, it is part of the South African higher education system and has a student enrollment of about 6,000.

In 1948, the government of Jan Christiaan Smuts was replaced by the National Party–led government of Daniel Malan following the defeat of Smuts's United Party in the national, whites-only elections of that year. This change would herald the beginnings of a racially segregated, highly oppressive, semi-fascist political, social, and economic structure that came to be called apartheid (Afrikaans for "separateness"). Of the various pieces of legislation that underpinned the development, over the years, of the apartheid system, two are particularly relevant: the 1959 Extension of Universities Education Act and the 1959 Promotion of Bantu Self-Government Act. The former forbade blacks from attending predominantly white universities without prior approval from the government, while the latter created pseudo-sovereign internal states called "homelands" for various black ethnic groups (out of the 13 percent black land reserves). Under the apartheid regime, therefore, building on the preexisting higher education system, there arose three sets of higher education institutions: one for blacks in the cities (such as the University of the Western Cape); one for blacks in the homelands (such as the University of the North); and one for whites (such as the University of Cape Town). The apartheid system, under the pressures of internal and external agitation and structural contradictions, eventually crumbled.

POST-APARTHEID SOUTH AFRICA (PASA)

In 1994, the apartheid system officially came to an end with the election of the African National Congress under the leadership of Nelson Mandela. This marked the second independence of South Africa (the first being its freedom from British colonial rule in 1910). How has the higher education sector fared in the new and still evolving, but radically different, political and economic climate in the post-apartheid South Africa (PASA)? It depends upon one's perspective. There is no question that in the central and most overriding task facing higher education in PASA, democratization, great strides have been made, especially at the level of enrollments. Institution after institution that had historically served an almost all-white student population have seen major demographic changes, so that black African students in some cases now approach a majority (Vergnani 1998).

Yet it is already clear that the road ahead is littered with daunting obstacles that are endemic to desegregating and decolonizing societies. Among these obstacles are democratizing student finance, combating the embezzlement and mismanagement of funds, ensuring the future of former apartheid black universities, implementing affirmative action policies at former apartheid white universities, ensuring curricular relevance, limiting brain drain among university personnel, restructuring higher education, and coping with the rising burden of state financing of higher education.

PART IV: THEMATIC PERSPECTIVES

The purpose of this section is to discuss from a historical perspective a number of issues that are of central concern today in African higher education, including equality of higher educational opportunity for women, the role of external aid in the development of African higher education, the direct role of higher education in the development process through community service, and the development of private universities.

Women's Access and Sex Equity

As early as 1933, a British government educational policy report (the Currie Report) advanced proposals concerning the education of women: "Women's education is retarded by the understandable reluctance of women to proceed overseas. Until there is in Africa provision for University Education in some form or the other, it will only be very rarely that a woman will proceed beyond the secondary stage" (Ashby 1966). Much progress has been made in extending higher education access to women since that report was issued. This fact is attested to by the increase in female participation rates at the tertiary level for Africa as a whole from 1970 (by which time most countries in Africa had experienced at least a decade of independence) to 1997 (the year for which latest data is available). In 1970, total female enrollment in tertiary institutions in Africa was 111,000. By 1997, it had reached 1,802,000, a 1,623-percent increase

Table 2.1. Women's Enrollment in Tertiary-Level Education by Percentage of Total Enrollment

Year	Africa	All Developing Countries	World
1970	23	29	38
1997	38	40	47
Percent Increase	65	38	24

Source: UNESCO 1999.

Table 2.2. Gross Enrollment Ratio in Tertiary-Level Education by Gender

	Africa		All Developing Countries		World	
Year	Female	Male	Female	Male	Female	Male
1970	0.7	2.4	1.7	4.0	7.1	11.2
1997	5.2	8.6	8.6	12.0	16.7	18.1

Source: UNESCO 1999.

(compared to a global increase of about 288 percent and a 761-percent increase for developing countries).

Absolute numbers provide a simplistic picture of these increases. It is necessary to consider female enrollment as a percentage of total tertiary-level enrollment and gross enrollment ratios (the ratio between total actual enrollments and the total estimated age group eligible for enrollment for a given educational level). From this perspective, one can see that progress has still been substantial, but not as significant as it seems from gross enrollment figures alone (see Tables 2.1 and 2.2).

Two other facts ought to be also noted: first, that the data does not include consideration of students who are studying abroad (though one can surmise that female participation in foreign higher education is likely to be even lower than that for local higher education, for both historical and cultural reasons). Second, it goes without saying that averages mask internal variations. Therefore, when one looks at individual African countries, the picture is highly varied. Consider the tertiary-level female gross enrollment ratios for the following countries for the year 1995: Chad: 0.2 percent; Burkina Faso: 0.5 percent; Lesotho: 2.5 percent; Egypt: 15.9 percent; Mauritius: 6.1 percent; Namibia: 9.9 percent; South Africa: 16.5 percent (figure is for 1994); Tanzania: 0.1 percent; and Tunisia: 11.6 percent (UNESCO 1999).

Still, whether one looks at individual countries or the continent as a whole, there is no question that considerable progress has been achieved in Africa in extending access to higher education to women since independence. Yet to say that much still remains to be done would be a gross understatement. Participation rates must improve until they reflect the population as a whole. This goal, however, is contingent on arriving at parity in enrollment levels at the secondary school level, which also remains to be achieved. Simultaneously, the widespread and persistent underrepresentation of females needs to be tackled, particularly in key areas of certain fields of study (for example, science and technology fields), in decision-making positions at the levels of both teaching and administration, in leadership positions, and in shaping the curriculum in terms of relevance to gender-related issues.

Considering that women constitute a majority of the population in most countries of Africa, there is need for a concerted effort to address all these problems. This should be done for human and civil rights reasons, to foster economic development, and to foster democracy. A dialectical relationship exists between expanding women's access to higher education and mounting an assault on patriarchy—the dominant principle governing social relations in Africa. Yet throughout the continent, patriarchy has been resurgent as women's (and children's) human and civil rights have been flagrantly violated on a massive scale.

External Aid and the Development of Higher Education

For any country, higher education is not only highly dependent on resources but is a relatively complex sector of the economy. By its very nature, higher education is a fusion of extremely heavy capital expenditures and highly labor-intensive processes such as teaching, learning, and research. Funding for higher education takes place within a context of fiscally burdensome and permanently recurrent budgetary allocations (for salaries, stipends, and utilities, for example). Not surprisingly, the development of modern higher education in Africa has always depended on external assistance. In fact, every single African country has been a supplicant, in one form or another, for such assistance (which, however, in the postindependence period has not been as forthcoming as originally hoped). Initially, such assistance came from the missionaries and the colonial administrations. However, during both the colonial period and throughout the postindependence period, other overseas actors and agencies have also played a highly critical support role. During the colonial period, overseas higher education institutions and overseas private philanthropic organizations played the most important support role. In the postindependence period, foreign governments, multilateral development agencies, and foreign scholarly societies also became central funding agents.

Overseas Higher Education Institutions: The Colonial Period

During the colonial period, the role played by overseas higher education institutions in the development of higher education in Africa took three basic forms:

- Through overseas training of African students
- Through externally run secondary school (and even university-level) examinations
- Directly through institutional affiliation and the granting of external degrees

In the absence of university-level higher education institutions in most of colonial Africa, many of the educated African elite who would come to provide leadership of the nationalist movements throughout Africa received their education at overseas higher education institutions. While overseas, they not only

had access to richly diverse curricula, they were also exposed to new and radical currents of political ideas (such as the Pan-Africanism of Marcus Garvey and W. E. B. DuBois) generated by a commingling of fellow overseas students from a variety of countries in the colonial empires (Adi 1998).

Not surprisingly, the rise of African nationalism was accompanied by demands for the establishment of higher education institutions in Africa itself. In fact, almost all the African nationalists prominently associated with the development of higher education in Africa (J. K. Aggrey, Nnamdi Azikiwe, Edward Blyden, Africanus Horton, D. D. T. Jabavu, and James Johnson) received their education overseas.

Overseas Private Philanthropic Organizations: The Colonial Period

The Phelps-Stokes Foundation holds a unique position among private philanthropic foundations responsible for the development of higher education in colonial Africa. For a short time, the foundation played an important role through the agency of the Phelps-Stokes African Education Commission. The commission was established in 1919 at the request of the Foreign Missions Conference of North America (prodded by the American Baptist Foreign Mission Society) and was charged with studying and making recommendations about the education of Africans in British colonial Africa.

The commission went to Africa in 1920; it was led by Dr. Thomas Jesse Jones (a white U.S. educator who was the executive secretary of the foundation and president of the Hampton Institute). Interestingly, Jones chose as his co-director a Ghanaian, James K. Aggrey. At the time of his appointment, Aggrey had been teaching for some two decades at Livingstone College in North Carolina. Both Jones and Aggrey were strongly influenced by the prevalent ideas of how best to educate African Americans, chiefly by ideas propounded by people such as Booker T. Washington and Chapman Armstrong, who emphasized practical (vocational) education rather than general academic education (King 1971).

Not surprisingly, the recommendations of the Phelps-Stokes Commission were not received with equanimity by everyone; they drew considerable criticism from sections of the black community on both sides of the Atlantic. In the United States, W. E. B. DuBois, Marcus Garvey, and the historian Carter Woodson accused the commission of advocating education designed to "create an obedient, docile, fundamentally conservative black underclass" (Hull 1990, 159). In Africa, James S. Thaele, a leading pro-Garvey African National Congress official in Cape Town, who himself had studied in the United States, described Aggrey as "a me-too-boss-hat-in-hand nigger" (Hill and Pirio 1987, 229).

Foundations that have been involved with higher education assistance in the postcolonial-period Africa include the Carnegie Corporation, the Edward W. Hazen Foundation, the W. K. Kellogg Foundation, the Ford Foundation, the John D. and Catherine T. MacArthur Foundation, and the Rockefeller Foundation. These foundations provide assistance either directly or, more commonly, through contracts with individual U.S. universities or through such U.S. organizations as the American Council on Education, the Institute of International Education (which also administers the Fulbright exchange program), and the African-American Institute.

In 2000, a consortium of four U.S. philanthropic foundations began an initial five-year partnership program (renewable for another five years) to assist select universities in a number of African countries, including Kenya, Nigeria, Mozambique, South Africa, Tanzania, and Uganda. The four foundations are the Carnegie Corporation, the Ford Foundation, the John D. and Catherine T. MacArthur Foundation, and the Rockefeller Foundation (Carnegie Corporation 2000).

Overseas Governments: The Post-Independence Period

The post-independence development of higher education in Africa, especially in the early years, was greatly assisted by external bilateral government support, without which African higher education would have not have seen as much progress as it has. During this period, higher education had not yet fallen into disrepute in policy circles at the World Bank and at United Nations agencies. The kinds of bilateral support received by higher education in countries throughout independent Africa reflected the complexity of that sector. That is, almost every aspect of higher education was targeted for support, including assistance with building construction, provision of student scholarships for staff development, payment of partial or whole salaries of local and externally recruited staff, assistance with logistical purchases (including library materials, computers, and lab equipment), and assistance with the establishment of programs of study.

Among the prominent country donors (and their relevant aid agencies) were Belgium, Canada (Canadian International Development Agency), former Eastern Bloc countries, France, Germany (German Academic Exchange Service), the Netherlands (Netherlands Universities Foundation for International Cooperation, International Training Center, Royal Tropical Institute, International Agricultural Center, and the Institute of Social Studies), Norway (Norwegian Agency for International Development), Sweden (Swedish International Development Authority), United Kingdom (the British Council, the Inter-University Council for Higher Education Overseas), and the United States (Agency for International Development).

Multilateral Agencies: The World Bank

The International Bank for Reconstruction and Development and its two associates, the International Finance Corporation and the International Development Association (often referred to collectively as the World Bank), and the United Nations Educational and Cultural Organization (UNESCO) are the two multilateral agencies that have played the most central role in the development of African higher education. These agencies have had a virtual monopoly on shaping policy on higher education among aid donors throughout the postindependence period. Unfortunately, from the perspective of the development of higher education in the developing world generally, and in Africa specifically, the outcome has been quite detrimental.

Up until the beginning of the 1960s, the World Bank did not provide loans for any purpose other than infrastructural development. However, as Jones (1992) explains, the Bank thereafter began to slowly enter the field of educational lending and eventually became the most prominent international provider of funds for educational development in Africa and elsewhere.

Even after lending to the educational sector was greatly expanded after Robert McNamara became president of the Bank in 1968, higher education remained a stepchild relative to the primary, secondary, and vocational sectors. McNamara insisted that development priorities should be based on addressing the needs of the poorest segments of society. Yet as Jones (1992) argues, the "basic needs" approach to development was more rhetorical than substantive. The misguided penchant for "rates of return studies" by economists at the World Bank (Lulat 1988) and the consequent conclusion that the highest rates of return came from primary-level education guaranteed the relative neglect of higher education.

With specific reference to the deteriorating economic circumstances of much of Africa in the 1980s, the Bank published an important policy document, *Education Policies for Sub-Saharan Africa: Adjustment, Revitalization, and Expansion* (World Bank 1988). The report proposed no change in the relative weighting in aid policy decisions. Instead, with regard to higher education, the bank called for such measures as privatization and institution of user fees. In 1995, the bank issued its *Priorities and Strategies for Education: A World Bank Review* (World Bank 1995), which stated:

> Basic education will continue to receive the highest priority in the Bank's education lending to countries that have not yet achieved universal literacy and adequate access, equity, and quality at that level. . . . As the basic education system develops in coverage and effectiveness, more attention can be devoted to the upper-secondary and higher levels. Bank lending for higher education will support countries' efforts to adopt policy reforms that will allow the subsector to operate more efficiently and at lower public cost. Countries prepared to adopt a higher education policy framework that stresses a differentiated institutional structure and diversified resource base, with greater emphasis on private providers and private funding, will continue to receive priority. (World Bank 1995)

The foregoing does not mean that there was no lending whatsoever for higher education purposes. The World Bank remains to date the single largest supplier of funds to African higher education. Yet its funding was much lower than it should have been if the World Bank educational lending had been informed by sound research on the relationship between development and education in general and between higher education and development specifically. The method the Bank uses to disburse loans is to select projects rather than sectors, which it finances jointly with the receiving country (an approach that itself is highly problematic). Taking the total global expenditure on all projects that the World Bank helped finance for the education sector as a whole during the period 1963–1990, allocation was only about 12 percent for postsecondary general education (Jones 1992, 137, 182).

As Africa enters the twenty-first century, however, there are hopeful signs that the World Bank and other institutions are beginning to question such relative neglect of higher education (Bollag 1998; World Bank 1999, 2000a).

UNESCO

UNESCO has also, until very recently, given priority to primary- and secondary-level education. Its sponsorship of the World Conference on Higher Education in 1998 offers some indication that its views in this regard are changing. UNESCO, in any case, is a financially poor agency, and its ability to provide financial aid to countries is extremely limited. While it does occasionally undertake "technical cooperation projects," these are generally financed through sources outside its own budget, such as the World Bank. African beneficiaries of these projects have included Ethiopia, Ghana, Kenya, Lesotho, Nigeria, and Zambia. However, UNESCO's greatest contribution with regard to the education sector generally, and higher education specifically, has been in the form of consultations, symposia, workshops, conferences, publications, and the collection of statistical data. Through these avenues, UNESCO has provided educators with benchmarks against which progress can be evaluated, targets to aim for, and opportunities for interchange of ideas among planners, practitioners, and funders.

With specific reference to Africa, one of the most important contributions UNESCO made in the realm of ideas was to sponsor in 1962 the first Africa-wide higher education conference of its kind. It was held in Tananarive and was appropriately titled Development of Higher Education in Africa. The conference looked at such issues as the role of higher education in economic and social development, higher education planning and financing, staffing, curricular choice and adaptation, inter-African cooperation, and the role of foreign aid in the development of higher education in Africa (UNESCO 1963).

An important theme in the pronouncements of African higher education leaders—supported by multilateral aid agencies such as UNESCO—has been the call for greater cooperation among universities in Africa. One very significant indirect outcome of the 1962 UNESCO conference was the birth of the Association of African Universities (AAU). The few heads of African universities present at the conference took the initiative to meet in Khartoum in 1963 to propose a draft constitution for an association of African universities that would promote cooperation among them and serve as a research clearinghouse for its members. The AAU was officially inaugurated in Rabat, Morocco, on November 12, 1967.

The next UNESCO conference dealing specifically with higher education in Africa did not take place until the 1990s, in preparation for the UNESCO-sponsored 1998 World Conference on Higher Education. The 1997 Regional Conference on Higher Education for Africa held in Dakar covered essentially the same issues as the 1962 conference, as well as more contemporary issues such as autonomy and academic freedom, sex equity, and information technology.

Of course, UNESCO has also sponsored a number of symposia, workshops, and special projects dealing with specific higher education issues, usually executed through its regional offices in Dakar, Nairobi, and Harare. Examples of these include the Project on Strengthening the Social Sciences in Africa (which included the formation of the African Council of the Social Sciences); the Seminar on Institutional Development of Higher Education in Africa (held in Lagos in 1991 in alliance with the AAU and with funding from the United Nations Development Program); University Twinning (UNITWIN), a project to promote networking among higher education institutions in the North and South); the Regional Project on Development of Learning/Training Materials in Engineering Education in Africa; infrastructural and curriculum projects to help increase the output of scientists and engineers; and so on.

Foreign Scholarly Societies

Informal (and sometimes formal) support has come to African higher education through membership of their staff in foreign scholarly societies, such as the African Studies Association (United States), the American Economic Association, and the American Association for the Advancement of Science. This support is essential not only for the personal academic growth of the individual staff member but also for the institution as a whole because it provides it with links to the international scholarly community. The importance of such international scholarly support will increase as African higher education develops its Internet connections (McMurtie 2000).

The aid described here has not been an unmitigated blessing. Especially in the postindependence era, the benefits of aid to African higher education have been questionable at times, especially when the aid does not serve its intended purpose, is too limited to be effective, or is misused. In recent years, the dire economic straits of many African countries have helped to highlight another kind of problem: the uselessness of aid when no local funds exist to permit the continued functioning of the aid project following its completion. Africa needs to develop a new aid model, one that involves not only capital expenditure support for a given project but also recurrent expenditure support on a diminishing shared-cost basis (for example, 100 percent support in the first year, 90 percent in the second year, and 80 percent in the third year) after completion of the project. There is a clear need for imaginative approaches to the aid relationship. Recurrent expenditure support does not necessarily have to come from a single donor; it could also come from a consortium of two or more donors. An excellent book on the general issue of aid to African education that is still very relevant today some fifteen years after its publication, sadly (suggesting unlearned lessons), is Hawes and Coombe 1986.

Community Service and National Development

When there is a crying need to solve so many urgent development-related problems, and when the universities are often the primary agents engaged in cutting-edge research (as they are in most African countries), community service must be a foundational pillar of the university's mission. This was emphatically acknowledged at the two major conferences on higher education that sought to influence the establishment and growth of higher education in Africa, the 1962 Tananarive Conference (UNESCO 1963), and the 1972 Accra Workshop (Yesufu 1973).

Community service is the extension of university expertise in the service of improving the quality of life of the community. It should be integral to all aspects of the university's mission, structure, and organization, including hiring and promotion, curriculum and teaching, and research and publications. In practice, however, African universities have not lived up to this definition of community service. With a few exceptions (such as running teaching hospitals and allowing public access to university library facilities), most universities have essentially been ivory towers.

However, there is now greater involvement of African universities in community service than in the past. A number of factors account for this development. First, the severe budgetary problems of the African university have pushed it in the direction of looking for ways to diversify its traditional source of funding support, which has led to involvement in entrepreneurial activities based on its expertise. Second, the continuing downward slide in faculty salaries in many African countries effected by the ravages of high inflation rates has pushed some faculty to engage in the increasingly lucrative cottage industry of "development consultancy" (in which one is paid in U.S. dollars). Paradoxically, the very actors that had once been an impediment to the use of the African university's expertise for development-oriented research, the foreign aid agencies, are responsible for the growth of this cottage industry. The general approach of external development agencies toward local research has been slowly changing. Many now increasingly feel that local expertise, when available, is more appropriate and cost effective. Third, the governments themselves have begun to adopt a more positive view of the university because many of the high-level personnel in government are now university trained, a vast majority of them at universities in their countries. Nonetheless, African universities have a long way to go toward being true community-service institutions.

Private Universities

If one excludes the educational institutions run by missionaries, the history of private educational enterprise in Africa is a short one. European countries have generally regarded educational provision as primarily the responsibility of the state, especially at the higher education level, a model they extended to their African colonies. It is not surprising, then, that one of the earliest private universities in Africa, the American University in Cairo, has its origins in the United States. It was established in 1919 and was accredited by the Commission on Higher Education of the Middle States Association of Colleges and Schools in the United States.

Even after independence, African countries did not encourage the establishment of private higher education institutions. In recent years, however, as a result of the enormous difficulties that public higher education has been facing, a number of African countries have begun to provide the legislative and evaluative mechanisms necessary to facilitate the development of privately funded higher education institutions. Examples in-clude Kenya, Nigeria, Uganda, and South Africa. This policy change has also been supported by external agencies such as the World Bank and UNESCO, which argue that African countries simply do not have the resources to meet the rapidly increasing demand for higher education and that private institutions are needed to step into the breach (Schofield 1996; World Bank 1994).

CONCLUSION: THE LEGACY OF HISTORY AND THE TYRANNY OF THE PRESENT

Higher education has come a long way from the time when much of Africa was ruled by Europe. Enormous progress has been achieved in quantitative terms. But higher education systems throughout much of Africa today are under severe stress.

Many African education institutions have experienced an enduring pattern of woes: crippling budgetary constraints; large-scale deterioration of physical infrastructure; overflowing classrooms; poorly equipped laboratories; intermittent supply of even such basics as water and electricity; shrinking and outdated libraries; widespread looting of library holdings; overworked and underpaid faculty who often must moonlight to make ends meet; inefficient administrations (many talented and able administrators have left for greener pastures); teaching, learning, and research that is bereft of even the most basic logistical support (such as chalk, textbooks, and photocopying machines); and government restrictions on academic freedom (Ajayi, Goma, and Johnson 1996; Amonoo-Neizer 1998; Assié-Lumumba 1996; Bollag 1998; Giudice 1999; Hoffman 1995–1996; Shabani 1995; UNESCO 1996; and Useem 1999b).

Modern higher education systems arrived in Africa amid a fanfare of great optimism. The sad truth is that much of that optimism is on the wane if it has not already evaporated completely, reflecting the collapse of civil society, the legacy of past higher education practices, and neglect of higher education by external aid agencies.

Few concerned with African higher education are willing to openly talk about the total collapse or near-total collapse of civil society in many African countries (defined here to mean all the major democratic social, political, and economic institutions). An inkling of the gravity of the situation can be assessed by comparing what the author of this chapter wrote eighteen years ago with what is happening today:

Nations such as those in Africa are saddled with a legacy of, among other things, steeply spiraling mass poverty; deep ethnic/regional conflagratory cleavages that threaten to destroy national integrity, heavily debt-ridden stagflation economies; endemic military takeovers; and a spreading pattern of gross violations of the mass of the citizenry's basic human rights by states dominated by increasingly cynical and corrupt elites. . . . Whereas the majority of the people in the WINs [Western Industrialized Nations] will continue to enjoy a materially superabundant life (based on an immensely wasteful system that requires two-thirds of the world's key finite resources to keep it going) the people of the African nations (i.e. those who will have survived the present large-scale famine ravaging huge areas in Africa and estimated to threaten nearly one-quarter of the entire African population with starvation) . . . will face even greater levels of deterioration in their standards of living. (Lulat 1985, 555)

If those were the circumstances of Africa eighteen years ago, the situation is now even more grim. Armed conflicts and civil wars are rampant. Even in the absence of armed conflict, many African states are reeling from the ever-mounting and crushing debt burden; an epidemic of the disease AIDS that has consumed millions of people and cruelly wrenched from millions of orphaned children their childhood (as they are forcibly thrust overnight into adult roles); the continuation of widespread kleptocratic corruption; spiraling mass poverty in the context of disintegrating stagflation economies; and massive and persistent gross violations of human rights of the citizenry. Tragically, large parts of Africa continue to be engulfed by widespread famines and floods of tremendous proportions. In other words, over the past eighteen years, the state of the African continent has become worse.

Among the higher education policies that have exacerbated these problems are the high cost of higher education, the ivory tower syndrome, and curricular shortcomings. Higher education in Africa has an extremely high unit cost, even when compared to other developing regions (World Bank 1988). Government after government are no longer willing or able to fund education adequately. This high unit cost is an outcome of a number of historically rooted practices, the most significant of which are:

- The wholesale transplanting of institutions from abroad, requiring the creation of physical infrastructures that were not organically linked to the local economy and society and therefore required huge capital and recurrent expenditures
- The decision to insist on free on-campus residence for all students, thereby requiring the building and maintenance of expensive dormitories as well as provision of taxpayer-funded board
- The decision to provide tuition-free education to all students, without even requiring a means test
- The decision to retain high salary levels (relative to salaries for similar positions in the rest of society) for teaching staff and administrators
- The use of higher education institutions as employment generators by governments
- The failure to maximize the impact of resources by not devising programs for nontraditional students (such as part-time, evening, and intersession students)
- The failure to engage in meaningful cross-border cooperation by developing regional higher education systems (rather than small, atomistic systems), thereby foregoing savings that arise from economies of scale, not to mention savings that accrue from the concentration of scholarly expertise

Compounding the difficulties stemming from the high unit costs has been the problem of the ivory tower syndrome that afflicts most universities in Africa today. Much in the same way that the physical location of these institutions has often been divorced from their geographic and economic environs, their activities have also been divorced to a considerable extent from

their sociopolitical environs. To date, there has been an inadequate effort made by African universities to institute measures that would permit them to institutionally integrate into the rest of society. The result has been alienation and distrust on the part of the citizenry, both ordinary people and ruling elites. Not surprisingly, higher education institutions have often become victims of politicization (with a consequent assault on autonomy and academic freedom) in the effort by the polity to demand accountability from universities. Many African universities have, at one time or another, seen an invasion of armed troops. Examples of countries that have seen their higher education institutions temporarily forcibly closed because of differences with the government (or sometimes the administration) in the 1980s and 1990s include: Algeria (March 1992); Burkina Faso (January 1999); Cameroon (April 1991); Congo (June 1990); Ethiopia (May 1989); Ghana (September 1999); Kenya (August 1982, November 1987, September 1992, June 1997, March 1998); Nigeria (May 1986, February 1988, June 1989, April 1990, May 1992, January 1993, December 1994, February 1997, June 1999, April 2000); Sierra Leone (January 1987, January 1990); South Africa (June 1984); Sudan (January 1982); Togo (February 1992); Zambia (November 1989, June 1990, April 1991); and Zimbabwe (October 1989, June 1998). These examples do not include cases where government forces have shot, abducted, or jailed students because of their outspoken views without closing the entire institution (Hanna 1975; Altbach 1989).

The most deleterious curricular shortcoming has been the insufficient emphasis on science and technology training. To date, African higher education systems have graduated far too few scientists, engineers, and doctors relative to the needs of the continent. This has contributed to the sense of the expendability of higher education in times of political and economic crisis, not to mention long-term debilitation of national development efforts.

Another major concern is the extent to which African higher education was put on the back burner in the 1980s and 1990s, with disastrous consequences. As the secretary general of the AAU, Narciso Matos, observed at the plenary session of the World Conference on Higher Education in Paris, "In spite of the crucial role of higher education, most agencies and African governments disengaged from the sector in the 1980s and early 90s on the argument that rates of social return in basic education are much higher than in higher education. Denied of funds, African higher education was brought to near collapse" (Matos 1998).

In delineating these major concerns, it is important to stress that while the present is always a product of the past, this does not mean that the present (or the future) must be a prisoner of the past. The rehabilitation of African higher education can be possible if it receives top priority from all concerned. The first task must be to restore higher education to its proper place in the educational pyramid of development planning, financing, and international aid.

Other pressing issues must also be tackled. These include confronting the issue of gender equity; the creation of doctorate-granting research universities, either nationally or regionally (Ajayi, Goma, and Johnson 1996); and a concerted effort to make the university more responsive to the needs of national development. The problem here is to strike a balance between particularistic and universal needs (Wandira 1977, 132).

When modern higher education arrived in Africa in the late nineteenth century, telephones, radios, television, photocopy machines, and videocassette players had not yet been invented. Whereas today all these inventions have become ubiquitously and seamlessly integral to the day-to-day activities of the educational enterprise in the West, this is not the case in Africa. The issue of integrating the new information technologies, such as the Internet, into higher education processes—as well as restructuring the traditional university model so that courses can be offered across traditional spatial boundaries—is crucial. The launch in 1993 of the University-based Critical Mass System for Information Technology (USIT) by the International Association of Universities (IAU) to help African and other developing countries enter the information age is one step in the right direction (Hayman 1993; Oilo 1998; Useem 1999a; Blurton 1999; and Jensen 1999).

The future of Africa at the dawn of the twenty-first century has never looked more bleak. Africa's circumstances are inextricably bound up with that of the rest of humanity. Consequently, only a concerted program of external assistance can break this conundrum. Fortunately, there are some in the West who are beginning to wake up to this fact, as evidenced in the recent initiatives of the United States philanthropic foundations. A peaceful, democratic, and prosperous African continent can mean nothing but good for the rest of the world.

REFERENCES

Adi, Hakim. 1998. *West Africans in Britain, 1900–1960: Nationalism, Pan-Africanism, and Communism.* London: Lawrence & Wishart.

Ajayi, J. F. Ade, Lameck K. H. Goma, and G. Ampah Johnson. 1996. *The African Experience with Higher Education.* London: James Currey, and Athens, Ohio: Ohio University Press.

Altbach, P. G., ed. 1989. *Student Political Activism: An International Reference Handbook.* Westport, Conn.: Greenwood.

Amonoo-Neizer, E. H. 1998. "Universities in Africa: The Need for Adaptation, Transformation, Reformation and Revitalization." *Higher Education Policy* 11, no. 4 (December): 301–309.

Ashby, E. 1966. *Universities: British, Indian, African—A Study in the Ecology of Higher Education.* Cambridge, Mass.: Harvard University Press, and London: Weidenfeld and Nicolson.

Assié-Lumumba, N'Dri T. 1996. "The Role and Mission of African Higher Education: Preparing for the 21st Century and Beyond." *South African Journal of Higher Education* 10, no. 2: 5–12.

Azvedo, M. 1970. "A Century of Colonial Education in Mozambique." In *Independence without Freedom: The Political Economy of Colonial Education in Southern Africa,* edited by Agrippah T. Mugomba and Mougo Nyaggah, 191–213. Santa Barbara, Calif.: ABC-Clio.

Berman, E. H., ed. 1975. *African Reactions to Missionary Education.* New York and London: Teachers College Press.

Blurton, C. 1999. "New Directions in Education." In *World Communication and Information Report, 1999/2000,* 46–61. Paris: UNESCO.

Bollag, B. 1998. "International Aid Groups Shift Focus to Higher Education in Developing Nations." *Chronicle of Higher Education,* October 30, A51.

Brown, G. N. 1964. "British Educational Policy in West and Central Africa." *The Journal of Modern African Studies* 2, no. 3: 365–377.

Burke, J. 1995. *The Day the Universe Changed.* Boston: Little, Brown.

Canfora, L. 1989. *The Vanished Library.* Berkeley: University of California Press.

Carnegie Corporation. 2000. "Four Foundations Launch $100 Million Initiative in Support of Higher Education in African Countries." Press Release, New York, April 24, 2000.

Ciment, J. 1997. *Angola and Mozambique: Postcolonial Wars in Southern Africa.* New York: Facts on File.

de Libera, A. 1997. "The Muslim Forebears of the European Renaissance." *UNESCO Courier* (February): 4–9.

El-Abbadi, M. 1992. *The Life and Fate of the Ancient Library of Alexandria.* Paris: UNESCO/UNDP.

Fraser, P. M. 1972. *Ptolemaic Alexandria.* Oxford: Clarendon.

Gourevitch, P. 1998. *We Wish to Inform You That Tomorrow We Will Be Killed with Our Families: Stories from Rwanda.* New York: Farrar, Straus & Giroux.

Guidice, B. 1999. "New Government in Nigeria Offers Little Hope to Academics: Universities Are Short on Funds and Overcrowded; Brain Drain Depletes Institutions of Top Scholars." *Chronicle of Higher Education,* August 13, A46.

Hanna, W. J. 1975. *University Students and African Politics.* New York: Africana.

Hawes, H., and T. Coombe, eds. 1986. *Education Priorities and Aid Responses in Sub-Saharan Africa.* London: Her Majesty's Stationery Office (for the Overseas Development Administration, U.K.).

Hayman, J. 1993. "Bridging Higher Education's Technology Gap in Africa." *THE Journal (Technological Horizons in Education)* 20, no. 6 (January): 63–69.

Hill, R. A., and G. A. Pirio. 1987. "'Africa for the Africans': The Garvey Movement in South Africa, 1920–1940." In *The Politics of Race, Class and Nationalism in Twentieth-Century South Africa,* edited by Shula Marks and Stanley Trapido, 209–253. London and New York: Longman.

Hoffman, A. 1995–1996. "The Destruction of Higher Education in Sub-Saharan Africa." *Journal of Blacks in Higher Education,* no. 10 (Winter): 83–87.

Hull, R. W. 1990. *American Enterprise in South Africa: Historical Dimensions of Engagement and Disengagement.* New York: New York University Press.

Jensen, M. 1999. "Sub-Saharan Africa." In *World Communication and Information Report, 1999/2000,* 180–96. Paris: UNESCO.

Jones, P. W. 1992. *World Bank Financing of Education: Lending, Learning and Development.* London and New York: Routledge.

Kelly, G. P. 1984. "Colonialism, Indigenous Society, and School Practices: French West Africa and Indochina, 1918–1938." In *Education and the Colonial Experience,* second revised edition, 9–32, edited by Philip G. Altbach and Gail P. Kelly. New Brunswick, N.J.: Transaction.

Kelly, S. 1993. *America's Tyrant: The CIA and Mobutu of Zaire.* Washington, D.C.: American University Press.

King, K. 1971. *Pan-Africanism and Education: A Study of Race Philanthropy and Education in the Southern States of America and East Africa.* Oxford: Clarendon.

Kitchen, H., ed. 1962. *The Educated African: A Country by Country Survey of Educational Development in Africa.* Compiled by Ruth Sloan Associates, Washington, D.C. New York: Praeger.

Lulat, Y. G.-M. 1985. "Zachariah's 'Plants' and 'Clay': A Rejoinder." *Comparative Education Review* 29, no. 4: 549–556.

———. 1988. "Education and National Development: The Continuing Problem of Misdiagnosis and Irrelevant Prescriptions." *International Journal of Educational Development* 8, no. 4: 315–328.

Lyons, C. H. 1970. "The Educable African: British Thought and Action, 1835–1865." In *Essays in the History of African Education,* edited by Vincent M. Battle and Charles H. Lyons, 1–32. New York: Teachers College Press.

Maier, K. 1996. *Angola: Promises and Lies.* Rivonia, South Africa: W. Waterman Publications.

Makdisi, G. 1981. *The Rise of Colleges: Institutions of Learning in Islam and the West.* Edinburgh: Edinburgh University Press.

Matos, N. 1998. Speech of Professor Narciso Matos, Secretary General of the Association of African Universities. In *Plenary: World Conference on Higher Education, UNESCO, Paris, 5–9 October, 1998.* Vol. V. Document no. ED-99/HEP/WCHE/Vol. V-NGO-2. Paris: UNESCO.

McMurtie, B. 2000. "America's Scholarly Societies Raise Their Flags Abroad: U.S. Associations Recruit Foreign Members and Start Efforts to Help Them." *Chronicle of Higher Education,* January 28, A53.

Mumford, W. B. 1970. *Africans Learn to Be French.* New York: Negro Universities Press.

Nwauwa, A. O. 1996. *Imperialism, Academe and Nationalism: Britain and University Education for Africans 1860–1960.* London and Portland, Ore.: Frank Cass.

Nzongola-Ntalaja, Georges, ed. 1988. *The Crisis in Zaire: Myths and Realities.* Trenton, N.J.: Africa World.

Oilo, D. 1988. *From Traditional to Virtual: The New Information Technologies.* Document no. ED-98/CONF.202/CLD.18. Paris: UNESCO.

Prunier, G. 1995. *The Rwanda Crisis: History of a Genocide.* New York: Columbia University Press.

Samuels, M. A. 1970. *Education in Angola, 1878–1914: A History of Culture Transfer and Administration.* New York: Teachers College Press.

Schofield, A. 1996. *Private Post-Secondary Education in Four Commonwealth Countries.* Document no. ED-96/WS-33. Paris: UNESCO.

Shabani, J. 1995. "Higher Education in Sub-Saharan Africa: Strategies for the Improvement of the Quality of Training." *Quality in Higher Education* 1, no. 2: 173–178.

Stockwell, J. 1997. *In Search of Enemies: A CIA Story.* Bridgewater, N.J.: Replica Books.

UNESCO. 1963. *The Development of Higher Education in Africa: Report of the Conference on the Development of Higher Education in Africa, Tananarive, 3–12 September 1962.* Paris: United Nations Educational, Scientific and Cultural Organization.

———. 1996. Working Group Lead Agency. Working Group on Education Sector Analysis. *Analyses, Agenda, and Priorities for Education in Africa: Review of Externally Initiated, Commissioned, and Supported Studies of Education in Africa, 1990–1994.* Working Group Series No. ED-96/WS/12(E). Paris: United Nations Educational, Scientific and Cultural Organization, published in association with Association for the Development of African Education, International Institute for Educational Planning.

———. 1999. *UNESCO Statistical Yearbook.* Paris: United Nations Educational, Scientific, and Cultural Organization.

Useem, A. 1999a. "Wiring African Universities Proves a Formidable Challenge." *Chronicle of Higher Education,* April 2, A51.

———. 1999b. "University of Zimbabwe Suffers as Economic and Political Turmoil Envelop the Country." *Chronicle of Higher Education,* August 13, A46.

Vergnani, L. 1998. "South African Universities Move to Cast Aside Legacy of Apartheid: Historically White and Black Institutions Face New Era of Recruiting Goals and 'Redress.'" *Chronicle of Higher Education,* September 4, A73.

Wagaw, T. G. 1979. *Education in Ethiopia: Prospect and Retrospect.* Ann Arbor: University of Michigan Press.

———. 1990. *The Development of Higher Education and Social Change: An Ethiopian Experience.* East Lansing: Michigan State University Press.

Wandira, A. 1977. *The African University in Development.* Johannesburg: Ravan.

World Bank. 1988. *Education in Sub-Saharan Africa: Policies for Adjustment, Revitalization and Expansion.* Washington, D.C.: World Bank.

———. 1994. *Higher Education: The Lessons of Experience.* Washington, D.C.: World Bank.

———. 1995. *Priorities and Strategies for Education: A World Bank Review.* Washington, D.C.: World Bank.

———. 1999. *Education Sector Strategy.* Washington, D.C.: World Bank.

———. 2000a. *Higher Education in Developing Countries: Peril and Promise.* Washington, D.C.: World Bank.

Yesufu, T. M., ed. 1973. *Creating the African University: Emerging Issues in the 1970s.* Ibadan: Oxford University Press.

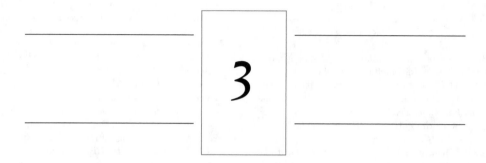

3

University Governance and University-State Relations

KILEMI MWIRIA

INTRODUCTION

In this chapter, university governance is understood to mean the formal and informal mechanisms that allow universities to make informed decisions and to take appropriate actions (World Bank 2000). At the institutional level, governance refers to local authority structures. These authority structures are influenced by the arrangements governing relations between universities and the wider society, mainly governments. This chapter is premised on the close relationship between what takes place within universities and their external relations with governments. Good governance is key in determining the pace and direction of African higher education development, particularly with regard to the improvement of the quality of the education provided by universities and to better management.

Because the author's experience is mainly in countries of Anglophone Africa, most of the examples in this chapter will come from these countries.

KEY DETERMINANTS OF UNIVERSITY-STATE RELATIONS

The Early African University as a "Foreign" Imposition

A good number of the governance-related shortcomings of African universities, in particular the dominance of governments in institutional decision making, have their roots in the way early African universities were founded. The African universities of the late nineteenth and early twentieth centuries were modeled on the style of the universities of their respective countries' colonial powers. For example, the early universities of Anglophone Africa adapted wholesale "the fundamental pattern of British civil universities in constitution, in standards and curricula, in social purpose. . . . They were to be self-governing societies. . . . And as for their social function . . . they were[,] as in England, to nurture an elite" (Ashby 1964, 18). Likewise, the universities

of Francophone and Lusophone Africa aimed to promote cultural and political assimilation of their graduates, allowing them to claim the right to French and Portuguese citizenship. Like their British counterparts, these universities became part of the French and Portuguese systems (Gaidzanwa 1995).

Such a founding philosophy has proved rather problematic for the good governance of universities and for the relations of universities with governments. First, the idea of autonomous institutions outside the control of the national leader was unacceptable to the emerging independent African leaders, many of whom came from the tradition of "the ruler knowing and presiding over all." For universities, matters were not made any better by their almost total financial dependence on government for both their development and recurrent needs. Unlike most African universities, universities in the colonial home countries benefited from endowments by individuals and private corporations. Thus, they have never been as dependent on state subsidies as have African universities. Even more important is the fact that although English and French universities continue to receive support from their respective governments, there are no formal structures for their control by government.

The extreme nature of the conflicts between African universities and governments is mitigated by the existence of long, well-established, and now largely acceptable conventions governing relations between autonomous universities and the state. It must also be remembered that a large majority of key government functionaries have attended or have had some experience with the workings of autonomous national institutions, including universities.

Second, the foreign origins of African universities have often meant that various interest groups perceive their role in national development differently. On the one hand, academics expect to enjoy academic freedom, often in its absolute sense. This implies their right to teach, research, and publish almost anything, notwithstanding the costs of such pursuits or the relevance for national development. The academic freedom argument has proved hard to sell to an African leadership that grapples with underdevelopment and that sees the most important function of the university as the alleviating of conditions of underdevelopment. In fact, some of the more well-known post-independence African leaders, most notably Kwame Nkrumah of Ghana, Julius Nyerere of Tanzania, and Robert Mugabe of Zimbabwe, were very clear about the need for African universities to devote themselves to addressing the most urgent needs of their respective countries. They urged universities to pay less attention to the pursuit of knowledge for its own sake in light of the fact that their nations' largely poor populations did not have any experience with university education and universities were unattainable to the majority of children. In keeping with such an understanding of the role of universities in national development, therefore, some African countries have closely tied their manpower requirements to university outputs. Piyushi Kotecha (1999, 18) has shown how the expansion of program offerings at the University of Botswana has been closely tied to the country's labor requirements. Thus, the government determines the overall structure of the university (including the structures of faculties and departments), curricular offerings, and projected staff and student numbers. Kotecha further notes that university implementation in these areas takes place in the context of national development plans.

Third, in keeping with the notion of absolute control of key national affairs, a good number of the African leaders found universities too visible and prestigious as national monuments to be given complete autonomy. They felt threatened politically by these institutions' leaders and their respective staff and student communities. It is partly as a result of this perceived need to keep a close watch over the affairs of universities that many African heads of state double as titular heads of their respective national universities. As chancellors of national universities, they have the power to appoint key university administrators and members of university governing boards, preside over the awards of degrees and diplomas, and directly or through their respective ministers of education appoint professors. African heads of state also appoint most of the key university administrators. These two factors have contributed to continuing tensions between African universities and their respective governments.

Finally, the elitist ethos of postcolonial African universities was later to pose serious governance-related problems for these institutions and their governments. Because the nurturing of an elite, or "future leaders," as university students were often referred to, called for a privileged lifestyle while at university, students have refused to accept that such luxuries are no longer affordable by their governments. Much of the tension between students and university administrations, on the one hand, and governments, on the other hand, has to do with the loss of the privileges African university students enjoyed in the 1960s and early 1970s.

GOVERNMENT CONTROL OF UNIVERSITIES AS A FACTOR IN UNIVERSITY-STATE RELATIONS

The enormous powers vested in the university chancellor have resulted in much friction between governments and members of university communities. The latter have complained that heads of state have authority over institutions that are supposed to be independent of the state and whose business they do not always understand. More important, they have pointed to incidences of undue and uninformed interference by chancellors in university decision-making processes. In fact, some African heads of state have forced public universities to enroll more students than they have capacity to adequately serve (Hughes and Mwiria 1990). Some university chancellors have ordered the closures of universities, while others have sought to directly influence curricular offerings. Kwame Nkrumah, Ghana's first head of state, warned University of Ghana academics that "if reforms do not come from within, we intend to impose them from outside, and no resort to the cry of academic freedom . . . is going to restrain us from seeing that our university is a healthy University [of Ghana] devoted to Ghanaian interests" (Ashby 1964, 92). In the same sprit, the University of Zimbabwe chancellor, President Robert Mugabe, informed the university community in 1983 that "higher education is too important a business to be left entirely to deans, professors, lecturers and university administrations" (Mugabe 1983, 2). Likewise, former Tanzanian president Julius Nyerere's Musoma-led Resolution of 1974 sought to draw the university into centralized government planning and even dictated admission conditions (Mkude, Cooksey, and Levey 2000, 1). According to this resolution, to be eligible for university admission, prospective students had to complete one year of compulsory national service, have a minimum of two years of satisfactory work experience, and provide a positive recommendation from an employer. The Musoma resolution also called for a review of university curricula and mandated the establishment of specific departments to address development needs.

A second manifestation of the strong hand of governments in university governance relates to the appointment of key university administrators by either the chancellor or the country's minister of education. In the most extreme cases, chancellors have appointed ruling-party functionaries to head universities, as happened in Dar es Salaam in 1970, when a former executive secretary of the ruling party was given the vice-chancellor position (Mkude, Cooksey, and Levey 2000, 1). These measures are aimed at consolidating the ruling elite's control over university business. In addition to the vice-chancellors, heads of state appoint their deputies, registrars, and, in a few cases, even mid-level officers, such as deans and heads of departments. In the more extreme cases, heads of universities change with a change in governments (World Bank 2000, 62). In many countries, the chancellor and his or her minister for education also appoint the key (and often a majority of the) members of university governing boards, most notably the university council. These nominees include the chair of the council, the country's education minister, permanent secretaries of the ministries that oversee universities, and vice-chancellors (rectors) and their deputies.

In some universities, there is provision for the representation of academic staff and students in university councils. However, in some of these cases, as in Zambia and Ghana, the elected representatives of these constituencies have to be approved by the chancellor (Mwiria 1992). At Makerere University (Uganda), the University of Botswana (Botswana), and the University of Nairobi (Kenya), more than half of university council members are directly or indirectly appointed by heads of state. This is one major reason for the relatively limited autonomy of universities in these and many other sub-Saharan African countries. In other cases, chancellors are able to send directives to the council through their key nominees, such as the education minister and vice-chancellor. In fact, the University of Zambia Act stipulates that "the Minister shall convey to the Chairman of the Council and the Vice Chancellor such general or particular party or government policies as may affect the conduct of the affairs of the University."

Such politicization of university decision making has given way to the use of considerations other than merit in selection of students, appointments and promotions of faculty and staff, curriculum design, the use of institutional funds, reform policies relating to rationalization, and related matters (World Bank 2000, 63). In extreme cases, as when universities operate under military dictatorships and other autocratic regimes, universities have suffered greatly from state interference in their affairs, especially with regard to the freedom to teach, research, and question excesses of such dictatorships. Fearful of the likelihood of increased political power on the part of academic staff and students, some of these governments have resorted to

> arbitrary arrests and prolonged detention without charge or trial; imprisonment under conditions that are cruel and degrading; restrictions on freedom of expression, assembly, association and movement; dismissal of staff; expulsion of students; university closures; banning of student organizations and staff unions; the prohibition of "political activity" on campus; discrimination against students on the basis of race, ethnic or regional origin; censorship of teaching and reading materials and manipulation of curricula. Lesser forms of coercion are also used as a means of intimidation, such as denial of promotions and tenure to outspoken academics; restrictions on travel abroad for research or meetings; refusal to grant scholarships to politically active students; and the requirement that students who have been implicated in political disturbances sign pledges of "good behavior" in order to resume their studies. (Africa Watch 1990, 1)

Academic repression has also been manifested in the government system of placing informers on campuses.

It has been argued that a strong government hand in the running of university affairs is not without some benefits for universities. This is because heads of states and ministers of education are in a position to approve government support for university programs and budgetary allocations. They could also approve allocation of land for institutional expansion, among other things. Likewise, ministerial powers could prove useful when it comes to institutional implementation of progressive government directives and key policies in times of emergency and the promotion of policies related to national integration and affirmative action. The challenge, however, is how to ensure that this strong government presence remains of value to both parties involved, not just the government.

THE CRISIS OF UNDERFUNDING

The relatively scarce resources available to African universities are at the root of strained relations between universities and their governments and poor institutional management. The almost total dependence on the state for funding has placed the typical African university in a particularly vulnerable position. First, most African governments have allocated a disproportionate share of their educational resources to primary education since the 1990s, often as a result of prompting by donors. The situation has been intensified by the implementation of structural adjustment programs that have resulted in substantial declines in the level of funding available to education in general and university education in particular. Heavy dependence on the state has posed a number of governance-related problems for universities. Partly because of the declining trend of most African economies, state funding to universities has been declining and is often unpredictable from one year to the next. This makes forward planning almost impossible, especially when the mode of funding is on a monthly basis, as at Makerere University in Uganda. More problematic, however, is the fact that because of declining funding, universities have been forced to cut down on some of their teaching and research programs, essential necessities (including transportation), and benefits previously enjoyed by students and staff. Many grievances of students and academic staff are a result of cutbacks in these privileges. However, academic staff have had more genuine reasons for complaining to governments than students, not only because of their poor salaries and other terms and conditions of employment but also because their respective teaching environments, their budgetary allocations for research, and other benefits (such as support for participation in conferences) have virtually disappeared.

A second funding-related tension has to do with the fact that in some countries, even when universities take the initiative to generate independent funding, they have to surrender these funds to relevant government departments (World Bank 2000). A third tension is that university budgets are often approved by government officials who may not have adequate appreciation of the funding needs of specific institutions. Fourth, the capital and operating budgets of most institutions are poorly coordinated, as evidenced by support for new buildings that are either never completed or are allocated no maintenance funds. In some cases, universities also lack the flexibility and autonomy to spend available funds in the best ways they see fit. For example, in some cases, unspent funds cannot be diverted to areas of greater need or to budget activities of the following year, a situation that sometimes results in unnecessary overspending to guard against the necessity of returning remaining funds to the treasury. Few African universities enjoy the autonomy to make important decisions on financial expenditure without consulting the government, which results in a great deal of inefficiency.

Universities have themselves contributed to intensifying funding-related tensions with both governments and their respective internal constituencies. In some cases, university demands may be unrealistic in the face of national underdevelopment and the miserable conditions in which the majority of the surrounding communities live. However, whereas accusations of wanting to engage in luxurious living in the midst of poverty may apply to some students, it is less the case for academic staff, a majority of whom can barely survive on their meager salaries. Governments also have reason to fault university administrations for not being particularly good managers of the available funds. There are many cases of universities spending on average more than 30 percent of their actual annual budgetary allocations, which has rendered government efforts to enforce rationalization impracticable. Certainly such overspending may have to do with the fact that the resources allocated to these institutions are too low. In many instances, however, overspending is often due to mismanagement. Cases of rampant misuse of institutional funds have been the subject of numerous auditors' reports in Kenya, Zambia, Ghana, Tanzania, and South Africa, to name only a few examples. In Kenya, the 1995–1997 report of the government auditor-general gave an account of a $1 million rip-off at one public university as a result of the payment of questionable allowances and exaggerated freight charges, concealment of highly valuable fixed assets from institutional records, unrecorded salary advances, illegal purchases and sale of vehicles, and false inventory entries and contract awards (Mwiria 1998, 44).

Institutional mismanagement is a consequence of a number of factors, including the appointment of unqualified political hirelings to manage institutional funds, the limited training opportunities available to poorly trained managers, the lack of policies that reward good performance and punish offenders, and the fact that university administrators can still obtain government funding, regardless of whether or not they deserve it, because of their strong contacts with relevant government officials. Donors are not blameless in this regard. Despite their talk of transparency and good governance, donors still fund institutions that misuse their donations. Some of these donors' criteria for selecting institutional projects for funding have been questionable. In some institutions, academics have benefited from donor support for their research projects, sabbatical and postdoctoral fellowships, and participation in international conferences either because of their close relations with respective donor officers or because of their gender. Finally, universities bear the blame for not taking enough initiative to generate independent funding. This is changing, however, as some institutions are now seeking ways to ensure their survival in the face of extreme underfunding.

THE STATE OF INSTITUTIONAL GOVERNANCE SYSTEMS

One of the major drawbacks of the system whereby the government appoints senior university administrators is that these appointees tend to be more accountable to the government than to their institutional constituents. In a bid to fulfill the expectations of government and in view of the fact that many of these appointees bypass more qualified colleagues to assume these senior positions, senior university administrators often resort to autocratic management styles. Such administrators are more prone to corrupt practices and may not allow for adequate opportunities for dialogue with their staff and students. In fact, some vice-chancellors have gone as far as muzzling student and

staff societies while establishing ruling-party branches on campus (Omari and Mihyo 1991). Nevertheless, there have been vice-chancellors who have defied the orders of government on matters that would have been damaging to their institutions. This has happened in Ghana and Zimbabwe, among other countries (Mwiria 1992), but such instances have been rare.

Second, in some universities, virtually all decision-making powers are concentrated in the office of the vice-chancellor or rector. Decision-making processes can thus often be very slow, resulting in major administrative inefficiencies. In some cases, the university vice-chancellor or rector has to approve expenditures of as little as $100, authorize staff travel to conferences, chair student and staff disciplinary committees and all appointment meetings, and take part in very minor administrative chores. In extreme cases, these university chief executives behave like autocrats who know everything, they withhold information from others and control resources, and they manipulate staff and student leadership (Mwiria 1998, 44). Sifuna (1999, 195–196) uses Kenya as an example of this management style in some African universities. He argues that most newly appointed university administrators in Kenya surround themselves with intellectual yesmen whose duty it is to spy for them.

University administrators have also been known to violate university statutes by establishing a model of decision making that concentrates all authority in the office of the vice-chancellor and by controlling information and withholding it from others. As a result, even their most immediate deputies are of almost no consequence; they are relegated to positions of subordinate, sycophantic advisers. Sifuna quotes an academic in one Kenyan public university who sums up the autocratic administrative behavior of some Kenyan public university vice-chancellors:

> The tendency for vice-chancellors to monopolize all aspects of decision-making has now been perfected in the creation of the Vice-Chancellor's Management Board whose powers seem too wide and are now gradually eroding the powers of senate on a number of critical areas. The senate is used for routine matters like approval of examination results. The terms and conditions of [the] service document is no longer respected. Issues like sabbatical and study leave may be granted depending on the chairman [vice-chancellor] of the Board's views about the applicant. In all public universities in Kenya, a management board has been established to assist the vice-chancellor in the running of the universities. In some of the universities the functions and composition of the boards are stipulated in the statutes while in others the boards are not constitutionally sanctioned and are handpicked by the vice-chancellor to ratify his/her personal decisions on the management of the university. In one of the universities, this management board is so much dreaded because of its unpopular decisions that it has been nicknamed the "Mafia Board." The popular view in most of the universities is that the management boards have usurped the functions and powers of senate in the running of universities. (Sifuna 1999, 196)

University administrators are also constrained by factors outside their control. Most of them lack opportunities for training in the area of governance, even though ongoing training is even more critical for them than for most academic staff, since a majority of them assume their positions without any prior administrative training and experience. A second handicap is the absence of modern information-management systems in most universities. This will become more critical as universities grow in size and find it increasingly difficult to organize basic institutional data manually (World Bank 1997).

A third problem relates to the fact that in most Anglophone universities, university administrators have to deal with both the academic and welfare concerns of students. This is less of a problem in Francophone universities, where these services tend to be handled separately (Gaidzanwa 1995). The overburdening of scarce university administrations with too many administrative responsibilities and inadequate administrative support structures creates additional challenges. Deans of faculties and heads of departments, for example, have to handle both administrative and academic matters *and* are expected to teach and conduct research. Yet these same academic administrators often undertake personal nonuniversity employment because they are so poorly remunerated.

INEFFECTIVE INSTITUTIONAL GOVERNING BODIES

In many African universities, senates, faculty boards, and heads of departments often rubber-stamp the wishes of university chief executives. There have been known incidences of some university chief executives arranging the appointment of professors, deans, and heads of departments who would simply sanction their decisions in the senate and who would victimize academic staff and students seen as critical of their administration. Citing the experiences of Kenya and Nigeria, Ibonvbere (1993) and Sifuna (1999) argue that many of those appointed to these administrative and professional positions are junior staff with limited professional experience. In other cases, professors are rewarded with dubious appointments with the sole aim of winning their cooperation in senate meetings, at which the discussions that take place are often mediocre and dishonest. Because a good proportion of these key administrators lack relevant professional qualifications, having been elevated to their positions for their loyalty to their appointers, they often use institutional resources to buy off academic staff and students. In Kenya, for example, among other misuses, university funds have been used for "the hosting by vice-chancellors of lavish parties and expensive breakfast and lunch meetings for academic staff with the aim of co-opting them as most of them cannot afford such luxury; the holding of senate meetings in expensive Mombassa beach hotels; funding ruling party candidates during local and national elections; rewarding loyal students and professors; setting up security arrangements on campuses; and for paying police informers" (Mwiria 1998, 44).

Even when it is less partisan, senate decision making is slowed down by its system of numerous and often uncoordinated committees. Tarpeh (1994) and Galabawa (1997) identify the inefficiencies of senate committees of most Anglophone universities, which include lethargy and delays in decision making,

waste of time and energy in the preparation of committee meetings and in the processing of related documentation, inability to make decisions on urgent matters without reference to a committee, and limited follow-up and accountability with regard to decisions. Senate committees have further been criticized for delving into minor and routine matters that could more easily be handled by relevant departments and individual lecturers, for being too large, for incorporating anybody who is head of a department without consideration of rank or professional experience, for holding unnecessarily long meetings, and for failing to implement decisions made during meetings (Galabawa 1997). Having said this, the senate committee system has the potential to enhance institutional governance, especially because committees can facilitate popular participation and the sharing of responsibilities by a relatively large academic community. The committee system also draws upon a large reservoir of expert knowledge within universities, which can be put to good use in the resolution of institutional problems. Finally, the senate committee system provides data on the internal operations of universities to a large segment of the university community and can promote the decentralization of decision making (Galabawa 1997).

Serving under the senate are the faculty boards, which are responsible for all administrative and academic affairs of the various university faculties. The chief faculty administrative officer is the dean. In many universities, deans are elected to their position. Heads of departments and directors of institutes also hold elective positions in a few institutions. It has been observed that deans, heads of departments, and directors of institutes could, if the environment permitted, contribute to the building of an institutional culture through their networks of relations with professors, students, and university support staff. However, several factors limit this potential. First, most university acts are not clear about the duties and job descriptions of these offices. Partly because of this ambiguity, their authority tends to be undermined by the central university administration and the senate committees (Galabawa 1997). Second, meetings of faculty boards and departments are often infrequent and irregular. When they take place, faculty representation is small and many of the decisions made, with the exception of those related to examinations, are not implemented by the senior university administration. Third, at the departmental and institute levels, respective heads or directors, most of whom hold nonelective positions, tend to make decisions single-handedly and present them to faculty boards as views of the majority, a situation which does not promote serious policy planning and strategic thinking. Finally, both deans of faculties and heads of departments (or directors of institutes) have at times victimized staff members who hold views contrary to their own, who are not supportive of the government's view, and who come from different regions of the country than their own. This is why some university academics argue for making the positions of heads of departments and directors of institutes elective. Such a system has its own drawbacks, however, including the possibility of introducing factional politics on campus, the possibility of young inexperienced scholars assuming these positions, and its impracticability in cases of very small departments.

THE INFLUENCE OF AFRICAN ACADEMICS AND STUDENTS

Most of the available literature on university governance and university-state relations in Africa identifies governments and university administrators as the main agents of the problem besetting African universities. Yet academic staff and students, who have often projected themselves as victims of institutional misgovernance and government interference, have also contributed to these conditions (Ibonvbere 1993; Munene 1997; Gaidzanwa 1995). Partly (but not exclusively) because of fear of victimization, academics have generally not done enough to challenge the status quo of government dominance in university governance systems or with regard to their own welfare issues. Zeleza (1996) argues that the dictatorial President Kamuzu Banda of Malawi was able to censor the Malawi university community so effectively only because academics ceded so much political space to the state and because some among them played a role in legitimizing Banda's autocratic rule. This experience has been replicated in many other African countries. Some of those co-opted by the state have served in various capacities, including as supporters of anti-university legislation, heads of government departments that suppress university autonomy, advisers to undemocratic national and university leaderships, and as ruling-party ideologues. Thus, many African universities have become fertile ground for the identification of academics who can be rewarded with lucrative jobs in government and in unproductive parastatals in return for their loyalty. Within the universities themselves, some academics even play the role of spies for government and the university administration, and others have turned out to be some of the most ardent critics of key tenets of university philosophy, in particular academic freedom.

Michael Chege (1996/1997) demonstrates how, at their most extreme, some African academics have sided with ruling authorities to organize systematic elimination of politicians or members of ethnic communities they see as being unsupportive of oppressive status quos. In a well-argued essay, "Africa's Murderous Professors," he gives a chilling account of the contribution of some Rwandan and Kenyan academics to the genocide of persons of Tutsi and Kikuyu ethnic backgrounds, respectively, by members of ethnic groups of the ruling elites. With regard to the 1994 Rwanda genocide, Chege describes how

> incitements to kill were spiced with history lessons of "well known" Tutsi treachery and exploitation of the Hutus. The radio's intellectual brain trust was made up of Ferdinand Nahimana, a professor of history at the Rwandan National University at Butare, and Casmir Bizimungu, a foreign minister of a former government. Indeed, so strong was the academic influence in these writings and broadcasts that, after the massacres, Emmanuel Bugingo, the new and irreproachable rector of the Butare campus, confessed that "all the killing in Rwanda was carefully planned by intellectuals and those who passed through this university." By the early 1990s, however, the question of government policy toward Hutu-Tutsi ethnic relations that engaged Belgian colonials

in the 1950s had come full circle. Particularly interested in these questions were professors Leon Mugesira and the aforementioned Nahimana. Their solution for Rwanda's 1993–94 crisis, and the manner in which they spread it, would have impressed Joseph Goebbels. The professors manufactured doctrines of Hutu ethnic supremacy depicting all Tutsis as a malignant cancer in the nation's history that deserved to be excised once and for all. As Mugesira told an extremist gathering in November 1992, "the fatal mistake we made in 1959 was to let the Tutsis get out. We have to act. Wipe them all out." (Chege 1996/1997, 34)

In most cases, the behavior of some co-opted African academics needs to be understood as a consequence of the dramatic deterioration of the material conditions of most African academics. In fact, some scholars see such deterioration in employment conditions as a deliberate government strategy to foster the cooptation of academics. Writing about Zaire, Coleman and Ngokwey (1993) argue that the effectiveness of the strategy of encouraging political complacency has rested as much on encouraging hopes among those waiting their turn as it has upon rewarding the converted. In addition, cooptation is made more possible by the fear of intimidation and actual victimization through termination of services or the use of force. But there are also many opportunistic academics whose main driving force is political.

It has also been shown that African academics can be as corrupt, nepotistic, competitive, sexist, and authoritarian as their counterparts in government or the university administration. There have been many incidences of academics dishing out favors, which include scholarships, opportunities for participation in conferences, allocation of consultancy and teaching assignments for which there is additional pay, and the granting of better grades, on the basis of the recipients' ethnic, racial, or geographical origins, religion, gender, and loyalty to the instructor. University deans and heads of departments have also been known to withhold information about academic conferences, fellowships, and research grants from their colleagues to ensure that those who benefit are either themselves or their cronies. Evidence of the ethnic favoritism of university governance is most apparent in the election of deans, a situation that has contributed to some university administrations wanting to revert to the system of appointing these administrators, as in the case of Zimbabwe (Murapa 2000). However, the use of appointees is often aimed at strengthening the hold of government and university administrators on academics. Gaidzanwa (1995) has also demonstrated how in some countries, such as South Africa, expatriate academics have been used to control local academics who stand up against poor institutional governance or in defense of the rights and welfare of academics. In South Africa, these expatriate academics are motivated by the relatively better employment terms and conditions compared to those of colleagues in their home countries. As a result, in addition to assuming administrative positions, many expatriates fail to participate in staff associations or protests and other alternative actions initiated by local academics. The situation is even worse when expatriate staff enjoy better employment contracts than locals, as is often the case, particularly in the historically black universities in South Africa, where such staff are beneficiaries of generous postdoctoral or sabbatical fellowships sponsored by external donor organizations.

Because issues of governance and the quality of university education are often inextricably tied, actions by academics that undermine the quality of education have intensified the governance crisis in numerous ways. First, when academics award grades on considerations other than merit, do not update their lecture notes, spend little time with students, focus on nonuniversity business, or receive promotions when they do not merit them, they introduce problems for university administrations. This is especially the case in these days of accelerated privatization of university education in which students are increasingly asking for "value for money." Governments are also requiring universities to be more accountable to the public by providing high-quality and relevant education. When universities fail to deliver on these expectations, tensions between the state and universities tend to be even more intense.

Students have played their own role in intensifying the governance crisis in most African universities. In some African countries, governments and university administrations have, surprisingly, had no problems identifying students who were willing to fight against progressive academics and fellow students. In some universities, students have been used by the ruling elites to demonstrate against demands for increased national and institutional democratization and have been used as security agents on campus. Such cooptation of students is becoming even more prevalent as many universities introduce cost-sharing measures and privatization of welfare services. Students from poor backgrounds have become easy prey for corrupt governments and university administrations. The politicization of universities along party, political, ethnic, racial, and other lines has encouraged these divisions in student politics, especially in Zimbabwe, Senegal, South Africa, and Kenya, to name only a few examples (Gaidzanwa 1995). In a good number of African universities, one finds a proliferation of student welfare associations modeled largely along ethnic, religious, and gender lines.

Students have also demonstrated a great deal of intolerance and undemocratic behavior toward those who hold contrary views to their own. Violent student demonstrations, which sometimes target innocent civilians, are familiar on African university campuses. Student violence has included verbal and physical abuse of other students, academics, administrators, and the general public as well as frequent destruction of property, including students' own facilities. Gaidzanwa (1995) cites, among other student excesses, female students beating up a hostel warden at Nairobi University, students flouting visiting regulations at residence halls at Dar es Salaam, student leaders accosting academic staff in Swaziland, violent demonstrations against innocent public bystanders by University of Zimbabwe students, and harassment of female students at most African campuses. Such behavior is antithetical to the widening of democratic space among the student community, as minorities may be afraid of being harassed and physically attacked if they exercise their democratic rights.

In some universities, such as those in Kenya, Nigeria, Ghana, and Zimbabwe, students have also been known to wage battles around issues of class backgrounds and gender. Gaidzanwa (1995) uses the experience of Zimbabwe and South Africa to demonstrate the widening divide between the majority of students who come from rural backgrounds and a minority from privileged urban backgrounds. This divide is not only manifested in the use of English language (and in different accents) but also in other behavioral trends, modes of dress, and student politics. Women and other minority students tend to be victims of the worst forms of harassment and subordination by their less tolerant and chauvinistic male counterparts. According to Gaidzanwa,

> The subordination of women students through verbal, physical and sexual harassment on African campuses shows the failure of students to deal with the politics of difference on campuses peopled by students of varying ethnic, class, gender and religious affiliations. Other incidents at universities such as that of Zambia and Cape Town also reinforce this observation. On these campuses, female students tend to be harassed and in the crisis cited in Zambia, Catholic students were harassed together with their religious leaders. The cultures of Southern African universities which stress macho sports such as rugby and soccer, coupled with beer drinking and the consumption of women or their harassment are antithetical to the widening of participatory and tolerant politics because most of the women, the religious and other minorities are often afraid of being harassed and physically attacked in the process of exercising their freedoms. This does not augur well for democratic governance in universities and it places university student politicians at par with their counterparts in national politics where observance of democratic norms and tolerance of difference is concerned. (Gaidzanwa 1995, 27)

Finally, given that university governance is largely concerned with overseeing academic programs, university administrators and relevant government officials are faced with enormous challenges when students care little about their education while at university. Cheating on examinations is rampant, a significant proportion of students do not attend lectures, many students hardly use existing library and laboratory facilities, and alcoholism and drug addiction are becoming more common aspects of student life. In South Africa, students have openly advocated being graduated without having put any serious efforts into their academic work, calling for a policy of "pass one, pass all" as a way of democratizing academic evaluation (Cross 1999).

STRENGTHENING UNIVERSITY-STATE RELATIONS AND INTERNAL UNIVERSITY GOVERNANCE STRUCTURES

A mutual and constructive relationship is in the interest of both governments and universities. Fortunately, some universities are beginning to experience less government control. Some African heads of states have recognized that the chancellorship of the university should be left to those who have a deep understanding of the functioning of those institutions and the time to devote to directing them. President Fredrick Chiluba of Zambia and former Tanzanian president Ali Hassan Mwinyi relinquished their roles as chancellors of their respective national universities. In these countries and elsewhere in Africa, eminent persons have been nominated to the position of chancellor following recommendations of university councils. In other countries, such as Nigeria, the only role the head of state plays is the role of visitor to the public universities. The newly drafted University Act in Uganda will give the country's head of state a similar role in its public universities. The new legislation also aims to reduce the power of the state over the appointment of senior university administrators and representatives of key university governing bodies. In most countries that have chosen this path, the positions of vice-chancellor, principal, dean, chair, vice-chair, and secretary to the councils are filled from a list of qualified persons generated through the active participation of the university community and university councils. Key university governing bodies also tend to be more balanced with regard to the inclusion of government representatives.

Governments will continue to have a major say in the running of universities as long as they meet the largest share of the financial needs of these institutions. However, members of the university community must have a voice, which does not necessarily rule out the decision-making role of governments. In Nigeria and most of southern Africa, the positions of vice-chancellors are advertised. The senate and the university council then prepare a shortlist of candidates that is presented to the chancellor or visitor, who selects senior executives from among those deemed acceptable to the university community. The university council and senate could play the same roles with regard to recruitment for positions of other senior administrators, namely those of the deputy vice-chancellors, registrars, and deans of students. Democratizing the way these positions are filled may increase the level of accountability of deans and heads of departments to their respective constituencies. However, there is a need to work out criteria for short-listing those eligible for election that are acceptable to all stakeholders, including the university administration. This approach will help mitigate the possibility that unqualified and inexperienced academics will assume these positions.

It is equally important to work out a clear mechanism for the separation of powers and devolution of responsibilities so that administrative authority is not concentrated in the hands of a few senior university administrators. Also critical is the creation of an appropriate staff development program for the benefit of administrative staff. While such systems exist for academic staff in some universities, there seems to be little interest in organizing similar training programs for university administrators. This is particularly urgent in view of the fact that most African universities are undergoing transformations that require skills that will improve their capacity to manage these changes. Management capacity should also be strengthened by improving management information systems. Better data management is essential in the areas of student and personnel records, financial accounts, payroll systems, utilization of space, management of institutional inventory, time-tabling, and course scheduling (World Bank 1997).

ESTABLISHING AND STRENGTHENING APPROPRIATE BUFFER BODIES

A second major reform measure is the creation and strengthening of the buffer bodies that are meant to act as intermediaries between governments and universities. Many African countries are now creating such bodies, while established ones can be found in Kenya, Nigeria, Ghana, Mozambique, South Africa, and Zimbabwe. Botswana, Tanzania, and Uganda have proposed the formation of such bodies in new, yet-to-be-implemented university acts. The main functions of these intermediaries are the coordination of overall university development, which includes accreditation of new institutions; oversight of university teaching and research programs, student admissions, and budget development; and the collection, storage, and analysis of basic data on national university systems.

The effectiveness of these buffer bodies is constrained by a number of factors. First, in many cases, both the actual establishment and the transfer of mediation powers to intermediary bodies have often been a rather slow process. Second, buffer bodies in some countries are filled with government nominees and are thus limited in their ability to perform a serious mediation role. In fact, in Zimbabwe it has been argued that the government's intention in creating the Commission for Higher Education (CHE) was to strengthen its control over the University of Zimbabwe. In Ghana, the government disbanded the National Council for Higher Education (NCHE) in 1982 because the views of the academics represented in it were considered to be more dominant than those of government (Mwiria 1995). A new body, the National Council for Tertiary Education (NCTE), has been created in its place (Benneh 2000).

Where intermediary bodies do exist, governments have not necessarily relied on them for guidance with regard to the allocation of resources or the overseeing of academic standards in the universities. In Kenya, vice-chancellors negotiate directly with the government, and the Commission for Higher Education (CHE) does not supervise public universities but instead focuses on private institutions. In some cases, however, the inactivity of buffer bodies may have more to do with the human and financial resources available for implementing their respective mandates.

Buffer bodies could be strengthened in a number of ways. There is a need for a legal contract between the government, the universities, and these organizations. These contracts should clearly spell out the acceptable levels of government involvement in the business of the buffer bodies and universities. Leaders of these bodies also need to enjoy some reasonable amount of power over vice-chancellors. This could be accomplished by placing such intermediaries in a position that is organizationally independent of the ministries of education under a department of university affairs. In Kenya, for example, vice-chancellors bypass the CHE secretary because they are at par in terms of rank. In fact, while the head of state appoints vice-chancellors, the education minister will appoint the CHE secretary if the proposed bill for governing the operation of CHE is approved by Parliament. Buffer bodies are also likely to have more authority over universities if those appointed to run them are nationally respected professionals and if no single interest group is dominant within them. It may thus prove worthwhile to include representatives of organizations that have a relationship to the university but no stake in its management. Finally, buffer bodies are more likely to convince governments of continued financial support if they have clearly worked out plans and accounting systems for the use of funds allocated to them (Saint 1992).

JOINT CONSULTATIONS AND SHARING OF PERSONNEL BETWEEN UNIVERSITIES AND GOVERNMENTS

Tensions between governments and universities could also be reduced through mechanisms for resolving conflicts. Many African universities have been closed down because governments and members of the university community lack the means to resolve their differences amicably. In this regard, the move to make university governing boards and intermediary bodies more representative is a positive first step. Equally necessary, however, are strong and representative staff and student associations. Unfortunately, this remains a weak area in most African countries, even though such associations are the most logical bridge between governments and members of university communities. If recognized by both parties, representatives of these associations, university authorities, and government staff could then set up special communication channels to deal with university emergencies (Saint 1992).

Informal meetings between government officials and members of the university community would also foster conflict resolution. It would greatly help state-university relations if heads of state and senior government officials, such as the head of the police, would visit universities from time to time. President Yoweri Museveni of Uganda, former Ghanaian leader Jerry Rawlings, and President Robert Mugabe of Zimbabwe found time to visit their respective national universities during times of crisis and candidly discuss the problems facing those institutions in light of the economic difficulties being faced by their respective countries. These visits greatly contributed to diffusing existing and potential tensions. Another time government officials might visit campuses is during university open days set aside for marketing universities to the wider public, as is done in some Kenyan public universities and at the University of Zimbabwe, among other institutions.

Given that one of the key areas of disagreement between universities and government relates to the mission of higher education institutions in national development, it is necessary for both parties to reach an agreement regarding these expectations. Representatives of intermediary bodies or special stakeholder committees could be well placed to organize consultations on the appropriate balance between university concerns about academic freedom and government calls for universities to train a needed labor force. A good example is the University of Dar es Salaam, which

> consults on a continuous basis with the Ministry of Science, Technology and Higher Education and with other government ministries and agencies through their respective officials and through meetings. At the individual level, this would normally involve the Vice-Chancellor, Minister, Permanent Secretary, Chancellor, Chairman of Council and its committees, and needless to say, the Presidents. Joint meetings include those of the University Council and its committees, the Higher Education Accreditation Council, and briefings given by the university to the members of the

National Assembly. However, a more recent development is the holding of annual consultative meetings on the UDSM transformation program, the first of which was held in September 1993. It was officially opened by the President of the United Republic of Tanzania and closed by the Chancellor of the university, and provided an opportunity for dialogue between the university management, faculties, academic staff and their association as well as external parties. This has become an annual event at which the transformation program is reviewed, discussed, and renewed. The proceedings of the Fourth Annual Consultative Meeting held in September 1997, for example, show that 127 participants attended it from the University, ministry, donor countries (Sweden, the Netherlands, Norway), other public universities in Tanzania and Eduardo Mondlane University in Mozambique. (Githinji 1999, 60–61)

Finally, a system in which governments and universities share personnel could go some way toward improving relations, since the two parties would have additional opportunities to understand each other better. This could be in the form of internships, guest lectureships and seminars, presentations by senior government officials, joint policy-oriented research, training of government personnel by universities, the hiring of university-based consultants by government, and joint meetings for the purpose of disseminating research findings.

FUNDING DIVERSIFICATION AND FINANCIAL AUTONOMY

Many of the tensions between universities and governments have their roots in the mode and levels of government financing of universities. Universities can do much to diffuse these tensions by identifying opportunities for independent financing. Makerere University in Uganda is perhaps the most successful in this regard, but many other universities are following suit. Universities are raising independent finances through the privatization of education services by admitting fee-paying students, by instituting cost-sharing measures, by renting university facilities to the general public, by renting commercial units, or by providing consultancy services, among other strategies. Although some of these measures have not been popular with students (especially those related to cost-sharing) and have been the cause of increased student unrest, they have contributed to the stabilization of universities in a number of important respects. Institutions that admit fee-paying students have fewer disruptions because those who pay want to finish their studies as quickly as possible. Additional income has also enabled institutions to meet some of their most urgent financial needs, especially those related to expansion and rehabilitation of the teaching and learning infrastructure. In terms of improved governance, additional income has meant more pay and benefits for academics, which reduces the incentive to strike for better pay from government because their own institutions are able to supplement government contributions.

Universities that are able to raise funding independently from the government are slowly winning the right to spend these funds without having to seek government clearance, which enhances possibilities for some long-term planning, especially if the level of the independently earned income can be predicted. However, long-term planning is more likely to benefit from a system of block grants allocated to universities in advance, as is the case in Ghana. Under such a system, governments can hold universities accountable because block grants place responsibility directly on the university management for initiative, innovation, and implementation of change (World Bank 1997). Among other things, flexibility in the use of funds would make it possible for universities to carry surplus from one year to the next, to decide on the most appropriate ways to allocate available funding, to determine salary structures for staff, and to generate additional income from private sources. Real progress, however, can be made only if universities put in place transparent systems of accountability aimed at reducing corruption and the misuse of institutional funds. Among other benefits, this measure will have the net effect of freeing more resources for university programs and the remuneration of staff.

Many of the problems associated with academic staff and students have their roots in the wider political and economic environments outside the universities. This is especially true of the apparent ethnic tendencies in university staff and student politics, as well as the gender-related conflicts cited earlier. Likewise, the tendency for academics and students to be easy prey for government functionaries has a lot to do with their relatively poor socioeconomic standing and lack of adequate remuneration. In the end, therefore, only increased democratization and economic progress can help alleviate many of the shortcomings in student and staff life on African university campuses. Nevertheless, there are interim measures that, while not entirely a solution, can promote a sense of accountability among students and staff. The first is increased democratization of university decision making while making an effort to keep partisanship out of university politics. Improved communication aimed at consensus building can go a long way toward achieving these goals. Second, merit considerations deserve more attention in the appointment of university administrators, promotion of staff, awarding of grades to students, and identification of beneficiaries for available training opportunities. In this regard, most appointing powers should be left to the institutions themselves through appropriate processes of transparent external and internal reviews and wide consultations. Once they are recruited, every effort should be made to ensure that the best staff personnel are retained. Improved terms and conditions of employment are a necessity for all staff, not only as a way of minimizing the possibility that staff will be used by politicians and university administrators to the detriment of good institutional governance but also because this may promote a stable university faculty.

Finally, in view of the difficulties faced by students around issues of welfare, it is necessary for university administrators to separate welfare and academic services. The best solution may well be the privatization of welfare services. The advantages of privatization of these services for universities include reducing the running costs of such services as catering while increasing their quality due to market competition, reducing the time university administrators spend on the administration of nonacademic programs, reducing tension between the university administration and students, and socializing students to become more independent and self-sufficient (Gaidzanwa 1995; Saint 1992).

IMPROVED COMMUNICATION

Promotion of dialogue among various university constituencies provides another opportunity to strengthen institutional governance. Functioning staff and student associations have the potential to contribute much in this regard. Regrettably, these are absent in most institutions or too weak when they exist. In addition, strong student and staff leaders often end up being victimized by the university administration. Working student associations are now particularly useful as student populations increase and as universities engage in privatization of educational and welfare services, giving students much more to protest.

Staff and student associations can enhance institutional governance in a number of important ways. First, they provide the opportunity for staff and students to discuss their welfare and related academic problems and to identify possible solutions in an organized manner. In this regard, they help restrain students from engaging in violent behavior or making unrealistic demands. Second, they provide a useful link between the student community and the university administration by allowing students an avenue for voicing their grievances in an organized way, by bringing students and administrators together, and by sending important signals to the administration about impending strikes. Finally, organized associations can enhance positive linkages between staff, students, and the wider society.

In addition to student associations, the dean of students could, if well supported, provide an important avenue for resolving student-related problems. However, in most universities, this position is relatively weak because students see deans as uncritical representatives of the administration, because deans are usually overwhelmed by large numbers of students, and because the position is marginalized within the university administrative structures (deans generally report to registrars or deputy vice-chancellors). Moreover, most deans of students do not possess much professional training and are rarely given opportunities for further training. In addition to regular training, the position of dean of students could be strengthened by elevating its status within the university hierarchy by making deans answerable to the vice-chancellor or by making the deanship equivalent to the position of deputy vice-chancellor. It is also important to make this position financially attractive to lure highly qualified professionals.

Dialogue and communication could be further promoted through impromptu informal meetings between university administrations and students. In this connection, the University of Ghana's elaborate system of junior common rooms and a residence board where senior administrators can interact with students and staff informally has done much to improve relations between the two groups (Mwiria 1992). Makerere University in Uganda has also used a system of communication rather effectively with regard to matters affecting both staff and students (Mwiria 1999). Beginning in the early 1990s, the university secretary's department has taken a number of measures to make the university administration more responsive to the needs of staff and students. In an effort to promote transparency in dealing with staff, top university administrators have made themselves more accessible to all staff who want to discuss any matters pertaining to their employment at the institution. The university has launched a weekly newsletter that summarizes information about staff appointments and promotions; important decisions reached by departmental, faculty, senate, and council meetings; student admissions; newly introduced programs; and other key developments. This publication has done much to reduce rumors, thus contributing to the promotion of transparency among members of the university community.

The university secretary's office has also established a system of quarterly management meetings with faculty and departmental administrators during which the vice-chancellor presents a situation report on institutional developments during the previous quarter. In addition, the university administration has initiated regular faculty visits to familiarize itself with events taking place at the faculty and departmental levels. Finally, the university administration has supported the idea of a strong academic staff association as the bridge between it and the academic community. This used to be a major area of weakness in the 1970s and 1980s, when Uganda was under military dictatorship. The Makerere University administration recognizes the presence and legitimacy of the staff and student associations by consulting its officials regularly on matters related to staff welfare. Thus, both the staff and student associations are represented in all the key university governing bodies. To ensure that tensions between administrators and students are kept to a minimum, the university administration holds regular dialogues with the leadership of the student association. From time to time, top university administrators arrange consultation meetings for the whole student population. The university administration also invites the minister of education to confer with staff and students on some of the problems they face at the institution and on the best ways to resolve them. Staff and students are now more prepared to cooperate with both the administration and the government. Students are also represented in smaller but critical committees such as the disciplinary and menu committees, and they are given the opportunity to voice their concerns on teaching and examinations and on any cases of unfair discrimination by staff.

THE FUTURE OF UNIVERSITY GOVERNANCE AND UNIVERSITY-STATE RELATIONS

Many of the changes that have taken and are taking place in African universities and at the level of university relations owe a great deal to the tide of democratization that has swept through the African continent since the fall of the Iron Curtain. For most African countries, there is likely to be no turning back from this wave of political liberalization. Under such circumstances, universities are more likely to continue experiencing positive change, especially with regard to institutional autonomy. This liberal outlook is sure to impact the way in which staff and students relate both to their respective institutional administrators and to their national governments. Such a democratic institutional culture will in turn impact national politics. Likewise, liberal politics will affect universities in ways likely to lead to more institutional accountability to governments and the wider public. This is

because more freedom will have to come with more responsibilities on the part of universities. Within universities, academics will want to know more about how available funds are spent; they will ask for quality education, especially as more university services become privatized; and they will insist on more decision-making power, including that related to the identification of senior university administrators. The increasing number of private universities in some African countries is likely to play an important role in influencing the pace and direction of institutional governance and university-state relations. As more youth and interested adults opt for private university education, governments will lose some of their power over public universities because they will no longer monopolize the provision of higher education. Governments may also be forced to provide more support for public universities to enable them to provide an education of a quality that can compete with private institutions. In fact, private universities have a definite advantage over public universities. They are more efficiently run because they are motivated by the profit motive and are free of political interference. To be competitive with the private sector, public university administrators have to be more efficient and innovative in their management styles, more democratic in their governance styles, and more concerned with issues of quality and relevance than ever before. They may very well be the ones to take the lead role in introducing reform without any urging by their respective governments, since politicians are more concerned about their increasingly competitive political turf. Forward-looking university leaderships could utilize this newfound freedom for the benefit of their institutions.

Also likely to influence the direction of change in universities is the behavior of both international and local donors with regard to decisions about which institutions and projects deserve their support. Partly because of calls for accountability by the taxpayers of the donor countries, donor countries are likely to be much more strict with their funding for African universities. Institutions associated with increased democratization and accountability for institutional funds are likely to be favored by donors who are asking for the same from governments. The same is true of both local NGOs and the wider public, which are increasingly becoming more aware, again due to increased democratization, of their role in keeping these national institutions functioning appropriately.

Regrettably, progress will be slow or nonexistent in a few African countries. This is especially the case in those countries under dictatorships. Economic underdevelopment, high illiteracy rates, and increased political apathy in some countries will also play a role in slowing progress toward better-governed and more accountable universities. The danger is high that these institutions will continue to be viewed as elitist citadels of little consequence to the lives of the majority of the African population. Overall, however, the drive toward positive change is stronger than that toward retrogression. In the areas of governance and university-state relations, factors external to universities, especially national politics and socioeconomic trends, will remain critical in determining the pace and direction of change. Any efforts aimed at reforming institutional governance structures must therefore reckon with the wider political and socioeconomic dimensions of African societies and their relation to

African university decision-making processes. Yet important changes must take place within the institutions themselves.

REFERENCES

Africa Watch. 1990. "African Universities: Case Studies of Abuses of Academic Freedom." Paper presented at the Symposium on Academic Freedom, Research and Social Responsibilities of the Intellectual in Africa, Kampala, Uganda, November 26–29.

Ashby, E. 1964. *African Universities and Western Tradition.* London: Oxford University Press.

Benneh, G. 2000. "An Overview of Tertiary Education in Ghana." Paper presented at the Foundation Partnership for Strengthening African Universities, Nairobi, Kenya, October 15–17.

Chege, M. 1996/1997. "Africa's Murderous Professors." *The National Interest* 46 (Winter): 32–40.

Coleman, J., and N. Ngokwey. 1993. "Zaire: The State and the University." In R. M. Thomas, ed., *Politics and Education: Case Studies from Eleven Nations.* Oxford: Pergamon Press.

Cross, M., ed. 1999. *No Easy Road: Transforming Higher Education in South Africa.* Cape Town: Maskew Miller, Longman.

Gaidzanwa, R. B. 1995. *Governance Issues in African Universities: Improving Management and Governance to Make African Universities Viable in the Nineties and Beyond.* Accra, Ghana: Association of African Universities.

Galabawa, J. 1997. "University of Dar Es Salaam Governance Structures, Organs and Role Offices: A Description of Salient Characteristics." Paper prepared for a regional dissemination workshop on the state of Kenyan public universities, Mombasa, May 28–31.

Girdwood, A. 1999. *Tertiary Education Policy in Ghana: An Assessment, 1988–1998.* Washington, D.C: World Bank.

Githinji, P. 1999. "Case III: University of Dar-Es-Salaam, Tanzania." In Svava Bjarnason and Helen Lund, eds., *Government/University Relationships: Three African Case Studies.* London: Commonwealth Higher Education Management Service.

Hughes, R., and K. Mwiria. 1990. "An Essay on the Implications of University Expansion in Kenya." *Higher Education* 19, no. 2: 215–237.

Hyden, G. 1991. "Academic Freedom in Africa: A Right Long Overlooked." Mimeo. Gainesville, Fla.: University of Florida, Center for African Studies.

Ibonvbere, J. 1993. "The State of Academic Freedom in Africa: How African Academics Subvert Academic Freedom." *Journal of Third World Studies* X, no. 2: 36–73.

Kotecha, P. 1999. "Case 1: University of Botswana." In Svava Bjarnason and Helen Lund, eds., *Government/University Relationships: Three African Case Studies.* London: Commonwealth Higher Education Management Service.

Mkude, D., B. Cooksey, and L. Levey. 2000. "UDSM-2000 and Beyond: A Situation Analysis of the University of Dar es Salaam's Institutional Transformation Programme." Mimeo. Dar es Salaam: University of Dar es Salaam.

Mugabe, R. G. 1983. "The Role of the University in the Process of Social Transformation." University of Zimbabwe Public Lecture Series, no. 1. Harare, Zimbabwe: University of Zimbabwe.

Munene, I. 1997. "The Struggle for Faculty Unionism in a Stalled Democracy: Lessons from Kenya's Public Universities." *Journal of Third World Studies* XIV, no. 1 (Spring): 91–114.

Murapa, R. 2000. "An Overview of Higher Education Reforms in Zimbabwe: Challenges and Prospects." Paper presented at the meeting of the Foundation Partnership For Strengthening African Universities, Nairobi, Kenya, October 15–17.

Mwiria, K. 1992. *University Governance: Problems and Prospects in Anglophone Africa.* AFTED Technical Note no. 3, Education and Training Division. Washington, D.C.: World Bank.

———. 1995. *Enhancing Linkages between African Universities: The Wider Society, the Business Community and Governments.* Accra, Ghana: Association of Africa Universities (AAU).

———. 1998. "Some Views on the Internal Culture of African Universities." *NORRAG News* (October): 44–45.

———. 1999. "Case III: Makerere University Uganda." In Svava Bjarnason and Helen Lund, eds., *Government/University Relationships: Three African Case Studies.* London: Commonwealth Higher Education Management Service.

Omari, I., and P. Mihyo. 1991. *The Roots of Unrest in African Universities.* Nairobi: Oxford University Press.

Republic of Zambia. 1987. *University of Zambia Calendar 1986–1987.* Lusaka: University of Zambia.

Saint, B. 1992. *Universities in Africa: Strategies for Stabilization and Revitalization.* World Bank Technical Paper no. 194. Africa Technical Department Series. Washington, D.C.: World Bank.

Sifuna, D. 1999. "The Governance of Kenyan Public Universities." *Research in Post-Compulsory Education* 3, no. 2: 175–211.

Tarpeh, D. N. 1994. *Study on Cost-Effectiveness and Efficiency in African Universities.* Accra, Ghana: Association of African Universities.

Task Force on Higher Education. 2000. *Higher Education in Developing Countries: Peril or Promise.* Washington, D.C.: World Bank.

World Bank. 1997. *Revitalizing Universities in Africa: Strategy and Guidelines.* Washington, D.C.: World Bank.

———. 2000. *Higher Education in Developing Countries: Peril or Promise.* Washington, D.C.: World Bank.

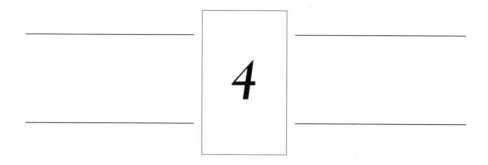

4

Financing and Economics of Higher Education in Africa

Maureen Woodhall

INTRODUCTION

Throughout the world—in both developed and developing countries—higher education has faced major economic and financial challenges in recent decades; demand has increased dramatically while resources have become more constrained. These challenges are particularly severe in Africa, where higher education institutions have faced stringent budget cuts and severe shortages of qualified staff despite rising public demand for access to higher education and improvements in the quality and equity of that education. In addition, economic changes have created demands for a more highly skilled labor force, more relevant scientific and technological research, and greater responsiveness to changing labor market needs.

There have been significant shifts in attitudes toward higher education in the past thirty years, on the part of both governments and international agencies and donors. Africa experienced a period of optimism and growth in the 1960s and early 1970s, when many African countries achieved political independence, responded to a deeply felt need to expand higher education (partly because of the need to replace expatriate staff by locally trained graduates), and increased budget allocations for all levels of education, driven both by rising levels of social demand and by research on the economic benefits of investment in human capital. This era was followed by a period of stagnant or declining budgets, as governments grappled with political and economic crises, wars and other emergencies, structural adjustment programs, and widespread poverty and unemployment. At the same time, many donors, partly in response to research on rates of return from primary education and to the arguments made at the 1990 World Conference on Education for All, switched emphasis away from higher to primary education. In the 1990s, a gradual shift in priorities again occurred, as increased emphasis on the "knowledge economy" and

research and activities for the 1998 UNESCO World Conference on Higher Education led to another reassessment of the role of higher education.

These changing attitudes have been reflected in a number of recent international conferences and publications on higher education. The World Bank published an influential report entitled *Higher Education: The Lessons of Experience* (World Bank 1994). A UNESCO conference resulted in the document *World Declaration on Higher Education for the Twenty-First Century: Vision and Action* (UNESCO 1998). These two agencies convened a Task Force on Higher Education in Developing Countries that reported in 2000 (Task Force 2000). In 1999, the Conference of Rectors, Vice-Chancellors, and Presidents of African Universities (COREVIP 1999), held in Tanzania, was entitled Revitalizing Universities in Africa: Strategies for the 21st Century. This chapter draws on information produced by these publications and conferences and on the activities of the Association of African Universities (AAU) and the Association for the Development of Education in Africa (ADEA) Working Group on Higher Education.

The chapter is organized in four parts. Part 1 summarizes the main conclusions from economic research on higher education, identifies key economic and financial issues facing African higher education, and considers proposals by the World Bank and other agencies to reform higher education financing. Part 2 reviews changing patterns of financing higher education and examines African experiences in mobilizing new sources of finance for higher education. Part 3 deals with the equity implications of these financing changes, particularly efforts to improve equity by providing financial support for students in the form of scholarships and student loans. Finally, part 4 considers requirements for successful financial diversification and examines recent experiences in tackling other issues raised in the debate on financing higher education, including ways of reduc-

44

ing costs, improving resource allocation, and strengthening institutional management and governance.

ECONOMIC RESEARCH ON HIGHER EDUCATION

The development of the concept of human capital in the 1960s led to extensive studies of the contribution of education to economic growth, the costs and economic benefits of education (using earnings differentials by level of education as a proxy for direct benefits), and rates of return on investment in education. (For a summary, see Psacharopoulos and Woodhall 1985.) This research demonstrated clearly that education is a profitable investment, both for societies and individuals, but that the benefits vary between countries, regions, and different levels of education. Economists have compared the returns to individuals (the private rate of return) and to society as a whole (the social rate of return), returns for different levels and types of education, and returns in different world regions. Estimates of rates of return now exist for more than fifty countries, including eighteen countries in sub-Saharan Africa. Over a twenty-year period, George Psacharopoulos published regular summaries and reviews of all known studies of social and private rates of return (see Psacharopoulos 1994 for a recent summary). On the basis of these reviews, the following general patterns can be identified throughout the world:

- Private rates of return are higher than social rates of return.
- The highest rates of return are usually for primary education, followed by secondary education, with higher education apparently being the least profitable investment in terms of social rates of return.
- The average rate of return for all levels of education is higher in developing countries than in industrialized economies.
- Rates of return for investment in education generally exceed the average social opportunity costs of capital [that is, the average rate of return to alternative social investments— 10 percent is usually used as an approximate yardstick], and in most developing countries, rates of return for education exceed average rates of return for physical capital.

Since Psacharopoulos was a senior economist in the World Bank for much of this period, his conclusions were widely quoted and had considerable influence, not only on World Bank lending policies but also on investment and aid strategies of other international agencies and donors. In particular, the conclusions of the World Bank study *Financing Education in Developing Countries* that "in most developing countries primary education should receive the highest investment priority" and "the present financing arrangements contribute to the misallocation of resources devoted to education" because higher education was "the relatively less socially efficient investment" (World Bank 1986, 9–10) contributed to the shift in donor priorities away from higher education and toward primary education. So pervasive was this effect that the Task Force on Higher Education notes that "the World Bank drew the conclusion that its lending strategy should emphasize primary education, relegating higher education to a relatively minor place on its development agenda" (Task Force 2000, 39).

Critics argued that estimates of the rate of return for education are seriously flawed. In particular, social rates of return underestimate the indirect benefits of education (sometimes called externalities or spillovers) to society that are not reflected in relative earnings. For example, the Task Force on Higher Education and Society argued that rate-of-return analysis "entirely misses the impact of university-based research on the economy—a far-reaching social benefit that is at the heart of any argument for developing higher education systems" (Task Force 2000, 39). In a detailed critique of rate-of-return studies in Africa, Paul Bennell lists a number of weaknesses, including inadequate or out-of-date information on earnings, and concludes that conventional patterns of rate of return "almost certainly do not prevail in sub-Saharan Africa under current labor market conditions" (Bennell 1996).

In the last few years, the balance has again shifted slightly, and the social benefits of higher education are now more fully acknowledged by donor agencies—not least because higher education trains the teachers, doctors, and other professionals who are vital for all other forms of investment. Nevertheless, the conclusion that private rates of return for higher education exceed social rates of return has significantly influenced the debate on how the costs of higher education should be financed and shared. Even though there is doubt about the accuracy of social rates of return, the evidence that university graduates can expect better job opportunities and higher lifetime earnings is widely used to support arguments in favor of more extensive cost sharing in higher education, particularly through the introduction of or increases in tuition fees and the use of student loans rather than grants or scholarships.

The argument that individual students or graduates should finance a greater share of the costs of higher education and that the share of the state should be reduced does not depend solely on rate-of-return analysis. Many studies have concluded that high dependency on state funding is simply unsustainable given the competing demands on often-declining government budgets in Africa. There are also powerful equity arguments in favor of changing the balance between public and private finance, since participation in higher education, which offers the prospect of higher lifetime earnings, is far greater among children who come from upper-income families from urban areas and who have access to higher-quality secondary schools than among the children of the disadvantaged rural poor. If, as is still true in most African countries, higher education is overwhelmingly state financed, then the result, according to the World Bank's 1988 study, *Education in Sub-Saharan Africa*, is that "income inequalities are increased by the sharply regressive effect of higher education expenditures; the system ensures that the rich get richer and the poor get poorer" (World Bank 1988, 77).

Apart from a substantial body of research on the financing of higher education, economic research has been done on costs and efficiency, both internal and external. Economists use the phrases *internal efficiency* to refer to relationships between inputs (both human and financial) and outputs (number of graduates, research outputs, etc.) within the university system (as reflected in indicators such as graduation, repetition and dropout rates, and student-staff ratios), and *external efficiency* to refer to relationships between higher education and the labor market (as reflected in employment and unemployment rates, shortages and utilization of graduates and highly educated workers, etc.) Research on costs of higher education has focused on the very high relative unit costs of university graduates in Africa, leading to the conclusion that "costs per graduate . . . are exorbitantly high. As a percentage of GDP (gross domestic product) per capita, which is a reasonable proxy for affordability, unit costs . . . of public higher education are between six and seven times more than they are in Asia and nine times more than in Latin America" (World Bank 1988, 75).

The conclusion that costs per student are "exorbitantly high" may appear perverse, given widespread evidence (for example, in surveys by the AAU) of inadequate university buildings, equipment, and libraries; overcrowding; academic brain drain due to declining staff salaries; and frequent references to a "crisis" in African higher education. (As one example: "the damage sustained by under-resourcing in universities during the years of economic decline, in almost all sub-Saharan African countries, has been massive and in some areas debilitating. In short there is a crisis" [Coombe 1991, 1].) The issue, however, is the high *relative* costs of university education in relation to gross national product (GNP) per capita or to unit costs of primary or secondary education. The World Bank's 1988 study quotes average unit costs of public higher education as a percentage of GNP per capita of 1,000 in Francophone Africa and 600 in Anglophone Africa (compared with averages of 118 in Asia and 88 in Latin America). A study of education financing in Uganda pointed out that in 1987–1988, the cost per student-year at the University of Makerere was more than 500 times the annual cost per primary school pupil (Kajubi 1992). These figures are based on research in the 1980s, however. Since then, many African universities have experienced massive increases in student numbers and a substantial decline in public expenditure for higher education. Yet the 2000 report of the Task Force on Higher Education quotes 1995 figures for tertiary expenditure per student as a percentage of GNP per capita that still show that the average for sub-Saharan Africa is five to six times the average for Asia and nearly ten times the average for Latin America (see Table 4.1).

The high relative unit costs in sub-Saharan Africa are compounded by high rates of repetition and attrition, leading to long average duration of periods of study and low graduation rates in many countries. Student-staff ratios are often low in sub-Saharan Africa in comparison with high-income countries, reflecting low teaching loads, which in turn are often the result of low salaries for academic staff, which forces university teachers to take multiple jobs. However, there are wide variations in student-teacher ratios between countries, institutions, and even departments in the same university. An AAU study of cost effectiveness found student-teacher ratios of 5 in Sudan and 19.2 in the Ivory Coast. In a single university in Nigeria, the ratio varied from 4.6 in the Faculty of Agriculture to 50 in the Faculty of Law (quoted in Saint 1992, 64). Student-staff ratios are even more distorted in the case of nonacademic staff, which in many universities outnumber academic staff, leading to a student to total staff ratio of 1 in some cases, which inflates costs per student and reduces

Table 4.1. Tertiary Expenditure per Student as Percentage of GNP per Capita, 1980 and 1995, by Region and National Income Levels

World region	1980	1995
Low- and middle-income countries	259	91
Sub-Saharan Africa	802	422
East Asia and Pacific	149	76
South Asia	143	74
Europe and Central Asia	67	36
Latin America and the Caribbean	19	43
Middle East and North Africa	194	82
High-income countries	39	26

Source: Task Force on Higher Education and Society 2000, 123.

expenditure on essential educational inputs such as books and maintenance of equipment.

Following extensive research on higher education in developing countries, particularly on the financing of higher education (see, for example, Ziderman and Albrecht 1995), the World Bank's policy paper on higher education (World Bank 1994) concluded that higher education does indeed face a crisis as a result of rapid growth in enrollments and stagnant or declining resources, leading to declining quality and low efficiency. The World Bank proposed four strategies for reform:

- Encourage greater differentiation of institutions, including the development of private institutions
- Provide incentives for public institutions to diversify sources of funding, including sharing costs with students, and link government funding closely to performance
- Redefine the role of government in higher education
- Introduce policies explicitly designed to give priority to quality and equity objectives (World Bank 1994, 4)

These proposals were reflected in the design of structural adjustment programs, adjustment loans for the education sector, and higher education reform projects financed by the World Bank and other donors in several African countries during the 1990s. These countries included Ghana, Malawi, Mauritius, Kenya, and Uganda. World Bank proposals are still being used to guide ongoing strategic planning in countries such as Mozambique and Tanzania.

CHANGING PATTERNS OF FINANCING HIGHER EDUCATION

Higher education in Africa is still mainly publicly financed and provided in public universities, but recent decades have seen two significant changes in many countries:

- The growth of private institutions in several countries
- Financial diversification in public institutions through introduction or increases in tuition fees and increases in nongovernmental sources of funding, including research and consultancy income and other forms of income generation

The Role of the Private Sector

Private higher education has traditionally played a much smaller role in Africa than in Asia or Latin America, but a study for the World Bank (Eisemon 1992) concluded that

> African governments that have allowed establishment of private institutions have been persuaded of [the] benefits [of] deflecting demand for higher education away from public universities and colleges that are under great financial pressure, and saving some foreign exchange. . . . Private higher education in African countries can help to accommodate some of the social demand for higher education and to diversify university systems, and thus merits encouragement by governments. (Eisemon 1992, 27)

Several countries have recognized the role that private institutions can play in meeting some of the excess demand for university or other postsecondary education and are now permitting or even encouraging the growth of private universities or postsecondary vocational institutions. New private universities have been established in countries such as Kenya, Mozambique, Sudan, Uganda, and Zimbabwe. In some cases, the growth in private enrollments has been dramatic. In Mozambique, for example, the location of some private institutions outside the capital city has helped to reduce the previous imbalance between the number of universities or colleges in the capital and those in the regions. However, the proportion of higher education students in private universities remains low, even in countries such as Kenya, where there has been considerable expansion. In contrast, more than half of higher education enrollments are in the private sector in many countries in Asia.

The growth of private institutions, which is a very recent phenomenon in Africa, raises the important issue of accreditation or other means of quality control. In Kenya, for example, the Commission for Higher Education (CHE) is responsible for accreditation of all new universities, private and public, and for overall planning and coordination of higher education. In other countries, a ministry of education or higher education has responsibility for accreditation or approval of private institutions. Establishing criteria for such accreditation is now a critical issue.

Cost Recovery

Another recent development has been the introduction of cost recovery, which is traditionally much lower in Africa than in Asia or Latin America. In the 1990s, governments made attempts to introduce cost recovery or cost sharing by establishing or increasing tuition fees, often as part of a World Bank higher education sector or structural adjustment credit. In Kenya, for example, tuition fees were first announced in 1989 but were never implemented due to political opposition and student unrest, despite the fact that expansion of student numbers from 8,000 in 1984 to 40,000 in 1990 imposed an unsustainable financial burden on government funds. The implementation of a fee of $260 per student, together with the introduction of a scholarship fund for needy students (which caters to no more than 20 percent of needy students), was one of the conditions of

a World Bank education-sector credit, but there were many implementation problems. One critic concluded that

> the bursary scheme is currently fraught with problems of fair allocation. What has come out quite clearly since the bursary scheme was started is that it lacks well-defined criteria and procedures for identifying the needy. The result of the present haphazard and uncoordinated process is that many who deserve a bursary do not get it, while some awardees have been proved not to be needy. (Orodhu 1995, 41)

This shows clearly that success in the implementation of cost recovery is crucially bound up with the adequacy of any system of financial support for students.

In countries such as Ghana and Uganda, the first step in reducing public subsidization of higher education and shifting part of the costs to students themselves was to withdraw subsidies for food and accommodation gradually and introduce charges. In Uganda, for example, the rising costs of student living allowances (known as *boom*) and subsidies for food and accommodation meant that these costs absorbed over 80 percent of the annual budget of the University of Makerere by 1988, which seriously undermined quality. However, when the government announced the abolition of living allowances and the introduction of modest charges for food and accommodation, there was fierce opposition, which was eventually overcome by a successful campaign to persuade the public that free higher education and highly subsidized food and accommodation for university students was neither sustainable nor equitable. The vice-chancellor at the time, Professor W. Senteza Kajubi, argued:

> Since parents who cannot afford to pay the high fees demanded even at the primary school have to withdraw their children, only to be taxed to support the lucky few who reach the university, it can be argued that free education, food, accommodation, 'Boom' etc. at the top, are a form of subsidy by the poor to the rich parents and their children. (Kajubi 1992)

Since taking the first tentative steps to introduce cost recovery in Uganda, the government and the University of Makerere have introduced far more radical measures, including a wide variety of programs to generate income. The task force report of 2000 describes how Makerere "moved from a situation where none of its students paid fees to one where more than 70 per cent do. Where previously the government covered all running costs, now more than 30 per cent is internally generated" (Task Force 2000, 54). The results include allocation of additional resources to academic infrastructure, libraries, and staff salaries, which in turn has improved quality and staff retention. The task force concludes that this experience at Makerere "puts to rest the notion that the state must be the sole provider of higher education in Africa" (Task Force 2000, 55).

Other Forms of Financial Diversification

Many universities have also tried to increase funding from private sources by introducing various ways of generating additional extrabudget revenue. A study of income generation in African universities concluded that

> little progress has been made in African universities towards financial diversification and income generation, although the potential exists. . . . Universities must become more entrepreneurial, cost-conscious and profit-orientated. . . . Donors can materially assist by funding and organizing programs to educate governments, universities and students on the need for reform, by supplying proven, computerized management information systems, and by supporting efforts to establish income generating activities. (Blair 1992, 48)

Some African universities have moved in the direction of becoming more entrepreneurial by organizing evening classes, in-service training courses for industry, and other market-oriented courses that charge full-cost fees; by increasing research income; by setting up consultancy units; by hiring university facilities for conferences; and by privatizing university bookshops or other services and running them commercially. William Saint's report for the World Bank (1992) describes initiatives in Botswana, Ghana, Kenya, Lesotho, Nigeria, South Africa, and Tanzania, including some unsuccessful examples. He quotes one study that concluded that little or no attempt is made to determine whether or not these activities generate a profit or even cover their costs in virtually all cases (Mbajiorgu 1991). Saint's overall conclusion in 1992 was that "little progress in diversifying the sources of higher education funding has been achieved over the past three years. Financial diversification remains an important goal, however, because it contributes to institutional stability." For the long term, Saint proposes a university funding pattern consisting of:

- 70 percent state funding, through a block grant based on a formula tied to enrollments
- 20 percent funding from students and their families, including scholarships provided by donors and the private sector and student loans
- 10 percent funding from income generation, fund-raising, and other sources

Saint notes that a fundamental requirement for financial diversification is that universities possess the autonomy to collect and manage their income. This is not the case in most universities, particularly in Francophone Africa, where universities are unable to operate their own institutional bank accounts. "As a result, income generation flows directly into the public coffers and universities have no incentive to diversify their financial base" (Saint 1992, 59).

FINANCIAL SUPPORT FOR STUDENTS

Financial diversification frequently involves shifting an increasing proportion of the costs of higher education from the taxpayer to students and their families. The effects of this change on access, equity, and equality of opportunity (for males and females, different social or income groups, urban and rural areas, etc.) depend on the type and level of financial aid available for students. Many African countries traditionally provided living allowances, as well as free higher education, but in recent years the increasing diversification of funding sources for higher education has been matched by a growing diversity of forms of student support, particularly the provision of more carefully targeted scholarships for the financially needy and other disadvantaged groups. In several countries, including Ghana, Kenya, Nigeria, and South Africa, student loans have been introduced.

There were many reasons for the increased interest in student loans and deferred payment schemes in the 1990s. Just as the combination of rising enrollments and financial stringency convinced policymakers that higher education institutions could not continue the old system of funding themselves, so systems of student support based entirely on grants have proved to be increasingly costly to governments and ultimately unsustainable. Grants have also been widely criticized on grounds of equity, since they mainly benefit children of upper-income families, who will, as graduates, enjoy higher-than-average earnings. Since grants are financed out of general taxation, they thus involve a transfer of income from the poor to the rich.

Political controversy frequently surrounds the question of student loans, and a number of critics have pointed to difficulties in implementing student loan programs, particularly in developing countries, even arguing at times that student loans are virtually unworkable in Africa. This has led to a considerable body of research on the experience of student loans in developing countries (see Woodhall 1992; Ziderman and Albrecht 1995). The International Institute for Educational Planning (IIEP) organized a series of international forums to review experience with student loans, including a forum devoted to student loans in Anglophone Africa (Woodhall 1991); Francophone countries have had little experience offering student loans.

Student loan schemes in Africa have a very mixed history. A few programs, such as the Tertiary Education Fund in South Africa (TEFSA), have proved popular and successful, although others, such as the Kenyan scheme, were largely unsuccessful in recovering loan repayments for many years. Considerable problems arose in Ghana, where student opposition to the introduction of loans contributed to the fall of the government in 1971 and to the abandonment of the scheme in the following year. This experience was often cited in the 1970s and 1980s to suggest that student loans were not feasible in Africa, but Peter Williams, who analyzed this early experiment in Ghana, concluded that failure to mobilize public opinion to see the advantages of student loans and a feeling among students that they were being made "scapegoats for the country's failure to control higher education costs" helped to explain the strong initial opposition to the scheme. But he argued that loans "seemed to have become accepted by the public at large and even student opposition was less vocal once the scheme was in operation" (Williams 1974). Loans were eventually reintroduced in Ghana, first in 1975 to help with the purchase of books, then in 1989 for living expenses. The current scheme in Ghana is unusual in that it is financed through the Social Security and National Insurance Trust (SSNIT); graduates' social security contributions are used to repay their outstanding student loans before they can become eligible for pensions or other social security benefits. A study of this scheme concluded that student loans are regarded as feasible in Ghana and as an essential part of the system of financial support for students who would not otherwise be able to afford to meet the costs of accommodation, food and books. Despite problems of poor rates of loan recovery in the past, the Government is optimistic that the new scheme, introduced in 1989, will achieve a higher rate of recovery because collection is linked to the social security and national insurance scheme. (Kotey 1992, 458)

Experience in Africa and in other regions suggests that there are at least six requirements for effective design and management of a student loan scheme:

- Efficient institutional management, including adequate systems for selection of borrowers, for disbursement of loans, for record-keeping, and for data storage and processing
- Sound financial management, including setting appropriate interest rates to cover inflation and thus maintain the capital value of the loan fund and cover administrative costs
- Effective criteria and mechanisms for determining eligibility for loans, determining appropriate subsidies, and assessing requests for deferral or forgiveness of loan repayments
- Adequate legal frameworks to ensure that loan recovery is legally enforceable
- Effective loan collection machinery, using either commercial banks, an income tax system (as in Australia, the United Kingdom, and several other developed countries), national insurance mechanisms (as in Ghana), or paycheck deduction (as in Kenya) to ensure high rates of repayment and minimize default
- Information and publicity to ensure understanding and acceptance of the terms for borrowing and repayment of loans

Increasingly, an effective system of student support that offers scholarships or loans for needy or other disadvantaged groups, including women and students from rural areas, is seen as a prerequisite for the introduction of tuition fees. Without adequate financial support, students from low-income families will be denied access to higher education or are likely to drop out because of financial problems. Too often in the past, policies on cost recovery or fees, on the one hand, and scholarships, loans, and other financial aid for students, on the other, were seen as separate issues. In reality, they are closely interrelated. An effective system of financial aid for students is an essential condition for ensuring an efficient, equitable, and sustainable system of financing for higher education.

One difficulty that has arisen in many countries is the identification of the most needy students in the absence of reliable means tests and accurate measures of family income. The Tertiary Education Fund for South Africa has developed quite detailed mechanisms for estimating students' family income. These determinations are made at an institutional level, but there are many problems involved and the measures are often crude. In some countries, universities use proxy measures, such as the level of fees in a student's previous secondary school, to provide a rough measure of family income. If selection of needy students is carried out at a local level, it may be easier to identify

low-income families and to keep track of students after graduation, although problems arise when communities or institutions adopt the attitude that all of their students are needy and claim that it is impossible to differentiate between various individuals' needs.

A major problem with student loan schemes in many countries has been the high levels of default. Ziderman and Albrecht (1995) concluded that in Kenya, the combined effects of interest subsidies, default, and administrative costs in the 1980s meant that loans were actually more costly than a system of direct grants would have been. This was partly due to the low rate of interest charged on student loans, which was much lower than inflation; administrative shortcomings, such as inadequate records; and legal problems, including the fact that uncollected loans could be written off after a number of years and employers had no legal authority to deduct loan repayments from an employee's salary. The collection of loan repayments was not taken seriously. The Kenyan government transferred the administration of student loans to commercial banks, but some bank administrators had an attitude that "It is not our money," which meant few efforts were made to collect repayments. Collection efforts have recently improved considerably, partly as a result of investment under a World Bank project to reform the student loan scheme, including

- Computerization of records
- Legislation to authorize employers to deduct loan repayments from graduates' salaries
- A large-scale public campaign to emphasize the need to repay loans

Problems with student loans still exist in many countries, notably problems of default caused by unemployment among graduates and the need for frequent recapitalization of loan schemes with long repayment periods and subsidized interest payments. Many countries, including Nigeria and Lesotho, discovered that so-called revolving funds for student loans simply absorbed more and more public funds rather than generating savings. However, some of the pessimism that surrounded student loans in Africa in the early 1980s has been overcome, and some programs and reforms that were introduced in the early 1990s are providing better results.

CONDITIONS FOR SUCCESSFUL FINANCIAL DIVERSIFICATION AND REFORM

International experience in both developed and developing countries suggests that the success of attempts to reform and diversify higher education financing depends on a number of factors, including institutional capacity and political will. Analysis of experiences in African universities can help to identify conditions under which financial diversification has been successful or has failed. In 1993, the AAU set up a Program on Higher Education Finance and Management to support and publicize research in this important area. A regional conference to launch the program included a review of the implications of financial diversification for African universities (Woodhall 1995), which identified three requirements for effective policies and mechanisms for cost sharing and financial diversification:

- A strong and appropriate institutional framework to administer income generation and cost recovery and to target financial aid effectively
- Powerful incentives for institutions and administrative bodies to ensure efficient management and collection of revenues
- A consensus among politicians, academic leaders, students, parents, and the wider community about the necessity and desirability of financial reform

The review concluded:

Experience suggests that success in financial diversification in African universities will depend on a) effective design and monitoring of programmes; b) capacity building to provide appropriate administrative, financial and institutional frameworks for effective management and monitoring; and c) consensus building, to ensure widespread understanding and acceptance of the benefits of such a policy for higher education institutions, students, employers, taxpayers and the community at large. (Woodhall 1995, 22)

A recent report by the Task Force on Higher Education analyzes how these requirements were achieved in one successful example—the dramatic financial diversification that has taken place at Makerere University in Uganda:

The reasons for Makerere's tradition-breaking accomplishment can be found in the interplay between a supportive external environment and an innovative institutional context. Among the most important contextual factors have been macroeconomic reform, which has led to steady economic growth . . . [and] political stability, which has strengthened the government's willingness to respect university autonomy. Inside the institution, much of the reform accomplishment can be ascribed to the energy and imagination of the university's leadership, their faith in the benefits of professional, participatory and decentralized management, their unambiguous sense of ownership of the reform process and their commitment to a tradition of academic excellence. The Makerere accomplishment has lessons for other universities in Africa that face similar resource constraints. . . . It dramatizes the point that a supportive political and economic environment is a prerequisite for institutional reform. It also demonstrates the variety of institutional factors involved in creating a management structure suited to ensuring the use of resources, not simply for broadening institutional offerings, but for creating the academic ethos and infrastructure on which the university's contribution to the public good depends. (Task Force 2000, 55)

The experience at Makerere shows that financial, managerial, and other kinds of institutional reform must go hand in hand. Such reforms may include:

- Curricular changes to increase the relevance and flexibility of courses, which increases external efficiency and makes it easier to generate income from part-time and continuing education market-oriented programs

- New mechanisms for internal allocation of resources, which can improve internal efficiency and provide incentives for departments to generate income
- Improved utilization of staff, such as increasing teaching loads while reforming or increasing academic salaries to increase staff retention and reward performance
- Introducing management information systems and capacity building so that university managers have more accurate information about costs and performance indicators such as wastage and graduation rates

Such measures can help universities address some of the other key issues identified in the debate on finance and economics of higher education in Africa. These include finding ways to:

- Reduce unit costs without lowering quality
- Increase internal efficiency by reducing repetition and drop-out rates
- Improve the use of existing resources, including staff and physical facilities
- Increase academic and financial autonomy of institutions while providing the information necessary to ensure accountability

There are a number of positive examples in all these areas. Institutional diversification, which the World Bank recommended in its 1994 policy paper on higher education, can be seen not only in the growth of private institutions but also in the growth of distance education. For example, by the mid-1990s, the Open University of South Africa enrolled 130,000 students at a unit cost of 50 percent of the unit cost of conventional universities in the country (Task Force 2000, 31). The ADEA Working Group on Higher Education (WGHE) commissioned surveys of distance-learning activities in higher education and published a directory that included programs in Botswana, Cameroon, Madagascar, Namibia, Nigeria, Tanzania, and Zimbabwe (ADEA WGHE 1998). Recent developments include the African Virtual University, which is supported by the World Bank, and a Francophone equivalent, Université Francophone Virtuelle, which is supported by the Agence de la Francophonie. Other attempts to increase diversification include the development of polytechnics or technikons in several countries. All these initiatives aim to meet some of the growing demand for private higher education at a lower unit cost than in conventional universities.

It is important to improve resource allocation to improve incentives and reward efficiency (World Bank 1994). In their review of university funding mechanisms, Ziderman and Albrecht (1995) distinguish between negotiated budgets, input-based funding formulas, output-based funding formulas, and quality, or student-based, funding systems. Almost all the African examples they cite are either of negotiated budgets (Ghana, Guinea, Kenya, Senegal, Sudan, and Tanzania) or input-based funding formulas (Nigeria and South Africa). The disadvantages of such systems, according to Ziderman and Albrecht, are that funding tends to be unstable; they offer no incentives to improve efficiency, since institutions often cannot keep any savings generated by better use of resources; and they offer no incentives to become more responsive to labor market or student demand.

There have recently been a few cases in which a government has introduced reforms of university funding mechanisms to increase institutional autonomy and provided incentives to diversify sources of funding and improve efficiency. Examples include the University of Eduardo Mondlane in Mozambique and Makerere University in Uganda.

South Africa has gone further, following the 1996 report of the National Commission on Higher Education (NCHE) and the 1997 Education White Paper, A *Programme for the Transformation of Higher Education*. It has attempted to devise and implement a new funding formula for all higher education institutions that incorporates steering mechanisms designed to encourage universities and technikons to achieve certain policy goals. These include increasing equity, internal efficiency, or quality; becoming more responsive to labor market or social demand; and introducing and improving strategic planning. The funding of institutions in South Africa will in the future include two elements: block funding, based on a funding formula, and earmarked funding, intended to provide steering to achieve specific policy goals, such as the allocation of funds to institutions for grants and loans under the National Student Financial Aid Scheme. A recent study by the Washington-based Institute for Higher Education Policy (IHEP 2000) on the use of steering mechanisms that included experience in other countries, particularly the United States, is intended to help in the design of the new funding system by the Department of Education and its implementation in a Pilot Project Consortium on Higher Education at two universities (Durban-Westville and Natal) and two technikons (ML Sultan and Peninsula).

This concept of government steering using financial and other incentives is quite different from the pattern of detailed government control of higher education that prevails in much of Africa. Frans van Vught distinguishes between two government strategies for influencing higher education: state control and state supervision (van Vught 1994, 331–332). The concept of government steering is also an integral part of state supervision, which is gaining acceptance in many countries, although it is still comparatively rare in Africa. The Task Force on Higher Education quotes an African expert who reported that "with the government in many countries having assumed the power to appoint and dismiss the Vice-Chancellor, governance in the universities has thus become a purely state-controlled system" (Task Force 2000, 62). Not only is such a system inconsistent with efforts to make universities less reliant on public funding, it provides no incentives for them to become more responsive to the market or to social demands. Neave and van Vught describe detailed state control of higher education as a "high risk venture" in a world of increasing volatility that requires flexibility and innovation in higher education systems (Neave and van Vught 1994, 315). They document a general movement in many countries, particularly in Europe, Asia, and Latin America, toward the state supervisory model. The four African case studies in their book (Ghana, Kenya, Tanzania, and Uganda) show that state control is still the norm. Kenya, for example, represents the "state control model *par excellence*" (Omari 1994, 72). However, all the African authors suggest that change is inevitable. In Ghana, university reforms introduced between 1988 and 1993 faced initial opposition, but the study

suggests that "with the softening of the initial government approach of insisting upon specific measures and implementation schedules and the increasing resort to reasoned negotiation of realistic outcomes with full university participation, a significant confidence-building process has begun" (Sawyer 1994, 48). Case studies in Tanzania and Uganda have also predicted that future relationships between government and universities are likely to change in both countries (see Sivalon and Cooksey 1994, and Eisemon 1994). Recent experience in Makerere, discussed above, shows that this is already happening in Uganda.

Another recent trend associated with the move toward greater financial diversification and institutional autonomy is a growing recognition of the importance of strategic planning. This was a major theme of the Conference of Rectors, Vice-Chancellors, and Presidents of African Universities in 1999. An analysis of the experience of Eduardo Mondlane University in Mozambique for the ADEA WGHE provides both positive and negative lessons. The study concludes that the efforts to build a process of participatory planning was difficult, but that

> it had the immediate advantage of widening awareness of problems, encouraging a greater feeling of "ownership" among students and academic and administrative staff, and gave to the major actors hands-on training in planning and budgeting . . . and provided an important stimulus to conduct necessary reforms. (Fry and Utui 1999, 19)

A recent article by the ADEA, summarizing a joint report by the AAU and the World Bank, concluded that "the process of renewal within African universities can only begin when universities themselves seize the initiative. . . . University management and academic staff must assume responsibility for their own future and take initiative on their own behalf" (ADEA 1999, 2).

This review of recent experience in African higher education shows that institutions are already undertaking new initiatives that include strategic planning, the generation of new sources of revenue, improvements in internal efficiency, a search for ways to reform curricula, and the introduction of new courses, including distance learning, in response to labor market and social demand. Experience shows, though, that these efforts will work best in a supportive environment. Governments and funding agencies can promote such an environment by designing effective systems of financial support for disadvantaged students, through funding mechanisms that encourage greater efficiency, and through management information and training systems that help institutions monitor the effects of financial changes and improve institutional management capacity.

REFERENCES

ADEA (Association for the Development of Education in Africa). 1999. "Higher Education in Africa: The Way Forward." *ADEA Newsletter* 11, no. 1 (January–March): 1–3.

ADEA WGHE (Association for the Development of Education in Africa Working Group on Higher Education). 1998. *Tertiary Distance Learning in Sub-Saharan Africa: Overview and Directory to Programs*. Washington, D.C.: World Bank, for ADEA Working Group on Higher Education.

Bennell, P. 1996. "Rates of Return to Education: Does the Conventional

Pattern Prevail in Sub-Saharan Africa?" *World Development* 24, no. 1: 183–199.

Blair, R. D. 1992. *Financial Diversification and Income Generation at African Universities.* Africa Region Technical Department (AFTED) Technical Note no. 2 Washington, D.C.: World Bank.

Coombe, T. 1991. *A Consultation on Higher Education in Africa: A Report to the Ford Foundation and the Rockefeller Foundation.* London: Institute of Education, University of London.

Eisemon, T. O. 1992. *Private Initiatives and Traditions of State Control in Higher Education in Sub-Saharan Africa.* Population and Human Resources Department Education and Employment Division (PHREE) Background Paper 92/48. Washington, D.C.: World Bank.

———. 1994. "Uganda: Higher Education and the State." In G. Neave and F. van Vught, eds., *Government and Higher Education Relationships across Three Continents: The Winds of Change.* Oxford: Pergamon Press, for the International Association of Universities (IAU).

Fry, P., and R. Utui. 1999. *Promoting Access, Quality and Capacity Building in African Higher Education: The Strategic Planning Experience at the Eduardo Mondlane University.* Washington, D.C.: World Bank, for the Association for the Development of Education in Africa (ADEA) Working Group on Higher Education.

IHEP (Institute for Higher Education Policy). 2000. *Funding South African Higher Education: Steering Mechanisms to Meet National Goals.* Washington, D.C.: Institute for Higher Education Policy.

Kajubi, W. S. 1992. "Financing of Higher Education in Uganda." *Higher Education* 23, no. 4: 433–441.

Kotey, N. 1992. "Student Loans in Ghana." *Higher Education* 23, no. 4: 451–459.

Mbajiorgu, M. S. N. 1991. "Innovative Responses to the Problem of Under-funding of Universities." Paper presented at the Economic Commission for Africa (ECA)/Association of African Universities (AAU) Senior Policy Workshop on Resource Mobilization and Financing of African Universities. Accra, Ghana, December 1991.

Neave, G., and F. van Vught, eds. 1994. *Government and Higher Education Relationships across Three Continents: The Winds of Change.* Oxford: Pergamon Press, for the International Association of Universities (IAU).

Omari, I. M. 1994. "Kenya: Management of Higher Education in Developing Countries—The Relationship between the Government and Higher Education." In G. Neave and F. van Vught, eds., *Government and Higher Education Relationships across Three Continents: The Winds of Change.* Oxford: Pergamon Press, for the International Association of Universities (IAU).

Orodhu, J. A. 1995. "Cost Recovery and Its Impact on Quality, Access

and Equity: The Case of Kenyan Public Universities." *Higher Education Policy* 8, no. 1: 40–43.

Psacharopoulos, G. 1994. "Returns to Investment in Education: A Global Update." *World Development* 22, no. 9: 1325–1343.

Psacharopoulos, G., and M. Woodhall. 1985. *Education for Development: An Analysis of Investment Choices.* New York and Oxford: Oxford University Press.

Saint, W. 1992. *Universities in Africa: Strategies for Stabilization and Revitalization.* Washington, D.C.: World Bank.

Sawyer, A. 1994. "Ghana: Relations between Government and Universities." In G. Neave and F. van Vught, eds., *Government and Higher Education Relationships across Three Continents: The Winds of Change.* Oxford: Pergamon Press, for the International Association of Universities (IAU).

Sivalon, J. C., and B. Cooksey. 1994. "Tanzania: The State and Higher Education." In G. Neave and F. van Vught, eds., *Government and Higher Education Relationships across Three Continents: The Winds of Change.* Oxford: Pergamon Press, for the International Association of Universities (IAU).

Task Force on Higher Education and Society. 2000. *Higher Education in Developing Countries: Peril and Promise.* Washington, D.C.: World Bank.

UNESCO. 1998. *World Declaration on Higher Education for the Twenty-First Century: Vision and Action.* Paris: United Nations Educational, Scientific and Cultural Organization (UNESCO).

van Vught, F. A. 1994. "Autonomy and Accountability in Government/University Relationships." In J. Salmi and A. M. Verspoor, eds., *Revitalizing Higher Education.* Oxford: Pergamon Press, for the International Association of Universities (IAU).

Williams, P. 1974. "Lending for Learning." *Minerva* 12: 326–345.

Woodhall, M. 1991. *Student Loans in Higher Education 3: English-Speaking Africa.* Paris: International Institute for Educational Planning (IIEP).

———. 1992. "Student Loans in Developing Countries: Feasibility, Experience and Prospects for Reform." *Higher Education* 23, no. 4: 347–356.

———. 1995. "Financial Diversification in Higher Education: A Review of International Experience and Implications for African Universities." *Higher Education Policy* 8, no. 1: 16–23.

World Bank. 1986. *Financing Education in Developing Countries: An Exploration of Policy Options.* Washington, D.C.: World Bank.

———. 1988. *Education in Sub-Saharan Africa: Policies for Adjustment, Revitalization and Expansion.* Washington, D.C.: World Bank.

———. 1994. *Higher Education: The Lessons of Experience.* Washington, D.C.: World Bank.

Ziderman, A., and D. Albrecht. 1995. *Financing Universities in Developing Countries.* Washington, D.C. and London: Falmer Press.

5

Private Higher Education in Africa
Six Country Case Studies

Bev Thaver

This chapter analyzes the growth of private higher education in six African countries in relation to some of the perspectives and themes identified in international literature on education. The first part offers a brief outline of some perspectives and themes as they arise in the literature. The second part provides a descriptive overview of the six country studies, outlining elements related to the size and shape of the private education sector. Following this, it draws together certain key issues from the country studies with perspectives from the literature. The third section provides a brief comparison of trends evident in the country studies with those emerging in the private higher education sector in South Africa. In my conclusion, I signal broad themes that hold implications for social policy in the field of private higher education.

The growth of private higher education in Africa, which has been spurred on by both local and global factors, is a very uneven process. The steady growth of the sector has resulted in myriad institutional types ranging from not-for-profit to for-profit, each providing a specific social function. While the former tend to be religious in orientation, emphasizing a strong moral discourse, the latter tend to have a business orientation and a strong market-related discourse. With the exception of South Africa, where the market discourse predominates, the six country studies are characterized by the competing discourses of religion and the market. The tensions that arise through these various discourses are mediated by the state, which is driven by the need to redress inequities in higher education.

PRIVATE HIGHER EDUCATION: INTERNATIONAL PERSPECTIVES AND THEMES

Several themes are evident in the international literature on private higher education. One way of defining the field is to declare a boundary line between public and private in the overall system of higher education. However, "institutions called pri-

vate and public are not always behaviorally private and public, respectively" (Levy 1986, 15). For example, the criterion of finance, which is often used to declare the boundary line, cannot be clearly deployed because "private universities may receive State subsidies; public ones may receive business contributions" (Levy 1986, 15). This ambiguity makes it difficult to clearly demarcate the public from the private in university education in Africa.

Besides the lack of definitional clarity, the meanings of private higher education shift from country to country. Private higher education in one country may not have the same meaning in another country. For example, the country-specific contexts result in private higher education institutions being accorded one status in one country and a different status in another country (Geiger 1986).

A further problem in defining the field is linked to the extent of state involvement in the private higher education sector. A common approach to defining the field is to cluster higher education institutions operating independently of state finance and to call them private higher education institutions. In other words, "an institution is private to the extent that it receives its income from sources other than the State, and public to the extent that it relies on the State" (Levy 1986, 16). However, attempts to understand the nature of state involvement in private higher education institutions highlight the complexity of the relationship. The state plays an influential role, either directly or indirectly, in establishing the conditions for the existence of private higher education institutions (Geiger 1988). For example, the growth of private higher education in India is linked to policy changes in higher education (Tilak 1999). The role of the state is a key factor in the shaping of private higher education institutions.

Reasons for the growth of private higher education institutions must also be examined. The need for education that cannot be filled by the public sector is referred to as demand-absorption

Table 5.1. Number of Private Higher Education Institutions, 2000 (or last known date)

Region	Country	Colleges	Polytechnic	Universities	Total
West Africa	Ghana	27	—	4	31
	Nigeria	2	1	3	6
East Africa	Kenya	—	—	8	8
	Tanzania	—	—	10	10
	Uganda	—	—	6	6
Southern Africa	Zimbabwe	3	—	4	7
Total		32	1	35	68

Source: Ministry of Education 1995; Nwamuo 2000.

(Levy 1986). Various scholars have deployed this perspective to analyze the rise of private higher education in Latin America (Levy 1986), Japan (Geiger 1986), the Philippines (James 1991), Kenya (Eisemon 1992), and India (Tilak 1996). Another motivation is the need for differentiated education (Geiger 1985; James 1991). Proponents of this view argue that the need for different education arises when certain groups in society make demands for alternative and specific types of education (Geiger 1985). For example, country studies in Mexico have focused on the theme of differentiation (Kent and Ramirez 1999). Another factor in the growth of private institutions linked to differentiated need is the demand for better education based on the claim that private institutions can provide a better-quality education than the public sector (Geiger 1985). Along with local factors, such as the social demand for higher education, the ideology of the market has also been cited as influencing the growth of the private sector. This is especially the case with for-profit institutions. From this perspective, private higher education is perceived as a marketable commodity that can be traded. This application of market ideology to higher education is related to the growing international emphasis on education as a key to economic growth (Altbach 1998). The combination of these factors has resulted in the international expansion of private higher education institutions.

Having outlined some of the themes from the international literature, it is important to identify the extent of the debate on private higher education in Africa. There is a paucity of literature dealing with this debate. A recent study found that no large-scale study has documented the establishment of private higher education institutions and their contribution to higher education in Africa (Nwamuo 2000). Nonetheless, country-based studies, including studies of Kenya (Eisemon 1992) and Ghana (Ministry of Education 1995b) and a recent study on private universities in Africa (Nwamuo 2000), have been conducted. In this literature, two themes are highlighted. The first focuses on the demand-absorption thesis. For example, Eisemon argued that one of the reasons for the growth of private higher education in Kenya has been an excess in the social demand for higher education beyond the public sector's capacity to provide it. He also notes that the growth of private higher education was "an outcome of the great expansion of public secondary and higher education in the late 1980s" (Eisemon 1992, 7). This expansion

could not be accommodated by the public sector, and subsequently private universities were permitted to develop.

A second view holds that the rise in private universities in Africa is related to the enhancement of access to higher education. A recent study identified a total of eighty private universities in Africa. Within a context in which fiscal constraints result in declining standards at public universities in Africa, arguments are being made for the establishment of new universities with fresh mandates and missions (Nwamuo 2000).

AN OVERVIEW OF THE COUNTRY CASE STUDIES

Because of the dearth of available data, this study has confined itself to those African countries with good primary data. The six countries that form the focus for this study are Ghana, Kenya, Nigeria, Tanzania, Uganda, and Zimbabwe. Drawing on primary data and commissioned reports, this chapter charts the expansion of the private education sector in the six countries (Table 5.1).

In all six country studies, the number of private higher education institutions has grown over the past few years. However, it is difficult to accurately chart the size of the private education sector in the different countries. In 2001, the six countries had sixty-eight private higher education institutions.

One of the difficulties in charting the size of the private higher education sector is that colleges are so amorphous in how they function. For example, it is not clear if all colleges operate at the higher education level. Furthermore, no clear boundaries exist between their function as providers of training, accreditation, and standards. Consequently, the figure of thirty-one private higher education institutions for Ghana should be treated somewhat cautiously. If the college and polytechnic types are excluded, the actual number of private universities in the six countries is thirty-five (Nwamuo 2000). Within this sector, countries in the East Africa region assume the lead (Table 5.2).

In order to assess the size of the private university sector, it is important to make a comparison with the number of institutions in the public higher education sector.

The number of private universities in the East African region is beginning to outstrip the number of public universities in the region. In all three countries, one finds evidence of a growing private university sector. However, this trend is not ap-

Table 5.2. Number of Public and Private Universities in Africa by Region, 1999–2000

Region	Country	Public	Private	Total
West Africa	Ghana	5	4	9
	Nigeria	35	3	38
East Africa	Kenya	7	8	15
	Tanzania	3	10	13
	Uganda	2	6	8
Southern Africa	Zimbabwe	4	4	8
Total		56	35	91

parent in Nigeria, which has a very large public university sector and a small private university sector. On the other hand, the number of private universities in relation to public universities is similar in Ghana and Zimbabwe. In Ghana, there are indications that some of the institutions with a college-type status have assumed a university status. For example, the institutions of Valley View and Central, which were recorded as colleges in the mid-1990s, are currently recorded as universities (Ministry of Education 1995b; Nwamuo 2000).

One of the indicators of the growth of the private sector is the size of enrollments in private higher education institutions. In Nigeria, a comparison of enrollments from a public with that of a private higher education institution reveals a sector that is rather small. For example, the University of Benin has a total enrollment figure of 24,320 (AAU/IAU 1999), whereas the estimated enrollment range for the Babcock University (a private university) is between 500 and 1,000 (Nwamuo 2000). Finally, the University of Zimbabwe has an enrollment of 12,938 students (AAU/IAU 1999), whereas the Solusi University (a private one) has 529 students (AAU/IAU 1999).

While the enrollments in the private sector are fairly small, the number of private universities in relation to that of public universities is fairly significant. With the exception of Nigeria, the number of public universities is being challenged by the increasing expansion of the private university institutions. Thus, the growth in the number of institutions in the six country studies has not kept up with increases in enrollment size in the private university sector in Kenya, Zimbabwe, and Nigeria.

INSTITUTIONAL TYPES

With the exception of the polytechnic institutions in Nigeria, three institutional types can be found in the private higher education sector: universities, colleges, and professional institutes or schools. In certain instances (for example, in Kenya), there is a commitment on the part of university leaders to promote private universities as teaching-research institutions. Both polytechnics (mainly in Nigeria) and colleges (in Ghana) run courses at diploma and certificate levels. In Ghana, certain professional and bridging degrees are awarded through the public university. A variety of foreign-based professional institutes in Ghana offer courses that lead to a professional qualification from British-based institutions (Ministry of Education 1995b).

Examples of the latter include the Chartered Institute of Management Accountants and the Chartered Institute of Marketing. A combination of these types exists in those countries that form the focus for this study. Further research is needed on the transferability among and articulation of these various institutional types.

Africa seems to have a preponderance of institutions with a not-for-profit status. Because a correlation often exists between financial status and program orientation, not-for-profit institutions tend to have a religious orientation (either Islamic or Christian), while for-profit institutions tend to take a secular approach. With the exception of the professional institutes, this religious orientation is also evident in the not-for-profit colleges, polytechnics, and universities.

PROGRAM FOCUS

Private higher education institutions offer a variety of programs at various levels. Within Ghana, colleges can be divided into four subsets, each with a specific program focus. The not-for-profit theological colleges offer programs in training for the priesthood at the certificate and diploma levels. A subset of religious colleges provide business programs that complement the religious studies component. These are offered toward degree-level courses, in partnership with the University of Ghana. A third subset of colleges has a vocational thrust, offering certificate courses in art and design, telecommunications, and automobile engineering. Finally, the colleges of professional studies (also referred to as professional schools/institutes) provide mainly professional training in accounting, management, business administration, and marketing through examinations run by the United Kingdom–based bodies (Ministry of Education 1995b).

In Kenya, Tanzania, and Uganda, the private universities offer a mix of programs that range from religion, science and technology, nursing, agriculture, and communication to various liberal arts and social science courses. Several of these programs are offered alongside a religious studies component.

Within all six countries, the not-for-profit institutional types with a religious orientation focus on either Islamic or Christian education. In certain instances, the religious content is combined with a secular focus. To this end, an Islamic perspective is incorporated in separate courses in certain disciplines at the Mbale University in Uganda (Useem 1999b). For example, the political science program offers a module on Islamic political thought, and in the social sciences the theories of Freud and Darwin are discussed alongside Islamic concepts of human personality and creation. This is similarly the case with not-for-profits that have a Christian orientation. Both involve promotion of religious epistemologies. Hence, an emerging theme in the private higher education institutions is a strong emphasis on moral ideas and values. However, this religious discourse is gradually being challenged by the market-economy discourse that undergirds the business studies courses prevalent in the for-profit institutions.

Several of the for-profit institutions offer special courses tailored to suit the needs of the market. Useem has argued that these institutions do not emulate the "supermarket model of a university, with programs in all or most fields" (Useem 1999a, A66). Instead, they offer select courses and consequently are better understood as "boutique" institutions. Their courses are uniquely designed, as in the case of Nkumba University in Kenya, to suit the business market. As such, a differentiated mandate is being promoted among the for-profit, secular, business-oriented private higher institutions. A similar case for differentiation could be made for the not-for-profit institutional types, with religion being the differentiated demand.

Two key elements tend to dominate the curriculum in private higher education institutions: religious training and business management courses. In the field of business studies, courses include marketing, administration, management, accounting, and banking and finance. These courses are offered at the certificate and diploma levels (in the case of Nigeria and Ghana) and the degree level (in the case of Kenya and Zimbabwe). The emphasis on business courses suggests an emerging market orientation. Although no data is available for Uganda and Tanzania, official pronouncements indicate movement in a similar direction (Useem 1999a).

FINANCING OF PRIVATE HIGHER EDUCATION INSTITUTIONS

Funding for private higher education institutions is drawn from a variety of sources in the six countries examined here. First, tuition fees are an important source of funding for these institutions. In data gathered on Kenya and Zimbabwe, there are huge variations in the fees of private universities in these two countries. The Catholic University in Kenya charges a tuition fee of $1,268, whereas tuition at the Solusi University in Zimbabwe costs $55 (AAU/IAU 1999). There is also significant variation between the fees for private and public institutions in the two countries. For example, fees at the Catholic University in Kenya are three times higher than those at the University of Kenyatta (where the annual fee is $415). On the other hand, in Zimbabwe, the private university of Solusi charges a minimal fee in relation to that of the University of Zimbabwe (where the annual fee is $272). While the fees at Kenyan private universities are much higher than those of public institutions, the trend is reversed in Zimbabwe. The high costs of education in Kenya may limit access to an elite class, as Altbach (1999) has pointed out.

A second source of funding for private institutions, especially the not-for-profit religious-based institutions, are subsidies from sponsoring organizations. Lower fees are made possible by a subsidy from the affiliated body, as in Ghana, Kenya, and Zimbabwe. Another example is the Islamic University in Uganda, where the original founder, the Organization of the Islamic Conference, has funded the university. These subsidies are linked to certain conditions that tie the local institution to the ideals and values of the foreign sponsoring body. In Uganda, for example, financial support from Saudi Arabia is tied to support for a fundamentalist form of Islam, in contrast to the more liberal version common in Uganda (Useem 1999b).

A third source of funding for private higher education institutions are loan schemes established with national and international higher education stakeholders. The higher education minister in Uganda has argued for greater involvement by the World Bank, specifically in the form of loans to the government that can be used to create a revolving fund for its private universities (Useem 1999a). Similarly, in 1998, Kenya's Higher Education Loans Board introduced loans for students at private universities using a family means test (Kigotho 1998). In Tanzania, the public and private higher education sectors have cooperated in developing a government-sponsored scheme to enable students to enroll in private universities (Useem 1999a). In Nigeria, a modified loan scheme operated by the Nigerian Education Bank has been implemented (Barrow 1996).

Besides actively establishing systems to channel financial support for private higher education institutions, governments assist private higher education institutions in other direct and indirect ways. The Ugandan government has assisted the Mbale University by donating 300 acres of land adjacent to the current campus in addition to a prime piece of property in Kampala, where the university is building office space. The aim is to generate income through rentals (Useem 1999b). On the other hand, while the Kenyan government does not provide any form of direct subsidy to private institutions, it has taken an active role in helping the institutions to finance themselves. In Kenya and Tanzania, the government has encouraged the private sector to invest in private institutions, and the Kenyan Commission for Higher Education urges the private sector to invest in and donate resources to the universities. In Tanzania, the government is cooperating with the private sector to develop systems in which government-sponsored students can enroll in private universities (Useem 1999a, A66). On the other hand, Nigeria offers no government support for private higher education institutions. For example, in Nigeria, private higher education institutions do not benefit from the public higher education tax fund established through a decree in 1993 (Barrow 1996). Finally, in Ghana, private institutions are "treated no differently from other private companies, receiving no special privileges as educational institutions" (Ministry of Education [Ghana] 1995, iv).

GOVERNANCE

In private universities, the apex of decision making rests with the board of trustees, followed by the university and academic councils (Nwamuo 2000). In these structures, the rector, as a founding member, has strong decision-making powers and determines their composition in ways that ensure that the private interest is paramount. The composition of these structures is determined by the private institution, unlike governance structures in public universities, in which the state exercises control over appointments of key figures to councils. In the country studies, control over decision making in both not-for-profit and for-profit institutions rests with individuals as representatives of either sponsorship bodies or shareholder interests.

A key issue in the governance structures of transnational institutions is whether or not their values and governance instruments respectively reflect and ensure their interest. Where local universities are affiliated to a transnational institution, the two sometimes share constitutional structures (Ministry of Education 1995b). As a result, the style and culture of governance in international institutions ultimately impact and shape the local institution. For example, certain local private institutions in Kenya and Uganda are accountable to transnational religious bodies. Similarly, when the composition of the governance structures reflects individual interests—as in the case of the for-profit institutions—administrators are accountable mainly to private shareholder interests. Most private institutions have the independence to appoint staff of their choice, unlike most public institutions. While the state does not control appointments, it could be argued that sponsorship bodies exercise some control over the nature of appointments if such appointments reflect the values and interests of the sponsoring organization. For example, Martyrs University in Uganda seeks to employ people who have internalized the university's vision (Useem 1999a).

In private institutions, autonomy is exercised also in relation to the content of programs. Data collected across the six countries indicate that while autonomy from the state is clearly exercised in relation to curricula, academic content is influenced by the affiliated body in the case of the not-for-profit institutions. For example, in Uganda, sponsorship from a parent body in Saudi Arabia is tied to the promotion of a fundamentalist form of Islam (Useem 1999b). In a similar way, the market motive influences the academic content of programs in the for-profit institutions. For example, the program fields at Nkumba University in Uganda have a strong business-oriented focus.

Compared to public higher education institutions, private institutions have more autonomy from the state. However, this does not mean that the state does not seek to monitor and shape the governance structures in private institutions (Geiger 1988). To the contrary, there have been attempts on the part of the state in some of the country studies to replicate public governance structures in private institutions. To this end, some states have advanced the idea of uniform and standard criteria for academic governance structures across public and private sectors. In Kenya, for example, private universities, which historically have based their governance structures on the transnational bodies supporting them, are supposed to model themselves on public universities (Ministry of Education 1995c). Similarly, one of the requirements for the establishment of institutional governance structures in Nigerian private higher education institutions stresses uniformity of administrative and management structures with those that exist in the public higher education sectors (Barrow 1996). In Ghana, this strategy of replication of governance systems may be constrained by the highly personal and individual style of management prevalent among the for-profit institutions there (Ministry of Education 1995b).

ACADEMIC STAFF

In all the country studies, the number of academic staff working full-time in private higher institutions is rather small. This pool of full-time faculty is complemented with part-time academics from public institutions. Private institutions tend to consolidate this small pool by offering competitive salary packages and work benefits that generally are higher than those at public institutions. Against a backdrop of poor salaries and work conditions in public universities, private universities are determined to make packages attractive for staff. The encouragement of research among faculty is another strategy. Much emphasis is placed on promoting a research culture so that staff can keep abreast of developments in their field (Useem 1999a, A66). A trend among the private universities is to devise strategies to attract and maintain staff. This is especially important in light of competition for faculty members with East African governments, which are anxious to strike a religious balance in their cabinets and official appointments (Useem 1999b).

With limited finances for the further expansion of full-time faculty, private institutions often recruit academics from public universities. This is the case in Ghana and Uganda, where full-time faculty are supplemented by academics from public universities who teach selected part-time courses. This practice of moonlighting is also prevalent within Ghana's private higher education sector (Ministry of Education 1995b). It is important to note that moonlighting ushers in its own set of tensions. Moonlighting staff are not bound by the same institutional loyalty as those who are working on a full-time basis. Private universities seek to cultivate and harness the energies of their own staff. For example, the Martyrs University favors staff who have "internalized the university's vision and can form the core of the institution" (Useem 1999a). Consequently, it has a policy of giving its graduates the first option for employment before it hires from outside.

REGULATION

The expansion of private higher education institutions has necessitated coordination and control by governments in countries throughout Africa (Altbach 1999). Various legislative frameworks have been established to regulate the higher education sector. In each of the country studies, the legislative framework varies from being rigid, as in the cases of Kenya, Tanzania, and Nigeria, to being extremely weak, in the case of Ghana.

Kenya has very stringent regulations that need to be met in order for a private university to be established. It has detailed laws and regulations about the processes by which private universities can be established. Private universities are established by a charter granted by the president according to the provision of the University Act. A number of stringent criteria must be met before the Commission for Higher Education will approve a charter. These relate to admission requirements, program length, qualification levels, enrollments, competence of programs, minimum academic qualifications for staff, infrastructural facilities, and ethical standards governing university staff members (Ministry of Education 1995c). Similar conditions exist in Tanzania under its Higher Education Accreditation Council (Nwamuo 2000).

In Zimbabwe, the National Council for Higher Education Act of 1990 empowered the National Council for Higher Education to receive and consider applications for the establishment of private universities and colleges. The council makes recommendations to the minister of higher education, and subsequently submissions are made to the president. Through this process, private higher education institutions are established as corporate bodies with their own charter. The regulatory elements of the charter identify criteria for the organizational structure of private institutions (such as vision and mission, membership, governance, staff appointments, and conditions of service), admission procedures, and the political rights and disciplining of students (Ministry of Education 1995a). In Zimbabwe, every private higher institution has to pay a registration fee and an annual subscription (the equivalent of about US$5) to a private college trust fund established by the Ministry of Education. The fund is to be used for "effective monitoring of courses/workshops for college principals and their lecturers" (Ministry of Education 1995a, 69).

The private higher education sector has been subject to rigid regulations in Nigeria. This has developed out of the individual interpretations of the 1979 constitution, which culminated in a proliferation of private universities. Within six months of the ruling, twenty-six private universities were established in Nigeria, allegedly "without due regard to issues of quality, adequate planning, and funding." It is claimed that only a few of these institutions showed some evidence of planning toward their objectives (Aliyu 1984, cited in Barrow 1996). The implications of this for the maintenance of academic standards, as well as economic factors such as the employability status of students from such universities, necessitated government intervention in 1984. Through a 1984 decree, the government abolished private universities and prohibited the establishment of new ones (Barrow 1996). However, by the late 1980s, the increase in the social demand for higher education necessitated a review of this regulation, and the Commission on the Review of Higher Education recommended a set of criteria for the establishment of new institutions of higher learning. Through a new 1992 decree, federal and state governments and other interested parties were permitted to establish higher education institutions, subject to certain legal criteria. These criteria include factors such as an academic structure and focus that caters to perceived needs; a vision and mission aligned with Nigerian social, political, and economic aspirations; and adequate financial resources. Further, the criteria include a "master plan" for infrastructural and program development; adequate teaching resources, facilities, and tools; an adequate enrollment base and administrative structure based on established norms; and a system for professional cooperation and affiliation. The regulations are fairly stringent and have a strong focus on quality assurance measures (Barrow 1996).

Ghana undertakes very little regulation of nonuniversity for-profit institutions. The Education Act of 1961 makes provision for the registration and regulation of all private tertiary institutions in Ghana, but it appears never to have been enforced. The private colleges are treated no differently than other private companies. In this sense, the government argues that no special privileges are accorded to private institutions (Ministry of Education 1995b).

With the exception of Ghana, where a legislative framework for private higher education institutions was established forty years ago, such structures have been introduced only recently in countries such as Kenya, Nigeria, and Zimbabwe. Their focus is varied: in Kenya there is a strong academic focus to the crite-

ria, whereas the focus in Nigeria and Zimbabwe is on financial stability and organizational structures, respectively.

KEY THEMES

Expansion and Differentiation

All six countries under consideration have shown a steady increase in the number of private higher education institutions. In Uganda and Kenya, the escalating demand for higher education has led senior higher education officials to advocate for the growth of a private university sector. In Uganda, legislation favoring the establishment of a National Council for Higher Education to act as an accrediting body for the private universities has been considered by the Parliament (Useem 1999a). Demand for higher education has outstripped supply in Zimbabwe as well (Ministry of Education 1995a). In the late 1980s, Zimbabwe witnessed a rapid expansion of A-level students that culminated in the application of selective entry criteria by the public university. However, the public sector was not able to meet this increase in demand in a swift way. This excess in the social demand for higher education resulted in revised legislation that empowered the National Council for Higher Education to receive and consider applications for the establishment of private universities and colleges (Ministry of Education 1995a). This was also the case in Nigeria after the implementation of a decree in 1992 that permitted the establishment of private higher education institutions. Indications are that Ghana has also witnessed increased growth in its private education sector.

The rise of private higher education institutions is linked to the needs of specific groups. In all six countries, private universities are related to various denominations of Christianity. For example, the Seventh-Day Adventist church has a presence in Nigeria, Ghana, and Uganda; the Methodist church has a presence in Ghana, Kenya, and Zimbabwe; the Catholic church has a presence in Kenya, Nigeria, and Uganda; and the Episcopal, Lutheran, and Pentecostal churches have a presence in Tanzania and Ghana. Although Christianity predominates, Islam also plays a role at the Universities of Zanzibar in Tanzania and Mbale in Uganda. It is clear that the social function of religious-based private higher education institutions is to provide professional training as well as to advance religious forms of knowledge at the university level. Arguably, the inculcation of religious values at the higher education level could be one way of challenging secular and westernized epistemologies that dominate the production of knowledge in higher education.

Financing of Private Higher Education

Private higher education institutions are self-financing and draw their funding from diverse sources. This diversity creates its own sort of tensions. For example, high tuition costs could limit access to an elite class of students (Altbach 1999). This would ultimately defeat one of the key "fresh missions and mandates" (Nwamuo 2000), which is to open up access to higher education. With regard to sponsorship from affiliated transnational institutions, indications are that finance is tied to certain conditions that ultimately place limits on the autonomy of the institution. In a similar way, loans from bodies such as the World Bank could influence the types of courses that students could undertake. Finally, direct governmental assistance for private institutions in all the country studies could provoke criticism that governmental support for private institutions undermines support for public institutions (Altbach 1999).

Ownership and Profits

In all the country studies, the majority of the institutions operate on a not-for-profit basis, while an emerging minority operates on a for-profit basis. The religious-based institutions have legal rights, which vary from country to country, that do not permit them to earn a profit, effectively guaranteeing them a high level of autonomy (Altbach 1999). In all the country studies, there is a range of Christian-based denominations; Uganda and Tanzania have an additional Islamic presence. These groupings either "own" or indirectly influence the course of decisions in these institutions.

Autonomy

In the country studies, both not-for-profit and for-profit institutions are relatively autonomous from state control, which does not mean that no laws govern their operations. Various legislative frameworks regulate the two education sectors in the different countries. With the exception of Ghana, which has very limited enforcement, the frameworks are fairly rigid in the cases of Kenya, Nigeria, Tanzania, and Zimbabwe. While the state sets the boundary for the operations of private institutions, they are also permitted a fair degree of autonomy (Altbach 1999).

Multinationalization of Higher Education

A key theme in the private higher education institutions in the six country studies, more especially in the for-profit sector, is the influence of market ideology on higher education (Altbach 1999). Private higher education is perceived as a marketable commodity that can be traded. In East Africa, evidence points to the emergence of secular-based private higher institutions with a for-profit motive that are managed by a new group of "education entrepreneurs" deploying market principles in education (Useem 1999a). This pattern of education entrepreneurship is evident at the University of Igbidion in Nigeria. The application of market ideology to higher education is related to a global ideology that defines education as a private good for economic growth (Altbach 1998).

COMPARATIVE TRENDS IN PRIVATE HIGHER EDUCATION

The rise of the private higher education sector in the mid-1990s in South Africa is linked to the country's racial legacy of apartheid. At this time, the predominantly white student population developed a demand for "better education." In the mid-1990s, "when black South Africans started flocking to the universities, white South Africans started leaving the universities and moved into private institutions" (Thaver 2001). This

phenomenon arose from the shifting political conditions as South Africa moved from an apartheid to a democratic policy framework.

One element of the democratic policy framework of the 1990s was the opening of higher education institutions to all students with the requisite entry requirements. This culminated in a shift in the color profile to one that was increasingly more black. However, at the same time, negative public perceptions developed regarding standards at public higher education institutions, which contributed to the flight of white students to private higher education institutions. It is important to note that private higher education institutions had begun to mushroom by the mid-1990s. These institutions had taken advantage of the conducive conditions ushered in by the new constitution of 1996, which acknowledged the right of everyone to establish independent educational institutions. As a consequence of these favorable conditions, several local and transnational institutions engaged in various twinning and partnership arrangements. The period of the late 1990s in South Africa was marked by the rapid growth of private transnational higher education institutions. Whereas factors such as excess and differentiated demand for higher education are key rationales for the rise of private higher education in the six country studies reviewed here, the need for "better education" within a racialized framework is a significant rationale in the South African context.

In South Africa, it is very difficult to clearly chart the size of the private education sector. A recent study conducted by the Education Policy Unit at the University of the Western Cape found that South Africa has approximately 323 such institutions (Mabizela, Subotzky, and Thaver 2000). This figure should be treated cautiously, as several of these institutions had initially been operating at a level beyond Grade 10 and then crossed over (with some of their provisioning) into the higher education level. The boundary line between further and higher education is thus ambiguous, making it difficult to accurately chart the size of the sector both in terms of the number of institutions and enrollments.

In terms of institutional types, the variety evident in the country studies is similar to that of South Africa. There, in addition to colleges, there are several international professional institutes, very similar to those in Ghana. For example, South Africa's Institutes of Marketing and Accounting also operate in Ghana. However, a key difference exists between the country studies and South Africa in relation to the size and presence of private universities. The private university presence in South Africa is exclusively comprised of transnational institutions. The country has no local private university presence.

Whereas not-for-profit institutional types with a religious-moral focus dominate in the six countries examined, for-profit institutional types with a business-management studies focus dominate in South Africa. In line with the profit motive, courses are only provided when there are sufficient students to generate a high return on the profit margins (Thaver 2001). Since they are mainly profit-making enterprises, course provision is subject to financial feasibility.

We can also see similarities in staffing trends. In the country studies, the pool of qualified staff is relatively small; hence there is much reliance on staff from the public institutions. This practice of moonlighting is also evident in South Africa. Although the private higher education sector is rapidly expanding there, it relies on a small pool of full-time staff. It complements this pool by drawing on academics from public institutions. In both the country studies and South Africa, this tendency to moonlight may have the effect of undermining institutional loyalty.

While several of the country studies are sustained through diverse sources of funding, this is not the case with the private higher education institutions in South Africa. Their primary source of income is through tuition fees, which are very high, thereby restricting access to education. Furthermore, unlike some other countries, private higher education institutions have not been able to muster much governmental support in South Africa.

Currently, the legal instruments governing private higher education in South Africa are the Higher Education Act of 1997 and the Higher Education Amendment Act of 2000. Both demarcate the boundaries for registration as a private higher education institution. At the time of this study, a detailed regulatory framework for the operations of private institutions was in progress.

CONCLUSION

This chapter has focused on private higher education institutions in Ghana, Nigeria, Kenya, Tanzania, Uganda, and Zimbabwe. Patterns from these country studies were then compared with those patterns that are emerging in the private education sector in South Africa. This comparative discussion has highlighted several broader themes that need consideration from a policy perspective.

One such theme is the role of the state in controlling higher education and private ownership, which can create tension between national socioeconomic priorities and private market priorities. The lack of accountability of private institutions poses a challenge for the ability of states to control the higher education systems in ways that can be beneficial to the society at large (Altbach 1999).

From this study, it is clear that global economic processes such as the deregulation of world markets and the increasing commodification of education have resulted in higher education being treated as an economic good. To this end, various transnational institutions are engaging in partnership arrangements with local private higher education institutions. This has resulted in the fragmentation and subsequent marketing of different elements of the academic program. African states are thus presented with the complex challenge of regulating their education sectors in the interest of national priorities that seek to redress colonial legacies within a context of fiscal constraints, decentralization, and globalization.

BIBLIOGRAPHY

AAU/IAU (Association of African Universities and International Association of Universities). 1999. *Guide to Higher Education in Africa.* London: Macmillan Reference Limited.

Altbach, P. G. 1998. "Themes and Variations in Comparative Perspective." *International Higher Education* 10 (Winter): 10.

———. 1999. "Private Higher Education: Themes and Variations in Comparative Perspective." In P. G. Altbach, ed., *Private Prometheus: Private Higher Education and Development in the 21st Century.* Westport, Conn.: Greenwood Publishers.

Barrow, M. 1996. "Developments in Private Post Secondary Education in Nigeria." In A. Schofield, ed., *Private Post-secondary Education in Four Commonwealth Countries.* Paris: UNESCO.

East African. 1999. "Private Universities Flourish Despite Their Prohibitive Costs." (October 11–17).

Eisemon, T. O. 1992. "Private Initiatives and Traditions of State Control in Higher Education in Sub-Saharan Africa." PHREE Background Paper Series PHREE/92/48. New York: World Bank.

Fielden, J. 1996. "World View: Change Out of Africa." *The [London] Times Higher Education Supplement* 26 (April): 16.

Geiger, R. L. 1985. "The Private Alternative in Higher Education." *European Journal of Education* 20, no. 4: 385–398.

———. 1986. *Private Sectors in Higher Education.* Ann Arbor: University of Michigan Press.

———. 1988. "Public and Private Sectors in Higher Education: A Comparison of International Patterns." *Higher Education* 17, no. 6: 609–711.

James, E. 1991. "Private Higher Education: The Philippines as a Prototype." *Higher Education* 21, no. 2: 189–206.

Kent, R., and R. Ramirez. 1999. "Private Higher Education in Mexico in the 1990s: Growth and Differentiation." In P. G. Altbach, ed., *Private Prometheus: Private Higher Education and Development in the 21st Century.* Westport, Conn.: Greenwood Publishers.

Kigotho, W. 1998. "Private Students Get Loans." *The [London] Times Higher Education Supplement* 13 (November): 10.

Levy, D. 1986. *Higher Education and the State in Latin America: Private Challenges in Public Dominance.* Chicago: University of Chicago Press.

Mabizela, M., G. Subotzky, and B. Thaver. 2000. *The Emergence of Private Higher Education in South Africa: Key Issues and Challenges.* Bellville, South Africa: Council on Higher Education, Education Policy Unit, University of the Western Cape, South Africa.

Ministry of Education [Ghana]. 1995a. "Private Tertiary Institutions in Zimbabwe: Case Study." In *Study on Private Tertiary Education in Ghana.* Ghana: Association of African Universities.

———. 1995b. *Study on Private Tertiary Education in Ghana.* Ghana: Association of African Universities.

———. 1995c. "Private Universities in Kenya: Case Study." In *Study on Private Tertiary Education in Ghana.* Ghana: Association of African Universities.

Nwamuo, C. 2000. *Report of a Study on Private Universities in Africa.* Ghana: Association of African Universities.

Thaver, B. 2001 (March). "The Local Conditions That Have Contributed to the Growth of Private Higher Education in South Africa." Paper presented to International Conference on Globalization, Cape Town, South Africa.

Tilak, J. 1996. "The Privatisation of Higher Education." In Z. Morsy and P. G. Altbach, ed., *Higher Education in an International Perspective: Critical Issues.* New York: Garland Publishing.

———. 1999. "Emerging Trends and Evolving Public Policies in India." In P. G. Altbach, ed., *Private Prometheus: Private Higher Education and Development in the 21st Century.* Westport, Conn.: Greenwood Publishers.

Useem, A. 1999a. "In East Africa, New Private Colleges Fill a Growing Gap between Supply and Demand." *The Chronicle of Higher Education* 46, no. 3: A65–A66.

———. 1999b. "Muslims in East Africa Develop Their Own Higher-Education Options." *Chronicle of Higher Education* 46, no. 13: A69.

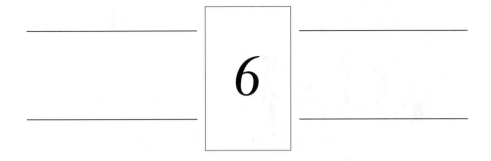

Foreign Aid Financing of Higher Education in Africa

Lynn Ilon

The story of donor assistance to African higher education is a story of waxing and waning resources and commitments. It is closely linked to the interplay of development ideology, the perceived role of education within that ideology, and the geopolitical position of Africa. Each of these forces has changed with the shifting political and economic climate of the world economy. As such, the story of why donor monies fell off during some periods and increased during other periods needs to be understood in the framework of evolving development ideology.

This chapter begins by delineating the geopolitical world ideologies of aid and various phases of aid orientation with respect to Africa. During these various stages, primary, secondary, tertiary, and informal sectors have each had their role to play.

Bilateral donors were largely guided or influenced by these trends but were by no means bound by them. Thus, the second part of the chapter explores deviations from dominant development approaches. It is within this larger picture that bilateral aid has taken place. Each of the bilateral donors has pursued a specific role and agenda within the dominant approach. Although bilateral agencies certainly followed the broader development ideologies, such aid also deviated from them when specific economic or political goals were being pursued.

Multilateral and bilateral donor assistance for education in Africa has largely come together in the most recent period. The emerging knowledge economy has brought to the forefront global issues of poverty, disease, and environment; awareness of these issues means that education for Africa is being viewed as both a good investment and a necessary humanitarian need. Multilateral and bilateral donors and philanthropic organizations have begun to refocus on Africa and, in particular, on the role of higher education in the continent. Whether historic "waxing and waning" will continue or whether this emerging period represents a fundamental shift in priorities, it is clear that agreement is emerging that higher education deserves immediate and substantial attention on the continent of Africa.

FOREIGN ASSISTANCE FOR EDUCATION WITHIN WORLD DEVELOPMENT APPROACHES

Education has played a very specific role in the history of foreign assistance to developing countries. During the early years of post–World War II development aid, education was not considered as a target. The predominant development theories of that time posited that the best investments were in "bricks and mortar," such as large infrastructure or building projects. Aid for education developed as a concern some time after the "human capital revolution" (Schultz 1961) and began in earnest in the 1970s. While bilateral aid has tended, in the broad sweep, to follow dominant development approaches, it deviated in significant ways, especially in the sector of education. In the era immediately following the independence of many African nations, education—particularly higher education—was viewed as a way to retain or strengthen the political (and, tangentially, economic) ties between former colonies and their colonial powers.

Foreign aid to Africa has had a complicated history. Although Africa has been and remains, by far, the poorest continent, it has had to struggle to claim a good share of development aid. The African continent received about 10 percent of total foreign aid to so-called less developed countries (LDCs) in 1974 (the earliest year that the Organization for Economic Cooperation and Development [OECD] has data). In the 1980s, aid to Africa accounted for between 16 and 20 percent of the foreign aid pie. This share rose to about one-third of all LDC foreign aid (exclusive of "countries in transition") in the 1990s. (In 1990, the OECD split its database for foreign aid. The two streams of data are now "less developed countries" and "countries in transition." All data quotes in this article derive from the "less developed countries" stream of data.)

Many tables in this chapter are taken from OECD statistics on donor aid. The Creditor Reporting System (CRS) from which this data is gathered is culled from some sixty-six agencies

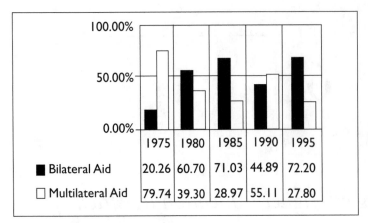

	1975	1980	1985	1990	1995
■ Bilateral Aid	20.26	60.70	71.03	44.89	72.20
☐ Multilateral Aid	79.74	39.30	28.97	55.11	27.80

Source: OECD CRS Data.

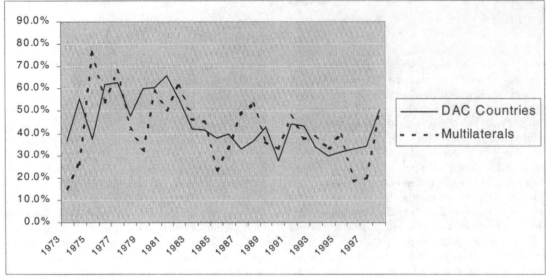

Source: OECD CRS Data.

FIG. 6.2. *Percent of Total World Aid for Education Flowing to Africa, Multilateral and Bilateral, 1975–1998*

worldwide, including bilateral and multilateral agencies. Bilateral agencies committing $100 million or more to postsecondary education in Africa from 1974–1998 were Australia, Canada, France, Italy, the Netherlands, Norway, Spain, Sweden, Switzerland, the United Kingdom, and the United States. Three multilateral agencies also contributed to African higher education over this period: the African Development Bank, the European Commission, and the World Bank.

Unfortunately, the OECD database does not cover philanthropic organizations, and historical data on aid from these organizations is not easily accessible. Some philanthropic monies have been committed to African higher education in the last forty years, but the sums are likely to be small when compared to total donor aid. According to the Carnegie Foundation's

Patricia Rosenfield, some Carnegie monies have been designated to African universities beginning in the 1930s. The Rockefeller and Ford Foundations began at later dates. Carnegie and Ford largely dropped out of funding African higher education in the 1970s and have only renewed their interest in the last decade.

A large part of education aid to Africa has come from multilateral agencies. Over the last twenty years, multilateral lending has accounted for about half of all aid to education in Africa, though multilateral influence is waning. From a high of nearly 80 percent of total education aid in 1975, multilaterals now account for less than one-third of the education aid to Africa. Further, special caution should be used in interpreting this data because the dollars reported in any given year were the *amount committed* in that year; a large commitment may be made in a

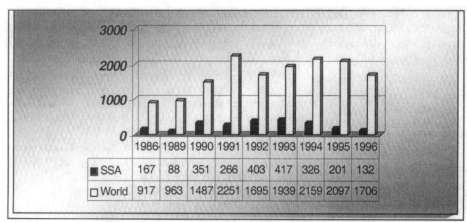

FIG. 6.3. *World Bank Loans to Education 1986–1996 (in millions of U.S. dollars)*

	1986	1989	1990	1991	1992	1993	1994	1995	1996
■ SSA	167	88	351	266	403	417	326	201	132
□ World	917	963	1487	2251	1695	1939	2159	2097	1706

Source: Bennell and Furlong (1997), table 4, p. 11.

given year, but actual expenditures could be spread over a number of subsequent years. Also, aid to Africa is characterized by "problems of absorption." That is, moneys committed are often never spent because bureaucratic problems exist either in the donor or recipient countries. Also, as noted by the Institute for Development Studies, some bilateral donors report only a fraction of their actual education spending in the OECD database (Bennell and Furlong 1977, 4).

Most of this aid has come from the World Bank's International Development Agency (IDA) loans. This agency loans at very low interest rates and concessionary terms to the poorest of the world's countries. Nearly all lending to Africa is IDA lending.

In sub-Saharan Africa, about half of all multilateral aid has derived from the World Bank; the European Union has picked up another 40 percent. In North Africa, the World Bank has undertaken no education lending that appears in the OECD data; Europe accounts for 84 percent of all education lending there. Even at that, the World Bank is Africa's largest education lender.

Donor aid comes from multilaterals (principally the European Commission, the World Bank, and the African Development Bank) and from the development assistance countries (DAC countries) within the OECD. They consist of the twenty-three DAC members: Australia, Austria, Belgium, Canada, Denmark, Finland, France, Germany, Greece, Ireland, Italy, Japan, Luxembourg, the Netherlands, New Zealand, Norway, Portugal, Spain, Sweden, Switzerland, the United Kingdom, the United States, and the European Commission.

By far, the predominant multilateral lender is the World Bank, which remains true to its original purpose of promoting market growth. It has viewed educational lending through the lens of economic theories of development. Education entered into the economic development equation around 1965, when theories of human capital began to seep into development aid. Since that time, lending by the World Bank has gone through several phases. Each took a different angle on how education best fits within market development.

The first phase of educational aid, the human capital period, theorized that education was predominantly an invest-

ment. Thus, educational aid ought to be targeted to those areas of the sector where the payoffs were highest. The next phase, structural adjustment, hypothesized that no aid (regardless of its projected returns) was very useful if the recipient country did not have fiscal policies that lent themselves to open trade and foreign direct investment. Phase three, called management and governance, built on structural adjustment initiatives and hypothesized that recipient governments had to have sound management and governance practices to absorb and maximize benefits derived from the growth generated by open markets (and, hence, educational investments). Phase four recognized that abject poverty and severe inequality hindered market development, growth, and stability. The final phase, just now coming into vogue, recognizes that knowledge will be a primary driver of new growth and sees development as linked to the ability to use and produce knowledge. While these phases overlap both in approach and in time, they serve as useful categories for charting World Bank education aid. Equally, they serve as guideposts for understanding thinking behind much bilateral aid because such aid is often based on economic interests.

PHASE ONE: HUMAN CAPITAL

The approach underlying the first wave of World Bank lending to education derived from a newly developed theory in economics known as human capital theory. This theory posited that individuals, families, companies, or countries could view education as an investment. The monetary and opportunity costs of education could, if properly guided, bring considerable returns in the form of increased productivity and earnings (Schultz 1963). This logic was applied to LDCs in many subsequent rate-of-return studies (Psacharopoulos 1973; Psacharopoulos and Woodhall 1985).

The view that education was an investment spurred two clear trends in foreign aid thinking. First, educational aid was quickly added to the mix of development aid. Beginning in the 1960s and increasing pell-mell through the 1970s as well as much of the 1980s, education became a larger share of the total aid package.

In their comprehensive article on foreign assistance to higher education in Africa, Eisemon and Kourouma chart many of the same trends in higher education financing. The human capital era is termed the "golden age" of assistance for university development:

> Educational expansion was the keystone of economic planning, of social policy and of strategies for fostering political development in African and Asian countries in the 1960s and 1970s. This was the golden age of foreign educational assistance aid and coincided with expansion of the higher educational systems in most of the donor countries. (Eisemon and Kourouma 1994, 276)

Early studies using human capital theory concluded that rates of return for education increased with higher levels of education (Schultz 1963; Renshaw 1960). Although later work on returns to education in LDCs contradicted this original conclusion (Psacharopoulos 1973), the continual increase of moneys for education in general meant an increase for higher education as well.

PHASE TWO: STRUCTURAL ADJUSTMENT

The rush to invest in education and the accompanying assumption that educational investment had potentially larger returns than infrastructural, or "bricks and mortar" investment, however, soon began to slow.

> The educational system developed along relatively high-cost lines which could not be sustained in the face of the economic deterioration of the 1980s. When government revenues ceased to expand and, in some cases, declined, cuts in education budgets became inevitable. The [World] Bank bears some responsibility for this situation insofar as it encouraged expansion of education systems beyond sustainable limits without seriously investigating the recurrent cost implications of its actions during the 1960s and 1970s. (Ridker 1994)

The result of substantial educational and other social-sector lending was increasing debt throughout Africa without the theorized "returns" on the investments. In 1970, public debt in sub-Saharan Africa was approximately $6 billion; by 1998, it had increased to about $170 billion (World Bank 1999). A new development approach began to blame the disappointing returns for public investment on the recipient country's financial policies. Investments, it was hypothesized, could not reap potential returns if the country did not manage its internal and external financial affairs properly.

In response, the World Bank ushered in new loan policies for the region. The era of structural adjustment lending began in the early 1980s; lending was premised on reduced public expenditures and increased trade "liberalization" by recipient countries.

In the design of these programs, achieving domestic and external financial stability was seen as an important ingredient for a sustainable rate of economic growth. The most significant aspect of the adjustment efforts of sub-Saharan African countries during 1986–1992 was the progress they made toward liberalizing their economies, with a view to enhancing incentives and the efficient utilization of scarce resources. (Nsouli 1993)

Tightening the fiscal belt had consequences. A World Bank review of human resource lending during this era acknowledged this crowding-out effect. The World Bank's "lending budget for the social sectors was constrained for several years to make room for structural adjustment lending. In reaction, it urged its borrowers even more forcefully than before to pursue internal efficiency and cost recovery" (Ridker 1994, 13).

The percentage of World Bank aid devoted to education began a long downward slide in about 1981 as the institution diverted funds to structural adjustment lending. Such loans favored "the efficient utilization of scarce resources" rather than increased spending on social sectors. According to Lancaster, "Adjustment lending came to average nearly a third of total [World] Bank operations in Africa in the years between 1985 and 1995" (Lancaster 1999, 197). Thobani (1984) led the way by recommending that public sponsorship of education be reduced and student fees be increased. This new logic introduced a definitive budget constraint to the educational investment equation. Mingat and Psacharopoulos quickly followed suit. Writing for the World Bank's *Finance and Development* journal, they recommended that publicly funded student subsidies be phased out (Mingat and Psacharopoulos 1985).

Eisemon and Kourouma call this period "Over Investment in Human Capital" (1974, 280), and attribute the change in trends to new research from the World Bank showing that higher education had lower returns than did investments in primary education (Psacharopoulos 1973). "So long as attention focused on the marginal returns to different educational investments measured in terms of increases in lifetime earnings, investments in higher education could not be justified on the basis of efficiency or equity" (Eisemon and Kourouma 1974, 282).

During this period of decreasing foreign aid to social sectors, higher education was hit hard. The World Bank recommended cuts to higher education (*Times Higher Educational Supplement* 1988; Ridker 1994), and higher education institutions began making cuts that would have a decade of consequences (MacGregor 1997; Ping 1995; Dickson 1988; Fatunde 1998). As Eisemon and Kourouma note, "Throughout the 1980s, the resource base to support higher educational institutions in many countries was eroded. In sub-Saharan Africa, for example, public expenditures for higher education, adjusting for inflation, increased at less than half the rate of enrollment growth in the period 1980–1987" (1974, 282).

Structural adjustment policies per se were not cited as the underlying rationale for decreased spending. Rather, higher education institutions were viewed by the World Bank as highly inefficient (World Bank 1988; Brock 1996), and it recommended that specific efficiency "norms" be adopted (Eisemon and Holm-Nielsen 1995). A rift developed between governments and donors over higher education aid (*Chronicle of Higher Education* 1988). The World Bank's report on education in sub-Saharan

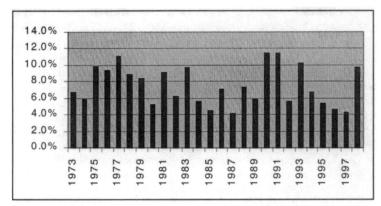

FIG. 6.4. *Percent of Foreign Aid to Africa Devoted to Education: 1973–1998*

Source: OECD CRS Data.

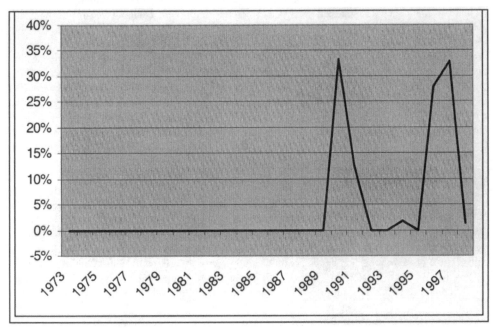

FIG. 6.5. *Percent of International Aid for Education in Africa Devoted to Postsecondary Education, 1973–1997*

Source: OECD CRS Data.

Africa (Moock 1987) was highly criticized by academics within Africa; the final version (World Bank 1988) added a section emphasizing the importance of higher education (Jacobson 1988). As a result, higher education was given a higher spending priority at the end of the structural adjustment period. In 1990, World Bank lending for postsecondary education had a temporary rise from its longtime base of zero. This rise, however, was short lived. Higher education was not to be a World Bank priority again until the gradual rise of the knowledge economy approach and the World Bank's concomitant emphasis on higher education.

The World Bank reported no spending on higher education until 1990. But a review of selected World Bank annual reports shows that some higher education spending was occurring as far back as 1976. It was not until the early 1990s, however, that such

Table 6.1. Spread of World Bank Funds to African Education by Subsector, Selected Years by Percentages

World Bank Report Year	Primary Education	Secondary Education	Higher Education	Other*
1976	13.9	29.9	14.5	41.8
1983	33.6	16.3	7.8	42.4
1993	22.6	13.2	20.3	44.0
1995	12.8	6.7	0	80.4

*Includes nonformal education, training, teacher training, and policy planning management
Source: World Bank Annual Reports, selected years.

spending began to be substantial as a proportion of total spending on education in Africa.

PHASE THREE: MANAGEMENT AND GOVERNANCE

Structural adjustment policies failed to pull Africa out of a severe economic decline. In a retrospective piece summarizing lessons learned and future directions on structural adjustment policies in sub-Saharan Africa, Nsouli (writing for the World Bank) concludes: "Quite often the progress made in putting in place [structural adjustment] reforms was hindered by a weak administrative and institutional base. . . . Good governance is an important element for the success of the adjustment effort" (Nsouli 1993, 22).

The bilaterals followed suit in rapid succession (Versi 1997). A Japan Foreign Ministry report stated that "the nation's foreign aid policy aims to encourage 'good governance' by developing countries in the long term, rather than merely meeting their immediate needs" (Washio 1993, 3). The U.S. Agency for International Development heralded "governmental capability" as a primary condition for development program success (Vondal 1991).

The philosophy of foreign aid to higher education moved with this larger development approach. "Donors moved 'upstream' into influencing policies affecting the higher education sector and 'downstream' into program and research funding affecting university training and activities of their staff," noted Eisemon and Kourouma (1994, 285). A Ford/Rockefeller Foundation report emphasized better management of university systems (Coombe 1991).

Spurred by criticism that higher education was suffering under structural adjustment, the World Bank put out its first policy paper on higher education in Africa in 1994 (World Bank 1994). The report emphasized the importance of examining higher education from an efficiency perspective and focused on reforming higher education systems and finding private funds to provide additional resources. Universities on the continent began to respond by asking for increased administrative control to divest themselves of "governance" problems endemic in their governments (Association of African Universities 1991). Some universities responded by emphasizing the need for better management processes and tools (Ingalls 1995; Nakabo 1999; and Biraimah and Ananou 1995) or more efficient use of resources (Liverpool, Eseyin, and Opara 1998).

PHASE FOUR: POVERTY AND MARKETS

Alas, even the addition of "good governance" policies to the liberalization and efficiency lending in the 1980s and early 1990s did not turn development around for Africa. By the mid-1990s, with a growing global economy, African economic growth had to take a new tack. The World Bank's HIPC [Heavily Indebted Poor Countries] Debt Initiative included support by the World Bank and the IMF to refinance HIPC debt through gold sales. The principal objective of the HIPC Debt Initiative is to bring the country's debt burden to sustainable levels, subject to satisfactory policy performance, to ensure that adjustment and reform efforts are not put at risk by continued high debt and debt

service burdens. The World Bank concluded, "Growth will not be sustained unless underpinned by investments in human and social infrastructure. . . . The Bank and IMF will strengthen the [debt reduction] Initiative by ensuring that department relief will target the poorest member countries" (World Bank 2000c).

Linking poverty needs ("human and social infrastructure") with market growth represented a new approach. Social-sector lending, largely neglected in structural adjustment policies, was now thought to be a prime target for new investment (*Business Africa* 1993). This new focus did not mean a repudiation of market-based development goals. Rather, stable markets were deemed to be a key factor in the reduction of poverty.

As the development approach moved to focus on the alleviation of poverty as a major strategy to build markets, universities in Africa once again had a difficult time justifying increased public expenditures (*Chronicle of Higher Education* 1993). In 1990, a conference in Jomtien, Thailand, became the base for a renewal of aid to education but an even deeper withdrawal of support for higher education. The Jomtien Conference (as it came to be known) and the highly limited moneys to universities in continuing World Bank loans caused considerable concern in Africa. "The suspicion is that donors wish to reallocate resources from higher to primary education and compel African governments to do likewise" (Eisemon and Kourouma 1994, 294).

The response by donors and African countries evolved into two related areas. First, universities in Africa began to emphasize the need for linkages among themselves and between the continent and universities in other international regions. In part, this recognition came before the recent emphasis on knowledge-value and was a response to shrinking budgets and investments (Vergnani 1991; Morna 1995). Second, it was recognized that technology was an increasingly good means of cementing these linkages, although the challenges were great (*Times Higher Educational Supplement* 1995; Useem 1999; MacGregor 1998). Several initiatives were implemented to increase connectivity for African universities (Cornwell 1998; Lubbock 1995; Kigotho 1997).

The focus on poverty and markets left African tertiary education short of donor assistance, although philanthropic agencies filled some gaps. The Rockefeller Foundation initiated its assistance to support dissertation work by African scholars, but most philanthropic funding agencies felt that support for the tertiary sector was a low priority in spending to reduce poverty. Other foundations did commit some money to higher education in Africa; about $5 million from the Carnegie Foundation went into African universities in the decade of the 1990s (Rosenfield 2000), and the Ford and Rockefeller Foundations also had continuing initiatives. So although bilateral and multilateral support was lacking, some philanthropic organizations put small amounts into African tertiary education during this period.

PHASE FIVE: THE KNOWLEDGE ECONOMY

The emerging emphasis on knowledge and its value is closely tied to markets and to poverty reduction efforts, but it still represents a distinct ideological era. "Knowledge is another important resource that the [World] Bank is helping to mobilize in support of accelerated poverty reduction in Africa" (World Bank

2000c). Africa's lag in development is now directly linked to a drain on knowledge resources (Kigotho 1999). As some analyzers have begun to acknowledge, "First-rate education and health care are vital investments in the assets [the poor] control: their own labor, enterprise and ingenuity" (*Times Higher Educational Supplement* 2000).

The juxtaposition of economic growth, poverty, and markets is relatively clear when viewed through the lens of a knowledge economy. The increasing market value of knowledge implies that diverse knowledge sources will take on increasing importance (Ilon 2000). Thus, the new development approach, while bowing to the realities of linkages between poverty and the market, has developed a second strand of thinking. Africa must be brought into the knowledge economy—both for its own growth and for the productivity of knowledge industries in wealthier countries.

Kaplinsky (1994) notes that knowledge inputs increase profits and productivity in even the poorest of countries and the most mundane of manufacturing processes. The full theory of knowledge and economics has yet to be articulated, including good working definitions of "knowledge" and "information."

The World Bank has a competitive advantage in knowledge. Aside from its considerable monetary resources, it has long been a storehouse of data, information, and publications, although some would argue that it falls short of a knowledge-building organization. It now has some 6,000 online reports with full access via the Internet.

The Bank's Indigenous Knowledge Project states that "it aims to facilitate a multilateral dialogue between local communities, NGOs, governments, donors, civil society and the private sector" (World Bank 2000d). One of the World Bank's background papers for the *1998/99 World Development Report* (World Bank 1998a) cites a good example of how local and diverse knowledge is used to help markets:

> As scientists at the Institut des Sciences Agronomiques in Rwanda and at the Centro Internacional de Agricultura Tropical in Colombia learnt, local women farmers have very valuable knowledge. The two or three varieties of beans considered by the scientists to have the most potential had achieved only modest increases in yields. They then invited the women farmers to examine more than 20 bean varieties at the research stations and to take home and grow the two or three they thought most promising. They planted the new varieties using their own methods of experimentation. Their selections outperformed those of the scientists by 60 to 90 percent. (World Bank 1999)

In 2000, for only the second time, the World Bank issued a policy report on higher education (Task Force on Higher Education and Society 2000). The report represented a "sea-change in thinking about higher education in the developing world" (*Times Higher Educational Supplement* 2000). The new report faced the challenge of how to reframe decades of work that had shown empirically that primary education was a better investment than higher education. Devoting an entire section to this discussion, the report concludes, "But the standard rate-of-return analyses stopped here, consistently failing to reflect that the benefits of higher education extend well beyond the incre-

mental earnings accruing to those individuals who receive it" (Task Force on Higher Education and Society 2000). Emphasizing the new knowledge economy, it adds that "statistical analysis, case study, and common observation all point to the fundamental importance of higher education to development" (Task Force on Higher Education 2000).

The task force viewed poorer countries as being at an increasing disadvantage in the stock of educated residents and the ability to produce new forms of knowledge:

> Countries that are only weakly connected to the rapidly emerging global knowledge system will find themselves increasingly at a disadvantage. The gap between industrial and developing countries in per capita incomes and standards of living will widen unless the corresponding gaps in knowledge and access to knowledge are successfully addressed. . . . Compared with investment in the production of goods, investment in the production of new knowledge yields potentially higher economic returns, but entails higher risks. For example, designing and marketing the best computer-operating system in the world is enormously lucrative; the second- and third-best systems are far less profitable. This would surely not apply in the case of steel mills, oil refineries, or food-processing plants. The winner-takes-all character of investment in knowledge demands a high level of existing knowledge and skills even to enter the fray. Few developing countries possess this knowledge. (Task Force on Higher Education and Society 2000)

Knowledge is another important resource that the Bank is helping to mobilize in support of accelerated poverty reduction in Africa. Ideas often matter as much as money—sometimes more: information is one of the most important resources in today's global economy, and the World Bank is ready to play a role. The World Bank has begun "stepping up support for higher education through programs like the African Capacity Building Foundation, the African Virtual University and the World Bank's World Links program" (World Bank 2000b). Joined by Canada, Ireland, Portugal, and the European Commission, the World Bank has developed the African Virtual University (AVU), which is run out of Nairobi, Kenya. The AVU is the Bank's major African initiative in higher education:

> AVU's curriculum includes foundation courses in calculus, differential equations, physics, chemistry, and statistics as well as courses in computers and engineering. . . . Recently, a curriculum task force was formed to structure a four-year undergraduate degree program in computer science, computer engineering, and electrical engineering. (World Bank 1998c)

In April 2000, four major U.S.-based philanthropic organizations launched a joint initiative to provide $100 million in aid to higher education in Africa (Carnegie Corporation 2000). The Ford Foundation and Carnegie Corporation have already committed nearly $1 million each to various African universities, while the Rockefeller Foundation has put additional funds into its initiatives on female education and support of dissertation work by African scholars. The MacArthur Foundation is at a planning stage for an educational initiative based in Nigeria.

Table 6.2. Recipients of Postsecondary Overseas Development Aid from Canada (by Percent)

Recipient	1970s	1980s	1990s	All Years
Cameroon	0.0	26.6	9.6	19.1
Kenya	0.0	15.1	24.1	15.7
Rwanda	9.9	19.9	0.9	13.8
Senegal	50.1	8.7	6.1	12.7
Ghana	0.0	0.3	16.6	4.6
Morocco	0.0	2.7	9.2	4.1
Other African countries	40.1	26.7	33.5	30.0
Total	100	100	100	100

Source: OECD CRS Data.

Table 6.3. Recipients of Postsecondary Overseas Development Aid from France (by Percent)

Recipient	1970s	1980s	1990s	All Years
Algeria	0	0	16.4	11.5
Burkina Faso	5.7	15.2	6.8	8.4
Cameroon	32.6	8.7	11.1	12.6
Madagascar	0	9.7	2.5	3.7
Senegal	41.1	8.1	3.4	7.9
Tunisia	0	0	38.7	27
All others	20.6	58.4	21.1	28.8
Total	100	100	100	100

Source: OECD CRS Data.

These effects are based on a recognition of the role of knowledge for the future of Africa and the critical role tertiary education plays in civil society. "Strong African universities can play a role in protecting basic freedoms, enhancing intellectual life, and informing policy making. This is clearly the right moment to have a 'bias for hope' and to increase support for their leaders" (Carnegie Corporation 2000). Likely, this is just the beginning of a new era. Poverty and markets are the driving forces behind emerging ideologies of development and foreign aid. But knowledge continues to hold a prominent place in recent efforts to reduce poverty, grow markets, and build a strong civil society.

DONORS DEFINE A ROLE FOR AID TO EDUCATION

Bilateral agencies have played a key role in education aid throughout Africa. As a general trend, higher education is garnering increasing support from donors. Still, higher education continues to receive sporadic support as a proportion of total education aid. In no year has postsecondary education received more than one-third of all education aid, and most years it received much less, averaging about 11 percent over the last 25 years.

A surprising amount of bilateral aid for postsecondary edu-

cation has come from Canada over the past two decades. Another fairly steady donor over the decades has been France. Other countries weigh in more sporadically. In the mid-1990s, Canada began to build local knowledge capacity by funding research and research dissemination in West and East Africa (Akhtar and Melesse 1994). In the Cold War era, the only other major donor to postsecondary education aid was Japan. Sweden put in a large amount in the 1970s but cut back substantially in the 1980s and 1990s.

Where did all that Canadian aid go? Table 6.2 shows that there was no definitive pattern. Senegal received the most postsecondary education aid in the 1970s, while Cameroon, Rwanda, and Kenya were the top recipients in the 1980s. The 1990s have favored Kenya and Ghana. Overall expenditure patterns are also inconsistent. About $161 million was spent in the 1980s, whereas much less was spent in the 1970s and 1990s ($30 million and $68 million, respectively).

Ideologies drove bilateral aid in Africa. While the underlying aid ideologies that were applied to education fit throughout much of the world, each bilateral donor felt it had a specific role to play within this world political and economic context. Bilateral aid put a template of sorts on the overall development approach and often determined where and in what amounts (if not always what types of) bilateral aid would be given.

COLONIAL TIES

A principal determinant of aid distribution continues to be linkages between former colonies and former colonial rulers. Political independence did not mean an end to economic and cultural domination. Education was a handy way of retaining these ties by integrating new elites into political, economic, and cultural practices and policies of the former colonial power (Altbach 1971). In so doing, former colonies routed their international linkages through their former colonial power, increasing the influence and well-being of the "mother" country. Most notable in the creation of these ties was bilateral aid from France.

The goal of French diplomacy in Africa has long been to maintain French influence in its former territories—in the words of several French scholars, "to transform a space of sovereignty into a zone of influence" (Adda and Smouts 1989, quoted in Lancaster 1999, 121). As a result, half of France's bilateral aid worldwide has been concentrated in Africa, and most of that has been concentrated in France's former colonies and other Francophone countries of the region (Lancaster 1999, 115).

Britain's colonial policies were guided by the notion that each country would reach independence eventually, but the timeline for that independence was always far into an unforeseeable future (Chikeka 1990). Nevertheless, most British colonies gained their independence between 1957 and 1965. Even into the 1970s, Britain continued to concentrate most of its aid within its former colonies. The exception was Mozambique (Lancaster 1999).

Higher education played a particular role in retaining these linkages. The elite of the former colonies were immersed in an education system designed to make them comfortable with, and increase their stake in retaining ties with, the former colonial

Table 6.4. Percent of Education Aid to Africa Devoted to Postsecondary Education, by Donor and African Region, 1980 and 1985

		Central	East	Egypt	North	South	West	Total
1980	France	31.1	0	0	0	0	68.9	100
1980	United States	0	0	94.8	0	5.2	0	100
1985	France	17	4.1	22.4	0	0	56.5	100
1985	Canada	50.5	6.6	0.1	0	0	42.7	100

Source: OECD CRS Data.

power (Altbach 1977; Mazrui 1975). Much of the postcolonial education aid "was intended to strengthen institution-to-institution linkages between universities in developed and developing countries" (Eisemon and Kourouma 1994, 277).

Moving beyond colonial ties has remained a slow, sometimes painful process for donor and former colony alike. The British policy of "no aid after independence" quickly gave way when both American and Canadian aid agencies made it clear that they were ready and willing to step into the vacuum (Lancaster 1999, 133).

THE COLD WAR

Another factor at play in bilateral aid was the Cold War. Schraeder, Hook, and Taylor (1998) analyzed aid patterns from the Cold War years of 1980–1989. They found that the "ideological stance" of recipient countries was a good predictor of aid targets for the United States, Japan, and Sweden. Whereas the United States and Japan primarily targeted capitalist countries, aid from Sweden was directed toward countries with socialist ideologies. Most bilateral donors left Francophone countries to the direction of France during the Cold War. France was only too happy to comply because this fit within its philosophy of maintaining cultural influence in its former colonies. French education aid was largely concentrated in Francophone West and Central Africa over the Cold War period.

Higher education had a special importance during the colonial period in that it had the ability to influence political socialization and win allegiances of Third World countries (Eisemon and Kourouma 1995). Nevertheless, given the predominant ideologies of structural adjustment and poverty alleviation, higher education was given very little priority during this period. In the years 1980 and 1985, only three countries recorded aid for postsecondary education. France remained heavily invested in West Africa and, to a lesser extent, Central Africa. The United States stayed away from higher education during this period, with the exception of a $27 million loan to Egypt in 1980. Canada maintained some interest in postsecondary education, putting most of its postsecondary education moneys into Central and West Africa.

MARKETS

The end of the Cold War ushered in a new era in which markets could be joined on a scale as never before. Suddenly,

the power of donor countries depended not so much on retaining influence in recipient countries as on establishing trade and markets. Markets took on new importance.

In sharp contrast to the preceding era when the West (especially America) sought to strengthen and enhance France's privileged role in Francophone Africa as a bulwark against communism, the end of the cold war seemingly has heightened economic and political competition among the Western powers. As a result, French policy-makers increasingly claim that the US and Japan, and to a lesser degree, Germany and Canada, pose potential economic and political threats to French interests in Francophone Africa. (Schraeder 1995, 540)

France, dominant in West Africa for many years, began to lose some ground in the region. In 1998, the United Kingdom entered West Africa, dedicating nearly half of its education aid there in 1998. Most education aid remained at the primary and secondary education levels, but the general trend can still be seen in postsecondary aid. Canadians gave large grants for postsecondary education beginning in 1985 and were later joined by Italy and the United States.

France, of course, was not the only donor that had to rethink its donor strategy in light of the end of the Cold War. For the United States, "the end of the Cold War may not have had an immediate impact on overall levels of aid to Africa, but it did affect which countries received it. Except for humanitarian relief, aid to several favorites of the past—Sudan, Somalia, Liberia, and Zaire in particular—was terminated" (Lancaster 1999, 90).

According to Owoeye and Vivekananda (1986), Japan's commercial interests were always predominant in determining aid recipients in Africa. Lancaster traces their entry into the donor club to Japan's concessional loan to Nigeria, designed to mitigate Nigeria's complaints about its increasing deficit to Japan. "By 1995, Japan was the fourth largest aid donor in Africa, providing over $1 billion to the region per year" (Lancaster 1999, 167). Nevertheless, Japan is slipping in influence with respect to postsecondary aid, largely because other donors are entering or are increasing their involvement in the postsecondary sector. As a percentage of total postsecondary aid to Africa, Japan has slipped from 18.5 percent in the 1970s to 5.2 percent in the 1990s.

One of the most promising footholds for market growth emerged in the middle of the 1990s with the reemergence of South Africa as a player in the global market. Not waiting for the legal shift of power to majority rule, donors began a politically sensitive effort to enter the country through the back door (Marx 1992, 181). Education aid began to trickle in in 1990 and really began to boom beginning in 1995, the onset of the post-apartheid era.

One of the first concerns of foreign donors of aid for post-secondary education in South Africa was increasing equity and access to higher education, a strategy designed to emphasize political stability and bring growth in the market there (Herman 1995). But the process was not straightforward. Accelerating integration of black Africans into former white universities meant that the tertiary backbones of black South Africa were put at risk; formerly black universities could no longer attract the best black students (Loxton 1995; Vergnani 1999). In an effort to help black students participate in higher education, the European Union stepped in with a $20 million grant to pay their tuition and fees (MacGregor 1994; *International Trade Finance* 1995). Although equity represented the first goal of postsecondary education to South Africa, it is likely not the long-term goal. Not only does South Africa represent the largest potential market in sub-Saharan Africa; it is the gateway to the rest of the subcontinent. Decidedly, South Africa is beginning to influence the subcontinent's global economic linkages and markets in big ways (*Economist* 1995b).

Aid to South Africa from bilateral donors began in 1990 (at least aid that was recorded in OECD databases). During the four-year period from 1995 to 1998, aid doubled from the previous six-year period of 1990 to 1995. The biggest donor was the United States, which stepped in with nearly $20 million in grants in 1996, followed by another $8.3 million grant in 1997. Sweden has kept up a fairly constant stream of aid to postsecondary education since 1990.

CONCLUSION

The World Bank has recently renewed its emphasis on the importance of higher education to development. In a recent speech, World Bank president James Wolfensohn said that education must be placed "at the core of development" (Wolfensohn 2000). The linking of poverty reduction with market stabilization and the realization that diverse, often local, sources of knowledge now have real market potential mean that education aid has taken on additional significance from the way it was viewed in previous eras. The recent economic growth and/or recovery of major and emerging world economic powers means that the financial resources available for such aid and the market importance of such aid are increasing.

Africa remains the home of many of the world's poorest countries. With its massive environmental, health, and political problems, the ability to grow both consumption and production markets is at risk in the continent. At the same time, the continent represents huge, largely untapped markets of producers, consumers, and diverse thinkers. Investment in education, a major component of building stability, will play an important and increasing role in Africa's future. This new era may one day be labeled the "golden age" of foreign aid for higher education in Africa.

ACKNOWLEDGMENTS

My thanks to Bhaswati Bhadra for her many hours of data analysis, Preeti Shroff-Mehta for her usual fine editing and references, and Paul Gallina for structural and logical editing.

REFERENCES

Adda, J., and M. C. Smouts. 1989. *La France face au sud: Le Miroir brisé.* Paris: Karthala. Cited in Thomas Eisemon and Mourssa Kourouma, "Foreign Assistance for University Development in Sub-Saharan Africa and Asia," in Jamil Salmi and Adriaan Verspoor, eds., *Revitalizing Higher Education.* Washington, D.C.: World Bank, 1994.

Akhtar, S., and M. Melesse. 1994. "Africa, Information and Development: IDRC's Experience." *Journal of Information Science* 20, no. 5: 314–322.

Altbach, P. G. 1971. "Education and Neocolonialism." *Teachers College Record* 72: 543–558.

———. 1977. "Servitude of the Mind? Education, Dependency, and Neocolonialism." *Teachers College Record* 79, no. 2: 187–204.

Association of African Universities. 1991. "Study on Cost Effectiveness and Efficiency in African Universities: A Synthesis Report." Accra: AAU (mimeo). Cited in Thomas Eisemon and Mourssa Kourouma, "Foreign Assistance for University Development in Sub-Saharan Africa and Asia," in Jamil Salmi and Adriaan Verspoor, eds., *Revitalizing Higher Education.* Washington, D.C.: World Bank, 1994.

Bennell, P., and D. Furlong. 1997. "Has Jomtien Made Any Difference? Trends in Donor Funding for Education and Basic Education since the Late 1980s." Working Paper 51 (mimeo). Sussex: Institute for Development Studies.

Biraimah, K., and D. Ananou. 1995. "Sustaining Higher Education in Francophone West Africa: The Togolese Case." *Educational Forum* 60: 68–74.

Brock, A. 1996. "Budgeting Models and University Efficiency: A Ghanaian Case Study." *Higher Education* 32: 113–127.

Business Africa. 1993. "Tapping into Japanese Aid." *Business Africa* 2, no. 15: 1–31.

Carnegie Corporation. 2000. "Four Foundations Launch $100 Million Initiative in Support of Higher Education in African Countries." Available online at: http://www.carnegie.org/sub/news/partnership.html

Chikeka, C. 1990. *Britain, France, and the New African States: A Study of Post Independence Relationships, 1960–1985.* Lewiston, N.Y.: E. Mellen Press.

Chronicle of Higher Education. 1988. "Conference on Financing of Education in Africa Reveals Differing Views on Cuts for Universities." *Chronicle of Higher Education* 34 (February 3): A39+.

———. 1993. "Universities Urged to Take Steps to End Africa's Higher Education Crisis." *Chronicle of Higher Education* 39 (June 9): A31+.

Coombe, T. 1991. "A Consultation on Higher Education in Africa: A Report to the Ford Foundation and the Rockefeller Foundation." Mimeo, Department of International and Comparative Education, Institute of Education, University of London. Cited in Thomas Eisemon and Mourssa Kourouma, "Foreign Assistance for University Development in Sub-Saharan Africa and Asia," in Jamil Salmi and Adriaan Verspoor, eds., *Revitalizing Higher Education.* Washington, D.C.: World Bank, 1994.

Cornwell, Tim. 1998. "University of the Air Nears Black Off." *Times Higher Educational Supplement* 1343 (August 14): xi.

Dickson, David. 1988. "Conference on Financing of Education in Africa Reveals Differing Views of Cuts for Universities." *Chronicle of Higher Education* 34: A39+.

Economist. 1995b. "A New Scramble: Foreign Investment in Africa." *Economist*, August 12, 17.

Eisemon, T., and L. Holm-Nielsen. 1995. *Reforming Higher Education Systems: Some Lessons to Guide Policy Implementation.* Washington, D.C.: World Bank. Available online at: www.worldbank.org/html/extdr/educ/backgrnd/rhesys2.html

Eisemon, T., and M. Kourouma. 1994. "Foreign Assistance for University Development in Sub-Saharan Africa and Asia." In Jamil Salmi and Adriaan Verspoor, eds., *Revitalizing Higher Education.* Washington, D.C.: World Bank.

Fatunde, T. 1998. "When Demands Are a Part of Education: Deterioration of the Francophone University System." *Times Higher Educational Supplement* 1323 (March 13): 12.

Herman, H. 1995. "School-Leaving Examinations, Selection and Equity in Higher Education in South Africa." *Comparative Education* 31: 261–274.

Ilon, L. 2000. "Knowledge, Labor and Education." *Compare* 30, no. 3: 275–282.

Ingalls, W. 1995. "Building Consensus for Change: Developing an Administrative and Management Structure in a Southern African University." *Higher Education* 29, no. XX: 275–285.

International Trade Finance. 1995. "Zimbabwe Meets Commitments—Attracts Finance." *International Trade Finance* 234 (April 7): 10–11.

Jacobson, R. 1988. "World Bank Revises Report on Education in Africa to Emphasize Support for Financing of Universities." *Chronicle of Higher Education* 34 (January 27): A41–42.

Kaplinsky, R. 1994. *Easternisation: The Spread of Japanese Management Techniques to Developing Countries.* Essex, England: Illford.

Kigotho, W. 1997. "Internet Lifeline for a Continent." *Times Higher Educational Supplement* 1288 (July 11): v.

———. 1999. "IMF Links African Slump to Brain Drain." *Times Higher Educational Supplement* 1392 (July 9): 13.

Lancaster, C. 1999. *Aid to Africa: So Much to Do, So Little Done.* Chicago: Century Foundation.

Liverpool, L. S., E. Eseyin, and E. Opara. 1998. "Modelling for Resource Allocation to Departments and Faculties in African Universities." *Higher Education* 36, no. 2: 139–153.

Loxton. 1995. "South African Colleges Scramble to Accommodate More Students." *Chronicle of Higher Education* 41: A44.

Lubbock, R. 1995. "Faced with Daunting Challenges, Scholars in Africa Strive for Access." *Chronicle of Higher Education* 41 (June 9): A22.

MacGregor, K. 1994. "Bursaries or Bust in New Age." *Times Higher Educational Supplement* 1135 (August 5): 9.

———. 1997. "Natal Sheds Staff and Courses as Cuts Bite." *Times Higher Educational Supplement* 1289 (July 19): 11.

———. 1998. "Britain Promotes University Links." *Times Higher Educational Supplement* 1318 (February 6): 12.

Marx, A. 1992. "International Intervention in South Africa: The Difficult Transition to Development Assistance." *Journal of International Affairs* 46, no. 1: 175–191.

Mazrui, A. 1975. "The African University as a Multinational Corporation: Problems of Penetration and Dependency." *Harvard Educational Review* 42, no. 2: 191–210.

Mingat, A., and G. Psacharopoulos. 1985. "Financing Education in Sub-Saharan Africa." *Finance and Development* 22, no. 1: 35–38.

Moock, P. R. 1987. *Education Policies for Sub-Saharan Africa: Adjustment, Revitalization, and Expansion.* Washington, D.C.: World Bank.

Morna, C. 1995. "African University Leader Call for Broad Alliance to Promote and Protect the Cause of Higher Education." *Chronicle of Higher Education* 41 (February 17): A43.

Nakabo, S. 1999. "Statistical Data: The Underestimated Tool for Higher Education Management." *Higher Education* 37, no. 3: 259–279.

Nsouli, S. 1993. "Structural Adjustment in Sub-Saharan Africa." *Finance and Development* 30, no. 3: 20–23.

Organisation for Economic Cooperation and Development Creditor Reporting System (OECD CRS) Data. 2000. Available online at: http://www1.oecd.org/scripts/cde/viewbase.asp?DBNAME=cde_crs

Owoeye, J., and F. Vivekananda. 1986. "Japan's Aid Diplomacy in Africa." *Scandinavian Journal of Development Alternatives* 5, no. 4: 145–155.

Ping, C. 1995. "African Universities Beset by Financial, Social Calamities." *Black Issues in Higher Education* 12 (September 21): 34–35+.

Psacharopoulos, G. 1973. *Returns to Education: An International Comparison.* New York: Jossey-Bass.

Psacharopoulos, G., and M. Woodhall. 1985. *Education for Development: An Analysis of Investment Choices.* New York: Oxford University Press.

Ramphele, M., and H. Rosovsky. 2000. "Educated People Are No Luxury, They're Essential." *Times Higher Educational Supplement*, March 19.

Renshaw, E. 1960. "Estimating the Returns to Education." *Review of Economics and Statistics* 42: 318–324.

Ridker, R. 1994. "The World Bank's Role in Human Resource Development in Sub-Saharan Africa: Education, Training and Technical Assistance." Sector Study 13449. Operations Evaluation Department. Washington, D.C.: World Bank.

Rosenfield, P. 2000. Personal conversation with Patricia Rosenfield, director, Carnegie Corporation International Development Program.

Schraeder, P. 1995. "From Berlin 1884 to 1989: Foreign Assistance and French, American, and Japanese Competition in Francophone Africa." *Journal of Modern African Studies* 33, no. 4: 539–567.

Schraeder, P., S. Hook, and B. Taylor. 1998. "Clarifying the Foreign Aid Puzzle: A Comparison of American, Japanese, French and Swedish Aid Flows." *World Politics* 50: 294–323.

Schultz, T. 1961. "Investment in Human Capital." *The American Economic Review* 51, no. 1: 1–17.

———. 1963. *The Economic Value of Education.* New York: Columbia University Press.

Task Force on Higher Education and Society. 2000. *Higher Education in Development Countries: Peril and Promise.* Washington, D.C.: The World Bank. Available online at: www.tfhe.net/about/about.htm

Thobani, M. 1984. "Charging User Fees for Social Services: Education in Malawi." *Comparative Education Review* 28, no. 3: 402–423.

Times (London). 2000. "World Bank Enlists HE to Narrow Poverty Gap." *Times* (London), March 3.

Times Higher Educational Supplement. 1988. "World Bank's Africa Strategy Urges Staffing Cuts." (February 12): 10.

———. 1995. "Development Education: With Reviews of Instructional Materials." *Times Higher Educational Supplement*, November 10, 35–41.

Useem, A. 1999. "Wiring African Universities Proves a Formidable Challenge." *Chronicle of Higher Education* 45, no. 30 (April 2): A51–53.

Vergnani, L. 1991. "South Africa, Black Nations Develop New University Links." *Chronicle of Higher Education* 37 (July 10): A35.

———. 1999. "South Africa's Black Universities Struggle to Survive in a New Era." *Chronicle of Higher Education* 45, no. 27: A45–A46.

Versi, A. 1997. "Africa and Aid." *African Business* (January): 36–38.

Vondal, Patricia. 1991. "Social and Institutional Analysis in the African Economic Policy Reform Program." *Studies in Third World Societies* 44, no. 2: 61–78.

Washio, A. 1993. "'Good Governance' to Be ODA Criteria." *Japan Times Weekly International Edition* 33, no. 42: 3.

Wolfensohn, J. 2000. "A Time for Action: Placing Education at the Core of Development." Speech delivered at the World Education Forum, Dakar, Senegal, April 27. Available online at: www2.unesco.org/wef/en-news/coverage_speech_wolfen.shtm

World Bank. 1988. *Education in Sub-Saharan Africa: Policies for Adjustment, Revitalization and Expansion.* Washington, D.C.: World Bank.

———. 1994. *Higher Education: Lessons of Experience.* Washington, D.C.: World Bank.

———. 1998a. *World Development Report 1998/99: Knowledge for De-velopment.* Washington, D.C.: World Bank. Available online at: www.worldbank.org/wdr/wdr98

———. 1998c. "Knowledge for Africa: African Virtual University." Available online at: www.worldbank.org/wdr/wdr98/africa/bpafr9.htm

———. 2000b. "Knowledge for Africa: Knowledge for Development in Africa." Available online at: www.worldbank.org/wdr/wdr98/africa/bpafr1.htm

———. 2000c. "The World Bank Group in Africa: An Overview." Available online at: www.worldbank.org/afr/overview.htm

———. 2000d. "Indigenous Knowledge Program." Available online at: http://www.worldbank.org/afr/ik/default.htm

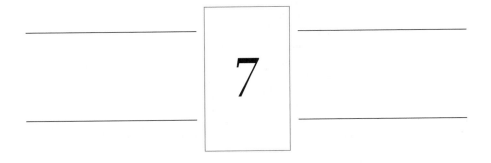

7

Massification and Future Trends in African Higher Education

RICHARD FEHNEL

Some African leaders deal in diamonds to finance wars of greed and are seemingly unmoved by appalling human tragedies on an unprecedented scale. Other leaders dream of a renaissance that will make the twenty-first century theirs. Meanwhile, the rest of the world speeds toward a new global economic order that may potentially cut Africa adrift and make it a Fourth World island with little economic intercourse with the rest of the world's economies (Castells 1998; Carnoy 1995a). The incongruity of these totally divergent realities makes one wonder whether there is any hope on the horizon for Africa—especially its sub-Saharan region.

A NEW ECONOMIC DEVELOPMENT STRATEGY FOR AFRICA

One can see a glimmer of hope, provided that new leaders with courage and conviction step forward to implement a different economic development strategy and provided they receive substantial support from their citizens and the global community. The underlying basis for hope is grounded in a strategy that combines realistic economic planning with bold new moves in human resource development. The broad outline of such a strategy was advocated in a recent study conducted by the African Economic Research Consortium (AERC) and the United Nations University. It is based on a model of development used by the so-called Asian tigers to move their economies from agriculture to a diverse combination of manufacturing, commerce, and knowledge industries (AERC 1998).

This model used a strategy that created regionally focused economic policies and built the physical and fiscal infrastructures necessary to launch sustainable, competitive entry into the global economy. An essential component to implementing this strategy is having a workforce capable of meeting the demands of a dynamic global marketplace. To develop such a capacity requires a balanced investment in education and training across

all education sectors as well as in the existing workforce. For many education leaders, who think primarily in terms of education production based on cohorts of school-aged children and school-leavers seeking access to postsecondary education and training, such a move is a major shift in human resource development planning. A strategic shift of this nature has been recommended in a recent report by the Task Force on Higher Education and Society (2000), which focuses on the developing areas of the world.

The relationship between economic development and a balanced investment across education sectors—with a growing focus on higher education—is, in the judgment of some economists and development experts, one of the key findings in recent decades. This finding signals a departure from earlier education policy for developing countries that put a higher priority on investment in primary education (Carnoy 1995b). It has led to a shift in education investment that is reflected in growth in enrollments in tertiary education, as reported in a recent analysis of education trends in Europe and North America (OECD 1999). This shift seems to be linked to the knowledge and information revolution and reflects the new reality that investments in the production of skilled workers yield greater economic returns for a country than investments in the production of goods (Serageldin 2000). Another recent study of global higher education also affirms the linkage between growth in the ratio of tertiary education enrollments and growth in national income (Task Force on Higher Education and Society 2000).

The AERC strategy would have African countries develop regional trade relations while building their human resource capacity through investment in education and training in areas valued by the global labor market. In time, as shown in Taiwan, Korea, and, more recently, in India, this strategy can lead to the gradual development of industries whose productivity will support a deepening and broadening of investments in human resources and infrastructure development, including physical infrastructure, such as roads and telecommunication facilities, and institutional infrastructure, such as financial institutions, courts, democratic structures, and educational systems. In a relevant comparison, Carnoy points out that Ghana and Korea were similar in population, gross national product (GNP), and percent of the budget invested in education in the 1960s. Then Korea made the long-term commitment to massify access to education at all levels and change curricula to put greater emphasis on math and science, while Ghana continued with basically the same education policies. Since the 1960s, the economic development plot of the two countries has sharply diverged. Korea has become an important player in the global economy, while Ghana languishes. Education policy is one of the key factors for the change (Carnoy 1995c).

THE IMPLICATIONS OF DEMAND: MASSIFICATION AND BALANCE

Can the AERC strategy of intense regional economic development and heavy investment in education—as the first phase of a globalization strategy—work in Africa? Yes, but it would require a commitment to mass education and training on a scale that is unprecedented for most of Africa. What do we mean by mass education and training? Basically, it means that a substantial percentage of the school-aged cohort has access to and participates in education through the secondary level and that the content of the education they acquire prepares them for a changing work environment, requires problem-solving skills, and uses math and science regularly. Additionally, it also means that a small but significant portion of the labor force (12–15 percent) attains postsecondary education and that much of the workforce has regular access to continuing education and training programs in order to keep abreast of changes in the knowledge base that are relevant to their industries. The focus on workforce development provides the balance that is missing in the human resource development efforts of most nations.

In other words, the demand for higher education and training by the traditional school-leaver cohort and by the workforce would be raised substantially above current levels, and the quality of education and training would likely need to change, as well, if sub-Saharan Africa is to prevent a further slide toward Fourth World economic oblivion.

DEMAND FOR EDUCATION FROM SCHOOL-LEAVERS

Table 7.1 compares education participation rates—that is, the ratio of the age cohort of a population that is educationally active to the total cohort of that age group—in three regions of the world (sub-Saharan Africa, East Asia, and Europe and Central Asia) and indicates that enrollments in all three levels of education in sub-Saharan Africa lag far behind enrollments of similar age cohorts in the other two regions. At the tertiary education level, only 3 percent of the college-age cohort in sub-Saharan Africa was educationally active in 1995, compared with 32 percent in Europe and Central Asia. Without a dramatic increase in participation in appropriate education and training activities throughout the entire education sector, sub-Saharan

Table 7.1. Education Participation Rates by Percentage of Total Population, 1995

Education Sector	Sub-Saharan Africa	East Asia	Europe and Central Asia
Primary	74	115	101
Secondary	25	64	83
Tertiary	3	7	32

Source: Task Force on Higher Education and Society 2000, 104, Table A.

Africa will not be able to develop the broad base of labor capacity needed for a place in the global economy.

In the remainder of this chapter, our emphasis will be on the tertiary, or higher education, sector. This is not to imply that the other education sectors are not a priority.

At present, the participation rate in tertiary education in sub-Saharan Africa lags far behind participation rates in other areas of the world that are characterized as "developing." One recent study puts the participation rate in the region at roughly 340 per 100,000 inhabitants. By contrast, the rate in East Asia is more than double that, while the rate in the higher-income countries of Europe and Central Asia is approximately 2,400 per 100,000 (Task Force on Higher Education and Society 2000, Table B). Another study covering roughly the same time period paints an even gloomier picture: the tertiary-level gross enrollment ratio in sub-Saharan Africa is 3.6 percent, as compared with 14 percent in Arab states, 10.4 percent in Asia, and more than 18 percent in Latin America (UNESCO 1998).

If sub-Saharan Africa embarks on a strategy of catching up with the rest of the global economy, it will need to at least double the tertiary-education participation rate. Data for 1995 shows that the total enrollment in tertiary education in sub-Saharan Africa is approximately 1.8 million, 1 million of which are accounted for by two countries—Nigeria and South Africa (Task Force on Higher Education and Society 2000). There is no doubt that the demand exists to double enrollment in tertiary education. The problem is on the supply side: most African countries do not have higher education access policies that would easily accommodate an increase in provision to secondary school graduates. Budgetary constraints under existing economic conditions make changes unlikely unless policies regarding the financing of higher education are changed.

WORKFORCE DEMAND

Some educational economists believe that at least 12–15 percent of a nation's workforce must have a higher education if it is going to compete in the new global economy and that a constant effort in continuing education must be made to keep this workforce abreast of changes (Sadlak 1998; World Bank 1998/1999). This represents the most daunting challenge for most African countries. Few African countries have a system for providing professional continuing education and training on a scale needed to double or triple the percentage of the workforce with higher education qualifications. Seeking to meet this demand requires a conceptualization of massification that is not currently under consideration in most African countries.

What might be the level of demand for providing education and training to sub-Saharan Africa's workforce? According to World Bank data, the total labor force for sub-Saharan Africa in 1997 was roughly 268 million (World Bank 2000a). Assuming a desired higher education qualification rate of 12 percent of the labor force, sub-Saharan Africa should have approximately 32 million persons with tertiary education in the labor force. Data on the educational attainment of the labor force in sub-Saharan Africa is not readily available, but the actual figure is not likely to be anywhere near this level. The International Labor Office report *Key Indicators of the Labour Market 1999*, a definitive source of information of this nature, suggests that the level of the labor force with tertiary education is less than 3 percent (International Labor Office 1999). The Task Force on Higher Education and Society report indicates that only 2 percent of the population over the age of 25 in sub-Saharan Africa had attained tertiary education in 1995 (Task Force on Higher Education and Society 2000). These estimates would suggest a shortfall of considerable dimensions. If only 3 percent of the labor force has tertiary education qualifications, there would be a gap of roughly 9 percent of the labor force, or approximately 24 million persons—more than ten times the current enrollment in higher education in sub-Saharan Africa.

These estimates of demand offer a broad perspective on massification and balance in education and training. Clearly a much more nuanced consideration of the relationship of the general strategy or approach to each nation's development goals is needed. Strategic choices will need to be made about the economic sectors that will receive attention; about the desire to have access to education and training equally available to all, irrespective of race, gender, ethnicity, and geographic location; and about the efforts needed to address the content issues of education and training programs.

Consequently, there can be little argument with the notion that sub-Saharan Africa must reconsider its education and training policies if the region intends to have a meaningful part in the global economy. The demand for access to education and training programs, as a function of both population growth and the changing nature of labor markets, has never been greater. Education planners and finance ministers are faced with tough choices ahead if long-term national and regional strategies are to be put in place.

SUPPLY IMPLICATIONS: GLOBAL TRENDS, OPTIONS, AND CHALLENGES

Tough choices are involved in facing up to the challenges of raising the rate of provision of education and training to internationally competitive levels. Clearly one option is to make sure that physical and human resources are used to maximum capacity. Some sub-Saharan countries, such as South Africa, have underutilized capacity. South African higher education institutions have responded by seeking new markets of learners, particularly among the workforce of industries that have shortages of trained personnel, and by opening branch campuses in parts of the country that have been underserved.

Another dimension of the maximization of the use of existing resources is to improve the efficiency of existing resources. Examples of such action would include increasing the throughput rate of students, decreasing the dropout rate, reducing or eliminating duplication of programs and courses within an institution or system, and reducing or eliminating programs with low demand and high costs that cannot be justified in cost-benefit terms. Governments can and should influence whether and how steps such as these might be taken by creating "steering mechanisms" in the funding arrangements between government and higher education institutions that lead toward the appropriate production of human resources necessary for economic and social development (Merisotis and Gilleland 2000; World Bank 1994). Such steering mechanisms should reinforce institutional strategic plans and are likely to promote the strengthening of higher education institutions in the long run. But, as some universities have experienced, the processes of reorienting academic programs away from traditional patterns of enrollments toward new programs that reflect new national needs sometimes create short-term instability in academic areas targeted for reductions in staff. Occasionally, departments and courses that are affected negatively seek protection behind cries of autonomy and academic freedom. It is at times like these that institutional governing boards and executives need to work collaboratively with policymakers and other education stakeholders to assure that institutional and national needs and actions are mutually supportive and that the steering mechanisms for institutional funding reflect these needs.

Making tough choices also means facing up to the realities that university graduates are underemployed or unemployed in some African countries. In some cases, this may be the result of supply exceeding demand; students and their parents sometimes make career choices that do not take into account where the growth of jobs may actually be occurring. Students may train to become doctors, lawyers, or preachers when the nation may need agronomists, economists, and mining engineers. In other cases, it may be that the nation's economy is in such bad shape that it lacks the capacity to employ new graduates in the fields necessary for economic growth. In still other cases, the problem may be that new graduates lack knowledge and skills appropriate to the current needs of the profession, reflecting curricular stagnation. Employers may be unwilling to hire new graduates whose training they know to be inadequate.

Whatever the reasons, many African countries have real problems matching supply to anticipated demand in terms of the output of higher education and training programs and the continuing education of professionals and skilled personnel. And it must be acknowledged that in some cases this mismatch exists because higher education institutions have failed to anticipate or respond to emerging trends.

GREATER INSTITUTIONAL DIVERSITY AND DIFFERENTIATION

Most African countries still have only one institution of higher education, a national university created shortly after independence as a symbol of freedom from a colonial past. Given the global proliferation of knowledge and information in all fields of study and the broadening of demand for access to information, many countries have found that a narrow base of providers is simply inadequate to keep up with changing demand for education. As a consequence, the development of greater institutional diversity through either vertical or horizontal differentiation is being turned to as a national strategy throughout the world (Task Force on Higher Education and Society 2000). In some cases, diversification is the result of "vertical differentiation" —that is, the creation of institutional separation between undergraduate and graduate or postgraduate teaching. In other cases, diversification is the result of "horizontal differentiation"—that is, the development of a wider variety of types of higher education institutions.

PRIVATE HIGHER EDUCATION

A notable development in horizontal and vertical diversification in recent years has been the expansion of private higher education providers throughout the world (Tooley 1999; World Bank 1994). In Chile, private institutions were introduced in the 1970s and now provide a large proportion of professional-level and graduate-level education, while in Brazil most of the nation's undergraduates are enrolled in recently created private universities (Task Force on Higher Education and Society 2000). Korea and Japan have also followed a path of increasing diversity through the introduction of private higher education. In Japan, more than three-fourths of all higher education students attend private institutions (James 1995). In many situations, the growth of private provision is the result of the failure of public institutions to address the demand for access to higher education. In other cases, the growth of private higher education reflects the growth in demand for more differentiated programs of study—created either by the rapidly changing character of the marketplace or, in some cases, demands for educational settings that cater to special groups, such as women or minorities.

Other forms of horizontal diversification have a somewhat longer history. The United States introduced a different type of institution in the middle of the twentieth century with the creation of the community college that offers both academic and vocational learning tracks. Experiments in the introduction of community colleges in other parts of the world have been less successful than the U.S. experience, but efforts continue. South Africa's Further Education and Training sector—which straddles to a certain extent the skills gap between secondary and higher education—has created the legal space for community colleges, but lack of financial resources in the public sector has limited the expansion of this postsecondary education sector.

DISTANCE EDUCATION INSTITUTIONS

The launching of the British Open University signaled the creation of still another type of educational institution—distance education. The University of South Africa (UNISA) has been in operation as a correspondence institution since the 1940s and is among the largest universities in the world. Both Anglophone and Francophone countries in sub-Saharan Africa have made extensive use of distance education for teacher training. The

successful rise of distance education has created another form of differentiation, the development of a "dual-mode" institution—that is, the expansion of programs offered by a residential university or polytechnic to include distance education. A recent survey of distance education programs in sub-Saharan Africa listed sixty-five dual-mode higher education institutions and sixty single-mode institutions, which serve mostly teacher-training needs (Roberts and Associates 1998). Unfortunately, the survey does not indicate how many learners are being served through distance education programs in Africa. These higher education institutions include both public and private providers as well as a few consortia of mixed public-private providers and NGOs such as the innovative African Virtual University project initiated by the World Bank in 1996.

UNIVERSITY COLLEGES

Efforts on the part of many American educational institutions to develop programs that meet the needs of working adults led to a different form of horizontal differentiation. In the 1970s, some universities created special colleges for working adults. Some states created special universities, such as Empire State College in New York, Governor's State University in Illinois, and Thomas Edison University in New Jersey. Most of these institutions experimented with modes of delivery and curricular innovations, including recognizing the value of learning through life experience by awarding credits for it. However, many of these efforts were constrained by traditionalists in academe who resisted such efforts.

CORPORATE UNIVERSITIES

The slow response by higher education to the accelerated demands for education and for training of the workforce led to the development of another type of educational institution, the "corporate university." Examples of this form of higher education provider have existed for many years in North America and Europe. Some estimates place the number of corporate universities in the United States at more than 1,500, with enrollments similar to that of the traditional, formal colleges and universities (Spender 1998). As a result of the spread of multinational corporations throughout the world, one can now find examples of corporate universities in Africa. In Nigeria, the Peugeot Corporation has started its own training program for engineers, information specialists, and managers because it cannot rely on public universities to provide qualified graduates. In South Africa, the petroleum industry, in partnership with South African and Canadian institutions of higher education, has started a corporate university to train employees for the industry throughout Africa. Part of the rationale for this move is that it is much more economical to provide training in Africa than in Europe or North America. In addition, the involvement of both South African and Canadian institutions means that it is more likely that the education offered in corporate universities in South Africa will be of high quality and will be culturally appropriate to the region; this might not be the case if students had to go elsewhere for their job-related education.

The rise of corporate universities and the spread of distance education has been greatly assisted by the availability of information and communication technology. In higher education settings, ICT covers a wide spectrum of applications, including, for example, computers in the classroom that may have Internet and/or intranet access, and synchronous and asynchronous instruction using various types of telecommunications, including satellite technology. Clearly, ICT is the most rapidly growing form of institutional diversification. This development is not limited to the United States; the worldwide market for online courses is estimated to be worth $10 billion annually (Cloete and Moja 2000). Intercontinental partnerships between institutions and corporations are being formed almost daily to meet the growing demand for courses offered using ICT as both a means of delivery and as the prime content of instruction—that is, the content of instruction is concerned with information and communication technologies and their applications. For example, the U.S.-based *Chronicle of Higher Education* reported on November 3, 2000, that a master's program through Global eCommerce will be offered through a joint venture of universities in Greece, the United States, Germany, Sweden, and the Netherlands (Ludwig 2000). In South Africa, many universities and technikons are now advertising online courses as a response to the penetration of the African higher education market by North American, European, and Australian "brick and click" institutions.

The growth in institutional diversity is also reflected in the tremendous differentiation in programs—that is, an increase in areas of study being offered by higher education institutions globally. This increase is driven by the exponential growth in knowledge production in recent years and the need for knowledge users to keep up to date. The increase in program differentiation is a response of educational institutions to the simultaneous demands to broaden and deepen areas of study and an increasing turn toward transdisciplinary study to deal with the complex and interrelated problems associated with globalization. This trend toward increasing program differentiation was identified as the result of several factors, including the growth of knowledge production outside the traditional venues of academe. Faced with a loss of monopoly in knowledge production, educational institutions have responded by increasing their involvement in knowledge dissemination. This has been done by looking for more "market niches" and engaging in research and education partnerships with the private sector (Gibbons 1998). Market niches may be specialized areas of study, such as ecotourism, that combine other fields of study in response to growing market demand; they may also address the unmet needs of target student groups, such as working adults, by offering educational services at times or in locations not served by the usual modes of program delivery.

"Mode 2" is a term used to describe a new pattern of knowledge production, dissemination, and utilization that emerged in the latter half of the twentieth century in which the key role of universities as producers of new knowledge through research was displaced by specialized think tanks and laboratories. In Mode 2 settings, the pursuit of knowledge is generally motivated by a desire to solve problems that have relevance to national needs. The pursuit of solutions tends to transcend the traditional disciplinary lines found in higher education, and the measure of success tends to be more concerned with applicability of the knowledge rather than traditional scientific tests of proof. This type of activity is fundamentally different than knowledge production during the Mode 1 period (Gibbons 1998). In Mode 1, knowledge production and dissemination was tightly organized around academic disciplines, which led to the development of universities that had a pivotal role in establishing the "rules" by which new knowledge and new knowledge producers were recognized.

However, with the advent of global communications in the mid-twentieth century, a merger of two distinct social phenomena—democratization and economic globalization—led to dramatic changes in expectations about how knowledge could be used to address broad social challenges (the call for relevance) as well as expectations about who could become knowledge producers and appliers (the call for massification of higher education) (Scott 1995; Kraak 2000). Gibbons sees this merger at the heart of the shift from Mode 1 to Mode 2 education that underlines the challenges facing universities throughout the world. The shift challenges traditional conceptions of the role of educational institutions and the notions of who should be educated, for what purpose, and by what means.

If universities are to carve a new role for themselves in the production and dissemination of knowledge, they must create new partnerships and new forms of organization. Those that have made such changes have flourished; those that have not have languished. The challenge for many African institutions is that they not only need to learn the new rules of engagement implied by Mode 2 conditions but they also need assistance in identifying and nurturing the alliances and partnerships Mode 2 requires. In many cases, these new partners may be foreign organizations, further complicating matters. And, in many cases, there is great concern that developing Mode 2 relationships will mean a loss of control and possibly a further vulnerability to brain drain.

In sum, growing demands for access to higher education globally have led to a variety of responses. Some of these responses can be seen in sub-Saharan Africa. Many of these options present huge new challenges to institutions, to higher education systems, and to conventional academic disciplines and professions, since they imply new patterns of organization and new or different purposes and expectations. However, unless there is a deliberate and intensified effort to increase the capacity of the tertiary education sector in Africa, these responses may have little impact.

AFRICA'S CHALLENGE: BUILDING APPROPRIATE HIGHER EDUCATION CAPACITY

The challenge facing Africa is how to build capacity in higher education systems to meet the demand for education and training required for participation in the global economy. As indicated earlier, fewer than 2 million students are enrolled in higher education in sub-Saharan Africa out of a population of approximately 627 million (World Bank 2000b). To meet the demand implied by education investments made in other countries that are moving from low-income, low-information industries toward information- and technology-based industries, sub-Saharan Africa must create space for new learners from the schooling sector and those from the workforce seeking a "second chance or a second bite" (OECD 1999). How many new spaces will depend on the specific economic sector strategies in different countries and the availability of financial resources within the region.

CAPACITY BUILDING AND FEES

This brings us to the issue of increasing capacity in the context of scarce government resources and other constraints. Perhaps the fundamental question is how to finance the costs of creating more capacity (Partnership for Capacity Building in Africa 1997). There are few choices:

- Cost sharing through the introduction of fees where none exist and raising fees where they already exist
- Generating more revenues from other activities to cross-subsidize capacity building of education and training programs
- Allowing private institutions to enter the arena of higher education provision

Many African countries need to consider introducing fees where none have traditionally existed or raising fees where they already exist. This is an area where politicians and institutional administrators fear to tread because of turbulent responses by students to the prospects of introducing or raising fees in the past. But it is an issue that must be addressed. In effect, African development is being held hostage by a tiny portion of the population, many from privileged backgrounds, who demand that their personal economic future be paid for by the masses who have little or no opportunity to participate in higher education themselves (Teferra 1999). For the most part, it is a worst-case scenario that is driven by uninformed self-interest. In Nigeria, for example, full-time residential students at the federal universities have successfully held off the introduction of fees for decades, even though part-time students and graduate students at these universities pay fees, as do all students at the state universities. In South Africa, on the other hand, student fees account for approximately 15 percent of the revenues received by higher education institutions. In 20 percent of Asian countries and more than 50 percent of Latin American countries, fees generate more than 10 percent of recurrent expenditures in higher education (World Bank 1994). In many countries, cost sharing has begun by eliminating government support for student accommodation and meals and privatizing these services.

The issue of fee payment must be examined in conjunction with bursary and loan policies so that truly needy students are not excluded from access to higher education. Furthermore, fee structures need to be considered in the context of human resource priorities to assure that scarce government resources are put to the best use instead of providing capacity in areas of study that add little value to development.

BUILDING CAPACITY AND GENERATING REVENUE

A major trend in higher education in much of the world is diversification of revenue generation beyond government subsidies. While research grants and contracts have always provided a modest source of income to universities worldwide, the development of these activities and contract education and training programs have become important sources of revenues to institutions and the means by which many have been able to improve quality and build staff and physical capacity. The "entrepreneurial university" is more than a catchphrase; it is a paradigm shift in the culture of educational institutions (Clark 1998). Aggressive development of a broad range of revenue-generating activities has changed the nature and stature of many institutions and has led government commissions to recommend policies that encourage and reward such activities (South African National Commission on Higher Education 1996; Dearing 1997). The most easily developed revenue-generating activity seems to be training programs for industry through courses outside of the regular academic curriculum. These programs have often been developed by individual instructors out of personal interest. What is interesting about this type of activity is that at many institutions in North America and Europe, it has evolved into new academic programs that in turn have generated additional government subsidies (Jongbloed, Maassen, and Neave 1999). The Virtual University of the Monterrey Institute of Technology, based in Mexico, enrolls about 9,000 degree students and 35,000 non-degree students throughout Latin America (World Bank 1999). This trend is emerging in many of the continuing education programs that are being developed by a few entrepreneurial institutions in South Africa and in the urban areas of Nigeria and Kenya.

On a different track, but within the same framework of income-generating activities, the strong movement by many Asian, European, and North American universities to enter into partnerships with the government and the private sector for research and problem solving is a clear indication of the economic value of these joint ventures (Clark 1998; Gibbons 1998). Moves such as these have been a way for universities to recapture a role in the production of knowledge. They have helped institutions find their way to a problem-solving paradigm of research, which, in many cases, has made their contribution to local and national development more productive and effective than the pursuit of "blue sky" research. An example of the double benefit of such undertakings can be seen in the Technology and Human Resources in Industry Program (THRIP) jointly developed by the South African National Research Foundation and the Department of Trade and Industry of the government of South Africa. THRIP brings together industry, academia, and research organizations by providing matching funds for approved projects (*Mail and Guardian* 2000). It is estimated that the program will provide more than $35 million this year to partners, including institutions of higher education, for industrial research. In 1991, the University of Tanzania began a process of revenue diversification and program review that has led to a major transformation of the institution and made it an attractive partner to donors and private investment (NUFFIC 1999).

Ventures of this type have also created opportunities and challenges around issues of intellectual property. Columbia University in the United States was projected to earn more than $144 million in 2000 from patents it has developed in partnerships with the private sector (Arenson 2000). While some regard this type of activity as another paradigm shift, the fact is that joint ventures of this nature have existed in Europe and the United States since the Cold War. However, they remain a new and underdeveloped trend in African higher education (Oni 1999). There is some concern that vigorous pursuit of "research for profit" and "cash-cow training programs" will dilute the core functions of higher education. However, these concerns need to be balanced against the grim realities faced by many African universities. The vital question is: What are the core functions of higher education institutions in Africa? Do they not include embracing activities—and responsibilities—that will contribute significantly, directly, and immediately to national and regional uplift? How many African universities can honestly claim that they are enhancing their capacity to contribute to national and regional development and can point to the bottom line to prove that diversification and growth of revenues justify this claim?

CAPACITY BUILDING AND PRIVATE HIGHER EDUCATION

International experience suggests that turning to private higher education is another option many countries have followed to increase system capacity. Within this option, several options exist. Governments in Kenya, Nigeria, and South Africa, to cite a few examples, have changed laws to allow private higher education institutions to come into being and to respond to the backlog of demand from both school-leavers and working adults. When Brazil and Peru made this choice, they created a significant increase in the supply of higher education opportunities for students—to the extent that more than 50 percent of the total tertiary enrollment in Brazil today is in private institutions. Korea made a similar choice in the late twentieth century, with the result that more than 50 percent of college-aged adults are now enrolled in postsecondary education programs, and of these more than 80 percent attend private institutions (World Bank 1999).

Another variation is to allow public higher education institutions to admit students beyond the numbers covered by government subsidies, provided these students pay their own costs of education. This is being done at Uganda's Makerere University and in some of the entrepreneurial universities and technikons in South Africa. In these cases, the financial cost of increasing capacity is borne by the student (or, more likely, by the student's employer), not by the state. Within two years of adopting this plan, a majority at Makerere University were private, fee-paying students (NUFFIC 1999). Because of cross-subsidization, the university was able to expand enrollment of state-supported students. In the United States, many state education authorities have found it much more efficient to subsidize students attending private institutions than to build and staff new publicly supported institutions.

Another option is the development of joint programs between public and private institutions, as has happened in South Africa. Such partnerships allow each institution to utilize its strengths, and by merging resources, to undertake what neither by itself had the capacity to initiate.

BUILDING STAFF CAPACITY

There is an urgent need in sub-Saharan Africa to build the capacity of academic staff to meet the growing demand for education. This involves more than simply pushing more graduate students through the education pipeline and into teaching and research positions, which in itself is a major problem, given the competition from government and the private sector and the threat of brain drain.

The greater challenge is to develop and retain an academic corps competent in the range of skills demanded in the transition from current economies and government practices to ones oriented more toward global engagement. These skills include problem solving, the ability to produce knowledge in the context of applications in real-life situations, the ability to work comfortably in several disciplines (transdisciplinarity), the ability to manage information, and the ability to work in cross-cultural settings and in flexible organizational arrangements (Gibbons 1998; Kraak 2000). The problem is that many in the current academic corps of African universities lack these skills and the opportunity or commitment to acquire them. The old practice of sending individuals abroad for training does not work in most cases. It is too expensive, often irrelevant, and generally impractical. These are not the skills that one can easily acquire by surfing the Internet, even if one assumes that a professor in the typical university in sub-Saharan Africa has access to the Internet.

Developing the academic corps necessary to lead the transformation of African higher education needs to come through creative arrangements with institutions among higher education providers and between higher education and the public and private sectors. Examples of such programs are beginning to be found and are generally supported through donor efforts, as in the example of the project involving the University of Cape Town and seven other African universities (West and Shackleton 1999). The African Economic Research Consortium (AERC) is another example of interinstitutional cooperation for the development of academic staff with support from the international donor community (World Bank 1999). The Association of African Universities, with donor funding, also supports faculty exchanges and joint research efforts. However, efforts such as these need to be implemented on a much larger scale if they are going to develop the critical mass of academic staff needed to support institutional capacity building throughout sub-Saharan Africa.

Assuming that it is possible to mount the efforts necessary to develop an appropriate academic corps, a major challenge facing many universities will be to retain personnel. There will be tremendous pressures for academic staff to leave and join private sector government programs, a form of "internal" brain drain. That threat can and must be met by creative commitments among universities and their new partners to share rather than compete in the utilization of human resources. All parties need to realize that short-term competition will cripple or kill long-term development strategies. New rules about leaves for faculty and staff, joint appointments, ownership of intellectual property, tenure, and other aspects of the academic life need to be developed, experimented with, and adapted if higher education expects to retain the best and the brightest. It can be done. After years of watching bright young men and women leave India for the promise of careers in the software industries of other countries, Indian institutions and corporations have found ways to reverse the brain drain and make it a "brain gain," creating what may become the most dynamic national software industry in the world.

STRATEGIC PLANNING

Making the right choice among options to create capacity may require careful and innovative strategic planning if institutions and their partners are to avoid costly mistakes and make decisions that can have immediate benefits to the institution, the nation, and the region. Evidence of the value of such planning can be seen in the dramatic cases of Spain and Finland, where joint ventures between government and higher education focused on the development of the telecommunication industries. Both countries have experienced significant economic growth in these industries, with notable positive spillover effects in other sectors of the economy (Castells 1999). While there is a growing awareness of the need for strategic planning, the actual practice of it by higher education institutions in sub-Saharan Africa is recent and therefore has not reached a level where coordinated strategic planning among universities and across national boundaries has begun (AAU 1995; Ekong and Plant 1996; Fry and Utui 1999; Task Force on Higher Education and Society 2000). However, coordination of a strategic nature will be necessary if financial support from governments, the private sector, and donors is to be secured at levels needed to transform higher education in the region.

INFORMATION AND COMMUNICATION TECHNOLOGY

The challenges faced by sub-Saharan Africa in meeting an agenda for massification and balance in higher education may be greatly facilitated by the rapid rise of information and communication technologies. Moneys that would have gone into brick-and-mortar projects can now be invested more directly into human resource development by relying on ICT to deliver content anytime and anywhere. ICT offers a way to leapfrog over years of staff and curriculum development, to assist scholars and researchers in the region to work together more closely, and to shape an agenda for learning, research, and problem solving that is appropriate for the region. Through ICT, multinational corporations operating in the region will be able to afford more investment in human resource development. Through such expansion, closer ties to the global economy will be realized. As Saint points out in his important study of tertiary education and technology in sub-Saharan Africa, ICT has the potential not only to make university campuses obsolete but also to bring university education within the reach of everyone who desires it (Saint 2000).

CONCLUSION

Higher education in sub-Saharan Africa has a vital role to play if this region is to remain an active partner in the global economy. International lessons demonstrate a close relationship between sustained investments in higher education and the growth of national income resulting from participation in the global economy. Investments need to be targeted to fit national and regional development priorities. They also need to include major commitments to upgrade the current workforce to secure the returns on productivity that are needed to sustain longer-term investments in education, training, research, and development.

Sub-Saharan Africa lags far behind other regions globally in terms of higher education. It has the lowest participation rate in higher education of any area of the world, while its workforce has the lowest level of tertiary education attainment. Action must be taken to expand the capacity of the region to meet unmet demand. Tough choices and strategic decisions will need to be made to raise the revenues needed to finance expansion of higher education throughout the region, to improve the quality of education in ways that are appropriate for meeting regional economic development policies, and to steer institutions, governments, and education consumers in directions aimed at uplifting the economy of the region.

Institutions will need to develop extensive new partnerships with each other and with the private sector, government agencies, and the donor community on a scale much greater than anything yet experienced in the region if a critical mass of education and training at a tertiary level is to be reached before it is too late.

Exciting trends are emerging in higher education around the world that have relevance for sub-Saharan Africa, some of which are already evolving in the region. These trends need greater support from the higher education stakeholder community—including the private sector and other end users of higher education's products and services—to propel them to a scale and a level of quality that can bring rewards to the region.

REFERENCES

AAU (Association of African Universities). 1995. "Report of the AAU/UNESCO/CHEMS Workshop on Strategic Planning in African Universities." Accra, Ghana: Association of African Universities.

AERC (African Economic Research Consortium) and United Nations University. 1998. *Strengthening Africa's Participation in the Global Economy.* Tokyo: AERC.

Arenson, K. 2000. "Columbia Leads Academic Pack in Turning Profit from Research." *New York Times*, August 2, 2000.

Carnoy, M. 1995a. "Education and the New International Division of Labor." In Martin Carnoy, ed., *International Encyclopedia of Economics of Education*, 2nd ed. Oxford, England: Elsevier Science.

———. 1995b. "Rates of Return to Education." In Martin Carnoy, ed., *International Encyclopedia of Economics of Education*, 2nd ed. Oxford, England: Elsevier Science.

———. 1995c. "Education and Technology Change." In Martin Carnoy, ed., *International Encyclopedia of Economics of Education*, 2nd ed. Oxford, England: Elsevier Science.

Carnoy, M., M. Castells, S. Cohen, and F. Cardoso. 1993. *The New

Global Economy in the Information Age: Reflections on Our Changing World. University Park: Pennsylvania State University Press.

Castells, M. 1998. *End of Millennium.* Vol. 3: *The Information Age: Economy, Society and Culture.* London: Blackwell.

———. 1999. *The Social Implications of Information and Communication Technologies.* Report prepared for UNESCO's World Social Science Report. Paris: UNESCO.

Clark, B. 1998. *The Entrepreneurial University.* Oxford: Pergamon, 1998.

Cloete, N., and T. Moja. 2000. *Vanishing Borders and New Boundaries in the Information Society.* Pretoria: Centre for Higher Education Transformation.

Dearing, R. 1997. *Higher Education in the Learning Society: Summary Report.* Norwich, England: The National Committee of Inquiry into Higher Education.

Ekong, D., and P. Plant. 1996. *Strategic Planning at Selected African Universities.* Accra, Ghana: Association of African Universities.

Fry, P., and R. Utui. 1999. *Promoting Access, Quality and Capacity Building in African Higher Education: The Strategic Planning Experience at Eduardo Mondlane University.* Paris: Association for the Development of Education in Africa Working Group in Higher Education.

Gibbons, M. 1998. *Higher Education Relevance in the 21st Century.* Washington, D.C.: The World Bank.

International Labor Office. 1999. *Key Indicators of the Labour Market 1999.* Geneva: ILO.

James, E. 1995. "Public-Private Division of Responsibility for Education." In Martin Carnoy, ed., *International Encyclopedia of Economics of Education,* 2nd ed. Oxford, England: Elsevier Science.

Jongbloed, J., P. Maasaan, and G. Neave. 1999. *From the Eye of the Storm: Higher Education's Changing Institution.* Dordrecht: Kluwer.

Kraak, A. 2000. *Changing Modes: New Knowledge Production and Its Implications for Higher Education in South Africa.* Pretoria: Human Sciences Research Council.

Ludwig, J. 2000. "A Digest of Recent Corporate News in Distance Education." *Chronicle of Higher Education,* November 3.

Mail & Guardian (Johannesburg). 2000. INNOVATIONS Supplement. September 15.

Merisotis, J., and D. Gilleland. 2000. *Funding South African Higher Education: Steering Mechanisms to Meet National Goals.* Washington, D.C.: Institute for Higher Education Policy; Pretoria: Center for Higher Education Transformation.

National Commission on Higher Education. 1996. *A Framework for Transformation.* Pretoria: National Commission on Higher Education.

NUFFIC. 1999. *The Financing of Higher Education in Sub-Saharan Africa: Results of Workshop Sessions.* April 21, 1999. The Hague: NUFFIC.

OECD (Organization for Economic Co-operation and Development). 1999. *Education Policy Analysis.* Paris: OECD.

Oni, Bankole. 1999. *A Framework for Technological Capacity Building in Nigeria: Lessons from Developed Countries.* Bremen, Germany: Institute for World Economics and International Management.

Partnership for Capacity Building in Africa. 1997. *Revitalizing Universities and Africa: Strategy and Guidelines.* Washington, D.C.: World Bank.

Roberts and Associates. 1998. *Tertiary Distance Learning in Sub-Saharan Africa.* ADEA Working Group on Higher Education. Washington, D.C.: World Bank.

Sadlak, J. 1998. "Globalisation and Concurrent Challenges for Higher Education." In P. Scott, ed., *The Globalisation of Higher Education.* London: Society for Research in Higher Education and Open University Press.

Saint, W. 2000. *Tertiary Distance Education and Technology in Sub-Saharan Africa.* Education and Technology Technical Note Series, vol. 5. Washington, D.C.: World Bank.

Scott, P. 1995. *The Meaning of Mass Higher Education.* Buckingham, UK: Open University Press.

Serageldin, I. 2000. "University Governance and the Stakeholder Society." Keynote Address at the International Association of Universities Conference, Durban, South Africa, August.

Spender, D. 1998. Keynote Address at the Annual Conference of the Council on Adult and Experiential Learning, Phoenix, Arizona, October.

Task Force on Higher Education and Society. 2000. *Higher Education in Developing Countries: Peril and Promise.* Washington, D.C.: World Bank.

Teferra, D. 1999. "Ideas for Financing African Higher Education." *International Higher Education,* no. 17 (Fall): 18–19.

Tooley, J. 1999. *The Global Education Industry: Lessons from Private Education in Developing Countries.* London: International Finance Corporation.

UNESCO (United Nations Educational, Scientific and Cultural Organizations). 1998. *Statistical Yearbook.* Paris: UNESCO.

West, M., and L. Shackleton. 1999. *USHEPiA: Building a Research Capacity in Africa.* Washington, D.C.: Association for the Development of Education in Africa Working Group in Higher Education.

World Bank. 1994. *Higher Education: The Lessons of Experience.* Washington, D.C.: World Bank.

———. 1999. *Knowledge for Development.* World Development Report. New York: Oxford University Press.

———. 2000a. *African Development Indicators 2000.* Washington, D.C.: World Bank.

———. 2000b. *Little Data Book 2000.* Washington, D.C.: World Bank.

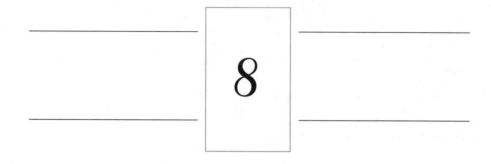

8

Women in Universities and University-Educated Women
The Current Situation in Africa

Eva M. Rathgeber

INTRODUCTION

In many countries in Africa, there is concern about how to better integrate women into social and economic development processes. Despite an increased emphasis on gender issues, the actual progress made by African women over the past two decades is still small in terms of real equity, access to power, and prestige in their societies. At a global level, the proportion of women enrolled in institutions of higher education grew from 44 percent in 1980 to 47 percent in 1995. However, in most African countries, female participation is still considerably below the global level (UNESCO 1999). Perhaps most important, although women are entering into higher education in increasing numbers, this has not resulted in an increased participation in formal labor markets, especially at professional and managerial levels. In most countries in Latin America, 25 percent or more of the administrative and managerial positions are filled by women, but few countries in Africa have achieved even 20 percent (United Nations 2000).

The status of women in African universities is a reflection of their situation in society. Women are underrepresented in African universities, and those who are able to pursue higher education concentrate in traditional "female" fields such as education, arts and humanities, and social sciences. In almost all countries, female teaching staff are few in number and comprise less than 10 percent of the faculty at the most senior professorial level. Female students are frequently subjected to sexual harassment or subtle downplaying of their skills and potential and are discouraged from entering fields dominated by men. When they graduate, women often have poor employment prospects and receive lower salaries and fewer opportunities for advancement. They frequently suffer discrimination in the workplace.

Significantly, many African women—whether university students or professionals in the workplace—accept this discrimination as "normal" and do little to try to change the situation (Nare 1995). In fact, while many educated women engage in various types of voluntary activities to improve conditions or create opportunities for poor women, few undertake systematic analysis of their own situation or try to put in place mechanisms to combat overt and widespread sexual discrimination and harassment in their societies. Most educated African women are strong supporters of "women in development," or giving women access to opportunities of all types. However, relatively few have moved toward the conceptualization of gender issues in a more holistic way that sees women's lack of opportunities as only one symptom of the structure of gender relations in Africa, a structure that is inherently discriminatory and frequently derogatory toward women. This chapter will explore this issue in detail, providing statistics and evidence of the current situation of women students in African universities and professional women in the workplace. The chapter will end with an examination of some strategies that could be used to improve the status of women students in the universities. It must be stated at the outset that the term "African" is used somewhat indiscriminately since, of course, differences exist among countries and institutions. By necessity, an overview chapter of this nature makes generalizations that could certainly be challenged in specific cases.

OVERVIEW

The past four decades have witnessed a massive expansion of African higher education. In 1960, sub-Saharan Africa had only six universities (excluding South Africa). Today, the region has more than 150, and the numbers continue to grow. Enrollment in higher education has increased dramatically as more students in almost every country have pursued the opportunity to further their studies at home. In addition, private colleges and universities have been established in many African countries. In East Africa (Uganda, Tanzania, and Kenya), there are now seventeen private universities with a combined student population of more than 15,000. Often these are small institutions with limited resources that are linked to religious organizations, but they are providing an alternative to overcrowded national universities. Finally, in the 1990s, evening classes and part-time learning became increasingly popular in Anglophone Africa, and distance education began to be seriously pursued by various institutions. While none of these initiatives has focused specifically on increasing the access of girls and women to higher education, all of them have played a role in increasing the absolute numbers of women enrolled in higher education in Africa.

In spite of the increase in student numbers and institutions since the 1960s, overall funding for education fell, especially in the 1980s and 1990s, as a result of World Bank–imposed structural adjustment programs. Even in the 1990s, when donors began to reinvest in primary and secondary education, a deep-seated reluctance to support higher education remained; it was seen as a "luxury" in countries that could not afford to provide even universal primary education. In the past two decades, African governments have increasingly regarded donor assistance as a necessary factor in any expansion of education facilities. Needless to say, this has strengthened the role of donors in setting the direction for African education at all levels. Perhaps for this and other reasons having to do with state control, African civil society has been less involved in education in recent years. The fact that civil society has so little direct contact with the universities has meant that these institutions have not felt a high degree of accountability to their clientele. At one level, this means that universities are less likely to design their programs to meet the needs of society and to make their students more employable. At another level, little public scrutiny of the universities takes place, with the result that discrimination against women can continue unabated.

UNESCO continues to be a major actor in analyzing and setting the directions for global education and education policy. Interestingly, UNESCO has never identified the gender relations of higher education as an issue for separate analysis. UNESCO has emphasized increasing female student intake, but it has not systematically advocated a critical review of the structure of the universities to recognize and understand the depth of discrimination against women, both as students and faculty. Because African universities were established and organized to meet the needs of male students, female students sometimes have a hard time "fitting in," especially in nontraditional areas of study. This cannot be corrected simply by recruiting higher numbers of female students and female professors, which could be done with affirmative action policies such as were adopted in the United States in the 1970s. It involves a much more fundamental rethinking of the gendered nature of the higher education process and the underlying assumptions that drive the behavior of both staff and students. A recent World Bank report on higher education in developing countries deals with the issue of gender with only five paragraphs on the "Problems Facing Women and Disadvantaged Groups" (Task Force on Higher Education and Society 2000, 41). This is not atypi-

cal of mainstream thinking about issues of gender and higher education in Africa. Women are seen as marginalized or as "disadvantaged," and it is thought that their problems can be solved by ensuring that more are offered places at universities.

While this is an important beginning, it does not address the more serious and difficult question of how to change the whole culture of university learning to make it more women-friendly, particularly in the natural and physical sciences. Such evidence as exists reveals that African men and women, especially those enrolled in the sciences, may have very different university experiences. Interviews in the 1980s with female medical students in Kenya suggested that even when women performed better than their male colleagues, their success was often attributed by male students to their alleged unfair advantage in dealing with medical school teachers, who were primarily male and were presumed to be sexually attracted to the female students (Rathgeber 1991).

Research in Cameroon suggested that women scientists managed to pursue their careers in science despite opposition from schools, universities, and bureaucracies (Woodhouse and Ndonko 1993). Far from being encouraged to study science, female students were subtly—and sometimes very directly—told time and again that science was not a suitable area of study for them. This attitude tends to be replicated in the workplace. Relatively few African women hold senior academic positions in science-related subjects. In turn, this means that young girls who want to pursue science have few mentors and role models.

WHAT ARE WOMEN STUDYING?

Table 8.1 shows that the number of female students enrolled in tertiary education (universities, teachers' colleges, professional schools, or other postsecondary institutions) varies significantly from country to country. In a few cases, the number of women enrolled in tertiary education is beginning to approach equity with males. In nine of the sixteen countries in Table 8.1, more than 40 percent of the students enrolled in postsecondary institutions are female. The relatively high participation of females in tertiary education in a few countries like Lesotho, Swaziland, and Botswana is explained by the fact that males have economic opportunities at a younger age (mostly in the mining sector), which encourages parents to keep daughters rather than sons in school. Overall female enrollment is approximately 43 percent for the sixteen countries in Table 8.1. Although more African women are attending tertiary institutions, they are still concentrated in traditional fields of study. This is seen clearly in Table 8.2.

Women are still concentrating in the traditional fields of education, humanities, and social sciences, although they increasingly are well represented in medical sciences. In most African universities, entry standards for admission into medical studies are among the most rigorous of all disciplines. While the number of women in health sciences is relatively high in several countries, the absolute number of students in medicine still tends to be quite small. It should also be noted that "medical sciences" includes nursing, and probably a high proportion of women students in this field are actually enrolled in nursing

Table 8.1. Enrollment of Students in Tertiary Education in Selected African Countries, 1994–1998*

Country	Year	Total Number of Students	Female Students	Percent Female Students
Lesotho	1996–1997	4,614	2,507	54
Swaziland	1996–1997	5,658	2,927	52
South Africa	1994	468,086	230,600	49
Botswana	1996–1997	7,275	3,449	47
Djibouti	1995–1996	130	61	47
Tunisia	1996–1997	121,787	54,278	45
Algeria	1995–1996	267,142	118,368	44
Egypt	1995–1996	850,051	352,902	41
Morocco	1994–1995	250,919	102,720	41
Zimbabwe	1996	46,673	17,016	36
Uganda	1996–1997	34,773	11,542	33
Burkina Faso	1994–1995	9,452	2,087	22
Ethiopia	1996–1997	42,226	8,524	20
Tanzania	1995–1996	12,776	2,075	16
Eritrea	1997–1998	3,096	410	13
Togo	1994–1995	11,173	1,487	13
Total		2,135,831	910,953	43

*Countries were selected based on geography, to provide an overview of the continent.
Source: UNESCO 1999.

programs. Finally, health sciences are often regarded as "soft" sciences because of the strong component of human interaction. Since numerous studies suggest that women are more attracted to subjects with a component of social usefulness (Wellcome Trust 1994; Erinosho 1993), it is not surprising that those who enter scientific fields are drawn toward health sciences.

An analysis of data from the 1980s showed that women enrolled in higher education tended to concentrate in non-scientific subject areas and that they were more likely to attend nursing schools, teacher-training colleges, or business education colleges than universities (Rathgeber 1991). To a considerable extent, they were guided in these choices by prevailing social expectations. For example, schoolgirls in Kenya were discouraged from attempting to excel in male-dominated subject areas. Even at the secondary school level, girls were encouraged by teachers to give equal weight to marital and career prospects when planning for their futures. Thus, they were socialized from an early age to accept constraints imposed by their future reproductive roles and to avoid careers that could conflict with motherhood. Research in Francophone Africa also found that female students were concentrated in the humanities and that, although women are prominent in agriculture in Africa, few females studied agronomy (Assié-Lumumba 1993). Some researchers also have found a relationship between social class origins and field of study. In Egypt, for example, middle- and upper-class women are more likely to study scientific and professional subjects, while lower-middle-class women enter humanities, social sciences, education, agriculture, and nursing (Cochran 1992). However, some changes are occurring. Recent work in Tanzania, Botswana, and Malawi showed that the number of women enrolled in agriculture diploma and degree

courses was gradually increasing and that institutions of higher education were making efforts to encourage women to study science. Sokoine University of Agriculture in Tanzania has a group of women researchers and academics that encourages young women at the secondary and tertiary levels to study agriculture- and forestry-related disciplines (Acker, McBreen, and Taylor 1998).

Nonetheless, it is striking that in all the countries listed in Table 8.2, with the possible exception of Algeria, only a small proportion of students enrolled in natural science programs are women. In all parts of Africa, it seems that natural sciences and engineering are rejected systematically as attractive courses of study by women. Algeria has a relatively high proportion of female university students (44 percent) but they make up only 36 percent of the total enrollment in natural sciences and 65 percent of the total enrollment in the humanities. Swaziland has 52 percent overall female enrollment, but women make up only 12 percent of the students in natural sciences. Uganda has 33 percent overall female enrollment, but only 16 percent of students enrolled in natural sciences are women, as compared with 40 percent enrolled in social sciences. Moreover, countries with very low levels of female enrollment seem to have lower proportions of women enrolled in natural sciences. This suggests that African women are even less likely to enroll in natural science programs in countries that have made little progress in increasing the numbers of women overall in higher education. Given the importance of science and technology to African development, this is an observation that should be taken very seriously by policymakers. A general shortage of scientists exists in Africa, though their skills are central in enabling the continent to participate in the ongoing information technology

Table 8.2. Percent Women in Fields of Study in Selected African Institutions of Tertiary Education, by Country

Country	Year	Education	Humanities	Social Sciences	Natural Sciences	Medical Sciences	Other
Algeria	1995–1996	25.8	65.4	46.7	36.3	49.9	54.9
Benin	1996	20.6	NA	19.9	12.6	24.3	13.2
Botswana	1996–1997	49.1	55.6	59.9	23.9	90.8	24.9
Burkina Faso	1994–1995	13.6	32.0	22.4	7.7	23.8	NA
Chad	1995–1996	4.9	14.8	12.9	5.6	NA	NA
Djibouti	1995–1996	61.1	NA	41.5	NA	NA	NA
Egypt	1995–1996	53.9	53.4	35.8	29.4	43.1	27.0
Ethiopia	1996–1997	22.7	34.6	26.7	12.1	17.1	NA
Gabon	1994–1995	22.3	32.6	35.9	NA	58.5	NA
Guinea	1996–1997	9.2	14.1	13.0	6.5	17.0	NA
Lesotho	1996–1997	70.9	64.4	45.7	31.3	NA	NA
Madagascar	1996–1997	35.5	65.5	46.2	29.9	47.2	NA
Morocco	1994–1995	30.6	51.2	41.7	28.4	49.3	34.1
Mozambique	1996–1997	30.2	27.4	18.5	20.0	56.1	NA
Namibia	1995	57.7	51.5	42.5	35.2	83.3	66.2
South Africa	1994	63.7	60.9	46.0	29.4	61.2	54.6
Swaziland	1996–1997	55.3	56.8	59.5	12.3	84.9	85.8
Togo	1996–1997	27.9	20.0	16.5	5.6	21.2	16.1
Tunisia	1996–1997	41.9	61.0	43.7	32.4	55.0	28.5
Uganda	1996–1997	29.1	38.3	40.4	16.7	31.0	50.2
Tanzania	1995–1996	18.1	NA	19.9	9.1	28.3	53.7
Zimbabwe	1996	46.0	28.1	41.5	14.0	38.5	20.7

NA = Data not available.
Source: UNESCO 1999.

revolution and in other aspects of globalization. However, very little public discussion has occurred about the low numbers of women engaged in science and technology, and no real efforts have been made by African university administrators to examine why women and girls reject these subject areas or whether it would be possible to redesign the curricula in natural sciences and engineering to make them more attractive to females. It is commonly assumed that women are simply "not interested" in these areas of study and that the fault lies with women themselves rather than with the way that these subjects are taught from secondary school onward—or with the kind of institutional environment within which the sciences are taught (for example, with very few female professors).

PROBLEMS FEMALE STUDENTS FACE

Most students enrolled at African universities still come from rural backgrounds. A study in Cameroon in the early 1990s showed that 77 percent of students originated from farm families. Research in Togo, Benin, Senegal, and Gabon also suggested that about two-thirds of university students came from rural backgrounds (Assié-Lumumba 1993). However, research in Nigeria suggested that just over half the students at one uni-

versity came from urban backgrounds and that women were slightly more likely than men to come from an urban background (Biraimah 1994). On the whole, however, the university provides the first exposure to new ideas for the majority of African students. This may be a factor in explaining some of the very traditional views held by male students about the status of women.

Since the late 1990s, numerous countries, including Tanzania, Kenya, and Uganda, have undertaken modest affirmative action programs; for example, by reducing university entry requirements slightly for females as compared with males. One unintended effect has been that some male students regard women as academically weaker and openly state this opinion, thus contributing to a generally negative atmosphere for female students. Nonetheless, female participation in higher education has increased in these three countries and efforts have also been made to encourage women to go beyond a first degree. For example, the directorate of postgraduate studies at the University of Dar es Salaam offers graduate scholarships for female students, and the gender management committee at the university has sponsored female academic staff for Ph.D. training (Mlama 1998).

Once admitted to university, female students face further

problems. Many African secondary schools are segregated by sex, so students often have little previous experience of attending classes with members of the opposite sex. At the university, female students may be subjected to sexual harassment, date rape, or, more commonly, constant verbal undermining or denigration. Male faculty members do not necessarily recognize the potentially damaging effects of remarks that may not be meant unkindly, such as references to women's lack of "interest" in certain subjects, to the importance of their roles as wives and mothers, or to their personal appearance. Most universities have inadequate or no systems in place to provide support or advice to female students in such situations. To begin to combat this situation, the Southern African Network of Institutions Challenging Sexual Harassment and Violence was formed in 1997. In South Africa, the Gender Equity Task Team of the Ministry of Education has identified sexual harassment as a major problem for female students.

The University of Dar es Salaam has also recognized this as a problem, but sexual harassment continues, despite its ongoing efforts to sensitize faculty and students. Penina Mlama notes:

> In a study by the Gender Dimension Task Force of the University of Dar es Salaam, an exposition of unfavourable male-female students' relationships is presented. The female student harassment includes character assassination literature . . . intimidation which includes preventing female students from wearing short pants, having non-University student boyfriends, entering male teachers' offices, taking four o'clock tea from the University Cafeteria or watching TV in the students' common room. . . . If girls perform well they are accused of having sexual relations with the male staff. The sexual harassment has unfortunately also included rape. Male staff are also reported to victimize female students when sexual favours are denied. (Mlama 1998, 480–81)

Female students find themselves unable to combat this treatment and usually suffer in silence. Since stereotyping about the "appropriate" roles of women is so widespread, in cases of less overt sexual harassment (such as sexual stereotyping), women sometimes have not developed sufficient analytical skills to understand that they are being denigrated in the larger society. In general, African universities have relatively few female faculty members and even fewer senior female faculty members who could help to reduce hostility toward women on campus (Makhubu 1998). Moreover, universities have been so beleaguered by financial problems for the past two decades that feminists have had difficulty convincing administrators to commit scarce resources to gender-related activities. Equity and fair treatment for female students have been considered at best a low priority and at worst a nonissue when libraries, laboratories, and faculty salaries have all been in need of additional resources. This problem is reinforced by the fact that most senior university administrators are male and have not had the personal experience of sex-based discrimination (Namaddu 1995).

Women academics in African universities are almost always concentrated in the lower ranks. Research in Kenya showed that men often move from one university to another to secure higher positions, but women usually stay in one institution because of the lesser mobility that is associated with their family responsibilities and ties (Kanake 1997). In the mid-1990s, there were only three female full professors at the University of Nairobi, and there were none at Kenyatta University (the largest and oldest public universities in the country). Female academic staff were concentrated in the lecturer, tutorial fellow, and graduate assistant categories, mainly in nonscientific areas.

Lydia Kanake's study of the Kenyan education system (1997) found that universities sometimes deliberately delay promoting their faculty members (presumably for salary savings). Although promotion criteria are laid down clearly, promotion committees do not always follow them, and personal relationships can become positive or negative factors in promotion decisions. The study concluded that promotion or appointment was linked with nepotism, ethnicity, political affiliations, and personal relationships with those in power. Scholarship, while important on paper, often counted for less in reality. Another Kenyan study, focusing on university libraries, drew the same conclusion: merit and experience were secondary, relatively inconsequential factors in promotion decisions, which were based primarily on ethnicity and personal relationships with the university librarians (*Daily Nation* 2000). In such a situation, women again are disadvantaged because they are less likely to have personal relationships with those in power and have less time for political activities because of their reproductive responsibilities.

HIGHER EDUCATION AND PARTICIPATION IN THE WORKFORCE

A serious problem faced by universities in almost all African countries is the high rate of unemployment of both male and female graduates. This has given rise to intense debates about the relevance of the university to the needs of the societies in which they are based. Despite visible evidence of serious graduate unemployment and underemployment, research suggests that investment in higher education is still a good choice at the individual level.

A recent study in Kenya found that rates of return for primary and especially secondary education are considerably lower than in the past (Appleton, Bigsten, and Manda 1999). Between 1978 and 1995, the private and social returns to secondary education fell by more than two-thirds, due to the fact that secondary schooling was expensive and the chances of finding employment declined as the Kenyan economy deteriorated. However, this did not hold for tertiary education. Although the numbers in the sample were small, the evidence suggested that private rates of return for university education were high. (This may have been part of the reason for immense public pressure for the expansion of the university system in the 1980s.) In general, rates of return for women were somewhat higher than for men at all levels.

The data suggest that higher education raises both the employment prospects and the social expectations of graduates. This seems to have different effects on men and women. For women, social expectations sometimes outweigh employment expectations. Even when women have successfully completed

Table 8.3. Responses by Men and Women as to Why They Prefer a Male Boss

Prefer a man because men are:	Do not prefer a woman because women are:
Hard working	Emotional
More professional	Petty
Able to handle crisis	Difficult to cheat
Considerate	Easily distracted
Tough	Known to hate fellow women who are smarter than they are
Decisive	More likely not to forgive easily
Forward-looking	Quick to misinterpret one's mistake as disobedience
More exposed to new ideas	Not always efficient (think of children and family all the time)
More impartial	
Always obeyed by everyone	
People who have high esteem	
Good negotiators	

Source: Abagi, Olweya, and Otieno 2000.

higher education, they are discouraged in some countries from participating in the labor force after graduation (Cochran 1992). Although this constitutes a significant loss of human capital for poor countries that have invested in the development of higher education systems, it reflects a set of entrenched social norms. Indeed, prevailing social norms still act as a disincentive to many African women who might otherwise pursue higher education or enter male-dominated fields of study. A recent study in Kenya (Kanake 1997) found that women and men often considered higher education as an impediment to a woman's marriage prospects. A female respondent at a Kenyan university explained:

> I got my Ph.D. and now my husband and I are separated. Things went on smoothly before I left for studies. When I came back, my husband started complaining that I was not taking good care of our children, that I spent most of my time in my academic work. . . . His parents said I would be unfaithful. Perhaps it was because I had a Ph.D. and he did not. (Kanake 1997, 22–23)

Melanie Walker quotes a respondent in a South African study of women academics:

> I wanted to get my Ph.D. and that was what ultimately caused the rift with this man who had asked me to marry him. I said we'll wait, it's not going to take that long, but he didn't want that, he just wanted a family, so I split. I don't regret it though. (Walker 1998, 342–343)

In most African countries, it is widely believed that men should be better educated than their wives; therefore, young women sometimes curb their ambitions to ensure their suitability as marriage candidates. This feeling prevails despite the spiraling cost of living and the increased necessity for families to depend on the incomes of two wage-earners. It is possible that the current economic hardships will have an impact on social attitudes toward female higher education, but the effects of this will only be felt in years to come.

Little is known about job productivity or satisfaction of African university graduates, but a 1982 study by the Eastern and Southern African Universities Research Program (ESAURP) surveyed 1,800 employed graduates in Kenya, Somalia, Swaziland, Tanzania, and Zambia and asked them to self-report their level of success in their work. Only 17 percent considered themselves to be above-average employees (productive and successful), while 42 percent considered themselves to be average and a surprising 41 percent considered themselves to be below-average employees. The highest number of graduates in this category were in medicine/health and business/administration (46 percent and 48 percent, respectively). Relatively fewer graduates in agriculture/veterinary sciences (26 percent) and education/teaching (26 percent) held this opinion of themselves (Maliyamkono et al., 1982, cited in Ishumi 1994). The results were not disaggregated by gender, but these figures present an interesting contrast with research among Nigerian university students reported by Biraimah (1994). More than 50 percent of her sample of male and female undergraduates fully expected to have successful high-status careers. This suggests that the actual experience of university graduates on the job may be markedly different from their expectations. This may be especially true for women because their chances for quick promotion are often poor once they enter the workforce. A recent study in Kenya based on a countrywide sample of almost 2,000 people and almost equally divided between men and women found that both sexes preferred male bosses and that this view was most strongly held by people with tertiary level education (Abagi, Olweya, and Otieno 2000). In investigating further, the researchers found the responses presented in Table 8.3 to be typical.

These results reveal the entrenched stereotypes and attitudes held by a cross section of the Kenyan population. However, the authors emphasize that the most conservative and traditional views were held by the most highly educated people in their sample, which suggests that professional women have a difficult time establishing their worth. The attitudes of workers toward female supervisors reflect the values that are part of contemporary Kenyan society. They seem to be shared in other African countries. Recent data for various African countries show that between 1985 and 1997, the proportion of women among

Table 8.4. Male and Female Participation in Research and Development by Category of Personnel in Selected African Countries, 1984–1997

Country	Year	Researchers		Technicians and Equivalent Staff		Other Supporting Staff	
		Total	F	Total	F	Total	F
Benin	1989	794	100	242	64	1,651	339
Burkina Faso	1997	176	34	165	16	439	NA
Burundi	1989	170	17	168	NA	476	NA
Central African Republic	1990	162	16	92	5	NA	NA
Congo	1984	862	NA	1,473	NA	NA	NA
Egypt	1991	26,415	NA	19,607	NA	56,274	NA
Madagascar	1994	159	45	483	175	405	85
Mauritius	1989	193	33	172	46	656	97
Nigeria	1987	1,338	NA	6,042	NA	5,500	NA
Senegal	1996	19	5	29	7	30	NA
South Africa	1993	37,192	NA	11,343	NA	11,929	NA
Togo	1994	387	NA	249	NA	837	NA
Tunisia	1997	1,145	NA	524	NA	2,011	NA
Uganda	1997	422	162	272	34	256	NA

NA = Data not available.
Source: UNESCO 1999.

administrative and managerial workers in the formal sector was usually below 20 percent. For example, in 2000, the percent of managers and administrators who were female in Mali was 20, in Egypt 16, in Zimbabwe 15, in Cameroon 10, and in Algeria, Nigeria, and Zambia 6 (United Nations 2000) (Table 8.4).

Many educated African women do not challenge the status quo and quietly accept discrimination in the professional workplace. This may be partly a result of traditional African belief systems that place great value on motherhood as a visible symbol of female maturity and status. In some African societies, after the birth of a first child, especially a boy, women are forever known afterward as Mama X (name of the child). In Swahili, the title of respect for any mature woman, mother or not, is "Mama." Consequently, African women, perhaps more than their counterparts in Europe and North America, feel a strong desire and social pressure to become wives and mothers (or at least mothers). However, this puts them into a vulnerable position professionally because men often argue that women are too preoccupied with affairs of the family to give full attention to their careers. Since both men and women place great value on "family"—and women are considered the rightful keepers of the family in terms of seeing to its daily maintenance—this creates a difficult position for professional women who, on the one hand, want to ensure that their family obligations are met and, on the other hand, need to put extra time and effort into their careers if they wish to advance. Of course, all professional women in every society face this dilemma, but it is arguably more taxing in the African context because prevailing social norms do not usually require males to share family maintenance responsibilities, except financially. Moreover, responsibility for extended families continues to be significant in African societies because

of the lack of pension plans or state health and welfare systems that could provide assistance to needy family members. Thus the family obligations of women often go far beyond simply caring for their own children.

PARTICIPATION OF WOMEN IN SCIENTIFIC AND ACADEMIC ADMINISTRATION CAREERS

Since relatively few African women study natural sciences, it is not surprising that they are underrepresented in scientific research institutions. Table 8.5 gives some indications.

It is evident that women are underrepresented in research and development institutions in Africa. The statistics are poor and it is hard to draw any firm conclusions, but perhaps most interesting is the fact that a large number of countries still do not collect sex-disaggregated data on researchers, technicians, and other science-related personnel in national institutions. Without this kind of information, it is unlikely that any affirmative action programs to increase the number of women scientists will be undertaken.

The situation in African universities is very similar (see Table 8.6). At the end of the 1990s, only 6 percent of the universities in the African Association of Universities were led by women. Thirty-seven percent of the 463 universities in the Association of Commonwealth Universities were led by women. It is clear that providing more female role models is a huge task in Africa even at the level of higher education administrators. In this respect, the work of the Forum for African Women Educators (FAWE), based in Nairobi, Kenya, has had an important impact by regularly bringing together senior female education administrators to assess and analyze this situation, produce statistics, and enhance awareness of and sensitization about women in higher education.

In many African countries, vice-chancellors at public universities are directly appointed by the government, sometimes directly by the head of state. Consequently, the possession of expertise, management skills, and even academic prominence may be overshadowed by political considerations. Appointment to head a university or college often is a reward for supporting the political goals of the government. Those recommending the appointments are almost always men, and they are likely to recommend other men, thus effectively eliminating women from consideration. In her study of the Kenyan system, Kanake (1997) found that there were no established criteria for the selection of vice-chancellors and that loyalty to the government, closeness to the chancellor (in the case of Kenya, the president, Daniel arap Moi), and the need to reward colleagues seemed to be important considerations. A study in Francophone Africa found that not a single government had appointed a female university rector as of the early 1990s. Similarly, few women were deans, vice-deans, or heads of departments, institutes, or research centers (Assié-Lumumba 1995).

Women academics themselves have done little to change the status quo. Few have lobbied and built sympathetic constituencies outside the university. This may be generally true of women in male-dominated fields. Two qualitative research studies based on interviews with female African scientists in Kenya and Cameroon suggested that women accepted male definitions of professional comportment, standards, and conduct when they completed their studies and entered their professions (Rathgeber 1985; Woodhouse and Ndonko 1993). Successful African women may be forced to adopt a male model of success to survive the rigors of scientific training and professional practice. In the Cameroonian case, women did not identify systemic obstacles or discrimination and saw their own success as based on personal determination and hard work within the context of their individual lives. Woodhouse and Ndonko note the failure of their respondents to identify the structural determinant of gender and its impact on their own academic progress and possibilities. Similarly, Walker found in her study of South African female academics that they ranked race and class higher than gender as obstacles to their success (Walker 1998). Again, this suggests that most African women are reluctant to question the status quo and generally are not engaged in bringing about structural change or social transformation. It is clear that this is an issue that requires further research.

INVOLVEMENT OF DONORS WITH AFRICAN UNIVERSITIES

Multilateral and bilateral donors have been involved with the development of African higher education from the onset of the postcolonial era, although they were more interested in primary and secondary education in the 1980s and 1990s. Recently, however, the pendulum seems to be swinging back toward postsecondary education. In early 2000, four American foundations (the Carnegie Corporation, the Rockefeller Foun-

Table 8.5. Academic Staff in Science* Departments of Selected African Universities by Rank and Gender

Country or City	Professors		Senior Lecturers		Lecturers	
	M	F	M	F	M	F
Botswana	7	0	15	1	47	1
Ghana**	73	1	136	17	294	40
Nairobi, Kenya	111	3	139	15	289	40
Lesotho	9	0	15	1	22	2
Malawi	24	1	45	7	64	13
Ibadan, Nigeria	134	6	169	25	174	38
Swaziland	6	1	18	0	42	11
Tanzania	56	2	101	3	137	10
Zambia	26	3	36	0	178	21
Zimbabwe	35	2	70	10	181	38

*Science refers to natural sciences, agriculture, engineering, earth and environmental sciences, mathematics, computer science, medicine, and veterinary science.
**Combines data from Legon, Cape Coast, and University of Science and Technology, Kumasi.
Source: Makhubu 1998, 511. Compiled from Commonwealth Universities Yearbook, 1993.

dation, the Ford Foundation, and the MacArthur Foundation) announced a partnership initiative intended to provide $100 million for African higher education over a five-year period. Their Partnership to Strengthen African Universities will help to establish links among education leaders across regional and national borders. Although the types of projects to be supported will vary according to the programs of each foundation, the criteria for selecting universities will include location in a country undergoing public policy reform, support for innovation and use of new technologies, strategic planning aimed at building national capacity for social and economic development, and creative, broad-based institutional leadership. While the early announcements of this initiative have not focused specifically on expanding opportunities for African women, it is highly likely that this will be a strong component of the new programs since the donors involved have an interest in the advancement of gender equity. The four American agencies all have good records in Africa of creating partnerships with local institutions rather than prescribing or dictating behavior. Nonetheless, the fact that foreign donors are so often the driving forces behind the introduction of equity issues in African universities is a sad reflection of the lack of priority given to the issue by university administrators themselves. Few senior-level university administrators have made a commitment to improving access and learning environments for women except in cases where they have been strongly encouraged to do so by the promise of outside funding. This suggests that the notion of gender equity has not really been accepted beyond the most superficial levels. There is no question that the financial resources of donors have provided a strong incentive to promote gender equity at African universities. Penina Mlama observes that although there have been many grassroots, national, and regional gender activists, "at times pressure had to come from donors of higher education who put gender as a string to funding. It is also no secret that a lot of the research on gender was done because that is where the donor funds were" (Mlama 1998, 474).

Finally, it is worth mentioning the concerted work of the Working Group on Female Participation, which is part of the Association for the Development of Education in Africa. Founded in 1990, this group is composed of African ministers of education and other senior civil servants, donor agencies, researchers, planners, and African NGOs. FAWE serves as the lead agency, and during the past ten years the working group has identified and supported collaborative efforts to build the capacity of individuals and private and public institutions to accelerate female participation in education at all levels. Although they have focused on primary and secondary education, FAWE has done an excellent job throughout Africa in raising the profile of female children and their educational needs.

DISTANCE EDUCATION AND THE POTENTIAL OF NEW TECHNOLOGIES

African students have been disadvantaged during the past two decades as inadequate funding has led to a decline in the quality of education and poor teaching and research facilities. This has been widely recognized and efforts are being made to redress the situation. However, these efforts are mostly donor-driven and do not necessarily reflect strong commitments from national governments to rebuild their university systems. In an era of spiraling health costs due to the HIV/AIDS pandemic and continued pressing needs in other sectors, it is unlikely that higher education will receive substantial infusions of funding from African national governments in the short term. This paints a pessimistic picture for the improvement of opportunities for African women. However, there is some potential for positive change with the growing prominence of computer-based information and communication technologies (ICTs).

New technologies are already having an impact in the improvement of library services and access to the global marketplace of ideas. During the 1980s and 1990s, most university libraries were unable to acquire sufficient books and periodicals to ensure that staff and students were abreast of current thinking and scholarship in their fields. Libraries were understaffed and lacked staff with communications technology skills. However, some corrective measures are currently underway. For example, the Kenya Institute of Management is coordinating the Kenya Education Network project, which aims to establish an online service library for universities in the region by 2004. Public universities will be able to join and get online references, abstracts, and catalogues as well as acquisition, school networking, and consultancy services (*Daily Nation* 2000). It is likely that this type of regional or centralized service will become more common and will eventually replace the need for universities to offer their own complete range of library services. As university fac-

ulty members become less isolated and more familiar with current thinking and practices in other institutions of higher education, it is likely that the culture of learning will be positively impacted and that this in turn will have beneficial effects for women students. At the very least, increased connectivity will enable female students and staff at different institutions in their own country and outside to communicate more easily, to share experiences, and to build solidarity.

The second area in which the increased use of ICTs can play a significant role is distance education. Distance learning has considerable potential in Africa, since telecommunications facilities are rapidly expanding, mostly through the introduction of mobile units rather than through land lines. Currently, most African distance education is still carried out using conventional text and correspondence methods. Many programs have also used audiocassettes, community radio, and sometimes television. Numerous African universities are beginning to offer distance education programs but few, with the exception of the World Bank–funded African Virtual University, have taken full advantage of ICTs. As this becomes more common, possibly with programs based at community telecenters, it will be easier for women in remote areas to upgrade their skills and their knowledge base by taking courses offered by the universities.

Can expanded distance education make a particular difference to women students? Karen Evans (1995) has identified cultural, attitudinal, situational, and institutional barriers that have made it difficult for women in many cultures to participate in tertiary education. Distance learning could help overcome some of these barriers, such as the need for women to live away from home and the disadvantages they face in coeducation classes. It would allow women to participate in learning programs from their own homes or communities, tuition fees are much lower, and they would be able to continue to meet family commitments. However, distance education for women, especially in the area of science and technology, can easily suffer from the same weaknesses as conventional university-based education in terms of curriculum design. To date, the experience has been mixed. For example, Tanzania established its Open University in 1994 and had established thirty-six regional study centers countrywide by the end of 1996. Plans are currently underway to use satellite technology to reach distance learners more efficiently (Mmari 1998). Nonetheless, the Open University's experience in attracting female students has not been markedly different from that of the traditional universities. Only 121 of its 958 enrollees in 1997 were female, amounting to approximately 13 percent. Indeed, this is lower than the figures for the University of Dar es Salaam. It is clear, therefore, that university administrators will have to make special efforts to attract female students to enroll in distance learning programs. This, in turn, is related to the need for university administrators to address the issue of low female enrollment in all academic programs in a more creative way.

CONCLUSION

Universities should be at the forefront of social transformation. They should lead the way in encouraging society to critically analyze existing practices and should bring forward ideas for alternative approaches. Virtually all African universities have been important sources of research about their own societies. However, as pointed out by Katherine Namuddu (1995), African universities have been inept at ensuring that the research knowledge generated by their own staff is used to bring about beneficial change in society. Even more significantly, they have rarely used that knowledge to restructure their own operations.

If African university administrators have a genuine interest in making their institutions more receptive and supportive of female staff and students, several strategies could be followed. Namuddu (1995) has argued for invoking affirmative action programs to do the following:

- Ensure that a predetermined quota of women is admitted into each course of study
- Purposefully search for qualified female applicants for each vacant position at the university
- Design bridging courses, focusing on content or coping skills, to eliminate the weaknesses women might have before they enter the university
- Put in place firm policies for detecting, reporting, and redressing sexual harassment by staff or students
- Identify good female students early and put them on the necessary track for staff development opportunities
- Ensure the purposeful and accelerated promotion of good female candidates into higher academic positions

These are standard techniques that have been used successfully in other regions of the world. However, they have received little attention from most African university administrators.

During the 1980s and 1990s, literally thousands of studies on gender issues were carried out by African academics. African universities now hold an immense and well-documented knowledge base on gender issues. Yet universities have done little to change their own practices vis-à-vis the status of female students and faculty; similarly, they have had little impact in changing social attitudes. If anything, African universities have tacitly endorsed some of the most conservative thinking about the role of women through their own poor record of appointing women into senior academic positions.

Some of the blame for this lies with professional and academic women themselves. Although many have participated in impassioned battles for better opportunities for poor women, few have ventured to seriously challenge the status quo in their own careers and lives. Most have accepted the second-rate position of women in politics, universities, and public service. For example, in 2001, Kenya had no female cabinet ministers and only two female permanent secretaries, yet this did not seem to be an issue of pressing concern for most educated women in the country. Most African women have chosen to focus their efforts and modest militancy on issues that are less politically contentious and are unlikely to bring them unwanted scrutiny from male colleagues or superiors. In a sense, this is a strategy of self-preservation, but unless educated women begin to analyze their own situations and recognize that women are being systematically discriminated against at all levels of society, it is unlikely that there will be dramatic changes in the status of women in African universities or society in general.

REFERENCES

Abagi, O., J. Olweya, and W. Otieno. 2000. *Counting the Social Impact of Schooling: What Kenyans Say about Their School System and Gender Relations.* IPAR Discussion Paper Series, DP 024/2000. Nairobi: Institute of Policy Analysis and Research.

Acker, D. G., E. L. McBreen, and S. Taylor. 1998. "Women in Higher Education in Agriculture with Reference to Selected Countries in East and Southern Africa." *Journal of Agricultural Education and Extension* 5, no. 1: 13–21.

Appleton, S., A. Bigsten, and D. K. Manda. 1999. *Educational Expansion and Economic Decline: Returns to Education in Kenya, 1978–1995.* WPS/99-6. Oxford: Centre for the Study of African Economies, University of Oxford.

Assié-Lumumba, N'Dri Thèrése. 1993. *Higher Education in Francophone Africa: Assessment of the Potential of the Traditional Universities and Alternatives for Development.* AFTHR Technical Note no. 5. Human Resources Division. Washington, D.C.: World Bank.

———. 1995. *Demand, Access and Equity Issues in African Higher Education: Past Policies, Current Practices, and Readiness for the 21st Century.* Association of African Universities, Joint Colloquium on the University in Africa in the 1990s and Beyond, Lesotho, January 16–20.

Biraimah, K. 1994. "Class, Gender and Social Inequalities: A Study of Nigerian and Thai Undergraduate Students." *Higher Education* 27 (1 January).

Cochran, J. 1992. "Western Higher Education and Identity Conflict: The Egyptian Female Professional." *Convergence* 25, no. 3: 66–77.

Daily Nation. 2000. "Alarm Over Library Services." *Daily Nation* (Kenya), August 14.

Erinosho, S. 1993. *Nigerian Women in Science and Technology.* Dakar: International Development Research Centre.

Evans, K. 1995. "Barriers to Participation of Women in Technological Education and the Role of Distance Education." Vancouver: Commonwealth of Learning. Available online at: http://www.col.org/barriers.htm

Ishumi, A. 1994. *Thirty Years of Learning: Educational Development in Eastern and Southern Africa from Independence to 1990.* Ottawa: International Development Research Centre.

Kanake, L. 1997. *Gender Disparities among the Academic Staff in Kenyan Public Universities.* Nairobi: Lyceum Educational Consultants.

Makhubu, L. P. 1998. "The Right to Higher Education and Equal Opportunity Particularly for Women: The Major Challenge of Our Time." In *Higher Education in Africa: Achievements, Challenges and Prospects.* Dakar: UNESCO Regional Office for Education in Africa.

Mlama, P. M. 1998. "Increasing Access and Equity in Higher Education: Gender Issues." In *Higher Education in Africa: Achievements, Challenges and Prospects.* Dakar: UNESCO Regional Office for Education in Africa.

Mmari, G. 1998. "Increasing Access to Higher Education: The Experience of the Open University of Tanzania." In *Higher Education in Africa: Achievements, Challenges and Prospects.* Dakar: UNESCO Regional Office for Education in Africa.

Namuddu, K. 1995. "Gender Perspectives in the Transformation of Africa: Challenges to the African University as a Model to Society." In *Women in Higher Education in Africa,* 17–57. Dakar, Senegal: UNESCO.

Nare, Z. C. 1995. "Being a Woman Intellectual in Africa: The Persistence of Sexist and Cultural Stereotypes." In *Women in Higher Education in Africa,* 1–11. Dakar, Senegal: UNESCO.

Rathgeber, E. M. 1985. "Cultural Production in Kenyan Medical Education." *Comparative Education Review* 29, no. 3: 299–316.

———. 1991. "Women in Higher Education in Africa: Access and Choices." In Gail P. Kelly and Sheila Slaughter, eds., *Women's*

Higher Education in Comparative Perspective. Dordrecht: Kluwer Academic Publishers.

Task Force on Higher Education and Society. 2000. *Higher Education in Developing Countries: Peril and Promise.* Washington, D.C.: World Bank.

UNESCO. 1998. "Higher Education and Women: Issues and Perspectives." ED-98/CONF.202/CLD.14. Available online at: www.unesco.org/education/educprog/wche/principal/women.html

———. 1999. *Statistical Yearbook.* Paris: UNESCO Publishing and Berman Press.

United Nations. 2000. *The World's Women 2000.* New York: United Nations.

Walker, M. 1998. "Academic Identities: Women on a South African Landscape." *British Journal of Sociology of Education* 19, no. 3: 335–354.

Wellcome Trust. 1994. *Why May Women Science Undergraduates Not Be Seeking to Take Up Careers as Scientists? A Scoping Study for PRISM.* London: Wellcome Trust.

Woodhouse, H., and T. M. Ndongko. "Women and Science Education in Cameroon: Some Critical Reflections." *Interchange* 24, no. 2: 131–158.

9

Tertiary Distance Education and Technology in Sub-Saharan Africa

William Saint

INTRODUCTION

At the beginning of the twenty-first century, sub-Saharan Africa confronts unrelenting pressure to expand access to tertiary education, despite a decline in the quality of education and the lack of funding possibilities. The symptoms of this fundamental imbalance between enrollments and funds are multiple: overcrowded classrooms, poorly equipped learning facilities, brain drain of academic staff, declining research output, frequent strikes and campus closures, outdated and irrelevant curricula, and high graduate unemployment. Fueled by population growth and increased access to primary and secondary education, the number of African students seeking entrance to tertiary programs will surge during the current decade. Under present circumstances, however, only a tiny percentage of them will be successful. Consequently, where democratic societies offer channels for anxious parents and expectant students to voice their frustrations, tertiary education will likely be—or continue to be—a volatile political issue. Now, then, is the time for governments to anticipate the rising chorus of such demands and take steps that will ease the pressures for access while upholding the national interest in high-quality tertiary education and responsible stewardship of national resources.

This chapter addresses the question of how African nations might improve the balance between access to tertiary education and funding for tertiary education without making further sacrifices in quality. The answer lies in the use of distance learning, complemented in some cases with a selective application of new information and communication technologies (ICTs). The following discussion provides an overview of tertiary-level distance learning and technology experience throughout sub-Saharan Africa and the world at large. It highlights the relevance of these experiences for African nations that are committed to achieving increased participation in the global knowledge-based economy of the twenty-first century. It concludes with various suggestions

about how distance learning and technology use at the tertiary level might be adapted and gradually expanded within Africa.

The term "tertiary" is used throughout the chapter in preference to "higher education" because "higher" often connotes university education. Use of the latter term runs the risk of excluding tertiary-level alternatives to universities, including distance education programs, where many of the more innovative developments are now taking place.

WHY DISTANCE EDUCATION?

The demand for tertiary enrollments in Africa is easily illustrated (see Table 9.1). Using demographic projections for the 18-to-23-year-old age cohort traditionally associated with tertiary education, and conservatively assuming continuity in the countries' current gross enrollment ratios, it is evident that at least sixteen countries of sub-Saharan Africa will need to double their current tertiary enrollments over the coming decade (i.e., grow at a rate of 7 percent annually) just to enable a constant share of their populations to pursue tertiary-level certifications. Unfortunately, the current HIV/AIDS pandemic in Africa, which accounts for 70 percent of all new AIDS cases in the world, will require many of these countries to produce even higher numbers of university graduates in order to maintain existing human resource capacities. Planning for academic staff at universities will need to be based on unprecedented assumptions about the rate of attrition. If these same countries would seek to improve their tertiary enrollment ratios by only a few additional percentage points, they would have to triple current tertiary enrollments by the year 2010. They are therefore prime candidates for distance education interventions.

The potential benefits associated with an expanded use of distance education in Africa are numerous. If adequately managed, distance education could enable an expansion of tertiary enrollments at less cost per student than under the traditional

Table 9.1. Tertiary Enrollment Projections for Sub-Saharan Africa, 1996 and Projected

Country	Tertiary Enrollments 1996[1]	Projected Population 2010[2]	Population Aged 18–23 2010[2]	Tertiary Enrollment Ratio 1995 (or latest year)[1]	Tertiary Enrollments 2010 (at Current Gross Enrollment Ratio)[3]	Tertiary Enrollments 2010 (Gross Enrollment Ratio + 50%)[3]
Angola	6,331	17,185,000	2,027,830	1.0	20,278	30,417
Benin	14,055	8,330,000	1,016,260	3.1	31,504	47,256
Botswana	8,850	1,992,000	249,000	5.8	14,442	21,663
Burkina Faso	8,911	15,928,000	1,895,432	1.0	18,954	28,431
Burundi	4,256	8,924,000	1,079,804	0.9	9,718	14,577
Cameroon	36,000	19,820,000	2,279,300	2.2	50,145	75,217
Cape Verde	*	541,000	63,297	4.2	2,658	3,988
C.A.R.	3,684	4,492,000	534,548	1.4	7,484	11,226
Chad	3,446	9,186,000	1,047,204	0.6	6,283	9,425
Congo	13,806	3,911,000	465,409	6.5	30,252	45,378
Dem. Rep. Congo	93,266	69,782,000	8,373,840	2.3	192,598	288,897
Equatorial Guinea	*	574,000	67,158	0.2	134	201
Eritrea	3,093	4,804,000	581,284	1.0	5,813	8,719
Ethiopia	35,027	89,515,000	10,115,195	0.7	70,806	106,209
Gabon	4,655	1,566,000	169,128	2.8	4,736	7,103
Gambia	1,591	1,523,000	175,145	1.7	2,977	4,466
Ghana	36,012	25,998,000	3,119,760	1.4	43,677	65,516
Guinea	8,151	10,428,000	1,209,648	1.2	14,562	21,774
Guinea Bissau	*	1,440,000	165,600	0.2	331	497
Ivory Coast	52,228	18,976,000	2,390,976	4.5	107,594	161,391
Kenya	43,000	38,869,000	4,936,363	1.6	78,982	118,472
Lesotho	4,614	2,927,000	336,605	2.4	8,079	12,118
Liberia	*	4,443,000	453,186	0.3	*	*
Madagascar	26,715	23,469,000	2,839,749	2.1	59,635	89,452
Malawi	5,561	14,154,000	1,712,634	0.6	10,276	15,414
Mali	*	16,733,000	1,974,494	0.8	15,796	23,694
Mauritius	6,746	1,306,000	118,846	6.5	7,725	11,587
Mozambique	7,143	25,048,000	2,955,664	0.4	11,823	17,734
Namibia	11,344	2,189,000	258,302	8.1	20,922	31,384
Niger	*	14,751,000	1,696,365	0.7	11,874	17,811
Nigeria	260,000	168,369,000	19,867,542	4.1	814,569	1,221,854
Rwanda	2,200	9,716,000	1,185,352	0.5	5,927	8,890
Senegal	24,081	12,241,000	1,432,197	3.4	48,695	73,042
Sierra Leone	*	6,056,000	696,440	1.3	9,053	13,580
Somalia	*	15,735,000	1,778,055	*	*	*
South Africa	617,897	56,613,000	6,170,817	15.9	981,160	1,471,740
Sudan	*	36,850,000	4,053,500	3.0	121,605	182,407
Swaziland	5,658	1,263,000	143,982	6.0	8,639	12,958
Tanzania	12,776	44,014,000	5,281,680	0.5	26,408	39,613
Togo	11,639	6,082,000	735,922	3.6	26,493	39,740
Uganda	30,266	30,137,000	3,556,166	1.7	60,455	90,682
Zambia	10,489	11,717,000	1,499,776	2.5	37,494	56,242
Zimbabwe	46,673	15,270,000	1,939,290	6.5	126,054	189,081

Notes:

*Data not available in *UNESCO Statistical Yearbook*. Asterisked figures were obtained from World Bank data.

[1] UNESCO 1998a.

[2] UN 1998. Medium variant figures employed.

[3] Author's calculations.

residential campus system. Greater flexibility in the design and delivery of curriculum content than is normally associated with classroom teaching enables distance education courses to adapt to specific student needs or work requirements, thereby enabling greater relevance. Distance education also accommodates the growing demand for lifelong learning more easily than residential programs.

Distance education offers other benefits as well. It can effectively reach those learners who have been denied access to tertiary education, such as women who are unable to attend traditional educational programs because of household responsibilities or cultural constraints, economically marginalized groups, refugees, and the incarcerated. Also, distance learning programs delivered by universities in the developed world through the Internet and supported by online virtual libraries are increasingly available at the postgraduate level to self-motivated students in Africa who seek postgraduate qualifications. As expanding tertiary enrollments generate a parallel need for additional numbers of academic staff, graduate training becomes more difficult to accomplish as the costs of overseas graduate training rise and donor funding of study fellowships declines. Under these constraints, internationally available "virtual" postgraduate programs can help to produce the needed increases in academic staff.

Distance education is the most modern form of educational delivery. It is a twentieth-century invention based on organizational structures and technologies produced by the industrial revolution. As we begin the twenty-first century, distance education is innovating rapidly and expanding around the globe. In the past, distance education was often viewed as inferior by much of the traditional academic community because it tends to have lower graduation rates and less direct interaction between teacher and student. Today, this no longer needs to be the case. Experience accumulated worldwide is contributing to more effective program design. It has repeatedly been demonstrated that there is no significant difference in student performance according to the teaching methods employed (Willis 1994, 42; Rumble 1997; Moore and Kearsley 1996, 99; Turoff 1997b). The choice of medium for educational delivery, therefore, depends mainly on the specific circumstances of the learning situation. However, mixed-media teaching has been shown to have greater learning impact than single-media approaches. Notably, it is not uncommon for well-designed distance learning materials to be used by lecturers and students in the classroom, thereby providing a boost to the quality of classroom instruction.

These benefits have made tertiary distance education the world's fastest-growing educational sector. Asia now boasts 3.5 million tertiary distance education students, with China alone accounting for 1.4 million (UNESCO 1998a). Latin America has more than 1 million tertiary-level distance education students, with particularly active programs in Brazil, Colombia, Mexico, and Venezuela (World Bank 1998a). The United States has more than 2 million distance education students, while Canada has half a million.

AFRICAN EXPERIENCE WITH DISTANCE EDUCATION

Distance learning and associated technology applications are not new tools for tertiary institutions in Africa. In Anglophone Africa, the University of South Africa (1998 enrollment 117,000) began in 1946 as a correspondence university and has evolved into one of the world's largest open distance learning universities. Botswana, Kenya, Malawi, and Zambia have used distance education for teacher training since the 1960s (John 1996). By 1985, there were twenty-five state-funded distance education institutions in the Anglophone countries of Africa (Murphy and Zhiri 1992, 7). The first Francophone experience in distance learning involved correspondence courses offered in 1970 by Marien Ngouabi University in Brazzaville. During the 1980s and 1990s, teachers updated their skills through distance education programs in Benin, Burkina Faso, Burundi, Cameroon, Central African Republic, Ivory Coast, Mali, and Togo. An experienced nongovernmental organization (NGO), INADES-Formation, established by Jesuits in 1962 and headquartered in Abidjan, now offers practical skills development for poor rural populations through distance education programs in twenty African countries.

More than 140 public and private institutions currently provide tertiary distance education services within sub-Saharan Africa (Roberts & Associates 1998, 9). These programs rely mainly on print media, supplemented by written assignments and face-to-face tutoring (Murphy and Zhiri 1992, 36). Some of them have also made creative use of national broadcast radio, audiocassettes, and, more recently, e-mail. The bulk of these programs provide training that enables in-service teachers to upgrade their skills. Other main uses are imparting business management or information technology expertise to employed workers. A recent survey of 143 tertiary distance education programs in Africa found that 52 percent of Anglophone programs and 67 percent of Francophone programs targeted teachers and school administrators (Roberts & Associates 1998, 13). Notably, 12 percent of programs in both language areas were aimed at university students—and this statistic is growing.

The same survey registered a slight difference between Anglophone and Francophone countries with regard to the use of telecommunications technology for distance education. Although print media were employed by virtually all Anglophone and Francophone programs, the former made comparatively less use of the Internet, but this situation is changing rapidly. A significant minority of Francophone programs employed the Internet to some degree but used it more for program coordination than for direct teaching. Satellite broadcast is now being used on a pilot basis by both Anglophone and Francophone participants in the African Virtual University project initiated in 1996 by the World Bank.

Outside the sphere of distance education, Internet connectivity is expanding rapidly but unevenly. All fifty-four African countries now have access to the Internet in their capital cities (Jensen 2002), but it is almost exclusively used by upper-class urban populations (Bamba 1999). Particularly active Internet markets are found in South Africa, Ghana, Senegal, Mozambique, Kenya, Uganda, Zimbabwe, and Ivory Coast. In early 1999, a survey of Internet capability at fifteen sub-Saharan African universities outside of South Africa that were considered to be among the more progressive in their use of ICT concluded that only four possess full Internet capability, including Web sites; six have limited Internet capability; three have e-mail only provided

Table 9.2. Tertiary Distance Education Enrollments in Selected
Countries, 1996

Country	Tertiary Enrollments[1]	Distance Learning Enrollments[2]	Percent Enrollments in Distance Education
South Africa	617,897	225,000*	36
Madagascar	26,715	7,864	29
Tanzania	12,776	2,836	22
Swaziland	5,658	450	7
Zimbabwe	46,673	3,473	7
Zambia	10,489	621	6
France	2,091,688	233,000**	11
Spain	1,591,863	104,429	7
United States	14,261,778	1,000,000	7
Mexico	1,532,846	103,913	7
United Kingdom	1,820,849	110,477	6
The Netherlands	491,748	25,051	5
Germany	2,144,169	55,000*	3
Thailand	1,220,481	456,313	37
Sri Lanka	63,660	20,601	32
China	5,826,636	1,422,900	24
South Korea	2,541,659	482,915	19
Indonesia	2,303,469	414,061	18

*Rough estimate based on several different sources.
**Ministère de l'Education Nationale, de la Recherche et de la Technologie,
June 1999.
[1]UNESCO 1998a.
[2]Author's calculations.

through a campus network; and two have limited e-mail capacity through individual connections in some departments (Materu-Behitsa and Levey 1998). The twenty-four federal universities in Nigeria are gradually becoming linked electronically through the Nigeria Universities Net (NUNet). A recent survey of Francophone universities indicates that at least eleven of them have full Internet access and maintain their own Web sites. International infrastructure in support of African Internet connectivity will improve considerably next year with completion of a sophisticated submarine optical fiber cable that will link Western and Southern Africa with Europe, Asia, and the rest of the world in 2004. This cable has the intrinsic ability to propel most of sub-Saharan Africa into the new millennium (Farrell 1999, 91). When this cable becomes operational, the main remaining constraints to African Internet connectivity will be national telecommunications monopolies and their outdated policies.

Today the landscape of distance education in Africa is changing rapidly. Experimentation with various distance learning methods is underway in a number of countries. Namibia and Ghana have formally declared dual-mode instruction to be their national policy. Botswana, Cameroon, and Zambia are using a university-based Internet system to support interactive regional study centers for distance learners (Pecku 1998). Tanzania, Botswana, and Zimbabwe have established new tertiary institutions

wholly dedicated to distance education. The Zimbabwe Open University already enrolls nearly 10,000 students in nine programs and recently launched a master's degree program in education for in-service teachers. Uganda enrolls 1,400 students in a bachelor's of commerce degree program given at a distance and is planning to expand into the areas of law, technology, and sciences. Nigeria's Center for Distance Learning (Abuja) offers B.A. and B.S. degrees in fourteen subject areas. Madagascar has pioneered the use of audiocassettes for university programs in law and the social sciences. Ivory Coast, Congo, Togo, and Benin are in various stages of setting up university-based distance education programs. In Senegal, distance education supports teacher training and master's degree programs in health and law (Republic of Senegal 1997). Several African nations use distance education on a scale that is proportionately greater than the way European or North American countries use it but less than that achieved by many Asian countries (see Table 9.2).

New information and communications technologies are contributing to these changes. The provision of distance education based on satellite transmission and interactive e-mail is being tested by the African Virtual University project sponsored by the World Bank and by the Université Virtuelle Francophone (Virtual Francophone University) supported by the Agence universitaire de la francophonie (AUPELF-UREF). The development of telecenters—public sites that offer fee-based access to telephones, fax, e-mail, and full Internet services—is growing in South Africa, Ghana, Nigeria, Senegal, and elsewhere. In some cases, telecenters are being expanded to offer access to learning (Farrell 1999, 95). The Confederation of Open Learning Institutions in South Africa (COLISA), a partnership of the country's three main tertiary distance education institutions, is developing Internet-based courseware, a Web-based student-teacher interaction system, and a series of local Internet access points for students (Farrell 1999, 99).

These developments have proceeded unevenly across the continent. As a result, individual countries vary considerably in their capacities to design, manage, support, and evaluate tertiary distance education programs. A survey of institutional capacities for distance education in twenty-two African nations indicates a fairly logical sequence to the development of these institutional capacities. The observations, summarized in Table 9.3, indicate that most countries possess university distance education units engaged in distance education based on printed materials, often with donor support. These core capacities later give birth to a greater diversity of provisions (for example, private providers) and a wider range of technology use (for example, radio, television, and the Internet). It is only at rather advanced stages of institutional differentiation that explicit governmental policies for distance education emerge, NGOs join the ranks of distance education providers, national professional associations for distance education take shape, and open universities are established. Institutional capacities for distance education are more differentiated, and therefore more developed, in Anglophone countries than in Francophone countries.

POTENTIAL BENEFITS OF TERTIARY DISTANCE EDUCATION FOR AFRICA

As the most modern form of educational provision, distance education at the tertiary level offers Africa the possibility of leapfrogging certain phases in educational development. Additionally, it creates the possibility of increased access to tertiary education at more cost-effective levels. An increase in mass education under the constraint of diminishing resources is a global phenomenon not limited to the African continent. However, these trends are more highly amplified in Africa. This provides an opportunity for Africa not only to tackle its tertiary education problems more effectively but also to contribute better solutions for the provision of tertiary education in other nations.

Tertiary distance education holds forth the promise of three primary benefits for Africa. These are increased access to education, improved educational quality, and more efficient use of limited resources. Each of these topics will be discussed in turn.

GREATER ACCESS

Distance education programs can increase educational access by reaching out to four groups commonly excluded from traditional education programs. These are secondary school graduates who fail to gain admission to the university, married women with household responsibilities, geographically isolated

or uprooted students (such as refugees), and economically disadvantaged communities. Of these, the largest and most rapidly growing group is composed of secondary graduates who were unsuccessful in the competitive admission process for tertiary education. Low tertiary enrollment rates mean high levels of exclusion. For example, in 1996, only 6,088 students of 22,477 qualified applicants (27 percent) were admitted to the universities in Ghana. In Uganda, just 6,000 out of 11,000 (54 percent) secondary school graduates who qualified for admission in 1996 were able to gain university entrance. In Nigeria, less than 20 percent of the 475,923 candidates for university admission in 1996–1997 were successful. With residential space at a premium, university aspirants increasingly view tertiary distance education as a viable alternative to residential instruction. The University of Swaziland, for example, has offered tertiary programs since 1995 through its Institute of Distance Education explicitly for university applicants who qualify for admission but who are unable to gain entrance because of lack of space and facilities. The number of students at the Institute grew from 100 in 1995 to 500 in 1999, a number that represents roughly 13 percent of total university enrollment in Swaziland.

Women currently comprise 35 percent of tertiary enrollments in Africa (UNESCO 1998a, 2–14) but only 23 percent of university students (UNESCO 1998b, 18). This sizable underrepresentation indicates a considerable potential for development gains stemming from increased participation rates by African women in tertiary education. Home-based study on a flexible schedule is well suited for women who also have family responsibilities and may be particularly appropriate for Muslim societies. This is seemingly borne out by tertiary distance education enrollment statistics from a variety of countries. In South Africa, for example, 70 percent of students at Vista University, a distance learning institution, and 50 percent of students at UNISA (University of South Africa), an open university, are women. In Namibia, 77 percent of distance learners are women. In Madagascar, 46 percent of distance education students are women. In Swaziland, the proportion is 44 percent. It should be noted, however, that the advantages of home study for women are contested by those who point to women's heavy home and agricultural responsibilities and argue that they must leave home in order to stand a chance of educational achievement.

Distance learning can extend tertiary education opportunities to students in rural areas, small towns, and refugee camps who do not have convenient access to tertiary institutions. For the isolated but motivated student, the savings can be considerable: they save travel time and travel expense and are able to continue earning a living while studying. In Thailand, for example, 70 percent of tertiary distance education students are located in rural areas (Dhanarajan et al. 1994, 43). For a portion of Africa's 6 million refugees, and for those who may also be displaced from their countries by social tensions and political instabilities, distance learning programs could help refugees obtain the skills needed for self-sufficiency and responsible citizenship. This is a challenge that has not yet been seriously confronted in Africa. Among the fundamental questions to be addressed are: Whose responsibility is it to educate refugees? What are the obligations of the home country and the host country? Who pays for their

Table 9.3. Capacity Development Sequence for Distance Education in Sub-Saharan Africa

Country	Tertiary Corr. Courses[1]	Univ. Has DE Unit[2]	Donor Project Exists[3]	MOE DE Unit Exists[4]	Univ. DE Res. Unit Exists[5]	Priv. DE Unit Exists[6]	Radio DE Courses[7]	NGO Involved in DE[8]	Univ. is ISP[9]	Strategy Paper Exists[10]	Natl. DE Assoc. Exists[11]	Univ. Provides Courses on DE[12]	TV DE Exists[13]	Open Univ. Exists[14]	Total
South Africa	1	1	1	1	1	1	1	1	1	1	1	1	1	1	14
Tanzania	1	1	1	1	1	1	1	1	1	1	1	1		1	13
Zimbabwe	1	1	1	1	1	1	1	1	1	1	1			1	12
Ghana	1	1	1	1	1	1	1	1	1	1	1	1			12
Zambia	1	1	1	1	1	1	1	1	1				1		10
Cameroon	1	1	1	1	1	1	1	1					1		9
Mauritius	1	1	1	1	1	1	1	1	1						9
Mozambique	1	1	1	1	1	1	1	1							8
Ivory Coast	1	1	1	1	1	1	1						1		8
Madagascar	1	1	1	1	1	1	1								7
Senegal	1	1	1	1						1	1	1			7
Kenya	1	1	1	1	1		1								6
Namibia	1	1	1	1	1	1									6
Burkina Faso	1	1	1	1			1	1							6
Togo	1	1				1		1	1	1					6
Nigeria	1	1	1	1					1						5
Benin	1	1	1	1						1					5
Botswana	1	1							1	1					4
Malawi	1		1					1							3
Sudan	1	1			1										3
Uganda	1	1	1												3
Ethiopia			1												1
Total	21	20	19	16	13	12	12	11	9	8	5	4	4	3	157

Key:
1. Tertiary correspondence courses are provided in the country.
2. University contains a unit responsible for distance education.
3. Donor supported project in distance education exists.
4. Ministry of Education contains a unit responsible for distance education.
5. University contains a unit that conducts research on distance education.
6. Private provider of distance education courses exists.
7. Distance education courses are offered via radio.
8. A nongovernmental organization provides distance education courses.
9. University is an authorized Internet Service Provider.
10. Government has issued a formal strategy statement for distance education.
11. A national professional association of distance educators exists.
12. A university-level course on distance education theory and methods is taught.
13. Distance education courses are offered via television.
14. An operational open university exists in the country.

education? One groundbreaking project in refugee education has been underway since 1994 at the Southern Africa Extension Unit in Tanzania. With assistance from the United Nations High Commission on Refugees, a distance education program has been developed for refugees from Burundi who are living in camps in Western Tanzania. The program offers basic English study to these French-speaking Burundians as well as secondary-level mathematics, history, geography, and Swahili. Its purpose is to prepare these refugees to take advantage of other educational opportunities available in Tanzania. At present, the program enrolls 800 students and has produced more than 2,000 graduates.

Where sufficient political will exists, distance learning can also be a viable option for impoverished or socially marginalized communities. In Thailand, studies show that family income levels of residential university students are four or five times higher than those of distance education students. Anecdotal evidence from Africa suggests that similar income disparities exist in a number of countries. In the highly competitive context of tertiary admissions, access by elites to private secondary schools or special tutors can make the difference between entrance and exclusion. Because it allows students to work and study simultaneously, and because it does not require the additional costs of campus residence, distance education offers an alternative pathway to tertiary training for students with limited financial means. Over time, it could contribute to a narrowing of the education gap among different ethnic groups and thus to a country's long-term political stability.

IMPROVED QUALITY

Distance education fosters educational quality and relevance in several ways. Because teachers and students are separated by distance, successful curriculum design requires clarity of communication, coherent logic, and good organization in its presentation. This increases the effectiveness of its pedagogy and, where the distance education courses are prepared by contracted classroom lecturers, often contributes to improved face-to-face instruction as well. In addition, by using standardized materials developed by subject experts, it promotes high-quality instruction and equitable provision of educational opportunities. Moreover, experience shows that where good instructional materials for distance education exist, classroom students quickly appropriate them as study aids, thereby helping them to improve their academic performance. In Namibia, South Africa, and Tanzania, distance education is being used to provide remedial or bridging programs to secondary school graduates who lack the necessary qualifications for tertiary admission.

When countries fall within the sphere of influence of multiple external distance education providers, quality control and certification of equivalence for degrees can be a challenge. This is the case in Mauritius, for example, where the Tertiary Education Commission has exhaustively reviewed distance education course offerings from Australia, India, South Africa, and elsewhere. Over time, however, the accreditation problem is expected to grow as international markets for tertiary distance education develop and become more competitive. Rather than become involved in ever-more-demanding efforts to determine

the equivalence of constantly shifting course offerings and content, the long-run solution is likely to be a certification of the demonstrated competencies of individual students on the basis of internationally accepted performance criteria. Many technical and professional fields have national qualification or licensing examinations that can effectively play this validating role for distance education graduates (Rumble and Oliveira 1992). Notably, the new Western Governors' University in the United States offers students the option of obtaining a degree entirely on the basis of self-study. The degree is awarded once the student has successfully passed a series of competency-based examinations. This approach seems certain to expand in the future.

Educational quality can also be enhanced by the prudent use of new information technologies to support classroom teaching in direct or indirect ways. Direct support to teaching occurs when lecturers can access the latest scientific information, well-developed syllabi, reference resources, effective learning exercises, and creative teaching aids via the Internet. Indirect support occurs when e-mail and the Internet are employed to nourish local research activities that positively impact teaching. In the quest for such benefits, the Senegalese national telecommunications company, SONATEL, is currently expanding Internet access for universities, training centers, and firms.

In the near term, the Internet's impact on African tertiary education is likely to be greater in research than in education (Langlois 1998). By allowing worldwide access to large amounts of relevant information, the Internet diminishes research costs and compensates for the shortage of books and scientific journals that often plagues university libraries. Through e-mail, it enables increased interaction among scholars and fosters the emergence of transgeographic research teams. The Internet also allows the rapid dissemination of research results while facilitating peer review (and therefore quality). Lastly, it helps to increase local research capacity by sharing equipment and facilitating the remote use of costly scientific instruments. One initial effort to tap this potential is Uninet, an academic and research network linking fifty-eight universities, polytechnics, and research centers (and 500,000 students and staff) in South and Southern Africa (Knoch 1997). A similar research networking initiative is being developed in Francophone Africa, called Réseau electronique francophone pour l'education et la recherche (REFER).

THE SPECIAL SIGNIFICANCE OF UNIVERSITY LIBRARIES

University libraries (and librarians) will be key actors in efforts to raise the quality of higher education and research through the application of new electronic technologies. The emergence of a global knowledge-based economy, together with the information and communications technologies that bring it into being, is expected to exercise a transforming effect on university libraries in Africa. Within a knowledge economy, value increasingly lies not in possessing information but rather in developing the capabilities to access it and adapt it for new applications (Gibbons 1998). Most knowledge produced globally is not produced where its application is most needed. The challenge is how to transfer knowledge that may have been produced anywhere in the world to places where it can be used effectively in a particular problem-solving context. Because Africa is not presently well equipped to participate in the global knowledge economy, developing the organizational and electronic capacities to identify, access, and adapt external knowledge for local problem-solving will produce developmental dividends. This has significant implications for universities and their libraries. In the coming years, educational institutions will progressively be able to generate income not from the knowledge they possess but from services structured around this knowledge. Libraries will play a fundamental role in this. For this reason, the role and function of the university library should be given particular attention during any university strategic planning process.

Libraries will become interactive information resource centers for the university and the surrounding community, providing both traditional and computer-based learning materials. They will merge gradually into electronically linked regional and global knowledge webs. Over time, they will take on the important role of electronically disseminating university research findings to a worldwide readership, thereby combating superficial impressions that Africa produces little new knowledge as a region. An initial foundation for such an electronic network for research information and dissemination currently exists in eleven Francophone countries, where universities have established Internet-linked multimedia resource centers under the SYFED-REFER program sponsored by the Agence Universitaire de la Francophonie. In addition, libraries may provide sites for specialized course delivery via the Internet or CD-ROM technology that are equally available to students and the public at large. In fact, this practice has recently been initiated by the University of Zimbabwe's Media Center in the area of biology. But for developing countries to benefit from the explosion in the production of knowledge and access to it, educators and researchers need to protect time-honored principles of full disclosure and free flow of scientific information and resist tendencies to convert every bit of information into a piece of marketable intellectual property (Darch 1998, 6).

For this transformation to occur, tertiary institution managers and library administrators will need to understand and support the evolution of the role of the library from handmaiden to full partner in the academic enterprise. Tight institutional budgets will need to favor acquisition of technology and training for library staff; academicians will have to cede some of their limited funds for the common good. As this electronic knowledge network is built up, library staff will become more active members of curriculum and research teams, identifying relevant knowledge and sharing it with the team. This implies a significant change in the job descriptions, employment qualifications, and professional status of African university librarians.

The road to such transformations will be difficult. On most campuses, academic and library staff lack an awareness of what ICT can do for them. Access to information about communication technology and even to computers is generally limited. A small but significant number of African university libraries have no functioning computers at all. They are often located in countries where governments remain suspicious of ICT. A larger group of university libraries possess a few stand-alone computers equipped with dial-up e-mail and perhaps a CD-ROM player. In most cases, this group is heavily dependent on

donor assistance for the maintenance and development of its technology. Consequently, this group's ICT gains are vulnerable to regression when donor financing ends. Only a very small number of university libraries—in Namibia, South Africa, Tanzania, Zambia—are linked to a local computer network with full connectivity to the Internet and can count on the necessary institutional support for sustainable ICT development. This number will increase with the completion of renovations at the Grande Bibliothèque at Cheik Anta Diop University of Dakar, Senegal. With funding assistance from the World Bank, this library will function as an electronic multimedia and information center for the university and serve as the Internet hub for a network of local libraries.

Even where university libraries possess some information technology, it is used very unevenly. An active minority of students are often the main users. There are two reasons for this. First, the technology is unreliable due to fluctuating supplies of electricity and to poor maintenance of equipment. The latter is due in turn to lack of know-how and the inability of meager library budgets to cover maintenance expenses for ICT. Second, very little training of library and academic staff in the use of these technologies has taken place. Consequently, few people know how to use the technologies or are able to teach others.

Development assistance agencies have much to contribute to library transformation, since they have access to the technical skills, experience, and funds needed to launch such a project. But to make effective and sustainable contributions, development partners must make a long-term commitment to library restructuring and to maintenance and development of the technology they install. Agencies often have erred in providing technological tools without considering their implications for maintenance costs and associated training needed for sustainability. Some of them have actually ignored the role of university libraries in their efforts to promote ICT use within African universities. They, as well as many university administrators, seem to believe that direct Internet access will eventually eliminate the need for libraries. This is not the case, even though the Internet may well lead to reduced centrality of the library as a physical facility even as it enhances the responsibilities of librarians themselves. University librarians must learn to play a different but important role, one that entails facilitating access to information, integrating and reorganizing it to meet academic needs, and encouraging the use of ICT for class assignments and research.

One urgent need is for a major reform in African training programs for professional librarians. Existing programs are outdated. Library reform experience from development partner countries can be a valuable contribution to this needed change. In this regard, schools of library science in five Francophone countries (Benin, Cameroon, Ivory Coast, Madagascar, and Senegal) are expected to participate in a program of continuing education in the use of computerized information networks known as FORCIIR (Formation continue pour l'information informatisée en réseau). Coordinated by the École des Bibliothèques et documentalistes de Dakar and supported by the French Ministry of Foreign Affairs, this program will provide students in these schools with supplemental distance education courses in the use of new information technologies to support university teaching and research.

COST EFFICIENCY

Distance education is cost efficient in four ways. First, it lowers the costs of tertiary education for students, who do not have to give up income from employment in order to study. Distance learners pay no residential fees or commuting costs. And as the practice of cost-sharing in tertiary education becomes more common in Africa, tuition charges for distance learning are expected to be less than those for residential instruction.

Second, distance learning often operates at more efficient staff-to-student ratios, thereby reducing the proportion of institutional budgets dedicated to staff salaries. Similarly, it minimizes the need for investment in costly physical facilities and in their maintenance, thus enabling more funds to be used in support of teaching inputs and learning activities. These efficiency gains, however, must be achieved through careful planning and creative management. They cannot be reaped by simply introducing distance education programs. Many factors combine in complex ways to influence the costs of distance education. For example, it is estimated that up to 100 hours of course design and development time are necessary for each hour of student learning time in distance learning courses, although this ratio varies widely in practice. In comparison, good-quality classroom teaching can be provided with ten hours of preparation time for one hour of learning (Rumble 1997). Other factors that condition course costs include the useful life of the course, the number of students enrolled, the type of delivery system used (costs rise sharply when a medium other than print is used), the nature of academic assessment, the kind and extent of student interaction, and the levels of expertise employed in the design, development, and delivery of courses.

Third, unlike the traditional campus model, tertiary distance education offers declining marginal costs. As enrollments rise, the cost per student goes down (although the costs per graduate may be high if the completion rate is low). Cost analysis of tertiary distance learning programs in Canada, Ireland, and Israel indicate that their unit costs per student are roughly equivalent to the unit costs of on-campus teaching in schools with enrollments as low as 3,000 (Daniel 1996, 62). In Kenya and Nigeria, B.Ed. degrees were offered at a distance for smaller enrollments while maintaining this cost-per-student advantage (Makau 1993; Cummings and Olaloku 1993). Taking into account the fact that the cost of telecommunications is falling dramatically and will soon cease to vary with distance (Cairncross 1995), the gradual incorporation of new technologies into the delivery of distance education could further increase its cost efficiency.

Fourth, distance learning is cost efficient because it employs a modular approach. Course materials can be updated or modified to suit particular types of students without the need to reproduce them in their entirety. This flexibility will become a more significant advantage as tertiary education in the twenty-first century confronts the challenge of serving an increasingly diverse pool of students with an expanding range of learning requirements.

WHAT IS THE MAIN CONSTRAINT TO ACHIEVING THESE BENEFITS?

Reaping the benefits of accessibility, quality, and cost efficiency outlined above is contingent on solid program management. In fact, distance learning programs generally require better management skills than traditional tertiary programs. With scattered students, dispersed part-time tutors, challenging logistics, unreliable communication services, time sensitivity in the production and distribution of learning materials, and detailed student records, successful distance education programs require a management team with above-average skills in organization, logistics, and problem solving. This management team need not be large, but it must be capable.

For the most part, distance education makes use of existing staff and facilities and therefore does not require major staff recruitment or expensive building campaigns. If desired, it can be managed through a relatively small coordinating unit housed on an existing university campus, as is the case of the National Distance Education Center in Ireland. Likewise, tutoring and academic support for students can be arranged by contracting experienced local teachers or other professionals on a part-time basis and by renting community educational facilities on evenings and weekends.

New information and communications technologies can contribute to making distance learning programs more manageable. Computerized management information systems are now available to support complex logistics, including inventory management and materials dispatch. Computerized management systems are also essential for the administration of student records —such as registrations, scheduling, grades, assessments, and credits acquired—in an era of lifelong learning. Projected developments in telecommunications technology and personal communication devices are expected to eventually do away with expensive in-house technology systems. Already, the skillful use of desktop publishing and laser-printing capabilities has reduced the need for extensive warehousing of instructional materials for many distance learning programs.

DEVELOPING NATIONAL POLICIES

Countries interested in developing their capacities to provide tertiary distance education will need to formulate policies to shape this particular subsector, to guide teaching and learning, and to develop policies for institutional development and capacity building. The purpose of national policy is to define public goals for a given sector and to chart a course for attaining them. Although few African nations possess a formally articulated policy to guide tertiary distance education, the existence of a publicly accepted strategy in this area has proven essential for setting priorities, marshaling resources, and launching meaningful initiatives.

Countries that have developed policy frameworks for tertiary distance education include South Africa, Madagascar, and

Mauritius. Their education policy statements are worth studying. Although national conditions will shape much of their specific content, all national education policies need to address four common questions.

Should Distance Learning Be a Separate or Integrated Part of the Tertiary System?

Experience teaches the value of integrating distance education fully within the existing formal education system (Willis 1994, 11). Where this is not accomplished, the danger is that distance education will remain undervalued and underused at the periphery of the educational system. Full integration helps to reduce inevitable resistance to innovation within existing tertiary institutions and does much to overcome the perception that distance education is inferior to residential instruction. Australia, for example, has been particularly successful at integrating distance learning with its tertiary system. As a result, it is common for students to take a mix of on-campus and distance courses. Dual-mode approaches that make use of existing academic staff and facilities reduce the competition for scarce resources often associated with the establishment of a new institution and erode staff resistance by offering opportunities for direct participation. Likewise, common admissions policies for residential and distance students, together with the award of a single institutional degree based on common standards, will do much to offset the notion that distance education is of inferior status.

Integration works best when some distance learning is undertaken by a number of students in most departments. At the University of Mauritius, for example, first-year students are taught at a distance and move to residential status only after successful completion of the first year of study. Other tertiary education systems that offer students a choice between residential and distance education, or a mix of the two, include Australia and Canada. This approach avoids attaching stigma or status to specific student categories by offering education through a mix of modes that spans face-to-face instruction at one end of the continuum and distance learning at the other. The student then chooses the particular mix of on-campus and distance education classes that he or she desires. Although the goal remains the achievement of fully integrated residential and distance learning programs, such integration has proven politically contentious within institutions because of the rigidities and resistance discussed above.

Should Access Be Open or Conditional?

When coupled with reports of widely varying quality in educational preparation at the secondary level, the multitude of aspirants to tertiary education in Africa suggests that admission to tertiary distance education programs should be selective, at least for the near term. Selectivity based on student qualifications or assessment of ability will make student numbers more manageable and enable higher pass rates, thereby contributing to the cost effectiveness of these programs. In the interests of fairness and equity, however, governments may wish to consider offsetting selective admissions with fully open entry to a qualifying or bridging course, which must be passed as a requirement for admission to the tertiary distance education program (Murphy and Zhiri 1992, 31).

What Technology Should Be Employed?

Numerous studies from around the world produce a consistent answer to this question: the medium of instruction does not make any important difference in student achievement, attitudes, or retention (Willis 1994, 42; Rumble 1997; Moore and Kearsley 1996, 99; Turoff 1997a). In fact, how the media are used has proven to be more important than which medium is selected. Furthermore, multiple media appear to be more effective than a single medium, with interactivity between students and tutors contributing a major boost to learning. Since the choice of technology does not influence learning, the factors of technology cost and maintenance become determining considerations. On this basis, print media are likely to remain the best choice for most of Africa. They are inexpensive, reliable, and widely accepted. They are readily used by students without requiring them to have access to specific equipment or services. At the same time, care is needed to avoid commitment to inflexible technologies chosen without reference to educational need and context, unexpectedly high operating costs, and underestimation of the needs for good pedagogical practice and strong student support systems (SAIDE 1999). For this reason, educational planning should be emphasized over technical planning in the early stages of program design.

How Can Distance Education Be Financed?

In many African countries, some degree of cost-sharing for tertiary distance education programs between students and government is an established precedent. This practice derives from an assumption that distance education students are employed and can therefore afford to pay a portion of tuition costs. In light of present limitations on the use of public assets to fund the expansion of tertiary education, this precedent is fortuitous and should be preserved. The extent to which the costs of distance education are shared between government and students varies considerably around the world (Mugridge 1994). Within Africa, annual tuition costs in tertiary distance education range from $40 in Madagascar to $180 in Zimbabwe, $185 in Tanzania, and up to $1,200 for an M.B.A. program in South Africa.

Private providers and their students can also carry a portion of the financial burden of tertiary distance education. A recent review of 143 tertiary distance education programs in sub-Saharan Africa found that 41 percent of sixty-six Anglophone institutions are privately operated. In sharp contrast, none of the sixty-seven Francophone institutions surveyed is privately managed (Roberts and Associates 1998, 12). In a context of limited government resources and technical capacities, such private programs can play an important role in expanding access to tertiary education, if educational, quality can be assured. One example is the new privately financed Mid-Rand University, located near Johannesburg, South Africa, which is planned to operate largely on the basis of distance learning programs. Another private tertiary institution, Africa University in Zimbabwe, is poised to initiate distance learning activities. Recognizing the value of such private initiatives, the International Finance Corporation has selected private higher education and distance education as areas of emphasis for its investments in the private sector.

World experience indicates that both governments and tertiary institutions tend to underfund distance education, thereby compromising its effectiveness. Underfunding is common in the provision of critical student support services, for staff training, and for professional development. One deterrent is that distance education normally requires considerable up-front investment to train staff, design curriculum, prepare materials, and acquire technology. Once these hurdles are passed, the comparatively modest recurrent costs of the program can usually be covered in large part by student fees.

This front-loaded expenditure profile suggests that tertiary distance education projects are ideal candidates for international development assistance. Development partners' funds can provide the seed capital and technical support to launch a distance learning program over an initial four-to-five-year period with the assurance that the program will become self-sustaining. As one reference point, a successful four-year capacity-building project in tertiary distance education that was undertaken by the government of Mauritius with funding from the Canadian International Development Agency cost approximately $500,000 in U.S. dollars.

POLICIES FOR TEACHING AND LEARNING

All effective distance learning programs depend on the three legs of good learning materials, effective student support, and efficient logistics (Daniel 1996, 40). The production of learning materials can be a costly activity and is therefore the area in which good management can do the most to reduce program costs. Recent experience in Kenya and South Africa, for example, suggests that it costs roughly $40,000 to develop each new tertiary course when satellite, computer, and CD-ROM systems are used. The purchase of existing course materials from another distance education institution can be a good strategy for beginning a distance education program, since the materials are proven, readily available, and likely to facilitate local accreditation. However, transporting an effective distance education course from one cultural context to another usually requires some retooling and adjustment. This should ideally be accompanied by a student performance feedback loop so course managers can ascertain whether the adapted course is working properly.

In the longer run, local production of course materials is frequently the best approach. In addition to possible cost savings, it is a good way to promote local staff ownership of the distance education program. In most cases, the buying of course materials is not an attractive option unless the number of students for the course is low and local course development costs are high (Rumble 1997, 90). Generally, the accepted practice is to produce learning materials through the use of design teams in which each member contributes a specific skill. Design teams vary in composition but often include a content expert, an instructional designer, a communications or media specialist, an editor, and a peer reviewer.

Student support is universally underscored as the most critical factor influencing student success (Keast 1997; Moore and Kearsley 1996). Timely feedback to students on their performance, on-site tutoring, and access to library and laboratory materials are essential for student achievement in tertiary distance education programs. Without such support, student drop-out rates will rise and eliminate any advantages of cost-effectiveness for distance learning. The estimated world average is a 40 percent drop-out rate for distance education students, although some feel that this rate is even higher; in Africa, the rate is often above 50 percent (Moore and Kearsley 1996, 158; Murphy and Zhiri 1992, 12).

The importance of student support to successful learning is illustrated by the following experience. When the University of South Africa discovered in 1986 that pass rates for its physics courses were only 20 percent, it responded by strengthening student support services. When the university offered second-chance assignments and more tutorial support and decreased the ratio of students per staff member from 201:1 in 1986 to 112:1 in 1997, the pass rate doubled to 40 percent (Cilliers and Reynhardt 1998). As a general guideline, twenty-five students per tutor is suggested for study centers that are easily accessible to students (Rumble 1997, 108). Where students are scattered and live in remote areas, smaller groups and more tutors will be needed. Notably, many distance education programs make evening and weekend use of the laboratories and classrooms of other public educational institutions for their tutorials and practical work, thereby eliminating the need for wholly owned facilities.

Efficient logistics is the third determinant of effective tertiary distance learning programs. Study materials must be distributed a in timely fashion. Feedback on student performance should be communicated without delay to sustain student motivation and guide learning. A well-managed system of student records also provides a solid foundation for efficient logistics. Fortunately, computerized management information systems (MIS) today make these tasks much easier and more accurate than when these records were maintained by hand. However, experience with MIS is not yet widespread in Africa (South Africa is an exception). Where it exists, inadequate computer maintenance has often interrupted system use and offset expected efficiencies. The inability of public institutions to pay competitive salaries and retain trained staff has been a second obstacle to expanded use of computerized MIS.

For tertiary distance learning to increase enrollments and broaden access, all tertiary academic programs will need to be converted into a modular/credit system. Under this system, a student earns a certain number of credits for each successfully completed course and receives a degree when the total number of required credits has been accumulated. Conversion to a modular/credit system is a laborious but vital process. The modular/credit system accommodates self-paced instruction, lifelong learning, and student mobility between residential and

Table 9.4. Internet Resources for Tertiary Distance Education

Institution (Country)	Website
Commonwealth of Learning	www.col.org
Consortium International Francophone de Formation à Distance	www.ciffad.francophonie.org
Global Distance Education Net (World Bank)	http://www1.worldbank.org/disted/sitemap.html
International Centre for Distance Learning (UK)	www.icdl.open.ac.uk
American Center for the Study of Distance Education (USA)	www.ed.psu.edu/acsde
South African Institute for Distance Education	www.saide.org.za
Tele-université Quebec (Canada)	www.teluq.uquebec.ca
Institute for Distance Education, University of Maryland (USA)	www.umuc.edu/ide
University of Wisconsin (USA)	www.uwex.edu/disted
University of British Columbia (Canada)	www.ubc.ca
Distance Education Center, University of Southern Queensland (Australia)	www.usq.edu.au/dec
Centre National d'Enseignement à Distance (France)	www.cned.fr
African Virtual University (World Bank)	www.avu.org
Université Virtuelle Francophone	www.uvf.org
Réseau Africain de Formation à Distance	www.bf.resafad.org
Distance Education and Training Council (USA)	www.detc.org
Fédération Interuniversitaire d'Enseignement à Distance	www.telesup.univ-mrs.fr/
Distance Learning Resources, Cornell University (USA)	www.sce.cornell.edu/dl
Service national d'information sur les outils pédagogiques multimédias pour l'enseignement supérieur, EDUCASUP (France)	educasup.education.fr

distance programs, and tertiary distance education cannot function without it.

POLICIES FOR CAPACITY BUILDING

Capacities for planning and for management are more important in distance learning than in traditional face-to-face education. This is because communication with a geographically dispersed student body is more expensive and time-consuming than in the classroom, and mistakes are therefore more difficult to correct. Yet the skills required to mount effective distance education programs are not hard to acquire. In most cases, several months of intensive instruction for academic staff who have prior teaching experience are sufficient. In addition, Internet-based courses in distance education techniques are increasingly available. The Web sites in Table 9.4 contain information and references on the organization and practice of tertiary distance learning. Many provide training materials or information on distance education training programs which are offered either in a residential setting or over the Internet.

Lessons from experience indicate that staff training often receives insufficient attention (Bates 1997, 11). Competent staff serve as the foundation stone on which all other distance education activities are erected. Yet, in the effort to get distance learning programs into operation, institutions often allocate insufficient preparation time and funding for staff training. A survey of distance learning experience in Senegal and Kenya found that many distance learning services, including student instruction, were provided by unqualified personnel (Chale and Michaud 1997). A good training program for distance education instructors will include:

- Practice in the design, production, and presentation of materials
- Ample hands-on practice with delivery technologies
- Practice with techniques in how to humanize a course
- Practice with techniques for facilitating student participation (Moore and Kearsley 1996, 152)

Learning by doing is the best path to skills development.

A fairly standard sequence of institutional capacity development can be discerned in sub-Saharan Africa. Just as a foundation must be built before walls can be erected and walls are needed before the roof of a house can be supported, a similar sequence of building blocks is needed when developing distance education programs. For example, it is possible to identify institutional capacity gaps for specific countries in Table 9.3. These gaps become prime candidates for capacity-building attention. For example, Ivory Coast might appropriately give its attention to establishing private distance education and university-based Internet service providers before considering more advanced initiatives. Likewise, universities in Mozambique and Senegal might consider establishing a distance education research unit as their next capacity-building step.

Partnerships are a particularly good way to build local capacities in distance education. Distance education is well suited to the use of institutional linkages and collaborative networks. Given the time and expense required to develop good course materials, it would appear to be an obvious solution for African universities to work together in producing these materials, perhaps in association with an experienced institution located outside the region. One current example is the RESAFAD program (Réseau Africain de Formation à Distance), which joins Benin,

Burkina Faso, Guinea, Mali, and Togo with a university support network in France to produce distance learning materials for the in-service training of primary and secondary education teachers. Another is the TELESUN program in Cameroon, in which five European universities collaborate with the University of Yaoundé in action research to test and validate a system of televised multimedia science teaching. Other examples include the sharing of course materials between the University of Nairobi and the Open University of Tanzania and a collaborative B.Ed. program between the Zimbabwe Open University and the University of Botswana.

In Southern Africa, a promising experience in regional partnership called TELISA is under way. It is led by Technikon, SA, South Africa's distance learning polytechnic, which enrolls 80,000 students and offers 220 different certificates and diplomas. This partnership, called the Technology Enhanced Learning Initiative for Southern Africa (TELISA), seeks to work regionally through public and private partnerships to expand community access to educational information technology and the Internet. Activities also include noneducational applications in the areas of business, marketing, and community development. TELISA is establishing information clearinghouses in Southern African countries to support educators' access via the Internet to curriculum information relevant to participating countries and institutions. In addition, it works with community groups to facilitate the introduction of online community learning centers and the training of local educators to improve access to skills and resources. Community centers are presently operational in Kgautswane, South Africa, and at the Institute of Extra-Mural Studies of the National University of Lesotho. Three others are under implementation in South Africa.

In practice, most new distance learning programs have benefited from a mentoring partnership with a more experienced institution. In some cases, local partnerships with private firms, such as network providers or equipment suppliers, could ease the management burden and provide valuable access to marketing expertise. Likewise, long-standing efforts to establish a regional open university serving all of sub-Saharan Africa may receive the necessary impetus as e-mail and Internet enable institutional partners to participate fully and effectively in such initiatives at an affordable cost. Notably, the creation of a regional open university was one of the few distance education recommendations presented in the World Bank's 1988 education policy paper for Africa. The idea remains valid today.

WHAT INSTITUTIONAL MODEL TO CHOOSE?

What institutional mechanisms can be employed to deliver distance learning services? Four possibilities exist. They are: dual-mode programs, single-mode programs, franchised international programs, and direct nonfranchised international programs. The advantages and disadvantages of each form will be discussed in turn. It should be noted, however, that many of these distinctions will blur and fade in practice: "Evidence from single and dual-mode universities, and from conventional campuses, suggests that we are approaching the point where there is no longer a clear division between conventional and distance education. University education will be conducted by various

means at different times and places according to the requirements of different groups of students" (Mugridge 1992, 154). Mirroring a similar trend in Australia, South African universities are increasingly operating on a mixed-mode basis in which students combine face-to-face and distance learning classes with on-campus residence. Yet even if such blurring of delivery modes occurs in practice, it is helpful to distinguish them as conceptual categories.

A dual-mode institution offers both classroom instruction and distance education programs. The dual-mode model appears best suited for enrollments in the 10,000–20,000 range. However, with capable management, the financial break-even point can be pushed down to enrollments as low as 5,000. Where traditional tertiary institutions can be persuaded to view distance education as a serious alternative of comparable quality, dual-mode institutions can also effectively serve enrollments of more than 20,000 students.

The dual-mode approach possesses numerous advantages. It makes use of and is supported by an existing academic community. Classroom and distance instruction are based on common materials, and performance is evaluated using common standards. It can be gradually introduced as resources permit. Where an academic credit system is employed, students can move back and forth between distance and classroom study or pursue a combination of the two. In smaller institutions, this approach enables a broadening of curriculum and allows courses to be taught when academic staff are on vacation or when academic positions are unfilled.

The main disadvantage of dual-mode instruction is that efforts to introduce distance learning approaches within traditional tertiary institutions based on face-to-face teaching are likely to encounter stiff resistance to change among the existing academic and administrative staff. In a number of African institutions, administrative rigidities, limited management autonomy, and lack of program flexibility add to the challenge of promoting such changes. Often, the inclusion of special performance criteria that recognize staff contributions to distance education programs, together with financial incentives for the additional time required, can help to overcome this conservatism.

Distance education within a dual-mode university can be organized in one of two ways. One is the specialist institute in which a core group of specialist staff, drawing upon content expertise from university departments, design courses, produce materials, and oversee their distribution and use. An effective example of this approach is the National Distance Education Center at Dublin City University in Ireland. A second approach is a coordinating unit that functions as a liaison between students and university departments that directly produce and offer distance education courses. This model has been employed at the University of Zambia (Ng'andwe 1995). Because it often lacks decision-making power within the institution, this latter approach has tended to be less effective.

The single-mode institution is a wholly dedicated distance learning institution. Where student admissions are not selective, this model is usually called an "open university." Its advantages include a strong specialist staff, the absence of institutional resistance to a new and different form of pedagogy, and the institution's potential to serve students from more than one country. Its principal drawbacks are that it requires a sizable initial investment to be properly established, that considerable political will needs to be mobilized to do this, and that its graduates may be viewed as inferior to those from the existing residential institutions. Single-mode universities currently operate in South Africa, Tanzania, and Zimbabwe.

Under a franchised international program, a foreign provider of distance education programs enters into partnership with a local tertiary institution to offer these programs on a joint basis. This is often done as a commercial venture. The local institution uses course materials developed and copyrighted by the foreign provider but takes responsibility for local logistics, student support, and management. The two institutions share the fee income. The franchise approach possesses four main advantages:

- It does not require much local expertise to get started and therefore can be initiated rather quickly.
- The course content may be more attuned to international trends and requirements.
- It may thus be easier to obtain course accreditation.
- It can be supported by international technical (and possibly even financial) assistance.

Among its disadvantages are that it may be less adapted to local needs, it may not be very accountable to local quality assurance mechanisms, and it may be more expensive than locally developed programs. One example of a franchised international program is the master's program in agricultural development offered by Wye College in the United Kingdom (UK). A variation on this approach is the in-service master's program in business administration contracted from the Open University in the United Kingdom by the governments of Eritrea and Ethiopia for their senior civil servants. The franchise model is quickly expanding. It was recently estimated that franchised courses now account for 140,000 foreign students and $410 million in revenue for the UK alone (Bennell and Pearce 1998).

Direct provision of distance learning from nonfranchised international institutions is only just beginning to emerge. In this case, an established distance learning facility or "virtual university" offers courses internationally, generally using the Internet and interactive e-mail. All that the student requires to gain access is a computer, a modem, an Internet connection, and a credit card. Master's programs in engineering transmitted to North American and Asian students via satellite by the National Technological University in the United States are one such example. In Africa, UNISA's new Web-based virtual university, called Students On-Line, can be reached by anyone on the African continent with an Internet connection. The range of directly provided international distance education courses is expected to expand rapidly over the next several years.

The advantage of this model is that little or no action is required by local governments or institutions. In addition, students can study without leaving home or job and without having to raise the funds necessary to study abroad. Its disadvantages are its possible lack of quality control and the associated risk of disreputable providers, possible differences in "educational culture" between sending and receiving societies (Moore 1994, 189), the absence of local tutorial support, and fee scales that may prevent access to all but the most wealthy students. In the long run, the risk of using nonfranchised international distance learning is that tertiary education may become another entrenched commodity that developing countries must import from the developed world, thus creating a new and more effective form of cultural imperialism. This possibility gives developing countries an added incentive to cultivate distance education capacities and to work together in doing so.

In selecting among these four institutional models, market analysis is recommended as an essential part of the planning and decision-making process. Typically, market analysis looks at four areas:

- Student demographics (age, geographic distribution, qualification desired, occupational interest, socioeconomic status)
- Competition (alternative services available to students and alternative delivery modes for providers)
- Regulatory environment (quality standards, licensing, accreditation, taxation, telecommunications)
- Students' ability and willingness to pay (Willis 1994, 79)

A market survey of a representative portion of the target population can yield essential information about the scope of demand for different course levels and the type of course content that is most sought after. The Bangladesh Open University, for example, interviewed 16,000 persons before finalizing its plans for course offerings. Because distance education requires a significant up-front investment in the development of course materials and tutorial support, market analysis is important to maximize the success of initial strategic choices and to reduce the possibility of misguided educational initiatives. Many of the established open universities, such as those in India, Hong Kong, and Bangladesh, have experience in conducting market analyses and could be contacted for guidance and technical assistance in this area.

WHAT MANAGEMENT CHOICES MUST BE MADE?

Once an institutional mechanism for the delivery of distance learning programs is chosen, an implementation framework is needed to manage day-to-day activities. This implementation framework should be guided by a mission statement that has been developed to orient the overall undertaking. Experience indicates that it is usually best to start with a small number of high-quality distance education courses that respond to significant areas of public demand identified by a market survey. Courses should be carefully chosen according to the country's employment needs and related job skills.

The biggest challenges to the establishment of distance education programs within existing tertiary institutions are attitudinal barriers and institutional resistance (Mugridge 1992, 54; Keast 1997, 42; Evans and Nation 1996, 150). Professional opposition arises from beliefs that educational quality will not be maintained, that students will not adapt, and the belief that time-tested methods are best. In addition, personal worries—such as fear of change and new technology, job insecurity, and concerns about professional reputation—also play a strong role. Institutional resistance emerges when established procedures must be changed, accepted standards are not applicable, organizational roles or units need to be transformed, or new entities might compete for limited budgetary resources. These are, in fact, exactly the types of changes necessary to establish distance education. In its fully developed state, distance learning requires a substantial change in academic culture from a tradition of individual scholarship, research, disciplinary orientation, and independence to a new culture characterized by an institutional mission, teamwork, interdisciplinary and problem-solving approaches, conflict resolution, management, and accountability. How can such changes in institutional culture be initiated?

When a traditional tertiary institution is involved in setting up distance learning programs, a senior-level "champion" is frequently required to initiate the necessary changes within a resistant academic culture (Moore and Kearsley 1996, 234). This is ideally a person of status and credibility who is persuaded of the merits of distance learning approaches. In addition, the change process can often be accelerated somewhat by clear policy statements from top political leaders and appropriate state interventions to underscore the government's commitment to the new policies.

In practice, much of an institution's resistance to distance learning may derive from rigidities in its operational setup and administrative procedures. These rigidities are bound up with the assumption that tertiary education is undertaken largely by students who have recently completed secondary schooling and who are now preparing to enter the workforce. These operational systems inhibit academic staff from exploring new approaches to teaching and learning in response to the growing diversity of student needs and circumstances. In this context, greater administrative flexibility is not merely a desirable "ideal." It is a necessary prerequisite for effective competition if tertiary institutions are to respond to the changing demands of individuals, companies, and governments that will be deciding whether or not to buy the institution's services.

What does a call for greater administrative flexibility mean? It means retooling procedures so that academic staff can allow students to do one or more of the following: register and enroll throughout the year; take courses of any length and accumulate credits toward broader qualifications; combine courses in different ways to create different learning programs; exit programs at many different points; postpone studies for any length of time; study at sites that are convenient and accessible (including home and the workplace); study at times of the day and week that fit with their lifestyles; write examinations and undertake other assessments throughout the year; and pay at different times and in different ways.

Assessments of experiences with distance education indicate that, in addition to insufficient administrative flexibility, several other mistakes are also common in the course of implementation planning. These include premature selection of technology; emphasis on technical planning and neglect of educational planning; failure to consider market-related factors, such as consumer demand, competing alternatives, and the regulatory environment; and insufficient identification and use of available program resources (Willis 1994, 69).

Only after a market-oriented educational plan has been drawn up should the choice of technology be addressed. The mix of technologies to be used for providing distance education is a key implementation decision, as it has direct implications for program organization, staffing, and costs. As noted earlier, the choice of technology has been shown to have relatively little effect on learning achievement. Thus, this choice should be guided by what works reliably in the local environment and by local costs. The choice of technology should be followed by a technology development plan that details infrastructure requirements, hardware needs, training necessities, cost estimates, and investment priorities for teaching, research, administration, and community service (World Bank 1998b, 32).

The next important set of management decisions shapes the program's organizational structure and staffing. These decisions should, to the extent possible, seek to build on existing strengths, recognize the need for industry and employer communication, and include some capacity for social marketing of the distance education programs. The value of a small coordinating unit staffed by specialists to national distance education programs located on the campus of an existing university, along the lines of the National Center for Distance Education in Ireland, has been mentioned previously. With regard to dual-mode initiatives, experience teaches that it is important for the head of distance learning programs to be accorded academic status equivalent to that of faculty deans, that the head have a seat in the institution's decision-making forum, and that a separate budgetary item for these programs be under the head's direct control. Without such safeguards, the distance education program will take much longer to establish.

Another lesson from experience is that effective implementation of tertiary distance education programs requires permanent attention to staff development. New roles and skills are necessary when academic staff move from teaching to tutoring. Identified training priorities include strategic management, instructional design, communications, oversight of trainers' methods, and pedagogical use of technology. It has been noted above that staff training is frequently underfunded in the effort to reduce costs, a practice that can be counterproductive. A shortage of trained staff and training capacities can lead to a transitional period of poor-quality distance education services. This, in turn, can undermine the initial credibility of a new program. One knowledgeable practitioner has suggested that each staff member should spend five days a year on professional development and another five days a year on technology skills (Daniel 1996, 157).

Various training programs for providers of distance education currently operate on the continent. Within Anglophone Africa, a diploma-level course in distance education is offered at a distance by the University of South Africa. A certificate-level course has recently been introduced by the Open University of Tanzania. Within Francophone Africa, preparations are underway at the Centre de Formation à Distance of the University of Benin, Togo, with support from a UNESCO chair, to offer a tertiary program in distance education. The RESAFAD program already offers a distance learning diploma program in multimedia communications.

Governance and accountability arrangements for tertiary distance learning programs are also important considerations and can produce a substantial payoff. High levels of participation by staff, employers, and students can generate more successful programs (Daniel 1996, 129). In South Africa and Indonesia, for example, active involvement by these groups in planning and evaluating distance learning programs has helped to increase their educational effectiveness. Where a team-based approach to course development is adopted, a more collegial style of institutional governance has proven to be preferable.

CONCLUSION

Distance learning that incorporates a judicious use of new information and communication technologies, especially as these become increasingly available in sub-Saharan Africa, promises to provide an important part of the solution to the continent's growing demands for expanded access to and improved quality of tertiary education. While each country will need to craft its own approach to the establishment of tertiary distance education programs and institutions, considerable worldwide experience is available to inform policymaking and planning in this area. This experience suggests that the following general guidelines can help African nations to build successfully the capacities they need to support effective tertiary distance education.

- Assess current good practice from other countries and develop explicit national strategies for tertiary distance education and associated technology development that are solidly based on existing local capacities (which in some cases are significant).
- Support this strategy with an aggressive start-up phase of institutional and human resource capacity-building activities that are incorporated within other education sector projects. Partnerships with overseas distance education programs and with local industry or other training institutions can improve the quality and efficiency of this process.
- Design or re-engineer organizational structures to accommodate the unique requirements of distance education. Capacities for course design, student support, learning assessment, and service delivery management should be among the essential considerations.
- Integrate distance education courses and certifications into the existing tertiary education system as fully as possible, recognizing that choices represent a continuum ranging from campus-based face-to-face teaching to home- or office-based learning by means of one or more media. For many African countries, a dual-mode approach in which distance learning programs are incorporated within existing tertiary institutions would appear to be the most cost-effective and manageable approach. This integration should also include acceptance of distance education degrees as employment qualifications for the civil service.
- Use printed materials as the main medium of instruction, invest in good-quality course design and study guides, and strive for strong and effective student support services.
- Use new information and communication technologies to improve management efficiency and enhance educational quality rather than to expand access; pay special attention to library transformation in this process.
- Limit course offerings to areas of high student demand and

develop only at the pace permitted by resource availability and management capacity.

THE FUTURE

What can African governments, and particularly their ministries of education, expect if they make an effort to develop their tertiary distance education capacities? Perhaps a glimpse of the future of global tertiary education will help to answer the question.

Tertiary enrollments will expand rapidly in the years ahead. The recent trend of tertiary enrollments in the developed countries toward massification will continue and expand to engulf the developing world as well. Lifelong learning will become the global norm as both countries and workers strive to build and maintain a competitive edge. Students of all ages will start, interrupt, and restart studies; pursue them on a full-time or part-time basis; and do so through a mix of self-study, digital learning, and face-to-face participation in learning activities. Learning will be greatly individualized and self-managed. For this reason, a highly professional student guidance system, in which personal counseling by tutors forms an important component of teaching, will become a central element in tertiary education.

Tertiary education in the future will be based much less on academic disciplines and more on transdisciplinary study. Great emphasis will be placed on one's ability to learn independently, communicate effectively with others, collaborate productively in teams and groups, show cultural and social sensitivity, demonstrate flexibility, and accept social responsibilities. Media competence will become a universally required skill. The goal will be to prepare students for a knowledge economy in which they will work in virtual (online) companies, organizations, committees, and project teams (Peters 1999).

Research will no longer be the domain primarily of universities, and it will diverge increasingly from the structures of university education. It will become an interactive undertaking involving many types of knowledge producers who work together in networked teams that form, dissolve, and regroup as needed to tackle complex transdisciplinary problems. Disciplinary science will gradually give way to "research in the context of application" aimed at understanding and manipulating complex systems (Gibbons 1998, 42).

New technologies will make university campuses obsolete. Students will use asynchronous multimedia communications delivered by the Internet and receive learning support through virtual libraries and online video conferencing. Students will design their own individual courses of study by selecting courses from a menu appropriate to their level of demonstrated learning. Education will be undertaken when the student has time available for study instead of when the student can meet at a certain time or a certain place. Courses will begin and end on a continual basis. Dull administrative tasks, such as paying fees, recording grades, monitoring attendance, assessing class participation, and charting progress, will be performed automatically. Software will operate on voice recognition systems. Students will use portable computers with high-speed wireless access to the Internet as their main study tools. In this way, tertiary education will become truly personal and truly portable, possibly within the next ten years (Downes 1998).

The crucial point to grasp from the vision presented above is that the development of national distance education capabilities is the stepping-stone by which all nations will proceed into this future.

ACKNOWLEDGMENTS

This chapter is reprinted from W. Saint, *Tertiary Distance Education and Technology in Sub-Saharan Africa*, ADEA Working Group on Higher Education (Washington, D.C.: World Bank, 1999). Francesca Purcell, Graduate Assistant at Boston College, assisted in the reorganization of the article for this book.

REFERENCES

Bamba, Z. 1999. "Using ICTs in University Libraries to Improve the Quality of Training and Teaching in African Universities." Paper presented at the Conference of Rectors, Vice Chancellors, and Presidents of African Universities, Arusha, Tanzania, February 1–4.

Bates, A. W. 1997. "Restructuring the University for Technological Change." Paper presented at the Carnegie Foundation Conference, What Kind of University? London, June 18–20. Copyright University of British Columbia.

Bennell, P., and T. Pearce. 1998. *The Internationalization of Higher Education: Exporting Education to Developing and Transitional Economies*. Brighton, UK: Institute of Development Studies, University of Sussex.

Cairncross, F. 1995. "The Death of Distance: A Survey of Telecommunications." *The Economist*, September 30: 64–66.

Chale, E. M., and P. Michaud. 1997. *Distance Learning for Change in Africa: A Case Study of Senegal and Kenya*. IDRC Study/Acacia Initiative. Ottawa, Canada: International Development Research Centre.

Cilliers, J. A., and E. C. Reynhardt. 1998. "Thirty Years of Physics at UNISA." *South African Journal of Higher Education* 12, no. 1: 174–183.

Cummings, C., and F. A. Olaloku. 1993. "The Correspondence and Open Studies Institute, University of Lagos." In Hilary Perraton, ed., *Distance Education for Teacher Training*. London: Routledge Press.

Daniel, J. S. 1996. *Mega-Universities and Knowledge Media: Technology Strategies for Higher Education*. London: Kogan Page.

Darch, C. 1998. *The Shrinking Public Domain and the Unsustainable Library*. Cape Town, South Africa: University of Cape Town.

Dhanarajan, G. 1994. *Economics of Distance Education: Recent Experience*. Hong Kong: Open Learning Institute Press.

Downes, S. 1998. "The Future of Online Learning." *Journal of Distance Learning Administration* 1, no. 3 (Fall). Available online at: http://www.westga.edu/~distance/downes13.html

Evans, T., and D. Nation. 1989. *Critical Reflections on Distance Education*. New York: Falmer Press.

———, eds. 1996 *Opening Education: Policies and Practices from Open and Distance Education*. New York: Routledge Press.

Farrell, G. M. 1999. *The Development of Virtual Education: A Global Perspective*. Vancouver, BC, Canada: Commonwealth of Learning.

Gibbons, M. 1998. *Higher Education Relevance in the 21st Century*. World Bank contribution to the UNESCO World Conference on Higher Education. Washington, D.C.: World Bank.

Jensen, M. 2002. "African Internet Connectivity: Information & Communication Technologies (ICTs), Telecommunications, Internet and Computer Infrastructure in Africa." Available online at: www3.sn.apc.org/africa

John, M. 1996. "Distance Education in Sub-Saharan Africa: The Next Five Years." *Innovations in Education and Training International* 33, no. 1 (February): 50–57.

Keast, A. 1997. "Toward an Effective Model for Implementing Distance Education Programs." *American Journal of Distance Education* 11, no. 2: 39–55.

Knoch, C. 1997. *Uninet—The South African Academic and Research Network*. IDRC Study/Acacia Initiative. Ottawa, Canada: International Development Research Centre.

Langlois, C. 1998. "University and New Information and Communication Technologies: Issues and Strategies." *European Journal of Engineering Education* 23, no. 3: 285–295.

Makau, B. 1993. "The External Degree Programme at the University of Nairobi." In Hilary Perraton, ed., *Distance Education for Teacher Training*. London: Routledge Press.

Materu-Bahitsa, M., and L. Levey. 1998. *Database of African Theses and Dissertations: Report of a Feasibility Study*. Nairobi, Kenya: The Ford Foundation.

Ministère de l'Education Nationale, de la Recherche et de la Technologie (France). 1999 (June). Personal communication with author.

Moore, M. G. 1994. "Is There a Cultural Problem in International Distance Education?" In M. M. Thompson, ed., *Internationalism in Distance Education: A Vision for Higher Education*. University Park, Pa.: American Center for the Study of Distance Education.

Moore, M. G., and G. Kearsley. 1996. *Distance Education: A Systems View*. Belmont, Calif.: Wadsworth Publishing.

Mugridge, I., ed. 1992. *Distance Education in Single and Dual Mode Universities*. Vancouver, British Columbia: Commonwealth of Learning.

———. 1994. *The Funding of Open Universities*. Vancouver, British Columbia: Commonwealth of Learning.

Murphy, P., and A. Zhiri, eds. 1992. *Distance Education in Anglophone Africa: Experience with Secondary Education and Teacher Training*. EDI Development Policy Case Series no. 9. Washington, D.C.: World Bank.

Ng'andwe, A. 1995. "Distance Education at the University of Zambia: Problems of Quality and Management." *Higher Education Policy* 8, no. 1: 44–47.

Pecku, N. K. 1998. *Survey of Current Status of Distance Education in Cameroon*. Vancouver, British Columbia: Commonwealth of Learning.

Peters, O. 1999. "The University of the Future: Pedagogical Perspectives." In Helmut Hoyer, ed., *The New Educational Frontier: Teaching and Learning in a Networked World*. Proceedings of the 19th World Conference on Open Learning and Distance Education, Vienna, June 20–24, 1999. Oslo, Norway: The International Council for Open and Distance Education.

Republic of Senegal. 1997. *Using Distance Education for Higher Education in Senegal*. Dakar: Department of Higher Education, Ministry of National Education.

Roberts & Associates. 1998. *Tertiary Distance Learning in Sub-Saharan Africa: Overview and Directory to Programs*. ADEA Working Group on Higher Education. Washington, D.C.: World Bank.

Rumble, G. 1997. *The Costs and Economics of Open and Distance Learning*. London: Kogan Page.

Rumble, G., and J. Oliveira. 1992. *Vocational Education at a Distance: International Perspectives*. London: Kogan Page.

SAIDE (South African Institute for Distance Education). 1999. "Distance Education and Educational Technology Choices in South Africa." Available online at: www.saide.org.za

Turoff, M. 1997a. "Costs for the Development of a Virtual University." *Journal of the Asynchronous Learning Network* 1, no. 1 (March).

——. 1997b. "Alternative Futures for Distance Learning: The Force and the Darkside." Keynote presentation at UNESCO/Open University International Colloquium on Virtual Learning Environments, Milton Keynes, UK, April 27–29. Available online at: http://eies.njit.edu/~turoff/Papers/darkaln.html

UN. 1998. *World Population Prospects: The 1996 Revision.* New York: United Nations.

UNESCO. 1998a. *Statistical Yearbook.* Paris: United Nations Educational, Scientific and Cultural Organization.

——. 1998b. *World Statistical Outlook on Higher Education, 1980–1995.* Paris: United Nations Educational, Scientific and Cultural Organization.

Willis, B., ed. 1994. *Distance Education: Strategies and Tools.* Englewood Cliffs, N.J.: Educational Technology Publications.

World Bank. 1994. *Higher Education: The Lessons of Experience.* Washington, D.C.: The World Bank.

——. 1988. *Education in Sub-Saharan Africa: Policies for Adjustment, Revitalization and Expansion.* Washington, D.C.: World Bank.

——. 1998a. *Knowledge for Development.* World Bank Development Report 1998/99. Washington, D.C.: World Bank.

——. 1998b. "Latin America and the Caribbean: Education and Technology at the Crossroads." Discussion paper (April). Washington, D.C.: World Bank.

Young, F., and I. Fujimoto. "Social Differentiation in Latin American Communities." *Economic Development and Cultural Change* 23 (April): 344–352.

10

The Language Predicament in African Universities

Damtew Teferra

INTRODUCTION

The continued use of Western languages as the medium of instruction at African institutions of higher education is both a remnant of colonialism and an effect of the current forces of globalization. Unfortunately, the impact of the prominence of Western languages, such as French and English, has received little attention in the research on improving the quality of African higher education.

A multitude of factors, external and internal, local and national, regional and global, constantly pose challenges to higher education in Africa. The litany of the challenges is rather long and is common across most of the institutions of the continent.

The most widely recognized and significant problems facing African higher education include poor and declining funding, escalating pressure to provide access, serious gender, ethnic, and geographic inequities, massive brain drain, and the general deterioration of the infrastructure of the institutions. These problems are so numerous, so complex, so overwhelming, and so extensively intertwined that it is often difficult to clearly isolate the causes from the symptoms that conspire against effective and equitable higher education on the continent.

Often, the most subversive elements are neither obvious nor clearly isolated. Instead, they are often shrouded by other problems. This chapter will focus on one of these hidden yet subversive elements that undermines the quality of higher education across Africa: the impact of Western languages as the medium of instruction in African higher education.

The existing body of literature does not seriously recognize, discuss, or even attempt to address the problem of Western languages as the instructional media in African higher education. In the literature to date, language is often relegated to the bottom of the list of problems that plague African higher education. Yet the problem of Western languages as instruments of educational delivery, and their impact on higher education on nations across

Africa have been clearly depicted in many of the chapters in this book. The pattern of the problem as depicted throughout this book sends a clear message to take the matter seriously and face the problem directly.

WESTERN LANGUAGES AS INSTRUCTIONAL MEDIA: THE INTERPLAY

More than half a dozen languages are currently in use in African higher education institutions: Afrikaans, Arabic, English, French, Italian, Portuguese, and Spanish. Except for Arabic (and, arguably, Afrikaans in South Africa), no native language, *sensu stricto*, is used as an instructional medium in African higher learning institutions. Overall, English, French, and, to some extent, Portuguese remain the major Western languages of instruction in African institutions of higher learning.

At a time when globalization has become a powerful force, the dominant position of European languages has become more accentuated and evident in Africa. English, in particular, has emerged more prominently than any other major European language, fueled by, among other things, the force of the Internet and the economic and cultural elements of globalization (Altbach 1987; Altbach and Teferra 1999).

The struggle for dominance among and between Western and native languages is a growing phenomenon in a number of African higher education institutions. There is an interesting trend toward a transition in the language used as the instructional medium in Rwanda, for instance, where the core of the leadership in government and power is changing. This is also the case in Sudan, where the political predilections are shifting, and in Equatorial Guinea and, to some extent, in Somalia, where perceived socioeconomic benefits appear to be dictating the choice of language for instruction.

Sudan has been attempting to shift its medium of instruction in its higher learning institutions from English to Arabic for quite some time. A recent government directive set Arabic as the primary language of instruction in all higher education institutions in the country, thus supplanting English. This decision by the Sudanese government has been the cause of acrimony and division within and outside the nation's universities.

Stemming from Belgian colonialism, French continues to be used as the language of instruction in Rwandan educational institutions and business transactions. For three decades or longer, many Rwandans sought refuge in Uganda, Burundi, Congo, Tanzania, South Africa, French-speaking West Africa, or Kenya, where they spoke English or French; their return has changed the linguistic landscape of the country. This difference in linguistic backgrounds has, Jolly Mazimhaka and G. F. Daniel report in Chapter 52, influenced a new language policy, which calls for the teaching of both English and French at all levels of education and the use of either language as the medium of instruction.

The situation in Equatorial Guinea depicts the complexities of utilizing multiple languages in one nation. Deborah Pomeroy (Chapter 30) notes that Spanish is the official language of Equatorial Guinea and that all schools there teach in Spanish, with the exception of the Nigerian Equatorial Guinean International School (which uses English) and the French School (which uses French). Until recently, French was considered the language of business in Equatorial Guinea, which is not surprising as the nation lies in the midst of Francophone Africa. In casual conversation, though, most adults speak their tribal tongues; for example, Fang or Bubi. In addition, those who were educated in the Soviet Union also speak Russian. And finally, the current language of economic empowerment is English. There is no official policy about English, but officials in several government ministries maintain that English is the language of the future. Many secondary schools have courses in English as well as French.

Until Somalia plunged into chaos and disintegration in the 1990s, Mohamed Nur-Awaleh observes in Chapter 56, higher education was available through one university and its six colleges. There were also seven specialized postsecondary schools, all of which were government based. Although institutions also delivered education in English and Arabic, the main language of instruction at the university was Italian.

These few examples illustrate the extent to which African institutions are melting pots of Western languages. The next section examines in greater detail how Western languages are faring as instruments of educational delivery in African higher learning institutions.

WESTERN LANGUAGES: THEIR EFFECT ON AFRICAN SCHOLARSHIP

The competency of a good number of African students in the Western languages, as examined below, leaves a lot to be desired. Many contributors in the chapters to follow claim that poor levels of proficiency with the language of instruction is a major factor in the declining quality of higher education in Africa. Some of the contributors also attribute the high student attrition rates to the inability of students to function effectively in the language of instruction. The following individual cases from the country chapters highlight the pattern.

Nigeria: Nigeria is the most populous African country, with a population of about 120 million. It also has the largest postsecondary enrollment in sub-Saharan Africa: nearly 1 million students are enrolled in over 200 postsecondary institutions, including forty-five universities. English is the official language of Nigeria and the language of instruction at all levels after the first three years of primary school. However, Munzali Jibril (Chapter 51) reports that proficiency in English has been on the decline at all levels of the educational system, and poor communicative competence is a major cause of failure in public examinations both at the secondary and the higher educational levels.

Mozambique: The language of instruction throughout the whole education system in Mozambique is Portuguese. Portuguese, which is also an official language of Mozambique, is spoken as a mother tongue by less than 1 percent of the population (Pierce and Ridge 1997). As Arlindo Chilundo reports in Chapter 48, the level of understanding of the language is often poor in both primary and secondary schools, leading to poor preparation at the pre-university level.

Guinea Bissau: Guinea Bissau also uses Portuguese, even though it is spoken by only 10 percent of the population. Julieta Mendes observes in Chapter 37 that students enter higher education institutions with a language handicap and concludes that this has been one of the underlying factors behind the low performance of students, especially in primary schools. Both the School of Law and the School of Medicine have enacted an additional full year of core courses to address language and other deficiencies.

Madagascar: The language of instruction for advanced secondary and university education programs in Madagascar is French. Since Malagasy is the first language of both teachers and students, however, it is not uncommon for class conversations to lapse into the lingua franca, presumably due to the poor French comprehension of students. There was an attempt during the 1970s to create an entire primary and secondary program in Malagasy. This ultimately proved unsuccessful, James Stiles reports in Chapter 42, because of a lack of finances and continued pressure from aid agencies to utilize a "global language."

Liberia: English is the medium of instruction in the Liberian education system. Patrick Seyon reports in Chapter 40 that the high repeater and attrition rates throughout the system are more closely linked to the language problem than to poor-quality teachers and the lack of instructional materials, which are often assigned the blame.

Ethiopia: With its more than 65 million people, Ethiopia stands as the third-most populous country in Africa. In Ethiopia, where about 50,000 postsecondary students were enrolled at the end of 2000, most institutions, particularly the universities, have what is called a "freshman program." The primary objective of the program, Habtamu Wondimu writes in Chapter 32, is to ameliorate academic deficiencies by improving students' English skills, since English is the medium of instruction in universities and other higher education institutions.

Kenya: In Chapter 38, Charles Ngome, quoting Mwiria (1993), reports that the failure rate of students in university examinations in Kenya is rising. The labor market continues to voice concerns about the poor quality of graduates from Kenyan universities. The decline in standards is further demonstrated by the university students' poor command of the English language, which is the medium of instruction in the Kenyan system of education.

Morocco: In Moroccan higher education, Arabic is the language of instruction for most disciplines in the humanities and social sciences, while disciplines in law and economics follow a bilingual Arabic-French pattern. Science- and technology-related disciplines have been taught exclusively in French. Mohamed Ouakrime observes in Chapter 47 that the total Arabization of the science-related disciplines at the secondary school level and their teaching in French at the university level negatively affected the experiences and outcomes of students who enrolled to study science. Although partial solutions to the problem have been devised, students' negative outcomes have translated into declines in enrollment at faculties of science and an increasing tendency toward humanities and the social sciences.

Mauritania: In 1999, Ahmed Kharchi notes in Chapter 45, the Mauritanian government reformed the educational system, specifically examining the medium of instruction. Kharchi, without specifically addressing the language situation, noted that the reform aimed to progressively create a unified bilingual system to replace the existing one, which was divided into two subsystems, one in Arabic and the other bilingual (in Arabic and French).

Namibia: Many students in Namibia, Barnabas Otaala writes in Chapter 49, have difficulty with English as the language of instruction, since English is often their second or third language. Consequently, they often experience difficulties in following lecturers and taking notes or engaging in discussions, at least initially. Regarding course materials, many textbooks do not include relevant local or contextualized issues or illustrations. In addition, the language of the textbooks may be too difficult for students to comprehend, considering that it is written in the students' second or third language.

Somalia: In Chapter 56, Mohamed Nur-Awaleh describes the multiplicity of Western languages as one of the problems Somalia continues to face at its postsecondary institutions. Somali, Italian, English, and Arabic are being used simultaneously in the different levels of education. This resulted, according to a 1983 World Bank report, in confusion and a breakdown of coordination among different levels of education (World Bank 1983). The multiplicity of languages in the rudimentary, fledgling, and strife-ridden postsecondary education in Somalia has compounded other problems currently affecting the system.

South Africa: With over half a million students in its universities and technikons, South Africa has the second highest student enrollment in sub-Saharan Africa (after Nigeria). In South Africa, one of the major challenges in higher education, George Subotzky holds (Chapter 57), is improving the graduation rates of students. He argues for better support measures to ensure that university and technikon students are equipped with the basic language and academic literacy skills that they so often lack as a consequence of poor-quality primary and secondary schooling.

Tanzania: In Chapter 60, Daniel Mkude and Brian Cook-sey, quoting studies on Tanzania conducted by Roy-Campbell and Qorro (1997), point out that English is progressively being eliminated from Tanzanian public life and that proficiency in English is diminishing. Secondary school teachers also report that although English is the official medium of instruction, they often feel obliged to resort to Kiswahili in order to establish meaningful interactions with their students. Students admitted to institutions of higher education are victims of this ambivalence of language policy; most have a low proficiency in spoken English, and their writing is barely understandable. College and university staff and external examiners have repeatedly complained that students' low competence in English has a negative impact on their learning process.

The extensive testimonies from all these countries must lead researchers to take the matter of language usage in higher education seriously.

- What issues does this consistent pattern affirm? What lessons should be learned from this pattern?
- What will be the consequences of this problem for education systems in individual nations in particular and for the continent as a whole?
- Given the current scenario, what are the perceived and real threats to African scholarship when the current systems rely predominantly on Western languages, Western knowledge and information, and Western products?
- What should universities, governments, donor organizations, and NGOs do to address the entrenched problem of deficient skills in Western languages that is intricately interwoven with educational quality, access, and success?

In nation after nation, the use of Western languages as instruments of educational delivery in African higher learning institutions has proved significantly problematic. These examples above and many others point to poor skills in instructional media as responsible for considerable failures in much of the continent's educational systems. Yet this factor still remains largely unacknowledged. Nations cannot afford to ignore imminent and real threats that slowly and covertly devour the fabric of their intellectual souls by preventing students and scholars from acquiring skills and knowledge. The language issue is one such threat that needs to be addressed. All countries should revisit the state of the language medium of instruction in their educational systems and tackle the problem at every level—from primary to university—if they intend to produce competent and confident domestically trained scholars.

As knowledge and training hubs for domestic educational, managerial, governmental, and business institutions, postsecondary institutions can be central breeding grounds both for mediocrity and for excellence. Poorly trained university graduates that go into teaching deliver even less competent students to universities, creating a continual cycle of mediocrity. In this way, the problem is not localized at postsecondary institutions but has ramifications that extend beyond the education system in particular into the nation and all of its institutions as a whole.

What should be done to start the complex processes of dealing with this huge problem? First of all, it should be firmly recognized—and acknowledged—that using Western languages as media of instruction in African higher education systems must be immediately reexamined.

The second step is to devise a variety of systematic strategies to address this complicated situation. Addressing the problem will be neither simple nor straightforward, but the complexity of the problem should not deter experts, policymakers, NGOs, and governments from dealing with it. The response to this complex and entrenched problem requires complex, well-informed, and sustained approaches. No matter how complex they may be, language issues, which are vital to effective instructional communication, are just too critical to ignore.

Two possible alternatives—developing vernacular languages for higher education and improving fluency in a Western language—are discussed below, but only the second one can be deemed currently viable. The development of local and regional languages to replace the Western languages as media of instruction in higher education appears to be untenable, at least in the near future. The stages of development of written vernacular languages, the political sensitivity associated with designating a particular vernacular language for instruction, the multiplicity of vernacular languages, the shortages of published materials in vernacular languages, the poor publishing infrastructure, and meager human, financial, and technical resources pose daunting challenges to advancing local and regional languages as the instructional medium in higher education institutions. Even with the political will and the financial capacity to do it, a number of factors would hinder this alternative. What follows is a brief examination of the possible challenges to the development of vernacular languages as media of education in Africa.

PROMOTING VERNACULAR LANGUAGES:
THE COMMON HURDLES

The development of vernacular languages as media of instruction is fraught with a multitude of problems—logistical, technical, political, financial, and emotional. These problems are discussed briefly in the following sections.

Multiplicity of Vernacular Languages

The complexity of language issues in Africa is compounded by its diversity. Today about 1,200 languages are spoken in sub-Saharan Africa alone. Nigeria, the most populous country in Africa, reports to have at least 400 vernacular languages in addition to English, Arabic, and Pidgin (Ufomata 1999). Tanzania, Ethiopia, and Zambia have one hundred twenty, ninety-nine, and seventy languages, respectively. Most of these languages have yet to develop into a written form and are far from being used as an instructional medium in lower schools, let alone in postsecondary institutions (Teferra 1999).

Africa's ethnic heterogeneity is reflected in language. Per capita, there is a wider range of languages spoken in Africa than in any other continent in the world. Ironically, there are also more French-speaking, English-speaking, and Portuguese-speaking countries in Africa than anywhere else in the world. In terms of ethnic units which use African languages as mother tongues, Africa is a continental Tower of Babel in all its diversity

(Mazrui and Mazrui 1998). This linguistic diversity, which further illustrates the rich cultural and ethnic diversity of Africa, has definitely made it difficult for most countries to designate and promote a few languages over any others.

Controversy Created by Designating
Vernacular Languages for Instruction

Designating vernacular languages as media of instruction is a very political and contentious matter. Such decisions are often so sensitive that they cause public outcry and stir violence. In countries where there are historically competing dominant ethnic or tribal groups, governments are often reluctant to pick one language as a medium of instruction for fear of offending any one of the other groups. For instance, the Igbo, Hausa, and Yoruba languages are widely spoken by large segments of the Nigerian population. The decision to select any one of these three major languages as the national language or the dominant language for education is politically difficult (Altbach 1999).

Contemporary scholars working in the field of language planning bemoan, however, the lack of status of vernacular languages, which are increasingly losing out to Western languages (Bloor and Tamrat 1999). In some countries, we also find competition among and between local, regional, and Western languages. Bunyi (1999) holds that in Kenya, for example, the regional language, Kiswahili, competes with English for emphasis in education.

In some cases, certain vernacular languages that had been widely and effectively used for a long time as media of instruction in schools, government, and businesses have seen their status downgraded, and this has generated a lot of debate. The use of Chichewa in Malawi (Ufomata 1999) and Amharic in Ethiopia (Bloor and Tamrat 1996; Teferra 1999) are examples of this shift.

In a few other cases, vernacular languages have been given firm recognition. In order to satisfy as many stakeholders as possible as well as help develop them, some countries have designated many vernacular languages as either official or national languages. For instance, South Africa now recognizes eleven official languages, each to be used as a medium of instruction. Namibia has given national status to thirteen local languages (Pierce and Ridge 1997).

What makes the issue of developing vernacular languages even more daunting is the presence of languages that cross borders. Somali, for instance, is spoken in Somalia, Kenya, Djibouti, and Ethiopia. However, the Somali language has not emerged as an important regional language in the same way that Kiswahili has, for instance. Political sensitivity and controversy continue to underline the issue of cross-border languages and their usage. Other languages, such as Hausa, Fulfude, Kanuri, and Kiknogo, also cut across national boundaries and are used for purposes of regional trade and cooperation (Heugh 1999).

Difficulties of Publishing and Writing

The selection of language scripts is also a controversial and political issue. In Ethiopia, there was a heated debate about whether to use Geez, Latin, or Arabic script to represent the languages that were designated as the media of instruction. Geez script, probably the only truly African script in existence, had been used in all Ethiopian schools until the beginning of the 1990s, when it was replaced in many parts of the country by Latin and, to a limited extent, Arabic scripts.

Many African languages do not lend themselves for use as a medium of publishing and education, having no written scripts, grammatical conventions, or standardized usage. Creating written forms for traditional languages makes the already complex and expensive process of curriculum development for the schools, as well as publishing for both educational and general purposes, much more challenging (Altbach 1999).

Africa has the least developed publishing infrastructure in the world. The major task of publishing is focused on the provision of textbooks and readers for primary and secondary schools. Books, periodicals, and other educational materials that are currently produced in much of the continent still require significant improvement. Furthermore, producing and publishing materials in many languages is often costly, complex, and logistically forbidding.

The multiplicity of languages, the problem of identifying a particular language as a medium of instruction, the stages of development of languages for writing and publications, the paucity of published materials, the poor vocabularies and grammatical conventions to convey ideas and concepts, and the poor infrastructure for producing, publishing, translating, and developing teaching materials locally will continue to be obstacles to the development of vernacular languages into a medium of instruction in education in general and higher education in particular. Moreover, the increasing globalization of the world has added another dimension to the already complex equation.

What Do We Learn from Others?

The challenges associated with providing educational materials in vernacular languages; the absence of an infrastructure that can produce, translate, and publish materials for higher education; and the many other issues mentioned in this chapter have hindered the emergence of a vernacular language as a medium of instruction in African higher education. Some North African countries that are working to establish Arabic as the sole medium of instruction in higher education may be the exceptions.

Similar initiatives in some non-African countries, such as Malaysia, can be instructive. English was the colonial language of Malaysia, which, through consistent and concerted policies, changed its medium of instruction in the universities to Bahasa Malaysia in the 1970s. Still, partly due to Malaysia's strong desire to become part of the international knowledge network and to secure its place in the increasingly global world, Malaysia is now shifting back to English in some areas.

Eastern Europe also provides some vivid examples of the evolution of languages, not only for use in education but also for use in governments, legal systems, and businesses. With the end of the Cold War and the breakup of the former Communist regimes, Eastern Europe has undergone dramatic changes. Rus-

sian is no longer the major language of business and communication in the former states of the USSR. As a matter of fact, countries such as Estonia, Latvia, Lithuania, Georgia, Azerbaijan, and Armenia either eliminated or downgraded Russian as a medium of instruction in favor of other languages. Hall and Thomas (1999) observe that after 1990, Mongolia also abandoned Russian for English as the first foreign language of students.

The decision whether or not to use a particular language as a medium of instruction is not just a matter of local predilections. It has become a matter that increasingly takes into account global and international influences and developments as well.

Caveat

The issue of languages is as complex as it is fundamental. The challenges listed above will continue to confront the emergence of vernacular languages into fully developed media of instruction in higher education. These challenges must not be used as an excuse for neglecting the development of local and regional languages, however.

Some countries and regions are better placed to capitalize on the current status quo. Northern and Eastern Africa—where Arabic and Kiswahili, respectively, are widely spoken, published, and used in business, education, and legal systems—may have a better chance of developing these languages.

Language is an important part of the cultural heritage of any nation, and it must be preserved, nurtured, and developed. African governments have to make conscious efforts to preserve and promote this heritage, even in the context of the tremendous challenges that accompany the language issue. There is no question about the paramount cognitive, cultural, and educational significance of vernacular languages.

CONCLUSION

The major purpose of this chapter is to underscore the prevalence of poorly developed Western language skills in African higher education institutions where Western languages continue to be the primary media of instruction. Since the development of vernacular languages faces the untenable challenges listed above, there is a strong need to undertake a major campaign to improve students' abilities to utilize the existing Western languages that continue to serve as instructional media in African higher education institutions. These improvements require a firm commitment and substantial input in terms of financial, logistical, and technical resources.

African universities rely on the knowledge system that has been developed in Western languages. The developed world, spearheaded by the West, produces a disproportionate share of knowledge, which is then conveyed in Western languages. African universities have neither the capacity to generate enough knowledge for their own consumption nor the infrastructure to process and translate outside sources—yet. Virtually all books, journals, databases, and other resources that are used at most African higher education institutions are imported, and these resources are communicated in Western languages. There is no way Africa could simply drop Western languages as media of instruction and embrace its vernacular languages overnight without losing access to important education resources produced elsewhere. In the age of the Internet, globalization, and expanding knowledge systems, driven by a few Western languages, no country can afford to remain shielded in a cocoon of isolation brought about by language limitations. Such isolation would prove both disastrous and, likely, impossible to achieve. The external forces are simply too strong for African countries to resist.

At the same time, countries should still make committed and sustained efforts to develop their own languages. The most viable and pragmatic approach, therefore, is to run a two-pronged initiative that both overhauls the use of Western languages and nurtures local and regional languages simultaneously. Working to improve the communication skills of students in Western-based instructional media while also promoting the development of local and regional languages remains a formidable challenge, however.

The harmony, balance, and coexistence of Western languages with vernacular languages should be contemplated within local, national, regional, and international contexts. The language issue needs to be perceived as a phenomenon of diverse variables that should be continually examined, tweaked, and guided. This may be easier said than done.

Up until now, the language problem has been largely recognized as a symptom of ailing African educational systems. Instead, the issue of language should be upgraded into one of the primary causes of declining educational systems across Africa. The problem must be recognized and isolated to garner greater levels of attention which would, ideally, result in more direct action. Recognition confers visibility, and visibility must lead to action. The inefficiency in the current use of Western languages and its impact on the accessibility and effectiveness of African higher education, and African education systems as a whole, is simply too significant to be considered simply as a symptom of other problems. The language problem should be officially declared as one of the main factors working against improvements in educational quality in Africa.

The extensive efforts that are currently underway to reinvigorate the state of higher education in Africa must seriously consider the impact of the language factor on higher education and also advance pragmatic strategies to deal with it. The role of NGOs, international organizations, major foundations, and governments in tackling this critical problem of educational delivery cannot be overemphasized.

REFERENCES

Altbach, P. G. 1987. *The Knowledge Context: Comparative Perspectives on the Distribution of Knowledge.* New York: State University of New York Press.

———. 1999. "The Dilemmas of Publishing in African Languages." In P. G. Altbach and D. Teferra, eds., *Publishing in African Languages: Challenges and Prospects*, 1–10. Chestnut Hill, Mass.: Bellagio Publishing Network, Boston College.

Altbach, P., and D. Teferra, eds. 1999. *Publishing in African Languages: Challenges and Prospects.* Chestnut Hill, Mass.: Bellagio Publishing Network, Boston College.

Bloor, T., and W. Tamrat. 1996. "Multilingualism and Education: The Case of Ethiopia." In G. M. Blue and R. Mitchell, eds., *Language and Education: British Studies in Applied Linguistics*, vol. 11, 52–59.

Bunyi, G. 1999. "Rethinking the Place of African Indigenous Languages in African Education." *International Journal of Educational Development* 19, nos. 4–5 (June): 337–350.

Hall, D., and H. Thomas. 1999. "Higher Education Reform in a Transitional Economy: A Case Study from the School of Economic Studies in Mongolia." *Higher Education* 38, no. 4 (December): 441–460.

Heugh, K. 1999. "Languages, Development and Reconstructing Education in South Africa." *International Journal of Educational Development* 19, nos. 4–5 (June): 301–313.

Mazrui, A. A., and A. A. Mazrui. 1998. *The Power of Babel: Language and Governance in the African Experience.* Chicago: University of Chicago Press.

Mwiria, K. 1993. *University Education in East Africa: The Quality Crisis.* Kenyatta University, Nairobi.

Pierce, B. N., and S. G. Ridge. 1997. "Multilingualism in Southern Africa." *Annual Review of Applied Linguistics* 17, nos. 4–5: 170–190.

Roy-Campbell, Z., and M. Qorro. 1997. *Language Crisis in Tanzania: The Myth of English versus Education.* Dar es Salaam: Mkuki na Nyota Publishers.

Teferra, D. 1999. "The Politics of Multilingual Education and Publishing in Ethiopia." In P. G. Altbach and D. Teferra, eds., *Publishing in African Languages: Challenges and Prospects*, pp. 75–109. Chestnut Hill, Mass.: Bellagio Publishing Network, Boston College.

Ufomata, T. 1999. "Major and Minor Languages in Complex Linguistic Ecologies: The Nigerian Experience." *International Journal of Educational Development* 19: 315–322.

World Bank. 1983. *Somalia: Education Sector Memorandum.* Washington, D.C.: World Bank.

11

Student Activism in African Higher Education

IRUNGU MUNENE

INTRODUCTION

Student activism has historically been a crucial aspect in student life in higher education internationally. Since the beginning of the modern university systems in the developed and developing world, university students have engaged in activist movements that have had a profound impact not only in the institutions but also in the wider sociopolitical terrain. Though largely ignored in academic studies, student activism remains one of the most enduring characteristics of African higher education (Federici and Caffentzis 2000). The history of African higher education shows that student activism has permeated the entire spectrum of the continent's higher education, including during the pre-independence period. Altbach (1981, 1989) has argued that two variables differentiate student activism in developing countries (including Africa) from the rest of the industrialized world: its endurance and its great sociopolitical impact. To better appreciate student activism in African higher education, it is important to define what it entails. A sufficient definition will also require that we delineate features that differentiate African activism from its counterpart in the developed world.

Activism is deemed to be any student revolt or unrest that "constitutes a serious challenge or threat to the established order or to ordained authority or norms" (Nkinyangi 1991, 158). This rebellion includes a wide variety of activities, including defiant political conduct, classroom boycotts, destruction of institutional property, attacks on college staff, and widespread riots leading to the injury of students and the general public. In the course of its evolution, one or more of these features of revolt have characterized student activism in African universities. This definition underscores the fluid nature of student activism on the continent. It is highly dynamic and potent, and localized institutional issues are heightened to the extent that they fuse with wider sociopolitical issues in the prevailing political dispen-

sation. Indeed, central to student activism in African higher education has been its political significance and social consequences, which have been given impetus by the single-party oppressive political regimes that have existed in much of the post-independence era.

Even with this definition, no satisfactory theory has been promulgated to explain the genesis, configurations, and outcomes of African student activism or even that of the rest of the world. Nevertheless, student activism in Africa differs considerably from activism in the advanced countries; student activism in Africa has shown a greater affinity to nationalism than has activism in developed countries. As will be shown later, African students have historically been in the forefront in the struggle for the continent's liberation from colonialism. Post-independence activism has also tended to follow this line of action; many student protests are concerned with safeguarding national identity and protecting the democratic rights of the citizens. Hanna (1979, 130) has noted that university students in Africa are concerned "with two great political issues: ethnic versus national considerations, and democratic versus authoritarian rule," which underscores the centrality of nationalism fervor. This contrasts sharply with the situation in developed countries, where such passion for liberation and national identity is not as prominent a feature of student activism.

Student activism is by nature oppositional (Altbach 1991, 248). In Africa, student radicalism has had a leftist orientation, as seen in countries such as Kenya, Tanzania, and Zambia, where Leninist and Marxist ideologies have been potent philosophical pillars in student protests in the recent past. In Western industrialized nations, Marxism has been a far less common feature of activism; student activism in the West has tended to focus on issues such as diversity, multiculturalism, and civil rights. Even the Western student protest movement in the 1980s against universities that held stocks in corporations that did business with apartheid South Africa was not marked by a Marxist ideology.

Student protest is socially accepted in the African political scene, enjoying a political legitimacy that is absent in advanced nations. The result is that African nations view the activism of African students much more sympathetically than industrialized nations view the activism of their students. In Kenya, for instance, students have on various occasions directly supported both the government and the opposition parties (with different consequences; Munene 1997). In either case, these activities have been deemed as legitimate political activity by the society. In contrast, students are not considered to be legitimate political actors in industrialized countries (Altbach 1991, 250). This demonstrates clearly how important historical context is to understanding the legitimacy accorded to student activism by a society.

The prominence of African student activism over its counterpart in the industrialized world is further accentuated by the reaction it provokes from the governing authorities. Generally, political authorities have a wide range of options at their disposal in dealing with student activism. These range from totally ignoring the protests, as is commonly the case in advanced nations, to brutally suppressing them, which is the common trend in Africa (Altbach 1991). This reaction in Africa is based on the prevailing belief that the student movement constitutes a direct threat to the prevailing political order. As will be discussed later, sub-Saharan Africa has had more than its fair share of brutal suppression of student protests. The outcome of such measures has been either to curtail the movement or, in most cases, to increase its size and level of militancy.

Viewed from an international context, student activism in Africa has had greater repercussions than movements in the advanced nations. The consequences of African student activism have at times been revolutionary, leading to fundamental changes. Student protests have effected major political realignments, including the overthrow of political regimes in some African nations. Such fundamental changes have rarely been effected by students in the developed world in the recent past (save for the 1960s in France and the United States). The potency of student activism is due to a number of factors: the absence of viable democratic structures and institutions, which increases the relative impact of an organized student body, the legitimacy accorded to students in politics, the close proximity of universities to the centers of political power (both of which are generally located in the state capitals), and the domination of the universities by students from the higher socioeconomic status, which affords them direct access to powerful segments in society (Altbach 1991, 258).

The rest of the chapter will be devoted to the examination of student activism in African higher education from historical and contemporary perspectives. The object of this analysis is to provide the broad political, social, and economic framework necessary for appreciating the context in which this activism has taken place. Additionally, this analysis will enable us to appreciate the genesis of the activism and demonstrate the extent to which institutional-based micro-level conditions work in conjunction with the socioeconomic macro-level environment to shape the general trend of the movement.

STUDENT ACTIVISM AND THE INDEPENDENCE MOVEMENT

Historical scrutiny of student activism in Africa shows that its political role can be traced back to the independence movement. Political mobilization of students in the colonial era gave way to a heightened political awareness that ultimately led to anticolonial sentiments both at home and abroad. Prominent among the student organizations that engaged in the independence struggle abroad was the West African Student Union (WASU). Founded in London in 1925, WASU became the most virulent critic of colonial excesses of the day, including racism, forced labor, land alienation, and export-oriented economic policies that transferred surplus goods from Africa to metropolitan Europe (Ayu 1986; Hanna and Hanna 1975, 52; Segal 1962, 230). It advocated a return of all alienated lands; the development of a diversified agricultural system, with an emphasis on local food production; a classless society; and mass education for all the colonized people. WASU's lasting legacy was its role as a training ground for Nigerian nationalists and its formulation of a detailed program that later became a model for Africa's decolonization.

Within the continent, too, students were engaged in anticolonial movements from Cape Town to Cairo and from Senegal to Sudan. In Mozambique, members of a national student organization (including such notable postcolonial leaders as Eduardo Mondlane, Joaquim Chisano, and Mariano Matsinhe) were instrumental in organizing the liberation movement and articulating the message of national freedom and resistance to Portuguese colonial rule (Mondlane 1983, 113–115). In the West African nation of Senegal, university students joined forces with trade unionists, emerging African businesspeople, and Islamic religious leaders to shape the nationalist course in the struggle for independence in the postwar period (Bathily, Diouf, and Mbodj 1994; Gellar 1982, 32). In the 1970s, African students from Zambia, Tanzania, and Uganda were active in the liberation movement to free the breakaway British colony of Southern Rhodesia (now Zimbabwe) as well as in independence movements in Angola and Mozambique (Lulat 1981, 250; Cefkin 1975).

Student activism in the colonial era is also credited with the emergence of the first generation of independent Africa's leaders. It is instructive to note that heads of states such as Kwame Nkrumah of Ghana, Jomo Kenyatta of Kenya, Modibo Keita of Mali, Kamuzu Banda of Malawi, and Nelson Mandela of South Africa were student leaders and activists in their university days. Student activism provided these future leaders with a forum and organizational base from which to articulate anticolonial sentiments and exercise their leadership capabilities.

Important as it is in the history of African higher education, pre-independence student activism was limited in terms of its impact when compared to the post-independence movement. To a considerable degree, its impact was constrained by the limited number of higher education institutions. This made higher education students an island of elites in a sea of illiterate masses. Not only were the students isolated geographically from the rest of the populace, they were also socially distanced from the ordinary citizenry by their new language, knowledge, and outlook. They articulated their ideas in the colonial master's language and often aspired toward a Western lifestyle. Federici observes that activism at this period was "the response of an educated elite to its marginalization within the colonial system" at a time when "leading sectors of international capital were preparing to come to terms with the end of colonialism and looked at formally educated Africans as future rulers" (2000, 90–91). This dynamic captures the sociopolitical reality of student activism in the colonial era. Because university students were culturally and intellectually distant from their local countrymen, their activism seemed to enjoy a wide measure of latitude for political initiative from the colonial governments. In contrast to workers' organizations, indigenous churches, and nationalist movements, which experienced substantial repression by the colonial governments, student organizations and their leaders were generally left to their own devices.

Nevertheless, pre-independence activism made important contributions. First, it demonstrated that university students could participate in the liberation of their colonized nations, just as could organizations such as trade unions and political parties. Second, it showed that students were willing to confront sociopolitical issues that had great implications for the wider transformation of society as opposed to being merely concerned with micro-level institutional issues. These attributes have continued to define student activism to this day.

STUDENT ACTIVISM IN THE POST-INDEPENDENCE ERA: THE 1960S AND 1970S

A remarkable feature of post-independence student activism has been the increase in its magnitude and scope. Nkinyangi (1991, 159–160) has estimated that student protests took place in twenty-nine countries between 1970 and 1979. This represents nearly three-quarters of the countries in sub-Saharan Africa. In the period 1980–1989, protests were recorded in twenty-five countries. These statistics underscore the frequency and the scope of activism on the continent, which contrasts with student activism of the earlier pre-independence period. Throughout the post-independence period, student political activism has come to occupy a significant place in the sociopolitical milieu of the continent.

Activism in the 1960s and 1970s was centered on issues that were more ideological and less institutional. The ideological basis of these protests revolved around widespread disenchantment with the post-independence state. A plethora of ideological issues preoccupied student organizations and their leaders, the most prominent being national development ideology, foreign relations, alignment with superpowers in the Cold War era, and the liberation of the southern African countries. Student protests around these issues brought them into conflict with government leaders and dramatically redefined student-state relations.

The ideological leanings of students contributed a great deal to Nigerian university student protest against their government's military pact with the British government in 1960. Students at Ahmadou Bello, Ibadan, Lagos, and Nsukka Universities formed a powerful national movement, the Nigeria Union of Students (NUS), which successfully campaigned against the Anglo-Nigerian Defense Pact. This pact would have led to the establishment of British military bases on Nigerian soil (*Africa*

Diary 1962, 375–376). This union was later blocked when the civilian government was overthrown by the military in a coup d'état in 1966.

In Zambia, similar protests took place in 1971 and 1976 when University of Zambia students clashed with their government over foreign policy. The 1971 riot, ironically, began as a demonstration in support of the Zambian government policy toward South Africa. However, when President Kaunda failed to condemn the police for the brutality they displayed after the demonstration resulted in a riot, the students accused the government of hypocrisy in its foreign policy toward apartheid (Legum 1972; Rothchild 1971). In the 1976 case, students demonstrated against Zambia's foreign policy toward the civil war in neighboring Angola (Burawoy 1976). Protests against foreign policies were also recorded in other independent countries. In Ivory Coast, students protested against President Houphouet Boigny's unilateral decision to welcome Indo-Chinese plantation owners to resettle in the country in 1961 (Zolberg 1975, 114–115). Students also held anti-imperialist demonstrations over incidents such as the killing of Patrice Lumumba in Congo; the Sharpeville massacre in South Africa; Portuguese brutality in Angola, Mozambique, and Guinea Bissau; and France's testing of atomic bombs in the Sahara desert (Ayu 1986, 80–81).

Foreign policy was not the only reason for student activism in this period. Far from it; students protested over a host of issues related to the sociopolitical and economic conditions internal to a particular country's development. In Kenya, University of Nairobi students engaged in protest each year following the 1975 assassination of the popular parliamentarian J. M. Kariuki, who was regarded as a spokesman for the masses. Ghanaian students, angered by the excesses of the military dictator Acheampong, questioned the legitimacy of his rule during student demonstrations in 1975 (Yeebo 1991, 108). In 1978, Nigerian students clashed with the government of General Obasanjo over the cost of education, which culminated in the "Ali must go" movement. This protest took off after eleven students were killed while battling police in Lagos and Zaria (Federici 2000, 105). Besides issues of development and accountability, students were also preoccupied with questions of Africanization, institutional governance, and neocolonialism. These issues precipitated student riots in Zaire, Senegal, and Ethiopia in the late 1960s and 1970s (Hanna and Hanna 1975, 72–75).

Probably the first, and most dramatic, illustration of the impact of student engagement in opposition politics involved student participation in the Ethiopian revolution of 1974 in which Emperor Haile Selassie was overthrown. The dramatic events in 1974 were the culmination of a series of protests against the policies of Emperor Selassie's regime by Addis Ababa University students that began in 1965. There were protests against the regime's policies every spring between 1965 and 1969, with the exception of 1967. In 1965, students marched in support of a land reform bill before Parliament; in 1966, they protested to close "a concentration camp" for indigents that the government had established outside Addis Ababa; and in 1968, they demonstrated against the increasing American influence at the university. In 1969, students focused their activism on the inadequacies of the educational system (Wagaw 1990, 1984; Grey 1979, 152–171).

Broadly conceived, student activism in African higher education in the 1960s and 1970s reflected student concern with the role of the postcolonial state. It also underscored their self-ordained role as a vanguard ensuring that political leaders did not veer off the path of national development as envisioned at independence. Protests about foreign policy sought to guarantee that political leaders did not capitulate to neocolonial interests. Their criticisms reflected their belief in students as the social conscience of society. In other words, university students regarded themselves as a legitimate political class protecting and advocating for the interest of the broader population. The absence of legitimate political opposition (most African countries had either become one-party political systems or military dictatorships) gave considerable legitimacy to this political role.

Thus, in contrast to the period from the mid-1980s to the present, in the 1960s and 1970s, student activism was driven by the broader sociopolitical concerns prevailing in society. Enjoying a high level of social prestige and living in relatively comfortable settings at academic facilities that were adequately supported, university students were less involved in university-level crises. Their attention was directed toward national, regional, and international issues centering on governance, academic freedom, and development ideology. Student writings and speeches reflected this situation and displayed a high degree of sophistication, intellectual refinement, and rhetorical complexity, as the following piece from the University of Zambia illustrates:

> Students have done it again. They have said "no" to [affiliation with] U.N.I.P. [United National Independence Party]. They have refused to be part and parcel of vague ideologies and vague intentions. They have refused to look at the world in terms of the "animal in man" because like the forces of history they have shown and will continue to show there is no such thing as evil interest in man. . . .
>
> It is the type of society that man is born into that determines what he will be. Capitalist society, as such, dehumanizes man, it creates artificial values in him and develops in him atomistic attitudes towards others. . . . If we seem to have Marxist views of everything it is because Marxism is a tool of analysis for the oppressed people. It is scientific and a product of long bitter developments of the capitalist system of production. (UZ *Spokesman* 1977, cited in Lulat 1981, 245)

Given statements such as these, it is hardly surprising that student protests invited the wrath of the political authorities. In many circles, students were regarded as the unofficial opposition and were accused of collaborating with foreign forces to the detriment of national interests. The crown and the gown could hardly coexist peacefully in the same political town, and collisions were inevitable. The nature and scope of student activism would shift dramatically in the period after 1980.

STUDENT ACTIVISM IN THE 1980S AND BEYOND

The contemporary period of student activism, traced from the beginning of the 1980s, is unique in several respects. First, it negates the myth that politics and education are distinct; activism in this period has brought to the fore the political reality that micro-level factors, operating at the institutional level, can fuse with broader national concerns such as the quest for political pluralism and economic decline to occasion changes of tremendous proportions. Second, and perhaps more important, student politics and activism have ceased to be governed overwhelmingly by larger national and international ideological factors and are now more focused on institutional and survival issues. The downward trend in the economic fortunes of the continent has been the social genesis of these transformations.

The 1980s marked a watershed in Africa's economic decline. As measured by changes in the gross domestic product per capita, over two-thirds of the countries in sub-Saharan Africa regressed economically during the period 1965–1989. This trend has continued to the present day. Angola, Uganda, the Democratic Republic of Congo (formerly Zaire), Zambia, and Madagascar are among the most critical cases (Elu 2000, 54). So great has been the economic decline that most countries in the region have been unable to deal effectively with their poor economic performance since the mid-1980s. Angola, Burundi, Cameroon, Republic of Congo, Sierra Leone, Democratic Republic of Congo, and Zambia registered relatively high levels of decline between 1987 and 1997 (Elu 2000).

A host of internal and external factors, beginning in the early 1970s, account for the dismal economic performance of the continent, which has resulted in unprecedented levels of poverty and economic stagnation. Internally, the countries in the region have witnessed widespread government corruption, poorly conceived national development policies, gross mismanagement of national resources and development programs, recurring droughts, internal conflicts, and extensive violations of human rights (Mbaku 1994). Internal factors have been exacerbated by external ones, such as unfair terms of trade with industrialized nations, increased oil prices, the decline in official development assistance, and unmanageable foreign debts (Elu 2000, 54). Added to these has been Africa's burgeoning population. Sub-Saharan Africa has the world's fastest population growth rate, and its fertility rate is the world's highest (World Bank 1999). As the economic fortunes of the continent have dwindled, poverty levels have increased; many nations are unable to provide adequately for basic needs such as health, education, water, food, and shelter, among a host of other needs.

As a way to ameliorate these adverse economic conditions, the World Bank and the International Monetary Fund (IMF) have, since the early 1980s, recommended specific policy reforms for African countries seeking financial assistance. These policy reforms, popularly known as structural adjustment programs (SAPs), have entailed the following measures:

- Cost-sharing in the provision of social services such as education and health
- Withdrawal of educational subsidies, including students' and teachers' personal allowances
- Cost-recovery schemes, including the introduction of tuition fees and accommodation and lodging charges in higher education
- Privatizing public-sector activities (World Bank 1991, 1989, 1988)

The implementation of these measures in higher education institutions has been a major cause of the new wave of student protests and unrest. Disaffection with cost-recovery schemes such as the introduction of fees and student loans has caused campus riots in Kenya and Zambia. The elimination of student personal allowances has led to campus closures in Kenya, Sierra Leone, Ivory Coast, and Senegal. Reforms directed at eliminating redundancy have been met with riots in Madagascar; university examination reforms in Mali have yielded similar protests. The most frequent source of protest has been the cost of privatized accommodation and lodgings. Universities in Ivory Coast, Kenya, and Nigeria, among others, have been rocked by violent student protest over the costs of food and accommodation (Kamotho 2000; Wekesa 2000; Bako 1994; Nkinyangi 1991).

Coupled with these tight fiscal and monetary conditions have been the increased enrollments that have characterized most universities in the region. The 1990s was marked by a dramatic increase in the number of students enrolled in higher education institutions. According to the World Bank (1994, 2), enrollment has been increasing at an average of 6.2 percent per year in the low-income countries and at 7.3 percent in the upper-middle-income countries. The experience of Kenya represents a typical case; enrollments in public universities exploded from 8,900 in 1985–1986 to more than 40,000 in 1997 (Republic of Kenya 1997, 221). Table 11.1 gives an indication of the enrollment trends of a number of sub-Saharan institutions between 1980 and 1990. Exceptional growth was observable in the Central African Republic, Togo, Benin, Burkina Faso, Niger, Cameroon, and Madagascar, all of which realized a 50 percent growth in enrollment or greater.

Rapid expansion in enrollment has been beneficial in that it has increased opportunities for higher education for groups that would otherwise not have had such access. Nevertheless, growth under worsening economic conditions, coupled with austerity measures, has led to a decline in per-pupil expenditures. The average expenditure in 1980 was $6,300; this figure had declined to $1,500 by 1990 (World Bank 1994, 2). Institutions operate under very adverse conditions; essential teaching and learning resources such as classrooms, equipment, and libraries are not only inadequate but also outdated. The academic staff have not fared well either. Morale has hit an all-time low, while brain drain has taken its toll on African institutions. Consequently, there has been a major decline in research output and the number of academic programs offered. The impact of these conditions has led to a major discrepancy between the institutional organization, planning, evaluation, and supervision that is required to fulfill the institutional missions and the challenges posed by increased enrollment (World Bank 1994; Assié-Lumumba 1993, 12–14). Declining conditions in universities have spurred discontent about student conditions, thereby creating a volatile environment:

Students in Africa are everywhere in ferment. Protests, demonstrations and riots have resulted in injuries, lockouts, even deaths. The virus of discontent has spread to Zaire, Congo, Cameroon, Nigeria, Benin, Senegal, Sudan and Zimbabwe. Underlying the upsurge of protests is not simply high spirits and political posturing but a fundamental revolt against teaching, poor conditions, unpaid scholarships, rising prices, lack of concern by those in charge and general deterioration of educational conditions. (Baffour 1989, 9)

Poor institutional governance and leadership have also contributed to student disaffection with the universities. The appointment of key university managers in sub-Saharan national universities has usually been the prerogative of the government. These appointments have often been based not on the appointees' academic excellence or administrative competence but on their personal loyalty to the appointing authority (Mwiria 1992, 5). Conscious that their continued stay in office depends on the goodwill of the government, these administrators tend to be more accountable to the state than to students and staff. In an attempt to fulfill the expectations of the government, these senior administrators have resorted to administrative high-handedness and authoritarianism. The prevailing administrative organization in many African universities, as a result, tends to be highly centralized, hierarchical, and rigid. Students have minimal or no say in decision making. In universities in Malawi, Nairobi (Kenya), and Zambia, student associations have been proscribed at one time or another (Ajayi, Lameck, and Johnson, 1996, 177–179; Mwiria 1992, 47; and Assié-Lumumba 1993). Students have also complained of victimization of student leaders by university administrations whenever they speak out. Given such limited scope for participation in university governance, the preferred way students have chosen to make themselves heard is to go on strike.

Poor institutional leadership has been exacerbated by heightened government infringement on academic freedom. Governments in sub-Saharan Africa have engaged in acts that have compromised the academic freedom of both academic staff and students. Governments have not taken constructive criticism of their policies kindly and have instead resorted to acts inimical to freedom of inquiry, such as banning public lectures on campus, proscribing staff and student associations, denying scholar-

Table 11.1. University Enrollment in Selected African Countries, 1980–1990

Country	1980	1987–1990	Growth in %
Benin[3]	4,000	8,883	122
Burundi[2]	1,900	2,762	45
Burkina Faso[3]	1,600	4,760	198
Cameroon[4]	11,500	34,000	196
Central Africa Republic[2]	1,700	2,600	53
Chad[1]	2,000	2,048	2
Gabon[2]	2,000	2,741	37
Madagascar[4]	22,000	37,181	69
Niger[3]	1,400	3,317	137
Rwanda[2]	1,200	1,650	38
Togo[2]	4,800	7,348	53

Note: 1 = small no-growth system; 2 = small but expanding system; 3 = small but rapid-growth system; 4 = large multi-institution system.
Source: Saint 1992, 69.

ships to vocal students, expelling student leaders, and using other forms of coercion (*Daily Nation* 2000; Nduko 2000; and Mwiria 1994). This sustained attack on academic freedom has accounted for a great deal of the tension between students and the government now prevailing in many countries in the region and has culminated in student riots. To a considerable degree, state infringement on academic freedom has mirrored the situation obtaining in the wider society. Until recently, many African governments allowed for no opposition, controlled the mass media, and had no mechanisms for checks and balances.

THE IMPACT OF THE CURRENT STUDENT PROTESTS

The sheer enormity and frequency of contemporary student protests has been the most significant defining feature in student activism since the mid-1980s. These protests have had immense political significance since activist students have forged alliances with other social groups that have been engaged in sociopolitical protests. In Ivory Coast, for instance, students in 1990 joined advocates of democracy and sections of the military to demand increased freedom of expression and a multiparty system of government at the same time as they protested the cost of food and lodging. Students also demanded the official recognition of the newly launched National Organization of Pupils and Students (Barrin 1990).

Nigeria is another country in which resistance to SAPs has been more organized and defiant and has had considerable political consequences. Defiance against World Bank and IMF conditions imposed on the country's higher education system began in earnest in 1986 and has escalated into a national crisis every year since. In 1988, students played the leading role in protests organized by workers and civil servants against the price of fuel, the cutting back of fringe benefits for civil servants, and the dissolution of the Nigerian Labor Congress. In 1989, dozens of students were killed while demonstrating against SAPs, and in the following year, the military regime killed or arrested hundreds of students protesting the $120 million World Bank Education Sector Loan to rationalize Nigerian universities. This was followed by a year-long closure of the country's universities (Caffentzis 2000, 16; Jega 1994; Bako 1994, 165–167). Of the loan conditions, the National Association of Nigerian Students (NANS) observed:

> Our struggle against the deadly piece of credit began by exposing its unpatriotic intentions and its deadly consequences. The conditionalities (cleverly disguised as "eligibility criteria") include a freeze on recruitment of all categories of staff, mandatory staff retrenchment, introduction of tuition fees, phasing out of courses [and] of remedial and pre-degree programs, commercialization of education, procurement of 60 percent of equipment from manufacturers approved by the "World" Bank, scrutinization of all curricula by the "World" Bank and mandatory importation of expatriate staff, whose salaries were to be heavily topped. (*Solidarity* 1990, cited in Bako 1994, 166–167)

Students viewed the SAPs as representing a total transfer of control (financial, managerial, and curricular) of Nigerian higher education to external and foreign agencies.

Students' expansion of mobilization around institutional welfare issues to protest against wider sociopolitical and economic concerns has also been recorded elsewhere in the continent. In Zimbabwe, student protests at the University of Zimbabwe over tuition fees in 1990 were accompanied by demonstrations against corruption in the government and its revolutionary pretenses (Cheater 1991). In Sudan, the struggle against SAP conditions on campus has merged with the struggle against the gradual Islamicization of education and the deteriorating state of the economy. Thus, violent student protests accompanied the 500 percent increase in the cost of sugar in 1988 and the shortage of essential commodities such as bread, sugar, and other staples (Al-Zubeir 1995).

While student collaboration with workers and pro-democracy activists is an understandable logical outcome of struggles against such harsh economic realities, their joining forces with the military forces against civilian regimes is worrisome; it negates the students' commitment to democratic governance and participatory democracy. In Zaire, in 1989, military forces sent to quell rioting university students ignored their orders and instead joined students in solidarity and demanded improved terms and conditions of service. Together, they attacked the Zairean TV station and looted shops belonging to Lebanese and West Africans. Similarly, students have supported attempted military takeovers of the government in Kenya (1982) and Benin (1989), played key roles in military coups in Sudan (1985 and 1989), and participated in Nigeria's six coups between 1966 and 1985 (Baffour 1989).

Clearly, the conditions prevailing on state campuses have given rise to circumstances in which military entry into politics has received broad-based student support rather than opposition. Even though such alliances portend very worrisome potential scenarios, they appear to be in line with the historical roles that African university students have come to play as future leaders and as guardians of the society against political oppression and manipulation by the ruling political class. The alliances also highlight the political vacuum in systems in which opposition parties have largely been outlawed; the military, organized groups of students, and trade unions are able to function as the unofficial opposition in such systems.

A strong sense of frustration and urgency explains the heightened level of violence that has characterized student protest in the SAP era. Violent and destructive demonstrations now distinguish student protests in most African nations. This violence has been accompanied by wanton destruction of property, numerous injuries, and, at times, loss of life. These consequences have not been limited to students alone but also have affected innocent members of the public. Such levels of violence in student protest are unprecedented and have become a source of concern to political authorities on the continent. In October 2000, Kenyatta University students in Kenya went on strike to protest high Internet charges on campus. In the course of the protests, the students caused extensive damage to university property and public vehicles on a nearby highway as they battled the police (*Daily Nation* 2000). Within the same month, students at the sister Egerton University set an administration building on fire as they protested against the poor living and academic conditions on campus (*Daily Nation* 2000). Earlier, in November

1997, three Kenyatta University students were killed as students and police engaged in a fierce battle outside the university precincts while students were on their way to the city center to protest against the declining conditions on campus.

At the University of Zambia's Lusaka campus, violent student protest led to the closure of the university in May 1986. During this incident, university offices were reportedly petrol-bombed by students. Among the demands of the protest were the unconditional release of a jailed union leader and improvement in food quality. Two years earlier, in 1984, students had fought pitched battles with the police following the requirement that they obtain a meal card to eat in the university cafeterias. The move was designed to eliminate the practice among students of bringing off-campus friends to eat free of charge at the cafeterias. In the course of the protests, civilians were injured when the military police prevented students from marching to the official residence of President Kenneth Kaunda to air their grievances (Mwiria 1992, 11–12).

The upshot of these conflicts between students and the state has been the gradual militarization of Africa's universities. Police intervention in university affairs has become a matter of fact in many institutions. The security arms of most universities are now managed by national police forces, which specialize more in gathering information about political aspects of student protest than in providing a safe environment for academic pursuits. Police informers have also found their way into classrooms and halls of residence. Since the mid-1980s, Kenya's public universities have been infiltrated by an elaborate network of police informers whose work is to monitor and report on student activities (Munene 1997). Some countries have seen more brutal police intimidation. Nigeria's repression of students has included the use of "secret cults," while Cameroon has used "self-defense groups" to intimidate student activists. These gangs of heavily armed students enjoy the protection of campus police as they break up student meetings, harass student leaders, and terrorize the general student population (Federici 2000, 100). Under these conditions, it is little wonder that state universities have continued to be the last vestiges of dictatorship even as African societies have experienced some relative measure of democratic reform through the adoption of multiparty political systems.

Overall, student protest has exacerbated the decline in educational quality. A major effect of these protests has been frequent university closures, which have ranged from a few weeks to more than a year. In 1986, the University of Madagascar was closed for six months after student riots. The University of Nairobi was closed for thirteen months in 1982 after students supported an attempted military coup. Between 1970 and 1988, the university was closed seventeen times for varied periods because of student demonstrations (Nkinyangi 1991). These closures have disrupted academic programs and have had a disastrous effect on the morale of academic staff. Furthermore, closures have been accompanied by the expulsion of student leaders (see *Daily Nation* 2000). These expelled leaders are usually labeled as troublemakers and are denied opportunities for further education and employment in their countries. Besides being a waste of valuable talent, it produces a crop of frustrated and disgruntled former student leaders in the wider society.

Student protests have also had a number of negative ramifications internal to institutional operations. They have led to the displacement of institutional goals. During conflicts, both administrators and students expend enormous time, energy, and resources first to outmaneuver each other and later to resolve their conflicts instead of working together toward the realization of the university's institutional mission. In addition, the protests have increased the costs of running the institutions. Damages resulting from student riots, rescheduling of the academic calendar, and payment of salaries to idle staff during university closures have raised the costs of operating institutions affected by student riots. Furthermore, such riots have eroded the credibility of the institutions in the eyes of potential donors, further curtailing the potential flow of the much-needed financial support.

Disruption of academic programs and the attendant repercussions offer a compelling case that academic management is in crisis. The long and short unscheduled university closures following riots interfere with academic programming and planning, which has spillover effects in secondary schools. In Kenya, for instance, because of the loss of one academic year in public universities due to student riots, graduates from high school had to wait for one year before they could gain admission to the institutions. Omari (1991, 3) rightly notes that the protests have ultimately led to "deprofessionalization of academia; loss of public esteem and respect for teaching staff; unnecessary changes in staffing of higher education; dislocations in planning for human resource development and deployment; loss of funding, consultancies, and intellectual contacts."

CORPORATIST INTERESTS OR POLITICAL CONSCIOUSNESS?

Scholars have debated the motivation underlying the widespread student protests that have occurred since the mid-1980s. Scholars at the World Bank (see, for instance, Saint 1992) have contended that student protestors represent an elite and privileged class that is trying to safeguard its favored status. University students, they claim, have enjoyed comfort and material status that are not available to the rest of the population. They have enjoyed free accommodation, lodging, and tuition, in addition to job guarantees at the conclusion of their studies. Generally, these benefits have not been made available to students in other colleges. Student protest over institution-specific issues such as food, accommodation, and learning facilities have given credence to this view.

Furthermore, the protests have occurred at a time when the democratization of access to higher education has been taking place. This process has enabled a greater number of students to enroll in higher education, thereby distributing elite privileges to a wider segment of the population. The combination of the increase in the number of university graduates and the declining economic performance of the continent has resulted in high levels of graduate unemployment and underemployment. These factors have been crucial in fueling student discontent in the universities. The discontent is an indication of the failure of universities to serve as vehicles for upward social mobility for students.

Other scholars have rejected this elite-corporatist thesis as the basis of student protests. In its stead, they have advanced the view that the students' behavior is premised on the desire for self-determination (see, for instance, Federici 2000, 101–102). The protest by the students, according to this group of scholars, is a challenge to the control of their country's most important institutions—universities—by external forces. Students contend that the control of the continent's universities and the determination of what is to be taught and how students should be treated should be a prerogative of the national governments, not international agencies, and that World Bank and IMF conditionalities violate these cardinal principles of self-determination in the development of national higher education. This view has been enhanced by the fact that students have struggled against cost-sharing schemes (as demanded in the SAPs) that mitigate against the democratization of access to public higher education. In addition, not all students have elite and corporatist leanings; on the contrary, many students hail from poor and disadvantaged backgrounds and risk going to jail or being killed in the course of protesting. Furthermore, when students collaborate with trade unions, opposition political parties, and other stakeholders in the struggle for social justice, they are protesting the loss of sovereignty in economic decision making at the national level. This orientation indicates a rising tide of political consciousness based on a critical examination of the prevailing conditions at the institutional level. Given these factors, the scholars propounding the self-determination thesis argue that it is untenable to postulate that students are driven only by elite and corporatist interests in their protests.

In the final analysis, both views are highly useful in understanding the motivations underlying student protests. Rather than view them as contradictory and mutually exclusive, it is more appropriate to regard them as complementary explanations. Students may react violently to safeguard their status and privileges as clients in the highest institutions of learning in their country and may also desire to be at par with their counterparts in the rest of the world. This is not only to be expected but is also quite rational. The significance of student protests in terms of class is reflected in the reaction of African governments to student grievances over food. Student protests over food underscore more serious problems, since "if students, an elite group, are improperly fed . . . it is a sign of food shortages throughout the country" (Rhoda 1986, 124).

On the other hand, student protests over institutional conditions and their collaboration with other social forces in society are clear testimony of the nexus between group interests and the desire for national sovereignty and self-determination in the context of globalization. The rising level of political awareness among students and their willingness to take risks in the quest for wider sociopolitical change exceed the goals of material comfort desired by an incipient elite class. The struggle for such large-scale change embodies a broader vision of a better life for a wider segment of society.

PROSPECTS OF STUDENT ACTIVISM IN AFRICA

The dominant role of student activism in the political landscape of African higher education in the last three decades cannot be gainsaid. The impact of the movement has extended far beyond the confines of the campuses. As the continent enters into the new millennium in the context of immense sociopolitical and economic transformations, it is pertinent to question whether the pace of student activism will continue to be sustainable in the foreseeable future. If events in the United States, Europe, Latin America, and Southeast Asia are anything to go by, then it is highly doubtful that the protest will grow in scale and scope or spawn dramatic sociopolitical changes in the coming years. A number of factors underlie this prognosis; the first is the macro-political context, while the second is the higher education context.

Central to the macro-political factors is the recent redemocratization of most national political systems on the continent since the early 1990s. Redemocratization refers to the reintroduction of multiparty political systems in countries in which a one-party system or a military regime was in power. The new political situation has created conditions that limit the scope and impact of student activism. No longer is the political landscape on the continent a vacuum devoid of opposition forces in the form of political parties and active civil societies. These oppositional forces have gradually replaced university students as the alternative voice for those that have hitherto been subjugated by the one-party state. In any case, these alternative groups are more sophisticated and have a higher level of legitimacy for active involvement in politics than university students could claim to muster. In countries such as Malawi, Nigeria, Zaire, and Zambia, opposition parties have replaced the authoritarian oligarchies that had dominated the political scene. Thus, it is not far-fetched to postulate that the emerging political reality has, to a considerable measure, accounted for the waning sociopolitical consequences of student activism, a situation likely to be more pointedly vivid in the near future.

The end of the Cold War has also hastened the stemming of the tide of student activism. The demise of the Soviet Union as a world superpower robbed students of an important reference point in their ideological war with capitalist-oriented nations. The collapse of the Soviet Union has been seen as a triumph of capitalism; most former Soviet republics and their allies in Eastern Europe now embrace capitalism and democracy as models of state economic organization and governance. The use of Marxist ideological doctrines had formerly created a powerful psychological atmosphere for student cohesion when they confronted an exploitive state. Without the ideological stimuli that the Soviet Union provided to the student movement, it is unlikely that left-wing student leaders will have the moral leverage or clout to spearhead protests using a Marxist frame of reference. Devoid of such a powerful ideological base and an ideologically committed leadership, student protests will likely be less vibrant in the future than they have been in the past.

Activism has a greater impact when students operate as a cohesive group. Recent transformations in higher education changed the homogeneous nature of student bodies. The first form of transformation has been the tremendous growth in student enrollments since the late 1980s. More and more students have gained admission into an increasing number of higher education institutions. This system-wide growth has been accompa-

Table 11.2. Enrollment Percentages in Various Disciplines in Selected African Countries, 1995–1996

Country	Total Enrollment	Education	Humanities	Social Sciences	Natural Sciences	Medical Sciences	Other
Algeria	267,142	0.7	13.4	25.0	49.8	10.0	1.1
Ethiopia	42,226	24.5	2.7	31.5	35.5	5.8	NA
Guinea	8,151	3.6	17.4	21.7	41.9	14.4	1.0
Mozambique	7,143	18.3	7.9	21.3	46.1	6.4	NA
Namibia	11,344	25.9	12.1	13.8	4.4	19.1	24.7
Nigeria	207,982	14.9	10.9	22.4	41.2	10.6	NA
Tanzania	12,776	14.3	NA	41.4	39.3	3.2	1.7
Zimbabwe	46,673	47.4	3.9	22.1	23.4	2.4	0.7

NA = Data not available.

Source: UNESCO 1999, 2:470.

nied by divisive diversification. The increased admission of nonelite students, such as part-time students, has meant that a large number of students operate outside the university for the greater part of their studies. This undermines the students' sense of being part of a unified community.

System growth and divisive diversification have been evident in the disciplinary fields as well as in institutional types. Traditionally, radical students have emanated from law, the social sciences (such as sociology and political science), and the humanities (such as literature, history, and philosophy), but with recent institutional growth and diversification, these disciplines have been eclipsed by the rapid enrollment in business-related and science and technology–related fields. Table 11.2 presents data on student enrollment in various disciplines in selected African countries in the 1995–1996 academic year. The data show that the natural and medical sciences have experienced increased enrollment when compared to education, the humanities, and the social sciences.

Closely related to this disciplinary diversification is institutional proliferation. In the last decade, Africa has become host to a wide variety of higher education institutions, both public and private. The era of countries being dominated by a single prestigious national university seems to have come to a close. The proliferation of institutions has made student unity harder to realize, since students in different institutions have dissimilar backgrounds, socialization, goals, and living conditions.

Another powerful institutional transformation affecting student activism has been privatization. Most African countries now have private universities and colleges, even though enrollment in such institutions may be small at the moment. The number of private institutions, however, is on the increase. A characteristic feature of these private institutions is the absence of student activism. Generally students in the private sector originate from the upper socioeconomic stratum in society. Furthermore, these institutions specialize in business-related and theological disciplines, which historically have had fewer linkages to radical activism. The combination of institutional selection and student self-selection tends to ensure that activism remains muted in private institutions. Where public and private institutions exist, it has been difficult for students to achieve

commonality over issues. A divided student body has less impact on the wider sociopolitical front. This will likely become more evident in the future, as privatization cuts across all aspects of higher education in both private and public institutions.

CONCLUSION

Student activism has been an important feature in African higher education. Student protest against sociopolitical and economic injustices began during the colonial period in the 1920s. Post-independence activism can be delineated in two sections. As we have seen, the period after independence in the 1960s to the late 1970s was characterized by student protest informed by deep ideological convictions that, at times, posed a direct challenge to the legitimacy of the state, especially in international relations. Activism in this period generally eschewed institutional issues, since students were assured of relative comfort while on campus.

The beginning of the 1980s to the present day, a period dominated by SAPs in African economies, represents the second phase of activism. Protests have often been driven by the deteriorating living and academic conditions in universities as a result of reduced funding following the implementation of SAPs. The mobilization of students around institution-based welfare issues has had implications beyond the confines of the campuses. In a radical challenge to the state, students have on many occasions collaborated with political parties, unions, religious organizations, and even the military in an attempt to effect political changes such as multiparty democracies or military coups.

The future sociopolitical potency of student activism remains in question. Wide-ranging institutional and social transformations may diminish the impact of such protests. The redemocratization of most national political systems has meant that students are not the only opposition force articulating issues on behalf of the masses. Opposition parties that are now functional in many states are often more articulate than students. Finally, universities have experienced growth, diversification, and privatization, all of which have made it more difficult to forge unity among students.

REFERENCES

Africa Diary. 1962. 11, no. 6, February 3–9.

Ajayi, J. F., K. H. G. Lameck, and G. A. Johnson. 1996. *The African Experience with Higher Education.* Athens, Ohio: Ohio University Press.

Altbach, P. G. 1981. "Student Activism in the 1970s and 1980s." In Philip Altbach, ed., *Student Politics: Perspectives for the Eighties,* 1–14. Metuchen, N.J.: Scarecrow Press.

———. 1989. "Perspectives on Student Political Activism." In Philip Altbach, ed., *Student Political Activism: An International Reference Handbook,* 247–260. New York: Greenwood Press.

———. 1991. "Students' Political Activism." In Philip Altbach, ed., *International Higher Education: An Encyclopedia,* 247–260. New York: Garland Publishing.

Al-Zubeir, A. 1995. "Sudan." In J. Daniel, N. Hartley, Y. Lador, M. Nowak, and F. deVlarning, eds., *Academic Freedom 3: Education and Human Rights.* London: Zed Books and World University Service.

Assié-Lumumba, N. T. 1993. *Higher Education in Francophone Africa: Assessment of the Potential of the Traditional Universities and Alternatives for Development.* Washington, D.C.: World Bank.

Ayu, I. 1986. *Essays in Popular Struggle.* Oguta, Nigeria: ZIM Publishers.

Baffour, A. 1989. "Students in Ferment." *New African* (London), May: 9–12.

Bako, S. 1994. "Education and Adjustment in Nigeria: Conditionality and Resistance." In Mamadou Diouf and Mahmood Mamdani, eds., *Academic Freedom in Africa,* 150–191. Dakar: CODESRIA Book Series.

Bathily, A., M. Diouf, and M. Mbodj. 1994. "The Senegalese Student Movement from Its Inception to 1989." In Mahmood Mamdani and Ernest Wamba Dia Wamba, eds., *African Studies in Social Movement and Democracy,* 127–168. Dakar: CODESRIA Book Series.

Barrin, J. 1990. "Marxism Is Losing Its Way on the African Continent." *The Manchester Weekly Guardian,* February 1–6, 16.

Burawoy, M. 1976. "Consciousness and Contradiction: A Study of Student Protest in Zambia." *British Journal of Sociology* 27, no. 1: 78–97.

Caffentzis, G. 2000. "The World Bank and Education in Africa." In Silvia Federici, George Caffentzis, and Ousseina Alidou, eds., *A Thousand Flowers: Social Struggles against Structural Adjustment in African Universities,* 3–23. Trenton, N.J.: Africa World Press.

Cefkin, L. 1975. "Rhodesian University Students in National Politics." In Judith Hanna and William Hanna, eds., *University Students and African Politics.* New York: Holmes and Meier Publishers.

Cheater, A. 1991. "The University of Zimbabwe: University, National University, State University or Party University?" *African Affairs* 90: 189–205.

Daily Nation. 2000. "How to End Unrest at State Universities." *Daily Nation,* November 27, 4.

———. 2001. "Varsity Suspends 11 More Students." *Daily Nation,* January 23, 4.

Elu, J. 2000. "Human Development in Sub-Saharan Africa: Analysis and Prospects for the Future." *Journal of Third World Studies* 17, no. 2 (Fall): 53–71.

Federici, S. 2000. "The New African Student Movement." In Silvia Federici, George Caffentzis, and Ousseina Alidou, eds., *A Thousand Flowers: Social Struggles against Structural Adjustment in African Universities,* 87–112. Trenton, N.J.: Africa World Press.

Federici, S., and G. Caffentzis. 2000. "Chronology of African University Students' Struggles." In Silvia Federici, George Caffentzis, and Ousseina Alidou, eds., *A Thousand Flowers: Social Struggles against Structural Adjustment in African Universities,* 115–150. Trenton, N.J.: Africa World Press.

Gellar, S. 1982. *Senegal: An African Nation between Islam and the West.* Boulder, Colo.: Westview Press.

Grey, R. 1979. "Education and Political Socialization." In Victor Uchendu, ed., *Education and Politics in Tropical Africa,* 152–171. New York: Conch Magazine.

The Guardian. 1990. Manchester, February 27.

Hanna, J., and W. Hanna. 1975. *University Students and African Politics.* New York: Holmes and Meier Publishers.

Jega, A. 1994. "Nigerian Academics under Military Rule." University of Stockholm Research Report, no. 3, Department of Political Science.

Kamotho, K. 2000. "Revealed: Rot behind Varsity Unrests." *East African Standard,* November 5, 381.

Legum, C. 1972. "The Year of the Students: A Survey of the African University Scene." In Colin Legum, ed., *Africa Contemporary Record,* A3–A30. London: Rex Collins.

Lulat, Y. G.-M. 1981. "Determinants of Third World Student Political Activism in the Seventies: The Case of Zambia." In Philip Altbach, ed., *Student Politics: Perspectives for the Eighties,* 234–266. Metuchen, N.J.: Scarecrow Press.

Mbaku, J. M. 1994. "Africa After More Than Thirty Years of Independence: Still Poor and Deprived." *Journal of Third World Studies* 11, no. 2 (Fall): 13–58.

Mondlane, E. 1983. *The Struggle for Mozambique.* London: Zed Books.

Munene, I. 1997. "Origins and Perceptions of Universities, Students and Students' Organizations of Kenyatta University Student Leaders." In Akim Okuni and Juliet Tembe, eds., *Capacity Building in Educational Research in East Africa: Empirical Insights into Qualitative Research Methodology,* 279–298. Bonn: Deutsche Stiftung für Internationale Entwicklung.

Mwiria, K. 1992. *University Governance: Problems and Prospects in Anglophone Africa.* Washington, D.C.: World Bank.

———. 1994. "Democratizing Kenya's Public Universities." *Basic Education Forum* 4 (January): 45–50.

Nduko, J. 2000. "Students' Rights and Academic Freedom in Kenya's Public Universities." In Silvia Federici, George Caffentzis, and Ousseina Alidou, eds., *A Thousand Flowers: Social Struggles against Structural Adjustment in African Universities,* 207–214. Trenton, N.J.: Africa World Press.

Nkinyangi, J. 1991. "Students Protests in Sub-Saharan Africa." *Higher Education* 22, no. 2 (September): 157–173.

Omari, I. M. 1991. *Student Unrest and Qualitative Improvements of Higher Education in Developing Countries: Notes for Discussion.* Washington, D.C: The World Bank.

Republic of Kenya. 1997. *Economic Survey 1997.* Nairobi: Government Printer.

Rhoda, H. 1986. *Human Rights in Commonwealth Africa.* Totowa, N.J.: Rowman and Littlefield.

Rothchild, D. 1971. "The Beginning of Student Unrest in Zambia." *Transition* 8 (December): 66–74.

Saint, W. 1992. *Universities in Africa: Strategies for Stabilization and Revitalization.* Washington, D.C.: World Bank.

Segal, R. 1962. *African Profiles.* Harmondsworth (Middlesex): Penguin Books.

UNESCO. 1999. *Statistical Yearbook.* New York: UNESCO Publishing.

Wagaw, T. 1984. *The Burden and Glory of Being Schooled: An Ethiopian Dilemma.* Proceedings of the Seventh International Conference of Ethiopian Studies, Institute of Ethiopian Studies, University of Addis Ababa.

———. 1990. *The Development of Higher Education and Social Change:*

25

An Ethiopian Experience. East Lansing: Michigan State University Press.

Wekesa, B. 2000. "Student Activism through the Years." *East African Standard,* November, 5, 381.

World Bank. 1988. *Education in Sub-Saharan Africa: Policies for Adjustment, Revitalization and Expansion.* Washington, D.C.: World Bank.

——. 1989. *Sub-Saharan Africa: From Crisis to Sustainable Growth.* Washington, D.C.: World Bank.

——. 1991. *Education and Adjustment: A Review of Literature.* Washington, D.C.: World Bank.

——. 1994. *Higher Education: The Lessons of Experience.* Washington, D.C.: World Bank.

——. 1999. *World Development Report, 1998/99.* New York: Oxford University Press.

Yeebo, Z. 1991. *Ghana: The Struggle for Popular Power. Rawlings: Saviour or Demagogue.* London: Beacon Books.

Zolberg, A. 1975. "Political Generations in Conflict: The Ivory Coast Case." In Judith Hanna and William Hanna, eds., *University Students and African Politics.* New York: Holmes and Meier.

12

Scientific Communication and Research in African Universities
Challenges and Opportunities in the Twenty-First Century

Damtew Teferra

INTRODUCTION

Scientific communication is the intellectual lifeline of scientists. It is a highway upon which knowledge, paradigms, and thoughts are formulated, shared, and disseminated. A sound scientific communication infrastructure ensures scientists regular and reliable access to current knowledge and information generated both internationally and locally. The presence of such a reliable infrastructure facilitates scientific research and encourages scientists to advance their quest for knowledge and remain on the frontiers of their disciplines.

The world is increasingly driven by information and knowledge made possible by breakthroughs in science and technology (S&T). As a result, the crucial role of S&T in national socioeconomic development has received increasing recognition and emphasis in those countries where most of these innovations were conceived. The level and extent of scientific and technological discovery have become an index upon which the social, economic, and political status of a particular country is gauged.

The West continues to dominate in the production, organization, packaging, and dissemination of most of the world's knowledge. As a consequence, it unilaterally controls and determines the nature, business, and rules of the game. The Third World, and Africa in particular, relies heavily on this knowledge: Africa produces only 0.3 percent of the world's "mainstream" knowledge.

In Africa, universities predominate in the production of mainstream science (Davis 1983). By and large, African universities constitute the most important knowledge capital of their nations. They are the national scholarly nerve centers where a critical mass of highly trained and educated individuals pursue their intellectual duties; they provide a hub for current scholarly, technical, and material resources. African universities are major movers and shakers when it comes to determining the intellectual, scientific, and scholarly direction and developmental agenda of their respective countries.

African universities and research centers—as major producers, consumers, and disseminators of scientific knowledge and information on the continent—are the foci where challenges as well as opportunities play themselves out. As a consequence, an extensive discussion of universities and their scientific communities is necessary to establish a better understanding of the state of scientific communication on the continent.

Because scientific research relies on access to and the flow of information, data, and knowledge, developing a research base on the scope of scientific communication is an important factor in the promotion of that research. As the capacity to generate knowledge in Africa is limited, it is crucial to have a good understanding of the underlying elements that either constrain or promote its development.

The avenues of scientific communication are expanding at a remarkable pace. The Internet, e-mail, online databases, and online journals are some of the new developments that are changing the scope of research development, research communication, and knowledge production and dissemination. These developments are likely to have a remarkable impact on countries of marginal scientific significance, among which many African nations find themselves.

The status of scientific communication in a nation relies predominantly on the maturity of scientific research in that country. As a consequence, discussions on the state of scientific communication naturally gravitate toward a close examination of the scope of scientific research. Hence, what follows is a brief examination of the scope of scientific research in Africa.

Various sources have been utilized in the course of preparing this chapter. Research reports, review papers, formal and informal interviews, and online resources were consulted. Moreover, this chapter relies heavily on nearly 100 open-ended survey responses that were gathered from universities in eight African countries.

THE SCOPE OF SCIENTIFIC ENDEAVORS IN AFRICAN UNIVERSITIES

In many sub-Saharan African countries, universities are among the most important scientific institutions. Frequently, they account for a significant proportion of national research expenditures, a relatively large share of the scientists engaged in research and development activities, and the bulk of the national production of influential scientific research (Eisemon and Davis 1993). An array of factors have shaped the development of scientific research in Africa that range from past history to current political and economic realities.

Magnitude of the African Scientific Community

Opportunities to develop a long-term commitment to an area of research with concomitant productivity appear to be related to the availability of a critical mass of colleagues in the same geographical region (Crane 1972). Africa has never had more than a miniscule fraction of this critical mass of scientists.

To begin with, there were very few African graduates at the time of the independence movements that began four decades ago. The continent had only six universities at the time of independence, and these enrolled only a handful of students (Yesufu 1973). Zaire, for example, reached independence without a single national engineer, lawyer, or doctor. Zambia had only 100 university graduates. The University of East Africa, serving Kenya, Tanzania, and Uganda, had a total of ninety-nine graduates in 1961 (World Bank 1991).

Starting nearly from scratch in the 1960s, African universities experienced impressive academic growth, though many observers feel that results remain unsatisfactory, that universities only partly fulfill development needs, and do not cope with the anguish that African states feel about their growing marginalization in the world's economic scene (Gaillard and Waast 1993). Even in this academic expansion, most university graduates come from the humanities and social science disciplines and not from science and science-based disciplines. The target set by African universities in 1961 to raise the total enrollment in the sciences to 60 percent still remains to be met in many countries in 2001. Universities are not producing enough scientific and technological manpower, one factor which is basic to the lack of progress in research and in the general utilization of S&T in development (Makhubu 1990).

In countries that have small scientific communities, the critical mass of the community is too small to permit the development of strong and viable local networks of professional communication in many scientific specialties. Working without the benefit of peers in one's own or related specialties is typical of members of small or isolated scientific communities (Eisemon and Davis 1989). The absence of a cohort of scientific communities impinges on the development of scientific culture in terms of research and communication. For instance, the challenges of maintaining unbiased, locally produced journals are exacer-

bated by this phenomenon. Stolte-Heiskanen (1986), who suggested the careful selection of experts to tackle personal and paradigmatic biases—by increasing the number of referees, for example—holds these improvements as considerably more difficult to implement in the relatively small and closed scientific communities on the periphery, such as those in Africa.

A scientific community that has a small critical mass often tends to have limited scientific interactions. When such a scientific community is a component of a country that is economically poor, politically unstable, and infrastructurally precarious, these engagements become even more constrained and undermined. Most of the African scientific community finds itself in this state.

In terms of quality, not only high school graduates—who have very little experimental scientific experience, if any at all—but also those who graduate with science degrees have limited practical knowledge and expertise. As secondary and postsecondary enrollments have increased dramatically and the financial state and commitment of governments have declined, the quality of academic institutions has suffered. Eisemon and Davis (1991) observe that many university laboratories in Africa cannot support undergraduate science instruction, much less provide what is needed for high-quality postgraduate training and staff research. In fields such as the natural, biological, agricultural, and engineering sciences, observers note that many basic requirements of postgraduate studies are almost entirely lacking.

In brief, the scientific community in Africa is small and precarious. Scholarly societies are very few in number, weak, or nonexistent in many disciplines. Research activities in Africa are limited, and the amount of knowledge that is considered mainstream is tiny. Locally based conferences, symposia, and other large-scale scholarly gatherings are limited in number and scope and are often inconsequential and insignificant.

"Brain Drain" and "Brain Hemorrhage"

Since independence, Africa has faced a very tumultuous time that has been replete with man-made and natural disasters. Civil unrest, economic depression, drought, famine, and disease prevented the emergence of a conducive environment for development in all walks of life. In fact, the primordial scholarly environment that emerged in the 1960s and the effort to establish a high-powered scholarly and civic infrastructure that had gathered some momentum lost its steam in the chaotic decades that followed. Out of the small, but vibrant, community of scholars that Africa managed to produce, many have gone overseas, forced by conditions at home to seek a better working and living environment elsewhere. This has resulted in a massive brain drain, while those who remained behind watched themselves become academically stagnated and incapacitated.

In 1998, nearly 120 doctors were estimated to have emigrated from Ghana; between 600 and 700 Ghanaian physicians are practicing in the United States alone. This represents roughly 50 percent of the total population of doctors in Ghana. It is estimated that about 10,000 Nigerian academics are now employed in the United States and that more than 1,000 professionals left Zimbabwe in 1997. Between 1980 and 1991, only

39 percent of Ethiopian students returned from studies abroad out of the 22,700 who left (Sethi 2000).

It is fair to project that the gravity of brain drain a country suffers is by and large inversely proportional to the socio-economic and sociopolitical health of that country. As a matter of fact, Africa seems to continue to generate an intense force that further exacerbates the gravity of the drainage (Teferra 2000).

The "universality" of S&T not only facilitated the exodus of scientists and technologists from the continent but also challenged the development of research, science, and technology there. This is a chronic problem of Third World countries that fail to ensure adequate working and living conditions for their experts. Although new information technologies may dampen scientists' and engineers' incentives to emigrate, the brain drain phenomenon is likely to continue in the absence of specific countervailing actions (Task Force on Higher Education and Society 2000).

In addition to brain drain, what is called "brain hemorrhage" has become a serious challenge to the revival of scientific life at African universities and research institutions. Most scientists who stayed on in their institutions became divorced from research and development activities due to the many challenges afflicting those institutions. Other scholars sought a market elsewhere, outside of the universities, where they could find better employment opportunities, either as consultants or as part-timers, and as a consequence neglecting their research duties. This has become a common phenomenon in many countries as private higher education institutions, which generally lack research components, expand. A good number of active researchers from the small congregation of experts are sucked into high-level leadership and bureaucratic positions in government and better-paying jobs outside government, often at the expense of their research duties. Later, many fail to keep up with developments in their own fields—the very expertise and achievement that presumably brought them to their elevated position.

The infrastructure that oversees and manages national research requires capable expertise that is able to moderate between the interests of scholars and their governments. In African countries, where governments play a crucial role in laying out policies and executing them, the organizational makeup of the bureaucracy as well as its expertise are critical. Shahidullah (1991) emphasizes the importance of leadership in governmental organizations for the development of S&T. Forje (1993) went further by squarely charging that governments are the "fundamental problems of S&T in Africa."

Given the multitude of challenges S&T and research face in Africa, it may come as no surprise that neither a sustainable scientific research infrastructure nor a successful scientific culture has emerged—yet. Hence, Africa remains far behind the rest of the world in generating, organizing, disseminating, and consuming scientific knowledge.

AFRICAN SCIENTIFIC KNOWLEDGE IN THE GLOBAL MARKET

Most developing countries spend only 0.5 percent or less of their GDP per capita on R&D, while developed countries spend 2 percent (Task Force on Higher Education and Society 2000).

Comparisons of national research expenditures as well as the production of mainstream research indicate that most Asian countries spend a much higher proportion of GNP for research than African countries. While the scientific output of most Asian countries increased faster than the growth of world mainstream science, often spectacularly, African science grew more slowly than world science (Eisemon and Davis 1992). As a matter of fact, the state of numerous African countries has worsened over the last two decades, creating a deteriorating environment that is not conducive to scientific and scholarly research.

Repeated pledges by most African governments to increase their expenditure in S&T have not been fulfilled, due to the multitude of sociopolitical and economic setbacks the continent has faced. At a UNESCO-sponsored conference in 1964, ambitious plans were drawn up to guide the region's scientific development for the next twenty years. The conference recommended the attainment of a ratio of 200 scientists and engineers per million population by 1980 (UNESCO 1964). The countries pledged to spend 0.5 percent of their GNP on scientific research. These commitments were twice as much as those projected for scientifically advanced, industrialized countries in the same period. Spending targets were set even higher ten years later, when African countries agreed to spend 1 percent of their GNP on S&T. Hardly any African country has followed the recommendations on the expenditures agreed upon at these major meetings, all of which significantly underscored the importance of S&T as instruments for development (Forje 1993). The woeful economic situation of most African countries during the 1970s and 1980s has meant a steady decline of both external and domestic financial resources for universities, resulting in funding levels that cannot match, in real terms, the requirements of critical inputs—equipment, books, and journals—to sustain acceptable standards of instruction, research, and service (Ajayi, Goma, and Johnson 1996).

Gauging African Scientific Output: The Hurdles

The *Science Citation Index* (SCI) remains one of the most common tools for measuring the output of scientific research based on articles published in reputable mainstream journals. Of the estimated 50,000 to 70,000 scientific journals published worldwide, SCI covers about 5 percent; almost all of them are published in scientifically developed Western countries (Eisemon and Davis 1993). Taking into account SCI's claims to have included 90 percent of all the important scientific findings in the world, the contribution of Africa is virtually negligible (Teferra 1995). As a matter of fact, Africa accounts for 0.4 percent of the world's R&D expenditure and produces 0.3 percent of "mainstream science" (Gaillard and Waast 1993).

However, the SCI has been criticized for its inappropriateness, ineffectiveness, and partiality as a measuring instrument for scientific output from developing countries as a whole and Africa in particular (Altbach 1987; Canhos, Canhos, de Souza, and Kirsop 1996; Eisemon and Davis 1989; Teferra 1995; Krishna 1997). The distinction between "mainstream" science and presumably "non-mainstream" science—a distinction operationalized by the choice of scientific periodicals indexed by international scientific information services—would seem to marginalize a good deal of respectable science produced in developing countries (Davis 1983). "Given the small size of scientific efforts in developing countries," Frame (1985) went on to question "how much of a contribution can indicators [like this] make to the improved management of the scientific enterprise?"

As a standard tool for measuring scientific productivity, the SCI relies heavily on quantitative figures. And yet quantitative data on scientific activity in sub-Saharan Africa are rare, and this is particularly true of time-series data (Davis 1983). A viable, reliable, and unbiased tool for measuring the scientific productivity of African—or for that matter Third World—institutions and their academic and research communities is woefully lacking.

We know that mainstream journals often do not publish much from or on Africa; hence, whatever is published is virtually ignored by major international databases. And yet measurements of scientific productivity continue to rely on these databases. The development of an appropriate scheme is long overdue, but work toward that end appears to be a long way ahead. The development of another functional and alternative discourse in the regime of scientific communication and scientific research requires a careful examination and thorough understanding of the manner, scope, and magnitude of these activities in Africa and the Third World in general.

Before a product can be measured, the elements to be gauged need to be clearly identified, the characteristics under which this product is manufactured well understood, and the condition by which it was formulated fully established. If we are to develop a better tool to assess African research productivity, it is crucial that we understand the manner in which African scientists communicate, establish the value of the products they produce, and pin down the factors that prompt or constrain their communication.

The knowledge base about African scientific communication is limited and narrow and lacks systematic survey (Alemna, Chifwepa, and Rosenberg 1999). Much of what is available exists in a format that is neither accessible nor well organized. Even though a number of initiatives have been launched and implemented to address this problem, there remains a substantial amount of work to be done before it can be dealt with satisfactorily and sustainably.

Given the status quo, one cannot help but wonder how national governments assess scientific productivity when they do not have an effective tool to measure it. What criteria do governments or other funding sources employ to assess merit in the absence of a sound instrument? Measurement of scientific productivity calls for a good grasp of the facets of scientific communication in various circumstances.

Time and again scientists in Africa, and in other developing countries, for that matter, have been involved in research that already had been addressed (or was being addressed), largely due to a lack of an adequate, reliable, and regular flow of knowledge and information to guide them to the frontiers of their specialties. Although supplying scientists with up-to-date information and knowledge is costly for institutions, to neglect to do so is equally costly. It is important to stress that the cost-, time-, and resource-saving features of an effective scientific communication infrastructure remain to be fully understood by African academic administrators, policymakers, and others.

It is thus of particular importance to countries with limited financial resources to clearly identify their most productive and efficient institutions while primarily taking into account the national interest. Without a tool that can effectively determine scientific productivity (even in highly advocated research areas of national significance), the allocation of resources to competing institutions and competing national interests will remain a challenge. The first and major step toward developing such a tool lies in a thorough exploration and understanding of the culture and manners of scientific communication in the continent.

Building Local Scholarly Entities: The Rationale

Science is generally considered to be a universal entity, and technology—its common derivative—a universal commodity. The role of S&T communication in a developing country is, however, slightly different from its role in developed countries. All knowledge is culturally specific, although certain fundamental characteristics are common to all human beings from the psychological and physiological perspectives. But since all human beings are not living in the same natural and cultural environments, the knowledge different groups of people acquire and the actions they base on that knowledge vary (Vilanilam 1993). Many scholars agree that the development of a national research culture is not a straightforward or simple process. They insist that the Third World needs to develop a strong infrastructure for knowledge creation and dissemination; for example, research and publishing (Shahidullah 1991; Molnar and Clonts 1983; Gaillard, Krishna, and Waast 1997).

The Third World greatly needs the scientific knowledge and technology produced in the West, but the Third World itself must have the scientists and technologies to understand, replicate, and organize this knowledge and technology within their own sociocultural context (Shahidullah 1991). The assumption that Western support would somehow give birth to a viable technological infrastructure is unattainable (Psacharopoulos 1980).

Gaillard, Krishna, and Waast (1997) argue that there is a dire need to develop national research communities in Third World countries in light of current developments in commerce and information exchange. Given the integration of research, industry, and trade organizations in the North and the emerging international regimes in intellectual property rights, it will become necessary for the South to develop local scientific potential in some of these crucial areas of research, such as agriculture and the biological sciences.

SCIENTIFIC COMMUNICATION IN AFRICA

The dissemination of knowledge—scholarly communication—is an increasingly complex phenomenon in the contemporary world. It involves many interrelated elements—the individual researcher or scholar who produces knowledge; the invisible college of peers who may assist in its creation or who provide commentary and evaluation; the mechanisms of publication such as journals, book publishers, and others; the libraries; and, increasingly, participants based on the new technologies, such as databases and reprographic agencies (Altbach 1987).

Scholarly journals in most fields—particularly in the sciences

—are the key element in the knowledge distribution network and are even more important than books. Even in an age of computer-based data networks, journals are the standard means of communicating the latest knowledge in most academic fields (Altbach 1987). This continues to be the case even in the West, where dramatic developments in the area of information and communication technology (ICT) have taken place and electronic journals are growing, and it remains abundantly true as well for the Third World, and Africa in particular, where such developments have had limited impact.

Journals constitute the lifeblood of the scholarly enterprise: they provide a medium through which scholars communicate and converse, ideas are circulated and consumed, and research results are disseminated and debated (Zeleza 1998). Thulstrup (1992) also underscores that the free transfer of research results through scientific journals to other researchers, as well as to a wider group of users, may still be the most important mechanism in the dissemination of all fundamental research.

A recent study substantiates that print-based journals are also the most prominent avenue of scientific communication in Africa. It also affirms that journals are the single most important communication media of surveyed scientists—seven in ten report that journals are their major avenue of scientific communication. The reasons attributed to the prominence of journals in the African scientific institutions are diverse, but they generally fall under five categories: accessibility, regularity, reliability, simplicity, and availability (Teferra 2002).

Exposure to current information is crucial to scientific endeavor and yet remains highly limited in Africa, where the resources for such undertakings are extremely meager. Faced by constant increases in subscription rates, which virtually double every six years, academic libraries everywhere have found it increasingly difficult to acquire a full range of publications (Zell 1998). Although the problem is widespread, the gravity of the plight is most critical in Africa, where libraries are in a state of misery; journal subscriptions are not renewed in the poorest countries (Gaillard and Waast 1993).

Given the small scale of research activity on the continent, it is hardly surprising that few scientific publications originate from Africa (Teferra 1995). According to an old report published by the African Association of Science Editors in 1990 (AASE 1990), Africa publishes a total of 150 or so scholarly journals. A recent report by Jaygbay (1998) notes that forty-eight sub-Saharan African countries account for more than 400 scholarly journals. (It is unlikely that this includes South Africa.)

International versus Regional Journals:
Access, Relevance, and Attitude

In Teferra's study, about nine in ten scientists reported access to international journals. This is another testimony to an already established fact: African institutions depend heavily on knowledge generated in Western institutions. But many in this study—about one in four—also indicated that their access to these journals is limited by footnoting their responses with "irregular," "incomplete," and "out of date."

The study found that regional journals are another resource for African scientists; half of the responding scientists confirmed

that they have access to these publications. Considering the widely held view that regional journals have limited distribution across the continent, this is a large proportion. It should be cautioned however, that one in four also remarked that they have limited and irregular access to these journals as well.

Many scholars and experts on publishing agree that scientific research outlets in Africa are limited and most of those that exist are precarious at best (Altbach 1998; Rosenberg 1999; Zell 1996). The irregularity of publication and uncertainty of nationally based journals have been widely written about; by Aguolu and Aguolu (1998) on Nigeria, Legesse (1998) on Ethiopia, Ganu (1999) on Ghana, Bakelli (1999) on Algeria, and others (Zell 1993, 1996).

It is interesting that the scientists surveyed in Teferra's study wrote rather positively about regional journals. Many underscored the considerable relevance of regional journals in addressing local and regional issues of common significance. Of those who responded, more than two in three (70 percent) wrote affirmatively, stating that regional journals are as important and relevant as other (similar and/or related) international scientific journals. Some of the responses include:

- [They are] very important in that they tackle the same scientific problems as we do. International journals are often too concerned with industrial science [and tend to be less relevant].
- Regional journals are more applied and display better understanding of the local problems and issues; international journals are theoretically more advanced, but are often impractical/too abstract.
- [They are] important because they [provide] an opportunity to have information on [related] work and also [help track] the names and addresses of the people who are working in the field.

In general, those who wrote affirmatively described regional journals as being a more practical, relevant, and important scientific communication medium that can help develop and promote common regional agendas and research interests.

In another study by Alemna, Chifwepa, and Rosenberg (1999), the majority of staff—just under 70 percent—at Ghanaian and Zambian universities considered African-published journals equally or more important than journals published elsewhere, with half (49 percent) rating them equally important. The reasons given were similar to those in Teferra's study: journals published in Africa are contextual, and the results presented and discussed are relevant to the African environment and conditions.

In Teferra's study, a few scientists dissented. They expressed reservations based on the irregularity, limited professional significance, limited breadth and coverage, and nonspecialized content of such journals. An organic chemist at University of Dar es Salaam wrote at length:

Let's be honest, international scientific journals are well established and the quality of information is often high and relevant to work in our field. Although I don't want to marginalise the importance of regional journals . . . every scientist tries (or should try) to reach the widest public and widest recognition as possible and therefore will try to get his work published internationally. A local journal will face the scarcity of high quality input, first because of research constraints and secondly because of the dilemma whether the scientist should publish high standard work in these journals with limited distribution (and initially maybe even limited quality) if he knows it can be published in internationally recognized journals.

A board member of an African scientific society based in the United States wrote, "In all honesty, the quality of education journals in Africa is substantially inferior to those in other regions and/or international ones."

Similar patterns were also observed by Alemna, Chifwepa, and Rosenberg (1999); they note that, as a whole, the academics interviewed in the study did not show any special interest in materials published in Africa and did not consider them vital for teaching and research. They preferred to read and be read in Western journals. Gaillard's comprehensive study (1991) of 766 scientists from developing countries found that one-quarter of the respondents also felt that national publications in their field were "not very important" or "not important" at all to research.

The most prevalent reason for not subscribing to regional and international journals is financial. Various other reasons include the scarcity of such journals nationally, their irregularity and unreliability (when they exist), and their tendency to be too general in content.

Electronic Journals: Awareness, Attitudes, and Perceptions of African Scientists

In the West, electronic journals have become increasingly important avenues of scholarly communication. Many journals now appear both in print (hard copy) and electronic format. In fact, some journals are now born electronic; that is, they are conceived and founded as electronic journals from the outset. Some of the major initiatives to acquire journals on the continent are electronically based.

Online journals are a new and rapidly developing phenomenon, and African experience with them is quite limited (ADEA 2000). This assertion is partly substantiated in Teferra's study, which reports that nearly nine in ten surveyed scientists said that they were "unaware of a journal which is no longer issued on paper, i.e., only available online" in their discipline. It should be underscored that a number of factors may have contributed to this negative response. Two in three of the respondents said they would publish in such journals because of their manageability, quality, speed, better access, and distribution.

Some also reflected misgivings about these developments, writing, "Computers are newcomers in most African countries, therefore the readership of such a journal will be limited"; "as many African institutions do not subscribe to [paid-up] online journals, it will not be useful for African institutions and their scholars"; "I do not think they will be available to most people in the Third World, even if they would be potentially available, in reality the telephone lines, power sources, [and] computers are not reliable, and computer networking may not exist"; and "I personally do not mind [publishing in online journals] but the published materials may not be available locally and this concerns me."

The major concern of African scientists with regard to online publishing is access—for themselves, their fellow scientists, and their institutions. As much as they affirm the significance of such journals and the medium of communication, they fear that they will be left behind, given the precarious infrastructure of most African institutions in providing these services. Others reflected their concerns about the quality and reputation of such journals.

Professional Conventions

Conferences, symposia, seminars, workshops, panel discussions, and conventions are the other major means of scientific communication. Such meetings are particularly important for disseminating useful information to professionals in a timely manner. They are often the first forums to disclose public information. They are live and offer opportunities to contest, criticize, affirm, or reject the methods and procedures that have been followed and the conclusions that have been drawn.

A good number of such meetings take place locally. Major scholarly gatherings on the continent are, however, few and far between. Most of the major and influential conferences take place in the developed countries. African scientists travel long distances to attend these meetings. As most African institutions have become increasingly desolate and poor, overseas travel has become practically impossible. Chatelin and Arvanitis (1988, in Gaillard and Waast 1993) observed that scientific meetings now receive less support from university administrations. Honoring an invitation to go abroad, they wrote, commits the scientist to hurdling a number of obstacles: exit visas, foreign entry visas, foreign currency, depleted travel budgets, and the administration's hint of suspicion that the trip is for pleasure or an unjustified privilege for a senior civil servant (Gaillard and Waast 1993). Even when support exists, many scientists are unaware of it.

The situation forces African scientists to stay put until the materials presented at such conferences are published in one form or another—often after an extended period of time. This is, of course, contingent upon the capacity of their libraries or departments to be able to trace these publications and the availability of resources to order them. In most cases, African scientists lack not only the resources to attend these meetings but also the capacity to track down the materials that were presented.

Conferences are important because they allow direct access to readership, in situ refereeing, less rigor and more ease in presenting materials, alternative avenues for presenting data that are not suitable for journal publication, and a relatively easy way to meet sponsors. Among the scientists surveyed, the most prevalent reason for not attending professional meetings rests on financial constraints. Other constraints include too many lecture hours, other career pressures, nonrelevance of the meetings, and the shortage of publishable and presentable materials.

Personal communication with colleagues and friends reveals that many less-than-deserving scholars and administrators travel to conferences abroad. In institutions where cronyism, favoritism, and nepotism are rampant, decisions involving such travel tend to be influenced by the whims of powerful and influential elements. Travel abuses by superiors and senior academic fellows are not infrequent—particularly when invitations are fully paid for. A few even describe conferences as "shopping opportunities" for the senior and powerful. In such cases, these individuals fail to represent the interests of their fellow colleagues, lack the ability to contribute meaningfully to the meetings, and, moreover, deprive the institutions of the potential benefits of the meetings.

Mwiria (2003) notes that many African academics can be as corrupt, nepotistic, tribalistic, and authoritarian as their counterparts in government or university administration. There have been many known incidences of academics dishing out favors such as scholarships, opportunities to participate in conferences, and allocation of consultancy and teaching assignments for which there is additional pay, on the basis of ethnic/racial/geographic origins, religion, gender, and demonstrated loyalty to the giver. Some of these misbehaviors are also noted by others (Teferra 2001; Murapa in Mwiria 2003). Mwiria goes on to say that university deans and heads of departments have also been known to withhold information about academic conferences, fellowships, and research grants from their colleagues in order to ensure that those who benefit are either themselves or their cronies.

To complicate the challenges of scholarly travel, some countries even impose restrictions on the free travel of their scholars. This is often imposed as a strategy to stem the tide of brain drain. For instance, the former Ethiopian regime imposed restrictions on scholarly travel by demanding bonds (guarantors) as a guarantee for their return. While the recent effort to reinstate the act in Ethiopia lost its momentum, a number of countries, such as Eritrea, are trying to legitimize the practice.

Using one's own resources to attend scientific meetings is out of the question for virtually all scientists, due to ever-declining salaries, declining values of local currencies, and inflation. With resources decreasing for most universities, requests for travel abroad are generally laughable, and scientists refrain from asking their institutions to sponsor them. As a consequence, African scientists continue to depend on external agencies for sponsorship to attend scholarly meetings, much as they do to undertake research activities.

In Teferra's study, 50 percent of the respondents reported external agencies as their most typical source for the resources to attend meetings. While three in five described a combination of sources, only one in five named their institution as their most typical source of funding for such activities. Respondents from Ethiopia (who make up 45 percent of the survey) and Mozambique depend heavily on external support, while those from Botswana—a fairly wealthy country—report their institution as the major funder of travel expenses.

The manner in which conferences and other scholarly gatherings are held has also evolved due to technological discoveries that have made distance a less significant variable in the communication equation. Virtual conferences are now the way of life in the West. E-conferences, video conferencing, conference calls, and other electronic-based avenues of hosting meetings have become simpler, easier, and cheaper, in addition to being time-savers. The technology that made this possible is still not widely or effectively utilized in Africa and the Third World in general. Even though ICT is expanding in Africa, the full-scale exploitation of such facilities and opportunities—which require a solid infrastructure, reliable service, and a bigger bandwidth—appears more than a little distant.

As communication technologies improve and expand on the continent, and as the effort to revitalize higher education and S&T gathers momentum (Task Force on Higher Education and Society 2000), it is hoped that the situation will improve and help to further scientific communication by way of meetings—both real and virtual.

CHALLENGES AND DILEMMAS IN SCIENTIFIC COMMUNICATION

This section explores the various avenues of scientific communication as well as the problems and challenges that African scientists constantly face.

State of Scientific Journals

African institutions that publish journals face a multitude of complex problems—obstacles so severe that very many African journals have never appeared beyond their maiden issue. As Zell describes it:

> Many new journals are started in Africa each year, a small number have been successful, have received international acclaim, and enjoy relative prosperity; but many others have sunk after the first issue, or have become dormant after only a year or two. Many have taken off with the best of intentions and sometimes fine first issues (though frequently with recklessly optimistic initial print runs) but have not survived beyond volume 1, number 1. (Zell 1996, 1)

According to an Ethiopian information scientist in Teferra's study, the challenges include "lack of adequate funding, overloaded editors, [and] inadequate marketing for journals to sustain themselves."

Many scientists do produce articles, but locally or nationally based journals do not appear to be their prime targets. Despite the generally stiff and unequally competitive environment of Western-based journals (Altbach 1998), African scientists often target these publications for their work, and with good reason. Western-based journals offer wider distribution, better reputation, better visibility and credibility, a higher chance of promotion, and better opportunities for cooperative initiatives.

Acquisition of Journals

Over the years, journal acquisition in most African universities has declined, due largely to escalating costs, declining funding, and foreign exchange regulations. A 1993 survey of thirty-one university and research libraries in thirteen African countries conducted by the American Association for the Advancement of Science (AAAS) revealed that all but three of the libraries had had a serious cut in their subscriptions to journals in the mid-1980s. The library at Addis Ababa University (Ethiopia), at the University of Nigeria, and the University of Yaounde's

Medical Library (Cameroon) had the highest cuts, canceling 1,200, 824, and 107 journals respectively, owing largely to foreign exchange regulations (Levey 1993). The University of Addis Ababa, which in 1983 had subscribed to 2,700 titles, received only 126 through funding from the Swedish Agency for Research and Cooperation with Developing Countries (SAREC) in 1993 (Patrikios 1994).

The University of Nigeria Library, for example, had virtually no subscriptions except the eighty journal titles acquired from the American Association for the Advancement of Science (AAAS). More than half the libraries in a study made by Levey (1993) subscribed to no more than 100 journals through their internal funding. Other sources also report many institutional medical libraries in Africa as having no current subscriptions. Some fortunate university libraries, such as the one at the University of Zimbabwe, managed to retain 72 percent of the titles it subscribed to in 1983 (from 3,100 to 2,240) with the help of donors (Patrikios 1994). Even Zimbabwe—not considered a typical African country, owing to its "thriving scientific and technical research and development base" (Hussein 1999)—faces financial difficulties in subscribing to and acquiring journals.

While resources for libraries have declined in most African universities, the cost of periodicals has soared dramatically. Today, it is common to find journals with annual subscriptions costing US$1,000, especially in the sciences (Zeleza 1996). A study by Birenbaum (1995) estimates that the cost of serials in North America increased 115 percent between 1986 and 1994; in that same period, the cost of monographs rose by 55 percent. Not only has acquisition capacity declined for African and other Third World countries, it has also declined for much more affluent U.S.-based research institutions, including those reputed for their acquisition capability. Birenbaum (1995) observes that serials acquisitions among members of the Association of Research Libraries, based in the United States, dropped by 4 percent; acquisitions of monographs dropped by 22 percent during that same period.

Editorial Predicaments as Constraints on Scientific Communication

On the editorial front, quite a large number of African editors lack the professional, technical, peer, and administrative support that exists in the West. The review process and the culture of unbiased critical judgment of scientific work are often not well developed in Africa. The small critical mass of scientists in most African countries does not lend itself to ensuring the anonymity of either reviewers or authors, and that can compromise both the integrity of the work and scholarly ethics. In the absence of specialists, editors may have to look for reviewers outside of the country. Yet communication between editors, reviewers, and authors is an extremely difficult task that can take many months, even years, on a continent that has a precarious communication infrastructure. Editors usually work alone, often without any secretarial or administrative support and in an environment that is neither conducive to nor appreciative of their efforts (Altbach 1987; Negash 1998; Teferra 1996; Thulstrup 1992).

The production quality of quite a large number of Afri-

can scholarly publications remains generally poor in terms of page layout and design, graphics, copyediting, print quality, and binding. Even though desktop publishing technology has significantly improved the quality and quantity of scholarly publications, the ease with which a "publication" can be put together has resulted in numerous shoddy and overdone designs (Teferra 1998).

Despite the multitude of challenges, many scientists in Africa produce knowledge, even though it is communicated poorly or in most cases not at all. While many publications are hindered by a shortage of publishable materials, many scientists carry with them stacks of data with good potential for publication. The latest survey on "gray literature" in Algeria, for example, revealed that research centers produced many kinds of materials (articles, proceedings, theses, reports, patents, software). But, unfortunately, the institutions and their staff do little or nothing to promote their papers (Bakelli 1999). Bakelli goes on to say that "a great quantity of scholarly knowledge is lost, forgotten and confined in research desks, laboratories or university library shelves. This is related to the authoring behavior. Our researchers," he adds, "are not trained to practice transforming 'gray literature' to 'white literature.'"

Ganu (1999), writing on the state of scholarly publishing in Ghana, concurs that, with five universities to cope with, the University Press is almost saturated with manuscripts that will remain in the queue for some time. He goes on to say that in spite of the large number of academics in the system, manuscript assessment continues to be a major source of delay that ultimately favors the piling up of "gray literature."

Very few universities possess their own presses. Even these lack the appropriate skills and managerial expertise to publish academic journals. The journals are often irregular, limited in circulation, and lacking in visibility. This heavily impinges on the marketability, distribution, and reputation of African journals, not only in the selective and highly competitive international knowledge market but even at home, where shortages of publications are rampant.

The publication of journals in an African context is oftentimes strongly associated with African institutions of higher learning—notably universities. The university faculty commonly makes up the core of the editorial board of whatever journals exist locally. Thus, much of what goes on in the university has a direct bearing on the lives of these journals. More often than not, running the business of a journal is the work of one person who acts as editor-in-chief, editor, messenger, copy editor, managing editor, technical editor, referee, designer, and negotiator (with printers, distributors, and university officials), often with little or no recognition, sympathy, and/or assistance from the university administration. A questionnaire circulated by Teferra to African journal editors who participated in a workshop, for instance, reveals that almost all the editorial offices of the representatives at the workshop had only two people working in them, of which most were amateurs (Teferra 1996).

No wonder such journals face numerous problems, from quality (design and layout) to production and marketing, from distribution and access to maintaining regularity. As traditional publishing activities shift toward the complex world of electronic publishing, it makes the duties, responsibilities, and qualifications of editors even more demanding—if not impossibly difficult. As Hussein (1999) firmly underscores, the electronic publishing world requires an editorial team that has skills in the production of HTML files, graphic files, Web pages, and electronic marketing. In addition, one must consider future electronic storage and archiving of journals, the shelf life of floppy and hard discs and CD-ROMs, the compatibility of software, and the creation and maintenance of stored materials and databases. Editorial bodies in Africa are by and large ill prepared to handle these complex activities.

Publishing efforts of African scientists are also constrained by a number of other factors: teaching overload, limited experience with scholarly writing, and lack of publishing knowledge.

Bias and Prejudice against African Science

Articles published by scientists working in laboratories in developing countries—even those included in international journals—are seldom cited or quoted in review publications. This is not the result of any true evaluation of the merit of such articles or the relevance of the topic to areas of interest to the reviewer but rather to the lack of visibility of the scientist and possible indifference to scientists from developing countries (Radhakrishna 1980). The scientists of these communities are caught in an especially vicious circle, because even when their findings are published in highly influential, prestigious scientific journals, their work is far less often cited than writings by their Western colleagues (Arunachalam and Garg 1985).

Bias and prejudice against African science, research, and publications have been widely reported and debated. Many hold that there is a general and consistently unfavorable attitude toward scientific activities and innovations on the continent. Some go even further and accuse Western scientific establishments of thinking that no good science emerges from Africa.

In Teferra's study, an Ethiopian plant ecologist reported that "articles published internationally are highly regarded. There exists serious bias against Third World science. In reality, quality does matter very little, rather where a particular material is published. I am a witness and victim of this bias." "There is a belief," a Botswanese geoscientist wrote, "that the local staff is less rigorously tested" which fosters the bias against African work. An Ethiopian botanist wrote "big bias against local indigenous materials [exists]." He added, "Any Third World person should be better than the First World person if they have to be taken seriously."

A Mauritian chemist admitting bias wrote, "Getting your paper accepted in an international journal, especially when all the work has been done locally" is a major challenge to publishing. A Ugandan chemist forcefully claimed, "Publishing in the Western journals is very difficult for any African-looking name." He went on to say, "We need African journal[s] that can publish our papers without checking to see whether the name is Western. Before this [happens], we will always find problems of publishing."

The bias—either perceived or felt—reported in this and other studies and expressed against local and regional journals in numerous private and public meetings impinges on the communication of scientific knowledge and consequently hinders its development in Africa. It is human nature to go for the best and avoid controversy—even over such issues as the academic quality of journals. But this discourse prevents high-quality work from being published in Africa by natives and nonnatives alike.

Time as a Productivity Factor

Overcrowding and escalating enrollments have become characteristic features of most African universities. This has resulted in teaching overload, leaving little time for research and publishing. The low salaries and inflation that prompt many to moonlight in various nonacademic institutions and postsecondary private institutions inside and outside academia now pose a serious threat to research productivity.

About one in four of the scientists surveyed in Teferra's study reported lack of time as one of their publishing challenges. They wrote, "I don't have enough time for research. The teaching load as well is too much!"; "No time to work on publication since a heavy teaching load"; "It is difficult to combine publishing, field research and teaching"; "Too much teaching/administrative work hampers publication productivity"; and "As everybody is tied up with teaching, little attention is given to promote scientific communication."

On the Electronic Front

Even though the global communication system has dramatically transformed due to developments in ICT that make communications ever easier, simpler, and cheaper, the African scientific community still lags behind the rest of the world in reaping these benefits. For example, approximately 55 percent of Internet users are in Canada and the United States, 24 percent in Europe, 17 percent in Asia and the Pacific, 3 percent in Latin America, and 1 percent in Africa. The number of personal computers per thousand inhabitants ranges from fewer than one in Burkina Faso and three in Zimbabwe to 27 in South Africa, 38 in Chile, 172 in Singapore and 348 in Switzerland. The price of a computer represents on average eight years of wages for a Bangladeshi but less than one month for an American (Hallak 2000). Africa has only 14 million telephone lines—less than most big cities in Europe and America (Barrow 1999). The statistics for Africa as a whole are downright depressing, and even the figures for universities are modest.

Limited access to new means of communication is a challenge frequently described by scientists. Some of the scientists in Teferra's study wrote "They are not readily available"; "[I have] limited access because it is owned by my institution, so [there are] several users!!"; "[The Internet] facility is not available to everyone"; "[There is] not much time available to use them, [because] they are shared resources"; "[The] will of other institutions and heads of offices determines [its usage]"; and "[I am] lacking [direct access] personally."

Other scientists described technical difficulties associated with accessing existing resources, including poor and slow telephone connections, lack of efficient administration and maintenance of the system, the constant need to upgrade software and hardware facilities, and an unreliable infrastructure and services. In particular, the problems associated with poor telephone communication are frequently observed. Frequent power interruptions, poor phone lines, and low bandwidth are some of the most common hurdles to electronic communication in African universities.

Some scientists wrote about the difficulties of tapping into and managing the vast resources on the Internet. Their challenges include "find[ing] the information I need without wasting too much time"; "updating my knowledge on how to use some of them"; "plenty of information, tiring to search"; "always new software on the market and lots to learn"; "time management"; and "finding enough time to really use them efficiently." An electrical engineer noted that "the major challenges for scientific communication in my institutions are limited flow of knowledge among experts in the field due to lack of culture, lack of the necessary resources (funds to get journals and access to the Internet), lack of understanding on where to find information specially on the Internet, inadequate time (most of our activities are routine and time consuming)."

DEVELOPMENTS AND OPPORTUNITIES IN SCIENTIFIC COMMUNICATION

This section discusses positive developments and opportunities in scientific communication in African universities. It also discusses the impact of ICT in improving the state of scientific communication on the continent as well as the spin-off from these developments.

Regional and International Initiatives

A number of initiatives—chiefly in the areas of publication and distribution—have been undertaken to address certain aspects of the problem of scientific communication in African institutions. These include the launching of the African Journals Distribution Program (AJDP) and the African Periodicals Exchange (APEX), the establishment of the African Journals Support and Development Center (AJSDC, after amalgamating AJDP and APEX), direct donor support and subsidies, and the organization of workshops and subsequent publications on the theme (Alemna, Chifwepa, and Rosenberg 1999).

A program called African Journals Online (AJOL), launched by the International Network for the Availability of Scientific Publications (INASP), is another such initiative. This program currently puts the table of contents, and in some cases the full text, of seventeen journals in science, technology, and medicine online (INASP 2000).

AJDP is one of the most creative initiatives "designed to support the distribution of African scholarly journals *within* Africa. The scheme's long-term objective is to make a contribution to the development and improvement of the quality of research in Africa through the provision of reliable and regular intra-African channels of communication" (Zell 1996).

Beginning January 2002, the poorest African countries, along with those in Asia and Latin America whose per capita income is under US$1,000, received free Internet access to nearly 1,000 research periodicals. This three-year initiative between six major publishing companies and the World Health Organization is expected to benefit much of Africa.

A joint cooperative initiative between four northern European and ten East African universities will use the Internet to provide full-text articles in two disciplines; development studies and business management. In the future, this initiative, known as SAP—Supply of Academic Publications to and from Universities in Developing Countries—which began in July 2001, aims to expand the content of the journals and the number of universities involved (Bollag 2001).

Cornell University also has a scheme to provide cheap digital journals to developing countries. Called the Essential Agricultural Library, the scheme mounts many years' worth of text from a large body of agricultural and life science publications on CD-ROMs. Universities and other research institutions in more than 100 developing countries are eligible to access the collection for under 3 percent of the estimated cost of subscribing to the journals (McCollum 1999).

SAREC and AAAS have been particularly supportive of many African universities in the acquisition of journals and other academic publications for a long time. While AAAS has been at the forefront of promoting CD-ROM support and to some extent improving infrastructure, SAREC has provided support in both the areas of acquisition and development of knowledge.

The African Virtual Universities (AVU) initiative, which is currently operating in a number of African countries, is attempting to address the issue of access to up-to-date journals through its digital library. Kenyatta University in Kenya, where the AVU project first started, is currently able to access more than 1,700 journals through the AVU digital library, and this number is destined to grow to over 2,400 journals (Eshiwani 1999).

In Francophone African countries, the Université Virtuelle Francophone (Francophone Virtual University), supported by the Agence Universitaire de la Francophonie (University Agency for the French-Speaking Community), has launched an online publication called *Médiathèque* that contains specialized bibliographies (of journals, theses, and full-text references) in medicine, agriculture, health, and computer science in order to disseminate scholarly work by the African scientific community (Saint 1999).

Electronic media have become a growing and important means of communication in African universities in particular and for the continent as a whole. It should not come as a surprise that universities tend to be the first place to acquire technologies, for they often have relatively better resources and the expertise to take advantage of them. This is particularly so in many developing regions, like Africa, where universities are the most important national scholarly institutions.

The Significance of ICT for African Scientific Communication

The unprecedented developments in ICT have been championed and celebrated widely. Even though Africa and its institutions remain far behind the rest of the world in terms of ICT access, strides made on the continent have been significant. Despite the numerous problems currently faced by both new and old communication avenues, a few institutions—such as universities and research establishments based in the capitals and some major cities, where the need and the know-how to run them exist side by side—enjoy better access.

In 1994, the world map of Internet connectivity showed only two countries in Africa, Egypt and South Africa having full access to the Internet. As a matter of fact, Jensen (1999) reported that forty-nine of fifty-four African countries have access to the Internet, predominantly in the capital cities. In November 2000, Eritrea became the last country to acquire Internet connectivity. There is increasing interest from the international community and donor agencies to assist in Internet development in Africa. At last count, there were roughly 100 such projects underway (Akst and Jensen 2001).

Currently, there is much room for optimism; Africa will soon be surrounded by a 32,000-kilometer ring of laser light as a new undersea fiber-optic cable—capable of carrying 40 gigabytes per second—is constructed. Experts say that this project, called Africa One, will plug Africa into the high-speed Internet. The project—which is projected to cost US$1.6 billion and aims to be completed by 2002—is expected to transform high-speed communication on the continent (Whitehouse 1999; Akst and Jensen 2001).

Computer density has attained a level of about one personal computer for every 300 people in Africa. Today, most African universities have basic e-mail connectivity, while universities in twenty-five countries have full Internet access, although this access is mostly restricted to staff and graduate students. Almost all universities have some form of Web presence, hosted either locally or elsewhere. However, the momentum toward increased access to universities and research institutions has not been followed by concerted action to improve content and enhance scientific communication and publishing (Adam 1999). The plight of higher education institutions outside the capital cities is generally similar across Africa, where the telephone, electricity, and other infrastructural services are poor. For example, among the six universities in Cameroon, only one has a properly equipped and modern computer center. The rest "barely have rudiments of information systems" (Njeuma et al. 1999). Whereas the metropole-to-metropole interaction between African scientists tends to be improving, the community of scholars away from the metropolis remain marginalized and isolated.

Use of computers has already reduced the drudgery in primary publishing—creating, copying, and appending manuscripts. The Internet has dramatically reduced the ever-increasing delay and inadequate communication in the peer-review process and in researcher-to-researcher contact. Before widespread use of the Internet, a paper article sent by mail from one African institution to another could take months. Now the same report takes ten minutes (Adam 1999).

Many reports indicate that African scientific institutions have benefited from ICT developments considerably. More than 80 percent of the respondents in Teferra's study rated ICT as either "very important" (54 percent) or "important" (26 percent). An electrical engineer wrote "Email and access to the WWW have dramatically improved my work and capacity to publish. I was able to buy books for teaching, have a look at courses delivered elsewhere to match it with my teaching, downloaded materials for students, etc. I use WWW as a basic research tool especially for getting new insights." An Ethiopian botanist wrote, "The email gives me more time for preparing my notes and for teaching, as it is quicker to use. It is also very fast and cheaper [to] read on screen and respond or write and send; in most cases printing is not needed, thus less costly." A Mozambican theoretical physicist concurred: "It represents a very fast source of new developments in my area. It puts me in contact with people skilled in my area and helps me use their experience in my teaching activities." According to a Tanzanian organic chemist, "I cannot imagine working without them. . . . They have virtually made my visits to the library obsolete and the preparation of teaching materials very easy."

An organic chemist at the University of Dar es Salaam described how the new communication media has been instrumental in research, teaching, and scientific communication: "In research [I use them as an] organising tool [and for] report writing" and in "teaching [for] development of teaching materials, future design of educational web-pages." Under the category of "scientific communication," he wrote, "Email has changed our scientific collaborations dramatically, communication by letters [has] been replaced by instant messaging."

Some also credit ICT with facilitating collaborative work and enhancing the ability to use time efficiently. A taxonomist at Addis Ababa University wrote, "Internet and email play a very important role. It is very important for collaborative purposes. For example we are concurrently undertaking a research project from three locations in Africa and Europe. . . . With projects that are launched from different countries, it is now possible to complete a three-month job in one week. Communication has been very smooth and fast."

An organic chemist at University of Dar es Salaam wrote along the same lines: "The Internet has optimised communication, which makes collaboration with other institutions abroad more viable. Certain analyses are done abroad" and this is communicated quickly, thanks to the Internet. He reckoned, "This communication leap has also increased the scientific credibility of African scientists."

Scholarly isolation has long been recognized as a serious challenge to the development of scientific research. Scientists consider the use of the new technology to be a mitigating force against this feeling of scientific loneliness. Many in Teferra's study indicated their positive perceptions of being part of the global scientific community: "Because we are communicating with the rest of our colleagues everywhere thanks to email [and the] Internet, we do not feel isolated." A mathematician from University of Namibia wrote, "[The introduction of ICT is a] major improvement, [and there is] no longer a feeling of isolation." A Mauritian physicist concurred: "[I do] not really [feel isolated] now that there is email and the web. I use that extensively."

CD-ROM Technology

CD-ROM technology was once considered a panacea for chronic shortages of S&T resources in African institutions because of its unique qualities of speed, power, durability, user-friendliness, ease of mailing, and simplicity. The technology possesses enormous potential for African researchers to gain access to scholarly data and literature. The disks can hold huge volumes of information and are inexpensive to ship yet do not require special handling, storage space, or the large drives necessary for magnetic media. The system is relatively inexpensive, even more so today as disk drives decline in price. It does not require an online telephone connection, and, equally important, power outages do not affect the disc or its memory. CD-ROMs are easier to read than microfiche or film, less difficult to store, and possibly more durable than fiche or film in difficult environments. Full-text compact discs might also prove more secure than print copy, for it is impossible to mutilate them by cutting out pages (AAAS 1990).

A CD-ROM service provides the academic and research community at the University of Dar es Salaam in particular, and Tanzania in general, access to current information and has relieved the isolation of scholars and scientists in that region. In fact, since the "service became operational, the Appointments Committee for Academic Staff no longer accepts complaints about lack of access to scholarly publications. Everyone on campus is expected to use the new service to improve their own scholarship" (Newa 1996).

The experience with CD-ROM technology at the University of Zimbabwe is similar. The primary effects of the medium have been to vastly increase access to and use of current health information sources, whether in the form of abstracts or full-text journal articles or segments from constantly updated textbooks. Along with this increase, there have been very significant changes in the information-seeking behavior of large proportions of the academic staff and the student body (Patrikios 1996).

A number of universities, institutions, and companies have been using CD-ROM technology to transmit, market, and/or exchange knowledge, information, and databases. Cornell University is one institution in the business of developing scientific knowledge mounted on CD-ROM technology exclusively for use in developing countries. Cornell's CD-ROM Essential Electronic Agricultural Library has the potential to contribute directly to the quality of research in Africa (Useem 1999). While CD-ROM technology remains an important avenue and resource for scientific communication (despite common complaints of costly subscription fees), its glamour seems to have been dampened by the rise and unprecedented growth of virtual technology.

CONCLUSION

The creation and dissemination of scientific knowledge is complex and is based on fluid and dynamic processes of which publishers, librarians, and scholars have very little awareness. Even those who posit the universality of scientific knowledge will concede that the processes of legitimization (peer review, citation, and indexing) and the socioeconomic conditions under which scholars carry out their sacred vocation (self-, corporate, and state censorship; language barriers; and societal pressures) vary enormously (Jaygbay 1998).

The world of scholarly communication described by Altbach in the 1980s has witnessed profound changes, even though the fundamental tenets that existed in the knowledge system remain basically the same. Scholars continue to do research and generate knowledge, the peer review process is still intact, the invisible college of peers remains the major force shaping and molding knowledge and perspectives, and journals, book publishers, scholarly societies, and libraries are still largely the major players in the business of the knowledge system.

That said, the world of scholarly knowledge and information has made significant strides in the last decade in a variety of ways. Among these strides, one of the most remarkable developments made possible by innovations in ICT with regard to scholarly communication is the emergence and proliferation of electronic journals. Needless to say, these developments in ICT have made an impact on every conceivable aspect of life, including the creation, organization, packaging, managing, distribution, and communication of knowledge and information. CD-ROMs, online databases, e-mail, the Internet, and other paraphernalia have made (virtual) communication simpler, quicker, and cheaper and have contributed to the unprecedented developments that shape communication in general and scientific communication in particular. These developments are widely and strongly felt in the West, where the scientific infrastructure is robust; financial resources are sufficient to pay for the services; technical resources are abundant to establish, run, maintain, and upgrade infrastructure; and the community of scholars is large enough to create a need for further improvement and flex strong academic muscles to demand and obtain them.

Although the environment in which African scholars generate knowledge, the medium through which they communicate it, and the sociopolitical landscape in which all these are grounded vary by country, the general trend and culture across these variables remain the same. Most African countries possess small and fledgling scientific communities that are often ineffective in the creation of the knowledge that is a prerequisite for communication and consumption. Africa has the smallest scientific community in the world; consequently, it contributes less than 0.5 percent of the total knowledge created in the world.

Print-based journals continue to be the most important and effective means of scientific communication in African institutions, though the difficulties of running them are rife. Africa's capacity to produce scientific literature is restricted by its capacity to produce a communicable product. This cuts at the heart of the issue of scientific communication. Unless there is a constant and reliable source of knowledge, it is futile to talk about its packaging. Unless there is a dependable source for a product, it is difficult to find patrons who want that product. Unless there is the capacity to provide products on a regular basis, the demand for that product, its source, and its packaging will have very little limited value and, ultimately, very little success.

As long as the Third World and Africa remain dependent on the West for knowledge and information, they will continue to follow the patterns of development set there. As long as print-based journals continue to be issued as they have been for generations, the best that African and other Third World countries may hope for is that the status quo will be maintained. But the status quo is under pressure from different fronts to change, particularly from the technology front, and Africa has cause for alarm, because those changes will be made without factoring in the needs of Africa or the Third World.

The scope and magnitude of scientific communication in Africa over the last few years have expanded and diversified. These developments have curbed the isolation of the African scientific community. There is a strong belief that a solid and reliable ICT infrastructure acts as a panacea to many of the deficiencies in scientific communication in particular and scientific research as a whole.

Although numerous initiatives—by international and non-governmental organizations, major commercial publishers, and Northern universities—to promote access to and delivery of both international and, to a limited extent, regional journals and publications have been made, a conscious and committed effort to revitalize the infrastructure and processes for the production and dissemination of knowledge in African universities must be sustained.

BIBLIOGRAPHY

AAAS. 1990. *Computer and CD-ROM Capability in Sub-Saharan African University and Research Libraries.* Washington, D.C.: American Association for the Advancement of Science.

AASE (African Association of Science Editors). 1990. *Directory of Scholarly Journals Published in Africa: A Preliminary Survey.* Nairobi, Kenya: Academy Science Publishers.

Adam, L. 1999. "Connectivity and Access for Scientific Communication and Publishing in Africa." Paper presented at the workshop on Scientific Communication and Publishing in the Information Age, Oxford, UK, May 10–12. Available online at: http://www.inasp.org.uk/psi/scpw/papers/adam.html

ADEA (Association for the Development of Education in Africa). 2000. *ADEA Working Group on Higher Education Report.* Working Group on Higher Education Meeting in Abuja, Nigeria, December 1–3, 1999.

Aguolu, C. C., and I. E. Aguolu. 1998. "Scholarly Publishing and Nigerian Universities." *Journal of Scholarly Publishing* 29, no. 2 (January): 118–129.

Ajayi, J. F. Ade, K. H. Goma Lameck, and G. Ampah Johnson. 1996. *The African Experience with Higher Education.* Accra, Ghana: Association of African Universities.

Akst, D., and M. Jensen. 2001. "Africa Goes Online." *Carnegie Reporter* 1, no. 2 (Spring): 2–8.

Alemna, A. A., V. Chifwepa, and D. Rosenberg. 1999. *African Journals: An Evaluation of the Use Made of African-Published Journals in African Universities.* Education Research, serial no. 36. London: Department for International Development, UK.

Altbach, P. G. 1987. *The Knowledge Context: Comparative Perspective on the Distribution of Knowledge.* New York: State University of New York Press.

——. 1998. "The Role and Nurturing of Journals in the Third World." In P. G. Altbach and D. Teferra, eds., *Knowledge Dissemination in Africa: The Role of Scholarly Journals,* 1–12. Chestnut Hill, Mass.: Bellagio Publishing Network, Boston College.

Arunachalam, S., and K. C. Garg. 1985. "A Small Country in a World of Big Science: A Preliminary Bibliometric Study of Science in Singapore." *Scientometrics* 8, no. 5–6: 301–313.

Bakelli, Y. 1999. "Scholarly Publishing in Algeria: Initiatives for Greater Accessibility by Scientists." Paper presented at the workshop Scientific Communication and Publishing in the Information Age, Oxford, UK, May 10–12. Available online at: http://www.inasp.org.uk/psi/scpw/papers/bakelli.html

Barrow, G. 1999. "Africa Gathers to Bridge Technology Gap." Available online at: http://news.bbc.co.uk/hi/english/world/africa/newsid_485000/485275.stm

Birenbaum, R. 1995. "Scholarly Communication under Siege." *University Affairs* (Association of Universities and Colleges of Canada) (August–September): 6.

Bollag, B. 2001. "East African Universities Will Gain Journal Access in New Online Project." *International Higher Education* 23: 8–9.

Canhos, V. P., D. A. L. Canhos, S. de Souza, and B. Kirsop. 1996. "Electronic Publishing and Developing Countries: Trends, Potential, and Problems." Paper presented at the Joint ICSU Press/UNESCO Expert Conference on Electronic Publishing in Science, UNESCO, Paris, February 19–23.

Crane, D. 1972. *Invisible Colleges: Diffusion of Knowledge in Scientific Communities.* Chicago: University of Chicago Press.

Davis, C. H. 1983. "Institutional Sectors of 'Mainstream' Science Production in Sub-Saharan Africa, 1970–1979: A Quantitative Analysis." *Scientometrics* 5, no. 3: 163–175.

Eisemon, T. O., and C. H. Davis. 1989. "Publication Strategies of Scientists in Four Peripheral Asian Scientific Communities: Some Issues in the Measurement and Interpretation of Non-mainstream Science." In P. G. Altbach, C. H. Davis, T. O. Eisemon, S. Gopinatthan, H. S. Hsieh, S. Lee, E. F. Pang, and J. S. Singh, *Scientific Development and Higher Education: The Case of Newly Industrializing Nations.* New York: Praeger.

——. 1991. "Can the Quality of Scientific Training and Research in Africa Be Improved? *Minerva* 29: 1–26.

——. 1992. "Strengthening Research and Training in Sub-Saharan African Universities." *McGill Journal of Education* 27, no. 2 (Spring): 122–149.

——. 1993. "Universities and Scientific Research Capacity." In Aqueil Ahmad, ed., *Science and Technology Policy for Economic Development in Africa,* 68–93. Leiden, the Netherlands: E. J. Brill.

Eshiwani, G. S. 1999. "Higher Education in Africa: Challenges and Strategies for the 21st Century." In P. G. Altbach and P. McGill Peterson, eds., *Higher Education in the 21st Century: Global Challenge and National Response,* 30–38. Annapolis Junction, Maryland and Boston, Mass.: Institute of International Education and the Boston College Center for International Higher Education.

Forje, J. W. 1993. "The Role and Effectiveness of National Science and Technology Policy-making Bodies in Africa." In A. Ahmad, ed., *Science and Technology Policy for Economic Development in Africa,* 12–30. New York: E. J. Brill.

Frame, D. 1985. "Problems in the Use of Literature-Based S & T Indicators in Developing Countries." In H. Morita-Lou, ed., *Science and Technology Indicators for Development.* Boulder, Colo.: Westview.

Gaillard, J. 1991. *Scientists in the Third World.* Lexington: University of Kentucky Press.

Gaillard, J., and R. Waast. 1993. "The Uphill Emergence of Scientific Communities in Africa." In A. Ahmad, ed., *Science and Technology Policy for Economic Development in Africa,* pp. 41–67. New York: E. J. Brill.

Gaillard, J., V. V. Krishna, and R. Waast, ed. 1997. *Scientific Communities in the Developing World.* Thousand Oaks, Calif.: Sage.

Ganu, K. M. 1999. "Scholarly Publishing in Ghana: Role of Ghana Universities Press." *Journal of Scholarly Publishing* 30, no. 3 (April): 111–123.

Hallak, J. 2000. "Global Connections, Expanding Partnerships and New Challenges: A Report Presented on the Occasion of the Conference." In Don Perrin and Elizabeth Perrin, eds., *Collaboration Beyond Borders*, 13. Washington, D.C.: UNESCO.

Hussein, J. 1999. "Science Journals in Zimbabwe: Will Electronic Publishing Improve Their Long Term Viability?" Paper presented at the workshop Scientific Communication and Publishing in the Information Age, Oxford, UK, May 10–12. Available online at: http://www.inasp.org.uk/psi/scpw/papers/hussein.html

INASP (International Network for the Availability of Scientific Publications). 2000. "African Journals Online: An Evaluation of the Pilot Project 1997/1999." Pamphlet. Oxford, UK: INASP.

Jaygbay, J. 1998. "The Politics of and Prospects for African Scholarly Journals in the Information Age in the Third World." In P. G. Altbach and D. Teferra, eds., *Knowledge Dissemination in Africa: The Role of Scholarly Journals*, 64–73. Chestnut Hill, Mass.: Bellagio Publishing Network, Boston College.

Jensen, M. 1999. "Information & Communication Technologies (ICTs) Telecommunications, Internet and Computer Infrastructure in Africa." Available online at: http://www3.sn.apc.org

Krishna, V. V. 1997. "A Portrait of the Scientific Community in India: Historical Growth and Contemporary Problems." In J. Gaillard, V. V. Krishna, and R. Waast, eds., *Scientific Communities in the Developing World*, 236–280. Thousand Oaks, Calif.: Sage Publications.

Legesse, N. 1998. "SINET: An Ethiopian Journal of Science—The Tribulations of an African Journal." In P. G. Altbach and D. Teferra, eds., *Knowledge Dissemination in Africa: The Role of Scholarly Journals*, 75–84. Chestnut Hill, Mass.: Bellagio Publishing Network, Boston College.

Levey, L. A., ed. 1993. *A Profile of Research Libraries in Sub-Saharan Africa: Acquisitions, Outreach, and Infrastructure*. Washington, D.C.: AAAS.

McCollum, K. 1999. "Cornell Offers Developing Nations Digital Journals on Agriculture." *The Chronicle of Higher Education*, December 3: A47.

Makhubu, L. P. 1990. "Universities and Institutions of Higher Education and Scientific and Technological Research." In A. A. Kwapong and Barry Lesser, eds., *Capacity Building and Human Resource Development in Africa*, 69–77. Halifax, N.S.: Lester Pearson Institute for International Development, Dalhousie University.

Molnar, J. J., and H. A. Clonts, eds. 1983. *Transferring Food Production Technology to Developing Nations: Economic and Social Dimensions*. Boulder, Colo.: Westview Press.

Mwiria, K. 2003. "University Governance and University/State Relations." In P. G. Altbach and D. Teferra, eds., *African Higher Education: An International Reference Handbook*. Bloomington: Indiana University Press.

Newa, J. M. 1996. "The CD-ROM Service for the University of Dar es Salaam." In *Bridge Builders: African Experiences with Information and Communication Technology*, pp. 13–25. Washington, D.C.: National Academy Press.

Njeuma, D. L., D. L. Njeuma, Herbert N. Endeley, Francis Fai Mbuntum, Nalova Lyonga, Dennis L. Nkweteyim, Samuel Musenja, and Elizabeth Ekanje. 1999. *Reforming a National System for Higher Education: The Case of Cameroon*. Washington, D.C.: ADEA, The World Bank.

Patrikios, H. A. 1994. "A Minimal Acquisitions Policy for Journals at the University of Zimbabwe Medical Library." In *Survival Strategies in African University Libraries: New Technologies in the Service of Information*, 93–99. Washington, D.C.: AAAS.

———. 1996. "CD-ROM for Health Information in Zimbabwe." In *Bridge Builders: African Experiences with Information and Communication Technology*, 27–44. Washington, D.C.: National Academy Press.

Psacharopoulos, G. 1980. *Higher Education in Developing Countries: A Cost-Benefit Analysis*. World Bank Working Paper, no. 440. Washington, D.C.: The World Bank.

Radhakrishna, ed. 1980. *Science, Technology, and Global Problems: Views from the Developing World—UN Conference on Science and Technology for Development, Kuala Lampur, Malaysia, 27–30 April 1979*. Oxford: Pergamon Press.

Rosenberg, D. 1999. "African Journals Online: Giving Journals Published in Africa a Presence on the Web." Paper presented at the Workshop on Scientific Communication and Publishing in the Information Age, Oxford, UK, May 10–12. Available online at: http://www.inasp.org.uk/psi/scpw/papers/rosen.html

Saint, W. 1999. *Tertiary Distance Education and Technology in Sub-Saharan Africa*. Washington, D.C.: The World Bank.

Sethi, M. 2000. "Return and Reintegration of Qualified African Nationals." Paper presented at the Regional Conference on Brain Drain and Capacity Building in Africa, Addis Ababa, Ethiopia, February 22–24.

Shahidullah, S. M. 1991. *Capacity-Building in Science and Technology in the Third World: Problems, Issues, and Strategies*. Boulder, Colo.: Westview Press.

Stolte-Heiskanen, V. 1986. "Scientific Assessment: Evaluation of Scientific Performance on the Periphery." *Science and Public Policy* 11, no. 2 (April): 83–88.

Task Force on Higher Education and Society. 2000. *Higher Education in Developing Countries: Peril and Promise*. Washington, D.C.: The World Bank.

Teferra, D. 1995. "The Status and Capacity of Science Publishing in Africa." *Journal of Scholarly Publishing* 27, no. 1 (October): 28–36.

———. 1996. "Workshop for African Journal Editors." *Bellagio Publishing Network Newsletter* 18 (November).

———. 1998. "The Significance of Information Technology for African Scholarly Journals." In P. G. Altbach and D. Teferra, eds., *Knowledge Dissemination in Africa: The Role of Scholarly Journals*, 39–61. Chestnut Hill, Mass.: Bellagio Publishing Network, Boston College.

———. 2000. "Revisiting the Doctrine of Human Capital Mobility in the Information Age." In Sibry Tapsoba et al., eds., *Brain Drain and Capacity Building in Africa*, 62–77. Dakar, Senegal: IDRC, IOM, and ECA.

———. 2001. "Academic Dishonesty in African Universities: Trends, Challenges, and Repercussions—An Ethiopian Case Study." *International Journal of Educational Development* 21: 163–178.

———. 2002. "Scientific Communication in African Universities: External Agencies and National Needs." Ph.D. dissertation, Boston College.

Thulstrup, E. W. 1992. "Improving the Quality of Research in Developing Country Universities." Document no. PHREE/92/52. PHREE Background Paper Series. Washington, D.C.: The World Bank.

UNESCO. 1964. *Outline of a Plan for Scientific Research and Training in Africa*. Paris: UNESCO.

Useem, A. 1999. "Wiring African Universities Proves a Formidable Challenge." *The Chronicle of Higher Education*, April 2, A51.

Vilanilam, J. V. 1993. *Science Communication and Development*. Newbury Park, Calif.: Sage Publications.

Whitehouse, D. 1999. "Circle of Light Is Africa's Net Gain." June 23. Available online at: http://news.bbc.co.uk/hi/english/sci/tech/newsid_376000/376016.stm

World Bank. 1991. *The African Capacity Building Initiative: Toward Improved Policy Analysis and Development Management*. Washington, D.C.: World Bank.

Yesufu, T. M. 1973. *Creating the African University: Emerging Issues of the 1970s*. Ibadan: Oxford University Press.

Zeleza, P. T. "Manufacturing and Consuming Knowledge: African Libraries and Publishing." *Development in Practice* 6, no. 4: 293–303.

———. 1998. "The Challenges of Editing Scholarly Journals in Africa." In P. G. Altbach and D. Teferra, eds., *Knowledge Dissemination in Africa: The Role of Scholarly Journals*, 113–38. Chestnut Hill, Mass.: Bellagio Publishing Network, Boston College.

Zell, H. 1993. "African Scholarly Publishing in the Eighties." In P. G. Altbach, ed., *Readings on Publishing in Africa and the Third World*, 20–30. Chestnut Hill, Mass.: Bellagio Publishing Network, Boston College.

———. 1996. *A Handbook of Good Practice in Journals Publishing*. Pilot Edition. London: International African Institute.

———. 1998. "African Journal Publishers in a Digital Environment." In P. G. Altbach and D. Teferra, eds., *Knowledge Dissemination in Africa: The Role of Scholarly Journals*, 85–97. Chestnut Hill, Mass.: Bellagio Publishing Network, Boston College.

13

African Higher Education and the World

Philip G. Altbach

From the beginning, African higher education has been influenced from abroad. Perhaps more than in any other part of the world, African universities are dependent on academic policies and practices elsewhere and follow curricular and other patterns from abroad. The origins of African higher education stem mostly from the policies of the colonial powers that ruled much of the continent during the nineteenth and twentieth centuries (Ashby 1966; Lulat 2002). In the postcolonial period, African higher education continued to be shaped to a considerable extent by foreign influences. At the beginning of the twenty-first century, globalization is an added influence. The theme of this chapter is the complex set of relationships that links African higher education to the outside world.

TWENTY-FIRST-CENTURY CONTRADICTIONS

A number of central factors underlie this analysis. Academic institutions must be part of a comprehensive set of national institutions that are aimed at nation building, the stimulation of a civil society, and educating the talent needed for African countries to succeed in a complex global environment. Although African universities are national institutions that are part of a global network, they must maintain their essential independence. Maintaining independence and autonomy in the context of globalization is a special challenge for Africa in the twenty-first century.

Globalization buffets African higher education in many ways. Some argue that it will bring Africa easily into the twenty-first century by opening societies to the contemporary trade in ideas as well as the trade in products. But the negative impacts of globalization are considerable and need careful attention. In many ways, Africa has as much to lose from the globalization of higher education and knowledge as it has to gain. For example, subjecting higher education to the strictures of the World Trade Organization (WTO) will take away from individual African na-

tions much of their power to regulate their own higher education institutions. They will have difficulties ensuring that emerging African higher education systems are not overwhelmed by institutions and programs that can be freely imported and exported under the WTO's regulations.

This chapter has as its underlying assumption the need for universities and other higher education institutions to be essentially autonomous yet integral parts of a national system of education that serves the public good. The ways in which academe interacts with global forces and institutions must be tempered by this basic commitment. It is increasingly difficult to maintain autonomy in a globalized world. The situation for Africa is particularly difficult because of the relative weakness of most African higher education institutions and the dependence on foreign funding for much of the research done in African universities.

CENTERS AND PERIPHERIES

Universities worldwide are part of an international knowledge system, and it is essential to understand the nature of this system and how specific countries fit into it. The largest and most powerful academic systems serve as centers, while most others are to some degree peripheral to these centers. Academic systems and institutions at the center have well-developed teaching and research facilities, funds for research, and a sizable scientific community, and they increasingly use English as their language of instruction and communication. At the beginning of the twenty-first century, the major English-speaking academic systems are the major centers of higher education and research. The United States and the United Kingdom, and to some extent Canada and Australia, are the most important constellations of academic power in the world today. Other large academic systems, including Japan, Germany, and France, also have the necessary infrastructures of research capability, knowledge dissemination, and large scientific communities to be centers in their own rights. They are at something of a disadvantage, though, in that they do not use English as their main language of teaching and scholarship. Consequently, they are increasingly being drawn into using English for communicating. The concentration of scientific power in a small number of countries characterizes the academic system of the twenty-first century. The United States accounts for close to half of the world's research and development (R&D) expenditures. When the other major Western industrialized countries and Japan are added in, this minority of rich countries provide 90 percent of world R&D funding allocated to higher education institutions. With more than 600,000 academics, the United States is home to the world's largest academic community, perhaps 25 percent of the world's total. Most of the world's dominant scholarly and scientific journals are published in English and edited in one of the main English-speaking countries (Altbach 1998b).

Much of the rest of the world is peripheral to these international centers. Even wealthy countries with large and well-equipped universities such as Denmark, the Netherlands, and Sweden are, in a sense, peripheral. Their academic systems look to the major centers for leadership, and their scholars publish in internationally circulated journals. Large and well-established universities in India and China are also peripheral (Altbach 1998a; Altbach and Selvaratnam 1989). Despite the existence of some world-class academic institutions, large numbers of scientists and scholars, and an active local academic community, India and China continue to look to the major international centers. They are, in many respects, gigantic peripheries.

Africa suffers from multiple peripherality. The continent looks to the major international centers for academic and scientific leadership. African academic systems produce little research, and there are only a few Africa-based journals. African universities cannot afford either the scientific equipment needed for research or the journals and databases needed to keep abreast of current world scientific developments. African scientific production hardly registers at all on the international stage. Many African universities are also peripheral to the academic institutions in their former colonizing countries. Anglophone African universities still look to Britain to some extent for leadership, while Francophone African institutions look to France and, to some extent, Canada.

TRADITIONS OF DEPENDENCE

African countries, with the exception of Ethiopia, have all experienced colonialism. For the most part, universities were established either by the colonial power or, when the universities were established after independence, with the guidance of the former colonizer. Further, almost all African universities were established in the latter half of the twentieth century, so they have not had time to build up their own academic traditions.

The colonial academic heritage is one of dependence, even subservience. Academic institutions have had to overcome this tradition to become fully independent (Lulat 2002). Throughout Africa, the basic academic institutional pattern was imposed

by the colonial power and the language of instruction was that of the colonizer, not an indigenous language. In Anglophone Africa, the universities were established by the British and were patterned on British models (Ashby 1966). French academic ideas and models are the sole patterns of university organization in Francophone Africa. Portugal exported its academic model to its colonies, although there was little emphasis on higher education. In all cases, it was not the goal of the colonial power to foster independent and autonomous academic institutions. Indeed, just the opposite was the case. The colonizers wanted the universities to be loyal to the colonial regime and to educate graduates who could take their places in the colonial administration, not in the front ranks of freedom struggles. Academic freedom was limited, and administrative structures ensured close ties to the government. Graduates were generally employed by the colonial governmental administration. It was assumed that the few graduates who required advanced training would go to the metropole for further study.

The pattern of colonial academic development remains largely unchanged in much of Africa. Governments have not encouraged universities to be autonomous and independent and in general have retained the tight controls they had during the colonial era. With just a few exceptions (such as in Tanzania), European languages continue to completely dominate higher education. In many ways, the subservient universities of the colonial era served the narrow interests of postcolonial governments. Many would argue, however, that both higher education and society would be better served by academic institutions that were more autonomous and more committed to academic freedom and innovation. It is significant that Ethiopia, which was never under sustained colonial domination, chose to use a Western academic model, mainly that of the United States, for its higher education institutions and has from the beginning used English as the medium of instruction in its university sector.

Metropolitan powers have remained powerful forces in their former colonies. Traditional academic links, including the presence of many graduates from metropolitan universities, the use of textbooks and curricular materials from the metropole, laboratory equipment, and other resources have helped to maintain close ties between African nations and their former colonizers. Foreign assistance programs aimed at helping and also maintaining strong links with higher education in the former colonies have also played a role. Without question, the colonial tradition of higher education has inhibited the development of fully autonomous and independent academic institutions in Africa.

GLOBAL ENTREPRENEURIALISM AND COMPETITION

The twenty-first century has the potential to be a period of unprecedented competition in higher education. As academe in many countries has had to become more entrepreneurial, universities have attempted to develop programs and structures that can earn income and reduce dependence on government funding (Clark 1998). This has meant that many academic institutions in industrialized countries have developed international strategies to sell educational products overseas, attract fee-paying foreign students, and in general to enhance their international profiles. Africa is inevitably seen as a market for educational programs and products from abroad. The current state of African higher education development does not—perhaps with rare exceptions in Egypt and South Africa—permit African institutions to be able to compete in the international higher education market.

Africa is at the beginning of this era of competition. So far, overseas educational providers have been interested only in South Africa as a market for educational exports, and this has created accreditation and control problems for the South African authorities. As other African countries begin to improve economically and as the demand for higher education increasingly outstrips the ability or willingness of governments to provide access, private and overseas providers will continue to enter the market. The competition for students, both in the distance education market and in the popular fields of business management and information technology, will intensify.

The private sector is becoming an increasingly significant part of the new competitive environment in higher education worldwide (Altbach 1999). Private higher education has come relatively late to Africa, although several countries, including Kenya, Uganda, and Zimbabwe, now have a significant private sector. Some private institutions are in the for-profit sector, while most are not for profit and are often linked to religious organizations. Overseas for-profit higher education providers are increasingly involved in transnational higher education enterprises, often in collaboration with local universities. There is no doubt that Africa will be affected by these trends in the near future. Aggressive private-sector marketing will inevitably become part of the African higher education landscape.

The challenge for Africa, as a recipient of the new entrepreneurialism in higher education, will be to assess needs, evaluate the overseas providers, and ensure that the public good is being protected in the context of providing access and opportunity. This will be a difficult task. Measuring the quality of educational programs is not easy, even within the borders of one country. It is much more difficult to assess programs offered by overseas providers, especially if they are provided through distance education. Africa is poorly equipped to assess and accredit its domestic academic institutions. Foreign providers will be even more difficult to evaluate.

As Africa develops and its higher education markets become more sophisticated, the pressures from abroad will intensify. It is possible that competition among African academic institutions will emerge as well. There is already a continent-wide market for professors, and many of the most talented academics prefer to teach in such countries as South Africa, Botswana, and Namibia, where salaries are relatively high and academic conditions are reasonably good. Student flow from one African country to another is currently very limited, but this may also be a future trend.

Worldwide, academe has become competitive. More than 1.5 million students study outside their home countries. There is an international labor market for the best professors. Academic institutions are increasingly offering academic programs and degrees outside their home countries. The Internet has made access to knowledge products worldwide much easier, and, as a result, such products are being internationally marketed. Foreign providers may wish to team up with African academic institutions or even private-sector firms to offer academic degrees or certificates. Africa will inevitably be affected by these, and other, competitive trends. It will be at a disadvantage in this international competition, but an understanding of the nature of this competition and the development of strategies to deal with it will be helpful.

THE ROLE OF RESEARCH

Research is one of the central functions of higher education. Many consider research to be the hallmark of the best universities and academic systems (Ben-David 1968). For Africa, research is an especially complex issue. On the one hand, there is a great need for Africa-based research—to understand and interpret African society and history; to gain insights into the problems, social and political, that African countries face; and to build up a knowledge base about all aspects of African society. There is also a need to do research from an African perspective on the physical and natural environment and to build research based on products that are of special importance to Africa. Medical research in areas of special concern for Africa, such as HIV/AIDS and other diseases endemic to the continent, is crucial. Furthermore, most African universities emphasize research and publication as a requirement for academic advancement and as a way to keep abreast of scientific developments. A commitment to research is very much part of the academic ethos in Africa.

The research enterprise itself and the communication of research is very much part of an international scientific network. Africa, as noted earlier, is peripheral to the world scientific system. Most research is done elsewhere, and the journals and databases that communicate science and scholarship are located in the major industrialized countries. The fact that African universities and scholars do not have any control in the research system and must conform to the norms of those who do control it creates problems for African research. African scientists must conform to the methodological orientations and dominant paradigms of those who control world science and scholarship. Moreover, major journals are often uninterested in publishing articles on African topics. The international gatekeepers of science may not find African work relevant. This often means that topics which are of special relevance to Africa may not be publishable in internationally circulated journals. Yet research that relates to local, national, and regional issues is most useful to African development.

African academics face the challenge of pursuing research that is relevant to the African context while at the same time conforming to the norms of world science. In addition, African universities generally lack much of the infrastructure necessary for research. Access to the main scientific journals is limited, and laboratory equipment, especially in fields that require expensive apparatus, is either inadequate or unavailable (Teferra 2002). Without participation in the mainstream of science and scholarship, Africans face great difficulties in their attempts to fully participate on the frontiers of research and scholarship.

Research is a central focus and value of higher education everywhere, and if African universities are to develop, they will need to continue to emphasize research. Yet they face the problems of how to carry out quality research in the context of scarcity of resources. African scientists and scholars will need to develop a mix of links with world science while at the same time focusing on local and national research needs. African universities will need to provide appropriate resources for research. An emerging model for research in African higher education has the best African universities focusing significant resources on research while other academic institutions will necessarily have a lesser research role. In such a differentiated academic system, which is emerging in most African countries, most postsecondary institutions will focus mainly on teaching and not on research (Task Force on Higher Education and Society 2000, 46–58). Africa faces special challenges in developing a sound economic model for teaching and research across its systems and especially in improving its research profile in the broader international context of research and development and the dramatic inequalities in research systems worldwide.

THE DIASPORA AND ITS ROLE IN AFRICAN HIGHER EDUCATION

There is an international network of academic talent. More than any time since the Middle Ages, when European scholars and students crossed borders to study and teach in academic institutions, contemporary academe is mobile and international. Africa is perhaps affected by this internationalism more than any other part of the world—and the impact is largely negative.

African scientists and scholars work all over the world. There is a significant African academic diaspora. It is estimated, for example, that there are more Ghanaian medical doctors working outside of Ghana than within the country. There has been an exodus of South African academics and professionals in many other fields to Europe and North America. Many of the best professors from Francophone African countries work in France, Belgium, or Canada. There is also a regional diaspora. Academics from some of the poorer African countries, such as Ethiopia, Malawi, or Zambia, can be found teaching in South Africa, Botswana, Namibia, or Zimbabwe, countries that have better academic facilities and higher salaries.

Poor working conditions, low salaries, societal unrest, and, in some cases, severe restrictions on academic freedom or even repression have all contributed to this exodus of African academics. The fact that African universities use English or French as the main languages of instruction makes it especially easy for local scholars to find jobs elsewhere.

Africa is, of course, not alone in facing a loss of academic talent. The global migration of highly educated people affects most of the world. North America, Australia, and the nations of the European Union have greatly benefited from an infusion of international brainpower. Immigration rules have, in many cases, favored this influx of educated people. Flows are highly complex. The "sending" countries are mainly, but not exclusively,

in the developing world. For example, while Britain receives many highly educated people from Africa, South Asia, and elsewhere, it also sends some academics to Australia, Canada, and the United States, where salaries are higher. South Africa, as noted earlier, sends talent to Europe and elsewhere while at the same time absorbing highly educated people from other parts of Africa. Egyptians are visible members of university faculties in many Arabic-speaking countries. Sometimes scientists and others who have migrated return home. Some highly educated Taiwanese who emigrated to the United States when there were few economic opportunities and political repression at home returned to Taiwan when conditions improved. With few exceptions, however, these complicated patterns and flows of migration work to the disadvantage of the developing world.

Given current conditions, a continuing flow from developing to industrialized countries is inevitable. Academic institutions can minimize the flow by offering the best possible working conditions at home. Insofar as possible, however, academics must have access to the latest knowledge from around the world and at least a modicum of laboratory and other equipment to make teaching and research possible. It is beyond the capability of African universities, as it is of most of the world's universities, to provide the most current and expensive laboratory apparatuses. Scholars and scientists who are able to work in an atmosphere of academic freedom and who are respected in society will be less likely to emigrate. Still, even with the best facilities and an appropriate academic environment, many of the best African scholars will likely choose to leave, lured by higher salaries and the chance to work at the frontiers of scientific discovery abroad.

A key challenge, under these circumstances, is to build links and relationships with the African diaspora, which is now spread worldwide. Developing a consciousness of the importance of the diaspora is an important first step. While there currently are many individual links and some efforts to build organized scientific links with the African diaspora, much remains to be done. Most academics have considerable loyalty to and affection for their home country, even if they have emigrated, and many are willing to contribute to academic development in their country of origin (Choi 1995). The understandable tendency to feel that those who have abandoned the homeland are somehow suspect needs to be eliminated, and efforts must be made to involve diaspora scholars and scientists in the development of African science and universities. There is, after all, a significant degree of patriotism and commitment to the country of origin among most expatriate scholars and scientists. Networks, joint research, visiting assignments, and many other models may be implemented to take advantage of a key resource.

EXTERNAL INFLUENCES: DONORS AND AUTONOMY

Foreign influences play a major role in African higher education. Not only are European academic models and patterns dominant but foreign assistance programs have a significant impact in Africa. Indeed, Africa is in this respect considerably more dependent than any other part of the world. It has been pointed out that foreign donors provide funding for most of the research done in African universities. Donors provide funds for scholarships, laboratory equipment, computers, and supplies, as well as for books and journals. Many African universities spend a considerable amount of time and energy seeking support from foreign organizations and governments.

This situation leads to imbalances in African academic development as well as an overdependence on foreign funding that is not sustainable and indeed may disappear with little notice due to changes in the priorities of the donor or in government policy. Dependence on donor funding reduces the autonomy of African universities as well and makes academic institutions and researchers subject to the priorities of the funders. The donors, whether private or governmental, have their own priorities and concerns, and these may not always coincide with what is best for African higher education and science. Some have argued that donor funding is little more than neocolonialism in a modern form (Mazrui 1984). While there is generally an appropriate accommodation of the interests of recipients by donors, the fact remains that the situation is essentially one of dependence.

There are many different types of foreign assistance in African academe. These include direct assistance to universities, departments, or individual scholars that may have considerable autonomy in their use of this help. Much more common are the myriad efforts that target particular programs and require careful coordination between the goals and funds of the external provider and the local institution or government. These programs range from specific research or teaching initiatives to initiatives to build the infrastructures and departments. Some, such as major World Bank–funded reform efforts, may have an impact on entire academic systems. Donors may provide scholarships or postdoctoral grants to African academics or they may build up the capacity of local institutions to offer advanced scientific training at home. The fact is that the priorities and conditions of the donors generally determine the nature of the programs.

Few, if any, African universities are in a position to reject external support in an effort to maintain their autonomy. The challenge throughout the continent is to balance the policies and concerns of local institutions and national governments with the priorities of external donors.

ENSURING THE FUTURE

This analysis does not present a very optimistic picture of the role of African universities in the contemporary global environment (Saint 1992). Africa is a small and relatively weak part of the global academic system, and it is impossible to keep out foreign influences in higher education and research. Indeed, even if it were possible to limit globalization in the economy, and this is doubtful, it is impossible to do this in higher education. Science and scholarship know no borders. Academe has always been international—even the powerful American university system was shaped by ideas from Germany in the nineteenth century and by England in the century before. The challenge for Africa is to somehow balance national priorities and needs with the global influences discussed in this chapter. In order to do this, the following factors should be kept in mind:

- The first step in solving a problem is recognizing it and understanding its parameters and scope—thus, the current circumstances and future prospects of specific academic institutions and postsecondary systems in Africa need careful analysis.
- Those responsible for programs and linkages between African institutions and governments and the rest of the world need to be aware of the challenges and pitfalls, as well as the opportunities, inherent in a basically unequal relationship. The relationship is inevitable, and even necessary, for African academic development, but it remains problematic.
- Donors must always be aware of their special responsibility to ensure that the programs and initiatives are based on mutual understanding and discussions among equals.
- The long-term implications and sustainability of programs and initiatives must be kept in mind. It may not be advisable to implement efforts that cannot be sustained.
- Links between Africa, Latin America, and Asia may help change the historical monopoly of Africa's exclusive relationship with Europe and North America. Broadening Africa's links may help bring a broader sense of globalization to the continent.
- The African diaspora can in many cases be a kind of buffer to the impact of globalization on African higher education and should be constructively involved in Africa's global reach.

Perhaps most important, Africans need to be cognizant of both the benefits and the challenges of the global environment of the twenty-first century. While it is not possible to shun the rest of the world, a realistic relationship with it can, in the long run, help African higher education constructively engage with and benefit from globalization.

REFERENCES

Altbach, P. G. 1998a. "Gigantic Peripheries: India and China in the World Knowledge System." In P. Altbach, ed., *Comparative Higher Education: Knowledge, the University, and Development*, 133–146. Greenwich, Conn.: Ablex.

———. 1998b. "The University as Center and Periphery." In P. Altbach, ed., *Comparative Higher Education*, 19–36. Greenwich, Conn.: Ablex.

Altbach, P. G., ed. 1999. *Private Prometheus: Private Higher Education and Development in the 21st Century.* Westport, Conn.: Greenwood Publishers.

Altbach, P. G., and V. Selvaratnam, eds. 1989. *From Dependence to Autonomy: The Development of Asian Universities.* Dordrecht, the Netherlands: Kluwer.

Ashby, E. 1966. *Universities: British, Indian, African.* Cambridge, Mass.: Harvard University Press.

Ben-David, J. 1968. *Fundamental Research and the Universities.* Paris: Organization for Economic Cooperation and Development.

Choi, H. 1995. *An International Scientific Community: Asian Scholars in the United States.* Westport, Conn.: Praeger.

Clark, B. 1998. *Creating Entrepreneurial Universities: Organizational Pathways of Transformation.* Oxford: Pergamon.

Lulat, Y. G.-M. 2003. "The Development of Higher Education in Africa: A Historical Survey." In D. Teferra and P. G. Altbach, eds., *African Higher Education: An International Reference Handbook.* Bloomington: Indiana University Press.

Mazrui, A. A. 1984. "The African University as a Multinational Corporation: Problems of Penetration and Dependency." In P. G. Altbach and G. P. Kelly, eds., *Education and the Colonial Experience*, 273–290. New Brunswick, N.J.: Transaction.

Saint, W. S. 1992. *Universities in Africa: Strategies for Stabilization and Revitalization*. Washington, D.C.: The World Bank.

Task Force on Higher Education and Society. 2000. *Higher Education in Developing Countries: Peril and Promise*. Washington, D.C.: The World Bank.

Teferra, D. 2002. "Scientific Communication in African Universities: External Support and National Needs." Ph.D. dissertation, Boston College.

PART 2

Countries

14

Algeria

AMAN ATTIEH

COUNTRY AND EDUCATION PROFILE

Algeria, whose official name is The Democratic Popular Republic of Algeria, is the second-largest country in the African continent. Lodged on the northwestern side of this continent, Algeria shares common borders with seven countries: Libya, Mali, Mauritania, Morocco, Niger, Tunisia, and Western Sahara. Only one-fourth of its 2.38 million square kilometers (918,923 square miles) is arable, and that land is confined to the country's northern terrain, which explains the concentration of population and higher education institutions there. In 2000, Algeria was estimated to have a population of 30 million with an average annual growth of 2.9 percent (Turner 2000, 134). In 1998, Algeria had a gross national product (GNP) of $46.5 billion, equivalent to $1,550 per capita (Europa Publications Limited 2000, 392).

Student participation in the education system follows the pattern of a pyramid. Nine years of compulsory school attendance, referred to as basic education, are followed by three years of secondary education. Basic education covers six years of primary and the first three of the six years of secondary schooling for ages 6 to 15. The robust 94 percent of the relevant school-age group enrolled at the primary level in 1996 (97 percent of males and 91 percent of females) drops to only 56 percent of the eligible age group (58 percent of males and 54 percent of females) at the secondary level (grades 7–12) (UNESCO 2000, 148). This brings into question the seriousness of educational authorities in enforcing compulsory attendance and developing a more meaningful way of reporting enrollment data to better ascertain the extent to which compulsory attendance has been achieved at the primary level. With respect to higher education, figures for 1996 show a further precipitous reduction of student participation, declining to only 12 percent of the relevant age group (14 percent for males and 9.8 percent for females) (UNESCO 2000, 156).

Illiteracy among the younger generation has decreased. In 1997, the average rate of illiteracy for the population's 15–24 age group was 8.7 percent among males and 19 percent among females. Illiteracy among the age group of 15 and above was 35.8 percent (24.5 percent among males and 47.3 percent among females) (UNESCO 2000, 132). Approximately 12.5 percent of the country's budget was dedicated to education in 1997 (Europa Publications Limited 2000, 398).

HISTORICAL BACKGROUND OF THE PRESENT EDUCATIONAL SITUATION

Higher education in Algeria has undergone several transformations in the last 200 years. Prior to the French invasion in 1830, Algeria enjoyed a number of institutions of higher learning that had a well-developed corpus of knowledge firmly rooted in the Islamic sciences and their ancillary subjects. Students who enrolled in these institutions, referred to in Algeria as *zaawiyahs*, streamlined through a centripetal education structure in which they acquired their preparatory training at the prestigious institution of the *madrasah* (equivalent to secondary school) following primary schooling at the *kuttaab* (Chabou 1988, 84). The *kuttaab*, a word whose root means "writing," offered students training in numeracy and literacy, which revolved mainly around the memorization and writing of the Koran but was broadened at times to include some of the most famous poems in Arabic literature. The outstanding pupils of the *zaawiyahs* traveled to the more distinguished learning centers of al-Azhar in Cairo, al-Qayrawaan in Tunis, or al-Zaytuunah in Fez, Morocco, for more advanced training in the Islamic sciences, which equipped them for positions in the administrative and judicial hierarchy of the Algerian Muslim courts. Overall, this tertiary system and the earlier levels of education were privately established through endowments and administered by a learned coterie of *ulama*, or the learned, whose professional respect was commensurate with their institutional affiliation. This cobweb-like education network ensured some degree of literacy among the masses, which was essential for a life of piety, a central notion in Islam, and served the economic needs of both the massive agrarian and the urban commercial communities. Reports indicate that when the French arrived in Algeria in 1830, the illiteracy rate was 30 percent, which was lower than that of France (Chabou 1988, 84).

The transformation caused by the French colonial power was abrupt and disruptive. The 1,000-year-old complacent Algerian educational tradition faced progressively stronger challenges and had to reckon with an alien, elitist structure, which culminated in the establishment of the University of Algiers in 1909. Attendance at the university was based on two premises. One was that students had to have successfully completed elementary and secondary *lycée* state education, which was aimed at bolstering the interests of colonialism and at teaching modern, secular subjects, with an emphasis on mathematics and the sciences. Second, the university was accessible only to the offspring of European civil servants and French military personnel. The situation led to a dual system of education: a *lycée* system for the colonialists and a religious system for the indigenous population. Historically, the relationship between these institutions was strained and inimical. The religious coterie and the Islamic learning institutions were upset with the widening influences of secularism and French cultural imperialism. The French colonialists, on the other hand, feared the indigenous education system would compete with theirs and therefore subjected it to strict legal and administrative control. Subsequently, by the 1920s, the Islamic learning institutions, together with their moral authority and the popularity of the *ulama*, began to dwindle in quantity and quality. They provided a very limited type of workforce whose qualifications restricted it to teaching in the traditional schools, performing religious functions as judges and scribes of the Shariʿa courts, or serving as bilingual translators and interpreters. Such training could not adequately meet the ever-increasing demand for the French language and for modern subject specializations in state institutions, nor could it serve the developing new market economy and industries of the French colonists.

For a long while, "public" and "private" education signified a reverse of the popular notions of these terms. The "public" education system established by the French government either excluded the Algerians or limited their access. Until 1895, the state schools were exclusive to European children and offered a curriculum identical to that of France. After that year, a separate school for Algerian children, earmarked for those whose parents were employees of and assistants to the colonial administration, was opened. The French government later made education more accessible to the Algerians, first through the segregated *lycée* schools at the pre-university level between the two world wars, and then through the unified comprehensive school system. But the schools still fell short of accommodating the age group of children who would feed into higher education (Chabou 1988, 84). Just before the Algerian war of liberation, there were only 1,000 Algerian university graduates, of whom 354 were lawyers and 165 were medical practitioners such as doctors, pharmacists, and dentists (El-Kenz 1991, 12–13). French public education for the indigenous population was very narrow in scope. Thus, the burden of educating most Algerians was placed on the shoulders of "private" endowed religious schools; that situation persisted until the dawn of the independence era. By then, the *zaawiyahs*, regrettably, had sunk to providing no more than rote memorization of the Koran (K. Megatali 2001).

LIMITATIONS OF THE DATA

The scarcity and inconsistency of data on the quantitative development of the various components of Algerian higher education is one of the limitations of this study. First and foremost, there are no complete historical or systematic figures published by any one source. To analyze the development of enrollment trends, one has to resort to comparing different datasets and sources to reconstruct the larger enrollment picture, which at times can be daunting, especially given the incongruity of the figures. Data for this chapter were aggregated from three sources (Wannas 1989, 165–167; UNESCO 1999a; BuʿIshshah 2000, 33). The second limitation is the discrepancy in the components that constitute a given referent. The third is the absence of a chronology of more detailed statistics of student distributions according to types of institutions and by level, gender, and region. Total enrollment figures not only obscure the attrition rate but do not allow one to follow a given student cohort and compute its dropout rate, particularly with regard to students studying in colleges or institutes where the choice of disciplines is limited. Moreover, data is not readily available regarding the trends of expenditures in higher education. All of this has hampered my effort to make better inferences and policy recommendations as guidance to outside donors interested in meeting specific needs in Algerian higher education.

AIMS OF HIGHER EDUCATION

In spite of these lacunae and discrepancies, the success of the Algerian government and people in widening access to education for Algerians in the last forty years has been remarkable. To achieve that, the government adopted four broad goals. Driven by the motto "democratizing higher education," to which successive governments after the war of liberation adhered, the first aim was to broaden access to higher education for the diverse groups that make up the social and cultural fabric of Algeria. Education, at least in principle, is now open to all able and competent individuals without regard to ethnicity, economic status, or social class. A second aim was to link higher education to the process of national development and production. This has meant focusing on generating adequate numbers of scientists, researchers, and teaching faculty directly involved in the development process by training competent individuals to feed sectors of the market economy vital to the nation's needs. A third goal was Arabicization. This has involved massive projects to rewrite the postsecondary education curriculum in Arabic for all disciplines and areas of study, and the use of Arabic as the medium of instruction. This aim also has significant cultural and historical overtones. By devising a content-based Arabic curriculum, modern Arabic would gradually reclaim its universal status by becoming once again a tool of research, science, and knowledge. This goal has not yet been completely realized, due to opposition to Arabicization among some groups. In contrast, the fourth goal of Algerianization seems close to being attained. Algeria's intensive efforts to multiply enrollments and train faculty in and outside the country have been fruitful. By the early 1990s, all the administrative positions and almost all teaching and research positions had been filled with Algerian nationals. This excessive zeal to Algerianize education employment has in some cases prevented recruitment of needed and better qualified non-Algerians (Saleh and Musa 1996, 362–364).

ACCESS TO HIGHER EDUCATION

To better appreciate current student enrollments, one has to use the baseline of 1962, the year of Algerian independence. Tables 14.1 and 14.2 show that, with the exception of 1993, there has been a spectacular and consistent increase in these figures through 1999. The highest increase averaged 62.2 percent per year in the years 1962–1965, when the newly independent state marshaled all its forces and resources, material and human, to expand the access to education essential for nation building and to compensate for past colonial iniquities. Despite these steady increases, the trend slowed down to an annual average growth of 28.5 percent for 1965–1970, to 22.9 percent for 1970–1975, and to 19.9 percent for 1975–1980. Then came a dramatic increase of a yearly average of 25.9 percent for 1980–1986, followed by a sharp decrease to 10.4 percent during 1986–1990 and 4.3 percent in 1990–1995, edging up slightly to 5.4 percent between 1995 and 1999. These figures, though impressive, still leave room for much improvement, considering that for every 100,000 Algerians, only 1,238 attended an institute of higher education in 1996 (UNESCO 2000, 156). When placed in comparative perspective, Algeria ranked fourth among all the African countries reporting this data in 1996, after Egypt (1,895 per 100,000), South Africa (1,841 per 100,000), and Tunisia (1,341 per 100,000) and had one-fourth the higher education enrollment rate of the United States (5,341 per 100,000). In terms of the male and female age cohorts for that year, Algeria ranked fourth (with 14 percent and 9.8 percent, respectively), after Egypt (24.2 percent and 15.9 percent), South Africa (18.0 percent and 16.8 percent), and Tunisia (15 percent and 12.5 percent) (UNESCO 2000, 156–157).

GROWTH OF FACULTY AND APPOINTMENTS

Democratizing and Algerianizing tertiary education have markedly impacted faculty development and recruitment. The large cohorts graduating from precollegiate levels naturally demanded a rapid expansion in the number of eligible faculty. While Algerians constituted only 10 percent of the faculty in 1962, this percentage soared to 98 percent in 1995 and has remained at that level, thus realizing nearly complete indigenization. The analysis of selective figures (Saleh and Musa 1996, 365) in Table 14.3 shows an average annual increase in the number of faculty of 323 percent from 1962 to 1979. This fell to an annual average growth of 13 percent from 1970 to 1986, tapering off to 10 percent between 1985 and 1995 and dropping 0.6 percent between 1995 and 1999, the first period of negative faculty growth since independence.

Table 14.1. Student Enrollment in Algerian Higher Education, 1962–1970

Year	Total	Male	Female (Percent)
1962	2,809	2,230	579 (21.0)
1963	3,853	3,039	814 (21.0)
1964	4,926	4,727	199 (4.0)
1965	8,053	6,422	1,631 (20.0)
1966	9,272	7,421	1,851 (20.0)
1967	9,720	7,500	2,220 (23.0)
1968	10,681	8,283	2,398 (22.0)
1969	13,830	10,422	3,408 (25.0)
1970	19,213	14,375	4,838 (25.0)

Source: Wannas 1989, 103.

Table 14.2. Student Enrollment in Algerian Higher Education, 1975–1999

Year	Total Student Enrollment	Percent Growth	Number Male	Number Female (Percent)
1975	41,847	114.3	NA	NA
1980*	79,351	89.6	58,337	21,014 (26.0)
1986	201,982	154.5	NA	NA
1987	203,529	0.8	NA	NA
1989	258,995	27.3	NA	NA
1990	212,413	10.4	NA	NA
1991	236,185	4.3	142,714	93,471 (40.0)
1992	257,379	1.7	150,451	106,928 (41.0)
1993	250,939	1.6	144,239	106,700 (42.0)
1994	252,334	0.2	145,080	107,254 (42.0)
1995	267,135	16.3	148,774	118,361 (44.0)
1999**	423,000	—	—	—

*Wannas 1989.
**Bu'Ishshah 2000, 33.
Source: UNESCO 1999b.

Table 14.3. Number of Faculty Participating in Higher Education in Algeria, 1962–2000, Selected Years

Year	All Faculty	Algerian Faculty	Percent Algerian Faculty
1962–1963	950*	95	10
1979–1980	7,900	5,315	67
1986–1987	12,000	10,210	85
1990–1991	15,171	14,167	93
1995–1996	18,000	17,640	98
1999–2000	17,480*	17,130	98

*Author's computation.
Source: Saleh and Musa 1996, 1:365.

Even though there are no causal explanations in the literature for this negative growth, one can surmise from broader political and economic dynamics that a conglomeration of factors have influenced the trend toward faculty retrenchment. One may be that some faculty sought to teach abroad in more financially rewarding countries due to the country's economic ills. Another is the massive exodus of Algerians escaping the country's bloody civil strife. From 1992–1997, more than 400,000 Algerians, mostly Francophone professionals, including university professors, fled the country (Associated Press 1997). The percentage of faculty who have fled is not readily available, although the exodus of faculty has increased since 1997 (A. Megatali 2001). Other faculty were either murdered by the militant Islamic groups or, if they were sympathizers of these groups, were detained by the government security forces ("Unholy Cycle of Abuse," 1–5; Europa Publications Limited 2000, 387–391).

Faculty retrenchment has undoubtedly affected the healthy overall student-to-faculty ratio of earlier years. In 1995, the student-to-faculty ratio was 17:1 (300,000 to 18,000) (Saleh and Musa 1996, 365), though there is a discrepancy in student enrollment figures (between 300,000 and 347,410) given by two different sources (see Table 14.2). This ratio has been progressively higher of late, reaching around 25:1 (423,000 to 17,130) in 1999 (see Tables 14.2 and 14.3). This has led to problems in overcrowded amphitheater seating during lectures in certain disciplines at some university institutes (Bu'Ishshah 2000, 33).

Appointments, remuneration, and promotion of faculty, who are considered civil servants, are standardized. The government meticulously specifies the qualifications, degrees, years of training, experience, service, research activities, professional development for each distinctive category, and rank on the civil servant ladder for each type and level of institution. Nonetheless, in the last decade, Algeria has experienced deteriorating standards due to nepotism and fraud (al-Sha'b 2000).

TYPE OF INSTITUTION, STRUCTURE, AND CURRICULUM

The type and structure of tertiary educational institutions fall into five categories (International Association of Universities 2001), though, for several reasons, it is not possible to delineate all institutional types with any precision. One is that the nature and function of some are ill defined. Another is the interchangeable use of different designations, particularly the laxity in the use of the terms "al-madrasah" in Arabic and the French "ecole," both of which are equivalents of the term "institute." Still another is the structural changes that higher education is continually undergoing due to policy and/or demographic changes and experimentation. This being the case, it is for example difficult to determine the exact number of Algerian universities. One source mentions twelve (Rhodes University Library 2002), while the Ministry of Higher Education lists ten universities and the United Nations lists thirteen (Ministère de l'Enseignement Supérieur et de la Recherche Scientifique 1999; Permanent Mission of Algeria to the United Nations 2001).

Algeria's universities, including the University of Islamic Sciences, are still strongly affected by the French model, both in structure and content. All but two, which concentrate on the hard-core sciences, offer the disciplines that typify a French university core. Each university is divided into faculties, the counterpart of colleges at American universities, which in turn are divided into academic departments. The educational reforms of 1971–1974, which aimed to create a more decentralized pattern of control and to encourage autonomy, replaced faculties with "institutes," only to have faculties reinstated again following a 1998 ministerial decree calling for the reorganization of fields of studies in universities under the umbrella of "colleges." It appears that enrollment figures, which declined steadily at some institutes, such as the former Institute of Historical Studies at the University of Algiers, during the last decade could no longer justify their existence as independent entities (Bu'Ishshah, 44–45).

The courses offered by the University of Annaba provide a good example of the more inclusive universities. These include the hard-core sciences, mathematics, engineering, medicine, law, economics, business management, the humanities, and the social sciences (Université Badji Mokhtar–Annaba 2001). The specific degrees awarded are determined by the field of study or discipline, not by the specific college.

Algeria's universities have three consecutive stages. The first, the undergraduate level, is divided into two concurrent cycles, which are generally parallel rather than sequential. One is the short three-year terminal track, in which successful students are awarded a *Diplôme d'Etudes universitaires appliquées* (DEUA). The second, longer cycle of four years affords students in-depth training in their specialties. At the end of this cycle, if successful, students obtain the more prestigious degree of *Licence* or *Diplôme d'Etudes supérieures* (LES or DES), comparable to the bachelor's degree in arts or sciences in the United States, leading to the next university stage. The professional training for the *Diplôme* in engineering and medical sciences— for architects, engineers, dental surgeons, pharmacists, and veterinarians—requires five years, while the *Diplôme* for medical doctors requires seven.

The second stage admits the most accomplished students with a LES or DES. It lasts at least four years and requires a thesis defense, after which students earn the *Magister*, which makes them eligible to apply for a university teaching post as a lecturer in their respective area of specialization. In comparison to the master's thesis at an American university, the Algerian thesis is generally a much more weighty and serious academic product, both in length and quality, with an emphasis on the establishment of new knowledge. In some cases, they are comparable to the doctoral thesis at some American universities.

The third stage, which usually takes three to five years, leads to the *Doctorat d'Etat*. Admitted candidates hold the *Magister*, and their academic activities do not entail studying specific courses. All their training is carried out through individual research under the supervision and direction of a professor who serves as a mentor. The defense of the thesis is open to the public.

Most of the universities administering these higher degrees are located in northeast, north central, or northwest Algeria, where the population is mostly concentrated in the arable highlands and close to the coastal plains.

Algeria's five university centers constitute the second type of postsecondary education. They have arisen as a timely response to the immense needs of the student population from the main universities, such as the University of Algiers, the University of Tlemcen, and the University of Wahran, and have widened access to those living in areas distant from the capital. At their inception, their programs of studies were usually limited in comparison to universities. Nonetheless, they focus on generating cadres of professionals and technicians who are able to respond to the social and economic needs of their respective geographical regions. Within the reaffirmed mission of democratizing education set out in the five-year educational plan of 1980–1984, a conscious effort was made to increase areas of specialization to meet the growing demands of a broadening base of individual interests. This phenomenal growth has forced some of the centers to become full-fledged universities, as in the case of the former University Center of Tizi-Ouzou, which recently became a university. It is more than likely that this metamorphosis will continue, while new centers will also be established.

A third type of higher education institution in Algeria is provided at the coveted Polytechnic Institute. Its aim is to give rigorous training in the theoretical and applied sciences. It admits qualified students who earned high grade point averages in the scientific baccalaureate, the national competitive secondary education exit exam. The curriculum of the Ecole Nationale Polytechnique includes the engineering sciences (electronic, electrical, chemical, industrial, mining, civil, hydraulic, mechanical, environmental), the basic and exact sciences, and foreign languages needed for research purposes. The polytechnics hope to play a leading role in the country's economic development.

The fourth type of postsecondary institution is exemplified in the National Institutes (Institut National), which do not have a uniform training period or structure. These institutes have proliferated in number and in the wide range of fields of study they offer. One example is the Institute of Technology of Education (ITE), which trains basic education teachers for the first five grades. Their number is dwindling, however, as the demand for rapid, intensive short-term teacher training that existed in the decade following independence no longer exists and current circumstances dictate the longer periods of training now being provided by the École normale supérieure. The rest of these training institutes, which form the majority, focus on science and technology. Their original mission, as defined a quarter of a century ago, was to optimize the educational training of students who did not pass the national competitive baccalaureate examination and channel them to basic, specialized training. In training qualified semiprofessional workers and high-level technicians who could be gainfully employed, these institutes would serve the nation's service, administration, industry, and agricultural sectors (International Association of Universities 2001). Training in these institutes lasted two and a half years and was mostly geared to basic and more practical instruction in fields of science and technology such as hydraulics, environmental sciences, economic sciences, agriculture, and paramedical training. Satisfactory conclusion of this course earned individuals a *Diplôme de Technicien supérieur*, which ensured that they could easily be absorbed in the market economy. The number of these institutes has decreased almost by half. Counting only those with the word "institute" in their title, one finds thirty-three in 2001 (Permanent Mission of Algeria to the United Nations 2001), compared to sixty-three approximately fifteen years ago (Wannas 1989, 84–87). It is not clear whether this indicates a change of status or merely changes in name.

Popular demand for more training and education, as well as the desire to move the concentration of students away from the traditional universities, propelled the authorities to further expand these institutes to offer a higher education track. As a result, some institutes now recruit baccalaureate students to study for a period of five years in the various engineering sciences, leading to a *Diplôme d'ingénieur*, which is comparable to a degree awarded by a university. In principle, no difference in quality control exists between the five-year engineering studies courses in these institutions and those in the university, save in administrative setup and financial responsibilities. While the universities are under the sole purview of the Ministry of Higher Education and Scientific Research, the national institutes are under the auspices of this ministry and the collaborative patronage of a host of other ministries, which number nearly as many as there are portfolios in the cabinet. These include the Ministry of National Education, the Ministry of Vocational Education, the Ministry of Agriculture, the Ministry of Industry, and many others. Currently, the shorter training period in these institutes and other postsecondary training institutions is gradually being phased out due to the fierce competition for work in the debilitated state economy, which in turn has prompted the government to deliberately raise standards and degree requirements for entry-level jobs (Rouwaq 2001).

The fifth type of postsecondary education institutions are the teacher training institutes. These institutes are referred to as École normale supérieure. They cater to the professional training of teachers who plan to teach at the nine-year basic education and four-year secondary schools. To enroll at this type of institute, students must have successfully passed the baccalaureate. Basic education teachers train for three years, ending with the *Diplôme de Maître d'Enseignement fondamental*, or for four years, ending with the *Diplôme de Professeur d'Enseignement fondamental*. Secondary school teachers train for five years, after which they obtain the *Diplôme de Professeur d'Enseignement secondaire*. The last year is normally reserved for professional training, when students enroll in a combination of pedagogical courses, both theoretical and practical, and acquire practical classroom teaching experience; the prior years are devoted to acquiring knowledge in their subject matter specialties.

The most recent of all these teacher training institutions is the University for Lifelong and Distance Education, which was established in the early 1990s. Its objective is to give full-time employees and workers who do not have a university education the opportunity to do so by upgrading their knowledge and skills during evening hours. It accepts students with the baccalaureate as well as those without it, provided they have had at least three years of secondary education and are at least 24 years of age. The university makes use of the already existing facilities at other universities. It has been reported that this university has had a rocky start due to inefficient administrative logistics, limited supporting services, low faculty incentives because of poor salaries, and obsolete curricula (Shrukh 1996, 448–451).

PRIVATE EDUCATION

Private education has so far played no role in Algerian higher education. This is mainly due to the permeating state ideology of socialism, which historically has perceived privatization to be inimical to the interests of nation building. The government asserted that state ownership and close administration of educational institutions would not only foster equal educational access across the ethnic, gender, social, and geographic divisions that have encumbered Algeria for so long but would also orient citizens toward obtaining the best possible education needed to stimulate the economy. The sluggish state of the Algerian economy for more than a decade—resulting from the accumulation of its outstanding international debt and the decreasing global demand for oil, hence the plummeting of the country's oil revenues and devaluation of its currency—has induced the government to try in recent years to encourage privatization by selling some of its manufacturing enterprises and production units to the public, but it has not yet planned similar measures in the area of higher education.

CONTROL OF THE EDUCATIONAL SYSTEM

The responsibility for formulating most educational policies and supervising their execution remains the prerogative of the national government. Its authority is embodied in several agencies with varying degrees of responsibility. Chief among these is the Ministry of Higher Education and Scientific Research (MHESR), established in 1971 to relieve the Ministry of National Education from the burden of phenomenal expansion in tertiary education. A minister who is a political appointee of the president heads the MHESR. Two officials serve the minister. One, the secretary-general (the equivalent of deputy minister), assisted by two *directeurs d'études*, is charged with handling the ministry's administrative functions pertaining to delivery of services and communication with regional educational authorities. The other, the cabinet head, assisted by seven officials (referred to as *chargés d'études*) and four *attachés*, is in charge of curricular matters, which are placed under the purview of five administrative units (known as directorates), each with its own director. These are the directorates of education and training; coordination, scientific research, and technological development; regulation and cooperation; development and planning; and fiscal affairs. Each directorate is in turn divided into several units, headed by a deputy director, which cover all aspects of curriculum, ranging from content, degree requirements, teaching methods, training, follow-up, and evaluation to documentation, appointments, promotion, and research (Ministère de l'Enseignement Superieur et de la Recherche Scientifique 1999). The minister appoints prominent scientific, educational, and research personnel, as well as renowned professors, who function in an advisory capacity and draw up the curricula and syllabi for different subject areas. After the minister endorses their suggestions, they become policy and are mandated at the provincial level.

The retrenchment of economic and productive enterprises, coupled with an ever-widening social malaise, brought about a dysfunctional administrative and academic state of affairs. In 1996, this prompted Algeria's president to establish the High Council of Education to advise him on restitution of standards and integrity to the university and higher education. This advisory body has been commissioned to study all matters relating to the teaching and learning process. It concerns itself, among other things, with continual assessment of national educational policy and planning through coordination, assessment, evaluation, follow-up, research, study, and exchange activities with regional and international bodies. This body is constituted of a complex network of vertical and hierarchical subunits representing a broad membership of experts in education, science, culture, and economics, as well as technocrats, the intelligentsia, trade unions, and parents' associations. All of the information gathered and reported to the president by this council is shared with the MHESR and other ministries, particularly the ministries for religious studies and vocational and technical education, which have jurisdiction over their institutions of higher learning.

Representatives of education at the provincial level are embodied in administrative entities called university academies, which are located in the eastern, western, and central parts of the country. They are entrusted mostly with enforcing legislation and decrees by continual evaluation of the educational démarche. Their spheres of responsibility include activating and coordinating all pedagogical operations; assembling, recording, and analyzing educational statistics; assessing the needs of the university academies; evaluating specifications for building facilities and all supporting units and services; and making informed recommendations for future planning and development (Jaami'at al-Jazaa'ir 2001).

Finally, one finds the internal administrative and organizational machinery of individual educational institutions. For example, the university is under the administration of a rector or chancellor, who is assisted by the president of the university, who in turn is assisted by a secretary-general and a number of vice-presidents. The president and his office personnel supervise the directors of all institutes and/or colleges, who oversee the department heads. The latter are the only elected administrators chosen from among the faculty by the faculty, while all others in the administrative hierarchy are government appointees. A corresponding internal organizational hierarchy, though not identical, is found in the polytechnics, university centers, and national institutes. The academic council is another internal body formed on university campuses to govern in an advisory function to the chancellor. It consists of administrative personnel and one faculty representative and it makes recommendations concerning course planning and logistics, research interests, and collaborative efforts with other institutions. There appears to be much duplication between the responsibilities carried out by this council and the university administrators, most of whom serve on it.

DECENTRALIZATION

It seems clear that the term "decentralization" is used differently in the Algerian educational literature than in most contexts. The government's control of the administration leads to the conclusion that there is little sharing of decision-making processes with educational authorities at the provincial and local levels. Matters that local authorities of postsecondary institutions can determine are limited in scope and carry little weight in the large picture. The upshot is that the whole enterprise is highly centralized, and regulated standardization is equated, at least in theory, to social equity and justice.

FINANCING AND PATTERN OF FUNDING

Higher education funding is also highly centralized: education is financed by the central government, while local communities play no direct role. The national government, via the education ministries and other ministries, is responsible for funding all aspects of education and providing free schooling for all registered students, including internationals. Each individual student is also entitled to a scholarship for living expenses. Additionally, the MHESR has built dormitory complexes and cafeterias on or in close proximity to the universities, constituting "university cities" where students, for nominal charges, receive food and board, not to mention other services. For the year 1999–2000, the government's total expenditure on higher education is estimated to be 7 percent of its GDP of 46.3 billion Algerian dinars (Energy Information Administration 2001; BuʿIshshah 2000, 33). Though the paucity of data since the 1990s has prevented one from observing accurate expenditure trends in the last decade, it is expected, based on past practice, demographics, and calls for reform, that expenditures will increase in the next decade (Metz 1994, 113).

LANGUAGE

It is known that language and ethnicity are closely intertwined. This clearly applies to the Algerian context. The two dominant languages, Arabic and Berber, were vehicles that expressed the ethnic identity of these respective groups. With the advent of colonialism, these languages had to reluctantly share their turf with a third encroaching language, French. The trilingual mélange has since remained constant, with each language signifying a certain social status or a given political or religious identity that is manifested in the dynamics of ideological movements on the national scene.

The medium of instruction in higher education has been based on the type of institution in question. The *madrasahs* and *zaawiyahs* have used Arabic in instruction since the middle of the eighth century, when Muslim Arab rule became firmly established in Algeria. French was the language of instruction at the University of Algiers and all the public schools at the precollegiate level, imposed as a deliberate, official policy intended to wipe out Arabic language and Arab-Islamic culture. Subsequently, French became the lingua franca among Arab, Berber, and French Algerians in most nonreligious circles. As a literary form and mode of written expression, the Arabic language ebbed tremendously during French rule. When Colonel Houari Boumediene, the second president, seized power in June 1965, 60 percent of Algerians could not read Arabic.

With the exception of journalism, intellectual production and discourse on most topics in print were typically in French. Academic, scholarly, research, and literary output was rarely written in Arabic (Muhammadi 1999, 65–70). Though common in many African nations, this Algerian phenomenon was unique among Arab states, including the other Maghreb countries of North Africa. Moreover, none of the various Berber languages, which existed mostly in spoken form, occupied a place or were studied in the religious or the state *lycée* schools.

The role of the Arabic language was to change immediately after independence in 1962. Arab nationalism had a strong impetus in reviving the Arabic language, particularly Modern Standard Arabic (MSA). After Arabic was declared, along with French, to be one of the twin official languages of the new republic, it was necessary to devise new curricula to reshape the emerging cultural identity in Algeria and the country's experience as an Arab, Islamic, and socialist nation. The speedy and intense undertaking of the Arabicization process took a toll on the country's national budget, particularly since faculty from different Arab countries were given lucrative remuneration to teach Arabic in Algerian schools and write textbooks and instructional materials in the new target language (Wannas 1989, 112–121).

Even though most of Algeria's curricula have been Arabicized, Arabicization took much longer to implement at the collegiate than at the precollegiate level. One reason is that the colleges were awaiting the enrollment of the first wave of graduates who had studied the Arabicized curriculum at the secondary level. Second, and more important, some Algerians have questioned the usefulness of complete Arabicization of the university curriculum in light of the Western domination of knowledge, particularly in science, technology, industry, and now in electronic communication. The debate continues. Many nationalists and various Islamic groups perceive Arabicization as reinforcing Algerian self-determination and national identity while also symbolizing its break from the legacy of French colonialism and present Western cultural imperialism. The other group argues that Arabicization would reshape the country into a self-besieged island, while a Francophone curriculum affords Algeria greater opportunities to ally itself with the global economy and new world order, a crucial determinant for the well-being of its ailing economy. The latter group includes many ethnic Berbers, whose persistence and frequent demonstrations forced the authorities to seriously consider the use of the Berber language in curricular offerings. After they applied tremendous pressure on the government through compelling arguments and somewhat militant collective activities, the Berbers succeeded in carving a place, albeit small, in the college curriculum. The University of Tizi Ouzou in the heartland of the Kabyle region now offers the Zouaouah dialect as part of Kabyle ethnic studies. As recently as October 2001, Algeria witnessed massive Berber demonstrations demanding that Berber languages and culture be accorded the same esteem as Arabic in the academy and elsewhere. These debates and events have postponed the target dates of complete Arabicization at the collegiate level (Metz 1994, 86–90).

Meanwhile, many Algerians have been evaluating the benefits of expanding the study of English at the university level in the last decade. This discussion has been gaining momentum, partly because many people recognize that English now functions as the lingua franca for global communication, banking, business, and commerce and partly because it is a neutral political symbol that is devoid of the negative connotations that have been associated with French in the Algerian experience. There have even been some debates among university students about whether or not to substitute English for French in teaching some science and technical subjects (A. Megatali 2001). It is telling that information about the Algerian institutes of higher learning is presented on their Web sites in English as well as in Arabic and French.

STATUS OF EDUCATIONAL RESEARCH

Educational research has received considerable support from the Algerian government. Much of the research is overseen at various official levels by national and regional institutional offices and bureaus. The MHESR directs much of the research and oversees formal agreements of collaboration with the individual universities and other higher education establishments to develop and carry out projects. Some research units deal with pedagogy, curricular material and textbook development, teacher and faculty training, supervision, and testing and evaluation for the purpose of improving the efficacy of internal structures and practices. Most research seems to concentrate on empirical and pragmatic studies that generate knowledge to help improve the various sectors of employment and the economy. More than fifty of Algeria's sixty-two research institutions are skewed toward the hard sciences, the applied sciences, and technology, the last two being closely related to boosting the health and productivity of the various sectors of the economy and environment.

However, the government's support of research activities appears to be more rhetorical than substantive when one examines faculty participation in research. Despite the ministry's emphasis on the significance of research for faculty rank, salary promotion, and development, it has adopted the long-time practice of automatic faculty promotion based on years of service, thus fostering apathy and disregard for the importance of research. Various studies also point to the low esteem that faculty and researchers are accorded; their work often is not appreciated and they lack the facilities needed to carry out their research. University libraries are still short of books, journals, and other acquisitions and are tremendously poor in electronic resources, particularly the Internet and commercial databases.

These ambivalent attitudes and adverse conditions, coupled with low salaries, have prompted those oriented toward research to move to other countries where material and moral rewards for research are much higher, causing successive waves of brain drain to Europe and the United States. Other faculty seek positions with the more lucrative salaries offered in the universities of the Gulf states. Consequently, higher education has increasingly been a bastion of poor research institutions. Algeria has been producing students without any, or with meager, research skills, even though the country remains in dire need of academic, empirical, and scientific experimentation to revitalize its weak domestic industry, improve productivity, and match its strong economic performance of the 1970s. According to President Abdelaziz Bouteflika (al-Sha°b 2000), economic stagnation

is the root of the political volatility that has been plaguing Algeria since the early 1980s.

ACADEMIC FREEDOM

Faculty research and the learning process are affected by the climate for academic freedom. Despite the lack of sources accounting for the number of faculty who have been harassed, detained, or murdered for exercising their academic freedom, human rights violations by the Algerian authorities and militant Islamic groups are well documented (UN Mission to Algeria 1998). Hundreds of thousands of citizens, including a large percentage of intellectuals and journalists, have been silenced since 1992. Algeria's armed security forces have used harsh measures, ranging from imprisonment to torture, disappearances, extrajudicial summary, and arbitrary executions, to silence public criticism of government policies and practices ("Unholy Cycle of Abuse"). Faculty members representing different discourse traditions, be they militant, secular, or traditional Islam, do not have free rein to express their views for fear of retaliation from the state authorities or various Islamic militant groups or even their own groups. This has led to an atmosphere of self-censorship in which learning is sterile and sanitized.

EDUCATION AND UNEMPLOYMENT

Another serious phenomenon in Algeria is the wide discrepancy between quantitative projections for human resource training set out in successive national development plans and the actual market needs for higher education skills. After many years of studying and training, many students (graduates and nongraduates) have found, particularly since 1988, that their skills are not in demand and cannot earn them gainful employment. International surveys (Energy Information Administration 2001) have reported that unemployment has now risen to around 30 percent. Official in-country sources estimate the number of unemployed Algerians to be around 2.5 million, one-sixth of whom are secondary and college degree holders, including not only graduates from the human and social sciences but also those trained to become doctors, engineers, and lawyers (Bu°Ishshah 2000, 33).

Dissatisfaction is equally widespread among current university students, who frequently complain that the buying power of their fellowships is being eroded at the same time that the maintenance of the university facilities and dorms has deteriorated and become substandard because of inflation and devaluation of the currency. Many are critical of the government's policies and its distribution of the country's wealth. Students have become very critical of the government's regimented fiscal policies and its withdrawal of education subsidies. Their economic alienation has led to a variety of demands, including the dismantling of the present governmental structure; the establishment of an Islamic state where the Shari°a governs all aspects of life; the revitalizing of secularism, pan-Arabism, and socialism; the strengthening of workers and unions; advocacy of human rights; calls for agrarian subsidies and reforms; and demands for the recognition of Berber identity and languages. As student groups expressed their lack of confidence in their government and questioned its legitimacy, their demonstrations, protests, strikes, and absences from classes became so frequent that the government at times ruthlessly manhandled them, creating cycles of violence between students and government. From 1990 to 1999, government retaliation was particularly harsh against student groups who were staunch advocates of the Salvation Front Party (FIS), which has been diligently toiling to create an Islamic republic in Algeria modeled after the government of Iran. When the FIS won national elections by a surprisingly wide margin, the army immediately seized power and ruled with an iron fist until February 1999, under the pretext that it was defending the fundamental principles of democracy, socialism, Arabism, and Islam upon which the Algerian nation was built. The government's tactic of intimidating students through imprisonment and execution only ignited more and more violence, which prompted many attempts to explain the cause of the civil disobedience that has beleaguered Algeria since 1988 (Mortimer 1991, 1993; alᶜAmmar 1996).

GENDER ISSUES

Even though female students face the same problems as their male counterparts, their participation in higher education has distinctive characteristics. One is the spectacular advance in their enrollment, which is stronger in some disciplines than others. The annual gradual but steady increase in female participation in universities since 1962 has led to an overall increase; by 1996, women accounted for 45 percent of students in higher education in Algeria (UNESCO 1999b, 213). Gender distributions among the university disciplines for 1996 show that females constituted 26 percent of students in education (pedagogy and teacher training), 65 percent in the humanities (fine arts, drama, religious studies, and theology scholasticism), 47 percent in law and the social sciences (including behavioral sciences, business administration, commerce, home economics, communication, and social services), 36 percent in the natural, engineering, and agricultural sciences (including mathematics, computer sciences, architecture, urban planning, transportation, and commerce), and 50 percent in the medical sciences (UNESCO 2000, 126, 160). Females constitute around 25 percent of faculty.

Much of the reason for this aggressive push for women's education is legislative. The Algerian Constitution of 1976 explicitly gives equal status to men and women. It prohibits any discrimination based on sex and guarantees women the same political, economic, social, and cultural rights as men. It recognizes the crucial role played by women in the war of liberation and further affirms that the objectives of the Algerian revolution cannot be fully realized without the full participation of women in the process of change and nation building and their full integration into Algerian society. This legislation was stated in more general terms and reaffirmed in the Constitution of 1989, but men have been given more social control over women since that time.

Despite these educational gains, the integration of women

in the workforce in public life is still poor. In 1977, 1982, and 1990, they comprised, respectively, only 6 percent (183,234), 7 percent (244,787), and 8.5 percent (360,000) of the working population. The situation is even worse in politics. Approximately twenty years after the war of liberation, in 1980, women filled only 1 percent of elected positions in municipal elections and 3 percent in regional elections. In 1981, there were only ten women among several hundred representatives in the National Day Assembly. Since then, several women have secured high positions in government cabinets and ministries and have won national elections, but they still occupy a marginal role in these institutions.

A host of factors obstruct a more accelerated rate of women's participation in Algerian society. One major factor has been the unhealthy economy, which makes competition for the limited employment opportunities fierce, exacerbating gender discrimination. Another is the ideological influence of the FIS, which opposes the public, secular image of women. Consequently, women have lost some of the earlier support they had from their husbands, fathers, and brothers, and even the government, in asserting their freedom of self-expression, which has either discouraged some from seeking employment or convinced them to assume their traditional role at home.

The ultraconservatives have also used several tactics of intimidation to deny women active roles in public life. Perhaps the most hideous are the fatal aggravated assaults against women, presumably by extremist fundamentalists, that led to the assassination of more than 190 women during the first nine months of 1995. Other violations against women range from abduction and rape to temporary marriages, physical beatings, and mutilations (UN Mission to Algeria 1998). The assailants interpret their actions as being authorized by the Shariᶜa because they are engaged in jihad against their adversaries and the enemies of Islam. University female students who do not conform to "Islamic" conduct and wear a veil have been targets of the terrorist tactics that occur in the university. There is a growing body of literature of women's personal stories of this kind of forced intimidation (Germain-Robin 1996). Some women have decided to fight such abuses through public protests or through their parliamentary representatives. The latter, depending on the political mood of the country, have at times been unresponsive to women's pleas that they reclaim the basic rights and freedoms to which they were entitled by Algeria's constitution. One such case was a demonstration sponsored by the *mujaahidaat*, the name given to female fighters who were actively engaged in the war of liberation, in 1983 in front of the national assembly. The event was a way for the women to voice their serious concerns regarding the newly enacted family code, which they believed subjugated women to men's control, thus depriving them of some of their previously recognized basic rights. In response, the police, acting on orders of the higher authorities, arrested 385 of them (Germain-Robin 1996, 55). Many women have avowed that they prefer being part of the workforce to being homemakers (Germaine-Robin 1996, 26–28). It has been reported by Amnesty International that the level of violence and number of murders and assassinations among the major parties to the conflict "diminished considerably in 1999," after President Bouteflika assumed power and scores of prisoners were released as a gesture of rapprochement with the militants.

EXISTING CHALLENGES AND RECOMMENDATIONS

Algeria's higher education challenges are as old as the MHESR, if not older. The following recommendations reiterate points made many times by Algerian and international educational experts, though Algeria has repeatedly failed to administer these prescriptions.

First and foremost is the pressing need to open access to schooling to the large segments of underprivileged in Algeria, particularly the rural population, the urban poor, and women, who have faced restricted access to primary and secondary schooling and, subsequently, to higher education.

Second is the necessity for better cooperation and coordination between the two major administrative entities of the educational enterprise, the Ministry of National Education (MNE) and the MHESR, which were separated in the 1970s. The territorial approach of each body has led to a progressively more strained relationship that has become detrimental to the national interest (Bu'Ishshah 2000, 94–95).

The third challenge is the ever-expanding intrusion of the centralized administrative bureaucracy. It is clear that all successive governments since independence have responded to Algeria's educational ills through building up an intricate system of hierarchical and vertical bureaus in the form of commissions, councils, committees, university academies, and, lately, the new National Council for Educational Reform. Attempts to solve timely issues or bring about reform have met with little success, problems have stagnated, and red tape has stirred popular resentment because it slows down the handling of every procedure. Algeria must undertake some serious rethinking regarding its style of administration. The country needs to experiment with other administrative models, particularly educational decentralization and privatization.

Fourth is a dire need for the qualitative strengthening of the curriculum, particularly in the humanities and social sciences. The knowledge base of the curriculum should strike a balance between fact finding, knowledge acquisition, and mere recall, on the one hand, and the training of students in research design, both qualitative and quantitative, on the other. Course materials, which are often outdated and are typically confined to a limited corpus, should be expanded to include more updated bibliographical listings and training in library research. Moreover, stronger links between school content, life education, and productive work need to be developed in practice, not just as rhetoric.

Fifth is the need to improve the quality of the faculty and allow teachers to exercise their prerogatives. One challenge is to enforce policies regarding the selection process for entry-level faculty, which is supposed to be based on one's qualifications and capability. Another is to encourage regular short-term in-service faculty training using stronger incentives that are coupled with accountability. Still another is to grant faculty autonomy and academic freedom to exercise more initiative in curricular matters, not just to fulfill certain bureaucratic functions and assigned tasks. A final challenge is to give greater weight to research in promotions and merit increases to encourage faculty to generate new knowledge.

A sixth recommendation is a renewed emphasis on the value of university education and degrees. Massive development in education has paradoxically created a devaluation of university degrees and the alienation of "surplus" graduates. Not only should degrees bring a respectable economic return, but university graduates should be recognized as having social and cultural prestige. Otherwise, political instability and violence are likely to continue (El-Kenz 1991, 13–14). In fairness, it must be stated that it is hard to imagine how Algeria's huge oversupply of graduates can be reduced in the next decade, particularly since signs of an economic rebound are meager and the expansion of higher education is continuing at a quick pace.

Seventh is the need to change attitudes toward the role of the library in education. There is an immediate need to upgrade the conditions of the poorly maintained libraries and their acquisitions and to encourage undergraduate students to continually consult academic books and journals, a precondition for conducting research.

An eighth goal is to give Algeria's universities academic autonomy. Since the 1980s, many institutions have been vulnerable to political pressures because of their lack of adequate funds at the expense of quality control. Some administrators have lost sight of their proper function and role as guardians of teaching and learning and have abused their positions by mistreating faculty, tampering with standards, and accruing personal material gains.

President Bouteflika candidly presented a litany of the problems that have been plaguing Algeria's universities in his keynote address at the graduation ceremony at the University of Houari Boumedien (al-Sha'b 2000). These include an unproductive administration style, personnel inefficiencies, violation of qualification standards in hiring and promotion practices for faculty and administrators, low educational standards for students, poor training in research skills, falsification of degrees and documents, bribery, nepotism, substandard support services (libraries, Internet, and digital technology), and, above all, poor and limited research publications.

Algeria today stands at a more positive juncture than it has for a long time. If President Bouteflika keeps his accord with the opposition and follows through on his rhetoric about educational reforms and development strategies, and if world oil revenues continue to improve the GNP, then higher education will likely witness positive changes. At the time of this writing, though, the majority of the Algerian citizens (beyond President Bouteflika's close supporters), particularly the various political groups and factions, are barely giving him a passing grade for his political, economic, and social policies. If positive changes, particularly the economic situation, are not observable in the coming two years, then the ills of higher education will likely worsen.

BIBLIOGRAPHY

al-'Ammar, M. 1996. "al-Jazaair wa al-Ta'addudiyyah al-Muklifah" [Algeria and the Costly Multiparty System]. In Sulayman al-Riyaashii, ed., *al-Azmah al-Jazaairiyyah* [*The Algerian Crisis*]. Beirut: Markaz Dirasaat al-Wihdah al-'Arabiyyah [Center for Studies of Arab Unity].

al-Riyaashi, S., ed. 1996. *al-Azmah al-Jazairiyyah* [*The Algerian Crisis*]. Beirut: Markaz Dirasaat al-Wihdah al-ʿArabiyyah [Center for Studies of Arab Unity].

al-Shaʿb (newspaper). 2000. July 9.

Amnesty International. 1997. *Amnesty International 1997 Report: Middle East and North Africa Regional Summary*. Available online at: http://www.amnesty.org/ailib.aireport/ar97/mdesum.html.

Associated Press. 1997. "Algeria: More Than 400,000 Fled Since Insurgency Began." AP Newswire Online, April 27.

BuʿIshshah, M. 2000. *Azamatu al-Taʿliim al-ʿAalii fii al-Jazaair wa al-ʿAalam al-ʿArabiyy* [*The Crisis of Higher Education in Algeria and the Arab World*]. Beirut: Dar al-Jil.

Chabou, M.-D. 1988. "Algeria." In T. Neville Postlethwaite, ed., *The Encyclopedia of Comparative Education and National Systems of Education*. Oxford: Pergamon Press.

El-Kenz, A. 1991. *Algerian Reflections on Arab Crises*. Translated by Robert W. Stookey. Austin: Center for Middle Eastern Studies, University of Texas at Austin.

Energy Information Administration (EIA). 2001. "Arab Maghreb Union." Accessed April 4. Available online at: http://www.eia.doe.gov/emeu/cabs/algeria.html

Europa Publications Limited. 2000. "Algeria." In *The Europa World Yearbook 2000*. London: Gresham Press.

Germain-Robin, F. 1996. *Femmes Rebelles D'Algérie*. Paris: Editions de l'Atelier.

International Association of Universities. 2001. "Higher Education Systems." Accessed March 7. http://www.unesco.org/iau/whed-2000.html

Jaamiʿat al-Jazaaʾir [The University of Algiers]. 2001. Accessed May 10. Available online at: http://www.univ-alger.dz

Megatali, A. 2001. Interview by author, Austin, Texas, May 7.

Megatali, K. 2001. Interview by author, Austin, Texas, May 15.

Metz, H. C., ed. 1994. *Algeria: A Country Study*. Washington, D.C.: U.S. Government Printing Office.

Ministère de l'Enseignement Supérieur et de la Recherche Scientifique. 2001. "Higher Education and Scientific Research." Accessed April 4. Available online at: http://www.mesrs.edu.dz/french/INDEX.HTM

Mortimer, R. 1991. "Islam and Multiparty Politics in Algeria." *Middle East Journal* 45 (Autumn): 575–594.

———. 1993. "Algeria: The Clash between Islam, Democracy and the Military." *Current History* 92, no. 570 (January): 37–41.

Muhammadi, H., ed. 1999. "ShayʾʾAn al-Adab al-Faransiyy." In *Fayd al-Ghorbah* [*The Deluge of Alienation*]. Cairo: al-Hayʾah al-Masriyyah al-ʿAmmah li-al-Kitab.

Permanent Mission of Algeria to the United Nations. 2001. Universities and Institutions and Research Centers. Accessed April 3. Available online at: http://www.algeria-un.org/msiepag

Rhodes University Library. 2002. "Directory of University Libraries in Algeria." Available online at: http://www.ru.ac.za/library/contacts/africa/algeria.htm

Rouwaq, J. 2001. Telephone interview by author, May 7.

Saleh, S., and Z. Musa. 1996. "Dawr al-Jaamiʿah wa al-Bahth al-ʿIlmiyy fii Tanmiyat Buldaan al-Maghrib al-ʿArabiyy" [The Role of the University and Scientific Research in the Development of the Arab Magreb, with Particular Reference to the Algerian Experience]. In Sulayman al-Riyaashii, ed., *al-Azmah al-Jazaairiyyah* [*The Algerian Crisis*]. Beirut: Markaz Dirasaat al-Wihdah al-ʿArabiyyah [Center for Studies of Arab Unity].

Shrukh, S. al-D. 1996. "al-Takwin al-Jaami ʿiyy al-ʿArbiyy al-Mutawaasil bi-Hasb al-khibrah al-Jazaaʾiriyyah" [Arabic Further Education Regarding the Results of the Algerian Experience]. In Sulayman al-Riyaashii, ed., *al-Azmah al-Jazaairiyyah* [*The Algerian Crisis*]. Beirut: Markaz Dirasaat al-Wihdah al-ʿArabiyyah [Center for Studies of Arab Unity].

Turner, B., ed. 2000. *The Statesman's Yearbook*. London: Macmillan Press.

UN Mission to Algeria. 1998. "To Assess Overall Situation in Algeria, U.N. Mission to Algeria Must Tackle Human Rights Issues." July 21. Available online at: http://www.hrw.org/press98/july/un-algr.htm

UNESCO. 1999a. *Statistics*. Accessed March 2001. Available online at: http://www.uis.unesco.org/en/stats/centre.htm

———. 1999b. *Statistical Yearbook*. Paris and Lanham, Md.: UNESCO Publishing and Bernan Press.

———. 2000. *Taqriir ʿan al-Tarbiyah fii al-Aalam* [*Report on Education in the World*]. al-Mukallis, Lebanon: Matbaʿat Hasiib Durghaam wa Awlaaduhu.

"Unholy Cycle of Abuse." 1996. *Middle East*: 1–8.

Université Badji Mokhtar–Annaba. 2001. *Les Facultés*. Accessed March 4. Available online at: http://www.univ-annaba.net/facultes.htm

Wannas, al-M. 1989. *al-Dawlah wa al-Masalah al-Thaqaafiyyah fii al-Jazaair* [*The State and the Question of Culture in Algeria*]. Tunis: al-Matbaʿah al-ʿArabiyyah [The Arabic Press].

World Bank Group. 2000. *Algeria in Brief*. Accessed May 20. Available online at: http://wbln0018.worldbank.org/mna/mena.nsf/Countries/Algeria/

Angola

PAULO DE CARVALHO, VÍCTOR KAJIBANGA, AND FRANZ-WILHELM HEIMER

INTRODUCTION

Angola is located in west central Africa. It has a surface area of 1,246,700 square kilometers (481,377 square miles) and a highly differential population density of, overall, about 6.6 inhabitants per kilometer. In 2000, its estimated population was 13.4 million, of whom slightly over 50 percent lived in urban areas—up to 4 million in and around Luanda, the capital. There are three major and six minor ethnic groups.

What is today a sovereign country was originally constituted through Portuguese colonial occupation at the beginning of the twentieth century, after about 500 years of Portuguese presence at certain coastal points and a process of territorial conquest which started in the nineteenth century. As a Portuguese colony, Angola experienced intense Portuguese settlement, the creation of an important population of mixed blood, and the systematic exploitation of "native labor." The late colonial period, 1961 to 1975, was marked by anticolonial war but simultaneously by considerable economic development, by political adjustments which implied full citizen status for all, and by incisive social transformations which led to "upward mobility" for significant numbers of the former "natives." At the same time, there was a sudden acceleration of the—until then hesitant—constitution of a social formation encompassing the territory as a whole. Independence came in 1975, after the collapse of the authoritarian regime which had existed in Portugal since the 1920s. Well over 90 percent of the white population left the country, which at first became a one-party state: the MPLA (Movimento Popular de Libertação de Angola), which had fought the Portuguese since 1962, was the only legally recognized political party. The MPLA's constitutional function was to lead the state, and it tried to put into practice a socialist system known as the People's Republic. The two other movements which had also taken part in the anticolonial war, the FNLA (Frente Nacional de Libertação de Angola) and UNITA (União Nacional para a Independência Total de Angola), were excluded from the political system and opted for armed resistance to the MPLA regime. The civil war, which started even before independence, was, until 1990, conditioned by the international conflict between East and West and by the regional policy of South Africa's apartheid regime. After a series of agreements among the parties involved in the conflict, elections held in 1992 led to the establishment of a multiparty democracy and the end of what was then termed the First Republic. The MPLA won the absolute majority and presently dominates Parliament and the government and maintains the presidency. Other parties—including the FNLA and factions of UNITA—are also part of the political system, but they carry little weight. However, immediately after the elections, UNITA's main body resumed its attempt to conquer political domination through military means, and civil war has been going on ever since. Although UNITA has been reduced over the last few years to waging guerrilla war affecting a number of rural areas, it is still accountable for heavy constraints on economic, social, and political development (see Heimer 1979; Gonçalves 1991; Roque 1993; Messiant 1994; Kajibanga 1996; Anstee 1997; Hare 1998; Jorge 1997, 2000; Kissinger 1999; Schubert 2000; Carvalho 2000a, 2000b; Hodges 2001). Early in 2002, the death of UNITA's historical leader, Jonas Savimbi, led to an almost immediate end of civil war and opened the way for an entirely new political dynamic, which has yet to be defined.

During the First Republic, the economic regime was one of state or collective property and centralized planning and control. The Second Republic began a process of stepwise liberalization of property regulations, possibilities for entrepreneurial initiatives, and rules for importation and exportation, while administrative measures such as the establishment of prices and exchange rates began to be loosened or abandoned. Under both regimes, the economy evolved around the offshore extraction of oil, which in 1999 made up for 87.2 percent of the budget revenues of the Angolan state. The second-most important source of revenue is the extraction of diamonds, followed at great distance by the production of timber and coffee. Since independence, there has been a steep decline in industrial production as well as in the production of cash crops, and the country is now a far cry away from its former self-sufficiency in food production. In 1999, the budget deficit of the Angolan state reached 7.8 percent of the gross domestic product (GDP). Over the last decade, the yearly revenue per capita decreased by about 47.5 percent. Credit is hard to come by, and there are no incentives to save. In 2000, 81.5 percent of the bank deposits were in foreign currency. The informal economy is essential for the survival of the population and absorbs most of the manpower; in Luanda, where the formal economy is strongest, the informal sector still represents 58 percent (see Meyns 1994; Roque 1991; Aguilar and Stenman 1993; Ferreira 1993–1994, 1999; Messiant 1994; Cerqueira 1996; Carvalho 1997; Rocha 1997; Queiroz 1998; Sousa 1998).

Poverty and social inequality indicators are extremely high. In the urban areas, about 40 percent of the population lives in absolute poverty; in rural areas, the figure is almost 80 percent (PNUD 2000). More than half the Angolan population is thus living below the poverty line. Sixty-one percent of the overall revenues are concentrated in the hands of the uppermost 20 percent of families, while the poorest 20 percent hold a total of 3.2 percent (PNUD 1999b, 20). The index of human development is very low; in 1999, its coefficient was 0.398, making Angola the 160th country in the world out of a total of 174 (PNUD 1999a).

While education in colonial Angola was, until 1961, well developed for the white population only and extremely limited for the "natives," it went through an almost explosive expansion from 1962 onward. It became pivotal for the upward mobility of mixed-blood and black Angolans and decisive for a rapid spread of the Portuguese language. After independence, Angola tried to boost education even more and, in addition to regular schooling, launched adult literacy campaigns during the first years. However, the combination of civil war and economic difficulties soon led to reverse effects. As a result, education has, in fact, been declining steadily over the last decades. About half the population is now presumed to be illiterate. The proportion of children entering school at the proper age is about 30 percent. School enrollment for the first six classes is about 50 percent, but only 30 percent survive the first four classes and 15 percent the first six classes—one of the worst situations the world over. The proportion of dropouts is such that the overall expenses per pupil are 2.5 times higher than the normal amount (Instituto Nacional de Estatística and UNICEF 1997). Despite all these shortcomings, postcolonial education—together with mechanisms such as radio and television, military service, and thriving Christian churches and communities—has been a powerful motor for the continuous spread of the Portuguese language, which is the only teaching language at all levels. Today, Portuguese is spoken by a majority of Angolans and has become the normal language of communication in all urban areas, where the younger generations are increasingly out of touch with the African languages spoken in the country.

This chapter will try to take stock of what has been achieved in higher education and what has not, conveying an idea of the shortcomings and inadequacies which at this stage are the overruling characteristics in this field.

THE HISTORY OF HIGHER EDUCATION IN ANGOLA

Although the beginnings of primary education in what is today Angola can be traced back to the seventeenth century, and although secondary schools began to appear early in the twentieth century, higher education was launched only toward the end of the colonial era. Catholic higher education for future priests started in Luanda and Huambo in 1958. In 1962, the Estudos Gerais Universitários de Angola were created in Luanda as part of the Portuguese university system, providing facilities for the study of agriculture, forestry, civil engineering, medicine, veterinary medicine, and education; in 1966, forestry and veterinary medicine were transferred to Huambo, education to Huíla (Oliveira and Leite 1972). In 1968, the Estudos Gerais became the autonomous Universidade de Luanda, launching study programs in the natural sciences (Luanda) as well as in geography, history, and romance languages and literature (Huíla). In 1972, 3,336 students attended this university, while 604 individuals from Angola attended universities in Portugal (Silva 1992–1994). At the same time, the higher ecclesiastical seminars of the Catholic church continued to function in Luanda and Huambo, and in 1962, the Catholic church opened an M.A. study program at its Instituto Pio XII for social work in Luanda.

When Angola became independent—that is, after the exodus of the Portuguese population had started—the Universidade de Luanda had twenty M.A. study programs (twelve in Luanda, six in Huíla, two in Huambo), 2,354 students, and 274 staff members. It was composed of six schools (faculties): science, economics, engineering, and medicine in Luanda; agriculture in Huambo; and arts/education in Huíla. From 1965 to 1975, the number of study programs had thus been multiplied by four, the number of students by 8.2, and the staff by 15.2.

Shortly after independence, all nonstate educational institutions were closed down, including the institutions of Catholic higher education. In 1979, the name of the university was changed to Universidade de Angola. In the following years, a law school and the corresponding M.A. program were created in Luanda. The school of arts was closed and was replaced by ISCED (Instituto Superior de Ciências da Educação), a school essentially designed to train secondary school teachers, which today exists in the cities of Benguela, Cabinda, Huambo, Luanda, Lubango, Sumbe, and Uíge and offers thirteen M.A. study programs (biology, chemistry, English language and literature, French language and literature, geography, history, mathematics, pedagogy, philosophy, physics, Portuguese language and literature, psychology, and sociology). In 1985, the university was renamed Universidade Agostinho Neto, after the first president of the republic (and simultaneously the first rector of the Universidade de Angola). Its statutory mission became the preparation of high-level cadres for the cultural, economic, and social development of the country.

As a consequence of the political developments of the early 1990s, the Angolan government conferred to the university, in 1995, a new legal status and organic structure. Its nature and mission were redefined in the UAN statutes as being those of "an

Table 15.1. Evolution of M.A. Study Programs at the Public University of Angola

Programs	1963	1968	1975	1980	2000
Agriculture & forestry	X	X	X	X	—[1]
Architecture	—	—	—	X	X
Biology	—	X	X	X	X
Biology for secondary teaching	—	—	—	X	X
Business sciences	—	—	—	X	X
Chemical engineering	X	X	X	X	X
Chemistry	—	X	X	X	X
Chemistry for secondary teaching	—	—	—	X	X
Civil engineering	X	X	X	X	X
Economics	—	—	X	X	X
Education/Pedagogy	X	X	X	X	X
Electrotechnical engineering	X	X	X	X	X
English for secondary teaching	—	—	—	X	X
French for secondary teaching	—	—	—	X	X
Geographic engineering	—	—	—	X	X
Geography	—	X	X	—	—
Geography for secondary teaching	—	—	—	X	X
Geology	—	X	X	X	X
Geophysics	—	—	—	X	X
History	—	X	X	X	X
History for secondary teaching	—	—	—	X	X
Information engineering	—	—	—	X	X
Law	—	—	—	X	X
Mathematics	—	X	X	X	X
Mathematics for secondary teaching	—	—	—	X	X
Mechanical engineering	—	—	X	X	X
Medicine	X	X	X	X	X
Mine engineering	X	X	X	X	X
Pedagogy	—	—	—	X	X
Philosophy for secondary teaching	—	—	—	X	X
Physics	—	X	X	X	X
Physics for secondary teaching	—	—	—	X	X
Portuguese for secondary teaching	—	—	—	X	X
Psychology for secondary teaching	—	—	—	X	X
Romance philology	—	X	X	—	
Sociology for secondary teaching	—	—	—	—	X
Veterinary medicine	X	X	X	X	—[1]

[1]Does not function because its installations were destroyed by the civil war.
Source: DPSE 1965 and 1969; Ministério da Educação 1978, 1992; UAN 1998, 1999a.

entity of public law, having statutory, scientific, pedagogical, administrative, financial and disciplinary autonomy, designed for the formation of high level cadres in the different fields of knowledge."

In 1998, the Universidade Agostinho Neto consisted of eight schools (*faculdades* and *institutos superiores*). It offered thirty-five M.A. study programs and forty-five optional specializations. Student enrollment reached 8,536, and the staff counted 736 members. Units of the university existed in seven provinces: Luanda, Benguela, Cabinda, Huambo, Huíla, Kuanza-Sul, and Uíge.

It must be emphasized that since colonial times, education in Angola has served to create and preserve social differences

and to consolidate social relations of domination (Heimer 1972, 1973; Carvalho 1989; Silva 1992–1994). This is particularly evident in higher education. Until independence, the vast majority of the students in higher education were Portuguese or their descendants; in 1974, only an estimated 5 percent were of other origins (USAID 1979, 62; Fundação 1996, 50). The reasons lay partly in social discrimination but mainly in the existence of fees at the level of secondary and higher education, which were far beyond reach for all but a few Africans.

After independence, education—from the elementary to the higher level—became free of charge and expanded considerably, while racial discrimination was eliminated. The result was a massive intake of students from all parts of society. This also applied to higher education, but here the rapid formation of new urban middle classes was soon felt: under the First Republic, they almost immediately constituted a "state-class" that controlled the political, administrative, military, ideological, and economic apparatuses and used education in their own class interest.

However, the introduction of mass education without adequate means to meet their needs, especially in terms of qualified teaching staff, together with the continuing civil war and economic difficulties, led after a few years to a substantial decline in the quality of the whole educational system, including the university, which, as a consequence, did not really serve the interests of the state-class. The first reaction was to create a huge system of scholarships for higher education abroad, fueled by foreign countries—especially, but not exclusively, those of Eastern Europe and Portugal—and by the Angolan state itself. This system, which often provided for scholarship amounts higher than university staff salaries, was inevitably put to use by the state-class, which succeeded in channeling toward this system proportions of the state budget considerably higher than those allotted to the university (Carvalho 1990).

Soon after the transition to the Second Republic, the decision was taken to replace this system with one that permitted and even fostered the establishment of private institutions of higher education that were in part indirectly fueled by the state (Messiant 1999). As early as 1992, the Catholic church launched Angola's first private university, the Universidade Católica de Angola, which began to function effectively in 1997 in Luanda and today offers M.A. study programs in law, economics, business, and computer sciences.

This precedent has to date been followed by the constitution of three "private commercial" universities. In 1999, the Universidade Lusíada de Angola was founded in Luanda as an extension of the private Universidade Lusíada existing in Lisbon; the study programs it offers so far are law, economics, business, and accounting. That same year, an Instituto Superior Privado de Angola opened its doors (also in Luanda) that provides study programs in pharmacy, nursing, physiotherapy, and dental medicine; in 2001, it began programs in architecture and urbanism, administration and business, communications and journalism, management, and computer sciences. In 2000, the Universidade Jean Piaget de Angola, an extension of the institution existing under the same name in Lisbon, opened its doors in Viana (on the periphery of Luanda); there, the programs are law, economics and business, engineering, nursing, medicine, psychology, and sociology; in 2001–2002, it offered programs in food engineering, civil engineering, architecture and territorial planning, social work, education and pedagogy, sports, and special education and rehabilitation.

All these universities are for-profit institutions and function on the basis of substantial fees paid by the students. While they to some degree make up for the shortcomings of the public university, they serve above all the interests of the state-class and of the new entrepreneurial class which the state-class has begun to engender.

In 1999, Universidade Nova de Angola was legally created by the Fundação Eduardo dos Santos, the foundation established by the president of the republic then in office and named after him. However, this institution has not yet begun to function, and its future is unclear at this stage.

In the meantime, the Universidade Agostinho Neto has announced plans for the creation of "centros universitários" for all geographical and cultural regions of the country, demonstrating a concern for the "cultural dimension of development" (Kajibanga 1999b, 2000a, and 200b). The declared intention is to "create opportunities for an outbalanced development of the country" (Universidade Agostinho Neto [UAN] 1999b).

TENDENCIES AND PATTERNS IN HIGHER EDUCATION

Policies of Higher Education

Shortly after independence, in 1977, the First Republic adopted a new educational system for Angola, which began to be implemented in 1978. This system provided for:

- A first level of basic education that consists of an introductory year and four years of elementary education (first to fourth forms)
- A second level of basic education that consists of a fifth and sixth form
- A third level of basic education that consists of a seventh and eighth form
- An intermediate level of education that offers two options: the pre-university cycle (three years, ninth to eleventh forms), which gives access to higher education, and the intermediate cycle *strictu sensu* (four years, ninth to twelfth forms)

This system was formulated by the MPLA and automatically endorsed by the government. Its intention was to generalize access to education in response to calls for social equality and national development. All educational institutions were to be state owned and state run as well as free of charge. The expectation was that all children would complete at least the first level of basic education. Links between schools and local communities were postulated, as was a functional role of education for agricultural and industrial development (Sousa 1997, 48–54; MPLA 1977, 122–125). The university was to maintain its role of serving development through the preparation of an educated elite and at the same time constitute a support for the political system and a symbol of national sovereignty (Fundação 1996, 50–51).

The lines to be followed by the university were detailed by the MPLA in 1981 (MPLA 1981, 122–125). For the ensuing five years, they were to be the following:

- Preparation of a plan for the overall reform of higher education and its stepwise implementation
- Establishment of a system of selecting students
- Intensification of exchanges with other universities in order to improve teaching through the collaboration with foreign staff (mostly from socialist countries)
- Establishment of links between teaching and research, involving the students
- Establishment of priorities for teaching and research in fields of paramount importance for the social and economic development of the country

In keeping with the last goal, special attention was given to the role higher education could play in the acutely felt need to accelerate economic development (Ferreira 1999, 45–52, 207–210). Direct involvement of the university in economic production was demanded by the ruling party, MPLA, implying a high priority for technical and agricultural studies and a downgrading of social and human sciences (Sousa 1997). In this context, the university's tendency to become an elite institution was criticized, and it was postulated that it should give access to everybody who could demonstrate adequate capacities or aptitudes. The subordination of all university teaching to Marxism-Leninism as an analytical theory and a research methodology was a matter of course.

In 1992, the transition to multiparty democracy led to important changes in government policies concerning higher education. The wave of political and economic liberalization reached the university almost immediately, abolishing its ideological framework. The new constitution confirmed the paramount importance of education, conferring authority for all basic decisions on this subject to the Parliament. This organ gave the matter high priority, and early in 1993 it organized a roundtable which produced a project for a new educational system (Projecto de Lei de Bases do Sistema de Educação). The structure proposed there consists of four subsystems:

- Pre-primary education
- General education—primary and secondary cycles
- Technical and professional education—professional training and secondary professional cycle
- Higher education—the university is to have a graduate (B.A., M.A.) and a postgraduate (*mestre*, doctorate) cycle; in addition, shorter "polytechnic" study programs are to be introduced

As a consequence of these options, education in Angola has been, and still is, going through a period of transition in which the new structures have been introduced step by step while the old ones still exist, although more and more residually.

Over the last fifteen years, since before the end of the First Republic, a number of studies were published (see Varii 1985; Fundação 1987; Fundação 1996; UNESCO 1993; MPLA and UAN 1999) and several conferences on the situation of higher education in Angola were held (First, Second, and Third Conselho Universitário in 1984, 1986, and 1988; Forum on the UAN and Higher Education in 1998) with the goal of improving public policies in this field. Early in 2000, the MPLA organized an in-depth debate on the subject and concluded that improved higher education required the following:

- Correct educational policies and sustained public and private investment in education
- Close links between teaching and research
- The development of scientific and technical study programs essential for development, with special attention to agriculture, veterinary medicine, and business management
- Development of higher education in the country itself, with studies abroad limited to postgraduate programs essential for development in Angola

Except for the latter, all these conclusions had already been adopted in the 1980s but never implemented. For three reasons, the year 2000 marks a decisive turn in Angolan policies concerning higher education:

- The huge volume of resources previously channeled toward studies abroad will from now on be made available for the development of higher education in the country.
- The appearance of private universities brings very considerable pressure to bear on the state, in the sense that it must now adopt more adequate and efficient policies for public higher education.
- A new concern with trans-, inter-, and multidisciplinarity and with studies better adjusted to the realities in Angola—and Africa in general—has triggered a far-reaching process of restructuring all study programs.

Financial Resources and Management of Higher Education

In the present system of higher education in Angola, there is a clear distinction between policy decisions and policy implementation. At the level of policy decisions, the institutional actors are Parliament, the government as a whole, and the Ministry of Education. More concretely, the parliamentary committee on education, culture, science, and technology, the government, and the minister of education are here the most salient entities. On the level of policy implementation, public and private universities under the new constitution have autonomy in organization, teaching, and research. In the future, there will be a council of rectors, meant to coordinate policy decisions among the universities themselves and even to adopt common rules and measures.

At this stage, the financial resources of higher education have four sources: the state budget, student fees, contributions from private and international donor organizations, and paid services to individual or corporate users.

The public university depends overwhelmingly on the state budget. Every year, it is granted a recurrent budget and a capital budget. The former is granted directly to the university by the government and has four main components: personnel expenses, purchase of goods, payment of services, and other expenses. The first component always constitutes more than 80 percent of the overall budget (Ministério da Educação 1992; MPLA 2000), although the adjustment of salaries constantly lags far behind the constant increase in the cost of living. Also, year after year the ordinary budget proves insufficient for even the most basic needs.

The capital budget is granted by the Ministry of Education and administered by the university. Like the recurrent budget, it does not provide funds for research, an activity which, as a consequence, has been extremely limited (Camarada 1992; Kajibanga 1998, 1999a). In fact, poor financial resources have practically reduced the university to teaching, that is, the bare essentials of study programs.

The weak economic performance of the country and the expenses of the continuing civil war have led to significant re-

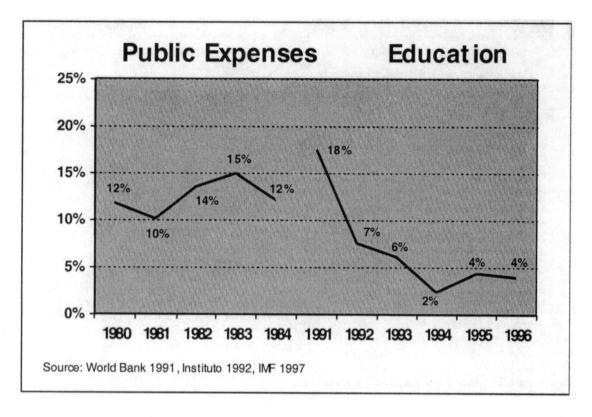

FIG. 15.1. *Percent of State Budget Allocated to Higher Education in Angola, 1980–1996*

ductions in the proportion of the overall state budget dedicated to education expenses.

Figure 15.1 illustrates the enormous oscillations in and the drastic overall decrease of the share allotted to higher education in the state budget. The obvious conclusion is that the declared policy decisions on education have not been put into practice in Angola, which has clear implications for the country's development.

Student fees constitute, almost by definition, the main financial resources for the private universities, though not much information on their financial situation is made available to the public. The fact that they exist and multiply demonstrates, of course, that they count on the growing purchasing power of the state and entrepreneurial classes in Angola—enough to justify initial investments from abroad (generally Portugal). As to the Universidade Agostinho Neto, it has just started new evening study programs meant for jobholders, which require fees.

The public university and some private universities have benefited from contributions by sponsors operating within the country, such as the oil and diamond companies, as well as from diverse international entities. The Universidade Nova de Angola counts on contributions from an Angolan foundation (Messiant 1999).

There are some revenues from services, such as permitting the use of installations and equipment by other institutions, the production of teaching material, and others; however, these possibilities are as yet poorly explored, mainly for the lack of legislation on the subject.

Institutions of Higher Education

In 2001, the following institutions of higher education existed in Angola:

• Universidade Agostinho Neto: Luanda, Benguela, Cabinda, Huambo, Lubango, Sumbe, Uíge (public)
• Universidade Católica de Angola: Luanda (private)
• Universidade Lusíada de Angola: Luanda (private)
• Universidade Jean Piaget de Angola: Viana (private)
• Instituto Superior Privado de Angola: Luanda (private)
• Universidade Nova de Angola: (private; has not yet started to function)

The Universidade Agostinho Neto is still by far the most important higher education establishment in Angola. It is true that over the years it has suffered from blatantly insufficient financial resources as well as from infrastructures—including libraries, laboratories, workshops, and student dorms—which are often in a state of extreme neglect. On the other hand, during the 1990s, the university expanded into a network which today spreads over most of the country—although the minor campuses are, at this stage, generally limited to the human and social sciences, which are less demanding in terms of resources. At present, the university is composed of the following schools:

- School of Natural Sciences, Luanda: biology, geographical engineering, geophysics, geology, physics, mathematics, chemistry
- School of Agrarian Sciences, Huambo: agronomy, veterinary medicine
- Law School, Luanda (extensions in Cabinda and Lubango): law
- School of Economics, Luanda (extensions in Cabinda and Sumbe): economics, business sciences
- School of Engineering, Luanda: architecture, electronic engineering, civil engineering, computer engineering, mechanical engineering, chemical engineering, mining
- Medical School, Luanda: medicine and surgery
- School of Education, Benguela: education; training for secondary school teachers in French, geography, history, mathematics, psychology
- School of Education, Huambo: chemistry, education, English, French, geography, history, mathematics, psychology (does not function because of war damage)
- School of Education, Luanda: education, English, French, history, mathematics, philosophy, Portuguese, psychology, sociology. Extensions in Cabinda (education, history, psychology), Sumbe (education, psychology), and Uíge (education, psychology)
- School of Education, Lubango: biology, chemistry, education, English, French, geography, history, mathematics, Portuguese, psychology
- Nursing School, Luanda: nursing

In 2002, a second (and autonomous) public institution of higher education is to be created, the Instituto Superior de Ciências Sociais e Políticas. It is to be located in Luanda and will launch study programs in the social sciences, strategic studies and international relations, the mass media, political economy and business management, political science and political marketing, and public administration.

As to private universities, the situation is as follows:

- Universidade Católica de Angola, Luanda: business sciences, computer sciences, economics, law
- Universidade Jean Piaget de Angola, Viana: business sciences, economics, engineering, law, medicine, psychology, sociology (in 2002, study programs in architecture and urban planning, civil engineering, food engineering, social work, teacher training for technical schools, special education and rehabilitation, and sports are to be launched)
- Universidade Lusíada de Angola, Luanda: accounting, business sciences, economics, law
- Instituto Superior Privado de Angola, Luanda: administration and management, architecture and urban planning, information and management, journalism and mass media, nursing, dental medicine, pharmacy, physiotherapy
- Universidade Nova de Angola, Luanda: study programs in the fields of humanities and technologies to be launched in 2002

It must be emphasized that in all universities, the curricular structure is similar to that in Portugal and other European countries. There are at present no B.A. programs (*bacharelatos*), only M.A. programs (*licenciaturas*), which last four to five years. The structure also provides for *mestrados*, that is, post-M.A. programs leading to an academic degree (*mestre*) in its own right, which is at the same time a step toward the Ph.D. (or M.D., etc.) degree; however, as of early 2002, no post-M.A. programs are functioning in Angola.

Access to Higher Education

For all institutions of higher education in Angola, access supposes the completion of the secondary (intermediate) cycle; that is, the eleventh form of the "pre-university" cycle or the twelfth form of an "intermediate" cycle. In addition, all private universities organize preparatory (*propedêutico*) years which students have to pass before they are admitted to the M.A. study programs. Furthermore, the Universidade Católica de Angola does not admit students who are older than 25 years.

The demand for access to the Universidade Agostinho Neto has always been far higher than its capacity to accommodate students, because it has for a long time been the country's only institution of higher education and because it is free of charge. As a consequence, since independence, it has been necessary to select the best candidates among those possessing the formal qualifications year after year. The selection system and criteria have changed over the years: since 1992, the rector of the UAN has had the authority to establish the admission criteria. A *numerus clausus* was established for all study programs and specific admission exams were defined for each program. Authority for defining the core subjects and the system of these exams (one or more tests) was conferred to the different schools. Since 1999, the *numerus clausus* has been established by each school. For access to admission exams, an additional criterion was adopted: an overall mark of fourteen (on a scale of twenty) at the secondary/intermediate level.

For access to the private universities, the essential condition is the payment of a monthly fee ranging from US$200 to US$350: at the Instituto Superior Privado de Angola, the fee is US$200 for the polytechnical study programs and US$250 for programs in the field of health care; the Universidade Católica de Angola has established a uniform fee of US$250 and the Universidade Lusíada de Angola a fee of US$350; at the Universidade Jean Piaget de Angola, it is US$350 for medicine, US$300 for nursing and engineering, US$200 for the (compulsory) preparatory year, and US$200 for all other study programs.

Staff and Students

Tables 15.2 and 15.3 show the evolution of the numbers of university students in 1964–1971 and 1977–1998.

The tables illustrate a stepwise increase, year after year, in the number of students in higher education until independence. At that time, there was a sharp (73 percent) drop in student numbers at the university, mainly due to the fact that most of the white population left in 1975 or shortly thereafter but also due to the closure of all other institutions of higher education. From 1977 onward, the student population increased again, and in 1998 it was double what it had been at independence. The

Table 15.2. Students in Higher Education during the Colonial Period in Angola, 1964–1971

Study Program	1964	1965	1966	1967	1968	1969	1970	1971
Universidade de Angola	418	477	607	827	1,074	1,570	2,125	2,435
Agriculture and forestry	38	36	38	40	55	71	90	91
Natural sciences[1]	—	—	—	—	63	135	236	231
Education	91	32	22	53	75	160	152	180
Economics	—	—	—	—	—	—	210	243
Engineering[2]	180	242	298	400	464	586	649	774
Veterinary medicine	26	37	56	70	78	99	118	122
Medicine & surgery	83	123	163	214	283	394	520	549
Arts[3]	—	7	30	50	56	125	150	245
Catholic Seminars	89	79	92	95	104	121	145	131
School of Social Work	24	28	7	67	74	66	79	94
Normal[4]	—	—	—	—	—	27	20	8
Total	531	584	706	989	1,252	1,784	2,369	2,668

[1]Biology, chemistry, geology, mathematics, physics
[2]Civil, electrotechnical, mechanical, mines, industrial chemistry
[3]Includes teacher training
[4]Teacher training
Sources: DPSE 1965, 96–97; 1966, 96–97; 1967, 96–97; 1968, 89; 1969, 95; 1970, 91; 1971, 87; 1972, 87.

Table 15.3. Fields of Study of Students in Higher Education in the Postcolonial Period, 1977–1998*

Field	1977	1997	1998
Natural Sciences (Luanda)	404	665	713
Agriculture (Huambo)	86	300	290
Law (Luanda)	—	891	1,134
Economics (Luanda)	172	1,115	1,201
Engineering (Luanda)	78	621	428
Medicine (Luanda)	260	506	672
Education (Benguela, Huambo, Luanda, Lubango)	109	3,818	4,098
Total	1,109	7,916	8,536

*Universidade Agostinho Neto only
Sources: Ministério da Educação 1978, 9; UAN 1998, 83; UAN 1999a, 14.

average yearly rate of growth was 10.2 percent after 1977, while it had been 27.6 percent before 1974.

Beyond these global indicators, one has to look at important changes which occurred with regard to the distribution of students over the different areas of study. During the colonial period, the proportion of students in engineering and medicine represented between 49 percent and 65 percent of the total student population; after independence, this figure immediately dropped to 39 percent in 1977 and has been steadily decreasing ever since, reaching 14.2 percent in 1997 and 12.9 percent in 1998. In the latter year, the humanities held the highest proportion of students, followed at a distance by the technical sciences, economics, law, medicine, natural sciences, and agriculture, as shown in Figure 15.2.

In other words, students in economics, the humanities, and law represent almost two-thirds of the university students in Angola, while the share of natural and life sciences is rather limited. This corresponds not only to the preferences of the students but also to the poor conditions prevailing in the latter sciences, due to scarce or nonexistent investments and, in the case of agriculture and forestry, the impact of civil war. Whatever the explanation, this distribution runs counter to the declared policies of the Angolan government.

Overall, about 60 percent of university students in Angola are men. Studies in the technical sciences, especially in engineering, are overwhelmingly a male domain, while there is a strong female presence in the life sciences and (to a lesser degree) the humanities.

The students in the age group of 21 to 30 years represented 44 percent of enrollments in 1998. However, while the corresponding proportions were significantly higher during the colonial period and grew steadily over time (from 59 percent in 1964 to 74 percent in 1974), they decreased after independence. In short, the student population has become considerably older as a by-product of a policy of giving access to larger numbers of candidates; in 1998, as many as 10 percent of the university students were 40 or more years of age.

As to teaching staff, the most recent information available refers to the situation in 1998 and thus includes only the Universidade Agostinho Neto. That year, the staff at that university numbered 736, 10 percent of whom were foreigners. There was a strict hierarchical stratification: 11 percent were full professors, 7 percent associate professors, 21 percent assistant professors, and 61 percent teaching assistants. Only the first two categories were composed of Ph.D. (or M.D., etc.) holders. That year, the student-teacher ratio was 11:6.

For the private universities, all of which are of very recent creation, available statistics are as yet highly fragmentary and sometimes of doubtful reliability. All of them taken together rep-

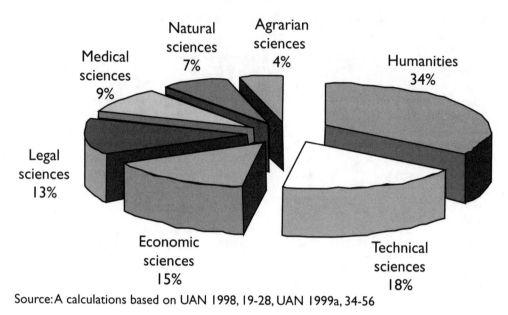

Source: A calculations based on UAN 1998, 19-28, UAN 1999a, 34-56

FIG 15.2. *Student Enrollment in Various Fields of Higher Education, Angola 1998*

resent only a small fraction of higher education in Angola. The figures for the Universidade Agostinho Neto can come close to reflecting the overall situation.

Student Associations

University students in Angola started to organize themselves while the decolonization process was still underway. A politically independent Association of the University Students of Luanda was created in 1974 but ceased to exist by mid-1976 because of adverse political conditions (AEES 1983, 8). In 1979, under the name Association of Higher Education Students (AEES), so-called dynamizing groups were constituted in the different schools of the university, starting in engineering, medicine, and the natural sciences. These groups had a status similar to that of labor unions; they were supposed to defend the interests of students and guarantee their "active and conscious" participation in the solution of academic problems (AEES 1983, 9–11). Their activities, which included seminars on higher education and student movements that were held from 1977 to 1982, had an important mobilizing impact on the students and led to the transformation in 1983 of the AEES into an effectively countrywide organization. In line with the political regime of the First Republic, it was the only student organization existing, and it worked within the prevailing system.

In the process of the political transformations initiated in 1992, the AEES fell apart. In its place, autonomous student or-

ganizations were constituted in each school of the Universidade Agostinho Neto and then became affiliated with a newly constituted umbrella association, the Angolan Students Union (UEA), which brought together student organizations from all levels of the educational system. The university student organizations represented the student body in all organs of the Universidade Agostinho Neto.

Although university students in Angola can be said to be highly mobilized, and despite the fact that even in the private universities, nuclei of associations were constituted almost immediately, the UEA officially ceased to exist in 2000. The dominant reason was probably heavy pressure from the main political parties to replace the one overall organization with different organizations that were linked to different parties. In addition, attempts by student leaders to use the associations for their personal benefit played an important role in the demise of the organization. At present, the future of student associations is uncertain.

PROBLEMS AND CHALLENGES

Political Interference

One of the main problems that has faced higher education in Angola since independence has been frequent interference from institutions that hold political power.

Until 1992, the only existing university had the status of a public entity dependent upon the Ministry of Education. Its dependency was political as well as administrative. Its rector and vice-rectors were appointed by the president of the republic upon the recommendation of the ruling party, the MPLA; the rector had the political status of a vice-minister. The directors of the different schools were appointed by the minister of education, also upon the recommendation of the MPLA. The university was supposed to

• Apply the policies and guidelines of the MPLA
• Plan and implement government policies in the field of higher education
• Guarantee teaching, research, and the diffusion of scientific knowledge

A good indication of how far political interference actually went is the fact that the ruling party intervened, formally or informally, in the hiring and firing of each member of the teaching staff (UAN and UP 1996). For the social and human sciences, only party members of solid Marxist-Leninist conviction were appointed. In these sciences, even the teaching programs were established by the so-called ideological department of the MPLA and usually corresponded to what was taught in countries such as the Soviet Union or Cuba. In short, the university was strongly conditioned by Angola's affiliation to one of the two blocs of countries which then existed.

The political changes introduced since the early 1990s led to profound transformations in this situation. In 1995, extensive legislation was approved that conferred full autonomy to the university, which ceased to be institutionally subject to orders from the MPLA or the Ministry of Education. A system of internal democracy was introduced, guaranteeing free elections of all organs and officeholders by the teaching staff. The latter was guaranteed that the selection process would be based exclusively on academic merit.

The new legislation was applied immediately, and all the elections it stipulated were held. However, because the new framework diminished the authority of the Ministry of Education without really clarifying the relationship between university and government, a conflict arose as early as 1996. The government suspended the elected rector of the UAN in 1997, in 1999 appointed a temporary board of commissioners, and in 2000 issued a Statute of Higher Education which considerably strengthened government control over public as well as private universities. This meant a return to a legal situation that made considerable political interference possible in higher education. However, in an unprecedented act of independence, the Supreme Court ruled in July 2001 that the suspension of the elected rector had been unlawful, so that institutional interference may in the future become more difficult. Even in 2001, the directors of all schools of the Universidade Agostinho Neto—except for the law school—are MPLA militants and members of the MPLA cells of their respective schools; they have to report to these cells as well as to the MPLA Central Commission on Higher Education, from which they receive guidelines.

The whole process can be understood against the background of the control the MPLA exercised over public education during the First Republic and tries to maintain in the Second Republic. In line with the organizational model of

Marxist-Leninist parties, one of the commissions functioning at the level of the Central Committee of the MPLA is in charge of controlling the university. While it is certain that Angola is no longer a one-party state, the MPLA is largely dominant and is set on retaining as much power as possible through organizational mechanisms which have not changed radically. This system of interlinked government and party interference in higher education constitutes a major problem and is clearly detrimental to the development and consolidation of the sector (Kajibanga 1998).

Problems of Quality

A second challenge which higher education in Angola faces is that of its pervasive low quality. A number of indicators allow us to assess and explain the severe shortcomings in efficiency and productivity.

The list should start with the insufficient scientific training of the teaching staff. One indication of this is the extremely limited number of conference papers and publications produced by the faculty of the Universidade Agostinho Neto. In 1998, a total of 49 conference papers (most of them not presented in writing), 5 articles in scientific journals, and 12 books (9 were readers for students; only 3 reflected research results) were produced (UAN 1999a, 34–56). Another indicator is the refusal of many teachers to openly discuss their teaching curricula (contents and bibliography), which in many instances have not been updated since the 1980s (and in a few cases since the 1960s) in the social and human sciences. This means that often the Marxist-inspired programs of the First Republic are still in use. The lack of scientific quality is also illustrated by the fact that an important part of the teaching staff, including full professors, do not hold academic degrees above the M.A. level (UAN 1999a, 11).

In addition, the overwhelming majority of the teaching staff, including that of the schools of education, have either insufficient pedagogical preparation or none at all. In 1997, UNESCO and UAN held an international seminar on this problem and recommended a number of measures, none of which has been implemented so far (UNESCO and UAN 1997; MPLA 2000, 9–11). This deficiency is the main cause for the highly inadequate systems teachers use to evaluate students.

Both shortcomings—the scientific and the pedagogical—are linked to the low salaries of the teaching staff, which to a significant extent explain their low professional motivation and force many instructors to accept additional jobs, regularly or occasionally, outside the university (on the permanent increase in cost of living in Angola and the increasing inadequacy of public salaries, see Ferreira 1992, 1993–1994; Aguilar and Stenman 1993; Carvalho 1995–1996, 1997, 1999; Instituto Nacional de Estatística 1996; PNUD 2000). In the realm of higher education, corruption, present everywhere in contemporary Angola, is particularly salient (see Carvalho 1994, 1998; Júnior 1994; Ministério da Justiça 1990, 1996; Gonçalves 1999; Andrade 1999; Ngonda 1999; Rocha 1999a, 1999b; Sousa 1999). Except for a minority of brilliant students, admission to study programs is obtained by bribes varying from $300 to $2,000, payable to the faculty members who are in control of the admission process. By the same token, "buying one's way through the program" is fre-

Table 15.4. M.A. Degrees Conferred by the UAN

School	1980–1991	1998
Natural Sciences	183	49
Law	221	40
Economics	461	27
Education	204	24
Agriculture	172	10
Engineering	338	9
Medicine	491	4
Total	2,070	163
Average per year	173	163

Sources: UAN 1999a, 22; Ministério da Educação 1995, 50.

quently the logic followed after admission: staff members often sell teaching materials or give private lessons to their students; payment is made either in money or in services of all kinds (including sexual) rendered by the student or his or her relatives and friends.

Low salaries and poor working conditions have led the union of university teachers and the union of university employees to organize a number of strikes since 1996 (Rocha 1997, 40; MPLA 2000). These constituted the main reason for the limited number of classes taught in most study programs. In the 1990s, classes were taught for only four to six months instead of nine, so that the total number remained far below what UNESCO and other international bodies stipulate for M.A. programs and sometimes even below what is the established minimum for B.A. programs.

At the same time, the majority of the students are not in the "regular" situation of being able to fully concentrate on their studies. In 1998, 68 percent of students held full-time jobs outside the university, and 4 percent were in the armed forces (UAN 1999a, 112).

The precarious and often calamitous state of the existing infrastructures; the lack of adequately equipped libraries, laboratories, workshops, and the like; and the scarcity of teaching materials of all kinds contribute to the overall qualitative shortcomings of the university.

Yet another set of reasons stems from the mismatch of academic programs to the economic, social, and cultural realities of the country, in particular to the kinds of human resources needed (Guerreiro 1985; Delors 1996, 121–123). This also holds true for private universities, which more often than not copy the model of their Portuguese "mother universities" or of the Universidade Agostinho Neto.

All this entails negative consequences, measured in part by the success/failure rates of the students. In 1998, a total of 7,502 candidates presented themselves for the annual exams at the Universidade Agostinho Neto, but only 1,291 of them, or 17 percent, passed. As a result, only 24 percent of the students matriculating at that university, or less than one in four, were allowed to go on to the next year of their respective study programs (MPLA 2000). Of course, the statistics available have to be interpreted against the background of the above-mentioned corruption.

The accumulation of these kinds of circumstances means that a very small proportion of students actually finish their study programs and obtain the M.A. degree.

As shown in Table 15.4, higher education in Angola has produced only 2,070 holders of an M.A. degree in twelve years (1980–1991)—an average of 173 per year. In 1998, this figure was even lower, and the 163 successful students represented only one-third (32.7 percent) of those who had been attending the final year of the respective study programs that year. Even these poor results are obtained only at the cost of students staying in the study programs much longer than the regular four to five years—sometimes up to twice as long. As mentioned above, no holders of post-M.A. degrees have been produced so far.

Another measure of quality is the low level attained by those who have successfully concluded the M.A. study programs. On this point, no data exists, but from all that has been described above, it is clear that critical observers are entitled to hold very low expectations.

All in all, it is evident that, contrary to the declared policy of giving high priority to higher education to facilitate development, the quality of this sector is among the lowest on the African continent. As a consequence, "The low efficiency of the educational system increases the mass of unemployed and underemployed, penalizes the economic productivity of the country, weakens the purchase power of the salaries, devalues the human resources, and limits the indexes of competitiveness of the enterprises" (Rocha 1997).

The low quality of higher education is the main reason many Angolans go abroad for their B.A./M.A. studies—mostly to the United Kingdom, the United States, France, Portugal, Brazil, South Africa, and Namibia. The second reason is the wish to escape military service. In addition, there are those who go abroad for post-M.A. studies because these do not (yet) exist in Angola. In addition to the above-mentioned scholarship system, the financial basis for studies abroad has been scholarships granted by foreign institutions of all kinds, but such studies are increasingly funded privately by families who belong to the state-class and the entrepreneurial upper class. No figures are available, but it is certain that the number of students who study abroad after taking the M.A. is at least many hundreds, perhaps even several thousands. A certain proportion of those who obtain foreign diplomas do not return to the country, but here again no figures are available. As far as is known, there is practically no outward migration of holders of Angolan university diplomas to take jobs abroad.

Creation and Use of Human Resources

Until the end of the 1980s, a university diploma obtained either in Angola or abroad automatically guaranteed a good or at least reasonable job in Angola. Since then, the situation has changed drastically for a number of quite diverse reasons. One reason is the low quality of higher education in Angola and the ensuing low prestige of university diplomas. Another reason is the fact that in the service sector (including public administration), jobs are more often than not acquired according to criteria other than merit and competence. A third reason is the decline of the formal economy, which is linked to the low salaries paid in this sector. These circumstances have led to two consequences for the holders of university diplomas—increasing unemployment and transition into the informal sector of the economy. Seventy-two percent of the workforce in Luanda has left the formal economy since independence (Sousa 1998, 35).

Only an estimated 0.4 percent of the Angolan population of 19 or more years of age hold higher education diplomas; they are predominantly male and live in urban areas (Instituto and UNICEF 1997, 54–56). Unfortunately, data on their employment situation exist for Luanda only (Sousa 1998, 18–20). In 1995, 2.4 percent of the economically active population of the Angolan capital and 2.6 percent of the employed workforce held university diplomas. Their proportion was roughly equal in the formal and the informal sectors of the economy. Twelve percent of the holders of such diplomas were unemployed. Beyond the reasons given above, this situation reveals the absence, or the lack of effectiveness, of government policies for high-level human resources (i.e., those individuals with university diplomas) based on merit and competence and in line with developmental needs (Carvalho 1995–1996), and this despite the existence of legislation on the integration of university diploma–holders into the job market.

In this context, the several thousand holders of foreign university diplomas are in a particularly difficult situation. Most of them, though by no means all, obtained their diplomas in former socialist countries during the First Republic and are now faced with the problem that their studies are often considered to be of lesser value. All holders of foreign diplomas are in a position of disadvantage vis-à-vis those who studied in Angola while they were already employed. There is no obvious overall solution to this problem.

Scientific Research

During the First Republic, the task of organizing scientific research was attributed to different ministries as well as to the Universidade Agostinho Neto, where the National Center for Scientific Research (CNIC) was created. Under the Second Republic, this structure was slightly altered by the creation of the Ministry of Science and Technology in 1997; the CNIC was attached to the new ministry.

Under the First Republic, the investment in scientific research was low. In the field of social and human sciences, the MPLA undertook or commissioned some research along Marxist lines; research outside the party was obliged to follow the same methodology, and alternative approaches were violently suppressed, in extreme cases through police intervention. Generally, research was held in low esteem. All this resulted in the absence of a tradition of research and in an almost total lack of links between university teaching and research—which is well illustrated by the fact that in several cases, teaching staff have reached the highest hierarchical level without ever having carried out research. Self-evaluations by the Universidade Agostinho Neto paint a somber picture of the research aspect of higher education, underlining the reasons why it has not been significant: lack of laboratories and research centers, lack of financial resources, lack of stimuli for research in the legal statutes

governing the career of the teaching staff, and the nonexistence of a school of social and human sciences (UAN 1979, 1987).

The situation has remained very much the same under the Second Republic, except that now there is relative methodological freedom (though political and ideological pressures persist). In 1999, the Unversidade Agostinho Neto approved a resolution on the creation of centers of scientific research and postgraduate (post-M.A.) teaching, but this document has not yet been implemented. Thus, higher education in Angola continues to neglect both actual research and the creation of research competence. The few scientific research projects which have been undertaken in Angola in the 1990s are, without exception, due to individual initiatives and are funded by resources mobilized by the researchers themselves, which are normally from extra-university sources.

SUMMARY AND CONCLUSIONS

Higher education was introduced in Angola in the 1950s and 1960s while it was still a Portuguese colony, through the initiative first of the Catholic church and then of the colonial state. Access was then heavily conditioned by social origin: students were overwhelmingly white. At independence, in 1974, there were about 4,400 students in Angolan higher education.

After independence, the public university, now Universidade Agostinho Neto, grew steadily. In 1998, it had roughly 8,500 students and almost 750 teachers in thirty-five M.A. programs running not only in the capital, Luanda, but also in a number of other cities. From 1999 onward, a total of five private universities were launched.

In all policy statements issued by the Angolan government, high priority is given to education in general and higher education in particular. However, the actual investment in this field lags far behind declared intentions and has even been decreasing since 1992, ranging at present well below the averages of countries in sub-Saharan Africa and developing countries in general.

The quality of higher education in Angola is very low. Three-quarters of the students do not pass their annual exams, have to repeat greater or lesser parts of the programs, or drop out.

The role the university plays in the development of the country is highly debatable. Overall, higher education in Angola not only reflects the profound political, economic, and social crisis of the country but can be seen as a mechanism that contributes to the reproduction of the prevailing logic of disorder.

The main challenge faced by higher education in Angola at this stage is that of solving serious problems of quality. The preconditions for this endeavor are:

- A firm political decision to use resources to educate Angolan students at home rather than abroad
- Freedom of scientific thought and academic activities for teachers, researchers, and universities
- Adequate infrastructures for teaching and research, particularly libraries, laboratories, and workshops
- Research centers that are adequately equipped and staffed
- Updated teaching programs that are adapted to the realities of the country

- Teaching and research priorities which are a function of the developmental needs of the country
- Training of the teaching staff in educational theories, methods, and techniques
- An attitude of social and academic responsibility on the part of the students
- A national policy of human resources that favors scientific and professional competence
- Salaries in line with the social importance of higher education
- Reintroduction of ethics into the university system through persistent routing out of corruption

BIBLIOGRAPHY

AEES (Associação dos Estudantes do Ensino Superior). 1983. *1ª Conferência nacional dos Estudantes do ensino superior. Documentos.* Luanda: Associação dos Estudantes do Ensino Superior.

Aguilar, R., and A. Stenman. 1993. *Angola 1993: Back to Square One?* Gothenburg: Department of Economics, Gothenburg University.

Andrade, Vicente Pinto de. 1999. "Corrupção e crescimento económico." Public lecture in series on A promoção de uma gestão pública, ética e transparente, Luanda.

Anstee, M. 1997. *Órfão da guerra fria. Radiografia do colapso do processo de paz angolano. 1992/93.* Porto: Campo das Letras.

Camarada, C. 1992. "A universidade. Aspectos para reflexão." Conference at the Centro Universitário do Huambo.

Carvalho, P. de. 1989. *Struktura spoleczna spoleczenstwa kolonialnego Angoli.* Warsaw: Institute of Sociology of Warsaw University.

———. 1990. *Studenci obcokrajowcy w Polsce.* Warsaw: Institute of Sociology of Warsaw University.

———. 1993. "Velhos dogmas no ensino." *Correio da Semana,* December 19, 7.

———. 1994. "Valores e aspirações de duas turmas de jovens do ensino médio de Luanda." In *Paix, Progrès et Démocratie en Angola,* 63–75. Paris: Éditions du Centre Culturel Angolais.

———. 1995–1996. "Reflexões sobre Política Salarial." *África* (São Paulo) 18–19, no. 1: 257–268.

———. 1997. "Política cambial selectiva." *Ngola—Revista de Estudos Sociais* (Luanda) 1, no. 1: 217–247.

———. 1998. "A adaptação ao meio académico e o sucesso escolar." Paper presented to the Fórum sobre a Universidade Agostinho Neto e o Ensino Superior em Angola, Luanda.

———. 1999. "O impacto da crise político-económica angolana na qualidade de vida das populações." Paper given at colloquium on Vencer a Fome e a Miséria, Luanda.

———. 2000a. "Guerra e paz aos olhos dos luandenses." In *La Réconciliation en Angola. Une Contribution pour la Paix en Afrique Australe,* 92–110. Paris: Éditions du Centre Culturel Angolais.

———. 2000b. "Natureza do conflito angolano." In Ismael Mateus, Reginaldo Silva, and Bernardo Vieira, eds., *Angola. A festa e o luto. 25 anos de independência,* 87–99. Lisbon: Vega.

Cerqueira, J. 1996. "Probabilidades económicas dos angolanos a curto e longo prazos." In *Les Perspectives de Reconstruction de l'Économie de l'Angola,* 57–72. Paris: Éditions du Centre Culturel Angolais.

Delors, J., ed. 1996. *Educação: um tesouro a descobrir. Relatório para a UNESCO da Comissão Internacional sobre Educação para o século XXI.* Porto: Asa.

DPSE (Direcção Provincial dos Serviços de Estatística). 1965, 1966, 1967, 1968, 1969, 1970, 1971, 1972. *Estatística da Educação. Ano lectivo 1964/65* (1965/66 etc.). Luanda: Direcção Provincial dos Serviços de Estatística.

Ferreira, M. E. 1992. "Despesas militares e ambiente condicionador na política económica angolana (1975–1992)." *Estudos de Economia* 12, no. 4: 419–438.

———. 1993–1994. "Performance económica em situação de guerra: o caso de Angola." *África* (S. Paulo) 16–17, no. 1: 135–156.

———. 1999. *A indústria em tempo de guerra (Angola, 1975–91).* Lisboa: Edições Cosmos & Instituto de Defesa Nacional.

Fundação, C. G. 1987. *Universidade Agostinho Neto. Estudo global.* Lisbon: Fundação Calouste Gulbenkian.

Fundação, G. T. 1996. *Contribuição para a revitalização da Universidade em Angola.* Porto: Universidade do Porto.

Gonçalves, J. 1991. *Angola a fogo intenso. Ensaio.* Lisboa: Cotovia.

Gonçalves, M. 1999. "Eficácia jurídica dos instrumentos legais no combate à corrupção: procuradoria Geral da República, Tribunal de Contas e Alta Autoridade Contra a Corrupção." Public lecture in series on A promoção de uma gestão pública, ética e transparente, Luanda.

Guerreiro, M. G. 1985. *A Universidade. Factor de desenvolvimento e mudança.* Faro: Universidade do Algarve.

Hare, P. 1998. *Angola's Last Best Chance for Peace: An Insider's Account of the Peace Process.* Washington, D.C.: United States Institute of Peace Press.

Heimer, F. W. 1972. *Educação e Sociedade nas Áreas Rurais de Angola. Resultados de um inquérito.* Vol. 1. Luanda: Missão de Inquéritos Agrícolas de Angola.

———. 1973. "Estrutura Social e Descolonização em Angola." *Análise Social X,* no. 40 (1975): 621–655.

———. 1979. *The Decolonisation Process in Angola: An Essay in Political Sociology.* Geneva: Institut d'Études Internationales.

Hodges, T. 2001. *Angola from Afro-Stalinism to Petro-Diamond Capitalism.* Oxford: James Currey and Bloomington: Indiana University Press.

Instituto Nacional de Estatística. 1996. *Perfil da Pobreza em Angola.* Luanda: Instituto Nacional de Estatística.

Instituto Nacional de Estatística and UNICEF. 1997. *MICS. Inquérito de Indicadores Múltiplos.* Luanda: Instituto Nacional de Estatística and UNICEF.

Jorge, M. 1997. *Pour Comprendre l'Angola.* Paris: Présence Africaine.

———. 2000. "O conflito em Angola: natureza e perspectivas." Paper presented to the colloquium on La Réconciliation en Angola: une Contribution pour la Paix en Afrique Australe, Paris, Éditions du Centre Culturel Angolais.

Júnior, S. 1994. "Crise no ensino. A corrupção segue dentro de momentos." *Correio da Semana* 3, no. 43 (October): 23–30.

Kajibanga, V. 1996. "O Estado pós-colonial e a questão da defesa nacional." Paper presented to the Simpósio sobre a Defesa Nacional, Luanda.

———. 1998. "Liberdades Académicas e Instituição Universitária em África." Opening conference at the Fórum sobre a Universidade Agostinho Neto e o Ensino Superior em Angola, Luanda.

———. 1999a. "Ensino Superior e Dimensão Cultural do Desenvolvimento." Paper presented to the Semana Social "Educação para a Cultura da Paz," Luanda.

———. 1999b. "Culturas Étnicas e Cultura Nacional. Uma reflexão sociológica sobre o caso angolano." Public lecture at the Universidade Católica de Angola, Luanda, for the 2° Encontro Internacional dos Delegados da Igreja Católica dos Países Lusófonos.

———. 2000a. "Sociedades Étnicas e Espaços Socioculturais. Uma contribuição ao estudo das culturas étnicas e da cultura nacional em Angola." Public lecture at the Africa Institute of the Russian Academy of Sciences and at the School of Arts of Lomonosov University, Moscow.

———. 2000b. "Tradição, educação e dimensão cultural de desenvolvimento. Notas avulsas para uma perspectiva sociológica do caso angolano." Public lecture at the Semana Científica da Universidade Jean Piaget de Angola.

Kissinger, H. 1999. *Years of Renewal.* New York: Simon & Schuster.

Messiant, C. 1994. "Angola: Les voies de l'ethnisation et de la décomposition." *Lusotopie* 1–2: 155–210.

———. 1999. "La Fondation Eduardo dos Santos (FESA): autour de l'investissement de la société civile par le pouvoir angolais." *Politique Africaine* 73: 27–44.

Meyns, P. 1984. "O desenvolvimento da economia angolana a partir da independência: problemas da reconstrução nacional." *Revista Internacional de Estudos Africanos* 2: 121–161.

Ministério da Educação. 1978. *Princípios de base para a reformulação do sistema de educação e ensino na R.P.A.* Luanda: Ministério da Educação.

———. 1992. *Exame sectorial da educação.* Luanda: UNESCO, UNICEF, Ministério da Educação.

———. 1995. "Plano Quadro de Reconstrução do Sistema Educativo (1995–2005)." Unpublished manuscript. Luanda: Ministério da Educação.

Ministério da Justiça. 1990. *Estudo sobre o fenómeno da corrupção.* Luanda: Ministério da Justiça (draft).

———. 1996. "O fenómeno corrupção e sua influência na educação." Paper presented to the conference on A educação em Angola. Para uma melhor qualidade de ensino, Luanda.

MPLA (Movimento Popular de Libertação de Angola—Partido do Trabalho). 1977. *Orientações Fundamentais para o Desenvolvimento Economico-Social no período 1978/1980.* Luanda: Secretariado do Comité Central.

———. 1981. *Orientações fundamentais para o desenvolvimento económico-social. Período 1981–1985.* Luanda: Secretariado do Comité Central.

———. 2000. "Diagnóstico e perspectivas do desenvolvimento do ensino superior." Luanda: MPLA (draft).

MPLA and UAN. 1999. *Proposta de política de expansão geográfica da Universidade Agostinho Neto.* Luanda: Universidade Agostinho Neto.

Ngonda, L. 1999. "A percepção da sociedade civil sobre o fenómeno da corrupção." Public lecture in the series on A promoção de uma gestão pública, ética e transparente, Luanda.

Oliveira, C., and F. Leite, eds. 1972. *Legislação Universitária. Parte geral. 1930–1971.* Luanda.

PNUD (Programa das Nações Unidas para o Desenvolvimento). 1999a. *Relatório do Desenvolvimento Humano. 1999.* Lisbon: Trinova.

———. 1999b. *Relatório do Desenvolvimento Humano. Angola 1999.* Luanda: PNUD.

———. 2000. "Políticas de Redução da Pobreza. Procurando a Equidade e a Eficiência." Luanda: PNUD (draft).

Queiroz, F. 1998. "A economia tradicional e a transição para a economia de mercado." Paper presented to the 1as Jornadas sobre Economia de Angola, Luanda.

Rocha, M. A. da. 1997. *Economia e Sociedade em Angola.* Luanda: Luanda Antena Comercial.

———. 1999a. "Subsídios para uma análise sobre a corrupção em Angola." Public lecture in the series on A promoção de uma gestão pública, ética e transparente, Luanda.

———. 1999b. "A corrupção e o seu impacto no desenvolvimento económico de Angola." Public lecture in the series on A promoção de uma gestão pública, ética e transparente, Luanda.

Roque, F. 1991. *Economia de Angola.* Venda Nova: Bertrand.

———. 1993. *Angola: Em nome da Esperança.* Venda Nova: Bertrand.

Schubert, B. 2000. *A Guerra e as Igrejas. Angola 1961–1991.* Basel: Schlettwein.

Silva, E. M. da. 1992–1994. "O papel societal do sistema de ensino na Angola colonial (1926–1974)." *Revista Internacional de Estudos Africanos* 16–17: 103–130.

Sousa, C. de. 1999. "O Papel dos tribunais no combate a corrupção." Public lecture in the series on A promoção de uma gestão pública, ética e transparente, Luanda.

Sousa, J. P. D. Araújo de. 1997. "A educação e o Desenvolvimento Endógeno em Angola. Evolução, problemas, perspectivas." M.Sc. dissertation, Universidade Portucalense.

Sousa, M. A. de. 1998. *Sector Informal de Luanda. Contribuição para um melhor conhecimento.* Luanda.

UAN (Universidade Agostinho Neto). 1979. "Perspectivas sobre a Investigação Científica e o desenvolvimento da República Popular de Angola." Unpublished manuscript. Luanda: Universidade Agostinho Neto.

———. 1987. "A Investigação Científica na Universidade Agostinho Neto." Unpublished manuscript. Luanda: Universidade Agostinho Neto.

———. 1998. *Relatório de actividades. Ano civil de 1997. Plano de acção 1997–2001.* Luanda: Universidade Agostinho Neto.

———. 1999a. *Relatório de actividades. Ano civil de 1998.* Luanda: Universidade Agostinho Neto.

———. 1999b. "Política de expansão geográfica da Universidade Agostinho Neto." Unpublished manuscript. Luanda: Universidade Agostinho Neto.

UAN (Universidade Agostinho Neto) and UP (Universidade do Porto). 1996. *Contributos para a revitalização da universidade em Angola.* Porto: Universidade do Porto.

UNESCO. 1993. *Estudo sectorial do ensino superior.* Luanda: UNESCO.

UNESCO and UAN. 1997. "Pedagogia universitária nos países africanos de língua portuguesa." Unpublished manuscript. Luanda: UNESCO and Universidade Agostinho Neto.

USAID. 1979. "A Report to the Congress on Development Needs and Opportunities for Cooperation in Southern Africa." Annex A: "Angola." Unpublished manuscript. Washington, D.C.: United States Agency for International Development.

Varii. 1985. *Ensino superior na República Popular de Angola. 1975 a 1985.* Luanda: Ministry of Education and Universidade Agostinho Neto.

16

Benin

Corbin Michel Guedegbe

INTRODUCTION

Benin, known as Dahomey until 1975, is a former French colony that became independent in 1960. It is located in West Africa and shares boundaries with Burkina Faso and Niger to the north; Niger and Nigeria to the east; and Togo to the west. Its southern limit is defined by the Atlantic Ocean. The total area of Benin is 112,334 square kilometers (43,372 square miles). The total population is estimated at 5.6 million. Approximately 90 percent of the workforce is engaged in agriculture, Benin's major economic activity. The country, which has an average adult literacy rate of 66 percent and a gross enrollment ratio of 78 percent in primary education, belongs to the Least Developed Countries group on the basis of gross domestic product per capita and its human development indicator. The official language is French and the national currency the CFA franc (1 CFAF = .01 French franc).

As regards its political history, the country experienced a period of instability between independence in 1960 and 1972, with several military coups during that period. After 17 years of one-party rule following the 1972 coup, the country entered a new era with the beginning of the democratic process in 1990.

Benin's higher education system has been shaped by its French structure. It is a public system controlled by a single university system and has gone through several stages. Though, to a certain extent, it has contributed to meeting the human resource needs of the country, the education system has been facing serious difficulties that have caused a deterioration of its internal and external efficiency. National and international developments require the system to adapt to the requirements of the evolving socioeconomic environment.

HISTORICAL BACKGROUND OF POST-SECONDARY EDUCATION

As was the case with other French colonies in Africa, during the colonial period (1890–1960), Benin had no higher education system. Colonial subjects were trained in France and later in Senegal at the Dakar University when that institution was established after World War I. Since the headquarters of the regional colonial administration was in Dakar, this university served as a de facto regional center for Francophone West Africa.

After independence, the history of higher education in Benin went through several phases, including the creation of a preparatory first year in letters in Porto-Novo and the establishment of a joint higher education institution with neighboring Togo in the late 1960s, with one branch in each country (arts and letters in Togo and sciences in Benin). In general, students spent the first two years in either branch, which were affiliated to French universities, and were sent to Dakar or France to complete the first degree (*licence*).

In 1970, Benin decided to create its own university. Named Université du Dahomey at the time of its creation, it became Université Nationale du Bénin (UNB) in 1975 after the country changed its name from Dahomey to Benin. The university, which was established by presidential decree on August 21, 1970, is different from the Université du Bénin, Togo's national university.

Benin's higher education system is mostly a public and central system. The UNB caters to most of the demand for post-secondary education in the country. However, the late 1990s saw the emergence of private institutions, which are becoming a major feature of the system.

STRUCTURE

On the basis of their mode of admission, UNB institutions can be divided into the following categories:

- Institutions of general education with open access. Anyone with the *baccalaureat* (secondary school leaving certificate) can enroll in these institutions. There is no restriction to admission. These are:
    a. Faculty of Letters and Human Sciences
    b. Faculty of Sciences
    c. Faculty of Law and Economics
- Institutions of professional education with selective access. Applicants must have the *baccalaureat* and pass an entrance exam. These institutions have admission ceilings. Students who enroll are generally awarded a full scholarship and do not pay any tuition. Until the mid-1980s, there was only one admission stream, which was very competitive. Now, in addition to this admission mode, most of these institutions also admit a second group of students on the basis of a test. This category pays for full "private" tuition. The institutions concerned are the following:
    a. National Institute of Economics
    b. National Institute of Public Administration
    c. National Institute of Youth and Physical Education
    d. National Institute of Social Work
    e. Faculty of Agronomy
    f. Faculty of Medical Sciences
    g. University Polytechnic College
    h. Teachers College: one advanced, and three lower levels.
- Postgraduate and affiliated institutions. They are the following:
    a. Regional Institute of Public Health
    b. Institute of Arabic Languages and Civilizations
    c. Beninese Center for Foreign Languages
    d. Institute for Advanced Studies in Mathematics and Physics
- Service institutions. These are:
    a. University Library
    b. National Center for Student Welfare
    c. The SYFED Center, which has been established as a component of the Université des Réseaux d'Expression Française, UREF (University of the French-speaking Networks)

The creation of the selected access institutions in the late 1970s stimulated demand for higher education because these schools had a professional orientation and offered better job opportunities to their graduates. But enrollments increased at the open access institutions in the 1980s, particularly at the Faculty of Law and Economics (FASJEP), where the number of students increased five times. In 1999, with 6,193 students, FASJEP enrolled 38 percent of all UNB students. When we add the students enrolled in letters or related fields, about 65 percent of all UNB students are enrolled in nonscientific fields offering very limited job opportunities.

As a whole, UNB is composed of 19 institutions scattered on 6 campuses. The main campus, Abomey-Calavi, is located 8 miles from Cotonou, Benin's major city.

Table 16.1. Student Enrollments in Higher Education, Benin, 1970–1999

Year	Enrollments
1970	350
1975	1,896
1980	3,390
1986	7,253
1990	9,201
1995	11,007
1996	11,227
1997	14,055
1998	14,486
1999	16,284

Source: Services de la Scolarité (Admissions and Records), Rectorat, Université Nationale du Bénin, Campus d'Abomey-Calavi, Bénin, 2000.

STUDENTS

Table 16.1 presents the evolution of enrollments from 1970 to 1999. Enrollments have grown considerably since the university was established in 1970. They grew from 350 students in 1970 to 7,253 in 1986, 11,007 in 1995, and 16,284 in 1999 (which includes 3,346, or 20.5 percent, women). Student enrollment in higher education represents only 1 percent of the age group. In 1999, the three so-called classic faculties (letters and human sciences, economics and law, and sciences) enrolled a total of 12,925 students, or 79 percent of the entire university.

Students have always been a powerful force both on campus and in society. Students in Benin have a long history of activism and unrest closely related to the country's political and economic climate. The one-party regime that ruled the country from 1982 to 1989 endeavored to control student movements by banning all associations and imposing a national students' association, the Coopérative Universitaire des Etudiants (Student University Cooperative), which is affiliated with the ruling party. With the emergence of the democratic system of government in 1990, the focus of student activism has remained closely related to Benin's economic and political life and people's insecurity about their future. Several student organizations have been established. Students very often go on strike and hold demonstrations to demand improved living conditions and more jobs from public authorities. Students are now free to hold such demonstrations as long as they do not break any law regulating such actions. Student activism has caused serious disturbances on campuses which have had a negative impact on the quality of education, since they have often resulted in government's decision to close down the university for several days or even months.

ACADEMICS

Table 16.2 presents the evolution of the number of academics since 1992. From 614 in 1992, the number decreased to 559 in 1994, remained stable until 1997, and reached 638 in 1999.

Table 16.2. Faculty and Teaching Staff in Higher Education, Benin, 1992–1999

Year	Professors	Assistant Professors	Teaching Assistants	Others	Total
1992	88	272	194	60	614
1993	88	284	196	35	603
1994	90	287	150	32	559
1995	67	266	228	0	561
1996	81	304	177	0	562
1997	85	346	170	0	601
1998	88	357	165	0	610
1999	101	371	166	0	638

Source: Services de la Scolarité (Admissions and Records), Rectorat, Université Nationale du Bénin, Campus d'Abomey-Calavi, Bénin, 2000.

Due to financial constraints, the government stopped recruiting new civil servants (academics are civil servants in Benin) for several years. New recruitment resumed only recently.

In general, assistant professors are those holding the *Doctorat de troisième* cycle (doctorate) and professors are those holding the *Doctorat d'Etat* (doctorate). The last category (teaching assistants) is composed of those who do not have the doctorate yet. They are graduates of UNB or foreign universities and are recruited by the Ministry of Education upon the recommendation of the university. They mostly perform teaching activities, pending the award of a scholarship to complete their doctorate abroad. Due to the current financial difficulties, however, this scholarship program was stopped for more than ten years and was resumed timidly only in the mid-1990s. Thus, many of these teaching assistants could never obtain the doctorate, which is a necessary condition to become a full member of the academic profession.

Benin is a member of the CAMES, the Council for Higher Education in Africa and Madagascar, and thus applies the CAMES standards and norms of the academic profession. CAMES is an association of seventeen countries which have agreed to adopt common standards for their higher education systems as far as degrees, curriculum, and faculty promotion are concerned. The agreement creating CAMES was signed by seventeen heads of state and governments in Lomé, Togo, on April 26, 1972. The current members of CAMES are: Benin, Burkina Faso, Burundi, Cameroon, Central African Republic, Chad, Congo, Cote d'Ivoire, Gabon, Guinea, Madagascar, Mali, Mauritania, Niger, Rwanda, Senegal, and Togo.

The CAMES promotion system is based on productivity (publications). On an annual basis, each university submits its candidates for the various ranks. The appropriate CAMES committees meet to review the nominations according to the rules in force. For the highest rank (*Professeur Agrégé*) and in some disciplines (law, medicine, economics, and political sciences, for example) a competition is held every two years.

The prevailing concerns in the academic profession that affect the quality of the system are the following:

- The situation of the large number of teaching assistants who are still waiting to complete their doctoral studies.
- The academic promotion system, which is perceived as unfair by faculty members who obtained their doctorate outside the French system. Under the single doctorate system adopted by France a few years ago, the Ph.D. and the new doctorate are considered to be equivalent and normally entitle one to apply and compete for the hierarchical academic titles determined by CAMES.
- The large number of part-time teachers. The part-time faculty represents a considerable proportion of the entire faculty. Most of them are government employees working in state or parastatal organizations. They have various qualifications and constitute the bulk of the teaching staff, particularly in selective-access (professional) sections of UNB. Although they help reduce the shortage of faculty, they cannot perform beyond a certain level. It is obvious that UNB will find it difficult to have a full-fledged academic profession with a high degree of professionalism as long as such a considerable proportion of the teaching staff is part-time.

FINANCING

The government allocates more than 30 percent of its total budget to education. With less than 2 percent of the total student population of the entire educational system, higher education consumes 20 percent of the total education budget. Higher education is financed almost exclusively by the government; it also benefits from foreign assistance programs for specific activities. Most of the budget of higher education goes to faculty salaries, student scholarships, and other subsidies. Only a small portion (about 4 percent) is allocated to research and equipment. This situation accounts for the fact that libraries, labs, and equipment are often inadequate and insufficient. Foreign financial assistance was instrumental in establishing the university and was provided mainly by France and Canada. Other countries such as Belgium and the Netherlands have assisted in the areas of teaching and research.

EFFICIENCY

The degree program in the university follows the French system and is organized in three cycles. The first cycle lasts two years, at the end of which successful students obtain the *Diplôme Universitaire* (diploma). The second cycle also lasts two years and leads to the *Licence* degree (associate degree) after the first year and the *Maitrise* degree (bachelor's) after the second year. In the institutions of specialized training, the first cycle can last up to three years and the second cycle up to two years, with each cycle leading to a terminal degree. The third cycle (leading to the doctorate) has been recently established for a few disciplines. In addition to the Faculty of Medicine, where students graduate as medical doctors, the university has already awarded doctorates in economics, law, mathematics, and physics in conjunction with foreign universities.

Internal Efficiency

Internal efficiency refers to the relationship between a system's (or subsystem's) outputs (learning achievements) and the corresponding inputs that went into creating them. The internal efficiency of the Benin higher education system is considered to be very low. Only a small percentage of students graduate, particularly in open-access institutions. Promotion and graduation rates are better in selective-access institutions (Lamoure 1990). This low internal efficiency is partly due to the fact that UNB has not yet succeeded in controlling student flow. Wastage and repetition rates are high and lead to an artificial inflation of numbers. As a consequence, the average length of study is incredibly high. It is estimated that an average of eleven years is needed to produce a four-year graduate at UNB.

Recent statistics indicate that, as a whole, from 1993 to 1998, out of 100 students registered, about 54 percent successfully completed their academic year (moving to the next year or completing their degree), 33 percent repeated their academic year, and 13 percent were expelled from the university. The performance of the "faculties" (whose students have a 51.5 percent overall completion rate) is lower that that of the specialized institutions (whose students have a 66.2 percent completion rate).

The administration has not been able to track enrollments accurately for years. The computerization of admissions and records, which is currently in progress, will make it possible to control the flow of students and improve the external efficiency of the system.

External Efficiency

The external efficiency (or external productivity) of an educational system is the relationship between the cost of producing learning results (outputs) in a particular period and the cumulative benefits (individual and social, economic and noneconomic) that subsequently accrue from these learning results over a long period.

The external efficiency of higher education in Benin is considered to be low because these cumulative benefits have decreased over the years. One major feature of the deterioration of external efficiency is the current high rate of graduate unemployment. This is due both to lack of economic growth and to the irrelevance of many students' studies to real manpower needs and training.

ADMINISTRATION AND GOVERNANCE

The first decree organizing the university and higher education in Benin was signed by the president of the Republic in 1970. It was amended by another decree in 1973. Subsequent orders by the minister in charge of higher education and instructions by the university rector have regularly provided guidelines for implementing these decrees. Among these, one should mention Rector's Instruction No. 092/MEN/CAB/DC/R/UNB of February 13, 1991, relating to the organization and operation of the rector's office, and the Ministerial Order No. 0007/MEN/ CAB/DC/R/UNB/SG of July 5, 1995 relating to the organization of the election of deans of faculties.

The history of governance of the university system has been closely related to the evolution of the country's political situation. The 1972 military coup, which marked the beginning of the seventeen-year one-party rule, occurred only two years after the university was officially established. During that period, the university was under tight control and surveillance by the authorities. Many faculty members who did not share the prevailing political ideology were harassed and even imprisoned. The appointment of the senior management of the university (the rector and his deputy, the general secretary, and the deans and heads of specialized institutions) was the exclusive prerogative of the government. Autonomy and academic freedom were very limited, a fact that led several faculty members to leave the country. This political interference was a real obstacle to academic, financial, and administrative accountability and thus to good governance in higher education.

Since the advent of the democratic process in the early 1990s, the situation has been gradually changing. The rector is still appointed by the government, but deans are now elected by their peers. Professors now enjoy substantial academic freedom, which is very conducive to the development of academic activities.

A SYSTEM IN CRISIS

Benin's economic situation and the performance of its higher education system show clearly that, just as in the majority of other countries in sub-Saharan Africa, higher education has failed to contribute effectively to national development. A study conducted in 1992 (Guedegbe 1994) revealed that the majority of academics surveyed admit the existence of a crisis within higher education. They consider "deteriorating working conditions" to be the major characteristic of this crisis, followed by "the mismatch between training and the manpower needs of the national economy."

Indeed, Benin's higher education system is in serious crisis today. The system lacks resources, is both internally and externally inefficient, and faces increasing demands while resources are dwindling. Economic difficulties, the requirements of a Structural Adjustment Program administered by the International Monetary Fund, and the 50 percent devaluation of the CFA franc (the common currency of most Francophone African countries) in 1998 have considerably limited resources available to higher education in Benin (Guedegbe 2000). As a consequence, the academic environment has been weakened and there has been a climate of instability on campus. This is a multifaceted crisis stemming from a diversity of problems and constraints, including an obsolete institutional framework, uncontrolled student flow, low teaching quality, insufficient infrastructure and equipment, insufficient financial resources, and poor working and living conditions for students, faculty, and administrative staff (Agbodjan 1997).

Students have reacted to this crisis through a series of protests and demonstrations mostly aimed at obtaining improved conditions and better job prospects.

The need of many faculty members for a nonacademic external career is another indication of the crisis and a sign of the vulnerability of the academic environment. This situation results from many factors, including:

- The decline of living standards of the professorate due to economic crisis and increasing costs of living
- The prestige, power, and financial benefits attached to government positions
- The development of the utilitarian conception of higher education

The external career drive has increased the cosmopolitan orientation of the faculty and reduced their commitment to their academic work. Their ability to accommodate two apparently contending aspects of their dual role (the internal academic one and the external one) is strongly determined by their perception of the current crisis. Since a committed and dedicated faculty is necessary for the effective development of higher education in the institutional and national contexts, it is necessary that academic environments be improved and strengthened. Efforts are underway to limit the negative impact of external careers on normal higher education activities. One such measure is the above-mentioned rector's decision concerning the election of deans, which stipulates that the post of faculty dean is incompatible with any external function.

ADDRESSING THE CRISIS: HIGHER EDUCATION REFORM

So far, the government has made sporadic attempts to address the crisis in education. However, these efforts have not led to major changes because of a lack of financial resources and lack of determination to achieve actual reform (Chede 1989a; Chede 1989b). The government recently took a major step by commissioning a comprehensive external review of the higher education system. The audit addressed both policy issues regarding the relationship between higher education and development in general and internal questions specific to the institutions of higher education. It analyzed the overall functioning of the university (structures, teaching, research, financial management, personnel management, and student services) as well as the university's relations with the state and made recommendations to address the various issues identified, which concern all aspects of higher education. Among the external factors affecting higher education in Benin, it highlighted the failure of the authorities to reconcile a planned approach to higher education and moves toward a more liberal economy (Ministry of Education 1999a, 1999b).

DIVERSIFICATION OF ACCESS: PRIVATIZATION IN BENIN HIGHER EDUCATION

Privatization will undoubtedly be one of the major features in the evolution of higher education in the years to come. It is a response to the inability of public higher education to respond to the changing needs of the labor market or to provide short-term training programs (Guedegbe 1999). Technological development in Benin has generated a growing need for specialized skills that the university, in its current organization, cannot meet. Private institutions are filling this gap. As has been mentioned earlier, the democratic era has promoted a free market economy and thus established an environment conducive to private enterprises.

Many private primary, secondary, and vocational institutions have been established. The same trend has appeared in higher education in the last five years. A recent study (Gnansounou 1998) identified twenty-seven private higher education institutions with enrollments ranging from 20 to 521 students, even though no such institution existed in the early 1990s. Most of these schools are located in the country's major city and are rather small institutions offering two-year courses in industrial, business, and secretarial areas. Some of them are affiliated to foreign higher education institutions (mainly in France) and provide joint higher-level courses. The private higher education institutions in Benin together enroll about 2,700, which represents 16 percent of enrollments in higher education in the country, and employ about 670 teachers and 236 administrative staff. Most of their teachers work part-time and come from the UNB or the civil service.

A decree by the Ministry of Education regulates the creation of all private educational institutions, from primary to higher education. It sets conditions for opening and managing these institutions. This decree does not seem to be adequate for higher education, which needs a specific one. One burning issue is the accreditation of private higher education institutions. Recent debates between the university and the owners of these institutions about the quality of the education and training they provide—as well as the areas which are considered to be too sensitive to be dealt with in private institutions without control, such as the training of nurses and medical lab technicians—indicate clearly that there is need for specific regulations. Pressure exists from both the university and the private sector to solve this issue.

CONCLUSION

Established in 1970, public higher education in Benin has gone through different stages. It has been and is still the major provider of high-level trained personnel in various development sectors. Thirty years of experience running a public, national, single-university system have indicated strengths and weaknesses of such a system faced with the challenges of a different nature, stemming from the gradual universalization of higher education within the context of globalization. It is now evident that the survival of this system as a viable development tool for the country will depend on the ability of the education sector to bring about the necessary reforms that will enable it to meet the current and coming challenges that are unavoidable, due to evolving changes in the internal and external environments. The reforms to be effected must be founded on comprehensive reviews of the system, such as the one conducted in 1998, and on a participatory approach involving all stakeholders.

Among the challenges to be addressed are the reorganization of the current public university system and the drive toward growing privatization. It has become obvious that the public system lacks the flexibility required to respond to the individual and social needs in the country, especially given the challenges of poverty alleviation in a context of globalization. Alternative approaches, such as the ones offered by private higher education, are necessary. The recommendations of the recent comprehensive audit of the public higher education system offer a context for carrying out a profound reform of education in Benin. Success will depend on the willingness, as well as the ability, of the authorities to bypass resistance and opposition and implement these much-needed changes.

BIBLIOGRAPHY

Agbodjan, J. P. 1997. *Higher Education in Benin: A Study Conducted in Preparation of the Donors Round Table on Education.* Cotonou, Benin: UNDP and Ministry of National Education.

Chede, A. G. L. 1989a. "La fonction sociale de l'Enseignement Supérieur au Bénin." *Ehuzu* (April): 3443.

——. 1989b. "Le Mal-Développement de l'enseignement supérieur au Bénin." *Ehuzu* (May): 3464.

Gnansounou, S. C. 1998. "A Diagnostic Study of Private Higher Education in Benin." Cotonou, Benin: Ministry of National Education, USAID.

Guedegbe, C. M. 1994. "The Professorate and Academic Life in Africa: A Case Study of the Academic Profession at Benin National University." Ph.D. dissertation, State University of New York.

——. 1999. "Higher Education Reform in Benin in a Context of Growing Privatization." *International Higher Education* (Summer): 16. Available online at: http://www.bc.edu/bc_org/avp/soe/cihe/index.html

——. 2000. "Currency and Crisis: Higher Education in Francophone Africa." *International Higher Education* (Winter): 3. Available online at: http://www.bc.edu/bc_org/avp/soe/cihe/index.html

Lamoure, J. 1990. *L'enseignement supérieur au Bénin: bilan et perspectives.* Cotonou, Benin: UNESCO/UNDP.

Ministry of National Education. 1999a. *Proposals (Draft) for Reform of the Benin National University: Audit Report.* Vol. 1: *Proposals.* Cotonou, Benin.

——. 1999b. *Proposals (Draft) for Reform of the Benin National University: Audit Report.* Vol. 2: *Annexes.* Cotonou, Benin.

17

Botswana

Sheldon G. Weeks

INTRODUCTION

The former British protectorate of Bechuanaland became Botswana at independence in 1966. As of its last census in 1991, the country was one of the largest in area and one of the most populated of the 71 so-called small states with populations below 1.5 million (of which thirteen were in Africa). The population in Botswana has grown from an estimated 450,000 in 1966 to an estimated 1.7 million in 2001.

In 1983, Botswana had the highest gross national product (GNP) per capita (at $920) of the eleven Southern African Development Community countries, which had an average GNP per capita of $324, excluding South Africa, which then had a GNP per capita of $2,550 (Makoni 1994, 179). This relative wealth has fueled a variety of developments in what has become known as the most stable democracy and most rapidly growing country in Africa. Botswana has been able to diversify its economy, moving beyond its dependence on cattle and marginal agriculture, since the discovery of diamonds in the mid-1970s and the development of nickel-copper matte, soda ash, coal, and limited high-cost tourism, mainly in the Okavango Delta (Salkin et al. 1997). In 2000, per capita income was around $2,000, unemployment was 16 percent, there were approximately 260,000 formal-sector jobs, and the government's foreign reserves totaled $6.4 billion (Gaolathe 2001).

Botswana is one of the few third world countries with a hard currency strategy and minimal exchange controls (Hope and Somolekae 1998). Despite its relative prosperity, Botswana, caught in the geopolitics of Southern Africa, was economically dependent on South Africa and remained a member of one of the oldest customs unions in the world. Botswana was a "frontline" state opposing apartheid in South Africa and supporting independence for Zimbabwe (achieved in 1980) and Namibia (achieved in 1990) (Edge and Lekorwe 1998). An expanding economy and a stable government have made possible a steady growth in Botswana's educational system. Botswana has gone from being one of the poorest countries in the world to a middle-income nation (Holm and Molutsi 1989; Salkin et al. 1997).

DEVELOPMENT OF TERTIARY EDUCATION

We can identify seven stages in the development of the University of Botswana (UB). The first stage was the establishment of the University of Basutoland, Bechuanaland, and Swaziland (UBBS), which grew out of negotiations in 1962 that approved the transformation of a Catholic institution at Roma in Lesotho into UBBS. With the assistance of the Ford Foundation and the British government, the facilities were purchased, and the university opened in 1964 with 188 students. After the independence of Lesotho and Botswana in 1966, UB reached the second stage in its development. The university first awarded degrees in 1967 (replacing those that had been awarded previously by the University of South Africa in Pretoria, South Africa). The University of Botswana, Lesotho, and Swaziland (UBLS) was funded equally by the three governments. The infrastructure was initially established in Lesotho, with Botswana offering only extramural and education courses and Swaziland specializing in agriculture. Following an enquiry in 1970, university planners agreed to develop the infrastructure at each campus equally.

The university reached stage three in 1975. While a working group was preparing a report on the devolution of UBLS into three university colleges, Lesotho nationalized the campus at Roma and created the National University of Lesotho. Students from Botswana and Swaziland were sent home. This step was the outcome of political interference and resulted in an exodus of students from Botswana and Swaziland, the establishment of a law program in Swaziland, a program in social sciences in

Botswana, and, soon after, the creation of the University of Botswana and Swaziland (UBS). This arrangement continued until separate universities were agreed to in Botswana and Swaziland (stage four) in 1992.

The precipitous collapse of UBLS because of national political agendas in Lesotho has resulted in extreme caution on the part of planners and decision makers in Botswana. As Jakes Swartland commented, "the faith in regional cooperation was shattered when they took the NUL out of the tripartite UBLS" (Swartland 1997).

In 1992, the University of Botswana was in the midst of a major building program, including construction of a science faculty with six well-developed departments, seven new halls of residence (intended to house 1,600 more students), a main cafeteria, departments of educational technology, computer science, humanities, and social science, as well as administration buildings. A Center for Continuing Education was built in Francistown, while a research center was established in Maun (Weeks 1993). Under the National Development Plan (NDP7), the university expanded from 2,700 students in 1990 to 6,500 by 1997 (Republic of Botswana 1991). The university has continued to grow, reaching 10,000 students in 2001 under the National Development Plan 8 (NDP8) (Republic of Botswana 1997). It is expected to grow to 15,000 students by 2009. Additional facilities developed in Gaborone in 2001 include a new Center for Continuing Education, major extensions to the university's library (increasing its capacity to 500,000 volumes), new student hostels, and an Olympic-sized swimming pool.

With increased revenues from diamonds and other resources, Botswana was able to launch an effective training plan for high-level human resources. Where scholarships are not available from donors, the government has sponsored students to study at the University of Botswana, in Southern Africa, in Europe, in North America, in Australia, and in New Zealand, especially in specific areas in which training is not available within the country or region. The majority of university graduates find employment fairly quickly. Contrary to the earlier views of Colclough (1988), Botswana has not experienced the "higher education paradox" in which the further expansion of tertiary education actually makes the constraints caused by shortages in skills worse.

In the decade that followed Zimbabwe's independence in 1980, Botswana tried to establish links for undergraduate training in veterinary science at the University of Zimbabwe. At first, Botswana was told that space was not available. The government of Botswana then bought a large house in Harare and converted it into dormitories. The University of Zimbabwe then insisted that this house be placed in its "pool," as it would not permit segregation by citizenship. Next the university refused to accept more than two or three students a year from Botswana, arguing that there was insufficient space for Zimbabweans. This position was supported by a resolution in the Parliament of Zimbabwe. Efforts by the Ministry of Education in Gaborone to purchase another house in Harare to offer to the University of Zimbabwe were rejected by the Ministry of Finance and Planning in Gaborone. The faith of people in regional arrangements had again been shattered (Swartland 1997).

HISTORY OF COOPERATION: STAGES

One of the major areas of cooperation in higher education under the South African Development Community (SADC) was the establishment of the Southern African Center for Cooperation in Agriculture and Natural Resources Research and Training (SACCAR). SACCAR offers two-year master of science programs in land and water management, animal science, crop science, and agricultural economics at Sokoine University of Agriculture in Morogoro, Tanzania; at Bunda College, University of Malawi; the University of Zambia; and the University of Zimbabwe. The key to the success of these programs over the years has been sustained support from donors in North America and Scandinavia. SADC has contributed about 10 percent of the costs, and 90 percent has come from donors (mainly USAID and SIDA). This has kept the program afloat (Nkambule 1997).

The sixth stage in the development of UB came with the first democratic elections and the establishment of the new South Africa in April 1994. South Africa joined SADC, opening the possibility of new arrangements and new forms of cooperation between universities in Botswana and in South Africa. The seventh stage was reached in 1997 with the signing of a SADC Protocol on Education and Training, which officially endorsed the creation of centers of excellence, the exchange of students and staff, and the exploration of new forms of cooperation (Mbuende 1997). One interesting decision, which has already been implemented in South Africa, was that fees for students from SADC countries should be the same as for citizens (even though some South African universities now charge a substantial international student fee). The University of Botswana has implemented this policy at the graduate level only.

It is interesting to note that the three BOLESWA nations (Botswana, Lesotho, Swaziland) each still have only a single national university, while elsewhere in Africa, universities—both public and private—have proliferated (Coleman and Court 1993; Girdwood 1997; Saint 1992; Sifuna 1997).

There are many more tertiary institutions in Botswana than UB. The key educational and health training institutions all are affiliated with UB, and their certificates and diplomas are awarded by the university. These affiliated institutions are a significant innovation in tertiary education which has received wide recognition (Hopkin 1993, 1996).

Of the six colleges of education, two were established before independence in 1966. The oldest is the Lobatse Primary Teachers College, which began in 1947 at Kanye and moved to Lobatse in 1956. It became a college of education in 1996. The other primary teachers' college that opened before independence was located at Serowe; the college, which was for females only, commenced operation in 1963 and became a college of education in 1997. The other two teachers' colleges are at Francistown (opened in 1968) and Tlokweng (opened in 1984). The two secondary teachers' colleges are at Molepolole (opened in 1985) and Tonota (opened in 1990). In addition, nine health training institutions are affiliated with UB.

In 2000, the Ministry of Education transformed its six vocational training centers into tertiary technical colleges and opened a new one in Gaborone to help absorb the "double output" from

Table 17.1. History of Cooperation in Higher Education in Botswana, 1964–1997

Stage 1:	January 1, 1964: Opening of the University of Basutoland, Bechuanaland, and Swaziland (UBBS).
Stage 2:	1966: With national independence of Basutoland, Bechuanaland, and Swaziland from the United Kingdom, UBBS becomes UBLS—the University of Botswana, Lesotho, and Swaziland.
Stage 3:	October 20, 1975: Withdrawal of Lesotho and the establishment of the National University of Lesotho (NUL) and, as a consequence, the University of Botswana and Swaziland (UBS).
Stage 4:	October 23, 1982: Formal inauguration of the University of Botswana (UB).
Stage 5:	1982–1994: Various efforts of cooperation between universities in the Southern Africa region explored; some are effective, while others collapse.
Stage 6:	1994–1997: The new Republic of South Africa is established and joins the South African Development Community; the first Center of Excellence is agreed to at the University of Botswana.
Stage 7:	September 8, 1997: The signing in Blantyre, Malawi, by the SADC's heads of state of a protocol on human relations and training, set to be ratified by each nation and confirmed at further annual meetings.

secondary schools. This was the result of the closing of Tirelo Setshaba (National Service) (Molefe and Weeks 2001). In spite of all these changes, Botswana has been able to enroll only 6 percent of the tertiary age group in further education, compared to 10 percent in the developing world and 50 percent in the developed world. Only 2 percent of the population has completed tertiary education, compared to 26 percent in high-income countries.

Distance education has remained underdeveloped in Botswana. Since 1998, the government has moved to provide adequate services at the pre-tertiary level by establishing the Botswana College of Distance Education and Open Learning (BOCODOL). It has depended on the university to provide distance education at the higher levels through its Center of Continuing Education (CCE). The university introduced a Certificate of Adult Education in 1983 and then certificates and diplomas in accounting and business studies (CABS/DABS). In the 1990s, "Learning Centers" were opened by the university in most major centers in the country to support CABS and DABS. Only in 1999 did the CCE begin to service the wider needs of Botswana society. Its first step was to provide primary teachers with opportunities to upgrade their qualifications.

The stages in the history of cooperation in tertiary education in Botswana are summarized in Table 17.1.

STRATEGIC PLANNING

Strategic planning is more developed in Botswana than in most African countries. This planning includes six-year rolling plans and occasional reviews of different sectors. Botswana currently is carrying out its eighth National Development Plan and in 2002 will be preparing for its ninth plan (Republic of Botswana 1997). The current planning cycle goes from 1997 to 2003. UB is firmly rooted in the national approach to planning, so it is constrained by the state's allocation and commitment of resources.

When the study that produced *Report of the Review Commission of the University of Botswana* (University of Botswana 1991a) was being made, the 1991–1996 plan for the university was already set. It was difficult to make any major alterations in the university during this period, even though only one faculty (out of four, at that time) had done any rigorous planning.

UB obtains both its capital and recurrent budgets through the rolling national development plans and the annual budget cycle. Though the university is in the center of the fastest-growing city in Africa and is the only university in a stable and wealthy country, its needs have not been matched through existing expansion. In the last decade, the university has constructed facilities for four major faculties (science, humanities, social sciences, and education) and is currently planning a major complex for its Faculty of Engineering (the former polytechnic run by the Ministry of Education) that will move it to the main campus. The 240-student graduate student village is probably the best such facility south of the Sahara. New buildings for the Faculty of Business are also now being planned as part of NDP8, which will commence in late 2002.

The university still has a long development agenda, including a multipurpose hall, a second graduate student village, new buildings for the faculties of humanities and education, a cultural complex (which will include a museum and theater), and other required facilities. Current shortages in space have forced the university to provide offices for new staff in temporary camps and forced more students to live off campus than is considered desirable (approximately 50 percent, whereas the goal was to have only 30 percent living off campus).

As the only university in Botswana, UB has continued to receive favored treatment by the government. Until 1999–2000, the university underspent its budget by more than $4 million a year (or nearly 10 percent of the budget). This was due to salary savings caused by unfilled vacancies. In 1999–2000, significant salary increases eroded this surplus. The "government subvention" to the university has increased significantly each year. In 1998–1999, it was approximately $40 million, which was increased to $50 million in the following year. Approximately 20 percent of the university's annual budget has been raised from tuition fees and other revenue (mainly from the refectory, the residences, and the bookstore). The average cost per student per year of $6,000 is highly subsidized. In 2000, UB's assets were valued at approximately $150 million. A new UB Foundation has been established to seek funds from the private sector to support new initiatives at the university.

There have been two key reviews of Botswana's education system; the first was in 1977, while the second was in 1993 (Republic of Botswana 1977, 1993, 1994, 1997; Weeks 1993, 1995b). Both were supportive of the tertiary education system and UB. The second National Commission for Education and the Revised National Policy on Education both called for increased access and the creation of a Tertiary Education Council (TEC).

NATIONAL SERVICE (TIRELO SETSHABA)

Tirelo Setshaba began with 28 volunteers in 1980 (Fako, Selabe, and Rowland 1986). By 1997, the program involved 6,300 participants and cost more than $10 million a year (Mudariki, Ndzinge, Tsayang, and Weeks 1997). Botswana established a unique form of national service that was non-military, civilian-based, and designed to place individual participants in institutions such as primary schools, village courts, and health clinics while they would live with host families in the community where they were assigned.

Tirelo Setshaba was intended to absorb all Form V school-leavers, but it fell far short of this goal as the output of the educational system rose. By 1999, the program had space for only half of O-Level leavers. The program was also designed to promote national development and a commitment to rural development among the future elite of the country. By the late 1980s, though, more and more participants were being placed in urban villages and towns, a move required by the rapid expansion of the scheme, which negated the original objectives (Molefe, Mudariki, Tsayang, and Weeks 1997). The scheme was also intended to be a thirteenth year of students' education, but this objective was never achieved (Molefe and Weeks 2001).

In 1999, the government of Botswana decided that it would terminate Tirelo Setshaba as of April 2000. Though on the surface this would result in significant savings, the termination of national service had many hidden costs. For example, the end of Tirelo Setshaba doubled the number of students seeking places in tertiary education to include both those finishing their national service and the group finishing Grade 12 in November 1999. The number seeking entrance to further study thus escalated from around 12,000 to more than 20,000. UB agreed to take up to 700 more students than the 2,800 it normally would have admitted in August 2000. This has resulted in significant overcrowding at the university, since its facilities were not expanded to meet this demand. The Ministry of Education has pledged to find places for 3,000 more students overseas, but the A-Level requirements elsewhere have made this goal difficult to achieve. As a consequence, some students have been sent to inferior private institutions in Malaysia and South Africa, from which a few of them have demanded repatriation.

THE UNIVERSITY OF BOTSWANA

UB acquired its third vice-chancellor on February 1, 1998. The foundation vice-chancellor when the university opened in 1982 was John D. Turner, an education professor from the United Kingdom. The position was localized in 1984 when Thomas Tlou, a professor of history, became the second vice-chancellor. In 1997, after thirteen years of service, Professor Tlou announced his intention to retire from the position and return to teaching and research.

The new vice-chancellor, Sharon Siverts, is an educator from the United States. Her appointment was made by the chancellor, Sir Ketumile Masire, the former president of Botswana, who retired from politics in March 1998. Professor Siverts stands out as a head of an African university and of one of the 468 Commonwealth Universities. She comes to UB from the University of North Dakota and Metropolitan State College in Denver, Colorado. She served in both institutions as the vice-president for academic affairs.

Vice-Chancellor Siverts has not received 100 percent support at UB. Unknown members of UB Council have leaked negative information about the appointment to the press. Lebang Mpotokwane, who is chair of the UB Council, has had to defend the appointment twice publicly. The concerns raised relate to delocalizing the post, using too-stringent criteria, ignoring competent Botswanians, failing to search for a candidate from within Southern Africa, and the award of a generous salary supplement. Some critics have argued that the post should be readvertised. Mpotokwane defended the council's action, stating that it was committed to maintaining the position at the professorial level and preserving university autonomy; that the methods used to recruit the new vice-chancellor had been transparent; that the salary supplement had been approved by government; and that it was too late in the appointment process to reopen the search.

Vice-Chancellor Siverts assumed leadership of a university in transition. Since 1995, three new faculties have been created to supplement the existing faculties of education, science, and humanities and social sciences. The new faculties are in engineering and technology, business, and the school of graduate studies. In addition, the Botswana College of Agriculture, which awards degrees through UB, functions as an eighth autonomous faculty. Five of the eight deans are citizens (including the first female deans). A new Faculty of Health Sciences will be provided for in the National Development Plan 9 (NDP9). A special pre-medical program was launched in 2000–2001. Of the approximately 700 academic staff, 57 percent are citizens. The university aspires to be a center of excellence in Southern Africa. Some of its programs have already been recognized by SADC, the United Nations, and other bodies.

Faculty from Central, Eastern, and Western Africa have moved to UB seeking better working conditions. Many of these same faculty have then moved again to tertiary institutions in Namibia, South Africa, or elsewhere, where they win promotions, tenure, and support for buying a house (options not available to expatriates in Botswana). Vacancies exist at the university, particularly at the senior level. As a consequence, existing staff have been overloaded and the university has underspent its budget. New staff-to-student ratios during NDP8 (from 1:12 to 1:15) may exacerbate these problems.

Though currently most graduates eventually become employed, the Ministry of Finance and Development Planning is concerned about the overproduction of graduates, particularly in the social sciences.

MISSION, VISION, AND VALUES

The vision of UB is to "be a leading academic center of excellence in Africa and the world" and to "advance the intellectual and human resource capability of the nation and the international community." The declared "values" of the university are designed to facilitate the achievement of these objectives. The key contradictions are:

- a combination of ample yet insufficient funding from the government. The government perceives itself as being generous, but the rapid growth of the university and resulting increases in resource requirements have outstripped its level of funding.
- a policy of recruiting staff development fellows from new graduates with B.A.s instead of mature people who have achieved their M.A.s.
- the baseline for staff is the M.A., while in all world-class universities, it is the doctorate.

During the 1990s, the UB Council resisted raising the required base level for staff from the M.A. to the Ph.D., with serious unintended consequences for the university. This policy can only serve to perpetuate mediocrity instead of promoting excellence.

ORGANIZATIONAL TRANSFORMATION OF THE UNIVERSITY

In 1990, a major review of the organization, management, structure, and statutes of UB was initiated. This led to the formation of seven task forces and other ad hoc working groups on the future of the university. Their recommendations were considered by planning committees, the senate, and the council and were integrated into proposals for a new university management structure.

The review of UB (University of Botswana 1991a) attempted to set some guidelines for shifting from a small university on a conventional British model to a larger institution with 10,000 students by 2003. One major recommendation was the introduction of a system of directors (on more of an American model) to cover computing, finance, institutional information, research, and student affairs. The seven task forces that were set up in 1992 following the review and the council's formal response (Turner 1991b) were originally intended to report in sixth months but continued to meet years later (Ingalls 1995). This process reflects not only extreme caution, leading to a snail-like pace of change, but also the desire on the part of key participants to maintain collegial relationships and consensus on change. This caution may be related to being the only national university in a small state, but it also reflects a desire to avoid the precipi-

tous mistakes observed in other countries. For example, if UB is to establish a university press, it must succeed, not start and then flounder. But the unintended consequence of being overcautious is inaction.

UB follows a consensus style of collegial management (Ingalls 1995). This process of consensus building is related to the traditional structure of decision making in the country, the *Kgotla*, or meeting of the people with the chief. Ingalls was so impressed with UB's management style that he concluded his article by observing that

> the process of consensus building at the University of Botswana can serve as a model for other African institutions attempting to reform their administrative structures and management practices. If they do, they may take a giant step forward towards solving many of the problems which prevent them from contributing fully to the economic growth and development of their nations. (Ingalls 1995, 284)

The reverse side of the coin is found in delays in decision making related to the desire to avoid making mistakes, a sensitive caution but one that may result in procrastination. This caution results in a tension between the vision and the process required to turn that vision into reality. Other examples are the failure to create a university bookstore rather than a "textbook shop" for students only, and the postponement of a decision to establish a university press of Botswana. The bookstore is scheduled to be privatized in 2002. Funds have finally been set aside to launch the press, perhaps as early as 2002.

A tension also exists between perceived capacity and actual capacity for the university to accomplish its objectives. Though UB has expanded 200 percent in size between 1991 and 2001, and localization (replacement of foreigners by citizen staff) is running now at over 50 percent, the majority of staff are hardworking and committed but are young and have yet to acquire broad experience. In addition, very few have yet to achieve promotion beyond senior lecturer. Whether they will be able to resist the continued pressures to adopt "managerial efficiencies" and do more with less in the next six years remains to be seen.

UB's new statutes and restructuring plan were approved by the Council in August 1998 and implemented in 1999. The major features of the plan are the creation of a third deputy vice-chancellor (for student affairs) and eighteen director positions (constituting a third level in the administration, separate from the seven faculties led by deans).

The new management structure includes the following directors:

- Directors for Public Affairs, Legal Counsel, Institutional Planning, and Internal Audit report to the Vice-Chancellor.
- Directors for Academic Services, Student Welfare, Careers and Counseling Services, and Culture, Sports and Recreation and Health Services report to the Deputy Vice-Chancellor for Student Affairs.
- Directors for Financial Services, Human Resources, and Campus Services and Information Technology report to the Deputy Vice-Chancellor for Finance and Administration Directors.
- Directors for Academic Development, Library Services, Continuing Education, Research and Development, and the Harry

Oppenheimer Okavango Research Center report to the Deputy Vice-Chancellor for Academic Affairs.

The major change in the university structure was the elimination of the old positions of registrar and bursar. Of the eighteen new director positions, five embodied new functions, while the rest involved reorganization of existing activities. The new directors (with the exception of the librarian and two others whose duties have not changed) had to apply for the positions when advertised. To increase accountability and performance, directors serve on a renewable contract for three years at a time. As a consequence, the top three levels of management are composed of people on contract.

The university has embarked on "semesterization" (a shift from examining full courses once a year to every semester), but this has been delayed until 2002 because of complications. Other issues on the agenda to be addressed as part of semesterization include policies to allow students to repeat a course instead of repeating the whole year, which is extremely wasteful; a review of the role of external examiners (senior academics from another university who review academic standards, writing, coursework, and examinations once a year); a review of the current system allowing students to assess staff (each course taught); the strengthening of a pan-university Communication and Study Skills Center; and new policies on the computer networking of the university, consultancy work, and sexual harassment.

STATISTICS

The student population of UB in 1999–2000 by faculty is shown in Table 17.2. Table 17.3 shows the citizenship status of faculty and staff. Overall, Botswanan citizens occupy 85 percent of positions at the university but occupy 53 percent of the lecturer and senior lecturer positions and only 16 percent of professorships. This is a source of frustration to those Botswanan staff who feel foreigners are keeping them in the lower ranks. UB has a strong staff development program, which in 2000 supported more than 130 fellows in their studies for higher degrees around the world.

THE DEVELOPMENT OF GRADUATE STUDIES

Graduate studies have been extremely slow to develop at African universities. Where they have started, they have been fraught with problems related to shortages in qualified senior staff, declining financial resources, and inadequate library, computer, and other facilities (Coleman and Court 1993; Girdwood 1996; Saint 1992, 1993; World Bank 1994).

> When they were of good quality, the M.A. programs were particularly useful in preparing candidates for more advanced graduate work abroad. However, some of the graduate programmes were launched prematurely and proved to be of dubious quality. There was also a danger of incestuous inbreeding and of lifetime parochialism . . . [and] there are pronounced limits to the utility and prudence of an institution using its own postgraduate programs for the development of its own staff. (Coleman and Court 1993, 262–263)

Table 17.2. Distribution of Students by Field at the University of Botswana, 1999–2000

Business	685
Education	1,879
Engineering and Technology	998
Humanities	1,629
Science	1,354
Social Sciences	1,231
Graduate Studies	419
Continuing Education	1,966
Total	10,161

Source: University of Botswana 2000, 43.

Table 17.3. Distribution of Staff by Citizenship Status at the University of Botswana, 1999–2000

Staff Category	Citizen	Expatriate	Total
Academic	397	300	697
Support	1,487	42	1,529
Total	1,884	342	2,226

Source: University of Botswana 2000, 44.

The struggle to develop tertiary education facilities in Africa, with their significantly higher costs compared to primary education, has resulted in a focus on the provision of undergraduate programs—at the certificate, diploma, and degree level—to the neglect of postgraduate programs. Support for graduate studies overseas was readily available from a variety of aid donors and was deemed desirable and preferable—a hidden negative judgment on local capacity and standards, perhaps reflecting a colonial appraisal of local capacity (Nwa and Houenou 1990).

Sub-degree-level studies have all too easily absorbed university-level resources in Africa, and certificates and diplomas continue to be offered by universities because they may be more cost effective and of a higher standard than could be obtained at other tertiary institutions in the country. That this focus must shift, particularly the need to extend courses up from diploma to degree and to postgraduate studies and research, remains to be fully recognized (Dubbey 1994; Husen 1997).

This contradiction in the growth of African universities is exposed most dramatically by the situation in South Africa, where in 1990 the historically black universities produced 74 percent of the undergraduate diplomas and only 5 percent of the master's and doctoral degrees, compared to the historically white universities in South Africa, which offered only 7 percent of the diplomas and 85 percent of the master's and doctoral degrees (Wolpe 1995, 282). Wolpe recognizes the links and synergism between graduate programs and research; strong research programs are needed to attract graduate students. I would add that a university in the process of transformation from an undergraduate college to a full university requires strong graduate programs to attract and hold quality staff. UB, for example, has been short up to thirty staff at the professional level over the years.

The process of change from an undergraduate college to a university is not automatic. The first step is the presence of a strong undergraduate department before graduate studies are introduced. "Prematurity in the introduction of graduate studies, most typically in response to strong indigenous pressures, but occasionally as a result of expatriate zeal and Foundation encouragement, [has] proved to be a common problem" (Coleman and Court 1993, 50). Coleman and Court recognize the importance of in-country graduate programs, given the

> imperative of establishing educational and cultural independence; the essentiality of indigenizing the curriculum content and research locale, and this can best be achieved by a Ph.D. programme *in situ*; and the importance of the indigenous professoriate being able to participate in advanced graduate instruction as part of their own professional development. While recognizing the weight and validity of these reasons, others argue that at few places in the developing world are there yet the human and infrastructural resources to mount a high quality Ph.D. program that commands a competitive prestige in the world university market place; such programs should be initiated only when the institutions themselves are fully developed. (Coleman and Court 1993, 263)

At UB in 1990, out of 884 graduates, 39.7 percent received certificates and diplomas, 53.5 percent received degrees, and only 6.8 percent received postgraduate diplomas and master's degrees—but only 0.7 percent of this small group took master's degrees (University of Botswana 1992, 35). Does this mean the university was then comparable to a historically black university in South Africa? Not really, because the political, social, and economic context of development in Botswana is entirely different from South Africa. By 2000, the proportion of master's graduates had risen to 4.2 percent while undergraduate diplomas and certificates were still 50 percent of a total of 2,730 graduates.

Botswana has enjoyed wide support from the world community for upper-level undergraduate studies (most science students went abroad to complete their undergraduate degrees in engineering, medicine, veterinary medicine, pharmacology, and so on). The need for graduate studies at UB was not recognized in the early 1980s (Turner 1984; Setidisho and Sanyal 1988). Extensive opportunities were available for UB graduates to enroll in higher degree programs in North America, Europe, Australia, and New Zealand under full scholarships paid for by the host countries. Since 1993, key donor agencies and nations have tended to phase out aid agreements with Botswana because of the perception that Botswana had become a middle-income or wealthy nation and therefore no longer required such assistance (Hopkin 1993; Burchert and King 1995). This has caused planners and decision makers in Botswana to reassess what they will pay for graduate studies. UB, where a master's degree may cost one-third of what it costs for a program in North America or Europe, is now considered an attractive alternative. It appears that graduate degrees at UB, given the performance of past master's students and the positive assessment of external examiners, are now seen as equal to or better in quality than those attained at many universities abroad.

In addition, some donors have recognized UB as a "center of excellence" and an approved destination for third-country training (for example, the Canadian International Development Agency has paid for Namibians to study in Botswana instead of going to Canada, and the German Academic Exchange Service has offered scholarships for graduates of other African institutions to study in Botswana in the sciences). A key example of this is the African Economic Research Consortium (AERC), which began in 1988 and in 1994 launched a collaborative master's program for Anglophone Africa that involves eighteen universities in thirteen countries and sponsors 150 students in a two-year master's program at six universities, including UB. Evaluations of these programs have recognized an important "cascading effect" on the quality of undergraduate economics education (Fine, Lyakurwa, and Drabek 1994; AERC 1996).

Graduate studies at UB commenced in the early 1980s with the introduction of M.A. programs in religion, English, and African languages and literature. This was followed by a new M.Ed. graduate program introduced during the sixth National Development Plan (1984–1990), but enrollment ranged between only six and eleven students. In the seventh National Development Plan (1991–1996), the establishment of master's programs across the university was given a green light (University of Botswana 1991b). But only a few programs developed that attracted students, sponsorship, and international recognition: the master's programs in education, environmental science, business administration, and library and information studies. As a result, planned growth in graduate enrollments and output did not occur.

A variety of factors combined to curtail the rapid growth of graduate studies at UB during the late 1980s and early 1990s. Running through all of them is the impact of the university's firm commitment to strive for quality, excellence, and the highest standards attainable in its academic programs.

In the early 1980s, UB designed and implemented a two-year master's degree program, coordinated until April 1996 by a committee of the senate, the University Graduate Studies Committee. Though a high degree of flexibility has been maintained in implementing these programs, especially with regard to the number of courses, the course equivalents, and weighting of dissertations versus research papers, all programs have balanced out as nine full-course equivalents over two years. In contrast, many master's degree programs in Europe and North America can be completed in one year and are therefore more attractive to sponsors and students.

Though the first graduate programs in religious studies, education, and environmental science received support in the mid-1980s, this quickly evaporated when the Ministry of Education and other bodies responded to major offers to train to the master's level in the United States and the United Kingdom. The program in religious studies ceased, the master's in education was suspended, and the intake in environmental sciences dropped to one student. This situation changed in the 1990s with the shift in priorities from overseas to in-country and third-country training at the master's level, and the recognition of "centers of excellence" (such as the master's degrees in economics, business administration, and library and information studies). In the late 1990s, there was a marked growth and interest in graduate study at UB, not only from the other fourteen SADC countries, but also from Kenya, Uganda, Ethiopia, Cameroon, Nigeria, Ghana, and Sierra Leone.

The demand for places in UB has resulted in designing master's programs that teach between 4 and 8 P.M., thus allowing for part-time students to participate. These students commute as far as 200 kilometers daily to attend classes at least two days a week. In this way, the university has tapped a local market and responded to a local need. Most part-time students are self-sponsored—and one or two have even rejected government sponsorship because they only received 75 percent of their salary over two years. For programs like the M.B.A. and the M.Ed., the demand far exceeds the number of places available—even though little has been done to market these programs.

Because UB has been seen primarily as an undergraduate college, it has had difficulty attracting and holding qualified senior staff. The ability of a department to launch and sustain graduate studies is dependent on the presence of such staff. The rapid growth of undergraduate student numbers in the university has resulted in the expansion of key departments and a significant increase in the number of senior positions (a small department of nine is allowed only two professors, while a large one of more than twenty-four may have five or more).

UB has not been immune to the "structural adjustment" problems faced by universities elsewhere in the world—or the "McDonaldization" of higher education (Berman 1995; Currie 1995; Hartley 1995; Ronan and Ronan 1995). With the introduction of master's programs, some staff have ended up teaching and supervising more students without any additional rewards, as graduate studies may have been imposed in addition to their already existing undergraduate commitments. At UB, this is a structural problem related to the recruitment of new staff and the synchronization of staff development for citizens, as many departments have an approved establishment but may have unfilled positions. The difficulty the university faces in the recruitment of professorial staff exacerbates this problem. As a consequence, some staff appear to be doing more for less, but not because of the extensive cuts to higher education that have been experienced elsewhere (Welch 1996).

The senate and council approved general regulations governing M.Phil. and doctoral studies at UB in 1992. The Faculty of Education and the University Graduate Studies Committee approved the admission of the first doctoral student soon afterward in 1992. This student was not permitted to register, even though she had full sponsorship from a foreign donor and was eminently qualified, because the Faculty of Education and the Department of Educational Foundations had not passed any special regulations to govern the M.Phil. and Ph.D.; nor had they demonstrated that they had the capacity (number and quality of staff, library, computer, and other resources, and so on) to commence doctoral studies. It was also claimed that M.Phil. and Ph.D. programs needed to be advertised before students could be enrolled.

In 1995, the University Graduate Studies Committee approved the admission of 2 students to enroll for a master's of philosophy (M.Phil.) in Mathematics and a Ph.D. in natural products chemistry. These two students were registered in January 1996. Special regulations for these programs were approved

by the Board of the School of Graduate Studies only in mid-1996. The science faculty has taken the lead in establishing research-based programs for the M.Phil. and Ph.D. programs in environmental science, chemistry, mathematics, physics, and the biological sciences. Currently the Faculty of Humanities has added doctoral programs in history and library and information studies, and the Faculty of Education has added doctoral programs in adult education, mathematics and science education, and educational foundations. Of 500 graduate students in 2001, only twenty-three are enrolled in seven of ten approved M.Phil. or Ph.D. programs, while the rest are spread across nineteen master's degree programs. More graduate students could be enrolled at both levels, but difficulties in obtaining sponsorship curtail opportunities.

The School of Graduate Studies was approved by the UB Senate in March and the UB Council in July 1994. The university moved with all deliberate speed to establish the school. The position of dean was advertised in 1995 and the vacancy filled from within the existing university establishment in April 1996.

The university's intention was to support M.Phil. and Ph.D. studies only when it was assured that excellence could be achieved through a critical combination of staff (particularly senior staff) and resources (library, computer, laboratory, and so on). The university is attempting to ensure that no mediocre programs are introduced. The process of review through departments, faculties, the School of Graduate Studies, the Academic Policy Review and Planning Committee, and the senate and council may result in delays, but it also ensures that rigorous attention has been devoted to new initiatives and that broad consensus is reached on their introduction.

In the future, the university will tend to support programs that are part of building "centers of excellence." One program that had won international support, the postgraduate diploma in population and sustainable development based in the Faculty of Social Sciences, commenced in 1995 but was phased out in 2001 because sources of external funding ceased. This program was supported by the UNFPA Global Program in Population and Development and was transferred to UB, following intense competition, from the Institute of Social Studies in The Hague. In 1995, it enrolled twenty students from seventeen countries in Africa and Asia. This program had links with other programs in Chile, Egypt, India, Morocco, and the Netherlands. Major donor support to graduate programs had been provided by the UNFPA Global Program in Population and Development (for the Postgraduate diploma in population and sustainable development) and by the Belgian Government (to support SADC scholarships for the M.P.A. and the M.Sc. in applied microbiology). In 1999–2001 their gifts accounted for 50 percent of the moneys donated to UB.

It is anticipated that other programs will be developed in association with the regionalization of programs through SADC. Another example of an initiative that will most likely have wide support when it is introduced at UB is the AERC doctoral program in economics (Coleman and Court 1993; Fine, Lyakurwa, and Drabek 1994). It is anticipated that by the year 2002–2003 (the end of NDP8), approximately seventy-two students will be enrolled in various doctoral programs at UB. The African Regional Postgraduate Program in Insect Science (ARPPIS) could also come to Botswana. It is an example of pan-African coopera-tion in graduate studies (Aboderin 1995).

One striking aspect of the master's programs at UB, at least so far, has been their high rate of retention. This may be attrib-uted to the entry standard that has been adhered to—at least a 2.0 or better grade point average in the first degree. In most programs, the retention rate from the first to second year has been at least 90 percent, and the completion rate has been nearly as high. Even part-time students, who are the most likely not to pass and complete, have been doing very well. The one exception is the M.B.A. program, which was designed as a three-year, partially modular, program for part-time students, who have been more likely to withdraw and fail than in other pro-grams.

One initial objective that was part of NDP7 planning in 1990 was to externalize or place in a distance education mode some of the master's programs. However, this has not hap-pened, despite encouragement and support for this option by the Ministry of Education. Delays have been experienced be-cause the Center for Continuing Education was without profes-sorial leadership and the staff to support a distance M.Ed. The ministry, demonstrating the frustration with these delays, ar-ranged for the support of the Overseas Development Administra-tion in London and the University of Bath to develop a master's degree in educational management and administration in a part-time, three-year modular with a lower entry standard but three exit points (advanced certificate, advanced diploma, and M.A.). The Ministry of Education in Gaborone proceeded in anticipa-tion that UB would take over and implement the Bath program in 1996. This did not happen, though, since it could not be implemented in its original form. The Bath degree had been developed to serve the needs of expatriate staff in international schools around the world. It is also not customary practice for one university to adopt in toto the academic content of another university. Issues of comparable standards achieved in the two programs and the lower entry standard employed to admit stu-dents for the Bath degree had to be carefully evaluated. The Faculty of Education implemented its M.Ed. "flexi-mode" in 2000 and now has twenty students enrolled.

In order for a new master's program to be accepted by the university, a department has to demonstrate through a market survey that enough demand for the course exists within the country. This entails canvassing various ministries and obtain-ing letters of commitment to sponsor students. When the De-partment of Mathematics in the science faculty tried to launch an M.Sc., it was not endorsed because it was unable to demon-strate support for such a degree within the country. It has since been recognized that with approximately one-third of the mas-ter's students coming from outside Botswana, support by other governments and donors for a master's program at UB should be accepted. For instance, the master's in applied microbiology, which commenced in 1997, received extensive support from other African nations.

Another program that was supported by the university as part of NDP7 (but which was delayed in starting until August 1996) is the master's in nursing science. This program was approved by the various committees and the senate in 1994 and should

have started then, but it was not endorsed by the council on the grounds that the first degree was a B.A. (in nursing education) and not a bachelor's in nursing science. The council believed at the time that a master's in nursing science must have a bachelor degree in nursing science as its foundation, but has since re-versed this decision and recognized that the B.A. in nursing edu-cation was of sufficient quality to prepare students for a master's in nursing science.

An unexpected consequence of the move to formally launch the School of Graduate Studies has been the decision by the UB Council to gradually phase out the Center for Graduate Studies in Education (CGSE) in the Faculty of Education. The CGSE was created in 1990 as part of NDP7 and was administered by a director who was an associate professor and was also given the responsibility of coordinating research for the education fac-ulty (Youngman 1994). Other faculties did not have a full-time salaried coordinator of graduate studies. The Faculty of Educa-tion justified this position on the grounds that its master's program was cross-departmental—it even included one depart-ment in the humanities faculty—while other master's degrees were based solely in individual departments. This faculty-wide master's was cost-effective because it avoided duplication (stu-dents undertook a common core course in research methods and integrated foundations) and the unified first year led to more than ten specializations during the second year (some of which were also cross-departmental, such as research and evaluation). With the creation of the School of Graduate Studies, the council did not believe the university could afford two coordinating bod-ies. In spite of the growth of master's programs and the rapid rise in student numbers, coordination of programs remains the re-sponsibility of staff members selected to serve this role in each department. Of twenty coordinators of higher degrees, only one receives an allowance—the M.B.A. coordinator—because it is a generic degree across three departments.

UB's commitment to quality in its higher degrees is reflected in its desire to maintain two-year master's programs. Through-out all the changes that have taken place during NDP7 and that are planned in NDP8, no one has proposed that the length of time taken to complete the master's for full-time students be reduced, even though staff are aware that students complain about this duration, particularly those who know people who have gone abroad and completed a master's in as little as nine months! It is as if any change that might be interpreted as low-ering standards is non-negotiable. At the same time, increasing interest exists in modularization and in finding ways for students to progress by semester instead of by year. New regulations in 2001–2002 will allow exceptional students to complete a mas-ter's degree in three semesters.

Currently, the resources made available to graduate stu-dents appear liberal, as conditions are far better than many other "majority world" (Third World) nations. Yet the resources do not match those available for graduate students in the first world, such as those for teaching assistantships, laboratories, comput-ers, carrels, office space, and funds for research and to attend conferences. Teaching assistantships have yet to be established (it is currently illegal for students who are not citizens to work); although there are graduate student computer laboratories, the number of computers available is limited; there are very few carrels and no offices for graduate students (there is a shortage of offices for staff); and, unless they are provided by a sponsor or aid donor, there are no UB funds for graduate students to purchase laptop computers, to attend conferences, or to support their field research. The challenges to the university, as it increases 50 percent in size over the next five years, are to find ways to develop graduate studies, to provide the resources required, and to maintain a leading edge and its recognition as a center of academic excellence.

STUDENT POWER

Student power in Botswana generally reflects the personalized needs of self-seeking and opportunistic student leaders. Playing a leading role in the Student Representative Council (SRC) is perceived as a training ground for future involvement in national politics. The key political parties (in power and opposition) both maintain ties with individual student leaders and manipulate student politics. What is at stake are not issues but the ability to maintain power and control. During the 1990s, this resulted in direct confrontations both with the university administration and state authorities. Twice the university was closed when the education minister employed powers granted to him under the University Act. This makes for a very different picture compared to student activities in neighboring countries and as found in the literature (Altbach 1998, 117–129). In the March 2001 SRC elections, the Botswana National Front (the opposition party in parliament) won all the SRC positions.

Student demonstrations and strikes usually begin with a common grievance over the issue of food and then quickly escalate to other issues. Rarely have the UB students demonstrated in solidarity with students anywhere else in Africa or the world. Social problems derived from the wider society continue to trouble the university. In the past decade, the SRC has tended to organize a strike in mid-February (now called "national students' day").

Botswana, long promoted by the northern world as a stellar example of a stable democracy at work in Africa, is not free from confrontations. An example from 1995 will document the course of one confrontation. On February 16, 1995, trouble began when University of Botswana students marched to Parliament and then stormed the parliament building with other demonstrators. On their way from Parliament, protestors smashed vehicles, shops, and other buildings. While in a democracy everybody has the right to protest, nobody has the right to destroy other people's property. Police, an anti-riot unit, and the Botswana Defence Force were posted around Gaborone and Mochudi to restore order. UB was closed at 1 P.M. on February 17, 1995, by order from the government, following a declaration from the education minister, Dr. Gaositwe Chiepe, under the powers vested in her under Section 5(3) of the University of Botswana Act (CAP57:01). The minister stated that the closure, the first time the government used this clause to close the university, was caused by an "illegal demonstration staged by the students of the University of Botswana who caused unprovoked malicious damage to both private and public property and vio-

lently invaded the National Assembly while in Session." The closure applied to all students and classes but not to university staff, who were instructed to "continue with their normal duties" by the then vice-chancellor, Professor Thomas Tlou.

The SRC took the government to court seeking the reopening of the University of Botswana. The government won its case and handed the powers back to UB and the vice-chancellor in mid-March 1995. The government then overruled this decision and decreed that the university remain closed. They then moved to arrest student leaders for their part in the illegal demonstration, and decided to keep the university closed to avoid further demonstrations and student-led strikes.

RESEARCH CAPACITY

One of the jewels in UB's crown was the National Institute for Development Research and Documentation (known as the NIR). The NIR was established in 1975 and during its first decade earned an international reputation with more than eighty publications (Morapedi 1987, 415–422). Its research foci were land and environment, education and society, health and nutrition, issues of migration and settlement, and rural development. NIR became a darling of international aid donors. As it entered the 1990s, resources began to decline, staff changes undermined productivity, and finally it was changed in the late 1990s to the Directorate of Research and Development and then in 2001 to the Department of Research and Development, with only a few staff members.

The demise of the NIR has been accompanied by the rapid growth of a major research center in northern Botswana. At the end of February 2000, the UB officially launched the Harry Oppenheimer Okavango Research Center (HOORC) at Maun in Ngamiland. The Center moved into its new facilities outside of Maun in March 2001.

The Okavango Research Center has been operating since late 1994 under the leadership of Professor Lars Ramberg. In 2000, the center had eight academic staff and ten support staff and planned to build up to twenty-four academic staff and thirty support staff over the next five years. In addition, graduate students and postdoctoral researchers from UB and universities around the world are attached to the HOORC and participate in its research programs. The center has established significant links with various universities in Southern Africa, Europe, and North America and is part of various research networks in Africa. The center also maintains a herbarium and a library. The Okavango Research Center's current focus is on natural resource management in the region, in particular hydrology and water management, ecology, international resource policy and law, social aspects of natural resource management, and tourism management.

THE PRIVATE SECTOR

Botswana still has only one national university. The main contribution to tertiary education by private institutions is in the field of business and computer studies; key international players are Damelin from South Africa and NIIT from India. The government is not averse to sponsoring students to attend private institutions and might give its full support to a new initiative.

In 2001, a small group of private entrepreneurs will open the first private tertiary institution in Botswana in Francistown. They believe that the time is ripe because of the expansion of senior secondary schools and UB's limited capacity to meet the demand for further studies. They hope to attract people forced to retire at 60 who still have a lot to contribute to the development of the nation through education and training. The new college will begin by offering foundation-year courses, particularly in the sciences.

Staff, including citizen staff, often leave the university for employment in the private sector because it offers higher salaries, particularly in computer science, accounting and management, and economics. Even other parastatals can offer salaries that are up to twice those provided by UB.

THE CREATION OF A SECOND UNIVERSITY

In Botswana, the establishment of a second university by the government remains a political issue. The national committee on a vision for 2016 (fifty years after independence) deferred a recommendation on the establishment of a second university until that date. In its long-term planning (called "Beyond 10,000" or 10,000 students), UB identified at least twelve new academic programs that the university could launch within current structures. The working group felt that the establishment of a second university remained a decision of the government and was a matter for the Tertiary Education Council to act upon. It was suggested that the need for a second university should be reviewed at the end of NDP9.

The development of tertiary institutions affiliated with UB should continue. The satellite campus model may be used by the university to guide developments over the next decade, with some of the affiliated colleges of education eventually becoming "university colleges." This could lead to full independence and a proliferation of universities in Botswana by 2020.

These moves will not mollify those politicians and others from the northern part of Botswana (and from non-Setswana-speaking language groups) who seek recognition, development, and prestige through having their own university. Currently the government operates a number of technical colleges and two colleges of education in the north. UB has the Okavango Research Center and a number of extension centers in the north. The presence of these tertiary level institutions in Francistown and Maun will not in the long run delay the demand for regional parity and a second university. Moves to establish a second university are bound to happen before 2016.

THE FUTURE OF THE UNIVERSITY OF BOTSWANA

By the year 2016, UB will likely have achieved the following goals, in my estimation:

- The university will have achieved wide international recognition as a premier university in Africa. It will also be playing a major role within the SADC region.
- The university will be less reliant on government subsidies

and more active in fund-raising through projects, consultancies, course fees, sponsored courses, and other means. The new UB Foundation will play a critical role in this process.
- There will be 80 percent localization in all aspects of university functioning, while 20 percent high-level expertise will be retained to ensure the international character of the university.
- The university will be providing high-quality and well recognized degree-level education in all major disciplines. Undergraduate certificate and diploma programs will have been phased out completely (except where no other tertiary institution is able to offer them), and graduate programs will have expanded to take their place.
- The university will have a very strong research base by virtue of postgraduate research programs in all areas in which demand exists. This will be projected to meet the needs of the country and beyond.
- The university will have a fair number of chairs in several areas, endowed by multinational industries, international organizations, and philanthropists.
- The university will have international linkages with other universities and research and development organizations with mutual memoranda of understanding.
- The university will be able to boast at least ten centers of recognized academic excellence.
- All staff and students will have easy access to computer facilities and enhanced connectivity.
- Distance learning will have embraced modern technologies to enhance education delivery.

LIFELONG LEARNING AND THE FUTURE

A culture of lifelong learning will eventually be established in Botswana. In-service training is already pervasive and supported by employers. Lifelong learning in the future should encompass university education and graduate studies, since people will perform better on the job if they are able to retool every few years (Walters 1999).

Which level of education contributes the most to development? Indices from economists have generally favored primary education. The arguments and methodologies behind such conclusions have been found to be fallacious, but the new interpretations are not widely accepted. One problem is that rates-of-return analyses for higher education are not broken down to differentiate between the impact of undergraduate and graduate studies. If, as is claimed, it is more profitable to invest in higher education, is it possible that graduate studies are an even better investment? An assessment of social reality may end up favoring graduate studies. Research and development that comes from graduate studies may be found to contribute the most to development rather than primary or secondary schooling or undergraduate studies.

WHAT IS OUR IMAGE OF THE FUTURE?

Are we moving in Africa to solve the problems that trouble the world—problems of agricultural productivity, population control, cultural survival, language maintenance, equitable distribution of wealth, and the maintenance of peaceful and harmonious societies? Will all aspects of life be enhanced by technology? We make certain assumptions about the role of tertiary education in development and the enhancement of the quality of life. Only time will tell if they are valid. In Botswana, less than 4 percent of the tertiary age group is enrolled in any form of education. In the future, one-third of the relevant cohort will have access to further education (instead of the 7 percent today). This will require the development of open access as opposed to the current limited and elite access. The dilemma of standards versus opportunity for all will remain. It will be challenged by worldwide qualifications available and verified on the World Wide Web.

A shift will occur in the future related to who controls universities in Africa. The consumers (students) and the creators (academics) who can facilitate will have greater influence and control than administrators and staff. This will be affected by supply and demand. Demand will likely increase for "vocational" courses. (The success of Phoenix University in the United States is an example of this shift.)

In the future in Africa, the costs of tertiary education will be covered from new sources and through new mechanisms. The new models could include the use of vouchers, free access (benefits greater than the costs), an income-tax surcharge, and other means.

The form and content of tertiary education will change as a result of globalization. Education will be more relevant and practical, will build on experience, and will support insightful learning. Research and development will still take place in academic centers, but it will also take place at home and in the field. "I think, therefore I am" will become "I think, therefore I create, I write, I communicate." The paralyzed French author who wrote his book *Butterfly, Bell and Candle* by blinking his eyelid has shown us what might be achieved.

SUMMARY AND CONCLUSION

In the past two decades, the University of Botswana has grown into an impressive institution that now ranks as one of the best in Southern Africa. It has enjoyed the advantage of being the only national university in a small state—a state that was both stable and had sufficient resources to support rapid development. The university has benefited from strong and consistent support from the government and from having the means to build a significant infrastructure and to attract and hold quality staff from throughout Africa and the world. The ethos of the university has been to move with caution and to attempt to avoid the mistakes that have been made in higher education elsewhere in the continent that have resulted in overcrowding, inadequate staff and facilities, falling standards, and a general demoralization and decay. In this, the university has been successful. At the same time, this pace of development has caused the university to miss opportunities and fail to develop its full potential. But the accomplishments of the last twenty years outshine the problems and contradictions that remain. The challenge for the future remains to continue to develop capacity at all levels. A university can never stop progressing.

REFERENCES

Aboderin, A. 1995. *On the Feasibility of Inter-university Cooperation in Joint Graduate Training and Research in Africa.* Accra: Association of African Universities.

AERC (African Economic Research Consortium). 1996. *An African Based Doctoral Program in Economics.* Nairobi: African Economics Research Consortium.

Altbach, P. G. 1998. *Comparative Higher Education: Knowledge, the University and Development.* Greenwich, Connecticut: Ablex Publishing.

Burchert, L., and K. King, eds. 1995. *Learning from Experience: Policy and Practice in Aid to Higher Education.* The Hague: Centre for the Study of Education in Developing Countries.

Colclough, C. 1988. "Higher Education Paradox in African Development Planning." In Ansu Datta and Kenneth King, eds., *Botswana: Education, Culture and Politics,* 99–117. Edinburgh: Centre of African Studies.

Coleman, J. S., and D. Court. 1993. *University Development in the Third World: The Rockefeller Experience.* Oxford: Pergamon Press.

Currie, J. 1995. "Globalization Effects on Academic Work: Case Study of One School in an Australian University." Paper presented at the Comparative and International Education Society Annual Conference, Boston, Massachusetts.

Dubbey, J. 1994. *Warm Hearts, White Hopes: Memoirs of a British VC in Malawi.* Pretoria: West Penrose Books.

Edge, W. A., and M. H. Lekorwe, eds. 1998. *Botswana: Politics and Society.* Pretoria: J. L. van Schaik Publishers.

Fako, T. T., B. B. Selabe, and M. J. Rowland. 1986. *The Principle and Practice of Tirelo Setshaba: A Comprehensive Evaluation of the Botswana Community Service Scheme.* Gaborone: Government Printer.

Fine, J. C., W. Lyakurwa, and A. G. Drabek, eds. 1994. *PhD Education in Economics in Sub-Saharan Africa: Lessons and Prospects.* Nairobi: East African Publishers.

Gaolathe, B. 2001. *Budget Speech, 5th of February.* Gaborone: Government Printer.

Girdwood, A. 1997. "The University in Africa: Evolving Roles and Responsibilities." In K. Watson, S. Modgil, and C. Modgil, eds., *Educational Dilemmas: Diversity and Debate.* Vol. 2: *Reforms in Higher Education,* 250–258. London: Cassell.

Hartley, D. 1995. "The 'McDonaldization' of Higher Education: Food for Thought." *Oxford Review of Education* 21, no. 4: 409–423.

Holm, J., and P. Molutsi, eds. 1989. *Democracy in Botswana.* Gaborone: Botswana Society and University of Botswana.

Hope, K. R., and G. Somolekae, eds. 1998. *Public Administration and Policy in Botswana.* Kenwyn, South Africa: Juta.

Hopkin, A. G. 1993. "Botswana the Blessed? Aid to Education in Botswana." *Mosenodi: Journal of the Botswana Educational Research Association* 1, no. 1: 51–62.

———. 1996. "External Examining and Moderating at the University of Botswana." In P. T. M. Marope and S. G. Weeks, eds., *Education and National Development in Southern Africa,* 85–100. Gaborone: Saches.

Husen, T. 1997. "Quality in Higher Education: Conceptual Framework and Operational Criteria." In K. Watson, S. Modgil, and C. Modgil, eds., *Educational Dilemmas: Diversity and Debate.* Vol. 4: *Quality in Education,* 30–41. London: Cassell.

Ingalls, W. B. 1995. "Building Consensus for Change: Developing an Administrative and Management Structure in a Southern African University." *Higher Education* 29, no. 3: 275–285.

Makoni, S. 1994. "Economic Co-operation and Development in Southern Africa." In S. Brothers, J. Hermans, and D. Nteta, eds., *Botswana in the 21st Century,* 169–181. Gaborone: Botswana Society.

Mbuende, K. 1997. "SADC Summit to Review and Rationalise Programmes." *The Botswana Guardian*, September 5, p. 3.

Molefe, D., T. Mudariki, G. Tsayang, and S. Weeks. 1997. "Maximising Learning Opportunities for Tirelo Setshaba (Botswana's Unique Non-Military National Service)." *Journal of Research in Post-Compulsory Education* 2, no. 1: 69–81.

Molefe, D., and S. G. Weeks. 2001. "National Service—Is It a Thirteenth Year of Education? The Rise and Fall of an Innovation in Botswana." *Africa Today* 48, no. 2: 105–126.

Morapedi, N. T. 1987. "The Role of the National Institute for Development Research and Documentation (NIR, University of Botswana) in Improving the Research Environment in Botswana." In Robert Hitchcock, Neil Parsons and John Taylor, eds., *Research for Development in Botswana*, 415–422. Gaborone: Botswana Society.

Mudariki, T., S. Ndzinge, G. Tsayang, and S. Weeks. 1997. *Evaluation of Tirelo Setshaba: Final Report.* Gaborone: Government Printer.

Nkambule, N. 1997. Interview with the author, August, Gaborone.

Nwa, E. U., and P. Houenou. 1990. *Graduate Education and Research and Development in African Universities.* Accra: Association of African Universities.

Republic of Botswana. 1977. *Education for Kagisano: Report of the National Commission on Education* and *Volume 2: Annexes.* Gaborone: Government Printer.

———. 1991. *National Development Plan 7, 1991–1997.* Gaborone: Government Printer.

———. 1993. *The Report of the National Commission on Education, 1993.* Gaborone: Government Printer.

———. 1994. *The Revised National Policy on Education.* Government Paper no. 2. Gaborone: Government Printer.

———. 1997. *National Development Plan 8, 1997–2002.* Gaborone: Government Printer.

Ronan, N. J., and C. H. Ronan. 1995. "One More Time: How Do You Finance Higher Education?" *Mosenodi: Journal of the Botswana Educational Research Association* 3, nos. 1 and 2: 55–64.

Saint, W. S. 1992. *Universities in Africa: Strategies for Stabilization and Revitalization.* World Bank Technical Paper no. 194. Washington, D.C.: World Bank.

———. 1993. "Initiating University Reform: Experience from Sub-Saharan Africa." *Zimbabwe Journal of Educational Research* 5, no. 1: 1–20.

Salkin, J. S., D. Mpabanga, D. Cowan, J. Selwe, and M. Wright, eds. 1997. *Aspects of the Botswana Economy.* Gaborone: Lentswe la Lesedi and Oxford: James Currey.

Setidisho, N. O. H., and B. C. Sanyal. 1988. *Higher Education and Employment in Botswana.* Paris: International Institute for Educational Planning, UNESCO.

Sifuna, D. 1997. *The Crisis in the Public Universities in Kenya.* In K. Watson, S. Modgil, and C. Modgil, eds., *Educational Dilemmas: Diversity and Debate.* Vol. 2: *Reforms in Higher Education*, 219–229. London: Cassell.

Swartland, J. 1997. Interview with the author, January, Gaborone.

Turner, J. D. 1984. "The Role of the University of Botswana in Meeting National Manpower Requirements." In M. Crowder, ed., *Education for Development in Botswana*, 225–236. Gaborone: Botswana Society and Macmillan Botswana.

University of Botswana. 1991a. *Report of the Review Commission of the University of Botswana.* Gaborone: University of Botswana.

———. 1991b. *Decisions of the University of Botswana Council on the Report of the University of Botswana Review Commission.* Gaborone: University of Botswana.

———. 2000. *UB Annual Report 1999–2000.* Gaborone: University of Botswana.

Walters, S. 1999. "Lifelong Learning within Higher Education in South Africa: Emancipatory Potential." In Crain Soudien and Peter Kallaway with Mignonne Breier, eds., *Education, Equity and Transformation*, 575–587. Hamburg: UNESCO Institute for Education and Dordrecht, the Netherlands: Kluwer Academic.

Weeks, S. G. 1993. "Reforming the Reform: Education in Botswana." *Africa Today* 40, no. 1: 49–60.

———. 1995a. "Educational Research Policy and Planning: A Third World Perspective." In Shirley Burchfield, ed., *Research for Educational Policy and Planning*, 32–39. Gaborone: Macmillan Botswana.

———. 1995b. "Executive Summary of the Second National Commission on Education's Recommendations and Those of the Revised National Policy on Education: Government Paper Number 2." *Mosenodi* 3, nos. 1 and 2: 84–102.

Welch, A. 1996. *Australian Education: Reform or Crisis?* Sydney: Allen and Unwin.

Wolpe, H. 1995. "The Debate on University Transformation in South Africa." *Comparative Education* 31, no. 2: 275–292.

World Bank. 1994. *Higher Education: The Lessons of Experience.* Washington, D.C.: IBRD and World Bank.

Youngman, F. 1994. "The Role of the University in Developing Educational Research Capacity and Influencing Educational Decisions." In S. Burchfield, ed., *Research for Educational Policy and Planning*, 195–235. Gaborone: Macmillan Botswana.

18

Burkina Faso

WENDENGOUDI GUENDA

INTRODUCTION

Located at the heart of West Africa, Burkina Faso is a Sahelian country with an area of 274,000 square kilometers (105,874 square miles). It is a landlocked country with limited natural resources. Burkina Faso has experienced rapid rural and urban population growth; exploitation of arable lands, vegetation cover, and water resources; erosion and reduction of soil fertility; and the threat of desertification.

The population of Burkina Faso is estimated at about 12 million people. More than 50 percent are women, and 52 percent are under fifteen. The population has a density of 39.3 inhabitants per square kilometer, a birth rate of 45 per 1000, a death rate of 16.4 per 1,000, a population growth rate of 3 percent per year, and an estimated average life span of 52.2 years. About 4 million people in Burkina Faso are immigrants. The working population makes up 54 percent of the population, with 92 percent working in agriculture and 2 percent in industry. The country's gross domestic product (GDP) is $2,336 million. External debt was 55 percent of GDP in 1995, and 45 percent of the population live below the poverty line. This demographic has created a significant increase in demand for education at the primary, secondary, and higher education levels. Despite continuous efforts to increase enrollment, the school enrollment rate remains 40.92 percent in primary education but only 1 percent in higher education. According to the United Nations Development Program, the human development indicator for Burkina Faso is 0.276; the country is ranked 172 (out of 176) in the world.

The economy is dominated by the agricultural sector and the presence of a dynamic informal sector. Agriculture, which should be the driving force behind this economy, cannot produce enough surplus to feed the population or provide exportable goods to finance the development of the economy.

The political situation in Burkina Faso has been charac-

terized since 1991 by a pluralist and constitutional democracy; the president is elected by universal ballot and all the republican structures provided for by the constitution have been instituted. Political stability has fostered the country's development, which has been slow at times but steady in most of the sectors of Burkinabé society.

Burkina Faso has suffered from the deterioration of international economic conditions, which has brought about such problems as the drop in the price of raw materials, the increase of interest rates and national debt, and the subsequent devaluation of the CFA franc by 50 percent in 1994. This led the government to introduce a structural adjustment program (SAP) in 1990, aimed at boosting public finances and reviving the economy. The economic policy of Burkina Faso focuses on a permanent concern for subregional and regional economic integration, as shown by the involvement of the country in the West African Economic and Monetary Union (WAEMU) and the Economic Community of the West African States (ECOWAS), as well as by the efforts undertaken to liberalize the economy through the removal of regional and subregional customs duties.

HISTORY OF HIGHER EDUCATION

Higher education in Burkina Faso (formerly Upper Volta) dates back to April 24, 1961, when the government signed a cooperation agreement with France. This agreement led France to set up a Higher Education Center in Burkina Faso based on the model and quality of higher education in France.

The Institute for Teacher Training, created on October 20, 1965, marks the origin of higher education in Burkina Faso. This institution contained the Training Center for Secondary Education (CPES), which aimed to provide training for first-cycle secondary teachers.

CPES, the first university structure, later became the Higher Education Training Center of Ouagadougou (CESup), endowed with separate legal status and financial autonomy. At that time, CESup was made up of all the higher education and research structures of the country, including the University College of Humanities, the University Educational Institute, the University Institute of Technology (IUT), the Upper Volta Center for Scientific Research (CVRS), and the Center for Documentation and Educational Development. The CVRS withdrew from CESup on September 25, 1972.

CESup became a university by decree number 74-031/ PRESS/EN of April 19, 1974, and was renamed the University of Ouagadougou (UO). Its enrollments at that time were estimated at 374.

Since its inception, the University of Ouagadougou has undergone two periods of reform, in 1985 and 1991. The significant outcome of the 1985 reforms was the multiplication of institutes and schools within the university, including IUT, the Institute of Humanities (INSHUS), the University Institute of Languages, Literature and Arts (INSULA), the Institute of Mathematics and Physics (IMP), the Institute of Chemistry (INC), the Institute of Natural Sciences (ISN), the Institute of Rural Development (IDR), the Institute of Educational Sciences (INSE), the National Institute of Cinema (INAFEC), the College of Law (ESD), the College of Health Sciences (ESSSA), the College of Economics (ESSEC), and the College of Computer Science (ESI).

In 1991, these institutions were grouped into schools with the objective of increasing the usefulness and the performance of UO in light of national realities. Ultimately, though, these structures were once again decentralized in 1995–1996.

UO included three campuses in 1996–1997. The campus of Ouagadougou was made up of five faculties: humanities (referred to as FLASHS), science and technology (FAST), economics and management (FASEG), health sciences (FSS), and law and political science (FDSP). The campus of Bobo-Dioulasso included two institutes and one school: IUT, IDR, and ESI. The campus of Koudougou included the Teacher Training School of Koudougou (ENSK), aimed at training teachers, pedagogical advisers, and inspectors of primary and secondary schools.

Until June 1997, one rector supervised all three UO campuses. Since the 1997–1998 academic year, the Polytechnic School of Bobo-Dioulasso (UPB), which replaced the Polytechnic University Center of Bobo-Dioulasso, and the Institute for Teacher Training of Koudougou (ENSK) have each become autonomous structures, though they maintain multiple links with UO.

Since November 2000, UO has been divided into seven training and research units (Unité de formation et de recherche, UFR) and one institute: Literature, Arts, and Communication (UFR/LAC), Health Sciences (UFR/SDS), Exact and Applied Sciences (UFR/SEA), Economics and Management (UFR/SEG), Humanities (UFR/SHS), Legal and Political Sciences (UFR/SJP), Earth and Life Sciences (UFR/SVT), and the Burkinabé Institute of Arts and Trades (IBAM).

Private higher education is relatively new to Burkina Faso. The Higher Institute of Computer Sciences (ISIG), established in 1992, was the first private institution of higher education in the country. Since 1996, a number of institutions have opened, including the College of Applied Sciences (ESSA) in Bobo-

Dioulasso in 1996, the Training Center in Computer Science and Management (CEFIG) in 1997, the Private Polytechnic College (ISPP) in 1998, the College of Commerce (ESCO-IGES) in 1999, and the Free University of Burkina (ULB) in 2000.

REFORMS AT THE UNIVERSITY OF OUAGADOUGOU

Since its creation in 1974, UO has undergone three significant reforms. The first reform, in 1985, aimed at developing reduced services, better control of student enrollments, greater specialization in the individual institutions, and the development of four productive activities at the university. The outcome of this reform was the creation of nine institutions and four training colleges. The major problem of this reform, however, was the tendency to place too much emphasis on training in the first cycle, overlooking the need for a common core curriculum.

The second reform, which took place in 1991, focused on adapting training programs and establishing integrated services to replace the former isolated structures. The discussions leading to these reforms involved the government, parents, teachers, students, and trade unions. Planners sought to find an appropriate balance between the training profiles proposed by the university and the needs of the country. This reform resulted in better rationalization of the use of human and material resources available and the development of new training sections focused on technology and professionalization, but it met with resistance from the teachers' trade unions.

The third reform started in November 2000, during the breakdown of the 1999–2000 university academic year, which was marked by the lack of evaluation of the first four levels and the massive failure of the first-year class. Long strikes organized by students during this time were related to a national political crisis caused by the death of the journalist Norbert Zongo and to student demands for better material and financial conditions for their studies. A certain anarchy gained ground on the campus characterized by confrontations among student factions and between students and teachers. The university closed on October 6, 2000, and reopened in December. The reforms undertaken prior to reopening focused on managing the increased number of first-year students, professionalization, and improving the material and financial conditions of students and teachers.

Under these reforms, the university adopted new structures: training and research units that combine the fundamental training of faculties and the professionalization of institutes. Here again, the teachers' unions refused to be involved in the commissions charged with setting up the new structures, especially the training and research units replacing the faculties.

CAPACITY IN HIGHER EDUCATION INSTITUTIONS

Burkina Faso presently counts eleven higher training institutions. Three of them are owned by the state and the others by the private sector.

The state-owned institutions are:

• The University of Ouagadougou (UO), which is made up of seven UFRs and one institute. As of March 2001, UO enrolled

11,277 students and had 303 permanent and 175 part-time teachers.

- The Polytechnic University of Bobo-Dioulasso (UPB), which is made up of two institutes and one school. UPB has 370 students enrolled and 134 teachers.
- One high school: ENSK, which has 286 students and 60 teachers.

Private education institutions:

- The Free University of Burkina (ULB) at Ouagadougou, which has 135 students and 19 teachers.
- The Higher Institute of Computer Science and Management (ISIG), which has 550 students and 60 teachers.
- Private Polytechnic Higher Institute (ISPP), which has 279 students and 35 teachers.
- The Higher Institute of Technology (IST), which has 62 students and 24 teachers.
- The College of Applied Sciences (ESSA), which has 231 students and 38 teachers.
- The College of Commerce (ESCO-IGES), which has 300 students and 62 teachers.
- The Training Center in Computer Science and Management (CEFIG), which has 81 students and 28 teachers.
- The School of Sciences and Computer Technology of Faso (ESTIF), which has 43 students and 17 teachers.

The current institutions of higher education in Burkina Faso enrolled a total of about 14,000 students in 2000.

UO alone hosts 80 percent of the students of Burkina Faso, even though its real capacity is for only 8,000 students. The more than 4,000 students repeating the same class during the invalidation of the year 1999–2000 have added to the normal total number of enrollments. Table 18.1 shows the total number of students by gender during the period 1995–1996 to 2000–2001.

For over a decade, Burkina Faso has been involved in the promotion of new technologies in the field of education and in the development of an adequate administration. Thus the College of Computer Science was created in the 1990s and worked closely with institutions such as the Telecommunications National Office (ONATEL), the National Center for Information Processing (CENATRIN), and the General Delegation for Computer Sciences (DELGI). The private sector has also played a significant role in the development of computer science in Burkina Faso.

The field of computer science is developing throughout the world. Burkina Faso is no exception, since the computer is becoming more widely used in all economic sectors.

According to the National Office for the Promotion of Employment (ONPE), employment problems are linked to professional training. In order to benefit from an economic surge and to remain a source of skilled labor in the context of the West African Economic and Monetary Union (WAEMU), Burkina Faso should be more involved in professional training and recycling courses.

There are three kinds of training cycles:

- The first cycle includes the first and second years of university studies. Students who complete this cycle earn the general

Table 18.1. Student Enrollment by Gender at the University of Ouagadougou, 1995–2001

Academic Year	Gender		Total
	M N (%)	F N (%)	
1995–1996	6,339 (75)	2,086 (25)	8,425
1996–1997	6,112 (77)	1,856 (23)	7,968
1997–1998	6,061 (77)	1,809 (23)	7,870
1998–1999	6,764 (77)	2,049 (23)	8,813
1999–2000	7,993 (77)	2,407 (23)	10,400
2000–2001	8,678 (77)	2,599 (23)	11,277
Total	41,947	12,806	54,753

Source: Direction des Affaires Académiques et Scolaires, "Management for Academic and School Activities, 1995–2001," University of Ouagadougou, March 27, 2001.

study university diploma (DEUG), the PCEM in health sciences, or the DUTS in a professional area.
- The second cycle takes two years and corresponds to the completion of the bachelor's and the master's degrees.
- The third cycle includes two levels: the DEA, or the further university diploma in one year, and a *doctorat unique*, which takes three years. A third-cycle doctorate exists and is called *doctorat d'état* (state doctorate). The postgraduate doctorate will be replaced by the doctorate with a single thesis.

STUDENT ENROLLMENT

After the baccalaureate exam, the great majority of graduates attend university. Thus, the enrollment of students at UO is directly related to the total number of new baccalaureate holders. In 1990–1991, for instance, 1,210 new baccalaureate holders out of 1,575 enrolled at UO; in 1991–1992 they were 2,868 out of 3,093 enrolled; in 1992–1993, they were 2,673 out of 2,803 enrolled. The significant increase in the number of newcomers has also exacerbated a number of problems; for instance, the lack of space available to host a greater number of first-year students, and problems related to the organization of laboratory work and the supervision of students in general. Between academic years 1995–1996 and 2000–2001, total enrollment at OU increased from 8,425 to 11,277 (Table 18.1).

In 2000–2001, 97 percent of students were Burkinabé nationals; 3 percent were born elsewhere. The trend is toward enrolling fewer students who were not born in Burkina Faso; six years earlier, 10 percent of enrollees at OU were born elsewhere (Table 18.2). In 2000–2001, only one in four students was female, and fewer than one in four scholarship students was female.

Most students benefit from the support of the state in the form of financial assistance or a loan from the National Fund of Education and Research (FONER).

Table 18.2. Student Enrollment by Country of Origin at the University of Ouagadougou, 1995–2001

| Academic Year | Country of Origin | | | | | |
| | Nationals | | Foreigners | | Refugees | |
	M	F	M	F	M	F
1995–1996	5,712	1,883	602	198	25	5
1996–1997	5,369	1,634	724	218	19	4
1997–1998	5,515	1,641	530	164	16	4
1998–1999	6,241	1,863	510	182	13	4
1999–2000	7,417	2,225	566	180	10	2
2000–2001	8,429	2,543	242	55	7	1
Totals	38,683	11,789	3,174	997	90	20

Source: Direction des Affaires Académiques et Scolaires, "Management for Academic and School Activities, 1995–2001," University of Ouagadougou, March 27, 2001.

Table 18.3. Employees in Nonacademic Offices at the University of Ouagadougou, 2001

Services	Workers	Staff*
Rectorate	24	87
Bibliothèque Universitaire Centrale (Main Library)	9	22
Office du baccalauréat (Baccalaureate Office)	7	9
Atelier central de maintenance (Central Maintenance Workshop)	2	20

*Administrative, technical, and support staff.
Source: Direction des Affaires Académiques et Scolaires, "Management for Academic and School Activities, 1995–2001," University of Ouagadougou, March 27, 2001.

The ratio of students to teachers varies tremendously from one institution to another. UO has the least favorable rate—one teacher for every twenty-four students. The Polytechnic University of Bobo-Dioulasso has the best ratio, with one teacher for every three students.

In 1998, a seminar entitled "The University of Ouagadougou in the 21st Century: In Search of Efficiency and Performance" observed that with the constant increase in student enrollment, the number of teachers required for efficient teaching is increasingly higher than the number of available teachers. For instance, laboratory work is crucial. During these exercises, students move from theoretical concepts into practice under the supervision of a monitor, who helps them assess their understanding and makes necessary adjustments. It is clear that such working sessions cannot be efficient when the ratio of students to supervisors is too high. Beyond twenty-five to thirty students, it is difficult to achieve the expected results from practical work.

ADMINISTRATIVE STRUCTURE

The administrative structure of state-owned universities can be seen in Table 18.3. The rector or chancellor is appointed by the government after being nominated by the minister of higher education. The rector runs the administration and supervises the functioning of all higher education institutions. The rector is assisted by a vice-chancellor and a secretary-general, who coordinate central services.

Table 18.3 shows the distribution of staff and employees in nonacademic departments of UO. Table 18.4 shows the distribution of all employees and students in the Research and Training Unit (Unité de formation et de recherché, UFR) at UO.

The directors of the UFRs, the institutes, and schools are elected within their structures and appointed by the minister of higher education.

The central services of UO are:

- Administration of academic activities
- Administering the Department of Student Orientation and Information
- Human resources management
- Administration of faculty promotions and relations with the African and Malagasy Council for Higher Education (also referred to as CAMES)
- Administration of the development of information and new communication technologies
- Administration of professional and in-service training
- Administration of pedagogical innovations
- Administration of studies and consultation
- Administration of planning
- Administration of finances

Table 18.4. Faculty and Students in Departments of the Research and Training Unit (UFR) of the University of Ouagadougou, 2001

Department	Full Professor	Associate Professor	Senior Lecturer	Assistant	Full-Time Teacher	Part-Time Teacher	Student
Sciences économiques et de gestion[1]	—	3	11	12	—	—	2,357
Sciences exactes et appliqués[2]	7	10	25	3	1	33	1,098
Sciences de la vie et de la terre[3]	5	9	17	2	1	57	1,371
Sciences juridiques et politiques[4]	1	2	15	3	2	21	1,526
Lettres, arts, et communication[5]	2	4	38	9	4	46	1,547
Sciences humaines[6]	—	6	37	4	1	—	2,356
Sciences de la santé[7]	7	19	22	21	—	18	1,150
Total	22	53	165	54	9	175	11,405

[1]Economics and Management
[2]Exact and Applied Sciences
[3]Life and Earth Sciences
[4]Legal and Political Sciences
[5]Literature, Arts, and Communication
[6]Humanities
[7]Health Sciences

Source: Direction des Affaires Académiques et Scolaires, "Management for Academic and School Activities, 1995–2001," University of Ouagadougou, March 27, 2001.

The related services are the maintenance center, the central library, the university bookshop, the university press center, and the baccalaureate office. The Teachers' Training School is run by a general manager, who is assisted by a general secretary, a manager for studies, and a manager for training.

Private higher education institutions in Burkina Faso have two types of structures. The Free University of Burkina Faso is run by a rector, who is assisted by an administrative director and a secretarial staff. The institutes and the higher private schools have a founder, who is assisted by an administrative official responsible for the functioning of the institution. The latter is assisted by an accountant, a secretary, and inspectors or supervisors of the various sections.

GOVERNANCE

The administrations of UO and Bobo-Dioulasso are basically made up of five levels of decision making: the board of directors, the university assembly (or the council in charge of training and university life), the university council, institutions, and departments.

The board of directors is comprised of the representatives from the Ministry of Secondary, Higher, and Scientific Research Education; the Ministry of Finance; the Ministry of Public Service; the Ministry of Health; the Ministry of Employment; the Chamber of Commerce; the administrative staff; the trade union movement; teachers; and students. Members of the board of directors serve for three years, and their terms are renewable only once.

The assembly of the university, the Council of the Foundation and the Life of the University (CFVU), is responsible for deciding university policy. This structure is academic and ad-

ministrative in its nature. No far-reaching decision can be taken without the agreement of the assembly. The rector summons the assembly of the university at least twice a year. The body discusses important issues, such as modification of texts and reform of the exam system. The members of the assembly are the directors; representatives of the teaching, administrative, technical, and laborers staffs; students; the CNRST (National Center for Scientific and Technological Research); the Ministry of Employment; the Chamber of Commerce; and, for consultation purposes, the directors of central services.

The council of the university, or scientific council, is a structure that is purely academic in its nature. It decides on university policy. Its members are a fixed number of the representatives of higher educational staffs (professors, associate professors, and assistant associate professors).

The rector or the chancellor supervises the running of all the institutions of the university. The rector is assisted in his function by the vice-chancellors. The secretary-general also assists in the management of the university. He supervises social services and is responsible for the administrative and technical coordination of activities and also higher institutions. The directors of the UFRs are responsible for the institutions and report to the rector.

Departments are the basic structures for academic activities. The department develops and manages training programs in the sections and specialties. The university is made up of education and research institutions and support structures, such as libraries and a university press. Each education and research institution is divided into departments, each of which is supervised by a coordinator who is a teacher. The head of department is responsible for relations with management. The institution itself is run by a team made up of a manager, a head of the institution, a

Table 18.5. Scholarship Status of Students at the University of Ouagadougou, 1995–2001

Academic Year	Scholarship N (%)	Non-scholarship N (%)	Wage-earners N (%)
1995–1996	2,553 (30)	5,342 (63)	530 (6)
1996–1997	2,167 (27)	5,167 (65)	634 (8)
1997–1998	1,806 (23)	5,522 (70)	542 (7)
1998–1999	1,682 (19)	6,433 (73)	698 (8)
1999–2000	1,625 (16)	7,903 (76)	872 (8)
2000–2001	1,765 (16)	9,003 (80)	509 (4)
Total	11,598	39,370	3,785

Source: Direction des Affaires Académiques et Scolaires, "Management for Academic and School Activities, 1995–2001," University of Ouagadougou, March 27, 2001.

deputy manager responsible for academic activities, and a main secretary in charge of the administration. Overall management is handled by the central administration under the supervision of the rector.

An investigation carried out in 1998 found that 56 percent of teachers thought that the management of the administration was not efficient. Faculty often complain about administrative bottlenecks, the lack of autonomy of the institutions, and the procedure by which the rector is elected.

FINANCING AND BUDGET

The state-owned universities have a budget based mainly on subsidies from the state, but public funds are insufficient to cover all of their operating expenses. Indeed, electricity, water, and telephone fees are very high and UO has difficulties paying them every year because of the permanent deficit. It is imperative to search for additional funds for the university. Some additional funds are currently provided by bilateral or multilateral cooperation and by resources generated by the university. Students provide a small but increasing proportion of annual university budgets. For example, during the period 1995–1996 to 2000–2001, the percentage of students on scholarship at UO decreased from 30 percent to 16 percent. Eighty percent of students in 2000–2001 were non-scholarship students, compared with 63 percent in 1995–1996 (Table 18.5). Enrollment fees help defray budgetary expenditures as well. In 2001, Burkinabé nationals and refugees paid enrollment fees of between $9 and $16 annually; other foreigners paid a substantially higher fee of $286.

In the past, currency devaluation has negatively impacted the monetary value of the budget. It is therefore necessary that the state provide for increases of more than 15 percent in order to maintain the university's purchasing power.

The total number of students at UO varied from 4,216 to 9,523 in 1995 and reached up to 10,000 in 1999. The increase in the number of students and the inadequate subsidy provided by the state forced the university to find better ways to manage its

resources to contribute to its own financing, especially through the university library, the university press, and the guest house.

The university can better manage the delivery of services to help overcome its chronic budget deficits. But contribution of these activities to budgetary relief is still weak, due in part to several constraints, including the lack of personnel and inadequacy of infrastructures.

The current enrollment fees for foreign students are high but are similar to the enrollment fees prevailing in the French-speaking universities of the region.

School fees of Burkinabé students were increased in October 1998 in an effort to improve financial resources. UO should strive to achieve consensus about future increases in enrollment fees. Indeed, UO may need to introduce training fees for first- and second-cycle students to offset the cost of laboratory equipment and supplies as well as the extra staff hours needed for training and supervision.

MANAGEMENT OF FINANCIAL RESOURCES

Despite the poor financial resources of UO, excellent management has enabled the university to function without experiencing a crisis. To upgrade the management of the university financial resources in an efficient manner, officials should be trained in administration and management. The training of managers, heads of services, and teachers should focus on the greater professionalism needed for sound operation of the university and the enhancement of its significance for civil society.

To reach these objectives, the university should reinforce both North-South and South-South cooperation by encouraging synergy in institutional capacities. Such cooperation should contribute to an increase in the technical and legal competencies of universities in developing nations and reinforce regional cooperation.

GRADUATE EMPLOYMENT

The state has long been the main employer in Burkina Faso. In the past, the relatively small number of university graduates meant that those who completed their studies could find a job immediately. But this situation has completely changed. An increasing number of graduates now find themselves jobless. The professional sections of the state-owned universities and private institutions have greater success in preparing students for employment than do other higher education institutions in the country. Those earning degrees in the humanities, languages, law, and economics find it most difficult to find employment after graduation. At present, graduates in the exact sciences and health are not having the same difficulty in finding employment.

A 1998 study of university graduates and former students at UO found that almost all the respondents (92.3 percent) thought that technological and professionalized sections were sufficiently represented at the university. Out of 91 former students, only one was an employer; the others were wage-earners (which helps explain why job creation is very low). Thirty percent were jobless, and 88 percent complained about the lack of association with former university students. Although 96 percent were ready to participate in such an association, UO has no structure for tracking the professional life of university graduates. The 1998 study confirmed the necessity of adopting a strategy to professionalize training areas and to address the problem of joblessness faced by its graduates.

LANGUAGE OF INSTRUCTION

Burkina Faso is a Francophone country. French is the language of the administration and all the training and research institutions. However, English is commonly taught as a second language in secondary schools and at the university.

RESEARCH AND PUBLICATION

Research is one of the fundamental missions of the university. In Burkina Faso, fundamental and applied research is carried out by teachers in all their fields of competence. In addition, the CNRST contributes to the agricultural and technological development of the country.

UO has a number of assets to promote research, including its experience in popularizing information, its publication infrastructure, and its skilled staff. Some laboratories and creative research centers need to be reinforced, and initiatives for the creation of new research structures should be pursued.

Teachers and researchers at UO have performed the best in the region on various tests organized by the CAMES. The CAMES is an institution made up of seventeen Francophone African countries that makes sound scientific analysis of the promotion files of the teachers and researchers in the subregion. Its evaluation of UO indicates that the university has a competent staff for the development of utilitarian research, but advanced research carried out by senior students under the supervision of teachers should not be neglected.

CONSTRAINTS OF UNIVERSITY RESEARCH

A document titled "Ten Measures to Revive the African University" published in 1993 by a team of African rectors identified a number of problems facing academic research in Africa. It found that teachers are overburdened; remuneration conditions are unattractive; colleges lack appropriate books, infrastructure, and scientific equipment; schools do not have enough research assistants; in some cases research is undertaken in an environment of hostility; many teachers/researchers are drawn away to high political or administrative positions; African researchers are isolated; and research is not properly valued.

All these constraints apply to UO. This explains why the utilitarian research carried out at the university seems to have a limited impact on Burkinabé society. This is particularly reinforced by UO's weak organization and coordination of utilitarian research, the lack of scientific equipment and specialized tools, and its insufficient funding for research.

To be efficient, academic research must be based on teamwork that involves research projects implemented by a group of teachers and students under the supervision of a senior researcher. Yet UO is characterized by individualism, especially for the faculties without collective research structures.

Some hoped that the creation of the position of a vice-dean responsible for research and development within each faculty from 1991–2000 would result in a greater coordination of research activities and a greater dissemination of research results nationally. But this did not happen. In fact, these services are now less operational. Research centers that focus on producing research based on utilitarian goals still do not exist at UO.

Most of UO's laboratories lack crucial scientific equipment; many have even more serious problems, such as the lack of necessary physical structures, including buildings. Sometimes research in Burkina Faso lacks the scientific documentation, including field investigation and sampling, that is necessary for quality research.

Research at UO is further hindered by the lack of financial resources. An examination of the university's budgets shows that the items devoted to research are not clearly delineated. This prevents the development of utilitarian research.

In 1996, Burkina Faso adopted a Strategic Plan for Scientific Research (PSRS) that set out the essential needs for the social development of the country and the well-being of the population. Research managed by the university correlates strongly with the priorities mentioned in the PSRS. If by "utilitarian research" one means the resolution of the daily problems that hamper the economic development of the country, one can say that UO is carrying out utilitarian research. But one should also keep in mind that the primary role of research in society is to plan for the future by integrating past and present data.

Unfortunately, however, results of university research relevant to social and economic development remain unknown to the public and to development stakeholders. The responsibility for the dissemination of research results not only belongs to the researchers; it also belongs to the authorities. UFR management should work with ministerial departments to ensure that research results are properly disseminated. The relevant authorities should encourage funding for the public dissemination of research findings in Burkina Faso. It is only then that university research will launch our country into the twenty-first century.

STATE OF PUBLICATION

Several publications in Burkina Faso publish academic research. These include *The Annual Annals of the University of Ouagadougou*, *The Annual Scientific and Technical Review of CNRST*, *The Half Yearly Review: CEDRES Studies*, and *The Annual Burkinabé Review of Law*. These publications have review committees that include professors from institutions in Burkina Faso and researchers from the CNRST.

POLITICAL INFLUENCE ON CAMPUS

Various political forces have an interest in the control of the university. One might say that the one who controls the university gains a political insurance for the future, since the students of today are the future leaders of tomorrow. It is therefore reasonable to think that all the political regimes that have held power in Burkina Faso have developed various strategies to gain political strength on campuses.

The ruling party, the other legally recognized political parties, and small political parties fight to gain or increase their influence on the campus by attempting to control the associations of students, teachers, administrators, technical staff, laborers, and, especially, the elected members of the administration. Because the government finances higher education, it reserves the right to oversee the administration and policies at the university, but the institutions enjoy some pedagogical and administrative autonomy.

The fact that the rector is a political appointee is seen by some as a threat to academic freedom. In this way, the ruling class subtly tries to assert control over the university. This can engender a tense political atmosphere. If the will of the state is completely disregarded when appointing the rector, however, there is a risk that the rector will be given too much power or that the government will abandon the university's needs and requirements.

During a seminar held in 1998 to discuss the lack of autonomy of academic institutions, some faculty suggested that information is not properly disseminated and that communication between the administration and personnel is inadequate. Do faculty (not to mention students) really know the university administration in terms of services and procedures that should be expected? Does a faculty member entering the university learn more about the administrative functioning of the institution each time he or she needs a specific service? In these conditions, they may not be aware of some administrative procedures.

Of course, the university faces some economic difficulties, but there are also human difficulties. These include habits, ways of thinking and acting that have become "second nature," and resistance to change. Yet the university is a changing environment that is undergoing steady evolution. The resolution of our problems depends on the ability of the staff to adapt themselves to change (the new technologies) and to the reform of the university. The future of the university depends on the commitment of the staff members, efficient and humane administration, good leadership, the ability to attract and retain good students (including women), and the good performance of the faculty.

Concerning private higher institutions, the influence of politics is perceptible, especially regarding statutory and pedagogical requirements vis-à-vis state dictates.

STUDENT ACTIVISM

In the state-owned universities, students are organized in associations. The two most structured of these are the National Association of Students (ANEB), which is a leftist association, and the National Union of Students of Burkina Faso (UNEF), which is a rightist association. In principle, the associations defend the material and moral interests of the students. However, the experience at UO in 1999–2000 demonstrated that student associations have some links with political parties. In that year, ANEB was the main leader of the group of student associations, and radical conflict with opposition political parties resulted in the suspension of academic activities and the invalidation of the year.

In private institutions, student associations are corporate by nature and tend to focus on opportunities for employment after graduation. Similar developments are taking place at the state-owned universities. Indeed, a club of student entrepreneurs was set up in January 2001 to develop the spirit of business initiative among students at public and private institutions.

The living conditions of students have some impact on their attention span and ability to understand lectures. Of course, the great majority of students face considerable hardships. Most of them do not have even the basics to feed and take care of themselves, let alone money for buying books and other pedagogical materials. In a country such as Burkina Faso, where the annual average income per capita is extremely low, families are generally unable to fund the education of their children. In these conditions, aid from the state, especially for student scholarships, is necessary for the viability of the higher educational system.

Burkina Faso has established criteria for financing students that take into account their social status. Thus, most of the students who receive a scholarship can benefit from financial aid amounting to $185 in order to cope with their basic needs.

CONDITIONS FOR FACULTY

The material and social conditions of teachers in Burkina Faso have declined. When UO was created, the financial situation of university teachers was quite good, but today the university is unable to retain teachers, especially in fields facing competition from the private sector. Wages and benefits have remained stable, despite the fact that inflation and devaluation have significantly reduced the standard of living for teachers. As a result, teachers resort to private courses, consultations, and other projects, which means they are less available to fulfill their research and educational responsibilities. Teachers face tremendous difficulties obtaining teaching materials and recent publications in their specialty, which are necessary tools for research and the renewal of the course content. They also have inadequate access to new information and communication technologies such as computers and cannot afford the fees for a long stay abroad for research and personal development. These are undoubtedly serious obstacles to pedagogical and scientific progress.

The degradation of the teaching profession has been exacerbated by the excessive valorization and remuneration of business professionals. Teachers have experienced a decline in social prestige that is disheartening and certainly has had an impact on their performance. Generally, teachers are neither admired nor respected by students, which seriously undermines the pedagogical relationship. If the teacher is not seen as a social resource, he or she will not be paid due consideration by the students. Moreover, appropriate libraries and laboratories for faculty research work are insufficient or nonexistent in many fields. For instance, UO has no doctoral program in applied rather than theoretical physics. UO has started to address these faculty problems and has obtained increased funding, especially for a sabbatical year and the reduction of required work hours.

Faculty in the private higher education sector are not yet involved in research.

PROSPECTIVE VISION OF HIGHER EDUCATION IN BURKINA FASO

By 2010, the number of students at UO could reach 22,000; by 2020, it could reach 58,000 (Université de Ouagadougou 1998). If the university's structures are insufficient to host 12,000 students today, how will it manage such growth then?

UO needs to create regional universities throughout Burkina Faso and to develop distance learning programs.

CONCLUSION

In Burkina Faso, higher education is dominated by theoretical training, which currently accounts for 80 percent of the students who are enrolled at the University of Ouagadougou, the country's most diversified campus. All the other institutions of higher education are specialized and represent only 20 percent of national enrollments.

The vision of the university should be changed to allow greater flexibility. Especially in this era of globalization, the university is compelled to prepare individuals to adapt to new circumstances. New information and communication technologies should be welcomed. People will need to overcome their fear of these new instruments, which should be developed widely and made accessible.

BIBLIOGRAPHY

Agbangla, C., and N. Charpentier. 1999. *Rôle et place de l'université dans la société du XXIe siècle face à la mondialisation.* Ouagadougou: Cinquième Colloque, Université sans frontière.

AESO (Association des élèves du secondaire). 2001. "Déclaration." *Sidwaya* 4214 (March 1): 18.

Badini, W. E. 2001. "Université de Ouagadougou: un syndicalisme dévoyé." *L'Opinion* 178 (February 28–March 7): 15.

Groupe ESCO-IGES. 2000. "Un établissement de rigueur pour les étudiants d'élite!" *Le Pays* 2203 (August 18): 15.

MESSRS (Ministère des Enseignements Secondaires Supérieur et de la Recherche Scientifique). 2000. Décret no. 2000-559/PRES/PM/MESSRS/MEF portant approbation des statuts de l'Université de Ouagadougou. Visa cf no. 8460, Décembre.

———. 2001. "Université de Ouagadougou: Le Ministre aux syndicats SNESS et SYNTER." *L'Observateur PAALGA* 5362 (March 19): 7.

Ouampeba, A. 2001. "Club d'entrepreneurs étudiants du Burkina." Lettre et déclaration d'existence, January 29, 2001, Ouagadougou, Burkina Faso.

Sawadogo, F. M. 1998. "Priorité à l'éducation et à la formation des jeunes: Forces et faiblesses de l'Université de Ouagadougou." *Afrique-Education,* no. 45 (May 1998): 22–24.

Sawadogo, L. 2000. "La réforme de l'Université de Ouagadougou." *Wattitingol* 7 (November–December): 6.

Semde, I. 2001. "Université de Ouagadougou: la nécessaire refondation." Interview du TRAORE A. S. Chancelier de l'Université de Ouagadougou. *L'Opinion* 178 (February 28): 16.

SYNTER (Syndicat National des Travailleurs de l'Enseignement et de la Recherche). 2000. *A propos de la refondation de l'Université de Ouagadougou.* Ouagadougou: Assemblée générale du syndicat.

Tia Luc, A. 2000. "L'Université de Ouagadougou: La refondation en marche, la vie reprend." *La Depeche* 33 (December): 3–21.

Traore, S. A. 2001. "Rapport explicatif de quelques aspects institutionnels et pédagogiques de la refondation de l'Université de Ouagadougou. MESSRS/UO/Chancellerie." Direction des presses universitaires, January.

———. 2000. "La refondation de l'Université de Ouagadougou." *Wattitingol* 7 (November–December): 7–13.

Toguyeni, Y. A., F. Sib Sie, and A. P. Ouedraogo. 1998. *Rapport de la sous commission Efficacité interne de l'Université de Ouagadougou.* Ouagadougou: OU/CRDI.

Université de Ouagadougou. 1998. "L'Université de Ouagadougou au XXIe siècle: à la recherche de l'efficacité et de la performance." Université de Ouagadougou, Centre de Recherche pour le Développement International (CRDI), Septembre 1998. Ouagadougou: Direction des presses universitaires.

19

Burundi

JUMA SHABANI

INTRODUCTION

Burundi is a small country of 27,834 square kilometers (10,747 square miles) located in Central Africa between Rwanda, Tanzania, and the Democratic Republic of Congo. In 1995, the population of Burundi was estimated at 6.06 million inhabitants and the gross national product (GNP) per capita at $160. During the period from 1985 to 1995, the average annual growth rates of the population and the GNP per capita were 2.5 percent and 1.3 percent, respectively (UNESCO 1998).

According to the human development indicator (UNDP 1998), Burundi was among the least-developed countries in the world in 1998, with a life expectancy at birth of 44.5 years, an adult illiteracy rate of 57.7 percent, and a gross enrollment ratio of 23 percent for all levels of education.

Burundi is an agricultural country which earns foreign currency mainly through the export of tea and coffee. Burundi became independent in 1962. Since October 1993, the country has experienced a civil war that has led to a significant degradation of the living conditions of the population.

It is generally agreed that higher education in Burundi was quite effective from its beginning in 1964 through the beginning of the civil war. It made a major contribution to the training of the personnel required to run the civil service and the semi-public enterprises and to develop the education system. Since October 1993, however, the country has been beset with a very profound sociopolitical crisis that has negatively impacted the country's social and economic development.

The efforts made for a few years both by national political stakeholders and Burundi's regional and international partners indicate that the country could enjoy peace and security in the near future. As soon as peace is restored, the government of Burundi will have to conceive and implement reconstruction, rehabilitation, and development plans. Higher education should occupy a central place in the proposed plans, given the ma-

jor role that it plays in the process of sustainable human development.

In this chapter, I analyze the situation of higher education in Burundi from its inception until June 2000. In particular, I examine the performance of the system, including its achievements and shortcomings. I also analyze the trends in and provide projections for the growth of student enrollment, the size of academic staff, and the size of educational budgets. From this analysis, I identify a few areas of concern that could be used to formulate a proposal for the reform of higher education in Burundi.

THE MAJOR STAGES OF THE DEVELOPMENT OF HIGHER EDUCATION IN BURUNDI

At the beginning of the 1960s, higher education in Burundi was composed of three institutions: the Institute of Agriculture of Ruanda-Urundi, the Institut Facultaire of Usumbura (University Institute of Usumbura), and the Faculty of Science of Usumbura. In 1962, Ruanda, Urundi, and Usumbura changed their names to become Rwanda, Burundi, and Bujumbura. In 1964, these three institutions merged to create the official University of Bujumbura, known as the Université Officielle de Bujumbura (UOB, Official University of Bujumbura).

In 1965, the teacher training college known as Ecole Normale Supérieure (ENS, Teacher's School) was created with the mission of training the teachers of junior secondary schools. In 1972, the national school of administration known as Ecole Nationale d'Administration (ENA, National Advanced School for Administration) was established to train civil servants.

In 1973, UOB, ENS, and ENA merged to create the University of Burundi. This fusion was not carried out immediately; the ENA was integrated into the Faculty of Economics and Administration of UOB in 1975, and UOB and ENS were merged in 1977.

At the beginning of the 1980s, four other nonuniversity higher education institutions were created to train the technical staff required by the civil service. These include the School of Journalism, the School of Commerce, the Institute of Town Planning and Development, and the Institute of Agriculture.

In 1989, these institutions were integrated into the University of Burundi. The major objective of this integration was to optimize the use of the resources allocated to higher education. In the process of integration, the School of Commerce changed its name to become the Institute of Commerce.

By June 2000, in addition to the University of Burundi, higher education was provided in the following public and private institutions:

Public Institutions. The institute for training high-ranking military officers, the national school for training police personnel, the institute of business management, and the new teacher training institute.

Private Institutions. The Seminary of Bujumbura, the Institute of Management and Control, and the University of Ngozi.

The current trend of development of higher education in Burundi indicates that the number of private institutions is likely to increase tremendously in the near future. Student enrollment in private higher education institutions represents more than 10 percent of the total enrollment today.

In this chapter, I will focus my analysis on the University of Burundi.

THE STRUCTURE AND ADMINISTRATION OF THE UNIVERSITY OF BURUNDI (UB)

Decree 100/178 of September 1989 on the reorganization of the UB indicates in article 2 that the missions assigned to the University of Burundi are:

- To provide at the highest level scientific and technical knowledge
- To promote scientific, literary, and artistic research
- To contribute to the social, economic, and cultural development of the country
- To contribute to the civic and moral education of the students

Since its inception, the UB has decided to focus on training the various categories of personnel required by the civil service. This mission has been achieved quite effectively. In contrast, the university did not obtain satisfactory results in the implementation of its research mission.

Regarding the participation of the UB in social, economic, and cultural development, the university does not have any institutional structure or program for the implementation of this mission. It should nevertheless be recognized that the university's teachers are a strong presence on various national advisory committees.

THE UNIVERSITY COUNCIL

The council of the University of Burundi involves representatives of the university community as well as those of the public and private sector.

In general, the president and the vice-president of the council are elected from among the members of the council who are external to the university. The council is composed of ex officio members, the rector, the vice-rector, and members appointed by the head of state on the recommendation of the minister of higher education; four representatives from public administration; two representatives from the private sector; two representatives from the administrative and support staff of the university; three representatives from the academic staff and/or researchers; and two student representatives.

The council has the authority to ensure the smooth functioning of the university. For this purpose, the council has the following assignments:

- To define general university policies and regulations
- To approve the accounts of the past year and propose a provisional budget
- To recruit and promote the academic staff
- To take necessary actions to develop and maintain university property in collaboration with the student welfare management services and other qualified state services
- To create new administrative and/or research units

THE ADMINISTRATIVE UNITS

The rector is responsible for the overall management of the university and administrative and academic matters. In addition, he or she supervises the student welfare management services and the teaching hospital. In case of emergency, the rector is allowed to take measures to ensure the smooth running of the university. These measures must be ratified or dismissed by the council.

The rector works under the supervision of the University Council and the minister in charge of higher education and scientific research. However, the minister can only cancel actions taken by the council that contravene a legal provision applicable to the university.

The rector is assisted by a vice-rector and three directors—the director in charge of academic affairs, of administration and finance, and of research—a team of advisers, and an advisory council called the Rectoral Council, which is composed of the three directors mentioned above, the director of the student welfare management services, the director of the teaching hospital, the deans of faculties and institutes, and student representatives.

The rector, vice-rector, and directors are appointed by the head of state upon the recommendation of the minister of higher education for a four-year term, which is renewable only once.

Before the sociopolitical crisis that started in October 1993, the general management of the university was quite effective. The few weaknesses observed in some units were caused by the following factors:

- The assignments entrusted to units and the mechanisms for monitoring and evaluating their performances were not clearly defined.
- The management capacity of some units was relatively low.
- The strategies used for communication and dissemination of information within the university community were not effective.

- Some regulations related to staff benefits were not implemented.

Since October 1993, the UB has been beset with student and staff strikes, the closing of the university, killings, delays in the implementation of the academic programs, and a high turnover among the university's senior management authorities. As an example, for the period from 1993 to 2000 there have been six successive rectors at the University of Burundi. In addition, the academic year 1999–2000 started only in April 2000 instead of in October 1999.

THE ACADEMIC UNITS

Today the University of Burundi is composed of eight faculties, five institutes, and the center for teaching languages (CELAB). These include: the Faculty of Law, the Faculty of Economics and Administration, the Faculty of Arts and Humanities, the Faculty of Psychology and Education, the Faculty of Science, the Faculty of Agriculture, the Faculty of Medicine, the Faculty of Engineering, the Institute of Commerce, the Institute of Agriculture, the Institute of Technical Training, the Institute of Physical Education and Sports, the Institute of Applied Pedagogy.

During the period 1989–2000 the development of UB's academic units was marked by two major events. First, nonuniversity higher education institutions were integrated into the university in 1989. This integration aimed at optimizing the use of the resources allocated to higher education. Today, eleven years after the integration of these institutions into the university, no evaluation has been carried out to determine if the objectives of integration were achieved, or if it is necessary to detach the institutes of commerce and agriculture from the university in order to reinforce the diversification of the higher educational system.

The second event was the creation of the Institute of Applied Pedagogy. One of the major problems facing the educational system in Burundi is the lack of qualified teachers for secondary schools. Indeed, the average annual growth rate of student enrollments in secondary schools was 12 percent from 1985 to 1992, whereas the capacity of the university for teacher training remained very low (République du Burundi 1993; UNESCO 1999). This situation compelled the government to carry out a massive recruitment of foreign teachers, who represented more than 40 percent of the total teaching staff for secondary schools in 1993–1994 (République du Burundi 1993).

Following the political change in 1994 in Rwanda, several teachers of Rwandan nationality resigned from their positions to return to Rwanda, thus creating several vacancies in the teaching staff positions.

The need for more teachers for secondary schools will sharply increase with the development of community schools. Consequently, the decision to create the Institute of Applied Pedagogy is a good strategy for training a critical mass of qualified teachers. Unfortunately, in the past the number of students directed toward teacher training programs has been very low and these students have been among the weakest candidates.

Each faculty or institute is managed by a dean who is appointed by the university council on a proposal from the rector after a consultation with the relevant members of the faculty or institute. The dean is appointed for a term of two years, renewable only once. However, in practice, some deans have been in office for more than two terms.

In the performance of his or her duties, the dean is assisted by an assistant dean (two in the case of the Faculty of Medicine). The assignments entrusted to the assistant dean relate primarily to the preparation of the course schedules and the exam calendar (Université du Burundi 1989). It is generally agreed that these assignments are inadequate, given the need for the faculties and institutes to revitalize and develop research, to strengthen staff development programs and linkages with the productive sector, and to improve the staff's pedagogical skills.

THE RESEARCH UNITS

The coordination of academic research was introduced at the university in 1978 with the creation of a publication and research unit supervised by the director of academic affairs (Université du Burundi 1989). The position of director of research was created in February 1985 to coordinate and monitor the implementation of the university's research policy.

In 1986, the University Council created the University Research Council, a consultative body in charge of the planning and supervision of all the research and publication activities. The university research policy makes provision for four categories of research (Université du Burundi 1989): research carried out to obtain an academic qualification, consultancy, research in a specific field, and pedagogical research.

The university's research policy does not make any distinction between fundamental and applied research. However, the various authorities at the university and at the national level constantly recommended that research programs should take into account Burundi's national needs and development priorities. This recommendation motivated the university to define five priority research areas. They are food self-sufficiency, health, the education system, the use of local materials in industry, and the analysis of international development trends and their impact on the national economy (Université du Burundi 1989). Unfortunately, the university did not define the research programs that should be implemented in these various areas.

The research carried out at the university makes only a minor contribution to the socioeconomic development of the country. This situation is mainly caused by the following factors:

- The training of researchers does not take account of Burundi's national development needs. One of the consequences of this situation is that it is difficult to mobilize a critical mass of researchers even in priority areas of development.
- The number of full-time researchers and laboratory technicians is very low.
- Inadequate public funds exist for research, and the implementation of research programs is frequently delayed. Indeed, in spite of the low level of the research budget, available resources are not always exhausted (Shabani 1995). It is also worth mentioning that practically all research activities that

require fieldwork have been suspended since October 1993 because of security problems.

Among the four categories of research recognized by the university, consultancy and pedagogic research are not taken into account in the process of staff promotion. This situation contradicts the university's desire to strengthen ties with the productive sector and its goal of improving the pedagogic skills of the academic staff.

The research centers are placed under the overall supervision of the director of research. In general, the research centers are created without preliminary feasibility studies. These centers should play a major role in the mobilization of the resources required for the promotion of postgraduate study programs and research. Unfortunately, the performance of the research centers at the University of Burundi is generally extremely low.

TEACHING AND RESEARCH SUPPORT SERVICES

These services, which include libraries, printing works, and the university bookshop, are placed under the general supervision of the director of research.

The university library network is composed of a central library and six faculty libraries. The budget allocated to the libraries for acquisition of books and periodicals decreased from 2.8 percent of the general operational budget in 1989 to 1 percent in 1993. The general operational budget is composed of the regular university budget, the budget of the student welfare management services, the budget allocated to scholarships, and contributions from external sources. Even though allocations for the library got smaller and smaller, the library was not able to spend all the funds in its budget for various reasons (Shabani 1995). The library budget is inadequate, especially if one refers to the recommendation of the Association of African Universities (AAU 1991) that 5 percent of the general operating budget be allocated to libraries.

The reduction of the budget allocated to the library system resulted in a decline in the number of books per student from sixty-five in 1989 to forty-six in 1993. In the early 1990s, the university libraries of the United States held an average of seventy-eight books per student (Saint 1992). The number of books per student is certainly not a solid indicator of the quality of teaching, especially in the case of the University of Burundi, where books are often acquired in the form of gifts or from orders placed by the academic staff for their teaching and research activities. Nevertheless, the number of books per student provides an indication of the resources available to the university to facilitate general access to knowledge.

OTHER SUPPORT SERVICES

The missions assigned to the student welfare management services (ROU) include management of student dormitories, catering and other social services for students, maintenance of the university buildings and property, and logistical support for the academic program.

The overall management of the ROU is entrusted to a director appointed by the head of state on the recommendation of the

minister of higher education. The director works under the supervision of the ROU's council and the rector of the university. The rector's supervision of student welfare management services usually consists of approval of its annual reports and bylaws and decisions made by the ROU's council prior to their implementation.

The staffing of the ROU is governed by the administrative and technical staff regulations of the UB and Burundi's labor regulations and laws.

The teaching hospital (Centre Hospitalo-Universitaire de Kamenge, CHUK) is also placed under the administrative supervision of the rector of the university, but its overall management must conform with the medical regulations governing hospitals and health centers in Burundi. The overall management of the CHUK is entrusted to a director appointed by the head of state on the recommendation of the minister of higher education. The director works under the supervision of the CHUK's council and the rector of the university.

The missions assigned to the CHUK cover training and staff development programs in health sciences, medical care, and research in health sciences.

The personnel of the CHUK is composed of employees from the Faculty of Medicine, who are governed by the teaching staff and the regulations of the university, and hospital staff, who are governed by the statutes of the CHUK. The working relationships between these categories of personnel are defined in a memorandum of understanding signed by the Faculty of Medicine and the hospital. The implementation of this memorandum is facilitated by the fact that both institutions work under the supervision of the rector of the university.

BILATERAL AND INTERNATIONAL COOPERATION

As indicated in Table 19.1, during the period from 1985 to 1996, several countries and organizations contributed to the running and development of the University of Burundi. Bilateral and international cooperation mainly consisted of the provision of foreign lecturers and professors, provision of scholarships for studies abroad, support for teaching and research programs, and procurement of scientific equipment and teaching materials.

In addition, from 1987 to 1992, a number of effective cooperation programs were established between higher education institutions in the Economic Community of the Great Lakes, which includes Burundi, Rwanda, and the Congo (formerly Zaire). These programs mainly focused on staff and student exchanges and joint research programs (Table 19.1).

Since the early 1990s, most of the cooperation agencies have gradually removed their support for postgraduate programs in which junior academic staff were allowed to spend four or five years in developed countries for Ph.D. studies. This change compelled UB to initiate a master's degree program in commercial computing and the so-called sandwich postgraduate programs in mathematical physics and medicine (programs in which a student who is enrolled at a university in his or her home country is jointly sponsored by a professor from that institution and a professor from an institution abroad).

Following the aggravation of the sociopolitical crisis since October 1993, all the cooperation programs implemented at UB

Table 19.1. Countries and Organizations That Contributed to the Running and Development of the University of Burundi, 1985–1996

Faculty/Institute	Countries	International Cooperation Agencies	Bilateral Cooperation Agencies	
Science	Belgium; USSR	UNESCO; United Nations University	Communauté française de Belgique[1]	AUPELF[2]
Engineering	Germany; USSR	UNDP	—	AUPELF
Economics and Administration	Switzerland	UNDP	—	AUPELF
Arts and Humanities	France	—	—	AUPELF
Medicine	France	—	—	AUPELF
Agriculture	Belgium	—	—	AUPELF
Psychology and Education	—	—	—	AUPELF
Law	Belgium	—	—	AUPELF
Institute of Technical Training	Canada; USSR	—	Communauté française de Belgique	—
Institute of Agriculture	Egypt; China	—	—	—
Institute of Commerce	—	—	—	—
Institute of Physical Education and Sports	—	—	—	—
Pedagogic Institute[3]	Belgium	—	—	—

[1]The French Community in Belgium.

[2]AUPELF stands for the Association des universités partiellement ou entièrement de langue française. In 1998, AUPELF changed its name to Agence Universitaire de la francophonie.

[3]In 1993, the Pedagogic Institute was replaced by the Institute of Applied Pedagogy.

Source: Annual Reports, University of Burundi.

were suspended in 1996. This suspension had not been lifted as of June 2000.

REQUIREMENTS FOR ENTRY TO THE UNIVERSITY OF BURUNDI

By the end of the 1980s, requirements for entry to the university were defined by Decree-law 1/105 of July 13, 1989, on the reorganization of the education system in Burundi. According to this decree, a student must have obtained an upper general secondary school-leaving certificate approved by a special committee set up by the minister of higher education to enter the university. This certificate is equivalent to the French *baccalauréat* (French baccalaureate) and the A-level in the British system.

For the polytechnic section, which provides undergraduate training programs in mathematics, physics, and engineering, students must also have passed an entrance examination in mathematics, though students enrolled in technical secondary schools were allowed to enter the university under special conditions defined by the minister of higher education.

Since the 1996–1997 academic year, students must also spend one year of military service within the national army before they are allowed to enroll in an academic study program. Since 1999, however, admission to university has been governed by a new decree that requires all students to pass a special university entrance examination. The pass rate from secondary to higher education in Burundi is high. If one considers only pub-

Table 19.2. Average Annual Growth Rates of Student Enrollments for Burundi and Sub-Saharan Africa, 1985–1993

Country	Level of Education		
	Primary	Secondary	Higher Education
Burundi	7.8	12.0	11.0
Sub-Saharan Africa	3.0	3.5	9.4

Source: UNESCO 1999.

lic secondary schools, this rate was estimated at 80 percent in 1993 (Republic of Burundi 1993).

TRENDS IN STUDENT ENROLLMENT

From Table 19.2 one can see that enrollment in sub-Saharan Africa increased more rapidly in higher education than in the other education sectors. This was not the case in Burundi, where the highest average annual growth rate was achieved in secondary education. This situation may be partly explained by the rapid increase in the number of secondary community schools.

The enrollment growth in higher education in Burundi was slightly higher than in sub-Saharan Africa. Considering that higher education increased faster in sub-Saharan Africa during

Table 19.3. Distribution of Enrollment by Level and Field of Study during the Academic Year 1992–1993

Area	Years 1 and 2		Years 3 and 4		Postgraduate Programs		Total	
	No. students	%	No. students	%	No. students	%	No. students	%
Arts and Humanities	1,945	66.4	624	49.6	0	0	2,569	60.3
Sciences	985	33.6	633	50.4	71	100	1,689	39.7
Total	2,930	100	1,257	100	71	100	4,258	100

Source: Annual Report of the Academic Unit, University of Burundi, 1994.

the period under review than in any other region, one can conclude that the average annual growth rate in Burundi is quite high. Actually, if the operation of the university had not been disturbed by sociopolitical crisis, it follows from Table 19.2 and the compound growth rate equation that the total enrollment would have reached 8,840 students by the year 2000.

However, despite rapid enrollment growth, other indicators show that the higher education system in Burundi is among the least developed in sub-Saharan Africa. For example, the gross enrollment ratio was 0.7 percent in Burundi, compared to 2.4 percent in sub-Saharan Africa and 51 percent in the developed countries. In addition, the number of students per 100,000 inhabitants was 65 in Burundi in 1990, compared to 162 in sub-Saharan Africa, which means that a young Burundian boy or girl was 2.6 times less likely to undertake higher education studies than another person of his age living in sub-Saharan Africa. At that time, the number of students per 100,000 inhabitants exceeded 5,000 in North America and 2,500 in most of the developed countries.

Considering the strong correlation between the development of a higher education system and sustainable human development, these figures suggest that the government of Burundi should continue to increase enrollment in higher education. However, because of the limited facilities available at the university and the lack of job opportunities in the civil service, it is necessary to encourage the development of other forms of higher education and to promote study programs that will enable graduates to create their own jobs instead of claiming existing ones as their right. In 1989, the civil service employed 92 percent of university graduates. Since 1993, the number of graduates has increasingly exceeded the number of jobs available in the civil service.

DISTRIBUTION OF ENROLLMENT BY LEVEL AND FIELD OF STUDY

From Table 19.3 one can determine that arts and humanities students represented 60 percent of the total enrollment. For Years 1 and 2, this percentage was 66 percent, double the number of students enrolled in science. However, for Years 3 and 4, enrollments in the sciences were slightly higher than those in arts.

Table 19.4. Academic Pass Rates at the University of Burundi for the Period 1990–1993 by Percent

	Year 1	Year 2	Year 3	Year 4	Average
1990–1991	57	69	79	95	70
1991–1992	53	56	85	95	76
1992–1993	63	81	84	94	73
Average	57.7	68.7	82.7	94.7	73

Source: Annual Report of the Academic Unit, University of Burundi.

All the existing postgraduate programs were in the area of science. The low enrollment in postgraduate programs reflects the general situation of French-speaking African universities. In most English-speaking African universities, enrollment in postgraduate studies exceeds 10 percent of the total enrollment. This partly explains why three Anglophone countries—Nigeria, Kenya, and Sudan—produced 70 percent of all the research papers published in sub-Saharan Africa (Saint 1992).

INTERNAL EFFICIENCY

Table 19.4 shows that for the period 1990 to 1993, pass rates at the University of Burundi were between 70 and 76 percent for the whole university, 53–69 percent for students in their first two years of study, and 79–95 percent for students in their third and fourth years. These rates indicate that the UB was quite effective in increasing pass rates in the early 1990s. In the other French-speaking countries, the pass rate rarely exceeded 25 percent for the first years (Saint 1992, 13). In Madagascar, for example, the first-year pass rate was estimated at 13 percent in 1990 (Salmi 1992).

During the period 1989–1993, the repetition and drop-out rates for the whole university were 16 percent and 6 percent, respectively. For the first-year programs, the repetition rate was 26 percent. These rates were quite low. Indeed, the repetition rate in 1989 exceeded 40 percent in Congo and was close to 50 percent in Madagascar (Saint 1992). In 1992, the drop-out rate at Makerere University in Uganda was 20 percent (Salmi 1992).

From October 1993 to June 2000, the UB was beset with student and staff strikes, campus closures, suspension of external

Table 19.5. Requirements for Recruitment and Promotion of Academic Staff

Rank	Degree required	Other conditions
Assistant	First-class honors	None
Senior Assistant	First-class honors	Three years of seniority in the rank of assistant
Lecturer	M.A. or equivalent degree	None
Senior Lecturer	Ph.D. or equivalent degree	None
Associate Professor	Ph.D. or equivalent degree	Three years of seniority in the rank of senior lecturer Publications
Full Professor*	Ph.D. or equivalent degree	Five years of seniority in the rank of associate professor Publications

*In addition to the above conditions, candidates in the Faculty of Medicine must pass the *concours d'agrégation* (certification examination) organized by the African and Malagasy Council for Higher Education.

cooperation, massive brain drain of academic staff, and difficulties in purchasing books and equipment, especially during the period of economic sanctions against Burundi. This situation led to a considerable decline in the quality of teaching and research.

REQUIREMENTS OF ACADEMIC STAFF FOR RECRUITMENT AND CONDITIONS OF SERVICE

The major stages of the career of the academic staff at the UB are assistant, senior assistant, lecturer, senior lecturer, associate professor, and full professor. The requirements for promotion to the various levels of the career are summarized in Table 19.5.

The wages, allowances, and other benefits granted to the personnel of the university are determined by the University Council. The current salary scale for the various personnel categories was approved in 2000. The salaries paid by the university to the teaching staff are quite high compared with salaries for other public services. For example, an assistant at the university earns almost twice what a civil servant with the same qualifications earns.

Monitoring and evaluation of the work completed by the academic staff are done through an annual performance evaluation and an evaluation for staff promotion. The form used for annual performance evaluation of the academic staff is inadequate. Indeed, five of the seven categories on the form are related to the achievements of the staff member in the social life of the university community. The evaluation should relate to all the assignments entrusted to the academic staff: teaching; research; contribution to social, economic, and cultural development; and participation in students' civic education.

According to university regulations, the minimal teaching load varies between 180 and 220 hours per annum, but no criteria have been set up for the evaluation of the pedagogical skills of the faculty, in particular the quality of the syllabi and the teaching methods used. The evaluation simply consists of checking whether or not the teacher completed the prescribed teaching load.

In contrast to the requirements for teaching, the regulations do not specify the time that teachers must devote to research, and no institutional structure has been set up to manage teachers' contributions to social, economic, and cultural development. All the faculties and institutes offer a class on civic education; this fulfills the requirement that educators participate in the civic education of their students. In general, however, no importance is attached to this course, which is often assigned to young assistants or to part-time teachers.

In order to make the annual evaluation of performance more meaningful and relevant, therefore, it is necessary to design new evaluation mechanisms that will take into account the assignments entrusted to the academic staff.

For the moment, the criteria used for staff promotion do not take into account pedagogical skills. According to the teaching staff regulations, the evaluation for staff promotion must take account of a teacher's academic qualifications, teaching load, research activities, publications, pedagogical skills, and seniority. For the moment, the criteria used for staff promotion relate only to the publications.

Teachers: Pedagogic Skills

Because teaching occupies a central place in the career of academic staff, it is necessary to extend the criteria used for evaluation and promotion to include teaching activities. Research carried out recently in the area of teaching and learning makes it possible to define a suitable pedagogical profile of a higher education teacher (Obanya, Shabani, and Okebukola 2000).

In general, university faculty do not undergo formal training in pedagogy. Consequently, it is necessary to provide them opportunities to acquire skills in teaching and learning. From 1988 to 1992, the UB organized several training workshops on teaching and learning for the academic staff, thanks to funds received from UNESCO and the World Bank.

Staff Development Programs

Continuing education is a right that is recognized for all categories of academic personnel. In 1993, the university devoted US$2,060 of its regular budget to staff development programs for administrative and technical staff and $28,830 to academic staff for participation in international conferences. These resources accounted for 0.26 percent of the university's general operational budget. This figure is inadequate, especially if one refers to the recommendation of the Association of the African Universities to allocate 5 percent of their general operational budget to staff development programs (AAU 1991). Moreover, during 1989–1993, the budget allocated to staff development programs was not exhausted (Shabani 1995).

Staff development programs in Burundi have benefited significantly from bilateral and international cooperation. During the period under review, major financial contributions came from several agencies:

- The Belgian agency in charge of development cooperation gave its former scholarship holders an opportunity to undertake a three-month research visit to a university in Belgium every three years.
- The United Nations Development Program (UNDP) provided funds to the Faculty of Economics and Administration to enable the staff to undertake short-term research visits to European universities.
- The French Cooperation supported short-term research visits of staff from the Faculties of Arts and Medicine to universities in France.
- The Abdus Salam International Center for Theoretical Physics provided support to staff from the Faculty of Science for short-term research visits to a research center located in Trieste and to a number of selected Italian laboratories.

In addition, the Faculty of Science organized several staff development activities from 1984 to 1992; in particular, weekly postgraduate research seminars in mathematics and physics, international workshops in mathematical physics, and postgraduate training courses in earth sciences.

Foreign and Part-time Teachers

From 1985 to 1993, the average annual growth rate of the academic staff at the University of Burundi was 8.6 percent, compared to 5 percent in sub-Saharan Africa (UNESCO 1999). This rapid growth contributed to a decrease in dependence on foreign teachers; their numbers fell from 54.9 percent in 1985 to 22.6 in 1993.

The government of Burundi gave a high priority to the training of teachers at the highest level. In 1994, 42 percent of the academic staff of the UB had a Ph.D. degree (Université du Burundi 1994), and 27.4 percent of the total academic staff had

Table 19.6. Growth of Faculty at the University of Burundi, 1985–1993

Academic Year	Total Academic Staff	Foreign Staff	Percent Foreign Staff
1985–1986	315	173	54.9
1986–1987	462	217	46.9
1987–1988	474	175	36.9
1988–1989	537	155	28.8
1989–1990	516	123	23.8
1990–1991	436	131	30
1991–1992	501	140	27.9
1992–1993	560	127	22.6

Source: Annual Report of the Academic Unit, University of Burundi, 1994.

been enrolled in postgraduate programs in developed countries at some point.

Unfortunately, since the beginning of the sociopolitical crisis in October 1993, most of the staff undergoing postgraduate training abroad have not returned to Burundi. Furthermore, from 1994 to 2000, a number of other university teachers left the country in response to the aggravation of the crisis and the suspension of bilateral and international cooperation in education. Those who did not leave the country entirely often spend most of their time teaching in Rwanda and the Democratic Republic of Congo, where they are paid an honorarium for the number of hours taught. While they are abroad, they keep their salaries and other benefits at the UB.

In addition to foreign teachers, the UB heavily relies on part-time teachers. During the academic year 1992–1993, part-time teachers represented 35 percent of the total academic staff. In the Faculty of Agriculture and the Institute of Commerce, the figures were 50 percent and 85 percent, respectively (see Table 19.6 for more).

In 1994, the staff composition at the UB was 13.3 percent assistant professors and full professors, 34.5 percent lecturers and senior lecturers, and 52.2 percent assistants and senior assistants.

ACADEMIC FREEDOM AND INSTITUTIONAL AUTONOMY

Academic freedom and institutional autonomy are essential requirements for a higher education institution to fulfill its mission effectively. Academic freedom is conceived as a set of rights and duties of university teachers, while institutional autonomy refers to the degree of freedom in the relationship between the institution and the government.

According to the recommendation concerning the status of higher education that the UNESCO General Conference adopted in 1997, academic freedom covers the right to carry out at least the following activities without any interference or fear:

Table 19.7. Structure and Growth Rate of the University's General Operational Budget, 1990–1993, by Percentage

Components of the Budget	1990	1991	1992	1993	Average Annual Growth Rate
External Cooperation	+30	+19	+22	+13	−15.8
University of Burundi	+29	+36	+30	+35	18.9
Student Welfare Management Services (ROU)	+17	+17	+18	+20	15.3
Scholarships	+24	+28	+30	+32	20.3
Total	100	100	100	100	—

Source: Financial Unit and Student Welfare Management Services, University of Burundi, 1994; and Ministry of Higher Education.

teaching, conducting research and publishing research results, designing curricula, being able to express uncensored opinions about the institution, and participating in professional bodies.

It is generally recognized that the exercise of academic freedom entails a number of obligations for teachers; in particular, the duty to teach students effectively, to be fair and equitable to all students, to respect ethical and professional standards, and to respond adequately to the needs of the society.

The rights and duties of the teachers at the UB are defined in the teaching staff regulations adopted in 1990. In general, the university and the government of Burundi ensure that the conditions required for teachers to fully enjoy academic freedom remain in place. In the past, the number of teachers who did not respect their duties was quite limited. Since the beginning of the sociopolitical crisis in 1993, however, an increasing number of teachers have granted advantages to certain students on the basis of their ethnic origin.

PUBLIC EXPENDITURE FOR HIGHER EDUCATION

The various indicators used to measure the financial outlay of a country for education—in particular, the public expenditure for education expressed as a percentage of the current or total government expenditure—show that the effort made by the government in funding higher education is quite high (République du Burundi 1993; Shabani 1998).

Moreover, the total public expenditure for education increased from 20.5 percent of current government spending in 1989 to 27.1 percent in 1993 (République du Burundi 1993). In sub-Saharan Africa, this figure was estimated at 17 percent in 1993. In 1993, the government of Burundi allocated 25 percent of total public expenditure for education to higher education, compared to 17 percent in sub-Saharan Africa (ADEA 1995; UNESCO 1999).

THE UNIVERSITY'S REGULAR BUDGET

The academic budget is composed of the funds received from the government and funds raised from tuition fees. To study the structure and the growth of the regular budget, I will divide it into the following four categories (Banderembako and Minani 1994):

- The pedagogical budget: teaching materials and teaching and learning activities
- The research budget: research activities
- The human resources budget: staff salary and benefits and staff development programs
- The budget for administration and general services

For the period 1989–1994, the human resources budget increased at an average annual growth rate of 25 percent. For the pedagogical and research budgets, this rate was −10 percent and −9 percent respectively. In 1994, the human resources budget accounted for 71 percent of the university's regular budget.

One can project from Table 19.7 that if the operation of the university had not been disturbed by the post-1993 sociopolitical crisis, the university's regular budget would have been equal to 3.2 times the 1993 budget by the year 2000 and that the budget would have been allocated as follows:

- Human resources: 83.7 percent
- Administration and general services: 15.6 percent
- Pedagogic activities: 0.4 percent
- Research: 0.3 percent

THE UNIVERSITY'S GENERAL OPERATIONAL BUDGET

This budget is composed of the following budgets that contribute to the general operation of the university:

- The university's regular budget
- The budget of the student welfare management services (ROU)
- The scholarship budget
- External cooperation contributions

From 1990 to 1993, the scholarship budget increased more rapidly than other components of the university's general operational budget. For this period, the average annual growth rate of the scholarship budget was 5.7 greater than the increase in enrollment. In absolute value, the scholarship budget represented 98 percent of the regular university budget in 1992.

During the period under review, the average annual growth rate of the cooperation budget was –15.8 percent. The cooperation budget's share fell from 30 percent of the university's general operational budget in 1990 to 13 percent in 1993. As indicated earlier, all the cooperation programs at the UB were suspended in 1996.

If a sociopolitical crisis had not disturbed the operation of the university, the scholarship budget would have been almost equal to the university regular budget by the year 2000 in absolute value.

CONCLUSION

It is generally agreed that the University of Burundi has been quite effective in training the workers needed to run the civil service. It has also made a major contribution to the social development of the country, in particular through the participation of the academic staff in the national advisory committees and on boards of directors of various semipublic enterprises.

The operation of the university has been significantly disturbed since 1993 by a sociopolitical crisis; in particular, through student and staff strikes, delays in various academic programs, closure of campuses, problems obtaining books and equipment, and a massive brain drain of the academic staff. All these phenomena have led to a significant deterioration in the quality of teaching and research.

As soon as Burundi finds peace, the government will have to conceive and implement reconstruction and rehabilitation programs in the various sectors of the national life. The education system will have to occupy a central place in this effort, given the central role in sustainable human development.

The analysis presented in this chapter indicates that reform of higher education should cover at least the following areas:

Access to Higher Education

The demand for access to higher education will increase tremendously following the rapid growth of secondary education enrollments and the anticipated massive return of refugees and displaced populations after a peace agreement is signed. It is necessary to identify the various systems and forms of higher education that should be established to respond effectively to the demand for access and other needs and challenges. The sociopolitical crisis in Burundi has led to the emergence of private higher education institutions. While encouraging this spirit of initiative, it will be necessary to set up effective mechanisms that guarantee the quality of higher education.

The Higher Education Financing Policy

The structure of the university's regular and general operational budgets indicates significant imbalances, in particular with regard to the budgets for human resources and scholarships. Projections of the growth of higher education budgets show that the current policy is not sustainable in the long run.

It is necessary to plan a national consultation to determine the nature and the scope of the reforms needed to make the higher education financing policy more viable and sustainable.

The University Academic Staff

In recent years, Burundi has experienced a massive brain drain of the university's academic staff. This phenomenon shows that the current teacher training policy, which consists in sending instructors abroad for several years, is not viable. The data available show that this policy is very expensive and is not sustainable in the long run. In addition, the training abroad does not always take into account Burundi's specific needs. This partially explains the difficulties in mobilizing a critical mass of experts even in the priority development areas. Therefore, it is necessary to consider other systems and forms of postgraduate training, in particular the so-called sandwich programs, which have given satisfactory results in some sub-Saharan African countries.

Poor working conditions have contributed significantly to the brain drain of academic staff. It is necessary to improve working conditions, including measures beyond a simple salary increase. The university should also design adequate strategies to facilitate temporary or permanent return of the highly trained national scholars and researchers living abroad. In this respect, the experience of the UNDP/TOKTEN (Transfer of Knowledge through Expatriate Nationals) program may be useful.

SELECTED BIBLIOGRAPHY

AAU (Association of African Universities). 1991. *Study on Cost Effectiveness and Efficiency in African Universities: A Synthesis Report.* Accra, Ghana: Commercial Associates.

ADEA (Association for the Development of African Education). 1995. *A Statistical Profile of Education in Sub-Saharan Africa, 1990–1993.* Paris: Gauthier-Villars.

Banderembako, D., and E. Minani. 1994. "Contribution à l'étude institutionnelle et financière de l'université du Burundi. Partie III: Le système de gestion du budget et du patrimoine de l'université du Burundi." Unpublished report. Bujumbura: Université du Burundi.

Ndayisaba, J. 1994. "Contribution à l'étude institutionnelle et financière de l'université du Burundi. Partie II: Les performances pédagogiques de l'université du Burundi." Unpublished report. Bujumbura: Université du Burundi.

Obanya, P., J. Shabani, and P. Okebukola. 2000. *Guide to Teaching and Learning in Higher Education.* Dakar: UNESCO-BREDA.

République du Burundi. 1993. "Stratégie de développement et de financement de l'éducation." Document provisoire. Ministère de l'éducation nationale, Bujumbura, September.

Saint, W. 1992. *Les universités en Afrique: Pour une stratégie de stabilisation et de revitalisation.* Banque mondiale, Document technique no. 194 F. Washington, D.C.: Banque mondiale.

Salmi, J. 1992. "Perspectives on Financing of Higher Education." *Higher Education Policy* 5, no. 2: 13–19.

Shabani, J. 1995. "Etude institutionnelle et financière de l'université du Burundi." Rapport intérimaire. Accra: Association of African Universities.

———. 1998. "Lifelong Higher Education for All in Sub-Saharan Africa." In J. Shabani, ed., *Higher Education in Africa: Achievements, Challenges and Prospects.* Dakar: UNESCO-BREDA.

UNDP (United Nations Development Program). 1998. *World Report on Human Development*. Paris: Ed. Economica.

UNESCO (United Nations Educational, Scientific, and Cultural Organization). 1998. *World Education Report 1998*. Paris: UNESCO Publishing.

———. 1999. *Statistical Yearbook 1999*. Paris: UNESCO Publishing and Bernan Press.

Université du Burundi. 1989. *25ème anniversaire rétrospective 1964–1989*. Bujumbura: Presses universitaires, Université du Burundi.

———. 1994. "Etude institutionnelle et financière de l'université du Burundi." Rapport préliminaire. Unpublished report. Bujumbura: Université du Burundi.

20

Cameroon

Dorothy L. Njeuma

INTRODUCTION

Cameroon is a bilingual country in Central Africa that uses English and French as its official languages. It covers a surface area of 475,442 square kilometers (183,569 square miles). Located between latitudes 4°N and 13°N of the equator and running from the Atlantic Ocean to Lake Chad, its climate and vegetation are varied as is its population, which is estimated at 15 million people who belong to more than 200 ethnic and linguistic groups.

Cameroon's economy is based primarily on agriculture; its main exports are cocoa, coffee, palm produce, bananas, tea, and rubber. Other natural resources include crude oil, natural gas, timber, and bauxite. The 1999–2000 World Development Report of the World Bank lists the gross national product (GNP) of Cameroon as $8.7 billion in 1998, with a GNP per capita of $610 and an annual growth rate of 6.7 percent. Life expectancy is 55 years for men and 58 for women. Adult literacy is estimated at 21 percent for men and 35 percent for women. About 47 percent of the population live in urban areas, compared with 31 percent in 1980, indicating a considerable tendency toward rural exodus.

Higher education in Cameroon dates only from 1961, after the country achieved independence. From one university in 1961, Cameroon now has seven full universities, six state-owned and one private. Of the state universities, one is English-speaking, one is Francophone, and four are bilingual (English and French). These institutions have a total student enrollment of about 60,000 students. There are also a good number of other postsecondary institutions that are not part of the university system. Some are public and some private; many of the private ones are running without formal approval.

In this chapter, I will examine higher education in Cameroon, discussing its historical background, its development, the challenges with which it has been faced, and the reforms that have been undertaken to respond to them.

HISTORICAL BACKGROUND

Higher education in Cameroon has been very significantly influenced by the country's colonial history. From 1884, Cameroon was a German colony. It was entrusted by the League of Nations to France and Britain in 1918 as one of the spoils of World War I. The bulk of the territory (more than 80 percent) was given to France, while the smaller part, constituting about 20 percent, went to Britain. The two trust territories thus had different colonial histories from 1918 to 1961 when, following a plebiscite supervised by the United Nations, the English-speaking Southern Cameroons decided to achieve independence by reuniting with the French-speaking Republic of Cameroon, which had gained independence from France in January 1960.

During the intervening period from 1918 to 1961, the British Southern Cameroons, which was administered together with Nigeria, followed the British system of education. Schools were run largely by the missions. The language of instruction was English, although a few selected indigenous languages were used in the first few years of primary school; the missions also used these languages for purposes of evangelization.

In contrast, the French trust territory (French Cameroons) developed a French system of education. The medium of instruction was French. Some selected indigenous languages were also used here in the first few years of primary school; these were also the languages of evangelization.

Upon reunification in 1961, Cameroon became a federation, consisting of West Cameroon (English-speaking, making up 20 percent of the population) and East Cameroon (French-speaking, constituting 80 percent of the population). English and French were named as the official languages in the constitution.

The different colonial legacies of the two federated states affected the development of higher education in the country as a whole. There were no postsecondary institutions in the country at the time of independence.

THE BEGINNINGS OF HIGHER EDUCATION IN CAMEROON, 1961–1973

With independence, the need was felt to provide tertiary education to train experts for the civil service, secondary schools, and teacher training colleges and for the development of agriculture, which was the mainstay of the economy.

With the assistance of UNESCO and the French government, the National Institute for University Studies was created in 1961. It became the Federal University of Cameroon in 1962, providing for degree programs in law, economics, the arts, the human sciences, and the pure sciences. At the same time, professional programs were created at the School of Administration and Magistracy (ENAM), the School of Agriculture (ENSA), the Military Academy (EMIA), and the School of Education (ENS).

In 1967, a new impetus was given to higher education. A Council for Higher Education was instituted to define policy and draw up a development plan. The years 1969–1971 saw the creation of new professional schools: the Business School (IAE) in 1968, the Medical School (CUSS) in 1969, the School of Journalism (ESIJY) in 1970, the International Relations Institute (IRIC), and the School of Engineering (ENSP) in 1971.

ENAM and EMIA were independent structures, separate from the Federal University. The university proper consisted of six specialized schools (ENS, ENSA, CUSS, ESIJY, IRIC, and ENSP) and three faculties (Arts and Human Sciences, Science, and Law and Economics). These institutions served the needs of students who had previously sought tertiary education abroad. Admission into the specialized schools was limited, and selection was based on an entrance examination. In contrast, entry into the faculties was open to all holders of the baccalaureate or the General Certificate of Education Advanced Level.

As these institutions were supposed to cater to English-speaking and French-speaking students, they were bilingual. Instruction was given in English or French, depending on the decision of the teacher. However, students were free to write their papers and examinations in English or French. In principle, this arrangement was expected to work out satisfactorily, since the teaching of the second official language was introduced in the secondary school curriculum across the whole country from 1961. Later on, this practice was extended to the last three years of primary school. English- and French-language courses were also offered at the university and were compulsory for all students. However, the practical reality turned out to be different. First of all, because the university was financed by France and run by French nationals, the programs were more like those of France and other Francophone countries. Also, because the greater proportion of the population is French speaking (80 percent), there was a preponderance of French-speaking teaching staff who were more familiar with the Franco-

phone system of education and taught in French. This situation created tensions, which led to demands for the creation of an English-speaking university to cater to the interests of English-speaking students. A more detailed presentation of the development of higher education in Cameroon is available in Gwei (1975) and Njeuma et al. (1999).

GOVERNANCE

France made a preponderant contribution to the conception and funding of higher education in Cameroon. When this is combined with the fact that Cameroon is more than 80 percent French speaking, it is understandable that the system of higher education strongly resembles that in France and other French-speaking countries, even if it has certain aspects that take account of the bilingual nature of the country and its complex colonial experience. For example, the program in law offers courses in the English and French legal systems.

From 1961 to 1973, the Federal University of Cameroon was administered and funded essentially by the French Foundation. The vice-chancellor, some of the administrators, and a sizable proportion of the academic staff (especially at the initial stages) were French. The contributions in finance and staffing to the university by the governments of France and Cameroon were negotiated on a yearly basis by a Franco-Cameroon commission, which met alternately in France and in Cameroon (Njeuma 1999).

By legislation introduced in 1967, the chancellor of the university, who was also the minister of national education, became the executive head of the university, with responsibility for its administrative and financial management and the recruitment of teaching staff. In practice, however, administrative and financial management was delegated to the vice-chancellor, who was therefore, up to 1973, the executive and academic head of the university. The minister of national education retained supervisory authority over the university. He or she recommended deans of faculty and directors of professional schools for appointment by the head of state. He or she also appointed heads of departments on the recommendation of the vice-chancellor, following election by teaching staff.

The university had a Governing Council, presided over by the vice-chancellor. All deans of faculty and directors of schools sat on the council, as well as representatives of the various grades of teaching staff from each faculty and school. A number of government ministries, including the presidency of the republic and representatives from the education, finance, public service, planning, and labor ministries, were also represented on the council. The Governing Council had responsibility for administrative and academic policy of the university, including recruitment, promotion and discipline of academic staff, and adoption of the budget. However, its resolutions had to be approved by the minister of education. Academic programs were drawn up by the faculties and schools, but they were approved by the minister of education. Matters of general policy were determined by government. The Ministry of National Education had a Department of Higher Education with special responsibility for following up matters related to tertiary education.

AUTONOMY AND ACADEMIC FREEDOM

Cameroon's government exercised considerable control over the university. However, the university itself had relative autonomy. The Governing Council, for example, had a preponderance of teaching staff. The content and execution of academic programs, as well as evaluation of students, rested with academic staff. Each faculty had a faculty assembly made up entirely of academic staff, as well as a council of professors, which consisted of the dean and all professors; this latter body was responsible for academic, research, and financial matters relating to the faculty, as well as proposals for recruitment, promotion, and discipline of teaching staff. Professional schools, in contrast, had a management board that included representatives from ministries and the private sector. These boards were responsible for the academic orientation of the school. The university had total responsibility for the management of its budget, with devolution to the level of deans, directors, and sometimes to heads of departments.

FUNDING

Subsidies from the state and contributions from the French government were the main source of funding for the Federal University. No tuition fees were charged, and students paid only a very small registration fee, which constituted a negligible proportion of the budget. Fairly adequate budgetary allocations were made to cover teaching, research, investment, staff salaries, and an elaborate welfare system for students.

As will be seen later, a significant proportion of the university's budget went to pay staff salaries and to provide for student welfare, such as scholarships and room and board. Decreasing amounts were available for infrastructural improvements and equipment for teaching and research.

TEACHING STAFF

Teaching staff of the university were classified in four grades: professor, associate professor, lecturer, and assistant lecturer. Recruitment into each of these grades was based on qualifications from the Francophone and Anglophone systems of education as specified by government decree in January 1969. Salary scales were also detailed in this decree, as well as criteria for promotion from one grade to the next. These were based primarily on publications and teaching experience. However, subjectivity in interpretation of the criteria soon created tensions, especially between those who had received degrees in France and those who had received them from other countries—such as Britain, the United States, Germany, and the Soviet Union. Moreover, as more qualified applicants became available, criteria for recruitment also changed. For example, by 1973, the university was no longer recruiting holders of master's degrees as assistant lecturers. Also, Ph.D. holders who previously had been recruited as associate professors were recruited as lecturers and later as assistant lecturers. Moreover, under an agreement between Cameroon and France, teaching staff of French nationality were recruited and classified according to criteria that prevailed in France.

STUDENTS

Students were admitted from the French-speaking and English-speaking systems on the basis of their end-of-secondary-school qualifications for faculties and an additional entrance examination for professional schools.

The open-door policy for admission into the faculties very quickly had unforeseen effects as enrollment figures rose astronomically with the creation of more secondary schools after independence. From 213 students in 1961–1962, the university had 5,533 students by 1973–1974, exceeding the figure of 5,000 for which the university was constructed (University of Yaounde Catalogue, 1984–1985). These students were taught by 357 staff, making a teacher-student ratio of 1:15. This would be considered a fair ratio; however, failure rates were quite high, especially in the Faculty of Science.

Students paid only registration fees, amounting to 3,300 FCFA (about $13) per annum. However, they received monthly stipends of 30,000 francs ($120 at the time) in the faculties, which was well above the minimum wage, while those in professional schools had up to 60,000 francs ($240). In addition, room and board were provided at highly subsidized rates. Students could buy meals for 85 francs (about 34 cents) and rooms went for 3,000 francs (or $12) per month, including water and electricity.

Students participated actively in the Students Union and were represented on the Governing Council of the University.

THE PERIOD 1973–1992

The year 1973 marked a significant transition in higher education in Cameroon. Following the referendum of May 20, 1972, the Federal Republic of Cameroon became the United Republic of Cameroon. The Federal University of Cameroon was consequently renamed the University of Yaounde in August 1973. With that transition came the end of the management of the university by the French Foundation. A new organizational structure and system of governance were instituted. An executive chancellor representing the government, different from the minister of national education, became responsible for the administrative and financial management of the university, with the vice-chancellor taking charge only of academic and research matters. However, the university still remained under the supervision of the minister of national education.

While student numbers were controlled in the professional schools through a selective entrance examination, enrollments in the faculties with no *numerus clausus* increased geometrically. A high proportion of the budget was allocated to student scholarships and welfare services. By 1974, the University of Yaounde had more than 6,000 students, of whom 3,693 were in the faculties. Classes were overcrowded, and the failure rate of students was rather high. There was also growing concern about the large numbers of graduates from the faculties who could not find jobs.

In December 1974, the Council on Higher Education, which was created in 1967, met for the first time. The major recommendations of the meeting of the council were:

Table 20.1. Students Enrolled in State Universities in Cameroon from 1961–1962 to 1998–1999, Selected Years

Year	Buea	Douala	Dschang	Ngaoundere	Yaounde	Yaounde I	Yaounde II	Total
1961–1962	—	—	—	—	213	—	—	213
1970–1971	—	—	—	—	2,011	—	—	2,011
1981–1982	—	343	617	—	9,462	—	—	10,422
1991–1992	52	1,062	518	327	32,327	—	—	34,286
1998–1999	5,380	11,376	8,776	3,082	—	21,273	10,657	60,544

Source: 1999 Statistical Yearbook of Higher Education in Cameroon, MINESUP.

- To envisage the creation of a University of Technology
- To professionalize training in the faculties
- To reduce student numbers in the faculties through selective admission and other measures
- To limit assistant lecturers to a contractual period (meaning that they would no longer have tenure)

Following these recommendations, the conditions for recruitment and promotion of academic staff became clearer and more streamlined. Tenured ranks were those of lecturer, associate professor, and professor. Criteria for promotion were specified, and nobody could skip a grade in the academic ladder. Assistant lecturers were recruited on contract for a period of two years, renewable twice; during this period of probation, they had to obtain terminal degrees and publish to be promoted to the tenured rank of lecturer, or they would be weeded out of the system.

Decree No. 76-462 of October 18, 1976, was very welcome as it provided special allowances for academic staff and defined their conditions of service. Special monthly allowances were instituted for academic staff, ranging from 100,000 francs ($200) for assistant lecturers to 150,000 francs ($300) for professors. Provision was also made for a special research allowance that ranged from 100,000 francs per annum for assistant lecturers to 200,000 francs per annum for professors.

In the quest for a University of Technology, four new university centers were created in April 1977 with specific areas of professional specialization: Buea University Center, which specialized in languages, translation, and interpretation; Douala University Center for business studies and teacher training in technical education; Dschang University Center, which specialized in agriculture; and the Ngaoundere University Center, which specialized in food science and food technology. The objective of these university centers was not only to create centers of excellence but also to spread institutions of tertiary education more evenly across the country: Buea is in the Anglophone zone, Douala in the economic capital on the coast, Dschang in the western grasslands, and Ngaoundere in the north. They were also intended to free up the University of Yaounde, which was heavily overcrowded with more than 8,000 students in 1977 on a campus intended for 5,000. A Universities Coordination Commission was also created, bringing together heads of university institutions to meet with the minister of national education and other ministries (presidency, prime minister's office, finance, planning, public service).

By 1979, new programs were drawn up and the duration of studies specified:

- Three years for the bachelor's degree
- One year for the master's degree
- Two years for the *Doctorat* (equivalent to the M.Phil.)
- Four years beyond the *Doctorat de 3eme Cycle* for the *Doctorat d'Etat*

Conditions of admission into faculties and professional schools, as well as regulations governing studies, were defined as a means of limiting student enrollment numbers. Candidates for admission into faculties and schools were to have spent no more than five years in the last three years of the secondary school cycle. They were to be at most 25 years old on January 1 of the year of admission, and they could not repeat any of the first two years of the bachelor's degree program more than once. Attendance at lectures, practicals, and tutorials was to be closely monitored, and absences were to be punished by prohibition from writing examinations or withdrawal of scholarships.

Although it was envisaged that the Council on Higher Education and Scientific Research would convene on an annual basis, the second meeting took place only in October 1982 (Ministry of National Education 1982). It announced the special recruitment of 1,700 university graduates and recommended, among other ideas, the creation of two-year postsecondary institutions to train midlevel technicians to promote economic and industrial development.

Despite the measures taken in 1979 to limit student enrollments, the population continued to rise at the University of Yaounde. By 1991–1992, the university had more than 32,000 students. Classrooms were overcrowded and teacher-to-student ratios were very high. Although the university had 735 teachers for the 32,327 students enrolled (giving a general teacher-student ratio of 1:44), the ratios were quite alarming in the faculties—1:252 in the Faculty of Science, 1:132 in the Faculty of Law and Economics, and 1:58 in the Faculty of Arts. Success rates reduced sharply and dropout rates increased.

Meanwhile, student numbers in the university centers were relatively low and, in some cases, facilities were not used to their optimum capacity. For example, the Buea University Center, which had capacity of 2,000, enrolled only 52 students (see Table 20.1).

Because of the elaborate student welfare system, budget priorities became increasingly distorted, with 43 percent of the

Table 20.2. Student Enrollment in Cameroon State Universities, 1992–1999

University	1992–1993	1993–1994	1994–1995	1995–1996	1996–1997	1997–1998	1998–1999
Buea	807	2,005	3,249	4,099	4,185	4,599	5,380
Douala	1,635	4,782	7,475	7,301	8,389	9,744	11,376
Dschang	2,092	1,824	2,248	3,711	4,880	7,342	8,776
Ngaoundere	776	789	950	1,225	1,526	2,039	3,082
Yaounde I	25,166	19,440	17,756	15,935	13,947	19,276	21,263
Yaounde II	13,279	9,586	8,382	5,874	5,747	6,265	10,657
Total	43,755	38,426	40,060	38,145	38,674	49,265	60,534

Source: Ministry of Higher Education 1999.

budget spent on student scholarship, meals, and housing and 46 percent on staff salaries. This left just about 10 percent for the university's primary mission of teaching, research, and contribution to national development.

The years 1990 and 1991 also witnessed considerable political unrest nationwide and calls for political pluralism. This activism found fertile ground in the universities, especially on the Yaounde campus. Meanwhile, with the onset of an economic crisis in the mid-1980s, the financial resources of universities dwindled; it therefore became increasingly difficult to continue to provide student scholarships and to subsidize meals and student housing. Student strikes became rife, encouraged by political activists.

THE 1993 REFORMS

In the face of these difficulties, the government decided to begin serious reforms of the university system. The initial plan, which was announced in May 1991 and confirmed in April 1992, was to transform the university centers in Buea and Ngaoundere into full-fledged universities. By January 1993, the reforms were extended by a series of enactments, which provided for the following:

- The creation of six universities: Buea, Douala, Dschang, Ngaoundere, Yaounde I, and Yaounde II. The two universities in Yaounde were the result of splitting the former University of Yaounde, and the other four converted former university centers into full universities. The immediate result of this move was to relieve the crowding at the former University of Yaounde and provide more variety and greater opportunities for university education. Buea was to be an English-speaking university, and the University of Ngaoundere a French-speaking one, as announced in 1991.
- Organizational structure and programs were to take into account the specificity of each university.
- The new universities were to operate on a semester course-credit system or on a modular system to allow for flexibility.
- Programs were to be made more varied and more professional in order to better respond to job market needs.
- Admission was to be selective, taking into account available resources, especially space.

- A more substantial registration fee of 50,000 francs (about $100 at the time) was introduced, and the system of scholarships was scrapped. The intention was to increase the participation of students in financing universities.

The details of these reforms are contained in the 1993 publication of the Ministry of Higher Education, *Higher Education Reforms in Cameroon*.

ACHIEVEMENTS

The reforms were seen in some quarters, especially among donor agencies, as an "expansion" of the higher education system at a time of severe economic crisis. However, they were imperative under the circumstances and had a number of positive effects.

Effective Decongestion

The reforms resulted in more rational use of the university centers created in 1977, which had not successfully relieved the crowding at the former University of Yaounde. Table 20.2 shows that enrollments dropped at the University of Yaounde after the 1993 reforms, while those in the new universities increased.

Improved Access

The reforms provided for a better geographical distribution of universities across the country. Universities are now closer to the homes of students.

This was an important factor in improving access to university education and has particularly enhanced the enrollment of female students. At the University of Buea, for example, female students now constitute 47 percent of total enrollment. Also, it has become easier for students who could not attend the lone university that existed before the reforms to gain admission into the universities in their regions.

Structural and Academic Specificity

The new universities were effectively given structural specificity in the enactments creating them. The University of Buea, for example, has a vice-chancellor as executive and academic head who chairs the senate. Its council is chaired by a pro-chancellor. Its language of instruction is English and the nomenclature of its degrees is that of the English-speaking university system: bachelor's degree, master's degree, doctor of philosophy, and so forth. It runs on the semester course-credit system. It has also retained its original specialization as a center for languages, translation, and interpretation.

In contrast, other universities, although bilingual—except in the case of Ngaoundere—have adopted the structure of Francophone universities, with a rector as executive and academic head who chairs both the senate and council. Instruction is in either English or French, depending on the teacher, while students can write papers and examinations in English or French as they choose. These operate in semesters, as well, but their academic structure is based on the system of course credits, on modules, or a combination of both. The nomenclature of their degrees is that of the Francophone university system: *Licence, Maîtrise, Doctorat,* and so forth. Each of the schools has maintained its specialization from prior to the reforms: Douala in business and the training of teachers of technical education, Dschang in agriculture, Ngaoundere in food technology, Yaounde I in medicine and engineering, and Yaounde II in law, economics, journalism, and international relations.

Academic Organization

The academic year is structured in semesters. Academic work is organized either on the credit system (in the case of Buea) or on the modular system (for the other universities). The flexibility of these systems allows students more freedom of choice of study programs. The programs are also more varied. A number of professional programs have been maintained or introduced—these include computer science, secretarial duties, journalism and mass communication, translation, interpretation, nursing, medical laboratory science, accounting, banking, finance, management, and women's studies.

The duration of studies is three years for the bachelor's degree, twelve to twenty-four months for the master's degree, and three to five years for the doctorate degree. Only one doctorate degree is now awarded, in contrast to the two granted before the reforms.

More Job Opportunities

The new universities have also created more job opportunities. From 1,164 university teachers in 1992–1993, there are now 1,792. This has lowered the teacher-student ratio, which makes for improved learning. More support staff have also been recruited.

More Rational Budgetary Priorities

One of the most significant achievements of the reforms has been the abolition of scholarships and the introduction of more substantial registration fees. The priorities of budget spending have turned away from student welfare to the more primary missions of the university, which are teaching and research. Com-

ing at a time when state funding of higher education had dropped by more than 70 percent, student registration fees have constituted a more substantial and a more reliable source of financing for universities, making up about 30 percent of their recurrent budgets.

PRIVATE HIGHER EDUCATION

In the years since 1990, there have been efforts in Cameroon to create private institutions that offer tertiary education. Among those that exist at present are the following:

- Advanced Institute of Information Science and Management (Institut Supérieur de Sciences Informatiques et de Gestion), Yaounde
- Advanced Institute of Management (Institut Supérieur de Management), Douala
- Advanced Institute of Development Information and Commerce (Institut Supérieur de Developpement Informatique et Commercial), Yaounde
- Advanced School of Management (Ecole Supérieure de Gestion), Douala
- Advanced School of Science and Technology (Ecole Supérieure des Sciences et des Techniques), Douala
- Adventist University, Nanga Eboko
- Bamenda University of Science and Technology, Bamenda
- British College of Professional Management, Douala
- Catholic University, Yaounde
- Groupe Tankou, Bafoussam
- Institute of Information Technology (Institut des Technologies de l'Informatique), Douala
- International University, Bamenda
- Nacho University, Bamenda
- PONAB Polytechnic, Bamenda
- Samba Advanced Institute (Institut Samba Supérieur), Yaounde
- Siantou Advanced Institute (Institut Siantou Supérieur), Yaounde

A good number of these private institutions are not authorized by the government because they do not meet minimum requirements regarding infrastructure, equipment, and staffing. Only a few have been approved; the others are nevertheless operating illegally. They charge tuition at rates that are more than five to ten times those of state universities. Many of them do not have full-time teaching staff of their own and rely mainly on lecturers of state universities. The quality of education they offer is thus often doubtful. Their attraction lies in the short professional courses that they offer in areas such as secretarial studies, insurance, accounting, banking, finance, commerce, management, journalism, information technology, hotel management, and electronics. They prepare students for the *Brevet de Technicien Supérieur* (Vocational Training Certificate) organized by the Ministry of Higher Education, as well as for other foreign diplomas.

A draft bill is in preparation to set general policy on higher education. This should address the issue of criteria for the creation and operation of private universities and institutes.

DIFFICULTIES

As can be seen, the objectives of the reforms have been largely achieved. However, some difficulties have been encountered in their implementation, especially with regard to funding, infrastructure, equipment, staffing, programs, overcrowding, and student performance.

Reduced and Irregular Funding

It was assumed that the subsidies that the former University of Yaounde and the university centers received from the state in 1991–1992 would be maintained after the 1993 reforms. This would have enabled the new universities to build new infrastructure, provide equipment, and improve teaching and research.

Unfortunately, state funding of universities dropped drastically in 1992–1993 and 1993–1994 and has remained low ever since. From a total overall budget of 47,756,000,000 francs for the university institutions in 1991–1992 (about $86,512,000 at the time), the figure dropped to 21,477,000,000 francs in 1992–1993 (about $42,924,000) and to 13,080,000,000 francs in 1993–1994 (about $21,160,000). This is a drop of nearly 74 percent in two years. The situation was made worse by the drastic salary cuts for civil servants in 1993, followed by devaluation of the CFA franc in February 1994. This is quite catastrophic, even if one considers the fact that the salaries of university teachers have been paid directly by the Ministry of Finance since November 1993. Subsidies for investment were not disbursed to the universities from 1992–1993 to 1998–1999. Those for recurrent expenditure were low and unpredictable until 1999–2000. In some years, the level of disbursement was as low as 25 percent (Njeuma et al. 1999).

Some universities, such as Buea and Dschang, have set up development funds as alternative sources of revenue. Although enthusiasm was high at the beginning, it has since waned. Surprisingly, students have actively protested against this initiative.

Reluctance of Students to Pay Fees

Fees paid by students currently constitute about 25 percent of the recurrent budgets of Cameroon's state universities. However, there has been considerable resistance on the part of students against paying the registration fees instituted in 1993. This is a regrettable attitude, when one considers that no tuition fees are actually charged. Besides, the sum of 50,000 francs is much lower than fees paid in most private nursery, primary, and secondary schools in the country. It is also only 10 percent of fees charged at the Catholic University and 20 percent of fees in other private postsecondary institutions.

Shortage of Infrastructure and Equipment

These factors contributing to reduced funding have meant that the infrastructure expected for the new universities could not be constructed, nor could new equipment be acquired. The consequent lack of lecture rooms, laboratories, and staff offices has not only rendered the problem of shortage of space very acute but has impacted negatively on teaching and research.

Negative Impacts on Research and Publications

Given their budgetary constraints, the new universities have focused on teaching and staff remuneration to the detriment of research, library acquisitions, books, and publications. Research projects have been financed largely by external grants.

Increased Student Numbers and Overcrowding

Meanwhile, student enrollments at the new universities have grown beyond their 1992–1993 capacities. The University of Buea, for example, had 5,380 students in 1998–1999, an increase of more than 250 percent since 1992–1993. The University of Douala has grown from 1,635 students in 1992–1993 to 11,376 in 1998–1999 without any additional buildings. Consequently, overcrowding has been transferred from the former University of Yaounde to the new universities.

Another factor that has contributed to the continuing rise in student numbers is the reluctance or inability on the part of administrative authorities to limit admission into the faculties, contrary to the stipulations of the reforms. Most universities continue to admit students far above their limitations of space, equipment, and even human resources, under pressure of demand for access and in an attempt to maintain or increase income from registration fees.

Reduced Staff Quality and Increased Brain Drain

Because of the relatively low remuneration following the salary cuts of 1993 and the currency devaluation of 1994, the universities have not been able to recruit qualified teaching staff. In fact, a good number have left the country for greener pastures since 1994. The universities have gone back to recruiting holders of master's degrees as assistant lecturers, a practice that was abandoned as far back as 1973. In some universities, assistant lecturers constitute up to 70 percent of the teaching staff. Lecturers transferred or appointed from the Universities of Yaounde I and II to other universities have sometimes refused to take up their new posts. Some universities rely to a significant extent on part-time teachers from other universities.

The negative effects of this situation on quality are quite considerable. Table 20.3 shows the evolution of teaching staff numbers in state universities from 1991–1992 to 1998–1999. Although the number of teaching staff has increased from 1,066 in 1992–1993 to 1,792 in 1998–1999, staff quality has declined significantly.

Tendency toward Uniform Programs

The 1993 reforms were intended to diversify higher education and provide more varied programs, which young Cameroonians had been seeking abroad in large numbers. It is estimated that more than 10,000 Cameroonians still pursue university studies abroad every year—in France, the United States, the United Kingdom, Canada, Germany, Italy, South Africa, Nigeria, and other countries. Unfortunately, because of the financial difficulties indicated above, it has not been possible, especially in the short period since the reforms, to provide professional training

Table 20.3. Teaching Staff at Cameroon State Universities from 1991–1992 to 1998–1999

Year	Buea	Douala	Dschang	Ngaoundere	Yaounde I	Yaounde II	Total
1991–1992	54	144	115	61	790	—	1,164
1992–1993	67	108	127	62	702	—	1,066
1993–1994	92	144	126	97	712	161	1,332
1994–1995	82	155	127	94	702	158	1,318
1995–1996	133	159	127	98	646	193	1,356
1996–1997	135	203	195	103	664	195	1,495
1997–1998	155	221	188	117	673	203	1,557
1998–1999	161	249	235	156	742	249	1,792

Source: Ministry of Higher Education 1999.

in such areas as medicine, engineering, and technology in the new universities. Besides, there is a tendency to standardize programs in all the universities, which goes against the spirit of the reforms.

Poor Student Performance

Failure rates seem to have remained high after the reforms. A number of factors are responsible for this. The new course-credit system and the system of modules and *unités de valeur* (course credits) are unfamiliar to students and even to some staff. Students are being required to pass in every single course, with no compensation allowed for grades obtained between courses. There are also no deadlines for registration; even where they exist, they are difficult to enforce. This leaves room for students to start attending lectures late. The rate of absenteeism is considerable, yet no sanctions are applied for absence from lectures, tutorials, and practicals. Students can repeat levels and courses as many times as they are able to persist, a situation that was highly regulated before the 1993 reforms. They are not required to buy books, and libraries are often equipped poorly.

All these factors contribute to the poor performance of students in examinations. As a result, the practice of repeat examinations—which took place before the reforms and which, in principle, is not provided for in the texts of the reforms—has been perpetuated. The repeat examinations may have their justification, but they place considerable strain on the teaching and administrative staff. In addition, as the examinations take place in September, teaching in the new academic year often starts quite late, quite often in late October or even in November. The persistence in this direction is unusual, seeing that repeat examinations were discontinued in secondary education in 1977. An evaluation of the 1993 reforms can also be found in Njeuma et al. (1999) and Tsala et al. (1998).

CONCLUSION

Higher education in Cameroon dates only from independence. It has been very significantly influenced by the country's Anglo-French colonial heritage, particularly by France. Started in 1961 with the schools of education as well as three faculties

to provide graduates for the public service, it expanded quite rapidly. A number of professional schools were created between 1968 and 1971. Although the university was under government control, it was given relative autonomy and academic freedom. An elaborate program of student welfare and an open-door policy for admission were put in place to attract students and to stem brain drain. Funding was fairly adequate, provided essentially by the state and the French government through the French Foundation.

However, with the withdrawal of the Foundation in 1973, problems began to emerge: inadequate funding and infrastructure, displaced budgetary priorities, uncontrolled student numbers, and overcrowding. The creation of four university centers in 1977 did not successfully relieve overcrowding at the University of Yaounde. More extensive reforms in 1993 created six state universities, which made for more equitable geographical distribution of tertiary education students, improved access, and brought more varied structure and programs. The new universities abolished scholarships, established a broader funding base through increased financial participation of the beneficiaries of higher education, and rationalized budgetary priorities. Private postsecondary institutions have burgeoned but are often lacking in quality.

Serious difficulties still pervade Cameroon's education system. These include reduced and irregular funding; student resistance to cost sharing; shortage of infrastructure, equipment, and books; reduced quality of staff; and poor implementation of some of the provisions of the 1993 reforms, which has exacerbated overcrowding and poor student performance. These problems need to be addressed in a more satisfactory manner.

REFERENCES

Ajayi, J. F., A. Goma, L. K. H. Johnson, and G. Ampah. 1996. *The African Experience with Higher Education.* Accra: The Association of African Universities.

Gwei, S. N. 1975. "Education in Cameroon: Western, Pre-colonial and Colonial Antecedents and the Development of Higher Education." Ph.D. dissertation, University of Michigan.

Ministry of National Education (Cameroon). 1974. *Actes du conseil de l'enseignment supérieur et de la recherche scientifique et technique.* Yaounde: University of Yaounde Press.

Ministry of Higher Education (Cameroon). 1982. *Actes du conseil de l'enseignment supérieur et de la recherche scientifique et technique.* Yaounde: Société de Production et d'Edition du Cameroun.

——. 1993. *Higher Education Reforms in Cameroon.* Yaounde: Centre d'Edition et de Production pour l'Enseignement et la Recherche.

——. 1999. *Statistical Yearbook of Higher Education in Cameroon.* Yaounde: Ministry of Higher Education.

Njeuma, D. L., H. N. Endeley, F. F. Mbuntum, N. Lyonga, D. Nkwete-yim, and S. N. Musenja. 1999. *Reforming a National System of Higher Education: The Case of Cameroon.* Paris: ADEA Working Group on Higher Education.

Njeuma, M. Z. 1999. "Territorial Regions: Pioneering Knowledge." In L. Holtedahl, S. Gerrard, and M. Z. Njeuma, eds., *The Power of Knowledge: From the Arctic to the Tropics.* Paris: Editions Karthala.

Tsala, G., et al. 1998. "Raport de sythèse sur l'evaluation de la réforme du systéme de l'enseignement supérieure." Unpublished manuscript. Yaounde: Ministère de l'Enseignement Supérieur.

University of Yaounde. 1985. *Annuaire de l'Université de Yaounde, 1984/85.* Yaounde: Société de Production et d'Edition du Cameroun.

World Bank. 2000. *Entering the 21st Century.* World Development Report 1999/2000. Oxford: Oxford University Press.

21

Cape Verde

RICHARD A. LOBBAN, JR., AND RICHARD LEARY

INTRODUCTION

The Cape Verde Islands are located some 300 miles off the western coast of Africa across the Atlantic Ocean from Senegal and at the same latitude as the Sahara Desert. The Portuguese first settled the nine islands of Cape Verde in 1462. They served as a regional center for the slave trade and small-scale plantation economy. Soon a mixed Crioulo population emerged from various African slave groups and Portuguese settlers. An eleven-year armed struggle (1963–1974) took place on the African coast and finally liberated the islands from Portuguese colonialism in 1975.

Resources on the islands are scarce. Most important, water is in short supply, which makes regular agriculture unpredictable and insufficient. Exports from Cape Verde include salt, animal hides, fish, bananas, and coffee. The key to the Cape Verdean economy is its strategic location, which makes it an important center of the region's trade. In addition, Cape Verde receives significant remittances from its very extensive diasporic population. Imports include manufactured items, fuel, and foodstuffs.

Although literacy and income in Cape Verde are very low by European standards, they are quite high relative to nearby African nations. The government mandates compulsory primary education for boys and girls from 7 to 14 years of age, but at least one-third of this age group did not attend school in the late 1980s. The attendance rate has improved since then, but the poor and rural adult population is 33 percent illiterate. The colonial inheritance in education has been truly damaging.

In fascist Portugal (1926–1974) itself, education was a low priority. The country had a high rate of illiteracy and low rates of primary education. On the eve of Cape Verde's independence, only 9.8 percent of the population in Portugal was in primary school, compared with about 19 percent in the United

States at that time. Meanwhile, Cape Verde had a primary enrollment rate of only 4.7 percent, and nearby Portuguese Guinea (Guinea-Bissau) had only 3.8 percent of its population in primary school. Both countries had only high schools and no universities at all then, as now.

Primary education enrollment increased dramatically in Cape Verde and Guinea-Bissau after independence. Although the Portuguese had left about 100 simple primary schools and two secondary schools in Cape Verde when they departed in 1975, this was vastly short of the country's needs then, not to mention today. Since independence, significant gains have been registered. Officially, illiteracy was to be eliminated completely by 1990 (improving from 28 percent in 1950 and 63 percent in 1970), and while some very poor or elderly people may have been left behind, full literacy has very largely been achieved at the primary level.

Gender inequality remains a problem in the education system. The presence of females in the classroom declines disproportionately as the grade levels advance. The government's compulsory educational policy for students 7 to 14 years of age remains in effect, but enforcement measures need to be strengthened, and reasons of failure because of poverty need further attention.

ISSUES IN POSTCOLONIAL CAPE VERDE

Among the many pressing issues in the twenty-five years of independence have been economic development, import substitution, diversification in the economy, and, especially, the emergence of multiparty democracy. Serious limits in the transportation, communication, and educational infrastructure have also been addressed with notable achievements, though considerable development needs remain. Cape Verde has no postsecondary university. The highest level in the educational system presently includes four secondary schools, one industrial school, and one commercial school. Despite this significant deficiency, many Cape Verdeans have undertaken postsecondary education and received professional degrees. Moreover, the government has active plans to redress this deficiency.

A subjective feature of elite and colonial values in education is a lingering inheritance that may be poorly suited to the practical concerns of educating a nation for democracy and development. For the largest part of the twentieth century, Portuguese colonial education featured values of racism and fascism that will require effort to eliminate. Many books are out of date. Rapidly changing technical fields are also quickly dated. Thus, another part of the future mission of higher education in Cape Verde will not only be bricks and mortar and faculty and staff, but a widespread national debate about the nature of the society Cape Verdeans wish to create and the kinds of courses and pedagogy that would be most suited to achieve this.

SECONDARY EDUCATION IN CAPE VERDE

Among the complex issues relating to the creation of secondary and higher education in Cape Verde are the costs to the nation of developing needed physical structures, teaching staff, and libraries. Issues of curriculum context are also being examined closely to ensure that the postsecondary system is not only cost effective but also relevant to Cape Verde's development needs. Another emotional and practical struggle has been to legitimate and standardize Crioulo orthography in schools and in a dictionary. Major steps have already been taken in this respect at the elementary levels, but it has yet to be determined at the postsecondary level whether instruction will occur in the nation's lingua franca of Crioulo (Kriolo), in the more formal Portuguese, the more universal English, or some combination of these languages. Courses in Cape Verdean Crioulo are periodically offered in American schools and community centers to a limited extent, but the debate about the role of Crioulo in postsecondary education in Cape Verde has hardly begun.

EDUCATIONAL RESOURCES

Other resources with implications for education in Cape Verde include a television channel with heavy Portuguese connections and two government-run radio stations. Newspapers such as *Semana*, *Terra Nova*, and *Voz di Povo* have been published, causing some anxiety from the government. The Cape Verdean Institute of Books and Records serves as the national publishing house. One may also visit the National Historic Archive for research. Portuguese books and other foreign-language books also have a small but established market. A new ethnographic museum of culture and history has opened on the Platô of Praia, and plans call for the creation of a small museum on each island. Plans to build an aquarium in Mindelo are advancing.

Educational resources for Cape Verde can also be derived from its membership in many international bodies, including the Organization of African Unity, the United Nations (especially United Nations Educational, Scientific and Cultural Organization, UNESCO; United Nations Development Program, UNDP; Food and Agriculture Organization, FAO; World Health Organization, WHO; and United Nations Children's Fund, UNICEF), and African Countries with Portuguese as the Official Language (PALOP). UNESCO projects have targeted technical and educational cooperation. The organization funded a project to support the computerization of the newsroom of the Cape Verdean national radio, which has a direct impact on public education and information.

Some private-sector companies have already introduced cooperative training to upgrade Cape Verdean education. A partnership between Toyota and the African Development Foundation offers training in technical maintenance, repair, inventory control, and entrepreneurship for its employees. Government planning agencies in the fields of banking, demography, health, taxation, law, housing, transportation, tourism, agriculture, marine resources, water conservation, drought relief, ecology, and energy also represent areas that not only need educated staff but also provide opportunities for training and supervised internships.

The former mission of United States Agency for International Development (USAID) to Cape Verde has, sadly, been closed down, but the Peace Corps continues to offer some training programs for Cape Verdeans. Formerly the Peace Corps was engaged in agriculture and public health, but at present they are more centered on the National Teacher Training School, which offers Teaching of English as a Foreign Language (TOEFL) programs. They are also creating curricular and teaching materials for Cape Verdean secondary education that should increase the demand for more postsecondary studies. Other Peace Corps projects are concerned with issues of city planning, environmental protection, and information technology.

Bilateral programs such as the Saint Francis Exchange Program (based in Hartford, Connecticut) seek to upgrade Cape Verde's medical training and other areas important to its national development. The Saint Francis program allows Cape Verdean doctors to travel to Connecticut and American doctors to visit Cape Verde. Some bilateral training between Cape Verde and the United States has also taken place in the area of narcotics and law enforcement. In addition, the European Economic Community has signed an agreement with Cape Verde that provides training upgrades in science, technology, law, and economy related to the very important Cape Verdean fishing industry. The World Bank is working in Cape Verde to support financial reform, including training in banking management and administration. These projects help to support a variety of infrastructure projects and public-sector capacity building. For example, the World Bank's International Development Association provides long-term credit at very favorable rates for developing nations, including Cape Verde.

The United States Information Agency has a modest project in Cape Verde and the Azores in a school partnership program that funds teacher and student exchanges at the secondary level. Other foreign governments such as Germany and Austria have been or will be expanding their involvement in primary education improvement. Some private foundations from these nations are also involved. Because of its former colonial ties, Portugal is involved in Cape Verdean development. A professional institute for bankers established in 1980 is sponsored by the Portuguese Bank Association. Such programs have expanded with the increased privatization of Cape Verde in the last decade.

Literacy in Cape Verde varies by class, gender, age, and by island. São Nicolau boasts the highest literacy at 77.3 percent, while Santo Antão has a rate of 74.7 percent. São Tiago, the capital, which has a large poor rural population, has only 41.4 percent literacy. According to 1990 data, Cape Verde has 64,895 primary school students, 97,401 preparatory school students, and 18,341 students enrolled in secondary school (Halter 1993). All islands are served by junior high schools, which offer classes through an equivalent of the 9th grade. In the Barlavento (windward, northern) group of islands, the Liceu Baltasar Lopes da Silva (Baltasar Lopes da Silva High School) in Mindelo, São Vicente, has functioned since independence. For the Sotavento (leeward, southern) group of islands, the main secondary school had long been the Liceu Domingos Ramos (named after a hero of the armed struggle), which is located in the Platô section of Praia, São Tiago. Even after running multiple sections per day, the school became so overcrowded that a second high school was built in the Varzea section of the capital. A smaller third high school extension was functioning at Achada to service the Prainha part of town.

Clearly, the demand and need for postsecondary education in Cape Verde is acute. According to UNESCO data, more than 60 percent of Cape Verdean teachers have only a primary education, and about 30 percent may have received no formal teacher training. The rapid growth of Cape Verde's population, which has substantially topped 430,000, makes the need for higher education facilities even more urgent, although the steady growth in the gross national product and in per capita income will help to make education funding and payment of tuition costs more realistic and possible.

By 1982, the number of secondary students had reached only 192; after a major mobilization, though, the number shot up to 6,439 by 1988 and to 18,341 by 1990. Enrollments have continued to escalate, underscoring the great need for further education for the now substantial number of Cape Verdean high school graduates. To a certain extent, one may consider that the last year of high school in Cape Verde is virtually equivalent to the first year of college. Consequently, one may imagine a further elaboration of this existing program while awaiting the development and construction of a freestanding University of Cape Verde. Night courses and/or extension courses could also make use of these existing facilities in the interim.

The seminary in São Nicolau also deserves mention here. Founded in 1866 to educate priests and missionaries for Cape Verde and Lusophone Africa, it also stimulated a measure of classical education and appreciation of arts and literature. However, the colonial and police authorities routinely suppressed Cape Verdean intellectuals and artists in their efforts to prevent any expression of pro-independence or nationalist sentiments. The seminary's limited resources proved to be something of an intellectual and literary oasis for Cape Verde and provided the educational foundation for some of the few Cape Verdeans who went abroad for further study in the nineteenth and early twen-

tieth centuries. The seminary's long history was finally terminated in 1971, with the opening of the Gil Eanes school in São Vicente. One of the functions of Gil Eanes was to train Cape Verdeans as functionaries in the colonial service in Africa.

CAPE VERDEAN DIASPORA

The principal source of postsecondary education for Cape Verde rests firmly on its most important export and resource, that is, the people themselves. As is true for many insular nations, a common survival mechanism is an exodus and resulting emergence of a diasporic community to make up for the deficiencies in natural resources, employment, and educational opportunities. The scholarly community has documented this centuries-long pattern of dispersal from Cape Verde, both for "pull" factors of a brighter future abroad and for "push" factors of escape from drought, poverty, and limited options. Consequently, Cape Verde may actually have more of its citizens, or at least more people of Cape Verdean nationality, in the diaspora than actually in the archipelago. Areas of significant Cape Verdean concentration include Europe (especially Portugal, Holland, Spain, and Italy); Africa (especially Senegal, Guinea-Bissau, and other Lusophone nations); and Brazil, Cuba, and North America (especially in southeastern New England). This unusual circumstance currently provides the most important source of postsecondary education for Cape Verde, since most of these lands offer educational opportunities that Cape Verdeans can utilize. On the other hand, many Cape Verdeans have limited language and job skills that limit their admission to higher education, even when residing in nations that may offer educational opportunities. Moreover, those who do gain higher education abroad are most often lost to the brain drain and return to Cape Verde not for employment opportunities but mainly for family visits or retirement.

To illustrate the importance of education abroad, it is important to note that all doctors and lawyers in Cape Verde have received their formal training outside of the archipelago. Those with advanced technical training, such as degrees in engineering and other academic fields, are likewise wholly trained in these diasporic areas. Important efforts are being made by the government to not only attract remittances from and incorporate diasporic Cape Verdeans into their homeland but also to attract them to return and help with national development, technological and skill transfer, and research and training projects.

CREATING A UNIVERSITY OF CAPE VERDE

In five centuries of colonial rule in Cape Verde, Portugal failed to draft any known plan for establishing a university for the archipelago. The first published intention to create such a university appeared in the 1962 program of the African Party for the Independence of Guinea and Cape Verde (PAIGC), which had been founded in 1956 under Cape Verdean leadership. Section VII.b.1 of the PAIGC program specifically calls for the creation of university education and scientific and technical institutes. This was principally authored by the PAIGC secretary-general and Cape Verdean revolutionary intellectual Amilcar Cabral, who had been trained as an agronomist at the University of Lisbon in Portugal. Presumably, the dream at that time was to build a joint university for Guinea-Bissau and Cape Verde, since a common political party linked the two nations at that time. Another early public reference to a Cape Verdean university emerged in the period after the overthrow of the colonial and fascist regime in Portugal in April 1974. In this case, a small group of Cape Verdeans then residing in Luanda, Angola, published a manifesto addressed to the Lisbon Junta of National Salvation that called for the creation of a university in the Cape Verdean archipelago. The Luanda proclamation of May 4, 1974, was signed by Cape Verdean geophysicist Humberto Duarte Fonseca and others, including Yolanda Morazzo, Edgar Gomes Santos, Alcides dos Santos Fialho, Alfredo Furtado de Azevedo, Manual Duarte, Antero Barros, and Francisco Correia (Lopes 2000).

Naturally, nothing could be done to realize this plan until independence was won in 1975. In 1978, João Manuel Varela reintroduced the idea of a joint Guinean–Cape Verdean university. Varela is presently the head of a maritime technical institute (ISECMAR) in São Vicente. But after political unity was fractured in a 1980 coup in Bissau, little further progress was made to create a University of Cape Verde (UCV) at that time. After the electoral defeat of the PAICV (the Cape Verdean successor party to the PAIGC) by the dissident Movement for Democracy (MpD) party in the early 1990s, MpD renewed the plan to establish the UCV.

Further legislative progress was achieved with the creation of the Higher Institute of Education (ISE) in 1995; the Higher Institute of Engineering and Maritime Sciences (ISECMAR) in October 1996; the National Institute of Agricultural Research and Development with Law in 1997; and the Higher Institute of Economic and Commercial Sciences (ISCEE) in 1998. In 1999, further legislation created a technical commission responsible for education that led to two legislative decrees in 1999 to create statutes allowing for teaching personnel in higher education and research. In June 1999, the Cape Verdean National Assembly, the nation's highest legislative body, added more detail to the proposed structure of Cape Verdean higher education regarding admission, grants, diplomas, and qualifications. These points were set out in a document of September 27–30, 1999, the "Basic Law for Higher Education," which itemized issues of planning in Cape Verdean higher education, as well as credentialing, funding, and consolidating the various institutes of higher education that were already functioning in the archipelago. Other work in the National Assembly in 1999 determined the strategic and financial planning of the UCV and the curricular plans of study and types of degrees to be awarded in the UCV. These include bachelor's, master's, doctoral, and honorary degrees.

The UCV was formally proclaimed to be in legal existence in the official bulletin of Cape Verde of August 7, 2000. The official objective of the UCV will be to create a center for the transmission and diffusion of culture, science, and technology. At this point in its establishment, the UCV is under the authority of Secretary of State for Education Filomena Delgado. The plan is to have a functioning UCV in two years.

Linkages have also been established between the incipient UCV and the University of the Algarve in Portugal, which has signed cooperative protocols in areas such as maritime sciences, electrical engineering, and computer sciences. The University of Evora in Portugal has signed a parallel agreement for postsecondary mathematics teaching. These arrangements are a truly important expression of the Cape Verdean government's interest in creating a postsecondary institution of education and training.

Presumably, curricula and related faculty from existing Cape Verdean educational institutions will be incorporated in the future programs of the proposed University of Cape Verde. The Ministry of Health and Social Affairs in Cape Verde presently conducts special training programs for nurses, laboratory technicians, and social workers. Specialized training is provided at the Maritime Training Center in Mindelo, and other training programs are offered at the Center for Administrative Training and Promotion. In 1985, the Cape Verdean government created the National Institute for the Study of Agriculture (INIA) to promote research in agriculture and some related social sciences. Other institutions include the Higher Institute of Education, the National Historical Archive (AHN) for archival and historical studies, and the Piaget Institute, a private university.

However, there is still a long way to go before the UCV becomes a reality. A long campaign of financial development and planning still needs to be conducted. Much work needs to be undertaken to recruit and train the administration, technical staff, support personnel, and faculty. Colleges and universities are notoriously expensive to operate, and there will also be struggles over the curriculum, not to mention the many political issues that need to be addressed to keep a university open and protect its intellectual autonomy. Certainly the need, potential, and interest for a University of Cape Verde is very high, but one cannot imagine that it will meet its target date for opening. The present expenditure of Cape Verde's national budget on education is 50 percent, but the funds are still mostly allocated at the primary level and, to a lesser degree, the secondary level. Sending students abroad on government money remains very expensive for Cape Verde; without a domestic university to absorb highly trained individuals, the rate and speed of the return on this investment is questionable. In 1980, about 688 Cape Verdeans were overseas studying at universities and technical schools. By 1982, this number had jumped to 1,000 and it has since more than doubled, according to some estimates. Although the number of students overseas on private funds is difficult to measure accurately, one study suggests that 10 percent of Cape Verdean students overseas are studying medicine; some of these students were studying on Cape Verdean funds (Lobban and Lopes 1995).

Meanwhile, until a university is fully functioning, work proceeds on many fronts. An exchange program has been proposed with Roger Williams University in Rhode Island. A Cape Verde Study Abroad Program with Rhode Island College (RIC) and the University of Rhode Island (URI) has been in place since 1997. The concentration of resources in oceanography at URI has also resulted in training programs for Cape Verdeans at their Narragansett and Kingston, Rhode Island, campuses. RIC also has a Cape Verdean Studies Special Collection that enjoys intense international use. The University of Ohio was engaged in a TOEFL program in Cape Verde from 1994 to 1997. The campuses of the University of Massachusetts in Boston and in North Dartmouth have also addressed Cape Verdean issues in various ways, especially because of the substantial Cape Verdean numbers in their own student populations. A great variety of Cape Verdean Web sites formally and informally contribute to the dissemination of knowledge about Cape Verde.

CONCLUSION

Postsecondary education in Cape Verde was virtually nonexistent for centuries. On the other hand, funding higher education study abroad was part of a deeply rooted system that valued education. Since secondary education was available only on a limited basis in Cape Verde, there was always a demand for more advanced studies. After independence, the number of students enrolled in secondary schools increased markedly. The demand for further studies began to be addressed with the establishment of several institutes of higher studies to train teachers, health workers, and businesspeople. The cost of foreign education was high, and the domestic demand increased further. Thus, in the 1990s, more concrete plans were made to initiate a freestanding university of Cape Verde. These plans are now very advanced and the future University of Cape Verde will integrate the former institutes and prepare a wide range of other programs for postsecondary education when it and its satellite branches open, probably in the first decade of the twenty-first century.

BIBLIOGRAPHY

Carreira, A. 1982. *The People of the Cape Verde Islands.* Hamden, Conn.: Archon Books.

Direcção Geral do Ensino Superior e Ciencia. 1999. *Forum Sobre o Ensino Superior em Cabo Verde.* Praia: Assembleia Nacional.

Duncan, T. B. 1972. *Atlantic Islands.* Chicago: University of Chicago Press.

Foy, C. 1988. *Cape Verde: Politics, Economics and Society.* London: Pinter.

Government of Cape Verde. n.d. "Proposta De Lei de Bases Do Ensino" [Basic Law of Higher Education]. Draft of the 33-article protocol creating and legitimating the proposed University of Cape Verde and its official and legal functions.

Government of Cape Verde. 1999. *O desenvolvimento do ensino superior em Cabo Verde.* Praia: Ministry of Education.

Halter, M. 1993. *Between Race and Ethnicity: Cape Verdean American Immigrants, 1860–1965.* Champaign-Urbana: University of Illinois Press.

Hamilton, R. 1975. *Voices from an Empire: A History of Afro-Portuguese Literature.* Minneapolis: University of Minnesota Press.

Irwin, A., and C. Wilson. 1998. *Cape Verde Islands: The Bradt Travel Guide.* Old Saybrook, Conn.: Globe Pequot Press.

Lobban, R. 1995. *Cape Verde: Crioulo Colony to Independence.* Boulder, Colo.: Westview Press.

Lobban, R., and M. Lopes. 1995. *Historical Dictionary of the Republic of Cape Verde.* Lanham, Md.: Scarecrow Press.

Lopes, J. V. 2000. "Criada Universidade de Cabo Verde." *Semana* (Praia), September 1, 5.

Macedo, D. 1983. "The Politics of an Emancipatory Literacy in Cape Verde." *Journal of Education* 165, no. 1: 99–112.

Meintel, D. 1984. *Race, Culture, and Portuguese Colonialism in Cabo Verde.* Syracuse: Syracuse University Press.

22

Central African Republic

GASTON M. N'GUEREKATA

INTRODUCTION AND HISTORICAL BACKGROUND

Landlocked in the heart of the African continent, the Central African Republic (CAR) is a former French colony. Previously named Oubangui Chari, the country has 3.2 million inhabitants unequally spread over 622,984 square kilometers (240,535 square miles). The average population density is 5.1 persons per square kilometer. Most of the population is concentrated in the cotton-farming areas of the northwest, in the capital city of Bangui, and in the Oubangui River catchment areas, where economic activities and the road network are relatively well developed. By contrast, the north and northeast are sparsely inhabited. About 45 percent of the population is under the age of 14, and 51 percent are female. The average annual rate of population growth is 2.5 percent. Sixty-three percent of the population is illiterate and over 75 percent of the young female population is illiterate.

The largely subsistence agricultural sector involves about 85 percent of the active population and provided one-third of the gross domestic product (GDP) in 1998. Cotton and coffee are the leading export crops. In 1998, diamond exports represented the leading source of national income (US$59 million), followed by cotton ($27 million). Timber also accounted for a substantial part of exports earnings.

GDP growth since the Central African Republic achieved independence has been irregular. After experiencing average annual GDP growth of 4.5 percent during the 1960s, when most economic activities were in the private sector, the GDP decreased by 3 percent annually between 1970 and 1981 because of poor economic management. Agricultural and industrial production increased in the mid-1980s in response to the rise in production prices for cotton, coffee, timber, and diamonds. Political turmoil between 1989 and 1993, along with army mutinies in 1996 and 1997, severely affected the economy. Since then, GDP growth has been fluctuating between 3.5 percent

and 5.2 percent a year. This has been related to a favorable international context and the structural adjustment program approved by the International Monetary Fund (IMF), which implemented long-term austerity measures. In 1999, another positive factor was a decline in imports, which were down 2.4 percent compared to 1998. Since it is landlocked, the Central African Republic assures its import-export flux through the neighboring countries of Cameroon (via road) and the Democratic Republic of Congo and the Republic of Congo-Brazzaville (via the Oubangui and Congo Rivers). Consequently, its economy depends largely on the political situation in these countries. For instance, since May 2000, there has been a severe oil shortage due to the civil war in the Democratic Republic of Congo. However, according to the Agence France-Presse news agency (October 15, 1999), quoting Central African and international experts of the Bank of Central African States, the economic perspectives for the year 2000 remained good.

The political situation in the CAR has been unstable since the mid-1960s. The country's first head of state, David Dacko, was ousted by a military coup in 1966. Jean-Bedel Bokassa, the new strongman, brutally ruled the country until 1979. During that period, the country experienced one of the most degrading and violent dictatorships ever in Africa. Bokassa crowned himself emperor during an extravagant ceremony that ruined the country's economy in 1976. In September 1979, David Dacko took over again with the military and political support of France. Two years later, General Andre Kolingba ousted Dacko and installed another military dictatorship, which lasted until the democratic election of Ange-Felix Patasse in 1993. Unfortunately, several army mutinies, along with economic mismanagement and political authoritarianism, severely jeopardized all of Patasse's promises of democracy.

The structure of the education system in the CAR is similar to that of other African countries formerly administered by France. Six years of primary school are followed by four years of lower secondary school leading to the diploma of the first-cycle studies. Then, students can enter the general upper secondary education or the technical high school in Bangui, both of which prepare students for the baccalaureate degree and entrance to postsecondary schools.

French and Sango, respectively, are the foreign and national official languages. However, despite attempts to promote and use Sango in schools, French remains the language of instruction at all levels of the education system.

Like most developing countries, the CAR faces powerful pressures to expand and improve its higher education sector. After achieving independence in 1960, the country had no university. Central African students expatriated, particularly to France, to obtain degrees in higher education institutions. In the early 1960s, the country shared with Gabon, Chad, and the Republic of Congo a common postsecondary institution: the Foundation for Higher Education in Central Africa (FESAC), created by France to provide a regional training infrastructure for people of the former colonies of the French Equatorial Africa. The CAR hosted the Agriculture Institute in Wakombo (105 kilometers south of the capital city Bangui), while secondary school teachers received their training at the School of Education in Brazzaville, Republic of Congo. A forestry program was offered in Gabon, and Chad hosted the zootechnics training for students coming from these countries.

The Wakombo site was chosen because the city sheltered a French agriculture center called the Wakombo Agricultural Research Center (CRA), along with a botanical center. High-level research was then conducted on tropical plants such as coffee, cocoa, and pepper trees. The center ran the *Cahiers de la Maboke*, a respected international journal published in collaboration with the French Museum of Natural History, from the mid-1940s to the nationalization of the center in 1966.

In December 1969, the dictator Bokassa created a national university in the country. Rulers of Gabon and Chad did the same in their respective countries, which led to the end of the FESAC.

CURRENT OVERVIEW OF THE HIGHER EDUCATION SYSTEM

At the beginning of the 2000–2001 academic year, the higher education sector in the Central African Republic consisted of only two public institutions, the University of Bangui and the National School of Administration and Judiciary (ENAM), and one private school, the International Preparatory College (College Preparatoire International, CPI). Approximately 6,500 students are enrolled in the postsecondary system. The whole system is under the umbrella of the Ministry of Higher Education and Scientific Research, except for the National School of Administration and Judiciary, which is under the control of the secretary-general of the government.

THE NATIONAL SCHOOL OF ADMINISTRATION AND JUDICIARY (ENAM)

ENAM is a professional school for future civil servants and magistrates. Due to the lack of job offers in public administra-

tion over the past two decades, the enrollment in the school has severely declined and the curriculum is now workshop-oriented for the benefit of public-sector workers.

THE INTERNATIONAL PREPARATORY COLLEGE (CPI)

CPI responds to the continuing demand for access to professional and technical training. The two-year college program leads to degrees in computer sciences, accounting, marketing, and secretarial careers. These diplomas are granted under the leadership of the University of Bangui. Despite the lack of tenure and qualified instructors, the college provides a high-quality education to hundreds of national and international students from Cameroon, Chad, Gabon, and the Democratic Republic of Congo. This is a typical example of a successful private higher education institution that needs to be encouraged and supported.

THE UNIVERSITY OF BANGUI

Mission, Objectives, and Governance

At the time the university was created in 1969, a major issue faced by the country was the provision of trained workers to gradually replace expatriates in the modern sector of the economy. The baccalaureate degree obtained at the senior level of the secondary school was the only requirement to admission to the university. However, some postsecondary training programs, such as medicine and management, required a special test before entering.

In 1980 and 1981, following the collapse of the empire established in 1976 by Bokassa and the restoration of the republican regime, the first reform in the higher education sector was adopted as a response to pressure from several national scholars who returned home from Europe. The mission of the university was redefined, but it was still based on the French model, including its strong research component. The new policy granted partial administrative and financial autonomy to the university. It provided guidelines for recruitment, tenure, and promotion of faculty as a particular body in the public administration. To stimulate and promote research, special monthly allowances were granted to faculty members. A Board of Trustees was created, supposedly to oversee general administration and planning of the university. However, as in France, higher education remains the responsibility of the government, and university officials have limited autonomy. The minister of higher education (who is also the chancellor of the university) has thus far been the true coordinator and decision maker, since the board has failed to meet. In 1987, following a recommendation of a national seminar devoted to higher education, a high commissioner was appointed within the head of state's cabinet with a broad mandate to direct and coordinate the national scientific and technical research policy, including research at the University of Bangui. However, the strong need to set up and improve research policymaking and implementation in the higher education sector has not translated into action; currently there is almost no research being done in the CAR. In the beginning of the 1990s, a call to address the social and economic development issues led the government to incorporate a service component into the mission of the university.

The University of Bangui is the major institution of higher education in the CAR. The rector (vice-chancellor) is the chair of the University Council and the highest decision-making authority of the institution. The council makes decisions on matters such as curricula, admission policy, degree requirements, faculty appointments, and promotion decisions. Faculty and student representatives, along with heads of schools and institutes, are members of the council. A representative of the Ministry of Higher Education also sits on the council, which meets twice a year.

In practice, academic freedom is respected in the CAR, if we understand this concept as the right of scholars to pursue their research and to teach and to publish without control or restraint by institutions that employ them.

In theory, the University of Bangui is granted limited administrative and financial autonomy. As mentioned earlier, the minister of higher education is the true decision maker in practice. For instance, university officials cannot hire a professor; the government does. The university's budget is centralized at the state level and fails to be fully executed each year. No university agenda can be implemented without the government's consent and support.

Teaching and Research Units

There are eight teaching units within the university:

School of Science. The School of Science offers four-year degree programs (master's degrees) in biology, chemistry, physics, mathematics, and geology. A five-year program in mathematics will be offered during the 2001–2002 academic year to prepare students for doctoral programs. The School of Science is one of the strongest schools with a good passing rate. Despite some problems with laboratory equipment, the quality of training is very high. Graduates from the school who travel abroad in pursuit of higher degrees in their respective fields are in general adequately prepared. In addition, many graduates currently hold a teaching position in the school.

School of Health Sciences. The School of Health Sciences runs two categories of programs: (a) The seven-year medical program leads to a diploma of Medical Doctor. Graduates in 1982 were the first doctors entirely trained in the country by national professors. Because of the delicate nature of the profession, it was a true challenge when the decision to run the program was taken. With the technical and financial support of the World Health Organization and accreditation from the Conference for Francophone Deans of Schools of Medicine (composed of representatives from France, Canada, and other French-speaking countries in Africa), which handled the dissertations jury, the quality of education was high in the beginning years. International students from several countries (Cameroon, Chad, Comoros, Congo, Benin, and the Democratic Republic of Congo) earned scholarships granted by international organizations to study medicine in Bangui. (b) The school also offers programs in nursing and trains personnel in various fields of health services.

The school has a huge impact on the health sector in the country: 85 percent of medical doctors in the CAR graduated from the school. After 25 years of existence, it is facing funding problems. Moreover, a number of its full professors are about to retire. Some are working off campus in better-paid jobs. The quality of education has been declining recently.

School of Law and Economics. This school is the second-largest one on campus. It started its activities in October 1970. At the present time, it offers four-year programs leading to the so-called semiprofessional master's degrees in both law and economics, with an emphasis on internships and general education as well. The master's degree in economics, for instance, has two concentration options: in Rural Economy (Economie Rurale) and Economy of Projects (Economie des Projets). Experts from businesses and industry are invited to give a talk at the annual scientific seminar to help students better understand the real problems in the sector before graduation. This reform has successfully brought well-prepared students onto the local job market and should be encouraged and pursued.

The school also organizes a short-term program of law for midlevel professionals in lawyers' offices and tribunals. It has not yet developed a sufficient collaboration with the National School of Administration and Judiciary (ENAM), which is unfortunate. These institutions should combine their human and financial resources to achieve their shared goals.

Numerous graduates from the School of Law and Economics are currently the nation's leaders. However, there are not enough tenured professors in the school. There is no doubt that the salaries at the University of Bangui are not attractive for economists and jurists. A number of faculty members have switched to careers in law during the past five years. Attempts to run a pre-doctorate program have also failed, basically because of the lack of qualified professors.

College of Letters and Human Sciences. This institution has the largest student enrollment. Programs include master's degrees in philosophy, sociology, history, geography, linguistics, English, and modern letters. Training in this college remains classical and has few links to the job market and the national social context in general. It is our belief that social scientists should play a key role in providing a better understanding of society's values and the form of democracy best suited to the country. Toward this end, this school should reform its training and research programs, address development issues, and promote an enlightened citizenship.

The Higher Institute of Rural Development (ISDR). The ISDR offers a short-cycle program for midlevel personnel in the rural development sector. In the past, the institute had regional prestige. It trained agriculture engineers for Gabon, Chad, the Republic of Congo, and the Central African Republic and received financing from the European Development Fund. The ISDR campus is located in an enjoyable and luxuriant forest region south of Bangui. For this reason, it is used to host several international conferences and workshops, including summer camps for American Peace Corps members. It is a potentially market-driven institute. Unfortunately, it suffers from a severe lack of financial input. Its distance from Bangui (100 kilometers) is a great handicap to its operation. Most of the faculty are now part-time employees who are faced with the weekly expensive and uncertain trip to the school. The university does not provide reimbursement for these trips. The implementation of a distance-learning program could provide a solution to this critical situation.

The University Institute of Management. The institute offers a four-year program in business administration. In the early 1990s, its graduates experienced employment problems. Complaints from employers included inadequate preparation of students. In response, the institute implemented reforms with the scientific support of the University of Paris XII, Val-de-Marne, to meet the expectations of the local job market. It also adopted a new flow chart that includes close supervision by a board of trustees with representatives from business. The institute also developed an excellent relationship with the private sector in which all students are granted internships in enterprises before graduating.

The Higher Institute of Technology (IST). The IST has trained numerous experts in mining and geology. With the strong support of Romania, the proportion of international students at IST has been very high due to the quality of education. At the end of the 1980s, the need for personnel in the mining sector declined in the CAR. The institute then adopted new short-cycle programs. It now provides training in electricity and telecommunications to midlevel agents of local plants. There is only one technical high school in the country. Since the first education project was implemented in the CAR with funding by the World Bank in 1972–1982, there have been no provisions to develop the technical curriculum or train technology teachers in the secondary schools. Consequently, the institute suffers a shortage of students and qualified professors. It also has inadequate facilities and obsolete equipment. As a result, the IST will not be able to implement other relevant programs without new physical and financial resources.

School of Education. This school provides training for secondary school teachers and other administrative agents who are serving in the Ministry of Education. Its infrastructure is adequate, but the school's enrollment is low given the shortage of teachers the country faces. The percentage of students preparing for a mathematics and sciences teacher's diploma remains insignificant.

The CAR has four research centers: the Institute for Applied Linguistics, The University Center of Documentation in History and Archeology of the Central African Republic, The Center of Francophone Research and Studies, and The Center of University Pedagogy.

The Institute for Applied Linguistics is conducting research and studies on Sango and other national idioms in collaboration with the International Society of Linguistics. Its works are of great interest for the country, since Sango is an official language that 85 percent of people use. The Institute also attracts international scholars interested in Sango and other African languages. For instance, a number of Peace Corps volunteers have been very interested in learning Sango at the Institute.

The other research centers are skeletal and could be more efficient if they were incorporated into the academic departments of social sciences or education, for instance.

Enrollment and Other Student Problems

Student enrollment in 1998–1999 was 5,486, which represented an increase of nearly 80 percent in three decades. Successive education reforms in the country had two major objectives:

- To increase the number of lower secondary school graduates (grades 7–10) and improve the quality of the curriculum for this educational level
- To expand and improve the quality of scientifically and technically trained (upper secondary school) graduates (grades 11–13)

Quantitative aspects of these objectives were partially achieved. Enrollment figures indicate that the number of students preparing for the mathematics and physical sciences baccalaureate degrees have significantly increased. Enrollment at the University of Bangui reflects this situation. The proportion of students in mathematics and sciences jumped to 35 percent in 2000, compared with 8 percent in 1981.

The percentage of female students remains very low. It varies from 3 percent in science to 16 percent in law and the human sciences. Young women are facing strong pressures in the society to leave school and take up their traditional role of housekeepers. Ethnic minorities, such as Pygmies and Bororo, are poorly represented in higher education. The government should address the endemic cultural and social problems that exclude minorities from the system. An equity policy must be implemented to encourage disadvantaged people to pursue higher education.

Despite numerous attempts to address the needs of the national economy, the University of Bangui still reflects the former French model with its emphasis on theoretical training. The academic programs do not meet the labor-market needs for midlevel personnel in the manufacturing and services sectors of the economy. In the humanities, some course contents do not reflect the CAR's national culture and environment. While the titles of some programs (technology, rural development, health sciences, and management) appear relevant, the reality is quite different. There is still some incompatibility between training and the knowledge of real problems that the country faces.

Curricula, Graduates, and Employment

The baccalaureate degree is the requirement to enter most programs. In sciences and mathematics, entering students are fairly well prepared. In medicine, business, and rural development, for instance, entering students need to pass a special test. Most of the curriculum at the University of Bangui is inspired by the French model. Courses run over a year and exams are usually given twice per semester. Students must obtain a total average grade of 10 over 20 in June to pass. There is a general retest in October. Failure to pass automatically cancels all grades obtained that year, even in courses in which the student received decent scores. The lack of flexibility in curriculum does not permit students to easily change their academic program and enroll in a new department. There is no opportunity for part-time enrollments. This rigid schedule prevents working people from attending the university to improve their skills and contribute more effectively to the development of the nation.

Because the university provides insufficient information and guidance service, students enroll in programs without any information about job opportunities. In the past, higher education graduates had no difficulty finding a job. This is no longer

Table 22.1. Fiscal Year 2000 Budget (in thousands of FCFA) in the CAR

Total National Budget (FCFA)	123,574,940
Running Expenditures	
Higher Education	1,165,620
Education (kindergarten, primary, secondary schools)	8,246,093
Scholarships	
University of Bangui	400,000
Total (in and out of state)	1,483,380
Investments	
Higher Education	162,000
Education (kindergarten, primary, secondary schools)	484,000
Total	11,941,093

Note: US$1.00 = FCFA 745.

Source: Loi des Finances RCA 2000

the case. Getting hired in a field related to one's training is now rare. Graduates from literature and social sciences have the worst track record. Medical doctors and teachers sometimes wait for years after graduation to find employment by the government (which remains the major employer in the country).

A large number of graduates travel overseas, particularly to France, to pursue higher degrees. Since 1994, with the devaluation of the national currency, it has become too expensive to study in developed countries. Students are now relocating to West African universities.

The quality of higher education in the CAR has declined in the last decade. Political turmoil, extreme financial difficulties, and long and frequent strikes are major factors that have contributed to this rapid deterioration. Any effort to improve higher education is intimately linked to the general economic and political situation in the country.

Funding and Financial Problems

Higher education in the CAR is basically financed publicly. In the 1970s, while the university was under French rule, France paid some expenses, such as French workers' salaries and office and other academic supplies. Since 1980, French public aid to higher education in the CAR has consistently diminished. It is now exclusively used to support French faculty. Due to extreme financial difficulties over the last ten years, the Central African government has been unable to face its responsibilities for the whole higher education sector.

During the 2000 fiscal year, the budget of the University of Bangui represented approximately 1.7 percent of the national budget (Table 22.1). The budget was primarily devoted to salaries and scholarships. No substantial investment was expected. There were 162 million Francophone Central African Francs (FCFA) supposedly allocated to investment. In reality, the money was used for facilities maintenance needs. As of October 2000, the government has still been unable to provide these financial resources.

Faculty and other university workers have not been paid for months. This situation has been the major source of several problems. Many professors choose to teach in private secondary schools or work in the commercial sector to meet their daily needs. Some of them have decided to relocate to developed countries for regular and higher pay. Corruption has been rapidly growing on campus, and the willingness of faculty to evaluate student work fairly has been jeopardized. Immediate consequences of this difficult situation have been poor training quality and low faculty performance. Students have also been at the mercy of professors in need. It is of great importance for the future of the higher education sector that the government promptly and steadily address faculty salary issues.

The lack of sufficient financial resources for higher education in the CAR is a direct result of the state of extreme poverty and great instability of the country. In August 2000, delays in pay for public-sector workers reached up to seventeen months. The country is still paying a high price for the 1996–1997 mutinies by the army. Private organizations and the international community in general are suspicious of the stated willingness of the government and leading political parties to put an end to their political quarrels.

After careful examination of the government's inability to adequately support academic activities at their institutions in the spring semester of 1995, university officials decided to develop market-driven activities to generate financial resources. For instance, the Higher Institute of Technology (IST), with expertise from the Polytechnic School of Yaounde in Cameroon, had planned to manufacture and sell cheaper satellite dishes within a not-for-profit university firm run by faculty and students. Students would then acquire technical skills and managerial experiences. Unfortunately, the government banned these initiatives without offering any other solution to the lack of funds for higher education.

Physical Resources and Facilities

At the time it was created, the University of Bangui could accommodate 300 students. They all enrolled in programs in mathematics, chemistry, biology, physics, law, economics, and literature. Due to a strong demand in other fields, more facilities had to be constructed.

In 1976, with the technical and financial support of the

World Health Organization (WHO), the School of Medicine was built with spacious classrooms, adequate laboratories, and office space for faculty and administrators. The school also used some facilities at the Bangui Pasteur Institute, which was part of the well-known French health research center, the Pasteur Institute.

While visiting the university in September 1981, just days after he took over, General Kolingba (the new strongman of the CAR) recognized the need for more classrooms. He decided to repossess a huge palace belonging to Emperor Bokassa and granted this property to the university. Renovations were rapidly executed to the so-called Kolongo campus, which was located in an area with no public transportation: garages were turned into rudimentary amphitheaters and bedrooms into offices. Unfortunately, the lack of electrical power and chalkboards made student learning quite difficult. During inclement weather, classes could not be conducted.

A library was constructed in the mid-1980s with a World Bank loan. It is a tiny facility containing more than 3,000 books and titles, most of them dated. With no computer, books can be found only through a tedious card catalog system. University officials have never solved the schedule and access problems frequently reported by students. Indeed, the library opens only during the public administration schedule while the majority of students are in class. Library clerks have refused to work on weekends or in the evening.

Along with the library, the World Bank financed a computer room with a dozen workstations in the Higher Institute of Technology (IST). The equipment was fairly up to date. A French instructor managed the computer room, and it had partial financial autonomy. It was a market-driven center that organized training sessions for private, as well as public service, workers. But the equipment was obsolete by 2000. With the government's consent, Coeur d'Afrique Association, a Central African nongovernmental organization, is planning to provide a campus network and the necessary connection to the Internet. This will reduce the intellectual isolation of the institution and provide access to the very latest information in science. It is well known that the Internet provides access to new and modern forms of teaching and learning, such as distance learning and teleconferences, from which developing countries can greatly benefit.

In general, the infrastructures and facilities of the University of Bangui are far from being sufficient and adequate. There is a great need for more classrooms, laboratories, and office space. Professors do not have office rooms. Consequently, extra-classroom activities such as office hours or conferences with peers are difficult or impossible to organize.

Since 1971, no substantial investment has been made to improve students' substandard living conditions. Student dormitories can hardly accommodate 250 people. Getting a room on campus is a challenge, especially for freshman students. Students cannot afford housing expenses in town. The university offers no student loans, and those students lucky enough to live on campus sometimes sublet their rooms to increase their income. The tiny cafeteria of eighty seats provides cheap but sometimes unhealthy food due to the inadequate funding by the state treasury. Sports facilities are limited to a soccer yard and a basketball court. University teams are usually trained in other public facilities off campus.

Research and Publishing

All higher education institutions in the CAR are teaching oriented. Research activities, even in the so-called research centers, are limited. In the 1970s, the University of Bangui published the *Annals of the University of Bangui*, which included articles in fields such as mathematics, physics, economics, and law. Even though it printed some good articles, the journal never gained an international audience.

The Research Institute for Mathematics Education published several preprints on Sango and mathematics. These works include the study of the impact of the national language, Sango, on students' learning of mathematics, as well as research on counting in Sango, mathematics and Central African culture, and other topics. But this institute is no longer active.

The department of geography created *Masaragba* (which means "rhino" in Sango) in 1992. *Masaragba* is a journal devoted to environmental issues. At the time it was created, this journal was a contribution of the University of Bangui to the United Nations Conference on Environment and Development in Rio de Janeiro, Brazil. It has been so successful that the editorial board continues to publish the journal with financial support from GTZ, a German nongovernmental organization.

Students in medicine, economics, rural development, geography, linguistics, sociology, and philosophy have conducted several theses and studies under faculty supervision. These papers remain internal documents and cannot be considered as research publications.

There is an extreme shortage of textbooks. In most cases, notes dictated by the professors during class are the only sources of information students have for a course. To compensate for the lack of books, some professors in various departments (law and mathematics, for instance) provide handouts of their own work. A typical example is the *Collection Matub* (Mathematics University of Bangui), a series of textbooks created by a professor in 1983 to serve as a useful aid for independent studies in calculus. This dated series, financed by the Agence Culturelle de Coopération Technique et Française, a Paris-based cultural agency, has been very successful.

Faculty Body

During the first decade of the university (1970–1979), the majority of faculty were expatriates. Competent professors from France and the Soviet Union held positions in the institution, basically in mathematics, physics, and chemistry. France appointed vice-chancellors and deans of schools. It was a period of grandeur, marked by funding from France, regular publication of the *Annals of the University of Bangui* containing high-level research articles, intellectual fervor on campus, and de facto recognition of the diplomas by France and other European countries.

In 1979, President David Dacko ousted Emperor Bokassa with the strong political and military support of France. Dacko fired the Soviet instructors and banned them from teaching in any school in the country. The French government withdrew most of its nationals, including the vice-chancellor. The University of Bangui then operated under the leadership of Central African administrators and faculty. The majority of the administrators and faculty were qualified scholars who had been teaching in French and Canadian institutions during Bokassa's dictatorship.

At the beginning of the 2000–2001 academic year, the faculty body had reached 300, including contractual and part-time instructors (Table 22.2). Only 5 percent are expatriates and nearly none are female. Half of the instructors have not earned a doctorate degree in their fields. As an institutional member of the African and Malagasy Council for Higher Education (CAMES), the University of Bangui should stop hiring candidates without doctorate degrees, banish positions of assistants, and give full opportunities to the assistants to earn doctorate degrees and be promoted. In the absence of a system of continuous faculty training and development, this problem remains to be addressed by the university's leaders. Most full professors are medical doctors who received tenure via the French medical board examination. Their promotions were not based on teaching experience or research capability. They are, however, respected as the first and brilliant generation of faculty who trained and tutored the hundreds of young medical doctors now running the health sector in the country.

Faculty salaries are low. On the other hand, teaching loads appear to be quite reasonable. They range from five hours per week for a full professor to eight hours for an assistant. Like all state employees, university faculty may be appointed to positions in other services. They must then keep a minimum of one hour teaching in their respective schools. This decision makes sense given the lack of faculty in most programs. It also keeps faculty in touch with their disciplines.

Appointments and Promotions

Appointments and promotions at the University of Bangui are handled in the same way as most universities that are members of the CAMES, with peer evaluation. There are, however, no advertisements on vacancies. Applications are reviewed by a departmental committee and a university committee appointed by the rector. The University Council then makes its recommendations. The minister in charge of public administration hires candidates retained by the University Council after recommendation by the minister in charge of higher education. The promotion process is identical.

Diplomas have been the major criterion for recruitment, while promotion decisions are based on teaching and publication. Violations of this process by politicians have often occurred. In order to prevent subjectivity and other frequent external pressures on decisions regarding promotions, and to stimulate faculty research performance, the University Council decided in 1994 to submit all dossiers for CAMES's approval. Based on some recent decisions, it seems that the government has adopted a different attitude. In August 2000, for instance, perhaps anticipating a strike that teachers' unions were preparing for October 2000, President Patasse surprisingly granted special promotion and tenure to all faculty members of the University of Bangui

Table 22.2. Number of Academic Staff at the University of Bangui, 1999–2000

Title	Number
Professors	5
Associate Professors	5
Assistant Professors	124
Instructors	75
Visiting Professors	8
Part-time Instructors	7
Expatriates	19
Laboratory Assistants	57
Total	300

Source: Rectorate of the University of Bangui, June 2000.

regardless of academic performance, peer evaluation, or even teaching effectiveness.

It is our strong belief that partisan political decisions cannot transform the university into a great institution. Some standards are needed for degree requirements regarding student performance, faculty qualification, and achievements. Quality improvement in higher education can be achieved only by rewarding merit and performance.

Political Activism and Other Issues

Protests and riots are frequent on the University of Bangui campus. Ironically, the university's founder, Emperor Bokassa I, was overthrown in a military coup that originated from student rioters who had been brutally punished in 1979. University officials, as well as education ministers, often lose positions after demonstrations on campus. Political parties and the government frequently manipulate education in general and the University of Bangui community in particular. Politicians court both student associations and faculty union leaders.

The first faculty strike, which happened in 1989, led to profound political changes in the country. Under strong pressures after the strike, combined with a disastrous economic situation, President Kolingba was forced to reinstall democracy in 1990 and to organize free elections two years later. In 1993, just days after he took office, President Patasse solemnly asked the student body to designate their representative to enter his cabinet.

Some demonstrations have been staged due to delays in payments of scholarships by the government. Since the opening of the university in 1970, these monthly scholarships have been seen as salaries rather than study allowances. When a student obtains a baccalaureate, it is not only a hope for her or his own future—the whole family celebrates the event, in part because a scholarship means immediate financial support for a student's relatives.

CLOSING REMARKS AND OBSERVATIONS

Higher education in the CAR is in crisis. Existing problems are multiple and complex. The system suffers severe deficiencies in quality and does not satisfy real labor-market demands.

economy has stagnated. Various governments failed to adequately finance the education system and to assure regular and decent pay to its workers. In the 1990s, schools were closed for two consecutive years. Academic years were shortened by numerous strikes by professors and students. No credible education policy has been implemented.

The new National Plan for the Development of Education (PNDE), to be implemented during the decade 2000–2010, is a unique chance for the country. It is an encouraging step, if it is financed and adequately executed.

Despite the lack of data and follow-up by the authorities, the continuous increase in student enrollment over three decades indicates that Central African youth are eager to learn. They are showing particular interest in mathematics, the sciences, and technical curricula. The majority of parents cannot afford to send their children to study abroad. It is unquestionable that the labor market would move into a better state with the advent of democracy and good governance. The government could then take the opportunity of the PNDE to implement a strong higher education agenda that includes the following:

- An effective autonomy of institutions. State control should not be understood to mean frequent intrusions by the government in academic, financial, and personnel decisions. The management of the University of Bangui has to be decentralized and entrusted to a strong and stable leadership.
- Sufficient funding. Without sufficient financial resources, higher education institutions cannot achieve their goals and objectives. In the context of financial autonomy, university managers should access specific and sufficient provisions in the state treasury for running expenditures. They must also be in control of internal incomes such as tuition and workshop fees.
- Privatization. The government should encourage private institutions, especially professional schools that run relevant training programs, by granting more scholarships to their students.
- Promotion of an entrepreneurial culture via relevant curric-

ula to encourage the creation of more productive jobs. Better information on the labor market should be provided.
- Redesignation of the process of appointment and promotion based on track records of teaching, research, and community service. This includes annual peer, student, and department evaluation. The faculty pay structure must be improved by considering salary increases and merit rewards.
- Promotion of a strong and stable leadership at the University of Bangui by assigning top administrative positions to respected scholars. The university is more than a knowledge creation and maintenance site. University faculty members in developing countries must mobilize people for scientific truth and technological progress. They should be role models and agents for change in their respective societies.
- A quality education should be constantly targeted through periodic evaluations of programs and all academic activities. University officials must encourage competition and reward merit and performance.
- All resources available via international cooperation agreements and in the private sector must be fully utilized.

REFERENCES

Banque Mondiale. 1995. *L'enseignement supérieur, Les leçons de l'expérience.* Washington, D.C.: Publication de la Banque Mondiale.

Ministère de l'Education Nationale, République Centrafricaine. 1999. *Plan national de développement de l'education* (PNDE), 2000–2010.

Programme des Nations-Unies pour le Développement. 1997. Projet CAF/97/021/A/08/13, Elaboration du PNDE, Seminaire national de validation du Plan National de Développement de l'Education, 21–23 Juillet 1999.

République Centrafricaine. 1969. Ordonnance 69.063 du 12 Novembre 1969 portant création de l'Université de Bangui.

———. 1985. Décret 85.264 du 21 Aout 1985 portant statuts de l'Université de Bangui et ses modificatifs subsequents.

———. 1997. Loi 97.014 du 10 Decembre (1997). Portant orientation de l'éducation en R.C.A.

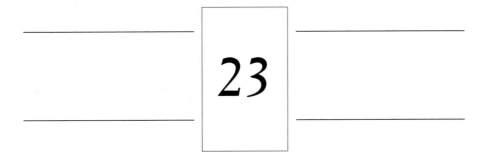

23

Chad

Mahamat-Ahmed Al Habo

INTRODUCTION

According to the human development indicators prepared by the United Nations Development Program, Chad is ranked 164th among the 174 countries surveyed. The majority of Chadians live below the poverty line, according to the World Bank. Although significant efforts and investments have been made to improve it, the illiteracy rate in Chad is still more than 80 percent. The proportion of students attending primary schools was 57.5 percent in 1997, while the overall schooling rate was 27 percent. There are significant regional disparities in rates of schooling.

In 1990, the Chadian government and its partners adopted a development strategy called Education-Training-Employment (Education-Formation-Emploi, or EFE). After a review in 1998, the strategy, made up of five programs corresponding to the five sectors of the educational system, was carried out through the year 2000. The strategy seeks to improve the efficiency of the educational system and to increase access to education. It targets various areas, such as teacher education, curriculum design, and the rationalization and management of the educational system. In spite of this mobilization, which is reflected more systematically in the priority given to education, efforts have yielded insufficient results so far.

Chad's educational system is faced with problems stemming from significant population growth and increased social demands for education. The expansion of the system has not met the desired expectations, and efficiency has been limited. Infrastructures are insufficient and often obsolete. The student-to-teacher ratio is very high, while the lack of qualified educators and managers, the outdated instructional equipment, and the inadequate quality of majors offered have contributed to the failure of Chad's educational policy. Technical education and vocational training, which are vital for national development, have

remained marginal; they suffer from an inadequate correlation between training and openings in the job market.

Higher education has been no exception to the problems of fulfilling the goals of all education sectors in Chad's educational strategy. Committed to improving the management of public resources in an attempt to meet structural adjustment programs, the Chadian government directed its attention to matters related to investment and basic education and failed to grant higher education the resources it needed to grow. EFE strategists decided to increase student enrollments, paying special attention to scientific and technological disciplines. The growth that followed 1992, particularly during 1996 and 1999, however, only exacerbated existing imbalances.

HIGHER EDUCATION AND THE RESEARCH NETWORK

The educational system in Chad was influenced by the French model, in which universities are under direct government supervision. As far as research is concerned, the Ministry of Higher Education and Scientific Research (Ministère de l'Enseignement Supérieur et de la Recherche Scientifique, MESRS) relies on a consulting body called the National Committee of Scientific and Technical Research (Comité National de la Recherche Scientifique et Technique, CNRST). The ministry has power over most educational institutions (universities, institutes, and centers) in which teaching and research activities are performed; some specialized professional institutions are supervised by other ministries.

The EFE strategy and the programs approved by the Chadian government during the States General for Education (Etats Généraux de l'Education), held in October 1994 in N'djamena, laid down the foundations for a new educational policy (Ministère de l'Education Nationale 1994a, 1994b). One of the objectives of the EFE National Program in connection with higher education and scientific research was to effect a moderate increase in the number of students in higher education. First-year enrollments could reach 1,800, and the overall number of students in higher education would be 4,000 by the end of 2001 compared to 2,800 in 1993–1994. The EFE also looked at ways of increasing student numbers at the institutions of a scientific and technological character, while controlling admissions of economics, law, and literary majors.

A closer link between education and the job market needs to be established for a better integration of graduates in Chad. The EFE proceedings recommended the creation of two-year study programs, continuing education for the training of civil servants, and measures to improve the student success rate at the University of N'djamena (NU, Université de N'Djamena) from 25 percent in 1989 to 60 percent in 2000. Recommendations also included a new scholarship policy that encourages admission into professional and scientific majors. The proceedings gave special attention to reinforcing Chad's higher education and scientific research infrastructure and to encouraging research that is relevant to issues related to the country's development. Generally, recommended policies addressed the issues of majors, curriculum, the revamping of the infrastructures and equipment, ways to win institutional support, and modification of policies related to scholarship awards.

Since 1992, the MESRS has not taken tangible measures to implement the EFE strategy because it lacks the means.

MESRS AND SCIENTIFIC RESEARCH

The MESRS is not responsible for all educational institutions. Some professional institutions are tied to other ministries, a fact which reduces the possibility of efficient coordination of the entire higher education sector. The institutions and independent organizations coming under the supervision of the ministry are NU, the Advanced Institute of Education (Institut Supérieur des Sciences de l'Education, ISSED), the National Center for Research Support (Centre National d'Appui à la Recherche, CNAR), the Sarh University Institute of Agronomy and Environment (Institut Universitaire des Sciences Agronomiques et de l'Environement de Sarh, IUSAE), and the Abeche Institute for Technical Sciences (Institut Universitaire des Sciences et Techniques d'Abéché, IUST).

The MESRS retains broad responsibilities in terms of implementing and evaluating government educational policy, setting up new universities, overseeing administrative management, designing manuals and didactic documents, defining appropriate pedagogy, and organizing examinations and entrance tests.

In the field of scientific research, the ministry is in charge of initiating, coordinating, and evaluating research programs in science and technology and comparing findings with other ministries. The ministry also has the task of training, employing, and promoting researchers in various specialties and publishing research findings.

In order to ensure the enforcement of its various prerogatives, the ministry has a board of directors. When need arises, the various administrative units of the ministry can resort to consulting organizations, such as the Commission for Authentication, Accreditation, and Degree Equivalency (Commission d'Authentica-

tion, d'Homologation, et d'Equivalence des Diplômes, CAHED), the National Committee for Scientific and Technical Research (Comité National de la Recherche Scientifique et Technique, CNRST), and the National Commission for Scholarships (Commission Nationale des Bourses, CNB).

INSTITUTIONS UNDER THE SUPERVISION OF THE MESRS

The institutions managed by the MESRS have limited infrastructures and means. Their output, as well as the quality of training they provide, is inconsistent.

N'DJAMENA UNIVERSITY

NU is composed of five schools: the School of Law and Economics (Faculté de Droit et Science Economique, FDSE), the School of Letters and Humanities (Faculté des Lettres et Sciences Humaines, FLSH), the School of Exact and Applied Sciences (Faculté des Sciences Exactes et Appliquées, FSEA), the School of Health Sciences (Faculté des Sciences de la Santé, FSS), and the National Institute of Human Sciences (Institut National des Sciences Humaines, INSH). Even though NU is a major university that hosts the vast majority of Chad's students, it is lacking in equipment and student supervision. The university is the subject of chronic conflicts that occur every year between the students (and sometimes professors) and authorities, a fact which adversely affects the normal functioning of the university. Despite such a difficult environment, the university has attempted to sustain itself and adapt to circumstances, namely through the creation of professional majors. However, research at NU is unorganized and very limited, and the university's documentation system does not meet the needs of either teaching or research.

The EFE strategy predicted a moderate increase in the number of students, with a goal of 4,000 students by the end of the century. The current increase has been significant; however, the 4,000-student target will not be reached unless the same increase rate is maintained (Table 23.1).

The university's board of trustees has total control in determining the quota of first-year enrollment and therefore the influx of new students. The schools apply admission quotas by selecting the new high school graduates based on their scores on core subjects. This system seems to be functioning satisfactorily. It is highly selective, since less than one-third of the students graduating from high school are admitted to NU. The schools' hosting capacity is the primary factor in determining quotas.

Creating a balance between majors is one of the objectives targeted by the EFE strategy; however, it is noteworthy that the increase in the number of students enrolled at the different specialties did not help in achieving the desired goals. While increases in scientific and technical majors and a decline in disciplines such as humanities, law, and economics were expected, the opposite has occurred since 1994–1995. The gap is growing wider, as more students are enrolling in the latter disciplines at the expense of the former.

Chad does not have enough high school graduates majoring in the sciences who earned satisfactory grades to fill the missing

Table 23.1. Student Enrollment at the University of N'djamena, 1994–1997

Institution	1994–1995	1995–1996	1996–1997
School of Law and Economics (FDSE)	792	916	1,021
School of Letters and Humanities (FLSH)	1,426	1,613	1,780
School of Exact and Applied Sciences (FSEA)	433	483	435
School of Health Sciences (FSS)	105	107	140
Total	2,756	3,119	3,376

Table 23.2. Faculty at the University of N'djamena, 1995–1996

Institutions	Faculty						Ratio*
	Total	Permanent	Part-time	Assistant	Lecturer	Students	
School of Law and Economics (FDSE)	51	12	39	6	6	977	1:81
School of Letters and Humanities (FLSH)	86	53	33	16	37	1,613	1:30
School of Exact and Applied Sciences (FSEA)	58	45	13	21	24	480	1:11
School of Health Sciences (FSS)	59	17	42	0	17	105	1:6
Total	254	127	127	43	84	3,175	1:25

*This is a ratio of permanent staff to students.

seats at the FSEA. Graduates with a D average outnumber those with a C average, and achievements of high school students in mathematics and physics are notoriously low, leading to a high failure rate in their first year at the university. In essence, the problem originates at the secondary school level, where scientific instruction is provided by an extremely limited number of qualified teachers.

Generally, the productivity of the university system is weak; limited portions of first-year students are able to obtain their bachelor's degrees, though the situation varies between schools and even between departments of the same school. NU is characterized by a high failure rate during final examinations, including among sophomores and juniors.

Student failure rates are due to several factors. First, the number of high school graduates is insufficient. Second, the conditions of student life are not conducive to learning: in certain schools (such as FDSE and FLSH), the scarcity of qualified teachers leads to poor supervision; small facilities force students to attend classes and practical courses outside amphitheaters and classrooms; libraries are poorly supplied; the university has no cafeteria or collective transportation; and there is no full-fledged campus. Third, teaching methods are generally inadequate, especially for first-year students.

The distribution of female students at NU remains quite unbalanced: women constitute 13.8 percent of students at FDSE, 14.9 percent at FLSH, 5 percent at FSEA, and 3.8 percent at FSS. The number of female students enrolled in scientific departments is particularly limited and does not exceed 15 percent at any institution. NU is consciously endorsing a policy to integrate women through a system of quotas in each department. The policy promotes recruitment of female high school graduates with lower scores than their male counterparts. This affirmative action policy certainly has shortcomings. In fact, the resolution of this problem lies upstream in high schools.

The faculty at NU is unequally distributed among permanent and part-time staff. In some departments, the number of temporary professors is around 50 percent. Similarly the teacher-to-student ratio reflects the discrepancy between schools. If we exclude the special case of FSS, where the number of students is strictly controlled, we notice that the ratio of permanent professors to students varies considerably between FDSE and FSEA (Table 23.2).

Despite concrete improvement over the last few years, faculty qualifications remain insufficient and deserve particular attention.

Since its creation, NU has had an implicit but fundamental mission of training civil servants. The majority of graduates have been employed in the Chadian civil service to fill teaching positions in secondary schools or assume administrative positions. However, to comply with structural adjustment programs, the Chadian government has frozen employment of civil servants for several years. This stagnation is not comprehensive, though; recruitment continues for graduates with very specific profiles in areas such as basic teaching and health.

NU was seriously affected by the policy of stagnation regarding recruitment. For fear of producing graduates doomed to unemployment, the university has considered orienting some of its majors toward employment in the private sector and self-employment. This situation explains the recent emergence of professional advanced specialties with new and specific curricula and the encouragement of professors to adopt new teaching methods. These recently created majors are not unique, though their organizational structure seems different. They share common characteristics in preparing students at various degree levels to assume jobs in the private sector. The majors are selective and all lead to a three-year degree. Combined with the already existing bachelor's degrees, they offer more options for students. The implementation of these majors was preceded by a pilot study among companies and nongovernmental organizations (NGOs) likely to recruit university graduates. Professionals are frequently called upon to share their knowledge with students and sponsor internships. These majors differ in terms of the balance between theoretical and practical experience and provision of initial (basic) education or both initial and continuing education. Similarly, they display certain particularities related to the length of the professionally oriented education, which starts at either the end of the first year of the common core program or at the end of the second year, if the common core is extended through the sophomore year.

Profession-oriented majors must be analyzed with particular attention, for they constitute a major factor in the development of higher education in Chad. Professionalization cannot be created by decree; it requires adherence to certain standards and principles. It is necessary to establish close relationships with employers in a carefully monitored dialogue that will lead to the participation of professional experts in the preparation and certification of various curricula. One cannot, however, ignore the fact that the education of professionals is costly; it requires increased training and significant material investment from companies that sponsor student internships. Professionalization also requires a profound change in the pedagogy at and the relations between the various educational partners (i.e., ministries and universities). The responsibility of the institution toward its students tends to increase in terms of employment. The objectives and commitments of each party must be clearly defined and quantitatively evaluated. The challenge of such regulations and requirements often leads to a reluctance to create majors that are too specialized.

Research

Research at NU is primarily conducted by doctoral students working toward their degrees. NU has almost no well-developed or organized research at the postdoctoral level. Only one school at NU has a research unit, a research laboratory, and a research program. Even at the individual level, research is almost nonexistent. The FSEA, an embryonic research entity, constitutes an exception in this respect. In fact, the FSEA research laboratories emerged thanks to collective projects undertaken in cooperation with multidisciplinary groups and various departments. Interuniversity agreements play an essential role in organizing research activity.

Even when motivation exists to conduct research in certain university departments, the lack of research facilities and resources, such as libraries and equipment, impedes researchers in all fields of expertise.

Student Services

NU's insufficient infrastructure is one of the major challenges that the university faces. The limited capacity for student housing seriously impacts the normal performance of the university.

NU's inadequate classroom facilities force classes to meet outside of the classroom. Students must study in severely overcrowded spaces. This situation is especially true for the FDSE and FLSH, where more than 80 percent of NU's students are registered. The FSEA, located in Farsha, enjoys more space because of the small numbers of students attending the school. The FSS, situated near the National Reference General Hospital in N'djamena (Hopital Général de Référence National de N'Djamena), also suffers from poor infrastructure. In fact, to realize the seriousness of this shortage, it is sufficient to note that NU was built in 1971 with the intention of hosting 600 students. In 1996, it had over 3,300 students but not a square meter had been added to the initial buildings, except for some small additions to the library, in the previous twenty-five years.

Other shortcomings are the absence of university cafeterias and the lack of public transportation for students coming from remote areas who are obliged to live far from N'djamena's city center. Hosting capacities for both students and teachers require emergency measures in this respect. The EFE strategy foresees a controlled increase of student numbers and the development of infrastructure to accommodate new students.

Scholarships are another source of problems. Sophomores and juniors are entitled to an unconditional grant. This right, which used to apply to all students, was eliminated for freshmen due to budgetary issues. Moreover, the Chadian government has a problem distributing grants on time. As a result, long strikes are conducted every year to protest this situation, thus impeding the normal operation of universities.

Library and Documentation Resources

The documentation system of the university consists of a central library and the school libraries that host the large collections of publications and periodicals. The central library hosts part of the documentation collection, namely research theses, memoirs, archives, cartography collections, and some periodicals. A small reference and reading room allows only limited access to these documents. Libraries located in schools constitute the essential part of the documentation system. The number of library seats is 70 at FDSE, 120 at FLSH, 70 at FSEA, and 30 at FSS. Moreover, the quantity of available volumes is not sufficient for the number of students, especially in terms of basic manuals. To avoid long waiting periods for books, students prefer to become members of private libraries.

University authorities have acknowledged that NU's libraries are not equipped for research activity and that specialized references are scarce and outdated. Many libraries were destroyed during the early 1980s in Chad, a time when universities were forced to close for long periods. Each library has an annual budget to renew their collections, which is run by the dean.

SCHOOL OF LAW AND ECONOMICS (FDSE)

The FDSE is the second-largest school at NU in terms of student enrollment and the last in terms of the total number of faculty members and permanent professors. The FDSE is divided into two departments: law and economics. It provides the best example of the hardships facing research professors in Chad today.

The increase in student enrollment at FDSE has been significant over the last two years, rising 29 percent, compared to an increase of 22.5 percent for the entire university. FDSE had the highest rate of student expansion. In the law department, the increase in student numbers was lower than in the economics department (19 percent, compared to 45 percent). This is contrary to the objectives set by the EFE, which called for a relative reduction in the number of students in FDSE.

The faculty at the FDSE are lacking in both numbers and training, despite some noticeable improvements. Because of the small number of doctors and the number of hours needed for student instruction, many fundamental courses are entrusted to part-timers.

The introduction of new subjects to FDSE is important. Until the last few years, the Chadian civil service authority recruited large numbers of FDSE graduates while ignoring the productive sector likely to benefit the country's development. This situation accounts for the generalist nature of degrees awarded, which undermines the importance of the disciplines such as private law (particularly business law and certain legal specialties and management disciplines), and the mismatch between degrees students earn and the specific skills needed by employers.

The absence of organized research in FDSE is another problem that needs to be addressed. Research in FDSE is carried out individually for degree purposes and is not published. Documentation resources are strikingly lacking and with the exception of the Consulting and Studies Office (Bureau d'Etudes et de Conseil), which launched some applied research projects over the last few years, there seems to be no real will to develop research activity.

THE SCHOOL OF LETTERS AND HUMAN SCIENCES (FLSH)

FLSH has the highest number of students and professors. The school is composed of eight departments: English, Arabic, Arab history, linguistics, history, geography, modern letters, and philosophy. Some of these departments already have or are in the process of creating professional majors.

The increase in student enrollment in FLSH over the last two years has lagged behind that at FDSE. FLSH has a wide pool of prospective candidates because the majority of high school graduates major in arts. This situation does not prevent the high rate of student failure in all departments, especially in the first year, with the exception of the Arabic department.

FLSH has launched new bachelor's degree programs in modern arts and geography with the goal of training future university professors. These programs, which are jointly conducted with NU, the University of Orleans, and the University of Avignon, also contribute to the training of students who plan to continue their graduate studies abroad. The modern letters degree, created in 1993–1994, trains students in French literature.

There are at least three bachelor's programs at FLSH: the Arabic language and literature major, ancient history, and applied linguistics. FLSH also offers a professional major that prepares students for jobs in information technology and communication. The major was launched in 1995–1996 and takes two years to complete.

Most FLSH departments lack clearly defined research policies. The research situation, however, is no better in FLSH than in FDSE, except in the linguistics department. Research in the other departments of FLSH is individual and degree oriented. Publications are very scarce.

THE SCHOOL OF EXACT AND APPLIED SCIENCES (FSEA)

The School of Sciences (FSEA) has fewer students than FLSH and FDSE but a larger faculty. The school is divided into six departments: biology, chemistry, technology, geology, mathematics, and physics. The FSEA started professional majors earlier than other schools after establishing its technology department.

FSEA is better organized than the rest of the university departments and is the only one committed to organized research. FSEA is also unique in favoring multidisciplinary subjects involving collaboration with other departments, an attitude that fosters institutional synergy.

The pattern of student enrollment at FSEA reflects its strict admission policy. Enrollment grew from 433 students in 1994–1995 to 483 in 1995–1996 then fell to 435 in 1996–1997. Despite recruitment through sponsorships and external interventions (which support nearly one out of every six first-year students), FSEA chose to control admission, hoping to improve the overall quality of the education it offered.

The faculty at FSEA is large compared to the number of students enrolled. Of the fifty-eight professors, twenty-four are associates, a sign of the higher qualification level of FSEA faculty compared to that of instructors in other schools.

All project engineers who have graduated with a FSEA degree since 1988 have been employed, either in teaching or maintenance positions. The prospecting for oil in Chad in the coming years is expected to encourage a major diversification in FSEA's employment profile.

Certain recent developments in research at FSEA have boosted its reputation within NU. The school has begun to organize research in laboratories on issues that are pertinent to Chadian national development. Such an initiative can only be beneficial to the university. Such research may gain credibility at the international level and would allow the university to establish relationships with other peer universities and private or public financial institutions. In this way, professors can also earn promotions and acquire international recognition.

SCHOOL OF HEALTH SCIENCES

The School of Health Sciences (FSS) was the last school to be created in NU. The school was established in 1990–1991, and its first doctoral students graduated in 1999. FSS was designed to provide Chad with qualified physicians, based on the awareness that most Chadian physicians graduating from foreign universities did not return to their homeland.

Access to the medical school has been very selective. The

entrance test for FSS previously took place every two years because of the school's low hosting capacity. This problem has been temporarily overcome, thanks to emergency measures allowing the school to switch to an annual entrance test in 1995–1996.

Selectivity at FSS is high, with as many as 557 candidates competing for about thirty seats in the first year. The number of seats open for competition is determined by FSS authorities in coordination with the planning unit at the Health Ministry, and is determined by the hosting capacities of the institution and the financial resources available for scholarships. All students are granted scholarships from the Chadian government in exchange for a ten-year commitment to serve in Chad's public health service.

FSS trains general practitioners who, in addition to their general medical training, acquire specific skills in surgery, gynecology, and obstetrics. NU has no medium- or long-term plan to establish new medical disciplines at the university. The FSS faculty is composed of about twenty permanent professors and forty part-time faculty.

The need for materials and equipment has been one of the major problems encountered by FSS since its creation. FSS does not meet the standards of actual medical schools in terms of facilities, equipment, or documentation.

On the bright side, FSS activities have not gone unnoticed by various international institutions. Organizations that have offered support to FSS include the World Health Organization (WHO), the European Union, the Association of Francophone Universities (Association des Universités Francophones), the Tropical Institute of Switzerland, and Doctors Without Borders, all of which are making efforts to help FSS meet its training objectives and improve its conditions. The most important technical support comes from the WHO, which is funding a position of study coordinator at FSS and training sessions for professors, opportunities to specialize abroad, and opportunities to participate in the accreditation exam organized by the accrediting body CAMES (Conseil Africain et Malgache pour l'Enseignement Supérieur).

THE NATIONAL INSTITUTE OF HUMAN SCIENCES

The Institute of Human Sciences (INSH) is the only institution that is totally devoted to research while being an integral part of NU. The INSH was created in 1961, reorganized in 1974, and annexed to the university in 1989. It has experienced serious operating difficulties in recent years.

The institute has ambitious plans, which include undertaking and coordinating research in the humanities that will promote Chad's economic, social, and cultural development; ensuring the evaluation of studies; initiating new studies; encouraging publishing; contributing to the training of specialized researchers in the field of social sciences; ensuring the inventory and classification of historical sites and monuments that have an archeological, artistic, or aesthetic value; and setting up guidelines for searches in coordination with concerned services.

The activity of the institute is mainly concerned with leading and realizing research projects, disseminating research results, and training researchers through internships, seminars, and conferences. The institute also has defined priority domains, namely education and training, health (human and animal), agriculture, and the environment. Judging by the number of its publications, INSH seems to have been more active in previous years than it is at present. In 2001 there was no evidence of the activities that are necessary to meet the requirements stipulated in its mission. In fact, INSH has been investigating new ways to revive its activity.

INSH is comprised of ten researchers who also hold teaching positions. However, despite efforts to define a common strategy, the institute remains mainly a center of individualized research projects rather than a research unit capable of structuring projects around major research themes. There is certainly a will to constitute research units and elaborate annual programs, but because of lack of funding, these efforts never reach the implementation stage. More serious problems stem from the fact that research projects are not coordinated within INSH. The various university schools also seem to ignore the institute. As long as NU is not adopting a collective view of the future of research in humanities and of the structures that need to be created, the fate of the institute seems uncertain.

THE ADVANCED INSTITUTE OF EDUCATIONAL HUMAN SCIENCES (ISSED)

The Advanced Institute of Educational Human Sciences (ISSED) is a public institution of higher education and research. It was established in 1989 to train high school teachers and was modeled after the National Institute for the Sciences of Education (INSE), which trains elementary education teachers. The mission of the institute also includes research in education and the elaboration of school curricula.

ISSED is an autonomous institution led by a panel chaired by a director. It has three departments: elementary, secondary, and educational research. The activity of ISSED is carried out by fifty instructors who hold advanced degrees and are trained researchers.

NATIONAL CENTER FOR THE SUPPORT OF RESEARCH (CNAR)

The National Center for the Support of Research (Centre National d'Appui à la Recherche, CNAR) is a public institution that reports to the minister in charge of higher education and scientific research. CNAR has a simple administrative structure that consists of eight full-time members.

CNAR was conceived in an original and unique manner. Its role is limited but essential. Indeed, CNAR supports research but does not initiate or elaborate any research enterprises. The center supports new research initiatives but has no researchers connected to it in any statutory way. CNAR is supposed to provide efficient support for researchers through funds tied to certain scientific projects. The center has been able to benefit from equipment that is not available to higher education institutions, including NU itself.

The mission of CNAR is to centralize, implement, and disseminate technical and scientific documentation on Chad that originates from national or foreign sources. It also designs computerized systems that allow the management of data and newly acquired books. CNAR has revitalized the technical and scientific atmosphere in order to enhance relationships between research, development, and training and the economic sphere.

CNAR supports research through the organization of seminars, colloquia, and roundtables. It also provides a structure designed to facilitate exchange between national and international researchers by implementing joint research projects and supporting specializations that are needed for the execution of current research programs. Finally, CNAR is developing a station to process satellite imaging pertinent to Chad.

CNAR has an important and diverse documentation collection that includes reference works, periodicals, reports, studies, microfiches, satellite images, CD-ROM documents, films, and maps. This collection, which is considered unique in Chad, constitutes a good information database for the research fields supported at the center. The center hosts twenty databases, including the database of the French CNRS (Centre National de la Recherche Scientifique). Considered to be a legal depository of national, scientific, and technical research findings, CNAR has supplied information on Chad to both the UN's Food and Agricultural Organization and the CIRAD (Centre de coopération internationale en recherche agronomique pour le développement).

In addition to the conference series organized by CNAR, the institute issues a number of publications, including *La Lettre de la Recherche et du Développement,* which is a liaison bulletin; the *Revue Scientifique du Chad,* which publishes scientific articles; and the *Travaux et Document Scientifique du Chad,* also a scientific publication. The *Revue Scientifique du Chad,* in particular, is likely to become a scientific journal of high caliber that will encourage Chadian researchers to publish their work.

INSTITUTIONS EXTERNAL TO THE MINISTRY OF HIGHER EDUCATION

In addition to institutions that operate under the responsibility of the MESRS, a number of other institutions of higher education that are devoted either to teaching or basic research fall under the responsibility of other ministries. Although these institutions vary in nature, they share the common characteristic of specialization within their domains.

NATIONAL SCHOOL OF ADMINISTRATION AND MAGISTRACY (ENAM)

The National School of Administration and Magistracy (Ecole Nationale d'Administration et de Magistrature, ENAM) reports to the government's general secretary. The school was created in 1963 to train administrative officials for the newly independent Chadian state. ENAM offers both initial and continuing education. The stagnation of recruitment in the public sector since 1992 has significantly impacted its graduates. The school has been operating at a slower pace than usual for a few years, focusing its activity mainly on continuing education.

The school's curriculum consists of three units. The first recruits high school graduates, the second recruits holders of a DEUG (General University Studies Degree), and the third recruits holders of a bachelor's degree. The period of study is two years, starting from the year of entry to ENAM. Since 1986, ENAM has produced 600 civil servants in all cycles and all specialties.

The flow of students, however, is very limited. ENAM presently has fifty to sixty interns undergoing training programs designed to meet immediate needs in the absence of a consistent educational policy for civil service in Chad. The teaching staff of ENAM is extremely reduced; it consists of two full professors and sixty part-time faculty who are either working as permanent civil servants, teaching on a regular basis at NU, or holding positions in the judiciary.

NATIONAL SCHOOL OF PUBLIC WORKS (ENTP)

The National School of Public Works (Ecole Nationale des Travaux Publiques, ENTP), created in 1966, is a public institution annexed to the Ministry of Public Works, Habitat and Transportation. ENTP has a regional vocation; it hosts students mainly from other Francophone African countries, such as Central Africa, Niger, and Gabon. Up to 1992, Chadian ENTP graduates were able to find work in the public service successfully. However, since 1992, ENTP has oriented itself to the private sector. The creation of the Office of Public Works, in spite of some difficulties, is undoubtedly a positive development.

Training at ENTP takes place in two cycles. The first cycle leads to a technical assistant certificate, the second to a technical engineering degree. To qualify for these degree programs, Chadian students must pass an entrance test and foreign candidates must be approved in a selection process. Both degrees require three years of study.

In 1999, twenty-five seats for the engineering program were offered to a pool of 800 candidates. The technical assistance program also has high criteria for selection; in 1999, it had thirty-six seats for 900 candidates. The stagnation of recruitment in the public service forced ENTP to change its training orientation toward the private sector and switch from an annual admission policy to a three-year policy. Cohorts are meant to follow one another without overlapping due to the limited number of seats.

ENTP did not facilitate research until the FSEA and the Research Laboratory on Renewable Energies and Local Materials were created, thus opening new possibilities for partnerships. The faculty at ENTP is composed of fifteen permanent and forty part-time professors and engineers and civil servants from the public works ministry.

Despite this promising progress, ENTP faces a number of obstacles. The first handicap is related to the regional vocation of the institute. In 1986, Gabon stopped sending its students to ENTP, while other countries, such as Central Africa and Niger, still send their students to ENTP but have not contributed financially to their education for several years. Despite the repeated promises of these countries to cover the payment deficit, Chad has been forced to finance these students from its own funds. The institute reflects the general lack of local expertise in certain areas, a problem that is exacerbated by the absence of adequate equipment for students to conduct practical projects.

PRIVATE HIGHER EDUCATION INSTITUTIONS

Private higher education in Chad currently involves two institutions with different vocations, the Advanced Management Institute (Institut Supérieur de Gestion, ISG) and King Faiçal University (Université Roi Faiçal, URF).

ISG was established in 1989. Unique in its genre, the institute has no competition from other institutions. Its programs oriented toward management and services are very diversified, ranging from CAP or BEP (Certificat d'Aptitude Profesionnelle, CAP, or Brevet des Etudes Professionnelles, BEP), which are equivalent to a high school diploma, to the vocational training certificate (Brevet de Technicien Supérieur, BTS). The institute offers majors in accounting, secretarial work, and commerce.

The institute also offers training modules that allow candidates without a high school degree to obtain their BEP. Short training courses in computers and advanced management modeled on the Western master's degree in business administration are offered to professionals who already have a higher education degree. The institute provides customized training in management and computer information systems. Internships are compulsory for students.

The institute has 400 students and interns throughout its various programs. Its faculty includes five permanent and thirty part-time professors. Most faculty members are also university professors at other institutions. The professional integration of graduates is generally successful since the acquired skills and training are adapted to the needs of the job market. Jobs offered for BTS holders mostly lead to midlevel career positions. This constitutes one of the strong points of the institute within the whole educational system. The utility of its graduates is demonstrated by the positive reactions of the job market. In terms of continuing education, the activities of the institute are also successful because the institute benefits from various contracts with the government, the N'djamena City Hall, and various businesses.

King Faiçal University (URF) admitted its first cohort in 1991–1992. The institution has acquired nonprofit status, making it eligible for state subsidies. The main objective of the university is to train Arabic-speaking professors to teach at Arabic-language schools in Chad. Another one of its objectives is to train senior administrators. URF is a member of the Islamic Universities Organization in Egypt and has many agreements with Arab universities in Egypt, Sudan, Libya, Algeria, and Saudi Arabia. URF is composed of two schools: the Arabic Language School (Faculté de Langue Arabe) and the School of Education (Faculté de Sciences de l'Education).

In 1996–1997, URF had 359 students. One hundred seven were registered at The Arabic Language School, 218 were enrolled in the School of Education, and another 34 were enrolled in the graduate Advanced Studies Program (Diplôme d'Etudes Approfondies, DEA). To be admitted, students need to have a Chadian high school diploma or its equivalent. It is noteworthy that ten percent of the students are internationals, representing about nine African neighboring countries—Cameron, Libya, Niger, and Sudan—and even remote ones such as Burkina Faso, Djibouti, Gambia, Ivory Coast, and Mali.

Faculty at URF includes twenty-three professors of diverse nationalities who hold Ph.D.s from various universities. URF is hoping to launch new specialties, especially in medicine, science and technology, agronomy, and Islamic Law (Shari'a). It is also hoped that MESRS will consider these requests and objectively evaluate their impact.

HIGHER EDUCATION IN CHAD: PERSPECTIVES

Higher education and research have suffered significantly from their neglect by the Chadian government. Despite some small success in certain units and research institutions at NU, the day-to-day management of these institutions is becoming increasingly difficult. The lack of financial means limits the activities of most research institutions. The positive evolution of the entire system will be impossible unless the government becomes an integral partner in the system through sponsorship and assistance.

New Policy for Higher Education

The creation of a ministry devoted exclusively to higher education and scientific research demonstrates the commitment of the Chadian government to research. The ministry has not been able, however, to give a real impetus to the sector or solve the essential problems that affect various structures of higher education and research. The ministry has been able, though, to establish two university institutes with a technological vocation. Again, due to lack of sufficient funds and human resources, the ministry's capacity to maneuver and manage university research remains inefficient.

One of the dimensions of managing the sector consists in laying out perspectives for the future of higher education and research. A policy designed to motivate institutions to focus on the establishment of national objectives is a real necessity. This will entail elaborating goals and principles that correspond to the main objectives of Chad's higher education research activities. Presently, however, Chad's research program has no precise deadlines. The country lacks a general strategy and a concrete approach for realizing its research objectives. Chad needs to implement the EFE strategy to ensure that there is a close relationship between education and the job market and to adapt higher education to the needs of the Chadian economy.

Higher Education and Research: Adapting to Economic and Social Change

Education is an essential ingredient for any national development program. The training of senior technical and administrative managers is of paramount importance, more so than at any other moment in Chad's history as a developing country. Sustainable human development cannot be envisioned without competent actors equipped with necessary know-how. The emergence of new technologies, formulas, and strategies to organize labor and production, worldwide exchange of various sorts, and the development of networks of interaction between social and economic actors all necessitate the mastery of technical knowledge as a way to bridge the gap between developed and developing countries.

Chad's seclusion needs to be overcome gradually. Highly qualified graduates capable of integrating African and international information and communication networks have an important role to play. Many African countries are already confronting this challenge. Chad has no choice but to break out of its seclusion. The quality of its graduates and their ability to adapt to complex organizations and advanced technologies are major assets. The university has to be a place for the creation and diffusion of the spirit of enterprise. It should also create motivation through its various units by offering informed expertise. To meet the economic and social needs of its partners, the university should forge new partnerships and tap new resources to supplement state subsidies.

Generally, Chad needs highly trained individuals whose competence corresponds to the prerogatives of development, as well as available jobs, especially in the private sector, keeping in mind the relative stagnation of recruitment in the public civil service. This situation requires a new orientation of certain disciplines in higher education. It also requires the participation of research professors in projects that are directly applicable to the country's development. Finally, it is in the interest of Chad that sufficient proportions of youth have access to higher education and to knowledge. Personal development is a right that should be based solely on the merit and aptitude of each student (Bendima, Yaya, Kimto, and Pierre 1996).

Higher education and research are strategic tools with which Chad can face the challenges of the twenty-first century. Intelligence is becoming the major capital of nations, a situation that brings higher education and research to the forefront as a priority and requires that the means for their establishment and development become available. However, this also implies that the university must be totally integrated in society and in the system of production, without any restraints. This fact means that higher education should be aware of its role as a vector for social, economic, and personal change and mobility and that its management should adapt to its new responsibilities.

Quality Issues

Higher education in Chad today is confronted by problems of mass education, yet it lacks the human and material resources needed to carry out that mission. One of the main orientations over the coming years should be toward loosening the constraints that impede educational development. This does not mean simply increasing educational capacity; it also means ensuring quality in all aspects of education. The development of higher education should emphasize improved orientation of students, stricter regulation of the academic experience, ongoing reinforcement of the training of research professors, and the design of an objective and equitable system for providing access to higher education for women. Other practices should include revamping educational programs through systematic follow-up and evaluation; creating schools with professional majors (Merlin 1998, 2000) that can lead to jobs in the private sector; introducing lifelong learning in higher education

through the diversification of access and the encouragement of nontraditional students; improving libraries, databases, and information technologies; and expanding and rehabilitating university infrastructures. Other priorities are decentralizing NU through the creation of university structures in major cities, using resources more intelligently by establishing a new policy for distributing scholarships, improving student life on campuses, professionalizing the management of higher education institutions (including the various ministries and institutes), and strengthening regional and international university cooperation.

The search for quality in higher education and research should become an imperative for national policy as well. Professionalism should be reinforced at all levels of Chadian education and administration.

The modernization of the faculty constitutes another major challenge. NU used to train graduates destined mainly for the civil service, but higher education now needs to focus on the training of graduates for jobs that are more likely to be in the private sector. The public sector and the private sector require workers with different sets of skills and knowledge bases. This does not mean that the university should abandon classical disciplines. The training of civil servants, including secondary school teachers and educational administrators, remains a necessity, particularly since the need for such individuals is increasing.

Creation of Professional Majors Oriented toward the Private Sector

The Chadian economy has been oriented toward the private sector in recent years. Public companies have been privatized and foreign businesses have moved into the country. New jobs, especially in the service sector, have been introduced. University curricula that have been oriented toward public administration and public companies should adjust for these economic changes and initiate new professional majors to train professionals in the private sector, NGOs and nongovernmental professions, and encourage self-employment. NU has already begun such initiatives by launching five advanced professional majors in three of its schools. Two university institutions for technical sciences with an orientation toward technological and scientific study that corresponds to the economic activities of their regions have been created. This orientation, which conforms to the EFE strategy, should be strengthened. Chadian higher education should envision the creation of professional university majors at all schools so that after basic training, higher education graduates can find positions in the business world.

The duration of training in these professional majors may vary according to the professional field and the qualifications sought. From general training, it is possible to move into a specialty which can be initiated at the beginning of the university experience, at the second or third year, and in some cases, even at the senior year. The initial training should never be isolated; it should always be supplemented with a broader and ongoing course of study.

Applied research is also an important aspect of education. Contact with businesses would help higher education professionals appreciate concrete difficulties encountered in the field and would contribute to dialogue on the dissemination of new technologies and processes.

CONCLUSION: WHAT WILL THE FUTURE HOLD?

Even though Chad is poor, the discovery and potential exploitation of oil reserves in the southern part of the country are expected to yield important development benefits. Chad's growth in the next few years remains closely related to the development of the rural zone. Industry and services will benefit from the proceeds of oil exploitation but are still not sufficiently diversified. In this respect, potential sponsors have expressed their willingness to invest in meeting the financial needs of the country.

Chad needs more than generous natural resources and subsidies from development partners, however. Since its independence, Chad has experienced a long period of political unrest, marked by violence and civil war, which has led to mistrust among its partners and foreign investors alike.

Over the last decade, Chad has been able to renew the development process. Chad's political stability, nascent democratization, improvement of public finances, and fostering of a free economy in which the private sector is considered a primary contributor to development all have provided a promising atmosphere for national development.

Education has an essential role to play in Chad's development process. Through education, Chadians have the opportunity to participate in the country's economic, social, and cultural development. Education has diverse objectives, but one of its primary goals is to train young graduates who can assume positions in the private sector and in administration. Another is to help graduates take initiative and create their own businesses.

The system of higher education and scientific research in Chad lacks an efficient infrastructure and clear objectives. Its existence depends on its public and private educational institutions, which generally remain unstable. Without dynamic and permanent research, higher education will simply be an extension of the secondary school system. Research must become a major dimension of the higher education system. Research should be oriented toward Chad's social and economic development, not based on individual interest, and the National Committee of Scientific and Technical Research (CNRST) should be involved in selecting and balancing research activities.

Achieving these goals will require the development of a national research policy to define the objectives of university and nonuniversity research; the creation of specific funds for the development of research; the development of research policies and specialized units devoted to these activities; the creation of mechanisms to motivate researchers; the organization of research around centers and teams; the initiation of research projects at the regional, national, and international levels; and the publication of research in accordance with international standards.

Research teams should be established at universities and compete for international research grants, and researchers should be encouraged to resume postdoctoral research activity with a decent reward system. The concerned ministries, in turn, should support and lobby for research projects that they deem to be important.

Selectivity and controlled admission of high school graduates, particularly at NU, is needed to establish an equilibrium between various institutions' hosting capacities and the requirements of Chad's job market. Decisions about how to achieve this balance should be the prerogative of universities without any external interference. Admission to schools of law, economics, literary, and human sciences should also be stabilized. More students, however, should be oriented toward scientific and technical majors. In general, Chadian higher education needs to encourage better planning of majors according to national needs (training managers instead of economists, training jurists in private law rather than public law, and training translators, interpreters, and tourism workers).

Infrastructure is another important element NU must address. At all institutional levels—the library, amphitheaters, laboratories, reading spaces, equipment, language laboratories, and didactic manuals and references—the university is lacking. Another problem is the need for an informed and efficient use of NU facilities that are not used for teaching or research. In this respect, new university institutions should be established in Sarh and Abeche, as well as in N'djamena, to alleviate overconcentrations of students at certain institutions. Scholarships should be awarded according to objective and fair criteria, and grants for study abroad should be limited to academic specialties that are not offered in Chad.

Certain competencies now need to be acquired by all students, regardless of their professional goals. These competencies are varied but are all related to communication. University graduates should be computer literate and should have a good command of English, which is the universal medium for communication in the business world. All university majors should provide for these needs starting the second year.

Communication and information technologies have other important implications for higher education and research, including distance education, connection of universities to the Internet, access to a wide spectrum of databases, and the possibility of exchange with universities worldwide. These should be a priority in higher educational policy over the coming years.

MESRS should prioritize certain improvements, such as reinforcing management efficiency, recruiting qualified personnel and training the present ministry staff to carry out its missions, establishing an information system to allow the ministry to carry out statistical and qualitative analysis and to better coordinate its various ministerial units (Ministère de l'Education Nationale 2001), passing new regulations for the establishment and evaluation of private university institutions, and strengthening the management capacities of the higher education institutions, particularly with regard to administrative and financial management.

BIBLIOGRAPHY

Bendima, S. A., M. Yaya, F. Kimto, and G. Pierre. 1996. *Diagnostic de l'enseignement supérieur et de la recherche scientifique et technique.* N'Djamena: Ministère de l'Education Nationale.

Merlin, C. 1998. "L'Enseignement Supérieur et la Recherche Scientifique. Diagnostic et Perspectives." Unpublished report. Secrétariat Exécutif du CONEFE (Comité National EFE).

———. 2000. *La professionnalisation des filières d'Enseignement dans* l'*Enseignement Supérieur (Rapport de mission)*. N'Djamena: Ministère de l'Enseignement Supérieur.

Ministère de l'Education Nationale. 1994a. *Actes des Etats Généraux de l'Education National: Rapport Général des Travaux*. N'Djamena: Cooperation Française et Ministère de l'Education Nationale.

——. 1994b. *Documents de la Stratégie EFE. Sous-programme Enseignement Supérieur*. N'Djamena: MEN.

——. 2001. "Données Statistiques sur l'éducation: 1999/2000." Report realized with help from UNDP, UNESCO, EFE. Housed at the MEN: Direction des Statistiques Scolaires. N'Djamena: MEN.

Ministère du Plan et de l'Aménagement du Térritoire. 1998. "Reformu-lation du Programme National EFE: Sous-programme." Unpublished ministry document. N'Djamena

Téguidé, S. D., R. Toraira, and B. N. Roné. 1998. "Proposition de stratégie pour l'éducation de base, secondaire et supérieur d'ici l'an 2015." N'Djamena: MEN (Direction des Projets Education).

UNESCO. 1998. "Vers un agenda 21 pour l'enseignement supérieur (Conférence mondiale sur l'enseignement supérieur: l'enseignement supérieur au XXI siècle, vision et action. Paris, 5–9 October 1998)." UNESCO working document: ED-98/CONF.202/CLD.19.

24

Comoros, Reunion, and Seychelles
Indian Ocean Islands

HASSAN EZ-ZAÏM

COMOROS

The Comoro Islands are located in the Mozambique Channel between northern Mozambique and Madagascar. The Federal Islamic Republic of Comoros gained independence from France in 1975. Two years later, two islands, Anjouan and Moheli, broke from the new republic, declaring their independence. Comoro Islands are stretched over an area of 2,170 square kilometers (838 square miles). The total population is estimated at 706,300 according to the 1999 census estimates (Maher 2001).

Postsecondary education in Comoros is public and limited to a number of programs in teacher training, agriculture, and health sciences and a business school, with an overall capacity of 200 students. According to a 1997 World Bank report, more than 1,000 students were estimated in 1995 to go overseas for university studies. Considering the stringent economic situation of the country, the government decided to provide scholarships solely from donors' funds (World Bank 1997). Over a period of fifteen years, a few institutions have been created, mainly in the areas of fishery, agriculture, trade, and health care. Vocational training is provided in six public institutions with a total capacity of 1,000 students (1997 estimates). Three of these schools, whose graduates have been employed in governmental agencies, have been closed down.

Postsecondary education is offered at the Official School (l'Ecole Officielle), which is based on the French education model. The Official School combines the pre-elementary, elementary, secondary, and higher levels of education. Up until the late 1980s, education was entirely public, and private schools emerged only recently. The languages of instruction in Comoros are French and Arabic. Table 24.1 shows the number of schools, teachers, and students in Comoros in 2000.

In an address at the 1998 world conference on higher education, the Comoros ministerial representative pointed out that the discrepancy between increasing numbers of high school graduates and the declining university infrastructure lead these graduates to leave the country, most of the time without the necessary resources to pursue their studies (UNESCO 1998).

Educational partners of Comoros include the World Bank, the United Nations Population Fund (Fonds des Nations Unies pour la Population, FNUAP), the UNDP, UNESCO, and UNICEF. Comoros also receives technical assistance from countries such as France and Belgium, as in the 1997 education reform project conducted with the World Bank.

One of the major problems that most African countries suffer is the high level of illiteracy, especially among females. It is difficult for higher education to develop and prosper in the absence of a viable primary and secondary educational system. This explains the high priority that most of these countries, Comoros among them, place on primary and secondary education. This priority can be seen at the level of reform programs as well as monetary resources devoted to both sectors. The case of illiteracy in Comoros poses a serious obstacle; more than one-third of school-age children have no access to six-year formal primary education, and only one in ten of those who make it continues to lower secondary education. Enrollment ratios at the primary, secondary, and postsecondary levels are estimated at 64 percent, 11 percent, and 2 percent, respectively. Attrition rates increase as the educational level increases; a cohort analysis reported by the World Bank shows that only 13 students persist to high school graduation out of 1,000 students entering Grade 1 (World Bank 1997).

Problems such as political reforms, economic adjustment programs, teacher strikes, lack of pedagogical tools, obsolete and insufficient infrastructure, all of which are coupled with poor management, add more obstacles to the development of the educational system.

REUNION

Brief Overview

Reunion is a 2,512-square-kilometer (970-square-mile) southern African island east of Madagascar. Reunion, or the Department of Reunion, is a French overseas department home to 732,570 inhabitants (July 2001 estimate). The population of Reunion is an ethnic mix of French, Africans, Chinese, Malays, and Malabar Indians. French is the official language and Creole is widely used.

Reunion, as is the case of other overseas departments, is a French territory governed by the same constitution and laws as France. Reunion, however, enjoys a status of relative organizational autonomy. Article 72 of the French constitution stipulates that "the territorial units of the Republic shall be the communes, the Departments, and the Overseas Territories. . . . These units shall be free to govern themselves through elected councils and under the conditions stipulated by the law." Although part of the African continent, Reunion has been insulated from the main regional geopolitical currents thanks to its status as an integral part of France (Legum 1992).

Higher Education in Reunion

Reunion has one medium-size university. In 1998–1999, the University of Reunion enrolled nearly 10,000 students in its two campuses at Saint-Denis and Saint-Pierre (Table 24.2). It has three schools (Law, Economics, and Political Science; Science and Technology; and Humanities) and five institutes: Technology Institute (Institut Universitaire de Téchnologie, IUT), Business Administration Institute (Institut d'Administration des Entreprises, IAE), Professional Institute of Food Industry (Institut Universitaire Professionnalisé Agroalimentaire, IUP), and the Teacher Training Institute. Moreover, the university hosts six services ranging from continuing education, documen-

Table 24.1. Number of Schools, Teachers, and Students in Comoros, 2000

Level	Schools	Teachers	Students
Pre-primary	—	600	17,778
Primary	327	1,508	78,527
Secondary			
General	—	591	21,192
Teacher Training	—	11	37
Vocational Training	—	31	126

Source: Maher 2001.

tation, job orientation, and career placement to health care and international relations.

The university has seen major developments since 1991 in terms of building expansion, student enrollments, creating teaching positions, and expanding degree options. The university offers thirty-one majors in the General University Studies Degree (*Diplôme D'enseignement Universitaire Général*, DEUG), twenty-one bachelor's degrees, and thirteen other graduate degrees. Other graduate degrees, especially at the master's level, are shared between Reunion University and the metropolitan universities of Marseille I, Marseille II, Avignon, and Toulon.

A financial aid system is available to students through state scholarships, departmental grants, and grants from regional councils; the latter are offered mainly to doctoral students. By virtue of the constitutional status of Reunion as part of France, Reunionese students have the possibility of applying to French schools and universities.

University Governance

The University of Reunion is a public institution as stipulated in the 1984 law. It has a president and four vice-presidents:

Table 24.2. Student Enrollment at the University of Reunion, 1989–1999

Program	Law, Economics, and Political Science	Science and Technology	School of Humanities
Basic Legal Qualification Degree			
(Capacité en Droit)	92	—	—
Undergraduate	2,375	2,182	3,771
Graduate	157	78	176
Total	2,624	2,260	3,947
Continuing Education			
Permanent Education Service	764		
Business Administration Institute	249		
Total	1,013		
Grand Total	9,844		

Source: Université de la Réunion.

the administrative council vice-president, the scientific council vice-president, the studies and university life vice-president, and the international relations vice-president. The management of the university is shared between the three university councils: the Council of Studies and University Life, the Administrative Council, and the Scientific Council. Administration, faculty, and students are proportionally represented in the governance of the institution. Members of the three aforementioned councils are elected according to a stipulated decree from 1985. Representatives of the personnel and faculty are elected for a four-year term while students and outside members of the university community are elected for a two-year term.

The Administrative Council is responsible for defining the pedagogical, scientific, administrative, and financial policies of the university. The Scientific Council is entrusted with making recommendations to the Administrative Council on issues related to research, technical and scientific documentation, and graduate curricula. Curriculum and student affairs are delegated to the Council for Studies and University Affairs.

Research and Partnerships

A total of 180 professors among the faculty of Reunion University are involved in research throughout the three schools. Research is geared toward reinforcing an international position within the Indian Ocean region and contributing to regional development. More specifically, research at the university revolves around four objectives: follow-up and development of training programs for researchers, the internationalization of research through cooperation with neighboring countries, the valorization of research activity, and, finally, the initiation of joint research projects.

The University of Reunion maintains various partnerships with organizations and research centers. The plethora of institutions with ties to the University of Reunion speaks of significant available collaboration venues. Among the local partners there is the University Institute for Teacher Training (Institut Universitaire de la Formation des Maîtres, IUFM), the Development Research Institute (Institut de Recherche pour le Développement, IRD), the International Center for Cooperation in Agronomy Development Research (Centre de Coopération Internationale en Recherche Agronomique pour le Développement, CIRAD), the French Research Institute for Marine Exploitation (Institut Français de Recherche pour l'Exploitation de la Mer, IFREMER), the France Weather Forecast Agency (Météo-France), the Research Office for Geology and Mining (Bureau de Recherches Géologiques et Minières, BRGM), the Institute for Earth Physics (Institut de Physique de Globe, IPG Paris), the National Institute for Health and Medical Research (Institut National de la Santé et de Recherche Médicale, INSERM), the Technical Center for Sugar Production (Centre Technique de la Canne et du Sucre), the National Institute for Statistics and Survey (Institut National de la Statistique et des Études, INSEE), the France Electricity Company (Electricité de France, EDF), France Overseas Radio/Television (Radio/Télévision France Outre-mer, RFO), and the Reunionese Water Observatory (l'Observatoire Réunionnais de l'Eau).

Moreover, the University of Reunion cultivates relation-

Table 24.3. Number of Schools, Teachers, and Students in Seychelles, 1996

Level	Schools	Teachers	Students
Pre-primary	35	180	3,262
Primary	21	577	9,886
Secondary			
General	NA	598	8,151
Teacher Training	NA	27	237
Vocational Training	NA	64	711

Source: Maher 2001.

ships with a number of industries in the field of nutrition and in the food industry. With a rich and varied network of partnerships, the University of Reunion devotes considerable efforts to the internationalization of research. The Scientific Council has determined five areas of research in this respect: multiculturalism, volcanoes and the climate, preservation of floral resources, literature and anthropology, and marine resources.

SEYCHELLES

Seychelles, an Indian Ocean archipelago, became a republic in 1976 after 162 years under British rule and some years under French rule prior to that. Seychelles covers an area of 455 square kilometers (175.8 square miles) and hosts a population estimated at 80,000 in 1999 (Europa 2001). While Creole is widely used, the official languages are French and English.

Seychelles does not have a higher education system. Seychelles Polytechnic, however, is a postsecondary institution which is largely funded by the Chinese government (Ministry of Education 1999). The Polytechnic offers three postsecondary programs: building construction studies, teacher education and community studies, and health care (Table 24.3).

In general, education in Seychelles is public; however, since 1994, two for-profit private institutions, the Seychelles College and Regina Mundi, were opened. The latter, opened initially as the Princess Elizabeth Nursing School, grants degrees in three areas of specialty: nursing (three years), dental therapy (three years), and dental technician (two years). Students wishing to pursue further studies have to leave for universities abroad.

Distance-education alternatives have been closely examined by the Seychelles government. A 1998 report prepared by foreign educational consultants might culminate in creating a distance-education unit (Murphy and Walker 1998). The Seychelles Polytechnic enrolls about 1,600 full-time students and 1,200 part-timers. Students who wish to pursue their studies travel mainly to the United Kingdom.

The government expenditure on education was estimated at US$29.3 million in 1998 (Maher 2001). Student per capita cost in public schools increased between 1992 and 1997 from US$832 to US$908. Seychelles, partners in education are UNICEF, UNESCO, the African Development Bank, the Nigerian Trust Fund, WFD Consulting Inc., USAID, and the governments of

France, Britain, and China. Other countries, such as Australia, India, and Cuba, offer university scholarships to the most meritorious students graduating from the Polytechnic.

Most changes and developments in the Seychelles educational system occurred through reform programs in 1978 and 1980 that were inspired by the British comprehensive school system.

The language of instruction in Seychelles begins as Creole in the first and second grades before French and English are introduced (Trayte 1999). The language of instruction has seen changes over time as rule by France and Britain changed hands. The British introduced English into the curriculum in 1880, and since then English and French have been the only two "official" languages of the country. As for Creole, it is still considered the language mostly used outside the classroom. In this respect, Seychelles endures the same problems as many African higher education systems in struggling between the inherited colonial languages and the mother tongue.

British lack of interest in the Seychelles over the 160 years of colonial rule is evidenced by the fact that no schools were run in an official and systematic way until 1947 (Franda 1982).

CONCLUSION

Higher education in the Indian Ocean Islands is in its infancy. Postsecondary institutions in these countries face a number of common and special challenges. As is the case with other African countries, they had to supply the necessary trained civil servants and fill government positions, meet the demands for advanced education in the context of an increasing student population, and deal with the lack of a critical mass of high school graduates to expand and develop the system. Yet on the whole, these institutions have been able to cope with these problems in the context of various social, political, and financial constraints and make the best of the available resources.

Because of the size of the countries and their small population, partnerships with foreign institutions and other cooperative initiatives remain crucial ways to confront the challenges of the present and the future.

BIBLIOGRAPHY

Constitution de la république française [Article 74]. http://www.conseil-constitutionnel.fr/textes/c1958web.htm.

Franda, M. 1982. *The Seychelles: Unquiet Islands.* Boulder, Colo.: Westview Press.

Legum, C., ed. 1992. *Africa Contemporary Record: Annual Survey Documents.* Vol. 23. New York: Africana Publishing Company.

Maher, J., ed. 2001. *The Europa World Year Book 2001.* London: Europa Publications.

Ministry of Education. 1999. "The Major Development of Education in Seychelles [1977 to 1998]: ADEA Prospective Stock-Taking Review." Paris: Association for the Development of Education in Africa.

Murphy, D., and R. Walker. 1998. "Distance Education in the Seychelles: Future Directions." The Commonwealth of Learning—Consultancy Report, Seychelles 1998. Available online at: http://www.col.org/Consultancies/98Seychelles.htm.

Trayte, S. K. 1999. *Seychelles: Country Guide Series Report.* Washington, D.C.: American Association of Collegiate Registrars and Admissions Officers.

UNESCO. 1998. *Conference mondiale sur l'enseignement supérieur: l'enseignement supérieur au XXI siècle—Visions et actions.* Vol. V: *Plénière.* Paris: UNESCO.

Université de la Réunion. "L'Université française de l'Océan Indien." Available online at: http://www.univ-reunion.fr/t1_presentation_universite/t1_avantpropos.html

World Bank. 1997. *Comoros: Third Education Project.* Report # PIC5055. Washington, D.C.: The World Bank.

25

Congo (Brazzaville)

GASPARD MBEMBA

INTRODUCTION

Congo is a central African country covering an area of 342,000 square kilometers (132,053 square miles). The population of Congo was estimated at 2.6 million inhabitants in 1995 with a 3.0 percent annual growth. Brazzaville, the country's capital, hosts more than 1 million inhabitants. The population in other cities, such as Pointe Noire (the economic capital), Dolisie (also called Loubomo), Nkayi, Impfondo, Owando, Makoua, and Ouesso, ranges between 10,000 and 500,000. The country's gross national product (GNP), estimated at US$1.88 billion in 1996, is based mainly on wood and oil production (Union congolaise 1999).

According to a report presented to loan providers at the 1997 Roundtable Conference on Education, Congo (Gouvernement 1997a), like most sub-Saharan countries, has been undergoing a severe economic downturn since the 1980s, with the population outstripping economic development. The private sector employs only 17 percent of the workforce; the rest are employed in the public sector. Congo is one of the most heavily indebted countries in the world, owing US$2,100 per inhabitant. In 1994, the economic crisis was sharpened by the devaluation of the national currency; debt service during this year exceeded 220 billion francs, which is more than half of Congo's GNP. On the social level, this situation has had a number of repercussions as signs of deterioration have begun to show on many social infrastructures, such as health services, education, and employment. Signs of economic downturn could be seen in the decrease of purchasing power, migration, decrease in salaries, absenteeism among civil servants, lack of motivation, and need for senior executives. The sociopolitical situation in 1993–1994 intensified the economic downturn. The government resorted to prospecting for new oil sites in an attempt to resolve the crisis. Unfortunately, two new wars were triggered in 1997–1998, hav-

ing an even deeper impact on the country. However, with the progressive restoration of peace and security to the region, a new phase of reconstruction and development has begun. It is within this context that our analysis of the Congolese higher education system will be situated.

GENERAL VIEW OF THE HIGHER EDUCATION SYSTEM

The Congolese educational system is composed of four different types of institutions: public, private, training schools, and continuing education. All these educational categories are stipulated in the September 1990 law related to education, which was modified by the November 1995 law (008/90) defining the organizational structures of the Congolese educational system. The law in question stipulates a number of dispositions, among which are equality in access, free public education, compulsory education between the ages of 6 and 16, the government's responsibility for the organization of education, and the recognition of the private sector. According to the same law, the educational system is structured around four levels: preschool, primary, secondary (junior and senior), and higher education. During 1995–1996, the total student community amounted to 715,000 for all levels; that is, 27.5 percent of the country's population. This number is three times the one recorded in 1970, when the student population at Marien Ngouabi University was estimated at 18,257.

With regard to preschool, primary, and secondary sectors, the legislation clearly defines their organization, functioning, access requirements, and degrees granted at the end of each level. However, despite the existence of a ministerial hierarchy for the higher education system and the nomination of a director-general on two occasions (1984 and 1998) to lead this sector, there exists no specific legal text that clearly defines the workings of higher education. Prior to the ratification of the Sep-

Table 25.1. Ratio of Students to Professors, by Institution, Marien Ngouabi University, 1997–1998

Institution	Number of Students	Number of Professors*	Student-Professor Ratio
Ecole Nationale d'Administration et de Magistrature (National School of Administration and Magistracy)	286	27	10.6
Ecole Normale Supérieur (Teacher's School)	647	78	8.3
Ecole Normale Supérieur Polytechnique (Advanced Polytechnic School)	316	31	10.2
Faculté de Droit (Law School)	1,527	33	46.3
Faculté des Lettres et des Sciences Humaines (School of Letters and Human Sciences)	5,799	126	46.0
Faculté des Sciences (School of Science)	1,526	85	18.0
Faculté des Sciences Economiques (School of Economics)	4,499	37	121.6
Faculté des Sciences de la Santé (School of Health Sciences)	312	49	6.4
Institut de Développement Rural (Rural Development Institute)	431	33	13.1
Institut Supérieur d'Education Physique et Sportive (Advanced Physical Education Institute)	232	30	7.7
Institut Supérieur de Gestion (Advanced Institute for Management)	269	21	12.8
Total	15,844	550	28.8

*Total permanent professors.
Source: Office of the Vice-President, UMNG.

tember 1990 law authorizing the private sector to operate educational institutions, Marien Ngouabi University was the only postsecondary institution. Thus, most of the existing legal texts are specific to Marien Ngouabi University.

Since the promulgation of the November 1995 law, higher education has been provided through both public and private institutions at the levels of advanced schools, university schools, and institutes. Most of these institutions are located in urban areas, mainly in Brazzaville and Pointe Noire.

PUBLIC HIGHER EDUCATION

Public higher education consists of two levels, university education and nonuniversity education. Congo has one state university, Marien Ngouabi University (Université Marien Ngouabi, UMNG), located in Brazzaville. The UMNG has retained, to a certain degree, the mission assigned to it since its creation by a decree on December 4, 1971. Its mission is to create and disseminate knowledge, train individuals, organize lifelong learning, and prepare individuals for leadership positions in various domains.

Today, a committee chaired by the minister of higher education and managed by a technical council led by the university president administers UMNG. The latter is assisted in his duties by a vice-president and a secretary-general. While the president assumes direct responsibility for units such as the president's cabinet and the accounting and audit unit, the vice-president is responsible for research, academic affairs, cooperation, the university library, curricula, and exams. The secretary-general is in charge of human resources, administrative and financial affairs, residential life, buildings, equipment, and maintenance.

Every school or institute at UMNG is managed by an insti-

tutional council under the chairmanship of the dean or director of the unit in question. An academic secretary, a central secretary, and an accountant assist each council chair, while heads of departments are responsible for their respective units.

The university president, the vice-president, the secretary-general, the deans, and the directors are nominated through the ministerial council. The minister of higher education nominates directors and academic secretaries while the faculty and personnel of the department council elect department heads. Nominations are finalized by approval from the minister.

UMNG has an open access policy. UMNG has developed in all respects except in certain fields; namely architecture, pharmacy, dental surgery, medicine, veterinary, fishing, and fine arts.

UMNG is composed of eleven institutions of higher education—five faculties, three schools, and three institutes. The faculties include the letters and human sciences (Faculté des Lettres et des Sciences Humaines, FLSH), economics (Faculté des Sciences Economiques, FSE), law (Faculté de Droit, FD), and health sciences (Faculté des Sciences de la Santé, FSS), while the schools cover the areas of national administration and magistracy (Ecole Nationale d'Administration et de Magistrature, ENAM), teacher training (Ecole Normale Supérieur, ENS), and the polytechnic (Ecole Normale Supérieur Polytechnique, ENSP). The institutes are in charge of rural development (Institut de Développement Rural, IDR), sports and physical education (Institut Supérieur d'Education Physique et Sportive, ISEPS), and management (Institut Supérieur de Gestion, ISG). Other than the institutes, which have their own buildings, all institutions are located in buildings inherited from the colonial period. These buildings were initially designed for purposes other than education, and they do not meet any university building standards. UMNG enrolls more than 18,250 students, employs 900 staff members, and has 725 permanent professors (of whom only 41 are women), resulting in a ratio of 25 students per professor (Gouvernement 1997b; Table 25.1; UMNG 1998a).

ACCESS AND DEGREES

The admission requirements of UMNG are determined by ministerial decree (Ministère de l'Education Nationale 1995). Generally, UMNG accepts candidates of Congolese nationality as well as foreigners having a high school degree (*baccalauréat*) or its equivalent in return for an application fee. The university also grants training opportunities to government employees meeting certain academic and administrative qualifications. The ministerial decree determines admission requirements for other university levels as well. Admission, which is dependent on institutional capacity, is free for most faculties, the School of Health Sciences being one exception. The latter, as well as the advanced schools and institutes, require an entrance test. These tests are monitored yearly through a ministerial agenda that grants 10 percent of the total seats to foreign students and free-*baccalauréat* candidates. In 1997, the number of foreign students had decreased; only 60 out of a total of 19,000 were international students.

With the exception of the School of Health Sciences, schools are organized into three cycles: a first two-year university cycle leading to a University General Studies Degree (*Diplôme des Etudes Universitaires Générales*, DEUG), a four-year cycle leading to the bachelor's degree, and a third cycle including the advanced studies degree (*Diplôme des Etudes Approfondies*, DEA), the specialized studies degree (*Diplôme des Etudes Spéciales*, DES), and the doctorate. In the School of Health Sciences, degrees are organized into three levels; a *license* prepared in three years, a doctorate in medicine obtained over six years, and a certificate of specialized studies (*Cértificat d'Etudes Spéciales*, CES).

In schools and institutes, studies are structured around a short three-year cycle and a long five-year cycle. These programs prepare students for professional degrees in a variety of disciplines, such as technology, teaching, counseling, engineering, management, and physical education. Advanced schools and institutes are authorized to provide a university education upon permission from the university scientific council. A case in point is the UNESCO chair for education hosted in a teacher training school, leading to a degree of doctorate or postdoctorate in advanced studies in pedagogy evaluation and assessment.

The UMNG delivers 140 degrees (UMNG 1998b), thus responding to career needs in national education, administration, rural development, technology, human sciences, law, and economics. Nonuniversity postsecondary education is provided mainly through vocational and technical schools, such as primary teacher schools (Ecole Normale des Instituteurs, ENI), the national school for administration and magistracy (Ecole Nationale Moyenne d'Administration et de Magistrature, ENMA), and the paramedical training school (formerly a medico-social branch of the Central African Foundation for Higher Education). The professors at these institutions are mostly graduates of UMNG, though they have no formal ties to UMNG itself.

PRIVATE HIGHER EDUCATION

Private initiatives are increasingly moving into higher education, providing mainly technical and professional training in such subjects as business management and office and computer skills. Over the last ten years, a significant number of private higher education institutions have been created, especially in Brazzaville and Pointe Noire. The increase in the number of these institutions, however, is not proportionate to the number of agencies that supervise and manage this sector. Authorization for private institutions to operate may be acquired in a number of different ways. For some institutions, permission is given by the minister of higher education. For others, it is the minister of technical and professional education, and in still other cases, it is the minister of labor. Private institutions function according to specific norms and standards and deliver their own specific degrees. Unfortunately, the lack of precise data on private higher education makes it impossible to give their exact number. However, there are four recently created institutions that should be mentioned: the Free University of Congo (Université Libre du Congo, ULC), the Paradox Institute, the Business Administration Institute (Institut de Gestion d'Entreprises, IGE), and the Advanced School for Business Management and Administration (Ecole Supérieur de Gestion et Administration des Enterprises, ESGAE).

The Free University of Congo is composed of three departments: food industry technology, international trade and management, and law. So far, the early graduates of the ULC have been successfully integrated into the job market; some graduates, though also successful, were forced to resume their studies at UMNG because of the war.

The Paradox Institute, which was started in 1996, hosted 525 students during the 1999–2000 academic year, of whom 300 were women. The institute offers a two-year Vocational Training Certificate (*Brevet de Technicien Supérieur*, BTS) in management and computers. Top graduates are also easily integrated into the job market. The IGE, enrolling 525 students (of whom more than 50 percent are female) and with a teaching body of 60 professors, offers the same two-year degree in office secretary skills and communication. It also offers bachelor's degrees in accounting, finance, management, marketing, and computer management technology.

The ESGAE offers three concentrations where candidates seek a two-year Vocational Training Certificate (BTS) in office secretary work, information technology, human resources management, financial management, company management, and planning. The school also offers a five-year engineering degree in the same areas except for the secretary and information management majors. To obtain the BTS, entering candidates must either have a *baccalauréat*, a *baccalauréat* equivalent, or enroll in one year of preparatory courses. For the degree of engineer, candidates need to have a bachelor's degree and pay annual fees. Since its inception in 1993, ESGAE has conferred 37 degrees in engineering and 490 bachelor's degrees, among which 290 degrees were awarded in the finance department alone. Available statistics on the evolution of this institution show, however, that the number of students has been declining over the last three years. In 1996–1997, 492 students attended ESGAE; that number had declined to 242 in 1999–2000. This is probably attributable to the situation of war that the country endures. Another explanation is a decrease in family income, which makes it difficult for families to meet the expenses of private education.

HISTORICAL PERSPECTIVE

Congolese higher education was born under the colonial administration with the establishment of a basic structure, between 1958 and 1960, for a higher education system throughout French Central Africa (Afrique Centrale Française, AEF). Indeed, 1958 saw the creation in Brazzaville of the Institute for Advanced Studies, followed in 1959 by the Center for Advanced Administrative and Technical Studies (Centre d'Etudes Administratives et Techniques Supérieures, CEATS). The latter included a literary major, a scientific major, and a training school for high school teachers. The aim of the colonial administration was to train a local body of administrative agents.

In 1960, the four French colonies of the AEF achieved their independence, and a year later a convention was signed between the republics of Chad, Central Africa, Gabon, Congo, and France, marking the creation of the Central African Foundation for Higher Education (Fondation de l'Enseignement Supérieur en Afrique Centrale, FESAC). Through this convention, an agreement for cooperation in higher education brought together schools and institutes established in each of the represented countries. Part of this network was the Higher Education Center in Brazzaville (Centre d'Enseignement Supérieur de Brazzaville, CESB), comprised of the Law School, the Advanced School of Science, the Advanced School of Humanities, and the Medico-social Department. In addition to the CESB, the network grouped the agronomy institutes of the republic of Central Africa, the Zoology School in Chad, the Polytechnic School in Gabon, and the Teacher School of Central Africa in Brazzaville.

The objective of this institutional network was to provide the newly independent countries with necessary middle- and top-level administrators. From the start, priority was given to the training of administrative executives at the expense of the productive sectors of the economy. To reach this objective, a strategy of distance education via correspondence was set up; it constituted the building blocks of what would later become the correspondence education service. In 1965, when the education system was nationalized through legislation, and with the retreat of an expatriate teaching body that belonged to various religious denominations, the need in the educational system for executives became pressing. In 1964–1965, there were 608 university students (Document Congrès 1989). The FESAC finally crumbled in 1971, under the pressing need of the newly established states to confirm their individual sovereignty, and also due to Congo's revolutionary policy. The foundation had trained approximately 1,480 students by mainly foreign educators.

Congo, which inherited the infrastructures established under the FESAC, inaugurated the University of Brazzaville in 1971 through presidential decree. The creation of the university resulted from the proceedings of the first seminar on education (1970), which generated a new concept: the People's School Manifesto. Advanced schools operating under the CESB were converted into schools: letters and human sciences, science, law, and economics. The legislation creating the university stipulated the same mission mentioned earlier, which is hardly different from that of the Association of Partially or Entirely French-Speaking Universities (Association des Universités Partiellement ou Entièrement de Langue Française, AUPELF), namely "the creation and transmission of knowledge, service to the community, and the exercise of the public service." Texts of a political nature also outlined the missions of the university; the People's School Manifesto issued at the conference of the president of the republic in 1972 insisted that "for each new society, [there should be] a new university." According to the idea of the People's School, the university, which is conceived in the form of an advanced professional cycle, structured into institutes and schools, had for its mission the training of national executives within the spirit of scientific socialism.

During the period between 1971 and 1983, the University of Brazzaville entered a period of restructuring. New institutions developed, such as the Advanced School for the Sciences of Education (Institut Supérieur des Sciences de l'Education, INSSED), which replaced the former ENSAC; the Rural Development Institute (Institut de Développment Rural, IDR); the Advanced Physical Education Institute (Institut Supérieur d'Education Physique et Sportive, ISEPS); the Advanced School of Legal, Administrative and Managerial Studies, and Economics (Institut Supérieur des Sciences Economiques, Juridiques, Administratives et de Gestion, INSSEJAG); the Institute of Health Sciences (Institut des Sciences de la Santé, ISA); the Advanced School of Technical Training (Ecole Normale Supérieure de l'Enseignement Technique, ENSET); and the Advanced Pedagogical Institute (Institut Supérieur Pédagogique de Loubomo, ISPL) at Loubomo, which replaced the department of technical teacher training that had operated within the INSSED since 1977. This period of restructuring is codified by a number of legislative texts issued through presidential decrees.

By 1977, the University of Brazzaville was renamed Marien Ngouabi University. Since then, a number of branches belonging to a single political party, the Congolese Labor Party (Parti Congolais du Travail, PCT), have started to take shape within the university; for example, the Committee of the Party (Comité du Parti, CP), The Youth of the Party (La Jeunesse du Parti), the Central Labor Union (Centrale Syndicate des Travailleurs), and the Women's Organization (Organisation des Femmes du Parti). This period was characterized by the predominance of political criteria in the nomination of senior university executives and faculty promotion. Consequently, university autonomy was affected and relationships between students and faculty deteriorated (UMNG 1992).

As the concept of the People's School began to take a more democratic turn, Congo was achieving the highest schooling rate among African countries. The number of students, especially in the schools, grew rapidly beyond the institutions' capacity, making obsolete all pedagogical efforts to provide a good education. Cases in point are the buildings of the ENS, which were initially established to host 300 students; actual student enrollment exceeded 1,000 because of the open access policy. The department of university social services is very active within

UMNG; unfortunately, increasing social and political pressures, which have seriously impacted the functioning of higher education, have made this service counterproductive, with costs exceeding benefits. Similarly, the organization of study programs at the university over the same period also saw a number of changes; in addition to restructuring degree programs, students were required to undergo an entrance test. The UMNG also adopted bylaws and effected a course credit system, and a correspondence study program was established.

This period also witnessed the graduation of the first cohort of rural development engineers, physical education inspectors and professors, and medical doctors and the organization of seminars on teaching methods (UMNG 1998f). The financial situation of university personnel and professors at UMNG witnessed significant improvement in 1985 as well, with the readjustment of salaries and the implementation of faculty promotions. In 1988, the INSSEJAG was divided into three schools: the law school, the School of Economics, and the advanced institute of management. This reorganization speaks of the failure of the concept of the People's School to achieve professionalization in higher education. The 1988 conference called for reflection on the entire educational system and suggested a number of measures—a total of 275 recommendations—to improve the situation of higher education. As a result, in 1990, the presiding committee decided to close down the ISPL and to confer its mission to the INSSED, which was in turn converted into a teacher training school. The correspondence study program was temporarily suspended due to financial difficulties, and the study programs at the level of schools were restructured one more time. A new law strengthened private higher education. Two recommendations adopted during the Sovereign National Conference of 1991 have been implemented at UMNG. The first called for the organization of a convention on university issues, and the second related to launching a doctoral program. Marien Ngouabi University acquired a new status with the promulgation of the 1991 decree; the INSS became School of Health Sciences in 1993; the INSET was converted into the National Advanced Polytechnic School in 1996; and UMNG adhered to the promotion standards of the Conseil Africain et Malgache pour l'Enseignement Supérieur (CAMES).

Over the same period, the necessity to take pressure off Marien Ngouabi University led to the idea of relocation of certain institutions such as the IDR, the ISEPS, the ENS, and the School of Sciences. The idea of relocation, however, fell prey to strong controversy and was finally abandoned. Certificate of Advanced Studies (CES) programs were initiated within the School of Sciences, followed in 1996 by two postgraduate degrees and a program at the School of Economics leading to a master's degree. Moreover, following an agreement between UNESCO and Marien Ngouabi University, a chair in the sciences of education was created at the teacher training school with a focus on pedagogy and evaluation. This program offered master's, doctorate, and postdoctorate degrees. A number of other activities supplemented the many changes that were taking place in higher education, namely the intensification of scientific activity through the creation of new laboratories, the publication of the annals of Marien Ngouabi University and

other specialized journals, the establishment of research teams and learning communities, the organization of seminars and conferences, and other scientific activities. At the administrative level, a number of positions were created to recruit new faculty members.

Thus, the evolution of Congolese higher education, in conjunction with the training of Congolese students abroad and thanks to national scholarships and international cooperation, has provided Congo with a cadre of political, administrative, and technical executives who ensure the functioning of higher education in Congo today.

PRESENT TENDENCIES AND FUTURE OUTLOOK FOR HIGHER EDUCATION

Congolese higher education over the last few years has been the subject of a number of reflections and consultations at different levels. The persistence of the economic crisis is exacerbated by the conflict-filled sociopolitical climate, the deterioration of working conditions, and the increasing number of graduates in a saturated job market. Within the higher education context in particular, changes in the educational situation are reflected in the preparation of the UMNG States-General (Etats Généraux), which is based on general assemblies organized throughout the country's educational institutions. The synthesis of the proceedings of these meetings awaits the occurrence of the university's general assembly. At the national level, the feasibility of the People's School plan was analyzed and evaluated at a 1988 meeting which determined the inapplicability of the project. The national Sovereign Conference of 1991 launched a more detailed analysis of the higher education situation and called for the organization of the UMNG States-General. The government presented a report at the roundtable conference in Brazzaville in 1997. At the subregional level, the University Presidents Conference of Central Africa, which took place in Brazzaville in 1996, adopted an action plan that stipulated a certain number of measures supporting the suggestions and recommendations mentioned in earlier meetings.

MISSION OF MARIEN NGOUABI UNIVERSITY

Despite the conflict-ridden sociopolitical context of the last few years, the quantitative development of Marien Ngouabi University has been maintained, and the training of senior executives is effective. This quantitative development, however, takes place in certain disciplines, such as humanities and social sciences, at the expense of scientific and technical departments. The success rate, which is generally mediocre, especially during the first years (10 to 30 percent), does not show any sign of improvement because of the low achievement level of entering students and the difficulties they face in adapting to new programs. Another part of the problem is the absence of effective student orientation and adequate pedagogical methods at UMNG. Quality is nevertheless maintained at an acceptable level, considering that a number of Congolese students who have graduated from UMNG have been able to pursue their studies successfully abroad. Other graduates have been able to

Table 25.2. Distribution of Faculty by Rank and Institution, Marien Ngouabi University, 1997–1998

Institution	Professors	Lecturers	Teaching Assistants	Assistants	Instructors	Total Professors*
Ecole Nationale d'Administration et de Magistrature	—	—	16	10	1	27
Ecole Normale Supérieur	—	2	55	20	1	78
Ecole Normale Supérieur Polytechnique	—	—	12	19	—	31
Faculté de Droit	—	—	25	8	—	33
Faculté des Lettres et des Sciences Humaines	2	14	75	35	—	126
Faculté des Sciences	3	14	55	13	—	85
Faculté des Sciences Economiques	—	1	20	16	—	37
Faculté des Sciences de la Santé	9	10	13	13	4	49
Institut de Développement Rural	—	1	21	11	—	33
Institut Supérieur d'Education Physique et Sportive	—	1	9	20	—	30
Institut Supérieur de Gestion	—	—	7	12	2	21
Total	14	43	308	177	8	550

*Total permanent professors.
Source: Office of the Vice-President, UMNG.

carry out their professional careers, while still others are leaders in the business community (Etats Généraux; UMNG 1998d). The plundering of the university's physical infrastructure, though, has seriously impaired educational facilities.

INSTITUTIONAL CAPACITY

Though a number of postgraduate institutions are supervised by the ministry in charge of technical education and professional training, public higher education remains, for the most part, under the supervision of the minister of higher education. A number of legislative texts issued to restructure the internal organization of higher education—for example, the 1976 decree defining the organization of Marien Ngouabi University—have been revised to provide for a better internal organization. These legislative modifications have touched on issues related to decision making and administrative, pedagogical, and research structures. Matters related to internal bylaws and the election of senior officials, except for the president, are still on the agenda of the UMNG States-General.

The situation of institutional capacity remains unsatisfactory, and despite some efforts to build new facilities, the infrastructures necessary to achieve sound pedagogical goals are ever more difficult to afford. There is dire need for new buildings and modern equipment to replace the facilities that were destroyed during the wars. Documentation resources also need to be supplied and modernized; the library collection that consisted of some 67,000 books and more than 627 periodicals before the 1994–1997 civil wars counts today 30,000 books and no periodicals except for donations through bilateral cooperation agreements. We strongly believe that the time has come to reconstruct UMNG, whose revamping has been a leitmotiv since the mid-1980s.

FACULTY

Both faculty and administrative personnel supervise students; in 1997–1998, the teaching community consisted of 550 professors, among whom forty-one were women. The distribution by rank is presented in Table 25.2, where one can see the low number of senior professors and the persistent predominance of teaching assistants.

A major concern related to faculty is recruitment policy, which over the last several years has not allowed for the renewal of the university teaching body, a number of whom are approaching retirement. In 1997–1998, the number of part-timers exceeded that of permanent professors, due to legislation limiting workload to three hours daily.

STUDENT ENROLLMENT

Despite the deterioration of the job market during the period 1963 to 2000, the yearly numbers of high school graduates did not decrease. The highest rates of demand for higher education are situated between 1972 and 1996. The number of high school graduates entering the university in Congo increased by a factor of five between 1976 (3,785) and 1997 (around 19,000). For every 100,000 citizens, higher education accounted for 555 students in 1985, 582 in 1991, and 703 in 1997 (UNESCO 1998; UMNG 1998c, 18, 20), which is a higher rate of admission than the average of 100 for every 100,000 inhabitants common for all sub-Saharan African countries. For comparison's sake, the annual increase in the rate of enrollment (on average 2.8 percent between 1991 and 1997), which is close to the rate of increase of the population (3 percent), remains; this is, however, lower than the rate observed in Senegal (4.2 percent be-

Table 25.3. Distribution of Students by Age Group and Institution, Université Marien Ngouabi, 1997–1998

Institution	Age Group				Total
	18–21	21–25	25–30	30+	
Ecole Nationale d'Administration et de Magistrature	—	—	7	279	286
Ecole Normale Supérieur	5	91	262	289	647
Ecole Normale Supérieur Polytechnique	20	174	109	13	316
Faculté de Droit	86	692	605	144	1,527
Faculté des Lettres et des Sciences Humaines	151	2,125	2,890	633	5,799
Faculté des Sciences	189	926	405	6	1,526
Faculté des Sciences Economiques	206	1,814	1,939	540	4,499
Faculté des Sciences de la Santé	21	117	91	83	312
Institut de Développement Rural	11	143	164	113	431
Institut Supérieur d'Education Physique et Sportive	4	39	82	107	232
Institut Supérieur de Gestion	25	177	58	9	269
Total	718 (4.5%)	6,298 (39.8%)	6,612 (41.7%)	2,216 (14.0%)	15,844

Source: Office of the Vice-President, UMNG.

tween 1985–1994) and in Ivory Coast (8.86 percent between 1985 and 1994) (UNESCO 1998).

The enrollment rate in Congo is five times higher than the average enrollment rate in other sub-Saharan African countries. At the national level, and despite the increasing number of private institutions that offer higher education, Marien Ngouabi University probably offers the most interesting and affordable education package.

High school graduates apply to national as well as foreign higher education institutions. The number of students enrolled in higher education over the last few years is decreasing compared to earlier years, except for the ENAM, the ISEPS, the ISG, and the FLSH. A case in point is the enrollment at the School of Economics, which decreased by 30 percent between 1997 and 2000, while the School of Sciences registered a 42 percent decrease from 1997 to 1999.

UMNG still follows a free access policy for Congolese and foreigners in accordance with a decree (MENRST/UMNG) stipulating the conditions of access to Marien Ngouabi University (Ministère de l'Education Nationale 1995). Once all requirements are met, candidates are eligible to benefit from scholarships and all other university social services, including accommodation, restaurants and social services, medical services, and athletic services. The management of scholarships and accommodation does not fall under the direct jurisdiction of the university but is the responsibility of the Offices of Social Affairs and University Social Services which are attached to the cabinet of the minister of higher education. The financing of university social services and the granting of scholarships suffer serious budgetary problems and are not always run in a systematic fashion.

The distribution of students by age group over the various higher education institutions for the academic years 1997–1998 (Table 25.3) shows that less than 5 percent are below 22, the legal maximum eligibility age for scholarships.

For the same academic year, 44.3 percent were aged between 18 and 25 years. Disparities between sexes are such that female students represent 24 percent of the student community. Although encouraging, this percentage remains well below that of men, and within scientific and professional disciplines these percentages vary between 16 percent (ENS) and 21 percent (ENSP). Private higher education accounts for more than 50 percent of female students; examples of such institutions are the ESGAE, the IGE, and the Paradox Institute.

A number of high school graduates seek opportunities to pursue their university studies abroad, for various reasons. In fact, the demand for higher education in foreign institutions has increased over the last few years because of the war situation, which has considerably disturbed the academic calendar and the functioning of UMNG. This also explains the difference between the number of students admitted in the *baccalauréat* and those actually applying to the university during this decade. Various studies agree that it is necessary to devise solutions for better control of student enrollment in order to improve the educational landscape and recover the quality of university education.

PROGRAM DIVERSIFICATION AND MAJORS

In terms of capacity and the conditions of student supervision, UMNG is totally saturated. Diversification of programs and disciplines might provide a solution. Considerable thought has been given to creating new programs and setting up new institutions, as higher education is in great need of expansion and regeneration in order to stand up to challenges both at the national and international level. Private higher education has already taken this direction, and it seems that this tendency will provide better chances for survival. Because of long-established traditions and conventions, UMNG is difficult to change and has few choices in this respect. The creation of other universities throughout the country would allow UMNG to maintain its status as the central metropolitan university. New institutions of higher education should focus on modern technical disciplines, and diversification should occur in teaching methods and techniques, including distance higher education. The correspondence study program operated by Marien Ngouabi University, which was been suspended for financial reasons by the decision of the directing commission in 1990, was highly appreciated by many Congolese students. Since then, UMNG, through its Teacher School, has been part of various programs of distance education in the French-speaking area. The reluctance to launch distance education is certainly not due to legal reasons, since this type of education is stipulated in the 1995 law. A recent decree dated June 1996, modifying the earlier decree dated in 1976 that organized the University of Brazzaville, also stipulates the creation of a department for distance higher education. Resuming distance higher education is also one of the recommendations of a subcommission of the UMNG States-General on education. A decree adopted during the ministers' meeting mentions the creation of new university institutions and a national center for higher education. Implementation of the higher education center project was impeded by the 1997 war, and the decision has been altered recently by the directing commission, which has blended the distance-education project into the continuing education program. Distance higher education worldwide, as mentioned in the Treaty of Masstricht, usually develops in relation to the development of new information and communication technologies. At this time, digital campuses and programs are being established in many sub-Saharan African countries. UMNG has been chosen to host the next gathering of CAMES and is planning new teaching methodologies. In this context, the revocation of distance education in Congo constitutes a failure vis-à-vis the aforementioned law outlining the use of distance education as a complementary solution to increasing demands on higher education. Such a solution is certainly realistic considering the actual limited capacity of the university. Yet the present pedagogical provisions for student supervision cannot assume the task of organizing distance-education programs with efficiency; UMNG should probably wait for a better opportunity to launch such a program.

MANAGEMENT AND COMMUNICATION

The management capacity of UMNG, which has been weak for years, has been improving in a satisfactory manner with the introduction of computer tools such as the Internet connection for the president's office. The use of computers has made significant changes on many levels, namely in facilitating salary management, data management, and the handling of various types of statistical tasks. The tendency toward using computers and information systems has continued to develop; now UMNG offers computer science majors. However, it does not have a computer information department, even though younger private institutions have integrated computers into their operations from the beginning both as a tool for management and as a discipline.

PARTNERSHIPS AND COOPERATION

Partnerships Policy

At the national level, partners of UMNG include institutions such as the Office of the President of the Republic, the Ministry of Finance and Civil Service, the Ministry of National Education, the University Health Center, the student associations (twelve), the labor unions (three), the students' parents associations, high schools, and certain businesses. Representatives of these various partners, with the exception of the students' parents associations, share in deliberation activities with the university administration; part of their task is to conduct negotiations related to the improvement of working conditions. The University Health Center is a full-fledged partner in the operation of programs at the School of Health Sciences and gives a good example of the close and strong links that can be maintained between institutions of higher education and the job market. Faculty members at the School of Health Sciences have double status, since they are also permanent members of the University Health Center. In certain businesses, student supervisors are sometimes compensated, which provides a good environment for student internships. Despite all the difficulties in implementing and honoring engagements between higher education and its different partners, the relation between these two worlds remains a very active one.

Cooperation

UMNG has signed more than sixty agreements with various research and educational institutions worldwide, especially with countries from Central Africa, Western Europe, and North America (UMNG 1998f). These agreements have allowed UMNG to launch many projects, such as joint educational and research programs, faculty workshops, seminars and conferences, field trips for professors, and the modernization and acquisition of equipment for laboratories. Presently, the majority of these agreements have fallen into disuse, either because the Congo has not been able to honor its part of the agreement or because implementation has not taken effect at all. UMNG still benefits from assistance provided by the French Cooperation and maintains relationships with various international organizations such as the Association of Partially or Entirely French-Speaking Universities—University of French-Speaking Networks (Association des Universités Partiellement ou Entièrement de Langue Française—Université des Réseaux d'Expression Française, AUPELF-UREF), CAMES, the Association of African Universities (AAU), UNESCO, NASA, the African Office for the Sciences of Education (Bureau Africain des Sciences de l'Education, BASE), the British Council, and the French-Speaking Belgian Community. In relation to the UNESCO chair at the School of Educational Sciences, preparations are underway for the opening of branch offices in neighboring countries in order to bring regional researchers together. Part of the goal is also to benefit from the digital campuses in Libreville and Yaounde.

PLANNING AND REFORMS

A number of problems reported in various studies of UMNG since the liberalization of education in Congo point to the lack of planning, the absence of a clear vision for the university, poor programming and student orientation (UMNG 1998e), and the lack of a precise policy on the part of the government. Because

Table 25.4. School Fees in Certain Private Institutions in Congo, in FCFA

Institution	Christ-Roi School		Actuelle School	Advanced School for Business Management and Administration		Paradox	Business Administration Institute	
Level	High School	Primary	Vocational Training Certificate (BTS)	Vocational Training Certificate for Business (BTSE)	Engineering Degree (DI)	Vocational Training Certificate (BTS)	Vocational Training Certificate (BTS)	Specialized Studies Degree (DES)
Annual Fees	3,000	2,500	10,000	30,000	30,000	10,000	75,000	75,000
Monthly Fees	12,000	10,000	25,000	30,000	35,000	28,000	275,000	310,000

Source: Institutions cited.

of these concerns, UMNG hosted the Canadian Program for the Institutional Reinforcement for Technology in French-Speaking Africa (Programme Canadien de Renforcement Institutionel en Matière de Technologie en Afrique Francophone, PRIMTAF). This program has sensitized higher education institutions to strategic planning and encouraged them to modernize programs and elaborate on and evaluate projects. It is obvious that such a program does not solve the problem of defining a clear policy to bring about changes that need to take place on the national level. The ENSP was the first institution to implement changes through strategic planning. The same process has to be extended to all institutions, in accordance with the new vision prescribed for higher education. Other reforms that have been implemented concern the extension of study periods from two to three years for short study programs and from four to five years for longer programs, switching the maximum age of eligibility for scholarships from 23 to 22, and annexing university social services to the office of the minister of higher education. A 1996 government decree authorized the privatization of higher education and the recognition of institutions meeting the agreed-upon criteria. High achievement levels are expected on the part of managers of all the newly established schools.

FINANCING AND RESOURCES

The state is the main funding source for Congolese public higher education; it devoted 34.4 percent of public spending to higher education in 1985. Congo was one of the leading countries in sub-Saharan Africa in terms of public resources allocated to this sector in the 1980s. Ten years later, this effort was significantly diminished, while in neighboring countries, funding for higher education had increased (UNESCO 1998). Other funding sources are UNESCO, the French Cooperation, AUPELF-UREF, and the AAU. According to Law 29-71, the University of Brazzaville is a legal entity endowed with public rights, legal capacity, and financial autonomy, all of which implies that the university is entitled to a budget from the state to meet its needs in terms of operating costs and equipment, and that it has a distinct financial structure, a separate accounting system, and a separate income and expense budget.

In reality, however, the implementation of the university budget does not follow this financial structure. Marien Ngouabi University operates mostly on financial income from external sources such as the state and, rarely, from nongovernmental sources. Since the publication of the 1985 and 1991 statutes, the total budget has increased significantly, yet a number of problems persist: the cost of personnel absorbs most of the state's subsidy, the university's income is insufficient, and the portion of the budget devoted to operating costs has consistently decreased. Presently, the main source of university income derives from rental of university facilities, such as dorms and amphitheaters, and income from students' medical expenses and fees. Student fees amount to US$654 per year for nationals and US$2060 for international students. Congo offers the lowest education costs for international students. During the academic year 2000, income generated by student fees covered barely 1.34 percent of the total budget.

With regard to the private sector, the 1996 decree regulating private higher education stipulates entitlements for state-provided contributions in financing certain categories of accredited private institutions; however, no private institution up to now has been able to benefit from this disposition. Most private higher education institutions survive on their own income, which is composed mainly of registration fees, which vary depending on the type of institution and the programs offered (see Table 25.4).

STUDY PROGRAMS

Pedagogical committees design UMNG programs with special attention to the missions and objectives of each department and in accordance with the general orientation of the university. These programs are submitted to outside institutions for deliberation and approval before they are put into practice.

Most of the study programs of Marien Ngouabi University have been approved by CAMES. Generally, the designers of study programs are inspired by their own training experience, which explains the problems of adaptation that high school graduates encounter during their first year at the university, as these majors do not result from an informed decision about what study programs are needed. Within Marien Ngouabi University, seven of the eleven schools offer professional training consisting of both theoretical and practical components. Generally this type of institution offers training of good quality. Table 25.5 presents all the programs of study offered at Marien Ngouabi University.

LANGUAGE OF INSTRUCTION AND ITS IMPACT

Congo is a French-speaking country; from kindergarten to university, teaching is carried out in French, which is the official language and a remnant of colonization. Students are required to learn French even before entering school, since success in studies depends on the mastery of this language at all levels of schooling. As language is the vehicle of culture, the status of French in modern-day Congo has a clear impact on all aspects of life. However, because French is not the native language and because there is a discrepancy between spoken and academic languages, some students find it difficult to succeed in their course of study.

RESEARCH AND PUBLICATION

Research is one of the main missions of Marien Ngouabi University; it is through research that faculty members become eligible for promotion by CAMES. Faculty members at UMNG are assigned a six-hour workload for full professors, an eight-hour load for teaching assistants, and a twelve-hour load for assistants. Faculty members are expected to spend the remainder of their time in research, for which they receive a research indemnity. Studies of the higher education system point to a need for legal texts to regulate the programming and evaluation of research activities. The only existing legal text in this respect is the law 15/98 related to the orientation and programming of technological and scientific development in Congo. This law assigns the General Delegation for Technological and Scientific Research (Délégation Nationale à la Recherche Scientifique et Technique, DGRST) as the national coordinator in terms of research; UMNG remains excluded in the absence of formal cooperative ties with the DGRST.

Within certain scientific departments, such as the School of Sciences, the School of Health Sciences, the Teacher School, and the National Polytechnic School, research activity is normally carried out in pedagogical and research laboratories on a multitude of topics such as biotechnology, chemistry, physics, materials science, physiology, nutrition, mechanics, electrical engineering, environment, education, and health care. In other institutions, research is organized at the level of centers and units for practical training, such as the anthropology laboratory, the legal studies laboratory, and the center for economic documentation. Students are involved in the activities of these research centers mostly at the dissertation-writing stage. However, the economic crisis, which has had a significant impact on research budgets, and the destructive impact of the civil wars over the last ten years have greatly slowed or totally stagnated the pace of activity at these research centers. After years of inactivity, the publication of university annals has finally been resumed. The lack of research publications is one of the major handicaps for researchers at UMNG and impacts their career advancement by CAMES.

In conjunction with the UNESCO chair in education, a journal is planned to provide publication opportunities for researchers. Thanks to this chair, a number of international conferences and seminars have been organized. Their proceedings, relating to the situation of education and teaching methodologies in central Africa, were published in 1997 and 1998. Table 25.6 presents data about research activity in certain institutions in 1998; that is, immediately after the 1997 war. A look at institutional work portfolios shows, with few exceptions, that it is within institutions where the number of full-time faculty members is high that scientific research activity is flourishing.

SPECIFIC PROBLEMS

Student Activism

Students are generally organized into associations recognized by a decree issued by the minister of the interior. The decree defines the status of the association, its political profile, and other activities related to it. These associations assume significant roles in negotiations with ministerial and university authorities, especially with regard to university social services. Since the dissolution of the single-party system, participation of these associations in university life is no longer officially based on their political color.

Politics and the University

Higher education in Congo has always benefited from the special attention of the nation's political leaders. Senior executives of Marien Ngouabi University are still active participants in the national life of the country. They are affiliated with the political parties of their choice, and a certain number of these executives are involved in other political spheres, such as assemblies or the government itself, where they serve terms of various durations. This situation is not without consequences for the functioning of the university, especially with regard to voting for budget cuts. However, in contrast to the time when the single-party system prevailed, the interference of politics in the functioning of the university is not as frequent as it used to be.

Graduates and the Job Market

Since the mid-1980s, and with the intensification of the economic crisis, government jobs have been suspended due to structural adjustment plans imposed by international financial organizations. While a number of postsecondary institutions have been closed down, UMNG continues to train an increasing number of graduates. Students from technical and scientific majors in either public or private institutions are more easily integrated into the job market than are their counterparts from other disciplines; this is the case for the ENSP, the ISG, and the ESGAE. Other institutions manage to integrate the world of

Table 25.5. Programs of Study at the Marien Ngouabi University, 1998

Institution	Nature	Degree Offered	Specialties
Ecole Nationale d'Administration et de Magistrature	Administration Legal Studies	Technical Degree Diploma	9 16
Ecole Normale Supérieur	General Education	High School General Education Teacher Certificate (CAPCEG)	6
		High School Teacher Certificate (CAPES)	7
		General Education Inspector Certificate (CAICEG)	6
		Pedagogical Advisor Diploma (DCPP)	1
		Technical High School Teacher Certificate (CAIEP)	1
Ecole Normale Supérieur Polytechnique	Industrial Techniques Technical Education	University Degree in Technology (DUT)	6
		Technical High School Teacher Certificate (CAPCET)	11
		Technical Teaching Diploma (CAPET)	4
Faculté de Droit	Law	DEUG 3-year Degree B.A.	2 2 2
Faculté des Lettres et des Sciences Humaines	Language & Literature Human Sciences Communication	DEUG 3-year Degree B.A.	10 10 11
Faculté des Sciences	Applied Hard Sciences	DEUG 3-year Degree B.A.	4 7 7
Faculté des Sciences Economiques	Economics	DEUG 3-year Degree B.A.	1 4 6
Faculté des Sciences de la Santé	Health Studies Medicine	B.A. in health studies M.D.	3 1
Institut de Développement Rural	Agricultural Techniques Agro-forestry	Rural Development Engineer Degree	3 1
Institut Supérieur d'Education Physique et Sportive	Physical Education & Sports	Pedagogical Advisor Certificate (DCPP)	1
		Physical Education Assistant Teaching Certificate (CAPAEPS)	1
		Physical Education Teaching Certificate (CAPEPS)	1
		Physical Education Inspector Certificate (CAIEPS)	1
Institut Supérieur de Gestion	Secretarial Techniques and Management	Vocational Training Certificate (BTS) 3-Year Degree	3 2

Source: Direction des Affaires Académiques, September 1998.

Table 25.6. Research Projects at the Marien Ngouabi University, September 1998

Institution	Research Labs		Scientific Output			Post-Graduate
	Existing	Operational	Pub.	Thesis	Dissert.	
ENAM	2	1	3	—	—	—
ENS	8	4	3	—	—	UNECSO chair
ENSP	1	1	3	—	—	—
FLSH	6	6	50	—	—	Project phase
FS	14	0	150	5	15	Project phase
FSE	1	1	12	0	0	Graduate International Program (PTCI)
FSS	4	2	55	23	35	Specialized Studies Certificate (CES)
IDR	2	1	12	—	20	—
ISG	1	1	9	—	—	—

Source: Department of Academic Affairs, UMNG, ENS.

trade, industry, and telecommunications. Most of the graduates of the Teacher School are hired in the private educational sector. A number of graduates of the Teacher School are recruited by the Ministry of National Education to serve as volunteers while awaiting their definitive integration as civil servants. During the academic year 2000–2001, the government offered 100 positions to these volunteers in response to a demand for jobs that is five times that number. Many graduates of professional training schools spend years without jobs; however, in the absence of statistics, it is not possible to determine the number in this category. Joblessness of graduates is a problem that touches every family today. People are increasingly conscious that the government is no longer the job provider it used to be. Students feel increasing pressure to take on more job-oriented majors, and graduates are required to create their own employment opportunities. Many are forced to leave the country in search of better work opportunities. This situation affects not only graduates of Marien Ngouabi University but also those with degrees from foreign institutions, in whom the government has made a significant investment. The economic situation, coupled with lower purchasing power, is at the root of the brain drain in scientific disciplines such as math and physics, to the point that the positions available exceed the number of applications; in other instances, there are simply no scholars with matching profiles to fill available positions.

PRESENT AND FUTURE CHALLENGES OF HIGHER EDUCATION

Higher education has a fundamental role in the development of countries, and as such it is confronted by various obstacles. At UMNG, there are difficulties in meeting the basic mission of the university because of the political and social contexts. This situation requires that higher education play a new role in contributing to the reconstruction of the country and the rebuilding of the national heritage destroyed by the wars. Its new mission also extends to renewing the physical, moral, and intellectual resources needed to reach these goals, especially by improving working conditions and devising new alternatives for development and peace. On another level, higher education needs to

adopt new and efficient management methods through the acquisition of new information and communication technologies. It also needs to be able to contribute to inevitable globalization at different levels, in addition to preserving cultural richness and diversity. The scarcity of job opportunities in the public sector points to the necessity of adapting graduate profiles to the private sector. This orientation necessitates the revision of study programs and teaching methods, the acquisition of new equipment, the training of personnel, and the replacement of aging faculty. Standards should be established about the maximum capacity of UMNG, especially with regard to the student-faculty ratio. Although adaptation of higher education to the requirements of the private sector is needed, it will also be necessary to safeguard the faculty from becoming totally involved in the entrepreneurial vocation of the private sector.

Choosing effective teaching methods is another challenge, considering the fact that expertise is lacking or simply undervalued at the national level. Other questions that need to be answered concern available financial resources; namely, how the private sector can be a good partner for public higher education, offer graduates potential career opportunities, and extend public higher education despite the decreasing public budget (Shabani 1998).

The future of higher education can only be conceived within a framework of diversification, in which Marien Ngouabi University is assigned a new mission and works in partnership with other well-performing private and public institutions of higher education within a clear legal framework that defines the orientation, the curriculum, the objectives, and the structure of Congolese higher education. A new mission statement for Marien Ngouabi University is to be presented during the University States-General (UMNG 1998a). The mission will focus on the training of graduates capable of contributing to the democratic life of the country, improving the human condition, meeting the challenge of privatization, and developing basic and applied research activities that are likely to lead to a dynamic relationship between research and development. The objective will be to serve Congo by using its own scholarly potential and providing required advice and expertise. This new vision seeks to adopt new technologies such as virtual libraries, databases, and other diversified research tools, all of which should prepare graduates for better integration into the private sector and enable them to meet the challenges of the modern world.

Despite significant efforts on the part of public authorities to promote Congolese higher education, Marien Ngouabi University suffers from many weaknesses. The immaturity of the private sector, the economic crisis, and the effects of the civil wars have combined to reduce the effectiveness of higher education's contribution to the development of Congolese society. However, with the progressive reestablishment of peace, there is hope that Congo will be able to reconstruct a modern higher education system, one that can cater to the immediate and long-term needs of the country through the provision of high-quality services.

REFERENCES

Gouvernement de la République du Congo. 1997a. "Table ronde du secteur de l'éducation, document de synthèse." Brazzaville, Congo: Secrétariat Général du Gouvernement.

——. 1997b. "Termes de référence de la consultation sectorielle sur l'éducation." Brazzaville, Congo: Secrétariat Général du Gouvernement.

Gouvernement de la République Populaire du Congo. 1989. "Document du 4e Congrès du Parti Congolais du Travail (PCT)." Brazzaville, Congo: Bureau Politique du Parti Congolais du Travail (PCT).

Ministère [français] des Affaires Étrangères, Ambassade de France Congo. 2000. *Agenda 2000.* Brazzaville, Congo: Ministère [français] des Affaires Étrangères.

Ministère de l'Education Nationale, de la Recherche Scientifique et Technologique. 1995. "Arrêté no. 1311, du 20 juillet 1995 fixant les conditions d'accès à l'Université Marien Ngouabi." Brazzaville: Ministère de l'Education Nationale, de la Recherche Scientifique et Technologique.

Shabani, J. 1998. "Enseignement Supérieur pour tous tout au long de la vie en Afrique subsaharienne." In J. Shabani, ed., *Enseignement Supérieur en Afrique: Réalisations, défis et perspectives.* UNESCO, Bureau Régional pour l'Education en Afrique.

UMNG (Université Marien Ngouabi). 1992. "Document des Etats généraux de l'ENS." Brazzaville: UMNG.

——. 1998a. "Document des Etats Généraux de l'UMNG: Rapport de la Sous-commission Pédagogie et recherché." Brazzaville: UMNG.

——. 1998b. "Document des Etats Généraux de l'UMNG: Rapport de la Sous-commission Pédagogie et recherché." Brazzaville: UMNG.

——. 1998c. "Document des Etats Généraux de l'UMNG: Rapport de la Sous-commission Pédagogie et recherché. Brazzaville: UMNG.

——. 1998d. "Document des Etats Généraux de l'UMNG: Rapport de la Sous-commission Historique de l'enseignement supérieur." Brazzaville: UMNG.

——. 1998e. "Document des Etats Généraux de l'UMNG: Rapport de la Sous-Commission Perspective de l'enseignement supérieur." Brazzaville: UMNG.

——. 1998f. "Rapport [non official] de la Commission de réflexion sur l'enseignement supérieur et la recherche scientifique au Congo." January. Brazzaville: UMNG.

UNESCO. 1998. *L'enseignement Supérieur dans le monde: Statistiques 1980–1995, document de travail de la Conférence mondiale sur l'enseignement supérieur.* Paris: UNESCO.

Union congolaise des banques. 1999. *Agenda 1999.* Brazzaville, Congo: Union congolaise des banques, 1999.

26

Democratic Republic of Congo (Zaire)

Matundu Lelo

OVERVIEW OF HIGHER EDUCATION IN CONGO

Higher education in Congo began and grew in the midst of initiatives that took place in Africa in the early 1960s. Prior to independence, Congo had two universities: Lovanium University (Université Louvanium), created in 1954 in Kinshasa (formerly Leopoldville), and the Official University (Université Officielle du Congo), created in 1956 in Lubumbashi (formerly Elizabethville).

The history of Congolese higher education can be divided into four major periods, beginning in 1954 (the date of the inauguration of the Lovanium University in Kinshasa) through the period of the States General on Education (Etats Généraux de l'Education) in January 1996.

1954–1971

This period is characterized by a certain degree of autonomy at the operational level. The two nonprofit public universities, Lovanium University (affiliated with the Catholic Church) and the Protestant Free University of Congo (Université Libre du Congo), were established respectively in 1954 and 1963. They were governed by autonomously elected administrative boards that included a representative delegated by the minister of education. The third university, the Official University of Congo at Lubumbashi, inaugurated in 1956, enjoyed internal autonomy in spite of the control exercised over it by the minister of education, who chaired the administrative board.

To allow for wider consultation and to provide better compatibility between academic and administrative goals, an interuniversity commission was created. The presidents of the three institutions formerly met under the presidency of the minister of education or his representative.

1971–1981

The concentration of power at the central level in August 1971 marked a major reform in Congolese higher education. The newly created National University of Zaire (Université Nationale du Zaïre, UNAZA) regrouped the entire existing network of universities under one system. The three existing universities were blended together and the faculty was reshuffled among the three institutions. The Advanced Institutes (Instituts Supérieurs) were reorganized in two main categories: Advanced Technical Institutes (Instituts Supérieurs Téchniques, IST) and Advanced Pedagogical Institutes (Instituts Supérieurs Pédagogiques, ISP). The Revolutionary Council (Conseil Révolutionnaire) became the only administrative body. This 1971 reform was driven by three main objectives: preserving national sovereignty, reinforcing national integrity at the level of teaching and research, and ensuring the rationalization and planning of training under a more efficient and unified leadership.

1981–1989

In an attempt to regain the autonomy which the universities lost in favor of the centralization initiative, they were divided again into three universities (University of Kinshasa, Kisangani University, and Lubumbashi University) and eighteen Advanced Technical Institutes, sixteen Advanced Pedagogical Institutes, and a School of Agronomy (Institut Facultaire des Sciences Agronomiques). The Revolutionary Council was split into three distinct units to fit the various categories of institutions: the University Administration Council (Conseil d'Administration des Universités, CAU), the Advanced Technical Institutes Administrative Council (Conseil d'Administration, IST), and the Advanced Pedagogical Institutes Administrative Council (Conseil d'Administration, ISP). From a legal point of view, each institution had the status of a nonprofit entity. Missions were devised for each program while maintaining the unity of academic principles for the entire higher education system. Similarly, university personnel were given a different status from that of civil servants. To support the efforts of the responsible ministry, five new special bodies were created to attend to the needs of this network: the Permanent Commission for Studies (Commission Permanente des Etudes, CPE), the Interdisciplinary Center for Development and Continuing Education (Centre Interdisciplinaire pour le Développement et l'Education Permanente, CIDEP), the Auditors Service (Collège des Commissaires au Comptes, CCC), the Bursar's Office (Intendence Générale, IG), and, finally, the University Press of Zaire (Presses Universitaires du Zaïre, PUZ).

This period was characterized by a series of events that proved to have considerable impact on universities. In 1984, a roundtable was organized to review and respond to the problems that resulted from the reforms of 1971–1981. Moreover, the speech of the president on December 5, 1984, opened investment in higher education to the private sector after a long period of government monopoly. The 1985–1990 five-year plan sought mainly to address questions raised during the 1984 roundtable and by the president's speech. The 1986 law related to national higher education reaffirmed the sovereignty of the government's higher education policy in all national general educational matters.

Since 1989

The governmental edict dated April 29, 1989, declaring the liberalization of universities gave a new orientation to the system. Any private party fulfilling the requirements of a legal entity could set up a postsecondary institution. In addition to removing the monopoly of the state over universities, the law introduced a number of significant new measures. It allowed for a new distribution of university branches and advanced institutes to other parts of the country. It also encouraged the principle of educational partnership, as it did for the primary and secondary school sectors. Such changes were motivated by a number of factors. First, the consecutive economic crises the country endured encouraged the disengagement of the state vis-à-vis higher education. For example, education appropriations decreased from 24.2 percent in 1980 (7.4 percent for higher education) to 7.9 percent in 1988 (1.5 percent for higher education). Second, there was increasing demand for higher education in Congo. In 1988–1989, while the normal university capacity was estimated at 9,927 at the public universities of Kinshasa, Kisangani, Lubumbashi, and the Yangambi Institute of Agronomy (Institut Facultaire des Sciences Agronomiques), the actual number of students was estimated at 27,166, resulting in a 274 percent saturation rate.

The country also needed to reduce regional disparities in enrollments. The city of Kinshasa, with only 10.4 percent of the population, was hosting 53.1 percent of the student population in 1989–1990. Meanwhile, other provincial universities such as the Upper Congo (13.8 percent population) and Katanga (13 percent population) hosted, respectively, 10.9 percent and 29.6 percent of the student population.

Education officials sought to find solutions that could make up for decreasing government subsidies. Studies carried out by the Project for the Improvement of Higher Education (Projet de Rationalisation de l'Enseignement Supérieur et Universitaire, PRESU) note that the "recent emergence of many private institutions [in Congo] is an indication of an excess in demand for higher education that could not be satisfied by the public system. It is also [an] indication that certain users are ready to pay for higher education services, which means that there are other means to finance higher education" (Eduplus 1991, 48).

The principles and structures implemented in the 1981 reform are still in force today. It should be noted, however, that prior to the government liberalization measures, a number of postsecondary institutions reported to other ministries, such as defense, finance and budget, public health, and labor. In addition, other private institutions operated under the leadership of the churches. These included the Kinshasa Catholic Faculty (Facultés Catholiques de Kinshasa), the Kinshasa Protestant Faculty (Facultés Protestantes de Kinshasa), and the Kimwenza Saint-Pierre Canisius School of Philosophy (Philosophat Saint-Pierre Canisius de Kimwenza). On another level, during the "political transition" period (April 1990 through May 1997), the ministry in charge of higher education created many university centers and public advanced technical and pedagogical institutes as a step toward the "redistribution" of institutions throughout the country.

The initiation of a multiparty political system during the early 1990s constitutes one of the most important developments in the history of Congolese higher education. Indeed, the proceedings of the National Commission on Education issued from the National Supreme Conference held in 1991–1992 brought resourceful solutions: the creation of an educational charter, reaffirmation of a commitment to educational partnerships, the return of institutions nationalized during the 1971 reforms to their initial owners, and the organization of a roundtable on education, namely the States General on Education. The latter took place in January 1996, and from it came the present Project of the New Educational System, which unfortunately has not yet been implemented due to the particular situation Congo has been enduring over the last few years.

PRESENT SITUATION AND TENDENCIES OF HIGHER EDUCATION

Structure, Organization, and Management

The general organization of the present university system is regulated by the October 1981 law, the provisions of which constituted the foundation of the 1981 reform that is still in force today. Over the years, it has been supplemented by other legal texts and regulations, such as law #86-005 dated September 22, 1986. Other governmental edicts were issued to support the existing legal texts; a case in point is the higher education liberalization law of 1989.

With regard to the current tendencies of universities and issues related to their organization and management, Debbasch affirms that "it is possible to isolate some problems that are encountered as fundamental themes to the sector of education."

Debbasch stresses four issues: the redistribution of power across the entire system, the structure of the institutions, the actual jurisdiction of institutions, and the management modes of institutions (Debbasch 1996, 12).

Under Congolese law, a plethora of decision-making channels and hierarchy structures exist. At the national level, various ministries intervene in higher education: the Ministry of Finance (Ministère des Finances), which deals with budget allocation and loan provision; the Ministry of Public Education Service (Ministère de la Fonction Publique), which has control over personnel; and the Ministry of Planning (Ministère du Plan), which is charged with issues pertaining to the planning of human resources.

The Ministry of National Education (Ministère de l'Education Nationale), the main body responsible for higher education in Congo, has five distinct services, each with specific objectives and each reporting to their respective hierarchical authorities: the Permanent Commission for Studies, a consultative body that specializes in academic problems; the Interdisciplinary Center for Development and Continuing Education, which offers continuing training for officials and links the university to the broader Congolese community through seminars and continuing education programs; the Bursar's Office, the technical and logistic unit that supports the efforts of universities and advanced schools to acquire scientific equipment, transport, supplies, and food, and to develop infrastructure and production; the University Press of Congo (formerly the University Press of Zaire), which is responsible for the publication of books and journals and operates in close collaboration with universities and other specialized services; and, finally, the auditor's service.

The administrative councils of the universities, the advanced technical institutes, and the advanced pedagogical institutes constitute other centers of control and decision making. In principle, these units hold extended powers over the administration of institutions. Their duties include the definition of general policies and objectives, control of financial management, approval of budgets, enforcement of regulations and bylaws, authorization of real estate sales and purchases, and control of receipts and expenses.

At the institutional level, universities and advanced institutes manage their own operational and investment budgets. Institutional decision makers are the council of the university/advanced institute, the managing committee, the university president, the directors of departments, the faculty or section council, and the department council.

In practice, though the 1981 reform calls for institutional autonomy, the government remains the major player in terms of educational policy. It decides on issues related to the organization of universities; the spreading of institutions, faculty, and institutes across the country; the definition of general measures and regulations applicable to educational institutions nationwide; the elaboration of the general development plan for higher education; and the coordination and organization of professors and administrative and technical personnel.

The structures of higher education institutions, as well as decisions concerning their geographical distribution, are decided at the governmental level. Matters such as the composition of institutions, their operating guidelines and organization, and the definition of legal frameworks all pertain to the government. Similarly, the definition of the types of institutional specialization and the creation of new schools or programs are handled by the government.

Due to the plurality of structures and decision-making niches, it is difficult to define the actual powers of a particular ministry. Such powers include control over finances, the management of institutions, and the coordination and hiring of different academic officials, personnel, and certain members of specialized services. The powers and tasks of the ministry in charge of education in this respect are extravagant.

University Autonomy

The autonomy of higher education in Congo can be measured at the pedagogical, financial, and political levels. Institutional autonomy is exercised mainly in four areas—student admission policies, the hiring of teaching assistants, choice of academic programs, and design of exams. Access to universities is free. However, the low capacity of existing institutions compared to the level of demand and the low purchasing power of most families severely limit access to universities. Universities have the prerogative to recruit teaching assistants within the limits of available budgetary positions and eligibility. Promotion beyond the rank of project manager requires the approval of the Ministry of Education. Application for promotion is filed through the administrative council of the institution. The government also defines the programs of study and the pedagogical norms. Programs and teaching loads are regulated and accompanied by implementation directives. Finally, while the details for exams are determined according to the academic examination code of each institution, the general provisions concerning the evaluation of students are determined directly by the government.

Two modes of financing exist—state subsidies and institutional revenues. State subsidies represent 90 percent of education funding and cover salaries, operational expenses, and grants. Institutional revenue, which accounts for no more than 10 percent of any institution's budget, is composed essentially of admission fees and income from services. Legal texts and regulations (including the October 1981 law on the organization of higher education, the September 1986 law on national education, and the April 1989 government edict opening higher education to the private sector) mention other possible sources of financing, such as contributions from parents, businesses, national and international organizations, and private donors. Contributions from businesses to universities generally occur informally through interpersonal relations. Contracts or collaboration agreements between universities and businesses are uncommon. The example of the University of Lubumbashi in Katanga and the General Mining Company (Générale des Carrières et Mines, GECAMINES) and between the University of Kinshasa and the water supply company (Régie Congolaise de Distribution d'Eau, REGIDESO) are exceptions to the rule. Similar initiatives have been fostered since the liberalization of universities, especially at the level of private provincial institutions such as the University of Mbuji-Maya and the Diamond Mining Company MIBA (Minière de Bakwanga, MIBA).

The multiplicity of decision centers to manage human resources and the complexity of procedures for budget and financing impede the autonomy of universities in Congo. Institutions have no real say with regard to allocation of available resources or the possibility of using their budget to take advantage of available opportunities. Certain revenues, such as registration fees, are centralized at the ministerial level, but no policy clearly determines the allocation of financial resources at the governmental level.

As for political autonomy, universities in Congo are all subject to the same general regulatory framework, which is applied without distinction nationwide. Despite the political advances since a new regime came to power in 1997, the situation has not really improved because guidelines have not been updated according to major changes that occurred.

University Management Modes

Individual Nomination and Election: Generally, the principle of election is not used to designate officers. The senior officials of the different departments—such as senior academic staff, members of the academic and scientific personnel, and managers of administrative and technical staff—are designated by the president of the republic or one of the ministers in charge of higher education.

Nomination of Senior Administrators: Normally, university presidents are nominated by members of the academic community. In the meantime, the president of the republic appoints the chancellor following a proposal by the minister. With regard to the nomination of assistants, positions that require a certain technicality or particular skills are chosen by the administrative officers. Examples of such positions are the general administrative secretary and the budget administrator.

Choice of Senior University Officers: University senior officers are usually chosen by the academic community but not necessarily from within the institution.

It is noteworthy that the dispositions of legal and regulatory texts are applied in a selective manner and on a case-by-case basis on the part of the authorities, especially in the private higher education sector.

PRIVATE HIGHER EDUCATION

Private higher education institutions have often served as pioneering postsecondary educational institutions in African countries. In fact, higher education in many African countries began in private institutions. Maugenest (1994, 175) confirms that "private higher education is not recent. It was the frame—at least as far as Congo and Lesotho are concerned—within which the first higher education system was introduced in these countries. The universities of Lovanium and Roma, which were nationalized by the new independent governments, constituted the embryos of the new state universities."

A retrospective look at private universities in Congo shows three institutional types that dominated the emergence of this sector after the first generation of universities.

Private Church-Affiliated Universities: The Catholic and the Protestant theology schools of Kinshasa are examples of private religiously affiliated universities. These were prohibited from operating within the campus of the National University of Zaire in 1974, when separate private university initiatives began. Other Protestant postsecondary theology institutes that emerged in that same period included the theology institute in Goma in the eastern part of the country.

Individually Supported Private Universities: Inspired by the clerical initiatives, many private universities emerged throughout the country around 1976 in response to both increasing demand for access to higher education and a desire to make a profit.

Private Provincial Community Initiatives: This new type of university was established in the early 1990s in response to a number of factors. These institutions—called community universities—operate in the provinces (nonurban areas) and combine aspects of the public and the strictly private sectors. They have communal rather than individual initiatives and operate as not-for-profit institutions. Moreover, they are financed by various private local entities. These bodies nominate the managers of the institution and ensure institutional control through a majority of delegates nominated in various positions throughout the institution's structure. This type of initiative was legally established by the government university liberalization decision of 1989. The government edict, dated April 1989, encouraged many initiatives to create private universities in provincial areas. Initiatives were often carried out with the help of religious denominations. According to the data of the Ministry of National Education, in 1996, there were 263 private educational institutions: 28.9 percent were approved; 32.3 percent were authorized to operate; and 38.8 percent were being considered for authorization.

Some of these universities proved to be of good quality. Cases in point are the private Catholic Theology Schools of Kinshasa (Facultés Catholiques de Kinshasa), the Bukavu Catholic University (Université Catholique de Bukavu), the Graben Catholic University at Butembo (Université Catholique du Graben), the Free University of the Great Lakes at Goma (Université Libre des Pays des Grands Lacs), the Protestant University of Congo at Kinshasa (Université Protestante du Congo), and provincial universities, such as the Kongo University (Université du Kongo, the former University of Lower-Zaire). Other examples of successful private initiatives are those established under the patronage of religious orders, such as Mbuji-Mayi University (Université de Mbuji-Mayi) and Cardinal Malula University in Kinshasa (Université Cardinal Malula de Kinshasa). Unfortunately, many recent universities do not meet required higher education standards because of their organization and the conditions within which they operate.

Tshibangu (1998, 43) notes that "it is real progress to move not only towards a larger general decentralization of our university system, but to liberalize its management as well. This will not only increase the number of institutions, but will create a wide competition which can only be beneficial for the country when conducted seriously."

Today, a clear definition of norms and regulations is needed to clearly outline the relationships between the private universities, the public universities, and the government and to integrate the entire higher education system into a national plan.

UNIVERSITY COOPERATION

Congolese higher education has a long tradition of forming partnerships with other institutions. Since the colonial period, exchanges have been initiated between educational partners through the local community, in colonial companies, and in religious denominations. Belgium, the former colonial power, ensured the integral exchange with the outside world. The Catholic Church took the initiative in most cases by creating a number of postsecondary institutions such as the Advanced School of Nursing (Ecole d'Assistants Médicaux) in 1935, the Medical Foundation of the Louvain University (Fondation Médicale de l'Université de Louvain) in 1937, the Advanced School of Administration and Commerce (Ecole Supérieure des Sciences Administratives et Commerciales) in 1947, the Agronomy Center at the University of Louvain (Centre Agronomique de l'Université de Louvain, CADULAC) in 1949, and the Lovanium University in 1954.

Soon after independence, educational partnerships became more diversified as international organizations such as the United Nations, UNESCO, UNDP, USAID, and private foundations became involved, all of which helped to sustain initiatives started at the time of colonization.

Since decolonization, Congolese institutions of higher education have witnessed increased participation at the subregional (Central African and Great Lakes), regional (African), and international levels. This trend continued until the 1980s, when a period of isolation of the Congolese university began.

Local university cooperation generally involves consultation and exchanges between public and private Congolese universities. Unfortunately, such cooperation, because it is informal and not institutionalized, is carried out most of the time on an individual basis.

Subregional cooperation brings members of regional organizations such as the Conference of University Presidents of the Member Countries of the Great Lakes Community (Conférence des Recteurs des Universités des Etats Membres de la Communauté des Pays des Grands Lacs, CEPGL) and the Conference of Chancellors and Presidents of Central Africa (Conférence des Recteurs et Chanceliers de l'Afrique Centrale, COREVIC) into contact with each other.

Regional cooperation was initiated by two of the most visible organizations in Africa; namely, the Conference of Presidents of French-speaking Universities (Conférence des Recteurs des Universités Francophones d'Afrique, CRUFA), created in Kinshasa in 1973; and the Association of African Universities (Association des Universités Africaines, AUA), started in 1967 in Rabat, Morocco. The first activity organized in Dakar, Senegal, by the CRUFA brought together the Association of Partially or Entirely French-Speaking Universities (Association des Universités Partiellement ou Entièrement de Langue Française, AUPELF) and the Higher Education Bureau in Dakar.

International interuniversity cooperation can be seen in the activities of AUPELF and the French-Speaking University Agency (Agence Universitaire de la Francophonie, UREF). Although Congo was a founding member of these two associations in 1961, the participation of the Congolese universities was reduced to eleven institutions, of which nearly half are from the private sector. Congo is also member of the International Association of Universities (Association Internationale des Universités, AIU), which is another example of international university cooperation.

Other educational partnerships consist of relationships that tie the university to its socioeconomic and professional environments; for example, partnerships between universities and industry (GECAMINES and REGIDESO) and with private nongovernmental organizations and foundations such as the Rockefeller Foundation, the Ford Foundation, the Friedrich Neumann Foundation, the Konrad Adenauer Foundation, and the Hans Seidel Foundation.

Bilateral cooperation between various countries has taken place since the early years of higher education in Congo. Cooperative ties were established with many countries, including Belgium, France, Germany, Canada, Poland, Romania, the United States, Brazil, the United Kingdom, and Japan.

Multinational cooperation was conducted through relationships with UNESCO, the former Agency for Cultural and Technical Cooperation (Agence de Cooperation Culturelle et Technique, ACCT), the UNDP, the UN Economic Commission for Africa, the Organization of African Unity (Organisation de l'Unité Africaine, OUA), the European Union, and the UN University.

SPECIFIC PROBLEMS OF CONGOLESE HIGHER EDUCATION

Congo's enduring political crisis, which has been raging for a decade now, has spared no sector of activity in the country. The entire educational system has felt the impact of the war. The interconnection of issues and their mutual impact makes it difficult, therefore, to isolate and treat problems separately.

The context of the war in Congo (1996–1997 and since 1998) has impacted higher education and provided issues for reflection.

Student Activism: A few facts about the development of student activism in Congo help to shed light on current trends. In 1964, students of the former University of Lovanium asked for more participation in the organization and operation of the university in the form of a co-management model and demanded the Africanization of the conception, orientation, and methodology of both teaching and research.

In 1969 and 1971—that is, between the two main reforms of 1967 and 1981—students pushed for many social reforms related to the improvement of campus living and working conditions and increases in educational grants.

During the 1990s, with the introduction of a multiparty system, students clashed with each other in interethnic confrontations. The disturbances were a reaction to the political confusion of the country after the second government of transition nominated many former close associates of President Mobutu. Students organized roundtables all across the country calling for improvements to the university system through more adapted teaching and research programs. Students also demanded the reform of financial and administrative management, improved use of the existing infrastructure and facilities, and funding to build new facilities (Ngoma 1994).

These student movements had a considerable impact on the university that can still be felt today. As a reaction to these movements, a number of drastic measures were taken. In 1971, universities were closed down and students were enlisted in the army. The position of political authorities became less flexible toward the university; they saw it as a potential source of opposition. Reforms targeting universities were aimed at controlling the campus rather than finding appropriate solutions to problems in the education sector. In this respect, the university was used to enhance certain political interests (Sabakinu 1991).

Graduate Unemployment and Brain Drain: Studies conducted by the World Bank have linked unemployment in developing countries, especially the sub-Saharan area, to the fact that Africa has been training too many senior officers at the expense of researchers, experts, and specialists who are likely to serve in the development process. The World Bank also noted that training often does not correspond to the development needs of these countries (World Bank 1988). Job opportunities for university graduates in a given country depend largely on the development of its economy, which explains the unemployment problem that Congo endures (Norro 1991).

To deal with the problem of graduate unemployment, the Project for the Improvement of Higher Education (PRESU) conducted a study. Focusing on university training and employment, the study was based on a comparison between the estimated employment needs from 1991 to 2009 and the number of graduates expected from universities and advanced schools during this period. The conclusions of this study show that the degree of the compatibility between the job market and university graduates varies according to discipline, the level of training, and the prevailing opinion concerning the quality of training of graduates (Semagroup 1991).

A clear quantitative distinction exists between the disciplines that have an appropriate number of students, those suffering excess enrollment, and specialties with a deficit of students. When evaluating quality, many parameters need to be considered: the lack of practical training, lack of management skills, insufficiency and even absence of candidates fulfilling the required conditions, and absence of confidence in the university system on the part of both graduates and employees.

To remedy these deficiencies, PRESU/World Bank made a number of suggestions. On the level of quantity, stress was put on balancing the excess and deficit in students across departments. Programs were revised and creativity was encouraged in order to improve the quality of the curriculum. Structurally, collaborative networks with businesses, government, and the university were highlighted. Since the recommendations have been formulated, ten years have elapsed and none have been implemented.

A decade ago, Congo counted 110,000 university graduates. All senior political and national positions were filled by university graduates. Graduates occupied between 5 and 15 percent of the positions of technical advisers, 80 percent of the public sector, and 60 percent of the private sector. Evidence of the quality of university graduates has also been proven at the international level. Many contributions to research, seminars, conferences, and scientific societies bear witness to that, and many Congolese scholars have been solicited for teaching positions abroad

(Tshibangu 1998). But at the present time, higher education has suffered as the entire Congolese social, sociocultural, economic, and political fabrics have changed.

The African Club pointed out during a meeting held at Lomé, the capital of Togo, that the 1980s witnessed an increase in unemployment rates, even for university graduates with advanced degrees. The Club's assessment of the situation and of the proposed solutions at that time match to a large degree the conclusions and recommendations made by Semagroup in 1991. Personally, I believe that change will come only with the reestablishment of the necessary balances at all social levels; namely, democracy, economy, and stability.

Research and Publication: Research is the second traditional mission of a university. Many initiatives have been undertaken in Africa since early independence to promote research, disseminate its results, and integrate it with developmental strategies. Organizational and political entities involved in initiating research activity include other African governments, UNESCO, the UN, the UN Economic Commission for Africa (Commission Economique des Nations Unies pour l'Afrique, CEA), the United Nations Conference on Science and Technology for Development (Commission des Nations Unies sur la Science et la Téchnologie au Service du Développement, CNCUSTD), the Organization of African Unity, and other African universities.

Research and publication in higher education benefited from special attention in the first years after independence. At the time, authorities put in place appropriate structures to promote research. Each school was assigned a vice-dean in charge of research, and new research centers were established. Codes and statutes to regulate research activity were created. Later on, in 1978, the Permanent Commission for Research (Commission Permanente de la Recherche, CPR) and the Permanent Commission for Studies (Commission Permanente des Etudes, CPE) were created. Their impact on the quality of training was undeniable.

The University Press of Congo, part of the Zaire National University, served as a point of reference within Africa as well as abroad. Its mission has been impeded because of budgetary problems caused by insufficient funds, inconsistency in budget allocation, and the multiplicity of decision-making centers involved in budget management. Publication was also affected by the negative consequences of various reforms and the degradation of the university. The lack of focus and motivation among, and even the vagrancy of, researchers encouraged the monopoly of political powers over researchers, who were subjected to exile and dependence on foreign countries. The current state of the university is largely a consequence of these political problems.

Political Instability and the University: The Great Lakes region has been confronted over the last decade with the most profound and complex crisis of its history. Many serious problems have emerged as a result of war, including forced movement of population and disturbances in the school system. Although university members and scientific experts from regional universities are sometimes consulted on an individual level, the university is not an actor in conflict resolution.

In the eastern part of Congo, universities are having a difficult time operating properly because of the 1996–1997 war, which brought the present government to power, and the war between Congo and its neighbors that began on August 2, 1998 (Matundu 2000).

A review of the best years of the university in Congo reveal that solidarity and interuniversity exchanges, or, even better, university cooperation were essential to higher education. African universities in general are under a moral obligation to come to the rescue of the Congolese university, which has been the victim of a long and enduring political crisis. Throughout the drafting of this chapter, as I collected data and conversed with members of certain Western institutions and individuals involved directly or indirectly in projects underway in Rwanda, Burundi, and Uganda, it was clear that universities in these countries are not as deeply affected by this crisis as in Congo.

THE WAY FORWARD IN THE MIDST OF CHAOS

Talking about the prospects of higher education in Congo is both easy and complex. It is easy to determine the problem if one considers the increasing volume of studies conducted on Congolese education. The bulk of these studies were conducted between 1971 and 1989, and their conclusions are found in the States General on Education carried out in 1996; the Congolese Project of the New Educational System; and the recommendations of the studies carried out between 1989 and 1991 by PRESU/World Bank, though these have not been totally implemented. Other data consists of reflections made either upon personal initiatives or upon request from international organizations dealing with higher education such as the UN, Western universities, or former educational partners of Congo.

At the same time, defining the prospects for higher education in Congo is difficult. The fact is, as Peter J. Murphy says, that "even if we were to investigate the prospects based on knowledge of past, present, and general tendencies," it is difficult to make projections about the future for Congo in its current situation (CEPES/UNESCO 1985, 37).

Urgent Measures: Immediate measures need to be carried out on three levels: structures and activities, financial and budgetary planning, and internal and external relationships.

With regard to the structures and activities of the university, the entire set of legal and regulatory texts that govern the university needs to be updated to ensure that the government treats public and private educational institutions equally. Such provisions should be able to assign private institutions nonprofit status so they can support the public sector. Higher education also needs to be able to foster an academic community through various religious, secular, and public networks. Autonomy is another vital element that must be restored to the university, and the government must become an equal partner instead of a bureaucratic director.

Budgets are vital for the efficient functioning of higher education. It is vital that universities be able to negotiate their funding through a contractual policy, on the basis of which any given institution can negotiate its budget using an institutional project that reflects the main objectives envisioned in the long term and covers all aspects of the institution's life.

Relationships and ties both internally and externally are of paramount importance to the university. The principle of educational partnership should be implemented through involvement of various actors in the educational process. Furthermore, cooperation should be promoted from a model in which each party is respected and recognized as an equal partner and in which the benefits are mutual.

The university in Congo should be able to anticipate rather than merely be subjected to events. Such a wish will be realizable if Congo relies on its most cherished resources the human element scattered worldwide, and on long-term investment. Despite the long and deep crisis that is tearing Congo apart, its higher education system still holds its position in the international university community and will hopefully reassume its national role with the help of university cooperation networks.

BIBLIOGRAPHY

CEPES/UNESCO. 1985. "La gestion de l'enseignement: le rôle des administrateurs." Bucharest, Romania. *ARTEXIM: Revue trimestriel du Centre Européen pour l'enseignement supérieur* X, no. 3 (July–September 1985).

Coupez, A. 1982. "L'utilisation des langues et ses problèmes." In *Cooperation et Choc de Civilization: Symposium. Bruxelles: Decembre 12, 1980.* Brussels: Académie Royale des Sciences d'Outre-Mer.

Debbasch, C. 1991. "L'administration de l'enseignement en Europe." In CNRS, ed., *Annuaire Européen d'administration publique.* Paris: Edition CNRS.

Eduplus. 1991. *Activités:* A.3.1. Suppl. 48.

Lamour-Rontopoulou, J. 1994. "L'université Africaine à la croisée des chemins." *Afrique contemporaine, La documentation française* 172, Edition Spéciale (4ème trimestre, octobre–décembre 1994): 149.

Matundu, L. 1995–1996. "Pour de nouvelles formules d'administration universitaire, une étude prospective sur les universités du Zaïre." Mémoire de Master en Gestion et Administration Publiques, Université d'Anvers.

———. 1997–1998. "La coopération universitaire: support de l'université pour la réalization de ses missions en période de crise. Une étude sur l'enseignement supérieur et universitaire en R.D. du Congo." Mémoire de D.E.S. en Coopération au Développement, ULB.

———. 1998–1999. "Coopération Universitaire et prévention des conflits dans la région des Grands Lacs." In *L'Afrique des Grands Lacs: Annuaire 1998–99,* 336–354. Paris: Centre d'Etude de la région des Grands Lacs, Université d'Anvers, l'Harmattan.

———. 2000. "Détérioration et coopération universitaire dans l'est du Congo." In *L'Afrique des Grands Lacs: Annuaire 1998–99.* Paris: Harmattan.

Maugenest, D. 1994. "L'Enseignement supérieur privé." In *Afrique contemporaine, La documentation française* 172, Edition Spéciale (octobre–décembre 1994): 175.

Ngoma, B. 1994. "Faut-il privatiser les universités officielles du Zaïre?" *Zaïre Afrique* 288 (October): 498–499.

Norro, M. 1991. "Les universités et l'avenir du Zaïre." Conférence donnée à Anvers, 21 Février.

Pool de Kinshasha. 1997. "Pré-rapport sur les travaux préparatoires à la rencontre Belgo-Congolaise sur la relance de la coopération universitaire." Unpublished report.

Sabakinu, K. 1991. "Le rôle du professeur d'université dans le Zaïre de demain." Paper presented at Association des Professeurs de l'Université de Kinshasa, message aux travaux de la Conférence Nationale Souvraine, Kinshasa.

Semagroup. 1991. "Activité C1. Adéquation Formation-Emploi: Synthèse, présentation condensée des résultats et recommendations." PRESU/World Bank.

Tshibangu, T. 1984. "L'Enseignement supérieur et le développement de l'Afrique d'ici l'an 2000." Dakar: Consultation UNESCO-BREDA.

—— 1998. *L'Université Congolaise: Etapes historiques, situation actuelle et défis à relever.* Kinshasa: Edition Universitaires Africaines, ACCT.

——. 1999. "L'université Africaine et l'humanisme spirituel et scientifique pour le XXI^{è} siècle." Paper presented at the symposium Jubilé 2000, Rome. September.

Tshibangu, T., ed. "La contribution de l'enseignement supérieur au développement des sociétés africaines." Part IV, ED-82/MINEDAF/REF. Paper presented at a meeting of African ministers of education, n.d.

UNAZA (Université National du Zaïre). 1980. "Bilan de la Cooperation: lors du 25ème anniversaire de l'ESU." Report written by the Direction of the Cooperation for the 25th anniversary of the Higher Education in Congo. Kinshasha: Direction de la Coopération.

UNESCO. 1986. *L'enseignement supérieur et universitaire du Zaïre, République du Zaïre.* Paris: Départment de l'Enseignement Supérieur et Universitaire, Paris.

——. 1999. *Annuaire statistique.* Berman Press. Tables II-18, II-19, II-15.

UNESCO/BREDA. 1987. *Amélioration et rénovation de l'enseignement supérieur en Afrique. Actes du Colloque.* Senegal: Breda.

UNESCO/CEA. 1986. "Recherche scientifique et formation en Afrique." Paper presented at Conférence intergouvernementale, Lagos, Nigeria: UNESCO.

World Bank. 1988. *L'education Subsaharienne: Pour une stratégie d'ajustment, de revitalization et d'expansion.* Washington, D.C.: World Bank.

Côte d'Ivoire

PASCAL VALENTIN HOUENOU AND YVELINE HOUENOU-AGBO
in collaboration with FÊTÊ ERNEST KOFFI, CATHERINE GUÉRINA COULIBALY,
AISSATA BOURGOIN TOURÉ, and TOHOURI BERNABÉ GOUZILIE

INTRODUCTION

Côte d'Ivoire is a Francophone country in West Africa with an area of 322,462 square kilometers (124,503 square miles). With a growth rate of 3.8 percent per year, the population was expected to grow from 10,815,000 in 1988 to 14,208,000 inhabitants in 1995, which translates to approximately 27 inhabitants per square mile. More than 48 percent of the population is less than 15 years old (Houphouët-Boigny and Mansilla 1999).

Since 1980, the country has undergone an economic, social, and political crisis which has had a drastic impact on higher education and affected the development of manpower, the quality of research, and the contribution of higher education to general social development. Despite significant policies, meetings, and workshops at national, regional, and international levels, it has become more and more difficult to preserve the gains achieved at the onset of independence in 1960. This chapter will provide information on the development of higher education in Côte d'Ivoire, taking into account its general purposes, its institutional capacities, its curriculum, its output, its research activities, the maintenance of equipment, cooperation with other institutions, and challenges for the future.

Higher education in Côte d'Ivoire is comprised of universities and schools. The schools are generally oriented toward professional training. The official language is French. Over sixty local languages or dialects exist. Languages or dialects such as Baoule and Dioula, respectively used in the east-central region and the north, are taught in the Faculty of Arts of the University of Cocody.

The first Higher Education Center was created in 1958 under a French government decree. This Center reached full university status in 1964. Today there are three universities in Côte d'Ivoire, two Regional Units of Higher Education in the cities of Daloa (west central region) and Korhogo (in the north), and

many research centers. In addition, the National Polytechnic Institute and other public and private schools contribute to higher education in the country. For the academic year 1996–1997, thirty-seven out of fifty-five private universities received the endorsement of the Ministry of Higher Education and Scientific Research (Ministère de l'Enseignement Supérieur de la Recherche Scientifique 1997a). Most of them are located in the Abidjan Region. The first American university should start its activities during the academic year 2001–2002 or 2002–2003 in Grand Bassam City.

HIGHER EDUCATION ORGANIZATION

To describe the organizational system of higher education, two main periods can be distinguished: from 1958 to 1992 and from 1992 to 2000.

The Organizational System from 1958 to 1992

According to the 1966 decree that organized the University of Abidjan, three central structures were created: the Council of Higher Education Teaching, the Standing Board of Higher Education Teaching, and the University Council.

The Council of Higher Education Teaching, presided over by the chief of the government, was assigned the following objectives:

- To develop the higher education development program in Côte d'Ivoire, taking into account the priorities defined by the government
- To come up with measures to ensure the implementation of the program
- To coordinate the proposals of all interested ministerial departments by hiring more faculty and raising the educational standards for full-time faculty members

The Council of Higher Education Teaching could call on the services of expert consultants capable of helping them examine the issues listed above.

The Standing Board of Higher Education Teaching is presided over by the national education minister. Its functions include coming up with budget proposals for different higher education teaching schools that make decisions about issues relative to school life, administration, the creation of chairs, and the organization of curriculum development.

The University Council's responsibilities include budget approval; the allocation of credits; the distribution of teaching programs; the regulation of courses, lectures, and laboratories; and the proposal of higher education teaching disciplines, certificates, and teaching and research institutes to the Standing Board.

The University Council is composed of the rector as president, the deans, two teachers' representatives from each faculty, and the university secretary-general.

In addition to these central structures, faculty assemblies were created, which were presided over by the dean of each facility. The assembly defines faculty tasks in order to develop harmonious teaching methods and compare the different teaching methods used (lecture, guided works, and lab work). Students' representative groups (nonstatutory) were created to eliminate the drawbacks of student misrepresentation and to facilitate information sharing and communication between teachers and students.

University management structures include the Information and Programming University Centre (CUIP) and the University Data Processing Centre (CUTI). CUIP is an ongoing think tank aimed at developing and integrating a system to manage the scheduling, control, functioning, and evaluation of university activities. CUTI was created in 1974; its objectives are to organize and coordinate various computer courses, and to develop a computer network and manage materials and staff.

The University National Social Centre (CNOU) deals with the everyday management of student social life. It is in charge of housing, cafeterias, payment of scholarships, transport arrangements, and the management of social services (health, sport, and leisure). At the time, three-quarters of Ivorian students were entitled to scholarships. Housing and cafeteria fees were relatively low, and transport was free of charge.

The Organizational System from 1992 to the Present

The reform law of 1977 was never really applied and the organizational system remained mostly the same until 1992. An increase in the number of students on the Cocody campus and frequent problems caused by inadequate facilities and infrastructure led the government to search for a way to apply the 1977 law and to call for an adjustment. Thus, the decentralization of the National University became a reality, and it was divided into three campuses: the University Center of Cocody, the University Center of Abobo-Adjamé (in charge also of the Regional Center of Higher Education of Daloa), and the University Center of Bouaké (in charge of the Regional Center of Higher Education of Korhogo). Each center was directed by a

vice-rector under the leadership of a rector who was the head of the national university.

In 1996, the three centers reached full university status and became the University of Abobo-Adjamé, the University of Bouaké, and the University of Cocody. In these universities, research and training units (UFR) replaced the faculties in order to better integrate research within the teaching structures (decree No. 96-611 of August 9, 1996). The universities follow complementary and multidisciplinary principles, but they may also have a primary vocation. Each university has at least the following administrative, financial, and technical services: management and financial services, university properties and maintenance services, data processing services, documentation, scientific information, publishing services, registration, reception, and information services. For the first time in Côte d'Ivoire, the universities were clearly oriented toward professional programs. The University of Abobo-Adjamé was the first to make significant progress by developing short- and long-term academic and professional training programs, aimed at lifelong development through an integrated, participatory, and interdisciplinary approach with the support of the productive or other development sectors. The university also launched research and development programs focused on solving environmental and food-related problems and on forest preservation.

As the universities were professionalized, the schools of engineering at Yamoussoukro were reorganized and took the name of Houphouët-Boigny National Polytechnic Institute (INP-HB). In addition, the development of private universities was encouraged by the government, as the national university was unable to integrate all the pupils who had completed their secondary education.

Historical Background, Current Trends, and Development of Research Policy

The document entitled "Actes des Etats Généraux de la Recherche" (Ministère de l'Enseignement Supérieur de la Recherche Scientifique 1999) is the latest report highlighting the research activities in Côte d'Ivoire. This report provides historical background, information on the number of national institutions involved in the research activities inside and outside universities, and information on schools and ongoing projects.

Between independence in 1960 and 1970, important national research centers were created, such as the Institut de Recherche Agronomique (Institute of Agronomy Research, IRAT) and the Centre Technique Forestier d'Abidjan (Abidjan Forestry Technical Center, CTFT). Their activities were mainly oriented toward agriculture and forest exploitation—wood, cocoa, and coffee for export—as well as food self-sufficiency (rice, animal husbandry, etc.). The development of a real national research policy started in 1971, as the country became convinced that science and technology were the pathways to the future. The first ministry in charge of research was created in 1971. Specific tools and methodologies for planning research activities were developed under the leadership of the new ministry; program commissions, budget commissions, and commissions for young and graduating researchers were inserted within existing institutions. At the same time, research concerns were tackled in sectors other than agronomy, such as ecology, technology, and oceanography. In 1991, the International Scientific Research Institute for Development in Africa (IIRSDA) was created.

At the beginning, the ministries in charge of research and higher education were separated. But since the 1990s, the two areas have been overseen by the same ministry, the Ministry of Higher Education and Scientific Research, which has five main functions: to help with national development, to anticipate events in the field of research and development, to help with training at the graduate and postgraduate levels, to develop databases and information systems, and to disseminate research results.

The National Education and Training Sectors
Development Plan (PNDEF), 1998–2008

Despite goodwill and relevant policies, the quality of the output from the universities has been declining in recent years. This is due to various factors, which include institutional capacities and social, economic, and political instability within the country. Higher education concerns are now focused on the following points: the weakness of managerial capacity; the inadequacy of training and educational programs regarding the needs of society; and the inadequacy of research programs and projects with respect to higher education policies, sciences, and technology. Based on such facts, and also on the Yamoussoukro Declaration of the head of state on August 26, 1995, the major challenge to the education sector as a whole is to prepare Côte d'Ivoire to enter the third millennium and to become a postindustrial society well aware of information, knowledge, continuous training, initiative, and creativity. To address this challenge, the priorities laid out in the Law on Education No. 95-696 of September 7, 1995, are the search for equity and qualified human resources and the development of a national scientific and technological culture. Consequently, a National Education and Training Sectors Development Plan (PNDEF, 1998–2008) was developed to enable each Ivorian to get access to education and training throughout his or her life. This objective should be implemented on the basis of the following:

- The reinforcement of capacity building in terms of plans, programs, and budgets
- The development of a new technology information system
- The elaboration and implementation of an action plan for decentralization of the management of higher education and of training and research programs to meet regional needs
- The privatization of selected activities or sectors of interest
- The implementation of a follow-up system

PNDEF estimated the cost for higher education at about $73,142,465 during 1998 to 2008. This plan includes improved quality of universities, institutional development, and new sector development including networking, the Internet, research and development, and documentation. Ongoing activities in higher education are based on PNDEF, but it is difficult to attract funds from donors, given the political situation and the drastic economic situation the country has faced since 1999.

INSTITUTIONAL CAPACITIES

The University of Abidjan was originally built for 6,000 students. Before 1990, some efforts were made to add several new buildings and classrooms. Unfortunately, the efforts were not sufficient to meet the real needs of the university. In addition, libraries are obsolete because the lack of significant funds has seriously affected their ability to acquire books and journals. Finally, equipment for teaching and research is obsolete or lacking in many cases, mainly in scientific units, despite the effort made by the government and donors to solve this problem. Personal computers have appeared on campus only recently. The National Research and Higher Education Federation (SYNARES) has initiated a project to make personal computers available to all academic staff. Only the University of Abobo-Adjamé has its own Internet system for students and teachers. Other universities will be provided with the Internet with support from the ministry in charge of higher education. The situation in the schools of engineering at Yamoussoukro was different and more sustainable; infrastructures were adequate for both administration and academic staff and students.

Human Resources

According to national and Conseil Africain et Malgache pour l'Enseignement Supérieur (CAMES) standards, there are four levels of academic staff: lecturers, senior lecturers, associate professors, and professors. Until 1988, the number of lecturers increased, followed by a significant decrease in 1990 when the University of Abidjan faced its first big crisis of demonstrations by students and staff. This decrease was followed by significant progress and then a new decrease in 1996. The decrease observed between 1988 and 1990 was the result of the private sector attracting more young graduates from national and foreign universities and the lack of funds to pay salaries for new lecturers. The government was forced to reduce salaries in 1992, which allowed them to recruit more people for almost the same level of budget allocation. From 1991 to 1996, progress was made in terms of recruitment of lecturers, but it seems that a new decrease is taking place as a consequence of lower salaries for lecturers. In the specific case of senior lecturers, their numbers increase as the number of lecturers decrease. This phenomenon is difficult to explain; perhaps some efforts were made by lecturers to publish research, which is one of the basic criteria for staff promotion.

Finally, the number of associate professors is not encouraging for the period after the year 1995, and the number of professors is very low. This tendency could affect the quality of teaching and research and reduce university capacity because of the number of highly qualified staff who are retiring from the universities. The government is aware of this situation and recently decided to raise the retirement age of professors and associate professors from 60 to 65.

In 1998, the total number of researchers working in national research institutes or centers was 219, representing 14.2 percent of the total research and development personnel in Côte d'Ivoire (Tapsoba 2000). Very few of them earn their Ph.D. or doctorate degrees. The situation regarding qualified researchers is not encouraging despite the development of relevant laboratories within the country.

Administrative and technical staff are inadequate in terms of both quantity and quality. The total number of personnel in all universities remained stable until 1995 (828 persons). After that period, only 412 remained in their positions. One could explain this decrease by the fact that after 1997, universities were not allowed to use nonacademic personnel on a part-time basis.

French cooperation is very active in helping to computerize the registration process and deans' offices, partly as a response to the call to participate in PNDEF. The lack of technicians—there were only 112 in the entire country in 1998, which represents 7.2 percent of the total number of research and development personnel (Tapsoba 2000)—is affecting research and training activities as well; qualified technicians prefer being recruited to the private sector, where good salaries are ensured. Consequently, universities are facing a significant maintenance problem.

Financing and Funding Patterns

Funding for higher education comes from the government, which contributes more than 95 percent of the budget. In 1997, the government contribution was $60,389,041 for the General Working Budget (BGF) of higher education: 39.2 percent ($23,668,493) for salaries, 25.2 percent ($15,209,589) for the management of institutions, 24.3 percent for student loans, and 11.3 percent ($684,931) for private schools. Private-sector contributions were minor. Including debt, the overall BGF of Côte d'Ivoire in 1997 was $1,857,671,233 and $926,849,315 without debt. The BGF for higher education corresponds to 3.2 percent of total BGF (including debt; 6.5 percent without debt). In 1997, the amount of the Special Budget for Investment (BSIE) to higher education was $11,071,233, which represents 1.9 percent of the national BSIE. This specific budget enabled the Ministry of Higher Education to provide more amphitheaters, classrooms, and laboratories, but it still could not meet all real needs in terms of facilities and equipment.

In fact, the dependence of universities and higher education schools on government funds causes many difficulties. Universities are now called upon to develop strategies to attract more funds from development banks, donors, the private sector, and school attendance fees. But one policy urgently needs to be addressed: although it seems incomprehensible under the financial circumstances, the government contributed $11,057,638 for training abroad during the last three academic years (1997–1998, 1998–1999, 1999–2000), according to Ministry of Higher Education statistics. This sum was spent on scholarships for only 1,469 students and represents $3,685,880 per year, or $7,527 per student, an annual cost that is very high compared to the working budget of some universities. For instance, the University of Abobo-Adjamé has a total working budget of $4,530,137. The average annual cost of school attendance is estimated to be around US$480; each student pays tuition fees of only $10 (2 percent of the estimated cost) in state universities or about $2,000 in private universities. The tuition fee of $10 is very low and students will not accept any increase right now, because their parents have paid between US$200 and US$500 each year for thirteen years to pay for their secondary studies.

The government has developed a student loan program. Decree No. 98-405 created a student loan fund for higher education training. Student loans can be used by successful applicants to pay their tuition fees for training in national higher education institutions or abroad.

CURRICULUM

During the 1990s, surveys indicated the need to review the curriculum within higher education institutions. These institutions are now adopting a curriculum based on a Unités de Valeur (UV) system, which is very close to the course-credit system of North America. The University of Abobo-Adjamé was the first to make significant progress in this approach and has been chosen as a pilot institution.

The curriculum corresponds to three levels of courses. The first level is a postsecondary two-year program called the *Diplôme d'Etudes Universitaires Générales* (DEUG). The second level, the *licence*, is a post-DEUG one-year program that corresponds to the bachelor's degree in North America. The *maîtrise* is a post-*licence* one-year program. The third level includes postgraduate degrees. The *Diplôme d'Etudes Approfondies* (DEA) and the *Diplôme d'Etudes Supérieures Spécialisées* (DESS) correspond to research or professional master's degrees (one or two more years after the *maîtrise*). There are two types of doctorate degrees: *doctorat de cycle* and the *doctorat d'etat*. Only the University of Abobo-Adjamé is developing a doctorate program that corresponds very closely to the Ph.D.

Course programs are mostly organized into semesters. Registration for a program occurs at the beginning of the academic year, usually in September or October.

At the undergraduate level, students are entitled to a maximum of four years to complete their study. One cannot apply for the *licence* program without the DEUG, or for the *maîtrise* without the *licence*, or for the DEA or DESS without the *maîtrise* or equivalent degrees. Evaluation usually takes place at the end of each semester. Before the new academic year, a second session of examinations is organized, usually in September or October, for the students who did not pass all their credits.

At all levels, practical work in laboratories is very important, especially in applied sciences faculties or units. But due to the drastic economic crisis and the rapid increase in the numbers of students, universities were forced to limit this activity to the second year of DEUG for those students who passed the theoretical exams.

ENROLLMENT AND OUTPUT

Enrollment

One can have access to an undergraduate program after completing six years of schooling at primary school, followed by another seven years at secondary school. In the academic year 1997–1998, 100,724 students were registered at the level of higher education. Eighty-one percent of them (82,173 students) studied at public institutions dependent on the Ministry of Higher Education. Of these, 66 percent of the students were in state schools and universities. Eight percent of the students studied in the state schools of technology (Houphouët-Boigny and Mansilla 1999). Student enrollment from 1991 to 1998 indicates that the number of students at the University of Cocody remains significant despite the creation of the universities of Abobo-Adjamé and Bouaké. Student enrollment is very high in the fields of law, economics, and arts training and research units (e.g., faculties). The University of Abobo-Adjamé is in charge of training first-year medical students for the whole country; over 2,000 medical students register each year, almost 40 percent of the students at the university as a whole.

At the level of professional schools, the number of students is quite stable because they generally recruit only the number of qualified persons needed by the private sector. Nevertheless, enrollment at the College of Education (ENS), where students are trained to teach secondary school, has been declining since 1987, from almost 1,500 students to less than 200. Therefore, the country is facing a lack of secondary school teachers while the number of pupils has been increasing steadily. This could affect the quality of teaching and the results in that sector. Efforts should be made to educate girls, whose annual schooling rate is 15 percent, and whose numbers are especially low in the domains of sciences and technology. Finally, the increase in the number of applicants for higher education institutions will go on for many years as a result of increase in the birth rate and the evolution of pupil populations at the primary schools (Houphouët-Boigny and Mansilla 1999). As a consequence of this fact and the economic crisis, public higher education institutions, which have proven to be unable to promptly respond to social trends, will face many difficulties in the future because of a lack of infrastructure and academic staff; private universities should be very interested in alleviating this deficiency.

Number of Students Graduating from Programs

The number of students who graduated from the higher education programs is not available on a regular basis, due to the crisis within the universities since 1990. Some information on the University of Abidjan-Cocody was given in the Association of African Universities report for the years 1987–1988, 1988–1989, and 1989–1990 (Nwa and Houenou 1990). At the University of Abobo-Adjamé, in the academic year 1997–1998, 198 students got their DEUG degrees, 113 passed their *licence*, and 151 received the *maîtrise*.

RESEARCH ACTIVITIES

Côte d'Ivoire has set up various national research institutes and centers for development, both inside and outside the universities, under the authority of various ministries and institutions, such as the Ministry of Higher Education and Scientific Research, the Ministry of Agriculture and Animal Resources, the Ministry of Public Health, the Ministry of Industry and Small and Medium Scale Enterprises, the Ministry of the Environment and Forest, and the Ministry of Development and Planning.

Research institutions include:

• National Scientific Associations such as Association Ivoirienne des Sciences Agronomiques (AISA) and Groupe Inter-

disciplinaire de Recherche en Sciences Sociales en Côte d'Ivoire (GIDIS-CI)
• Private-sector laboratories
• Nonuniversity national research centers: the Research Center of Oceanology, the Ivorian Tropical Technology Society, the National Research Centre of Agronomy, and others, such as the Laboratoire National d'Appui au Développement Agricole (LANADA), and the Laboratoire National d'Etudes et de Météorologie Appliquée (LANEMA).
• Foreign research centers: the Swiss Scientific Research Center, the Center for International Cooperation in Agronomic Research, the Tropenbos Foundation (Holland), the Association for Rice Development in West Africa, and the Pierre Richet Institute. These institutes usually work with national researchers or research centers.

Research activities are mostly conducted by national academic staff and researchers in fields such as agronomy, technology, oceanography, social sciences, economics, law, health sciences, biology, ecology and environment, civil engineering, education, and local languages. Despite a lack of facilities and appropriately allocated funds, some patents or other research outputs do exist—mainly in the field of agronomy—and are published in national, regional, or international journals or reviews. But it is not easy to get access to such information. The Ministry of Higher Education is planning to address this deficiency in information through a Scientific and Technological Institutions Directory. Access to the Internet should also improve this situation. A brief survey of research activities and programs in the country revealed that different research institutions often work on the same topic without any collaboration. This is not cost effective; duplication should be avoided.

Postgraduate programs exist but do not produce significant results in terms of theses. Because research activities were supported mainly by countries such as France until recent years, they focused on topics of interest to the North. While attempting to develop capacity and alleviate the lack of staff, universities were not capable of developing projects or searching for funds. With the exception of agronomy, relevant research was funded by international agencies on a bilateral or multilateral basis. Those agencies are now financing research activities through development projects at the level of the technical ministries rather than higher education and scientific research. Poor research activities are also due in many cases to the researchers' preference for consultancy; research has not been seen as part of institutional activities, and researchers and staff can individually and easily get more money as consultants, which helps to compensate for their low salaries.

MAINTENANCE OF TEACHING AND RESEARCH EQUIPMENT

Despite efforts of donors and the government to provide equipment and other facilities through the Special Investment Budget, the situation observed by Nwa and Houenou in their 1990 AAU report is still applicable: "Universities do not make allocations for maintenance of teaching and research equipment, particularly at the level of the academic units. Where allocations were made, several of the units did not seem to have record[s] of such allocations. Where records were available, some of the amounts were very small" (Nwa and Houenou 1990, 59). Maintenance of equipment remains one of the big challenges for universities in Côte d'Ivoire, which require not only adequate facilities but also qualified technicians with good salaries. Some attempts have been made to make shared facilities available to different users.

The Ministry of Higher Education is in charge of higher education policy, but each national institution has its own cooperation cell. Universities or higher schools have bilateral or multilateral partnerships with outside institutions or agencies. This relationship pertains to the development of staff and student exchange programs, joint research or training programs, and the shared use of existing facilities, such as equipment. Côte d'Ivoire universities are currently members of the Association of African Universities (AAU), the Conseil Africain et Malgache pour l'Enseignement Supérieur (CAMES), Conférences des Recteurs des Universités Francophones d'Afrique et de l'Océan Indien (CUFRAOCI), Réseau des Universités Francophones (RUF), and the International Association of Universities (IAU). In addition, higher education institutions have agreements with universities or agencies in Europe (France, Belgium, Spain, Germany, etc.), Asia (Japan and China), South America, North America (the United States and Canada), and Africa. Other agencies (United Nations Environment Programs, United Nations Development Programs, Food and Agriculture Organization, The World Bank, the World Health Organization, the African Development Bank, the International Development and Research Center, etc.) contribute to the development of capacity through research, management, and training activities. Cooperation with the North is very important; more than 100 agreements were signed by the University of Cocody, most of them with France. The activity is generally initiated by the universities or schools and sometimes by the Ministry of Higher Education; this is how the agreements between national Ivorian universities and state universities in Georgia and Michigan were signed.

South-South cooperation is well developed with countries such as Benin, Central Africa, the Republic of Congo (Congo-Brazzaville), Gabon, Niger, Senegal, Togo, Morocco, Algeria, Egypt, and Tunisia, but not always on the basis of formal agreements. Such cooperation benefits from UNESCO, Francophone, and AAU funds. Within Côte d'Ivoire, there is a great deal of national cooperation in the areas of staff exchange, training programs, and sharing of equipment. For this purpose, agreements have been signed, for instance, between the University of Abobo-Adjamé and INP and Groupe LOKO (this group is one of the most important private technology higher schools in Côte d'Ivoire).

Higher education faces the following problems regarding cooperation:

- Poor South-South cooperation
- Unsustainable (informal) relations within South-South research institutions and universities

- A lack of national projects and involvement in networking or in regional projects
- Strong dependence on the North
- Insignificant policies in the field of higher education

SPECIAL PROBLEMS

Special problems for Côte d'Ivoire include political activism, political interference in the universities, unemployment of graduates, and brain drain.

Student Political Activism

Over the decade 1970–1980, the major student union, MEECI (Mouvement des Elèves et Etudiants de Côte d'Ivoire), was affiliated with the political party PDCI, the party of President Houphouët-Boigny. Despite difficulties, the MEECI group was quite stable until 1990, when a new group, FESCI (Fédération Estudiantine et Scolaire de Côte d'Ivoire), arose as Côte d'Ivoire began its multiparty era. The first FESCI secretary-general was Ahipeaud Martial. The University of Côte d'Ivoire was often disturbed by demonstrations as students clamored for more freedom, more equipment, and social equity. But FESCI soon faced an internal division, which resulted in the emergence of two groups, headed by Blé Goude and Soro Guillaume, that fought to rule the movement. This situation contributed to the destabilization of the university as a whole. After the coup of December 24, 1999, the country was ruled by the military, which declared its intention to clean house, call for social equity, and organize democratic elections. The new government promised to allow students to contribute to all decision making. Despite military declarations, there was an unexpected violent crisis within FESCI, perhaps because political groups were trying to take control of the student groups, disseminate their ideas, and get students to vote for them. It is too soon to draw a clear picture of the situation; this should happen during the coming years.

Political Interference in the Universities

There is obvious political interference in the universities. Teachers and researchers are very active in politics. Politicians try to influence campuses. Sometimes teachers and researchers appear to be an advocacy group for the population of Côte d'Ivoire, or they are seen as masters influencing their students (Memel-Fote 1997). Until recently, SYNARES dominated the campus of Cocody and the country. After 1990, a new teachers' and researchers' trade union, Union Nationale de la Recherche et de l'Enseignement Supérieur (UNESUR), appeared, which was seen as being very close to the PDCI party that ruled the country until 1999.

A significant number of teachers and researchers from universities are members of political parties and often hold important positions in governments. In fact, most of the leaders of the important political parties come from the universities. Difficulties between academics and the government are almost constant because of the general socioeconomic situation that applies to

Table 27.1. Salaries of Higher Education Staff in Côte d'Ivoire Before and After 1992

Status	Salary		
	Before 1992	After 1992	Percent of salary lost
Lecturer	723	263	64
Senior Lecturer	984	286	71
Associate Professor	1,414	343	76
Professor	1,718	535	69

Note: US$1 = 450 francs CFA before 1992 and 730 francs CFA in 2001.

Source: Fraternité Matin, *Journal Fraternité Matin*, March 7, 2000.

them: inappropriate academic facilities and very low salaries. Because of the economic crisis and pressure from the World Bank and other international funding institutions in the context of the Structural Adjustment Program (SAP), Côte d'Ivoire is facing severe budget cuts. Consequently, the government cannot recruit more academic staff, and it was decided in 1992 to reduce the special salaries that had been given to teachers and researchers since the 1980s. This could explain the phenomenon of brain drain (Table 27.1).

Brain Drain

Brain drain depends on such factors as:

- Public policy, which is capable of destroying existing capacities, and, if poorly managed, can also generate brain drain.
- The power of Western capitalist countries to attract qualified labor from developing countries, causing the African intellectual elite to be attracted by the economic benefits that they can get when they emigrate.
- The events of globalization that favor mobility.

A significant number of papers addressed this issue at the Regional Conference on Brain Drain and Capacity Building in Africa, February 22–24, 2000, in Ethiopia, organized by the International Development Research Center of Canada, the Economic Commission for Africa, and the International Organization for Migration. Until recently, brain drain was a rare occurrence in Côte d'Ivoire (Houenou 2000). Now, however, the higher education and research sectors are being very negatively affected by this phenomenon. The quality of teaching is also affected, as the student-teacher ratio (more than 30:1 in many places) is high, except in higher schools of technology, or Ecole Normale Supérieure (ENS). Quality is also affected by the heavy workload, in terms of hours per week of undergraduate and graduate teaching, supervision of graduate research, administration, and outside commitments. Workload was the subject of a study funded by the Association of African Universities (Nwa and Houenou 1991), but it is very difficult to evaluate. Poor funding of universities and of higher education schools has a seriously debilitating effect on capacity building. Only 20 per-

cent of the academic staff needed, planned, or authorized annually by the Ministry of Labour since 1992 have been recruited. The relationship between this situation and the strategy of low salaries is obvious. Consequently, the problem of brain drain is likely to require urgent attention in the coming years. The new government decided in June of 2001 to reestablish lecturers' salaries to levels given before 1992. This will help to improve the quality of teaching and research, especially if the country also benefits from the special funds ($68,493,150) given by the African Development Bank (ADB) to African universities for capacity building in terms of equipment.

CHALLENGES FOR THE FUTURE

Future challenges for higher education in Côte d'Ivoire are the introduction of good governance; the sustainability and development of qualified manpower through appropriate, professionally oriented programs; and the development of private universities.

It will be a challenge to introduce a real managerial approach to make universities capable of contributing to local development and able to serve the community through professional programs and research and development. Capacity building of manpower depends on an adequate budget for salaries, availability of classrooms and functioning equipment, and other facilities (books and journals in libraries, computer facilities) that are lacking or of poor quality. The lack or deterioration of such facilities and the administrative inefficiency of recent years have resulted in lowered productivity on the part of staff and poor academic performance on the part of students.

During this period of structural adjustment, financial sustainability for higher education will be a major challenge for universities. This depends on having appropriate funds for programs. The main sources of higher education financing are the government and donors. Institutions have been receiving less than their budgetary requirements, which has resulted in a curtailment of training activities and fieldwork, and is adversely affecting the quality of education offered. Therefore, universities should make efforts to develop a sustainable system and diversify their sources of funding. The sensitive subjects of tuition fees and partnerships with the private sector must be addressed, as some donors appear to be suffering from fatigue. It is high time to explore new ways to attract funds for tertiary education. The only known case of such philanthropy is the funding given by President Houphouët-Boigny ($225,000) in 1980 to the Ivorian Association of Agronomy Sciences (AISA) to help it in developing its activities. It is obvious that growth and development cannot be sustained in societies that do not pay serious attention to research and development. Therefore, local graduate training should be promoted instead of sending students to universities in Europe for graduate study.

During the last decade, higher education authorities have used "admission criteria to correct inequalities, but such policies often involve important quality and efficiency trade-offs" (Eisemon et al. 2000). Because the high rate of population growth affects staff development within the universities, higher education institutions in Côte d'Ivoire as well as other institutions in

Africa should be "aware of the potential of distance education in addressing educational challenges" (Darkwa and Mazibuko 2000). With the support of donors, the Ministry of Higher Education is leading an ongoing project to tackle this concern and create a virtual learning community. The development of private universities appears to offer a response to the need for social equity in accessing knowledge. Gender equity should be addressed, particularly in basic and natural sciences units.

Universities need to become more oriented toward professional training, develop a sound relationship with the private sector, help students use their education and skills to create employment, and promote small-scale enterprises. An international NGO, Junior Achievement, is now helping universities with the support of the government. Finally, the implementation of the PNDEF project will hopefully help higher education in Côte d'Ivoire make significant progress.

CONCLUSION

Developing a labor force to meet the needs of society is one of the contributions universities and other higher schools make to a nation. In this respect, the main challenge facing higher education in Côte d'Ivoire is related to the quality of output, which depends, in turn, on the quality of the administration, the academic staff, facilities, and teaching materials. Efforts should be made by all stakeholders—mainly the private sector—to preserve the gains achieved at the beginning of independence.

The implementation of the PNDEF strategy to meet new demands and challenges should facilitate the entry of higher education in Côte d'Ivoire into the third millennium with ease: the search for equity, the quality of teaching and research, and capacity building. But rapidly deteriorating socioeconomic and political conditions within the country are drastically affecting the quality of the training and research and are producing brain drain, a situation that must be addressed in the coming years.

REFERENCES

Darkwa, O., and Mazibuko, F. 2000. "Creating Virtual Learning Communities in Africa: Challenges for the Future." Available online at: http://firstmonday.org/issues/issue5_5/darkwa/index.html

Eisemon, T. O. 2000. "Increasing Equity in Higher Education: Strategies and Lessons from International Experience." Available online at: http://www.worldbank.org/html/extdr/educ/backgrnd/equity1.html

Houenou, P. V. 1998. "Stratégies de la Recherche Environnementales." Programmes National de Gestion de l'Environnement et des Ressources Naturelles. Rapport. Abidjan: Ministère du Logement, du Cadre de Vie et de l'Environnement.

———. 2000. Développement des capacités et exode des compétences: le cas de l'enseignement supérieur en Cote d'Ivoire. In Sabiou Kassoum, Pascal V. Houénou, Bankolé Oni, Meera Sethi, and Joseph Ngu, eds., Brain Drain and Capacity Building in Africa. Dakar, Senegal: ECA/IDRC/IOM.

Houenou, P. V., M. T. Tahoux, and L. Nago. 1995. Renforcement des capacités en matière de formation dans le domaine de l'interaction énergie-environnement: cas de l'Afrique de l'Ouest et du Nord. Rapport réalisé pour le compte de la Banque Africaine de Développement (BAD). Abidjan: BAD.

Houphouët-Boigny, D., and F. K. Mansilla. 1999. Femme et education scientifique: Cas de l'enseignement supérieur. Ouagadougou: Forum organisé par l'UNESCO.

Memel-Fote, H. 1997. "De la stabilité au changement: Les représentations de la crise politique et la réalité des changements." In Le Modèle Ivoirien en questions. Paris: Editions Karthala et ORSTOM.

Ministère de l'Enseignement Supérieur de la Recherche Scientifique (MESRS). 1997a. Plan National de Développement du Secteur Education/Formation (PNDEF). Volume 0 to IV. Abidjan: MESRS.

———. 1997b. Annuaire statistique de l'Enseignement Supérieur, année 1996–1997. Abidjan: MESRS.

———. 1997c. Les grandes rencontres de fraternité matin, lundi 27 janvier 1997. Abidjan: MESRS.

———. 1999. Actes des Etats Généraux de la Recherche. Abidjan: MESRS.

Nwa, E. U., and P. Houenou. 1990. "Graduate Education and R and D in African Universities." Report submitted to the Association of African Universities, Accra, Ghana. In author's possession.

Tapsoba, S. 2000. "Création et rétention du savoir en Afrique." In Sabiou Kassoum, Pascal V. Houénou, Bankolé Oni, Meera Sethi, and Joseph Ngu, eds., Brain Drain and Capacity Building in Africa, 18–34. Dakar, Senegal: ECA/IDRC/IOM.

UNESCO. 1998. Enseignement supérieur en Afrique: Réalisations, défis et perspectives. Bureau Régional de Dakar: UNESCO.

University of Dar es Salaam. 1998. "The USDM Transformation Programme." Proceedings of the Fifth Annual Consultative Workshop. Council Chamber 17th–18th September.

Djibouti

Nabil Mohammed with Damtew Teferra

INTRODUCTION

Djibouti covers an area of 23,200 square kilometers (8,958 square miles) and lies at the Horn of Africa. It borders the Gulf of Aden and the Red Sea and is tucked between Eritrea, Ethiopia, and Somalia. Today, Djibouti is considered a major transit point and a communication hub for the Horn of Africa.

According to a UN (1998) estimate, the population of Djibouti in 1999 was estimated at about 629,000. Unlike other countries in sub-Saharan Africa, the population of Djibouti is predominantly urban. Three-quarters live in towns and cities and over two-thirds of the population is concentrated in the capital, Djibouti.

BACKGROUND OF THE EDUCATIONAL SYSTEM

The Djiboutian educational system is modeled after the French system, adopting the same pedagogical model and administrative structures. As a consequence, the system is expensive to operate and is probably inadequate and irrelevant to the socioeconomic development of the nation.

The educational system has not been adapted to local needs because of its closer link with the French system in terms of academic schedule, programs, pedagogical approach, administration, and teacher training (MEN 1999; UNDP 1999). Moreover, low funding, budget cuts, and delays in the payment of salaries have hampered the progress of the system. The number of qualified Djiboutian staff is too small, and there is a high demand for qualified personnel from foreign countries. Some French-speaking countries, such as Algeria, have already signed agreements to send personnel to address this issue.

The literacy rate is very low at 48.4 percent (MEN 1999), with a significant gender disparity of 73.3 percent for men and 43.1 percent for women (Direction Nationale de la Statistique 1997). The average Djiboutian receives only 3.6 years of educa-

tion. The system contains six years of primary school followed by seven years of secondary school that consists of two cycles: four years in the first cycle and three years in the second cycle. Students can be registered for primary school at the age of 7.

The secondary school graduation rate currently is 58 percent. The number of students attending secondary school has increased considerably since the country's independence in 1977 (Table 28.1). Upon graduation, secondary school students are awarded a high school general certificate of education called the *baccalauréat*. The *baccalauréat* is a requirement for admission to higher education institutions and universities.

Table 28.2 provides figures of students registered for the *baccalauréat* and the estimated number of those students who are eligible for higher education. The number of enrolled students and eligible candidates has increased over the years.

There is a high student attrition rate, which is indicative of a poor education system. As a result, only 8 percent of students registered in the first year of primary school move on to complete their *baccalauréat*. The overall attrition rate from primary school to the end of secondary school is very high at 92.3 percent. The attrition rate at the end of the primary school alone is over 58 percent. At the end of the first and second cycle of the secondary school, attrition rates run as high as 53 percent and 48 percent, respectively. In addition, the drop-out rate is disproportionately high for female students.

THE STATE OF HIGHER EDUCATION

Higher education is currently one of the priority areas of government policy. One signal of this prioritization has been agreements and partnerships with French universities to improve the quality of instruction in Djibouti. Diplomas granted at Djiboutian institutions are recognized in France, and students can apply to French universities to further their studies.

Still, higher education in Djibouti is in its infancy, and the

Table 28.1. Trends in Student Enrollment in Secondary Schools in Djibouti from 1993–1994 to 1997–1998

1993–1994	7,296
1994–1995	8,182
1995–1996	8,917
1996–1997	9,812
1997–1998	10,976

Source: MEN 1999.

Table 28.2. Students in Djibouti Registered for the Baccalaureate and the Estimated Eligible Candidates

Year	Candidates for Baccalaureate	Eligible candidates for higher education
1998–1999	650	377
1999–2000	798	463
2000–2001	859	498
2001–2002	961	557
2002–2003	1,083	626
2003–2004	1,232	714

Source: MEN 2000.

country has no university in the strictest sense. In order to strengthen the capacity of secondary school teachers and promote the replacement of French teachers by Djiboutians, several two-year higher degrees programs—equivalent to an associate degree (*Diplôme d'Etudes Universitaires Générales*, DEUG) and DEUG MIAS (*Mathematiques, Informatique et Applications aux Sciences*; Mathematics, Computer Science and Scientific Applications)—hosted at the Center for Training National Education Staff (Centre de Formation des Personnels de l'Education Nationale, CFPEN), have been launched with the financial and technical support of the French government. During these two years of studies, all students get a scholarship equivalent to US$340 per month.

Another higher degree, the vocational training certificate (*Brevet de Techniciens Supérieurs*, BTS), was created with the objective of providing highly trained staff in the areas of economics, management, and computer science. Students in these programs receive a stipend of US$120 per month. Upon completion, diplomas are granted by the French universities that oversee the training program.

Associate Degrees (DEUG de Lettre and DEUG MIAS)

Since 1990, the CFPEN has organized two types of training: DEUG de Lettre (general university studies diploma) and DEUG MIAS (*Mathematiques, Informatique et Applications aux Sciences*; Mathematics, Computer Science, and Scientific Applications). DEUG de Lettre is a two-year program students enter after the *baccalauréat* and offers students two options from which they choose their studies.

Courses are primarily taught by French professors. Some of these professors are based in Djibouti, while others are visiting professors from the University of Montpelier (France) who teach two to three weeks a year. This faculty exchange was made possible by an agreement between the CFPEN and the University of Montpelier.

To bring relevance to Djibouti's regional and environmental context, the DEUG de Lettre program has been slightly modified from the original version at the University of Montpelier. For instance, in order to provide students with a sound understanding of the subregion's literature, special courses on the languages and literature of the Horn of Africa have replaced Latin courses.

Moreover, important courses in history, geography, and Arabic are offered with a specific focus on regional and environmental context. Since the introduction of this training option, 114 students have obtained their DEUG, and 23 students were expected to graduate in 2000.

The DEUG MIAS was created in 1996 with the support of the Distance Education Center of Besançon (Centre de Télé–Enseignement de Besançon) in France. The DEUG MIAS covers two years; each year is composed of eight courses distributed across two semesters.

Vocational Training Certificate (Le Brevet de Technicien Supérieur)

Le Brevet de Technicien Supérieur (BTS) is a two-year professional program that began in 1990 to train qualified staff to meet Djiboutian economic realities and to replace French technical assistants with well-trained Djiboutian staff. The programs include accounting, management, secretarial science, international trade, computer science, and tourism. Between 1990 and 1999, a total of 302 students were trained and 173 graduated, a success rate of 57 percent. Ninety percent of the graduates find jobs in Djibouti.

The total number of students enrolled in BTS programs in 1999–2000 was 134. The number of students has multiplied eightfold from 17 in 1990 to 137 in 1997; the most significant increase occurred in 1993–1994.

Infrastructure

CFPEN's library, with more than 10,000 books, covers a wide variety of subjects from the sciences, literature, and philosophy to civilization, religion, sociology, and pedagogy.

In addition to an audiovisual facility, CFPEN's twelve computer stations also offer DEUG MIAS students access to the Internet and individual e-mail accounts at its computer center.

RESEARCH AND CAPACITY BUILDING

Statute and Organization

The Advanced Institute for Scientific and Technical Study and Research (Institut Supérieur d'Etudes et de Recherches Sci-

Table 28.3. Staff of Institut Supérieur d'Etudes et de Recherches Scientifiques et Téchniques

Department	Staff and qualifications	No.	Sex	Age
Life sciences	Ph.D. in Plant Biology and Physiology	1	M	<40
	M.A. in Soil Sciences	1	M	<40
	Engineer in Agronomy	1	F	<35
	Technicians	4	3M, 1F	<35
	Agricultural laborer	3	M	40
Hydrogeology	Ph.D. in Hydrogeology	1	M	<40
	M.A. in Hydrogeology	1	M	45
	Technicians	2	M	<40
Hydrochemistry	Ph.D. in Hydrochemistry	1	M	<40
	Technicians	2	1M, 1F	35
Energy	M.A.	1	M	45
	Technicians	3	M	<35
Geology	Ph.D. in Geology	2	M	40
	B.A. in Geology	2	M	45
	Technicians	4	M	<35
Human Sciences	Ph.D.	1	M	32
Administration	NA	40	20M, 20F	35

Source: Institut Supérieur d'Etudes et de Recherches Scientifiques et Téchniques.

entifiques et Téchniques, ISERST) is the only research institution in the country.

ISERST is a governmental institute under the authority of the president of the republic through the Ministry of Presidential Affairs and the secretary-general of the government. Its mission is to develop and coordinate research, studies, and scientific and technical activities in order to promote their application to the economic and social development of Djibouti.

ISERST performs technical and scientific research in areas of national priority, such as soil sciences, ecophysiology, agronomy, renewable energies and energy conservation, hydrogeology, hydrochemistry, geology, and social sciences. The institute consists of six departments: hydrogeology, geochemistry, life sciences, geology, energy, and human sciences. Scientists who work at the institute hold various degrees relevant to each department. These departments are linked to one another through the Interdisciplinary Program for the Environment.

ISERST has an International Scientific Council composed of international researchers. Its role is to provide advice about the implementation of the institute's programs. Faculty in ISERST's departments (Table 28.3) have expertise in the areas of water, energy, soils, and crops research. The institute has a total of sixteen researchers (five of whom have a Ph.D. degree).

MODE OF OPERATION

As there is no science and technology university, there are no linkages made between research and education. Research and education are administered by two separate offices: the office of the president of Djibouti and the Ministry of Education.

Research is generally constrained by underfunding and budget reductions. The operating budget for research is negligible compared to budgets earmarked for salaries. As a result, the institute is obliged to generate its own funds through donations and from revenues for services rendered to the private sector.

As the only institute in charge of all national research problems, ISERST is too overwhelmed to pay close attention to educational problems. Just as the higher education system in Djibouti is poorly developed and provides only limited training expertise, research, too, is very limited. Nevertheless, some students who are based in French universities and some French professors have carried out significant research, particularly in the areas of history, sociology, and religion.

Generally, researchers at ISERST publish the results of their investigations in specialized international journals. ISERST also publishes a biannual journal entitled *Sciences and Environment* (*Sciences et Environnement*), which publishes articles contributed by both foreign and local authors.

LANGUAGES

Djibouti became independent from France in 1977. While the national languages are French and Arabic, French is the sole language of instruction during all six years of primary school; Arabic is taught as a subject. Unfortunately, instruction in Arabic is inefficient because of inadequacies in the program and poorly qualified staff. Local languages are not used as a medium of instruction.

Dependence on foreign financial support has imposed constraints on matters such as the language of instruction, the curriculum, and the sustainability of the instructional system. It is obvious that restricting the language of instruction to one particular language, in this case French, in an English- and Arabic-speaking region both limits the exchange of skills and development of linkages with regional universities, and impedes employment opportunities in other countries in the region.

STUDY ABROAD

An estimated 865 Djiboutian students are currently studying in foreign countries on government scholarships, up to 70 percent of whom are based in France. In 1999, the total yearly cost of foreign study to the government was about US$4.34 million (MEN 1999), which is very high in the context of the current financial state of the country.

Some of the students studying abroad return home with a variety of credentials equivalent to the DEUG, the *Licence*, the Master's degree, and the DEA; with two, three, four, and five years of higher education studies, respectively. Reliable statistics on their numbers and areas of studies are unavailable. Owing to the current difficult economic situation of Djibouti, most graduates prefer to stay in the country of their studies, which in most cases is France.

In order to address the challenge of this brain drain and enhance the national capacity of a highly skilled labor force, the government began creating a university in 2000.

DEVELOPMENT PROSPECTS

The political will to establish a university in the country was expressed during the last presidential election, in 1999. The new university was to start in September 2000 in collaboration with French universities and deliver diplomas after two years of education.

The university was expected to have three institutions: Djibouti's Institute for Higher Education (Institut de Formation Universitaire de Djibouti, IFUD), the Djiboutian Advanced Institute for Business (Institut Supérieur des Affaires de Djibouti, ISAD), and the Djiboutian Advanced Institute of Technology (Institut Supérieur de Technologie de Djibouti, ISTD).

CONCLUSION

Higher education is a new priority for Djibouti. The main objective of the educational system until now was to train teachers to meet the urgent demands of secondary school enrollments and to replace French technical assistants with Djiboutians.

As the only French-speaking country in the region, Djibouti suffers from isolation from the Anglophone and Arab countries of the region. Djibouti does not have any meaningful relationships or linkages with universities in the region in the East, in the Horn of Africa, or in Arab countries. This linguistic isolation has been a serious constraint to networking with other regional institutions and exchanging skills.

The high rate of employment for students trained in the country is certainly a success. The new trend of adapting and designing programs and curricula in line with Djibouti's socioeconomic realities appears to have provided good employment opportunities that are in sync with the market demand for trained domestic employees.

The commitment of the government to establish a university faces serious challenges, many of which may seem initially insurmountable, such as a lack of qualified staff to manage such an institution without resorting again to external support.

REFERENCES

Direction Nationale de la Statistique. 1996. "Enquête Djiboutienne auprès des Ménages." Ministère du Commerce et du Tourisme. Djibouti: Direction Nationale de la Statistique.

MEN (Ministère de l'Education Nationale). 1999. "Réflexion préliminaire à la tenue des Etats Généraux de l'Education Nationale en République de Djibouti." Document d'Orientation. Djibouti: Ministère de l'Education Nationale.

———. 2000. "Service de planification DGEN." Djibouti: Ministère de l'Education Nationale.

UNDP (United Nations Development Programme). 1999. "Coopération au Développement Bureau de Coordination Résident du Système des Nations Unies." Rapport. Djibouti: UNDP.

UN (United Nations). 1998. *World Population Prospects: The 1998 Revision.* Volume II: *Sex and Age Distribution of the World Population.* Djibouti: UNDP.

29

Egypt

MOHSEN ELMAHDY SAID

HISTORICAL BACKGROUND

Egypt's higher education system may be considered the oldest education system in the world. The world's highest educational ranking in the second millennium B.C. was granted from Oun University, northeast of Cairo. In the next millennium, in about 300 B.C., the educational center of the nation moved to Alexandria. Al-Azhar, an Islamic establishment in Cairo for well over 1,000 years (established in A.D. 975), was primarily dedicated to teaching Islamic religion and studying the Quran. It took about seventeen years to build Al-Azhar Mosque (A.D. 971–988), which was then used as the center of the educational establishment. Modern Egyptian education, however, started in the time of Mohamed Ali Pasha (A.D. 1798), who established many schools of engineering, medicine, law, and other subjects. At that time, distinguished graduates were sent to western Europe, in particular to France, to pursue higher education. Upon their return, they contributed to the advancement of the education system in Egypt.

In 1908, a national university was established in Egypt. Later, in 1925, this national university was merged into a public university, and in 1940 it was named after the late king of Egypt Fouad El-Awal. In 1953, after the Egyptian revolution, it was named Cairo University. The number of universities has continued to increase ever since.

Modern education in Egypt was formally established in 1923, when the first constitution stated that "primary education is compulsory for all Egyptian children." In 1952, the government of the revolution undertook the development of unified primary compulsory education.

Egypt participated in the ratification of the World Agreement on Economic and Social Rights, and the contents of that agreement have become part of the state's laws. In 1971, the constitution was amended to read: "The state guarantees equal opportunities for all citizens." In the same year, another amendment stated that "all citizens are equal before the law, regardless of their responsibilities, duties, sex, origin, religion or belief." In order to carry out these two articles, a constitutional framework was set up for the entire education system that included the following principles:

- Education is a fundamental right.
- The state is responsible for providing education for all and will supervise education to ensure its equity.
- Education in public institutions (state-run institutions) is free at all levels.
- Literacy is a national responsibility.
- Both primary and preparatory education are compulsory.

In 1981, a law was passed by the Egyptian parliament that made preparatory education and nine years of basic education compulsory. In 1988, however, a new law was passed requiring eight years of basic education as compulsory, changing the terminal year from Grade 6 to Grade 5. In 1999, yet another law announced the duration of compulsory education to be nine years, six years at the primary level and three years at the preparatory level, returning to the original system before the 1988 law. Although the 1988 law was meant to reduce the cost of compulsory education because of the inability of the system to maintain the level of investment needed, the consequences for the education system as a whole were quite harmful. The number of secondary school students doubled in the year Grade 6 was eliminated, and overcrowding of students entering the university six years later caused many problems. Overcrowding of students continued for many years. The current education system is still suffering from the consequences of this action. Failing students, together with the newly admitted students, contributed to the large number of students in successive years.

Because one of the strategic and prime mandates of the Egyptian government is to admit all students who move from secondary into tertiary education, the number of students admitted to higher education institutions nearly doubled. Yet the infrastructure in government institutions was not ready to accommodate this sudden increase in the number of students. Poor and limited facilities and overcrowding led to the deterioration of the average quality of higher education graduates, though the "above average" students graduating from the system perform well according to international standards. The number and performance of Egyptian graduate students accepted and admitted yearly to top ranking universities in the United States, Europe, and other countries worldwide support this argument. Over 1,000 postgraduate students are supported annually by the Missions Department of the Ministry of Higher Education (MOHE), which has a budget of 1.25 billion EGP (U.S.$290 million) during the government's current five-year plan (1997–2002).

Approximately one-third of Egypt's students enter general secondary schools, the traditional route to university. Almost 70 percent of students are channeled into technical secondary education, but less than 20 percent gain employment when they leave. The low employment rate for graduates demands that the relevance of technical education be reconsidered, including the possibility of merging the two tracks into an effective unified education system with internal options for matching student abilities with learning opportunities. To start with, ambitious reform plans, partially supported by the World Bank, the European Union, USAID, and others, are currently being implemented. The reform plans aim at channeling approximately half of the students admitted to secondary education into general secondary schools during the period 2002–2007. This secondary education reform measure will create further overcrowding, further burdening the higher education system as a whole.

BACKGROUND ON EGYPT'S RECENT ECONOMIC STATUS

During the second half of the twentieth century, Egypt's economy was overburdened by three wars that exhausted the greater part of its resources. Since the wars have ended, economic reform plans have been the main object of successive governments. In the 1990s, however, the Egyptian government made wide-ranging economic reforms that moved the country toward a more competitive market-based system. The initial phase of reform involved removing many of the distortions in the price system and impediments to trade and investment. The results were positive on the macroeconomic level. Egypt's budget deficit was brought down, liquidity creation was managed, inflation was reduced, exchange-rate stability was maintained, external reserves were increased, and growth was accelerated. The second phase of the reform effort focuses on the microeconomic level by deepening structural reforms to induce a strong and sustainable supply-side response from the private sector.

In recent years, real GDP growth has been rising steadily; in 1998–1999 it was estimated at 6 percent. The accelerated growth is largely attributed to the increasing participation of the private sector in economic activity and the government's commitment to reform. Government investment in infrastructure to improve the country's productive capacity has also contributed to economic growth.

The Egyptian authorities have been particularly successful in containing the budget deficit (now 1.0–1.3 percent of GDP). The same applies to control of monetary growth and domestic inflation, which remained at 3.8 percent in 1998 and 1999. It should be noted, however, that Egypt's fiscal deficit increased significantly in 1999, reaching 4.2 percent of GDP, partly as a result of an increase in public expenditure on large national projects. But Egyptian authorities have reiterated that fiscal discipline will be restored mainly through better tax administration and higher income from privatization on the revenues side. More recently, however, the last quarter of 2000 and the beginning of year 2001 witnessed a sudden devaluation of the Egyptian pound vis-à-vis the U.S. dollar by nearly 20 percent, which is expected to negatively impact the country's economic stability.

OVERALL EDUCATION STRUCTURE

When talking about higher education, one has to consider the rest of the educational ladder prior to higher education. Students coming out of preschool education (nurseries and kindergartens) are all streamed into six years of primary education, followed by three years of preparatory study, completing the basic compulsory education. After six years of primary education, the system streams the student either into the regular three-year preparatory program or into a vocational preparatory program, which also lasts for three years. Graduates may exit directly to the labor market or may continue for three years of vocational-technical secondary education before entering the labor market. The system also enables outstanding students from the vocational-technical secondary stream of education to join the nonuniversity stream of higher education. On the other hand, students who complete the three years of regular preparatory study may be channeled into four different streams of three-year secondary education programs; namely general, industrial (three- and five-year programs), agricultural and commercial, and vocational-technical. Graduates of five-year programs have better chances of getting into university education and receive better offers and opportunities from the labor market than graduates from the three-year programs. Entrance to secondary education streams is based on the grades achieved in the preparatory phase. Those who complete one of the four streams of secondary education, however, have the following options.

Graduates from general secondary education are streamed directly into four-, five-, or six-year programs of university education, whereas graduates from the other three streams are all channeled into nonuniversity education. In this case, students have the option of enrolling in two-, four-, or five-year programs offered in middle and higher technical institutes. Graduates from general secondary education can join the nonuniversity stream of middle and higher technical institutes when their grades do not meet the requirements for university enrollment. Industrial, agricultural, and commercial secondary school graduates can enter university, provided they score a grade of 75 percent and pass a general entry exam set for each of the three streams of secondary education. Although admissions are limited, the flexibility of the system allows equal opportunities to all students graduating from secondary education. In the 2000–2001 academic year, only 326 students were able to meet the enrollment criteria for university education.

Table 29.1. Adult Literacy Rates in Egypt by Gender, 1986–1999

Year	Literacy Rates among Males	Literacy Rates among Females
1986	62.2	38.2
1990	64.5	44.8
1996	71.0	49.8
1999	76.0	55.0

Source: Central Agency for Public Mobilization and Statistics (CAPMAS), September 2000.

LITERACY RATE VERSUS ENROLLMENT

In 1992, the president of Egypt declared that education is essential for maintaining strong economic growth and sustainable development and for building strong communities and a cohesive society. Extensive efforts have been made by the government to improve literacy rates and the education sector as a whole. The total literacy rate increased from nearly 50 percent in 1986 to more than 65 percent in 1999, an average annual improvement of more than 1 percent (Table 29.1).

POPULATION GROWTH VERSUS ENROLLMENT

Nearly all the population is enrolled in the education system in the age group for whom education is compulsory. About 62 percent of the population in the 12–14 age group is admitted to secondary education. Gross enrollment as a percentage of the population varies between 98 percent and 107 percent in the compulsory education age group. The lower percentage (less than 100 percent) indicates that not all the population of the age group is enrolled in compulsory education, whereas the higher percentage shows that population from higher or lower age groups are enrolled with the regular age group.

In higher education, however, the total population belonging to the 18–22 age group is nearly 6.9 million students and the total enrollment of undergraduate and postgraduate students in public and private universities, including higher education institutions, is nearly 1.29 million students; about 19 percent of the eligible age group are enrolled in postsecondary institutions. If part-time students (numbering about 250,000) are included, the total number of students rises to nearly 1.53 million, giving an enrollment ratio of approximately 22 percent. It is evident that the higher education enrollment rate in Egypt is comparable to those of most Organisation for Economic Cooperation and Development (OECD) countries (Task Force on Higher Education and Society 2000). Egypt has ambitious plans to raise the enrollment rate to between 25 and 30 percent during the coming decade. To reach this figure, however, extensive funds need to be raised.

PATTERNS OF STUDENT ENROLLMENT GROWTH

Since 1990, the government has increased its pre-university education budget by 150 percent in real terms. This has helped to bring about nearly universal access at the basic level and an enrollment rate of 62 percent at the secondary level. Combined with an age group whose enrollments are expanding, this success has created strong demand for postsecondary education. As mentioned earlier, a total of approximately 22 percent of the 18–22 age group (about 1.53 million students, of which about 40 percent are female) were enrolled at that level in 1998–1999. Three-quarters attended universities, and 25 percent were enrolled in nonuniversity institutions. The overwhelming majority (about 99 percent of all students) attended public institutions. It is worth mentioning that the number of female students enrolled in Egyptian universities and institutes has been continuously increasing as the literacy rate among females has increased (on average from about 30 percent to 50 percent over the last twenty years).

UNIVERSITY ENROLLMENT

Egypt's higher education system is comprised of twelve public universities (spread over twenty individual campus sites) and private universities (four of which are for-profit and one of which, the American University in Cairo, is not-for-profit). Many applications are pending with the Ministry of Higher Education to open additional private for-profit universities/institutions (French, British, and German universities are among the pending requests). The Ministry of Higher Education is setting up the regulatory measures and criteria to establish private universities and is continually refining them based on the experience gained from working with the already established ones. Table 29.2 includes a list of all of Egypt's public and private universities, indicating their year of establishment, locations, and the number of faculties or institutions, which are classified into two categories — science and technology (S&T) and humanities and social sciences (H&SS). Al-Azhar University, an Islamic university, is included separately in the table because it is not under the administration of the Ministry of Higher Education.

Table 29.3 shows the numbers of undergraduates who completed a degree for the period 1988–1989 to 1998–1999. The numbers of students who earned postsecondary degrees for the same period is shown in Table 29.4. Table 29.5 gives a breakdown of the total annual budgets of public universities for the fiscal years 1988–1989 through 1999–2000. The percentage of the budget increase in 1991–1992 (35 percent) was the highest increase during the last twelve years. The lowest annual increase, in 1997–1998 (4 percent), has been followed by a steady annual increase of about 10 percent.

The ratio of newly admitted male students to female students in Egyptian public universities is nearly 2:1, whereas this ratio is nearly 1:1 for enrolled and graduated students. It is interesting to note that the highest number of newly admitted students is in Al-Azhar University, which is comparable in size of enrolled students to Cairo University, the largest and oldest university in Egypt (SCU 1999).

Table 29.6 includes the number of colleges and institutes in Egyptian universities in 2000–2001 classified in accordance with the specializations of the eighteen sectors identified by the Supreme Council of Universities (SCU). A total of 268 colleges and institutes exist. Humanities and Social Sciences constitute

Table 29.2. Public and Private Universities in Egypt, 2000–2001

| | | | No. of Faculties/Institutes | | |
University	Year Established	City/Town	Science and Technology	Humanities and Social Sciences	Total
Public University System					
Cairo	1908	Cairo	22	21	43
Alexandria	1942	Alexandria	13	14	27
Ain Shams	1950	Cairo	8	9	17
Assiut	1954	Assiut	9	9	18
Tanta	1972	Tanta	10	11	21
El-Mansoura	1972	El-Mansoura	10	11	21
El-Zagazig	1974	El-Zagazig	15	15	30
Helwan	1975	Helwan	6	12	18
El-Menia	1976	El-Menia	8	10	18
El-Menoufia	1976	El-Menoufia	7	9	16
Suez Canal	1976	Suez Canal	12	10	22
South Valley	1994	South Valley	7	10	17
Total			127	141	268
Al-Azhar University					
Al-Azhar	A.D. 975	Cairo	9	13	22
Private University System					
American University in Cairo (AUC)	1919	Cairo	2	2	4
Sixth of October	1996	Sixth of October City	7	4	11
Misr for Science and Arts	1996	Sixth of October City	2	1	3
October for Science and Technology	1996	Sixth of October City	6	2	8
Misr International	1996	Cairo Ismailia Road	2	2	4
Total			19	11	30

Source: Supreme Council of Universities, September 2000.

the largest number of colleges and institutes and absorb the largest number of students. Colleges of Law and Commerce also have high enrollments. Graduates from those three specializations have a great deal of difficulty finding adequate job opportunities in the labor market and constitute one of the major challenges to the reform program.

Well over 250,000 part-time students are currently registered in public universities, further burdening the higher education system. The 55 percent increase in the 1995–1996 academic year dropped steadily and became constant at 13 percent during the 1998–1999 and 1999–2000 academic years. This trend reflects the government's intention to control the expansion of education at this level.

POSTGRADUATE ENROLLMENT

The total number of students enrolled in and graduated from postgraduate studies in Egyptian public universities during the period 1998–1999, including Al-Azhar and the academies and institutions, is nearly 135,000 students, and the corresponding number of graduate students is about 26,000. Private universities, with the exception of the American University in Cairo (AUC), have not yet started their postgraduate studies, since many of them have yet to graduate their first batch of undergraduate students. AUC does not offer Ph.D. programs, but it has a very successful and well-established Department for Public Services (DPS) that offers many courses of continuing educa-

Table 29.3. Undergraduate Student in Egypt Admitted to and Enrolled in Undergraduate Programs and Number of Completed Degrees, 1988–1989 to 1998–1999

| | Undergraduate Studies | | |
Academic Year	Admitted	Enrolled	Graduated
1988–1989	75,375	484,206	90,452
1989–1990	66,990	467,611	94,300
1990–1991	69,949	443,120	94,211
1991–1992	74,310	431,863	92,488
1992–1993	110,333	471,358	88,542
1993–1994	131,007	519,536	81,320
1994–1995	148,378	597,964	85,609
1995–1996	237,873	755,606	103,963
1996–1997	268,967	926,325	118,309
1997–1998	240,904	1,043,765	139,631
1998–1999	221,530	1,167,891	216,226

Source: Supreme Council of Universities (SCU), September 2000.

Table 29.4. Number of Students Who Earned Graduate Degrees in Egyptian Institutions of Higher Education, 1988–1989 to 1998–1999

Academic Year	Diploma	M.A. & M.Sc.	Ph.D.	Total
1988–1989	9,539	5,158	2,108	16,805
1989–1990	10,636	5,859	2,054	18,549
1990–1991	10,632	4,471	2,185	17,288
1991–1992	11,899	4,495	2,128	18,522
1992–1993	12,745	4,741	2,176	19,662
1993–1994	14,118	5,053	2,324	21,495
1994–1995	13,923	5,342	2,597	21,862
1995–1996	13,937	5,388	2,508	21,833
1996–1997	15,513	5,329	2,455	23,297
1997–1998	17,050	5,154	2,744	24,948
1998–1999	16,280	5,240	2,600	24,120

Source: Supreme Council of Universities (SCU), September 2000.

tion and training to the Egyptian community at large. In addition, AUC and the majority of Egypt's public universities offer regular degree and nondegree programs at the postgraduate level.

NONUNIVERSITY ENROLLMENT

The nonuniversity stream of education absorbs a significant portion of the student population enrolled in tertiary education. Egypt has fifty-one public nonuniversity institutions, of which forty-seven are two-year middle technical institutes (MTIs) and four are four- or five-year higher technical institutes (HTIs). Table 29.7 shows students graduated from both technical and commercial MTIs, given by gender, during the period 1987–1988 through 1997–1998. There were approximately 111,500 MTI students in 1998–1999, mostly enrolled in the nonindustrial or technical specializations (48,200) or industrial disciplines (48,100). The rest are enrolled in MTIs providing training in hotel and tourism services (2,200), and faculties of education (13,000). There was a steady increase in enrollment prior to 1996–1997 and there has been a slight decrease since 1997–1998.

GOVERNMENT EDUCATION EXPENDITURES

As stated in Egypt's constitution, the government is responsible for offering the Egyptian population free education at all levels. Table 29.8 gives a summary of annual government expenditures by level of education during the period 1990–1991 to 1998–1999. Expenditures are classified into three groups: primary and preparatory, higher education, and other types. Primary and secondary education expenditure is divided among the Ministry of Education, governorates, and the Islamic schools. Higher education expenditures—subdivided into Ministry of Higher Education, nonuniversity, university, and Al-Azhar University expenditures—are given separately, as well. The total government education budget in 1998–1999 was more than triple the 1990–1991 budget.

STRENGTHS AND WEAKNESSES OF HIGHER EDUCATION IN EGYPT

The strengths of the Egyptian higher education system include its strong human resources, consisting mainly of university professors; the large variety of educational and research disciplines; and the existence of institutions with long experience in higher education. Weaknesses fall mainly into two main categories: a very heavy workload for faculty, which has a direct consequence on the average quality of graduates, and inefficiency. For instance, in the academic year 1974–1975, there were 4 assistants to 1 staff on average. In 1987–1988, however, the ratio was approximately 1 assistant to 1 staff, whereas in 1998–1999, about 0.6 assistants were available for each staff member. Limited financial resources, overcrowding, inadequate infrastructure, undertrained faculty members in some areas, poor instructional materials and equipment, and lack of modern education technology also contribute to the low quality of graduates. Inefficiency is manifest in the absence of a sustainable financial policy, poor accountability, and lack of a formal assessment and accreditation mechanism. Accordingly, Egyptian higher education faces a number of challenges:

- System-wide governance and management
- Quality and relevance at the university level
- Quality and relevance at the middle technical level
- Fiscal sustainability of publicly financed enrollments

Each of these challenges will be briefly discussed below (MNSHD 2000).

GOVERNANCE AND MANAGEMENT

The governance and management framework suffers from four fundamental deficiencies:

Table 29.5. Expenditures by Public University for Fiscal Years 1988–1989 to 1999–2000 in Million L.E.

University	1988–1989	1989–1990	1990–1991	1991–1992	1992–1993	1993–1994	1994–1995	1995–1996	1996–1997	1997–1998	1998–1999	1999–2000
Cairo	161	259	233	445	465	585	643	724	840	893	944	1,130
Alexandria	104	115	154	180	232	253	269	325	344	390	460	482
Ain Shams	142	159	162	212	263	286	337	384	465	522	566	604
Assiut	73	95	98	158	191	197	159	206	256	244	311	278
Tanta	62	68	78	86	118	126	141	164	206	213	276	259
El-Mansoura	84	80	134	133	149	159	196	274	326	317	292	408
El-Zagazig	103	115	130	164	199	214	244	290	337	330	352	391
Helwan	55	60	71	83	99	100	128	165	199	157	190	221
El-Menia	32	39	41	48	70	70	84	108	123	134	133	168
El-Menoufia	44	46	60	58	87	100	101	110	152	149	163	167
Suez Canal	29	42	51	72	95	89	107	110	132	138	164	158
South Valley	–	–	–	–	–	–	49	79	102	129	134	131
Total Public University Budget	889	1,078	1,212	1,639	1,968	2,179	2,458	2,939	3,482	3,616	3,985	4,397
% Budget Increase	–	21	12	35	20	11	13	20	18	4	10	10

Note: US$1 = 3.4 L.E.

Source: Supreme Council of Universities (SCU), September 2000.

Table 29.6. Number of Colleges and University Institutes by Sector, 2000–2001

Sector	Number of Colleges	Number of Institutes	Total
Engineering	19	1	20
Medicine, Physiotherapy, Nursing	26	5	31
Agriculture	17	1	18
Veterinary Science	11	—	11
Pharmacy	11	—	11
Basic Science	18	1	19
Dentistry	7	—	7
Genetic Engineering & Biotechnology	1	—	1
Statistical Sciences	1	—	1
Music	1	—	1
Artistic Studies	6	—	6
Physical Education	17	—	17
Education	28	2	30
Political Science	1	—	1
Law	11	—	11
Arts, Humanities, & Social Sciences	37	22	59
Commerce & Business Administration	18	—	18
Computer Science & Informatics	6	—	6
Total	236	32	268

Source: Supreme Council of Universities, September 2000.

Table 29.7. Graduates from Technical and Commercial MTIs, 1987–1988 to 1997–1998

Year	Graduates from Technical MTIs			Graduates from Commercial MTIs		
	Males	Females	Total	Males	Females	Total
1987–1988	10,292	1,839	12,131	—	—	—
1988–1989	10,524	2,404	12,928	19,750	10,289	30,039
1989–1990	10,696	3,059	13,755	12,664	9,567	22,231
1990–1991	10,276	2,925	13,201	12,577	9,036	21,613
1991–1992	11,927	3,394	15,321	13,049	10,466	23,515
1992–1993	12,090	4,598	16,688	15,156	14,541	29,697
1993–1994	8,054	3,390	11,444	8,170	9,758	17,928
1994–1995	7,352	3,954	11,306	6,687	9,934	16,621
1995–1996	5,585	4,573	10,158	4,314	7,850	12,164
1996–1997	14,903	12,152	27,055	10,141	20,079	10,141
1997–1998	29,887	20,526	50,413	34,044	44,987	79,031

Source: Ministry of Higher Education (MOHE), October 1999.

- Complex and antiquated legislation and institutional organization
- Inefficient mechanisms for allocating resources and inefficient funding patterns
- Absence of structures to control quality
- Inadequate strategic planning and management, at both the systemwide and the institutional levels

LEGISLATIVE AND INSTITUTIONAL FRAMEWORK

The present legislative framework is not adequate for the challenges faced by a modern higher education system. Because it does not allow for diversification in the provision or financing of higher education, it is very difficult for private institutions to operate in Egypt. In addition, the Egyptian constitution man-

Table 29.8. Government Expenditures on Education by Level in Million L.E.

Education Level	1990/91 Actual	1992/93 Actual	1994/95 Actual	1996/97 Actual	1998/99 Budgeted
Primary and Secondary	2,813	4,499	5,720	8,068	9,540
Central Ministry (MOE)	348	825	882	1,249	1,459
Governorates	2,260	3,326	4,234	5,923	7,097
Islamic Schools (Al-Azhar)	204	348	605	896	984
Higher Education	1,707	2,485	3,352	4,550	4,223
Central Ministry (MOHE)	127	222	328	542	375
Nonuniversity Institutions	—	—	—	—	691
Universities (excluding Al-Azhar)	1,438	2,069	2,751	3,581	2,632
Al-Azhar University	142	194	273	427	525
Other	262	157	1,830	2,462	1,176
Total Education Expenditures	4,782	7,141	10,902	15,080	14,939

Source: Ministry of Finance (MOF), Ministry of Education (MOE), and Ministry of Higher Education (MOHE), 1999.

dates that education in all the country's educational institutions be free in all its different stages.

Another important issue that needs reform is the lack of full autonomy of individual institutions. For example, Egypt's ratio of administrators to teaching staff is high by international standards (4:3). As a result, the share of public spending devoted to actual teaching is low. University officials cannot readily remedy this, however, as personnel management is constrained by regulations similar to those in the civil service. Salaries are not linked to performance, and once an appointment is made, termination is very difficult. In addition, Egypt has no mandatory retirement age, which has led to a relatively skewed age distribution, an inverted pyramid of senior faculty members with fewer junior teaching staff to meet the teaching, tutoring, and contact needs of the majority of students. Nearly all full-time faculty members are permanent from their first appointment.

Administrative arrangements as stipulated in Egyptian legislation need to be reconsidered. The governance of the sector involves two separate frameworks and is ruled by two separate sets of legislation, one for the university sector and one for the nonuniversity sector. The university sector has a governance advisory body known as the Supreme Council of Universities (SCU), chaired by the minister of higher education that, in theory, is independent of the ministry. A similar but far less autonomous body exists for the higher technical institutes in the nonuniversity sector, with the same chairmanship. Intermediate nonuniversity sector institutions such as MTIs have no such body and are governed directly by the Ministry of Higher Education. All major decisions concerning admission levels and standards, definition of programs and curricula, creation of new academic positions for the recruitment and appointment of faculty, allocation of resources, establishment of academic stan-

dards, and the assessment of those standards are made by the Ministry of Higher Education through the SCU.

RESOURCE ALLOCATION MECHANISMS AND FUNDING PATTERNS

Rigidities and inefficiencies exist at the system-wide level and at the institutional level. First, at the national system-wide level, the mechanism for determining educational needs and public resources to fulfill those needs is inadequate. Education programs are determined by the SCU, recurrent financial resources by the Ministry of Finance, and investment resources by the Ministry of Planning. All need stronger planning and joint coordination. In the absence of a funding formula, budgets of universities are determined by the Ministry of Planning and Ministry of Finance based on individual discussions about and needs assessments of each university. The Ministry of Higher Education plays a minor role in this budgeting process. Furthermore, no effective policymaking advisory bodies exist to inform the government about resource allocation, coordinate with other institutions, or assist decision makers in planning system development. The SCU and the Ministry of Higher Education have no technical secretariat to carry out policy analysis or advisory functions, to guide system development, or to periodically monitor program quality and performance of graduates.

Second, at the institutional level, the resource allocation process is outdated and needs restructuring. Financial resources mainly are limited to government funds, student enrollment fees, funds obtained from centers of excellence established in some institutions to provide community services and/or research and consulting services, and funds obtained from joint research activities. Institutions have very limited authority over internal reallocation of resources among budget categories. Within universities, inadequate budgeting practices provide few incentives to be efficient or improve quality, and the present governance structures do not motivate senior managers to make the best use of resources. The presidents, vice-presidents, deans, and heads of departments have a very limited scope to manage budgets in an innovative way. These budgets are allocated in a line-item format, with very limited room for transfer between budget categories except, in most universities, by the authority of the president himself—even on minor matters. Uncertainty about the amount of government allocations and the size of the student intake at the beginning of the academic year prevents rational institutional budgeting.

QUALITY ASSURANCE MECHANISMS

A mechanism to measure educational outcomes is lacking, both for individual faculty members and at the program or institutional level. There is no mechanism in place to evaluate teaching, either for specific or for collective purposes. There are insufficient criteria for assessing performance, particularly teaching. Chairs and deans are not empowered to take any meaningful action in response to evidence of poor performance by their staff.

With respect to quality assurance in general, except for some individual and isolated initiatives, limited expertise exists for developing strong performance standards, and generally there is no readily available data to use as indicators of educational quality. Most academic departments do not seem to be focused on evaluation of student problems or their reactions to their learning experiences. And when specific instances of creative and responsive program innovations emerge, they receive little institutional support.

STRATEGIC PLANNING AND MANAGEMENT

Over the last thirty years, several institutional attempts have been made by successive education ministries to develop strategic plans, none of which was implemented satisfactorily because of limited funding and the general culture of management and strategic planning. Nor have the governing bodies of the higher education sector (such as the Ministry of Higher Education and SCU) and universities developed modern management information systems to assist them in strategic planning and resource allocation. Although these bodies gather many statistics, they make little use of them. Most statistics are collected and transformed manually, although there have been some limited individual initiatives to computerize and automate the process. Cairo, El-Mansoura, and Assiut Universities have already established information technology centers and have started to build their own modern management information systems.

QUALITY AND RELEVANCE AT THE UNIVERSITY LEVEL

An alarming figure in undergraduate university statistics is the number of repeaters that encumber the system year after year. For example, the success rate of engineering students at Suez Canal University in the first year is 60–65 percent, and of those who complete the first year, 80 percent graduate on time. This suggests that neither the existing student selection criteria nor the process of locating students to programs is very robust. Other contributing factors may also be the absence of a credit system and the fact that failure in some courses requires repeating them in a full year and, in some faculties, repeating all the courses.

Clearly, not every student is gifted with the abilities needed to succeed at the university level. Selection processes need to be able to sort students on the basis of characteristics that are stronger predictors of success. These could, for instance, be foundation knowledge, competency in study skills, writing ability, intellectual ability, motivation, and English language proficiency, especially in programs where some courses are taught in English, such as medicine and engineering. Private tutoring is a service that only a few academic staff members in some faculties offer to university students and for which they are remunerated accordingly. A medical student can reportedly spend as much as 6,000 L.E. per course for private tutoring (US$1 is equivalent to 3.4 L.E). The extent to which this service is in demand suggests that either the students find themselves insufficiently prepared for their courses or that they find the instruction they receive in their courses inadequate. Another factor is the high dependence of students on private lessons during secondary education, which can continue, with negative consequences, to the tertiary level.

EDUCATIONAL INPUT

Low quality and relevance can be attributed to deficiencies in educational inputs and in educational processes. Weaknesses in educational inputs can be classified in two groups related to infrastructure and academic staff.

Infrastructure

The size of Egypt's higher education system poses special challenges in making substantial investments in its infrastructure, operation, and periodic maintenance. Also, the combination of inadequate libraries and ineffective integration of information technology in the educational process contributes directly to low quality in higher education.

The lack of an overall technology plan: At the system and the university level, the short-term funding model and the lack of an articulated acquisition and replacement plan have led to an inconsistent and unproductive approach to the implementation of information technology. The lack of a governance structure is clearly tied to the lack of a technology plan; the two processes must go hand in hand to achieve desirable and measurable results.

Information technology and the Internet: Within individual universities, there is a shortage of modern information technology for teaching, libraries, and research. At the national level, Egypt's twelve universities are connected to the Egyptian University Network (EUN), with the SCU acting as the hub. The SCU, in turn, is connected to the Internet and acts as the Internet Service Provider (ISP) for the universities. However, no content (research material, library catalog, or learning media) is available through the EUN.

Libraries: Low rates of stock replacement and a high proportion of outdated content have contributed to the current low use of libraries. Weak management means that their improvement is less likely to be made a financial priority. Existing network structures for access to Egyptian and international research databases are poor and/or unaffordable, as are systems for the supply of primary documentation identified through secondary bibliographic databases. Access to the Internet is either direct for faculty and researchers or, with the help of library intermediaries, is extremely patchy. Perhaps related to this is the still-pervasive tendency toward administrative and physical fragmentation of library facilities rather than operation using economies of scale. University libraries have separate identities, maintained separately at faculty and/or departmental levels, and they do not share resources. Thus, Egypt's twelve public universities have more than 200 libraries, often with poorly maintained buildings and equipment. An automated library system linking all the eighteen faculties of engineering in the twelve public universities was established under a World Bank–financed project for the development of Engineering and Technical Education in Egypt (ETEP), but further expansion of the library network is still needed.

Academic Staff

Academic staff are adversely affected by selection and recruitment practices, academic qualifications and competencies, and remuneration and other incentives.

Selection and recruitment practices: The main method of hiring academic staff in the current system is to draw from the pool of graduating students at the bachelor's level. This is a problem for four main reasons. First, hiring appears to be an incentive to encourage and support strong students rather than a meaningful exercise to meet program needs or advance strategic development plans. Second, there is little injection of "new blood" into the system and hence little variation in the models of teaching and research that students might have been exposed to if they obtained their degree elsewhere. Third, as it draws from a very narrow pool of candidates, it limits the possibilities of identifying and hiring the most qualified individuals. Fourth, it assumes that high academic standing at the undergraduate level will be a reliable predictor of a solid performance as a researcher and teacher.

Academic qualifications and competencies: Often graduate students who lack experience and expertise serve as undergraduate teachers. Since 1975, Egypt has had a limited program of pedagogical training for three to four weeks for new faculty members. Participation in this program is mandatory for anyone seeking promotion from lecturer to assistant professor. The main deficiency of the program is the lack of its continuity in the area of development of teaching skills of faculty members. It also limits the development of pedagogical competencies of faculty members to the outset of their career, with no obligation and/or commitment to further develop their teaching skills.

Remuneration and other incentives: Salaries of academic staff are very low. Across the ranks, the salary scale consists of a base (which is the same for all within a rank) plus additional increments, the amounts of which vary depending on the number of years of experience and on extra tasks that staff undertake. Senior administrative staff (deans and chairs) receive negligible monetary compensation for taking on administrative positions. By law, all faculty members are allowed to hold other jobs. Junior staff (below the level of assistant professor) are allowed to tutor but not to work as consultants until they are in the third year of their hire. Staff often take advantage of this situation and seek other part-time employment opportunities in order to augment their income. Having two and sometimes three jobs contributes to high rates of absenteeism, particularly in the professional programs.

Faculty members appear to have very limited access to public funds to support their scholarship. Research funding from the Academy of Scientific Research, even on a competitive basis, is reportedly extremely limited, as is financial assistance that would help staff establish links with international scholarly communities. With the exception of one- to two-year scientific mission programs, faculty and staff receive no paid sabbatical leaves, and no systematic incentive process serves to encourage professional development. Faculty members, however, are entitled to a total of up to ten years of unpaid leave from their universities or institutes to work in other local or foreign universities or even in industrial enterprises during the course of their academic career.

EDUCATIONAL PROCESS

Educational process issues can be grouped in eight categories:

- Teaching methods
- Workload/teaching loads
- Working conditions
- Promotion of staff, assessment of performance, and accountability
- Responsibilities of academic staff
- Use of modern educational technology
- Research and development
- Activities of students

A brief account of each category follows.

Teaching Methods

It is very difficult to use teaching strategies other than the well-established traditional lecturing style because of

- The large number of students that a lecturer has to instruct
- The limited acquaintance with and support for new teaching technologies among many top-level administrators and their reluctance to accept these strategies as more appropriate for learning
- The limited financial resources available to acquire new teaching aids
- The limited space and facilities available to facilitate innovation

Workload and Teaching Loads

The normal workload allocation (eight hours per week for full professors, ten for associate professors, and twelve for lecturers) is particularly problematic for individuals who teach courses basic to all departments within a faculty. This leaves little time to prepare for teaching. If lecturers (who comprise nearly 44 percent of the academic staff holding a Ph.D. degree) were to teach only their allocated twelve hours a week and take the same amount of time for preparation, this would account for roughly two-thirds of their week. A new rule was issued a few years ago stating that staff members are obligated to carry up to 2.5 times their normal teaching load. Very limited remuneration is given to all staff members on a monthly basis (a fixed amount based on rank), irrespective of the overload, as long as it is within this ratio. Since a growing number of academic staff take on additional jobs outside the university for one or two days a week to supplement their income, it can be assumed that at least 44 percent of faculty spend little time on course preparation or on their other academic duties.

Working Conditions

The work environment for the academic staff in the majority of faculties does not appear to be conducive to either innovative teaching or to carrying out research. Office spaces are neither sufficient nor adequately utilized. As a rule, universities do not provide academic staff with computers. Also, the limited availability of qualified laboratory technicians is a source of major concern to faculty, particularly in disciplines that depend on laboratory equipment for teaching and research.

Staff Promotion, Performance Assessment, and Accountability

The majority of academic staff are hired for permanent (tenured) positions on the merit of their undergraduate academic standing without particular consideration for actual competency, or even potential ability, in teaching or conducting research. Only two formal promotion exercises are carried out during the entire career of an academic. No mechanisms such as merit pay are used to differentiate individuals and to reward superior performance. Promotion occurs in five-year intervals between each rank (from lecturer to assistant professor and from assistant professor to full professor). It is carried out through education-sector committees appointed by the SCU and includes representation from most senior staff (full professors who have been in the rank for at least five years), and involves an external peer-review process (within Egypt). Egypt uses neither regular student course ratings nor other mechanisms, such as peer evaluations or teaching portfolios, that could provide a measure of the quality of teaching. Nor are there any internal or external measures of accountability, such as annual reporting by staff of the work they do. It is true that academic staff members are poorly paid and are not offered many incentives, but they are not accountable for their time or productivity as long as they are present in their assigned lectures.

Academic Staff Responsibilities

In addition to the heavy teaching load, academic staff, particularly full professors, are overburdened by diverse responsibilities other than teaching. The SCU appoints around 120 promotion committees and each consists of at least three full professors. Senior academic staff provide the membership for many other committees, further making them less available to be actively and fully involved in undergraduate teaching and research. Moreover, participation in these committees places a heavy demand on the time of senior staff, which they might otherwise dedicate to advancing their scholarship.

Use of Modern Educational Technology

Egypt can point to few examples in which modern educational technology has been directly integrated into the course curriculum and used in a manner that would promote enhancement and extension of the course material beyond the lecture hall. Lack of financial resources makes it difficult to meet the needs for better equipment, access to networks and the Internet, professional development, expert assistance, and incentives. Students complain that universities are not offering them the opportunity to employ modern technology to further their learning and critical thinking skills. Most students also complain about the lack of sufficient computing resources, the limited access to the Internet, and the limited opportunity to learn new computing skills. These students feel it is essential for them to have these skills if they are to be prepared to effectively compete in the job market.

Research and Development

The general environment in the majority of universities does not foster research productivity or innovation by staff members. University research and development activities are highly dependent on individual faculty members, some of whom produce and publish research work of high international standard. The main incentive for the majority of faculty members to initiate and publish research is to fulfill the requirements for promotion rather than to produce quality and innovative research. Inadequate equipment and testing facilities, limited funds allocated for research by the university, absence of remuneration for conducting the research, and the deficiency in the relationship between industrial enterprises and universities to support research are among the factors affecting the quality and quantity of research produced by Egyptian universities. High-quality research work cited internationally from Egyptian universities is relatively sparse and disproportionate to the large number of faculty members working in Egyptian universities.

Student Activities

The higher education system in Egypt provides legal channels for students to organize their diverse activities through student unions. These student bodies are selected in each college through annual elections. College and/or university administrations ensure that the election process is secure and that candidates have no history of extreme political or religious tendencies or criminal conviction. Students have the freedom to practice in a wide variety of activities within university and college campuses. Activities related to political parties are not encouraged on the premises, but political culture and debates related to current and ongoing hot issues are welcomed and encouraged. On-campus peaceful demonstrations, which are fairly common, have elicited no objections from administrations at colleges and universities. However, off-campus demonstrations have been resisted and discouraged by administrations because of the possibility for violent and destructive actions, either by students themselves or external actors.

Another important student body established by the government is the Center for Leadership Preparation. The objective of the center is to prepare potential students for future leadership of the country. During mid-term and summer vacations every year, groups of students join this center for one to two weeks. Political debates with ministers and/or government officials, cultural meetings with eminent personalities in diverse fields, and social and athletic competitions are among the activities practiced in the center.

QUALITY AND RELEVANCE AT THE MIDDLE TECHNICAL LEVEL

The most dramatic example of mismatch between training and labor markets occurs in the case of the MTIs, which enroll too small a share of students (less than 10 percent) for the needs of a modern economy. The graduates of the MTIs have the worst employment rate in the nonuniversity sector (over 60 percent remain unemployed for at least two years). Because the quality of education provided in these MTIs is miserable, a vicious circle results:

• An insufficient number of mid-level technicians is produced.
• Graduates are not sufficiently prepared for employment at their level.
• The jobs for which they were supposedly trained are taken by graduates from higher-level schools (higher technical institutes or engineering schools) at a much higher unit cost to the state.

The causes of this unfortunate state of affairs may be attributed to the following factors:

• Lack of relevant mission and sufficient enrollments
• Inadequate governance framework
• Economically irrelevant academic programs
• Poorly trained teaching staff working under difficult conditions
• Outdated facilities and equipment
• Barriers to student transfer or progression

What follows is a brief description of each of these causes.

Lack of Relevant Mission and Sufficient Enrollments

The MTIs have existed for fifty years, but their mission, strategy, and philosophy have not undergone significant changes since

then. MTIs suffer from inadequate maintenance of equipment and facilities and outdated materials. Training of the teaching staff has been neglected over the years, leaving faculties unqualified for the requirements of a modern economy. Many of the forty-seven MTIs are small (50 percent have fewer than 2,000 students, and 25 percent have fewer than 1,000 students), and they suffer from a serious image problem in their communities.

Governance Framework

The Ministry of Higher Education has total central control over the management of MTIs. Even the purchase of simple equipment or basic maintenance expenditures needs to be authorized by the ministry.

Economically Irrelevant Academic Programs

The academic programs in the MTIs should reflect the labor-market need for mid-level personnel in the manufacturing and service sectors of the economy. While the titles of many of the programs (such as computer systems, information technology, production technology, and mechatronics) appear relevant to those needs, the reality is very different. The poor quality of curricula, learning materials, and laboratory equipment, as well as the low educational attainment of teachers, contributes to the overall poor quality of education in these institutions. The preparation of technicians and mid-level personnel requires serious rationalization and reform to make the system more relevant to the needs of the economy. The MTIs and HTIs lack even limited autonomy in developing programs based on market needs.

Poorly Trained Teaching Staff Working under Difficult Conditions

Many MTI instructors have no work experience outside of their institute and receive little or no in-service training during their teaching years. They are considered employees of the Ministry of Higher Education and are even less well paid than university professors, despite having a heavier teaching load. Moreover, MTI faculty members work under difficult conditions, including poor-quality infrastructures and teaching facilities. There is no apparent system of institutional accountability—of faculty to MTI administration, personnel to administration, or personnel to faculty.

Outdated Facilities and Equipment

Many of the MTI facilities are decaying (some have had to close due to safety considerations) and most of their equipment has become obsolete. Major rehabilitation and renovation is needed.

Lack of Policies for Student Transfer or Progression

Currently, MTI students have no way to transfer to universities, though there are some very limited pathways for these students to gain access to higher technical institutes. The barriers to university transfer are understandable, given the generally low standards for admission to MTIs and the low quality of training that students receive. Nevertheless, the lack of a rational policy for transfer could become problematic as the quality of MTIs improves. A national qualifications framework needs to be established to resolve this issue.

FISCALLY SUSTAINABLE ENROLLMENTS

In 1997–1998, 5.9 percent of the Egyptian GDP was allocated to education, a level equal to the OECD average. Of that amount, 28 percent was allocated to higher education. Overall expenditure on education as a proportion of the GDP has grown from 3.9 percent in 1991 to 5.9 percent in 1998. In spite of the expansion of public spending on education in Egypt (in both absolute terms and as a proportion of the GDP), the growth in the higher education student population has caused a decrease in per-student resources at that level.

During the period of rapid growth in the 1990s, the real resources per student in higher education provided by the government dropped in constant 1999 pounds from EGP 6,600 in 1992–1993 to an estimated EGP 4,000 in 1998–1999, an average of 8 percent per year. This reduction in resources has had a major impact on the quality of instruction and facilities. To raise higher education per-student expenditures to 1993 levels (which would require a 5 percent annual increase in per-student expenditures through 2008–2009) in a climate of rising enrollments, a major reallocation of resources in favor of higher education would need to occur. Although the president and the government have emphasized the importance of higher education to Egypt's development, such efforts will be fiscally and politically difficult to undertake if public funds continue to be the sole source of finance. Currently, the Egyptian constitution requires the provision of "free education" at all levels, making it difficult to charge tuition. For long-term reform planning, change of the constitution to allow for (at least partial) financial contributions by students in support of their higher education cannot be ruled out.

The very size of the Egyptian higher education system poses special challenges to the provision of quality education. Egypt has one of the world's largest higher education systems. In 1998–1999, it enrolled some 1.28 million students and employed more than 47,700 faculty members. It is projected from data of previous years that the number of students will increase at an annual rate of at least 4 percent (MNSHD 2000). Although Egyptian's population growth rate has slowed considerably in the last decade, the cohorts entering higher education and the labor force grew rapidly and will continue to do so, given the high birth rates of past years. Thus, enrollment in higher education grew at the high annual rate of 17 percent during the period 1992–1993 to 1998–1999. Under conservative assumptions that take into account the changes in secondary education under the Secondary Education Reform Program (SERP), rapid (but not quite the rate of the last decade) growth in enrollment is expected to continue, roughly at 5–6 percent per annum over the period to 2009 (MNSHD 1999). Put another way: given the high population growth, to simply maintain the share of the 18–

22 age group at its present 19 percent level would require on average an additional 60,000 new enrollments each year over the next ten years. It is therefore clear that increasing the share to at least the 25 percent level over the next ten years (an ambitious government reform target) will considerably add to new enrollments each year, requiring major investments that are beyond the capacity of the government alone.

REFORM ACTIONS

A review of the previous reform initiatives and the government strategy for current and future reform actions is essential to complete the picture. It is a fact that fierce competition and rapid change are the main features of the new global community. To stand a chance in this competitive environment, conventional reform methods must evolve. A totally different "leap approach" has to implemented—that is, large steps must be taken to accelerate progress—if developing countries such as Egypt are to narrow the gap in educational standards between themselves and developed countries. With the progress made in communications and information technologies, developing countries now have a golden opportunity to implement the leap approach. Egypt has already committed itself to the global village by signing binding international agreements that have already started to take effect.

THE ENGINEERING AND TECHNICAL EDUCATION PROJECT (ETEP)

Through the Ministry of Higher Education and its Projects Implementation Unit, the Egyptian government implemented a World Bank–financed project for the development of engineering and technical education over a period of seven years (1992–1998). The funding of the project included U.S.$30.5 million from the World Bank, complemented by the equivalent of U.S.$14 million in local currency from the government. The project's goal was to improve and strengthen engineering and technical education in Egypt. To respond to this challenge, the stated objectives of the project were 1) to improve the quality and occupational relevance of engineering education in Egyptian universities; and 2) to improve the quality of secondary and postsecondary technical education in Egypt by supporting the development of a new, more effective, type of technical education institution, which would meet the growing demand for better-prepared and more-qualified technical teachers.

Two project components were established to implement the reform program under the ETEP. A brief account of the achievements of each project component follows (Said, Anis, and El-Said 1999).

THE ENGINEERING EDUCATION DEVELOPMENT PROGRAM (EEDP) COMPONENT

Over a period of six years, many activities were implemented:

- One hundred fifty-nine projects were commissioned on a competitive basis to establish laboratories and new programs and to train staff/technicians, among other tasks. Peer evaluation committees reported a 97 percent success rate on implemented projects.

- Over 15 percent of the engineering staff members were involved in the developmental activities of EEDP.
- Model curricula were developed for six basic and engineering sciences courses and were disseminated among all the eighteen faculties of engineering.
- Links between academia and industry were supported.
- Pilot modern instructional tools (in electronic format) were developed.
- Institutional self-evaluation and quality assurance mechanisms were introduced as a first step toward the establishment of an accreditation mechanism (and were pilot implemented at three facilities).
- A comprehensive engineering education database accessible to all engineering faculties was established.
- Library automation and Internet/Intranet connectivity linking the eighteen engineering faculties was established.

THE TECHNICAL TEACHER EDUCATION DEVELOPMENT PROGRAM (TTEDP) COMPONENT

Concurrently, with the implementation of EEDP, many components were established under the TTEDP component:

- Two Industrial Education Colleges (IECs) were established to produce integrated teacher graduates capable of teaching theoretical and practical subjects in an integrated manner.
- Teacher training and development centers were established in both IECs.
- Infrastructure was refurbished and developed, and seventy-six laboratories and workshops were equipped in both IECs.
- One hundred eighty courses were developed in ten specializations employing more than sixty-five local experts from universities, technical institutes, and industry, complemented by international assessment through the British Council.
- Core staff members were trained in Holland and England (thirty-one students were granted a master's degree, and seven students were sent through the Missions Department of the Ministry of Higher Education to complete their Ph.D.).
- In-service training programs for teachers were implemented.
- Internet labs and library automation were initiated in both IECs.
- Multimedia-based courseware and up-to-date instructional materials (some in electronic format) were provided for both IECs.

GOVERNMENT REFORM STRATEGY

After the successful completion of the ETEP project, recent government actions geared toward building political consensus on issues critical to the higher education reform in Egypt have created a climate that is conducive to further concrete reform efforts. The government has come to realize that the growing globalization of trade, finance, and information flow is intensifying competition and is increasing the danger that Egypt will continue to fall behind its competitors. Implications of the in-

formation revolution and the knowledge economy need to be factored into Egypt's development agenda. Encouraged by the success of an increasing enrollment in primary education (to almost 100 percent) and the ongoing enhancement of learning and the teaching of IT skills through reforms in secondary education, the government is building on these efforts by improving the quality of education and opportunities for lifelong learning in harmony with worldwide directives (UNESCO 1998).

In response to the challenge of arresting the declining quality of higher education, in 1997 the new Minister of Higher Education nominated a national Higher Education Enhancement Program (HEEP) Commission, which consists of prominent members from the academic community, industrialists, and members of parliament. The 25-member commission formed six subcommittees with more than fifty other members from different disciplines and backgrounds, such as representatives from public and private universities, higher education institutes and training centers, the industrial and business sectors, and other stakeholders concerned with higher education. Each committee had a specific topic to address and held monthly meetings and public hearings that involved major stakeholders to build national consensus for the reform program, which is meant to provide answers for the issues identified in the critical review section.

In the preparation phase for the development of the reform program, several events took place. Study tours to Scotland and France in January 1998 (El-Sharkawy, Anis, and Said 1998) and to Australia and New Zealand in April and May 1999 (Elsalmi 1999) were arranged by the World Bank for some members of the national HEEP committee (the author of this chapter took part in both study tours). The study tour members received valuable firsthand information on higher education reform experiences in the host countries and reported on the findings, lessons learned, and proposed recommendations for the anticipated Egyptian higher education reform. The main reason for visiting the selected countries is that they have all been recently involved in the implementation of reform plans (Dearing 1997; Allport 1998), which enabled the guests to learn from recent reform experiences. Although there are various cultural and educational differences between Egypt and the countries visited, reform initiatives and implementation experiences remain similar and instructive.

Another important activity that took place in June 1999 involved the organization of an international symposium in collaboration with the World Bank. The event was prepared with the objective of learning about the main worldwide trends and important issues in the development of higher education from a select group of internationally known reformers in such areas as quality, diversification, economics, and financing alternatives. For this reason, five higher education specialists of broad international experience were invited by the World Bank to address the symposium on major issues that influence higher education reforms. An exchange of views and ideas between national and international experts regarding the formulation of a general policy and a strategic framework for higher education reforms proved to be very fruitful for the development of Egypt's reform plans. The proceedings of the symposium were published in two volumes (National HEEP Committee 1999; MNSHD 1999).

In the course of preparing for the reform framework, the National HEEP committee members focused on higher education issues. The committee has reviewed and taken into consideration many valuable ideas included in three of the World Bank reports directed toward reform of higher education in the twenty-first century (World Bank 1998b), quality assurance in higher education (World Bank 1998c), and the financing and management of higher education (World Bank 1998a).

The outcome of this process of planning for reform was a national conference in Cairo on February 13 and 14, 2000, at which more than 1,200 participants came to a consensus on a declaration recommending legislative, financial, and structural reform of higher education. Proceedings of the conference contained comprehensive information on all the studies, reports, and proposals developed over the past two years to address the various reform issues under consideration (National HEEP Committee 2000). The prime minister and the president endorsed the declaration. Press reviews and public reactions to the declaration have propelled the reform initiative into almost a movement, with the public calling on the government to act on the declaration. Some negative reactions among staff members on certain issues have been voiced in Egypt's newspapers, but the stage has been set for Egypt to begin to engage in meaningful and necessary higher education reforms.

The declaration's reform agenda is ambitious. The government is seeking to address the issues raised by the conference and has started work on their sequencing and logical articulation. Among the key areas highlighted for reform are:

- Development of a unified framework for higher education (including new legislation)
- Establishment of a new Supreme Council of Higher Education, asserting the principle of institutional autonomy
- Establishment of a National Quality Assurance Committee with specific guidelines for periodic evaluation
- Establishment of a funding formula with block grants and a higher education "master plan" at the national level, including the reform of admission policies
- Plans for changes to improve educational inputs (information technology, libraries, hiring of teaching staff, improving teaching methods) and criteria for the development of new academic programs and curricula (for example, responsiveness to society's needs, attainment of standards, and community orientation)
- Development of middle technical institutes and higher technical institutes, the former through a clustering of the existing institutes into regional polytechnics that will be both affiliated with one of the regional universities and associated with a regional industry

Other goals for government intervention include the establishment of a National Qualifications Framework (NQF), centers of excellence and multimedia centers, and the Egyptian Open University. Another goal is to improve graduate studies and research through improved infrastructure such as labs and equipment. The development of an NQF would add to the robustness and flexibility of the education system and was one of the essential recommendations of the National HEEP conference. Seamless transfer from one stream of education into the other is the main feature of the NQF, provided that the academic level set for the other stream is attained through a common degree or exam. Twenty-five projects were endorsed for implementation by the National HEEP conference. The list contains the intended impact of each project on five main issues—access, quality, efficiency, relevance, and governance and finance—and on the main entities concerned with the implementation of each project.

INSTITUTIONAL CAPACITY ASSESSMENT

It is essential to carry out an institutional capacity assessment study to ensure that bodies that implement reform projects have the required capacity measures for the successful implementation of the project. The institutional capacity analysis focuses on issues such as organizational settings; leadership and management; financial, material, and human resources; and other key work practices. The main purpose of this effort is to identify capacity gaps and propose alternatives. An institutional capacity study was carried out to assess the government agencies and institutions that will be involved in the implementation of the twenty-five projects endorsed by the HEEP conference. The report containing the study incorporates responses to all of the above activities (Said 2000).

HIGHER EDUCATION ENHANCEMENT PROGRAM (HEEP)

The conference declaration reform program is ambitious and requires extensive and diversified financial support. The Egyptian government has sought a commitment from the World Bank to continue its support for the education sector at large, thus extending its support of primary and secondary education to include tertiary education. Over the past decade, the World Bank has supported the Egyptian government in its attempts to reform the education sector at large. The primary and secondary education programs are currently being implemented with World Bank and European Union support (MNSHD 1999).

In the World Bank endeavor to support the Egyptian government in the implementation of its current reform initiative, most—though not all—of the conference recommendations will be supported by the proposed HEEP project. This strategic choice results from the objective urgency of alleviating many of the problems faced by Egypt's education system, the fact that many of these problems are interrelated, and the government's and the national HEEP committee's strong desire to implement a comprehensive reform program. Furthermore, this broad convergence of views provides the umbrella under which an overall reform program can be financed by the government, the World Bank, and other donors to act as a catalyst to the overall reform process. The European Commission (EC) and USAID have already expressed an interest in supporting reforms in the MTI and teacher training subsectors, respectively.

Specifically, the HEEP program will directly address:

- The antiquated system-wide governance and management framework
- All issues that affect the low quality and relevance of university graduates

• All issues that affect the low quality and relevance of MTI graduates

Another critical issue, the fiscal sustainability of publicly financed enrollments, is an ongoing issue that will be the subject of further discussions and continuing dialogue. It is essential, however, that the government decide on what its enrollment targets will be and how it will finance them. The government leadership has often declared that the intention is to provide all secondary school graduates with higher education opportunities. It is expected that improved access will result from an increase in selected public-sector capacity based on more efficient use of existing capacity, such as in MTIs, distance education, and an increase in private-sector capacity.

CONCLUDING REMARKS

Egypt has already started implementing its major reform plans for the education sector at large. The success or failure of the reform process in general, and HEEP in particular, will greatly depend on how the various government agencies, institutions, faculty members, and students will operate under the proposed reform plans. A fundamental change in how higher education operates and in the attitude toward change itself is needed to create the appropriate environment for development. The reform of higher education is an ongoing process that cannot be achieved simply by issuing laws, orders, or recommendations. It can only be sustained and implemented successfully if all stakeholders involved are committed to the anticipated change. Everyone has a fundamental role to play in supporting higher education reform and Egypt's plans for development (Said 1999).

Many of Egypt's proposed reform projects require minimal or no extra funding by individual institutions. In the newly emerging global world, Egypt must meet international standards and practices related to higher education if it is to face the main challenges of overcrowding and improving the quality of graduates.

REFERENCES

Allport, C. 1998. "Thinking Globally, Acting Locally: Life Long Learning and the Implications for University Staff." Keynote address presented at Re-working the University, a conference held at Nathan Campus, Griffith University, Australia, December.

Dearing, R. 1997. "Higher Education in the Learning Society." Report for the National Committee of Inquiry into Higher Education. Norwich, England.

Elsalmi, A., ed. 1999. "Higher Education in Australia and New Zealand: Lessons Learned." Study tour report presented to the World Bank Human Resources Group, Middle East & North Africa Region.

El-Sharkawy, A., I. H. Anis, and M. E. Said. 1998. "Higher Education in Scotland and France." Study tour report presented to the World Bank and the Egyptian Ministry of Higher Education.

MNSHD (Middle East and North Africa Sector for Human Development). 1999. Secondary Education Reform Project (SERP). Arab Republic of Egypt, Project Appraisal Document. World Bank.

——— 2000. "Higher Education Enhancement Program (HEEP)." Arab Republic of Egypt, Project Concept Document. World Bank.

National HEEP [Higher Education Enhancement Program] Committee. 2000. "Higher Education in Egypt." Proceedings of the National HEEP Conference, February 13–14. Egyptian Supreme Council of Universities (SCU) and MOHE.

National HEEP Committee and The World Bank. 1999. Higher Education Enhancement Program. International Symposium, June 24, Cairo. Vol. 1: *Excerpts*; vol. 2: *Monographs.* Cairo: World Bank Print Shop.

Said, M. E. 1999. "Higher Education Vision for the 21st Century: A Future Outlook." Keynote paper presented at CAINET99 Fourth Internet Conference and Exhibition, Cairo.

———. 2000. "Institutional Capacity Assessment of Government Agencies: Institutions Selected to Implement the Proposed Development Project HEEP." A World Bank Report.

Said, M. E., H. I. Anis, and M. K. El-Said. 1999. "Implementation Completion Report: The Arab Republic of Egypt, The Engineering and Technical Education Project (ETEP)." Report No. 19445 of World Bank Human Resources Group, Middle East & North Africa Region.

SCU (Supreme Council of Universities) Statistical Department. 1999. *Annual Statistics.* University Education Development Research Center, Ministry of Higher Education. 7 vols. Cairo.

Task Force on Higher Education and Society. 2000. *Higher Education in Developing Countries: Peril and Promise.* Washington, D.C.: The World Bank.

UNESCO Declaration. 1998. "Higher Education in the Twenty-first Century: Vision and Action. Proceedings of the World Conference on Higher Education, October." Available online at: http://www.unesco.org/education/wche/pdf/participants_doc.pdf

World Bank. 1998a. "The Financing and Management of Higher Education: A Status Report on Worldwide Reforms." A World Bank Report.

———. 1998b. "Higher Education in the 21st Century." A World Bank Report.

———. 1998c. "Quality Assurance in Higher Education: Recent Progress, Challenges Ahead." A World Bank Report.

30

Equatorial Guinea

DEBORAH POMEROY

INTRODUCTION

To understand higher education in the Republic of Equatorial Guinea, it is helpful to understand the geographic, historical, cultural, political, and economic context of this tiny African nation, population 600,000, that lives in an area of 28,050 square kilometers (10,830 square miles). These factors give rise to some of the unique challenges for higher education in the country. This chapter lays out these contextual factors, presents an overview of education in Equatorial Guinea, and describes the national university, La Universidad Nacional de Guinea Ecuatorial (UNGE). I also describe the Spanish distance-learning university, Universidad Nacional de Educacion a Distancia (UNED), and other higher education institutions in the country.

Equatorial Guinea lies between Gabon and Cameroon on the coast of central West Africa. The republic includes a large mainland province in which Bata, the nation's largest city, is located. In addition, the republic includes several islands, the most significant of which is Bioko. It is the largest island (2,020 square kilometers; 780 square miles) in the Gulf of Guinea and is the location of Malabo, the national capital. Bioko is much closer to Nigeria and Cameroon than it is to the mainland province, and its separation from the greater population and land mass of the mainland creates many challenges.

The two predominant cultural and linguistic groups of Equatoguineans, the Fang on the mainland and the Bubi on Bioko, are descendants of the great waves of Bantu migrations (Diamond 1997; Vansina 1989). The Fang have a very complex culture based on strong family ties. Their skills and cultural structure were initially suited to trading, at which they became quite successful. Their dependence on trade, however, created vulnerabilities that caused great hardship. Their relationship with the Spanish was generally one of suspicion, if not outright distrust (Fegley 1989). Since independence, most of the leaders in the nation have been Fang. Because of this, many Fang who work for the government, energy companies, and the national university now live in Malabo. The Bubi have a history of isolationism, a characteristic that protected them but also kept them out of the mainstream of national development. As Bioko was developed, however, a number of Bubi were able to gain relatively high levels of education and enter into strategic positions in the local economy.

In the early 1470s, Portuguese captain Fernao de Poo was the first European to discover and claim Bioko Island. In 1778, Spain gained control of the island and the mainland region by treaty. From 1827 to 1843, under an agreement, the British established Port Clarence, a naval base from which to deter slaving, the site of what has now become Malabo. The country remained under Spanish control until gaining independence in 1968 (Fegley 1989).

Macias Nguema led a peaceful transition into independence, but he turned into a dictator as his relationship with Spain deteriorated. In 1975, he closed schools, putting an end to formal education. Spain broke off diplomatic relations in 1977. All churches were forced to close in 1978. In 1979, the Macias regime was overthrown in a coup led by Col. Teodoro Obiang Nguema Mbasogo, his nephew. A U.S. State Department study noted that the terror of the Macias government "led to the death or exile of up to one third of the country's population" (U.S. Department of State 1989, 4). Multiple interviews and/or direct observation indicated that many intellectuals were especially targeted.

Following the coup, life in Equatorial Guinea slowly began to normalize. Relations with Western countries resumed. Some exiles returned, and several rounds of elections were held. The country, which has one dominant political party, remains relatively stable. Over the years, various Amnesty International reports (1996–2000) have expressed concerns about political repression and lack of freedom of speech. Equatorial Guinea is, however, slowly developing press and broadcast capacity. While local papers, including an opposition paper, are quite easy to obtain, international newspapers are unavailable. Access to the Internet is extremely limited because there are few phone lines and few servers, and service is limited. Very few individuals have computers, and even in Malabo there is only one business that provides public access to computers.

During the Macias years, Equatorial Guinea developed strong bonds with the Soviet Union, Cuba, China, and North Korea (U.S. Department of State 1989). Recent development of massive off-shore oil reserves, however, has moved the country toward the West, and the Corporate Council on Africa (2001) reports that Equatorial Guinea is forecasted to have the highest economic development of any country in the world in 2001. The development of these resources has brought major changes to Bioko, and oil found off Bata is bringing similar changes to the mainland as well. The infusion of energy money into the economy has created a demand for the development of banking, commerce, and education. With this new economic capacity, the country is slowly, but unevenly, emerging from years of neglect of, and in some cases damage to, its physical, social, and educational infrastructure.

With valuable resources come liabilities. Keeping the economy healthy and balanced in the context of the huge economic presence of the energy companies is a challenge. There are also powerful negative precedents in neighboring countries that must be overcome if Equatorial Guinea is to take full advantage of its petroleum wealth. Onishi (2000) points out a negative precedent in that neighboring countries have not fared well with such challenges. Despite the arguments of skeptics (Hecht 1999), Onishi says that government leaders are trying to avoid the mistakes of other African countries. This may be the ultimate challenge to the educational system.

GENERAL EDUCATION CONTEXT

During colonial times, formal education in Equatorial Guinea was exclusively a missionary function. Although there was a strong early Protestant presence on Bioko, Catholicism became the official religion under Spanish rule. Primary education provided by the missions was free and became available to children throughout almost all parts of Equatorial Guinea by 1943. Students wishing to pursue secondary education had to leave the country, since secondary schools were virtually nonexistent until after World War II (Fegley 1989). Despite this apparent lack of higher education opportunities, Spain had a policy that encouraged indigenous people to attain jobs in higher education and in well-salaried or civil service positions. As a result, Equatorial Guinea had one of the highest literacy rates and the highest per capita income on the African continent at independence (U.S. Department of State 1989).

Equatorial Guinea currently has a single public school system run by the Ministry of Education. The country is also home to a number of private and missionary schools. Some private schools, such as the Colegio Español (Spanish college), the French School, and the Nigerian Equatorial Guinean International School, are tuition schools run by foreign agencies. Others are totally independent. The missionary schools have a long history in the country and are highly respected. Most of these

independent schools use their own curriculum, though the schooling levels are comparable to those in the public schools.

The public educational program consists of five levels of mandatory primary schooling, culminating with a national examination. Following successful completion of the examination, children may enter secondary school. The secondary curriculum consists of seven levels, culminating with a pre-university year. After passing the seventh-level examination, students may take the university qualifying examination. A successful score on this examination entitles the student to acceptance at the university and enables the student to apply for scholarships to study at foreign universities. There are also a number of public polytechnic schools for vocational training.

Until 1993, the Spanish Cooperation gave direct assistance to public schools in Equatorial Guinea by providing curriculum, teacher training, and textbooks. At that time, the Spanish Cooperation shifted its focus to the Spanish missionary schools, Colegio Español and La Universidad Nacional de Educación a Distancia (the National University of Distance Education, UNED). While this has promoted more local control and ownership of schools, the transition and the loss of valuable resources to public schools have been difficult. Many Equatoguineans say that schools have declined in quality.

The Ministry of Education reports that students had a 10.1 percent rate of completion of secondary school in 1997–1998 (Asuma 2000). The general condition of the public school system is critical, though not for lack of caring by officials of the ministry. The schools lack trained teachers, and classrooms in city schools are extremely crowded, some with more than sixty children in a classroom. Younger children often sit three or four to a desk, and sometimes children must sit on the floor. Many buildings are in very poor repair, city schools run double shifts, and books, instructional materials, and equipment for the children do not exist. Most students go through twelve years of schooling without access to textbooks. Partly because of the lack of books and resources, and largely because of its inherited colonial traditions, the mode of instruction is almost exclusively lecture and recitation. Schools do not have special facilities such as libraries, laboratories, or gymnasiums. Conditions in village schools are worse. Mission schools and private schools provide significantly better learning environments and opportunities, but even these struggle to supply books and materials.

The national university (UNGE) trains teachers, but the Ministry of Education reports that it has a shortage of trained teachers. To fill the gap, the University hires uncertified teachers. Public school teachers receive very low salaries, and there are many reports of teachers holding two or three jobs to support their families. Many interviewees report that economic pressures on teachers have a profound effect on the quality of schooling. All evidence indicates that there is no apparent increase in funding for general education on the horizon, despite great increases in national wealth in the past few years.

HIGHER EDUCATION: LA UNIVERSIDAD NACIONAL DE GUINEA ECUATORIAL

La Universidad Nacional de Guinea Ecuatorial (UNGE), The National University of Equatorial Guinea, was founded in

January 1995. Its main campus is located on the site of the former National School of Agriculture. The main campus houses the central administration; the School of Agriculture, Fisheries, and Forestry; and the School of Arts and Social Science. A residence hall complex, with a housing and dining capacity for 200 students, is located about 1 kilometer (half a mile) from the main campus. The School of Administration and the Teacher Training School are on separate sites in Malabo. The university also has several programs in Bata: the School of Nursing, the newly opened School of Medicine, and a branch of the Teacher Training College (which trains instructors for the primary and early secondary levels only). The new School of Engineering and Technology is also located in Bata; it enrolled its first class in 2001. The facilities in Bata are all in separate locations. Now that the School of Engineering is completed, no additional schools have been scheduled for a while. The goal of the university administration is to consolidate and strengthen current programs rather than expand any further.

Programs

The School of Agriculture, Fisheries, and Forestry (Malabo): Agriculture was the first school of UNGE, having evolved from La Escuela Nacional de Agricultura (the National School of Agriculture). Because it is the continuation of a former school on the same site, the school has an established program and facility. Over the years, some of the professors have developed collections of indigenous specimens for laboratory use. According to the assistant director, the school used to enroll about 150 entering students each year, but intake has declined sharply because there are many new programs at UNGE and graduates are having difficulty finding jobs in related fields (Nchama 2000). The matriculation data in Table 30.1 indicates that all first-year students follow a common core of studies; students differentiate into specific programs in their second and third years. Of special interest is the fact that the combined second- and third-year enrollment in the specialties listed is only forty-three. This low number suggests major attrition in these programs. This conclusion is also supported by anecdotal accounts of students leaving school to take jobs in the energy companies.

This school runs a technical engineering degree program that requires three years of coursework and includes two summers of fieldwork, in addition to regular-term coursework. Students culminate their program with a six-month senior thesis project. The agricultural mechanics and fisheries programs consist of 286 credits, but the forestry utilization and agricultural utilization programs require only 170 and 183 credits, respectively. Petroleum technology credit requirements were not available. The director of the program explained that the difference in credit hours is due to laboratory or practicum experiences; each credit hour is equivalent to ten scheduled course hours. No electives are offered in any of these programs.

This school has a faculty of thirty-eight, three of whom hold doctorates. Other faculty members hold bachelor's degrees or technical engineering degrees. Because this is such an established program, the faculty have considerable experience supervising senior theses and research, though they do not have time or financial support for research of their own.

Table 30.1. Enrollment at the UNGE School of Agriculture, 2000–2001

Program	Matriculation 2000–2001
First-Year Common Core	51
Forestry Development	6
Petroleum Technology	14
Fisheries	12
Agricultural and Forestry Mechanics	6
Agricultural Development	5
Total	94

Source: Office of the Rector, La Universidad Nacional de Guinea Ecuatorial, Malabo, October 2000.

Table 30.2. Enrollment at the UNGE School of Arts and Social Science, 2000–2001

Program	Matriculation 2000–2001
Law	69
Political Science and Sociology	38
Information Science and Communication	16
Spanish Philology	10
Total	133

Source: Office of the Rector, La Universidad Nacional de Guinea Ecuatorial, Malabo, October 2000.

The School of Arts and Social Science (Malabo): The arts and social science faculty was assisted by five faculty members from the Spanish Universidad de Alcala (the University of Alcala) in designing this school's programs. Degree programs in law, political science, sociology, information science, and Spanish philology are five years in length and culminate in a bachelor's degree. The programs range from 240 credits for information science to 289 credits for law. These programs have no electives. Students are required to write a senior thesis in their final year.

This school is new and has not yet graduated a class. During their first year, all students take a common core of courses plus a few specialized courses. The sociology and political science programs share a common curriculum for three years, with specialization occurring only in the last two years. For this reason, the matriculation numbers in Table 30.2 are not separated for these two programs. The faculty reports that the law and political science programs have been growing since their inception due to greater job opportunities for graduates in these areas, while other programs are holding steady in their enrollment. The figures represent total enrollment in each of the program specialties.

The school has thirty-one faculty members; one holds a doctorate and the others hold a bachelor's degree. Several of the faculty members also teach at UNED.

The School of Administration (Malabo): This school runs

Table 30.3. Enrollment at the UNGE School of Administration, 2000–2001

Program	Matriculation 2000–2001
First-Year Common Core	18
Public Administration	14
Human Resources	3
Business Science	39
Tourism	NA
Total	74

Source: Office of the Rector, La Universidad Nacional de Guinea Ecuatorial, Malabo, October 2000.

three programs of three years' duration, each of which uses a common core curriculum for the first year. These programs encompass from 214 to 219 credit hours with no electives. In addition to the regular academic program, this school also runs a two-year certificate program in basic office skills. Table 30.3 shows the entering class enrollment in the first-year common core curriculum and the combined enrollment for the second and third year in the other programs.

In addition, the two-year Office Skills Diploma program that the school offers has an enrollment of twenty-five.

The faculty of the School of Administration includes one member with a doctorate; all others have bachelor's degrees.

The Martin Luther King, Jr. School of Teacher Training (Malabo/Bata): Since colonial times, the name of the teacher training school has changed several times, and it has had many different directors, but the location has remained constant. Initially, this was a boarding school, but now the school has evolved into one of the schools of UNGE. The teacher training school in Bata was founded in 1984. There are two diploma programs at the teacher training school: a two-year program culminating with a primary teacher diploma and the three-year bachelor's degree program for secondary teachers, which also includes a specialization in a specific area of study. Both programs include a teaching practicum. The fields of specialization are preschool education, primary education, foreign language, secondary basic arts, and secondary basic sciences. The program in Bata includes only preparation for primary and the early years of secondary teaching.

Malabo has twenty faculty members and Bata has thirty-five, including two with doctorates. In 2000–2001, Malabo enrolled 122 students. According to the administration, one of the difficulties facing the school is that many students come to the teacher training school only because they have no other job.

The School of Health and Environment (Bata): This school runs a three-year nursing program and currently enrolls forty-one students—twenty-nine men and twelve women. The nursing program is well established and is operated separately from the medical school.

The School of Medicine (Bata): This school is separate from the nursing school in facilities and administration. It opened in the fall of 2000 with a class of thirty students. The medical program is six years in duration and culminates in a degree of Doctor of Medicine. In addition to Equatoguinean faculty, the school has nine Cuban physicians who have come to Equatorial Guinea to teach. The school's curriculum is based on the Cuban model of medical training.

The School of Engineering (Bata): This new school was scheduled to open early in 2001. The program will be a three-year degree program and will include mechanical, electrical, and architectural engineering.

LANGUAGE

The vast majority of Equatoguineans are multilingual. Spanish is the official language of Equatorial Guinea, and all schooling is done in Spanish, with the exception of the Nigerian school, which uses English, and the French school, which uses French. Until the past few years, French was the language of business, since Equatorial Guinea is in the midst of Francophone Africa. In casual conversation, most adults speak their tribal tongues, such as Fang or Bubi. Those who were educated in the Soviet Union also speak Russian. At present, the language of economic empowerment is English. The government has no official policy about English, but officials in several government ministries maintain that English is the language of the future. Many secondary schools offer courses in both English and French. Equatorial Guinea's children's newsmagazine has feature stories in English, including grammar and vocabulary lessons. UNGE offers courses in basic and technical English. These courses are taught by nationals whose third or fourth language is English. Most of these teachers speak English but are not trained as teachers of English. Energy companies offer training in English, and some expatriates tutor or teach English. Since speakers of English are at a great advantage for employment in the energy companies, many are being drawn out of education and into more lucrative employment.

FACULTY AT UNGE

The following data is interpreted from lists of faculty and their hour assignments. There are four classifications of faculty:

- Special (teaching less than 8 hours)
- Part-time (minimum of 8 hours teaching; 12 total hours on campus)
- Full-time (15 hours teaching; 25 total hours on campus)
- Exclusive (15 hours teaching; 25 total hours entirely within a single department) (See Table 30.4).

In some cases, faculty split their time between schools; their contributions to both schools would be reported as part-time.

The university administration is very conscious of the limitations of the university. The vision of the university at this time is to develop collaborative relationships with other universities that will enable UNGE to strengthen its programs and faculty. The university would like to provide faculty with more opportunities to achieve higher levels of education and would like to see more full-time and exclusive faculty in the schools who would have time for research. As of now, no research is being conducted by faculty, due to lack of time and lack of training through advanced degrees. The university sees the instituting of

Table 30.4. Distribution of Faculty at UNGE

School	Special	Part-Time	Full-Time	Exclusive	Total
Letters and Social Science	0	27	1	3	31
Administration	19	9	3	0	31
Agriculture, Fisheries, and Forestry	4	16	7	11	38
Teacher Training at Malabo	13	6	1	0	20
Teacher Training at Bata	2	10	17	6	35
Medicine and Nursing	*	*	*	*	*

*This data was not available.

Source: Office of the Rector, La Universidad Nacional de Guinea Ecuatorial, Malabo, October 2000.

senior dissertations as the first step toward institutionalizing research at UNGE.

TECHNOLOGY

Despite the high level of interest by administrators, faculty, and students, UNGE has only very rudimentary technological facilities. As of November 2000, the entire university had only one Internet connection, and that was in the rector's office. The two schools on the main campus each had a computer; but other schools have no computers. There is a very limited computer laboratory with three functioning units on the main campus, but none of them is networked. UNGE has relied mostly on cast-off computer equipment, wiped clean of software, that is provided by the oil companies. Unfortunately, this kind of donation causes frustration, since many units are slow and hard to fix, and they are incompatible with each other and with more current software. There are also inconsistencies between the Spanish and English keyboards.

FACILITIES

The library facilities at UNGE are very limited, and books are not available for loan. On the main campus, the library contains approximately 3,500 books in a small room with limited student capacity. The teacher training school has a similar collection, housed in a nice, spacious room. The School of Administration has only a few hundred books in a small room. Most of the books in the libraries are multiple copies of course texts for students who cannot afford to buy their own texts. The United States Embassy in Yaounde is donating $19,000 to UNGE for its library.

In general, the university facilities are clean and the grounds are trim. The buildings on the main campus are generally well maintained. Classrooms at the main campus are quite adequate in size and furniture, but they lack audiovisual equipment. The science laboratories have limited water and electricity and are very poorly equipped. The other Malabo sites are barely adequate; they need basic equipment and what they have is in need of repair. The teacher training school has eight classrooms, an office, a library, and no laboratories. The School of Administration has five classrooms, a library, and an office. One of its classrooms has eight very old manual typewriters for the office skills diploma program.

The main campus has little room for growth, and the separation of facilities makes for inefficient use of teaching and administrative resources. The campuses are not networked (only the main campus has a computer), and they have few phones and fax machines. Written messages between campuses in Malabo must be hand delivered. Communication between Malabo and Bata is very limited. Because of this lack of basic technology, coordination and information flow between campuses is exceedingly difficult.

FINANCES

UNGE is nationally supported at an average of 97 percent of its operating expenses. The remaining 3 percent comes from aid, grants, or revenues generated by partnership activities and from the small registration fee paid by students. An example of external aid was the 50-50 split between UNESCO and the government of Equatorial Guinea to pay for a central administration building in 1998.

The following are the principal factors that contribute to the financial challenges of the university. According to the United Nations Development Program's *Human Development Report 2000*, Equatorial Guinea's national expenditure on education is about one-third of the average of developed nations. Virtually all of the university's financial support comes from this small national education budget. At the same time, the public school system, which is in desperate condition, competes for that same segment of the national budget. The university is developing needed new programs for medicine and engineering, but its equally valuable existing programs are in need of significant improvement. The satellite schools of the university have no computers; some don't even have fax machines. While there are signs of increased funding for the university (for example, the development of new programs, the acquisition of a few new computers for the central administration, and the purchase of a new van), it appears that the overall financial condition of the university is critical.

PARTNERSHIPS

UNGE has partnerships with La Universidad de Alcala de Henares in Spain, the University of New Mexico (UNM), and Arcadia University (formerly Beaver College) in Philadelphia. The partnership with La Universidad de Alcala includes planning of the curriculum, training of faculty and administrators, modernization of the library, and courses in Spanish for foreigners. Faculty from Alcala have helped some of the UNGE faculty review curriculum with the goal of bringing it up to Spanish standards. UNGE faculty and administrators have also visited Alcala for workshops and training.

The partnership with the University of New Mexico started in 1996. In 1997, Mobil Oil financed a trip for thirty faculty and administrators from UNGE to the UNM for six weeks to study university functions. Mobil also provided a scholarship for two UNGE faculty to study at the UNM for nine months. The universities have a plan for further partnership activities, but it has not been funded to date.

In 1999, Arcadia University and UNGE signed a partnership. Since 1998, Arcadia's Bioko Biodiversity Protection Program (BBPP) has invited UNGE students and faculty to participate in its annual expeditions into the Gran Caldera de Luba to conduct a census of the seven species of monkeys on the island. During these expeditions, UNGE participants received training and worked alongside American students and faculty. All UNGE participants were briefed on findings and received reports of the expedition. Technical assistants from the Ministry of Forestry also participated in these expeditions. As a result of this participation, several university graduates are now employed by BBPP, and one has begun to write his own grant proposals.

Bioko Island has been identified as part of the Guinean Forest "hot spot," one of the earth's most valuable regions for biodiversity preservation and, hence, a natural draw for scientists. Having established relationships with UNGE and with various ministries in Equatorial Guinea, Arcadia has acted as a facilitator between UNGE and research scientists from other universities such as Tulane University and New York University, who are eager to undertake research in Equatorial Guinea. As part of its commitment to UNGE, Arcadia faculty are channeling all research through UNGE and making sure that UNGE's faculty and students receive training. As much as possible, Arcadia is making sure that reference specimens remain at UNGE. Arcadia University has hired UNGE faculty and students to assist in gathering data for its own various conservation projects. The goal of these collaborations is to help establish a culture of research in the country. This is especially difficult in a country in which the method of instruction requires rote learning and the use of inquiry or problem-solving strategies for instruction is alien. To address this problem, Arcadia is beginning initiatives directed toward education.

Arcadia faculty have been working with the administration and faculty of UNGE to develop a study-abroad site for American students through Arcadia's internationally known Center for Study Abroad. Courses in this program will be taught by

distance, using computers, and by tutorials. UNGE faculty members will be paired with American professors, and UNGE students will be paired with American students. All students will earn Arcadia credit. The goal of this program is to help UNGE faculty and students develop a culture of teaching and learning based on an international standard of quality in their own country while also providing a rich African learning experience for American students.

As for other partnerships, UNGE also has a working partnership with Spain's National University of Distance Education concerning the use of facilities and is also developing a partnership with the University of Ghana.

HIGHER EDUCATION: UNIVERSIDAD NACIONAL DE EDUCACIÓN A DISTANCIA (UNED)

UNED is the largest university in Spain, with branches all over Spain and in other countries. Equatorial Guinea has branches in Malabo and Bata that have an annual intake of about 500 students. UNED offers higher education to students over 25 years old at no cost to participants.

UNED offers five-year programs culminating in a B.Sc. in law, political science, sociology, educational science, Spanish philology, history, or philosophy. In 2000, UNED began to offer master's programs and currently has two students enrolled at this level. The schools also offer doctoral programs in law, sociology, anthropology, and educational science. So far, UNED has only one doctoral graduate in anthropology. In 2000–2001, UNED enrolled about ten students in doctoral programs.

By far the largest UNED program is educational science. Students can take all five years through UNED; or, because the programs are almost identical, they can complete three years at UNGE and, after passing an examination, move over to UNED for their last two years. Even though successful completion of the first three years at UNGE certifies one to teach, many students elect to continue their education at UNED for placement on a higher salary scale and for better teaching jobs.

Students who come to UNED from UNGE cannot receive credit for their UNGE coursework. Students taking UNED courses can study independently or attend evening classes conducted by Equatoguinean tutors. The tutors lecture and provide feedback on student assignments, but all grades are based solely on student performance on a written examination given by Spanish professors who come to the country to administer the test. Papers are read and evaluated by the professors back in Spain. All courses are taught in Spanish.

Applicants must have passed the university qualifying examination given at the end of secondary school. The only limiting factor to enrollment is the matriculation deadline. Students pay no tuition or book costs; 100 percent of the funding comes from the Spanish Cooperative.

FACILITIES

In Malabo, UNED is located in space on the main campus of UNGE. It maintains its own office and library, and the program utilizes UNGE classroom space in the evening. The lending library is well furnished and contains more than 10,000 volumes. Due to competing needs for facilities, it is expected that UNED will soon vacate the UNGE facilities.

Faculty

UNED programs have two different kinds of faculty support. Regular course professors in Spain design the courses and select materials, and they are responsible for student evaluations. In addition, there are tutors on site in Equatorial Guinea. These tutors are Equatoguinean nationals who have completed at least a bachelor's-level degree at UNED or an equivalent internationally recognized degree. The tutors are responsible for conducting lectures, leading discussions, and helping students prepare for examinations.

Technology

Currently, the director of UNED has a computer. It has not yet been connected to the Internet because of the possibility that the office will be relocated. UNED is considering a plan to open a program in computer technology in Bata next year.

FOREIGN UNIVERSITIES

Whenever possible, students with academic potential elect to study abroad. Such study is possible through scholarships offered by foreign countries or agencies, which are administered by the government of Equatorial Guinea, or through personal funding. Equatorial Guinea has no program of national scholarships for foreign study. Several Equatoguineans reported that once a student has received a scholarship for international study, he or she may not receive additional scholarships for further study. This has the positive effect of spreading around opportunities, but it also has the negative effect of reducing talented students' access to advanced degrees.

CONCLUSION

Equatorial Guinea is a relatively new country with only thirty-four years of independence from colonialism, twenty-one of which were dominated by a brutal dictatorship. It is a country that until the past few years was struggling with extremely limited resources. Its intellectual and economic traditions were defined by colonial values rather than its own cultural values. It is slowly but surely developing national institutions that arise from its own values while at the same time being thrust into the global economy. Equatorial Guinea is trying to balance the need for modern technologies, yet it is grappling with a rudimentary communication system. The government is faced with the need to balance the economy between the wealth coming from the energy companies and the modesty of its other resources. It is also faced with the competing needs of two geographically distant and different regions. In 2000, in an attempt to equalize access to the government, officials from all of the state ministries moved their operations to Bata for a period of time. While this balances the needs of the different regions of the country, it makes access to officials in Malabo more challenging.

Another challenge is that despite an increasing American corporate presence on Bioko and the expectation that it will soon expand on the mainland, there is virtually no infrastructure for foreign business visitors or tourism in Equatorial Guinea. The few facilities that exist are in heavy demand; furthermore, there does not appear to be any government incentive to support tourism.

Several challenges face higher education in Equatorial Guinea. One challenge concerns the language of instruction. The fact that education for qualified students is provided free of charge from both UNGE and UNED is a tremendous benefit. That education, however, is in Spanish, while most of the good jobs require English. Most English speakers are moving into the business sector, so the availability of qualified English teachers for the public schools and UNGE is limited.

The condition of general education also has a very serious effect on higher education. Students from public schools arrive at the university level with no laboratory experience, with very limited access to books, and with an education based almost exclusively on recitation. This naturally limits the level and type of coursework that can be offered.

Meeting the demands of the growing economy offers another major challenge for the national university. As Equatorial Guinea moves rapidly into the global marketplace, demand for a well-educated workforce is increasing. While many UNGE faculty members are very dedicated, their general lack of advanced degrees is a major limiting factor for the university.

Even though it is not yet a decade old, Equatorial Guinea's national university is slowly working on coordinating and strengthening its curriculum and on developing programs that meet the needs of the country. With limited resources, the university is slowly trying to reach into this new century with new technology while at the same time trying to make do with antiquated equipment. It is competing with other sectors for financial resources and, even more important, for the intellectual talent of the nation. Drive, desire, and ability are immediately evident to anyone who spends time with educated Equatoguineans. The challenges in education in Equatorial Guinea ultimately boil down to financial, material, and technical resources and the opportunities to use them.

ACKNOWLEDGMENT

The author wishes to thank Dr. Gail Hearn, professor of biology at Arcadia University, for her valuable editorial assistance in the preparation of this chapter.

REFERENCES

Asumu Mongo, A. 2000. Data prepared for interview with Ministry of Education.

Clist, B. 1998. "Nouvelles données archéologiques sur l'histoire ancienne de la Guinea-Equatoriale." *L'Anthropologie* 108: 213–217.

Corporate Council of Africa. 2001. "Equatorial Guinea: A Country Profile for U.S. Businesses." Washington, D.C.: Corporate Council of Africa. Available online at: http://www.africacncl.org/programs/EGGuide.htm

Diamond, J. 1997. *Guns, Germs, and Steel.* New York: W. W. Norton.

Fegley, R. 1989. *Equatorial Guinea: An African Tragedy.* New York: Peter Lang.

Hecht, D. 1999. "Gushers of Wealth, But Little Trickles Down." *Christian Science Monitor,* July 7, 21.

Myers, N., R. A. Mittermeier, C. G. Mittermeier, G. A. B. da Fonseca, and J. Kent. 2000. "Biodiversity Hotspots for Conservation Priorities." *Nature* 403, no. 6772: 853–858.

Nchama, N. N. M. 2000. Interview with author.

Onishi, N. 2000. "Oil Riches, and Risks, in a Tiny African Nation." *New York Times,* July 23, A1–A6.

U.S. Department of State, Bureau of Public Affairs. 1989. *Background Notes: Equatorial Guinea.* Washington, D.C.: State Department.

U.S. Department of Energy, Energy Information Administration. 1999. *Equatorial Guinea.* Washington, D.C.: United States Energy Information Administration.

Vansina, J. 1990. *Paths in the Rainforest.* Madison: University of Wisconsin Press.

Eritrea

CHERYL STERNMAN RULE

INTRODUCTION

After years of colonization, federation, annexation, and, finally, a thirty-year war of secession from Ethiopia, Eritrea celebrated its independence on May 24, 1993. Since then, Eritrea has set about the arduous task of rebuilding—and, in many senses, building anew—its infrastructure, economy, and government. Among the most pressing needs was to train Eritrea's citizens in the art of nation building. To that end, the University of Asmara, the nation's only university, was reorganized, restaffed, and, in essence, rebuilt from the inside out. The Asmara Teacher Training Institute (TTI) and the Pavoni Technical Institute (PTI) now work alongside the university to educate students for their roles as participants in a new democracy.

I am including information about the TTI and the PTI because they require a high school degree for admission and thus qualify, in the strictest sense, as institutions of higher education. Further, students tend to attend these institutions directly after completing their secondary education. The Eritrean Institute of Management and the Mai Nefhi Training Center for Public Administration are different types of institutions that offer training to civil servants and government officials, but these do not fall under the rubric of higher education. Regarding the country's four technical schools, Shannon (2000) notes that "there are no other technical 'colleges' like the PTI. It is the most advanced and the highest academic/technical level of education right now. That may change in the near future, but I've heard nothing concrete on that front. The four other schools are of the 12+1 sort, offering a diploma; while [the PTI is] a 12+3, offering an advanced diploma." However, many Eritreans, including an Eritrean member of the USAID staff in Asmara, consider the University of Asmara to be "the only institution of higher education in Eritrea."

HISTORY OF THE UNIVERSITY OF ASMARA

In 1890, the King of Italy issued a decree declaring Eritrea an Italian colony. During World War II, in 1941, the British, who defeated the Italians, established a protectorate over Eritrea. The United Nations (UN) federated Eritrea with Ethiopia in 1952. This union lasted until the early 1960s, when Ethiopia dissolved the UN-sponsored federation and annexed Eritrea (Connell 1992).

According to the "Brief History of the University of Asmara" (University of Asmara, 1997), the University of Asmara was founded toward the latter half of the federation period, in 1958. Originally named the Holy Family University Institute by the Camboni Sisters Missionary Congregation, the institute's original goal was to prepare students for university study in Italy. After it was accredited by the Superior Council of the Institute of Italian Universities in 1960, the institution officially changed its name to the University of Asmara in 1964. Courses were originally conducted in Italian (1958–1963), then English and Italian (1964–1974), and, finally, in English alone (1975 on).

In 1990, as Eritrea's war of liberation entered its final stages, the Ethiopian government dismantled the university and relocated its faculty, staff, students, and resources to Ethiopia. In essence, the university was "reduced to ground zero" (Rotella 2000). The following year, with the war officially over, the Provisional Government of Eritrea (PGE) established the University of Asmara as an autonomous institution. Because so many of the former faculty members were unqualified for university teaching, the new university administration, backed by the PGE, dismissed one-third of them and reassigned them to other jobs in Eritrea. In 1993, the university was shut for six months not only to be reorganized but also to give administrators time to recruit qualified individuals, largely from the Eritrean Diaspora, to join the faculty (Useem 1998). When the university reopened its doors later that year, the formidable task of positioning the institution at the center of national development began in earnest.

Admission

Secondary school in Eritrea runs through the eleventh grade. In the spring of their final year, high school students sit for the Eritrean General Certificate Examination, known colloquially as the "matric" (short for matriculation). All students who fail to achieve the 50 percent minimum passing score must immediately enter eighteen months of military service training. According to the Ministry of Education (Eritrea Profile 1995), those who pass the exam

> will receive a one-year preparatory course which qualifies them to join the university. At the end of the year, however, they will sit for an examination for the entrance of the university. Students who pass the entrance examination will continue their university education without interruption provided they do their national service duty after finishing their university studies. Students who do not pass the university entrance exam are given the opportunity to obtain a certificate or diploma or its equivalent through vocational training or other courses.

Fewer than 10 percent of those who seek admission to the university are granted a spot. Tuition at the institution is free.

Mission, Size, and Programs

According to a document entitled "Mission and Objectives of the University of Asmara" (University of Asmara 1997–1998),

> The mission of the university is the discovery, generation and dissemination of knowledge in the service of society. In fulfilling this mission, the University of Asmara aspires to become a national centre of higher learning and scientific inquiry, a genuine seat of freedom, tolerance and culture, and a powerful catalyst for change and social progress. As an integral part of the Eritrean community, it will always endeavor to serve the needs of society, strive to address itself to the challenges facing our people and contribute to the solution of the problems afflicting our country.

The university currently offers bachelor's degree programs in the following fields: science, health science, arts and social sciences, business and economics, agriculture and aquatic science, law, engineering, education, and the freshman program. According to documents provided by the United States Agency for International Development (USAID) in Asmara, the freshman program, enrolling 1,152 students (1999–2000), is the largest, while the law program, which enrolls 124 students (1999–2000), is the smallest. The university's total student enrollment in degree programs increased from 2,836 in 1995–1996 to 3,912 in 1999–2000, an increase of 28 percent in four years. In addition, the university awards diplomas (432 students in 1999–2000) and certificates (125 students in 1999–2000) in select fields. In all, the Bachelor of Arts (12 fields), Bachelor of Education (9 fields), Bachelor of Science (14 fields), and Bache-

lor of Law (1 field) degrees, as well as diplomas (15 fields) and certificates (7 fields), are awarded.

In 1994, the university awarded 46 degrees and 80 diplomas (Semere 1994). By 1999, the number of degrees awarded increased more than tenfold. That year, more than 800 students graduated from the university: 550 with degrees, 109 with diplomas, and 151 with certificates (Yisak 1999). In 1999–2000, total enrollment at the institution topped 4,500.

Research

Because the administration devoted the majority of the university's start-up resources and energies to teaching, research activities are still in an "embryonic" stage (Yisak 1997). According to a university document entitled "Strengthening Research," there are only three "major" research themes currently being pursued: geophysics, medicinal plants, and materials science, all within the College of Science. Over the next five years, the university plans to expand its research activities and to initiate multidisciplinary research projects. In the interim, university officials acknowledge that "the research infrastructure of the UA . . . is almost nonexistent" ("Strengthening Research," 2).

As more and more faculty members return from study leaves abroad and acquire the necessary qualifications and analytic tools to design and pursue meaningful research agendas, the university plans to strengthen its research focus. Officials are well aware of the need to strengthen this sphere of the university's offerings. "Strengthening Research" provides lofty notions about what needs to be done: "new research facilities will be established"; "small existing ones will be strengthened through acquisition of major laboratory equipment"; the need for additional space for equipment will be addressed "by building new rooms or refurbish[ing] existing space"; and "a high power computerized data base needs to be established." While these goals are impressive in scope and admirable in direction, there is little evidence that firm steps have yet been taken to address these obvious deficiencies.

THE UNIVERSITY AT THE NUCLEUS OF NATIONAL DEVELOPMENT

The University of Asmara is the most prominent feature of the national development landscape in Eritrea today. Education in Eritrea is "viewed not as an end [in] itself but rather as a strategic tool for development" (Yisak 1998, 1). As the president explained,

> Our economic policy places special emphasis on the development of national scientific and technological capabilities through the strengthening and expansion of existing institutions including the university. The development of knowledge-intensive, export-oriented industries coupled with the promotion of appropriate up-to-date technology transfer are essential components of the national development policy and strategy. Like all African countries[,] the special situation in which we find ourselves makes the role of the university as a development engine more important

than is the case elsewhere especially in the industrialized nations. (Yisak 1999, 4)

To be sure, students in Eritrea attend the university as much to serve the needs of their burgeoning country as to fulfill their personal ambitions or families' dreams.

One challenge is female participation in higher education. A quick look at enrollment figures (University of Asmara 1999) reveals stark differences in male and female patterns of participation in Eritrean higher education. In 1991–1992, female students accounted for 577 (19.6 percent) of 2,942 students enrolled in the university's day and evening programs. In 1998–1999, they accounted for 540 (13.5 percent) of 3,994 students, a 6 percent decrease over a seven-year period. In other words, while the total enrollment at the university increased by 1,052, the number of female students actually decreased by 37 over this same period. This gender imbalance is mirrored in the academic and administrative staff. In 1991–1992, 3 (4.8 percent) of 62 academic staff members were women, compared with 24 (10.7 percent) of 223 in 1998–1999. Of administrative staff members, the numbers are significantly higher, though not necessarily "better." In 1991–1992, 183 (60 percent) of 305 administrative staff members were women, compared with 199 (55 percent) of 359 in 1998–1999. Thus, while women have held a majority of staff positions (except in 1995–1996, when they held 48 percent of such positions) since 1991, these positions are less prestigious and influential than academic posts, as is true at institutions of higher education in general.

In considering these figures, one might be tempted to assume that girls are conspicuously absent from Eritrea's educational system as a whole, but that is not the case. While women are underrepresented in Eritrean higher education, both as students and as faculty members, girls make up a healthy proportion of primary and secondary school enrollment. According to UNESCO (1999), girls accounted for 44–45 percent of total primary school enrollment for each year between 1991 and 1996. They represented 42 percent of total secondary enrollment between 1993 and 1996. Why, then, do they account for less than one-fifth of the student body at the university?

The answers, which are varied and complex, merit a far more detailed discussion than this chapter can provide. In brief, Eritrean girls tend to interrupt their schooling in their teenage years to marry and have children. Daily tasks such as hauling water, grinding grain, and washing clothes occupy the great part of their days and lives. Given long-ingrained cultural norms and the harsh realities of living in one of the world's poorest nations, the gender disparity among students enrolled at the University of Asmara is hardly surprising. What is perhaps surprising is the near-egalitarian status women held as soldiers during the 30-year guerilla war. They have struggled to maintain a firm footing in these new roles; however, Eritrea remains a highly male-dominated society. The exception is the Kunama ethnic group, a matriarchal tribe located largely in the western lowland areas. For a further discussion of gender issues in Eritrea, see J. Rude (1996).

Another challenge is access. The need to increase women's access to higher education in Eritrea has already been addressed, but broadening access to all sectors of the student population, particularly to those from Eritrea's multiple ethnic groups, is another high priority.

By any standard, Eritrea is a tiny nation. Yet its population of 4 million is remarkably diverse. Roughly half of its population is Christian and the other half Muslim. The country boasts nine ethnic groups—the Afar, Bilen, Hadareb, Kunama, Nara, Rashaida, Saho, Tigre, and Tigrinya—and as many languages. Each of these groups occupies distinct areas of the country, from the Afar in the lowland areas along the Red Sea coast to the Kunama in the western lowlands to the Tigrinya, who are predominant in Asmara and much of the eastern highlands. The university's population does not, however, reflect this diversity. In fact, the overwhelming majority of students at the university are Tigrinya males (Yisak 2000). Given that the Tigrinya group accounts for only 50 percent of all Eritreans (CIA 1999), their disproportionate representation in the elite sector of higher education will only widen the gap between the haves and the have-nots in the future. Only by increasing access to education for all people, from women to members of underrepresented ethnic groups, will Eritrea be able to improve the circumstances of members of its population in equal proportion.

Setting aside gender and ethnic considerations, even the brightest secondary school students find that landing a coveted spot in the university is enormously difficult. Of 11,000 high school students across the nation who took the matriculation exam in 1993, only 611 (5.6 percent) qualified for admission to the university (Eritrea Profile 1994). This number hovered around 10 percent in 1998 (Useem 1998). And gaining a spot in the classroom is just the beginning. In 1994, the attrition rate of entering freshman was 25 percent (Semere 1994); the attrition rate for women was even higher.

The faculty at the University of Asmara suffers not only from a gender imbalance but also from a lack of doctorally trained academics and a shortage of Eritrean-born teachers. In a speech at the World Conference on Higher Education in Paris, Dr. Wolde-ab Yisak acknowledged this severe limitation, noting that "one of the critical bottlenecks to the university's development plans has been the shortage of qualified academic staff and its excessive dependence on expatriate staff" (Yisak 1998, 3). In 1991, only 8 (12.9 percent) of 62 faculty members held doctorates. In 1994, the university recruited over 50 new faculty members, 37 of whom held Ph.D.s (Eritrea Profile 1994). By 1998, this figure had increased to 85 (38.1 percent) of 223. The numbers, however, belie the reality that a larger percentage of faculty members with doctorates are expatriates. In 1999, 210 faculty members taught at the university; 90 held Ph.D.s. Of these 90, only 38 (42 percent) were Eritreans (Yisak 1999). The Department of Marine Biology illustrates this problem vividly. Of the 10 faculty members with teaching and research responsibilities in 1999–2000, only one—the sole expatriate in the department—held a doctorate.

Another of the university's most pressing challenges is the dire lack of space. While the campus was originally designed to handle 1,700 students, enrollment in the 1999–2000 academic year exceeded 4,500. "The sheer absence of physical facilities is . . . limiting our ability to expand access to the university rather severely" (Yisak 1999, 6). According to one student, life at the university will improve significantly "when there [are] enough facilities" for all enrolled at the institution.

POINTS OF CONTENTION

A key problem, and one that invariably impacts morale on the campus, is low and divergent faculty salaries. In 1998, professors who earned roughly $400 per month spent half their earnings on rent and the remainder on food (Useem 1998). Fringe benefits, such as health insurance and contributions to retirement accounts, simply don't exist, and faculty have no union or staff association. Moreover, because many faculty members are expatriates, sponsored by various international funding agencies, their salary scale is not standardized. Local faculty members earn what the Eritrean government can afford to pay them, which is often far lower than what other governments are able to pay. Teachers from India, for example, make up a large proportion of the expatriate faculty at the university. Many of them are provided with subsidized housing in addition to higher salaries.

Another point of contention is top-down governance. At the helm of efforts to revitalize the university and address its numerous, complex challenges is Dr. Yisak, the institution's 56-year-old president. A few months after independence, in September 1993, Dr. Yisak assumed the presidency of the University of Asmara as a member of the Eritrean People's Liberation Front (EPLF).

By all accounts, Dr. Yisak is a strong leader who maintains tight control over his institution. In fact, leadership at the university seems synonymous with presidential leadership; shared governance is not widely practiced at this institution. Yet whether the president's tight control over all matters—from the most essential to the most mundane—is helping or harming the institution depends largely on one's perspective.

According to a former associate professor of mathematics, the university "is run on hierarchical and authoritarian lines . . . [in which] all authority flows from, and through, the university President" (McConnell n.d.). He cites the president's decisive authority in routine personnel decisions, his firm hand in budgetary matters, and his overinvolvement in mundane tasks such as requests to replace a broken blackboard as examples. Useem (1998), too, noted that "staff members and students complain that the administration is too centralized, particularly in the hands of Wolde-ab Yisak, the university's president." She cites the president's involvement in—and, according to some, orchestration of—student elections as an example. Yet while described as authoritarian by some, others note that Dr. Yisak is a significantly more "complex" leader than he may seem (Rosen 2000).

Revealingly, numerous interviews turned up no mention of any other leaders—either faculty members or administrators—at the university. While an Academic Senate does exist, the president leads this body as well.

STRATEGIC PLAN, 1995–2010

The University of Asmara's strategic plan is grounded in three interwoven principles: relevance (to local needs), quality (through selective linkages), and sustainability (based on partnerships rather than on donor-driven programs).

The Dual Linkage Model

Due to the scarcity of trained professionals and academics, which is directly related to Eritrea's colonial history and its prolonged war of liberation, quality at the university hinges, for the time being at least, on a series of formal linkages with universities abroad and, more important, on tenable partnerships with government and community agencies at home.

Linkages with local government and community agencies form the heart of the university's strategic plan. In an effort to strengthen ongoing national development initiatives, the university is building "durable partnerships with the public and private sectors" as well as with the community, referred to as the "University's stockholders" (Yisak 1998, 2). Each faculty member belongs to a steering committee along with community leaders in the relevant field. Members of the Faculty of Business and Economics, for example, participate on steering committees with "representatives of the financial sector . . . [such as] the banks, insurance companies, the Ministries of Finance, Trade and Industry, Tourism and the Chamber of Commerce." These steering committees identify problems to be addressed in the short, medium, and long term; determine "the level(s) of skill and the desired professional profile needed to tackle the identified problem(s)"; facilitate and coordinate "joint research activities through freely sharing information, facilities, [and] personnel"; "serve as an internal quality assurance unit to assess the functional standards" of teaching and research programs; and enable the university "to participate in the preparation and review of the sectorial strategic development" (Yissak 1998, 2–3). These local linkages, in short, ensure that the university's teaching and research remain "relevant and responsive" to all sectors of the nation's development agenda.

The second aspect of the dual linkage model is international in scope. The university's partnerships with institutions of higher education in Europe, the United States, India, and Australia, as well as its alliance with the association of Eritrean scholars in the diaspora, are aimed at improving educational quality and enhancing the qualifications of the faculty. There are several reasons for this external focus:

> Eritrea is a very small nation; its economic prosperity must, therefore, be based on [an] export oriented economy. If it is therefore to survive in a highly competitive open market, emphasis must be made on investment producing very high quality workmanship through high quality education. Efforts are being made through the university's external partnerships to inject high quality in our academic [programs] through the transfer of technology, training and through relevant research activities. (Yisak 1998, 3)

In 1999–2000, the Department of Agriculture was linked with both the Agricultural University of Norway and Wageningen Agricultural University in the Netherlands. The College of Arts and Sciences was linked with the University of North Carolina, the University of California Los Angeles, and the University of Florida in the United States. And the College of Education was linked with the Royal Danish University of Education in Denmark. These linkages, which are funded by the governments of Norway, the Netherlands, the United States, and Denmark, respectively, represent just six of the more than twenty-seven linkages the University of Asmara currently maintains with foreign institutions (USAID 1999/2000).

These linkages are designed to benefit both the University of Asmara community—students and faculty alike—and the foreign institutions themselves. Senior professors from the linked institutions come to Asmara for one semester or one year in order to teach and learn. They contribute their skills and knowledge to the community by joining local steering committees, identifying research questions for graduate students, supervising lecturers and other junior faculty members, and teaching courses. For example, the University of North Carolina at Chapel Hill and North Carolina Central University

> have been essential in enhancing the capacity [of] the University of Asmara to fulfill its mission mandated by the Government of Eritrea. The student/faculty exchange aspect of the linkage has produced four faculty members (two in public administration, two in journalism) to teach at the University of Asmara. Currently, four other Eritrean students are training at UNC-CH to become professors of journalism, geography, and anthropology. Therefore, the self-sufficiency of these departments within the University of Asmara has improved considerably as a result of this linkage (http://cehd.ewu.edu/cehd/faculty/ntodd/GhanaUDLP/EritreaUNC.html)

Visiting faculty members also gain valuable firsthand knowledge by studying local conditions. Eritrea's proximity to the Red Sea means that marine biologists from the Netherlands, for example, can study Eritrea's coastline for their own research even as they contribute their knowledge and skills to the university community. Eritrea's status as a new nation also means that political scientists who come to the university are able to gain as much scholarly knowledge through living and working in a fledgling country as they are able to contribute to it, or so it is hoped.

The linkages have yielded some additional benefits, including material resources and international goodwill. Partner institutions have provided the university with laboratory equipment and textbooks, both of which are in devastatingly short supply (Useem 1998). Moreover, in 1995, researchers from three Israeli universities pursued a joint voyage with their counterparts at the University of Asmara to study Eritrean coral and other natural treasures of the Red Sea. According to the *Jerusalem Post*, Israeli researchers considered the excursion "a breakthrough in relations between the two countries" (Siegel 1995, 12).

The flip side of the linkage is that Eritreans are afforded the opportunity to pursue their advanced degrees at partner institutions. Both active junior faculty members and recent university graduates who have exhibited superior performance and promise have benefited from these programs. (Graduates must complete at least two years of teaching service upon their return.) Of the 200 sent abroad for graduate work, 47 have returned with their master's degrees and 11 with their doctorates. Of those still in the pipeline, 39 percent are pursuing doctorates and 61 per-

cent are pursuing master's degrees. These external linkages are an efficient way to improve the credentials of the Eritrean faculty members, thereby increasing the ratio of Eritrean to expatriate teachers who hold advanced degrees. Presently, each link has a budget of 500,000 naqfa (roughly $52,000–58,000) or more per year. Most, and in some cases all, of the funding for these programs comes from international aid organizations. The USAID, for example, funds the university's linkages with American institutions.

Finally, the linkage system aims to create, in the words of the university's president, a "reverse" brain drain (Legum 1996). Instead of watching the university's best and brightest graduates disappear into more developed countries, the university is bringing top-notch faculty members to its doorstep and encouraging them to work closely with Eritrea's budding academicians. The ultimate goal is, of course, to inspire the newly trained Eritreans to stay in their country and pass on their knowledge to the next generation of students.

The most obvious question at this point is what impact, if any, these linkages have on the quality of education. The impact on individuals—both Eritreans who go abroad and foreigners who come to Asmara—is great. From fostering intercultural understanding to giving individuals the opportunity to study in a foreign land, the potential for personal enrichment is significant. Yet translating these personal benefits into concrete, positive impacts on students and, by extension, on national development, remains unproven at this early stage.

Further, the dual-linkage model has yet to be "fully validated," while the nature of the partnerships is doubly "skewed" (Yisak 1998, 4). In the local sphere, the university has far greater intellectual, and, presumably, monetary, capacity than the community agencies with which it collaborates. Yet in the international sphere, the partner universities in the developed countries have significantly more resources—monetary, educational, research-related, and programmatic—than the University of Asmara. In other words, the local linkages are skewed in the university's favor and the external linkages are skewed toward the university's partners. Achieving relative equilibrium on both fronts is necessary lest "suspicion and distrust" take hold among the various participants (Yisak 1998, 4). Finally, once equilibrium is established, the university must prove to its constituents, both local and external, that this model is producing concrete advances for the students and, ultimately, the nation.

MOVING TOWARD A COMMUNITY COLLEGE SYSTEM

To increase access to the great number of students who wish to pursue postsecondary education but who cannot garner a place in the university, the administration, with the support of the Italian government, is devising a system of junior colleges akin to the American community college system. This multicampus system will complement the University of Asmara, which plans to phase out its one-year certificate and two- to three-year diploma programs and concentrate instead on research-based graduate and postgraduate training. While the timeline is vague (even more so given the recent political instability and widespread destruction of buildings), six junior colleges, which will be located in various regions of the country, will award certificates and diplomas in natural and paramedical sciences, teacher training, social and management sciences, marine and maritime sciences, agricultural sciences, and technology. Graduates of these junior colleges could eventually, if they choose, apply to the University of Asmara to pursue advanced training.

OTHER POSTSECONDARY INSTITUTIONS

Several other institutions play a role in the Eritrean system of higher education, including the Asmara Teacher Training Institute (TTI) and the Pavoni Technical Institute. A teacher training college was established in Asmara in 1946 during the British administration with an enrollment of fifteen student teachers. "The admissions requirement . . . was the completion of at least the second year of middle school and a pass in the entrance exam" (Taye 1991, 57–58). Over the next several years, this college, which trained the majority of primary and secondary school teachers in Eritrea, tightened its admissions standards and began to admit only those who had completed the eleventh grade. Once the federation with Ethiopia was dissolved and Haile Selassie annexed Eritrea in 1962, the teacher training college was incorporated into the Ethiopian system.

After the Eritrean struggle for independence began in 1974, the teacher training institute was closed for six years. This decision came at a high cost to Eritrea's educational system, as Taye explains: "According to the plans of the Department of Teacher Education, the Institute could have trained about 400 prospective teachers in its pre-service [program] and about 10,000 teachers in its service [program] each year, as [had been the case] in the teacher training institutes [in] other parts of Ethiopia" (Taye 1991).

In 1995, a new teacher training college opened in the capital. The Asmara Teacher Training Institute offers training for primary school teachers only. "It admits secondary school graduates for a one-year course. At the end of this course, trainees are awarded a primary school certificate." Teachers and school directors can also update their training by enrolling in in-service courses held during the summer vacation (UNESCO 1995–1996).

According to *Eritrea Profile*, more than 440 teachers graduated from TTI in 1999. These graduates presently serve throughout Eritrea as primary school teachers.

The Pavoni Technical Institute (PTI) is a private technical college funded by the Gruppo Missione Asmara (GMA), an Italian nongovernmental organization. According to a former consultant to the PTI (Cairns 2000), the institute was originally set up to offer high school graduates advanced training in machine-shop technology. Specifically, the curriculum was designed, in collaboration with the University of Asmara, to prepare students to become machinists, machine-shop supervisors, and machine-shop instructors. It enrolled its first students in October 1996. Tuition is free.

Students must pass their matriculation exams in order to be admitted to the PTI. While the institute formerly maintained its own strict application process, the Ministry of Education now decides which students will attend the school (Shannon 2000). Upon completing the three-year program, students earn a certificate or advanced diploma. Officials at the university hope that some students may qualify as pre-engineering candidates for the mechanical engineering program (Cairns 2000).

The PTI has a budget of approximately 6 million naqfa (roughly $600,000–700,000), all from the GMA and the European Union. While the Eritrean government does not monetarily support the PTI, it does play a supervisory and evaluative role in certain areas of the Institute's operations.

In 1999, the PTI administration worked closely with the University of Asmara and the Ministry of Education to study the accreditation process to make PTI a technical college. The ministry has also asked the PTI to improve and expand its offerings with computer classes, physics and chemistry laboratories, and computer numerical controlled (CNC) machines. The computer lab, according to Cairns, is in place, and proposals for the other projects have been submitted for ministry approval (Cairns 2000).

Female participation at the PTI is low. In 1996, two (11 percent) of eighteen students were female, and both dropped out soon after entry. The class of 1997 had twenty-eight students, of whom two (7 percent) were female; one has since dropped out. And in 1998, four of twenty-four (17 percent) students were female; two are still in attendance (Cairns 2000).

THE IMPACT OF POLITICAL UNREST ON THE UNIVERSITY

On May 6, 1998, tensions erupted between Ethiopia and Eritrea over several disputed border areas and, according to some, tariffs, currencies, and access to the sea (Radin 2000). The intermittent fighting culminated in a full-scale war that reached its peak in May 2000. On May 19, 2000, the university officially closed its doors several weeks before the end of the academic year "as thousands of students packed up to join the army" (Agence France-Press 2000). According to one department head, "The President and the government he represents . . . made it very clear that [the] university should stay open and teaching/research activities [should] continue as [they had] before the war broke out. But . . . the university community and especially the students couldn't concentrate on their schooling" (Pedulli 2000).

Many students who had already completed their military service training, and many faculty members as well, joined the Eritrean Relief and Rehabilitation Commission (ERREC) to assist with internally displaced persons. Others assisted the government in conducting surveys assessing damage from the war. Some students and faculty members worked together to register casualties and monitor the conditions in the most heavily damaged war-torn areas.

CONCLUSION

The Eritrean system of higher education is a work in progress. The University of Asmara is growing both in enrollment and in size, and its administration has taken concrete steps to improve the qualifications of its faculty members. While its shortcomings—cramped quarters, extremely limited access, and a strictly hierarchical administration, for example—can be quickly enumerated, its plans for the future are ambitious and well conceived. Whether the new community college structure means that the university will soon offer advanced degrees, as is hoped, remains to be seen. Technical education, such as that provided by the TTI and the PTI, provides a worthwhile alternative to students seeking to further their practical skills and help rebuild a nation still visibly devastated by war. Yet vision, confidence, and careful planning can take the system only so far. Political stability and funding for new programs and facilities will ultimately determine whether Eritrea will achieve its dream of providing high-quality advanced education to all citizens who desire it.

REFERENCES

Agence France-Press. 2000. "Eritrean Students Demand to Fight for Nation." May 19.

Cairns, J. 2000. Personal communication, April 23.

Central Intelligence Agency. 1999. *The World Factbook 1999*. www.cia.gov/cia/publications/factbook/er.html

Connell, D. 1992. "Eritrea's Path to Independence." *The Christian Science Monitor*, January 15, p. 10.

Eritrea Profile. 1994. "Rebuilding the University." *Eritrea Profile* 1, no. 37 (November 26). Available online at: http://www.eritrea.org/cgi-local/epelectronic.cgi?v=02&is=02&ank=EFFCI#EFFCI

——. 1995. "Ministry of Education Issued on March 25, 1995 the Following Statement." *Eritrea Profile* 2, no. 2 (March 25). Available online at: http://www.eritrea.org/EIB/control/main.html

——. 1999a. "Dr. Wolde-ab Again Lays Stress on Relevance, Quality in University Education." *Eritrea Profile* 6, no. 28 (September 18): 4–8.

——. 1999b. "More Than 440 Graduate from Teacher Training Institute." *Eritrea Profile* 6, no. 27 (September 11). Available online at: http://www.eritrea.org/EIB/Eritrea_Profile/vol06/27/EP062709119906.html

Legum, C. 1996. "A Model Third World University." *Eritrea Profile* 2, no. 50 (February 24): 5.

McConnell, Alan. n.d. "Observations on a Stay at the University of Asmara." www.geocities.com/~hornafrica/eritrea/education/u/works/auniversity1.html. Accessed on July 5, 2000.

Pedulli, M. 2000. Personal communication, June 16.

Radin, C. A. 2000. "Horn of Africa War Has Deep Roots." *The Boston Globe*, May 24, p. A2.

Rosen, R. 2000. Telephone interview, July 26.

Rotella, S. 2000. Office of the President, Riverside Community College District. Telephone interview, April 20.

Rude, John C. 1996. "Birth of a Nation in Cyberspace." *Humanist Magazine* (March/April).

Semere, A. 1994. "Better Hopes for Asmara University." *Eritrea Profile* 1, no. 26 (September 10). Available online at: http://www.eritrea.org/EIB/control/main.html

Shannon, J. 2000. Personal communication, July 12.

Siegel, J. 1995. "Scientists Sail With Eritrean Colleagues." *The Jerusalem Post*, June 8, p. 12.

Taye, A. 1991. *A Historical Survey of State Education in Eritrea*. Asmara: Educational Materials Production & Distribution Agency.

UNESCO (United Nations Educational, Scientific and Cultural Organization). 1995–1996. "Eritrea—Educational System." Available online at: http://www.unesco.org/iau/cd-data/er.rtf

University of Asmara. 1997. "Brief History of the University of Asmara, 1958–1991." Available online at http://www.eritrea.org/EIB/Education/ASM_UNI.HTML#BriefHistory

——. 1997–1998. "Mission and Objectives of the University of Asmara." Unpublished document provided to the author by Laurie Kessler, Asmara.

——. 1999. "Statistical Summary: Students and Staff at the University of Asmara, 1991/92–1998/99." Unpublished document.

——. n.d. "Strengthening Research." Unpublished document.

USAID. 1999. Global Education Database. Available online at: http://www.usaid.gov/educ_training/ged/hrml. Accessed in 1999.

——. 1999/2000. "Institutional Linkages." Unpublished document, Asmara. In author's possession.

Useem, A. 1998. "Eritrea Strives to Transform a Struggling University into a Vital Institution." *The Chronicle of Higher Education*, May 29, p. A47.

Yisak, W. 1997. Sept. 24. "University of Asmara Developing Educational Partners." Keynote address at a forum for historically black colleges and universities, Washington, D.C., September 24. Sponsored by the U.S. Agency for International Development (USAID), by the President of the University of Asmara, Wolde-Ab Yisak. Available online at: www.asmarino.com/asmarino/AsmaraUniv/AsmaraUnivNews1.htm

——. 1998. "The Role of Higher Education in National Development." Speech at the World Conference on Higher Education, October 5–9. In Vol. V of *Higher Education in the Twenty-first Century: Vision and Action*. Paris: UNESCO.

——. 1999. "Opening Address by Dr. Wolde-Ab Yisak, President of University of Asmara, on the 29th Commencement Ceremony of the University." *Eritrea Profile* 6, no. 28 (September 18).

——. 2000. Telephone interview, May 1.

32

Ethiopia

HABTAMU WONDIMU

INTRODUCTION

Ethiopia has a population of 63 million, of which 60 percent is illiterate and 44 percent is below 15 years old. The primary-school-age (7–14 years) population is 12.61 million and the secondary-school-age (15–18 years) population is 5.58 million (CSA 1998). The under-20 population is 34.86 million. About half of the population is female. Average Ethiopian life expectancy at birth is 50 years. About 90 percent of the labor force works in agriculture and related sectors, and 85 percent resides in rural areas.

Primary education enrollment (Grades 1–8) in 1998–1999 was 5.7 million; secondary enrollment (Grades 9–12) was 530,000. Hence the gross enrollment ratios at the primary and secondary education levels were 45.8 percent and 9.7 percent respectively (MOE 1999). Ethiopia's higher education (postsecondary) enrollment rate is below 1 percent of the expected age group.

A BRIEF HISTORY OF HIGHER EDUCATION

Modern education in Ethiopia formally started only about 100 years ago, while modern higher education began with the founding of the University College of Addis Ababa on March 20, 1950. The College of Agriculture and Mechanical Arts, the College of Engineering in Addis Ababa, the Institute of Building Technology, Gonder Public Health College, Theology College of Holy Trinity, Kotebe College of Teacher Education, and the Polytechnic Institute at Bahir Dar were opened in the 1960s (see Table 32.1). In the 1970s and 1980s, new institutions were built, existing ones were reorganized, and a few high schools and vocational technical schools—Jimma and Ambo Agricultural Colleges, Addis Ababa College of Commerce, and Wondogenet College of Forestry—were upgraded at this time.

In 1961, most colleges in the country were reorganized under the Haile Selassie I University, with the main campus at the former palace grounds in Addis Ababa. With the beginning of a socialist revolution in 1974, the name of the university was changed to Addis Ababa University (AAU). Since the mid-1990s, AAU has been limited to the campuses in Addis Ababa and Debre Zeit. The former branches of AAU outside Addis Ababa have become separate universities or independent colleges.

Though there have been efforts to establish higher education institutions (HEIs) in the peripheries of the country, most institutions are located in the central, north, and northwestern part of the country (mainly in Addis Ababa, Bahir Dar, Mekelle, Alemaya, Awassa, and Jimma).

The University College of Addis Ababa had less than 1,000 students and less than 50 teachers in the late 1950s. Most of the teachers were foreigners. In the past 50 years, the university has experienced large growth in enrollment, diversity and levels of programs, size of the staff, budget, and research output. AAU celebrated its fiftieth anniversary in December 2000.

INSTITUTIONS AND PROGRAMS

Until early 2000, there were two universities and seventeen colleges in Ethiopia. AAU and Alemaya University of Agriculture (AUA) are the largest and oldest institutions in the country. Alemaya College of Agriculture became a university in 1985.

In this chapter, programs refer to areas of study (a major or concentration). These include such areas as biology, chemistry, accounting, economics, plant science, electrical engineering, nursing, and psychology.

There are more than fifty diploma programs, which run for two or three years. These include accounting, banking and finance, animal health, library science, nursing, building technology, general agriculture, secretarial science, laboratory technology,

Table 32.1. Enrollments and Academic and Support Staff of Higher Education Institutions in Ethiopia, 1998–1999

Institution and Year of Foundation	Total	Female	Graduates	Academic Staff	Support Staff
Addis Ababa University (1950)	10,448	1,475	1,855	750	1,688
Addis Ababa College of Commerce (1979)	1,977	842	737	77	88
Alemaya University of Agriculture (1954)	2,185	168	542	162	590
Ambo College of Agriculture (1979)	471	108	170	42	189
Arba Minch Water Technology Institute (1986)	829	38	74	69	208
Awassa College of Agriculture (1976)	768	117	219	95	259
Bahir Dar Polytechnic Institute (1963)	630	39	500	60	121
Bahir Dar Teachers College (1972)	1,070	102	62	64	171
Dilla College of Teacher Education and Health Sciences (1996)	1,215	187	101	87	183
Ethiopian Civil Service College (AA*) (1994)	1,602	161	371	116	126
Gonder College of Medical Sciences (1955)	821	155	183	89	345
Jimma College of Agriculture (1979)	504	107	207	51	191
Jimma Institute of Health Sciences (1982)	1,826	273	283	228	319
Kotebe College of Teacher Education (1969)	590	274	325	93	196
Mekelle Business College (1991)	621	110	107	38	93
Mekelle University College (1993)	642	44	47	68	83
Nazareth Technical College (1993)	807	44	201	110	197
School of Medicine Laboratory Technology (1997, AA*)	101	23	38	3	NA
Wondogenet College of Forestry (1977)	238	10	89	26	114
Total	27,345	4,277	6,111	2,228	5,161

Source: EMIS 1999. * = Addis Ababa

and sanitary science. Ethiopia has more than sixty undergraduate programs that run for four to six years. These include biology, chemistry, physics, mathematics, statistics, geography, history, psychology, English, accounting, management, economics, business education, various engineering programs, law, sociology, political science, veterinary medicine, educational administration, medicine, public health, and various agricultural programs. About fifty graduate programs run for two or more years and include medical specializations and various agricultural, engineering, and social science programs. These programs are offered by the institutions listed in Table 32.1. The graduate programs are offered only at AAU and AUA.

In addition to the nineteen institutions listed in Table 32.1, there are four junior teacher education colleges (Abbi Addi with 455, Awassa with 691, Gonder with 633, and Jimma with 474 students). There are also fourteen teacher training institutes (TTIs) with an average enrollment of 550 students each. The TTIs are postsecondary-level training institutes run by the regional governments. The one-year program prepares graduates to teach in the first cycle of primary education (Grades 1–4). Junior college graduates (trained for two years) can teach in the second cycle of primary education (Grades 5–8). All the institutions mentioned above are funded by the government. In addition, one can attend a postsecondary professional training institute such as a nursing school, the Bank and Insurance Institute, the Police College, the Mass Media Institute, and the Ethiopian Airlines Pilots and Technicians Training Center. The total enrollment of these institutes is below 2,000.

Since the mid-1990s, new private colleges have been ac-

credited by the Ministry of Education. The four officially recognized colleges are Unity College in Addis Ababa, Alfa College of Distance Education, People to People College in Harar, and Awassa Adventist College. Each of these colleges, except the Unity College, has about 2,000 students. Unity College has about 5,000 students. Their programs include business studies (accounting, management, law, and economics), auto mechanics, and agriculture.

A large number of secondary school leavers are looking for training opportunities, and the demand for skilled labor exists in many areas. Hence the chances are high that more private colleges will be opened that focus on areas with the best employment possibilities. Of course, this is possible only if a supportive environment exists in terms of government policies, investment, and accreditation.

It is the policy of the government and the Ministry of Education to group higher education institutions by regions and then to develop universities. In April 2000, coordinating offices of universities at Awassa, Bahir Dar, Mekelle, and Jimma were established and presidents appointed. The head offices of the universities are in these towns; the colleges in those towns and their vicinities will be under them. For example, Awassa College of Agriculture, Dilla College of Teacher Education and Health Sciences, and Wondogenet College of Forestry will be under the University of Southern Ethiopia (Awassa). Bahir Dar Teachers College and Bahir Dar Polytechnic Institute will be under Bahir Dar University. The same will hold for Jimma and Mekelle Universities. It has not been decided yet if the junior colleges of teacher education will be under the universities. It is likely that the junior colleges and the TTIs will continue to function under regional education offices, since they cater to primary-level teachers and primary education is under the jurisdiction of the regional governments.

In Ethiopia, diploma programs take two or three years and first-degree programs take four to five years, except medicine, which takes six to seven years. The AAU and the AUA have graduate programs (mainly master's levels) that run for two years. The Ph.D. (offered in such areas as biology, chemistry, and the English language) and specialty programs in medicine (surgery, pediatrics, etc.) take three to five years after the M.A. or the M.D. Graduate programs started in Ethiopia in 1978 with the establishment of the School of Graduate Studies in the AAU. The graduate programs started without additional resource allocations. Those programs consumed the resources (including staff and faculties) of the undergraduate programs and hence have negatively affected the quality of undergraduate education.

Various policy documents (e.g., education and training policy documents, Ministry of Education reports, and party programs) indicate that the objectives and functions of higher education institutions in Ethiopia are the following:

- Educate, train, and provide skilled labor
- Seek, generate, and cultivate knowledge (including research)
- Promote the development and adoption of science and technology
- Preserve and foster the progressive culture of various ethnic groups in Ethiopia
- Provide various community services supporting the socioeconomic development of Ethiopia

Higher education institutions throughout the country run degree and diploma programs, undertake research, and provide some extension and consultancy services. Though the achievements and failures of these efforts generally are not critically assessed, all indications suggest that the institutions are meeting expectations in teaching, research, and providing services to the community. The graduates of the institutions are now running many governmental and nongovernmental organizations in the country. The overwhelming majority of the teachers in advanced primary and secondary schools are graduates of higher education institutions in Ethiopia.

CURRICULA AND THEIR IMPLEMENTATION

The teaching staff of each institution design a package of courses for each diploma or degree program. The package must be approved by the relevant bodies of each institution. All courses have titles, numbers, credit hours, descriptions, outlines, and lists of references.

Sometimes politicians and academics complain about the lack of relevance of some curricula to the Ethiopian situation. Some argue that the curricula are copied from the developed countries with little modifications. Due to pressures from the political systems and from within, colleges revise their curricula periodically every ten to fifteen years. In the past twenty-five years, with the changes of governments, the curricula of most higher education institutions have been revised at least twice.

Most higher education institutions, particularly the universities, have what is called a freshman program. The primary objective of the program is to introduce students to the higher education system and to ameliorate academic deficiencies in areas such as English-language skills, basic sciences, and quantitative methods. The program in each college is directed toward the primary concentration areas (social sciences, agriculture, or natural science). Students select their major in the middle or at the completion of the freshman program.

Except in specific Ethiopian-language programs (Amharic, Oromiffa, and Tigrigna), the language of instruction is English. All higher education institutions operate on a semester system. There are two semesters in a year and each semester is sixteen weeks long (from registration through final examination). Students are required to carry a load of fifteen to eighteen credit hours per semester. A credit hour is one lecture hour (usually fifty minutes) of instruction per week for sixteen weeks. Students must have attended more than 75 percent of the classes to sit for final exams. Students registered for a two-year diploma program have to take 60–74 credit hours and receive a cumulative grade point average (CGPA) of at least 2.0 (C average). Students registered in four-year degree programs such as biology, economics, or psychology have to complete 128–144 credit hours and receive a CGPA of 2.0 and above. All failed courses (Fs) must be repeated until the student receives a passing grade.

Courses include general education, electives, and major area courses. The major area courses often account for about 50 percent of the total requirements, about sixty credit hours in degree programs and twenty-four credit hours in diploma programs.

Students are required to take twenty-four to forty-two credit hours for the completion of a master's program. A CGPA of 3.0 (B average) is required for graduation. Most graduate programs require that students write a master's thesis and defend it in public (AAU 1987; AUA 1994).

Freshman courses and some of the other courses have textbooks that are distributed individually or are shared by groups of two or three students. Many courses use reference sources, reading materials, and handouts. Teachers and students often complain about the lack or shortages of textbooks and up-to-date and relevant reading. The situation for laboratory equipment and chemicals is similar.

Lectures, group discussions, exercises, fieldwork, paper writing, student presentations, and laboratory work are used as methods of instruction. The dominant method of instruction seems to be the lecture method. Students are assessed by quizzes, midsemester exams, papers, presentations, and final examinations. When the class size is large, teachers tend to use objective types of examination such as multiple-choice, true-false, matching, and fill-in-the-blank tests. In graduate classes and when the size of the class is small (below forty), essay examinations are used more often.

In general, the grading system used throughout the country is as follows:

- Scoring 90–100 percent is excellent, a letter grade of A (4 points)

- Scoring 80–89 percent is very good, a letter grade of B (3 points)
- Scoring 70–79 percent is good, a letter grade of C (2 points)
- Scoring 60–69 percent is satisfactory or pass, a letter grade of D (1 point)
- Scoring below 60 percent is failing, a letter grade of F (0 points)

Teachers are expected to use the above system or use the normal curve distribution of grades. But experience shows that the discretion of individual instructors and the culture of various departments or colleges seem to be more operational.

Most programs require that the graduating students write senior essays or undertake projects that reflect some professionalism. A grade of C and above is expected on such projects. Earning a semester and/or a CGPA below 2.0 puts students in warning, probation, or dismissal status, depending on the level of the score.

ADMINISTRATION OF HIGHER EDUCATION INSTITUTIONS

Since 1994, each higher education institution has organized a board, a senate (if a university), academic commissions, and department councils. These bodies form the hierarchy of administration, with the Ministry of Education on top. From 1977 to 1991, the Commission for Higher Education (CHE) supervised and coordinated higher education institutions. The Higher Education Institutions Board reviews and adapts the plans and budgets of each institution to be submitted to the government, approves and then evaluates the implementation of educational programs, and prepares and submits suggestions to the Ministry of Education concerning the staff and students of the respective institute in the region. The members of the board are a representative of the Ministry of Education (chair); the heads of the region's education, health, agriculture, and planning offices; and a few relevant others (including heads of institutions) assigned by the Ministry of Education (Council of Ministers 1994; FDRE 1999).

The academic commission (AC) of each college faculty deliberates on and submits proposals about programs, plans, courses, certification, promotions, and students' status. The members of the AC are the head of the institution (chair), deputy heads of the institution, heads of departments, the registrar, and three elected representatives of the academic staff. The ACs of a few colleges also include the dean of students and the research and publications officer as members.

The department councils are composed of all full-time academic staff and are chaired by the department heads. The council prepares and submits recommendations to the AC concerning programs of study, curricula, courses, staff promotion, research projects, teaching materials, and examinations. The AC deliberates and makes decisions or recommendations to higher bodies, depending on the issue and its jurisdiction.

The universities have senates, which fall in between the boards and the ACs in their powers and duties. The presidents of the universities chair the senates. Two vice-presidents (academic and business), the deans of faculties, the directors of research institutes, the registrar, the research and publication officer, and elected representatives of the academic staff of each faculty are the members of the senate (AAU 1987).

Each of the above administrative bodies creates various committees to help them perform their duties. The most common and active committees include student affairs, staff development and promotions, and research and publication committees. Several activities are handled by standing or ad hoc committees.

The presidents and vice-presidents of the universities and the deans of the faculties are appointed by the government directly or through the Ministry of Education. The appointed officials are usually senior staff members of the institution. The department heads are elected by the department's council or are appointed by the deans of the faculties, depending on the institution. Until 1993, the deans of faculties and heads of departments were elected by majority vote of the college AC and departmental meetings.

STUDENTS

For the past 15 years in Ethiopia, an average of 60,000 students have completed their secondary education and taken the Ethiopian School Leaving Certificate Examination (ESLCE). The ESLCE serves as a certificate of secondary education completion and as an admission test for higher education institutions. Only about 10 to 15 percent of those who complete high school education are admitted to higher education diploma and degree programs each year. In 1999, new admissions to diploma programs, including teacher education programs, were 5,154; 7,199 were admitted to the degree programs. These figures include applicants who completed secondary education before 1999.

Admissions to higher education institutions are processed through the Ministry of Education, a tradition started by the CHE. Applicants are required to have completed their education and have earned a GPA of over 2.0 in the ESLCE in five subjects, including English and mathematics. Also, five passes in any of the following or equivalent foreign examinations are acceptable: the General Certificate of the University of London; the Cambridge Overseas Certificate; the West African School Certificate; or the Oxford Examination, with a GPA of 2.0 in English, mathematics, and any three of the most relevant subjects with the highest scores.

These are the criteria in principle. But the GPA cutoff points are determined every year based on the space available and the number of applicants. Hence, there were times when only those applicants with a GPA of 3.2 and above were accepted for degree programs and only applicants with a GPA of 2.6 and above were admitted to the diploma programs. Those not admitted to the regular programs can apply to the extension (continuing education) programs. The extension programs also have space limitations and grade-point restrictions.

Students completing secondary education in the peripheral and rural areas of the country, where the quality of education is lower, especially in terms of the qualification of teachers and adequacy of facilities, generally do not earn many high scores.

Table 32.2. Students Enrolled in Regular Programs of Education in Ethiopia by Field of Study, 1999*

Fields of Study	Diploma	Undergraduate	Graduate	Total
Agriculture	1,540	1,712	73	3,325
Engineering and Technology	746	3,218	50	4,014
Medical Science	1,487	1,900	231	3,618
Language Studies	—	682	76	758
Pedagogical Sciences*	289	2,667	61	3,017
Law	86	806	—	892
Natural Science	—	3,950	195	4,145
Commercial and Social Sciences	2,376	5,022	178	7,576
Total	6,524	19,957	864	27,345
Female in percentages	25.86	11.56	7.18	14.10

*Enrollment in junior teacher education colleges is not included.
Source: MOE 1999.

Hence, a proportionally large number of students are admitted to higher education institutions from the central and urban areas rather than peripheral and rural areas.

The criteria for admission to a graduate school are a bachelor's degree with good grades and a passing grade on the entrance examination administered by the faculty or the department concerned.

The admission rate for women has been only about 15 percent for the past several years. Some efforts have been made to improve the rate of female admission by lowering the admission cutoff grade point by 0.2 (for example, admitting boys with 3.0 and girls with 2.8 GPA to the same program). This affirmative action has improved women's admission rate but has not resulted in significant changes; the attrition rate of this group is higher than average. A preparatory program composed of a few months of skills development in language (English), quantitative methods, note-taking, and studying skills would be helpful to women in this group and to those coming from disadvantaged areas. One or two weeks of pep talks and "assertiveness training" are inadequate to help such students succeed in college.

All regular students are provided with free room and board. Only continuing education students (who take classes on weekends or during evenings) pay for application, registration, and tuition. Ethiopian tuition fees have been increasing over the years. One credit hour at Addis Ababa University in the 1998–1999 academic year costed Birr 32 (US$4). The fees for foreign students are about double.

There were 27,345 regular students in the institutions of higher learning in the 1998–1999 academic year. Females accounted for 15.64 percent of the students. (See Table 32.1 for enrollment by specific institutions.) The number of graduates in 1999 was 6,111, of whom 14.1 percent were women.

The number of enrollees and graduates have been increasing in the graduate programs of the AAU and the AUA. For instance, the two institutions had 657 enrollees and 136 graduates in the 1990–1991 academic year. Only fifty-one women were enrolled and nine were graduated during this period (EMIS 1994). By comparison, there were 634 enrollees and 201 graduates in 1994. Enrollments in 1998–1999 by field of study and gender (MOE 1999) were:

- In social sciences (geography, history, social anthropology, and demography): 71, with 4 females.
- In business and economics (economics and local development studies): 77, with 8 females.
- In education (curriculum, educational planning, and psychology): 61, with 4 females.
- In medicine (obstetrics and gynecology, pediatrics, surgery, etc.): 227, with 23 females.
- In natural science (biology, chemistry, statistics, etc.): 195, with 12 females.
- In engineering (civil, electrical, etc.): 50, with one female.
- In language (English, Amharic, linguistics, etc.): 76, with 7 females.
- In information science: 30, with 3 females.
- In pharmacy: 4, with no women.
- In agriculture (agricultural economics, horticulture, animal production, agronomy, etc.): 73, with no women.

Out of the total of 864 graduate students, only 62 (7.18 percent) were women. Engineering, agriculture, and pharmacy had the least or no female enrollment.

Current and reliable data are not available concerning employment and unemployment situations in Ethiopia. However, crude estimates are that there were a little more than 500,000 public employees and close to 1 million job-seekers in 1998 (Habtamu 1999). Of the job-seekers, only a very small number (perhaps less than 10 percent) are diploma and degree holders. The demand for engineers, accountants, medical professionals, managers, economists, agriculturists, and qualified secondary school teachers is high. The number of students enrolled in the continuing education programs (evening and Ethiopian winter season) was 24,960; 5,712 (22.88 percent) of them were women.

It is important to note that most women are enrolled in social and pedagogical sciences and in diploma programs. (See Table 32.2 for details concerning the broad fields of study and enrollment sizes.)

The attrition rate among higher education students has been 10–15 percent for the past several years, with the first year representing the largest share (Abebayehu 1998).

Most of the campuses of higher education institutions have student councils that mainly deal with cafeteria, dormitory, and recreational issues. In earlier days, particularly in the late 1960s and early 1970s, student unions played a significant political role in the country. The councils were active in struggles for democracy and in advocating respect for human rights and socioeconomic changes.

Some reports show that the main problems of students include economics (lack of finances for clothing, school materials, and recreation), lack of textbooks and adequate reference materials, and emotional and health problems (MOE 1989). Many students also complain that they are not admitted to the program of their first or second choice. Hence, it will take a while for many to develop the interest in their areas of admission (major field of study).

ACADEMIC AND SUPPORT STAFF

Higher education institutions recruit their own staff based on certain criteria. The criteria for the selection of applicants for teaching posts vary from faculty to faculty, but mainly include a high GPA (usually above a CGPA of 3.0), inclination and/or experience in teaching and research, and two or three letters of recommendation from instructors. Some faculties might require passing interviews to be conducted by an ad hoc committee established for staff recruitment.

Once employed, the teachers are assessed at the end of every semester (twice a year) by their students, colleagues, and the department head. The teacher must receive an above-average rating to continue their employment. Contracts are renewed every two years. Those teachers whose performance falls below average for two consecutive semesters will not have their contracts renewed. In the past five years, several contracts have been terminated due to low evaluations by students at the AAU. Higher education institutions give academic ranks of graduate assistant, assistant lecturer, lecturer, assistant professor, associate professor, or professor to all teaching staff. Professional librarians also have ranks similar to those mentioned above. Ranks and promotions are based on academic qualification (degree held), number of publications in reputable journals, years of service, teaching effectiveness, and services provided to the community. Often the hardest criterion to fulfill is publication. Salaries of instructors are based on their ranks. Many instructors complain that their salaries are too low. A full professor is paid about US$350 per month. The presidents, vice-presidents, deans, directors, and heads of departments receive additional allowances. Expatriate teachers have advantages of housing, travel, and other allowances.

As observed in Table 32.3, there were 2,228 teachers in higher education institutions in 1989–1999. Of those, 134 were expatriates. Most of the teachers have ranks of lecturer and below. The professors and associate professors were only 2.29 percent and 6.78 percent respectively. Over 66 percent of the instructors had a master's degree or a doctorate. The rest had a

Table 32.3. Teaching Staff by Academic Rank in Ethiopian Institutions of Higher Education, 1998–1999

Rank	Number	Percent
Professors	51	2.29
Associate Professors	151	6.78
Assistant Professors	391	17.55
Lecturers	895	40.17
Assistant Lecturers	147	6.60
Graduate Assistants	224	10.05
Others	369	16.56
Total	2,228	100
Females	137	6.15
Expatriates	134	6.01

Source: MOE 1999.

bachelor's or equivalent degree. Out of the total teaching staff, only 6.15 percent were women.

Full-time teachers are expected to carry a load of up to twelve credit hours per semester. Two to three hours of laboratory work is equivalent to one lecture hour. If an instructor has an officially recognized research project, he or she will be expected to carry only nine credit hours per semester.

The academic staff members of most institutions have the freedom of conducting research in any area of their choice, to teach students about course-relevant controversial issues, and to disseminate findings which are "not contrary to the morality, law and order or the security of Ethiopia" (AAU 1987, 73). Teachers are awarded sabbatical and research leaves, particularly if they are working in the universities. The leaves are granted to those persons who have effectively served the institution for seven consecutive years (in the case of sabbatical) or four consecutive years (in the case of research) and intend to continue their employment with the institution. The theoretical retirement age is 55, but most instructors, particularly those with higher ranks, continue their employment until they are 65 years old if they are in good health.

Academic staff members are expected to exhibit proper behavior and conduct that gains the respect of the community at large. Any breaches of discipline or duties are usually investigated by disciplinary committees established by the head of the institution. Usually the members of the committee are other teachers. Penalties include warnings, reprimands, fines taken from salaries, postponement of promotion to the next rank, and even dismissal (AAU 1987).

Quite a large number of academic staff quit the teaching profession and take other jobs or go abroad for training or other reasons. Though the number varies from institution to institution, Dejene and Yohannes estimate that about 50 percent of skilled workers migrate (Dejene and Yohannes 1998). These researchers and Seyoum Teferra (1997) reported that political instability and political persecution, low salaries and poor living conditions, lack of freedom and poor working (teaching and research) conditions are the main causes for this brain drain (as push factors). The pull factors include higher wages, better living and working conditions, better career and skill opportunities, intellectual freedom, and the political stability of the receiving (developed, mainly Western) countries.

Most teachers belong to the Ethiopian Teachers Association through their institution's teachers' association. The associations hold meetings, conduct conferences, and sometimes publish newsletters. The roles played by associations in bargaining for salaries, benefits, better working situations, and academic freedom have been limited for the past several decades. Various Ethiopian governments have been interested in these associations and have influenced them in ways suitable to the status quo. In 1994, the existing government fired forty-one teachers from the AAU who were considered strong critics of the government. Many of them were in the leadership of the AAU Teachers Association. Opponents of the status quo have been crushed or at least controlled in direct and indirect ways since the 1970s.

The lack of better democratic practices (wider participation, open discussions, transparency, accountability), poor salaries and other benefits, inadequate teaching and research conditions, the large weight given to student evaluations, and direct interference of the government in the activities of the institutions affect the commitment and contribution levels of the academic staff in a negative way. It is worth noting that "teaching effectiveness" is assessed by summing student evaluations (50 percent), colleague evaluations (15 percent), and evaluations by department heads (35 percent). Most staff are unhappy that student evaluations have so much weight. A weight of about 25 percent might be considered adequate.

There were 5,161 support staff (sometimes called administrative and/or general service staff) working in higher education institutions in Ethiopia in 1998–1999 (Table 32.1). These are employees engaged in services that involve the student cafeteria, janitorial services, finance, security, water supply, telephone, electricity, bookstores, archives, publications, and various clerical and manual services. Those providing professional and subprofessional services accounted for only 13.04 percent of the total supportive staff. Support staff do not directly participate in teaching or research activities. In 1998–1999, 48.36 percent of the support staff were females. Most of the support staff have a primary education or less: 16.92 percent had an education level above the twelfth grade.

Employment, promotion, retirement, and discharging of support staff are governed by the rules and regulations of Ethiopia's civil service agency. Their retirement age is 55 years. Many complain about their low salaries, leading a number to quit jobs in higher education and take better-paying jobs. Higher-paying jobs are available in international and nongovernmental organizations and in private businesses.

Table 32.1 shows the number of support staff in each institution. Addis Ababa University accounts for 33.66 percent and 32.71 percent of the academic and support staff, respectively, of the country's higher education institutions.

RESEARCH

The broad aims of research in HEIs are generating knowledge, making teaching more relevant, integrating theory with practice, evaluating and upgrading curricula, and addressing the felt needs of the society. The academic staff are expected and often required to do some research work. The work is done individually, in teams, or as research units (institutes). Some expatriate scholars, individually or in collaboration with Ethiopian researchers or institutions, also participate in research. The general understanding is that the academic staff of HEIs in Ethiopia spend 75 percent of their time in teaching and 25 percent in research activities. Those working in research institutes spend 25 percent in teaching and 75 percent in research work.

The Institute of Ethiopian Studies (IES), the first research unit in the country, was established in 1963. In 1999, there were six well-established research units within higher education institutions. These were the IES, the Debre Zeit Agricultural Research Center (under the Alemaya University of Agriculture), the Geophysical Observatory, the Institute of Development Research, the Institute of Educational Research, and the Institute of Pathobiology. The main purposes of these institutes are to promote research in their areas of mandate, provide fora for the exchange of views and information, and conduct research. They usually initiate, coordinate, and direct research projects; they also disseminate research findings through journals, various publications, workshops, seminars, and conferences. Each institute is managed by a director and its own board of advisers. The board of advisers usually includes around seven selected representatives from relevant faculties.

The scientific and reputable journals published by research institutes, professional associations, or colleges are:

- *Bulletin of Chemistry*
- *Ethiopian Journal of Agriculture*
- *Ethiopian Journal of Development Research*
- *Ethiopian Journal of Education*
- *Ethiopian Journal of Health Development*
- *Ethiopian Medical Journal*
- *Ethiopian Pharmaceutical Journal*
- *Journal of Ethiopian Law*
- *Journal of Ethiopian Studies*
- SINET: *Ethiopian Journal of Science*
- ZEDE: *Journal of the Association of Ethiopian Engineers and Architects* (Bekele 1996)

Though they are not considered as reputable yet, the Ethiopian Economic Association and Ethiopian Languages and Literature also publish serious research works. Many social science researchers also take advantage of the *Eastern Africa Social Science Research Review*, a reputable journal published by the Organization of Social Science Research in Eastern and Southern Africa (OSSREA). OSSREA is housed on the main campus of Addis Ababa University.

The reputability of journals is determined by the senates of each university, based on recommendations from their standing committees on research and publications. The criteria used include: a clear policy and guidelines for contributors, the existence of competent editorial and advisory committees (boards), a competent editor, anonymous peer review, and regular publication. The journals associated with the AAU are assessed every two to three years by the standing committee composed of seven members from various disciplines. The research and publications officer is the secretary of the committee. Usually, the dean of the School of Graduate Studies chairs the meeting. The same committee also assesses and decides on the quality of teaching materials, new textbooks, and major research proposals for funding.

Hundreds of studies have been conducted by the instructors of higher education institutions in Ethiopia. I would like to group the research works into six categories and indicate only a few of the areas studied.

- *Agriculture:* Animals and plant production, food, crop production and protection, horticulture, dry land biodiversity, resource conservation, use of improved agricultural technologies
- *Engineering and technology:* Energy sources, water resources, appropriate technology, irrigation engineering, foundation problems
- *Health sciences:* Common diseases, hygienic and sanitary conditions of specific communities, animal health and various diseases, epidemiology of schistosomiasis and leishmaniasis, food and nutrition, sexually transmitted diseases and HIV/AIDS, prevalence of asthma, eczema, hepatitis, measles, respiratory infections
- *Natural sciences:* Characteristics of the flora, fauna, and fish of Ethiopia, birds, worms and parasites, medicinal plants, geology, natural products chemistry
- *Social sciences:* Drought and famine, urban and rural poverty, history and languages of various ethnic groups in Ethiopia, socioeconomic situations, food aid, the land tenure system, legal and administrative problems, social values, child-rearing practices, problems of settlement, street children
- *Pedagogical sciences:* Curricula, learning problems, problems of testing, teacher education, implementation of education policies, quality of education, vocational education, special-needs education, literacy programs

The funds for the research work come from the government budget and donors. The contributions of some Scandinavian and European countries and the United Nations (UN) are immense. Reliable data are not available on the specific contributions of each country or agency regarding research projects.

Several reports (e.g., Habtamu 1990; Endashaw 1996) show that the "culture" of research is not as well developed as the higher education institutions desire. Lack of adequate finances, overloading of competent staff with teaching and administrative responsibilities, low salaries of teachers (which push them to look for other part-time work), inadequate research facilities, and the lack of adequate fora for the dissemination of research findings are some of the major problems reported. Many senior researchers also complain that there is no dialogue between researchers, policymakers, and those using research findings.

FINANCING HIGHER EDUCATION

Higher education in Ethiopia was and is financed mainly by the government. The funds for the capital and recurrent expenses are provided to institutions through the Ministry of Finance. However, some amount of assistance comes from various UN agencies and other bilateral donors, such as countries and organizations.

The amount of the recurrent budget allocated to the insti-tutions of higher education has been increasing every year. About 12 percent of the education budget is set aside for higher education. For instance, it was about Birr 97 million for 1996–1997 (US$11.8 million), Birr 145 million for 1997–1998 (US$17.7 million), and Birr 200 million for 1998–1999 (US$24.4 million). Out of the recurrent budget, about 50 percent is allocated for salaries (MOE 1998 and 1999).

The UNDP (United Nations Development Program), UNESCO (United Nations Educational, Scientific, and Cultural Organization), UNFPA (United Nations Population Fund), the World Bank (International Development Agency), SAREC (Swedish Agency for Research Cooperation), SIDA (Swedish International Development Agency), the British Council (United Kingdom), Germany, Sweden, the former Soviet Union, and others have assisted the higher education system through grants, experts, provision of consultancy, scholarships, loans (SIDA for construction and equipment), books, and equipment (Habtamu 1994). Some institutions have collaborative and twinning arrangements with universities abroad, particularly with those in the United States, the United Kingdom, Germany, Sweden, and Norway. Examples include partnerships between Alemaya University of Agriculture and Oklahoma State University, the AAU and Karl Marx University in Germany, Kotebe College of Teacher Education and University of East Anglia, and the AAU and the University of London.

As indicated earlier, the Ethiopian government pays for the food, residence, and health care of the students in regular programs. Addis Ababa College of Commerce is the only one that does not have students in residence. It provides each student Birr 120 per month (US$14.60) for ten months as a subsistence allowance. The new education and training policy (TGE 1994) and various documents of the Ministry of Education (e.g., MOE 1997) indicate that students will be sharing the costs for their education in the near future. Loan systems, paying by service, scholarships, and other arrangements are being considered. With the existing high level of poverty (more than 50 percent of the total population is below the absolute poverty line), regular drought and famine, inequity in access to good secondary education between regions and areas, and increasing youth unemployment, the implementation of a cost-sharing scheme in the near future would cause serious controversy. The author recommends thorough studies, open debates, transparency, clear understanding, and preparation of detailed guidelines before the implementation of such a policy.

CURRENT AND FUTURE CHALLENGES

Ethiopia is a large country with a population of some 63 million, most of whom are young. Primary-, secondary-, and tertiary-level participation rates are only 45.8 percent, 9.7 percent, and below 1 percent, respectively. Primary and secondary school enrollments in 1998–1999 were 5.7 million and 520,000, respectively. The demand for tertiary-level education is very high. The author estimates that about 90 percent of Ethiopians who complete high school would like to go to colleges and universities if opportunities were available. Compared to many developing and sub-Saharan African countries, the enrollment of 27,345 and the investments made by the Ethiopian government in higher education are small. Major socioeconomic development cannot be expected without adequate skilled labor in Ethiopia.

Enrollments have been increasing every year by about 10 percent for the past twenty-five years. New institutions have been established and new programs have been started. Existing programs have been upgraded and others have been discontinued. For instance, the college at Dilla was established in 1996 and Mekelle University was established in 1993. Kotebe College of Teacher Education is phasing out its degree programs except in health and physical education, and Bahir Dar Polytechnic Institute has been upgraded to offer degree programs and is phasing out some diploma programs it used to offer. Also, Addis Ababa University undertook a program evaluation in 1999 and is in the process of reorganizing itself and modifying curricula. It is expected that some faculties will be merged with others.

There is no question that it is necessary to make curricula more relevant, modify some programs, and reorganize institutions. But serious and objective studies, public discussions, and involvement of the stakeholders would be highly beneficial to these efforts. Unfortunately, most of the changes made by the AAU, Kotebe College of Teacher Education, and other institutions have lacked the benefits of these exercises.

Ethiopia needs highly competent labor in the economic, agricultural, social, and political spheres. Institutions of higher education have a major responsibility in the development of the skills needed for various sectors. In addition to small enrollment figures, the higher education sector has several problems. Some of the problems include (a) the lower quality of education as reflected by the lower qualification of many teachers, crowded classes, and limitations of teaching materials; (b) the lack of participatory leadership, transparency, and accountability from the Ministry of Education to the bottom units; (c) the discouraging research environment as reflected by lack of funds and bureaucratic red tape in releasing funds; (d) the significant rate of brain drain and rapid turnover of the teaching staff.

The government and the Ministry of Education have declared that there will be four "additional" universities (existing colleges grouped by regions) and that all the universities will have charters and some amount of administrative autonomy. The idea of regional universities, which started with the previous socialist government, could be supported in principle. However, questions about the availability of resources to allocate and decision-making powers of each university and the units under them need to be looked at more seriously. Though they are state institutions, the extent of the interference from the government and limitations placed on the teaching faculty's participation in decision making in internal affairs would have to change to foster the healthy and productive development of the sector.

Encouraging the establishment of private colleges (for example, by providing land for free and duty-free importing of instructional materials) and expansion of distance-education programs that are still at inception stages are other major activities that the development of the sector requires. In 1996, the education faculty (AAU) started distance-education programs with the support of the USAID. An African Virtual University Unit has also been established in the Science Faculty of the AAU with the assistance of the World Bank and UNESCO. Though the possibilities for accommodating a few more students and

those at the periphery seem promising, it is too early to make critical comments regarding these efforts. Distance learning and private colleges require flexibility, commitment, clear guidelines, and support. Since their advantages are immense, the encouragement of private higher education institutions and distance education deserves serious consideration by the government, the Ministry of Education, higher education institutions, stakeholders, and the community at large.

Finally, the author would like to point out that there is and has been some "distance" between the political systems and higher education communities (teachers, students, and the support staff), particularly with the Addis Ababa University. Making use of rapidly developing knowledge and technologies in the world and the reduction or resolution of the vast problems of the country—such as poverty, food shortages, recurrent drought and famine, environmental degradation, social conflicts, illiteracy, diseases, and rapid population growth—require collaborative efforts and significant human resource development. The institutions that could play significant roles in this regard need a democratic working atmosphere, relatively adequate resources, and stability. They need to participate in the leadership of the country. Dialogue within and outside institutions, elections of competent and visionary leadership, closer relationships among the stakeholders, and some degree of freedom and trust between policymakers, decision makers, and communities of higher education institutions are highly recommended.

REFERENCES

AAU (Addis Ababa University). 1987. *Senate Legislation of Addis Ababa University*. Addis Ababa: Addis Ababa University Printing Press.

Abeyayehu, A. 1998. "Problems of Gender Equity in Institutions of Higher Education in Ethiopia." In Amare Asgedom, William Cummings, Derebssa Dufera, Johnson Odharo, Habtamu Wondimu, and Girma Zewdie, eds., *Quality Education in Ethiopia: Visions for the 21st Century*. Addis Ababa: Institute of Educational Research/Addis Ababa University.

Aredo, D., and Y. Zelalem. 1998. "Skilled Labor Migration from Developing Countries: An Assessment of Brain Drain from Ethiopia." In Senait Seyoum and Alemayehu Seyoum, eds., *Human Resources Development in Ethiopia*. Addis Ababa: Ethiopian Economic Association.

AUA (Alemaya University of Agriculture). 1992. *Annual Research Report of the Alemaya University of Agriculture*. Alemaya: AUA.

———. 1994. *School of Graduate Studies Catalogue 1994/95*. Alemaya: AUA.

Bekele, E. 1996. *Biannual AAU Research Book: With Highlighted Information on Twenty Years of Research Activities at AAU*. Addis Ababa: AAU Printing Press.

Commission for Higher Education. 1985. *Higher Education in Ethiopia: Special Issue*. Addis Ababa: Artistic (in Amharic).

Council of Ministers. 1994. "Administration of National Higher Education Institutions Located in Regions." Regulation No 197/1994. Addis Ababa: Berhanena Selam.

CSA (Central Statistics Authority). 1998. *The 1994 Population and Housing Census of Ethiopia: Results at Country Level*. Addis Ababa: CSA.

EMIS (Education Management Information Systems of the Ministry of Education). 1994. *Basic Education Statistics*. Addis Ababa: EMIS/MOE.

FDRE (Federal Democratic Republic of Ethiopia). 1999. "Bahir Dar/

Mekelle/Southern Ethiopia/Jimma Universities Establishment Regulations." Addis Ababa: Berhanena Selam.

Higher Education Institutions. 1984–1992. Catalogues (e.g., Addis Ababa University, Aleyama University of Agriculture, Kotebe College of Teacher Education, Addis Ababa College of Commerce).

Ministry of Education. 1989. *Education Policy Study.* 3 vols. Addis Ababa: Education Materials Production & Distribution Agency (in Amharic).

——. 1996. *Education Sector Development Program, 1997–2001.* Addis Ababa: Ministry of Education.

——. 1997. *Future Direction of Higher Education.* Addis Ababa: Ministry of Education (in Amharic).

——. 1999. *Education Statistics Annual Report, 1998–1999.* Addis Ababa: Educational Management Information Systems, Ministry of Education.

Teferra, S. 1992. "Brain Drain among Academics in Two Higher Education Institutions in Ethiopia." *The Ethiopian Journal of Education* 13, no. 2: 1–37.

TGE (Transitional Government of Ethiopia). 1994. *Education and Training Policy.* Addis Ababa: Education Materials Production & Distribution Agency.

Wondimu, H. 1990. *Research and Development Priorities in Higher Education Institutions.* Addis Ababa: Higher Education Main Department.

——. 1994. "Education, Training and Manpower Planning and Policy in Ethiopia." Paper prepared for the UNDP Ethiopia. Addis Ababa: UNDP.

——. 1999. *Ethiopia's Educational Policy Reform and the Trends on Human Resource Development: Some Observations.* Addis Ababa: Forum for Social Studies.

Gabon

VINCENT MINTSA MI-EYA

INTRODUCTION

The Central African Higher Education Foundation (Fondation de l'Enseignement Supérieur d'Afrique Centrale, FESAC) was inaugurated in Brazzaville by a decree issued by the conference of the heads of states that formerly constituted the French African Equatorial Federation (Fédération de l'Afrique Equatoriale, AEF). Through this decree, signed on December 12, 1961, the conference adopted the charter for the organization of higher education in Central Africa. The foundation was situated at the same location of the former Technical and Administrative Center created in 1959 in Brazzaville. The foundation covered only the former territories of French Equatorial Africa, to the exclusion of Cameroon (which was administered under French supervision) and the Belgian Congo (Zaire) (Mintsa 1994).

Higher education institutions were distributed throughout the various newly established states. Gabon hosted a Polytechnic Institute in Libreville. Chad was home to the Veterinary and Zoological Institute and another law school in N'djamena (formerly Fort-Lamy). The Central African Republic hosted the Agronomy Institute of Wakombo, and Brazzaville (Congo) hosted the Higher Education Center for the humanities, sciences, and other disciplines.

Because it was scattered over many countries, this university network could not survive the independence movements of the various new nation-states. These movements gave birth to national universities in each of the former colonies that achieved independence from French colonialism. In Cameroon, the University of Yaoundé opened its doors in 1962, while the National University of Gabon was created in 1971. Between 1962 and 1970, all central African countries started converting various educational institutes into national universities.

The structure of the universities in the subregion of Central Africa illustrates how higher education institutions have been conceived according to Western vision and norms. Whether Belgian or French, these models have been reproduced mechanically.

THE NATIONAL UNIVERSITY OF GABON

The university model that is the legacy of the colonial tradition is a centralized and unified institution with top-down hierarchy. It is an institution that cherishes centralization excessively and abhors delegation of powers. It is conceived in the image of an absolute monarch who is jealous of his prerogatives, particularly with regard to conferring degrees and validating expertise. Contrary to this type of university, a traditionally African university should be one that is conceived as an organized means toward achieving a specific goal, led by a determined community.

In 1970, Gabon offered education at three institutional levels: higher education institutes of letters, law and economics, and sciences. Five years later, these centers were turned into schools and advanced schools of human sciences, law and economics, sciences, medicine, magistracy, engineering (Libreville), technical teacher training, forestry, and administrative assistant training.

The National University of Gabon, renamed Omar Bongo University (OBU) in 1978, was not decentralized until 1986, when the University of Technical Sciences of Masuku in Franceville was created. The latter marked a new orientation in the scientific and technical training offered by the school of science and the national school of engineering at OBU.

Gabonese higher education has multiple objectives that revolve around four main ideas. First, Gabon can no longer afford to live on a subsistence economy. Gabon should be able to produce industrial goods not only to meet its needs but also to take part in the general development exchange with other countries. To achieve this objective, Gabon should acquire the infrastructure of industrial countries, for which a university is essential.

Second, the university has to shape Gabonese identity, restoring its dignity and providing Gabon with the freedom to decide its destiny. The university should actively contribute to challenging the visible and invisible colonial mentality based on exploitation, assistance, submission, and resignation.

Third, the university should answer a number of urgent demographic questions that are crucial to the development of Gabon. Gabon has to figure out how to increase its population, distribute it evenly over the various regions, increase productivity, and thus achieve development.

Finally, higher education should ensure literacy and universalize education. It should generate and disseminate knowledge in order to eradicate illiteracy, which is responsible for most conflicts, wars, and lack of understanding.

Enrollment at OBU is estimated at 2,000, while the University of Technical Sciences of Masuku (Université des Sciences et Techniques de Masuku, USTM) hosts 700 students. The two institutions employ 600 permanent professors, including eighty French professors, twenty Canadians, and more than seventy contractual professors of different foreign nationalities. The student-professor ratios are generally good, yet the faculty structure is quite hierarchical: a few university professors, a modest number of assistant professors, and a considerable number of assistants (more than 57 percent of the total) (Ministère de l'Education Nationale 1983).

Although the number of administrative and technical personnel seems imposing with 272 at OBU and 96 at the USTM, the percentage of Gabonese employees is very limited, especially at the level of supervision: 78 at OBU and 52 at UTSM.

In terms of curriculum, the sociology and humanities curricula have been supplemented with more specialized training oriented toward development. In this respect, the university has become more realistic about meeting the professional needs of the country through providing better training for graduates.

Gabonese higher education is faced with significant obstacles, including limited financial means, which hinders all initiatives for reflection or adaptation; insufficient library resources, which are crucial to any institution of higher education; diminished prospects of employment, with civil service opportunities being decreased in compliance with structural adjustment programs imposed by international organizations such as the International Monetary Fund; the lack of an active economic structure; a crisis in the university over its mission and legitimacy; and the absence of any research activity.

POSTSECONDARY EDUCATION

Generally, the enrollment capacity of secondary education is satisfactory, with Gabonese schools hosting about 50 percent of the population eligible for higher education (54,000 students with 25,000, or 47 percent, in the private sector). Specialization in secondary school does not take place until the tenth and eleventh grades (Ministère de l'Enseignement Supérieur 1998).

In addition to public institutions, Gabon has private Catholic and Protestant institutions, schools organized by the Christian Alliance, and nonaffiliated private schools. Among the public schools, eight are run under agreement with France and enroll both Gabonese and foreign students. The organization of the national exam creates a distinction between good high schools and second-tier institutions. The former attract the best students by enforcing high admission standards, while the latter adopt an open-door policy to fill empty seats. This situation favors certain institutions while it discredits others. It also leads to a regionalization of institutions in terms of the quality of education. High schools in cities tend to set higher requirements than their rural counterparts.

Access to basic education is free to all, yet schooling of females in Gabon is significantly lower in comparison to schooling of males.

Technical and professional education seems to be the impoverished child of the Gabonese educational system. Conceived in a period when job opportunities were widespread, technical and professional education was considered a way out for dropouts as well as a good means of development for the tertiary industrial sector. The increased enrollment in this area in recent years has contributed to the regression of technical/professional education; the number of graduates grew dramatically, the quality of supervision declined, and job opportunities became scarce.

TEACHER TRAINING

Training of schoolteachers is conducted at a primary teacher training school and two secondary teacher schools (Ecole Normale Supérieure, ENS). The latter are entrusted with training teachers for both general secondary education and secondary industrial and technical education (Ecole Normale Supérieure d'Education Technique, ENSET). Gabon presently has no separate pedagogical training program for the technical sector.

Generally, the Gabonese government actively solicits teacher candidates. Prospective primary and secondary teachers benefit from financial incentives as soon as they are admitted to a training school, a fact which makes the profession more attractive. Classes are relatively small, with fewer than thirty students per class and even less in certain sections of the ENS and ENSET. At the level of secondary education, the high number of foreign professors (more than 80 percent in mathematics) constitutes a concern for the national authorities, who are striving to achieve the nationalization of education.

In terms of capacity, the number of rooms and school benches in the primary sector is less than the number of admitted students. The deficit of labs and science rooms is also significant in the secondary sector.

The primary-level school-teaching body is very insufficient, both in quality and number, while secondary-level teachers in certain disciplines such as French, mathematics, and physics are limited in number.

The entire Gabonese educational system has a poor graduation rate and serious problems with students failing, dropping out, and earning poor grades. Because of these problems, teaching methods need to be reconsidered, and scientific teaching pedagogy needs to be reinforced from as early as primary school. In this respect, the establishment of a kindergarten system was launched in recent years. Similar efforts should be sustained and those involved should learn from the mistakes that have plagued the primary and secondary school system.

The overall high school graduation rate is considered to be low, given that few candidates sitting for the exam obtain their degrees. Professors in the higher education sector are generally unsatisfied with the average level of education of high school graduates entering the university.

The overall number of high school graduates (totaling 2,090 in 1999) was composed of 1,305 majoring in literature, 785 majoring in science, and 112 majoring in math and physics. These figures do not meet the national need, especially for science teachers (Office of the Baccalaureate, 1999).

PRESENT SITUATION AND CHANGING STRUCTURES

Three axes of reform have been identified in Gabon—pedagogy, administration, and finances. Reform measures addressing human and physical resources might result in significant immediate improvements in management, while long-term measures will be concerned with the structures of the educational system, redesigning curriculum, and training a Gabonese teaching body.

The general reform of the university system should be implemented through the application of the higher education reform law. To increase internal productivity and reduce the problems facing higher education, the system needs to be adjusted for both better selection and orientation of students and a reevaluation of pedagogical methods.

Moreover, initiatives by the private sector to set up higher education institutions should continue. Indeed, private higher education offers an alternative and could be a valuable asset for higher education in general. Private higher education can increase enrollment, expand higher education without further cost to the state, help generate graduates with specialized skills, and diversify programs, thus filling gaps in the national educational system.

FINANCING

Gabonese higher education is structured on the classical model in which the state is the main funding source. The management of such a model necessitates heavy investments to establish and maintain basic infrastructures and equipment and to provide salaries to faculty and administrative personnel. The state finances up to 95 percent of the cost of each student. A generous financial aid system, which consumes up to 40 percent of the allocated budget, provides scholarships, room and board, and medical care. Enormous pressure in recent years has been put on the higher education system to stretch the available resources even further. Fees collected from students represent about 3 percent of the total budget (Ministère de l'Enseignement Supérieur 1997).

To diversify their resources and reduce their total dependence on the state, Gabonese higher education institutions are struggling to attract donations, generate revenues, and make students share in the cost of their education. Yet the results of such efforts fall far short of Gabon's overall needs.

CURRICULUM AND LANGUAGE OF INSTRUCTION

Students are admitted to universities after having successfully passed their high school exam, with either a degree type A or B for the school of letters, law, or economics, or type C, D, or E for the schools of medicine, science, or the polytechnic school. A special exam is organized for Gabonese citizens aged at least 22 with a minimum of two years of professional experience.

After two years of study, a university student is awarded an associate degree of arts or science (*Diplôme d'Etudes Générales Universitaires*, DEUG). A bachelor's degree requires four years, while the doctorate in medicine requires seven years of study. Engineering schools award a degree in engineering after five years of study and an advanced technical degree after three years.

The syllabus in Gabon is in French, which is both the language of instruction and the official national language.

SCIENTIFIC RESEARCH

Many changes have taken place since 1976 in terms of scientific and technical research at the level of national educational structures (between universities and advanced schools). These changes reflect the concern of the government that research be current and relevant to the economic, social, and cultural development needs of the country.

A university oriented toward development must devote resources to both research and teaching. The competence and expertise that universities possess in scientific and other domains should be put to work for the improvement of the community's life. While fundamental research should be preserved, applied research should be increasingly enhanced. Important financial resources should be allocated to researchers to enable them to reach their assigned objectives.

Many research projects can contribute to the enhancement of the university. Research on the integration of Gabonese languages into the educational system could help promote an understanding of the evolution of our cultures through the ages, safeguard our cultural values, and encourage Gabon's transition to modernity. Archeological radiocarbon dating can provide important insight into the anthropological history of Gabon. Many studies conducted at the school of medicine and health sciences at the Masuku University of Science and Technology (Université des Sciences et Techniques de Masuku, USTM) on certain tropical diseases have been very encouraging. Efforts are being made at USTM and the Polytechnic of Masuku to improve land fertility through fertilizers, while the schools of science are conducting important soil studies.

Faculty and researchers publish in international and African journals according to their specialty. Universities also host publications such as the Anglophone journal WAVES and the *Annales de l'Université Omar Bongo*, published by OBU.

SPECIFIC UNIVERSITY PROBLEMS

After independence was achieved, student associations were generally affiliated with a single political party. Relationships between these associations and the higher education administration were based on a spirit of solidarity and support for the political actions of the government. With the introduction of the multiparty system, these relationships have become increasingly tense, and conflicts have resulted in strikes and violence. Student activism is moving increasingly toward general political protest. Strikes and frequent university closures have also jeopardized South-South cooperation.

Gabon has experienced employment saturation in sectors that are not deemed essential for the country, while other crucial domains suffer the lack of an educated workforce. Dropouts from both universities and high schools regularly join the considerable mass of the unemployed. Consequently, females are often drawn into prostitution, while males regularly become addicted to drugs and alcohol.

Gabonese higher education, in this respect, can bring significant changes through continuing education and cooperation with other sectors of society. Among the employed, only 5,000 (16.7 percent) of the 30,000 civil servants work in jobs that correspond to their expertise. Gabon also relies heavily on foreign workers in many sectors.

PRESENT CHALLENGES FACING GABONESE HIGHER EDUCATION

The crisis of Gabonese higher education is manifold and is apparent on many levels: financial, institutional, administrative, pedagogical, and political.

While government efforts are vital on the financial and material levels, they have focused on the social aspect of student life instead of supporting efforts to improve pedagogy and research. University facilities and equipment are generally insufficient and small, and their construction often remains unfinished.

Gabon is highly centralized in terms of administration. Consequently, research faculty at the National Center for Scientific and Technological Research are unable to cooperate fully due to bureaucratic barriers that make the existence of cooperation with other academic institutions impossible.

Higher education in Gabon is characterized by poor grading procedures, inadequate orientation, and low levels of academic support. Students are faced with an inefficient system that fails to confirm and validate their efforts and competence.

In addition, Gabon has no clear focus on making its scientific research policies compatible with the national priorities for socioeconomic development and for the promotion of the significant biodiversity of the Gabonese ecosystem. There is a real need for scientific journals and equipment to promote both teaching and research activities.

Gabonese higher education has often been subject to the wrath of political figures, including intervention of the state in the academic affairs of universities. This situation has destroyed all notions of academic freedom. Above all, the Gabonese university is in dire need for creative ideas to rescue it from its heavy bureaucracy and sluggishness.

In summary, the crisis of Gabonese higher education is manifested on essentially two levels: the quality of education and the quality of research. There is an urgent need to address Gabon's educational mission and the compatibility of its higher education system with the national development needs. The number of university graduates is rising and the deterioration of relationships between the student associations, staff and faculty unions, and university administrators can be very detrimental if not addressed properly. Other issues that must be addressed are the conditions of service and the competence of administrative, academic, and research personnel.

CONCLUSION

Higher education in Gabon has contributed significantly to national development, especially through the training of competent graduates operating at all levels of public and private administration. However, the recent rise in student numbers and the lack of sufficient funds are negatively affecting the quality of both teaching and research. There is general agreement, though, that higher education constitutes a national investment whose benefits are felt at all levels of society, despite the scope of the crisis and the decrease in efficiency.

The establishment of a network of cooperation between the university and other poles of social development is the only way to steer higher education into providing a good education to students and to provide faculty and researchers with the necessary tools to carry out their duties.

Gabon should undertake significant conceptual and institutional reforms in education. In so doing, particular attention should be paid to the impact that globalization and the market economy are having on the job market. Other factors that need to be considered are the rapid development of knowledge and the advent of communication technologies.

BIBLIOGRAPHY

Campus Perspectives. 1999. "Quelles orientations après le bac?" *Magazine de l'Etudiant Africain* (June 1999).

Ministère de l'Education Nationale. 1983. *Compte Rendu des Etats Généraux de l'Education: Libreville, Gabon*. France: Berger Levrault Editions.

Ministère de l'Enseignement Supérieur. June 1997. "Première session du Conseil National de l'Enseignement Supérieur." June. Unpublished paper. Libreville, Gabon.

———. 1998. *Grands Choix de la Politique Scientifique et Universitaire au Gabon à l'aube du 21ème siècle: Actes des Etats Généraux, Volume 1 and 2, 3–6 mars 1998*. Libreville, Gabon: Imprimerie Louis.

Mintsa mi Eya, V. 1994. "L'Enseignement Supérieur au GABON." Unpublished paper presented at the University of California.

UNESCO. 1992. "Principaux enjeux et problèmes prévisibles de l'Enseignement Supérieur en Afrique au XXème siècle, 28 février–1er Mars 1991". Unpublished report. Dakar, Senegal: UNESCO.

———. 2000. "Projet d'appui a l'élaboration d'un programme de réforme et de développement de l'Education: Mars 2000". Unpublished report. Dakar, Senegal: UNESCO.

34

Gambia

KABBA E. COLLEY

INTRODUCTION

Higher education in Gambia is very different from higher education in most African countries. This is because no system of higher education existed in Gambia until five years ago. To understand the evolution and current state of higher education, one must understand the context in which it evolved. This chapter begins with a discussion of the socioeconomic, political, and historical context of higher education in Gambia. This discussion is followed by a brief review of indigenous education and the introduction of Western education. The role of early missionaries and the colonial government in shaping education in Gambia is then discussed. The rest of the chapter focuses on education in Gambia during the postcolonial period and the evolution of Gambian higher education from that period to the present day.

SOCIOECONOMIC, POLITICAL, AND HISTORICAL CONTEXT

The country of Gambia is located on the west coast of Africa between the 13th and 14th parallels. Its area is approximately 11,295 square kilometers (4,361 square miles), and it is surrounded by the Republic of Senegal on all sides except on the Atlantic Ocean. Gambia's population is 1.2 million, with an annual growth rate of 3.6 percent (based on 1993 census figures) and an estimated per capita income of US$800 (Government of Gambia 2000). Most Gambians live in rural areas and are employed directly or indirectly in the agricultural sector. The backbone of the Gambian economy is the production and marketing of groundnuts (peanuts), a legacy of the colonial era. Other important agricultural activities include fishing, cotton production, cattle rearing, and horticulture. The country's gross domestic product (GDP) is US$400 million, with agriculture

accounting for 30 percent, industry for 15 percent, and tourism and other service sectors for 55 percent (UNDP 1999).

Gambia's official language is English, another legacy of the colonial era. However, the use of English as a lingua franca in all schools and colleges has been seen by most people as positive because it is an opportunity to speak an international language and to become more functional in a global economy.

Historically, Gambia consisted of all the land into which the River Gambia drains, which is often referred to as Senegambia. It existed as part of the Great Empires of the Western Sudan, which declined in the thirteenth century (Faal 1991). As a part, albeit a small one, of those empires, it was greatly influenced by that period in history. That history is beyond the scope of this chapter, but it has been extensively researched and analyzed by other scholars (Clarke 1994; Faal 1991; Davidson, Buah, and Ajayi 1990; Diop 1987; Davidson 1984, 1985; Rodney 1983; and Du Bois 1965). After the decline of the Great Empires, the land and its people came under the domination of the Portuguese, the French, and the British. The latter established the colony of The Gambia and ruled it for about 300 years, until February 18, 1965, when the colony became independent.

Prior to colonial rule, the peoples of Africa, particularly in the Senegambia subregion, enjoyed a rich system of indigenous education. The main purpose of this system was to produce a person who was well rounded and able to carry on the traditional values of the older generation. It was highly functional and relevant to the individual and society. From birth to maturity, children were guided by the elders of the extended family. The traditions, customs, and moral values of the society were passed on through stories, ceremonies, games, and practice. The child acquired knowledge and skills by participating in daily work and assisting in the production of goods and services. Specialized training was provided through on-the-job experience or an apprenticeship system that involved working under the tutelage of a master craftsman or craftswoman for extended periods until competency was achieved.

Besides basic education and skills training, indigenous education also included various forms of higher education. According to Ajayi, Goma, and Johnson, "Indigenous higher education produced and transmitted new knowledge necessary for understanding the world, the nature of man and woman, society, God and various divinities, the promotion of agriculture and health, literature and philosophy" (1996, 5). Higher education was reserved mainly for rulers and priests, and the selection process was elaborate. The course of study varied according to the culture and language of the recipient, and teaching and learning was conducted through attachment and apprenticeship. The existence of an indigenous higher education system in Africa, particularly in the Senegambia subregion, has been well documented by Diop. In his book *Pre-Colonial Africa*, Diop noted that a thriving intellectual life existed in Western Africa that was very much influenced by Islam (which came to Western Africa in the early part of the eleventh century through trade, conquest, colonization, and missionary activities).

According to Diop, "In Africa, the language of higher education was Arabic, as was Latin for Europe of the same period. The Koran was the equivalent of the bible; it was the principle text to be studied, the one from which all others derived. It contained the sum of all that existed, past, present and future, the whole universe" (1987, 177). Although indigenous higher education was mainly driven by religious factors and in some ways catered to the ruling classes, it provided opportunities for many to acquire advanced knowledge and skills. It was well suited to the needs of the society. It was relevant and contributed to the stability of the society.

The coming of the European slave trade destroyed indigenous higher education by depopulating many parts of Africa, particularly Senegambia, and robbing the area of its best human and natural resources. Although the European slave trade ended centuries ago, the long-term impact is still being felt. This is because very little was done to address the educational question during the colonial period that followed the end of the slave trade. This is particularly true when one examines the history of Western education in colonial Gambia.

WESTERN EDUCATION IN GAMBIA: MISSIONARY INFLUENCE

The history of Western education in Gambia can be traced as far back as 1823. During this period, a working party of missionaries from the Society of Friends in London arrived in the capital, Banjul (formally called Bathurst), to carry out missionary work (Gray 1966). The head of the mission was Hannah Kilman, the widow of John Wesley, founder of the Methodist New Connection. Kilman and the sisters of her party settled in Banjul, where they opened up a girls' school. They taught scripture, reading, writing, cooking, and needlework. The brothers of the mission started a boys' school in Cape St. Mary and instructed their students in plowing and other farming techniques. The Sisters of Friends were followed by Methodist, Anglican, and Roman Catholic missions. The latter two missions opened

up schools in the Upper River Division (URD) of the country. (Gambia is divided into five administrative divisions; the URD is located in the interior of the country about 280 miles from the capital.)

One of the main goals of Western education was to Christianize the Gambian population. However, some missionaries, such as the Society of Friends, provided their students with agricultural and technical training. Others missions were interested in producing a "Western 'black coated worker' for whom there was only a limited scope in The Gambia, with the consequent denigration of the dignity of the tiller of the land" (Southorn 1952, 226). The introduction of Western education in Gambia was met with different responses from the population. For instance, some parents refused to send their children to mission schools because they feared that their children would become alienated from their traditional African values and culture. Others welcomed the idea because sending their children to school meant they could have a brighter future. The colonial government did not provide any financial support for education during this period. As a result, all the schools were run and financed by the missions. Most of the schools were located in Banjul and its surroundings and catered mostly to the local inhabitants and recently freed slaves. The curriculum was heavily influenced by Christian values, and the medium of instruction was English. The speaking of local languages was forbidden on school premises. Children learned more about the history and geography of the British Empire than they did about their own country. The system of indigenous education, which had not recovered from slavery, was assaulted once more by the missionary influence. Any chance of it evolving into a more sophisticated system of higher education (as in Timbuktu) was lost. The fear of many parents that traditional values and culture would be lost was being realized.

The provision of higher education from a Western perspective was never the intention of the British colonial government. According to Rodney, "Africans were being educated in colonial schools to become clerks and messengers. Too much learning would have been superfluous and dangerous for clerks and messengers. Therefore, secondary education was rare and other forms of higher education virtually non-existent" (1983, 267). The fact that education was considered dangerous is echoed by Ajayi, Goma, and Johnson: "At all events the prevalent attitude of the colonial regimes was to neglect education or seek to limit its provision. Neglect or restriction was evident at the elementary level, more severe at the secondary level and virtually total at the level of higher education" (1996, 28). From the above, it is clear that higher education was never a priority of the British colonial government. As a result, when independence came, newly independent countries such as Gambia did not have any higher education policy or infrastructure upon which to build.

EDUCATION IN GAMBIA AFTER INDEPENDENCE

Gambia has been independent for thirty-seven years. In 1970, the country changed from being a parliamentary democracy with a prime minister and the Queen of England as its head of state to a republic with a president as the head of state. Sir

Dawda Jawara, a Gambian trained in Scotland as a veterinarian, became the first president. From 1975 to 1980, the Gambian government implemented a major five-year development plan. The main objective of the plan was to reduce the disparity between urban and rural incomes through greater concentration of resources in the rural sector (Government of Gambia 1975). To achieve this objective, the government relied on the philosophy of "Teseto," or self-reliance. People were urged to participate in all levels of decision making in order to become self-reliant. Massive spending on development projects was carried out. Top priority was given to projects in the rural areas. In theory, the plan contained some positive elements; however, its implementation was widely criticized. According to McPherson and Radelet, "The planned development expenditure was too large and too poorly managed to produce a long-term positive effect on economic growth and development" (1989, 4).

It is important to note that the Jawara regime inherited not only an economic and political system that was based on the domination and exploitation of the Gambian people but also an educational system designed to maintain and perpetuate that system. Higher education was not a priority of postcolonial Gambia since there were more immediate needs to be met. During this period, several reasons were given by the government and aid agencies as to why higher education was not a priority. The most common one was that it could not afford a higher education system due to the country's size and limited economic resources (Njie et al. 1989). Furthermore, the critical mass of students, faculty, and staff needed to meet the demand for a higher education system was lacking. In addition, it was felt that a higher education system in Gambia would benefit only the few. Investment in basic primary education was considered to be more realistic and cost effective because it would benefit more people. However, despite all the rationalizations for not having a higher education system in Gambia, some felt the real reason was that the government feared it would lead to an educated citizenry that would eventually become politicized and challenge its policies.

In July 1981, the Gambian Field Force (the country's only paramilitary defense force, which had about 800 men), discontented with the country's economic situation, organized an unsuccessful coup d'état, which led to the intervention of Senegalese troops. President Jawara was restored to power by the Senegalese government, and in return he signed a confederation agreement known as the Senegambian Confederation. The main objective of the confederation was to establish a monetary union and a common defense and foreign policy between the two countries. The confederation was short lived and was eventually dismantled in 1989 due to differences between the two countries about its implementation.

A second five-year development plan was implemented from 1981 to 1986. The government again promised to "eradicate poverty, hunger, ignorance and disease, and build a nation of free, prosperous, and self-reliant people" (Government of Gambia 1983, vii). Although many Gambians responded to the call for self-reliance, the country was still suffering from widespread poverty, hunger, disease, and corruption at the end of the plan period. Massive government spending without a corre-

sponding increase in revenue created a major budget deficit and forced the country to borrow money from foreign sources to finance the economy. Foreign borrowing created a huge debt burden for Gambia and made the country more dependent on foreign assistance. Rampant corruption in both the public and private sectors during the plan period, coupled with the rising cost of oil, falling groundnut prices, and periods of drought, led to serious economic crises and political instability. This continued for years.

In 1987, the government convened its First National Conference on Education to discuss the worsening education crises in Gambia. The conference was attended by more than 250 delegates representing teachers, students, parents, administrators, policymakers, religious organizations, private companies, various government departments, nongovernmental organizations, and donor agencies. The main issues discussed at the conference were access to education, the shortage of qualified teachers, the role of secondary technical schools, nonformal education, examinations, curriculum, language policy, and the education of girls. After the conference, the Gambian government formulated its Third Education Policy for the period 1988 to 2003. In it, the government acknowledged for the first time the need for a policy on higher education in Gambia. It clearly noted:

> Given the increasing trend to make training more functionally relevant and the tendency the world over to increasingly reduce public subsidy of university education and the resulting increase in university fees for overseas students as well as the limitations on the placement of overseas students in such universities because of increasing local demand, the time has now come within the broad objectives of this policy period for [the] Government to clearly define a policy on higher education. (Government of Gambia 1988, 42)

One of the strategies proposed in the Third Education Policy (1988–2003) to address the higher education question was the establishment of a nucleus for a University of The Gambia at Gambia College. This meant using existing programs at Gambia College, building them up, and eventually turning them into degree programs. In addition, the policy noted that such programs would focus on areas that are critical to the human resource needs of Gambia, such as agriculture, education, public health, and nursing. Another strategy proposed by the policy was to collaborate with an overseas university on establishing a national university and to set up a multidisciplinary team to study the matter.

The idea of using Gambia College as the launching pad for a University of The Gambia did not materialize. One reason for this could be lack of or difficulty in finding a potential donor or partner. It could also be political. As is usually the case with large projects in Gambia, competition for control (especially because of the prestige and power associated with a national university) may have delayed or even killed the idea.

In July 1994, junior army officers led by Lieutenant Yaya Jammeh (a member of the presidential bodyguard) overthrew the Jawara government, charging it with corruption and mismanagement of public funds. Lieutenant Jammeh and his Armed

Forces Provisional Ruling Council (AFPRC) suspended the constitution and issued a four-year timetable for a return to civilian rule. However, because of pressure from Western governments and foreign donors, the AFPRC shortened its timetable for return to civilian rule to two years.

In August 1996, a referendum on a Draft Constitution of the Second Republic was held. About 80 percent of the registered voters voted in favor of the new constitution. In September of the same year, presidential elections were held and four main political parties contested the elections. The Alliance for Patriotic Reorientation and Construction led by Lieutenant Jammeh (who resigned from the military) won 56 percent of the votes, and Jammeh was elected the first president of the Second Republic.

Jammeh's Second Republic has inherited many of the social and economic problems left behind by the Jawara government, such as widespread poverty, unemployment, an inadequate health care system, a declining education system, huge foreign debt, and an economy based on foreign aid. Since coming to office in 1996, the government of the Second Republic has pledged to fight corruption and restore confidence in the government. It has also undertaken some economic and social reforms. However, there have been allegations of corruption and mismanagement of public funds (*New African* 1997), and some Gambians believe that the Second Republic has brought little change in their lives. It is against this background that higher education has evolved.

HIGHER EDUCATION IN GAMBIA

Higher education as defined by the establishment of educational institutions that offer bachelor's degrees, master's degrees, and doctorates did not exist in Gambia until 1995. Prior to this period, the only way a Gambian could pursue higher education was to enroll at a postsecondary institution or to travel abroad and attend a college or university. The main postsecondary institutions of learning in Gambia are the Gambia College and the Gambia Technical Training Institute (GTTI).

Gambia College was established in 1978 as a result of the consolidation of Yundum College (the country's first postsecondary institution), which consisted of a School of Education and a School of Agriculture, and two other postsecondary institutions (Gambia School of Public Health and the Gambia School of Nursing and Midwifery). Presently, the admission requirements for Gambia College vary from school to school. For instance, in the School of Education and Agriculture, programs leading to a certificate require four General Certificate of Education (GCE) ordinary-level (O-level) credits, while the Highest Teachers Certificate and the Higher Diploma in Agriculture require applicants to have five credits.[1] Admission to the School of Public Health, the School of Nursing, and the Midwifery Program is based on five O-level credits, including the English language and a core science subject. To be admitted to the Midwifery Program, candidates must complete the nursing program and have five years of work experience.

Gambia College offers programs leading to a certificate or diploma. The programs are primary education, middle school education, general agriculture, animal science, agricultural education, agricultural extension, cooperatives, public health, nursing, and midwifery. The duration of study varies according to program. For instance, the primary education program lasts two years, while the middle school program lasts three years. The program in general agriculture leads to a two-year certificate or a three-year higher diploma. The program in animal science and cooperatives lasts two years, while agricultural education and agricultural extension require three years of study. The public health program leads to a Higher National Diploma in Public Health and the West African Health Examination Board Diploma. The duration for this program is four years. The nursing program lasts three years and leads to the Certificate of State Registered Nurse; certified nurses with five years of experience are eligible for the Certificate of State Certified Midwife.

In 1990, the total student enrollment at Gambia College was 350, the majority of whom were enrolled in the School of Education (World Bank 1990). The total number of faculty members at the college was forty-three in 1993. Of these, seven were principal lecturers, twelve were senior lecturers, twenty-two were lecturers, and two were assistant lecturers (Government of Gambia 1994). Up-to-date data on student enrollment and characteristics for Gambia College are hard to come by. However, according to a source from the college (personal communication 2000), eighteen students were enrolled in the School of Public Health and thirty-eight students in the School of Nursing and Midwifery in 1999.

The Gambia Technical Training Institute was established by an Act of Parliament in 1980 as part of the Gambia World Bank Education Project. It was opened in 1983 and offered full-time, part-time, extended-day, and day-release courses in the following disciplines: building construction, carpentry and joinery, commerce, masonry, general engineering, automotive engineering, electrical engineering, mechanical engineering, plumbing and gas fitting, refrigeration and air conditioning, instructor training, and computer studies. The duration of study varies from one to three years. Admission to the GTTI is based on a selection examination developed by the institute and/or achievement of O-level credits. The graduates of the GTTI take an internal examination to meet the requirements of the National Training Standard and/or external examinations leading to the City and Guilds of London Institute Certificate, the Royal Society of Arts Certificate, or the Pitmans Certificate. The annual enrollment in 1987 was 505 students (Directorate National Vocational Training Program 1987). The number of full-time faculty at the institute in 1993 was seventy, including one teacher educator, six department heads, seven principal instructors, eleven senior instructors, twenty-nine instructors, and sixteen assistant instructors (Government of Gambia 1994).

Other than Gambia College and the GTTI, one can study at the Management Development Institute (MDI) and the Rural Development Institute (RDI). Both of these postsecondary institutions were set up in the 1980s to prepare a cadre of trained professionals who would be able to provide leadership in the implementation of the Gambian government's economic and social development plans. The main purpose of the MDI is to provide professional development courses for middle- and upper-level managers, administrators, auditors, accountants, and technicians in both the civil service and the private sector. Other than professional development courses, the MDI also offers diploma programs in business administration, management, and accounting. The admission requirements for the diploma program are four O-level credits.

Although the MDI focuses mostly on the training of civil servants and private-sector employees, it also provides research and consultancy services. Current data on student enrollment and characteristics are inaccessible. However, a review of government estimates and recurrent revenue and expenditure for 1993 to 1994 showed that the MDI has one principal management trainer, three senior management trainers, seven management trainers, and three assistant management trainers (Government of Gambia 1994). The MDI is funded by the World Bank/International Development Association and the government of Gambia.

The RDI is the only postsecondary institution located in rural Gambia (Mansa Konko, about 115 miles from the capital). The purpose of the institute is to train community development agents who will work with rural communities and help them improve their living conditions. Admission to the institute is based on performance on the O-level examination (a minimum of three credits, including English language) and a commitment to serve in a rural area. The training program usually lasts for two years and includes courses in community development, rural sociology, economics, project planning and management, youth work, social psychology, rural engineering, adult education, appropriate technology, agriculture, horticulture, cooperatives, home economics, health, bookkeeping, administration, and English. Graduates of the RDI are awarded the National Certificate in Community Development and are usually employed by the government as community development assistants upon recommendation by the Department of Community Development.

Data on enrollment trends in the postsecondary institutions are hard to obtain. However, Gambia College and the GTTI have enjoyed increased enrollment in the past decade and should continue to do so, mainly because there is a huge demand for the programs offered at these institutions (for example, a demand for teachers, nurses, health workers, agricultural workers, carpenters, welders, masons, electricians, and mechanics). In the past, the MDI had limited enrollment because the pool from which it draws its students—that is, government departments and the private sector—sent only a limited number of their employees at a time because of funding limitations. However, this is changing because the government and the private sector have recognized the need for a well-trained workforce. In addition, aid agencies such as the World Bank, the European Union (EU), and the United Nations Development Program have been pushing for a well-trained workforce as a precondition for continued economic support. In the 1980s, RDI enjoyed steady enrollment. During this period, there were many rural development projects, and government policy was very much in favor of training a "cadre of development workers who, given adequate support and covering as wide an area as possible, will enable the people to help themselves promote change" (Government of Gambia 1978, 7). In the 1990s, most of the policies and programs that created the need to train rural

development workers were suspended or stopped due to lack of funding.

Because all the postsecondary institutions in Gambia are government funded and run, all the administrators, faculty, and support staff are government employees. Except for Gambia College, which is headed by a principal, all the other postsecondary institutions are headed by directors. Gambia College and the GTTI both have a board of governors that is appointed. The principal or director is responsible for the day-to-day administration of the institution and is supported by an assistant principal or director. The heads of departments or divisions are responsible for the implementation of programs in their departments. Most of the postsecondary institutions receive some form of assistance from outside sources (e.g., UNESCO, World Bank, EU, and overseas universities) in the form of technical assistance. It is important to note that Gambia College and the GTTI are set up like colleges and therefore have organizational structures similar to colleges found in other African countries, while the MDI and the RDI are set up to look like corporate training institutes. They have a very limited number of faculty and students.

In order to receive higher education (sometimes called further education) beyond the postsecondary level, Gambian candidates must attend foreign colleges or universities. Although Gambian students are known to live in every continent, most pursue higher education at colleges and universities located in West Africa, the Commonwealth, Western Europe, the United States, the former Soviet Union, Eastern European countries, and the Middle East.

To be admitted to foreign colleges or universities, Gambian candidates must not only fulfill the admission requirements of the host college or university, they must also have sponsorship. Sponsorship usually takes the form of grants or scholarships provided to the Gambian government by the host country. The Ministry of Education, through a national scholarship board, administers grants and scholarships for higher education. The process is as follows: first one applies to and is accepted to a university, then one applies to the government for a scholarship. Sometimes government scholarships are predetermined and a candidate may end up accepting a scholarship outside his or her field of interest. Other than the national scholarship board, individual government departments offer fellowships to their employees for further training abroad, usually through some type of bilateral foreign aid. The allocation of scholarships, grants, and fellowships has been criticized by some Gambians who believe that those who are awarded scholarships are not always the most qualified. Although most Gambians who received higher education during the period 1965–1988 did so with the aid of government scholarships, grants, or fellowships, it is important to note that some Gambians have managed to study abroad with help from parents or relatives living abroad. There are also those individuals who work, save their money, and fund their own higher education abroad.

Although an externally oriented higher education system benefited Gambia by producing a class of trained professionals, the system also created several problems for the country. The first problem was that some who were foreign educated were unable to apply their knowledge and skills successfully in Gambia. This is because the type of training provided was not always the most appropriate or relevant to the needs of the country. For instance, there were cases of foreign-trained doctors who were never allowed to practice on the citizens of the host country. When they returned and started practicing medicine, their lack of hands-on experience proved fatal in many cases.

The second problem created by an externally driven higher education system was brain drain. This is the loss of trained human resources to host countries because the foreign-trained person finds it more attractive to stay and work in the host country than to return home. Sometimes it is a personal choice not to return home after receiving training; other times, the persons may fear political persecution when they return home. Data on the number of foreign-trained Gambians who have joined the brain drain pool is hard to find. However, it is believed that the number is in the thousands, most of whom are in the United States, the United Kingdom, and Scandinavia. The effects of the brain drain include heavy dependence on expatriates to run government projects. Although expatriates are well trained, they may not have a sufficient understanding of the people and culture of country they are hired to serve. Other consequences of the brain drain are the low number of scientists, doctors, engineers, and architects per capita and the low number of high school and postsecondary teachers, artists, writers, economists, lawyers, and entrepreneurs.

The third problem that is created as a result of an externally based higher education system is loss of foreign exchange. Every year that Gambia sends students abroad for training, the country is gambling its foreign exchange, because it does not know whether it will get a return on this investment. Data on the amount of money Gambia spends on higher education is very sketchy. However, a study by Njie et al. (1989, 1) noted that "between 1981 and 1985 approximately $3,000,000 was spent to train 40 Gambians to the Bachelor of Science level (BS) in the United States." In a time of rising tuition costs in most foreign universities, it will be very difficult for the government to continue to sustain a higher education system that is externally oriented.

In response to the problems cited above, a Second National Education Conference was held in 1995. The major concerns of the conference were basic education and life skills; technical, vocational, and scientific education; and planning, management, and capacity building. During the conference, a strong appeal was made for the establishment of a higher education system in Gambia: "The time has come within the broad objectives of this policy period for Government to clearly define a policy on higher education in order to chart the way forward in this particular crucial area of education" (Government of Gambia 1996, 43).

A clear policy on higher education in Gambia has yet to be developed by the government. However, a University Extension Program in cooperation with a Canadian university has been established as an interim arrangement before the establishment of a University of The Gambia. In addition, a Commission for Higher Education in Gambia has been formed. The members of the commission include the permanent secretary for the ministry of education; the heads of Gambia College, GTTI, MDI, and RDI; the coordinator of the University Extension Program;

and five members of the public. The functions of the commission are

> to formulate and implement proposals aimed at establishing The University of The Gambia by October 1997, develop a structure for governance and administration purposes, prepare a database of Gambian managers, academics, administrators and other professionals for the University, prioritize areas of study based on the high level of human resource needs of the country, facilitate the integration of The University Extension Program into the university and determine the role that existing tertiary institutions might play and what contribution they could make in the development of the university. (Government of Gambia 1996, 43)

The Commission for Higher Education in Gambia will eventually be succeeded by a Council for Higher Education that will be an autonomous body with expanded roles and responsibilities regarding the establishment and management of a higher education system.

THE UNIVERSITY EXTENSION PROGRAM

The University Extension Program (UEP) was started in November 1995. It is a collaborative effort between the Gambian government; the Nova Scotia Gambia Association (NSGA), a nongovernmental Canadian organization; and St. Mary's University, which is located in Halifax, Nova Scotia, Canada. It is an arrangement in which St. Mary's University will provide undergraduate training to qualified Gambian students in Gambia at a cost affordable to the government. Funding is mainly provided by the Gambia government. However, NSGA, the Canadian International Development Agency (CIDA), and other Canadian nongovernmental organizations have also pledged their support. The main program offered is a Bachelor of Arts degree. There is no Bachelor of Science program yet because laboratory facilities have not been established. Most of the students admitted to the program have A-level passes or hold professional certificates with work experience.

In 1999, the UEP graduated its first cohort of students. Graduates who earned B.A. degrees from St. Mary's University included five in English, twenty-six in international development, thirty-one in economics, nine in mathematics, three in geography, and six in history. Most of the graduates were males; only eight females earned B.A.s. This raises an important question about equity in higher education in Gambia: Why are so few women enrolled in the UEP? The answer to this question remains to be discovered. Perhaps a clear policy on higher education would provide guidelines on how to achieve greater gender equity.

Currently there are 250 students enrolled in the second cohort of students. Seventy-six of these students are self-funded and the rest are on some type of government scholarship. So far, forty-one St. Mary's University faculty have participated in the program, twenty-six of them with doctorates, two with twenty years of university teaching experience, fourteen with prior experience teaching in Africa, two former academic vice-presidents, three deans, about twelve former department chairs, and one Rhodes Scholar (St. Mary's University 2000).

In addition to the UEP, the Gambian government is implementing the first phase of the University of The Gambia (UoG). As of 2000, three schools have been established. They are the School of Arts and Sciences, the School of Health Sciences, and the School of Agriculture (*Chronicle of Higher Education* 2000). Admission requirements to the UoG are five O-level credits, including English language, mathematics, and a core science subject. Data on student enrollment, number of faculty, administration, supporting staff, academic programs, teaching, research, and funding sources are unavailable at this stage. The establishment of the UoG is a bold and exciting step. However, this step raises some important questions:

- What will be the relationship between the UEP, the UoG, and existing postsecondary institutions in the country?
- How will they be harmonized into a coherent higher education system?
- How will such an institution be economically sustained and protected from political interference?

These are important questions that remain to be answered.

THE FUTURE OF HIGHER EDUCATION IN GAMBIA

As can be seen from this chapter, higher education in Gambia does not exist in a vacuum. Rather, it is and continues to be shaped by the socioeconomic, political, and historical realities of the country. In this chapter, I have traced the evolution of higher education in Gambia by examining its history. I believe that the two are inseparable. The chapter demonstrates that colonial Western education in Gambia was never intended to benefit the country. Consequently, the leaders of the country who took over after independence inherited a system that did not promote higher education. The leaders of post-independent Gambia shied away from establishing a higher education system in the country because it was considered expensive and to some extent elitist. However, after more than thirty-five years of nationhood, this argument has started to wither away. The alternatives to not having an internally based higher education system in Gambia are too expensive. Educating Gambians abroad is expensive and unsustainable in the long term. In addition, this practice has created a brain drain on the country's human resources that has serious long-term economic and social consequences for the country. Also, as the world's economies become more integrated, competitive, and technologically driven, only those countries that are able to harness their human resources to meet their specific needs will ultimately succeed.

The government of Gambia's Second Republic has decided to advance higher education in Gambia because the country's external and internal reality demands it. The collaboration between the Gambian government and St. Mary's University is a step in the right direction. However, an important question can be asked: How sustainable is this collaboration? Past experience has shown that such partnerships, positive though they may be, do not last very long and usually die when funding runs out. Until Gambia is able to develop a university system based on its own idiosyncratic needs, resources, and realities, outside influences will continue to mold the country's vision of higher education.

NOTE

1. The GCE stands for General Certificate of Education. It is a regional examination administered by the West African Examination Council (WAEC) to all high school leavers in Anglophone West Africa (Gambia, Ghana, Liberia, Nigeria, and Sierra Leone). The GCE is offered at the ordinary level (O-level) or advance level (A-level). The O-level version of the examination is for those in the twelfth grade, while the A-level is for those in the fourteenth grade or in a college preparatory program. Students taking the GCE O-level examination can obtain a passing score, a pass with credit, or a pass with distinction. Most universities and colleges in Anglophone Africa, the Commonwealth, and some Western European colleges recognized the GCE certificate for university or college admission. The number of subjects and level of passes required in the O-level and A-level vary from institution to institution. The GCE was inherited from the British colonial system of education and has since been reformed to meet the needs of participating countries.

REFERENCES

Ajayi, J. F. A., L. K. H. Goma, and G. A. Johnson. 1996. *The African Experience with Higher Education.* Accra, Ghana: Association of African Universities.

Chronicle of Higher Education. 2000. "Bulletin Board." *Chronicle of Higher Education* XLVI, no. 20 (January 21): B18.

Clarke, J. H. 1994. *Christopher Columbus and the Afrikan Holocaust: Slavery and the Rise of Capitalism.* Brooklyn, N.Y.: A and B Publishers Group.

Davidson, B. 1984. *The Story of Africa.* London: Mitchell Beazley Publishers.

———. 1985. *Africa in History.* London: Granada Publishing.

Davidson, B., F. K. Buah, and J. F. A. Ajayi. 1990. *A History of West Africa 1000–1800, New Edition.* Essex: Longman.

Diop, C. A. 1987. *Precolonial Black Africa.* Brooklyn, N.Y.: Lawrence Hill Books.

Directorate National Vocational Training Program. 1987. *Annual Report of Training Activities 1986–87.* Banjul, Gambia: National Vocational Training Program, Office of the Vice President.

Du Bois, W. E. B. 1965. *The World and Africa: An Inquiry into the Part Which Africa Has Played in World History.* New York: International Publishers.

Faal, D. 1991. *Peoples and Empires of Senegambia: Senegambia in History, AD 1000–1900.* Latri Kunda, Gambia: Saul's Modern Printshop.

Government of Gambia. 1975. *The Five Year Plan for Economic and Social Development 1975–76 to 1978–80.* Banjul, Gambia: Government Printers.

———. 1978. *Rural Vocational Training Project Document.* Banjul, Gambia: President's Office.

———. 1983. *The Five Year Plan for Economic and Social Development 1981–82 to 1985–86.* Banjul, Gambia: Government Printers.

———. 1988. *Education Policy, 1988–2003.* Sessional Paper no. 4. Banjul, Gambia: Book Production and Material Resource Unit.

———. 1994. *Estimates of Recurrent Revenue and Expenditure 1993/94 with Estimates of Development Expenditure 1993/94.* Banjul, Gambia: Government Printer.

———. 1996. *Revised National Education Policy, 1988–2003.* Banjul, Gambia: Book Production and Material Resource Unit.

———. 2000. *Fact Sheet: The Gambia at a Glance.* Available online at: http://www.gambia.com/govt/paper/whitepaper.html#factsheet

Gray, J. M. 1966. *A History of the Gambia.* London: Frank Cass & Co.

McPherson, M., and S. C. Radelet. 1989. *Economic Reform in the Gam-*

bia: Policies, Politics, Foreign Aid and Luck. Cambridge, Mass.: Harvard Institute for International Development, Harvard University.

New African. 1997. "Gambia's Missing Million." New African (January): 10–13.

Njie, N. S. Z., J. Manneh, W. Clarke, and J. Murdock. 1989. A Proposal for Strengthening Gambia College: A Program to the Year 2000. Brikama, Gambia: Gambia College.

Rodney, W. 1983. How Europe Underdeveloped Africa. London: Bogle-L'Ouverture Publications.

Southorn, L. 1952. The Gambia: The Story of the Groundnut Colony. London: George Allen & Unwin.

St. Mary's University. 2000. "St. Mary's University Extension Program in the Gambia." Available online at: http://www.stmarys.ca/administration/publicaffairs/gambiagrad/background/background.html

UNDP (United Nations Development Programme). 1999. Human Resources Report 1999. New York: Oxford University Press.

World Bank. 1990. Staff Appraisal Report: The Gambia Education Sector Project. Report no. 8359-GM, Population and Human Resources Operations Division, Sahelian Department, African Region.

35

Ghana

Paul Effah

GENERAL OVERVIEW

The tradition of higher education in Ghana is a proud one. Ghana's higher education sector was originally centered in universities and coped with fewer numbers; in spite of the limitations associated with the model it inherited, it became one of the best systems in Africa using resources available in the 1950s and early 1960s. Ghana initially put an emphasis on basic education because it was felt that it was the best way to raise the general level of performance in the economy. It is now increasingly clear that developing countries cannot effectively adopt and apply modern technology, or even make contributions of their own to development, without adequate higher education institutions.

The experiences of the developed and quickly developing countries point to a positive correlation between higher education, particularly science and technology, and economic growth and development. Indeed, a recent study emphasized that "sustainable poverty reduction will not be achieved without a renaissance in the higher education system of developing countries" (Ramphele and Rosovsky 2000, 7).

Following trends in most parts of Africa and beyond, higher education in Ghana has been undergoing profound changes, particularly during the past two decades. Caused by both internal and external factors, the essential problem is that enrollments are growing at a much faster rate than expansion in physical and academic infrastructure, in part because of dwindling resources.

Ghana's economy is largely dependent on the agricultural sector, which contributed 40.5 percent to the gross domestic product (GDP) in 1998, followed by services (32.1 percent) and industry (29.4 percent) (ISSER 1999). Therefore, when cocoa prices plummeted by 40 percent and gold prices reached their lowest level of $253 per ounce in 1999—while at the same time crude oil prices increased by almost 100 percent to hit over $23

per barrel—foreign inflows dwindled to the lowest levels since the introduction of the government's Structural Adjustment Program in 1983. In spite of these externally induced problems, ISSER's "The State of the Ghanaian Economy in 1999" indicates that the economy on the whole performed satisfactorily well in 1999. The GDP growth rate of 4.4 percent was, for example, marginally lower than the 1998 rate of 4.7 percent, while the budget deficit increased slightly from 6.3 percent of GDP in 1998 to 6.5 percent in 1999 (ISSER 2002, 2).

Although on the whole the GDP grew by 4.4 percent in 1999, this fell short of the 7–8 percent annual growth rate target set in *Ghana's Vision 2020*. In terms of demographic trends, the population of Ghana increased from 4.1 million in 1948 to 12.3 million in 1984. According to the recent figures released by the Ghana Statistical Service, Ghana's population was 18.4 million in 2000. The per capita gross national product (GNP) in 1992 was $450 and has since declined to hover around $400 (ISSER 2000, 2).

The *Ghana Human Development Report* (UNDP 1997) sums up the effect of these developments on education in Ghana as one of rapid expansion of facilities and numbers without commensurate improvements in quality. The development report also indicates that 67 percent of women and 40 percent of men cannot read and write, pointing out that educational subsidies benefit the better-off more than the poor.

Despite these very difficult circumstances, the higher education sector has responded in creative ways to the pressing needs of the Ghanaian society, particularly since reforms initiated by the government in 1987.

Beginning with a brief history of higher education in Ghana, the remaining sections of this chapter discuss the major challenges facing tertiary education in Ghana as well as steps being taken to address them. In the process, a number of various suggestions are made.

BEGINNINGS OF HIGHER EDUCATION IN GHANA

By 1924, Achimota College had been established in the Gold Coast (now Ghana) to provide education from kindergarten through first-year university courses in engineering. To the extent that it was engaged in the provision of some university courses, Achimota College may very well qualify as the first higher education institution in the Gold Coast. However, no policy on higher education was formulated and no institution of higher learning was established in the Gold Coast until the appointment of two high-powered commissions—the Asquith and Elliot Commissions—by the government of the United Kingdom in 1943. The Asquith Commission, under the leadership of Cyril Asquith, inquired generally into higher education in the colonies, while the Elliot Commission, under the leadership of Walter Elliot, made recommendations specifically on higher education in West Africa (Odumosu 1973). Both commissions reported in 1945.

The Asquith Commission had no doubt that a university should be established in the Gold Coast. As with universities it envisioned for other colonies, the commission took for granted that the university best suited for the Gold Coast should be run as much as possible like an English university. This explains the view held by the Asquith Commission that the universities to be established in the colonies should be fully residential, multi-faculty centers of research and self-governing societies demanding from their students the same requirements and standards as British universities (Odumosu 1973).

It is not surprising that English became the medium of instruction in the Gold Coast. The Elliot Commission recommended the establishment of one university college each in Nigeria and the Gold Coast. On the basis, however, that secondary school teaching was not sufficiently widespread or of a quality that could sustain the numbers required for a viable university in both Nigeria and the Gold Coast, a minority report argued for the establishment of only one institution of university rank to serve the whole of British West Africa (cited in Daniel 1997).

Although inclined to proceed on the basis of the minority report, the British government gave in to pressures from the people of the Gold Coast and the country's willingness to make financial contributions. By an ordinance on August 11, 1948, the University College of the Gold Coast was established and formed a special relationship with the University of London. In 1961, by a parliamentary act of independent Ghana (Act 79 of August 22, 1961), the University College attained sovereign university status with powers to award its own degrees.

The reasons for modeling the University College of the Gold Coast on British universities are not very far-fetched. As a result of nationalist activities manifested in various forms of agitation for political independence, self-government for the colony had become imminent by the mid-1940s. Training men and women to take over from the colonial administration was therefore a top priority for the British government.

The second institution of higher learning in the country was the Kumasi College of Technology, which was established in October 1951. Moses Antwi has chronicled the various stages of the college in *Education, Society and Development in Ghana*

(Antwi 1992). Officially opened in January 1952, the Kumasi College of Technology was upgraded in 1961 to university status as the Kwame Nkrumah University of Science and Technology. Following the change of government in 1966, its name was changed to University of Science and Technology. In 1998, the name of the university was reverted by a parliamentary act (Act 559 of 1998) to the Kwame Nkrumah University of Science and Technology (KNUST).

The establishment of a third institution of higher learning at Cape Coast was not unrelated to developments in the lower levels of education. The Ten-Year Plan for Education Development drawn up in 1946 by the colonial government, the Accelerated Development Plan of 1951, and the subsequent Education Act of 1961, which made primary and middle school education free and compulsory, provided for a wide expansion and improvement of primary, secondary, and technical education and teacher training, all of which required a massive increase in the number of professional teachers. The University College of Cape Coast (UCC) was established in 1962 to meet this urgent demand. Originally designated the University College of Science Education, the University College of Cape Coast was established "in special relationship" with the University of Ghana until it gained its full university status and became the University of Cape Coast by a parliamentary act in 1971 (Act 390).

Two new universities—the University for Development Studies (UDS), headquartered in Tamale, Northern Region, and the University College of Education of Winneba (UCEW)—have been established since 1992. Beyond improving access, UDS was established to introduce new action-oriented degree programs in areas of development priority, to emphasize practical field training, and to adopt community-based educational systems and problem-based learning approaches. The university's principal objective in this regard is to address the deprivations and environmental problems that characterize northern Ghana and rural areas throughout the country. The UDS was expected to have campuses in four administrative regions in northern Ghana (Brong Ahafo, Northern, Upper East, and Upper West), and it was also established to ensure equity in the spatial distribution of universities since the other public universities had been located in the south and central parts of the country.

Established in special relationship with the University of Cape Coast in 1992, the UCEW is an amalgamation of previously diploma-awarding institutions under the Ghana Education Service located at Winneba, Kumasi, and Mampong.

Besides increasing access, the extreme pressure to train professional teachers for basic education created by the constitutional requirement for free, compulsory, and universal basic education (FCUBE) largely accounted for the establishment of UCEW.

CURRENT TRENDS AND CHANGING PATTERNS IN TERTIARY EDUCATION

By the early 1980s, the need for reforming Ghana's educational system had become apparent. In an address at a national workshop on educational reforms on January 14, 1987, Professor N. K. Dzobo, one-time dean of the Faculty of Education at the

University of Cape Coast and chairman of an education committee in 1973, expressed strong sentiments that put the need for educational reforms in historical perspective. He said:

> In spite of the bold educational innovative measures of the 1920's and of the subsequent ones, Ghana's formal educational system remained western and predominantly academic and elitist. As a result of the Accelerated Development Plan for Education in 1951, the pre-university educational system has become increasingly dysfunctional as it turns out a lot of school-leavers who have no marketable skills, neither do they have the mind to go into self-employment ventures. These school-leavers could see no bright future for themselves and they come to constitute a veritable economic and social problem for our society to solve. (N. K. Dzobo, quoted in Ministry of Education 1998, 12–13)

Consequently, Ghana introduced new educational reforms in 1987 to remedy the deficiencies of the country's educational system. The reforms sought, among other things, to

- Increase access to education at all levels to provide expansion and equity
- Improve institutional infrastructure, pedagogic efficiency, and effectiveness
- Expand school curricula to provide for academic, cultural, technical, and vocational subjects
- Change the structure of education by reducing the length of pre-university education from 17 to 12 years.

Basic education, defined as six years of primary school and three years of junior secondary school, was made compulsory for all children (to be followed by a three-year senior secondary school), while all postsecondary education was classified as tertiary education.

The reforms at the tertiary level were preceded by the appointment of a University Rationalization Committee (URC) by the government of the Provisional National Defence Council (PNDC) chaired in 1987 by Deputy Secretary of Education Esi Sutherland-Addy. The URC report formed the basis of the government white paper on the reforms to the tertiary education system in 1991, which sought to achieve eleven policy objectives, including the following:

- Expand access to tertiary education, including a significant increase in the proportion of women students
- Establish a stable and sustainable system for funding tertiary education
- Reverse the declining quality of education and restructure enrollment and output in the provision of skills in science, technology, social sciences, and humanities in relation to national needs
- Create institutional capacities for monitoring quality and evaluating policy in the tertiary education sector (Ministry of Education 1991)

MAJOR ISSUES IN TERTIARY EDUCATION

Tertiary education in Africa faces serious challenges. These have been aptly summed up by John S. Daniel:

The Higher Education crisis has five components: inability to accommodate the volume and variety of student demand; education is too costly and not sufficiently relevant to the labor market; teaching methods are too inflexible to accommodate a diverse student body; educational quality is not assured; and the university sense of academic community is being eroded (cited in Saint 1999, 1).

One may add inadequate funding to this list. In the sections that follow, these challenges are discussed, beginning with the need to expand access.

ACCESS TO TERTIARY EDUCATION

Available statistics suggest that there has been a significant expansion in enrollment at the tertiary level since the beginning of the educational reforms in Ghana. Enrollment in universities, for example, increased by 165 percent from 11,857 in 1991–1992 to 31,460 in 1998–1999. The polytechnics registered an increase from 1,558 in 1993–1994, when they were upgraded to tertiary status, to 12,926 in 1998–1999, representing an increase of 730 percent. The phenomenal increase in enrollment in the polytechnics was due partly to the opening of two new polytechnics at Sunyani and Koforidua in 1996 and the introduction of more programs.

Within a period of thirteen years—from 1983 to 1996—total enrollment in universities and polytechnics thus increased by 162 percent. This figure would have been higher if enrollment in other tertiary institutions, such as the Institute of Professional Studies and the Ghana Institute of Languages, had been taken into account. It is important to note that there were no admissions into the universities in 1995–1996 academic year because of the closure of the universities following a strike by the University Teachers Association of Ghana (UTAG) to back its demand for improved conditions of service.

Enrollment of women as a percentage of total enrollment increased in the universities from 21 percent in 1991–1992 to 26 percent in 1998–1999. The figures for the polytechnics for 1993–1994 and 1998–1999 were 16 percent and 21 percent, respectively. In spite of the expansion in enrollment at the tertiary level, the participation rate for the 18–21 age group in tertiary education is less than 3 percent in Ghana, compared to participation rates of between 30 and 40 percent for the corresponding age groups in the developed countries.

Figures available from the Secondary Division of the Ghana Education Service (GES) show that there were 57,708 final year students in public senior secondary schools in the 1996–1997 academic year, while 83,198 candidates from both public and private senior secondary schools were available to write the university entrance examinations (UEE) in 1997. Of this number, only 9,730 were shortlisted. The UEE was abolished in 1999 when it was observed that there was a higher degree of correlation between the performance of students at the UEE and the level of attainment at the senior secondary school certificate (SSSC) examination. Starting with the 1999–2000 academic year, university admissions have been based on the performance of students at the SSSC examinations.

Given the current demographic trends in Ghana, it is clear

that the demand for tertiary education can no longer be met within the existing policy framework. Within the West African subregion, Ghana, with a population of 18.4 million (about 4 million more than the estimated population of the Ivory Coast) had a tertiary enrollment of 36,000 in 1996, representing 69 percent of the Ivory Coast's enrollment of 52,228 (Saint 1999). Expanding access to tertiary education is rather urgent. A key issue to address in meeting this need is distance education.

Serious discussions about the introduction of distance education in Ghana did not begin until about the late 1980s. Distance education is, however, not entirely unprecedented, having been tried in a variety of forms by the Institute of Adult Education of the University of Ghana since the 1960s. Distance education has the advantage of offering flexibility in course design and delivery. Experiences from Africa and beyond also show that it can reach more students, particularly women, than the conventional methods and at a lower cost per student.

Distance education did not succeed in Ghana in the past because it was not adopted as a national strategy. In addition, it was developed to the exclusion of improvements in information and communications technologies. It is not enough to design and write course materials for distance education. Such a system also requires an adequate information and communications infrastructure. Both teachers and students should not only be computer literate but should also have access to computers and the relevant software packages.

Ghana has adopted a dual-mode approach, which combines on-campus instruction with distance education. A national coordinator was appointed in 1994, while a National Council for Distance Education was established in 1995. With the exception of the University for Development Studies, all other universities are expected to participate in the distance education programs. Lecturers have been commissioned to write course materials. Although implementation has generally been slow, the University College of Education of Winneba has already admitted its first batch of students into the distance education program.

Further progress in the implementation of distance education will depend on the realization by all stakeholders that distance education is one of the key routes for expanding education, particularly at the tertiary level. More commitment to the implementation of distance education is required of all stakeholders. University teachers and administrators also have an important role to play in ensuring that the necessary academic infrastructure is in place.

If effectively implemented, distance education will remove the barrier that residential accommodation for students currently places on enrollment. It must be emphasized, however, that distance education should supplement the traditional method of instruction. It cannot be a replacement since it will take some time to generate the necessary confidence in the distance education system and provide the required infrastructure.

As part of the tertiary education reform program, polytechnics have been upgraded to tertiary status and two new universities have been established by the government. In spite of these measures, access to tertiary education is still limited. These institutions have come to face the limitations of physical and academic infrastructure that complicate expansion in the older

tertiary institutions. About 60 percent of qualified applicants do not gain admission into tertiary institutions.

One approach that has been increasingly explored in many parts of Asia and Africa since the 1980s is the development of private tertiary institutions. It is estimated that about half of South Africa's tertiary students are enrolled in private institutions, for example.

In Ghana, there has been an upsurge in the desire, particularly by religious bodies, to establish private universities. By August 2000, the National Accreditation Board had granted accreditation to eleven private tertiary institutions to offer degree programs in religious and theological studies, administration, and accountancy, among other subjects.

Feverish preparations are being made by the Catholic, Protestant, and Muslim communities in Ghana to establish their own universities. The acid test is whether or not the private universities will break new ground in the delivery of instruction and management of tertiary education. The advantage they have in this regard is that it is possible to introduce innovations in course design and delivery and to respond to changes in the labor market more quickly because they do not have the institutional history of the traditional universities.

It would be a pity if the private universities being established by the religious bodies perpetuated the old model of campus universities, only to be stifled by lack of funds and eventually to be absorbed into the public stream, as has been the history of some previous private secondary schools in the country. Although it is too early to tell, there is not much evidence from the discussions so far that the religious universities would be markedly different from the established traditional institutions.

Every encouragement should be given to the private universities by the government to enable them to expand access and reduce pressure on the public universities. Moreover, they should be given incentives to be creative in their approach to education.

While inadequate student numbers were a source of concern in the 1950s and early 1960s, early signals in the 1980s suggested that the residential system inherited from the British system, which features full board and lodging facilities, could no longer be sustained. Student numbers had far outstripped the capacity of the existing physical infrastructure. Although nonresidential status had been introduced in the universities to cope with the expansion, students who were admitted on a nonresidential basis ended up squatting in the halls with their friends, stretching the facilities to their limits. It took a real battle with the student body in the mid-1980s for the government to divest itself from feeding students in the residence halls. Further policy changes were effected in the 1998–1999 academic year when, as part of new cost-sharing measures introduced by government, students were made to pay residential facilities user fees ranging from $15.40 to $23.10 per academic year.

Student contribution toward residential facilities has encouraged private companies to provide hostels on all campuses. During 2002, following discussions with the Social Security and National Insurance Trust (SSNIT), universities signed agreements with that organization for the construction of hostels on the various campuses. At the University of Ghana, some alumni have also agreed to contribute 1 percent of their salary over a period of three years to finance the construction of a 500-room

Jubilee Hall to mark the fiftieth anniversary of the university. If these positive developments continue, there will be substantial residential accommodations to allow for considerable expansion of access at the tertiary level.

To expand access further, particularly for people who are unable to leave their workplaces, provision of part-time and work-study programs has been explored. The establishment of UCEW has been timely in this regard. A number of the university's programs, particularly at the certificate and post-diploma levels in education, are run during the long vacation. The University of Cape Coast has introduced a master's degree program in educational administration for teachers and other education officials within the Ghana Education Service on a similar basis. The School of Mines of the Kwame Nkrumah University of Science and Technology at Tarkwa also has a master's degree program for professionals that is run on a part-time basis. Such a mix of opportunities in a variety of educational settings has the advantage of making tertiary education accessible to many more people.

ISSUES OF QUALITY AND RELEVANCE

Ghana has enjoyed the reputation of having one of the most highly developed and efficient educational systems in sub-Saharan Africa. In recent times, however, this reputation has been questioned.

There are several measures of quality. These include students' performance on standardized tests, the quality of teachers, students' exposure to current knowledge and information, academic expenditure per student, student-teacher ratios, and the general state of the learning environment.

Compared with the student-teacher ratio of 12 to 1 for the sciences and 18 to 1 for the humanities approved by the National Council for Tertiary Education (NCTE), statistics from the Committee of Vice-Chancellors and Principals show ratios in the universities as high as 30 to 1 for the sciences and 40 to 1 for the humanities. The situation has been worsened by the difficulty of attracting young lecturers as the current teaching staff ages. Data on teaching and research staff at the University of Ghana, Legon, for example, show that only 0.3 percent are under 30 years old; 15.1 percent are between the ages of 31 and 40; 40.2 percent are between 41 and 50; 33.4 percent are between 51 and 60; and 11 percent are above 60 years old (University of Ghana 2000). An analysis of existing vacancies in tertiary institutions makes the situation even worse. About 40 percent of faculty positions in the universities and more than 60 percent of those in the polytechnics are vacant.

In terms of public expenditure per student, the costs computed by a Committee on the Evaluation of Tertiary Policy Objectives, commissioned by NCTE, worked out to $918 for the universities and $230 for the polytechnics for the 1997–1998 academic year (NCTE 1998), which is lower than the $1,000 per student considered the threshold below which delivering adequate education in today's world becomes difficult (Partnership for Capacity Building in Africa 1997).

Although there has been considerable improvement in infrastructure in most tertiary institutions through credit and support from donor agencies, inadequate physical and academic facilities still remain one of the factors affecting quality in tertiary institutions in Ghana.

Measures to improve quality in the tertiary sector would have to be pervasive, including improved conditions of service to attract and retain staff, expansion in physical and academic infrastructure, introduction of new information technologies, improvements in library facilities and services, and the introduction of well-structured plans for staff training and professional development. The establishment of staff development units in tertiary institutions to provide training in pedagogy, curriculum development, testing, and evaluation would also enhance effectiveness of teaching and learning.

Educational institutions should also be assessed for their degree of relevance. Relevance can be looked at from several angles, including the point of view of the training institutions, the beneficiaries (the students and their families), the government, the public and private sectors of the economy, and the society in general. In whatever form it is provided, education must have a human mission—that is, the goal of accomplishing something for society. This reinforces the idea that "education that is worth the name should have two distinct and yet complementary foci; on the one hand, it should be expected to enhance the individual's awareness of his community and its needs, and on the other, it should provide the urge to act in such a way as to contribute to the consolidation and promotion of the community's well-being" (Dickson 1986, 4).

Tertiary education should strive to meet national development objectives outlined in Ghana's Vision 2020 document. It should also prepare students for their personal development and for the labor market, which, in the present modern economy, also means preparation for the globalized market. The interests and survival of the training institutions are also important. Above all, the tertiary sector should be able to assist society to identify its problems and to help address them.

Several authors have commented on the type of education that Britain bequeathed to its former colonies. Lord Bowden, for example, expressed regret that Ghana did not have an earlier opportunity to learn from other university systems, bemoaning that "perhaps because the [British] universities had nothing to do with the creation of wealth, they were content to be centres of privilege and they boasted that they had nothing to do with industry or commerce" (1997, 18). And yet history is replete with examples of how partnerships between universities and industry have helped to promote economic growth and development. Even more significant is how trained middle-level technical labor has served as a catalyst for industrial development. Graduates of the *école polytechnique* of France, as well as those of *Technische Hochschulem* of Germany, now technical universities, both of which are reputed for their ability to teach practical skills, have helped transform the industries of France and Germany (Bowden 1977). For this reason, T. M. Yesufu (1973) notes that graduates produced from the universities modeled along those in Britain tended to be highly academic and generalist in character and deficient in professional and practical skills.

The educational reforms introduced in 1987 have initiated significant changes in curricula. The NCTE has developed standards and norms for the universities and polytechnics. The ratio of arts courses to science courses has been set at 40 to 60; the ratio of male students to female students has been set at 50 to 50; and the enrollment growth rate has been set at 10 percent for the universities and 15 percent for polytechnics.

Ghana has not yet reached the goal it set for the ratio of arts to science courses. In 1999, 12,288 out of 31,501 students in the universities (39 percent) were offered science-based courses, while the corresponding figures in polytechnics were 6,382 out of 12,963 (49 percent), as against the national target of 60 percent.

The major constraints on science education are inadequate laboratories and workshops and an insufficient number of qualified science and mathematics teachers. One of the measures that has therefore been proposed to address the situation is the training and motivation of science teachers through the introduction of incentives such as higher incremental salary credits (NCTE 1998). It is worth noting that the introduction of the senior secondary school system has begun to address this problem. A larger number of science students are now graduating from these schools, which could lead to increased enrollment in science at the tertiary level if the necessary resources are provided.

The establishment of Science Resource Centers by the Ministry of Education and the institution of a Science, Technology, and Mathematics Education clinic for girls as an activity of the Ghana Education Service have both begun to produce positive results. In order to address the issue of gender disparity in enrollment at the university level, particularly in the sciences, Professor J. Anamuah-Mensah has recommended the reintroduction of remedial teaching which was formerly offered to females with poor grades (1995, 21).

Although still grappling with problems, the establishment of the University for Development Studies has begun to make a positive impact on the communities within northern Ghana. If it is well organized and integrated, and if its innovative mission and focus are maintained, the university is capable of producing practical professionals who are socially oriented as effective development agents for the twenty-first century.

Polytechnic education is also being restructured and upgraded to produce the middle-level technical labor power that the country needs for development. Because technical and vocational education have not been emphasized and have suffered shortages of equipment and qualified staff, and because they have not been properly integrated into the educational system, these two types of education have not flourished in Ghana in the past. Before the commencement of the educational reforms in 1987, there were only twenty-four technical institutes, compared with 240 secondary schools in Ghana.

The new educational reforms have introduced significant changes. Emphasis is now being placed on technical and vocational education. Technical syllabi and examinations at technician and trade levels for programs in construction and electrical and mechanical engineering have been localized, and polytechnics now offer Higher National Diploma (HND) programs.

Although the focus of polytechnic education is clear—to train practical-oriented middle-level technical staff—the lack of avenues for academic progression has been one of the major disincentives for polytechnic education. Integration of polytechnic education into the tertiary system will allow for easier transfer of credit and further progression. The introduction of a two-year post-diploma degree program at the UCEW Kumasi campus in technical and vocational education will partially satisfy this need.

Graduate unemployment, which was not considered a problem in the early 1960s, has become an issue in recent times. In the past, the public and civil services could absorb the relatively small number of graduates who were turned out each year by the universities. The public sector is now saturated, while the private sector is growing at a very slow pace. Finding jobs has become a problem, particularly for graduates in the general arts and humanities. The education service is perhaps the only sector that still has vacancies, but even here, graduates who want places in the cities are often disappointed, as vacancies exist primarily in the rural areas.

Many graduates in recent times have pursued additional professional courses in such areas as accounting and marketing or have enrolled in postgraduate programs to enhance their marketability. One possible solution to this problem is to diversify curricula to reflect labor-market demands more closely. Another is to train students for self-employment by equipping them with practical and entrepreneurial skills, as the UDS and polytechnics have been mandated to do.

FUNDING TERTIARY EDUCATION

By far the most serious challenge facing higher education in Ghana, as elsewhere in Africa, is inadequate funding. Tertiary education institutions in Ghana are funded largely from government sources. Over the past decade, education's share of the government's discretionary budget has not exceeded 40 percent. On average, the tertiary education subsector's share has been about 12 percent of the total recurrent education budget. For example, in 2000, education's share of the government's approved discretionary budget was $204,824,621 (32 percent). Of this amount, $23,870,359 (12 percent) was allocated to the tertiary sector.

The approved recurrent budget for universities in 1998 met about 50 percent of their estimated requirements. The corresponding figure for the year 2000 is 56 percent. In the case of the polytechnics, the improvement was significant, from about 30 percent in 1998 to 58 percent of estimated requirements in 2000. In spite of these increases, the 2000 budget still leaves serious institutional budgetary gaps. (See Table 35.1 for details.)

Given trends in the global economy, particularly the drop in the prices of cocoa and gold, major foreign exchange earners for Ghana, and competing demands from other sectors of the economy such as health and agriculture, tertiary education cannot expect to receive higher funding levels from government in the coming years. The indications are that the quality of tertiary education may be compromised unless the sources of funding are diversified.

At several forums, including the National Education Forum held in November 1999, stakeholders in Ghana's education system have agreed on the need for cost-sharing in tertiary education. Government policy on cost-sharing is defined in the White Paper on the Reforms to the Tertiary Education System: "It is intended to develop a system of cost sharing between govern-

Table 35.1. Recurrent Budget Estimates for Universities and Polytechnics in Ghana, 2000

Institution	Estimated Requirement (Units in US$)*	Amount Granted (Units in US$)	Percentage of Requirement Granted
Universities			
University of Ghana	10,318,233	6,329,543	61.34
Kwame Nkrumah University of Science and Technology	9,521,265	5,297,720	55.64
University College of Cape Coast	5,530,265	3,003,068	54.30
University for Development Studies	1,792,600	1,188,907	66.32
University College of Education of Winneba	4,682,476	2,123,708	45.35
Total Universities	31,844,839	17,942,946	56.34
Polytechnics			
Accra	109,342	54,209	49.58
Kumasi	105,061	55,749	53.06
Takoradi	102,366	52,207	51.00
Ho	70,888	50,359	71.04
Cape Coast	57,536	26,643	46.31
Tamale	65,066	44,045	67.69
Sunyani	71,873	45,277	63.00
Koforidua	33,003	20,020	60.66
Total Polytechnics	615,135	348,509	56.66

*Bank of Ghana Mid Rate in August 2000: US$1 = ¢6,493.36.

Source: National Council for Tertiary Education 2000.

ment, the student population and the private sector," although tuition is free for Ghanaian nationals (Ministry of Education 1991, 8). Although the principle of cost-sharing has been accepted by most stakeholders, its implementation has often been problematic. The introduction of academic facilities user fees, ranging from $44.66 for humanities to $100.10 for medicine during the 1999–2000 academic year, led to student protests and demonstrations and the closure of the universities. Under pressure from students, the government granted a rebate of 30 percent on the fees. The students were not satisfied, and the matter was further taken to Parliament by the National Union of Ghana Students (NUGS) for resolution.

Given that fewer than 3 percent of the 18–23 age group have access to tertiary education in Ghana, the assertion by Damtew Teferra that "a strong case can be made by pointing out that poor tax payers should not have to subsidize the education of the children of the affluent" is very pertinent (1999, 7). Difficult as it may be to implement, contributions from students toward the use of academic and residential facilities can improve the provision of tertiary education in Ghana.

The emergence of private tertiary institutions—which have already been accredited in Ghana by the National Accreditation Board—has strengthened the case that students and parents who are capable and are willing should pay fees in public tertiary institutions, in spite of government's tuition-free policy. This system has been tried with some degree of success in Uganda. The possibility of its implementation in Ghana should be explored. It is necessary, however, to ensure that deprived regions, the poor, and women are not disenfranchised in the process.

A major landmark in the history of education in Ghana was the establishment in 2000 of an Education Trust Fund by the government. Under this fund, an amount equivalent to 20 percent of the prevailing rate of the Value Added Tax collected (12 percent) is paid into the Ghana Education Trust Fund for educational purposes. The fund is intended to supplement the provision of education at all levels by government, to develop and maintain educational infrastructure, to provide supplementary funding for the granting of scholarships to gifted but needy students and of loans to students, and to offer grants for research and for the training of exceptional students to become teachers (Ghana Education Trust Fund Act 2000, Act 581).

Over the years, the government has also instituted scholarships and grants for students with exceptional academic promise, as well as other groups of students required to fulfill identified labor requirements of the country. Postgraduate and disabled students also benefit from the scheme.

Public interest in the provision of scholarships has been rekindled in recent times. Of particular importance is an educational fund established by Otumfuo Osei Tutu II, the Asantehene, the traditional head of the Ashantis. District assemblies, business entities, and traditional authorities are all establishing scholarship schemes in their respective areas. This is a positive trend that many hope will be sustained.

Introduced over a decade ago, the policy on student loans has had mixed results. It has enabled genuinely needy students to maintain themselves at the university and, more recently, at the polytechnics and other tertiary institutions. On the other hand, the program has accumulated a substantial amount of debt for the Social Security and National Insurance Trust (SSNIT), the operators of the scheme, because of the government's inability to pay the agreed-upon interest on the loans and the low rate of loan recovery. The scheme has also put a lot of pressure on workers' contributions, which are primarily meant to fund pension and other social security benefits.

Student numbers increased from 8,138 in 1989 to 50,000 in 1999, while the average loan increased from $7.70 to $154 per student during the same period. Interest on student loans is subsidized by the government. While the prevailing interest rate is about 22.3 percent, students are granted the loan at the rate of 10 percent. Using the total of 50,000 students and the subsidy of 12.3 percent on the interest rate, the government's subsidy on interest for the 1999–2000 academic year alone worked out to some $954,822.

The student loan scheme should be reviewed and made self-sustaining. The possibility of establishing a company to operate the program on behalf of SSNIT should be explored. Although the introduction of guarantors has improved loan recovery, the use of private agencies to locate students and to recover loans on behalf of SSNIT would further facilitate loan recovery. The existing law, PNDC Law 276 (1992), should also be reviewed to make it obligatory for organizations that employ students after graduation to deduct their loan payments from their paychecks on behalf of SSNIT.

At one of the forums on funding tertiary education held at Akosombo in 1997, the ideal distribution of contributions by government, students, the private sector, and tertiary institutions was determined to be 70, 10, 10, and 10 percent, respectively. If these levels were accepted for implementation by all stakeholders, tertiary education would see considerable improvement.

In Ghana, collaboration between tertiary institutions and the private sector has not been exploited effectively. Several such possibilities exist, including the establishment of joint research projects, appointment of visiting professorships from business and industry, the design of training programs to suit the specific needs of industry, and industrial training and apprenticeship for students of tertiary institutions. While universities and polytechnics would receive additional income and enrich their programs with industrial know-how, business and industry would improve their products by using new knowledge and technology through collaboration.

Some argue that the business of the university is to teach, research, and provide public services—not to make money. But without compromising the central mission of the university, it is possible to engage in income-generating activities that also promote the aims of the academic enterprise. Income generation has not made much impact in tertiary institutions in the past because it has not been pursued professionally. It is possible to generate income from alumni, consultancies, and other business ventures. The construction of Jubilee Hall at the University of Ghana from contributions of alumni suggests what alumni can do if they are effectively mobilized.

Income-generating activities would enable institutions and faculty to have access to additional income; they would also enhance institutional and individual capabilities and promote efficiency and harmony.

STRUCTURE, ADMINISTRATION, AND GOVERNANCE

Tertiary institutions in Ghana have a two-tier, or bicameral, system of governance. They have councils vested with overall responsibility for matters relating to finance, development, appointments, and discipline. In addition, senates or academic boards are responsible for all academic matters. A typical University Council consists of a chair and three other members appointed by government; the vice-chancellor; representatives of faculty, students', and workers' associations; and alumni, as well as representatives from the Ministry of Education in some cases.

Although the private sector does not have representation in its own right on most councils, appointments made by government normally reflect the interests of business and industry. A representative of the National Council for Tertiary Education or Ministry of Education, the pro-vice-chancellor, the finance officer, and the registrar, who is the secretary, generally attend council meetings. The titular head of the university is the chancellor. Until the 1992 constitution came into effect, the chancellor was the head of state.

The general management of tertiary institutions is undertaken through an elaborate system of committees and boards. The details of this system are set out in the statutes of the respective institutions. The basic unit in a university is the department, which is normally headed by a professor on rotational basis for a two- to three-year period. A combination of departments with related interests and activities constitutes a faculty, which is headed by a dean, who is normally elected from among the academic staff of the faculty.

Student administration is organized through student representation on the Students Representative Council, which is campus-wide, and the Junior Common Room, which is hall-based. The National Union of Ghana Students (NUGS) and, more recently, the Ghana National Union of Polytechnic Students (GNUPS) operate on a national level.

The minister of education has ministerial oversight of all levels of education. A National Council for Tertiary Education advises the minister on all matters relating to the development of tertiary education and also serves as a buffer between the government and the tertiary institutions. The universities and polytechnics also have the Committee of Vice-Chancellors and Principals and the Conference of Polytechnic Principals, both of which are nonstatutory bodies that serve as forums for informal consultation on matters of common interest to their respective institutions.

Until the government divested itself of managing student board plans in the mid-1980s, issues relating to board and lodging constituted a major source of strikes and student demonstrations. Following the introduction of the new educational reforms in 1987, issues relating to cost-sharing have been high on the agenda of student protests. In 1999, the NUGS protested an increase in the academic facilities user fees paid by students, which led to the closure of the universities.

As far as academic staff and other workers of the university are concerned, one major source of conflict has been poor salaries and conditions of service. To back their demands for better salaries and conditions of service, the University Teachers Association of Ghana struck for nine months in 1995, followed by a Polytechnic Teachers Association of Ghana (POTAG) strike in 1997 for similar reasons.

Conflict also arises from the relationship that exists between the university and government, especially with regard to the central issue of academic freedom and autonomy. The concepts of freedom and autonomy are indispensable values in the process of knowledge creation and the dissemination and application of research, which are the core functions of the university. Freedom and autonomy imply that universities have the freedom to select their students, appoint and remove staff, determine the content of academic programs, and control standards independently of government interference.

At times in the past, the government attempted to press unpopular measures on the university. In the 1960s, for example, the government decided to appoint "special professors" directly responsible to the president, who was also the chancellor. Attempts were also made to control the appointment of heads of departments (Ajayi, Goma, and Johnson 1996).

By and large, it can be said that the institutional structure, the legal framework provided for in acts and statutes, and the substantial amount of authority vested in the elaborate system of committees and boards insulate the academic community from outside forces and interference. Research can be conducted in any area without external constraints, while professors are free to express their views on any matter, whether it be academic or nonacademic. Ample evidence of academic freedom and autonomy abounds in Ghana, as reflected in inaugural speeches, interfaculty and valedictory lectures given by the academic community, and public discussions and publications.

The academic community, however, often raises some concerns in relation to academic freedom and autonomy. The academic institutions are unhappy about the situation in which they are often asked to conform to rules and regulations imposed by ministries and government departments.

Many also feel that the Ministry of Education does not have the expertise needed to handle issues affecting the higher education sector, which is much more complex than basic education. While one school of thought advocates a separate ministry for higher education, another believes that an easier option is to appoint an experienced desk officer for higher education in the Ministry of Education.

While recognizing that government intrusion into academic institutions could stifle them, absolute institutional autonomy is not possible so long as the government continues to fund higher education. In a period in which resources are increasingly scarce and institutions are being urged to cut down waste and to do more with fewer resources, the need for efficient management of resources will continue to be emphasized. The government will continue to give general direction for both public and private tertiary institutions through the appropriate agencies.

RESEARCH: CHALLENGES AND DILEMMAS

Research forms an integral part of the mission of the university. In fact, it is so important that it is often acknowledged as the hallmark of the university. Apart from helping to retain faculty and to train academic and professional staff, its importance lies in the fact that it is the process through which new knowledge is transmitted to society. Michael Daxner has stated the point forcefully: "The university of the future will be largely defined by its research or there will be no university" (Daxner 1999, 59).

In the view of David Balme, the first principal of the University College of the Gold Coast (now Ghana), if a university tried to solve an applied problem without relating it to basic scientific theory, the answer it would give would be a bad one and the university would have betrayed the trust reposed in it (Sey 1989).

Two broad categories of research may be identified; namely, basic and applied research. Basic research is experimental or theoretical work undertaken primarily to acquire new knowledge. This is important if the university is not to be starved of knowledge. But equally important is applied research, which is original investigation directed toward a specific practical aim or objective (OECD'S 1993 Frascati Manual, cited in Daxner 1999, 61).

There is a further debate about the desirability of creating teaching universities. The basis of this debate is the exponential expansion in enrollment at the tertiary level, which has led some to believe that creating purely teaching universities might address the problem. Examples of cases in which excellent teachers have either been dismissed or denied promotion because of poor performance in the area of research have been cited in support of this argument. In most universities in Europe and Africa, contract appointments require academic staff to advance their subjects by research, teaching, and extension, in that order of emphasis, which reflects the importance of research. Teachers at purely teaching universities might become stale in the present knowledge-based and globalized economy if they do not undertake research.

There are other forms of tertiary institutions than the university; colleges, polytechnics, and other tertiary institutions are not as heavily research based. A vocational institution at any level would be preoccupied with the promotion of teaching and learning and the transmission of practical knowledge directly related to occupations or jobs, while a polytechnic would primarily offer a wide range of knowledge and expertise covering theoretical and practical experience.

In a lecture entitled "The University: Does it Have a Future?," Professor Henry Wasser of the City University of New York emphasized the uniqueness of the mission of the university, noting that "except for its core function which is uniquely its own, any one or even all its functions can be discharged by other bodies" (Wasser 1996, 10). A university may farm out remedial or adjunct teaching to other tertiary institutions but not its research function, which remains central to its mission. A university that functions only on knowledge generated by other institutions cannot long survive.

The economic importance of research cannot be underestimated. It is estimated that Canadian university research adds around $15.5 billion each year to Canada's economy (in Canadian dollars) creating approximately 150,000 to 200,000 jobs (Association of Universities and Colleges of Canada 1998).

In the early years of Ghana's independence, a good number of locally trained graduates were awarded scholarships to pursue postgraduate programs abroad. After graduation, many of these students had the opportunity to publish aspects of their research work. Besides the availability of avenues for publication, a system of apprenticeship through which younger academic staff served their research tutelage under more experienced academics existed. Research was largely the fundamental type strongly influenced by the scientific community through the process of peer review and assessment and funded at the institutional level through the University Research and Conferences Committees.

During the last two decades or so, the overall research performance of African universities as a whole has been clearly deficient (Ajayi, Goma, and Johnson 1996). Research output and the generation of new knowledge have lagged far behind the training accomplishment of the African universities (Saint 1992). The reasons include the lack of clearly articulated educational and research priorities at both national and institutional levels (Kwapong 1979); increasing involvement of academic staff in undergraduate teaching because of the growing numbers of students, making it increasingly difficult to undertake research; lack of opportunities for sabbatical leave, conferences, and seminars; and a general lack of strong academic leadership in various departments, faculties, and research units (Ajayi, Goma, and Johnson 1996).

By far the biggest obstacle in the area of research appears to be financial deprivation. It is estimated that only about 0.1 percent of GNP is spent on research in Africa, compared to about 2 percent in the developed countries (Saint 1992). Annual budgetary allocations for research in most African universities are generally small, ranging from 0 percent to 3.8 percent (Ajayi, Goma, and Johnson 1996).

Available data on expenditures on research and development in Ghana show a declining trend from around 0.7 percent of GNP in the mid-1970s to 0.1–0.2 percent of GNP in 1983–1987 (More 1989, cited in Biggs, Shah, and Srivastava 1995). There is little or no evidence to suggest that this trend has changed. Estimates from the 2000 tertiary-sector budget show that an amount equivalent to $1,392,499 (22 percent of its approved budget) was allocated to the University of Ghana's ten research institutes for their operations. The corresponding figures for the eight research institutes of Kwame Nkrumah University of Science and Technology was $291,375 (5.5 percent), compared with $102,104 (3.4 percent) for the three research institutes at University College of Cape Coast (NCTE Budget 2000).

Academic staff also receive research allowances to assist with their research activities. Since March 1, 2000, this allowance has been increased from $92.40 to $338.81 per annum.

Individual researchers and departments depend more on their own resourcefulness for research activities. Some have been more enterprising in this respect and have been able to attract more funding for research than others because of the nature of academic leadership they offer and their relative research capabilities.

Although salaries of academic staff have seen some improvements during the past decade, a relatively poor salary structure still persists. Using salaries of academic staff in selected African countries, Bankole Oni shows that the pay package for the average Ghanaian professor is about 8.7 percent of that of her or his counterparts in South Africa and 10 percent of that of counterparts in Zimbabwe (Oni 2000).

A comparative salary analysis undertaken by a Salary Review Commission in the Civil Service and other sectors in Ghana in 1993 revealed that salary levels in sectors such as energy, finance, revenue collection, and media were all higher than those of the universities (Salary Review Commission 1993). As a result, some individual researchers and departments have tended to concentrate on consultancies, which more often serve the narrow professional interest of the researcher (Ajayi, Goma, and Johnson 1996).

Postgraduate training in universities in Ghana is still at its lowest ebb after three to four decades of their existence. Out of a total enrollment of 11,865 at the University of Ghana for the year 2000, only 1,265 (10.66 percent) are pursuing postgraduate studies. At the University of Cape Coast, postgraduate students represent 6 percent of total enrollment.

To promote research, a list of issues needs to be considered; correct policy orientation, vision and leadership, institutional changes of a far-reaching nature, empowerment of researchers, creation of space for young talent, and adequate funding are among the most critical ones (Bandaranayake 2000). One way of overcoming the difficulty of finding outlets for publication of research results, particularly for young academics, is to attach the younger professors to senior colleagues through a system of apprenticeship or mentoring to give them the necessary experience and help them gain local and international recognition (Effah 1998).

One of the initiatives taken in recent times is an assessment of the capacities of universities and research institutions with a view to identifying and promoting efficiency in operations and prospects for income generation. A number of research institutions, such as the Council for Scientific and Industrial Research, the Ghana Atomic Energy Commission, and the Ghana Academy of Arts and Sciences, are contributing to the quest for knowledge and improvement in the quality of life of the people. The United Nations University Institute for Natural Resources in Africa, based at the University of Ghana, is also strengthening the capacities of research institutions and is coordinating research and advanced training in the use and management of Africa's natural resources. Universities need to strengthen their links and collaboration with governmental, nongovernmental, and research institutions and with donor agencies to promote intersectoral and interdisciplinary research, avoid duplication of efforts, and, in the process, enhance research output and dissemination and application of research results.

BRAIN DRAIN

Another problem that has increasingly become one of the critical issues in Ghana and many developing countries in recent times is brain drain—the loss of qualified and talented professionals to other countries. Brain drain constitutes a significant financial and economic loss for the African continent and is incapacitating Africa's public and private sectors. According to ACP-EU (African Caribbean and Pacific—European Union) reports, Africa lost 60,000 professionals (doctors, engineers, lecturers, etc.) between 1985 and 1990, which has cost the continent an estimated $1.2 billion. The net effect is a loss of human capital and a loss of knowledge and critical capacities in all sectors.

Against the backdrop of the continuing trend in human capital flight from the continent to developed countries and the implication of this for development capacity, the question of brain drain and capacity building was adopted as the theme for a regional conference held in Addis Ababa, Ethiopia, on February 22–24, 2000. Available statistics confirm that many Ghanaian professionals are in other countries developing the social capabilities of their host nations. Although the issue of the flight of human capital has affected almost all professions, it is critical in the case of medical doctors. In 1998, for example, nearly 120 doctors were estimated to have emigrated from Ghana. Between 600–700 Ghanaian physicians, representing about 50 percent of the total population of doctors in the country, are known to be practicing in the United States alone. The situation with other professions may be equally alarming but may not have been highlighted because of lack of sufficient data.

The causes of brain drain include poor working conditions, inadequate remuneration, lack of equipment, lack of employment benefits and job security, political instability, limited opportunities for postgraduate studies (particularly in scientific and technological fields), and the increasing mismatch between training programs and labor-market demand.

When governments and families invest in human capital through training and education, they expect some return on their investment after the individual who has received the training becomes economically active. Seen in this regard, brain drain is an economic loss. Countries have therefore worked to implement strategies to counteract this loss, including:

• Restrictive policies, such as written agreements to serve for a specified number of years and compulsory national service
• Incentive policies designed to make emigration less attractive
• Policies designed to tax the individual migrant or host country to compensate the country of origin for the loss of human capital

These policies have generally not been very effective for a number of reasons. Restrictive policies are only temporary deterrents for migration, incentive policies are difficult to sustain because developing countries are not in a position to offer salaries and infrastructure comparable to the developed countries, and compensatory policies are problematic because of the difficulty in quantifying the loss to the country of origin in monetary terms.

Some have proposed a new approach, referred to as "brain gain strategy," involving two options—the return and the Diaspora options.

The return option, which has been implemented in Africa since the 1970s, involves attempts by countries to encourage their highly skilled expatriates to return home. Within the framework of the International Organization for Migration (IOM), qualified African nationals have been helped to return to Africa. The program has helped more than seventy Ghanaian professionals return. Although some success has been achieved, Ghana, as with most other countries in Africa, has not been able to implement the return option effectively because of the difficulty matching the salaries and infrastructure available in the more developed countries.

The Diaspora option is based on network approaches. It sees brain drain not as a loss but a potential gain to the country of origin. Highly skilled expatriates are looked upon as a pool of potentially useful human resources for the country of origin. Through a network of connections, this strategy gives expatriates the opportunity to transfer their expertise and skills to the country of origin without necessarily returning home permanently.

To take advantage of expertise and skills of Ghanaian professionals worldwide, a number of actions need to be taken:

• Set up a mechanism for taking an inventory of Ghanaian professionals outside the country that indicates their skills and areas of specialization. The Ghanaian embassies and missions abroad, as well as universities and other research and tertiary institutions, could assist in this regard.
• Adopt a more aggressive policy of networking with intellectuals who have migrated. To this end, encourage formation of expert groups abroad to be linked with existing networks.
• Link educational institutions to the system of diasporic networks and promote teaching, learning, research, and distance education through information communications technologies such as the Internet and teleconferencing.
• Encourage ministries, departments, and agencies to use the services of Ghanaian professionals abroad through such schemes as short stays, technical assistance, sabbaticals, and consultancies.

FUTURE DEVELOPMENTS

The foregoing discussions point to two main conclusions. One is that the growth and development of the economy of Ghana is inextricably linked to developments in its tertiary education system. The other is that the demands and pressures placed on tertiary education are bound to be complex and far-reaching in the twenty-first century. There are major obstacles to overcome. The Task Force on Higher Education and Society (2000) has identified, among other obstacles, absence of vision, lack of political and financial commitment, a knowledge gap between developed and developing countries, and attraction to wealthier countries arising from globalization.

As pressure on the demand for tertiary education mounts due to changing demographic trends, and financial resources continue to dwindle, quality is likely to be compromised. Three broad strategies are immediately required. The first is a repositioning of tertiary education to reflect the priorities of all its stakeholders. Second, a conscious effort should be made to increase resources available to tertiary education. Third, resource utilization, which is often taken for granted, needs to be significantly improved.

As a reminder, some of the critical steps that need to be taken are to

- Improve academic and physical infrastructure
- Review curricula and programs to meet the changing needs of society and the labor market
- Recruit, motivate, retain, and develop qualified staff
- Increase access, paying particular attention to women and the economically and socially disadvantaged
- Promote science, technology, and research
- Strengthen institutional management and governance
- Diversify sources of funding
- Introduce a mix of opportunities and course offerings to cater to the needs of working people

In the new millennium, the indications are that there will be a gradual shift from the public sector to the private sector as the driving force of economic growth. This will demand a qualitative change in the output of tertiary education institutions.

Distance education should become a more important supplement to the traditional mode of instruction. These projects cannot be undertaken to the exclusion of improvements in information technology, which must be integrated into the tertiary education system to take advantage of developments in the globalized economy.

If Ghana's concern is sustainable development, then improving tertiary education is a necessity. The government's commitment and role as a facilitator in promoting tertiary education will be increasingly crucial in the years ahead.

REFERENCES

Ajayi, J. F. A., L. K. H. Goma, and G. A. Johnson. 1996. *The African Experience with Higher Education*. Accra: AAU (Association of African Universities).

Anamuah-Mensah, J. 2000. *The Race against Underdevelopment: A Mirage or Reality*. Accra: Ghana Universities Press.

Antwi, K. M. 1992. *Education, Society and Development in Ghana*. Accra: Unimax Publishers.

Association of Universities and Colleges of Canada. 1998. *Higher Education in Canada: A Tradition of Innovation and Success*. Ottawa: Association of Universities and Colleges of Canada.

Bandaranayake, S. 1999. "Social Science Research in Sri Lankan Universities." *The Bulletin of Current Documentation of the Association of Commonwealth Universities*, no. 139, 11.

Biggs, T., M. Shah, and P. Srivastava. 1995. *Technological Capacities and Learning in African Enterprises*. Washington, D.C.: World Bank.

Bowden, L. 1977. "The Role of Universities in the Modern World." Paper delivered at the R. B Baffour Memorial Lectures, Kumasi, University of Science and Technology.

Daniel, G. F. 1997. "The Universities of Ghana." In *Commonwealth of Universities Yearbook, 1996/97*. London: Association of Commonwealth Universities.

Daxner, M. 1999. "Strategic Partnership in European Higher Education." In G. B. Freedman and G. A. Goerke, eds., *The Future of International Higher Education: Directions and Opportunities*. Vol. 1,

49–92. Houston: Institute for the Future of Higher Education, International Higher Education Monograph Services, University of Houston.

Dickson, K. A. 1986. "The Challenges of Education." In *Education, Human Values and Nation Building*. Proceedings of the Ghana Academic of Arts and Sciences, XXV, 1–16.

Effah, P. 1998. "The Training and Development of Academic Librarians in Ghana." *Library Management* 19, nos. 1 and 2: 37–41.

ISSER (Institute of Statistical, Social and Economic Research). 1999. *The State of the Ghanaian Economy in 1998*. Legon: ISSER, University of Ghana.

———. 2000. *The State of the Ghanaian Economy in 1999*. Legon: ISSER, University of Ghana.

Kwapong, A. A. 1979. *Higher Education and Development in Africa Today: A Reappraisal*. The J. B. Danquah Memorial Lectures, Twelfth Series, March. Accra: Ghana Academy of Arts and Sciences.

Ministry of Education. 1991. "The White Paper on the Reform to the Tertiary Education System." WP No 3/91. Accra: Ministry of Education.

———. 1998. "A Decade of Educational Reforms: Preparation for the Challenges of a New Millennium." A background paper prepared for the Ministry of Education by the Forum Technical Committee, November, 12–13.

NCTE (National Council for Tertiary Education). 1998. *Report of the Committee on Evaluation of Policy Objectives of the Reforms to the Tertiary Education System*. Accra: NCTE.

National Education Forum. 1999. *A Background Paper Prepared for the Ministry of Education by the Forum Technical Committee*. Accra: National Education Forum.

Odumosu, T. P. 1973. "Government and University in a Developing Society." Public lecture delivered during the University of Ife tenth anniversary celebrations, October. Ibadan: Abeodun Printing Works.

Oni, B. 2000. "Capacity Building Effort and Brain Drain in Nigerian Universities." Paper presented at the Regional Conference on Brain Drain and Capacity Building in Africa, Addis Ababa, February.

Partnership for Capacity Building in Africa. 1997. *Revitalising Universities in Africa: Strategy and Guidelines*. Washington, D.C.: World Bank.

Ramphele, M., and H. Rosovsky. 2000. "New Report on Higher Education in Developing Countries." *International Higher Education*, no. 20 (Summer): 7–8.

Salary Review Commission. 1993. "Report of the Review of the Salary Review Commission." November. Accra.

Saint, W. 1992. "Universities in Africa: Strategies for Stabilization and Revitalization." World Bank Technical Paper No. 194. Washington D.C.: World Bank.

———. *Tertiary Distance Education and Technology in Africa*. Washington, D.C.: World Bank.

Sey, S. 1989. *Tributes to David Mawbray Balme*. Accra: University of Ghana, Legon.

Task Force on Higher Education and Society, World Bank. 2000. *Higher Education in Developing Countries: Peril and Promise*. Washington, D.C.: World Bank.

Teferra, D. 1999. "Ideas for Financing African Higher Education." *International Higher Education*, no. 17 (Fall): 7–8.

UNDP (United Nations Development Programme). 1997. *Ghana Human Development Report 1997*. Accra: UNDP.

University of Ghana. 2000. *Basic Statistics*. Legon, Ghana: University of Ghana.

Yesufu, T. M. 1973. "Emerging Issues of the 1970's." In T. M. Yesufu, ed., *Creating the African University: Emerging Issues of the 1970's*, 37–87. Ibadan: Oxford University Press.

36

Guinea

SORIBA SYLLA WITH HASSAN EZ-ZAÏM AND DAMTEW TEFERRA

INTRODUCTION

Guinea became an independent state on October 2, 1958. The country has a land mass of 245,857 square kilometers (94,926 square miles) and a population estimated at 7.6 million. Fifty-one percent of the population are female, 46 percent are under the age of 15, and life expectancy is estimated at 45.91 years. During the 1990s, the country witnessed a massive influx of refugees escaping armed conflicts in Liberia, Sierra Leone, and Guinea Bissau.

Guinea has five regions: Lower Guinea, Middle Guinea, Highlands Guinea, Forest Guinea, and Conakry, the capital city. Despite its huge water, soil, and mineral resources, Guinea remains among the less developed and highly indebted countries with an income per capita estimated in 1997 at US$570. About 40 percent of the population live below the poverty line (about US$300 per capita). Guinea's difficult economic situation originates in its political history. As France started the decolonization process, offering its colonies the choice to become independent or remain as part of France, President Sékou Touré declared the country's wish to be independent. Taking this decision as a personal affront, France, under de Gaulle at the time, destroyed all records and equipment before leaving the country, cut all financial aid, and established customs duties on Guinean goods (Theobald 1960). It was not until the François Mitterand government that cooperative ties were restored between the two countries.

The government liberalized the economy in 1985. The macroeconomic policies adopted then, however, have worsened economic difficulties and social problems, resulting in unemployment and widespread poverty. This situation is also aggravated by difficulties linked to the drop in the value of bauxite in the world market, a mineral that accounts for up to 97 percent of Guinea's export revenue. Two-thirds of the world's bauxite is mined in Guinea (Oliver and Crowder 1981). The rising price of petroleum products and military conflicts in neighboring countries since the beginning of the 1990s have made Guinea's situation increasingly difficult.

THE STATE OF EDUCATION

Despite the progress made since the 1990s, the level of education in Guinea remains low. In 1999, the rate of schooling at the primary level was 57 percent and adult literacy was 36 percent with significant variations by sex, region, area of residency (84 percent in Conakry and 38 percent in the Highlands Guinea), and community. The schooling rate is estimated at 65 percent for boys and at only 37 percent for girls (Ministère 1999).

The low level of education is caused by several factors: poor infrastructure, shortages of equipment, and lack of teaching personnel and administrative staff at various levels of education. The government undertook major reform programs to increase access to education and improve the quality of teaching. An education revitalization program was initiated in 1990 in order to implement reforms at the level of primary education. In 1995, the university, with the assistance of the World Bank, launched the Country Assistance Strategy (CAS), which called for higher education reform "in light of severe shortcomings in the adequacy of higher education training vis-à-vis economic development needs and high unit cost" (World Bank 1995a).

THE SUBSECTOR OF HIGHER EDUCATION

In 1962, the Polytechnic Institute of Conakry (IPC) was the first institution to be established to train engineers and administrative staff to meet the economic and social development of the nation. From the 1970s onward, several institutions oriented primarily toward agriculture were established. Their number grew rapidly to reach nearly forty by the early 1980s. This significant increase was accompanied by very high enrollment (approaching 20,000 students by 1984), particularly in agronomy. Despite this growth, the absence of financial viability undermined the quality of learning and compromised the reputation of the higher education system.

In reaction to this situation, the government launched important changes to reduce the number of institutions that existed in the mid-1980s. Another initiative gave universities effective autonomy in terms of administrative and financial affairs. Currently, the higher education system of Guinea consists of two universities (the University of Conakry and the University of Kankan) and three professional institutes, which have been annexed to the universities (the Institute of Education, the Institute of Agronomy and Veterinary Sciences, and the Institute of Mining and Geology).

THE OBJECTIVES OF GUINEAN HIGHER EDUCATION

The system that includes higher education, science, and technology in Guinea has four main objectives designed to meet the social and economic development needs of the nation. First, higher education aims to train students for highly qualified professions in science and technology. Second, it has the task of producing, conserving, and disseminating scientific and technical information. Third, higher education strives at technology innovation and transfer to meet the community's needs. Finally, it serves as a tool in promoting scientific, technical, and cultural cooperation in Africa and internationally.

The first research institution, established in 1922, was affiliated with the Pasteur Institute in France. Since independence, several other research institutions have been created through international cooperation. They conduct applied research in a number of fields such as agriculture, marine biology, fishing, building materials, energy, traditional medicine, and the environment. Unfortunately, the development of many research centers could not be sustained due to lack of financial support.

Higher education, as a subsector of the national education system, includes teaching institutions, scientific and technical research centers, and the institutes of information and documentation. The Ministry of Higher Education and Scientific Research is responsible for the coordination, supervision, and implementation of educational policies. Problems facing this subsector are multifaceted: they consist of a lack of resources at the institutional, material, human, and financial levels. Consequently, the administrative performance, the supervision of training, and the quality of education and scientific production are low.

ADMINISTRATION AND GOVERNANCE

Until 1986, all institutions were controlled and managed by the central government. As part of the government's liberalization policy, private higher education institutions became part of the educational landscape in the second half of the 1980s.

A private school of economics and two colleges of economics and computer science were created. Several other postsecondary schools, focusing particularly on professional training in computer sciences, business administration, and technical areas, were opened as well.

Reforms initiated by the government conferred great autonomy on public institutions even though the state continues to be their principal funding entity. Appropriate procedures have been put in place to ensure more autonomy for public institutions, and participatory governance is encouraged within the institutions.

Two administrative bodies manage the implementation of national policy in matters of higher education: the Department for Scientific and Technical Research and the Department for Higher Education. These organs are responsible for ensuring the coordination, evaluation, and follow-up of the subsector. For lack of appropriate operational resources, the efforts of these departments remain ineffective.

INFRASTRUCTURE AND EQUIPMENT

The shortage of resources and equipment and the poor infrastructure pose serious problems to higher education and scientific research. The ratio of students to teacher varies from 28 to 1 at the Institute of Education to 52 to 1 at the Boké Institute of Mining and Geology, the University of Kankan, and the Institute of Agronomy Science of Faranah. The existing infrastructure needs to be fully utilized to admit many more students as there is a serious disparity between the social demand for higher education and real capacity of universities.

On another level, laboratories endure shortages in equipment and chemicals for experimentation. However, there is a noticeable effort to equip institutions with microcomputers and to provide training to students and teachers. Internet access, a project still at its infancy stage, is expected to be extended to all universities and research centers. The government is involved in the construction and renovation of buildings within several institutions.

Institutions of higher education and research have libraries and reading rooms within schools. There are also four specialized documentation centers containing over 41,000 books, more than 9,300 senior student theses, and 1,200 periodicals. Library resources for the institutions, however, remain insufficient.

TEACHING AND RESEARCH STAFF

In 1999, universities employed 325 administrative staff members. Higher education institutions have relatively few senior professors. In 1999, there were 717 full-time professors (among whom only a little more than one-third held a Ph.D.). Of these, eleven professors had a rank of full professor or lead researcher and sixty-eight had a rank of *Maîtres de Conference*. About 300 part-timers were hired to meet the shortage of professors. Among these there were some sixty expatriates working on long- and short-term contracts. Thus, in 2000, some 1,000 teachers were employed to teach 14,000 students with a ratio of about 14 students per teacher.

The IPC is a major institute that enrolled about 13 percent (1,021) of Guinean students in 2000. It employed eighty-five faculty members, among whom there were six full professors (two Guineans, four foreign), forty-eight lecturers (six Guineans, forty-two foreigners), thirty-one assistant professors, fifty assistants and laboratory technicians, thirty-seven part-time faculty members, and fifteen administrative staff members (CITEF 2000).

Scholarships through international cooperation are made available to support teachers training abroad. There is a need to put in place and to implement a national policy of teacher training and encourage faculty to exchange knowledge with their colleagues from other countries.

FINANCING

The financing of higher education and scientific research is guaranteed essentially by public funding of development and investment through the national budget. In addition to state funding, universities are working to generate funds through consultancies, collecting course fees, and other activities.

Expenses for the education sector in general fell from 28.3 percent of the national budget in 1970 to 8.9 percent in 1990. In 1991, as the program for education adjustment was launched, the budget was raised to 22 percent. Since then it has been above the 20 percent mark.

The higher education budget dropped from 29.3 percent in 1990 to 22.5 percent in 1992. It has remained between 17 percent and 20 percent since 1996. In 2000, higher education and scientific research received 26.33 billion Guinea francs, which represented 25.8 percent of the total budget of the national education sector. Of these, 3.4 billion francs were allocated to salaries.

The amount of student scholarships increased from 34 percent of the annual higher education budget in 1995 (World Bank 1995a) to 55 percent of the current total university subsidies, while training and research funding is allocated only 7.8 percent of the higher education budget. Private-sector participation in the financing of higher education needs to be investigated.

Almost 76 percent of the financial resources of higher education are channeled into salaries in research institutions. Research projects financed through bilateral and multilateral assistance approach 65 percent of the overall funding allocated to research institutions. Since the beginning of 1999, a project financed by the Guinean government and the World Bank has allocated research funds on a competitive basis.

Although the government encourages higher education institutions to develop income-generating activities, no major progress is being made in this respect. Until 2000, higher education institutions were capable of contributing only about 10 percent to their budgets.

The funding of higher education and scientific research lacks efficient management. The problem is primarily the disproportionate budget allocation for scholarships and salaries compared to that devoted to teaching, research, and teacher training and development. Furthermore, external financing from development partners is concentrated mainly in the University of Conakry. In this respect, the IPC maintains close relationships with businesses and industries through student internships and the services it provides. The IPC partners are involved in degree evaluation, definition of program objectives, funding of certain activities, and creation of laboratories. On the international level, the IPC has diversified its cooperation with Russia, and other partnerships have been established with countries such as Côte d'Ivoire, Mali, Germany (Gesellschaft für Technische Zusammenarbeit, GTZ), UNESCO, and the International Development Research Center (IDRC).

The funding problems of Guinean higher education have been the focus of the 1995 CAS reform. At the time, the per-student unit cost was estimated at $1,420 per academic year. Despite this relatively high cost, the academic programs offered were of low relevance and created only a small number of qualified students. Scholarships and salaries were absorbing significant portions of the subsidy, causing inefficient and inequitable higher education practices and high overhead costs. Thus, the CAS called for four measures to balance the budget:

- Mobilization of private income (student fees, evening classes)
- Leasing of university services to the highest bidder (contracting a private catering company for the university's cafeteria)
- Reducing the amount of scholarships (controlling admissions)
- Increasing the output of teaching and administrative personnel (cutting down overtime payments and increasing teaching hours) (World Bank 1995b; see Table 36.1)

In addition to balancing the higher education budget, the CAS strategy had another important priority—the reallocation of part of the cost savings from the higher education budget to finance the expansion of primary and secondary education (World Bank 1995b).

ENROLLMENTS

The high school degree is the minimum requirement to enroll in higher education. A high school graduate must also sit for a university entrance test. The entrance test results serve as a way to select students for enrollment. The demand for university access is so high that it cannot be entirely satisfied. Every year, only one-third of the candidates who sit for the entrance test are admitted. Student enrollments by institution for 2000 are given in Table 36.2.

The rate of student success within higher education varies from 62 percent to 87 percent, depending on the school. The attrition rate varies from 27 percent at the Polytechnic Institute and 26 percent at the School of Medicine to 6 percent at the Boké Institute of Mining and Geology. In most universities, the majority of students write their senior thesis in six months to two years after completion of their coursework.

Guinea counts today 14,000 students for a population of 7.6 million. To put this figure in some regional perspective, Senegal has 25,000 students for 7.9 million inhabitants, Côte d'Ivoire has 60,000 students for 13.7 million inhabitants, and Tunisia has 120,000 students for 7.3 million inhabitants.

Despite the fact that budget cuts and the imposition of tuition fees are having an impact on student enrollments, the idea of cost sharing seems to be the best sustainable way to improve the situation of higher education in African universities. Barry, Selassie, and Konate (2001) point out that despite lingering

Table 36.1. Cost Savings and Resource Mobilization Measures in Guinean Institutions of Higher Education, 1996–1999 (in thousands of U.S. dollars)

Measure	Description	1996	1997	1998	1999	Total
Overtime payments to teachers	80 percent reduction over 2 years	86	173	173	173	605
Use of contract teachers	60 percent reduction over 2 years	65	130	130	130	455
Day laborers	30 percent reduction over 2 years	38	77	77	77	269
Cost recovery: Evenings	Increase of 100 students per year	80	160	240	320	800
Cost recovery: Regular	Increase of 100 students per year	40	80	120	160	400
Scholarships	5 percent annual reduction	195	381	557	724	1,857
Cafeteria	25 percent savings	500	500	500	500	2,000
Total		1,004	1,501	1,797	2,084	6,386

Source: World Bank 1995a.

Table 36.2. Student Enrollment in Tertiary Education in Guinea by Institution, 2000

Institution	Enrollment
University of Conakry	8,000
University of Kankan	2,400
Faranah Higher Institute for Agronomic and Veterinary Sciences	1,700
Institute of Mining and Geology—Boké	700
Manéah Teacher Training School	1,200
Total	14,000

budget fallout, tuition fees are the best way to reduce budget pressures on the government. Similar initiatives are likely to increase competition between programs of study, raise standards, and increase the number of applicants (Barry et al. 2001).

MAJORS AND DEGREES

Several programs are offered in the two universities and three institutes, ranging from classical curricula such as philosophy and history to contemporary ones such as computer science.

University of Conakry

The University of Conakry has four schools and one polytechnic institute. The four schools are the School of Law, Economics, and Business; the School of Humanities and Journalism; the School of Natural Sciences (physics, mathematics, biology); and the School of Medicine, Pharmacy, and Dentistry. The Conakry Polytechnic Institute (Institut Polytechnique de Conakry, IPC) offers three majors in civil engineering (buildings, hydrotechniques, and bridges and roads), three majors in chemical engineering (food technologies, organic substance technology, and inorganic substance technology), two majors in electrical engineering (electric energy and electromechanics), and three majors in mechanical engineering (thermal machinery, automobiles and trucks, and paving equipment).

The university offers a general university studies degree (*Diplôme des Etudes Universitaires Générales, DEUG*) after two years of coursework; a higher technician diploma after three years of coursework and training (*Licence*); and bachelor's degrees after four years of coursework, practical training, and a thesis. The university also offers master's degrees in environmental studies, physics, and other areas. The doctorate in medicine is granted after five years of studies, one year of practical training, and one year of thesis writing. The IPC programs extend over a period of ten semesters that is divided between laboratory work, course projects, final-term projects, internships, and on-site visits.

In some schools, concern for relevance between the curriculum and the job market has been growing, and as a result, programs have been designed to train students to become professionals in fields needed in the job market such as business management, journalism, and tourism. The University of Conakry has created a unit to help integrate graduates into the job market and follow up on employment records.

University of Kankan

The University of Kankan has two schools: social sciences and natural sciences. The social sciences school has programs in economics, sociology, history, and philosophy, while the natural sciences school provides programs in mathematics, physics, and biology. Kankan University offers a B.S. after four years of study.

Boké Institute of Mining and Geology

The Boké Institute offers programs in fundamental sciences such as mathematics, physics, chemistry, geology, mining, and management. Students graduate from the institute with a degree in one of three majors: engineering, mining, or geology.

The Agronomy and Veterinary Institute of Faranah

The Agronomy and Veterinary Institute offers graduate degree programs in agronomy, veterinary sciences, and rural economy.

The Institute of Education Science

The Institute of Education Science has programs to train primary and high school teachers as well as continuing education programs for school administrators. The institute delivers two types of diplomas: a two-year certificate and a four-year diploma in education.

GENDER ISSUES

The proportion of female students at the universities is low. At the Polytechnic Institute, for example, there were about forty-seven students in 2000, all of them males. After some progress during the 1970s when female students represented 19.4 percent of the student population, the rate fell below 6 percent at the beginning of 1990, and reached 10 percent in 2000. In 1995, female participation in higher education was estimated at 6 percent out of the total enrollment, with the female adult illiteracy rate reaching a towering 87 percent out of a total male/female illiteracy rate of 76 percent (World Bank 1995b). From the standpoint of equity, only 2 percent of potential female students from rural zones are enrolled in institutions of higher education, compared with 20.8 percent of potential female students from urban areas.

The numbers for the female proportion of the teaching staff are even more dismal. At the University of Kankan, for instance, only 2 out of 100 professors were female. Female professors represent only 4 percent of the full-time faculty. At the University of Conakry, the percentage of females in management and supervisory positions is 25 percent at the central administration level, 30 percent at the School of Law and Economic Science and Administration, 15 percent at the School of Medicine, 12 percent at the School of Human Sciences, 6 percent at the School of Natural Sciences, and only 3 percent at the Polytechnic Institute.

CONCLUSION

In the increasingly global economy characterized by the expansion of commerce, finance, and science and technology, Guinea, like the rest of African countries, faces the threat of marginalization unless it prepares itself for the challenge. Countries in the same position as Guinea can cope with the increasing marginalization only if they are capable of producing a skilled workforce. In order to do that, the government needs to place a high priority on the education sector.

The objectives of higher education are now concerned with ensuring the quality of the programs that exist, increasing access to institutions of higher education, addressing issues of gender equity within higher education, and establishing a very strong link with the private sector.

In the foreseeable future, emphasis will be placed on the improvement of the quality of teaching to increase the competencies of university graduates and reduce unemployment. For that purpose, universities are engaged in a revamping of their curricula and launching graduate studies to upgrade the skills and knowledge of the faculty. In the same vein, a project for a new library network with state-of-the-art equipment in information technology is planned.

To play its role effectively, the Ministry of Higher Education and Scientific Research has to reevaluate the capacity of institutions and formulate and reconceptualize national policy to focus on the development of higher education and research. The ministry also needs to establish appropriate ways to evaluate the activities and outputs of education and research programs.

Several strategies are under consideration to increase access to higher education, such as distance learning, the creation of community colleges in several parts of the country, and support of the development of private universities and colleges.

BIBLIOGRAPHY

Annuaire de l'Université de Conakry. 2000. *Editions universitaires.* Conakry: Université de Conakry.

Barry, A., T. S. Abebayehu, and K. Adama. 2001. "The Surge for Cost Sharing in Higher Education in Africa." *CCGSE Newsletter* 14, no. 1 (Spring). Center for Comparative and Global Studies in Education, SUNY–Buffalo.

Ministère de l'enseignement pré-universitaire. 1999. "Données statistiques enseignement primaire Années scolaires, 1998–1999." Unpublished report.

CITEF (Conférence Internationale des Formations d'Ingénieurs et Techniciens d'Expression Française). 2000. "Enseignement supérieur technique francophone (Asie et Afrique): Guinee." Available online at: http://francophonie.w3sites.net/guinee.html

Oliver, R., and M. Crowder. 1981. *The Cambridge Encyclopedia of Africa.* London: Cambridge University Press.

Theobald, R., ed. 1960. *The New Nations of West Africa.* New York: H. W. Wilson Company.

World Bank. 1995a. "Good Practice Example of Least Cost Analysis: Guinea Higher Education Management Support Project." Report: SAR# 14895-GUI. World Bank document.

———. 1995b. "Staff Appraisal Report: Republic of Guinea—Higher Education Management Support Project." Report # 14895-GUI. World Bank document.

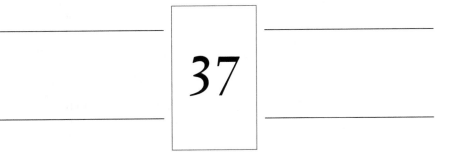

Guinea-Bissau

JULIETA MENDES

INTRODUCTION

Guinea-Bissau, a small country of approximately 36,125 square kilometers (13,948 square miles) with a population of about 1.2 million inhabitants, is located on the west coast of Africa. It is bordered by Senegal (to the north) and the Republic of Guinea–Conakry (to the east and west). Guinea-Bissau achieved its independence from Portugal in 1974 after eleven years of struggle led by the African Party for the Independence of Guinea-Bissau and Cape Verde (PAIGC).

Guinea-Bissau is among the poorest countries in the world. It ranked 168th of the 174 countries listed in the Human Development Index (IDH/UNDP 2000), scoring 0.343 against an average in sub-Saharan Africa of 0.456. The gross national product (GNP) per capita dropped from $240 in the 1980s to $180 in 2000. According to a report by IDH and the United Nations Development Project, 49 percent of the total population are considered poor and 29 percent live in absolute poverty. Guinea-Bissau's general illiteracy rate is about 80 percent and reaches as high as 90 percent among women. Economically the country is a member of the West Africa Economic and Monetary Union (UEMOA), which is made up of the Francophone countries of Africa. Its monetary unit is the CFA franc.

From 1974 to 1999, Guinea-Bissau was ruled by PAIGC. The first multiparty and democratic elections took place in 1994. In June 1998, Guinea-Bissau was brutally shaken by a conflict that lasted for eleven months and ended in the removal of Joao Bernardo Vieira from the presidency. A Government of National Unity was established to prepare the transition to another round of democratic elections, which took place in November 1999. This election brought to power the Party of Social Renovations (PRS), with Koumba Yala Kobde Nhanca as the president.

HISTORICAL BACKGROUND AND EVOLUTION

During the Portuguese colonial period, the school system as a whole was geared to serve the "selected few." Education was restricted to the children of the colonial masters and their followers. Secondary education was confined to the main cities; postsecondary education was nonexistent. The official colonial language, Portuguese, was and still is the language of instruction. Being able to speak and read Portuguese remains a privilege reserved for a small minority; current estimates indicate that only 10 percent of the population are able to read and write Portuguese at a functionally acceptable level.

Development imperatives—namely technical and scientific progress and the need to reaffirm national identity and cohesion—place higher education planning and development among the biggest challenges facing Guinea-Bissau.

The first attempt to create a postsecondary education system in Guinea-Bissau was initiated by the Ministry of Justice in 1979 with the establishment of a law school to train professionals for the administration of justice.

A few years later, a school of education was established to free the country from its dependence on Portuguese training for secondary school teachers. This effort lasted for some years, with different state institutions creating training centers to respond to their perceived needs and running them according to their own vision.

Higher education in Guinea-Bissau is not well organized and is not managed in an integrated manner. Initiatives in the field are not geared to respond to strategic planning. The country does not have a human resources policy, so training at all levels suffers from lack of coherence and coordination. As it exists in Guinea-Bissau, higher education cannot be called a system in the conventional sense of the word. No complementarity

Table 37.1. Higher Education Enrollments in Guinea-Bissau, 1997

School	Number
Medicine	64
Law	300
Education	400
Nursing	120
Sports	84

Source: INDE 1997.

exists among the five centers of higher learning or between these centers and the school system. Guinea-Bissau's higher education caters to about 1,000 students distributed among the five centers (Table 37.1).

On average, three years of training is required before a degree is awarded at the associate level. (This is the case for the schools of education, nursing, and sports.) Law students study for five years, leading to a bachelor's degree. Medical students need seven years, including an internship, to achieve a *Medicina geral*, which is equivalent to an M.D.

So far, all postgraduate studies must be undertaken abroad, since Guinea-Bissau has made no arrangements for long-distance training, such as virtual universities or the like. Cuba, Guinea-Bissau, and Portugal have signed an agreement to automatically recognize degrees from Guinea-Bissau's schools of law and medicine and their corresponding partners in Cuba and Portugal.

In the mid-1980s, the Ministry of Agriculture, recognizing the fact that agriculture is the most important sector of the economy—even today, agriculture contributes 61.3 percent of the country's GNP and employs more than 70 percent of its workforce—decided to create a school of agriculture. Backed by the Swedish government, the government established the Olaf Palme Center in Buba. Though the center did not continue for long, it left behind some important related structures, including the Research Center for Agricultural Development (INPA) and the Research Center for Fisheries (CIPA). Fortunately, these research structures have survived and play a very important role in providing data and information that is critical to understanding the evolution of the sector.

In 1999, the Government of National Unity issued a decree that placed all existing centers and every activity related to education and training under the coordination of the Ministry of Education. This is a landmark decision in the evolution of postsecondary education, a move that I hope may lead to a more effective and efficient plan for higher education development. As a matter of fact, in the same year, a steering committee for the creation of a national university was set up in Bissau at the National Institute for Research (INEP), a center of excellence known at both national and international levels. Created in 1984, INEP hosts the only public library in the country.

INSTITUTIONAL CAPACITY

The schools of law and medicine, the two most important institutions of higher education, are almost completely finan-

cially dependent on foreign assistance received through bilateral cooperation arrangements with Portugal and Cuba, respectively. Staff also depend to a great extent on foreign technical expertise. Most of the senior faculty at the School of Law are Portuguese. Likewise, all senior medical faculty members are from Cuba, with the exception of the nursing school, which employs mostly local staff. Dependence on foreign expertise will likely prevail for some time since Guinea-Bissau has no replacement program or plans to attract national expertise from its Diaspora. Very few graduates with a doctoral degree live in the country, but the few nationals that do are underpaid and have very poor working conditions.

Guinea-Bissau's financial and technical dependency is not without its problems, including systematic delays throughout the school year. This is especially true at the School of Medicine, where the school year is sometimes cancelled because of the lack of teachers and discrepancies in the school calendar. In addition, even some expatriate teachers are not adequately qualified.

CURRICULUM DEVELOPMENT

In terms of its curriculum, Guinea-Bissau normally borrows or copies international standards from parent institutions in Portugal and Cuba with no major changes. But the trend is toward developing curriculum internally. For example, the curricula at the School of Nursing and the School of Education are partly developed at the national level with the technical assistance of Cuba and Portugal. By and large, institutions of higher education are not structured or fully equipped to conceive or plan their own curricula. This means that often there are discrepancies between curricula and the labor needs of the country or with Guinea-Bissau's customary laws and practices.

Another problem is related to the language of instruction. Portuguese is functionally spoken by only 10 percent of the population, so many students enter higher education institutions with a language handicap. This has been an underlying factor in the low performance of students, especially in primary school. Both the schools of law and medicine have added an additional full year of core courses to address language and other deficiencies.

STUDENT POLITICAL ACTIVISM

One cannot talk about student political activism in Guinea-Bissau. Since the higher education institutions are lacking in self-identity, it follows that students generally do not see themselves as a class. This lack of consciousness makes students an easy target for political manipulation by the different political parties. Student unrest is normally related to late scholarship payments, but this only affects a minority since the majority of students are self-supporting.

BRAIN DRAIN

Brain drain is one of the pressing issues facing Guinea-Bissau. Because of the unstable economic and political climate within the country, some students choose to remain abroad instead of returning to Guinea-Bissau after completing their studies. A related problem is the flight of experienced professionals from the country, especially from the civil service. The biggest challenge facing capacity-building efforts in Guinea-Bissau is the retention of skilled labor.

The limited career prospects and high job insecurity in Guinea-Bissau are related to constant shifts in government, or its composition, and the politicization of work life. Placement even at the managerial level is often related more to political affiliation with the party in power than to issues of competence or seniority. This tendency was aggravated by the June 1998 conflict, which forced massive displacement of the population into neighboring countries, including European countries, as refugees. Many professionals among those displaced have decided to stay and work in these host countries. So far, no study has been conducted to estimate in hard figures the extent of the brain drain or the flight of expertise from Guinea-Bissau. But it is clear that the country as a whole, and the public service in particular, are suffering from a serious shortage of qualified workers and that the situation has deteriorated during the last few years.

UNEMPLOYMENT

Unemployment affects a significant number of postsecondary school leavers in the 15–39 age group. This cohort represents 34 percent of the total population and 73.1 percent of the active workforce. The majority in this age group have very limited academic or technical training. Their unemployment rate is estimated at 12 percent.

The number of students trying to enter the labor force increases yearly as more students do not find placement after completing the eleventh grade of high school at the few vocational-technical schools or other academic centers. Scholarships are very scarce, especially since the fall of the Eastern Bloc cut off a major source of scholarship funds for Guinea-Bissau. This situation leaves many young people on the streets, which increases crime within this age group, especially in the main cities and towns in Guinea-Bissau.

Law school graduates are the hardest hit by underemployment for reasons related to the concentration of public services in Bissau. The job market for lawyers has become congested in Bissau, while judiciary personnel are grossly underrepresented in other regions of the country. This situation will possibly change in the near future, since a major effort is underway to decentralize the public administration, especially the judiciary services and the administration of justice. In contrast, graduates from the schools of education and nursing, for example, find immediate placement—not because of more attractive salary or work conditions but because education and health services and structures are more developed and decentralized.

RESEARCH

Scientific research has not been a major activity for higher education institutions. Initiatives on the part of some ministries have not had a major impact because there is not enough dissemination of research results.

Research in the social sciences is more structured and is mainly conducted by INEP. Some research activity, thematic in nature, is also conducted by the National Institute for Education and Development (INDE) research programs on curriculum development, pedagogical strategies, and production of textbooks.

INEP is the only research institution adequately structured and organized to undertake publishing. Every six months, INEP publishes a magazine of Guinean studies, Soronda, but it has rarely been able to meet this deadline, due to financial constraints. Besides Soronda, INEP also publishes romances and novels written by independent authors under Kacu Martel and Lala Quema Editions. Kacu Martel has been instrumental in promoting research and the development of national literature.

Despite these efforts, research results have very little impact on training institutions or on policymaking. This lack of responsiveness has also negatively impacted the dissemination and application of research results. In contrast, international organizations are regular clients of INEP. They regularly request and pay for INEP's services. Its research results are often incorporated in development projects and programs in Guinea-Bissau.

PRESENT AND FUTURE CHALLENGES

Within the framework of national education reform in Guinea-Bissau, decree 6/99 of March 12, 1999 established the University of Amilcar Cabral. The government of Guinea-Bissau signed a protocol with the Universidade Lusofona de Humanidade e Tecnologia of Lisbon to provide technical support to the steering committee helping to set up the university. The committee submitted a draft proposal to the government on May 31, 2000. This document is presently under revision, and the final version was to be submitted in February 2001.

The government's current priority seems to be the restructuring of existing training institutions and the strengthening of some training centers, upgrading them to the level of full-fledged institutions of higher learning. Another priority is to develop curricula and programs in fields relevant to development needs of the country. In addition, a commission has been formed to formulate a policy that will allow the country to plan its human resource development in light of international and national developments and needs. However, in the absence of a national plan for human resources development and a national manpower training policy, the country urgently needs to devise a strategy that would encourage professional training centers to adapt their course offerings to the needs of the labor market and to individual needs. This will require a real partnership between all parties concerned.

It is urgent that a system of higher education be established in Guinea-Bissau under the responsibility of an institution that will ensure the coordination of all activities related to training in postsecondary education and promote the creation of national capacities in training and in scientific and applied research.

The university should champion the creation and maintenance of the required critical mass for national development. Because it is a center of knowledge, the university—in partnership with other training institutions, public or private, and civil society—should play a major role in improving the quality of education at all levels of society. In the short run, the university should promote the restructuring of the educational system based on a vision that corresponds to the needs and aspirations of the society. The university should become directly accountable for the success and failure of national development strategies.

CONCLUDING REMARKS

The task of creating a university to address present and future challenges is critical to Guinea-Bissau at this stage in its development. It is clear that a country cannot continue in this day and age without its own system of higher education.

Priorities should be realigned. The country must address this crucial sector for national development if it is to face the national, regional, and international challenges created by the current world order. However, Guinea-Bissau cannot accomplish these tasks without the assistance of other governments, institutions, and development partners that can provide the assistance necessary for the creation and development of University of Amilcar Cabral.

REFERENCES

Análise do Ensino Básico. 1994. (1991 a 1997/98) e Previsão para horizonte 2000—Apoio a Educação Firkidja—Men—Bissau—Maio.

Anuários Estatisticos de 1995/96 a 1998/99 Gabinete de Estrudo e Planificação.

Declaração de Politica Educativa. 1998. Men—Maio.

Documento de Estratégia Nacional de Redução de Pobreza. 1997.

Estudos Prospectivos a Longo Prazo. 1997. NLTPS—Guinea-Bissau 2025 "Djitu TEN." INEP/MIN. PLANO.

INDE (Institut national pour le développement d'éducation). 1997. Bissau, Guinea Bissau.

Note sur la situation socio-économique en Guinea-Bissau CNUD. 1999. Septembre.

Plano de Acção. 2000. 2000–2001 Men—Julho.

Plano Nacional de Desenvolvimento. 1998–2002.

Plano Quadro de Desenvolvimenti de Educação. 1993/94.

Relatório Nacional. 1997. De Desenvolvinenti Humano Guinea-Bissau.

United Nations Development Programme. 2000. Human Development Report 2000. New York: United Nations Development Programme.

38

Kenya

CHARLES NGOME

INTRODUCTION

Higher education encompasses not only the future potential of a country but also its present realities. The importance of higher education in enhancing adequate and proper training cannot be overstated, as it is expertise and technology that differentiate between the developed countries and developing countries such as Kenya. Unfortunately, in Kenya, as in other African countries, higher education is in deep crisis. A review of pertinent data shows declining public expenditures on higher education, deteriorating teaching conditions, gross overemployment in universities, decaying educational infrastructure and facilities, an increasing rate of unemployment among university graduates, a mass exodus of experienced and competent lecturers, shortages of adequate training opportunities for thousands of young people seeking higher education, the absence of academic freedom, and a decline in the quality of university graduates.

This adverse situation in higher institutions of learning could have been minimized if institutions had recognized the symptoms early enough and embarked on a restructuring project by putting in place mechanisms to broaden their income bases and mount a strong and effective managerial system that would have insulated these institutions against their current predicament. Although they are belated, several strategies and reforms that seek to salvage the universities have been set in motion. The private university sector is also responding to the crisis by offering a real alternative; private education is now an important component of higher education in Kenya. This chapter deals with the size, scope, and nature of postsecondary institutions of higher learning in general but focuses mostly on university education.

Kenya is a country of about 28.7 million people (14.5 million females and 14.2 million males) that is situated on the east coast of Africa. The country's population has experienced a growth rate of 2.9 percent per annum, having grown from 21.4

million in 1989 and 15.3 million in 1979. Close to 2.1 million people live in Nairobi, the capital city (Republic of Kenya 2000). The country is made up of more than forty different ethnic groups that vary in size from a few thousand to several million members. The four largest ethnic groups are the Kikuyu of the central province, the Luhya from western province, the Kalenjin of the Rift Valley province, and the Luo of Nyanza Province. These four groups plus the small ethnic groups constitute about 98 percent of the population. The remaining 2 percent is composed of Indian, European, and Arab immigrant communities. Most children from these immigrant communities attend several international primary and secondary schools located in the country before proceeding to overseas universities. Although Kenya is a multiethnic country, Kiswahili, a language that is spoken widely in the country, is the lingua franca, and English is both the medium of instruction in the Kenyan education system and the country's official language.

Agriculture is the mainstay of Kenya's economy. It contributes roughly one-third of the gross domestic product, employs more than two-thirds of the country's labor force, accounts for about 70 percent of export earnings (excluding refined petroleum), provides the bulk of the country's food requirements, and supplies a significant proportion of raw materials for the agricultural resource–based industrial sector. Throughout the 1990s, the growth in the agricultural sector was poor due to unfavorable weather conditions, corruption, poor governance, and low international prices for tea and coffee, which are Kenya's leading export earners. For example, the sector grew by only 1.3 percent in 1999, down from the already poor 1.5 percent recorded in 1998. Consequently, the 2.8 million peasant families who hold more than 60 percent of the arable land (estimated to be 19 percent of the total national land area of 57 million hectares) are very poor (Republic of Kenya 2000). The remaining 81 percent is arid and semi-arid land inhabited by pastoralists whose livelihood hinges on livestock and frequent migration in search of pasture and water. The majority of the pastoralists are poorer than the peasant farmers due to frequent loss of their livestock to drought and cattle rustling. Overall, 52 percent of the Kenyan population live below the poverty line. Though the country's annual per capita income is US$280, there is a significant gap between rural and urban incomes: the average monthly income for rural and urban Kenyans is US$13 and US$29, respectively.

The children of pastoralists participate in all levels of education (primary, secondary, and postsecondary) very poorly. Female children of pastoralists generally perform worse than boys. By contrast, children of peasant backgrounds from agriculturally productive zones of the country where gender parity has been attained at the primary school level show less inequality. The problem of underparticipation in education among the children of nomadic communities has a historical dimension. The missionaries whose work was inextricably linked to the development of schooling in Kenya, as in other African countries, concentrated in agriculturally productive areas. Consequently, pastoral communities in semi-arid and arid areas lagged behind in school participation. At independence in 1963, the Borana, Rendille, and Somali pastoralists of North Eastern Province had a gross enrollment ratio of only 2 percent at the primary school level. The enrollment of the Turkana, Samburu, Maasai, and various Kalenjin pastoralists of the Rift Valley province was 39 percent. The school participation rates of these pastoralist groups were below the national average of 58 percent and far below those of the educationally advantaged agricultural zones of Central and Western provinces, which were 94 percent and 71 percent, respectively (Republic of Kenya 1964a).

Since independence, Kenya has made some notable progress in the provision of education for all. The gross enrollment ratio at the primary school is presently estimated at 87.1 percent, and national literacy levels have risen considerably. The literacy rates of women increased from 10 percent in 1960 to 60 percent in 1998, and the literacy rate of men rose from 30 percent to 82 percent during the same period (Republic of Kenya 1998). In spite of this significant progress, primary school completion rates are less than 50 percent. They usually range between 43 percent and 46 percent. This shows that there are substantial rates of repetition and of drop-outs. The arid and semi-arid regions that were disadvantaged during the colonial era are as much as 50 percent to 60 percent below the national average of primary-school-age group enrollment. These zones are also characterized by a relatively low percentage of female enrollment. The national gross enrollment rate at the secondary education level oscillated from 30 percent to 18 percent between 1989 and 1999. This low enrollment is a reflection of the poor transition rate from primary to secondary school, which is currently 46 percent. The undercapacity at the secondary education level means that schools cannot absorb up to 50 percent of those who complete primary education, despite the fact that the student-to-teacher ratio is only 17 to 1 in secondary schools.

HISTORICAL OVERVIEW OF HIGHER EDUCATION

The foundations of higher education in Kenya were laid at Makerere in Uganda during the colonial era. In 1937, the de la Warr Commission recommended that Makerere College, which had been founded in 1922 as a technical college, award diplomas to East Africans. In 1949, Makerere became a university college of the University of London, following the 1943 report of the Asquith Commission on Higher Education.

The first Kenyan higher educational institution was the Royal Technical College of East Africa. The college was opened in Nairobi in 1956 to provide instruction in courses leading to the higher national certificate offered in Britain and to prepare matriculated students through full-time study for university degrees in engineering and commercial courses not offered by Makerere College. As it admitted its first students, the need was felt for expert advice on the pattern of higher education in East Africa. This led to the appointment of a working party in 1958, which recommended that the Royal Technical College be transformed into the second international university college in East Africa. In 1961, the Royal Technical College was renamed the Royal College of Nairobi and turned into a university college. It offered Bachelor of Arts and Bachelor of Science general degrees and the Bachelor of Science in engineering degree of the University of London. In 1963, when Kenya attained its independence, the Royal College became the University College of Nairobi and joined Makerere and Dar es Salaam Colleges to form the Federal University of East Africa. After the dissolution of the University of East Africa in 1970, Kenya, Uganda, and Tanzania set up their own national universities. In Kenya, the University of Nairobi was created by an Act of Parliament in 1970. Kenyatta College, a teacher training institution situated on the outskirts of Nairobi, became a constituent college of the University of Nairobi in 1972. Since then, the government of Kenya has established five other public universities. While Moi University at Eldoret in the Rift Valley province was established on the recommendation of the Presidential Working Party of 1981, Kenyatta University College (which was elevated to a full-fledged university in 1985), Egerton University (1987), Jomo Kenyatta University of Agriculture and Technology (JKUAT, 1994), and Maseno University (2000) were started by presidential decree.

OVERVIEW OF THE SIZE, SCOPE, AND NATURE OF POSTSECONDARY INSTITUTIONS

Although the pace of developing higher education was painfully slow during the colonial era, higher education has developed tremendously since independence. Kenya has six public and thirteen private universities with an enrollment of about 50,000 students. Roughly 80 percent are enrolled in public universities, while 20 percent of the total university student population attend private universities. Of the thirteen private universities, only five are accredited: Daystar University, United States International University-Africa (USIU-A), Scott Theological College, Catholic University of Eastern Africa (CUEA), and the University of Eastern Africa at Baraton. Each of these institutions except Scott Theological College offer postgraduate programs. The other eight private universities are mainly small religious institutions that award degrees through larger universities based in the West (mainly the United States): the Nairobi International School of Theology (NIST), Africa Nazarene University, Kenya Highlands Bible College at Kericho (KHBC),

Table 38.1. Undergraduate Student Enrollment at Kenyan Public and Private Universities 1996–1997 through the 1999–2000 Academic Year

Universities	1996–1997		1997–1998		1998–1999		1999–2000	
	M	F	M	F	M	F	M	F
Public	24,624	10,228	27,586	10,940	28,231	12,339	28,502	12,773
Private Accredited	2,534	2,676	1,971	2,053	2,942	3,090	3,217	3,785
Other Private	558	196	671	275	667	292	746	377
Total	27,716	13,100	30,228	13,268	31,840	15,721	32,465	16,935

Source: Ministry of Education, Science, and Technology, Statistics Section, 2000.

Table 38.2. Undergraduate Admissions in Engineering and Technical-Based Degree Programs in Kenya's Public Universities by Gender, 1997–1998

	Male		Female		Total Number
	Number	Percent	Number	Percent	
Architecture	44	88.0	6	12.0	50
Civil Engineering	86	93.5	6	6.5	92
Mechanical Engineering	72	96.0	3	4.0	75
Electrical Engineering	51	87.9	7	12.1	58
Computer Science	50	78.1	14	21.9	64
Total Number	303	89.4	36	10.6	339

Source: Joint Admissions Board Records, University of Nairobi, 2000.

Pan African Christian College (PAC), East Africa School of Theology (EAST), Nairobi Evangelical Graduate School of Theology (NEGST), the Methodist University at Meru, and St. Paul's United Theological College. Table 38.1 shows the undergraduate enrollment at public and private universities from academic years 1996–1997 to 1999–2000.

In spite of this massive expansion, gender and regional imbalances have shaped and continue to shape the development of higher education in Kenya, as in other African countries. The proportion of female enrollment declines as girls and women move up the educational ladder. As a result, female students make up only about 30 percent of total enrollments in the public universities. Female students' underrepresentation is higher in engineering and technical-based professional programs, as shown in Table 38.2. This scenario is reversed in the accredited private universities. Gender parity is evident in all the accredited private universities, where women comprise 54.5 percent of the 1999–2000 total student enrollment. Most women enroll in private universities because they fail to secure admission into the public universities, owing to their poor performance on the Kenya Certificate of Secondary Education; and because the course offerings in the private institutions are in the social sciences, education, arts, business administration, accounting, and computer science.

The majority of these female students, like their male counter-

parts, are drawn from the high-potential agricultural districts that have been historically favored in accessing Western education. Entry into higher education institutions is based on performance on the Kenya Certificate of Secondary Education (KCSE). This is in accordance with the 8-4-4 system of education: 8 years of primary, 4 years of secondary, and 4 years of university education. The minimum requirement for university admission is a mean grade of C+ in the KCSE examination. Ministry of Education, Science, and Technology statistics indicate that an average of 150,000 students sits for the Kenya Certificate of Secondary Education annually. Public universities admit roughly 10,000 students; about 3,000 students join private universities. Private universities and diploma-granting institutions admit students who cannot secure admission into the public university system. By the late 1990s, about 5,000 students were traveling outside the country each year for university education, mainly on self-sponsorship, to the United States, India, Britain, Canada, Australia, Russia, South Africa, Germany, and France.

Students who travel abroad, particularly those meeting minimum admission requirements, would attend local universities if facilities were available. A development in that direction has been initiated. Some public universities are entering into agreements with reputable middle-level colleges to offer courses under their accreditation. Jomo Kenyatta University of Agriculture and Technology (JKUAT) has been a pioneer in this new venture. The university has signed several agreements of cooperation with various institutions, including the Kenya School of Professional Studies, Nyanchwa Adventist College, Karen Cooperative College, and Loreto College, Msongari, to provide JKUAT certificates, diplomas, and degrees in Information Technology and Management. Also, several middle-level institutions that have been offering tuition for diplomas, and degrees offered to external students by foreign universities (from mainly Britain and the United States) are expanding such services by incorporating universities from South Africa. The Kenya College of Accountancy is developing a collaboration with the University of South Africa (UNISA) to serve as a learning center for students wishing to pursue UNISA degrees.

More than 60,000 students enroll in middle-level colleges, a sector of the Kenya educational system situated between secondary and university levels of education. The middle-level colleges cater to a variety of postsecondary career courses leading to certificate, diploma, and higher diploma awards. This array of institutions offer training courses in many fields, including teaching, agriculture, medicine, water treatment and management, civil aviation, banking, catering, computer science, commercial studies, and tourism. These middle-level colleges are owned by both the government and the private sector. By 1990, Kenya had about 160 middle-level colleges (Commission for Higher Education 1990), but in 2000 it was estimated that the country had more than 250 such colleges.

While Kenya displays a fairly well-developed institutional infrastructure in terms of the number of middle-level institutions, most of them suffer from a lack of adequate resources to perform their functions effectively. For technical and other types of training that rely on the availability of equipment, there have been numerous complaints that theoretical teaching (the "talk and chalk" method) has come at the expense of the acquisition of practical skills due to a lack of tools, equipment, and materials for practical training (Republic of Kenya 1999). The private sector has often complained about a serious mismatch between the curricula of most middle-level colleges and the demands of the market. Although the middle-level colleges form an important level of tertiary education in the country, on the whole they are poorly coordinated and neglected. The Commission for Higher Education that has authority to make policy for these institutions has contributed to making them irrelevant to modern job-market demands by failing to provide for quality assurance for the programs offered.

ADMINISTRATIVE STRUCTURE

All the public universities in Kenya are headed by the president, who serves as the chancellor. The president appoints vice-chancellors and principals of the universities' constituent colleges. These appointees owe their positions to their loyalty to the head of state who appoints them. Because of this mode of appointment (external imposition), vice-chancellors do not command the respect of their peers within the university community. The president also nominates most members of the university council. The council is composed of academic staff, students, the minister of education, and the permanent secretar-

ies of the ministries of education and finance. University councils are charged with the responsibility to formulate policy, create faculties and departments, and approve university staff appointments. The university senate is responsible to the council for academic affairs and for the financial and administrative management of the university. Senates are presided over by vice-chancellors and are dominated by heads of departments, who are potential vice-chancellors. Under the senate, faculty boards and departments oversee instruction and administer examinations. Except for the faculty deans, staff, and student representatives on university councils, all the other officers are appointed.

The recent creation of management boards to assist vice-chancellors in the running of public universities has resulted in overlap, duplication, and ambiguity in the university management structure. In some of the universities, the functions and composition of the management boards are stipulated in the institution's statutes; in others, the management boards are not constitutionally sanctioned and are appointed by vice-chancellors to ratify personal decisions about the management of universities. In most of the universities, management boards are assuming the functions and powers of senates in administering universities (Sifuna 1998).

The councils carry their nonacademic matters through a series of committees (which include the tender, housing, statutes, staff discipline, student discipline, staff appointments, and honorary degrees) chaired by different members of the council. The functions of these committees are defined by the councils.

Although university councils are supposed to assist university authorities in the running of the universities, most matters concerning appointments, promotions, and contracts are single-handedly dealt with by most vice-chancellors and principals without regard to due process. This centralized system of university governance, in which power and authority are concentrated in the hands of vice-chancellors, poses problems that border on mismanagement and abuse of public offices. On the other hand, management by the committee system tends to slow down decision-making processes.

CURRENT TRENDS AND CHANGING PATTERNS IN HIGHER EDUCATION

In this section, I discuss the financing and funding patterns of university education, staffing in public universities, income-generating activities, and private universities.

FINANCING AND FUNDING PATTERNS OF UNIVERSITY EDUCATION

The Genesis of Cost Sharing

Until the early 1970s, university education in Kenya was free. The full cost was borne by the government. In the mid-1970s, undergraduate students received a government loan to finance their education, covering tuition, accommodation, subsistence, and books. The recovery procedures for these loans were poor; thus, the original concept of developing a revolving fund from which more students would benefit was thwarted.

During the 1991–1992 academic year, the government introduced a cost-sharing scheme that required students to pay direct fees of US$80 (Kshs. 6,000) and a new student loan of about US$280 (Kshs. 21,000) per annum. All students were eligible for the loan regardless of their economic status. A bursary system was introduced to cater to those unable to raise the direct charge. Through it, full or partial bursaries were made available to needy students. Students from the public universities mobilized for a showdown with government and university authorities in which they demanded that the previous system of financing university education be maintained. The government responded by closing down the institutions. In 1995, the university financing system was revised. The direct charges were increased from US$80 to US$107 annually per student and total charges were raised to US$667. Student loans were consequently increased to US$560 and, most fundamentally, were no longer available to all students but were to be means-tested. Except for the cost of tuition, these changes transferred the responsibility for food and boarding from the government to the shoulders of parents and students. The most serious challenges to any means-tested loan system lie in getting needy applicants. Developing such systems is difficult even in industrialized countries in which a majority of people file income information with the tax authorities annually. The task is daunting in developing countries where large numbers of families, even the economically able ones, are likely to apply for loans and bursaries and operate in a semi-subsistence mode that makes verifying income and wealth data extremely difficult. A higher education system financed by the entire population but available to only a tiny minority has a highly regressive fiscal impact (Assié-Lumumba 1994).

The Unit Cost System

Funding of public universities in Kenya is currently based on unit cost. This is defined as the amount of money a university spends on one student per year per degree program. The current unit cost of US$1,600 is comprised of tuition of US$1,147 and catering, accommodation, and other costs that amount to US$453. The government's capitation per university is computed by multiplying the total number of students in the university by US$933, which is the government's annual grant per student. The present unit-cost system, which was computed in 1995 using figures from the 1991–1992 audited accounts of universities, is grossly inadequate as a basis of funding universities. The method does not take into account differential costs of the various degree programs. It actually introduces inequity in the funding of universities by the government. Universities that offer more science and technology programs are disadvantaged compared to those that host predominantly arts-based programs, since the same unit cost is used for all programs and the former are more expensive than the latter.

Moreover, it costs US$2,427 to train the cheapest degree student; the most expensive costs US$6,207. Consequently, all public universities are at present seriously underfunded. The underfunding of public universities has made it difficult for them to provide quality education, meet payroll expenses, provide benefits, make pension contributions, and fulfill other con-

Table 38.3. Cumulative Recurrent Deficits for Kenyan Public Universities

Year	Deficits in Kenyan shillings	Deficits in U.S. dollars
1991	222,705,554	2,969,407
1992	310,858,544	4,144,781
1993	216,326,145	2,884,348
1994	147,715,640	1,969,542
1995	135,313,271	1,804,177
1996	503,280,783	6,710,410

Source: Ministry of Education, Science, and Technology, Statistics Section, 2000.

tractual obligations and has also created phenomenal brain drain. The depth of the financial crisis afflicting Kenya's public universities is reflected in the chronic financial deficits shown in Table 38.3. The brief reprieve of 1994–1995 notwithstanding, the deficits keep rising because essential services must be kept afloat.

The most serious omissions in computing the unit-cost system of funding were in regard to postgraduate students, catering costs, and accommodation costs. Postgraduate students were not taken into account in calculating unit cost. Consequently, there is no direct government capitation for postgraduate students at present. This is in the context of the policy to strengthen postgraduate enrollment to at least 10 percent of the total university student enrollment and enhance research output. Since the unit cost was defined as the amount of money a university spends on one student per degree program, it did not include catering, accommodation, and other incidental costs that students incur. These critical issues should be considered in computing a viable unit cost as a basis for public funding of university education in Kenya.

STAFFING IN PUBLIC UNIVERSITIES

The presence of a skilled workforce is the critical factor of production in any organization. The public universities have two cadres of staff: academic staff and support staff.

An appropriate ratio of students to academic and support staff is essential in evaluating resource utilization in any university. The ratio is supposed to be favorable to allow the university academic staff to have adequate contact hours with their students as a means of enhancing high-quality education. Similarly, universities should posses enough support staff to offer necessary support services to both lecturers and students. Table 38.4, which includes data on the staff-to-student ratio in all public universities in Kenya, reveals that there is absolute overemployment.

The ratio of support staff to students is about double that applicable in other universities. Applying a realistic ratio of 1 to 6 indicates that the University of Nairobi is overemployed by about 2,517 support staff. The current academic establishment is based on Full-Time Student Equivalents (FTSE), which were

Table 38.4. Staff-to-Student Ratios in Public Universities, Kenya, 1994–1997

University	Ratio of Academic Staff to Students			Ratio of Support Staff to Students		
	1994–1995	1995–1996	1996–1997	1994–1995	1995–1996	1996–1997
Nairobi	1:9	1:9	1:9	1:3	1:3	1:3
Jomo Kenyatta University of Agriculture and Technology	1:9	1:9	1:9	1:3	1:3	1:3
Moi	1:12	1:6	1:6	1:4	1:3	1:3
Egerton	1:14	1:14	1:14	1:4	1:3	1:3
Kenyatta	1:16	1:14	1:14	1:4	1:5	1:5
Maseno	1:18	1:12	1:12	1:3	1:3	1:3
Average	1:13	1:12	1:12	1:3	1:3	1:3

Source: Commission for Higher Education, 2000.

computed using academic staff-to-student ratios agreed upon by the Commission for Higher Education (CHE) in 1994. The staffing ratios used in public universities are lower than similar ratios used in other countries. The case for reviewing the staff-to-student ratios of these institutions is overwhelming. If one applies a ratio of 1 to 18, which is the average in the Commonwealth universities, then the University of Nairobi is carrying an excess of 739 academic staff members (University of Nairobi 1999). The strain of gross overemployment at the University of Nairobi applies to all public universities in the country.

Public universities in Kenya can no longer sustain the burden and inefficiency of overemployment and underproductivity. This challenge has to be addressed by determining the appropriate staffing needs and improving the remuneration package for those who will remain. This will both eliminate unnecessary personnel costs and motivate and retain competent staff.

INCOME-GENERATING ACTIVITIES

Kenya's public universities are currently facing a major financial crisis that is characterized by shrinking revenues from the government, staff overemployment, escalating debts and deficits, limited alternative sources of funds, inefficient methods of collecting fees from students, low returns from full-cost recovery units, poor fundraising, and use of a defective unit cost as a basis for providing budgetary allocations. Faced with this deteriorating financial climate, the public universities are bridging the shortfall by mounting income-generating activities. These have primarily involved using university facilities and expertise by expanding enrollment of self-sponsored students, initiating business ventures, and organizing consultancy services.

Privatization of education in the universities and expansion of self-sponsored students through the introduction of parallel and external degree programs have been two of the most visible initiatives. Parallel degree programs admit students who meet the minimum admission criteria (an average grade of C+ or better) but usually have lower grades than their counterparts in regular programs whose fees are subsidized by the government.

While most of the regular students in lucrative fields such as medicine, pharmacy, law, architecture, and engineering are admitted with an average grade of A-, the parallel degree program accommodates students with lower grades. As a result, the program has drawn criticisms from the general public and regular students who contend that the programs are essentially money-making schemes that relax admission criteria as long as the applicant can afford the fees. These criticisms notwithstanding, the parallel degree programs are making public universities more attractive because their entry requirements are flexible, students have a choice in the courses they want to pursue, and they can complete the programs faster. In addition, these programs also cater to the working class, since they are offered tuition in the evenings and on weekends. Primary and secondary school teachers attend residential teaching/learning sessions during the months of April, August, and December when schools are on holiday.

Some faculties in these institutions are generating revenues through the parallel and external degree programs, while others are either running at a loss or have failed to attract any enrollment. The University of Nairobi has an enrollment of about 3,000 self-supporting students (although it has capacity for 3,000 more); Kenyatta University has roughly 2,000.

One worrisome issue, however, concerns the question of equity. Most of the students enrolled in these programs are from rich families. In the context of declining levels of state subsidies and scholarships for students admitted to public universities, the wholesale privatization of education costs is likely to exacerbate social inequality by excluding poor students and socially disadvantaged groups from participating in higher education.

Maseno University, which took the challenge of generating supplemental sources of income through its Investments and Economic Enterprises (IEE) program in 1994, has registered losses on its farm, bookshop, and photocopy services; but the program made a profit on its guest-house, housing, and transport services. A comparison of the aggregate income-generating unit's revenue with total expenditures, however, shows a negative profit trend. In the 1998–1999 fiscal year, for example, total permanent personnel compensation in the income-generating units was US$78,667 as compared to the total net profit of US$48,000. In the 1997–1998 fiscal year, total personnel compensation amounted to US$69,333, whereas only US$42,667 had been realized as the total net profit from all the income-generating units (Gravenir and Mbuthia 2000). Thus, the sustainability of the income-generating units at Maseno University is questionable. Due to overestablishment, efforts made to diversify sources of income for the university have been undermined by the lack of economies.

The organization of consultancy services as a way of diversifying funds for universities has not been very successful, although a number of lecturers from these institutions are deeply involved in consultancy assignments for various organizations. Most of the academics engaged in consultancies work entirely for their own benefit and often at the expense of their employer (the university) in terms of lost time and free access to university facilities. For universities to make a breakthrough on this front, they will have to negotiate skillfully with both the lecturers and the organizations for which they consult. Even then, until university authorities demonstrate some degree of accountability and transparency in how they manage university funds, lecturers will continue to avoid having their consultancies channeled through universities.

PRIVATE UNIVERSITIES

The growth of the private university sector in Kenya has been fueled by several factors, including the limited opportunities available in public universities; the constant closures of state-funded universities; the need to complement government-managed higher institutions of learning; and the determination by some religious organizations to open higher learning institutions largely for their followers.

Kenya is one of the few countries in Africa that has a well-developed private university system. The University of Eastern Africa, Baraton, which is located in the Rift Valley; and the Catholic University of Eastern Africa, Daystar University, and the United States International University (USIU-A), all located in Nairobi, are the major private universities operating in Kenya. As already stated, the country has nine other religious-based institutions that have very low enrollments.

The CHE, which is the intermediary body between universities and the government, has the overall responsibility of licensing private universities. CHE categorizes these institutions into three main areas: registered private universities, accredited private universities, and private universities operating on the basis of a letter of interim authority. CHE formulates procedures for the establishment and accreditation of private universities. For example, one of the rules requires a private university to have at least fifty acres of land before it can be accredited. Such a regulation may have been relevant when universities were meant to be sprawling campuses with high student enrollments. However, given how information technology has changed the approach to learning, universities no longer require so much space. This requirement impedes the development of private universities in Kenya and should be discarded. Most of the other requirements also demand an unrealistically high standard of university education. If applied to the letter, few universities,

including the more established public institutions such as the University of Nairobi, would qualify for accreditation (Mwiria and Ngome 1998, 38).

Private universities in Kenya offer several visible advantages. Since admission to public universities is extremely competitive, these institutions have provided school-leavers a second chance to benefit from university education at no extra public cost. For those already on the job market who want a university education, private universities are the perfect choice, making it possible for them to enroll for classes on weekends and evenings and offering them the flexibility of enrolling during those semesters when they are able to raise fees. This feature is now being replicated in the public universities. Young school-leavers whose parents can afford the fees of private institutions often prefer them to public universities because they are able to enroll in university earlier and complete their studies in a much shorter time than if they were to attend the less flexible state universities. Some private universities are performing better than most public universities because they are characterized by better management practices, planning strategies, and processes and by better utilization of available resources and facilities. They employ few full-time faculty but engage part-time faculty when the need arises, and they separate catering from academic services. Such efficiency contributes to a certain level of cost-effectiveness. Overhead in most private universities is kept to a minimum. The large academic and administrative staff that one finds in Kenya's public universities is not characteristic of private universities. Some private universities are generally better run than the public ones, a situation which is helped by the lack of political interference in their management.

To a limited extent, some of the private universities offer a better-quality education than their relatively bigger and public counterparts. The USIU-A library has a better collection of journal subscriptions than most public university libraries. Public universities no longer subscribe to many of the current journals in various disciplines of study. Moreover, students and staff at private universities have more access to computer facilities and related technology than do their counterparts in public universities. Private universities are also providing leadership in some aspects of higher education. Unlike public institutions, which are often characterized by a duplication of existing degree programs, some of which open few opportunities for postgraduate employment, the prominent private universities are making an effort to respond to market forces, even though their programs remain limited to the social sciences. As an example, the University of East Africa, Baraton, was the first higher education institution in Kenya to offer a community health degree in 1987, following the recommendation of the Nursing Council of Kenya. The University of Nairobi emulated Baraton and launched a similar program.

The leading four private universities (USIU-A, Catholic, Baraton, and Daystar) generate substantial income from student fees. As profit-making institutions, fees are charged strictly in accordance with market forces on the basis of full cost recovery. On average, tuition in these private universities for two semesters is about US$1,800. USIU-A, the most expensive private institution of higher learning in Kenya, charges approximately US$2,800 for students from Kenya, Uganda, and Tanzania but charges students from other countries US$4,008. The remaining nine private universities charge some tuition fees, but not enough to sustain their operations. Consequently, most of them rely on external donors. Financial support from donors includes the construction of physical infrastructure, donations of teaching and learning materials, and provision of scholarships.

These factors notwithstanding, it should be noted that the standard of education offered in the majority of the smaller private universities is relatively poor for five reasons. First, many of the students who enroll in these institutions have lower academic qualifications than their counterparts in public universities. Second, programs in private institutions are concentrated in narrow areas, often with heavy religious overtones. None of them offer courses in disciplines such as engineering, physical science, or medicine because of the costs involved in mounting these programs. Third, even in the more successful private institutions, because of the profit motive, weak students are encouraged to continue their enrollment until they graduate. Thus, the more rigorous lecturers who demand what they consider to be minimum standards from their students find themselves excluded from these schools. Fourth, the quality of education offered in these institutions could also be lowered by the fact that private universities invest little in research programs. This impacts negatively on their postgraduate programs. Fifth, inefficiency in the management of private universities results from the significant influence of religious bodies in some of these institutions. In some of these institutions, the religious affiliation of potential employees may be more critical than their professional competence.

PROBLEMS AND CHALLENGES FACING THE UNIVERSITY SYSTEM

In this section of the chapter, I discuss student political activism, political interference in universities, unemployment among university graduates, the poor state of research teaching and publishing, the problem of brain drain, and the poor physical infrastructure, instructional facilities, and quality of education at Kenyan institutions of higher education.

Student Political Activism

Political activism among Kenyan students has been one of the most visible features of higher education in the country due to the government's mismanagement of public affairs. Although Kenya inherited a well-tailored liberal constitution from its British colonial masters, the state amended and manipulated it to protect and expand the office of the presidency. This process of creating an authoritarian state in Kenya started in 1964 when the Kenya African Democratic Union (KADU) dissolved itself voluntarily and joined the Kenya African National Union (KANU), thus making Kenya a de facto one-party state. Efforts to organize new parties, such as the Kenya Peoples Union (KPU), which was banned in 1969, were violently thwarted. To legalize repression, the government passed the Public Security Act in 1966, which authorized detention without trial. Any outspoken members of Parliament were silenced, reducing that in-

stitution to a rubber stamp for government policies. The government also took steps to curtail the autonomy of all independent centers of power, such as the Central Organization of Trade Unions (COTU), and expected unthinking loyalty from the populace. These authoritarian measures were a precursor to the massive corruption that followed. The economic decline that has dogged Kenya since independence and the struggle to economically empower the government's key cronies raised the degree of corruption to unprecedented levels.

In the absence of mechanisms for checks and balances and autonomous associations in civil society capable of providing a counterbalance to the state, students and faculty have played a vital role in galvanizing opposition to the status quo. When Jaramogi Oginga Odinga, opposition leader of the Kenya Peoples Union, which was challenging government corruption, monopolization of power, and its arbitrary excesses, was prevented from giving a public lecture at the University of Nairobi in 1969, students boycotted lectures, arguing that the government was interfering with their right to receive ideas. Such protests have characterized the student-state relationship in Kenya. Institutions of civil society in Kenya are either banned or are rendered politically impotent through incorporation into the existing state structures.

The antagonistic relationship between the university and the Kenyan state has been exacerbated by the economic crisis afflicting the country. Public universities have been hit hardest by this crisis and the government's neoliberal economic responses. The massive student enrollment in these institutions has intolerably overstretched the capacities of the universities' physical infrastructure and instructional facilities. Student riots that have rocked universities have been prompted by unfavorable living conditions on campus and by poor library services. The continuing economic downturn and twenty years of structural adjustment have increased the poverty level in the country and undermined students' confidence in the capability of the state to deliver on its economic promises. Consequently, university protests have addressed issues facing not only universities but the country as well.

Student activism in Kenya has been facilitated by vibrant campus associations. Student associations have provided a platform that has enabled them to address collective grievances and organize demonstrations against the government without fear. To stem student activism, the government has tended to proscribe student organizations. The students' organization of Nairobi University (SONU), the Nairobi University Students' Union (NUSU), and the National Union of Kenya Students (NUKS) have all been unconstitutionally deregistered by the Registrar of Societies. Efforts to form the National Union of Students of Kenya (NUSKE), a gathering of students from Kenyan polytechnics, teaching colleges, and universities, have also been frustrated by the Registrar of Societies. Student newspapers have not been spared either. They have been proscribed from criticizing the government and from extolling causes such as good governance, fair land distribution, and proper management of public resources. The newspapers proscribed include *Sauti ya Kamukunji*, *Campus Mirror*, *Azimio*, and *Mzalendo*. Intensified repression against student activism notwithstanding, students in Kenya have maintained a remarkable degree of resilience by creating and recreating student associations whenever existing ones are banned or coopted.

Since their establishment, public universities have been closed many times due to student activism. The frequent closures have impacted negatively on the universities' academic standards. Academic calendars in public universities provide for an academic year divided into two semesters of seventeen weeks each. The many closures make this impossible to achieve. Unfortunately, in most of the universities, efforts are never made to make up for lost time by prolonging the academic term. Partly because of these regular closures, the Commonwealth Association of Architects, which has accreditation with more than 145 schools in former British colonies, deregistered the University of Nairobi's architecture school. Students who qualify in architecture from the University of Nairobi, therefore, must strive for additional qualifications to acquire international recognition as qualified architects.

Although neither the Kenyan laws nor the parliamentary acts that established the public universities in Kenya confer on the local administrators (called chiefs) the powers to keep a register of attendance for university students, whenever students have been sent home following closures, they have been compelled to report to the local government administrators twice a week.

During the current multiparty era in Kenya, the trend toward multiplication of student organizations along tribal lines has fragmented university students into competing camps that support ethnically based political parties rather than remaining autonomous and objectively critical with the ultimate aim of helping the country.

Although the current political wave of democratization in Kenya owes much of its success to the pivotal role played by student activism, that achievement has come at a price. The list of university students who have been expelled, jailed, exiled, killed, and denied employment after graduation or who have prolonged the normal length of studies because of their activism is quite long. Sometimes students have inexplicably destroyed people's property and inflicted untold damages on university facilities. Such activism has stretched the resources of universities and undermined their ability to provide quality education.

Political Interference in the Universities

The repressive and authoritarian political culture in the wider Kenyan society can be seen in the universities. The various statutes that regulate public universities in Kenya allow the government direct control of these institutions. The statutes provide that the president of Kenya is automatically the chancellor of the public universities unless he or she decides it fit to appoint other people to those positions. As chancellor, the president appoints chairpersons of university councils, their deputies, their honorary treasurers, and ten other members of the council in every public university to represent the government. All these appointees owe their allegiance to the president, not to the visions and missions of the universities that they are appointed to serve.

The president also appoints vice-chancellors. The vice-chancellors in turn fill the positions of heads of departments and director of institutes with their own nominees. Although each faculty in theory should hold open deanship elections, most have long dispensed with any form of democracy because of interference by vice-chancellors.

This administrative control has allowed the government to exercise undue interference in the smooth running of public higher institutions of learning in Kenya. Political patronage, rather than competence and merit, characterizes most of the senior appointments and promotions and all the decision-making processes. The government uses these control mechanisms to silence and dismiss dissenting lecturers and students and to reward its supporters. This has affected the integrity of most departments, since unqualified people hold influential positions. Kenyan public universities are thus tied to the vagaries of politics and the state.

Efforts to institute change continue to be thwarted by the government and vice-chancellors. In 1993, faculty members of all the public universities tried to take advantage of Kenya's new era of multiparty democracy to seek the registration of the Universities' Academic Union (UASU) but were denied the right of association by the government. Union leaders were sacked and bundled out of the university houses following a long strike that paralyzed the university system between 1993 and 1994.

The president's control of the university system also extends to teaching and research. Even though the country is now a multiparty democracy, all research proposals by faculty members and graduate students must be approved by the office of the president. To attend a seminar or a workshop abroad, lecturers require special clearance, again from the office of the president. It is apparent that the freedom to propagate ideas and freedom of conscience at the public universities are in serious jeopardy. Unwarranted government interference and abuse of academic freedom have eroded the autonomy and quality of the higher learning institutions. The situation is a liability to the whole country because it affects the quality of the professionals coming out of the country's universities.

Unemployment among University Graduates

When Kenya attained independence in 1963, a massive expansion at all levels of the formal education system took place in response to an acute shortage of manpower to facilitate the process of Africanization. That expansion followed a general consensus that a direct relationship existed between education and economic growth. Kenyans widely assumed that if education could produce the skilled labor so desperately required by a developing country, then the pace of economic development could be accelerated.

Following the disbanding of the University of East Africa in 1970, the University of Nairobi, which had been its constituent college, became an autonomous university through an act of Parliament. Since then, the country has established five public and thirteen private universities with a combined student population of about 50,000. As already noted, the basis of expanding the university system was the need to meet the requirements for

Table 38.5. Estimate of Demand for and Supply of University Graduates in Kenya, 1964–1970

	Demand	Supply	Shortfall– or Surplus+
Science-based occupations (doctors, engineers, graduate science teachers, geologists, etc.)	3,108	1,773	–1,335
Other occupations requiring specialized training (graduate art teachers, librarians, lawyers, etc.)	1,667	803	–864
Occupations in nonspecialized degrees (administration in government, business executives, etc.)	836	2,061	+1,225

Source: Republic of Kenya 1964b.

a skilled workforce. Available evidence, however, shows that the labor market for university graduates had already surpassed the capacity of the economy to provide the kind of occupations for which they had trained by the mid-1970s. Except in a few areas, education for labor development met its objectives a few years after independence, as shown in Table 38.5.

The output of graduates subsequently increased with the opening of more universities. The National Manpower Survey of 1986–1988 revealed that, even for specialized degrees, output had surpassed the demand for graduates in the labor market. The massive expansion of university education in Kenya is more a response to the demand of private individuals than to labor requirements. The Kenyan government has pursued populist policies by succumbing to private demand.

University expansion in Kenya has also been characterized by concentration in only a few disciplines. Between 1985 and 1993, more than 69 percent of graduates studied only four degree courses: Bachelor of Education, Bachelor of Arts, Bachelor of Science, and Bachelor of Commerce (Delloite and Touche 1995).

Due to constrained economic growth and the massive expansion of university education over the last twenty years, employment opportunities have not kept pace with the increasing number of graduates from the universities. This situation is aggravated by student overenrollment in arts programs. If current economic trends in the country continue, the unemployment problem among Kenyan graduates is likely to worsen.

The Poor State of Research, Teaching, and Publishing

A major factor that distinguishes universities from other institutions of higher learning in Kenya is the extent of work and research output, particularly in the form of published journal articles. In the 1970s and early 1980s, the volume of research

carried out at the University of Nairobi, the oldest and biggest public university in the country, was among the highest in Africa. Unfortunately, this is no longer the case. The state of research in Kenya's public universities today is characterized by financial constraints, inadequate staffing, inadequate resource materials, poor utilization, and minimal dissemination of research findings.

One of the key factors that has stunted the growth of research in the Kenyan university system is lack of adequate research funds (University of Nairobi 1999). The massive expansion of university education in the country from the mid-1980s to the 1990s took place without a proportionate rise in the physical resources available to universities. Such a decline in per capita funds has forced universities to curb their expenditures on staff development, equipment, and research. The large portion of support (although inadequate) for postgraduate and staff training and research work comes from donors and international organizations, including German Academic Exchange Services (DAAD), the Sasakawa Foundation, the International Development Research Center (IDRC), the Ford Foundation, the Carnegie Foundation, the Canada International Development Agency (CIDA), Gandhi Smarak Nidhi Fund, the German Foundation for International Development (DSE), and the International Center for Insect Physiology and Ecology (ICIPE). To illustrate the positive impact that international organizations can have on research and publishing activities in Kenya, the case of ICIPE will suffice. Based in Nairobi, Kenya, ICIPE was established in 1970 as an advanced research institute amid growing global concern about the misuse and overuse of synthetic pesticides. The center collaborates actively with over eighty partners throughout the world, including the University of Nairobi, Kenyatta University, Moi University, and Egerton University in Kenya. Through its African Regional Postgraduate Programs in Insect Science and Dissertation Research Internship Program, fifty-six lecturers drawn from the four Kenyan universities successfully completed their Ph.D. degrees between 1983 and 1999. Several Kenyan lecturers have also benefited from ICIPE's professional development programs (particularly its postdoctoral fellowship and the visiting scientist and research associateships), which enable established scientists to take up short-term assignments in ongoing research projects and enhance ICIPE's capacity in research planning and evaluation. Lecturers and postgraduate students who conduct research through ICIPE publish their research results in international journals dealing with entomology and crop protection.

Lack of adequate qualified researchers constitutes the second major constraint to the expansion of research. The economic crisis Kenya has been experiencing has engendered an unfavorable working environment in most universities. The remuneration packages that lecturers receive cannot guarantee them even the basic minimum living requirements. Therefore, the majority of academics are deeply demoralized. Some of the most competent lecturers and researchers have been forced to abandon universities for greener pastures abroad or to join the private sector. This exodus of the best brains from the universities has meant that only a few lecturers can handle research methodology courses effectively. Research output has also been curtailed by the significant expansion of university education, which has thrust heavy undergraduate teaching responsibilities and supervision of graduate students on the existing faculty, including well-established researchers.

The insufficient supply of material resources, scholarly literature, and equipment for research are major areas of deficiency. University libraries do not have funds to regularly purchase any research journals or hard copies of research papers. Access to databases in all disciplines is extremely limited.

Equipment for the science-based departments is an absolute prerequisite for research. However, in most departments, equipment is simply not available or is obsolete. Those working in disciplines that require consumables such as chemicals are constantly facing shortages. Most buildings that house student laboratories are dilapidated.

Poor utilization and dissemination of research findings also inhibits research. Because research has very limited influence on policy formulation in Kenya, the government has downplayed its importance. The poor dissemination of research findings is partly due to the lack of research journals in Kenya and Africa. After the collapse of the East African community in 1977, the East African Literature Bureau, which had been committed to publishing academic books and journals, also folded. Since its demise, no comparable publishing firm has shown any interest in publishing academic books and journals, which are considered to be money-losing ventures. This situation is aggravated by university authorities who promote less-qualified lecturers as long as they are loyal to the administration, its cronies, and the government. Consequently, there is little motivation to undertake research, since most promotions no longer reward research and publications.

Brain Drain

Like most other African countries, Kenya has inadequate pools of qualified professionals. The mass exodus of highly educated Kenyans from the country started in the mid-1980s and reached its peak in the 1990s. Most Kenyans emigrate to the United States, Canada, Australia, Europe, and to Southern African countries (Botswana, Lesotho, Swaziland, Namibia, and South Africa). Although data on brain drain is difficult to obtain, a 1998 study by Carrington and Detragiache (quoted in Downes 2000) showed that 6,912 Kenyans with tertiary-level education emigrated to the United States in 1990. This loss of human resources has seriously affected the quality of staff in the universities. Apart from the loss of skilled workers from these institutions to other regions, the universities are generally unable to attract high-caliber faculty to their institutions or to retain them. Due to various factors, lecturers are poorly remunerated. Most lecturers' pre-tax earnings range from US$250 to US$300 a month. Such salaries do not provide lecturers with even the bare minimum living requirements of food, education for their children, secondhand clothes for the family, and electricity bills. Academics who have remained in Kenya's universities try to supplement their university income by moonlighting. The practice of moonlighting takes many forms. Teaching on a part-time basis in private universities and consultancy work are favorites, but lecturers also engage in selling goods, operating food kiosks, and

other jobs. The evident consequence of moonlighting is that lecturers are forced to neglect their professional duties.

The situation has been worsened by the somewhat inhibiting environment in institutions of higher learning in Kenya, which has limited the space necessary for critical academic pursuits. This is reflected in the regular and unscheduled closure of public universities, intimidation of teaching staff and students who exhibit independence, politically motivated promotions of academic staff, and admission of underqualified students due to political pressure. As already pointed out elsewhere in this chapter, part of the devastation of the university system in Kenya has to do with the repressive political culture that has been fostered by the government's appointments of cronies to the vice-chancellorship positions. These vice-chancellors subvert both the spirit and tradition of democratic and accountable conduct of university affairs because they are more responsible to pressures and demands from without than from within the university. Vice-chancellors have surrendered the autonomy of universities to the government and connive in the flouting of university statutes by taking government directives. In response to this authoritarian culture in the universities and their deteriorating earnings, the most qualified lecturers have deserted the universities for better-paying jobs outside the country.

The brain drain from Kenya's universities has had a detrimental effect on the quality of education provided by these institutions, since those who emigrate are among the best trained, most experienced, and most productive scholars in their disciplines. As a result of this, the number of lecturers who hold Ph.D. degrees has declined in Kenya. At the University of Nairobi, only 40 percent of the teaching force hold Ph.D. degrees; 33 percent of the faculty at Kenyatta, 32 percent of the faculty at Moi, and 19 percent of the faculty at Egerton have Ph.D.s Although the possession of a Ph.D. degree is often a benchmark qualification for most university lecturers internationally, the converse seems to hold for Kenya. Because of this situation, the once internationally extolled higher institutions of learning such as the University of Nairobi, which was a center of serious scholarship and teaching in the 1960s and 1970s, are today more or less existing on past glory. The conditions of other public universities in the country are even more appalling than those at the University of Nairobi.

Mismanagement of Meager Resources

The fiscal crisis in the public universities is worsened by the misappropriation of meager resources. As students continue to live and study under deplorable conditions, the top administrators in the universities are annually accused by the Auditor General Office of mismanagement of funds and of having their priorities upside down. During the 1995–1996 financial year, Maseno University lost over US$666,667, most of it through rip-offs and false allowance payments. This same culture of corruption is partly responsible for the stalled projects that were begun in the mid-1980s in most of the universities. Projects whose construction was directly supervised and executed by donors were completed as scheduled. For example, at Egerton University, the posh Utafiti Hostel Complex for international research students and the Agriculture Resources Center that the United States

Agency for International Development (USAID) built were completed on time. However, the extension of the Agriculture Resources Center, which was being managed by the university, stalled largely due to misappropriation of funds (*The Standard*, October 12, 1996).

In spite of such rampant corruption and the availability of evidence documenting it by the Auditor General Office, vice-chancellors, principals of university constituent colleges, and other senior government operatives (commonly referred to as "politically correct people") are never arrested and prosecuted for blatant theft from the public and the government.

Inadequate Physical Infrastructure

Underfunding of public universities has seriously affected all facets of education in Kenya and lowered the quality of education. Although facilities are of decisive importance for any university to realize its mission, the facilities and the physical infrastructure of the public institutions of higher learning in Kenya are ranked last in the priorities of planning. The massive student enrollment in these institutions has overstretched the capacities of existing libraries, lecture halls, science laboratories, dormitories, and dining halls.

Egerton University, which has an enrollment of about 8,000 diploma and undergraduate students, has nearly the same facilities that were designed for only 1,600 diploma students before this former agricultural college was turned into a university by an act of Parliament in 1987. At Kenyatta University, lecturers in the Faculty of Education are forced to repeat the same lectures to as many as three or four groups of students because of the lack of lecture halls of adequate size; in other cases, some students listen to their lecturers through the window (Hughes and Mwiria 1990, 228). In such situations, students cannot concentrate on their studies well. Due to this unfavorable learning environment, teaching at Kenyan public universities is not the interactive affair that it should be. Rather, it has largely become the boring repetition by most lecturers of notes from papers that have yellowed with age.

Lack of maintenance of the existing facilities, inadequate as they are, has accelerated their decay. Most buildings in the public universities and their constituent colleges are in dire need of maintenance. The state of science laboratories and engineering workshops is dismal. They are dilapidated and lack chemicals and adequate and up-to-date equipment due to lack of funds and irresponsible planning. In science programs, it is not unusual for a class of more than sixty students to share twenty microscopes, meaning that only a few can learn how to use this basic scientific tool properly. In view of these circumstances, lecturers no longer attach much seriousness to laboratory practicums, and where they do take place—for example, in faculties of engineering—technicians do the work as students watch. This style of teaching does not permit students to understand the principles that govern experiments in the areas in which they are specializing or acquire skills they will later apply in the day-to-day challenges after graduation.

Services in Kenya's public university libraries have also deteriorated. The bulk of the books that are available are outdated and inadequate. Moreover, most of these libraries have no hold-ings list for journals and the catalogues and shelf holdings often do not match. In addition to the laxity and inadequacy of library staff, shelving is so poor also because some selfish students mix up textbooks of different disciplines so they are only accessible to themselves. Scarcity of relevant reference materials for students has led to the rise of vandalism in the libraries. Unable to photocopy required chapters or pages from reference books, some students simply tear them off to survive the cutthroat competition for the few useful books. A 1997 survey of university libraries in Africa revealed that lecturers at Kenyatta and Moi Universities use material that dates back to the 1950s. This means that courses they teach are out-of-date (Rosenberg 1997).

This sad state of affairs, coupled with the flight of the best lecturers from the institutions of higher learning in the country, has contributed to the declining quality of university education. The failure rates of students in university examinations has risen. The labor market exhibits concern regularly over the poor quality of graduates from the state universities. The decline in standards is further demonstrated by the university students' poor command of the English language, which is the medium of instruction in the Kenyan system of education (Mwiria 1993).

CONCLUSION

The basic thesis of this chapter is that the university system in Kenya is in a crisis that affects its ability to accomplish its role in society. A major indicator of the crisis facing universities is brain drain, which has seriously affected the quality of staff. The level of dilapidation of the physical infrastructure, the acute shortages of equipment, the misappropriation of the meager resources available, political interference, and frequent university closures are all manifestations of this crisis, which has considerably lowered the quality of education offered. If the public universities were business concerns, they would have been put into receivership many years ago.

Although universities have responded to this crisis by attempting to diversify their income-generating activities, changing staffing levels, and improving their efficiency and effectiveness, these institutions continue to accumulate debt. This shows that no matter how hard they strive to create the institutional capacity to generate alternative sources of funds, it would be unrealistic to expect Kenya's universities to become financially self-sufficient.

REFERENCES

Abagi, O. 1999. "Resource Utilization in Public Universities in Kenya: Enhancing Efficiency and Cost-Recovery Measures." Research Report. Nairobi: Institute of Policy and Analysis Research.

Assié-Lumumba, N. D. 1994. "Demand, Access and Equity Issues in African Higher Education: Best Policies, Current Practices and Readiness for the 21st Country." Paper prepared for the Donors to African Education Working Group in Higher Education.

British Council. 1996. "Report on Socio-economic Study of Access to University Education, Performance, Equity and Gender Issues." Unpublished research report. Nairobi.

Commission for Higher Education. 1990. "The Directory of Postsecondary Institutions and Courses (Excluding Universities) in Kenya." Nairobi Commission for Higher Education.

Delloite and Touche. 1995. "Graduate Labour Market Study for the Commission of Higher Education (2nd draft)." Unpublished research report. Nairobi.

Downes, A. 2000. "University Graduates and Development." In R. Bourne, ed., *Universities and Development*. London: Association of Commonwealth Universities.

Gravenir, F. V., and E. K. Mbuthia. 2000. "Generating Supplemental Sources of Income by Universities in Kenya: A Case Study of Maseno University." Unpublished paper prepared for conference on higher education, Kenyatta University, Nairobi.

Hughes, R. 1987. "Revisiting the Fortunate Few: University Graduates in the Kenyan Labour Market." *Comparative Education Review* 33: 583–601.

Hughes, R., and K. Mwiria. 1989. "Kenyan Women, Higher Education and the Labour Market." *Comparative Education* 25: 177–193.

———. 1990. "An Essay on the Implication of University Expansion in Kenya." *Higher Education* 19: 215–237.

Irungu, M. "The Struggle for Faculty Unionism in a Stalled Democracy: Lessons from Kenya's Public University." *Journal of Third World Studies* XIV, no. 1: 91–114.

Mwiria, K. 1993. "University Education in East Africa: The Quality Crisis." Unpublished paper. Bureau of Educational Research, Kenyatta University, Nairobi.

Mwiria, K., and C. K. Ngome. 1998. "The World of Private Universities: The Experience of Kenya." Northern Policy Research Review and Advisory Network on Education and Training (NORRAG), University of Edinburg, London.

Republic of Kenya. 1964a. *Report of the Kenya Education Commission.* Nairobi: English Press.

———. 1964b. *High-Level Manpower Requirements and Resources, 1964–1970.* Nairobi: Government Printer.

———. 1998. *National Primary Education Baseline Report.* Nairobi.

———. 2000. *Economic Survey 2000.* Nairobi: Government Printer.

Rosenberg, D., ed. 1997. *University Libraries in Africa: A Review of Their Current State and Future Potential.* London: International Africa Institute.

Sifuna, D. N. 1997. "Crisis in the Public Universities in Kenya." In K. Watson, C. Modigil, and S. Modigil, eds., *Reforms in Higher Education.* London: Cassell.

———. 1998. "The Governance of Kenyan Public Universities." *Research in Post-compulsory Education* 3, no. 2: 175–211.

Sifuna, D. N., and K. Mwiria. 1993. "Key Obstacles to the Development of African Universities." *Journal of Third World Studies* X, no. 2: 199–227.

University of Nairobi. 1999. "Report on Rationalization of Functions and Staff Rightsizing." Unpublished report prepared to guide management and planning for the University of Nairobi resources.

39

Lesotho

MATORA NTIMO-MAKARA

INTRODUCTION

The Kingdom of Lesotho, a former British protectorate, is a small enclave surrounded by the Republic of South Africa with an area of 30,355 square kilometers (11,720 square miles). It is predominantly highlands and mountains. The whole country is at the height of over 1,500 meters above sea level. Only 9 percent of its land is arable. Lesotho has a temperate climate.

According to the 1996 census, Lesotho's population stood at 1.96 million. With an annual growth rate of 2.6 percent, the current estimate of Lesotho's population is just over 2 million. The proportion of females to males is 51 percent to 49 percent. Eighty-one percent of the population live in the rural areas, while 19 percent live in urban areas. The average household size is 5.2 persons. Lesotho's literacy rate for ages 15 and above is 83 percent; literacy is highest among females (93 percent).

ECONOMY AND EMPLOYMENT

Lesotho basically has a subsistence economy; farming constitutes the major activity for most people, particularly in the rural areas. The country's natural resource base is generally poor. Lesotho's major natural resource is its highlands water. The Lesotho Highlands Water Project is a water export scheme through which surplus water is channeled through tunnels into the Vaal catchment area, which is in the industrial heartland of the Republic of South Africa.

In 1997, the per capita income was estimated to be $650 and the annual inflation rate stood at 7.8 percent (Kimane, Ntimo-Makara, and Molise 1999, 3). Slow economic growth and rapid population increases have resulted in high unemployment. It is estimated that only 45 percent of the working-age population is employed; 30 percent of the employed population is working in South Africa, especially in the mines. Lesotho's public service employs 28.7 percent of formal-sector employees, and the rest work for manufacturing companies. The private sector is very small. Because of Lesotho's geographic position, its economy is strongly linked to its economically stronger neighbor, South Africa. As a result, all the external forces that come to bear on the South African economy in turn impact Lesotho, sometimes to its advantage and other times to its disadvantage.

EDUCATION

Western-style education was introduced in Lesotho by missionaries in the early 1830s. The education system is modeled on the British system and consists of three major tiers—the primary, secondary, and tertiary/higher education levels.

The major higher education institutions are mainly owned by the government. Free primary education was introduced in Lesotho in 2000 and then only for the first two years of primary education.

THE SCOPE, SIZE, AND NATURE OF HIGHER EDUCATION IN LESOTHO

Higher education in Lesotho is broadly defined to include both university and tertiary-level education. In other words, it covers all post–high school education with a minimum duration of at least two academic years.

Lesotho has one university, the National University of Lesotho (NUL). In addition, it has close to twenty tertiary-level institutions, the most important of which are the National Teachers' Training College (NTTC), the National Health Training Center (NHTC), the Lesotho Agricultural College (LAC), the Lesotho Institute for Public Administration and Management (LIPAM), Machabeng College, and Lerotholi Polytechnic (LP). These are either owned or are heavily subsidized by the government of

Lesotho. Lesotho also has a network of private tertiary institutions with academic orientation ranging from business (seven) to technical/vocational (four) and religion (four). The proprietors include businesspeople, churches, and other civil organizations. In addition, a cluster of foreign institutions have emerged in Lesotho that provide tertiary and higher education in a range of areas.

THE NATIONAL UNIVERSITY OF LESOTHO (NUL)

The National University of Lesotho was born out of the small Catholic University College (later known as Pius XII University College), which was founded in April 1945 by the Roman Catholic Hierarchy of Southern Africa. Before this time, Basotho students used to go to South African institutions for most of their postsecondary and higher education. Pius XII prepared students for external degrees under the auspices of the University of South Africa (UNISA). Thus, the validation of programs and other logistics related to the academic operations of the college were undertaken externally in an effort to ensure quality. In 1954, the college was granted associate college status by UNISA, giving it more responsibility for tuition and examinations. Students were drawn from Lesotho (Basutoland), Botswana (Bechuanaland), Zambia (Northern Rhodesia), Zimbabwe (Southern Rhodesia), Malawi (Nyasaland), South Africa, and Namibia (South West Africa). From the late 1950s well into the early 1960s, the college experienced very serious financial problems, mainly because of its denominational character. This made it very difficult for international donor agencies and other foundations to grant the college any funding. By the early 1960s, the Catholic Church; the college's authorities; the Ford Foundation; the governments of the former British High Commission Territories of Basutoland, Bechuanaland Protectorate, and Swaziland; and the United Kingdom entered into serious negotiations to turn Pius XII College into an independent, nondenominational University of Basutoland, Bechuanaland Protectorate, and Swaziland (UBBS).

Economic considerations also came into play in determining this arrangement. It was reckoned that it would be cheaper to have one institution serving Botswana, Lesotho, and Swaziland rather than have each one run its own institution of higher learning. This was also in line with the British approach toward the University of Makerere, which served the three East African British Territories.

UBBS came into being in 1964. At this time, the student body had grown to about 190 and was almost 20 percent female. With the three high commission territories' attainment of independence in 1966, UBBS became the University of Botswana, Lesotho, and Swaziland (UBLS). The first UBLS degrees and diplomas were conferred in 1967.

The tri-national character of UBLS disintegrated in 1975 when it could no longer withstand the political strains that often beset such regional institutions as national interests become overriding factors in the partnerships. The same thing happened with the University of East Africa and the university that served Northern Rhodesia, Southern Rhodesia, and Malawi. Up to this point, the university had operated from its main campus at Roma in Lesotho. The NUL was established as an independent entity on the Lesotho campus of the UBLS on October 20, 1975, by the National Assembly of Lesotho.

NUL VISION AND MISSION

Initially, NUL's major focus was on providing basic training leading to production of skilled workers for the emerging civil service and the education sector. With time, demands have become diverse and now include areas such as health, agriculture, business and industry, and computer technology.

The institution has adopted the strategy of offering full-time and part-time programs, using distance teaching and learning modes to reach as many people in need of higher education as possible. It also operates a strong outreach and community service program, mainly through the Institute of Extra-Mural Studies.

ADMINISTRATION AND GOVERNANCE

In this section, I will explore administration and governance patterns within Lesotho's tertiary institutions. The major ones (NTTC, NHTC, LIPAM, and LAC) operate directly under relevant government ministries of education, health, public service, and agriculture, respectively, and are subject to government regulations. Academic staff are appointed by the Public Service Commission. This often results in serious problems of inefficient teaching and administration and general instability within institutions. Bureaucratic processes have frustrated proper functioning of these institutions. An attempt has been made through the Lesotho College of Education Act of 1998 to bestow some degree of autonomy on the colleges, particularly with regard to academic matters such as curriculum, examinations, and recruitment of appropriate staff. These institutions are affiliated with the university through appropriate faculties. The affiliation instruments emphasize NUL's responsibility in ensuring quality in the institution's academic programs. They still use their academic boards and other committees for internal affairs.

NUL is an autonomous institution and grants its own degrees. It is governed by a council that is made up of appointees of the head of state (who is also the chancellor), the senate, the congregation, the student union, nonacademic staff, and external members with wide experience from universities outside Lesotho. The council is responsible for overall policy matters.

The university's day-to-day administration is handled by the top management, consisting of the vice-chancellor, the pro-vice-chancellor, the registrar, the bursar, and the university librarian, guided by the provisions of the Acts and Statutes.

The university senate is responsible for academic policy and all academic matters. There is also representation from the affiliated tertiary institutions.

At the faculty and institute levels, the deans and directors manage the respective units. They are elected into these positions on a rotating basis and are assisted by the heads of departments and faculty tutors.

The dean of student affairs and her team of wardens, counselors, nurses, sports coaches, and a doctor work closely with both the management and student representatives.

STUDENT GOVERNANCE: THE STUDENTS' UNION

The student union was established under the National University of Lesotho Act in 1976. Paragraph 27(2) of the NUL order clearly states that "the Students Union shall not be a servant or agent of the Council or the University." All students of the university are members of the student union. The union receives a subsidy from the university to operate. It is audited annually, and the audited report is subject to the council's approval. The student union is under the general leadership of an elected Student Representative Council (SRC). Members of this council represent students on all major university committees, including the senate and the council. More or less similar arrangements exist in the other tertiary institutions, though it is a bit difficult to have organized structures like the SRC in the less formalized institutions.

Student activism on and off campus is not as strong as it was in the late 1960s into the late 1980s, when political struggles for liberation were strongest not only within Lesotho but across the region. Lesotho was in turn centrally situated to provide a convenient place from which to have a closer look at unfolding developments within South Africa. Students participated in demonstrations and all sorts of democratic activities. Students were eager to have their finger on the political pulse of the country and the region in order to influence and shape the future.

Currently, student activism tends to focus on their institution's administration and internal management of their affairs (both academic and nonacademic). Because the national government sometimes makes unpopular decisions regarding disbursement of students' personal and book allowances, students have also demonstrated against the government.

INSTITUTIONAL STRUCTURE AND CAPACITY

NUL consists of seven faculties, four institutes, the deanship of student affairs, and the library. The faculties are:

- The Faculty of Agriculture, which offers undergraduate and postgraduate programs with combinations in agriculture economics and rural sociology, animal science, crop science, soil science, and resource conservation. As part of its expansion, the faculty plans to introduce degree programs in forestry, agricultural education, food science, and technology/home economics.
- The Faculty of Education, which prepares professional personnel for the education system through undergraduate and postgraduate programs.
- The Faculty of Humanities, which offers programs in the humanities.
- The Faculty of Law, which currently offers a bachelor's degree in arts and law and a master's degree in law.
- The Faculty of Science, which offers only general Bachelor of Science and Master of Science degrees. The faculty has

recently started offering two new programs, a Bachelor of Technology in electronics with computer technology and a Bachelor of Technology in computer systems. It is anticipated that the faculty will establish closer working relations with the Lerotholi Polytechnic, which has hitherto been working more closely with South African technikons.
- The Faculty of Social Sciences, which offers a whole range of programs in the social sciences, with postgraduate programs in selected areas.
- The Faculty of Health, which has just been founded as the National Health Training Center (NHTC). For now, it offers subdegree programs in general nursing, medical laboratory science, pharmacy, public health, anesthesia, and psychiatry. The faculty has also assumed the role of leading and coordinating other health training institutions, such as three nursing training colleges.

The University has four institutes, which are mainly research oriented. These are the Institute of Education, the Institute of Extra-Mural Studies (which also operates an outreach program), the Institute of Southern African Studies, and the Institute of Labor Studies.

ADMISSIONS REQUIREMENTS AND ENROLLMENT

As a matter of policy, admission to NUL is open to any qualifying candidate regardless of age, sex, race, nationality, or religious affiliation. All new entrants to degree programs must have at least passed Cambridge Overseas School Certificate in the first or second division and must also have a credit in English language and an aggregate of no more than thirty-four credits.

For years, NUL has experienced the problem of low student intake into science programs because very few high school graduates have managed to earn the required credits in O-level mathematics and science subjects. In order to address this problem, the university is running a Pre-Entry Science Program (PESP) in which prospective science students come to the university some three months before the start of the first semester and receive special intensive lectures in mathematics and basic sciences. Those who pass the tests administered at the end of the course are registered for the first year of the Bachelor of Science program.

During the academic year 1999–2000, overall university enrollments stood at well over 2,800 students. This number includes both full-time and part-time students mainly based within the Institute of Extra-Mural Studies. About 80 percent are full-time students, while 20 percent are part-timers.

Basotho students constitute 94 percent of undergraduate students. Nonlocals, mostly from other African countries, account for about 6 percent.

Table 39.1 shows that more Basotho females than males enrolled in the education, social sciences, and humanities (arts) programs. The numbers were balanced in the law programs, while more males than females enrolled in the pure science–based programs. Overall, females accounted for 56 percent and males for 44 percent of NUL's enrollment. This trend is common across the undergraduate and postgraduate programs.

Table 39.1. Full-Time Basotho Students at the National University of Lesotho by Faculty and Gender, 1997–1998

Faculty	Certificates and Diplomas		First Degrees		Postgraduate Courses		All Courses		
	Male	Female	Male	Female	Male	Female	Male	Female	Total
Education	20	18	151	335	9	11	180	364	544
Social Sciences	22	10	271	321	2	—	295	331	626
Humanities	6	20	96	158		1	102	179	281
Law	—	—	104	105	—	—	104	105	209
Science	—	—	174	113	—	—	173	113	286
Agriculture	—	—	37	28	1	1	38	29	67
Total	48	48	833	1,060	12	13	892	1,121	2,013

Source: National University of Lesotho education statistics, 1997.

The explanation for the gender imbalances across programs could be the historical, cultural, stereotypical, and attitudinal factors that mean some females feel more at home with nonnumerical and nonscientific disciplines.

According to the 1999 Lesotho population data sheet, total enrollment for NTTC that year was 948, with a 73 percent female population, while 1,509 were enrolled in technical and vocational schools, of whom 43 percent were female.

THE POSTGRADUATE PROGRAMS

Enrollments in postgraduate programs are still very low. During the 1998–1999 academic year, the number stood at thirty-four students. Of these, twenty-three were registered in education programs (seven for the postgraduate certificate in education and sixteen for a master's degree). Women accounted for 61 percent of the postgraduate students.

The major reason for low postgraduate enrollments is the shortage of qualified staff to service the programs, particularly for the supervision of dissertation writing. For this same reason, the university still has not ventured to open up these programs for part-time study. Another critical factor is that as the major formal-sector employer in Lesotho, the government, as a matter of policy, does not necessarily reward higher qualifications beyond the first degree. This dissuades more people from taking the trouble to pursue further educational qualifications. Because of this policy, it becomes difficult for potential candidates to negotiate leaves to take classes, which forces them to resign from jobs to pursue their studies. However, in a country in which unemployment is so high, people do not want to risk losing their jobs by resigning. For the majority of university students, securing a loan from the National Manpower Development Secretariat (NMDS) is the only way to finance their studies. As a matter of NMDS policy, one has to first repay the loan upon completing a program before he or she can be granted another loan to pursue further studies. Because of the relatively low salary packages, it often takes students quite a while to repay, and sometimes they lose interest in continuing their education.

PART-TIME STUDY PROGRAMS

NUL and a few local tertiary institutions offer part-time study programs for candidates who, for one reason or another, cannot afford full-time study. The reasons include the following:

- Lesotho's high level of poverty, which makes it difficult for most candidates to afford the ever-rising cost of education (fees, books, equipment, etc.).
- The country's high unemployment rate, which means that people who are already in jobs do not want to risk resigning, especially given the high possibility of not being reabsorbed after completion of further study.
- The limited capacity of existing institutions to accommodate all qualified candidates. Most tertiary institutions, including NUL, cannot accommodate a good number of the full-time students in residential halls.

NUL offers a limited number of part-time certificate, diploma, and degree programs in business, education, and media. These programs are offered through a collaborative effort between the institutes and relevant faculties; the former handle administration and the latter are responsible for the academic aspects of the programs.

The programs are offered through a combination of distance education, block residential sessions (face-to-face tuition when students are on campus for a specified block period of a month or two), and direct-contact sessions with lecturers. Enrollment in part-time programs at NUL currently numbers about 1,000 students.

NTTC also offers in-service programs for teachers needing qualifications. The other local tertiary institutions do not offer part-time programs.

Distance education limits students to the use of printed media, given the lack of appropriate technology and communication networks in Lesotho. The mail delivery system still encounters delays, especially in the more rural parts of the country, leading to late submission of assignments and feedback. These and other related factors dissuade many potentially capable candidates from participating since they cannot afford the expenses of traveling to the nearest towns in which education centers are based.

LANGUAGE OF INSTRUCTION

English is the language of instruction in Lesotho, except in French- and Sesotho-language courses, in which English is used alongside the languages being taught. This policy applies to all tertiary and higher education institutions, whether they are public or private. Many students have been denied access because they lack a credit pass in English.

STAFFING

NUL has a teaching staff of about 216. Non-Basotho staff, the majority of whom hold professor or senior lecturer status, make up 26 percent of this figure. Most of them come from other African countries.

Although the university has a thriving staff development program, the institution is faced with a serious problem of not being able to retain most of them after they complete their training. The staff turnover is very high, since people resign to seek more lucrative jobs with better salary packages in the private sector and in South Africa. Even the nonlocal staff stay only a few monhs or years in Lesotho and pass on into South Africa.

The peculiar situation at NUL is that it has twice as many nonacademic support employees as it has academics. The financial resources of the university are, therefore, mainly devoted to nonteaching-related personnel costs. More than 60 percent of the institution's subvention goes to staff costs. This imposes limitations on the creation of additional teaching positions to enhance its academic programs. As indicated above, some postgraduate programs have been suspended due to shortage of academic staff. The ratio of academic staff to students in some faculties is 1 to 120.

To ensure that their interests and general welfare are protected, university employees have organized themselves into three staff unions:

- The Lesotho University Staff Union (LUTARU) for the academic staff, which includes teaching, research, library, and extension staff
- The Senior University Staff Union (SUSU) for senior university administrators, which includes the administrative assistant, assistant registrar, and senior assistant registrars
- The Non-Academic Workers Union (NAWU) for all other support staff

Following years of serious and often confrontational encounters, management and the unions negotiated and agreed to set regular, officially scheduled consultative meetings where issues can be thrashed out so as to avoid crisis situations that would disrupt the normal running of the institutions.

FINANCING AND FUNDING PATTERNS

Higher education in Lesotho is substantially financed by the government. The university gets about 90 percent of the funds it needs from the state. In 1999, the NUL budget amounted to M104,008,240 (1 Lesotho maloti (M; *pl.* maloti) = approximately US$0.10). About 78 percent went to personnel costs, leaving very little for development. The government supports capital projects and provides financial support to students through a loan program administered by the NMDS. Students repay the loans as soon as they have completed their studies and found jobs. Those who find employment outside the country must repay 100 percent of the principal, those who work in the private sector must repay 65 percent of the full loan amount, and those working in the public sector only need to repay 50 percent of the principal. Much of the money the university makes comes from student fees.

The NUL fee structure is very low compared to institutions in South Africa, where fees stand at seven times as much. For instance, tuition fees for Basotho students range from M3,500 per annum for arts students to M3,960 for science students, while foreign student rates stand at M11,665 per annum for arts students and M12,250 for science students. Although the quality of facilities and equipment at NUL is far below that of its South African counterparts, the university is engaged in ongoing negotiations with the government to increase fees at least fivefold. This would still be very modest given the amounts NMDS is prepared to pay for education outside the country.

Almost all of the studies on financing within the higher education subsector in Lesotho (including the World Bank Study 1984; Sims 1989; Fielden et al. 1995) have expressed concern about the deficiencies in the management of finances, especially at NUL, which is currently facing an unprecedented financial crisis. Problems included implementation of projects for which budgeting had not occurred. Similar studies were conducted within the public tertiary institutions by other consultants sponsored by the government and some of its development partners. These institutions also face similar financial management deficiencies. All of these commissions have recommended the institution of efficient and effective financial management strategies and serious cost-saving measures. The situation has not improved much. Most institutions are still in financial crisis despite their efforts to redress the situation.

Private-sector financial support to NUL is very limited. The university is devising strategies to forge partnerships with the private sector by seeking its input in curriculum reviews so the university can offer programs the private sector can support.

In a further effort not to rely entirely on government subsidy, the university has set up the NUL Consultancy Unit to negotiate consultancies for university staff with governmental and nongovernmental agencies. Part of each consultancy fee (40 percent) is paid into the university fund; the consultants retain 60 percent for each project they undertake.

Some donations in cash or kind have come from the international donor community. Prominent among these donors have been the British government, the World Bank, and the Netherlands government.

ALTERNATIVE TERTIARY AND HIGHER EDUCATION PROVISION BY FOREIGN INSTITUTIONS

In the past five years, Lesotho has experienced a trend of "mushrooming" institutions that facilitate provision of tertiary and higher education by their own home institutions outside of Lesotho. The government had to intervene to curb this ad hoc development by insisting that such institutions should at least be legally registered, while efforts are being made to develop a clear policy that would facilitate their being professionally vetted. The current lack of control has increased the competitiveness between local institutions and these new establishments. Most of them are distance-education institutions based mainly in South Africa. Examples include the Open Learning Group (OLG), which is not a school but an institution that acts as a channel to offer distance education by South African universities and technikons in countries outside South Africa. These institutions include the University of Potchefstroom, Port Elizabeth; the University of South Africa; and Rand Afrikaans University. In 2000, enrollment in these institutions stood at around 700. Other institutions operating in Lesotho originate from outside the African continent. Newport University is a legally registered institution in the state of California. It has a physical base in Lesotho and serves as an extension of its South African–based operation. The school currently enrolls about 400 students. British institutions also offer distance-education programs in Lesotho. Examples include the College of Preceptors, which concentrates on teacher education, and City and Guilds of London, which mainly provides for technical training. The Zimbabwe Open University is charged with regional coordination of the Commonwealth Youth Program, which is locally coordinated by the Institute of Extra-Mural Studies of NUL and is accredited by the Zimbabwean University. Ireland established the Center for Accounting Studies and continues to oversee its operations as a way of assuring quality.

A second category is composed of South African institutions that do not have agencies in Lesotho but are in direct contact with students who study part-time and go for block residential periods (ranging from a few weeks to a month) on the main South African campus. Such universities include the Universities of Orange Free State, the Western Cape, Natal Durban-Westville, and South Africa.

These institutions have filled a gap and are meeting the demand that NUL and the local tertiary institutions cannot. The limited capacity of the existing institutions makes it difficult to accommodate all candidates; moreover, NUL has tended to be conservative and has not quite opened up to attract and accommodate more students. Some constraints on NUL's expansion include:

• NUL's stringent admissions criteria, which require credit passes in English and/or mathematics regardless of the program for which an individual candidate has applied
• A lack of bridging programs. Potential entrants into science-based programs are taken through a six-month Pre-Entry Science Programme (PESP) to enhance their knowledge and skills, but no bridging programs exist in other disciplines. Therefore O-level results remain the only basis for screening candidates for admission.
• The delay by universities, NUL in particular, in diversifying courses and broadening the conventional university academic programs (often prompted by shortage of both physical and human resources and the necessary equipment)

In contrast, quite a number of international institutions with connections to Lesotho have some degree of flexibility with regard to both admissions criteria and student registration for studies, thereby eliminating the idea of closing dates. Even the decision regarding a student's course load rests with the student in consultation with tutors. Newport University, for instance, gives credit for work experience and specific workshops and short-term training programs in which candidates have participated. This generally leads to shortened periods of study.

These institutions also attract candidates because they offer a variety of programs that the local schools have not fully provided. These include human resource development and management, chartered accountancy, marketing, security studies related to policing, correctional services, traffic safety, computer technology, and advanced management.

MODE OF DELIVERY

Contact sessions are held countrywide at nearby selected centers with an academic adviser in Lesotho to guide and motivate students through their studies. Another way to deliver information is through correspondence programs with a backup of extensive instructional materials and regular workshops. In other institutions, classes are scheduled throughout the day and students work out their individual timetables and attend lectures at times that best suit them. One important challenge facing all these institutions is the production of appropriate teaching and learning materials that are affordable for students.

DISADVANTAGES RELATED TO THE INTERNATIONAL INSTITUTIONS

In 1998, the Ministry of Education commissioned a study by Setsabi and Matsela to evaluate Newport University. The commission generally reported positively about Newport. Similar institutions might also achieve similar results, but the necessary studies have not been conducted.

Despite Newport's high marks, local professional circles generally feel that these institutions are seeking to rip off Basotho with exorbitant tuition fees and expensive study materials without regard for quality of education. Many regard the flexibility in their admissions criteria as an indication of their willingness to compromise quality. Others argue that the majority of students admitted into these programs would never have qualified for admission to their main campuses in South Africa, even though students' examination papers are compiled and moderated by the lecturers of the accrediting institutions.

Because the NMDS is reluctant to give financial support to Basotho students enrolled in these institutions, their students generally have to support themselves. The probability is therefore high that the cost of tuition, books, and other related expenses will cause many students to drop out. Students working with overseas institutions often find that foreign exchange rates are far too high for them.

Institutions such as OLG operate a loan scheme through Edu-loan, a company registered in Lesotho that makes it financially viable for students to further their studies. For students who are becoming teachers, the Ministry of Education has provided support that encourages them to stay in the programs.

INFLUX OF BASOTHO STUDENTS INTO SOUTH AFRICAN INSTITUTIONS

When South Africa achieved democracy in 1994, opportunities that had previously been denied to the majority black population there started to open up to them. This included gaining access to higher education provided in the traditionally whites-only universities and technikons. Other black candidates from neighboring countries were also given the opportunity to enroll if they qualified for admission. This has contributed to an influx of Basotho candidates entering South African institutions, especially since local institutions cannot accommodate all qualifying candidates. Moreover, the former white South African institutions had superior programs, resources, facilities, and staff, which make them attractive to students.

The government of Lesotho pays out millions of maloti to South African institutions to support the education of Basotho students. According to the current NMDS statistics, about 2,400 Basotho students are currently enrolled in universities and technikons. The government pays at least M20,000 per annum in tuition fees per student. This amount excludes a stipend. In comparison, NUL charges about one-seventh this amount. South Africa has always argued that foreign students in its institutions are highly subsidized and ought to be charged more.

INSTITUTIONAL LINKS

NUL has a tradition of forging and maintaining links with other universities worldwide. The links with overseas institutions mainly concentrate on academic matters such as staff training.

The links with universities and other institutions in the subregion are the most useful in helping NUL grow and ensure academic excellence and quality in its work. Examples of the institutions that have links with NUL are the Universities of Botswana and Swaziland (which have historical connections and share a common culture), the University of Cape Town, the University of Fort Hare, the University of Wits, the University of Natal, the University of Western Cape, the University of Orange Free, and UNISA. The university has greatly benefited from its membership in international associations such as the Association of Commonwealth Universities (ACU), the Association of African Universities (AAU), and the Association of Eastern and Southern African Universities (AESAU). Cooperation at this level facilitates staff and student exchanges, external examinerships, and joint research projects. A similar pattern of cooperation has emerged between local tertiary institutions and their counterparts in South Africa, Botswana, and Swaziland. Regional initiatives such as the SADC (South African Development Community) Protocol on Education and Training are intended to provide a logistical framework to facilitate cooperation among regional institutions. One significant provision of the protocol is its concept of centers of specialization, which calls for institutions to specialize in specific areas and serve as a resource for the region. This arrangement would work to put countries' limited resources and facilities to maximum use.

THE STATE OF RESEARCH AND PUBLISHING

Research is one of the three major functions that all academic staff are expected to undertake, along with teaching and community service. The expectation is highest among staff who work in the full-time research institutes (Institute of Education, Institute of Labor Studies, and Institute of Southern African Studies), since they are required to do less teaching. In addition to its research activities, the Institute of Extra-Mural Studies engages in outreach activities in communities throughout the country. It also provides part-time programs in business and adult education. The bulk of NUL's research output comes from the institutes. The areas covered include the social sciences, education, law, humanities, and the sciences. Research is essentially development oriented and seeks to address pertinent problems facing Lesotho.

Some money is budgeted to facilitate research within the institutes. However, the institutes also have to seek funding by writing and selling project proposals to the donor agencies, to industry, and to the government. The university's budgeted research funds are disbursed by the Research and Conferences Committee, which is chaired by the pro-vice-chancellor. This fund can be accessed by any member of staff who submits a solid proposal. All proposals are screened by the committee. The fact that this fund has never been exhausted in any given year is seen as an indication that staff members are not undertaking as much research as they could.

Commissioned research is also conducted by the various units of the university. The government of Lesotho and international agencies are the university's major research clients. Civil society organizations in the Lesotho Council of Non-Governmental Organizations (LCN) have received help in conducting needs assessment and evaluation studies. The NUL Consultancy Unit facilitates and coordinates staff consultancy efforts. The unit sells the university's research capacity to potential clients who, in turn, contract members through this unit to undertake research.

Individual staff members also seek funding on their own to undertake research, though there is little evidence of this taking place in the tertiary institutions, except when studies are commissioned for outsiders to undertake research to inform curriculum reviews and other transformative processes through donor funding.

Research and development is a critical area for cooperation between institutions at the regional level and beyond. But Lesotho can meaningfully participate only if it develops a national research council to regulate, coordinate, and oversee the conduct of research. One of the problems that Lesotho has faced has been external researchers coming into the country to conduct research and departing without leaving even a copy of their findings for the country's records. These guests could also involve local researchers and help build Lesotho's research capacity. All this could be facilitated by a research council. The idea of establishing a council has been talked about for the past twenty years, but bureaucratic hurdles in the government and within educational institutions have frustrated progress on this project.

PUBLISHING

To encourage publishing by its staff, NUL has helped establish several journals, some of which are departmental, faculty, and general university journals. These include the *NUL Journal*, the *Law Journal* from the law faculty, and *Mohlomi Journal* in the history department. The National Teacher Training College has also established its own journal, *The Lesotho Journal of Teacher Education*, to facilitate publication by both NTTC staff and other educators.

The Institute for Southern African Studies (ISAS) operates a documentation and publishing unit. Staff or any interested persons can have their work published through ISAS. Faculty continue to publish in the reputable journals throughout the world, and their output has increased significantly in recent years.

POLICIES ON HIGHER EDUCATION

Lesotho has no clearly articulated and documented general policy on higher education and training. This includes tertiary-level education. This condition has resulted in a disorganized and unsystematic development of the subsector. Without any legal framework governing tertiary and higher education, it is difficult for the Ministry of Education to effectively control and monitor the subsector. The government has recently decided that a process should be set in motion to facilitate the establishment of a higher education council or commission that will be responsible for all issues relating to tertiary and higher education. One of the positive decisions by Lesotho's government has been its recent establishment of a Department of Tertiary and Higher Education within the Ministry of Education. Its major responsibility is to coordinate and facilitate development of policies for all tertiary education and training.

Historically, provision of higher education in Lesotho has been the monopoly of government. However, more private efforts are being made to provide education. This falls within the realm of those issues that need a declared policy to guide and regulate them. This is the most immediate challenge facing the government, since private education provision is currently unregulated.

CHALLENGES AND PROBLEMS FACING
HIGHER EDUCATION IN LESOTHO

Lesotho's higher education subsector faces serious problems that need urgent attention. They include:

- The lack of policy governing higher education. Lesotho needs a national council for higher education that would coordinate all matters relating to this subsector.
- The lack of a national development plan to guide training priorities.
- The lack of an adequate accreditation system. At present, Lesotho has no national evaluation tool for international/foreign certificates but depends on the Human Science Research Council (HSRC) in South Africa for assessments.
- The inequitable distribution of institutions of higher learning within the country. Institutions are concentrated in the capital city, Maseru, and a few district headquarters in the lowlands. The rural mountain population is greatly disadvantaged. Thus, potential candidates in these areas are actually denied easy access to higher education.
- Overpopulation and the high population growth rate (2.6 percent annually), which cause the whole education sector to be overstretched. There is an ever-increasing demand for higher education, and existing institutions can no longer cope. Other limitations on institutions are that they cannot offer the whole range of specializations from which people want to choose. This is in part due to economic reasons, since it is very expensive to provide the requisite facilities, equipment, teaching, and learning materials. Consequently, students often opt to enroll and register in South African institutions, thereby diverting scholarship funds to sustain them during their training in South Africa.
- Brain drain, since the country's retention level of highly trained and qualified personnel is very low. The South African job market provides handsome salary packages, with which Lesotho's economy cannot compete. So the capacity of institutions is continuously eroded. Even those who study and qualify in South African institutions seldom return home after completing their studies, because they are absorbed by the South African job market.
- The lack of gender equity in higher education. Gender balance has to be promoted in enrollments across disciplines. This requires a deliberate effort by the institutions themselves and by all stakeholders. Many in Lesotho still think that technical and science subjects are for males and that females have to settle for the so-called soft subjects.
- The qualitatively poor secondary and high school subsector, which does not produce qualified candidates for higher education. Many candidates have a difficult time passing English, the major language of instruction, so most of them fail to qualify for admission into higher education. Bridging programs are needed before entry into tertiary or higher education institutions. These are bound to be very costly.
- The HIV/AIDS epidemic, which is decimating the pool of potential candidates for higher education. Lesotho needs to incorporate an education component in the existing curriculum at this level and lower to sensitize students to the disastrous consequences of this disease for the whole nation.
- The lack of quality assurance and control. This problem has yet to be adequately addressed. Induction programs for newly recruited staff and continuous upgrading of staff are crucial in this regard.
- The dependence of Lesotho's universities on government subvention. Several recommendations have been made in the past to encourage institutions to forge viable strategies to secure funding from industry and the private sector and to engage in income-generating activities by marketing their own services.

• The lack of credit transfer mechanisms between Lesotho institutions and those in South Africa and beyond. This will require standardization of programs. The implementation of the SADC Protocol on Education and Training is likely to ensure that this happens.

The phenomenon of globalization poses a special challenge and in some ways a threat to small and poor states such as Lesotho, which has a very modest tertiary and higher education subsector. However, it has broken down barriers among and between countries so education can be accessed globally across frontiers. This has both advantages and challenges for educational institutions, which have to ensure that they measure up to expectations on the global stage.

CONCLUSION

Lesotho has only one university, but it has a network of more than twenty tertiary institutions. Some are run by the government, while others are operated by private organizations, including churches. Special mention has been made here of those institutions that are either NUL affiliates or have a special working relationship with the university.

Another critical factor that needs special attention is the intensifying process of establishment of foreign institutions in Lesotho that are extensions of South African universities and technikons, which are not currently regulated. This practice brings into question the quality of education in Lesotho. At the same time, this development is viewed positively by many, who feel that these schools are filling a gap and believe in the ability of the existing local institutions to satisfy the demands for higher education.

NUL has several development projects lined up. The institution needs to find alternative means of funding so it can reduce its almost total dependence on government funding. The prospect of privatizing the university has not been fully explored, but it is perhaps a viable option.

REFERENCES

Fielden, J., A. Schofield, D. Berube, R. Blair, A. Crompton, M. Mofolo, and D. Tarpeh. 1995. *Cost Containment Study at the National University of Lesotho.* London: Commonwealth Higher Education Management Service.

Kimane I., M. Ntimo-Makara, and M. Molise. 1999. *Socio-Cultural Phenomena Related to Population and Development in Lesotho.* Maseru: Ministry of Economic and Planning.

Lerotholi Polytechnic. 1999. Calendar.

Lesotho College of Education Act. 1998.

Lesotho Institute of Public Administration. 1989–1990. Prospectus.

Makoa, F. K. 2000. "Divestiture and Dependence: Reflections on Lesotho's Privatization Programme." In K. K. Prah and A. G. M. Ahmed, eds., *Africa in Transition: Political and Economic Transformation and Socio-political Responses in Africa,* 119–138. Addis Ababa: OSSREA.

Malie, E. M., N. Gebre-ab, A. S. Hartwell, V. P. Machai, S. M. Mokete, I. L. Monese, M. R. Montši, A. Motanyane, M. Motselebane, A. P. Nyenye, M. M. Tiheli, M. T. Motsoene, W. L. Perry, and E. M. Sebatane. 1982. *The Education Sector Survey: Report of the Task Force.* Maseru: Ministry of Education.

Matsela, Z. A. 1986. *Case Study of Lesotho's Higher Education Institutions.* Maseru: UNESCO.

Matsela, Z. A., O. M. Seheri, S. Baholo, C. M. Bohloko, M. M. Maloba, and W. M. Buku. 1978. *Report on the Views and Recommendations Regarding the Future of Education in Lesotho.* Maseru: Lesotho Government Ministry of Education.

Ministry of Education. 1999. Report of Stakeholders Workshop on Higher/Tertiary Education, August 31, Lesotho Sun–Maseru.

National Teachers Training College. 1997. Calendar.

National University of Lesotho. 1992. Order no. 19.

———. 1994–1995. *Faculty of Agriculture Student's Handbook.*

———. 1997–2000. Calendar.

———. 1999–2000. "Creating Effective Educational Opportunities for Basotho." Vice-Chancellor's Annual Report to Council. Volume I and II.

———. 2000a. "National University of Lesotho: A Brief Profile." Roma: Development and Planning Office.

———. 2000b. *Newsletter Information Flash,* vol. 7, no. 1 (April 1).

———. 2000c. *Vision 2000 Plus.* Roma: Development and Planning Office.

Ntimo-Makara, M. 1999. "Academic Quality: Critical Issues for the National University of Lesotho." Paper presented at the Lesotho National Commission/NUL Faculty of Social Sciences Regional Workshop on Relevance and Quality in the Formulation and Implementation of Socially Sustainable Development Programmes, Maseru Sun Hotel, Maseru, August 24–26.

O' Neil, M. 1990. *Effective Teaching and Learning at NUL.* A Report on a British Council Consultancy. Maseru: British Council.

SADC (South African Development Community). 1977. "Protocol on Education and Training."

———. 1993–2003. "Long Term Strategy for the Human Resources Development Sector." Mbabane: SADC Human Resources Sector.

Setsabi, A. M., and Z. A. Matsela. 1998. *Report of the Newport University Study Commission.* Maseru: Ministry of Education.

Sims, G. D., E. S. Baholo, N. S. Ndebele, M. Shattock, and A. Wandira. 1989. "Report of a Review Commission for NUL."

UNFPA (United Nations Population Fund) and Government of Lesotho. 1996. *Programme Review and Strategy Development Report.* Maseru: Ministry of Development Planning.

40

Liberia

PATRICK L. N. SEYON

OVERVIEW AND CONTEXT

Liberia was founded in 1822 by the American Colonization Society to settle freed American slaves. Liberia's population subsequently included slaves recaptured from slave ships that operated along the West African coast. It declared itself independent in 1847, becoming modern Africa's oldest republic. One of the two African countries not formally colonized by a European power, Liberia was ruled continually by American settlers until 1980, when a military coup brought Master Sergeant Samuel K. Doe, an indigenous Liberian, to power. He was a member of the Krahn ethnic group, one of sixteen in Liberia. The Krahn account for approximately 90 percent of the Liberian population. Variously estimated at between 2.5 and 3 million, Liberia's annual population growth rate is 3.3 percent, one of the highest on the African continent. Life expectancy is estimated at between 50 and 56 years.

Liberia has a dual economy based on a subsistence agrarian sector (with some cash cropping) and a modern monetary sector, operating basically on the export of raw materials. The principal foreign exchange earners are iron ore and rubber. Wood, coffee, cocoa, gold, and diamonds are Liberia's other important exports. Liberia's gross domestic product (GDP) per capita has been variously estimated at between $386 and $500. Liberia also has a dual currency system: the U.S. dollar, which was Liberia's adopted currency before 1980, is used alongside the Liberian dollar, which has a floating exchange rate of 45–75 Liberian dollars to 1 U.S. dollar. The government is the largest employer, but since the war (1989–1997), unemployment has shot up to 50 percent and underemployment has skyrocketed.

English is the official language of Liberia. It is used for instruction in school from the primary level through college. According to UNESCO (1999), Liberia's literacy rate is 46.6 percent. There are four major indigenous language groups, of which Kpelle is the largest; it is spoken by 22 percent of the population.

Even though Liberia's most recent education plan before the outbreak of the war, the National Education Plan of 1978–1990, called for expanding access to formal education, only 36 percent of the eligible school-age children were enrolled by 1988. Enrollment at the primary level had already begun to decline. Between 1984 and 1987, primary enrollment fell 27 percent (IEES 1988). During the war years, the public school system shut down and only a few missionary schools operated in Monrovia, the capital. Since the end of the war in 1997, enrollments have not reached their prewar levels at the primary and secondary levels. Shortages of schools and teachers and inadequate funding are responsible for Liberia's low school enrollment. Donor support for education, a major source of funding on which the Liberian government depends, declined dramatically by the mid-1980s and has all but dried up since the war. The World Bank, the African Development Bank, and the International Monetary Fund (IMF) were Liberia's principal educational supporters.

These developments have directly and indirectly impacted higher education in Liberia. Up to the end of the 1980s, there existed in Liberia a sort of higher education "system." However, the war that ripped Liberia apart destroyed the education system, leaving it a "mess" and a "system of problems" (Ackoff, Finnel, and Gharajedaghi 1984, 21). This study examines the "mess" in the context of some of the historical, economic, social, and political forces that have shaped postsecondary education in Liberia for the past century and a half. This approach benefits from the suggestion that "many of the current policy problems in higher education [in developing countries] have their roots in historical precedents, social traditions and values, and political imperatives" (Ransom, Khoo, and Selvaratnam 1993, 3).

At the start of the twenty-first century, the keys to sustainable development in Africa in general, and Liberia in particular, are human resource development and institution building. The critical institution in the process is the university. The centrality of the university in developing human capacity is universally acknowledged. It is not just Thomas Huxley's (1900) "factory of new knowledge." It is also the engine that drives the modern, or postmodern, world. As Jaroslave Pelikan has pointed out, "A modern society is unthinkable without the university" (1992, 13). Ismail Serageldin, the director of the technical department of the Africa region for the World Bank, notes that "strong universities are vital for enhancing African capacities to plan and manage national affairs." He adds: "Without academically and financially viable universities, Africa's future will be forfeited" (1992, vii).

These concerns raise an interesting set of questions regarding Liberia and its higher education system. Have things fallen apart in Liberia because it lacks an "academically and financially viable" university education system? Or are there other variables that can explain the Liberian situation? What if, for example, the university in Liberia was "academically and financially viable" but still lacked an enabling social and political environment and political commitment and support for the university project, or "the idea of the university" (Jaspers 1959; Newman 1976; Pelikan 1992)? Could it still deliver on providing "capacities to plan and manage" Liberia's national affairs? Could the university system in Liberia pass Altbach's (1998) test, for example, of "championing academic freedom" and the larger framework of freedoms of which academic freedom is a part, if in fact it operates in an oppressive, authoritarian context? Last, but not least, what if the university is mistaken for an *institution* instead of an *idea* (Pelikan 1992)? Can its mission in Liberia be properly understood and evaluated as providing or failing to provide "capacities to plan and manage [Liberia's] national affairs"?

These questions guide the inquiry into the university project in Liberia, which begins with the social context of education in Liberia. As Pelikan (1992, 137) has pointed out, one cannot "ignore the context of society within which [the university] lives and without which it could not exist." This analysis of context is followed by a brief historical review, which will demonstrate that the sponsorship and implementation of the university project by external forces have created huge problems for Liberia. Even when African states made efforts to create the "African university" (Yesufu 1973) and to make it the engine for Africa's socioeconomic and political development, the university in Liberia lacked the political support from the ruling elite needed to make it a "development university" for Liberia (Seyon 1973). Next, the current situation is described, followed by examination of issues such as policy reform, curriculum, funding, governance, research, and challenges for the future.

THE CONTEXT

Liberia has twin contexts—Africa and globalization—that have impacted the university project, and against which the challenges that lie ahead for postsecondary education in Liberia should be assessed. Liberia projects contradictory images to the world. The country is simultaneously Africa's oldest republic and its oldest one-party state. It has one of Africa's oldest modern universities, yet it is non-African for all practical purposes. It conducted supposedly democratic elections in 1997 that put a warlord into power, without democracy, and is mired in crises stretching back more than a century. Aspects of this context are relevant to the university project in Liberia, and they are examined briefly below.

Since the second half of the nineteenth century, the Liberian ruling class has shown little interest in "the idea of the university." Instead, it was outsiders such as the originator of the college project, Prof. Simon Greenlead of Harvard University, who "believed that the great need of [Liberia] was a literary and scientific college" (Allen 1923, 15). Part of this lack of enthusiasm for higher education was associated with the denial of such education to the freed slaves who settled in Liberia after they were in the United States. For example, Edward Wilmot Blyden, who was born in the Dutch West Indies and served as president of Liberia College, was denied admission to Rutgers University and other universities "because of the color of his skin" (Ajayi, Goma, and Johnson 1996, 17). The externally determined provision of higher education for Liberia did not necessarily incorporate what Liberians perceived as the function to be served by such education. This external support very early established Liberia's dependency on external forces not only for financial and other support, but, equally important, in determining the curriculum and hiring the faculty. In the 1880s and 1890s, and again in the 1920s and 1930s, both Liberia College and Cuttington College experienced temporary closures when overseas support was held up. (In the 1980s, a dramatic drop in support for education in Liberia by the World Bank, African Development Bank, and the International Monetary Fund led to an equally dramatic decline in government funding for all levels of education.)

In addition, the Liberian ruling elite did not make a connection between higher education and national development. Nor was there strong popular demand for higher education in Liberia during the last half of the nineteenth and first half of the twentieth centuries. As Hoff explains: "Liberia's circumstances during the first part of the nineteenth century inevitably retarded the spread of convictions, held by enlightened leaders, that higher education was necessary to national growth. . . . Popular sympathy for the cause of higher education was almost lacking" (1962, 52).

Nonetheless, a clash took place between internal and external forces over the curriculum for higher education in Liberia. Between 1862 (when Liberia College was founded) and 1890, a lively debate occurred about whether or not to establish a nonsectarian West African University. Among the influential participants was Edward Wilmot Blyden of Liberia. Blyden advocated for an institution whose African teachers "would have great influence in exposing and correcting the fallacies upon which our foreign teachers have proceeded in their utter misapprehension and, perhaps, contempt of African character" (Ajayi, Goma, and Johnson 1996, 19–20).

In his 1881 inaugural lecture at Liberia College, "The Aims and Methods of a Liberal Education for Africans," Blyden argued against the inclusion of modern European civilization in the curriculum of the West African University. This was because the period covered the trans-Atlantic slave trade and "theories—theological, social and political—[which] were invented for the degradation and proscription of the Negro." Instead, he chose the classics, because they "were capable of providing intellectual nourishment . . . without . . . race poison." To the classics, he wanted to add Arabic, mathematics, and major African languages (Ajayi, Goma, and Johnson 1996). Unfortunately, Blyden did not stay long enough in the presidency at Liberia College to implement his program. He left in 1884. But his imprimatur of a classical curriculum and liberal education stayed with the college until it became a university in 1951.

Although it was formally an independent country, Liberian's state-run higher education program was affected by the European conquest and colonization of Africa in the second half of the nineteenth century. Liberia adopted the European colonial model for governance of the African territories it acquired (Liebenow 1986) and imposed this model on its program of higher education. In this context, the state required the total submission of the "colonized" and was ruthless in punishing those it perceived as a challenge to its authority. Similarly, "The Laws of Liberia College" required students to subscribe to the following oath in order to be admitted: "I promise, on condition of being admitted as a member of Liberia College, . . . to obey all the laws and regulations of this College; I will faithfully avoid . . . disrespectful conduct to the Faculty, and all combinations to resist their authority" (Hoff 1962, 113). Those refusing to subscribe were denied.

The college laid down detailed rules and regulations that totally controlled every aspect of the students' lives, including when they were away from the campus. A student could be punished by expulsion for the mere act of treating any of the laws and regulations "with reviling or reproachful language, or by being guilty of any kind of contempt of their person or authority" (Hoff 1962, 115). The status of the students at the college was no different from that of the colonized in the state.

The combined effects of a lack of popular support and demand for higher education, the adoption of a classical curriculum, and the authoritarian governance structure meant that an innovative system of higher education, such as the land grant college system in the United States, could not have emerged. Instead, the college or university served to pass on ancient "truths" to its submissive students and did not become Huxley's "factory of new knowledge," challenging established order and orthodoxies, exploring new horizons in search of new truths, and creating new worldviews. These functions were reserved for the future.

Globalization imposed modernization imperatives and incorporated Liberia into the world capitalist system. The country specialized as a supplier of raw materials (mainly rubber and iron ore) and cheap labor, at wages of 50 cents per day, while serving as a market for imported manufactured goods. U.S. investment in Liberia, starting with Firestone in 1926, grew to $500 million by 1980. Like most exploited countries, however, Liberia grew "without development" (Clower, Dalton, and Harwitz 1966). Social inequality flourished. Literacy, which once stood at 80 percent, is now down to 46.6 percent; infant mortality rose; and life expectancy has fallen from 56 to 46 years (UNESCO 1999).

Modernization spurred Liberian nationalism and demands for fundamental human rights. This provided the moral, sociopolitical, and legal basis for the oppressed majority indigenous peoples to demand their civil liberties in the 1960s and 1970s, and Liberia experienced its first military coup in 1980. Instead of the good life that modernization promised Liberians, social, economic, and political conditions in Liberia plummeted rapidly following the coup. Human rights, civil liberties, and democracy were pushed aside and subordinated to the great power interests of the Cold War. Liberia served as the regional headquarters of the Central Intelligence Agency and Voice of America for Africa and the Near East. That gave it a strategic and military position in U.S. foreign policy and the Cold War (Schraeder 1994). For that reason, the United States supported the brutal military dictatorship of Samuel K. Doe, which paved the way to the civil war of 1989–1997.

During the 1980s, Liberia swung from a one-party state to a military dictatorship. By the 1980s, the general consensus was that Africa was in crisis. Liberia's eight-year factional war, which killed 250,000 and displaced two-thirds of its population of 2.5 million, epitomized Africa's crises (Seyon 1998; World Bank 1989; Davidson 1992; Hawk 1996; Ayittey 1999; Roberg 2000). In this context of totalizing power and authoritarianism, ethnic violence and civil wars, and superpower rivalry, the university in Liberia came under sustained violent attack by the state, sometimes encouraged or supported by the superpowers. Twice, in 1979 and 1984, Liberia's leading institution of higher education, the University of Liberia, was closed by the government due to student protests. A 1984 raid on the campus led to the death of at least two students, the rape of others, and the wounding of hundreds. Student leaders were arrested and threatened with summary executions. This was in the heyday of the Cold War, and the university was seen by the superpowers as the critical institution, next to the state, for socializing, controlling the minds, and winning the hearts of Africa's youth and future leaders to their particular brand of ideology. Thus, the scramble for control of the university in Africa became as fierce, if not more so, as that for Africa in the late nineteenth century. The university was perceived by Africa's political elite (who sometimes were semiliterate military dictators) and their superpower patrons not as a mere contender for "power" through stirring up popular revolts but also an extension of what President Ronald Reagan called the Soviet "evil empire." Under the expansionist doctrine, any faculty and student voices on the campuses raised against oppression and tyranny, whether for legitimate causes or not, were suspect and were met with merciless repression. Democracy and human rights became dirty, politically incorrect code words for socialism or communism.

This context bred contempt for intellectuals and the university, particularly for those advocating social transformation, economic equity, democracy, and human rights. This anti-intellectualism, together with the ideology that investment in higher education did not yield higher returns than investment in elementary and secondary education, led to the abandonment of development of the university in Liberia.

At the same time, the context of globalization contributed to a modernization mission for the university that was not without contradictions (Schraeder 2000). The mission included (a) transforming and "modernizing" African local cultures; (b) helping to create rational, impersonal modern nation-states; (c) preparing the formerly colonized exploited peoples to participate in the world capitalist economy; and (d) producing the high-level managerial and technical skills needed to operate and industrialize the new states. But that mission has been made extremely difficult, if not impossible. Local African cultures and the university itself may be too weak to successfully resist the forces of globalization threatening extinction, at worst, and irrelevance, at best (Sklair 1991; Schugurensky 1999). There are three fundamental factors, which, in combination, make the modernization mission nearly impossible. First, the African ruling elite lack the political will and commitment to carry out the project. Second, the university lacks both the capacity and resources to carry it out (Castells 1993). Third, external forces, particularly the World Bank, undermine development and the university in Africa (Assié-Lumumba 1993; Ajayi, Goma, and Johnson 1996).

Where does all of this leave "the idea of the university" in Liberia and Africa? Can the modernization mission assigned the university be achieved in these contexts, and how then is the university to proceed? The partial answer is for the university to do what it is best capable of doing. And that is to focus almost exclusively on the most central of the mission's modernization goals: providing the high-level labor power, equipped with scientific and technological skills and knowledge, for efficient management of the state and higher labor productivity and research. All this will serve as the engine powering rapid economic growth and modernization. Jacques Hallak states the case when he writes:

> There are five "energisers" of human resource development: education; health and nutrition; the environment; employment; and political and economic freedom. These energisers are interlinked and interdependent, but education is the basis for all the others, an essential factor in the improvement of health and nutrition, for maintaining a high-quality environment, for expanding and improving labor pools, and for sustaining political and economic responsibility. (Hallak 1990, 1)

It remains to be seen whether the university in Liberia can enter postmodernity, leapfrogging over modernity, to become Clark Kerr's "multiversity" (Kerr 1963). Will it have the freedom or autonomy, the political commitment, and the financial support needed to pursue its mission unhindered?

HISTORICAL BACKGROUND

From 1862 to the mid-1980s, higher education in Liberia centered around three institutions: Liberia College, precursor to the University of Liberia, Liberia's oldest public institution of higher education; Cuttington Collegiate College, precursor to Cutttington University College, a private college supported by the Board of Missions of the Episcopal Church in the United States; and Liberia's second public postsecondary institution, the William V. S. Tubman College of Technology, incorporated in 1978, formerly Harper Technical College, which was founded in 1971. Four private institutions claimed junior college status by the mid-1980s: Ricks Institute (now defunct), Zion Academy (now Zion Community College), Monrovia College, and the

College of West Africa (IEES 1988). In addition, there are two public Rural Teacher Training Institutes (RTTIs): Kakata Rural Teacher Training Institute (KRTTI) and the Zorzor Rural Teacher Training Institute (ZRTTI), which are supposed to be postsecondary but have not adhered to their formally stated mandate. Two additional postsecondary training institutions are the Mano River Union Forestry Training Institute and the Tubman National Institute of Medical Arts. Since the mid-1990s, Monrovia College has been raised to a four-year liberal arts college and has been renamed A.M.E. University (it now has financial support from the African Methodist Episcopal Church in the United States), and a new institution, also private and supported by the Catholic Church, Don Bosco Technical College, has been established.

LIBERIA COLLEGE/UNIVERSITY OF LIBERIA

Higher education started in Liberia with the establishment of Liberia College in 1862. A group of philanthropists known as the Trustees of Donations for Education in Liberia, representing the Massachusetts Colonization Society (MCS), based in Boston, Massachusetts, established the college. The MCS was the Massachusetts branch of the American Colonization Society (ACS).

Even though the Liberian legislature passed an act to establish the college, funding for construction of buildings, equipment, library resources, and faculty salary was provided by the Trustees of Donations up to 1878 (Hoff 1962). As noted earlier, the college offered a classical liberal arts program. Except for the inclusion of Arabic, the curriculum did not include courses directly related to the social, economic, political, and historical conditions of Liberia and Africa until 1951, when the college was raised to a university, and it hardly did so even then.

In this college, the Trustees of Donations felt that the Africans could demonstrate to a doubtful world that they were capable of intellectual pursuit, a proposition considered laughable in the Western world at the time. It is, therefore, no surprise that the broad mission of the college, as envisioned by the trustees, was to provide "any desirable number of students, a thorough literary, scientific, and professional education" (Allen 1923, 5). Ultimately, the graduates from the college were to become leaders of the state and church in Liberia. This mission was achieved; the college produced six of Liberia's presidents and a host of high-ranking officials of both the state and church.

The issue of adapting the college to the needs of Liberians claimed the attention of the trustees between 1880 and 1885. A study was done to adopt the model of the Hampton Institute in Virginia and to add a Normal Department and an Agricultural and Industrial Department. A proposal was adopted in 1884 to reorganize the college into three departments: the Elementary Course, the Scientific Course, and the Classical Course. The Trustees of Donations stated: "These will reach the masses of the youth, preparing intelligent laborers, efficient teachers, and fitting the few for the professions" (Allen 1923, 55). The Trustees of Donations decided that Liberia College would do for the Africans in Liberia what Hampton Institute was doing for the Native Americans in Virginia. Financial support for higher education in Liberia continued to be provided by the Trustees of

Donations, although the needs of the University of Liberia far exceeded its level of support.

Located in Monrovia, Liberia's capital, the University of Liberia, successor to Liberia College, was founded in 1951. Its charter states that the mission of the university included, among other goals, the creation of an institution of higher learning to provide professional training in all disciplines to all, Liberians and non-Liberians alike, and to provide an environment in which knowledge could be pursued "in an atmosphere of academic freedom" for its own end and could be used to remove the barriers inhibiting full development of Liberian society (Hoff 1962, 120).

The university offers a total of thirty-two degree programs in its five undergraduate colleges and four graduate programs. The five undergraduate colleges are Liberia College (College of Social Sciences and Humanities); William V. S. Tubman Teachers College; T. J. R. Faulkner College of Science and Technology; the College of Business and Public Administration; and W. R. T. Jr. College of Agriculture and Forestry. Postgraduate degrees are awarded in the following schools and colleges: the A. M. Dogliotti College of Medicine, the Louis Arthur Grimes School of Law, the School of Pharmacy, and the Regional Planning Program.

Liberia's war of 1989–1997 left the university in total ruins. Efforts have been underway since 1991 to restore university facilities. Estimates of necessary repairs and renovations made in 1991 put the cost at over $20 million, and the current government, which came to power in 1997, has paid very little attention to the needs of the institution by providing the necessary funds. The war-related damage to the institution has set it back for at least a half-century, if not more. Many of the senior scholars who fled the country due to the war are unlikely to return. The current staff work six to eight months before they receive one month's pay, which is less than $50.

CUTTINGTON COLLEGIATE AND DIVINITY SCHOOL/CUTTINGTON UNIVERSITY COLLEGE

In 1888, the Board of Missions of the Episcopal Church in the United States established Hoffman Institute in Harper City, Maryland County. A year later, a divinity school was added, and the institute was renamed Cuttington Collegiate and Divinity School, in honor of R. Fulton Cutting, treasurer of the Board of Missions, who provided the initial amount of $5,000 to set up the school. Like Liberia College, the college offered a classical liberal arts program. From 1929 to 1948, the college was closed principally for financial reasons. In 1949, it was relocated to Suacoco, central Liberia, its present campus, which is about 120 miles northwest of Monrovia. Its mission statement provides for the creation of a liberal arts college to prepare students with a "strong Christian character" to enter the marketplace or pursue graduate studies.

The college's curriculum now offers twelve bachelor's degrees in education, humanities, social sciences, nursing, sciences, and theology. Its Rural Development Institute offers a two-year associate degree in agriculture with a major in plant or animal science (Snyder and Nagel 1985).

Cuttington University College was also not spared by Libe-

ria's war and suffered extensive damage to its physical plant. It did not operate during the war years. Prior to the war, the institution was primarily supported by a subsidy from the Liberian government. Since the war, it has received unfulfilled promises from the government and no cash.

HARPER TECHNICAL COLLEGE/WILLIAM V. S. TUBMAN COLLEGE OF TECHNOLOGY

By the close of the 1960s, Liberia was experiencing phenomenal economic "growth without development" (Clower, Dalton, and Harwitz 1966), and concerns were raised about the need for an institution that would train middle-level technicians and technical teachers for elementary and secondary schools—a need considered critical for national development and one that was not being met by the two existing institutions of higher learning. This led to the establishment of the Harper Technical College (HTC) in 1971, which was later incorporated as the William V. S. Tubman College of Technology in 1978. Politics interfered and the college was located in a remote area, away from industries that may have cooperated with and used its graduates. Furthermore, the college was poorly equipped and serviced and lacked qualified faculty, technical laboratory equipment and library resources, and adequate electricity and telecommunication services (Snyder and Nagel 1985, 99–100).

The curriculum of the college included training in civil, electrical, industrial, and mechanical engineering and technical teacher training. In addition to the problems noted above, the project faced an uncertain future because the government counted on a loan from the World Bank for its support that did not materialize. The college struggled to survive up to the war of 1989–1997. After the war ended, it did not reopen.

CURRENT TRENDS AND CHANGING PATTERNS

No functioning national body presently sets national higher education policies or supervises and evaluates their implementation in institutions of higher education in Liberia. Higher education operates more or less on a free-market basis; demand drives the establishment of institutions of higher learning and the state exercises minimum control. This is a system-wide phenomenon. Even though the state provided subsidies to private elementary, secondary, and postsecondary institutions, between 1970 and 1984, government-managed schools accounted for only 66 percent of the total of 1,084 schools that served only 32 percent of eligible school-age children (Snyder and Nagel 1985, 48). By 1987, the percentage of government-managed schools had dropped to 60 percent and had deteriorated dramatically during the war years in the 1990s, when most public schools ceased functioning. This has left considerable room for churches and individuals to set up schools, many of which are of questionable standards.

In 1984, the Ministry of Education held a National Policy Conference on Education and Training. One of the policies growing out of the conference was the establishment of a Commission on Higher Education (Ministry of Education 1984). The commission was legally authorized in 1985 but was not established until 2000. Among its functions, the commission was to serve as the accrediting board for colleges and universities, to disburse government subsidies to accredited institutions, and to set uniform standards for admission and transfer of credits from one institution to another.

For now, the University of Liberia and Cuttington University College operate autonomously of the Ministry of Education and set their own policies. They conduct their own admissions examinations and have worked out arrangements for transferring credits to and from each other. The candidates for the examination must have a high school certificate and pass the national examination. The University of Liberia tests in math and English, while Cuttington University College tests in more subjects. Because Cuttington University College is a private institution, it is free to admit only those who pass its entrance examination, whereas the University of Liberia, under political and public pressures, conditionally accepts students who pass one subject and score high enough on the other to undertake remedial work. The William V. S. Tubman Technical College accepts only those students who meet its admissions requirements.

Because there is no national coordinating body, both the University of Liberia and Cuttington University College have undertaken ambitious expansion plans. The University of Liberia's ten-year long-range plan (1976–1987) envisioned relocating the institution to a new campus about seventeen miles outside the city, where there is adequate land for expansion. By 1983, the College of Agriculture and Forestry had been relocated to the new campus, its facilities having been completed with funds provided by a loan from the World Bank. The College of Science and Technology had started its move. Three of the graduate programs—medicine, law, and pharmacy—were to remain on the Monrovia campus. But it was doubtful by the end of the 1980s whether the two institutions could implement their ambitious development plans. Snyder and Nagel reported:

> Both these institutions have expansionist intentions, but both face crippling financial constraints. Their current programs are jeopardized by unmaintained facilities, limited instructional materials, and inadequate and uncertain operating funds. Research activities are negligible, and library holdings are limited and disappearing. Because there is little coordination of tertiary education in Liberia, these institutions face their problems independently. (Snyder and Nagel 1985, 96)

The war has put on hold for the immediate future any efforts to implement the development programs of the leading institutions, despite the country's dire need of trained labor for reconstruction and development.

Three other issues need to be addressed: internal efficiency, external efficiency, and access and equity. The definition of internal and external efficiencies put forth by IEES (Improving the Efficiency of Educational Systems) for Liberia states:

> An EHR [education and human resource] system is externally efficient to the extent that education and training can contribute to sustained economic and social development, build knowledge and skills geared to specific employment opportunities in the economy, and are balanced in terms of type and quantity of output. A system is internally efficient to the extent that it optimally allocates and uses available resources for improving the quality and increasing the quantity of education. (IEES 1988, 9)

First, it should be noted that a country such as Liberia, with a high illiteracy rate, gains in social development with any amount of higher education received by its members, even if it is not directly employed in economic activities. The absence of current data and systematic record keeping make assessing the internal and external efficiencies of Liberian higher education difficult. Analysis of articulated linkages between specific higher education programs and labor-market demand in Liberia is also lacking. The exception here may be the links between teacher training and the demand for qualified teachers and medical education and the demand for doctors in Liberia.

By the close of the 1980s, certain programs at the University of Liberia showed signs of being both internally and externally inefficient. The high remediation rates of students who are admitted conditionally (which was as high as 70 percent), the high attrition rate (which was as high as 60 percent in some programs), and the small percentage completing their studies in four years all suggested internal inefficiency. For example, between 1983 and 1987, only about 15 percent of those admitted to Teachers College at the University of Liberia graduated, and the percentage of graduates in the college dropped by 40 percent in the same period (IEES 1988). Teachers were attracted by higher-paying jobs elsewhere and did not stay in the classroom. It was no fault of the training institution that the unattractive conditions of service led to teachers leaving schools. At the same time, the annual output of 253 teachers for all the teacher training institutions was not enough to satisfy the high demand for qualified teachers by the system. Shortages of qualified faculty, instructional materials, laboratory equipment, and supplies, as well as deteriorating classrooms, added to the problem of internal inefficiency for the University of Liberia.

The issue of access and equity may not seem a problem on the surface. For example, no formal barriers restrict admission of any group to schools. Primary and secondary education in public institutions is free. However, parents have to contribute about $157 annually to buy uniforms, books, and supplies. For a country with a prewar gross domestic product (GDP) variously estimated at between US$386 and US$500 per capita, that is a major problem. Also, no formal barriers restrict admission of women to higher education in Liberia. Yet the small number of women completing high school limits their representation in postsecondary education. For example, between 1981 and 1987, when government-managed secondary schools accounted for 60 percent of total enrollment, women accounted for 38 percent (Snyder and Nagel 1985). But only a small fraction completed secondary school and sought admission to the universities. Churches have established high schools in rural areas which are better equipped and staffed than public high schools. These church schools cater to their members' children and charge little or no tuition fees. The result is that students from these schools outperform their counterparts from the public schools on the entrance examinations at the universities and are more likely to gain admission. Higher education is becoming more accessible to the children of the majority of the people who live in the rural areas and is serving as a social lever.

GOVERNANCE

Higher education in Liberia is decentralized. Each institution of higher education is autonomous and operates under a charter provided by the state. A board of trustees provided for under the charter governs each institution. The minister of education represents the state on each board, but he has no veto power. At the University of Liberia, the governance structure is elaborate. Below the board, which has overall policy responsibility, is an administrative council. The council consists of all academic and administrative officers, two elected faculty representatives, and two elected student representatives. The council serves in an advisory capacity to the president of the university, and oversees the day-to-day operation of the institution. In addition, the university has a faculty senate that deals with academic matters. It consists of heads of academic programs and associate and full professors. The promotion of faculty, the approval of new programs, and the awarding of degrees are among the matters the senate handles. Finally, the university has a general faculty assembly, which meets two or three times a year to handle general faculty matters. This structure assures a measure of inclusion and democratic governance at the institution. The board of trustees exercises veto power over policy decisions taken by the various governing bodies. This has been a source of friction between the board and the faculty and students. Cuttington University College operates under a similar structure.

INSTITUTIONAL CAPACITY AND STRUCTURE

By the close of 1989, when the war broke out, enrollment in all the universities, colleges, and training institutes totaled close to 10,000. The majority, about 7,000, were enrolled at the University of Liberia and Cuttington, with the rest spread among the technical and rural training institutes. By 1999, enrollment at the University of Liberia had swollen to 10,000, even though most programs were operating at less than their prewar capacity, due to shortage of faculty and lack of laboratory equipment and space. Cuttington has not reached its prewar enrollment of more than 1,000, and most of the other colleges and institutes are closed. By 1998, the system was producing more than 800 graduates, double the 1988 figure of about 400. At the top of the system are the state and private universities, followed by colleges and training institutes.

FINANCING AND FUNDING PATTERNS

The absence of current data for the decade of the 1990s creates difficulty in reporting patterns and forces us to rely on data from the 1980s. It is not likely that the state will fund higher education the way it did in the prewar decades. For one thing, the funds are not available; for another, the state has no commitment or willingness to continue that pattern of funding. Before 1962, operating funds for the University of Liberia were included in the budget of the Ministry of Education and the minister had to approve disbursements. That has since changed, and subsidies from the state for the institutions of higher education go directly to their governing boards. However, for budgetary purposes, the figures are included in the budget of the Ministry of Education. Thus, for the 1986–1987 fiscal year, for example, the ministry's budget of US$36.2 million shows subsidies to the University of Liberia of US$5.32 million (14.7 percent); the William V. S. Tubman College of Technology received government subsidies of US$873,000 (2.4 percent). Out of the general allotment of $1.96 million for subsidies for private and church-supported institutions, Cuttington University College received US$650,000, or 33 percent of the total. This subsidy from the state accounted for 75 percent of the operating budget of the institution.

As noted earlier, the state provides subsidies to private and church-operated postsecondary institutions. It also provides financial aid to students attending these institutions to cover half the cost of tuition and textbooks. This policy is less likely to be continued for the reasons stated above.

Students and parents have shared the cost of higher education from the time the University of Liberia was established in 1951, even though tuition and fees have been kept low and affordable. Student and parental contributions together have accounted for about 10 percent of the operating budget of the institution, even in the postwar period. As the state is hard-pressed for funds, more and more of the cost of higher education will be shifted to students and their parents in the foreseeable future. Some analysts suggest that "tuition should be increased to shift more of the responsibility for investment in higher education from the government to the student and family" (IEES 1988, 43). This may turn back the clock on the gains made in access and equity in the 1970s and 1980s, which would have dire socioeconomic and political consequences.

LANGUAGE OF INSTRUCTION AND ITS IMPACT

As indicated earlier, English is the official language of Liberia, and it is used as the language of instruction from primary through postgraduate education. Most children entering school come from homes where one of Liberia's indigenous languages is spoken. They spend two to three years in pre-elementary school, where the substantial portion of the curriculum is devoted to learning English (Leinhardt 1985). While a systematic study has yet to be undertaken, there are signs that the high failure rates on the national examinations and the entrance examinations at the universities may be related to English-language deficiencies. The high repetition and attrition rates throughout the system may also be linked to the language problem, although poor-quality teachers and lack of instructional materials are often assigned the blame.

SPECIAL PROBLEMS

The only islands of democracy in the ocean of authoritarian, personal rule in Liberia were the campuses of the universities throughout the 1970s and 1980s, as is the case today. The universities set up student multiparty participatory democratic institutions and structures for student governance. Campus newspapers took the national government to task on national policies ranging from domestic to foreign affairs. And in a one-party state in which opposition was considered treason, the students became the de facto opposition. Such activities, considered by the state to be subversive, did not go unnoticed. As noted earlier, twice, in 1979 and 1984, the University of Liberia was closed by the government.

Fundamental policy differences existed between the state and the universities. Each president or head of state felt that he was ruler of the state and institutions of higher education. As such, they interfered in matters that faculty considered purely academic, for example academic promotion. Any criticism of the government on such matters or policy meant a direct affront to the president. Such activities therefore constituted grounds to discipline the offenders, whether they were editors of campus student newspapers or professors who wrote and published papers or made speeches. Also, there was the feeling that because the state provided the funding for the institutions, the faculty and students had no right to bite the hand that fed them by being critical of the government. College and university campuses became ideological battlefields between the ruling political elite, on the one hand, and the faculty and students, on the other. At issue was the demand by the state to have the university teach "state defined knowledge and truths," particularly in the social sciences and humanities. During the 1980s and early 1990s, many students and faculty lost their lives due to sustained violent attacks by African states on the university (Atteh 1996).

The government's case was not helped when it had to reduce funding to the university, due in part to the poor performance of the Liberian economy as a result of the world recession at the time. Between 1970 and 1980, Liberia lost 40 percent of its purchasing power because of the decline in demand for its primary commodities, mainly iron ore and rubber (Atteh 1996). The students interpreted the reduction as punishment for their political activism.

Under external pressures from the World Bank, a policy shift in funding higher education also contributed to the state's problems with faculty and students. Economists from the World Bank informed Liberia and other African states that investment in primary and secondary education yielded higher returns than investment in university education, which was seen as elitist, since it was catering to a small number of students, and expensive. The policy choice was clear: if Liberia wanted rapid economic growth and development, then it should invest its scarce resources in primary and secondary education. Since the World Bank was a major source of funding for investment in education for Liberia, its views could be ignored only to the detriment of the state. Tertiary education received the lowest funding level (14 percent) of loan support to Liberia for investment in education from the World Bank in 1972; the level declined dramatically to only 4 percent by 1984. Liberia, misled by the World Bank, ignored UNESCO's research report that "the correlation between investment in higher education and the level of social, economic, and cultural development is well established" (Snyder and Nagel 1995, 18).

CURRENT AND FUTURE CHALLENGES FACING THE POSTSECONDARY SYSTEM

A number of important studies on improving education in Liberia were undertaken in the mid- to late 1980s that made recommendations that were not implemented due to the outbreak of the war in 1989. The problems that were identified then have since reached crisis levels. Among the studies were *Towards the Twenty-First Century* (Gongar, Snyder, Mintah, and Bropleh 1984), *Towards the 21st Century: An Extension of the University of Liberia's Long-Range Plan* (University of Liberia 1984), *Education and Training Sector Assessment* (USAID 1985), *The Struggle Continues! World Bank and African Development Bank Investment in Liberian Educational Development* (1971–1985) (Snyder and Nagel 1986), and *Education and Human Resources Sector Assessment* (IEES 1988). The first major challenge for Liberian education, which is highlighted in these studies, is to develop a systematic approach to education in Liberia. Some of the problems encountered by the institutions of higher learning, such as poorly prepared students, remediation, and high attrition and repetition rates, are linked to the poor quality of teachers, lack of adequate instructional materials, and poor facilities at the elementary and secondary school levels. Clearly, a system approach is needed to resolve these problems effectively and efficiently. The system approach will also solve what Snyder and Nagel (1984) identified as a "loosely coupled system," in which, among other things, there is loose coordination (or absence of it), units act independently of each other, production is unrelated to demand, and output displays redundant and poor quality.

Once a system approach is adopted, the next challenge is redefinition of the mission of the university so that, among other things, it can be Kerr's "multiversity" and Huxley's "factory of new knowledge." But the knowledge sought or created should not be for its own end. It should serve to address the poverty, diseases, and ignorance of Liberian society and assist Liberia in its transition from war to peace, from dictatorship to democracy, and from underdevelopment to modernity. University scholars, the Liberian ruling elite, and the international community, particularly the scholarly community, need to work together on this endeavor.

Third, redefinition of the mission of the university brings to the fore the critical issue of state-university relations and autonomy. The indispensability of the university to Liberia's national development will require that the Liberian ruling elite provide the necessary autonomy and financial and other support for its efficient and effective operation. Liberia's lack of a democratic tradition and environment will make this a particularly challenging undertaking. The university cannot wrap itself in the cloak of autonomy to avoid accountability to the people and state, which pay its bills. At the same time, the state cannot adopt the attitude that the university cannot be critical of its policies. Nor can the university, under the cloak of "academic freedom," so politicize itself that it cannot carry out its functions of instruction and research. A definite line separates academic freedom and accountability, on the one hand, and political interference, on the other. That line should be recognized and honored by all the stakeholders in the university project.

Fourth, Liberia's universities face the challenge of funding. If investing in human resource development is investing in a country's future, as Jacques Hallak (1990) has pointed out, then Liberia needs to adopt investment in education, particularly higher education, as its highest-priority national policy. This is not an either/or proposition between elementary and secondary education, on the one hand, and higher education, on the other. Both are needed, and a balance must be struck between the two levels. The scientists, engineers, doctors, agronomists, and other high-level technical and managerial personnel needed for national development cannot be produced at the elementary and secondary level, yet if a sound foundation is not laid there, the university will be powerless to produce them.

Imaginative and creative ways will have to be found to fund higher education, which is a public common good. Proposals to shift more of the cost to students and their parents will only create an obstacle to access and equity for those who are unable to pay. A variety of financial aid and student loan packages can be put in place. For example, before the war, graduates of the medical college, because their education was so heavily subsidized by the state, were required to serve for one year in the rural countryside before they could earn their diplomas and transcripts. As it turned out, the students loved the practicum, and people in the countryside benefited from health services that would have been unavailable otherwise. A similar plan for teachers could be implemented. A version of the U.S. Peace Corps and Job Corps programs could be adopted to fund higher education in Liberia.

STATE OF RESEARCH AND PUBLISHING VERSUS TEACHING

The state and external supporters of higher education in Liberia have shown little or no interest in providing funding for research. Additionally, the shortage of qualified teachers burdens faculty with heavy teaching loads, which leaves them little or no time for research. Before the war, the University of Liberia published two journals, one in law and the other in the social sciences and humanities. Both have been discontinued since the war. This raises the fundamental issue of relevance, which has become a double-edged sword. In the 1970s and 1980s, the issue of relevance had to do with whether the university was addressing the problems of the common African peoples. Since the consensus was that the university was not doing this, the solution was to "indigenize" the university (Yesufu 1973). The issue of relevance today for the university in Africa is whether it is doing anything of value that is not being done elsewhere more efficiently and cheaply so it can justify its existence (Schugurensky 1999). This raises three questions:

- Is the university in Liberia and Africa to be the mere consumer of and conveyor belt for knowledge produced and packaged in the advanced capitalist world?
- How relevant is that knowledge to the solution of the social, political, and economic problems of the common African peoples?
- Can the university serve the function of Huxley's "factory of new knowledge"?

The relevance of the university in Liberia and Africa will ultimately depend on the last question. For example, in prewar Liberia, herbalists had more effective therapies for malaria, hypertension, and other diseases than Western therapies, but there was no support for research to study the chemical properties of the herbs they were using. Indigenous agronomists knew which crops were disease resistant and the type of soil that would best grow such crops, but Western university-trained crop and soil scientists disregarded this knowledge because it was considered "primitive" and could not produce better results. In the world knowledge economy (Altbach 1998), unless the university can undertake such basic research to justify its existence and demand for support, it runs the high risk of becoming "irrelevant" (Schugurensky 1999). Liberia and other African states may not see the linkages between basic research and development and national economic growth, but they need to pay attention to the advanced industrialized countries, such as the United States and Japan, which are spending huge sums on research and development to fuel their growth.

CONCLUSION

This study has reviewed the state of higher education in Liberia for the past century, paying particular attention to the University of Liberia, Cuttington University College, and the William V. S. Tubman College of Technology. Over the period of study, Liberia has made remarkable progress toward meeting its human resource needs for development. This is reflected in the quantitative growth in degree programs, student enrollment, and the number of institutions claiming to be colleges and institutes. But this quantitative growth has not been accompanied by a corresponding qualitative improvement. Funding and research, as well as current and future challenges, need to be taken into consideration to improve the system.

Unfortunately, this study confirms the Improving the Efficiency of Educational Systems 1988 report, *Education and Human Resources Sector Assessment*, which noted:

Currently, EHR [education and human resources] activities are failing to be the stimulus for social and economic development that they should be and that they were planned to be. In fact, the formal education and training system is in danger of becoming a negative factor for development because of reduced internal efficiency and an inability to produce the types and quality of graduates required for Liberian development. Within the government accounts, education and training activities are in danger of becoming more significant as income transfer programs to civil servants and teachers than as investment activities in the skills and knowledge of the nation's citizens. (1988, 51–52)

Fewer resources are being provided in 2001 than in the 1970s and 1980s, even though the decline in support to higher education had begun by the mid-1980s. The facilities destroyed during the war have not been restored, and the government shows no interest in or commitment to doing so. In the final analysis, Liberia's "mess" has worsened, and "the idea of the university" is at great risk of death, leaving the Liberian people with no effective institution with which to build their future.

REFERENCES

Ackoff, R. L., E. V. Finnel, and J. Gharajedaghi. 1984. *A Guide to Controlling Your Corporation's Future.* New York: Wiley.

Ajayi, J. F. A., L. K. H. Goma, and G. A. Johnson. 1996. *The African Experience with Higher Education.* Accra: The Association of African Universities.

Allen, G. W. 1923. *The Trustees of Donations for Education in Liberia.* Boston: Thomas Todd Company.

Altbach, P. G. 1998. *Comparative Higher Education: Knowledge, the University and Development.* Greenwich, Conn.: Ablex.

Assié-Lumumba, N'D. T. 1993. "Higher Education in Francophone Africa: Assessment of the Potential of the Traditional Universities and Alternatives for Development." AFTHR Technical Note No. 5. The World Bank.

Atteh, S. O. 1996. "The Crisis in Higher Education in Africa." *Issues* 24, no. 1: 468–477.

Ayittey, G. 1999. *Africa in Chaos.* New York: St. Martin Griffin.

Carnoy, M. 1995. "Rates of Return to Education." In M. Carnoy, ed., *International Encyclopedia of the Economics of Education.* 2nd ed. Oxford: Pergamon.

Castells, M. 1993. "The Informational Economy and the New International Division of Labor." In M. Carvy, ed., *The New Global Economy in the Information Age.* University Park: Pennsylvania State University Press.

Clower, R. D., G. Dalton, and M. Harwitz. 1966. *Growth Without Development: An Economic Survey of Liberia.* Evanston, Ill.: Northwestern University Press.

Davidson, B. 1992. *The Black Man's Burden.* New York: Times Books.

DeMars, W., S. Talbott, and J. M. Weinstein. 2000. "The Crisis in Africa." *World Policy Journal* 27, no. 2 (Summer): 1–25.

Domatob, J. K. 1996. "Policy Issues for African Universities." *Issues* 24 (Winter/Spring).

Gongar, E. O., C. W. Snyder, Jr., S. Mintah, and A. Bropleh. 1984. *Towards the 21st Century: Development-Oriented Policies and Activities in the Liberian Education System.* McLean, Va.: Institute for International Research.

Gray, J. 1998. *False Dawn: The Delusion of Global Capitalism.* New York: New Press.

Hallak, J. 1990. *Investing in the Future.* Paris: International Institute for Educational Planning.

Hawk, B. 1996. "African Universities in Crisis." *Issues* 24 (Winter/Spring).

Hoff, A. A. 1962. *A Short History of Liberia College and the University of Liberia.* Monrovia: Consolidated Publication Incorporated.

Huxley, L. 1900. *Life and Letters of Thomas Henry Huxley.* 2 vols. London: Macmillan.

IEES (Improving the Efficiency of Educational Systems). 1988. *Education and Human Resources Sector Assessment.* Tallahassee, Fla.: Learning Systems Institute.

Jameson, F. 2000. "Globalization and Political Strategy." *New Left Review* (July/August): 49–68.

Jaspers, K. 1959. *The Idea of the University.* Translated by H. A. T. Reiche and H. F. Vanderschmidt. Boston: Beacon.

Kerr, C. 1963. *The Uses of the University.* Cambridge, Mass.: Harvard University Press.

Liebenow, J. G. 1986. *African Politics: Crises and Challenges.* Bloomington: Indiana University Press.

Leinhardt, G. 1985. "Liberia." In *The International Encyclopedia of Education.* Oxford: Pergamon.

Newman, J. H. 1976. *Idea of the University Defined and Illustrated.* Edited by I. T. Ker. Oxford: Clarendon.

Pelikan, J. 1992. *The Idea of the University.* New Haven, Conn.: Yale University Press.

Ransom, A., S. Khoo, and V. Selvaratnam. 1993. *Improving Higher Education in Developing Countries.* Washington, D.C.: The World Bank.

Roberg, R. I. 2000. "Africa's Mess, Mugabe's Mayhem." *Foreign Affairs* 79, no. 5 (September/October): 47–61.

Saint, W. S. 1992. *Universities in Africa: Strategies for Stabilization and Revitalization.* Washington, D.C.: World Bank.

Schraeder, P. J. 1994. *United States Foreign Policy toward Africa: Incrementalism, Crisis and Change.* Cambridge: Cambridge University Press.

———. 2000. *African Politics and Society.* Boston: Bedford/St. Martin's.

Schugurensky, D. 1999. "Higher Education Restructuring in the Era of Globalization: Toward a Heteronomous Model?" In Robert F. Arnove and Carlos Alberto Torres, eds., *Comparative Education.* Lanham, Md.: Rowman & Littlefield.

Secretariat of Education and Scientific Research (Libya). 1995. *Statistical Reports on Universities and Higher Technical Institutions.* Tripoli: Secretariat of Education and Scientific Research.

Serageldin, I. 1992. "Foreword." In W. S. Saint, *Universities in Africa: Strategies for Stabilization and Revitalization.* Washington, D.C.: World Bank.

Seyon, P. L. N. 1973. "The University of Liberia." In T. M. Yesufu, ed., *Creating the African University.* Ibadan: Oxford University Press.

———. 1977. "Education, National Integration, and Nation-Building in Liberia." Ph.D. diss., Stanford University, California.

———. 1997. "Rebuilding the University of Liberia in the Midst of War." *International Higher Education* 8 (Summer): 2.

———. 1998. *Quick Fixing the State in Africa: The Liberian Case.* Working Paper no. 217. Boston: Boston University, African Studies Center.

Sherman, Mary A. B. 1990. "The University in Modern Africa: Toward the Twenty-first Century." *Journal of Higher Education* 61, no. 4: 363–385.

Simpson, E. 2000. "Knowledge in the Postmodern University." *Educational Theory* 50 (Spring): 157–177.

Sklair, L. 1991. *Sociology of the Global System.* Baltimore: Johns Hopkins University Press.

Smith, A., and F. Webster, eds. 1997. *The Postmodern University? Contested Visions of Higher Education in Society.* Buckingham: Society for Research into Higher Education Open University Press.

Snyder, C. W., and J. Nagel. 1985. *The Struggle Continues! World Bank and African Development Bank Investments in Liberian Educational Development.* McLean, Va.: Institute for International Research.

UNESCO. 1998. *World Education Report 1998.* Paris: UNESCO.

———. 1999. *Statistical Yearbook.* Paris: UNESCO.

University of Liberia. 1984. *Towards the 21st Century: An Extension of the University of Liberia's Long-Range Plan.* Monrovia: University of Liberia.

USAID. 1985. *Education and Training Sector Assessment.* Monrovia: Ministry of Planning and Economic Affairs/USAID in Liberia.

Whitehead, A. N. 1929. *The Aims of Education and Other Essays.* New York: Macmillan.

World Bank. 1988. *Education in Sub-Saharan Africa: Policies for Adjustment, Revitalization and Expansion.* Washington, D.C.: World Bank.

———. 1989. *Sub-Saharan Africa: From Crisis to Sustainable Growth.* Washington, D.C.: World Bank.

———. 1991. *The African Capacity Building Initiative toward Improved Policy Analysis and Development Management in Sub-Saharan Africa.* Washington, D.C.: World Bank.

———. 1997. *World Development Report 1997: The State in a Changing World.* Washington, D.C.: World Bank.

———. 1998. *World Development Report 1998/99: Knowledge for Development.* Washington, D.C.: World Bank.

Yesufu, T. M., ed. 1973. *Creating the African University.* Ibadan: Oxford University Press.

Libya

ALI EL-HAWAT

INTRODUCTION

Libya, located in north Africa, is a country of more than 5 million people. The Libyan economy depends primarily upon revenues extracted from the oil sector. At close to US$9,000, Libya's per capita GDP is one of the highest in Africa. Higher education in Libya includes three major sections: (a) university education, which lasts four to seven years, after which students graduate in various fields of knowledge; (b) university vocational and technical education, which lasts three to five years, at the end of which graduate technicians are assigned to work in development projects; and (c) advanced postgraduate studies, which prepare students for M.A., M.Sc., and Ph.D. degrees in humanities and physical sciences, as well as various other professional diplomas.

The main objectives of higher education can be summarized in the following points: satisfaction of society's needs for a qualified labor force in the various fields of specialization and areas of knowledge; performance of basic and applied research and experiments which lead to the advancement of the sciences, arts, and technology; the promotion of the Third Universal Theory, which constitutes the political philosophy of the Libyan society; the promotion of Arabic-Islamic culture, which constitutes the Libyan heritage and history; and organization of conferences, seminars, and symposia, as well as the maintenance of strong academic ties with research centers and universities abroad.

University education includes a wide range of fields of study, such as basic sciences, humanities, languages and literature, engineering, industrial, medical and agricultural sciences, economics and commerce, environmental studies, and Islamic and international civilization studies.

Undoubtedly, higher education in Libya has achieved great accomplishments both quantitatively and qualitatively and has contributed to building up modern Libyan society. Libyan universities and higher education institutions were established in order to teach, train, and educate generations of employees and specialists in various fields of life in modern Libyan society.

In addition, modern education, including higher education and all the money and effort it requires, is and always will be a life necessity called for by the moral and social responsibility of the state, as it is necessary in order to continue to build up the modern state and society and achieve social and economic development.

Despite all the accomplishments already achieved, the development of higher education in Libya faces many challenges imposed by social and economic conditions. These challenges and difficulties influence higher education's internal and external efficiency. In addition, Libyan higher education has to cope with many new roles and functions that have emerged as a result of the changing world situation in the twenty-first century. Perhaps the most important among these roles and functions are the following: discovery of Libya's future needs; advancement of knowledge for human development and welfare; contribution to the capacity to build intellectual, cultural, and civil participation; contribution to the building of a learned society (the university community) that can provide cultural innovation and emotional richness; contribution to national efforts to eradicate poverty and to help marginal groups to be linked to the national development process; and contribution to building bridges of peace and cultural dialogue among various peoples and cultures in the world, especially among younger generations.

BRIEF HISTORY OF UNIVERSITY EDUCATION AND ITS GROWTH

After Libya's independence in 1951, its first university, which formed the foundation of the Libyan University, was established in Benghazi. It was called the Faculty of Arts and Education and was followed in 1957 by the establishment of the Faculty of Sci-

Table 41.1. Libyan Universities and Number of Faculties, Locations, and Number of Students Enrolled, Academic Year 1994–1995

University	Faculties	Students	Location
University of El-Fateh	11	51,561	Tripoli
The Arab Medical University	3	1,716	Benghazi
University of Gar-Yunis	6	24,453	Benghazi
The Great El-Fateh University for Medical Sciences	4	4,712	Tripoli–Misrata
Omar El-Mukhtar University	5	4,072	Bayda
Naser University	5	5,823	Khoms–Zlaitin–Tarhuna
El-Jabal El-Gharbi University	6	6,118	Nalut–Zintan–Yefren–Gheryan
Seventh of April University	6	11,135	Zawia–Zawara–Ajeelat–Subrata
University of Sabha	7	6,041	Sabha–Obari–Brak–Ghat–Merzeq
El-Tahadi University	10	5,032	Sirt–Hoon–BaniWalid–Misrata
University of Darna	6	4,490	Darna–Tubrok
The Open University	3	15,067	Tripoli and other locations throughout the country
El-Najim El-Sata University	Specialized Oil University	1,101	Brega Oil Terminal
Total	72	141,321	

Source: Secretariat of Education and Scientific Research 1995.

ence in Tripoli. At that time, the university's main objectives were no more than training teachers for intermediate and secondary education levels and training employees for various government jobs.

This single small university expanded gradually. Thus, in 1957, the Faculty of Economics and Commerce was founded in Benghazi, followed by the Faculty of Law in 1962. Later, in 1966, the Faculty of Agriculture was established in Tripoli. By 1967, the Libyan University witnessed further expansion as it annexed both the Faculty of Higher Technical Studies and the Higher Teachers Training college, both in Tripoli. The Libyan government founded both colleges in agreement and cooperation with UNESCO. These two colleges became the Faculty of Engineering and the Faculty of Education, respectively.

In 1970, the Faculty of Medicine was founded in Benghazi, and in the same year, another independent faculty, already in existence under the name of the Islamic University in Al-Bayda, was incorporated by the Libyan University under the name of the Faculty of Arabic Language and Islamic Studies. In 1987, this faculty ceased to exist, and its departments were annexed to the Faculty of Arts and the Faculty of Law at Gar-Yunis University in Benghazi. In 1972, the Faculty of Oil and Mining Engineering was founded in Tripoli, then moved in the late 1970s to Brega Oil Terminal Complex in the Brega area.

In 1973, the Libyan University was separated into two independent universities. These were known as the University of Tripoli and the University of Benghazi. Later these universities were renamed: the University of El-Fateh in Tripoli and the University of Gar-Yunis in Benghazi. All colleges operating in Tripoli became a part of the El-Fateh University, and all colleges operating in Benghazi became part of the Gar-Yunis University.

This partition of the Libyan University was in response to the expanding number of faculties and increasing generations of students. Taken together, both universities had more than fifteen faculties, covering various branches of knowledge. Further expansions have taken place since 1974, and this will be explained later.

Due to the increasing number of students enrolling in higher education since 1981, the university was restructured and the number of universities expanded to thirteen in 1995, consisting altogether of seventy-six specialized faculties and more than 344 specialized scientific departments. Three of these universities are specialized, namely the Arab Medical University in Benghazi, the Great El-Fateh for Medical Sciences in Tripoli, and El-Najm El-Sata (a specialized oil and mining University) in Brega. Table 41.1 shows these universities, faculties, locations, and the number of students enrolled in the academic year 1994–1995.

Some consider this number of universities excessive for a population as small as Libya's (about 5 million, according to a 1995 census). In addition, the thirteen universities demand huge financial resources which Libya can no longer afford due to the decrease in oil prices and international inflation. Recent privatization measures and policies, which have been taking place in Libya since the early 1990s, have led to a reduction in the number of universities from thirteen to nine.

As a result of the growing number of university students and the resulting pressure on the public budget, Libya's higher education policy allowed the local public administration (Shabiat), and the private sector to establish university colleges and higher education institutes. It should be noted here that the local administration must manage financial resources for its higher education institutes from local community sources, and, in the case of the private sector, the state assumes no financial obligations at all. Private higher education institutes must be totally financed by individual or group investors.

While this policy is considered an innovation in higher education, it triggered a wide debate among policymakers as well as in Libyan society at large. The main view is that a country as rich as Libya, with a small population, should finance all social services, including higher education. Furthermore, higher education should be under the state's control, and the state should not allow profits, markets, or wealthy people to control higher education in the private sector.

The problem is not whether the state is capable of financing higher education. The real problem is that in a three-year period (1997–2000), the local administration authorities (Shabiat) established more than five private universities. The question that arises is this: Do these private universities have the necessary technical resources, professors, and textbooks? It is feared that these new universities are no more than high schools offering low-quality education. Permitting the local community and the private sector to establish higher education institutions is a good step toward the spread of higher education, but the process should be studied carefully and must follow the standards set for higher education by the university.

VOCATIONAL AND TECHNICAL HIGHER EDUCATION

In 1980, Libya evaluated its whole educational system and found out that student admissions in universities were very high in the pure academic studies: social sciences, literature, law, and the arts. On the other hand, admissions were very low in basic sciences, technology, and engineering. This imbalance did not help Libya's industrial development. Libya's advancement into the developed world required a highly specialized labor force as well as technical experts. In 1980, as a result of this unbalanced situation, Libya came up with what was known as the New Educational Structure for higher education. This new educational structure required the establishment of technical and vocational education on the university level, in what became known in Libya as the Higher Technical and Vocational Institutions. These institutions were among the main types of higher education. Schooling at this type of higher education lasts three to five years. Graduates of these institutions are meant to hold technical positions in the area of industrial and agricultural production and services. In addition, a number of other technical institutions on the secondary education level are known as Secondary Technical Institutions (LNC 1998).

During the academic year 1995–1996, there were about fifty-four higher technical and vocational institutes, but in 1999–2000, this number increased to eighty-four, as shown in Table 41.2.

Expansion has taken place in the universities and higher vocational and technical higher institutes since 1973. In the academic year 1999–2000, the number of students in universities grew to 204,332, and 64,970 students were enrolled in higher technical institutes for a total of 269,302 students. The number of teachers in universities reached 4,907, and the number of teachers in higher technical institutes reached 4,898. At the higher technical institutes, many instructors are trainers and not teachers in the academic sense. They are, however, classified in statistical data as teaching staff members.

University faculties, as well as the higher technical institutes, are scattered all over the country. This distribution facili-

Table 41.2. Higher Technical and Vocational Institutes in Libya, 1999–2000

Type of Institute	Number	Number of Students
Polytechnic	23	13,432
Specialized Higher Institutes	25	17,938
Higher Institutes for Trainers	9	6,714
Higher Teachers Training Institutes	27	26,886
Total	84	64,970

Source: Secretariat of Education 1999, 3.

tates local learning and vocational training opportunities for students. It is not necessary to move to major cities in Libya. In addition, such higher education centers are seen as centers of social change and cultural development by the local population.

POSTGRADUATE STUDIES

For over a decade, postgraduate studies have been an important part of Libyan universities' activities. M.A., M.Sc., and Ph.D. programs are offered in various fields of knowledge. These postgraduate programs are mostly concentrated in big universities, particularly Gar-Yunis University and El-Fateh University. Since 1973, 1,992 students have obtained M.A. or M.Sc. degrees from Libyan universities, mostly from Gar-Yunis and El-Fateh Universities. During the same period, however, only about 100 students have attained Ph.D.s, and they are specialized in Arabic language and Islamic studies and humanities. Libyan universities have not yet started Ph.D. programs in science, technology, and engineering. Table 41.3 shows M.A., M.Sc., and Ph.D. enrollment in the Libyan universities during the academic year 1999–2000. Based on this table, it is evident that Libya has achieved great success in establishing postgraduate studies; the total enrollment number in these programs is estimated at 6,587 students.

Postgraduate studies in Libyan universities cover a wide range of areas of knowledge, but these programs are very much dominated by Arabic, Islamic studies, social sciences, and humanities.

About 10 percent of M.A. or M.Sc. students are from Arab, Asian, and African countries. These students will, upon completion of their studies, return to their home countries and contribute to their country's development and prosperity. Libya is proud that it can play such a role in international education and take the lead in creating greater understanding and cooperation in the world.

UNIVERSITY STUDENTS AND FIELDS OF STUDY

During the past two decades, university education has developed and expanded rapidly. The number of university students was estimated at 13,418 during the academic year 1975–1976.

Table 41.3. M.A., M.Sc., and Ph.D. Enrollment in Libyan Universities, 1999–2000

University	Higher Diploma	M.A.	Ph.D.	Libyan Board of Medicine	Total	Percent
El-Fateh	—	1,260	16	—	1,276	19.4
Gar-Yunis	158	1,183	73	—	1,414	21.5
Omar El-Mukhtar	—	18	—	—	18	0.3
Naser	—	328	—	—	328	5.0
Sabha	—	50	—	—	50	0.8
Seventh of April	—	752	11	—	763	11.6
El-Tahadi	—	13	—	—	13	0.2
Postgraduate Academy for Economic Studies	—	1,225	—	—	1,225	18.6
Specialized Medical Studies	—	—	—	1,500	1,500	22.4
Total	158	4,829	100	1,500	6,587	
Percent	2.3	73.31	1.52	22.77		

Source: Libyan National Center for Educational Planning 2000. It should be noted that the specialized medical studies are not postgraduate studies, but courses of study to prepare for the Libyan medical examination board or studies for medical diplomas and specialization in specific diseases.

Table 41.4. Student Enrollment in Higher Education in Libya, 1975–2000

Year	Number of Students in Universities	Number of Students in Higher Technical Institutes	Total
1975–1976	13,418	—	13,418
1980–1981	19,315	1,130	20,445
1984–1985	32,770	3,080	35,850
1989–1990	50,475	3,916	54,391
1992–1993	101,093	12,921	114,014
1993–1994	116,473	16,912	133,385
1995–1996	160,000	28,106	188,106
1996–1997	160,112	54,080	214,192
1997–1998	168,123	58,512	226,635
1998–1999	165,447	58,877	224,324
1999–2000	204,332	64,970	269,302

Source: Secretariat of Education and Scientific Research 1995; Abdull-Wahab 1996; National Center for Educational Planning 2000.

This number had increased to 269,302 students by the academic year 1999–2000. This quantitative development in enrollment is evidenced by Table 41.4.

The growth in female student enrollment in higher education is a positive aspect of the Libyan educational policy. The number of female students has increased dramatically. During the academic year 1980–1981, there were only 405 female students, about 21 percent of the total student enrollment. During the academic year 1999–2000, the proportion of female students reached 51 percent, in addition to the number of female students enrolled in higher technical institutes. This growth in the number of female students can be seen in Table 41.5.

Discipline experts have not conducted any studies concerning distribution of student enrollment in Libyan universities. However, there appears to be an imbalance between enrollment in humanities and arts and enrollments in basic sciences and technology. Approximately 35.4 percent of students aged 18 to 24 are enrolled in universities and higher vocational institutes; that is, 4,270 students per 100,000 of the population. UNESCO considers this rate as the highest among the Arab countries. The enrollment rate of 15 percent in higher institutes and 85 percent in universities indicates the imbalance between the number of theoretical or academic university students and the number of vocational and technical university students. In light of these facts, the general secretariat of education and scientific research took steps to increase admissions in higher vocational institutes. It is expected that this rate will reach 70 percent by the year 2010. The total number of students registered at all educational levels in Libya was 1,786,270 in 1996, an increase of 24 percent. This number represents 40.3 percent of the population.

Data reveals that 65.8 percent of students are registered in literature, arts, and humanities. Only 21.7 percent are registered in basic and engineering sciences. The number of students admitted to basic and engineering sciences decreased to 17.9 percent, while the number of literature, arts, and humanities students grew to 70.4 percent of the total. The number of of students admitted to sciences and engineering is low compared to some other Arabic countries, such as Jordan (25.2 percent) and Iraq

Table 41.5. Female Students in Libyan Universities, 1980–2000

Year	Number of Students		Total	Percent Female
	Male	Female		
1980–1981	15,259	4,056	19,315	21
1991–1992	40,094	32,805	72,899	45
1992–1993	52,568	48,525	101,093	48
1993–1994	64,069	52,413	116,482	45
1994–1995	—	—	160,000	NA
1995–1996	66,775	60,499	127,274	47
1996–1997	90,112	70,000	160,112	44
1997–1998	—	—	168,123	NA
1998–1999	81,807	83,640	165,447	51
1999–2000	—	—	204,332	NA

Source: General Secretariat of Education and Scientific Research 1996, 8; Libya National Center for Educational Planning 1999, 201–213; El-Hawat 1997; Secretariat of Education 2000, 1–5.

(23.7 percent) (UNESCO 1994). Admissions for the academic year 1995–1996 reached 9,301, only 30 percent of which were in science and technology. The number of students at higher vocational institutes rose from 16,912 students in 1993–1994 to 28,106 students in 1995–1996. It is expected that admissions to higher institutes will continue to rise, reaching 100,000 by 2010.

The fifty-one higher vocational institutes founded in 1996 are divided into the following groups, according to specialty: the first group has eleven teacher training higher vocational institutes; the second group has eight higher institutes for training technicians and instructors; the third group has twelve higher institutes for technical and industrial sciences; and the fourth group has twenty specialized higher institutes.

Admissions to these institutes for the academic year 1995–1996 were as follows: 23.3 percent in teacher training institutes, 9.4 percent in higher institutes for training technicians and instructors, and 21.1 percent in higher institutes for technical and industrial sciences (polytechnics). The remaining students go to specialized higher vocational institutes. It is assumed that 38.8 percent of these students specialize in technical and industrial fields (Abdull-Wahab 1996).

MANAGING AND FUNDING THE HIGHER EDUCATIONAL SYSTEM

The university is managed by the university's People's Committee, which is led by a secretary (dean), who is chosen from among the committee members. Faculties are managed in the same way (i.e., each faculty has a people's committee, which is led by a secretary who is chosen from among the committee members). Also, each head of department is a member in the faculty's People's Committee, and each secretary of a faculty's

People's Committee is a member of the university's People's Committee. The students are also members of People's Committees. They handle many matters relating to students' lives, associations, and unions in the universities.

The higher education system is under the authority of the state, yet universities have independent administrations and committees, as well as independent budgets and finances. As in many developing countries around the world, education in Libya is financed by the public budget. In 1998, the budget allocated for education represented 38.2 percent of the national budget (National Authority for Information and Documentation 1999).

In 1996, Libya's investment in education was one of the largest among the developing countries. Although no details are available concerning the higher education portion of the country's budget, it was estimated to be approximately 0.4 percent of GNP in 1992, and gross expenditure is estimated at Libya $42 million, according to ROSTAS (Regional Office for Science and Technology for the Arab States) sources in 1995 (Abdull-Wahab 1996).

The expansion in higher education has been rapid as measured by the number of registered students at universities and higher technical institutes and the establishment of more university faculties and higher technical institutes. This expansion and growth has put pressure on available financial resources, in addition to the effects of the decrease in oil prices since the early 1980s and rising international inflation. This continuous expansion in higher education requires an increase in budget expenditures, which is difficult to accomplish except at the expense of other sectors. Thus, scientific studies are being carried out to find ways to share the financing of higher education.

The Open University is the only institution in the Libyan higher education system that depends to some extent on tuition fees paid by students; it also earns income from the sale of books and scientific materials. The other universities and higher technical institutes depend completely on the country's national budget. Consequently, Libyan educational authorities are seriously considering alternative sources of finance. For this reason, Libyan educational policymakers have allowed the formation of private higher education institutes through what are known as educational cooperatives (*Tasharukiat Talimia*). They are also conducting studies to find out the best forms for partnerships between the public and private sectors to finance higher education. Great consideration is being given to establishing partnerships with nongovernmental organizations (NGOs) in Libya.

As stated earlier in this chapter, there is great debate in Libyan society concerning the financing of higher education. Many think that the state should finance all levels of education. Private use of resources will mean that many low-income families cannot send their children to universities and Libya's higher education will become an elite education. It will also contribute to widening the gap between the rich and the poor. If this happens, higher education will violate the principle of equal opportunities and mass education, a principle that has been a significant element of Libya's general social policy since the 1970s.

Contrary to this view, some people think that higher education should be financed privately and that these policy measures will improve the quality of higher education while reducing the growing number of university students who find their education irrelevant and end up unemployed. Whatever the arguments are, it is evident that Libya's higher education system needs re-planning in organization, curriculum, and financial resources in order to minimize pressure on the national budget. A great deal of research and analysis also needs to be done in order to determine what the social and economic needs of Libya will be in the coming decade.

Since 1975, computers have played an important role in managing and modernizing Libya's higher educational system. Computers have facilitated many tasks, including the quick announcement of admissions results for secondary school graduates. Computers also help in activities related to registration and admission examinations, the preparation of detailed statistics concerning the number of students, the recording of examination results, and the preparation of reports and futuristic studies relating to these institutions.

METHODS FOR EVALUATING THE PERFORMANCE OF UNIVERSITY EDUCATION

Since 1980, Libya has aimed at introducing a number of philosophical and structural amendments to the educational system known as the New Educational System. These included the recomposition of higher education goals to serve society and fulfill its needs in terms of social, economic, and human development in light of the demands of the twenty-first century and in correspondence to job-market requirements. Structural amendments also included finding more scientific and functional links between secondary education curricula and programs of specialization in scientific departments at university faculties. This led to the innovation of specialized secondary schools, which gradually replaced the traditional secondary education so that studies at a secondary school directly correspond to a specialization in the university or higher technical institute.

The continuous evaluation of university programs led to the creation of a number of new specialization fields in various scientific and technological fields. This was accomplished through the expansion of specialized university faculties, higher technical institutes, and scientific departments. Libya is committed to periodically amending and developing university education through specialized committees in order to meet the needs of Libyan society in the twenty-first century.

There are no specific methods, either of in-service or continuous training, to develop efficient university teaching staffs and employees because there are no regulations imposed on them. However, the universities, in cooperation with national, regional, and international organizations, such as the Arab Union for Technical and Vocational Education, UNESCO, ALECSO (Arab League Educational, Cultural, and Scientific Organization), and ISESCO (Islamic Educational, Scientific, and Cultural Organization), organize training courses in the fields of higher education, management, computer sciences, and educational technology and services from time to time. The objective of this type of training is to provide the administrative staff with modern and up-to-date skills in the management of higher education. Teachers have no training courses or in-service training unless they attend seminars or conferences in Libya or abroad.

Libya's higher education system has developed a complex organization, requiring the extensive modernization of Libyan universities, through the following research studies:

- Studies of the internal and external efficiency of higher education systems
- Research to establish new departments and faculties
- Review and evaluation programs carried out in university faculties and departments concerning the university's appropriateness, size, location, and development in the future

Libyan universities also need to establish mechanisms for the following aspects of higher education management:

- Continuous evaluation of the quality of higher education
- Gradual transformation of the higher education system from a traditional to a more modern system
- Continuous support of higher education and the development of forms of partnership with the private sector without affecting the principle of equal opportunity for education
- Development of training programs for newly appointed teaching staff, particularly in the areas of teaching methods, educational technology, and evaluation of student achievement

LIBYA'S HIGHER EDUCATION: ACHIEVEMENTS AND CHALLENGES

Libya's higher education institutions have made significant progress, both quantitatively and qualitatively, and have contributed to the establishment of a modern state in Libya. Universities and higher institutes have been established to prepare, train, and qualify successive generations of public officers and experts in modern Libyan society. Such graduates have gradually replaced the expatriate employees and experts who used to run the country. Moreover, higher education has greatly contributed to the establishment of the concept of citizenship. It is also credited with broadening Libyan citizens' horizons to the point where the problems of Libya—and the world—are sensed and given due concern.

Despite all its achievements, Libyan higher education still confronts problems, challenges, and criticisms that are precipitated and exacerbated by social and economic circumstances. As defined by an Arab expert, these problems are due to the fact that "the significant quantitative development achieved was not coupled with another qualitative one. Besides, the numerous education reform efforts that Arab higher education underwent were predominated by traditional inclination, copying and the transfer of foreign models. They were not characterized by innovation, creativity and adaptability to the requirements of the social and economic contemporary Libyan environment" (Nofal and Kmal 1990).

Nevertheless, the biggest problem facing Libya's higher education is the quality of its graduates and the lack of conformity of their number and training with the requirements of social and economic development and the labor market. This problem is further complicated by multiple social factors and pressures, particularly the increasing social demands for university education. University enrollment is considered valuable in and of itself, regardless of its feasibility or its effect on life and regardless of the quality of the certificate obtained by the graduate. In addition, there are no clear assessments of the need for skilled labor. This is combined with a surplus of graduates in certain specializations, such as human sciences, arts, law, and economics, which results in unemployment and acute shortages in other specialties, such as technology. It also leads to the importation of foreign labor in many economic sectors, particularly the oil industry, construction, and high-technology sectors (Nofal and Kmal 1990, 20).

The relationship between Libyan higher education and development stems from the role played by scientific research in development. It may be said that the relationship between scientific research and the developmental process is still feeble and fragile. Most developmental projects rely on scientific research conducted abroad by international companies and foreign experts. These projects are entirely dependent on foreign production.

Many industrial and agricultural projects have been designed and implemented with little or no participation from Libyan experts. This is due to a lack of experience in such fields or to a policy of abdicating responsibility to foreign interests. When Libyan experts do participate in projects such as local assembly processes, the provision of local counseling and design eases the use of local industrial inputs and experiences.

Nevertheless, most projects take the form of comprehensive contracts and are concluded with little participation from Libyan universities, research centers, and national scientists. This arrangement leaves Libyan society dominated by the shackles of importation and dependence on foreign resources. Such approaches will lead to the suppression of local creative activities and indigenous technology.

Some researchers attribute the weak link between higher education and development to the following causes and factors:

- A shortage of qualified personnel who are capable of using modern technologies
- An insufficient number of specialized institutions which foster research activities and the required updating of technical skills
- A shortage of information and expertise to facilitate the understanding of what is needed in the technological field to meet national priorities
- A shortage of expertise in applied fields and in the merging of science and technology in the developmental areas of education and industry
- Insufficient coordination and collaboration between universities and their respective research centers and between industries and governmental institutions
- Lack of collective work between Libya and other countries, especially Arab countries, with regard to coordinating and managing the process of transferring and using knowledge and technology

The majority of research conducted by university professors has little to do with local development. The main purpose of such research is to qualify for promotion in universities. Development, with all the problems it entails, does not seem to attract Libyan researchers' attention, due to the continuous reliance on foreign expertise, especially in industrial and higher technological projects.

Social Challenges

Higher education institutions face increasing social demand. This is attributed to rapid population growth, particularly in the 18- to 23-year age group, as well as to the widely held belief that university education is valuable, regardless of usefulness or quality. Libya's higher education system, like those in other Arab countries, is powerless against this crisis. To impede social demands on higher education, they set standards and rules of admission, but such steps are often ineffective. Most Arab states ultimately enroll increasing numbers of qualified students in various faculties every academic year. Despite this great quantitative expansion, the ratio of university students to the population and to the corresponding age group is still very low. Unless Arab countries set admissions polices that are linked to the requirements of development and the labor market, Arab universities, including those in Libya, will continue to produce huge numbers of jobless students. Such students accumulate in already congested administrations and form a pool of disguised unemployment.

This is coupled with the centralization of Arab higher education in capitals and big cities, which weakens its contribution to developing rural areas and agriculture and encourages emigration from the rural to the urbanized areas, minimizing equality of opportunities. Though many Arab countries, including Libya, embarked on opening universities and higher institutes in rural areas and small towns, this step will jeopardize higher education if it is not carefully considered and planned. Such universities are normally established at a quick pace and under social pressure without consideration for the basic requirements of university work, particularly scientific work. These universities, colleges, and institutions tend to produce graduates whose education is mostly inadequate, inflicting negative results on society rather than bringing positive results. Nevertheless, in many cases there is no escape from this option, and this is probably the only way higher education will reach rural areas in Libya and similar Arab countries.

Economic Challenges

Higher education continues to face financial and economic challenges due to the increasing need for funding, the various expansions of universities and the increase in the number of students, the reduction of the annual budgetary and developmental allocations to higher education as a result of austerity, the rationalization of expenditures, and a scarcity of financial resources. This has led in recent years to a vicious circle that affects overall academic and nonacademic performances. The system is no longer capable of producing highly qualified students and is less capable than ever of participating in the kind of scientific research that is linked to social and economic development. Faced with these hardships, Libya must consider finding new means of financing higher education; otherwise it will continue to be incapable of adapting to increasing social demand and unable to satisfy the developmental requirements embodied in competent human resources. It is also expected that expenditure on higher education will increase until Libya spends all that it can but will still not achieve these goals. All research and studies conducted on the economics of education, and higher education in particular, stress the need to reconsider the traditional modes that dominate the planning and managing of higher education in Libya. This might require a restructuring of the entire higher education system as well as the introduction of new and modern modes unfamiliar to Libyan society.

Planning Challenges

Higher education faces an obvious imbalance in specialization, which is marked by a significant increase in humanistic sciences, arts, and law and a decline in admission to basic sciences, engineering, technology, and advanced technical sciences. It is a history that goes back to the original philosophy of Libya's educational system, which was developed in the 1960s during the early years of independence. This philosophy made a distinction between material matters and the soul. Consequently, the curriculum was classified into units corresponding to spiritual elements without considering the personality or mind as a comprehensive, unified entity. Pedagogical philosophies in the 1960s adopted this trend under the influence of classical European educational traditions, or by what is known in the history of education as the Latinate educational model. The outcome of such thought in Libya's education has been that curricula in universities and secondary schools, as well as students' minds and personalities, suffer divisions and conflict between what is known in Arab universities as theoretical colleges and scientific colleges.

There is a great need to revise these divisions so as to prepare the student for life using a complete and comprehensive educational curriculum comprised of sciences, arts, and spiritual and technical disciplines. These needed abilities can only be obtained if there is a complete and comprehensive university curriculum that encourages clear thinking and creativity and enables students to deal with the local and the global, the simple and the complex, all at the same time.

As stated earlier, data presented by Dr. H. Abdull-Wahab indicates that specialists in basic and technical sciences constitute barely one-third of enrollment rates, whereas specialists in humanities constitute two-thirds of students. This is a reflection of an imbalance in the structure of scientific fields of specialization in Libyan universities. Moreover, it is out of line with the demands of the labor market and development, which require cadres of specialists in basic, technical, and engineering sciences. In fact, the lack of scientific resources in Libyan universities constitutes an obstacle for the many students wishing to study basic sciences, medicine, engineering, and electronics. This situation requires creative consideration in order to address the imbalance existing in scientific disciplines.

The most important challenge facing Libya's system of edu-

cation and its ability to adapt to the requirements of economic development is the relationship between the educational plan and the economy. For this reason, Libya has tried during the past few years to link higher education policies with those of development, the economy, and the society. Policymakers have tried, at least theoretically, to make their educational plan include higher education and render it part of the general development plan (El-Hawat 1997). Nevertheless, despite this theoretical commitment, there is still disparity in the points of view of the educational planner and the economic planner. For example, the educational planner looks at education as a comprehensive cultural project that prepares the individual behaviorally, professionally, and culturally, whereas the economic planner usually considers education, and higher education in particular, as an investment project only, one that is concluded and accounted for when expenses, profits, and losses are assessed.

Generally speaking, the following problems should be addressed within the framework of the relationship between educational planning and economic planning:

- Inadequate educational statistics and data
- Insufficient information about the labor force needs
- Lack of understanding between economists and financial experts
- Insufficient legislation that promotes a reciprocal relationship between educational and economic planning

Information, Technology, and Globalization

Libyan higher education enjoys huge buildings and advanced machines and technologies in its universities. Despite this relative progress, it is clear that modern information technology and globalization will impose a new situation on the field of education and higher education in particular. Universities in Libyan society will have to change their philosophies, curricula, and educational technology in order to enter the twenty-first century.

Traditional educational institutions, professors, and students have now realized some of the changes brought about by modern technology and globalization. Educational and learning processes can take place outside the boundaries of universities, and the traditional concept of the university can be developed and renewed, if not completely changed.

LIBYA'S HIGHER EDUCATION: ALTERNATIVES, CHOICES, AND FUTURE DEVELOPMENT

Some of the challenges and obstacles facing Arab higher education cannot be dealt with in this study. But all point to the same question: What is to be done by those in charge of Libya's higher education to adjust the system to the new social and economic situation in the country? In particular, how will they deal with the fact that rapid communication and globalization have dissolved geographic and social disparities among people, be they students, citizens, or workers in the labor market? Answering such questions necessitates setting new plans and strategies for higher education. It also necessitates adopting an innovative approach and bringing about a fundamental educational reform that springs from the idea that higher education should not necessarily be organized according to the traditional form currently prevailing in Libya; it should not necessarily be managed by the government and funded entirely by the state. Rather, higher education and its institutions ought to be patronized by nongovernmental bodies and by projects under the direct auspices and supervision of the state. New educational strategies must be built on a conviction that social and economic development depends on improving the quality of education at all levels and linking it with the labor market. Educated individuals should have broad knowledge and be prepared to be creative, capable of creating job opportunities for themselves and fellow citizens. That is to say, education must work to prepare self-confident individuals who can discover the unknown, embark on adventures, and strive to develop both themselves and their country. This kind of citizen will not be produced under the existing traditional educational system, which emphasizes its own reproduction and consecrates, under existing traditional educational technologies, recitation and stereotyped thinking and conduct.

Building the individual of the twenty-first century requires an educational system that is free of traditionalism; that is characterized by modernity, flexibility, and a vision for the future; and that gives due consideration to individual differences among students and among groups and the various social categories constituting the society. It is the responsibility of the state to promote and support all levels of education and fund them, even partially, because education, good education, constitutes the hope that Libyan society will survive in the twenty-first century. This stance rejects all calls that advocate that the state abandon higher education and limit admission opportunities. If these things were to happen, higher education would serve only certain financially powerful classes and elites. This contradicts, in basic ways, democratic educational principles, as well as social justice principles, which rely on education as an instrument for social mobility.

Development in the twenty-first century will require a literate and educated society, one of experts capable of creativity and innovation, capable of working in complex and highly technical institutions. This issue is very important, especially when we realize that Libya is building a modern industrial society that depends on science and well-educated workers. It is impossible to produce a skilled labor force for a modern economy based on science, technology, and information if higher education does not adapt to the labor force and the population as a whole. This requires the introduction of structural and qualitative changes to Libya's higher education system to render it more efficient and better able to adapt to the needs and requirements of development in the twenty-first century. These issues will require extensive planning and the efforts of institutions, work teams, experts, and scientists. Nevertheless, there is a dire need to diversify higher education institutions and programs. This innovative trend could be justified by the following facts:

- Higher education is one of the keys to confronting today's challenges.
- Higher education institutions and other academic and profes-

sional institutions are essential to development and to the implementation of developmental strategies and policies.
- There is a need for a new vision of higher education that combines global aspects of education with an adaptability to satisfy the demands of society. This new vision focuses on principles of enriching academic life and the relative independence of university institutions with a special emphasis on the principle of social work. (UNESCO 1995, 19–20)

The necessary diversification of programs and higher educational institutions should occur in the following fields:

First: Universities must be restructured in order to provide for advanced specialized programs directed toward basic, scientific, and applied research. Talented students and those who do well in their final year of secondary school will be streamed to such universities, which ought to be funded by the state.

Second: Universities or university colleges should be opened whose purpose is to train the labor force. Such universities should not focus on advanced scientific research necessarily; rather, they should focus on linking themselves directly with the demands and requirements of the labor market. The average student should be admitted to these universities side by side with those with advanced academic abilities. This trend demands that offices be created to guide students to universities in accordance with their abilities. A student is not to be admitted on the basis of his or her general grade average only, as is the case now in Libya and in most Arab countries. These universities can be established through combined governmental and nongovernmental efforts or they can be established in the form of a private educational institution, whose capital is to be sold in the form of accessible shares to public and private institutions and individuals.

Third: A comprehensive university, which is formed by merging academic and technical institutes into one single institution and which provides short-term and long-term programs, should be opened. The comprehensive university's aim is to develop technical training and improve its effectiveness by linking itself with scientific research and by linking scientific research with the needs of development as well as with the labor market and production processes. Such an experiment was successful in Germany (Nofal and Kmal 1990).

Fourth: Top priority should be given to institutes contributing to and participating in society. In a world characterized by rapid scientific and technological progress, sciences deserve significant attention from the government and other financing and technological bodies, as should those fields serving development and society. These funding bodies might find themselves torn between giving priority to areas whose social return is higher in the long run and meeting social demands for higher education under harsh budgetary conditions. The government sometimes solves this problem by creating open-door institutes and distance learning alternatives, the return on which has been quite good in many countries in the world. Another available alternative is private support, but this alternative alone is not enough. The state must perform the role of promoter. The university must assume responsibility for mobilizing financial, technical, and human resources and establishing the structures necessary for providing the required professional cadres of technicians, researchers, and operators. The university must also provide for less-respected fields and specializations, which are liable to be neglected, and generate the knowledge and expertise required in various economic sectors.

Fifth: One of the vital fields of investment (public or governmental), lies in organizing incentive-inducing structures (including the efficient dissemination of information about the cost efficiency of institutes), so as to harmonize between the need to achieve a certain level of efficiency and the need to avoid any interference that might bring about opposite results, such as suppressing innovative institutes and educational services provided through the private sector.

Sixth: In certain situations, alternative ways to provide higher education must be given priority. For instance, the need for qualified personnel possessing special abilities can be satisfied by introducing and providing shorter programs for the higher level of education, requiring two or three years instead of five or seven years in technical institutes, the open university colleges, and other open universities. The feasibility of such programs has proven to be good, particularly when concentration is directed to fields of great demand, whose graduates can easily find their way in the labor market.

Seventh: Groups lacking in representation, such as rural students or students belonging to vulnerable groups, should be seen as potential investments. The role of the state is required, since it is the instrument for establishing equality and social justice. Considerable investment on the part of the state should be directed to these groups so that a balance is achieved and the entire society participates in the process. National unity and a spirit of social justice are among the supreme goals of Libyan society.

Eighth: Priority of investment should be given to professional guidance in high school to familiarize students and their families with educational and professional horizons of higher education. By participating in sound decisions, the state can create more effective coordination between higher education and job opportunities.

Ninth: Cooperative higher education programs based on combining study and work and encouraging cooperation between educational and production institutions should be established. The advantage of this kind of education is that it realizes numerous goals, such as reducing the abstract theoretical aspect that dominates most of the curricula in Libyan higher education institutions. Also, strongly linking education with the labor market gives opportunities to working individuals whose circumstances would not otherwise allow them to continue their studies.

Tenth: Citizens who can participate financially in the setting up of such educational institutions should be encouraged to establish nongovernmental universities and colleges or higher institutes. The state may also cooperate. The state may provide a piece of land, buildings, and equipment, whereas private institutions or individuals may fund educational programs and pay the teaching staff. Such universities could be established in the form of cooperative educational institutions. That is to say, its capital is in the form of salable shares. This university receives tuition from the students and engages in investments in both the private and public sectors.

Eleventh: A national higher education fund with capital from the state and donations from public and private institutions and individuals should be established. This fund may establish universities, colleges, and higher institutes; grant loans to talented or needy students; and fund academic research that is linked to the requirements of economic and social development in Libya.

Twelfth: The scientific, technical, and administrative measures of evaluating university curricula should be revised so that due consideration is given to the quality and level of education, as universities attempt to respond to social demands for higher education.

Students ought to be trained and prepared to work and live in a society that is linked to and interacts with the world in all its complexities. The student should be able to preserve a proud cultural identity within and against globalization, the influx of information, and the transfer of ideas, values, and culture by means of modern mass media. Such innovation and reform in the field of education require revising higher education philosophy so that it encourages and enriches university life while promoting creativity, liberal thinking, and genuine scientific research. What jeopardizes Libya's higher education is not globalization or mass media, but rather intellectual stagnation, seclusion, and fear of innovation. Higher education philosophies should aim to broaden students' perspectives, developing their various abilities and instilling confidence in their identity, culture, and historic foundations. Had this process already taken place, students would be able to deal with globalization, sciences, and the entire world with confidence and pride in identity. This can only happen, however, when traditional approaches to university planning are abandoned and the university becomes a big laboratory of experimentation. The university must create an atmosphere that induces self-confidence and pride in national cultural identity while at the same time interacting openly with global culture, in all its modes and forms.

Finally, stagnation and isolation mean slow death, while education and knowledge mean a good and prosperous life for all individuals that allows them to participate in developing their society and retain a position and role in human global civilization.

CONCLUDING REMARKS AND RECOMMENDATIONS

Modern higher education was established in Libya in the middle of the twentieth century with one college. At present, there are more than 50 colleges, 270 departments, and 80 higher technical institutes that teach more than 200,000 students. This higher education system has both successes and challenges in internal and external efficiency.

In this context of analyzing and evaluating the relationship between higher education and the needs of development in the twenty-first century, including human and cultural development, it is clearly evident that Libya's system of higher education, and education in general, will need to be reformed in order to meet the country's future needs and cope with the changing nature of the global situation. It is clear that Libyan higher education must further examine its philosophical assumptions and make further changes to its educational curriculum, teaching technology, scientific programs, and types of specializations. This conclusion is drawn from the following facts:

- Higher education in Libya, as well as in many other developing and Arab countries, will have to deal with a wide range of obstacles, problems, and issues as it enters the twenty-first century. Some of them are local in nature (social demands on higher education, financing the expansion and growth of higher education, the quality of graduates, needs of new Libyan industrial labor market). Other obstacles and challenges are international (globalization, structural adjustments, the environment, cultural dialogue among the peoples of the world).
- Higher education cannot remain traditional in theory and practice. It has to be altered in its scientific programs and training in order to suit the needs of students, national society, and global culture.
- Higher education in Libya should not retain a single model of public higher education; rather, it must be changed into a partnership model, which depends not only on the efforts and financing of the state but also the private sector and NGOs, taking into consideration that the state is the first party responsible for higher education.

It should be noted also that the Libyan higher education system has to cope with many new roles and functions which have appeared as a result of the changing world situation in the twenty-first century. The data gathered in this research project shows that the most important among these roles and functions are the following:

- Discovery of future needs
- Contribution to the building of capacity in intellectual, cultural, and civil participation
- Contribution to the building of a learned society or "university community" that can provide cultural innovation and emotional richness
- Contribution to the national socioeconomic plans that Libya intends to carry out, especially in the coming plan (2001–2005)
- Contribution to the building of bridges of peace and cultural dialogue among various peoples and cultures of the world, especially among younger generations, who are the actual citizens of the twenty-first century

Our analysis and evaluation in this study leads to the conclusion that before Libya's higher education can take any role in future development, it must reform its management and develop its learning process, especially with regard to the following points:

- It must develop a long-term plan to supply universities and higher technical institutes with teachers and professors. Libya will need at least 10,000 university teachers in the coming twenty-five years if the rate of student enrollment is sustained as it is now.
- It must develop a plan to train university staff and provide training that covers the whole process of higher education, especially planning, administration, and economy of education, within the context of Libya's socioeconomic development in the future.

- It must provide training focused on educational management, with due consideration to the pedagogical and supervisory functions of the staff concerned with the overall process of higher educational planning and administration.
- It must enable grassroots organizations, parents, community leaders, investors, and voluntary organizations to become effective partners in planning, management, and implementation of higher educational policy programs at the local level. This is very important because, at present, Libya is allowing the establishment of private higher education institutes on the local level of communities, small towns, and villages, for the purpose of mass higher education (Hallak and Gothman-DURET 1990, 10–12).

Note: The ideas, conclusions, and judgments presented in this study do not represent, by any means, those of the official Libyan authorities and do not establish any legal, moral, or financial obligations on the Libyan State.

BIBLIOGRAPHY

Abdull-Wahab, H. 1996. "An Overall Evaluation of Higher Education System in Libya." Unpublished UNESCO technical report, Paris, February (in English).

AEGEE (Association des Etats Généraux des Etudiants de l'Europe). Europe. 1998. *The Future of Higher Education: A Student's Vision.* Brussels: AEGEE Europe.

Al-Seed, M., K. E. Shaw, and A. Wakelam. 2000. "Issues of Educational Administration in the Arab Gulf Region." *Middle Eastern Studies* 326, no. 4 (October) (in English).

Delors, J. 1996. "Learning: The Treasure Within." Report presented to UNESCO by the Chairman of the International Commission on Education for the 21st Century, Paris.

El-Hawat, A. 1995. *Higher Education in Libya: Reality and Future Perspectives.* Tripoli: Tripoli's Scientific Library (in Arabic).

———. 1996. "Postgraduate Studies in Libyan Universities." Working paper presented to a consultation committee at the National Center for Educational Planning, Tripoli (in Arabic).

———. 1997. "The Situation of Higher Education in Libya and Its Relationship to Development and the Labor Market: A Case Study." Study prepared for the Arab League Educational, Cultural and Scientific Organization (ALECSO), Tunis (in Arabic).

———. 1990–2000. Fieldwork on Libyan Higher Education. Author's personal collection.

———. 2000. "Higher Education and Human Development." Study prepared for the Arab League Educational, Cultural and Scientific Organization (ALECSO), Tunis (in Arabic).

———. ed. 2000. "Postgraduate Studies in Libya and Abroad: The Current Situation and Future Prospects." Report prepared by a team from the University of Alfatah (in Arabic).

El-Khawas, E. 1998. "Quality Assurance in Higher Education: Recent Programs—Challenges Ahead." Paper presented to the conference Higher Education in the 21st Century: Vision and Action, UNESCO-Paris, October 5–9.

Hallak, J., and Gothman-DURET. 1990. *Development of National Capacities for Training in Educational Planning and Administration: The Training Design and Policy of the IIEP.* S113. Appendix 4. Paris: IIEP (in English).

Khater, A. 1998. "UNESCO Mission to Evaluate Libya's Scientific Research Activities and Post-Graduate Programs during the Period 14–27 Executive Summary." June. Unpublished report (in English).

National Authority for Information and Documentation (Libya). 1999.

Libya: Report of Human Development 1999. Tripoli: National Authority for Information and Documentation Publishing (in Arabic).

National Center for Educational Planning (Libya). 1999. *Development of Education and Vocational Training in the Great Jamahiriya (1969–1999).* Tripoli: Secretariat of Education Publication (in Arabic).

———. 2000. "Financing Higher Education in Libya." In author's possession (in Arabic).

National Commission for Education, Culture and Science (Libya). 1998. *Higher Education and Prospects of Development for the 21st Century.* Libya's National Report, presented at the conference Higher Education in the 21st Century: Vision and Action, UNESCO-Paris, October 5–9 (in English).

Nofal, M. N., and M. R. Kmal. 1990. "Higher Education in the Arab World: Future Vision." *Arab Journal for Education* 10, nos. 1 and 2 (December) (in Arabic).

Rex, N. 1998. "Mobilizing the Power of Culture in Higher Education." Paper presented to a Free Roundtable at the conference Higher Education in the 21st Century: Vision and Action, UNESCO-Paris, October 5–9 (in English).

Secretariat of Education (Libya). 1999. "Higher Education and Scientific Research in the Great Jamahiriya." Report presented at the First Islamic Conference of Ministries of Higher Education and Scientific Research, Toward a Strategy to Develop Science and Technology in Islamic Countries, Riyadh, Saudi Arabia, October (in Arabic).

Secretariat of Education and Scientific Research (Libya). 1995. *Statistical Reports on Universities and Higher Technical Institutions.* Tripoli: Secretariat of Education (in Arabic).

Srkiz, F. 1998. "UNESCO Mission to Evaluate Libya's Postgraduate Programs in Social Sciences during the Period 22–27 June 1998: Executive Summary." Technical report (in Arabic).

UNESCO. 1991. *The Role of Higher Education in Society, Quality and Pertinence, UNESCO, Non-governmental Organizations, Collective Consultation on Higher Education.* New Papers on Higher Education (1) Meeting Documents, Paris, April 8–11, UNESCO-Paris.

———. 1995. *Research in Changing and Developing Higher Education.* Paris: UNESCO Publishing (in Arabic).

———. 1998a. *Higher Education in Africa: Achievements, Challenges and Prospects.* Dakar: Regional Office for Education in Africa (in English).

———. 1998b. *Higher Education in the 21st Century: Vision and Action.* Proceedings of the World Conference on Higher Education. Paris: UNESCO Publishing.

UNESCO and the University of Tokyo. 1997. "Report of the Roundtable on the Relationship among Research, Policy and Practice in Higher Education." Tokyo, September 3–5 (in English).

UNESCO Regional Office for Arab States. 1998. *Preparatory Conference on Higher Education in the 21st Century.* Beirut: UNESCO Regional Office for Arab States.

42

Madagascar

JAMES STILES

INTRODUCTION

Madagascar is the fourth-largest island in the world and the last significant land mass to be inhabited by humans (Dewar 1997). The country is home to a diverse population of unique flora and fauna, which partially explains why Madagascar has captured the imagination of explorers, naturalists, and the scientific research community over the past four centuries. Located 250 miles east of Mozambique and South Africa in the Indian Ocean, Madagascar represents the eastern edge of African culture and the western edge of Austronesian culture. Its population surpassed 15 million in 2000. The country has one of the highest birth rates on the African continent (3.3 percent per year). The vast majority of individuals (75 percent) live in small, relatively isolated villages and are engaged in subsistence farming.

Madagascar's diverse climatic zones allow it to grow a wide variety of agricultural products. The country exports rice, coffee, vanilla, and cocoa. Recent years have seen advances in the industrial and service sectors as foreign capital has arrived to take advantage of the well-educated population and relative stability of the government. Madagascar's per capita gross national product (GNP) is $250. Three-fourths of the population live below the poverty line.

When the Organization of African Unity (OAU) was being formed, Madagascar lobbied to have the name be the Organization of African and Malagasy Unity. This proposal is indicative of the country's sense of being a land apart. It is a place of contrasts, where various cultures have come together to form a unique cultural mix. The Malagasy have been heavily influenced by the outside world but have continually adapted what they have expropriated from the influences of successive generations. The history of the education system is parallel to the development of the nation as a whole. To understand the higher education challenges and opportunities in Madagascar, it is necessary to understand the context of its peoples, history, and language.

PEOPLE AND CULTURES

Uninhabited until the seventh century A.D., Madagascar's oldest known inhabitants were probably Malay-Indonesian sailors who migrated either directly from the east or from colonies on the nearby African coast. Later waves of African peoples, who came as both immigrants and slaves, have created a rich cultural diversity that evolved into some eighteen cultures, including the Sakalava in the north, Merina and Betsiléo in the central highlands, Betsimsaraka in the east, and Mahafaly in the southwest. The geographical isolation of the island, its mixture of Asian and African ancestry, and its contact with Arab and European cultures have produced a strong sense of unity among its people. Significantly, a common language, Malagasy, has always linked the populace. This Austronesian language evolved from language roots similar to the languages spoken today on the island of Borneo (known today as Kalimantan).

While the cultures of the island are distinct, a recent issue of the journal *Ethnohistory* cautions against approaching Malagasy cultures with preconceived notions of ethnicity and difference. The central highland cultures of Merina and Betsiléo identify most strongly with the original Indo-Malay settlers, and other cultures tend to identify more strongly with African peoples, but these conceptions of culture are inextricably linked to the domination of the country first by Merina royals and then by French colonizers (Lambeck 2001; Bloch 2001). However, as Maurice Bloch states, this does not imply that the cultural differences are completely constructed. These cultural identities are not based upon clearly delineated lines of ethnicity or origin. Rather, these differences must be understood within the Malagasy context in terms of how one moves through life and relates to one's ancestors (Bloch 2001). The relationship to one's ancestors and family is central to an understanding of contemporary Malagasy culture, even for the Westernized Christian intellectual classes. The far smaller familial group exerts a more significant impact on the contemporary person, connecting the contemporary Malagasy to the larger "cultural" group of Merina, Sakalava, and so forth.

HISTORY

Madagascar became a crossroads for Arab traders and others attracted to its strategic location and abundant agricultural products as early as the fourteenth century. In the late eighteenth and early nineteenth centuries, the central highland Merina began to unify the country under the rule of King Andrianampoinimerina (1787–1810) and his son, Radama I (1810–1828). Eager to end Madagascar's flourishing slave trade, Great Britain recognized Radama as the "King of Madagascar" and provided him with military technology. While the trade in slaves did not end either internally or externally, Radama used the military technology and recognition of his title to subdue most other cultures and create a unified Merina state with a capital in the central highlands city of Antananarivo. The British, in return, were allowed to use the Malagasy Indian Ocean ports and to send missionaries from the London Missionary Society (LMS).

The presence of LMS teachers, preachers, and artisans had significant consequences for the technological and educational development of the nation. While its main goal was evangelization, the LMS also brought artisans who introduced cut-stone masonry, brick making, large-scale irrigation, printing, and other technologies. With the goal of instructing the Malagasy people in their own language, the missionaries applied to King Radama for permission to create a fully written version of the language, convincing him to romanize Malagasy. Teaching and preaching in Malagasy rather than in English enabled the missionaries to reach a much wider population in their schools and churches and also served to displace some of the resistance to the presence and rising prominence of the foreign Christians (Brown 1995). The more advanced Malagasy students served as monitors for the beginning students and in turn became master teachers in their own right. In this way, the LMS and the Merina nobles created an educated class of Malagasy who would become preachers, teachers, and court functionaries.

After a brief period marked by the expulsion of foreigners and a return to isolation under Radama's successor, Queen Ranavalona I (1828–1861), Westerners were welcomed back. In 1866, Christianity became the official state religion after the conversion of Queen Ranavalona II. During this period, other European missionary groups were also active in Madagascar, and both the British and French governments used eastern and northern ports for trade.

After its return, the LMS founded three institutions of higher learning, a Normal School for Boys to train schoolteachers (1862), the LMS College to train pastors and court functionaries (1870), and a Normal School for Girls (1872) (Koerner 1999). The Lutherans, Anglicans, and Roman Catholics also started religious training institutes during this period (Brown 1995).

The LMS College was an impressive brick building with three large wings, and its lecture halls could hold 100 students.

By 1880, more than 400 graduates of the three LMS colleges had formed a network of Malagasy education and religious leaders (Koerner 1999). Student enrollment in the schools of the combined Protestant missions increased from 40,000 in 1880 to more than 134,000 in 1894. This latter figure, combined with the 34,000 Catholic school pupils, meant that by the end of the century, "the bulk of the population [in the central highlands] had at least some grounding in basic education" (Brown 1995). This was a surprisingly high level of literacy compared with other African nations, and is a testament to the LMS practice of turning responsibility for leading schools and churches over to the Malagasy people (Raison-Jourde 1991).

Madagascar became a French protectorate in 1885. After an Anglo-French treaty dividing up Indian Ocean interests, it became a full colony of France in 1895. General Joseph Gallieni, who had previously subdued much of Indochina, became governor-general of Madagascar. He was an ardent anti-cleric and consequently did not feel predisposed to favor French Jesuit interests over those of the Protestants, allowing both to continue their educational, medical, and religious work. While Gallieni permitted the continued use of the Malagasy language in schools, he decreed that the French language must also be taught. French soon became an important force in the newly colonized nation, and the ability to speak French became a prized attribute.

Gallieni's successor, Victor Augagneur, feared the power of the Malagasy-controlled schools and sought through a series of laws to diminish their power and prestige. He restricted access to the Colonial Professional College (a training ground for government functionaries) to students from colonial schools, mandated increased use of French, and forbade teaching within church buildings. These actions forced the closure of many church schools and set back education in Madagascar for decades. It was not until the 1930s that education levels returned to their precolonial levels (Koerner 1999).

Advanced education during the colonial period included the religious seminaries, the Colonial Professional College, and the Medical School of Béfalatánana, which was founded in 1896 to train medical personnel who would work under physicians trained in France. Additionally, some students continued to travel to Europe for advanced education, a practice begun as early as 1821 that was supported by foreign governments, missionary organizations, and private funds. Substantial numbers of students studied abroad. For example, at the dawn of independence in 1961, there were 576 Malagasy students studying in France, half of whom were on scholarships from the government (Koerner 1999). During World War II, access to European universities was impossible. Citing the need for legal clerks and lawyers, Malagasy jurists organized courses in law and established the Law Examinations Center. After the liberation of France in 1945, the center affiliated with the law faculty at the University of Aix-Marseilles; during the following decade, it was transformed into the College of Law (1955). Companion institutions of science (1954–1957) and letters (1959) were also formed during this period.

The end of the war led to increased calls for independence, and an armed opposition became more organized. France attempted to devise a semi-autonomous relationship between itself and Madagascar but eventually bowed to Malagasy demands for full independence. On June 26, 1960, independence returned to Madagascar, though this did not bring the end of French involvement. As part of the negotiated independence agreement, France continued to exert a strong influence over sectors such as education. Close relations with France and involvement of many French nationals in the affairs of the country marked the history of the first republic (1960–1972) under President Tsiránana.

One year after independence, the first true university was formally organized by merging the independent faculties of law, letters, and science and technology with the formerly independent medical school. The university enrolled 1,130 students during its first year (Secretariat d'Etat aux Affaires 1972). The campus was constructed on the edge of the capital city, Antananarivo, although the medical faculty remained at a separate campus. The French education ministry appointed the rector and all teaching staff of the new university, passing over many qualified Malagasy intellectuals who could have served in these roles.

The medical school curriculum was restructured to enable students to earn a full medical degree. Initially students studied during the first and last years in Antananarivo and spent the middle four years in France. Over time, facilities and personnel in Madagascar were upgraded so that full medical education could occur in Antananarivo (Burgess and Study Committee on Manpower Needs and Educational Capabilities in Africa 1965). At the same time, the government created four other institutions of learning and research: the National School of Public Administration, the National School of Public Works, the National School of Applied Agricultural Science, and the Institution of Social Advancement (Koerner 1999).

The student body at all of the institutions reflected the hegemony of the central highland cultures over the nation's other groups. The highland cultures (Merina and Betsiléo), which together made up 38 percent of the overall population, comprised 95 percent of the student body. Only 5 percent of students came from the remaining cultures, which account for 62 percent of the population. The existence of this division between the cultures of the central highlands and all other cultures (who are referred to as *les côtiers*, or people from the coast) is a central characteristic of the country and has impacted all areas of society. The differences in access to education for highland and *côtier* cultures helped to bring about the decentralization of the university that would begin after the formation of the second republic in 1978.

In one sense, the continued reliance on France paved the way for stability during the first decade of Madagascar's independence, but it also led to continued resentment from ardent nationalists. Nationalist sentiment and the economic difficulties of the early 1970s led to student strikes and a popular uprising that ushered in an interim government under Prime Minister Ramanantsoa (1972–1975), a former army general. The interim government used anti-French sentiment to replace French nationals with Malagasy colleagues in education, government, and civil society. Three years later, following the assassination of the newly elected president, General Didier Ratsiraka founded the socialist Second Malagasy Republic (1975–1989).

The assembly of the Second Malagasy Republic passed Law 78 040 (July 1978), which called for the decentralization, democratization, and Malagasization of the government and educational system. Malagasy was recognized as the official language of government and education, although French was retained for higher education and diplomacy. Using Malagasy served the explicit goal of rejecting France and the French, but it also elevated the conceptualization of Malagasy culture and served to further nationalist sentiment and support. After decades of being explicitly taught that their language, literature, and history were inferior to those of France, many Malagasy understood that using their own language was an important step in reconceptualizing what it meant to be Malagasy.

The law had far-reaching effects for higher education. It called for the division of the university into six regional university centers, one for each province. This division occurred initially in name only but eventually led to the current system of six separate universities (Rambeloson-Rapiera 1992). The movement of Malagasization called for replacing French nationals with Malagasy professors. While not all foreigners were forced to leave, the balance of power shifted as more and more positions were given over to Malagasy intellectuals. French remained the primary language of instruction in the universities, but Malagasy gained new prominence as departments of Malagasy literature, history, and culture were added at Antananarivo. Recognizing the student activism that helped create the Second Malagasy Republic, university leaders included faculty and student groups in discussions of how the university would serve the needs of the new nation (Rajaoson 1985).

Under President Ratsiraka, the government turned away from France and Western nationalized industries and attempted to encourage Malagasy culture. However, the demise of the Soviet Union, growing economic uncertainty due to the diminution of rice as a primary source of export income, and rising unemployment prompted another round of student strikes and general unrest in 1989. These pressures and events led to a new constitution and the third republic. In 1991, Albert Zafy, a professor of medicine, was elected president. President Zafy's government attempted to federalize the government, decentralizing power away from the capital and creating a federation of six provincial governments. The constitutional removal of President Zafy led to an election in 1996 in which the final two candidates were again Zafy and Ratsiraka. The election brought the return to power of President Ratsiraka, who became an advocate of privatization and decentralization.

Madagascar has recently experienced a decade of economic restructuring, expansion of the private sector, and a general opening up to a wide number of external forces. The government has been fairly stable for the past decade, and the country is preparing for a national election. Student and faculty activism continue today, as evidenced by the student strikes prior to a major referendum on further government decentralization in 1998 and the near strike of the teaching staff in June 1999.

Table 42.1. Academic Programs Offered at Madagascar's Public Universities, 1999

University	Law, Economics, and Sociology	Letters and Humanities	Science	Teacher Education	Polytechnic	Other
Antananarivo	4	9	3	8	9	Medicine and Agronomy
Antsiranana	0	1	1	3*	4	—
Fianarantsoa	1	0	2	3	0	—
Mahajanga	—	—	1	—	—	Medicine and Dentistry
Toamasina	2	4	0	0	0	Customs
Toliara	0	5	2	1	0	Marine Sciences

*Teacher education for technical education positions.
Source: MCU 1999 and MINESUP 1999.

Intercultural differences continue to surface in moments of crisis, such as the arson fire at the former royal palace complex in 1995, but are usually left smoldering below the surface.

LANGUAGE OF INSTRUCTION

Language is a central issue in Madagascar's educational history and current pedagogical context. When the nation was unified in the nineteenth century, the Merina dialect became standard Malagasy. While some regional dialects remain, one can converse throughout the country if one speaks standard Malagasy. It is a language with rich written and oral traditions (Dumont 1996).

During the colonial period, Malagasy continued to be spoken in all but official settings, except when French was used as a means of exhibiting one's education and class. French became the language of advancement during the colonial period and "the uncontested language of prestige" (Dumont 1996, 22).

In 1976, Malagasy became the language of instruction in primary and lower secondary public schools and French became a compulsory second language (Rakotondrazaka 1994). French is the language of instruction and examination for advanced secondary and university programs; Malagasy and a third language are compulsory. However, as Malagasy is the home language of both teachers and students, it is not uncommon for class conversations to lapse into the lingua franca. The results of this bilingual education can be quite powerful. The most adept students gain proficiency in at least two languages, but it can also lead to a disjuncture for less able students who grow up with partial knowledge of two different languages but a true mastery of neither.

Dominique Dumont (1996) illustrates how different actors involved with contemporary Malagasy culture offer different discourses on the language of instruction and how these multiple perspectives have shaped the reality of education and advancement. Dumont conjectures that the Merina may advocate education in Malagasy, knowing that they possess the resources and traditions to ensure that their children will be educated in both languages. The côtiers may hope to challenge Merina access to and advancement in higher education through the use of French, rejecting standard Malagasy, which they equate with Merina power. Postcolonial France has a strong commitment to maintaining French in the Francophone community as a way of maintaining its historical role as a world power. Finally, she suggests that America may be encouraging the use of Malagasy as a way of supplanting the attachments to France. Regardless of the political viewpoint, the issue of language of instruction and the resulting bilingualism of the populace will remain a potent factor for the foreseeable future.

STRUCTURE OF HIGHER EDUCATION SYSTEM

A separate Ministry of Higher Education (MINESUP) directs higher education in Madagascar. The prime minister, who is appointed by the president of the republic, appoints the minister of higher education. MINESUP is responsible for six public universities and numerous public institutes and research centers and is jointly responsible with other ministries for eleven other schools of advanced education. In 1992, it began to offer certification to private higher education institutions, sixteen of which have been certified. This range of institutions offers the Malagasy public a diverse set of educational options.

PUBLIC HIGHER EDUCATION

The first public university in the new Malagasy Republic was built in the capital city soon after independence. By the 1970s, this placement of the university in Antananarivo, traditional center of Merina power, became a topic of contention (Rajaosan 1985). The peoples in the other five provinces, frustrated by the hegemony of the central highlands, demanded that higher education be decentralized beginning in the mid-1970s. The original University of Antananarivo remains the largest and most diverse institution, while the other five regional universities are considerably smaller and offer programs that capitalize on particular strengths and opportunities of the area (Table 42.1).

The regional universities suffer from brief histories, fewer financial resources, and geographic isolation from the capital. Each regional capital is served by the national airline, but each has a considerably smaller population than and lacks the diverse intellectual life of Antananarivo. These factors make it more difficult to attract and keep teaching and administrative personnel. While the constitutional decentralization was intended to devolve power to the six provinces, much of the activity in the country still originates, or must flow through, the capital city. Decentralizing the university has increased access in other regions, but the regional universities lack resources to truly be classified as such. In his study of intercultural communication, *Meanings in Madagascar* (1999), Øyvind Dahl cites this solution to the problem of access to higher education as indicative of the Malagasy desire to preserve *fihavanana*, or mutual harmony, which is an important central concept in Malagasy life. Even though the resources to create the regional centers did not exist, they were established in part because of this desire to avoid conflict at all costs.

Regional universities tend to offer only beginning courses in given subject areas. Students interested in pursuing advanced work must travel to the capital city. All university students seeking doctoral degrees must enroll at the University of Antananarivo, with the exception of those working toward the doctorate in medicine or dental medicine; these two degrees may also be earned at the University of Mahajanga.

The levels and degrees in Malagasy education follow a French pattern, with three levels of university education. First-level students in the arts, sciences, law, and technology require at least two years of study to be granted a university diploma (DEUG, DUES, and so on). Students must pass a set number of courses and yearly exams in order to advance to the next year or level. The second level of university education requires a year of specialized study beyond the DEUG (or equivalent), which leads to a *license* (associate degree), and an optional additional year of study leading to a *maîtrise* (bachelor's). Third-level doctoral study lasts at least three years beyond the *maîtrise*. Two postgraduate degrees are awarded at the end of each of the first and second years of doctoral study, a *Diplôme d'Etudes Approfondies* (DEA) and a *Diplôme d'Etudes Supérieures* (DES). Submission of the thesis no earlier than the third year leads to a doctorate, *doctorat de troisième cycle*. Studies in medicine and dental medicine require at least eight and five years of study, respectively (UNESCO 1999).

Up until 1992, students could repeat a particular year of a single program up to six times while continuing to receive scholarships. Now a student may repeat the same year only twice. Failure on the third try means an end to government grants and one's academic career.

UNIVERSITY GOVERNANCE

MINESUP appoints a rector who governs each university with two constituent councils, one for administration and the other for academic affairs. The administrative council works with the rector to examine and approve the university's budget, fix the rules and regulations of the institution, and ensure the efficient conduct of business affairs. Together with the academic council and the rector, it works to define the principal activities of the university, plan for the education and training of faculty, and rule on proposals for new academic programs.

The academic affairs council concerns itself primarily with issues of pedagogy and research. It is responsible for conditions of access and has principal responsibility for supervising and overseeing programs and for guaranteeing the quality of research and teaching activities. The academic affairs council includes faculty members from various disciplines who provide guidance on the overall management of the academic enterprise (UNESCO 1986).

PUBLIC RESEARCH INSTITUTES AND RESEARCH CENTERS

The other institutes attached to MINESUP comprise a mixture of degree- and nondegree-granting institutions and other research organizations.

There are two higher institutes of technology (IST), one in Antananarivo and the other in Antsiranana. These institutes offer programs in civil and industrial engineering; the Antananarivo IST also offers programs in management, marketing, and accounting and is developing a new program in transportation management and logistics. The ISTs are seen as engines of growth for the developing nation and attract students interested in practical education. They maintain close ties with local industry in order to fund internships and provide students with job contacts and career information. Enrollment at the two schools has grown from roughly 175 students in 1993 to 550 in 1998.

Madagascar was an early proponent of distance education and is the only Francophone country in sub-Saharan Africa to develop an organized program at the tertiary level. The history of the program reaches back to pre-independence days when initial study in law occurred via a distance arrangement with the University of Aix-Marseilles (Saint 1999). In 1992, the government reorganized the program into the National Center of Tele-Teaching in Madagascar (CNTEMAD). Today it offers degree and nondegree courses to students in twenty regional study centers and consists of two years of pre-university-level courses for students without a baccalaureate and five years of university-level programs in law and management. CNTEMAD concentrates on practical business-related skills. It encourages students to form study groups and offers short-term internships with local firms. Teaching occurs using locally produced texts, audiocassettes, and radio programs. In 1997, nearly 8,000 students registered in university programs. Of these, 60 percent were male and 70 percent were registered in Antananarivo (MINESUP 1997). Degrees are awarded at both the first and second level, but the higher degrees are more vocationally oriented than their equivalents at the university. To date, CNTEMAD has awarded more than 3,900 degrees, and the examination success rate in 1997–1998 exceeded 50 percent. The program has received support from UNESCO and the French government. Graduates of CNTEMAD have been accepted into third-level university programs in France (Saint 1999).

Other centers directly under MINESUP include the National Center for Teaching English (CNELA), which offers nondegree courses in the study of English; two research centers, the National Institute for Nuclear Science and Technology (INSTN) and the Botanical and Zoological Park at Tsimbazaza (PBZT); and two new agencies to serve the wider higher education community, the National Evaluation Agency (AGENATE) and the Office of Communications for the Universities (MCU). Several of these centers have begun to experiment with profit-making ventures, such as offering short courses in English or specialized programs for business.

COLLABORATION WITH OTHER MINISTRIES

MINESUP supports eleven educational institutions in concert with other government ministries, including the National Institute of Accounting Science and Enterprise Administration (INSCAE), the National School of Administration (ENAM), a Military Academy, and institutes and centers for police, customs officers, court officials, geographers, and others. Among these institutions, INSCAE most closely resembles those programs in the public university system.

Madagascar and the World Bank created INSCAE in 1981 to provide students with the most up-to-date education in the field of financial management. Jointly supervised by MINESUP and the Ministry of Economics and Finance, it has evolved into a school that specializes in finance, entrepreneurship, and general management. It is a quasi-private institution that receives only 10 to 15 percent of its operating funds from the state. The remaining income comes from student tuition, special courses sold to businesses, consulting contracts undertaken by faculty and students, and direct support from international agencies. INSCAE is perceived by many to be one of the best educational programs in the country, but it is also the most expensive. Facilities are modern, clean, and well-equipped, with ready access to computers and language labs. However, the steep costs and high entrance requirements put it out of the reach of most students. Organizationally, a professor of management serves as general director of INSCAE. Its administrative council includes representatives of both ministries, the teaching faculty, and private enterprises.

PRIVATE HIGHER EDUCATION INSTITUTIONS

Private education has a long tradition in Madagascar. According to the recent report on human development by the UN and the government of Madagascar, roughly half of the 60,000 students in the second cycle of secondary schools attend private institutions. Religious seminaries to train clergy are operated by the Roman Catholic Church and at least four different Protestant traditions.

Fostering the growth of private higher education was one of the higher education reforms advanced at the beginning of the third republic. Since the 1960s, private institutions have been engaged in secular advanced education, though on a much smaller scale than the public system. New government guidelines offered the public certification of educational purpose and the resources of these private institutions. The guidelines were meant to ensure that these institutions were offering valid educational programs. Additionally, these measures sought to bring the private sector into dialogue with MINESUP and the public universities and offer opportunities for cross-sector cooperation.

Sixteen institutions have formed agreements with MINESUP and are part of the Association of Private Establishments of Higher Education in Madagascar (AEESPM), which was created

in 1995. Certification by MINESUP allows private institutions to participate in certain activities of the ministry (internships, grant programs, and some scholarship assistance). None of the current establishments have a current enrollment beyond 500 students, but they represent a growing and vibrant component of the overall system of higher education. These institutions range in subject matter and length of program from the eight-week School of Professional Agriculture at Bevalala (EPSA) to the Higher Institute of Communications, Affairs, and Management (ISCAM), which offers a four-year program of study in management and business (MCU 1999). The program of study at ISCAM overlaps with the programs at INSCAE and the IST, but it lacks the resources of the former and the low cost of the latter. What it does offer is open access to all students who can afford the tuition.

In terms of governance and organization, some schools resemble the organization of the universities, while others organize themselves along a business model with a CEO style of management. Most of the schools maintain close partnerships with particular industry groups and focus on connecting students with future employers.

STUDENT ENROLLMENT

Like other African countries, Madagascar has struggled with a greater demand for education than can be supported by the economy. The early 1990s found the public university system in disarray. There was widespread student unrest, productivity had dropped, and students on scholarship were able to repeat courses as many as six times (Koerner 1999; Viens and Lynch 2000). In 1993, these problems led to a series of systematic reforms sponsored by the new government of President Zafy and supported by international monetary institutions. As detailed in Table 42.2, enrollments in the public university system were reduced from around 33,000 in 1993 to fewer than 19,000 four years later. A more selective admission process was introduced, and the number of times a student could repeat an academic year was reduced to two (Viens and Lynch 2000). Enrollments were decreased in all but the two smallest universities. Mahajanga actually grew during this period due to the introduction of a successful program in dental surgery and an increase in the enrollment of foreign students, principally from the Comoros.

It is estimated that 2.5 percent of the traditional college-aged population are enrolled in tertiary education, but it is unevenly divided across the country (INSTAT 1999). In the province that includes the capital city of Antananarivo, the enrollment rate in tertiary education approaches 6 percent of the total student-aged population but hovers at no more than 1 percent elsewhere in the country. Table 42.3 displays the 1997 population for the six provinces and their percent of the national population total, as well as the enrolled student population and percentage of total enrolled students at the university within that province. This table should be read carefully, as not all students at the university in Antananarivo are from that province, but it does indicate some of the differences in scale that exist for the peoples from the various provinces. During the colonial period, census figures were gathered according to the cultures in the nation. Since

Table 42.2. Change in Enrollment at Madagascar's Public Universities, 1987–1997

University	1987	1990	1993	1994	1997	Percent Change 1987–1997
Antananarivo	26,592	27,680	24,038	19,865	12,431	–53
Antsiranana	867	882	783	887	865	0
Fianarantsoa	1,845	2,022	2,066	1,518	1,628	–12
Mahajanga	1,038	1,257	1,560	1,526	1,463	+41
Toamasina	3,081	3,472	2,603	1,719	1,411	–54
Toliara	1,683	1,733	2,152	1,422	1,147	–32
Total	35,106	37,046	33,202	26,937	18,945	–46

Sources: MINESUP 1997; Banque des Données de l'Etat 1992.

independence, population figures have been gathered only by province.

Girls have been educated alongside boys since the introduction of formal education in Madagascar in the nineteenth century. While cultural barriers continue to exist, females accounted for 46 percent of enrolled university students in 1996–1997, reflecting the strong role of women in Malagasy society. The near parity of Malagasy females in higher education stands in stark contrast to UNESCO's 1990 assessment of average female enrollment in sub-Saharan countries, which then stood at 18 percent (Mulli 1995). Looking at enrollment across academic subject areas, this balance of females and males is consistent, with the exception of engineering and agriculture. Only 30 percent of the enrolled students in these fields are women (UNESCO 2000).

Total current student enrollment in private higher education is more difficult to assess. Most institutions have quite small enrollments of 100–400 students. The 1997 MINESUP Annual Report estimated private enrollment at 1,500 students but failed to provide any detail. The actual figure is probably closer to 4,000–5,000 students.

ADMISSION TO HIGHER EDUCATION, TUITION, AND SCHOLARSHIP ASSISTANCE

Admission to the public universities and most private institutions of higher education requires the student to have passed his or her baccalaureate at the end of secondary school. All students who pass the baccalaureate are assured a place at one of the universities, but the most competitive programs (such as law, management, medicine, and the sciences) also have entrance exams that applicants must pass. Although economic and educational choices have increased for young people, 80 percent of students who obtain their baccalaureate continue to enroll in the university (Rakotondrazaka 1994). The pass rate of the baccalaureate varies from year to year and may serve as a way to control access to the university. In 1996, the pass rate was 25 percent; in 1997, it was 32 percent, and in 1998 it was 30 percent. Table 42.4 displays the varying pass rates for the six regions of the country for 1997.

Tuition has always been charged at the six public universities, but it is modest by American standards. Malagasy students pay only US$4–$8 tuition per course, but they lack many of the

Table 42.3. Population by Province and Enrollment at Madagascar's Universities, 1997

	Provincial Population		University Enrollments in Province	
Province	In Thousands	Percent of Total	Enrolled	Percent of Total
Antananarivo	4,163	30	12,431	66
Antsiranana	1,063	8	1,411	7
Fianarantsoa	2,931	21	1,147	6
Mahajanga	1,583	11	1,628	9
Toamasina	2,276	16	1,463	8
Toliara	1,986	14	865	5
Total	14,002		18,945	

Source: INSTAT 1999.

Table 42.4. Regional Baccalaureate Pass Rates at Madagascar's Universities, 1997

Region	Attempted	Number Passed	Percent Passed
Antananarivo	18,612	6,641	36
Antsiranana	2,519	744	30
Fianarantsoa	4,633	1,065	23
Mahajanga	2,478	746	30
Toamasina	3,596	918	26
Toliara	2,344	803	34
Total	34,182	10,917	32

Source: MINESUP 1996–1997.

student support services that exist in other countries. Students who are not able to live with their families must find housing and work to support themselves. Tuition at private and semi-private institutions (such as INSCAE or the IST) is not subject to government regulation and is therefore significantly higher. The range of tuition reflects the range of private institutions in the market, but it can be as high as $100 per course. For a student taking a full-time load of four or five courses, this tuition rate presents a high bar to pass. Consequently, the better private institutions tend to be populated with students from wealthier homes and families.

Students enrolled in the universities and ISTs are eligible for public scholarship grants administered by MINESUP. Students can receive grants as long as they meet eligibility requirements and continue to make progress toward a degree. The reduction of overall enrollment since 1993 has allowed the scholarship money to be spread more widely. The percentage receiving scholarship support has risen from 51 percent in 1994 to 74 percent of students in 1997. Grants are listed as covering one-third, half, or full assistance; however, one source lists maximum grants at only $9 per month. While this rate would cover tuition and direct expenses, very little money would be left over for living expenses.

TEACHING AND ADMINISTRATIVE PERSONNEL

The decrease in the number of students at the universities occurred at the same time as an increase in the number of faculty members. Between 1993 and 1997, there was an overall growth in teaching professionals of 26 percent, with the lowest growth rate at the largest campus and higher growth rates at the other five. This inverse growth pattern for students and faculty has resulted in drastically reduced student-to-faculty ratios. In 1993, there was an average student-to-faculty ratio of 47 to 1; this was reduced to 22 to 1 by 1996. This ratio is still alarmingly high and is cited by students as one reason why they pursue private higher education.

Faculty at the universities are predominantly Malagasy citizens, although roughly 10 percent of the teaching staff were foreign nationals in 1997. Roughly half of these were French nationals, while the remaining faculty were from Germany, Great Britain, Russia, China, and elsewhere (Rambeloson-Rapiera 1992). Women have made significant inroads into faculty positions, accounting for 31 percent of all teaching staff.

All faculty are appointed and promoted by the Ministry of Higher Education. Because they are a part of the government bureaucracy and are thus subject to external review by the ministry, promotion can be quite difficult to achieve on the basis of qualifications alone (Rambeloson-Rapiera 1992). Faculty report that being part of the federal bureaucracy imposes difficulties on the academic culture. The ministry, rather than academic officers, sets salaries and working conditions. It can be difficult, or impossible, for a chairperson to shift a department's academic priorities and procedures, and firing a poorly performing faculty member is virtually impossible.

Faculty members have strong ties to politics and the political system. Two of the three elected presidents of the republic have been university professors (Tsiránana and Zafy), and many serve or have served in the assembly. While professors are among the highest-paid civil servants, the rate of pay ($150–$360 per month) does not go as far as the average annual income of the country might suggest. A modest one-bedroom apartment in the capital could cost as much as $400 per month. Frustrated with low pay and inadequate resources, talented professors have left

the university and ventured into the private industrial sector. Private higher education also offers faculty members from the university the opportunity to increase their salaries by offering courses at these schools. University professors were offering courses at each private institution the author visited. Students complain that these courses mean that faculty devote less time and energy to their university courses. While the teaching corps increased during the 1990s, the number of administrative staff shrank by 5 percent. The student-to-administrator ratio (6 to 1) remains high relative to other countries.

ACADEMIC CULTURE AND BRAIN DRAIN

Given the history of student and faculty unrest and the Malagasy tradition of expository speaking (known as *kabary*), faculty describe the academic atmosphere as generally free of undue influence from the administration or government. The Association of University Faculty jealousy guards faculty rights and privileges but also at times can impede reforms of department chairs and others. There are five daily newspapers in the capital city, and there is open criticism of the government. But outside of these more formal opportunities for disagreement, the cultural norms of expression tend to support indirect rather than direct face-to-face criticism (Dahl 1999).

The brain drain that so often plagues developing countries is counterbalanced by very strong family ties and the strong presence of a middle class within Malagasy culture. According to one U.S. State Department official, Madagascar has one of the highest rates of return for students who study abroad. While there are Malagasy individuals who marry and settle in Europe, America, and other countries, the majority return home at the end of their training. The French government has been a strong supporter of repeated short-term intellectual exchanges with Madagascar. These exchanges serve as an additional enticement for Malagasy to return home after their university studies.

FINANCING

The 1997 budget for higher education was nearly $11 million. This figure is nearly double the $5.6 million budget of 1992 (INSTAT 1999; Koerner 1999). This was a period of high economic growth as Madagascar began its transition from a quasi-socialist economy to an open market economy. The share of the federal budget devoted to higher education increased from 1.3 percent in 1994 to 1.8 percent in 1997. During this same period, the percentage of the total budget devoted to primary and secondary education rose from 1.4 to 4.8 percent of the federal budget.

In its 1999 Annual Report, the Ministry of Higher Education stated that it plans to study whether or not the current apportionment of expenditure is in concert with the long-term goals of the country. Direct educational expenses currently account for 38 percent of the budget, followed by salaries for administrative and technical personnel at 21 percent, student assistance at 20 percent, and general administration at 11 percent. By 2005, the ministry intends for programmatic and expenditure plans to be rationalized and to be serving the goals set out during this study period.

RESEARCH

Malagasy researchers face the lack of adequate equipment, funds, time, and documentation to conduct research (Rambeloson-Rapiera 1992). During the later years of the second republic, university facilities suffered from severe neglect and fell into disrepair. The government has begun the process of refurbishment of research labs and libraries to provide better research space with support from donor nations (Japan, France, and the U.S.), but poor facilities, limited resources, and geographic isolation continue to limit research opportunities. However, even with these shortages, the research enterprise is strong, due to its early history, relations with donor nations (particularly France), and the rich natural environment of the island.

The contemporary research enterprise benefits from the history of active research in French, English, and Malagasy since the nineteenth century. The LMS published *The Antananarivo Annual* from 1875–1900, detailing their missionary activities but also including articles on natural history, geography, census statistics, weather, and Malagasy culture, folklore, and traditions. Malagasy authors were always represented in this extraordinary journal. In 1902, the French government formed the Académie Malgache as a scientific and research center on the model of the Académie Française. The bulletin of the academy continues to publish articles on a wide number of subjects and disciplines and has served as a principle journal for academic research. An international colloquium in September 2002 is planned to celebrate its centennial.

This history of past research efforts conflicts with the idea that universities in developing nations should focus their limited research dollars only on those projects that can create jobs and develop the marketplace with a direct impact on the country's development. At the 1998 UNESCO conference on Higher Education in Paris, Minister for Higher Education Joseph Sydson raised a defense of academically oriented research programs. "For us, the universities must continue to engage in their original vision of teaching and basic research in core academic subjects. While it is important to engage the private sector and meet the needs of employers, the goals of higher education must not be completely subordinated to the needs of the marketplace" (Sydson 1998, author's translation).

The experience of environmental and biological research efforts offers perhaps a balance between these sometimes competing interests. Malagasy researchers in biology, natural history, and environmental areas have worked alongside foreign researchers eager to explore, and sometimes exploit for economic benefit, Madagascar's rich ecosystems. Beginning in the 1970s, American and European researchers formed partnerships with Malagasy nationals to preserve and study the nation's vanishing rain forests. In the process, many Malagasy researchers have pursued advanced education in their sponsors' host countries and returned to continue researching this unique environment. American universities such as Duke, the State University of New York at Stonybrook, Cornell, and the University of Michigan now have long histories of partnership and training. The Japanese have sponsored research in the areas of shrimp and rice cultivation, and the French maintain strong ties with Malagasy researchers in many fields.

One aspect of the modern academic research enterprise unfamiliar to most Malagasy academics has been the competitive peer-reviewed proposal process common in Britain, France, and the United States. As part of the second Education Sector Development Project (CRESSED II) in 1992, the government and the World Bank undertook an innovative project to improve the state of research in higher education and give Malagasy scholars experience in this kind of peer-reviewed environment. The bank provided a loan of $5 million to the Malagasy government as seed money for a new foundation for higher education. The money is managed by a separate organization and came to be known as the Fund for the Development of Higher Education (FDES). MINESUP appointed the executive director and provides the operating funds for the FDES office, but the director is responsible to an executive council comprised of representatives from government, industry, and all sectors of higher education. While the design was meant to make the director of FDES independent of control by MINESUP, the reality is that the higher education community is a small one, and true independence may take time to develop.

The FDES funds three kinds of proposals: curriculum development, applied research, and institutional development. Faculty and administrators from any institution (public or private) may propose projects using publicly available guidelines based on competitive grant processes used in Europe and America. The institution forwarding the proposal, the FDES staff, and an independent panel of scientific experts review the proposals. They are then brought to the council for approval or rejection. The executive council (EC) makes all decisions on grants awarded.

An international panel of academicians comes to Madagascar twice a year to review the program's procedures and practices. Participants, who are sponsored by their respective governments, include representatives from France, Germany, Great Britain, Italy, Mauritius, and the United States. Their role is to ensure that the published guidelines of the program are followed and that it is managed according to international scientific community standards. The international panel makes reports to the FDES staff, the EC, MINESUP, and their respective embassies on the management of the program, areas that need improvement, and progress made.

The proposal standards are rigorous and represent a new level of detail and sophistication for the Malagasy academic community. The FDES staff conducted a series of open meetings and training sessions, some of which became quite contentious when faculty expressed dismay at the complexity of the blind peer-review process. Proposed projects may seek as much as $100,000 in funding from FDES, but they must be made in partnership with industry, commerce, and/or higher education institutions abroad. This particular stipulation has been a cause of conflict in the university community. The World Bank's stipulation was that these partnerships were to encourage the academic and business communities to work for the betterment of the society, but the FDES seems to favor certain disciplines or types of projects over others.

In the first round of proposals (awarded in September 1999), nine of the thirty-five proposed projects received funding. Most of the successful projects were examples of curriculum development, including the creation of a new program in international banking at INSCAE and a restructuring of the communications programs at the University of Antananarivo to reflect changes in the demands of commerce and the changing nature of media.

It appears that projects funded through this mechanism will continue to focus on economic development, but this may free up support for research in other areas in the future.

NEW INITIATIVES

In June 1999, MINESUP released its annual report on its accomplishments of the previous year and plans for the future. The accomplishments highlighted (diversification of higher education offerings, reorganization of research support, modernization of the management of the ministry, and renovation of university facilities) are really first steps toward future goals rather than concrete accomplishments. But without those first steps, opportunities for teaching and research would never be realized. The current plan for improvement MINESUP has established includes some needed reforms of the system, but it is unclear whether higher education will look very different at the end of this planning phase in 2005. Some of the stated objectives include:

- Development of professional and distance education opportunities. In 1999, the new University for the Indian Ocean (a joint effort of the governments of Mauritius, Reunion, and Madagascar) was launched. MINESUP plans additional joint efforts in the future. In the area of professional education, the universities and CNTEMAD will work on efforts to develop specific courses in management and finance for particular sectors of the economy (such as health care and transportation), and the ISTs will continue to expand their offerings of targeted engineering and technical programs. These efforts may bring additional revenue into the institutions as they target sectors of the economy that are growing and are in need of skilled personnel.
- Improvement of the management of human resources. In order to meet increased demand from students, it will be necessary to shift resources from administrative and technical personnel to the teaching staff, whether through voluntary departure, retirement, education, or professional retraining of current administrative and technical staff. This shift could prove very difficult. Like most bureaucracies, there is an entrenched sense of entitlement in the administrative ranks, and change will come slowly. It is not likely that large numbers of the technical staff will be retrained or educated so that they can take on teaching duties.
- Strengthening of documentation, information, and communication. The Office of University Communications (MCU) was created to increase knowledge of, and communications about, higher education's teaching and research efforts. Recently relocated to a large central office downtown, it has begun to publish guides to public and private educational opportunities and limited edition publications of research by faculty. It provides meeting and lecture space for academics as a way to encourage cross-disciplinary communication and has

launched a new internship program with the local business council.

- Rationalization of the expenditures of MINESUP. With a new plan in place, MINESUP has stated that the current funding priorities may change.
- Creation of a system of internal and external evaluation of programs, teaching quality, management, budgetary performance, and overall evaluation. MINESUP has asked all programs and institutions to devise an internal plan for evaluation and has created a National Evaluation Agency (AGENATE) to begin the process of external evaluation. The creation of AGENATE highlights the complexity of the new environment for higher education. The agency was formed in 1998 with the support of the Cooperation Française and the World Bank. In its first year of operation, the staff went to France to study and be trained in the French evaluation system. While the Malagasy higher education system is based upon the French system, it has matured differently, and the present-day realities of each are quite different. The staff is also interested in other forms of evaluation; it has investigated the American accreditation system to determine what elements of each might be incorporated into a system that best serves Madagascar's needs. The largest hurdles may lie ahead when AGENATE begins to try to implement an evaluation system where none has existed previously. The executive director and her team are attempting to create a model of evaluation that reflects the realities of the country but which will be perceived as valid and reliable by the developed world.

The private sector continues to evolve and change. Because of the small size of individual institutions, private and quasi-private institutions are nimble and can more easily capitalize on new ideas and trends. As the economic base of the country diversifies, private-sector higher education shows every indication of continued expansion. Among the Malagasy, several of the private institutions already have stronger academic reputations than their counterparts in the public sector. The government's endorsement of the institutions was seen by many as a sanction for the continued growth and development of this sector. The quasi-private institutions, such as INSCAE and the ISTs, are the institutions that are attracting the most external funding and attention. Because of their strong relationships with the business community, they have access to resources unavailable to the public sector.

CONCLUSION

The higher education system in Madagascar is grounded in a strong intellectual history and culture. The country has a tradition of valuing education and the unique blend of cultures that has brought Madagascar to its present position. It is this blending that provides the country with its greatest promise and its greatest dangers.

A commitment to family and country tends to encourage young Malagasy to return home at the end of their university studies abroad. The ability of the Malagasy to absorb external (African, Asian, Arab, and European) influences and transform them into something new has allowed the nation to transcend the differences that existed, and continue to exist, among the various cultures within the larger society. As a nation of cultural diversity, it struggles with the question of how best to live together as one nation and offer the same opportunities for all.

The opening of Madagascar's economy offers great hope for the future. The educated population will be attractive to businesses in the lucrative information marketplace. Three years ago, the government opened the markets for cellular telecommunications and Internet access to private competition. The success of these businesses may pave the way for additional service-economy business in the information age. As it has in the past, the country is increasing access to foreign capital, trade with other nations, and the Internet and has a renewed emphasis on teaching English, all of which could have an impact on increasing support for the higher education sector. Whether the structures of the old socialist-based government will change quickly enough to support these new businesses and organizations remains to be seen.

Madagascar remains a place filled with promise, one open to new ideas and willing to incorporate foreign ideas into the fabric of the nation. But the question for higher education is whether the promises can be fulfilled and whether the country can pull together for the advancement of all, or whether old hierarchies and relationships will continue into the future.

ACKNOWLEDGMENTS

The author wishes to acknowledge the many contributions of Randall D. Bird of Harvard University in the preparation of this chapter. Additionally I would like to acknowledge the many Malagasy researchers, students, and administrators who shared their experiences with me throughout my ten-month stay. Special thanks are extended to my sponsoring agency, the Maison de la Communication des Universités, and its executive director, Violette Ramanankasina. Any errors in this essay reflect not their teaching but the comprehension of the author.

REFERENCES

Banque des Données de l'Etat. 1992. "Madagascar en Chiffres." Statistical report. Antananarivo: Republic of Madagascar, 40–41.

Bloch, M. 2001. "The Ethnohistory of Madagascar." *Ethnohistory* 48, no. 1–2: 293–299.

Brown, M. 1995. *A History of Madagascar.* London: Ipswich Book Company.

Burgess, E. W., and Study Committee on Manpower Needs and Educational Capabilities in Africa. 1965. *French Education Policy in Sub-Saharan Africa and Madagascar.* New York: Education and World Affairs.

Dahl, Ø. 1999. *Meanings in Madagascar: Cases of Intercultural Communication.* Westport, Conn.: Bergen and Garvey.

Dewar, R. F. 1997. "Madagascar." In J. Middleton, ed., *Encyclopedia of Africa South of the Sahara.* New York: Charles Scribner & Sons.

Dumont, D. 1996. "Le problème de la langue d'enseignement." In F. Deleris, ed., *Madagascar 1995: le Maraism,* 115. Paris: L'Harmattan.

Secretariat d'Etat aux Affaires, Etrangères, France. 1972. "Structures et statistiques dans quatorze ètats Africains et Malgache." Paris: Secretariat d'Etat aux Affaires, Etrangères.

Hagström, S., and A. Steen. 1995. *The University in Africa in the 1990's and Beyond: The Changing Role of the University.* Stockholm: Universitetskanslern.

INSTAT (Institute National de la Statistique). 1999. *Second Report on Human Development in Madagascar.* Antananarivo: INSTAT and PNUD.

Koerner, F. 1999. *Histoire de l'enseignement privé et officiel à Madagascar (1820–1995): les implications religieuses et politiques dans la formation d'un peuple.* Paris: Harmattan.

Lambeck, M. 2001. "Reflections on the 'Ethno-' in Malagasy Ethnohistory." *Ethnohistory* 48, no. 1–2: 301–307.

MCU (Maison de la Communication des Universités). 1998. *Monde Universitaire Malagache.* Antananarivo: Ministère de L'Enseignement Superieur.

———. 1999. *Etablissements d'enseignement superieur prives agrees par l'etat.* Antananarivo: Ministère de L'Enseignement Supérieur.

Mulli, V. 1995. "Enhancing Women's Participation in Teaching, Research and Management of Higher Education: The Case of Nairobi University, Kenya." In Dyenaba Barry, ed., *Women in Higher Education in Africa,* 69–81. Dakar: UNESCO-BREDA.

MINESUP. 1997. *Annuaire statistique de l'année 1996–1997.* Antananarivo: Ministry of Higher Education.

———. 1999. *Rapport d'activités.* Antananarivo: Ministry of Higher Education.

———. 2001. Ministry of Higher Education Web Site, Department of Math and Information Technology. Available online at: www.refer.mg/edu/minesup. Accessed 2001.

Raison-Jourde, F. 1991. *Bible et pouvoir a Madagascar au XIXe siècle: invention d'une identité chrétienne et construction de l'etat, 1780–1880.* Paris: Karthala.

Rajaoson, F. 1985. *L'enseignement supérieur et le devenir de la société Malgache.* Antananarivo: Université de Madagascar.

Rakotondrazaka, R. 1994. "Madagascar." In T. Husén and T. N. Postlethwaite, eds., *The International Encyclopedia of Higher Education,* 3550–3556. Oxford: Pergamon.

Rambeloson, J. 1995. "Women in Antananarivo University." In Dyenaba Barry, ed., *Women in Higher Education in Africa,* 82–94. Dakar: UNESCO-BREDA.

Rambeloson-Rapiera, J. 1992. "Madagascar." In W. Wickermasinghe, ed., *Handbook of World Education: A Comparative Guide to Higher Education and Educational Systems of the World.* Houston, Tex.: American Collegiate Service.

Razafindrakoto, A. 1980. "Madagascar: A Case Study." In UNESCO, ed., *Educational Reforms: Experiences and Prospects.* Paris: Unipub.

Saint, W. 1999. "Distance Education: The Solution to African Tertiary Education Problems?" *Association of African Universities Newsletter* 5, no. 3: 1–2.

Sydson, J. 1998. Remarks by the Minister of Higher Education, Madagascar. In *L'ensiegnement supérieur au XXIe siècle: Vision et actions.* Proceedings of the UNESCO World Conference on Higher Education. Paris: UNESCO. Available online at: unesdoc.unesco.org/images/0011/001172/117228f.pdf. Accessed 2001.

Tarpeh, D. N. 1994. *Study on Cost Effectiveness and Efficiency in African Universities: Phase II—An Overview.* Accra: Association of African Universities.

UNESCO. 1986. *EDUCAFRICA: Case Studies on Higher Education in Africa.* Dakar: UNESCO.

———. 1999. "Madagascar Education System." Available online at: www.unesco.org/iau/cd-data/mg.rtf. Accessed 2001.

———. 2000. *The Right to Education: Towards Education for All.* Paris: UNESCO.

Viens, D., and J. Lynch. 2000. *Madagascar: A Decade of Reform and Innovation in Higher Education.* Washington, D.C.: The World Bank.

43

Malawi

Joseph P. A. Chimombo

INTRODUCTION

In this chapter, the term "higher education" is used to refer to all postsecondary educational institutions in Malawi. These higher education institutions are comprised of teachers' training colleges, technical colleges, nursing and agricultural institutions, and the country's two universities, the University of Malawi (UNIMA) and Mzuzu University. Although this chapter mentions other postsecondary institutions, its focus is university education because the universities enroll the majority of tertiary students and include all the disciplines that fall under the postsecondary institutions. Since Mzuzu University has only recently been opened, this chapter concentrates on UNIMA, which is the oldest and the largest institution of higher education in Malawi.

SOCIOECONOMIC CONTEXT

Malawi is a landlocked country in Southern Africa that is bordered by Tanzania in the southwest, Zambia in the west, and Mozambique in the southwest, south, and east. A British protectorate, Malawi gained independence in 1964 under the leadership of Dr. Hastings Kamuzu Banda. A 1998 population census indicated that 9.8 million people lived in Malawi, of whom 52 percent were female. The largest contribution to the gross domestic product (GDP) comes from agriculture (at 35.2 percent), followed by government services (14.5 percent), manufacturing (13.2 percent), and distribution (11.6 percent). Agriculture (mainly tobacco, tea, groundnuts, and cotton) yields 92 percent of the country's export earnings. More than 80 percent of the people live in rural areas; 73.3 percent of that group is involved in agriculture-related work.

A comprehensive labor survey (Malawi Government 1997) showed that most UNIMA graduates were absorbed by government and parastatal organizations. Overall, 52 percent of profes-

sionals and 79 percent of subprofessionals worked in government. Out of this workforce, only 16.6 percent of the posts went to women. The study also showed that 70 percent of doctors, 50 percent of surveyors of standards, 33 percent of architects, 31.5 percent of accountants, 23 percent of engineers, and 22 percent of farm managers were non-Malawians. Thus, while UNIMA was established to respond to the demand for professionally trained workers, the fulfillment of this objective is far from ideal. The country still faces a crisis of human resource development. A recent civil service census (Malawi Government 1995) indicated that the proportion of civil servants possessing postsecondary qualifications was only 5 percent out of a total of 112,975 civil servants, while 17 percent of civil servants had only a primary-level education and 19 percent of them had no formal educational qualification at all.

HISTORICAL BACKGROUND OF EDUCATION IN MALAWI

Education in Malawi dates back to the colonial era and the work of early missionaries. With the arrival of the Free Church of Scotland of the Livingstonia Mission at Cape Maclear, the first primary school was founded in 1875. However, until 1926, when the first government Department of Education was set up, the colonial administration played only a peripheral role in education, allowing each missionary group to design curricula for its own schools and examine its own students without any standardization across agencies. This neglect of the education sector by the government was to persist well after independence and is responsible for many of the present problems of education in Malawi. The tardy provision of education left Malawi without sufficient numbers of adequately trained people to hold responsible positions in the civil service when independence was declared in 1964.

Although UNIMA is a post-independence phenomenon, the need for the university was felt as far back as when Dr. Robert

Laws dreamed of developing Livingstonia Mission to university college status. However, the dream was not to become a reality until much later. It was during his detention in 1959 that Dr. Banda included the establishment of a university as one of the priorities of independent Malawi. Following a recommendation of the American Council on Education in 1963 (American Council on Education 1964), Malawi's Parliament passed the University of Malawi Act in October of that year. Teaching at the new university started on the Chichiri campus in September 1965.

From the onset, the policy goal that underpinned higher education in Malawi was to establish a university that would meet the economic and cultural needs of the country. Thus, UNIMA was to educate, train, and produce local manpower for medium- and high-level managerial positions both in government and the private sector. In addition, UNIMA was established to provide quality and relevant university education, initiate educational and industrial research for the benefit of the entire education system and the world of work, and promote dialogue and exchange of information between the university and the public sector.

UNIMA started with five institutions: Bunda College of Agriculture, Chancellor College, the Institute of Public Administration, Soche Hill College of Education, and the Malawi Polytechnic. Soche Hill College and the Institute of Public Administration were amalgamated when Chancellor College moved to Zomba in 1973. With time, the three colleges— Bunda, Chancellor, and the Polytechnic—expanded in both program and infrastructure. A fourth college, the Kamuzu College of Nursing, was added in 1979 to train nurses. More recently, in 1995, the College of Medicine was added to UNIMA for the training of doctors. Prior to that, Malawi's government had been sending students to the United Kingdom for their pre-clinical studies. The establishment of the College of Medicine meant that there was no longer the need to send students abroad, since students could undertake both pre-clinical and clinical studies at UNIMA.

ACCESS

University education in Malawi is still extremely competitive due to the very limited places offered to qualifying students each year. This is because the physical facilities at the university and the financial resources have not been expanded to respond to the increasing population of eligible candidates for higher education. Tertiary education also admits a very small proportion of the eligible school population. Only a total of about 1,000 places are offered every year at the five constituent colleges of UNIMA, for example. The World Bank (1995) observed that the 7,500 places available in all tertiary institutions only represented a mere 0.3 percent of the total number of students enrolled at all levels of education. The actual gross enrollment ratio has stagnated at 0.5 percent of the appropriate age group.

University enrollment growth is negligible when it is compared to the growth of enrollment in the secondary sector. The higher education sector in Malawi is therefore under strenuous pressure from the demand exerted by a quickly growing secondary school sector. As a result, the university continues to adhere

to a very rigorous selection system that depends on one's results from the Malawi School Certificate of Education (MSCE) examinations. However, there has been a growing lack of confidence in the MSCE results because of massive leakage of examination papers. Indeed, this leakage led to the cancellation of the 2000 MSCE. As a result, a university entry examination has been used together with the MSCE results as a selection instrument for the past four years.

Since the country's industrial base is expanding, albeit slowly, and since the loss of trained university graduates due to death and other factors is on the increase, it is imperative that university education be expanded. The recent opening of the Mzuzu University is expected to provide some relief for this problem of limited access. The Mzuzu University also hopes to enhance access to university education through distance learning, which has not been offered by UNIMA. Thus, distance education is not yet an established system of educational delivery in Malawi's higher education sector.

One area in which limited access to university education has created a major bottleneck is secondary school teacher training. It was found to be impossible to create adequate room for the training of teachers within the existing framework, despite the many projects at Chancellor College to expand the number of education students. To overcome this problem, a separate college exclusively for the training of secondary school teachers was established at Domasi in Zomba.

Domasi College of Education, which was established in 1993, has helped to reduce teacher shortage in the secondary school education subsector. The shortage of teachers grew from 700 in 1992 to 2,000 in 1997 and 8,000 in 1998. Since 1995, Domasi has been producing an average of 250 diploma teachers in the areas of the natural and social sciences and languages. The college's number of graduates must, however, increase for two reasons: the government has a plan to supply qualified teachers to community-supported day schools and rapid expansion is taking place in the education sector.

EQUITY

Another area of concern is the inequitable distribution of limited university positions between regions, districts, men and women, the rich and the poor, and rural and urban communities. Currently, the percentage of females selected for university education is only about 25 percent (Ministry of Education 1997a). The current selection policy does not use a quota system, at least for the districts, but considers academic performance only, mainly the MSCE results. This may not result in equitable distribution of these positions. This policy may tend to favor certain groups of students. Although there is an affirmative selection policy for women, its results need to be examined since so few women are receiving university education. Recent initiatives to increase the proportion of women are a positive development. Persons with special needs should also benefit from strategies such as the affirmative selection policy. It should be pointed out that the bias toward male enrollment in the university reflects the situation at both the primary and secondary school levels. Fundamental underlying cultural and economic factors in the education sector must be dealt with if female participation in higher education is to improve (Chimombo and Chonzi 2000).

Given Malawi's industrial needs, some have argued that the government should establish a scholarship system for deserving students. A scholarship scheme and loan facilities properly handled by financing agents would ensure that needy students would be able to attend university, while safeguarding merit requirements for tertiary education. One way of administering the scholarship would be to announce the areas in which the scholarships are available and let students compete for the awards, though this may not address the equity issue in the manner that many people have wished.

CURRENT TRENDS

The major development in higher education in recent times has been the establishment of the Mzuzu University (MU) in 1998. MU can be said to be a product of the increase in democracy that Malawi experienced in the mid-1990s under its new government. The major focus of MU is the production of secondary school teachers. The university hoped to make a fresh start and thereby avoid some of the problems that existed at UNIMA. It was also expected that MU would lead to competition with the existing university and would encourage and promote excellence in the delivery of higher education in the country.

It is too early to assess whether or not these objectives have been achieved by the new university. However, while the opening of MU has eased the problems of access a little, the major criticism raised against the new institution has been that it was opened while the government was failing to deal with the many problems in the already existing university. To many, MU may turn out to be another political white elephant. It is ironic that a whole new university should have started offering subjects that were already being offered at UNIMA. What is happening in reality is that most of the lecturers at Chancellor College are being hired to teach at the new university, thereby creating more problems for the faculty of education at Chancellor College.

Other efforts have been undertaken at UNIMA to complete the process of decentralization so that its five constituent colleges can become separate universities. The major problem with the central office in Zomba has been duplication of work, which is also a problem at college levels. Educators hope that once decentralization occurs, the colleges will be able to chart their own course of expansion in response to the needs of the market and attract funding through sponsorship from industry, thereby increasing access.

The institutions of higher education in Malawi have made headway on informatics and CD-ROM capacity. Most of their administrative functions are computerized, including student records and the university payroll. The libraries at Bunda College of Agriculture, Chancellor College, the College of Medicine, Kamuzu College of Nursing, and the Polytechnic have recently begun to use information technology, such as CD-ROM searches and the Internet, for information requests, research, teaching, and study. The libraries have also created local databases using CDS/ISIS software. These databases can be ac-

cessed from all college libraries and university research centers. The National Documentation Center of the Department of Research and Environmental Affairs provided the database structure to facilitate networking of information resources. In 1994, UNIMA established an e-mail network that is separate from other Internet service providers in the country. This e-mail project has now been superseded by full Internet connectivity, set up with assistance from the Sustainable Development Network Program, a United Nations Development Program–supported project. While the use of information technology has expanded very rapidly in recent years, the institutional capacity for managing this process remains very weak. Access to services such as the Internet can be extremely slow in Malawi. There is also the issue of sustainability of such services. Although cost effective, subscriptions for CD-ROMs and other subscriptions require foreign exchange. Serious commitments need to be made if these initiatives are to survive beyond the project levels.

Clearly, the University of Malawi has made headway in the use of information technology. Every effort is being made to introduce and promote information technology in the university. The University Computers Networking Group includes representatives from all colleges in Malawi and seeks to coordinate networking efforts. However, little information technology resource sharing is occurring because departments and colleges of the university function independently and often have computer hardware that is not available outside their area or to students or other staff.

CAPACITY AND STRUCTURE

As noted above, UNIMA's internal organization is characterized by a federal structure composed of five constituent colleges. Each college is headed by a principal, who is assisted by a vice-principal, a registrar, a bursar, deans, and a librarian.

Chancellor College is the largest constituent of the UNIMA colleges. It has the largest student body as well as the largest faculty. The newer colleges of nursing and medicine have relatively fewer students.

The central administration (popularly known as the University Office) is located in Zomba and is headed by the vice-chancellor, who is supported by the following senior staff members: the university registrar, the university librarian, a finance officer, an estates development officer, and the university research coordinator. The college registrars, bursars, and librarians are also representatives of the university registrar, finance officer, and university librarian, respectively. This arrangement creates a dual loyalty problem as these officers are operationally accountable to their respective principals but look to the University Office for promotion and transfers (MIM 1997). The highest body is the University Council, which provides overall policy guidance to UNIMA.

UNIMA employs large numbers of nonacademic staff, especially to operate municipal and student welfare services and care for the campuses. The staff-to-student ratios in the 1998–1999 academic year ranged from 1 to 3 in the departments of French and the classics at Chancellor College to 1 to 44 in the math and science department of the Polytechnic. Apart from the Polytechnic, which also registered high ratios of 1 to 21 and 1 to 23 in accountancy and business studies, respectively, staff-to-student ratios are generally very low in the other departments of UNIMA; Chancellor College has the lowest ratio. With 1,550 students and 145 academic staff and 358 support staff, Chancellor College operates with one staff person for every three students. Records from the registry showed that there were 112 staff in maintenance, 96 in the café, and 41 in security departments. There is wide variation across colleges and faculties in UNIMA's operations. This largely arises from the lack of substantive government guidance in the development of university education in Malawi.

FINANCING OF HIGHER EDUCATION

Money for student fellowships constitutes 12.3 percent of public expenditures on higher education in Malawi. This is the highest expense after salaries (at 37.7 percent), which means the scope for reducing such public expenditure is particularly broad. Thus, this statistic suggests the urgent necessity for UNIMA to institute reform measures, including a reduction in the proportion of boarding students, privatization of unconventional functions, and reduction of nonteaching staff. The expanded support roles beyond the traditional functions, which lead to an unwieldy common service and a bloated central administration (MIM 1997), have led to a reduction in the university's ability to reward its employees.

It can be clearly seen that although the primary education sector received the largest share of public education funds compared to the other levels (it received 60.2 percent of the education budget in 1999), the real unit cost is lowest at the primary level. In 1996–1997, for example, a secondary school student was six times as expensive as a primary school student and a university student was 153 times as expensive as a primary school student. Thus, despite recent progress in primary education funding, public financing of education still favors the secondary and tertiary levels. Given the fact of unequal participation in education among the various groups in Malawi, this means that the poor do not benefit much from higher education in Malawi.

In a report on who benefits from public spending on education, Castro-Leal (1996) observed that the poorest quintile received a 9 percent share of secondary education expenditures and only 1 percent of the share of tertiary education spending. In contrast, the richest quintile received a 39 percent share of secondary education and a 58 percent share of tertiary education spending. Clearly, large inequities in resource allocation exist between the various levels in the education sector of Malawi. The high subsidies to public university students are therefore not only an inefficient educational investment; they are also regressive. This is because the most affluent households that benefit from higher education expenditures are also the most powerful politically; education assistance reinforces their economic and social advantages. Unit costs are inflated by the failure to make the best use of expensive teaching personnel and physical facilities, which is reflected in light teaching loads, in limitations of class and laboratory hours to a restricted portion of the day, and

in the idleness of the entire physical plant and staff for almost three months every year.

CURRICULUM

UNIMA offers undergraduate and postgraduate studies in various fields. These include general degrees in social science, science, and humanities, as well as specialist degrees in agriculture, education, medicine, nursing, and engineering. The language of instruction in UNIMA is English. In fact, English is used as a medium of instruction from the fifth grade in Malawi public schools, while it is taught as a subject from the first grade.

The eleven faculties of UNIMA offer courses at the diploma and degree levels, with opportunities for graduate studies. Diplomas requiring three and four years of study, respectively, are awarded in business studies and nursing. Bachelor's degrees requiring four years of study are offered in agriculture, the humanities, the social sciences, education, and nursing. Whereas the original thinking on higher education in Malawi favored a liberal education, the 1980s saw a definite shift toward specialization. Degree-level courses in engineering were introduced at the Polytechnic, an honors degree was offered in some subjects at Chancellor College, and increased opportunities for higher degrees were created across the board.

The period also witnessed a greater emphasis on the training of secondary school teachers in response to the requirements of the Ministry of Education, Science, and Technology. Master's and doctoral programs of two to four and three to five years, respectively, are offered to suitable candidates in fields of study in which qualified staff are available. Although UNIMA establishes its own awards, it maintains, through external examiners and academic consultants, the highest standards in the interest of its own professional and academic reputation.

Technical education is also offered to students in a range of subjects at three government and two government-aided technical colleges. These colleges offer a four-year apprenticeship course, followed by three years of alternative institutional and industrial training. Primary school teachers are trained at five teachers' training colleges, and teachers for secondary schools are trained at the faculty of education of UNIMA and, more recently, at the Domasi College of Education and at Mzuzu University.

There has been growing concern over the fact that many of UNIMA's degrees are of little relevance to most employers (Moyo 2000). It seems that the absence of a well-articulated counseling program in secondary schools means that a number of students enter college and commence studies with little or no thought about the relevance of the eventual qualification. It would be safe to say that this also arises from the deteriorating standards in the whole education system and from the fact that the education system is mainly exam oriented. Malawi has witnessed a downward trend in performance on the MSCE from a pass rate of 33 percent in 1996 to 28 percent in 1997, 16 percent in 1998, and 13 percent in 1999. But the aim of higher education institutions should be to produce students who can do more than simply pass exams; they should also produce mature, capable, and thinking professionals. This means that we must think not only about appropriate teaching and learning styles but also about the nature of the curriculum and how it is assessed. As the needs of professionals change, as new technologies and methodologies arise, concomitant changes in the university's program structures and syllabi are needed. The increased unemployment among the graduates of UNIMA may be explained by the lack of linkage between higher education and employers and by the production of poor-quality graduates (Thomas et al. 2001).

Our teaching needs to be oriented toward an emphasis on finding solutions to the problems in an actual working environment. In response to a tracer study, graduates of UNIMA made two criticisms about the nature of the curriculum. The first was that the teaching of vocational subjects was too academic and did not pay sufficient attention to the legitimate intellectual demands of the professions. The second was that the graduates lacked cultural and aesthetic development (Dubbey 1989). The message from the graduates was that, in addition to the knowledge and the development of the academic and analytical ability gained, graduates also needed to develop more cultural awareness. Thus, university education must seek not only to provide better prospects for students who pursue nonvocational programs but also to look for ways to improve the cultural education of all students, whatever their subject areas.

Unfortunately, liaison with industry and other key groups about the development of the university has not been a priority in Malawi. While it can be acknowledged that the unfavorable economic crisis is partly responsible for the poor state of the university, a lack of clear awareness among key groups in society about the potential contribution of the university is also a factor. Interaction among the various stakeholders in education in Malawi is needed to bridge the gap between the university's curriculum and the world of work. Understandably, some are concerned that "many students end up in jobs that have nothing to do with the subjects they studied in college" (*Nation* 2000). It would be prudent here to note that bottlenecks exist in Malawi's examination-oriented system of education from the primary school level through to university levels. These bottlenecks need to be removed if we are to improve graduates' employment prospects.

RESEARCH AND PUBLICATIONS

According to Carr and Kemis (1986), one can undertake three types of higher education research: technical research to improve the effectiveness and efficiency of educational practice for professional development; practical research to transform consciousness; and emancipatory research to bring reform. Using this model, a significant amount of higher education research in UNIMA is practical; that is, research that seeks to transform "the what" of teaching. There is a dearth of emancipatory research that could be used for purposes of reform. Answering the legitimate question of why there have been few emancipatory research studies in higher education in Malawi, Dzimadzi (2000) offers three main explanations. The first is what he describes as the elitist nature of higher education. Although higher education institutions exist in various communi-

ties, Dzimadzi notes, they are still considered ivory towers far removed from the communities they should serve. This problem is even more pronounced in a country such as Malawi, where the percentage of college-trained personnel remains very low. Second, Dzimadzi points to the inadequate theoretical grounding of higher education institutions in Malawi. Because of its relatively new nature, the field of education does not have many experts, especially in the developing world. As such, research in higher education, for the most part, does not emanate from the scholarly interests of individual researchers but from national, regional, and international networks of agencies that have specific research concerns. This lack of theoretical grounding and restricted freedom of inquiry has largely contributed to the dearth of studies in the field. The last problem is the underdevelopment of postgraduate programs in Malawi. UNIMA is predominantly an undergraduate institution, and the development of postgraduate education has had to struggle against a rigid institutional pattern. Although the faculty of education, for example, has been under pressure to mount programs such as the University Certificate of Education and the honors program in education to produce postgraduates in education, the level of rigor in these programs has not been robust enough to attract large-scale funding.

Allocation to research has also been cut severely in recent times. In 1999, for example, only 0.7 percent of the UNIMA budget was allocated to research and publications. Since a significant part of postgraduate training involves student participation as apprentices in faculty research and ultimately the undertaking of a dissertation project, graduate education has suffered. Moreover, unlike the universities in the developed world, acquisition of tenure is not dependent on faculty research productivity (Dzimadzi 2000). As a result, in the absence of a supportive environment with research incentives, academics have little motivation to engage in strenuous research activities. Nonetheless, it cannot be denied that higher education in Malawi and elsewhere is a source of analytical perspectives on social problems and their possible solutions, which are independent of and are often a useful pluralistic counterpoint to political and religious authorities. Higher education institutions also provide a mechanism for indigenous self-expression, help to conserve and adapt local traditions and values, and constitute important symbols of national prestige and achievement. But these contributions are not possible without sufficient funds for research in Malawi.

Lack of research support also jeopardizes Malawi's long-term ability to take advantage of the worldwide advancement in scientific and technological knowledge. The country needs substantial capacity to absorb and utilize new knowledge. This capacity is in large measure developed through the operation of indigenous postgraduate teaching and research programs. The central point is that without local mastery of the underlying science of such development and an ability to adapt knowledge to local problems and conditions, the potential benefit to developing countries of these intellectual advances will likely be lost in large measure and certainly will be late in arriving. University-based programs of basic and applied research and of postgraduate education are essential for the mastery of science and technology. As Delors et al. (1996) observe, they are the key to sophisticated assimilation of humanity's exploding stock of knowledge and technology. They are a necessary condition for Africa's escape from intellectual dependency.

OTHER SOCIAL PROBLEMS

Dzimadzi (2000) observes that at its inception, UNIMA was handled with "kid gloves." This approach, though flawed, had the advantage of protecting the development of the budding university. The major drawback for Malawi, however, was that this approach eventually degenerated into political suppression of academics by a one-party dictatorship. After mid-1975, the political situation in Malawi was turbulent and UNIMA was badly affected by this. Political interference in university affairs became routine. A number of expatriates and local staff of the university were forced to relinquish their posts. Many Malawian lecturers, such as Jack Mapanje, were detained without trial for long spells, and many more disappeared from the scene. Any academics who sought to do "revolutionary" research were labeled "confusionists" and suffered enormous consequences. The result has been that UNIMA has always been reluctant to offer courses that raise consciousness and arouse criticisms against authorities. Even subjects as innocent as philosophy and psychology had to be introduced in the university under a fictitious subject called "human behavior" (COMESUN 1995). It is not surprising, therefore, that student activism was almost unheard-of in Malawi from the time UNIMA was established until the time democracy was born. The few students who tried to express their views were quickly targeted and most of them were detained. It is only in recent times that students have had a chance to fight for their rights or exercise their freedom of speech.

The repressive political environment undermined critical thinking in the university, which is detrimental to the cultivation of an individual's mind. Intellectuals need a supportive and fertile climate if they are to contribute to the growth of knowledge, but this has not been present in Malawi for the past three decades. Despite changes in the political atmosphere, the situation of academic freedom is still wanting in many ways in Malawi. Faced with this situation and a funding crisis, the result has been that many experienced academics have moved or are moving elsewhere in search of better working conditions, thus eroding the critical mass Malawi needs for research and teaching. Further, erosion of salaries and deteriorating working conditions have forced those academics who have persevered to engage in extracurricular activities to earn additional income. This has resulted in reduced student contact hours. UNIMA has lost about one-fourth of its staff because they have gone to look for greener pastures. It is ironic that the university should be losing staff when the country still relies on expatriates for most of its top management jobs.

With the onset of multiparty politics and democratization in the country, however, both students and staff in the university have become more aggressive in their demands for administrative transparency and better working conditions. But the fact that Malawi experienced a strict dictatorship for more than thirty years means that it will take time before people in Malawi can begin to fully enjoy the fruits of democracy.

FINANCING AND FUNDING PATTERNS

Financing university education is one of the serious problems currently facing UNIMA. Largely as a result of the accelerated training programs that it was mandated to deliver, the original funding for the university was centered on government financing. There was also heavy government involvement in the choice of what programs to run right from its inception. Consequently, UNIMA has not had any independent sources of income, let alone ideas on how to run its financial affairs. Just as secondary education has been based on the provision of bed space in addition to classroom space, the university has not been able to separate the academic from the housing requirements of the students. As a result of this, the provision of tertiary education has become highly unaffordable even to the government. The result has been that while the major portion of money allocated has gone to salaries, there has been a corresponding decrease in the provisions of other services within the university. The university is now faced with a situation in which grants from the government can no longer adequately meet the cost of running the university.

Over the years, primary education has enjoyed the largest share of Malawi's education budget. However, despite the few numbers of students in the university, the proportion of the education budget allocated to the university sector has consistently been higher than that allocated to the secondary sector and teacher training colleges.

The competition for dwindling resources has further been intensified by the shift in priorities away from higher education in favor of primary and secondary education. This competition has become even more intense with the opening of the Mzuzu University. The financial crisis facing the higher education sector manifests itself in the declining relevance and quality of education and research. Inadequacy of instructional and research materials has also resulted in increased tension between staff, students, and university management. In view of the current economic problems, it has become increasingly difficult for the university to implement its programs. In particular, conflicts over room and board for students have become especially cumbersome. Strikes and misunderstandings among students and even staff have unfortunately disrupted the university programs at times. This is a serious concern as it inevitably affects the quality of university education. In fact, frequent disruptions are one of the reasons for UNIMA to opt for the semester approach, since it has had such difficulty adhering to traditional college calendar terms.

The education ministry has recently developed financial strategies for reducing and recovering costs and has also increased student fees. Thus, there is the problem of a government policy aiming at a major increase in overall national student numbers at the same time that it is reducing funding per student.

Malawi's decision to share the costs of higher education with students was made in 1985 in response to the World Bank's condition of the institution of fees for an education credit and as part of a broader cost-recovery initiative in the education sector, which also saw an upward revision of secondary school fees. Prior to 1985, Malawian higher education students did not pay anything toward their education. Instead, they were paid allowances for incidental expenses, in addition to receiving free board and lodging (Dzimadzi 2000). The initial contribution being made by students in 1985 was about US$50. As expected, the student contribution has been increasing over the years in response to inflation and rising operational costs. In the face of financial difficulties, the university has been seeking other ways of generating funds and streamlining its activities. This was the main reason for commissioning the Malawi Institute of Management in 1997 to study ways in which the university's financial status could be improved. One important recommendation this study made was that UNIMA should charge fees for university education in the range of $2,700 per semester per student.

It was not surprising, therefore, that UNIMA, in collaboration with Malawi's government, raised the student contribution from about $40 to $575 at the beginning of the 2001 academic year, representing an increase of 1,500 percent. This led to widespread student unrest and public outcry. Even when the figure was reduced to about $310, students were still unhappy with the massive increase in fees. It was felt that the revision ignored the economic standing of the average Malawian. Although the government offered a student loan option, it was generally felt that the decision was taken without wide consultation and debate or consideration of more equitable ways to fund the rising cost of higher education in Malawi.

It should be pointed out that asking students and their families to share the cost of tertiary education does not mean that the government should lessen its financial support to higher education. Rather, promotion of broader financial participation should be seen as one way by which the government can help ensure that financial flows to higher education increase, which is necessary for its revitalization and ultimate expansion.

POLICY, PLANNING, AND REFORM

The 2000–2012 Policy Investment Framework for Malawi (PIF) identifies seven main areas for policy and planning in higher education: access, equity, quality, relevance, management, planning, and finance (Ministry of Education 1997b). The main objective in terms of access is to raise the participation rate of the relevant age group (18–23 years) in tertiary institutions from the current 0.3 percent to 1 percent. The strategies envisaged for achieving this policy objective are the optimal use of physical and human resources, the mounting of distance education so that distance-education students comprise 15 percent of the total tertiary education population by 2012, and the encouragement of private initiatives such that 15 percent of tertiary students will be studying at private institutions by 2012.

In terms of equity, the objective is to increase the proportion of female students from the current 25 percent to 50 percent by 2012 and to increase the proportion of female students in non-traditional areas from the current 28 percent to 40 percent over the same period. It is also hoped that tertiary institutions will increase the participation of students from disadvantaged groups to at least 15 percent of total enrollment. These goals are to be achieved through the provision of scholarship awards to needy students, the introduction of gender sensitization programs, and the provision of physical facilities that will be accessible to students with special education needs by 2007. To improve quality, tertiary institutions should collaborate with the government to improve the motivation of teaching and research staff by increasing their real wages by 70 percent of the 1997 value by 2002 and thereafter by 50 percent in real terms over the next two five-year periods. Other strategies to improve quality include strengthening staff development, increasing allocation to non-salary expenditures, improving assessment procedures, expanding the number of graduate programs so that 10 percent of full-time students will be postgraduates by 2002, and increasing allocation to research and publications from the 1997 level of 2 percent to 10 percent by 2012.

In terms of the management, planning, and financing of the higher education sector, the government needs to initiate appropriate legislation to promote the decentralization of public university administration and the strengthening of institutional governance by 2001. Tertiary institutions should also be required to take appropriate measures to strengthen their institutional planning capacities and promote collaboration between the university and the Ministry of Education on matters related to higher education. Such plans and strategies will require the establishment of efficient management information systems by 2002.

Under the PIF, tertiary institutions would be required to take appropriate action to promote the cost-effective use of available resources. This will entail devising strategies to enhance their capacity to diversify their revenue sources and introduce appropriate cost-sharing measures as a way of reducing government expenditures on higher education. These objectives should be achieved through an increase in the ratio of lecturers to students from 1 to 10 in 1997 to 1 to 25 by 2012, and an increase in the ratio of support staff to students from 1 to 4 in 1997 to 1 to 15 by 2012. Tertiary institutions would be required to privatize welfare services so that students would cover the full cost of boarding expenses by 2002. By that year, 20 percent of all full-time students will be expected to pay full economic fees, and an additional 50 percent will be expected to pay 50 percent of these fees. Other strategies include the introduction of a housing scheme for faculty who have no homes of their own. It should be pointed out here that by June 2002, most of these strategies had not yet been effected. Welfare services had not been privatized, the housing scheme had not been introduced, and although there had been an increase in the number of students (especially in the Faculty of Education), none of the students were paying full economic fees.

In summary, the recent call by the international community for Malawi to reorient public finances in favor of basic social services and the resulting emphasis on the need for the university to pay more attention to maintaining standards while limiting unsustainable budgetary expansion have forced UNIMA to adopt innovative reforms. However, some of these policy initiatives do not go far enough to ensure that tertiary education offered at universities is socially relevant or that the ability to participate in that education is fair and equitable. The stipulation of 1 percent coverage of the appropriate age group, for example, cannot guarantee that higher education will adequately contribute to national development. Further, the vision enshrined in these policy directives does not seem to have been developed on the basis of a proper understanding of the problems of the tertiary sector. Despite complaints about the large size of the university's staff (MIM 1997), for example, the PIF stipulates an increase of the ratio of support staff to students from 1 to 4 to 1 to 15, and it is not clear whether this includes the privatization of nonconventional functions. In addition, the PIF lacks the details necessary to facilitate a proper implementation of the proposed strategies.

CURRENT CHALLENGES

When nonsalary inputs to higher education dwindle, the most immediate consequences are that research ceases and instruction is reduced to little more than rote learning of theory from lecturers and notes on chalkboards. As a result, the skills most relevant to development, those acquired when theory is confronted with the exigencies of the real world, are not learned. Malawi is thus falling farther behind in its ability to generate knowledge and innovation, despite the increasing numbers of higher education graduates.

This chapter shows that, as presently conceived and managed, UNIMA is in a crisis involving direction, internal organization, resources, and relevance. UNIMA also seems to have been operating in a paradoxical situation. While the student-to-teacher ratios suggest that there is room for expansion of student enrollment, enrollments cannot expand without an increased investment in teaching and other learning facilities. Furthermore, colleges are operating at various levels of development. On one hand, the university is unable to recruit and retain qualified lecturers. Some departments are resorting to using unqualified lecturers to take charge of teaching. On the other hand, the university's few qualified lecturers are engaging in unofficial consultancies from which the university does not benefit. These factors and a host of other internal efficiency problems lead to serious concerns about the quality (in terms of both substance and relevance) and quantity (in terms of both numbers and distribution) of learning being provided by UNIMA (MIM 1997). These are challenges that are likely to face the university for some time to come.

An examination of the higher education literature reveals that the problems identified in this chapter are not unique to Malawian higher education. As Saint (1992) observed, the emergence of global markets has created a competitive worldwide economic system characterized by the rapid generation of knowledge and technological innovation, which has changed local labor markets and the kinds of skills required of graduates. Within Africa, population growth rates and increased access to education have boosted the social demand for higher education, leading to rising university enrollments (Saint 1992). The challenge for African universities, and Malawi is no exception, is to respond to the rising demand that higher education be offered with little or no increase in public expenditures while maintaining or improving educational standards.

The major challenge that remains arises from the fact that implementing the various reforms proposed above will involve balancing the economic considerations of education planning in light of Malawi's specific circumstances. This requires analytical and planning capabilities, which are exceedingly scarce. We are optimistic that this is possible, but only if we begin to regard the university as the key partner in the formulation of lasting reform solutions through research and other forms of collaboration that the nation requires. Ensuring that money is made available for research will be a challenge to both government and universities.

THE WAY FORWARD

It is important to recognize that UNIMA has made enormous contributions toward human resource development in Malawi. The majority of Malawians in positions of leadership are former students of the University of Malawi. Certainly Malawi cannot do without this institution. In spite of whatever political or social upheavals Malawi may experience, UNIMA will continue to make a vital contribution to the economic development of the country. For it to remain at the service of this nation, it needs more than goodwill from the general public, however. It also needs committed staff (COMESUN 1995).

One of the major shortcomings in the provision of higher education in Malawi is the small number of postgraduate programs. If African countries are to come to terms with their problems, the provision of postgraduate programs is unavoidable. Further, the provision of postgraduate training courses in Africa might be more relevant and cost effective compared to the training of people abroad. Postgraduate programs can ease the problem of staffing in the university, since postgraduate students may be asked to assist the full-time staff in offering tutorials.

In addition to cost sharing, universities could be financed in two other ways. Either universities should continue to operate as not-for-profit entities in which the goal of financial management is to balance each university's annual budget, or universities have to become highly entrepreneurial and become oriented toward generating income. Given the present tough austerity measures being imposed by most governments, there seem to be more possibilities in the direction of the latter option if our universities are to continue to be centers of academic excellence, as long as this change does not jeopardize the quality of education and research produced. It is also necessary for the university to concentrate on those activities which are central to its mission of advancing knowledge and promoting understanding by engaging in university teaching and research that is responsive to the needs of Malawi and Africa. It is imperative that we explore other arrangements for discharging nonacademic functions that take up a large percentage of the university budget, such as room and board for the students and security. It is high time we detach ourselves from an obsession with the provision of boarding facilities for students and the associated idea that quality education can only be provided in boarding facilities. Provision of boarding facilities in secondary schools is largely responsible for the lack of expansion of that sector. But the best way to provide these services is to let the private sector supply them or let students be responsible for their own accommodation. While recognizing that the majority of Malawians live below the poverty line, it is possible that with careful thinking, realistic levels of cost sharing can be worked out and implemented.

The advent of new possibilities for communication through computers, in particular, has created a potential for the internationalization of research and academic cooperation in general. In spite of some skepticism as to whether previously announced revolutions in the styles and methods of teaching and learning have really taken place, the possibilities for interactive online research, documentation, and teaching may very well bring significant changes in the educational process, especially at the higher levels. African universities cannot afford to remain behind in these developments.

According to Delors (1996), universities have four key functions: to prepare students for research and teaching; to provide highly specialized training courses adapted to the needs of economic and social life; to be open to all, so as to cater to the many aspects of lifelong education in the widest sense and to international cooperation; and to be able to speak out on ethical and social problems as an entirely independent and fully responsible institution exercising a kind of intellectual authority that society needs to help it to reflect, understand, and act. Higher education must continue to play its part in creating, preserving, and passing on knowledge at the highest levels. UNIMA has a particularly vital role to play given the current problems in the education sector of Malawi. Although the number of places in higher education is limited everywhere, it is important for higher education to unite equity with excellence. Universities must lead the way by trying out new methods of teaching new groups of students, recognizing the diversity of their backgrounds, understanding the various skills acquired outside formal learning systems, and promulgating, through the training of teachers and teacher trainers, new approaches to learning. The many innovative approaches being tried in Malawi's education system require the services of a well-articulated university research program.

The university must continue to be the fountainhead at which growing numbers of people, who find in their own sense of curiosity a way of giving meaning to their lives, may slake their thirst for knowledge. By calling universities to be places of culture and learning open to all, this chapter lends support to the affirmation of Delors et al. (1996) that the major task of the university is to participate in the major debates concerning the direction and future of society.

REFERENCES

American Council on Education. 1964. *Education for Development: Report of the Survey Team on Education in Malawi.* Zomba, Malawi: American Council on Education.

Carr, W., and S. Kemmis. 1986. *Becoming Critical: Education Knowledge and Action Research.* Philadelphia, Pa.: Falmer Press.

Castro-Leal, F. 1996. *Who Benefits from Public Education Spending in Malawi? Results from the Recent Education Reform.* World Bank Discussion Paper no. 350. Washington, D.C.: The World Bank.

Chimombo, J., and R. Chonzi. 2000. *School Dropout and Teenage Pregnancy: Its Causes and Magnitude.* Report Prepared for the Rockefeller Foundation. Zomba, Malawi: CERT.

COMESUN (Commission for the Establishment of the University in the North). 1995. *Report on the Establishment of a University in the North.* Submitted to His Excellency The President Mr. E. Bakili Muluzi. Lilongwe, Malawi: The Commission for the Establishment of the University in the North.

Delors, J., I. Amagi, R. Careris, F. Chung, and M. Manley. 1996. *Learning: The Treasure Within.* Report to UNESCO of the International Commission on Education for the Twenty-first Century. Paris: UNESCO.

Dubbey, J. 1989. "The Purpose of the University." Address by Dr. John M. Dubbey, Vice-Chancellor of the University of Malawi, to the Congregation held in Zomba on November 4.

Dzimadzi, C. 2000. "The Status of Educational Research and Its Role in Facilitating Institutional Reform: The Case of the University of Malawi." Paper presented at the Joint Review of the Malawi Educational Sector at the Malawi Institute of Management, 2–15 October. Zomba, Malawi: CERT.

Malawi Government. 1995. *Civil Service Census.* Reports on census results. Lilongwe: Government of Malawi Census.

———. 1997. *Manpower Survey of Malawi.* Lilongwe: Government of Malawi.

Ministry of Education. 1997a. *Education Statistics for Malawi.* Lilongwe: Ministry of Education.

———. 1997b. *Education Sector: Policy Investment Framework.* Lilongwe: Ministry of Education.

MIM (Malawi Institute of Management). 1997. *University of Malawi Reform Study: Problems and Opportunities Identification and Operations Assessment.* Lilongwe: MIM.

Moyo, E. H. 2000. "Of Graduates and Their Degrees." *The Nation Newspaper,* 7 June, p. 7.

Saint, W. 1992. *Universities in Africa: Strategies for Stabilization and Revitalization.* World Bank Working Paper 194. Washington, D.C.: The World Bank.

Thomas H., J. Chimombo, D. Hall, and R. Mwanditt. 2001. "Skills for Development—Skills for Employment: Links between Higher Education and Employers and Recognition of Educational Qualifications in Malawi." Report submitted to Department for International Development (DFID), U.K.

World Bank. 1995. *Malawi Human Resources and Poverty: Profile and Priority for Action.* Washington, D.C.: World Bank, Southern African Department.

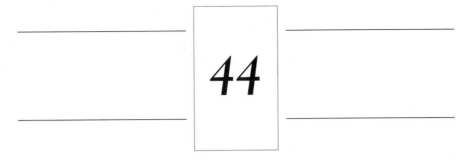

Mali

Diola Bagayoko and Moussa M. Diawara

INTRODUCTION

The September 2000 World Bank report on the Republic of Mali notes that Mali is a 1,240,190-square-kilometer (478,840-square-mile) landlocked country south of the Sahara that is covered by the desert for 60 percent of its land area. It is vulnerable to drought and is subject to declining soil fertility, deforestation, and desertification. Its population was estimated at 10.9 million in 1999 with a 2.8 percent population growth rate per year. Social indicators are very low: 70 percent of the population lives below the poverty line, life expectancy at birth is 50 years, and the overall illiteracy rate is 68 percent. In Mali, 80 percent of the workforce is engaged in agriculture or farming-related activities. Cotton, gold, and livestock constitute the main exports for Mali. The country's main trading partners are Ivory Coast, France, Senegal, and Belgium.

A stark description of Mali is provided by the World Fact Book, published annually by the U.S. government (CIA 2001). According to this report, children younger than 14 years old constituted 47 percent of Mali's population in 1999. Clearly, this has significant consequences for all cycles of education in Mali. Of Mali's 5 million people, slightly more than half are male.

HISTORICAL OVERVIEW OF POLITICAL AND GENERAL EDUCATIONAL CONTEXTS

Great empires existed in Mali from the twelfth century through the end of the sixteenth century, including the Empire of Mali and the Songhoi Empire. In particular, the Empire of Mali is credited with the establishment of the former University of Timbuktu, a generic name for several universities, though the most famous of them was that of the city district known as Sankore. The Songhoi Empire presided over the most celebrated era of the existence of the university in the sixteenth century. The faculty and students of this international university included representatives from many parts of the world. Two of the most famous faculty members of the time were Ahmed Bagayoko and his former student, Ahmed Baba, both of whom were from Mali. Baba, according to Joseph Ki-Zerbo (1978), is reported to have written up to 700 publications, some of which exist today. Arabic was the language of instruction in Timbuktu. The Web site of the Embassy of Mali in Washington (2001) provides informative summaries on the geography, the history, the economy, and the culture and people of Mali.

While higher education flourished in Mali from the thirteenth to the sixteenth century, an invasion from Morocco led to the destruction of the University of Timbuktu and its library in 1591. From the seventeenth century to the colonization of Mali by France in the late nineteenth century, religious education in Arabic was all that remained. It mainly took the form of apprenticeships and could be found in most cities, with emphasis on Djenné, Timbuktu, and Gao in the north; Mopti, Ségou, and Bamako in the south; and Kayes in the west.

During the colonial era, from the late nineteenth century through 1960, higher education was nonexistent in Mali. A very small number of students participated in formal, primary, and secondary education in French, which was of limited scope by design. In the colonial era, a few individuals pursued postsecondary education outside Mali, mostly in Senegal (at the University of Dakar, currently known as the Cheikh Anta Diop University) and in France.

After achieving independence from France in 1960, Mali embarked on a series of educational reforms that continue to date. From 1962 to 1968, the first government of independent Mali embarked on a massive schooling campaign at all educational levels. More schools were built to bring education to the general population at the primary and secondary levels. At the tertiary level, specialized schools of higher education were established. They included the National School of Engineering (ENI); the Ecole Normale Supérieure (ENSup), for the training of high school teachers and other professionals; the National School of Administration (ENA); the School of Medicine and Pharmacy; and the Rural Polytechnic Institute (IPR).

Other institutions dealt with the training of technicians, artists, accountants, primary school teachers, and so forth. The language of instruction remains French. The mission of institutions entrusted with basic personnel training (for example, of technicians, primary teachers, and artists) did not generally include research. Even though their graduates had received postsecondary education, some of these basic training institutions admitted students who had not earned a high school diploma (a baccalaureate). In the years following independence, Mali relied heavily on France, the former Soviet Union, Canada, Belgium, and several Eastern countries for higher education training.

Ample evidence exists that higher education institutions in Mali fulfilled their training mission from 1962 to the late 1980s. However, the high unemployment rate among college graduates in the late 1980s is one of several indicators that the undemocratic and repressive practices of the military regime have added to Mali's overall economic difficulties.

A military regime dominated in Mali from 1968 to 1991. Accounts of the profound and deleterious impact of this regime can be found in numerous reports and studies of international and other external organizations (such as the U.S. State Department, Amnesty International, the World Bank, and the United Nations). Education suffered greatly under this regime. Enrollments continued to grow rapidly and to outstrip governmental efforts to address educational needs throughout this period. For example, no new secondary schools were built by the military regime in twenty-three years. According to the Global Education Database (USAID 2000), the number of primary schools grew from 1,063 in 1975 to only 1,514 in 1991. This rate of growth more than doubled during 1992–1997, when 922 new schools were constructed.

The dictatorship was toppled in 1991 under pressure from popular movements, but the result of decades of wanton neglect had severely hurt the quality of education. The fear of persecution on the part of schoolteachers and higher education professors, and frequent failure of institutions to pay teachers and professors in the 1980s, were pernicious problems. When one takes into account the overall high unemployment rate in these years, it becomes clear why Mali experienced the flight of many young teachers and professors.

Since 1992, Mali has established a multiparty system that guarantees individual liberties, a free market economy, and a free press. The U.S. State Department (1998–2000) has ranked Mali high in recent years for its model implementation of a democratic form of government. Protection of individual liberties, true freedom of the press, and the credible and continuing decentralization of the administrative structures are proof of economic and legal environments conducive to a free market economy. They are among the very positive signs that portend a promising future for Mali, despite the disturbing statistics cited above. This democratic system is unleashing creativity and potential that will steadily bring Mali to a much brighter future.

The rapid growth rate of primary and secondary school enrollment must be placed in a broader context. From 1989 to 1996, primary school enrollment ratios were below 50 percent; less than half of prospective primary school students were actually enrolled in primary school. Net enrollment ratios were 21.8 percent and 23 percent in 1990 and 1991, while gross enrollment ratios were 26.7 percent and 28.8 percent, respectively, in those years. (A net ratio is obtained by dividing the number of primary school students who are of the official primary school age by the size of the official primary school age group and then multiplying the resulting quotient by 100.) In 1996, in contrast to the very low primary school enrollments in the waning years of the military regime, net and gross enrollment ratios were 38.2 percent and 46.7 percent, respectively.

HIGHER EDUCATION IN MALI, 1996 TO PRESENT

The above picture of general, political, and economic conditions in Mali in the late 1980s explains in part the genesis and persistence of activism in education in Mali. Specifically, higher education and secondary school students have regularly embarked on annual stoppages or strikes. This student activism helped to encourage a popular uprising. Popular protests escalated when the military regime was reported to have resorted to massacre in 1991. In response to the continuing protests by students, by labor, and by other groups, a military coup toppled the 23-year-old military regime in 1991. With the support of the international community, the coup leaders swiftly and credibly moved to prepare the ground for democratic elections in 1992. The end of the Cold War altered the priorities of the world's economic and political powers. Consequently, unconditional external support for many dictatorships largely evaporated. Democracy was established in Mali in 1992 with the election of a president and parliament. While the transition military group addressed some of the financial demands of the students, stoppages and strikes continued to plague the new democratic regime. Some academic years have been lost due to the large numbers of days when no classes were held. These occurrences applied not only to higher education but also to public secondary education.

Located in the capital city of Bamako, the University of Bamako (UB) was known as the University of Mali until May 2002. It is the latest example of successive reforms of the education system in Mali since 1962. It currently enrolls 25,000 students (Table 44.1). In the early 1990s, a study group started planning for the establishment of the university. The resulting restructuring of higher education brought together the existing schools and institutes of higher education, some of which were decades old. During the process, some new colleges were established within the university. While the University of Bamako (then the University of Mali) was formally established in 1993, it opened in the fall of 1996. The folding of the previously existing institutions into the university has been a gradual process that should be nearly complete in 2001.

The UB and its constituent institutions have been the only higher education bodies in Mali since independence, but efforts are now underway to establish several private higher education institutions. The master's degree in business administration of the University of Quebec at Montreal (initiated in September

2000) and the Centre Universitaire Mande (operationally established in 2000) also have collaboration agreements with UB, but it is too early to assess the possible long-term impact of these private efforts.

GOVERNANCE AND STRUCTURES OF THE UNIVERSITY OF BAMAKO

UB is a public institution endowed with financial autonomy under the supervision of the Ministry of Education. The university is governed by a policymaking board known as the University Council. The administration of the university is led by a chief executive officer, the rector. The major academic structures of the university, which are in charge of the tripartite mission of instruction, research, and service, are colleges, schools, and institutes. The term "institute" in this context is closer to that of "school" or "college" rather than "center." At this level, governance is shared by an assembly (a policymaking entity) and an executive office led by a dean. In a manner very similar to the operation of American institutions, faculty members are meaningfully involved in decision making at the level of schools, colleges, and institutes, particularly within their academic departments.

UB is comprised of the following major academic structures (acronyms represent the French names of the structures): four colleges (the Faculty of Medicine, Pharmacy, and Odonto-Stomatology, FMPOS; the Faculty of Science and Technology, FAST; the Faculty of Law and Economics, FSJE; and the Faculty of Literature, Languages, Arts, and Humanities, FLASH); three institutes (the Institute of Management, IUG; the Higher Institute of Training and Applied Research, ISFRA; and the Rural Polytechnic Institute of Training and Applied Research for the Integrated Development of the Sahel Region, IPR/IFRA); three schools, equivalent to specialized schools or colleges (the Ecole Normale Supérieure, ENSup, for training high school teachers and others; the National School of Engineering, ENI; and the National School of Administration, ENA, similar to the FSJE); and the Central Library. The library is not yet built or equipped with information and communication technology (ICT) resources, books, or journals. Its construction is provided for with funds through a loan the government of Mali received from the World Bank in December 2000. Planning has been underway since 2001.

MISSION OF THE UNIVERSITY OF BAMAKO AND DEVELOPMENT

The mission of the university is to provide instruction, research, and service. The very names of the schools, colleges, and institutes recognize the pivotal importance attached to the role UB is expected to play in national development. This mission includes:

- The training of basic technical personnel (with two-year associate degrees)
- The production of bachelor's degree holders for most facets of the public and private sectors

Table 44.1. Student-to-Faculty Ratios at the University of Mali, 1996–2001

Year	Number of Students	Number of Faculty	Student-to-Faculty Ratio
1996–1997	10,775	433	25:1
1997–1998	13,900	471	30:1
1998–1999	18,682	534	35:1
1999–2000	19,714	538	37:1
2000–2001	25,000	—	—

Source: Diawara and Bagayoko 2000.

- Graduate education for the production of new knowledge and the training of research scholars
- The delivery of extensive services to the Malian, regional, and international communities, with explicit attention to the needs for socioeconomic development

The role of the university as an engine for development is apparent in its organization and operation. Judicious coupling of the instructional and research component of the mission and of the service component is illustrated through the following examples:

- Units of studies and of production in various structures (faculties, schools, institutes) are also centers for research and service delivery to the community.
- Businesspeople are represented on UB's council, while many training and professional development courses take place in companies themselves.
- Some research projects are aligned directly with the search for solutions to development issues. Examples include the studies of the Niger River and the genetically driven development of high-yield and climatically adapted varieties of some cereals.

STUDENT ENROLLMENT AND RELATED ISSUES

UB's student population has been growing rapidly, but the number of professors at all ranks has not kept pace. The result is a growing student-to-faculty ratio (Table 44.1).

Difficulties directly related to the growth of the student-to-faculty ratio include the pressure on existing facilities, the increased teaching and grading load of the faculty, the decrease of research time and of research productivity, the decrease of services delivered to the community, and the dampening of collaborative efforts. The above picture is compounded by the approximately 5,000 new high school graduates who entered UB (then the University of Mali) in fall 2000. The relatively large numbers of students per faculty member are staggeringly high for some colleges. Ratios at FSJE and FLASH, for example, exceed 100 to 1. The disaggregated enrollment figures in Table 44.2 illustrate this point.

The disproportionately large enrollments in FSJE and FLASH can be traced to orientation practices in high school. Malian high schools offer three different paths to incoming

Table 44.2. General Census of Students and Faculty Members at the University of Mali, 1999–2000

Institution	Number of Students	Percentage Female Students	Number of International Students	Number of Faculty Members
Faculty of Law and Economics (FSJE)	6,607	28	106	45
Faculty of Literature, Languages, Arts, and Humanities (FLASH)	5,530	27	17	54
Faculty of Medicine, Pharmacy, and Odonto-Stomatology (FMPOS)	3,329	27	493	105
Faculty of Science and Technology (FAST)	2,004	9	130	51
Institute of Management (IUG)	796	57	36	29
National School of Engineering (ENI)	664	5	130	73
Rural Polytechnic Institute of Training and Applied Research for the Integrated Development of the Sahel Region (IPR/IFRA)	440	10	64	85
Ecole Normale Supérieure (ENSup)	264	5	0	83
Higher Institute of Training and Applied Research (ISFRA)	80	4	0	13
Total	19,714	19	976	538

Source: Diawara and Bagayoko 2000.

Table 44.3. Total and Female Enrollments in Higher Education in Mali, 1970–1996

	1970	1975	1985	1991	1994	1996
Total Enrollment	731	2,936	6,768	6,273	8,249	13,674
Percentage Female	—	—	13	14	15	19

Sources: Global Education Database, USAID, and UNESCO.

tenth graders: exact sciences (i.e., mathematics, chemistry, and physics), biological sciences, and letters and humanities. The high school curricula for these three options are drastically different. The exact sciences path, for instance, entails competitive mathematics courses up to calculus and several years of physics and chemistry. Consequently, once a student opts for the letters and humanities path in the tenth grade, he or she is basically out of the science, mathematics, engineering, and technology (SMET) tracks at the college level. The deep anxiety associated with the lack of employment prospects for numerous graduates of FSJE and FLASH is believed to be one of the contributing reasons for the conflicts, including strikes, in Malian higher education. Any long-term solution will require action at the high school level, including the provision of incentives to increase dramatically the enrollments in the paths for exact and biological sciences.

The above enrollment pressures somewhat overshadow the underenrollment of female students in the Malian education system. In 1999–2000, the ratio of the total number of female students at the University of Bamako to that of male students was less than 1 to 3 (Diawara and Bagayoko 2000). Hence, female students constituted less than 25 percent of the university's total enrollment (Table 44.3). Naturally, this picture is a reflection of the gender disparity at the primary and secondary levels. While we lack the space to delve into this matter adequately, we should underscore its detrimental effects on the economic, political, social, and cultural activities of Malian society.

SUMMARY OF PROBLEMS OF MALIAN HIGHER EDUCATION

The sources of the difficulties facing UB include the severe limitations of financial and other resources and the poor facilities and equipment. These limitations are accentuated by the magnitude of Mali's developing educational needs. More than twenty years of military regime did not favorably affect the socioeconomic or political conditions. With the advent of democracy, Mali is engaged in the task of development in a fashion that is expected to earn the support of partners around the world.

The magnitude of the student enrollment explosion at UB was difficult to forecast. The 1999 World Bank publication *Tertiary Distance Education and Technology in Sub-Saharan Africa* estimated the student population at the university would reach 23,694 in the year 2010, but it passed the 25,000 mark in fall 2000. One aspect of the enrollment issue, the utterly disproportionate numbers of non-SMET majors, is the result of policy errors. Basic development needs and the growing scientific and technological advances in the global market should have sufficed to identify and deal with this overproduction of graduates with little or no prospects for gainful employment in the public or private sectors, in or outside Mali.

Until 2000, Mali had a very generous scholarship system that supported secondary and higher education students. From the point of view of some international agencies, these scholarships constituted a disproportionately large portion of the limited funds allocated to education in general. The position of these agencies was easy to understand, given their nearly unanimous neglect of higher education in developing countries and their focus on primary education (Bollag 1998) through the late 1990s. Hence, some of them called these expenses misallocations. At the urging of some development funding agencies, including the World Bank, Mali restructured its scholarship system in 2000. It is too early to predict the long-term results of the changes. Savings from scholarship costs are expected to be invested in the enhancement of the quality of higher education (World Bank 2000a).

In 1997, Mohamed Diarra made a comprehensive assessment of "Educational Costs and Cost Recovery in Developing Countries" based on the case of Mali. In his work, macroeconomic considerations lead to the need to reduce or control the growth of scholarships. Extensive surveys of stakeholders in Mali suggested the possibility of recovering 10 percent of the per-student cost, provided it is phased in gradually. In its May 5, 2000 issue, the *Chronicle of Higher Education* asked international experts to discuss the issue of "Tuition Rising World Wide" (Woodward 2000). Their conclusion was that, given the limitations in appropriations by legislatures and the cost of higher education, the rise in tuition is practically unavoidable unless the quality of education is to be sacrificed. They noted that it was critically important for higher education institutions in the United States and elsewhere to ensure continued access through scholarship programs. Many institutions and countries judiciously take needs and merit into account in the allocation of scholarships. The 2000 restructuring of scholarship programs in Mali seriously limited them at the secondary level and placed greater emphasis on merit at the university level.

The shortage of qualified instructors and researchers in Mali has several roots. One major cause is the flight of faculty members during the twenty-three years of military rule, particularly during the last decade. This exodus was caused by a pervasive fear of persecution, the regular nonpayment of monthly salaries by the military regime in the 1980s, and the overall poor conditions of work and living standards in Mali as compared to other countries in the region or the world. Further, the devaluation of the national currency in 1994 added to the difficulties related to retaining or recruiting qualified university faculty members and researchers (Guedegbe 1996).

Another difficulty that is relatively common in developing countries stems from overreliance on legislative acts or governmental decrees in matters of university governance or policymaking. Naturally, these acts and decrees do not allow timely adaptation to the changing regional and global trends. Even though a credible decentralization is ongoing in Mali, the university still has to contend with a multitude of governmental decrees, laws, and bureaucracy that constrain its autonomy. For instance, the currently prevailing "hierarchization" of higher education in Mali provides for the various ranks of faculty members in a manner that does not permit proper attention to equity in personnel matters. Equity is not equality. Rather, it entails a comparison of individual productivities. For a faculty member, this productivity can be measured in terms of the amount and verifiable quality of teaching and grading, research, and related publications; service on committees; the production of pertinent

scholarly reports; grant writing for instructional, research, or infrastructure development purposes; and the delivery of professional services to the community at large. The 1992 legislation for the "hierarchization" of higher education, for instance, spells out the number of hours of instruction for the various ranks. An accompanying bill addressing benefits for faculty members limits to three months the length of time a faculty member may travel for study or research purposes, without even giving administrators the option to exercise discretion.

In the U.S. academic system, faculty members are ranked as assistant professor, associate professor, and professor. At UB, the hierarchy is as follows: assistant, maître assistant, maître de conference, and professeur (Diawara and Bagayoko 2000). The current policy at the university makes it mandatory for new faculty members to report directly not just to their respective department head but also to senior faculty members. The implications of such a system are twofold. First, very few senior faculty members at the university conduct bench research. Young faculty, who are sometimes at the cutting edge of scientific discovery, are thus asked to report to people who may have little to contribute to their field or to academic expansion. Such a situation puts junior faculty members, who have much to contribute, in a political corner; this could adversely affect their motivation and self-esteem. In addition, the higher officers of the educational system in Mali and the university administration have yet to completely resolve the difficulties involved with diploma equivalency. Consequently, in the interest of academic freedom and success, the standards for tenure and promotion of faculty at UB could benefit from some improvement.

Isolation; a relatively rigid administrative system; the lack of facilities, particularly of equipment; the inadequacy of the time devoted to research; and the insignificance of the value of research productivity in the prevailing evaluation schemes for structures and for faculty members are some of the reasons why those who wish to do research still face many challenges at UB. A minority of faculty members continue to make contributions to the production of new knowledge, as called for in the mission of the institution. With the support of an apolitical organization of professionals called MaliWatch, FAST, with the assistance of the UNDP's Transfer of Knowledge through Expatriate Nationals (TOKTEN) project, hosted the First Malian Symposium for Applied Sciences (MSAS) in fall 2000. The published proceedings of this symposium (Fad 2000) are a testament to the potential for research productivity by scholars in Mali and by expatriated Malian nationals.

THE UNIQUE PROBLEM OF EDUCATION IN MALI

The desire of young people to leave Mali, with no intention of returning in many cases, is widespread. While there could be several reasons for this migratory behavior, two important ones are (a) the annual and almost ritualistic interruptions of study cycles caused by student (and recently faculty) strikes and the related losses for students as compared to their peers in other countries; and (b) the increasing unemployment rate of college graduates.

This outward migration further compounds the classic flight of some well-trained scholars. Whatever the reasons may be for the continual strikes in Malian education, it seems clear that Malians have to make a choice between ending them or risking further compromise of the future of this landlocked country that is battling against desertification and poverty and their attendant ills.

Because of strikes, students in Mali have not been in school for the full academic year since 1991. This situation has resulted in the delayed administration of standard tests and, consequently, the delayed potential admission of Malian students to colleges and universities overseas. Further, Malian pre-college education is not currently meeting the minimum 780 hours of study per academic year (World Bank 2000a) recommended by UNESCO. In such a situation, strikes exacerbate an already poor state of affairs. In the process of education and research, there is no substitute for adequate time on tasks (Bagayoko and Kelley 1994). It cannot be overemphasized that the government of Mali, the leaders of political and labor organizations, parents, school administrators, and students must all fulfill their respective responsibilities in the search for a viable solution to these crises and find a way to achieve an immediate and definitive end to such strikes. In the absence of such a solution, the flight of the general school-age population is likely to increase, as is the flight of well-trained individuals. The future of Mali is at stake.

NATIONAL EDUCATIONAL PLANNING AND IMPLEMENTATION

Since 1996, Mali has embarked on a decade-long national program for the development of education (PRODEC). PRODEC (Ministry of Education 2000) is a continuing reaffirmation of the top-priority status of education in Mali, including higher education. This national planning and implementation effort has so far followed all the steps needed for success. In particular, the initial consultation with stakeholders in and outside Mali was thorough and transparent. The analysis of strengths, weaknesses, opportunities, and threats was thorough and addressed internal and external factors and trends. The vision, mission, and objectives that resulted from these efforts are well aligned with the priorities of Mali as a developing country, and the selected "priority directions" are congruent with realities in Mali and the trends in the region and the world.

The dynamic nature of PRODEC is partly signified by the continual actions of an interministerial group led by the Ministry of Education, which has been charged with implementing and updating it. Furthermore, significant allocations of national resources continue to be made to ensure successful implementation. By the seriousness and thoroughness of its approach, PRODEC underscores the cardinal importance attached to education in Mali. Several sections of the PRODEC report focus on higher education. It significantly undergirds several other activities, generally supported by external sources, to build or to enhance higher education infrastructure and quality in Mali.

A UNIVERSITY-WIDE REFORM PROJECT: TOKTEN/TALMALI

The extreme shortage of qualified teaching and research personnel, particularly at a time when student enrollment is rap-

idly increasing, is a key problem that engenders many other difficulties at UB. Starting in 1998, the United Nations Development Program (UNDP) funded the Transfer of Knowledge Through Expatriate Nationals (TOKTEN) project to assist the university. In 1999, the United Nations Educational, Scientific, and Cultural Organization (UNESCO) joined UNDP in funding Talents of Mali (TALMALI) to supervise research at selected units of the university.

In particular, TOKTEN/TALMALI, Phase I conducted more than eighty missions of instruction, supervision of research, and studies of program development. The duration of the missions varied from one week to one month. The July 2000 issue of *TOKTEN Info*, a comprehensive brochure periodically published by the project, provides complete details about these missions and the beneficiary academic units. Qualified expatriate consultants from around the world performed these missions. Several thousands of students directly benefited from these missions.

According to the independent external evaluation completed in September 2000 (Diawara and Bagayoko 2000), the joint TOKTEN/TALMALI project has so far been executed in an exemplary fashion and has met the objectives to the extent it was possible to do so within the first three years. The evaluation report recommended that funding be immediately and vigorously sought to continue the project for four more years to help institutionalize the gains of the first three years of the project. While significant funding by UNDP (more than $310,000) and UNESCO (more than $65,000) permitted the maintenance and the enhancement of the quality of instruction, of learning, and of selected research projects, much remains to be accomplished.

In the area of scientific research, for instance, TOKTEN is endeavoring to strengthen the linkages and collaborations between UB and several governmental research institutes, including the National Research Center for Science and Technology, the Rural Economy Institute, and the National Institute for Public Health Research. The establishment of relationships with institutions of expatriate nationals and others for the promotion of research is a key objective of TOKTEN/TALMALI.

Although the TOKTEN project has been a success, its future is doubtful unless a number of unresolved issues are soon addressed. These include the resistance from some faculty members to the idea, the management of overload and release time for local faculty members and the related salary problems, and the disruption of teaching, learning, and research activities due to strikes (Diawara and Bagayoko 2000).

EXTENSIVE AND INTENSIVE INTEGRATION OF TECHNOLOGY: USAID AND AAAS PROJECTS

Mali is one of the twenty-one African countries to which the Mickey Leland Initiative of the United States Agency for International Development (USAID) brought Internet connectivity. The related objectives of the Leland Initiative are to "create an enabling policy environment," to "create a sustainable supply of Internet services," and to "enhance Internet use for sustainable development" (USAID 1995). The initiative was launched in 1995–1996. A recent and far-reaching development in Mali consists of the building of a local area computer network (LAN) in all UB facilities, connecting these LANs into a university-wide intranet, and linking this infrastructure to the Internet. In late 2000, USAID provided more than ninety personal computers in support of the functional operation of this important information technology infrastructure. The use of a wireless approach in building UB's intranet circumvented current difficulties associated with the telephone system in Mali.

It is difficult to overemphasize the importance of the above infrastructure, given that the various colleges, schools, and institutes of the university are at different locations throughout the capital city of Bamako. One institute, the Rural Polytechnic Institute, is in a different city altogether. The potential benefits of the intranet for UB's administrative, programmatic, instructional, research, and service functions are immense.

As part of the implementation of the TOKTEN project, UB conducted a mission to the United States in late 2000. Contacts with the American Association for the Advancement of Science (AAAS) led to the inclusion of the university in the ongoing pilot study AAAS has been carrying out with some African universities. Instant and asynchronous access to journals, research, and other learning resources is critically important for university faculty members and graduate students. It is difficult to appreciate this importance without comparing the easy and comprehensive electronic searches to manual literature searches. Major journals and magazines, notably *Science*, *Nature*, and the *New Journal in Physics* are readily accessible online.

GOVERNMENTAL EFFORTS FOR INFRASTRUCTURE ENHANCEMENT

The Ministry of Education and the government of Mali seem cognizant of UB's dire need for funding in general, and for infrastructure enhancement and expansion in particular. Pursuant to the implementation of the national PRODEC Plan, Mali obtained a $45 million loan from the World Bank in 2000. The terms of this loan reflect not only the general objectives and implementation strategies of the nation's Ten-Year Plan, but also directly address goals that are specific to the university and that are priorities of TOKTEN/TALMALI. For instance, the terms call for a phasing out of secondary-level scholarship and the investment of the savings from the reduction of higher education scholarships into physical, personnel, and programmatic enhancements germane to the promotion and maintenance of quality in higher education. These terms also call for greater and transparent accountability, an enhanced assessment of learning outcomes as an important part of accountability, and credible efforts toward the reduction of the gender disparity that currently prevails in Malian education. According to the terms of reference, "support for higher education will be completely revisited under the program, with construction of a central library, support for science education, and research." The library is expected to take full advantage of information and telecommunication technologies (World Bank 2000a).

GENERAL REFLECTIONS

The 1999 "Education Sector Strategy" of the World Bank (1999) states: "But whatever the education situation and needs in a country, access to quality teaching and learning must be a pre-eminent concern." The problems and the key role of higher education in Africa have been comprehensively addressed by Dr. Narciso Matos (1999), the former secretary-general of the Association of African Universities (AAU). His cogent arguments indicate that the problems identified at UB, except for the frequency of student strikes, are common to other universities in developing countries. Other international education reports provide comprehensive strategies whose proper implementation could address higher education needs in Africa. The ongoing developments in Mali could have useful lessons for other countries.

A July 2000 publication of the United Nations University (UNU) in Tokyo, Japan, underscored the urgency of national planning and implementation and of subregional, regional, and global collaboration to maximize the benefits related to "opportunities for Africa in the Information Economy." In fact, since 1997, the World Bank, the AAU, and others have been advocating "strategic planning as the first most important step African Universities must take to regain initiative and shape their future." William Saint (1999) also stressed this need. A thorough exploration of possibilities available to UB through the use of information and communication technology (ICT) should consider substantive collaborations with other African universities, the UNU, the African Virtual University (Saint 1999), the Francophone Virtual University (Saint 2000), and expatriate nationals and their institutions.

The limitations of financial and other resources—as well as the growing needs in terms of student enrollment, instructional quality enhancement, and improved research productivity—strongly suggest the need for a bold and innovative utilization of ICT. The financial limitations cannot be downplayed, despite the fact that some instances of misallocations of resources may exist and could be corrected. ICT innovation will require proper planning and professional, transparent, and accountable implementation. This point is underscored to counter conclusions drawn from some haphazard applications of technologies that have not worked; conclusions based on these nonprofessional approaches should not be used to block what is perhaps the most promising and accessible route to a much brighter and sustainable future.

CONCLUSION

Frequent and annual stoppages by students and faculty members seem to have contributed to the delay of a promising future for education in Mali. In a way that is common in some other developing countries, higher education in Mali has growing and crying needs, on the one hand, and limited financial, human, and infrastructure resources, on the other. This seemingly gloomy picture may yield to a more flourishing future, however, due in part to PRODEC and some accompanying external assistance provided by UNDP, UNESCO, USAID, the World Bank, and others—provided the people and the government halt the disruptive stoppages. The young University of Bamako, with the TOKTEN, the wireless network built by USAID, and the modern library provided by the World Bank, is indeed on the threshold of capitalizing on ICT to solve old problems, particularly if international funding agencies over-come their early reservations about funding higher education in developing countries, particularly in Africa. The April 2000 an-nouncement by four major U.S. philanthropic foundations of the launching of a $100 million program to support such goals (Carnegie Corporation 2000) is perhaps a prelude to a needed focus on higher education.

REFERENCES

Bagayoko, D., and E. L. Kelley. 1994. "The Dynamics of Student Re-tention: A Review and a Prescription." *Education* 115, no. 1: 31–39.

Bollag, Burton. 1998. "International Aid Groups Shift Focus to Higher Education in Developing Nations." Global Higher Education Ex-change Web site. Available online at http://www.ghee.org/Resources/Inst-Stud%20Fin/Fin-Chron1articles/fin-chron-10-30-98-1.htm

Carnegie Corporation. 2000. "Four Foundations Launch $100 Million Initiative in Support of Higher Education in African Countries." Available online at: http://www.carnegie.org/sub/news/partnership.html

CIA (Central Intelligence Agency, United States). 2001. "World Fact Book: Mali." http://www.cia.gov/cia/publications/factbook/geos/ml.html

Cogburn, D. L., and C. N. Adeya, eds. 2000. "Exploring the Challenges and Opportunities for Africa in the Information Economy." The United Nations University (UNU), Tokyo, Japan.

Diarra, M. C. 1997. "Educational Costs and Cost Recovery in Develop-ing Countries: The Case of Mali." Ph.D. diss., Louisiana State Uni-versity.

Diawara, M. M., and D. Bagayoko. 2000. "Evaluation of TOKTEN/TALMALI." Report submitted to UNDP, UNESCO, and the Uni-versity of Mali. In author's possession.

Embassy of Mali, Washington, D.C. 2000. Mali Embassy Web site. Available online at: http://www.maliembassy-usa.org/

Fad, S., ed. 2001. *Proceedings of the First Mali Symposium on Applied Sciences (MSAS 2000)*. Held at the University of Mali, Bamako, Mali. Oulu, Finland: Oulu University Press.

Guedegbe, C. M. 1996. "Currency and Crisis: Higher Education in Francophone Africa." *International Higher Education* 3 (Janu-ary): 3. Available online at http://www.bc.edu/bc_org/avp/soe/cihe/newsletter/News03/textcy2.html

Ki-Zerbo, J. 1978. *Histoire de l'Afrique Noire, D'Hier à Demain*. Paris: Hatier.

Matos, N. 1999. "North-South Cooperation to Strengthen Universities in Africa." Available online at: http://www.aau.org/english/docu-ments/nscoop.htm

Programme Décennal de Développement de l'Education-PRODEC. 2000. Ministry of Education, Bamako, Mali. Summary available online at: http://www.anaisbko.org.ml/reformes/educ.html

Saint, W., ed. 1999. *Tertiary Distance Education and Technology in Sub-Saharan Africa*. Washington, D.C.: Association for the Develop-ment of Education in Africa.

USAID (U.S. Agency for International Development). 1995. The Leland Initiative: Africa Global Information Infrastructure Project. Available online at http://www.usaid.gov/leland/project.htm#Q.%20Exactly

———. 2000. Global Education Database published by UNESCO. Available online at: http://www.usaid.gov/educ_training/ged.html

U.S. Department of State. 1998–2000. Annual Country Reports: Mali. Available from the U.S. Department of State, Washington, D.C.

Woodward, C. 2000. "Worldwide Tuition Increases Send Students Into the Streets." *Chronicle of Higher Education* (May 5), A54.

World Bank. 1999. *Education Sector Strategy: The International Bank for Reconstruction and Development*. Washington, D.C.: The World Bank.

———. 2000a. Report no. PID2864. "Mali-Education Sector Invest-ment. Reference Terms for a $45 Million Loan for Educational Re-forms, in General, and the Construction of the Central Library of the University of Mali, in Particular." Available from the Ministry of Education, Bamako, Mali. Contact person: Barthelemy Togo. Also available online at: http://www-wds.worldbank.org/servlet/ WDS_IBank_Servlet?pcont=details&eid=000094946_00071906410472

———. 2000b. Mali Country Office Site. Available online at: http://lnweb18.worldbank.org/AFR/afr.nsf/

45

Mauritania

AHMED KHARCHI

INTRODUCTION

The Islamic Republic of Mauritania is a vast desertlike country over an area of 1,031,700 square kilometers (398,341 square miles) that has a population of a little over 2.5 million. The steel industry, which used to constitute the main source of income for the country, has diminished since the mid-1980s due to a decrease in demand and increased price competition in the international market. The fish industry, which has replaced steel as Mauritania's major economic activity, generated 57 percent of export income in 1995. Animal breeding is a widespread activity that earns about one-quarter of the gross domestic product (GDP). Agriculture is a major economic activity in the southern part of the country, in the Senegal River Valley. Foreign development aid constitutes about one-quarter of Mauritania's GDP.

With an average life expectancy of 53.5 years and a per capita income of US$410, Mauritania is relatively well off compared to other underdeveloped countries. The drought the country has endured over the last two decades has had a deep impact on rural areas, forcing a large number of people to move to urban centers. The rapid increase in the number of city dwellers has aggravated the problems of unemployment and poverty in the city, where the standard of living was already generally low. Mauritania's long-term development prospects depend to a high degree on its human capital. Mobilizing this capital necessitates funding the educational sector and establishing curricula and programs oriented toward development.

THE MAURITANIAN EDUCATIONAL SYSTEM

The Mauritanian educational system is the responsibility of the Ministry of National Education (Ministère de l'Education Nationale, MEN) and has four levels: basic, secondary, technical, and higher education. The ministry is in charge of the

national educational policy at all levels: designing programs, organizing exams, defining admission criteria for educational programs under its authority, and granting, renewing, or suspending scholarships. Traditional education, as well as some specific higher education institutions, do not come under the MEN's responsibility.

TRADITIONAL EDUCATION

Traditional education existed in Mauritania for centuries, provided by *mahadras*, which are either situated within the old cities or migrate with nomads' encampments. Funded mainly by students' parents, *mahadras* provide an education in Arabic that includes language instruction, Islamic theology, literature, and linguistics.

The secretary of the state in charge of alphabetization and original education (Secrétariat d'Etat chargé de la Direction de l'Alphabétisation et de l'Enseignement Originel) is in charge of overseeing the *mahadras*. The office conducted a survey that registered 1,728 *mahadras* enrolling 88,920 students (MEN 2000).

BASIC AND SECONDARY EDUCATION

Basic education, which extends over six years, is followed by an entrance examination that students must pass to move on to the secondary level. One of the main concerns of the public authorities has been the rapid increase in enrollment percentages. Because of this policy, the overall primary school gross enrollment rate increased from 41 percent in 1985 to 85 percent in 1995. This led to a large increase in student numbers at the secondary level, which saw an increase in its enrollment rate from 11.5 percent in 1985 to 13.7 percent in 1998. Secondary education is comprised of two levels: junior high school (four years) and senior high school (three years). By the end of the secondary school cycle, students must sit for the *baccalauréat* examination in order to enter the university.

In 1999, the government undertook a reform of Mauritania's educational system. The reform aimed at progressively creating a unified bilingual system in place of the existing one, which is divided into two subsystems, one totally in Arabic and the other bilingual (Arabic and French).

The technical education sector, on the contrary, has evolved at a very slow rate, estimated at about 1 percent. This sector is comprised of junior high and senior high technical colleges. An estimated 1,677 students, 30.5 percent of whom were females, were enrolled in this sector in 1998–1999.

HIGHER EDUCATION

Historical Overview

Mauritanian higher education was launched with the creation of a professional school, the National School for Administration (Ecole Nationale d'Administration, ENA), in 1966. ENA ensured the training of high- and mid-level officials for public administration. By 1970, a new professional school, the Teacher Training School (ENS), was set up to train secondary school teachers.

The creation of two other institutions followed a few years later. These were the Advanced Institute for Islamic Studies and Research (Institut Supérieur d'Etudes et de Recherches Islamiques, ISERI), established in 1979, and the Advanced Center for Technical Education (Centre Supérieur d'Enseignement Technique, CSET) in 1980. In response to the growing number of students and a decline in grants for study abroad, the government created Nouakchott University (NU) in 1981. Nouakchott University has two schools: the School of Law and Economics and the School of Letters and Humanities. The university was first located temporarily within the buildings of ENA and ENS. It recruited its candidates mainly among high school graduates with a major in literature. In 1986, the Advanced Scientific Institute (Institut Supérieur Scientifique, ISS) was created to host science majors.

The primary mission of ENA was profoundly modified, thus becoming the continuing education center for public administration personnel and relinquishing its facilities to NU. ENS followed suit, and its building became the School of Technical Sciences in 1995 (Faculté des Sciences Techniques, FST).

More institutions for both education and research have been created in recent years, including the Mauritanian Institute for Scientific Research (Institut Mauritanien de Recherche Scientifique) in 1974, the Arab and Islamic Sciences Institute (Institut des Sciences Islamiques et Arabes) in 1979, and the National Institute for Medical Specialties in 1997.

STATE OF HIGHER EDUCATION

The mission of higher education in Mauritania is threefold:

- To maintain, develop, and disseminate Mauritanian culture, as inspired by the spiritual values of Islam

- To train senior leaders and ensure their efficiency through ongoing adaptation of teaching methods to new scientific and technical developments and current transformations of social life
- To promote the development of scientific research

The Office of Higher Education at the MEN is in charge of defining educational objectives, organizing and developing higher education, supervising pedagogical evaluation, and controlling institutions of public higher education. The office is also in charge of implementing study-abroad programs, which is becoming its major task.

The current university system in Mauritania includes six postsecondary institutions: Nouakchott University, the Teacher School, the National Institute for Medical Specialties, the Arab and Islamic Sciences Institute, the Advanced Institute for Islamic Studies and Research, and the Higher Education Technical Center. The responsibility for these institutions is spread between the MEN and other ministerial departments. Other units are devoted solely to research, as is the case with the Mauritanian Scientific Research Institute.

Nouakchott University is the only university in the country and the major higher education institution in Mauritania, both in terms of human resources (students and personnel) and infrastructure. NU was created in 1981 as a public institution with judicial and financial autonomy. The mission of NU consists of training executive managers, contributing to scientific research, and promoting and developing Arab and African cultural values in partnership with other universities.

UNIVERSITY ORGANIZATION

The University Assembly includes members from every university department and representatives from the student body, the external legislative body, the MEN, and the Ministry of Finance. Members serve for a period of three years. The assembly, led by the university president, is the deliberating organ that defines the main orientations of the institution, including the organization of courses and programs, the establishment of bylaws, and the management of budgets. The assembly has a right to bring in additional temporary members as needed. The MEN reserves the right to approve, authorize, suspend, or abrogate decisions voted by the University Assembly.

NU is administered through the president's office, and includes the office of the university library, the information and technology center, the social services office, the center for the reinforcement of teaching second languages (Centre pour le Renforcement de l'Enseignement des Langues Secondes, CRELS), and central services (human resources, accounting, external relations, and supplies and equipment). The president, who is appointed by the ministerial council, is assisted in his duties by the University Assembly and a general secretary.

Each of NU's schools—the School of Law and Economics (FSJE), the School of Letters and Humanities (FLSH), and the School of Technical Sciences (FST)—is administered by deans, vice-deans, and a general secretary, and each has a deliberating body operating under the direction of the dean.

Table 45.1. Degrees Granted by Institutions Overseen by the Ministry of National Education, Mauritania, 1993–1998

	1993	1994	1995	1996	1997	1998
School of Letters and Humanities (FLSH)	165	196	224	235	185	199
School of Law and Economics (FSJE)	356	364	469	484	512	556
School of Technical Sciences (FST)	—	—	—	—	—	10
Total University	521	560	693	719	697	765
Teacher Training School (ENS)	58	29	45	76	102	210
Advanced Center for Technical Education (CSET)	46	33	48	49	52	76
Total	625	622	786	844	851	1,051

Source: MEN 2000.

FLSH has seven departments (Arabic, French, English literature, history, geography, philosophy, and interpreting), four administrative services, two research laboratories (geography and history), a center for documentation, and a library. History, geography, and philosophy majors are offered in both French and Arabic. FSJE has four departments, a research and study center, a library, and four administrative services. The FSJE bachelor's degree is divided between two years of general studies and two final years in majors such as public-sector economics, private-sector economics, public law, and private law. These majors are taught in both Arabic and French. Table 45.1 shows the number of degrees granted at NU from 1993 to 1998.

THE ADVANCED INSTITUTE FOR PROFESSIONAL STUDIES (ISEP)

After its creation in 1991, ISEP (Institut Supérieur d'Etudes Professionnelles) became an extension of the School of Law and Economics. Admission to the institute requires successful performance on an entrance test. The institute offers three majors: accounting management, commercial and financial management, and the barrister profession (Certificat d'Aptitude à la Profession d'Avocat, CAPA). Access to the management major is open to students holding a science major baccalauréat. Studies are carried over two years of study, leading to a technical university degree (Diplôme Universitaire Technique, DUT). The entrance test for the law school is open to holders of a bachelor's in law or its equivalent for a study period of one year.

TECHNICAL SCIENTIFIC SCHOOL (FST)

FST was established in 1995 and has five departments (biology, chemistry, geology, mathematics and computers, and physics), six administrative services, research units, and a library. Unlike other schools, access to FST is based on a selection from only those applicants who have earned a baccalauréat in science. At the third year, students are oriented toward professional majors such as mining, geology, physics-chemistry, applied information methods for business management, water management, and nutrition science and technology.

TEACHER TRAINING SCHOOL (ENS)

ENS was set up in 1970 to train secondary education teachers. The school was reorganized in 1987 and again in 1995. ENS is a public institution that trains teachers and inspectors for junior and senior high schools, and ENS instructors. Access to the school is open to holders of two-year and four-year degrees. In 1999–2000, ENS enrolled 185 students. It is managed by a deliberative body headed by an executive committee consisting of the director of the school, the assistant director, and the managing accountant.

ADVANCED CENTER FOR TECHNICAL EDUCATION (CSET)

The mission of CSET (Centre Supérieur d'Enseignement Technique) includes the training of senior and mid-level technicians for industry and business, as well as the training of professors and instructors destined for the technical and professional educational sector. Students have to complete a two-year study period and they benefit from a scholarship. The management and admission structure for the school is similar to that of ENS and is open to holders of the technical-major baccalauréat. For the academic year 1999–2000, the number of students at the CSET was 116.

ADVANCED INSTITUTE FOR ISLAMIC STUDIES AND RESEARCH (ISERI)

Operating under the responsibility of the Ministry of Culture and Islamic Guidance (Ministère de la Culture et de l'Orientation Islamique, MCOI), ISERI was established in November 1979. The mission of the institute is to provide a modern Arabic and Islamic education and to conduct basic research in the domain of Islamic sciences.

The institute is led by a director, an assistant director, and a permanent commission. Faculty members are recruited on a contract basis after taking an examination designed by the ministry. Newly hired faculty members must undergo training at MCOI before starting their teaching duties. The period of study

Table 45.2. Student Enrollments in Higher Education, 1992–2000

Institution	1992–1993	1993–1994	1994–1995	1995–1996	1996–1997	1997–1998	1998–1999	1999–2000
School of Law and Economics	4,774	4,637	4,886	5,248	5,731	5,656	6,452	5,697
School of Letters and Humanities	2,232	2,170	2,376	2,558	2,664	2,467	2,896	2,998
School of Technical Sciences	—	—	—	—	708	718	820	886
Total University	7,006	6,807	7,262	7,806	9,103	8,841	10,168	9,581
Teacher Training School	143	138	112	111	101	132	230	185
Advanced Center for Technical Education	127	101	99	105	115	122	113	116
Advanced Institute for Islamic Studies and Research	—	—	—	—	—	—	—	845
Total	7,276	7,046	7,473	8,022	9,319	9,095	10,511	10,727

Note: For the academic year 1999–2000, foreign students represented about 6 percent of the total university student body.
Source: MEN 2000.

at ISERI is four years, leading to a single major. Acceptance is open to candidates holding a *baccalauréat*, while graduates of the *mahadras* have to pass an entrance test. ISERI had 845 students in the academic year 1999–2000.

THE NATIONAL INSTITUTE FOR MEDICAL SPECIALTIES (INSM)

Opened in 1997, INSM (Institut National des Spécialités Médicales, INSM) is under the responsibility of the health ministry. The institute is entrusted with training students for medical specialties such as surgery and pediatrics. The studies are conducted for a period of four years, and acceptance is made after successful completion of an entrance examination and in accordance with seniority criteria.

ARAB AND ISLAMIC SCIENCES INSTITUTE (ISIA)

ISIA, which is an extension of Imam Mohammed Ben Saoud University in Saudi Arabia, was created in 1979. In 1980, the institute opened a specialized program in the sciences of the Shari'a and provides the same programs as its partner institution in Saudi Arabia. To attend the institute, candidates from the *mahadras* must take an entrance examination. All successful applicants are provided grants.

MAURITANIAN INSTITUTE FOR SCIENTIFIC RESEARCH (IMRS)

IMRS (Institut Mauritanien de Recherche Scientifique) was established in 1974 to encourage research in the field of human sciences and to supervise the conservation of the Mauritanian cultural heritage. The institute is under the responsibility of the MCOI. A deliberating and executive body is responsible for the administrative matters of the institute, while a scientific council is in charge of its scientific orientation and the development of research programs. Researchers are recruited according to need and upon examination.

HUMAN RESOURCES

Students

The student population increased significantly from 1990 to 2000. This increase is due to three main phenomena:

- The number of holders of *baccalauréat* degrees increased from 1,737 to 3,137 from 1990 to 1998.
- Demand for local higher education increased on the national level due to the progressive decrease in the availability of grants to study abroad.
- The inefficiency of university studies and the failure to enforce university regulations about graduation deadlines encourage students to extend their period of study, thus contributing to a swelling of student numbers.

As is clear from Table 45.2, the distribution of students by discipline is quite irregular. Students are concentrated mainly in the disciplines of law, economics, and literature. For 1999–2000, students in law and economics accounted for 59.5 percent of the total number of registered students, while students majoring in science and technology represented only 10 percent of the student body.

PERSONNEL

Teaching Body

The teaching body includes full-time and part-time faculty members. While permanent professors are civil servants appointed through the ministry of higher education, part-timers take over courses in disciplines that cannot be taught by permanent professors.

The ratio of students to permanent faculty is particularly high for the university (except for the School of Science and Technology) and for ISERI (about 42 to 1 and 60 to 1 respectively). ENS and CSET have a ratio of students to permanent faculty of about 5 to 1 and 7 to 1, respectively.

Despite the significant increase in student numbers—from 7,046 in 1993 to 10,727 in 2000—the number of faculty has barely increased, moving only from 249 in 1993 to 304 in 1999.

The number of part-time faculty, however, is more significant, particularly due to the lack of recruitment of permanent faculty and to the concentration of faculty in specific disciplines. In certain departments, such as Arabic literature and law, full-time faculty have a weekly workload significantly lower than the average because of the large number of available teaching assistants.

Recruitment Requirements

After taking an examination, professors are selected and distributed over three categories (A1, A2, or A3) according to credentials and seniority. A fourth category (A4) can only be reached through seniority. No faculty member has been admitted in this category yet (Table 45.3).

Tenure

Once recruited, faculty members begin a two-year probation period. The faculty member could be tenured by the end of this period upon recommendation of the University Council if the faculty member meets the conditions set by the higher education commission. The latter is composed of twenty-two members (thirteen from level A3 and nine from level A2).

Administrative and Technical Personnel

NU has 280 administrative and technical employees (the largest of any Mauritanian institution), followed by the Teacher School, which has forty-two employees, and, finally, by the Advanced School for Technical Education (CSET), which has eighteen employees.

The same law that defines the general status of civil servants and contractual agents of the state governs administrative and technical personnel in higher education (law 93.09, 1993). It seems that a separate law needs to be drafted for these specific categories. Other regulatory acts define the organization and function of the disciplinary council for civil servants (August 17, 1994), define the composition and the functioning of the national examination commission (March 19, 1996), and pertain to the common system of administrative and professional examinations (April 19, 1998).

Categories of Administrative and Technical Personnel

Currently there are three categories of administrative and technical personnel: personnel recruited by the state and delegated to the university or institutes; personnel recruited by the institutions themselves; and part-timers.

Part-timers constitute a large portion of the personnel at NU. However, the number of part-timers cannot be easily determined because it fluctuates according to the needs of the institutions (Liot 1994).

Table 45.3. Recruitment Conditions for Each Level of Faculty Service

Level	Recruitment Conditions
A1	Holder of a graduate or postgraduate degree or equivalent
A2	Holder of a doctorate in law or economics, Holder of a doctorate in engineering or equivalent, or Holder of a postgraduate degree or equivalent
A3	Holder of level A2 with 4 years' experience in the same level, Graduate in law, economics or similar disciplines, Holder of a doctorate in literature, science, or equivalent
A4	Holder of degrees required for level A3 with at least 4 years' work in a higher education institution.

DEGREES AND THE JOB MARKET

Mauritania currently has no viable statistics on the integration of higher education graduates into the job market. The MEN has no structure to conduct such a survey.

However, the Commission for Human Rights and the Eradication of Poverty, which is a public agency in charge of integrating unemployed graduates, conducted a survey on this topic in 1999. The results showed a total of 2,952 graduates with no jobs, of whom 85.6 percent were male. Of these graduates, 77.6 percent had completed their studies in Mauritania and 95.3 percent held a bachelor's degree or equivalent. A large majority of unemployed graduates (50.8 percent) hold a degree in management, while 17.2 percent hold a law degree. Other unemployed graduates hold degrees in literature (16.2 percent), history and geography (7.5 percent), and the sciences (11.4 percent). The survey noted that the number of unemployed graduates has been on the rise since 1993. Among the graduates majoring in literature, the proportion increased from 13.3 percent in 1993 to 40 percent in 1998. This tendency follows a similar trend in the School of Law and Economics, where the rate of graduate unemployment reached 48 percent in 1997. The job market seems to be saturated with the increasing number of graduates from these two disciplines (Table 45.4).

FINANCING

Mauritanian higher education is public and free. The contribution paid by students is symbolic. Students are only expected to pay a $2.50 registration fee. The government subsidy is the main source of internal financing in terms of operating costs. Investment expenses have been allocated mainly through international cooperation contracts.

Table 45.4. Unemployed Graduates of Nouakchott University, 1993–1998

Category	1993	1994	1995	1996	1997	1998
School of Letters and Humanities						
Number of Graduates	165	196	224	235	185	199
Number Unemployed	22	34	50	67	68	82
Percent Unemployed	13.3	17.4	22.3	28.5	36.8	41.2
School of Law and Economics						
Number of Graduates	356	364	469	484	512	556
Number Unemployed	81	103	137	203	247	195
Percent Unemployed	22.8	28.3	29.2	41.9	48.2	35.1

Source: MEN 2000.

Table 45.5. Operating Costs for Higher Education in Mauritania, 1991–1998

Year	Percent of Gross Domestic Product		Percent of State Budget	
	All Education	Higher Education	All Education	Higher Education
1991	4.4	1.3	27.1	7.9
1992	4.4	1.3	26.5	7.7
1993	4.1	1.2	23.6	6.8
1994	4.3	1.2	28.9	8.2
1995	4.0	1.2	27.6	8.1
1996	4.0	1.3	28.0	8.8
1997	4.1	1.2	28.6	8.5
1998	4.3	1.2	29.2	8.4

Source: MEN 2000.

Table 45.6. Trends in Higher Education Funding in Mauritania, 1991–1998

Year	Total Expended (in UM*)	Government Budget (in UM*)	External Funding (in UM*)	Percent of External Funding
1991	180	0	180	100
1992	183	15	168	91.8
1993	158	0	158	100.0
1994	318	150	168	52.8
1995	235.8	9.5	226	96.0
1996	451.8	120.8	331	73.3
1997	70	0	70	100.0
1998	360	10	350	97.2

*UM = Mauritanian Ouguiya (national currency; US$1 = 230 Ouguiya), in millions
Source: MEN 2000.

Operating Costs

The MEN, through its higher education office (Direction de l'Enseignement Supérieur, DES), provides grants and finances study-abroad programs for Mauritanian candidates. Higher education institutions are public entities that enjoy legal status and financial autonomy. Government subsidies cover the total operating costs. Institutions can also benefit from budgetary extensions, which are crucial for universities, and which are disbursed from the general state budget (Table 45.5).

Budget Allocation

Financial resources for institutions come from three main sources: the ministry of finance, the state investment budget, and external support. Negotiations with finance ministry authorities are carried out during meetings for the allocation of annual budgets. The customary policy of the finance ministry has been to increase the budget allocation by 10 percent every year. After the allocation of the initial budget, negotiations take place over budgetary extensions to cover transfer of expenses related to social assistance and food expenses (Table 45.6).

External funding comes mainly from the World Bank, the French Cooperation, national and international organizations, foundations, embassies, and interuniversity cooperation programs.

Annual investments in NU amount to $1.2 million, mostly through the project for the support of general education (Education V), which is funded by the World Bank through the International Development Association (IDA). The investment program funded by IDA aims at increasing the hosting capacity of the university through the construction and renovation of a 5,000-square-meter area, of which 3,000 square meters has been allocated for new buildings. The investment also targets the strengthening of library resources, especially reference materials and equipment, the training and improvement of administrative personnel, and the creation of a pilot project to restructure the higher education system.

On another level, the program led by the French Cooperation was launched in 1998 and was planned for a four-year period. The program is meant to support three main areas: the

School of Sciences and Technology, the teaching of second languages, and the Information Technology Center.

Precise and accurate information on operating budgets is difficult to obtain from institutions because of the confidentiality that generally surrounds budgetary information in Mauritania.

External Financing

Mauritanian higher education has significantly benefited from external loans through bilateral and multilateral agreements from international organizations such as the World Bank, the African Development Bank, UNICEF, PAM (Programme Alimentaire Mondiale, World Food Program), the Investment and Development Bank (BID), and the Organization of Petroleum Exporting Countries (OPEC). France, Belgium, Japan, and Germany have also contributed to the higher education sector in Mauritania. Investment expenses for higher education during the 1990s were provided mainly through foreign loans.

University Financial Situation

The university subsidy for the year 1997 amounted to US$3,029,611. Registration fees represent less than 1 percent of NU's operating budget.

COLLABORATIVE INITIATIVES

Higher education institutions organize various international seminars and colloquia in collaboration with local and foreign partners. Examples of these include the international colloquium on the informal economy in 1988, which included scholars from various countries; the 1992 Forum on Partnerships, which was organized in collaboration with local businesses and the French Cooperation; and the 1995 international colloquium on the contribution of Arabs to Latin America, which was organized with the help of UNESCO. The university also hosts regular scientific events organized by local bodies.

Various agreements have been signed between Mauritanian higher education institutions and universities, schools, and institutes from Algeria, Belgium, Canada, China, France, Morocco, Saudi Arabia, Senegal, Spain, and Tunisia. These agreements have allowed for the exchange of research faculty and students with these countries.

STUDENT UNREST

While higher education institutions in neighboring countries are frequently paralyzed by internal political strife, which often leads to a succession of school interruptions, in general, Mauritanian institutions have been unaffected by such problems. The longest interruption occurred in 1992 and lasted about four months. In fact, every year has seen demonstrations and strikes. Student demands are generally of a social nature, mostly related to the quality of grants, social assistance, food services, and medical care.

CHALLENGES TO THE HIGHER EDUCATION SYSTEM

Mauritanian higher education has been developed without enough prior planning. Despite dire budgetary constraints, Mauritania chose to provide higher education to every high school graduate without any concern for the future of the graduates or their integration into the job market.

Higher education in Mauritania faces a number of difficulties that impede the fulfillment of its mission. Institutions and the national research institutes in Mauritania report to different ministries. Their autonomy from the ministries is very limited.

This situation leads to incoherence in the management and supervision of these institutions. Moreover, teaching and research activities are secondary to the agenda of some of the ministries responsible for higher education. The bureaucracy often creates obstacles to teaching and research efforts that require flexibility and a high degree of initiative to overcome. Most higher education institutions have split allegiances between the ministry to which they are attached and the Ministry of Finance, which allocates the annual subsidies.

Because the government designates all the executive managers, deans, and directors for higher education, structural changes are needed to allow institutions to develop a more autonomous relationship vis-à-vis the responsible ministries. Such changes should lead to more democratization in assigning key positions; for example, through elections based on objective criteria pertaining to seniority, rank, and through the requirements of each position.

Higher education institutions in Mauritania have no orientation for newly admitted students. Students enrolled for the first time have little information about the majors or courses that are offered. Catalogs are rarely published; even when they are, they receive little publicity. Students are thus led to register for programs without knowing the subjects taught and with no orientations about where such majors might lead. This leads a number of students to drop or change majors after the fact.

Because of the lack of a central structure for coordination, a number of Mauritanian institutions offer almost the same curriculum. This is the case for FSJE, ISERI, FLSH, and ENS. The absence of coordination between training and the job market constitutes a major problem. Some majors are developed without any regard for the needs of the country. Training is often inefficient and does not meet the requirements of employers. The private sector, which is expanding significantly, tends to be totally ignored. The creation of professional majors that are adapted to the needs of the market is an urgent necessity.

Pedagogical methods are generally characterized by the transmission of information that is barely current. The participation of professors is very structured, and recourse to audiovisual technology is very limited. Most instruction is lecture oriented because of the increasing number of students in classrooms. The lecture mode has increased at the expense of laboratory sessions.

Research activity was nonexistent until recently. Teams and laboratories have started some research activities. Examples of these are the laboratory for historical research and study, the research team on the humid zones based at the School of Sciences and Technology, and the research centers at FSJE and FLSH. Yet research activity remains embryonic and does not involve the majority of faculty members because of the absence of a coordinated national research policy and the lack of resources. As a consequence, there is no scientific production at the university and little interest is given to vital sectors of the economy such as fishery, agriculture, and animal husbandry.

The condition of research is closely linked to that of documentation. The documentary resources of higher education institutions suffer an acute lack of recent publications and specialized resources. Allocations for documentation remain very low.

A number of faculty members have left higher education for positions in the public or private sector. Moreover, professors who are delegated to other state institution or agencies continue to benefit from the job privileges while carrying their teaching responsibilities in a perfunctory manner. Mauritania needs to encourage loyalty within academia by motivating professors not to abandon their vocations as educators.

Administrative and technical personnel are not trained to manage higher education institutions. Personnel for universities and other similar institutions are hired among graduates of various majors that range from law and economics to literature. The recourse to part-time faculty is now widespread.

Government subsidies for higher education are already significant and cannot be increased, given the other developmental priorities of the country.

The resources provided to the various institutions are not only insufficient but are inefficiently employed. The budget allocated for grants, social assistance, and food services constituted 37 percent of the general budget of the university in 1997.

The increase in the university budget observed since 1999 covered grants, dissertation expenses, food, and housing at the expense of more cardinal needs such as the quality of teaching and documentary resources. The salary budget had also increased, reaching 43 percent of the 1997 general budget, reflecting overstaffing of both personnel and faculty.

A number of tenured faculty members have a workload that is lower than average. Overstaffing contributes to this problem. Yet another problem is the fact that faculty carry multiple responsibilities. For example, one may simultaneously teach, act as head of department, and serve as an adviser. The same situation is reproduced among administrative personnel; a number of them have no precise task.

The decrease in budget allocations for expensive services such as grants, social assistance, and food services cannot be achieved without political will on the part of both the government and university authorities. Fears of the repercussions of these measures constitute a major deterrent for such initiatives.

ENS and CSET are the only institutions that have appropriate physical buildings and equipment. When the university was created, it did not have its own location but was hosted in temporary buildings. The increase in student numbers, however, was not matched by development in the university's infrastructure. Libraries and documentation centers can no longer accommodate the large number of students. Currently, Mauritanian higher education officials and foreign funding bodies are working on a plan to expand university facilities.

Present funding mechanisms must be diversified. Government subsidies are becoming more and more difficult to obtain. Negotiations with the public authorities are strained, and the amounts granted are always below expressed needs. It is also important to keep in mind that foreign funding is not always guaranteed.

Higher education institutions should seek to generate funding by means of research partnerships with governmental agencies and through the private sector, collaborative initiatives, and consulting services. Part of the solution must also be the rationalization of expenses, including the reduction of expenses for grants and social services, while taking into account merit and the social situation of the student. Registration fees could also be revisited with a concern for the social situation of the students and the needs of the institution.

THE WAY FORWARD

The seclusion and lack of coordination between higher education institutions, the multiplicity of responsible ministries, the redundancy in curricula, and the lack of rational spending are among the key challenges Mauritania faces. In its effort to restructure higher education, the minister of national education created a pilot committee in June 1995 entrusted with designing the main framework for the restructuring of higher education. The pilot committee was composed of the principal actors in higher education and representatives of the faculty, and based its work on a number of reports and studies carried out by Mauritanian and foreign experts. The committee obtained funding from the World Bank for its work. The committee's report identified the following needs:

- Adaptation of higher education programs to the economic and social context through informed orientation
- Reinforcement of the teaching capacity of higher education institutions, especially in scientific and technical disciplines
- Better management of personnel and faculty members through a system that motivates and uses the full expertise of these human resources
- Reconsideration of funding issues in terms of rational expenses and determination of priority sectors
- Coordination among the various units of higher education at the level of internal relations as well as relations with the responsible ministries
- Promotion of scientific research and orienting it toward national development priorities

It is hoped that these recommendations will be implemented to ease the challenges facing higher education in Mauritania.

BIBLIOGRAPHY

Bailleul, André, et al. 1996. *Mission sur l'enseignement mauritanien.*
Banque Internationale d'Information sur les Etats Francophones. 2000. *Etude relative à la restructuration du secteur de l'Enseignement supérieur Mauritanien.*
Flacher, Jacques. 1994. "Rapport d'évaluation du système d'organisation de l'Université de Nouakchott."
Groupe de réflexion technique. 1989. "L'enseignement supérieur mauritanien: analyse critique et recommandations."

Groupe de travail sur la restructuration de l'enseignement supérieur. 1993. "Propositions pour une réforme de l'enseignement supérieur."

Liot, Colette. 1994. "Statut des enseignants de l'enseignement supérieur en Mauritanie."

MEN (Ministère de l'Education Nationale), Direction de la Planification et de la Coopération. 2000. Novakchott: Statistiques scolaires.

Niewiadowski, Didier. 1992. *L'enseignement supérieur en Mauritanie. Bilan économique et social 1999–2000*. Supplément du journal *Le Monde*.

46

Mauritius

R. Baichoo, S. K. A. Parahoo, and I. Fagoonee

INTRODUCTION

This case study presents an overview of the state of higher education in Mauritius. Particular consideration has been given to the University of Mauritius, which was the only institution of higher learning operational in September 2000.

The University of Mauritius (UM) is a relatively young institution. It enjoyed a monopoly in the provision of programs at the tertiary level until 1999. As such it has been privileged with a unique development path.

BACKGROUND

In the 1960s, Mauritius essentially had an agricultural economy. Its economic fortunes were linked to the sugar industry, which accounted for about 34 percent of gross national product (GNP). The sugar industry contributed more than 95 percent of total export earnings and provided over 50 percent of total employment. The economy was bleak at that time. Caught in a Malthusian trap of a rapidly expanding population, with about 30 percent of the population below the poverty line, there were few prospects for sustained economic growth and improvement in the standard of living.

Three decades later, the Mauritian economy has evolved considerably and is now cited as a "success story." With an annual rate of growth of over 5 percent and a per capita income exceeding $3,500, Mauritius has graduated to the group of upper-middle-income countries. A fair degree of diversification in its economic activities has been achieved, and agriculture, manufacturing, and tourism have emerged as the three pillars of the economy. A new pillar of the economy, the quaternary sector, which represents about 12 percent of total output, is being expanded in the hope of making Mauritius a regional financial hub. The fifth pillar that is emerging very quickly is Information and Communications Technology.

POSTSECONDARY EDUCATION IN MAURITIUS: AN OVERVIEW

Tertiary education in Mauritius (defined here as postsecondary education) is offered at various levels by a range of institutions in the public and private sectors. Though tertiary education within the public sector is provided essentially through UM, the Mauritius Institute of Education, the Mauritius College of the Air, and the Mahatma Gandhi Institute provide tertiary-level programs of study either on their own or in collaboration with UM, which to date is the only degree-awarding institution in the country. These four tertiary education institutions operate under the aegis of the Tertiary Education Commission, which assumes the responsibility for planning postsecondary education and training, allocating public funds, and promoting coordination among the different institutions. In early 2000, a University of Technology of Mauritius Act was passed in the national parliament, though this institution is not yet operational.

In addition to the publicly funded institutions, a number of private institutions run tertiary-level courses that are, more often than not, delivered in collaboration with overseas institutions. Furthermore, a significant number of Mauritians undertake their tertiary studies through enrollment in overseas institutions, either by traveling abroad or using the distance learning options that several overseas institutions are now making available to students.

UNIVERSITY OF MAURITIUS

Established in 1965 as the College of Agriculture, UM is the single largest local tertiary education provider. Initially established with three schools in the areas of agriculture, administration, and industrial technology, the university has today expanded to include five faculties; namely agriculture, engineering, law and management, science, and social studies and humanities. Furthermore, five centers have been created: the Center for Medical Research and Studies, the Center for Distance Learning, the Center for Information Technology and Systems, a Consultancy Center, and the recently established Center for Applied Social Research and the Virtual Center for Innovative Learning Technologies.

In response to the country's human resource development needs, the university has gradually shifted emphasis away from certificate and diploma-level courses and now concentrates mainly on degree and postgraduate programs. In 1999–2000, the total student population stood at 4,748, an increase of more than 20 percent over the previous year. Though overall enrollment shows a more or less even gender distribution (47 percent female), it is to be noted that gender distribution, not surprisingly, varies across faculties, with a predominance of male students in the Faculty of Engineering (76 percent) and a predominance of female students in the Faculty of Social Studies and Humanities (68 percent). Of the total student population, 28 percent were in programs in the Faculty of Engineering, followed next by the Faculties of Law and Management (19 percent), Social Studies and Humanities (18 percent), Science (15 percent), and Agriculture (10 percent). The policy now is to shift toward degree and postgraduate study programs; enrollments in certificate and diploma programs accounted for only 9 percent of total enrollment in 1999–2000. Of the student population, 81 percent registered for degree programs and slightly less than 7 percent were enrolled in postgraduate programs.

MAURITIUS INSTITUTE OF EDUCATION

Founded in 1973, the Mauritius Institute of Education (MIE) was initially charged with the development of teacher curriculum, curriculum research and development, and reform of the national examinations system. Today, the institute is focused predominantly on teacher education and runs four schools; namely applied science, education, science and math, and arts and humanities. The institute shoulders the responsibility of improving the quality, competence, and qualifications of teachers from pre-primary through secondary education.

Total enrollment at the institute amounted to 2,309 in 1999, with new teacher trainees numbering 706. Only 8 percent of students were pursuing the B.Ed. degree, which is run jointly with UM, and another 8 percent were enrolled in postgraduate certificate courses. The majority of students (54 percent) were registered for certificate and/or advanced certificate courses, while the remaining 702 students were registered for diploma courses. The distribution of enrollment according to gender was more or less equal.

THE MAHATMA GANDHI INSTITUTE

With the aim of promoting Indian culture and traditions, the governments of Mauritius and India ventured jointly to establish the Mahatma Gandhi Institute (MGI) in 1970. The institute set up four schools—Indian music and dance, fine arts, Indian studies, and Mauritian, African, and Asian Studies—and is responsible for running tertiary-level courses in Indian studies,

performing arts, fine arts, and Chinese and Mauritian studies. MGI offers a few degree courses jointly with UM.

The student population of MGI stood at 436 in 1999, of which 73 percent were female. The largest cohort belonged to the Department of Languages, which accounted for 55 percent, followed by the Department of Fine Arts (30 percent); the Department of Sanskrit, Indian Philosophy, and Hindu Theology (11 percent); and the Department of Indian Music and Dance (4 percent).

THE MAURITIUS COLLEGE OF THE AIR

In 1971, the Mauritius College of the Air (MCA) was established to promote education, arts, and science through the mass media. In 1985, with the reenactment of the MCA statutes, distance education was declared to be the main objective of the college. The college, which merged with the Audio-Visual Center of the Ministry of Education and Science in 1986, has until recently been involved in the production of educational programs for broadcast on radio and television that cater to the primary and secondary education sectors. However, the college has recently assessed the crucial need for instructional tools at the tertiary level and has ventured into collaborative efforts with different faculties of UM. This has led to the development of instructional materials with an emphasis on the Mauritian context, which in turn facilitates the students' familiarity with their subject and leads to more effective teaching and learning.

NEW TERTIARY EDUCATION INSTITUTIONS

During the last few years, Mauritius has witnessed a burgeoning of tertiary education providers, both public and private. These are the University of Technology of Mauritius (Université de Technologie, Mauritius, UTM) (public), De Chazal du Mée Management Business School (private), the French-Speaking Entrepreneurial Institute (Institut Francophone d'Entrepreneuriat, IFE) (public), Indian Ocean University (public), the Industrial and Vocational Training Board (public), and polytechnics (public).

UTM is a new institution that has recently become operational. It is scheduled to open with three faculties—software engineering, public policy and management, and tourism and hospitality management—with an enrollment of 800 students. The seven programs that will be offered are the diploma in public-sector administration and management, the diploma in human resource management, the B.Sc. (Honors) in information systems, the B.Sc. (Honors) in software engineering, the B.Sc. (Honors) in tourism and hospitality management, the B.Sc. (Honors) in public sector policy and management, and a master's in public administration.

TRENDS AND PATTERNS IN HIGHER EDUCATION: EMERGING ISSUES

Two main trends that seem to have emerged on the education scene in the past several years are the dependence on distance education and the introduction of quality assurance.

Distance Education

Changing political scenarios all over the world, the increasing responsiveness of governments toward the educational needs and aspirations of the masses, and the growing realization that education is one of the major means of ensuring the socio-economic well-being of individuals and of society have brought about challenges that have not been experienced by the educational system so far. Areas of challenge include:

- The emergence of a very large number of students who seek education of diverse types at all levels of instruction
- The realization that education and learning should serve socioeconomic purposes and be socially relevant
- The facts that the relative sluggishness of existing education provision has created a time lag of immense proportions and that much has to be achieved in a very short time to revise this lag
- The need to develop innovative systems of education that are supported by technology, since conventional approaches to education are too inadequate to meet the new demands

DISTANCE EDUCATION: THE MAURITIAN EDUCATION SECTOR

The earliest manifestation of distance education in Mauritius was the establishment of MCA in 1971. A focused effort to utilize distance education, however, appears to have been inspired by two reports, *Open Learning and Its Potential in Mauritius* by Lord Young, and *Distance Education for Human Resource Development in Mauritius: The Way Forward* by Prof. John Daniel, both of which appeared in 1989. The Master Plan for Education recognized distance education as a "major strategy in educational development" and stated the purpose of distance education explicitly as follows:

> Mauritius will use distance education extensively and will set up an appropriate reform system to: improve access to education and skills for new groups such as working people, housewives, school drop-outs, or those wishing to continue learning; raise the quality of education of students and teachers; and implement the identified training programs in a reasonable time frame and in a relatively economic manner.

The providers of Distance Education in Mauritius to date include MCA, which caters to the needs of primary and secondary schools students; UM, through its Center for Distance Learning, which caters to modules with large cohorts of students; MIE, which caters to the needs of teachers; and other institutions run on a for-profit basis that offer degree programs in association with overseas universities.

THE UNIVERSITY OF MAURITIUS AND THE CENTER FOR DISTANCE LEARNING

To increase access to education, UM set up the Center for Extramural Studies in 1993 in association with the Commonwealth of Learning. Viewed as a facilitator, the center, renamed in 1996 as the Center for Distance Learning (CDL), undertakes course-audit exercises to identify modules attracting large cohorts of students. With the assistance of the faculties, modules are developed and taught using mixed modes of delivery.

Distinctive Features of the Center

Functions: In cooperation with the various facilities, the Center identifies courses to develop. It then contracts with professors to develop the units, establishes course development teams, provides instructional design assistance to the development teams, produces the draft and the final versions, and prints the manuals. The Center divides the students into sections, contracts with tutors for the conduct of each section, provides orientation to ensure a consistent approach among the various tutors, and arranges and conducts the final examinations in such a way that the contents of the examinations remain secure.

Training: Intensive workshops in the philosophy of distance education and in the basic skills necessary for course development are offered to faculty at large with the assistance of overseas agencies such as the Commonwealth of Learning and the Canadian International Development Agency (CIDA). The strategy of pairing an academic from Mauritius with an overseas counterpart to receive hands-on coaching in course development has paid off.

Training was pitched at three main levels: general training for the UM community at large, specific training for the principals of the Center, and very specific training for academics involved in development of new courses. Everyone who receives this training has the potential to be a university resource. The CDL already functions as a resource and has designed its own training program for academics.

INITIAL PROBLEMS FACED

For Mauritius to become fully functional in distance education, more than just the installation of a distance education unit at UM was required. The academic infrastructure needed for distance education needed to be established. Thus, it was necessary to divide the traditional academic year into semesters, organize courses into modules, attach credit value for the modules, set up a sophisticated computerized student registration and listing system, and change course and program configurations to allow students to study courses outside their home discipline.

MANPOWER: RESISTANCE

UM has been a very traditional British-type university, and when distance education was introduced, resistance was natural. In fact, in the early stages of the distance education project, UM had to struggle to define how distance education would operate, given the university's organizational culture. In fact, there was a feeling that UM personnel were being pushed into the distance education project and pushed to make changes against their will.

Appropriate training, unflinching support from top management, and the strategic leadership style displayed by the present pro-vice-chancellor responsible for distance education have all enabled a cultural shift to take place.

MODE OF DELIVERY

The evolution and institution of a hybrid approach to teaching and learning in Mauritius, which is probably unique in the world, deserves attention. Distance education courses are designed according to student-centered teaching and learning principles, and regular sessions with a qualified tutor are built into the model for each course. The courses are part of the regular programs and are offered to full-time and part-time students on campus. The students are not required to attend regular classes. Instead, students rely on a carefully designed course manual and other learning materials, which are purchased by all students. Tutorials are held on a weekly basis at the rate of one hour per course. Although there are many tutorial groups for each course, students write a common final examination that adheres to existing university policies.

This hybrid model has allowed the retention of some traditional educational values while at the same time it has introduced the notion of independent learning and state-of-the-art approaches to instructional design.

When the hybrid model started on campus in 1994–1995, the total number of students enrolled was 646; within a period of six years, enrollment reached 4,722. To date, fifteen distance education modules have been taught.

CHALLENGES OF DISTANCE EDUCATION

So far, the role of CDL has been limited in scope because of its original conception as a "facilitator." Certain general developments in higher education have ushered in challenges of an unprecedented nature. Some educators hope that is one way to address these challenges. Through the process of industrialization, it has become apparent that a paradigm shift in education has occurred. The concept of one training and one job for one life has given way to the idea that one will have several jobs—and hence multiple trainings—in one's lifetime. Retraining has become a cottage industry in Mauritius.

Such needs could be addressed through the distance education that has been made possible with recent developments in technology, according to some educators. Audio conferencing with international agencies is now a reality at UM; video conferencing will soon be a reality within the university. UM is in the process of developing World Wide Web–based courses to take advantage of the full potential of distance education.

QUALITY ASSURANCE

The Mauritian Tertiary Education Sector

The global trend in quality assurance for education systems holds that responsibility lies with an institution itself to provide quality education and training that meets established standards. However, verification from an external auditor is an important way to monitor an institution's self-regulatory frameworks, mechanisms, and processes once they have been implemented.

The concept of quality is not a new phenomenon in Mauritian education. All stakeholders need to be assured about the standards, relevance, rigor, and recognition of tertiary-level courses on offer in Mauritius. In fact, when the Master Plan on Education was being drawn up in the early 1990s, the Working Group drew attention to the urgent need for explicit and methodological approaches to assure the quality and standards of tertiary education.

Ideally, each tertiary education institution should implement its own quality assurance mechanisms to justify and safeguard the quality of education offered; however, the individual progress of Mauritian institutions has been somewhat stunted to date. Most are caught up in the discussion phase. So far, only UM has taken the bold and active steps of developing plans and strategies for both institutional and academic audits. In this light, quality audits, quality assessments, and accreditation become essential, not only to confirm that the institution's responsibilities are being properly discharged but also to promote public confidence in Mauritian tertiary education.

The Quality Assurance Committee set up by the Tertiary Education Commission (TEC) has the task of steering the implementation of quality assurance systems and procedures in publicly funded tertiary education institutions, namely UM, MIE, MCA, and MGI. The schedule for setting up quality assurance systems and carrying out internal assessments and external quality audits suggests that the first round of quality assessments should be concluded by 2005, with recurrent assessments every five years thereafter.

The University of Mauritius

UM has come forward with its own quality assurance framework that aligns itself with the guidelines of TEC. This framework is a blueprint for action in anticipation of the quality audit scheduled for 2000–2001. Mechanisms have already been set up to evaluate the university's programs. Student feedback questionnaires have been developed and used on a one-year basis since January 2000. Once it is fine tuned, this evaluation will help in the continual improvement not only of programs offered but also of academic teaching techniques and future curriculum development. Some have proposed that this feedback mechanism be used to promote and reward excellent teaching by faculty members. Also, a standardized format has been developed for undergraduate and postgraduate programs of study, and an organizational chart has been designed to define duties and responsibilities of different levels of program coordinators.

Furthermore, the establishment of the University Quality Assurance Team (UQAT) has enabled the development of a number of interdepartmental programs, for example B.Sc. (Honors) Math with Computing, B.Sc. (Honors) Economics with Finance, and B.Sc. (Honors) Chemistry with Business Management. It has also made possible the establishment of a graduate programs committee to streamline all graduate programs offered on campus.

Despite severe budgetary limitations, workshops are being held as part of the staff development plan with a view toward enhancing teaching and learning for better-quality delivery and academic practice. Workshops on Research Methodology for Social Sciences have been introduced to provide academics with the necessary research skills to enhance the research culture at the university and to foster better dissertation supervision at both the undergraduate and postgraduate levels. These capacity-building workshops are conducted by renowned overseas experts and will be continued on an ongoing basis so that all academic staff will have an exposure to this discussion. They will include induction programs in teaching and learning in higher education and will typically be followed by a reflective portfolio in preparation for the optional Proficiency Certificate.

INNOVATIVE APPROACHES

In line with its strategic plan, UM is set on attracting new clientele and on shifting the boundaries between on-campus and off-campus education. With the assistance of cutting-edge technologies, UM plans to make use of the World Wide Web, which allows one to integrate text, audio, and video, both as prepared clips and as live interactive systems. The Internet also offers text-based interaction and access to educational resources of unprecedented magnitude.

In a not-too-distant future, UM should be in a position to provide online courses that will increase access to education, introduce flexibility of delivery, improve learning, increase cost effectiveness, and create a better multimedia learning environment.

The setting up of a Virtual Center for Innovative Learning Technologies (VCILT) will harness the existing resources and potential of the CDL with the Center for Information Technology.

PRIVATE TERTIARY EDUCATION PROVIDERS

The influx of overseas educational institutions offering tertiary-level courses through distance education and the growth of local private enterprises offering courses through franchise agreements mean that appropriate legislation and necessary regulatory frameworks are needed to ensure the quality and standards of their provisions. In 1996, Mauritius established the National Accreditation and Equivalence Council (NAEC) to regulate the private tertiary education sector, including accreditation of courses and registration of the institutions. Unfortunately, the council has so far limited its activities to the determination of equivalence and recognition of qualifications awarded by local and overseas institutions. Subject to the introduction of the appropriate legislation, all private, regional, and overseas institutions offering tertiary-level courses should be programmatically and institutionally accredited by the NAEC, thus ensuring an alignment of quality assurance mechanisms by all tertiary education providers in Mauritius.

Institutional capacity-building is being fostered at various levels and on various fronts. Regular workshops in teaching and learning strategies help to maintain improved standards. Workshops on quality assurance ensure that university provisions meet high-quality standards.

At another level, ongoing training for academic staff in innovative teaching and learning strategies is being provided under the Program for Institutional Technology Enhancement in French-speaking Africa (Programme de Renforcement institutionnelle en Matière Technologique en Afrique Francophone, PRIMTAF) and the Center for Implementation, Study and Resources for Distance Education Learning (Centre d'application, d'étude et de resources en apprentissage à distance, CAERENAD).

INSTITUTIONAL CAPACITY AND STRUCTURE

The surging demand for higher education and pressures to increase access have led senior management at UM to find ways and means to stretch existing resources to the limit. In 1992, the number of students who were admitted stood at 943, while total enrollment was 1,658. In 1998–1999, the number admitted rose to 1,451 and total enrollment came to 3,667; in 1999–2000, intake was 1,816 and total enrollment was 4,748; finally, in 2000–2001, there was an intake of 1,679 and total enrollment reached 5,406.

To cope with the increased demand for higher education, the government has provided UM with additional space and human resources. The university has also adopted measures that would lead to a more efficient use of its resources. It has adopted the mixed-mode delivery system with modules involving large cohorts of students. Flexible learning programs have been launched to allow full utilization of campus facilities during evenings and weekends.

A space audit conducted in 1997 at the request of the University Senate revealed that space was being effectively and efficiently used. At an organizational level, however, UM found that the centralization of all operations was leading to unnecessary delays. A measure of decentralization was introduced when the registrar's representatives (the administrative assistants) were posted at each of the faculties. This arrangement has relieved considerable pressure on central administration. Examinations and the day-to-day administration of faculty are now entrusted to the administrative assistants, who act on behalf of the registrar. Furthermore, many administrative decisions are now being made by faculty boards, which report their actions to the senate.

FINANCING AND FUNDING PATTERNS

Full-time courses meant for secondary school–leavers are free of tuition fees, but tuition fees are charged for part-time courses designed for people who are already employed.

As the university tries to accommodate increasing demands created by positive growth in student enrollments, it has had to confront inflation in running costs. Although the main source of recurrent education funding, accounting for 85 percent of total funding, comes from the government, this tends to be absorbed by running costs, leaving relatively little for academic improvement and development. The government grant amounts to only 0.5 percent of the country's GDP, and many argue that this figure should be raised. However, it is also debatable whether meeting the cost of the increased provision of tertiary education should be borne solely by the government.

At present, the university generates only 15 percent of its total funds, mainly through consultancy, student fees, and renting of premises. As almost three-quarters of the student population are enrolled in full-time courses, which are offered for free, the revenue generated from these students is restricted to registration, examination, and library fees. Furthermore, the bulk of receipts from student fees is generated from employed students who are undertaking in-service, part-time courses and from the recently introduced flexible learning programs.

The challenge is how to generate additional sources of funding to maintain, and ultimately improve, the quality and standards of courses offered, which have been the main pillar of strength for the university. The funding pattern is provided in Table 46.1.

Table 46.1 clearly shows a relative decline in government grants and a corresponding increase in income generated from students. This is a result of aggressive efforts by UM to offer unconventional and fee-based programs of study that cater to the training and retraining needs of the working population.

Fees generated from consultancy and research have dropped by 0.2 percent. With the appointment of a full-time consultancy manager, UM expected that such funds would increase, but many firms prefer to contact academics on an individual basis instead of going through the UM Consultancy Center. However, this area still represents a huge funding potential, and exploration of ways to make it more effective should be undertaken.

Salaries of academic and administrative staff constitute the main items of expenditure at UM. Academic and infrastructural development costs were met by grants from the Higher Technical Education Project Funds (HTEP) and capital funds. HTEP is a loan program of the World Bank that provides funds to upgrade the qualifications of academic staff. But the program has already come to an end, and UM now finds itself with an additional burden of having to help fund the studies of academics.

More and more attention has been focused on the cost of higher education in Mauritius. In fact, concern about a financial crisis at UM is widespread. General operating costs are increasing, as is enrollment, and there is great concern that the quality of education and services at UM will decline. In addition, UM has to compete for funds with other social services in Mauritius, which have expanded significantly over the past twenty years.

CURRICULUM DEVELOPMENT

The relevance of curriculum to a society's needs and to the legitimate aspirations of its people is a key concept in any educational mission, particularly at the tertiary level. It is of paramount importance that programs are not only socially relevant but are also of the highest standards. This requirement is achieved at UM through the Curriculum Development Committee. This committee is essentially a quality assurance committee that scrutinizes the program proposals of all faculties to ensure that they meet both the quality assurance standards of the university and international norms. The meticulous and systematic scrutiny by the committee and its contribution to aligning local programs with those of overseas institutions of interna-

Table 46.1. Funding Sources for the University of Mauritius, 1997–1999

Source of Funding	1997–1998 (percent)	1998–1999 (percent)
Government grants	83.6	83.1
Income from students[1]	12.6	13.1
Other sources[2]	3.8	3.6

[1] Includes lab fees, registration fees, etc.
[2] From consultancy and research.
Source: University of Mauritius, Annual Report, 1998–1999.

tional repute have increased student mobility, making the concept of cashing, accumulating, and transferring credits a reality.

The Curriculum Development Committee also comes up with various program proposals for faculties to implement. The following are some of the proposals that have been adopted by appropriate faculties:

- Innovative interdisciplinary programs that enhance the employability of students; for example, B.Sc. (Honors) in agriculture with management.
- Open, flexible programs to satisfy the training and retraining needs of the working population. Such programs are usually run after working hours to enable people to "learn and earn" at the same time.
- General Education Electives (GEEs) to "humanize" the academic contents of the program of studies.
- Transferable Outreach Skill Programs (TOSP) to enhance the employability of the students through a broadening of their academic experience on campus. Such programs, usually of ten hours' duration, aim at developing the "whole person."

The most recent proposal of the Curriculum Development Committee, which could be termed revolutionary, has been the creation of a Virtual Center for Innovative Learning Technologies. This project, which will provide courses on the Internet, has been approved by the senate and is currently being implemented.

SPECIAL PROBLEMS

Unemployment is a special concern facing students at UM. Massification of higher education, rapid technological change, and the neoliberal political and economic agenda have all contributed to an unemployment crisis.

Tracer studies conducted on past students tend to confirm a worldwide trend in graduate employment that has led to unstable employment situations, underemployment in certain fields, and a general mismatch between certain fields of studies and the demand for graduates. On the other hand, in certain fields, such as teaching, many graduates have been able to find work.

Conscious of these problems, the UM has restructured

Table 46.2. University of Mauritius Operational Procedures

Areas of Operation	Criteria	Mechanisms
Admission system	Merit	Admissions Office through computer listing
Recruitment and promotion of staff	Qualifications	Staff Committee
Dismissal of staff	Serious misconduct	Staff Committee
Programs of Studies	Quality assurance	Advisory Committee, Faculty Board, Curriculum Development and Distance Education Committee, Senate
Quality assurance (QA)	As established by QA agency in U.K.	University Quality Assurance Team and Faculty Quality Assurance Team
Course delivery	Checklist as given in guidelines	University Quality Assurance Team, Student feedback questionnaire
Examiners	Agreed standards, calibration	Moderators, external examiners
Student matters	Vary	Student adviser, counselor
University matters in general	Vary	Court of the university

many of its programs of study and has introduced others that will produce graduates who will:

- Be flexible and able and willing to contribute to innovation
- Be prepared for lifelong learning and be able to work in teams
- Be able to adapt to the internationalization of the labor market
- Be knowledgeable beyond their areas of specific expertise and understand multidisciplinary applications

In more practical terms, UM has introduced multidisciplinary programs.

STUDENT, FACULTY, AND STAFF ADMINISTRATION AND GOVERNANCE

As an autonomous body, UM has an organizational structure specific to itself. Although it was originally designed with a typical hierarchical structure, UM has responded to changing social requirements and needs. Its structure is now more facilitative than restrictive.

Most of the university's activities are conducted through committees, which can be statutory and nonstatutory.

The statutory committees are as follows:

- Senate: This is the supreme academic body. It makes important decisions and approves programs to be offered to students. It is also responsible for the maintenance of the standards of instruction, examination, and evaluation. It can appoint subcommittees to consider any matters referred to it.
- Faculty Boards: There is a faculty board for each faculty; currently, there are five faculty boards. Faculty boards coordinate teaching and research work at the faculty level, approve programs of study, and take an active part in the examination and evaluation process. They also act on any matters referred to them by the vice-chancellor and/or the senate.
- Court: This is another important committee, in effect a kind of annual general meeting in which the university presents its achievements and future plans to the public.

- Council: This is a high-level committee that deals with all matters relating to administration, finance, and general policies.

Other important committees are the budget and infrastructure committee, which considers all financial matters, and the staff committee, which manages recruitment and selection of staff. Nonstatutory committees are usually ad hoc.

ESSENTIAL FEATURES OF THE POWER STRUCTURE

Autonomy

UM enjoys autonomy in the sense that it enjoys relative immunity as a corporate entity from interventions by external agencies. In other words, UM is entitled to formulate its own policies and make its own decisions within the framework of the social responsibilities vested to it.

Although UM receives all its capital and recurrent funds from the government, it has jealously repulsed any threats to its autonomy. As specified in the University of Mauritius Act, UM's council and senate always have the final say in any matters affecting the university.

Autonomy with respect to the external environment of the university is secured by a variety of mechanisms (Table 46.2).

The various built-in mechanisms allow UM to operate with complete autonomy with regard to the external environment: decisions are collectively taken through considered deliberations and debates, and no one is able to influence decisions inappropriately.

A system of checks and balances is in place at UM that limits internal autonomy, whether through routine feedback on the academic program for students or interaction with academic peers and employers. Such a system of checks and balances operates because autonomy is compatible with accountability in the academic world. Various mechanisms such as internal and external audits and questions at the senate, council, and court ensure that academics, although vested with full autonomy, are still accountable for their actions or inactions.

Democracy

UM's decision-making processes are democratic in the sense that all decisions are taken collectively. The collegial nature of academic relationships makes this possible. Delegation of power, decision making through committee deliberations, the election of representatives of both academics and students to important governing bodies, decentralized decision making, internal debates, and discussions on long-term policies are essential features of UM's governance.

Accountability and Public Audit

The fact that UM is autonomous does not mean that it is unaccountable for its actions. Because it is a publicly funded institution, UM uses resources from the government. As such, it is answerable to the latter on how effectively and efficiently it is operating within the framework of the social mandate with which it has been vested.

RESEARCH AND CONSULTANCY

Although the overall staff-to-student ratio is roughly 1 to 18, some faculties are faced with exceptionally high ratios. For example, the Faculty of Law and Management has a ratio 1 to 30 at present. This obviously impinges on faculty research activities. Nonetheless, UM has introduced several incentives to encourage research. These include the recruitment of research assistants, the provision of research funds for recurrent and capital expenditures, partial funding for participation in conferences, and financial support for overseas research partnerships. Research grant schemes are also available to staff under the aegis of the Mauritius Research Council. These incentives have proven to be effective. The university's performance in research has consistently improved; sixty-eight academic staff are currently enrolled for M.Phil. and Ph.D. studies at UM.

A golden opportunity has been presented to academics to publish high-quality articles in the *University of Mauritius Research Journal*. Three volumes of the first issue were published in March 1999, incorporating twenty-six internationally refereed papers. The journal includes research in science and technology, law and management, and the social sciences. The second issue was in press in late 2000.

Additionally, UM opened the University Consultancy Center in August 1998 to facilitate the consultancy process, encourage academic staff to build ties with industry, and strengthen university-community links. During the financial year 1998–1999, sixty-six projects were undertaken involving sixty-three university staff members. The projects included training programs, studies, and reports which were commissioned by public-sector parastatal bodies and by the private sector, NGOs, and international bodies. The Faculty of Engineering led in the number of projects (41 percent), and the Faculty of Social Studies and Humanities was highest in project value (30.5 percent).

ACADEMIC LINKS

Since its inception, UM has developed and maintained links with high-profile universities in many countries. The fact that most Mauritians are bilingual has enabled UM to collaborate with Anglophone and Francophone countries. The university is a member of both the Association of Commonwealth Universities (ACU) and the Association of Partially or Entirely French-Speaking Universities (Association Francophone des Universités Partiellement où Entièrement de Langue Française, AUPELF).

In addition to more recent collaboration with Australian, Indian, and South African universities, UM has maintained strong links with British universities (including Lancaster, Nottingham, Newcastle, Manchester, Imperial College, and Reading) and French universities (including Paris, Aix-Marseille, Aix-en-Provence, and Bordeaux). Last year, UM signed a collaboration agreement with Universiti Putra in Malaysia and Temasek Polytechnic of Singapore.

UM runs bilingual courses, including a regional M.B.A. program, under the aegis of the University of the Indian Ocean (l'Université de l'Océan Indien). This partnership was set up by the Commission of the Indian Ocean (Commission de l'Océan Indien), which is funded by the European Development Fund. The university admits students from Comoros Island, Réunion Island, the Seychelles Islands, and the Malagasy Republic to these courses.

UM also offers scholarships to students from Mozambique, Kwazulu-Natal (South Africa), and Seychelles. In fact, UM is now focusing on regional cooperation with members of the Southern African Development Cooperation (SADC). At present, the university is pursuing discussions under the SADC Intra-Regional Skills Development Program to increase the number of collaborative higher education ventures.

CHALLENGES: CURRENT AND FUTURE

The challenges UM presently faces are plentiful. The internationalization of the tertiary education industry worldwide means that the university will face even more challenges in the near future.

The number-one challenge confronting the university is how to effectively address the education needs of Mauritius. Because of inadequate institutional capacity, the university cannot meet the present demand for higher education. Limited access for students (roughly 45 percent of applicants who qualify to enroll in a course are admitted) has pushed Mauritians toward educational institutions that provide access to correspondence courses of international universities. Increasing accessibility therefore remains a key challenge.

The mushrooming of tertiary education providers that are able to offer more competitive and rewarding packages than UM has created greener pastures not only for students but also for the university's experienced academics. In this light, academic staff development is becoming increasingly critical to staff retention. The World Bank's HTEP funding, which had been the primary source of funding for staff M.Phil./Ph.D. studies, was phased out in June 2000. UM will therefore have to seek alternative sources of funding to upgrade staff qualifications and skills. The lack of staff development funding, together with the current terms and conditions of employment, makes it difficult to attract and retain high-caliber academic staff.

The worldwide dilemma over whether to massify higher education or retain the elitist system of higher education has already reached Mauritius and is creating conflict about the driving concept and philosophy of higher education in Mauritius. Some hold that higher education should evolve into a market-driven and pared-down enterprise that is capable of restructuring itself in an entrepreneurial way. Others argue that higher education should be learner-centered, affordable, interactive, collaborative, and diverse and that it should be focused on life-long learning.

UM was first conceived of as a developmental university with a mission to prepare the elite to run the state after independence in 1967. The state was willing to finance higher education because it was seen basically as a service aimed at fulfilling its labor needs in the public sector. The scale of operation was small, so the cost of higher education did not represent a great burden for the public budget.

The industrialization of Mauritius during the last two decades has brought challenges to the original model of UM. The university is now more focused on serving the needs of the productive system in particular and of society in general. This shift means the government is no longer the main user of the higher education system, which is reflected in its unwillingness to finance higher education on its own.

CONSIDERATION OF FUTURE DEVELOPMENTS

The Mauritian economy has so far relied on a limited number of sectors for its economic growth, including sugar, textiles and apparel, and leisure and tourism services. With the creation of the Sugar Protocol and the Lomé Convention, Mauritius was able to achieve a high degree of capital and knowledge formation in the agricultural and textile sectors. However, global challenges such as the formation of trading blocs, the phasing out of the Lomé Convention, and the dismantling of the Multi Fiber Agreement, coupled with the emergence of high-quality and low-cost Asian competitors, are but glimpses of the increasing dangers of relying on growth in these sectors only.

The structure of the Mauritian economy is undergoing fundamental changes to maintain its competitiveness and growth. With a booming tourism industry and steady growth in international financial services within the offshore and banking sectors, Mauritius is expected to move further toward the provision of services. This structural change requires the development of existing service sectors and the leveraging of current knowledge capital in the agricultural and manufacturing fields.

In this light, the development of human resources will be critical in enabling the transition of Mauritius to a knowledge-based economy. Education is seen as the empowering tool that will create a highly developed human resource asset capable of driving capital formation in the transition from a small open economy with limited resources to a major regional player.

The challenge that lies ahead for tertiary education institutions in Mauritius is tough, but with an institutional framework that integrates and channels efforts in the right direction, Mauritius should be on its way to becoming a regional knowledge hub.

ACKNOWLEDGMENTS

The authors would like to thank N. Foondun for painstakingly typing our difficult-to-read handwritten notes. The views expressed in this paper do not reflect the official views of the University of Mauritius.

SELECTED BIBLIOGRAPHY

1999. "Mauritius Examinations Syndicate: Developments in Exams." *Mauritius Examinations Bulletin, Special Issue* (December).

ADEA Stocktaking Review in Mauritius. 1999. *Country Case Study on Access to Education and Training in Mauritius.* Tertiary Education Commission.

ADEA. 1998. "The Financing and Cost of Education in Mauritius." ADEA Working Group on Finance.

Indian Ocean University. 2000a. *Bulletin of Indian Ocean University.* 8 (January/February).

——. 2000b. *Bulletin of Indian Ocean University.* 9 (March/April).

CIDA (Canadian International Development Agency). 1999. "Open Learning: A Canada/Mauritius Link (CIDA Project)—Final Report on Education." Hull, Quebec: CIDA.

International Labour Office Task Force on Country Studies on Globalisation. 1999. "Studies on Social Dimensions of Globalisation: Mauritius." Geneva: International Labour Office.

Tertiary Education Commission. 1994. "An Integrated View of the Institutional Development and a Strategy for Implementation."

——. 1996. "University of Mauritius Graduate Survey: Main Findings."

——. 1997a. *Development of an Information Technology Strategic Plan for the Tertiary Education Sector 1997–2000.*

——. 1997b. "Annual Report and Accounts 1996–1997."

——. 1998. "Strategic Plan for the Tertiary Education Commission, 1998–2003."

——. 1999a. "Biennial Report on Tertiary Education 1997–1998."

——. 1999b. "A Framework for Quality Assurance for the Tertiary Education Sector."

——. 1999c. "Participation in Tertiary Education."

University of Mauritius. 1999a. *Annual Report: 1998–1999.*

——. 1999b. *University of Mauritius Strategic Plan (1999–2004).*

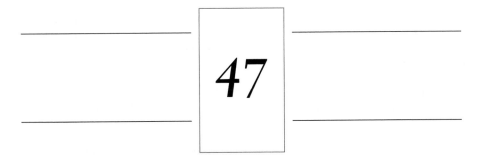

47

Morocco

MOHAMED OUAKRIME

INTRODUCTION

Morocco, with a population of just over 30 million in 2001 and an estimated 25.78 births per 1,000 inhabitants, suffers from all the ills of developing nations, such as illiteracy (over 45 percent); unemployment (over 16 percent); periodic droughts, which have serious negative effects on economic growth; and an endemic external debt of US$20 billion (1998 estimate) (MPEP 1998; MPEP 1999). Thus, Morocco, which devotes approximately 26.5 percent of its general budget to education, faces tremendous challenges that warrant the development of an educational system capable of effectively contributing to the necessary growth in its economy and to the sociocultural and economic promotion of those who participate in it. Institutions of higher education, in particular, are called upon to establish teaching and training programs likely to promote the development of knowledge, the advancement of research, and the training of the workforce.

Higher education in Morocco has had a long tradition, starting with the Qarawyin University, which was established in the ninth century (A.D. 859) in Fez. However, the Moroccan university, like universities in other African nations, is currently experiencing a period of crisis related to its growth; it is rather difficult to see the mid- and long-term consequences of this crisis. This crisis is exacerbated by the negligible attempts at reform that have been implemented since the mid-1970s and by the fact that all parties concerned in higher education have come to doubt the ability of the system as it stands to achieve the purposes that have been set for universities as institutions of learning and research. The recent political changes that have affected the country have initiated a national debate on education in general, and the changes due to take place as a result of the newly developed charter of education should have far-reaching effects on the Moroccan university.

HISTORICAL BACKGROUND

The history of higher education in Morocco seems to fit within the general pattern of the growth of universities in developing countries, particularly African ones (see for example, Court 1980; Reddy 1999). This pattern generally begins with a duplication of the colonial model. In the case of Morocco, the university was no more than an annex of the French Bordeaux University up to the late 1960s. Except in the Qarawyin, the organizational structure was modeled on the French system, with the same curricula, the same system of evaluation, and the use of French as the primary language of instruction. In the late 1960s and early 1970s, a series of reforms were carried out following the general educational policy of Moroccanization and Arabization. This led to the development of a so-called mixed bilingual (Arabic and French) system (with some remnants of the colonial model) and an attempt to develop a specific identity for the Moroccan university. Changes included the extensive Moroccanization of teaching and administrative staff and the use of Arabic as the language of instruction in a number of institutions, particularly the Faculties of Arts and Humanities and some disciplines in the Faculty of Law. (The term "faculties" is used here to refer to institutions.) These changes led to the emergence of a new Moroccan university, although the remnants of the colonial model, which has so thoroughly affected the organizational structure of higher education in Morocco, were still noticeable.

THE CHANGING MISSION OF HIGHER EDUCATION

The first mission assigned to the Moroccan university after independence was to meet the immediate national need for trained professionals (including teachers, engineers, doctors, and civil servants) to replace the departing French expatriates.

Until the late 1970s, this was the main function of institutions of higher education, which in some way explains the development of a system in which the definition of the needs of the country and training plans in terms of labor were the responsibility of civil servants in different government ministries. This also explains the later development of the system as a highly centralized and bureaucratic one in which decision making affecting the organization and governance of institutions of higher education is a prerogative of the governmental authorities in the Ministry of Higher Education (Ouakrime 1985).

By the end of the 1970s, a full Moroccanization of education, the administration, and other governmental agencies was achieved and it became more and more difficult for graduates to find employment, which had been guaranteed up to then. Thus, the initial mission of higher education became almost obsolete, and Faculties of Arts and Humanities, Law and Economics, and Science, in particular, came to be perceived as institutions designed to absorb the growing numbers of secondary school graduates and prepare them for second-rate employment at best and unemployment at worst. Although this situation is not particular to the Moroccan university, it does to a large extent explain the skepticism now spreading among members of the community that higher education has become unable to carry out its mission and that this is the main reason for the high unemployment rate of graduates.

ACCESS POLICY

The universal policy of open access to higher education immediately after the country's independence in 1956 was justified by the relatively small number of secondary school graduates and was initially designed to achieve two aims. The first one, as stated above, was to train as large a number of nationals as possible to take over positions occupied by French colonialists in different departments of the public and private sectors. The second aim was to accommodate one of the most important tenets of social justice, as was the case with all newly independent countries—that of providing education for all. Thus, a policy of open access was adopted in most institutions of higher education, qualified in some cases (such as in the Faculty of Medicine and the engineering schools) by the requirement that the candidate hold a baccalaureate secondary school degree in science or math. Faculties of arts and humanities and law and economics opted for an even more liberal policy by making access open to candidates without the baccalaureate if they passed a special competitive examination.

Soon, however, the pressure of numbers was used to justify the introduction of more stringent selection procedures (for example, the requirement of minimum grades in so-called major subjects such as math, science, physics, and chemistry and a competitive examination). Candidates for the faculties of arts and humanities, law and economics, and science were required to hold a "new" baccalaureate obtained on the year of application for registration. An immediate result of this policy was the exclusion of all candidates who, for some reason, had to interrupt their studies. In the 1998–1999 academic year, an attempt was made to abolish the "new" baccalaureate requirement in some institutions and to make access more open to nontradi-

tional students. However, the administrations of the institutions concerned have been reluctant to implement this decision on the ground that it leads to further pressure on already unfavorable staff-student ratios and scanty facilities.

This access policy resulted in the development of a dual system in which the first group of institutions ("specialized higher education") enjoy both highly favorable (up to 1 to 10) staff-student ratios and an adequate number of teaching/learning facilities, and a second group of institutions ("general higher education") have come to be perceived as institutions designed to absorb the huge numbers of arts and science baccalaureate holders and have poorer conditions.

OVERVIEW OF HIGHER EDUCATION

As mentioned above, the access policies adopted by different institutions in the system of higher education in Morocco have greatly determined their size, scope, and perceived functions (see Table 47.1). The development of a dual system that includes institutions of specialized higher education and institutions of general higher education, characterized respectively by a selective access policy and a relatively open one, has influenced the perceptions of stakeholders and general attitudes about the function of these institutions and their importance in the Moroccan university system.

THE NATURE OF INSTITUTIONS OF HIGHER EDUCATION

Three main factors have influenced the development of institutions of higher education in Morocco: historically, its colonial heritage, which contributed to the establishment of the initial rigid and bureaucratic pattern of organization; politically, the nationalistic orientation implied in the Moroccanization and Arabization of the educational system; and economically, changes in the perceived mission of higher education that have emphasized the necessity for the Moroccan university to serve the developmental needs of the country in the context of its socioeconomic reality.

In addition to Al Qarawyin University, which is considered the repository of a long-lasting cultural Arabo-Islamic heritage, three types of universities have been established, each of which corresponds to a specific stage in the development of higher education in Morocco. The first type is the established public institutions, which were set up immediately after independence or during the early and mid-1970s and have, as part of their developmental process, contributed to the labor-training mission that was initially assigned to the university. These institutions then concerned themselves with their own internal development through the restructuring of departments, the training of their own staff, and the development of new curricula and assessment procedures specific to each of them, thus establishing a relative independence vis-à-vis foreign modes of educational practice.

The second type of institutions is the newer public ones, established in the mid-1980s with the purpose of absorbing the ever-growing numbers of students and implementing a policy of relative decentralization that should promote further institu-

Table 47.1. Student Enrollment and Staff Size at Moroccan Universities by Gender, 1998–1999

Universities	Number of Institutions	Student Enrollment		Teaching Staff	
		Total	Female	Total	Female
Mohamed V Soussi (Rabat)	5	14,155	6,584	902	268
Mohamed V Agdal (Rabat)	5	23,944	11,458	1,184	325
Sidi Mohamed Ben Abdallah (Fez)	7	26,701	10,328	1,021	201
Qarawyin (Fez)	4	5,968	2,057	126	12
Mohamed I (Oujda)	4	19,246	8,432	589	76
Qadi Ayiad (Marrakesh)	8	32,414	11,955	1,251	232
Hassan II Ain Chock (Casablanca)	7	29,202	14,526	1,203	362
Hassan II (Mohammedia)	5	16,312	7,967	721	213
Ibn Tofail (Kenitra)	2	7,894	3,658	402	127
Abdelmalek Saadi (Tetuan)	6	9,929	4,683	550	101
Moulay Ismail (Meknes)	6	22,003	8,412	651	118
Ibn Zohr (Agadir)	4	11,205	3,982	451	87
Chouaib Doukkali (El Jadida)	2	7,796	3,562	440	97
Hassan I (Settat)	3	3,135	1,278	176	55
Total	68	229,904	98,882	9,667	2,274

Source: MPEP 1998, 367–368, 373.

tional autonomy in the long run. These institutions, although they are still in the process of establishing their own identity as centers of learning and research, are likely to constitute a motivating factor in the achievement of quality and excellence among institutions of higher education in the country.

The third type of institution, of which Al Akhawayn University is the only one at present, is the private not-for-profit schools. Al Akhawayn was opened in 1993 and was designed "as a Moroccan university, original in its organization and educational approach, using modern methods to disseminate Arab-Islamic and African culture, universal knowledge, science and advanced technology" (Al Akhawayn University 1993, 13).

Because of the highly American orientation of its organization and curricula, this university enjoys unprecedented prestige among Moroccan upper- and middle-class families and is likely to constitute a model for other schools in the future, particularly as it seems to "represent the ideal for most parents of students: American know-how, an American degree, and the avoidance of the dangerous acculturation associated with prolonged stay in the United States" (Coffman 1996, 4).

The private sector of higher education in Morocco is represented by a number of newly established profit-making institutions (higher institutes and schools), the first of which date back to the early 1980s. During the academic year 1997–1998, 8,500 students (3.38 percent of total enrollment in higher education) enrolled in 79 institutions of private higher education, of which more than 50 percent are located in Rabat, the capital, and Casablanca, the largest city in Morocco. As has been noted with ref-

erence to other contexts of higher education (see, for example, Giesecke 1999 on the case of central Europe), this sector, which has been established to relieve the public sector of some of the burden of the thousands of secondary school graduates, is characterized by instability and is highly dependent on the fluctuation of market forces. Its ability to compete with the public sector and obtain the degree of credibility that will allow its institutions to claim equal status with those of public universities has not yet been demonstrated.

SIZE AND SCOPE OF HIGHER EDUCATION

The rapid growth of the student population and the increasing number of institutions since the 1970s have been persistent features of Moroccan higher education and attest to the popular conviction of its usefulness to the socioeconomic promotion and well-being of the individual. In spite of the skepticism that has characterized people's perceptions of the ability of institutions of higher education to meet the expectations of those who benefit from this experience—particularly when a university degree has come to be perceived in the last two decades more as a "membership card of unemployed graduates' associations" than a "meal ticket"—the demand for higher education has not ebbed.

In the 1997–1998 academic year, 242,929 students (compared to 255,907 in 1998–1999) were distributed among 68 public institutions of higher education; of these, 60,601 were newly registered students (24.94 percent of the total number of stu-

Table 47.2. Student Enrollment in Moroccan Universities by Discipline, Nationality, Gender, and Academic Status, 1997–1998

Discipline of Study	Non-Moroccan	Female	New	Graduate	Undergraduate
Original education*	46	2,120	1,485	266	5,968
Law and Economics	643	45,205	29,291	2,734	106,565
Arts and Humanities	386	33,968	15,569	4,664	60,485
Science	546	13,274	10,261	4,644	37,748
Science and Technical disciplines	160	2,093	1,454	119	7,054
Medicine and Pharmacy	387	3,697	822	—	6,499
Dentistry	59	619	178	—	926
Engineering	36	370	80	416	1,205
Trade and Business Administration	71	645	409	—	1,422
Technology	66	762	1,052	—	1,957
Education	30	43	—	182	13
Translation	01	21	—	—	62
Total	2,431	102,817	60,601	13,025	229,904

*Religious and Arabic studies.

Source: MPEP1998, 367–368, 373.

dents in higher education). The largest proportion of such institutions are faculties of arts and humanities (14, or 20.6 percent), followed by faculties of science (11, or 16.2 percent). The largest proportion of students were enrolled in faculties of law and economics (109,299, or 45 percent), followed by those enrolled in faculties of arts and humanities (65,149, or 26.2 percent). The high percentage of students enrolled in faculties of law and economics may be explained by students' perceptions that a degree from these institutions, particularly in economics, will be useful when they try to obtain employment. However, this perception is often disconfirmed by the reality of the employment market and the growing number of unemployed graduates of all disciplines. These figures also emphasize the fact that institutions in which access is the least selective receive the highest proportion of students (over 71 percent). As a result, the perception about these institutions is that they are designed to absorb thousands of secondary school graduates, a large majority of whom (more than 70 percent) drop out or take more than six years to complete the four-year B.A. degree. This situation has contributed to the development of a feeling of frustration and despair among students and, to a large extent, justifies the continual state of tension caused by widespread student activism in the institutions concerned.

The figures in Table 47.2 confirm the existence of a dual system in Morocco in which institutions of "specialized higher education" (higher schools; and institutes of specialized disciplines, such as engineering, technology, business administration and management; and faculties of medicine and pharmacy and dentistry) that implement a highly selective access policy enjoy the privilege of favorable teacher-student ratios and a relative availability of facilities necessary for carrying out teaching/learning tasks. These institutions represent 29.41 percent of higher education institutions (20 of 68) for a student intake of 19,598 (8.06 percent of the total student population for the academic year 1998–1999). As the allocation of financial resources by the government to institutions of higher education is based

on the authorities' perception of the usefulness of certain fields of study for the strategic development aims of the country, it is easy to see the enormous gap in terms of unit cost between institutions that are classified as specialized higher education and other institutions, such as faculties of law and economics, arts and humanities, and science, which together received 216,840 students (89.26 percent of the total population) in the 1997–1998 academic year.

A new trend worth noting is that the rate of increase in student enrollment numbers has slowed down noticeably in the last ten years. The numbers from 1997 to 2000 clearly illustrate this pattern. Enrollment was 243,000 in academic year 1997–1998, 249,000 in 1998–1999, and 251,000 in 1999–2000.

Compared to rates that exceeded a 100 percent yearly enrollment increase in the 1970s, this stagnation is due to the relatively negative changes that have taken place in people's perceptions of higher education as a determining factor in the economic and social well-being of the individual. With few exceptions (institutions of specialized higher education and faculties of medicine, pharmacy, and dentistry), institutions of higher education are now viewed as producers of unemployable graduates. As a result, for thousands of secondary school graduates, the decision to enroll at university is made only when other alternatives are blocked.

An important consequence of the enormous increase in the number of students in higher education during the 1970s and early 1980s has been the growing pressure on institutions of higher education, as compared to institutions of special higher education. Whereas the latter still enjoy relatively favorable teaching/learning conditions, the former have reached the crisis stage reported for institutions of higher education in developing countries in Africa and elsewhere in the world. This crisis is manifested in unusually high student-teacher ratios and lack of basic equipment, library resources, and funds for research.

Another feature worth pointing out in relation to the student population in the Moroccan university is the alarmingly low percentage of students enrolled in graduate programs across the disciplines (2.5 percent in law and economics, 7.15 percent in the humanities and social sciences, and 10.95 percent in the sciences). The highest rates of students enrolled in graduate programs as a percentage of those enrolled in the same fields at the undergraduate level are recorded for the fields of education (182 of 195, or 93.3 percent) and engineering (416 of 1,621, or 25.6 percent). However, given that student enrollment in these two disciplines constitutes less than 0.25 percent of the total student population, we may consider that graduates in education and engineering are not representative of the graduate student population in higher education in Morocco. In fact, during the 1997–1998 academic year, the number of students enrolled in graduate study was only 5.36 percent of the number of students enrolled in undergraduate programs, hardly a rate to be proud of in a country that spends 7.5 percent of its general budget on higher education. However, the new reform project provides funds to set up research and development units, and there is hope that more graduate programs will be established in various disciplines and that a special financing scheme will be developed to provide minimum funding support to research projects submitted by these units. Because the proportion of students enrolled in graduate programs is an important indicator of the relevance and value of research in any system of higher education, the 5.36 percent rate of graduate students recorded for the 1997–1998 academic year does not do credit to a system that claims to have research high on its agenda.

Insofar as the participation of female students in higher education in Morocco is concerned, the figures for 1997–1998 yield an overall average rate approximating 43 percent. The highest percentages are obtained for disciplines as varied as law and economics (41.35 percent), arts and humanities (52.13 percent), medicine and pharmacy (56.88 percent), dentistry (66.84 percent), and trade and business administration (45.35 percent). The disciplines in the faculties of law and economics, arts and humanities, and science (31.31 percent) exhibit the highest levels of participation by female students. These are the disciplines that have traditionally attracted female enrollment in Morocco. Given the relatively small numbers of students in the other disciplines, we can safely assume that the high percentages of female participation recorded for specializations considered to be nontraditional, such as medicine and pharmacy, dentistry, and trade and business administration, are not representative of the pattern of female participation in higher education in Morocco. The more realistic figures for female participation of between 52.13 percent (arts and humanities) and 31.31 percent (science) seem to indicate a positive development regarding women's participation in higher education in Morocco relative to Africa and the Arab nations (see Mazawi 1999). Concern with women's contribution to Moroccan development is growing. A national charter for their integration in this process is being debated currently at all levels of Moroccan society. This positive trend is likely to further reinforce women's participation in higher education and their representation in the job market, particularly in areas which have traditionally been dominated by men. Although no statistical data exist to substantiate this, the impression is that far fewer females in Morocco pursue graduate education compared to females in Western countries.

The development of private institutions of postsecondary education has taken place in the last two decades and has been characterized by instability. These institutions are located in the main urban centers, particularly Casablanca and Rabat, where 49 of the 79 institutions that were functioning during the 1997–1998 academic year (62 percent) were located. They offer nontraditional courses, such as computer science, business administration, and management, with an emphasis on the perceived needs of the market.

Student enrollments follow the same pattern; private institutions in Casablanca and Rabat received 6,134 students out of a total of 8,500 (72.12 percent). In spite of the relatively high number of institutions, the student population in private higher education is less than 3.5 percent of the overall population of university students in the country. This modest rate may be explained by the relatively young age of private institutions of higher education, the instability of their situation, and, perhaps most important, the inability of a large proportion of Moroccan families to afford the fees charged by these institutions.

CURRENT TRENDS AND PROJECTED REFORMS

Past Reforms

Throughout its history, higher education in Morocco has undergone reforms initiated at different periods of crisis when the need was felt to introduce changes meant to contribute to the development of the university or to solve problems in the educational system. Although these reforms may have attenuated the acuteness of problems in some cases, they have actually reinforced a widespread conviction that higher education has generally been unable to meet the expectations of students, parents, and providers alike.

The first attempt to reform Moroccan higher education was carried out in 1975 with the promulgation of a number of legislative texts intended to constitute a framework for the development of a Moroccan university. The main aim of this reform was to move the system of higher education away from the rigid, bureaucratic, and undemocratic model inherited from the colonial era and to develop a more decentralized and representative one. It was also meant to define a new mission for higher education that was more consistent with the social, economic, and cultural needs of the country, particularly as the labor-training mission that had been assigned to it up to then was becoming obsolete.

The text of the 1975 reform provided a framework whereby institutions of higher education could enjoy some degree of autonomy through the establishment of governing bodies, such as the faculty councils and the university councils, which were made up of representatives of the faculty, students, the administration, and the community at large. However, due to a number of factors—such as restrictions on the role of the councils, the resistance to change demonstrated by representatives of the administration, and security concerns that led to a refusal to recognize the student movement and prevented student representatives from actually sitting on these councils—the role of these bodies was limited to a consultative one at best and a disciplinary one at worst.

The lack of planning for the reform and the resistance to change on the part of faculty and students prevented any effective changes in organizational structure and programs of study from actually taking place. Changes that were supposed to be implemented at the level of course content and assessment, for example, materialized in a mere change of course titles. Although no systematic evaluation of the impact of the 1975 reform exists, its implementation was limited to alterations in course titles, changes in assessment procedures that had more negative than positive effects, and a simulation of democracy in the management of institutions that led to even more frustration among the two groups most concerned—students and faculty.

A second attempt to introduce reform was carried out in 1981; it emphasized the need to introduce changes in the teaching programs and the assessment system to make students' experience of higher education more consistent with the perceived development needs of the country. However, as with the first attempt, teachers and students who had not been involved in drafting the reform project demonstrated so much resistance that the implementation of the changes relating to teaching and assessment was aborted.

The third attempt to reform the Moroccan system of higher education started in 1992 with draft proposals submitted by the Ministry of Higher Education and counterproposals submitted to the government by the teachers' union Syndicat National de l'Enseignement Supérieur (SNE-Sup). For the last eight years, heated debate has taken place concerning the mission of higher education and ways of making the university a democratic institution that promotes the social and economic needs of the individual as well as the development needs of the country. The debate has materialized in the drafting of a National Education Charter for the whole education system, which has received royal assent and is now being debated in the Moroccan parliament (COSEF 1999; MESFCRS 1999).

Reform within the National Education Charter

The component of the National Education Charter dealing with higher education is the result of reform texts drafted between 1995 and 2001. University faculty commissioned by the Ministry of Higher Education contributed directly and representatives of the teachers' union who sat as members of the national commission contributed indirectly to the drafting of the charter. The most important goal of the reform is to set up a system of higher education that is flexible enough to adapt to the rapid changes brought about by the process of globalization, better integrated into the socioeconomic environment, receptive to the contribution of other sectors, and effective enough to meet the needs of individuals and the community, but also designed in such a way that it lends itself to rigorous control and regulation mechanisms (e.g., internal and external evaluation, quality assessment procedures, etc.) aiming to assess its effectiveness and efficiency. Obviously, the implication here is that the present system of higher education lacks these qualities; hence, there is a need to introduce radical changes likely to contribute to the development of a system that exhibits the desired features listed above.

In order to achieve this general aim, the authors of the charter advocate a new, more rational and coherent approach to the governance of institutions of higher education and the establishment of institutions that will assume teaching and training roles consistent with the requirements of progress of knowledge and economic and social development. This also implies the design of a system based on competitiveness, diversification, and regulation and an institutional framework that allows for the involvement of the private sector as a contributing factor in the development of the university system.

The charter stipulates the need for the public and private sectors to cooperate with regard to institutions of higher education as embodied in three types of institutions: public universities, private profit-making universities to be established and managed by the private sector, and not-for-profit, fully autonomous universities that derive their funding from such sources as student fees, private patronage, consultancy, and renting of premises. From a functional point of view, two types of institutions are proposed: (a) Instituts Supérieurs d'Enseignement Fondamental (ISEF) and Instituts Supérieurs d'Enseignement Technologique (ISET); and (b) universities.

Instituts Supérieurs d'Enseignement Fondamental and Instituts Supérieurs d'Enseignement Technologique are colleges designed to absorb the initial intake of secondary school graduates, provide a common core program of general education that combines instruction and training over a period of two years, and provide students with basic intellectual, scientific, and technological knowledge that will enable them to cope with the potential demands of the job market. Students at ISEF will have three choices of majors: math, computer science, and physics; biology, chemistry, and geology; and humanities and social sciences and law and economics. Study programs at the ISET will emphasize professional and vocational skills with the goal of training skilled labor able to meet the immediate and long-term demands of the job market and be adaptable to technological innovation. After a two-year period, the performance of graduates of ISEF institutions will qualify them to either join the employment market as mid-level personnel or enroll in one of the universities for a B.A. degree in the discipline most compatible with their area of concentration during their first two years in postsecondary education.

Three kinds of universities are to be established:

- Public universities designed to carry out a teaching and research mission and assume a more active role in the development of higher education
- Private not-for-profit universities designed to stimulate competition among institutions of higher education and demonstrate high standards of quality likely to attract sponsorship and private funding
- Private profit-making universities to relieve the heavy burden of public universities and offer more diverse learning and training opportunities, thus contributing to the development of higher education and to the socioeconomic development of the country

Scientific research, both fundamental and applied, constitutes an important part of the higher education component of the national charter. Its basic aims are to contribute to the assimilation, mastery, and adaptation of science and technology and to foster the advancement of knowledge and the promotion of science and culture. The structural organization of scientific research is assigned to a number of national institutions, such as the Higher Council for Scientific Research and the National Foundation for Research, which are endowed with enough autonomy to establish a national research policy that takes into consideration economic priorities and the country's overall development strategy (MESFCRS 1997, 20).

Given the new emphasis on the autonomous and decentralized character of institutions of higher education, an important innovation in the higher education component of the national charter is the introduction of regulatory bodies responsible for establishing and ensuring standards of quality and fair competition through a process of evaluation and accreditation. One of these regulating bodies is the National Commission for Evaluation and Accreditation, which has been entrusted in the last two years with the task of assessing the training and research program proposals submitted for the establishment of graduate Research and Development Units. Although no systematic study has been carried out on the impact of the evaluation and accreditation work this institution has performed, the general impression is that teams of teachers whose proposals have not been accredited still demonstrate a lot of reticence toward this innovation. This points to the potentially negative reactions that some stakeholders in higher education are likely to demonstrate when various aspects of the new reform are implemented.

GOVERNANCE AND FUNDING OF HIGHER EDUCATION

The administrative aspects of the governance and financing of higher education in Morocco have always constituted controversial issues that have rather negatively affected the degree of success of the various reforms attempted so far. In this respect, the National Education Charter includes a number of changes that have already stirred heated debate, particularly about the nomination and election of members of university governing bodies and the introduction of some form of student fees to contribute to the financing of higher education.

THE ADMINISTRATION OF HIGHER EDUCATION

Ever since the inception of the Moroccan system of higher education, university presidents and deans have been nominated by royal decree upon recommendation by the Ministry of Higher Education. In spite of continual challenges to this procedure by the academic profession, presidents and deans have been accountable only to the government, represented by the Ministry of Higher Education, and political circumstances have been instrumental in the nomination or dismissal of these university officials. The higher education component of the newly drafted national charter deals with the issue in rather ambiguous terms. This controversy has been taken up in recent articles in the media, which points to the likelihood of very heated arguments and the need to reconcile relatively opposed views concerning the matter. Although the views held by different parties have not been made public, officials of the Ministry of Higher Education and parties allied with the government seem to opt for a procedure whereby university presidents, deans, and vice-

deans should be selected from a pool of applicants who fulfill criteria of suitability for each of the positions. Representatives of the academic profession, in contrast, aspire to a more democratic and transparent procedure in which university administrators would be elected by their peers and be held accountable first to the academic community. Debate about this issue is likely to continue before some form of compromise is reached.

The other bodies involved in the governance of higher education (e.g., university councils, which are presided over by presidents, and faculty councils and faculty scientific councils, which are presided over by deans) are made up of a majority of members elected by their peers, but the restricted consultative role that has been assigned to them thus far will also be an important issue for debate at the national level before a final decision is made about the adoption of the proposed National Education Charter. In addition, the form and extent of student representation in these bodies is also likely to constitute a "hot" issue on the agenda of the student movement and stakeholders in higher education who value democracy.

FINANCING HIGHER EDUCATION

In order to understand the resistance of authorities to a more democratic approach to the governance of higher education, it is important to bear in mind that the financing of the system has been a responsibility of the state throughout the history of the Moroccan university, which government officials believe is a justification of their claim to be sole managers of the funds made available to institutions. Resistance to change by members of the academic community in this respect is more related to the fear that job security—which has been guaranteed historically by the fact that as civil servants, faculty enjoy an automatic right to tenure—may be endangered. The government's demonstrated inability to maintain appropriate funding for all institutions of higher education may lead it to partially abdicate its responsibility and thereby lay the groundwork for the introduction of a contract-based recruitment and tenure policy. As job security is one of the most valued prerogatives of university teachers, this may lead the academic community to resist changes in the funding system of higher education.

Education in general, and higher education in particular, has always been free in Morocco. Moreover, it is only in the last ten years or so that restrictions on grants to students living with their families have been implemented and that the idea of students contributing financially to their studies has been alluded to in the various reform projects leading to the drafting of the National Education Charter. Given the fact that a large majority of Moroccan families are unable to financially contribute to the education of their children, a decision to introduce fees in higher education is likely to meet with staunch resistance on the part of those most concerned, namely students and their families. The national charter, although it does not provide details on the matter, stipulates that financially able families will be required to make a contribution and that some form of student loan system will be introduced.

Given the state's inability to maintain the required levels of financial support for higher education, it seems that the financing policy that has prevailed since the beginning of the

Moroccan university cannot be sustained anymore. Therefore, institutions will be called upon to seek other opportunities of funding and diversify their sources of financial income if they wish to enjoy the degree of independence to which they aspire. Some of the ideas suggested by Teferra (1999) for African higher education as ways to generate income have also been advanced (consultancy and technical services, cooperation with private businesses, effective resource-sharing mechanisms, and other income-generating programs) in the context of Moroccan higher education. This warrants the development of a new culture and new thinking which should contribute to the promotion of institutional autonomy and academic freedom.

THE ACADEMIC PROFESSION

Perceived Status

In spite of characteristics specific to the local Moroccan context, the situation of Moroccan academics is not very different from that described for academics working elsewhere internationally. The "rapid loss of status . . . [and] reputation among various professions [and] relative losses of income" reported by Enders (1999, 14) for academic staff in the European Union typifies the way Moroccan academics perceive themselves and, to a large extent, explains the lack of motivation that has been noticed in their attitude toward their profession. Moreover, the public perception that university teachers are responsible for what are considered to be falling standards, the failure of higher education to effectively prepare students for integration within the employment market, and some teachers' involvement in illicit dealings have led to public blame of the academic profession for the crisis of higher education.

The fact that university teachers are, as is still the case in many parts of the world, civil servants (*fonctionnaires*) makes their status vulnerable to political and socioeconomic circumstances that determine the overall status of the profession and its standing in the eyes of public opinion. For although they enjoy relative job security with guaranteed promotion and tenure, university teachers receive salaries that are far inferior to the salaries paid to people with equal qualifications in other professions, particularly in the private sector. As a result, moonlighting in private institutions and consultancy in the private sector have become additional ways to make ends meet. This situation accounts for the fact that the improvement of their material conditions has always been high on the agenda of university teachers, sometimes even at the expense of academic considerations.

The growing restrictions on government funding of higher education and the lack of opportunities to improve the material situation of academic staff have led to the search for alternative financing sources and institutional involvement in income-raising activities that would benefit both the institution and faculty. Such activities are distance teaching, consultancy work, teaching of courses (i.e., private teaching) in private institutions that are planned by universities and carried out by their teaching staff, research work commissioned and financed by agencies in the private sector, and publication of research using the universities' own word-processing and printing facilities. In this way,

faculty members involved in such activities would not have to look for moonlighting opportunities outside their institutions; these solutions would thus contribute to preserving what most professors still perceive as an honorable profession.

RESEARCH AND TEACHING

Research

In the new "alternance" government, a Department of State in charge of scientific research that is attached to the Ministry of Higher Education has been created. As a result, the budget allocated to higher education in 1998–1999 included an allowance exclusively reserved for scientific research (45 million Moroccan Dirhams, or US$4.5 million; CERSS 1999, 338). Moreover, the secretary of state for scientific research has declared before Parliament that decision makers agree that the development of scientific research calls for the constitution of consultative representative bodies to contribute to (a) planning scientific research and defining priorities and national programs; (b) coordinating and ensuring follow-up of state policy in scientific research; and (c) establishing institutions responsible for coordinating the various research programs (CERSS 1999).

At the institutional level, the status of research and the nature of research activities varies according to the type of institution concerned. Research, in comparison to teaching, has been accorded due importance in institutions of specialized higher education in which relatively adequate funding has been made available through projects and research contracts with the private sector, international development agencies, or foreign universities, particularly in France, the United States, and Germany. In contrast, research in institutions of the traditional type (for example faculties of science, law and economics, and humanities and social sciences) has generally been of the degree-seeking type in which individual teachers carry out research to obtain the *Diplome d'Etudes Supérieures* (DES, roughly equivalent to the M.A.) or the *Doctorat d'Etat* (Ph.D.) degrees for purposes of promotion from one administrative rank to the next. It is only in the last five years that teachers in these institutions have become more motivated to carry out research work other than the degree-seeking type, particularly as the new reform of higher education is meant to incorporate some form of evaluation of teaching and research when decisions related to promotion are being made. A further incentive for these teachers to get involved in research is the setting up of research and development units for graduate programs, of which 550 were accredited in 1998–1999 (CERSS 1999). The National Commission for Accreditation and Evaluation, an agency attached to the State Secretariat for Scientific Research, is entrusted with the task of making decisions about the accreditation of these units on the basis of evaluation reports submitted by academic "experts" who take into consideration a number of criteria that the agency itself defines. It is funded by the government and its role is likely to become more important with the introduction of the new reform, which emphasizes the processes of evaluation and accreditation. Overall, however, the rather insignificant status of research in institutions of higher education is reflected in the small number of research projects submitted in the humanities and social sciences and accredited by the newly established Program for Assistance to Scientific Research (PARS).

Difficulties with the publication of research work, which have been reported for most developing countries, are also a drawback of the system of higher education in Morocco. Generally speaking, Moroccan researchers who do not enjoy the privilege of belonging to an "old boy" publishing network find it difficult, sometimes impossible, to have their research work published. As publication facilities within the country are scanty and do not allow the desired dissemination of results, motivation to carry out research work is rather low and, as mentioned above, is often restricted to degree-seeking research.

Teaching

Ever since the creation of the Moroccan university, the recruitment of teaching staff has been carried out on the basis of degrees with little or no consideration for attested commitment to teaching or teaching performance, although most of the first faculty recruited to teach at the university had taught at secondary school. The almost total Moroccanization of teaching staff that was achieved through a "trainer training" program has led to a situation in which the junior faculty constitute a majority (71.13 percent in 1997–1998) in a system in which career advancement is a very slow process. This explains why less than 30 percent of the university faculty in Morocco have achieved seniority and reached professorship, a process that has, in most cases, been dependent on how early in his or her career the individual obtained the doctorate degree and on the subsequent number of years of teaching.

The system of promotion of faculty is an important issue that is still being discussed by the government and the teachers' union as part of the new reform. Whereas promotion within ranks was automatic after two or three years and promotion between ranks was conditional on obtaining a given degree (the equivalent of an M.A. for assistant lecturer and the equivalent of a Ph.D. for a lecturer), the new reform texts stipulate that both types of promotion be determined by the candidate's attested commitment to the institution (carrying out of administrative tasks, contribution to the image of the institution, etc.), teaching performance, and publication. These criteria are to be taken into consideration by the Scientific Council in decision making about the speed of promotion within ranks and promotion between ranks.

Another feature of higher education in Morocco is that staff development has been an alien concept to the Moroccan academic profession; it was only in 1997–1998 that a promotion procedure was introduced that took into consideration commitment to teaching as one of its criteria. Although lip service is paid to the need for faculty to update knowledge about their disciplines of specialization and developments in teaching and assessment methodology, concern with such issues is an individual matter and attempts to impose any form of staff development activities by the administration have been considered a breach of academic freedom.

Although no systematic study has been carried out to investigate the relationship between research and teaching, two opposite views prevailed before the introduction of both teaching and research as the two most important criteria in the promotion of teachers by the scientific committees of institutions of higher education. A first group held the view that "those who know how to, teach, and those who don't, do research," and a second group were of the opinion that "those who can do research, do, and those who can't, teach"! This has also led to the development of two subcultures within academia and antagonisms that are likely to be exacerbated if scientific committees that are responsible for making recommendations concerning the promotion of faculty are not attentive enough to the equal importance of research and teaching in institutions of higher education.

SPECIAL ISSUES IN HIGHER EDUCATION

Governance and Financing

A number of reform projects drafted since the beginning of the 1990s have culminated in the establishment of the National Education Charter, of which the higher education component is at present being debated among all stakeholders. In particular, a series of legal texts are in the process of becoming law and should result in an implementation of the reform starting from October 2000. A number of changes related to governance have been actually implemented beginning in the academic year 2001–2002. For example, the nine newly appointed university presidents have gone through a selection process in which the most important criterion considered by the selection committee was the quality of their project for the university that each was a candidate for.

An important innovation in this reform of higher education is the new system of appointment of university presidents and deans of faculties, wherein three candidates will be shortlisted for each position by a special committee before a final decision about nomination is made. However modest, this change is seen as a relatively democratic procedure in comparison to the old system in which university presidents and deans were nominated by royal decree on the recommendation of the Ministry of Higher Education.

A second innovation concerning the governance of higher education is that the management of universities is to become a responsibility of the president and a governing board, among whose members are representatives of both teachers and students who are elected by their peers. The president and the governing board will enjoy important decision-making prerogatives characteristic of autonomous and decentralized systems of higher education.

Financing higher education is an issue closely related to governance in that a democratic pattern of university management is dependent on at least some degree of financial autonomy. Given that the government has nearly always been the only provider of funds to institutions of higher education, it is easy to understand why the system has been so highly bureaucratic and centralized and characterized by rigid laws concerning the use of budget allocations across expenditure categories. A paradox worth noting in the context of higher education in Morocco is that since faculty are civil servants whose salaries have always been paid by the government, representatives of the profession tend to ignore the dependency of governance on financing, taking for granted the responsibility of the government but at the same time claiming autonomy for university institutions. Therefore, the relative abdication of financial liability by the authorities introduced in the new charter is likely to meet with strong resistance by the teachers' union, particularly in the case of vulnerable institutions, such as faculties of humanities and social sciences, in which opportunities to attract private funds are limited and expertise in the preparation of funding proposals is lacking.

The new charter has also introduced changes that imply that the taken-for-granted government financial support of the university will now take the form of a "budget" rather than an "allowance." This emphasizes the need for institutions of higher education to seek other sources of funding by attracting potential private funds, establishing consultancy services, hiring out facilities, and developing their own capacity to control their financial assets (Teferra 1999, 8). It also points to the need to address the very sensitive issue of charging fees, at the same time ensuring equity through some kind of "student-based fee policy that is tied to the family's ability to pay" (Hauptman 1999, 6), particularly since this criterion of equity is more and more a valued tenet in a country in which the winds of democracy are blowing.

Attrition and Unemployment

The extremely high attrition rates reported in the context of higher education in Morocco (up to 75 percent in some institutions) have been accounted for by a number of factors, such as lack of consistency between the student's choice of a discipline of study at the university and his/her real abilities as attested by his/her academic performance, inability to adapt to the rigorous demands of academic life, family and financial problems, and, most surprisingly, administrators' and teachers' concern with upholding standards. As a matter of fact, faculty and administrators in some cases take pride in the high rates of failure in their institutions, considering this to be an indicator of the "seriousness" of the assessment procedures and strict criteria they adopt for evaluating students. As a result, failure rates of 75 percent are a norm at the Moroccan university, particularly in the non-specialized sector, in which pass rates of more than 30 percent are often considered with suspicion by administrators and even faculty members. For students, repetition of courses has become a common feature of their experience of higher education. The average number of years a student takes to complete the four-year B.A. degree has been estimated at eight years. This has led to a drastic increase in the number of students repeating or even re-repeating the same year and has placed a heavy burden on institutions that were initially designed to accommodate no more than 20 percent of their present student population. This situation has also contributed to a feeling of frustration among students and their perception that the main aim of the system is to jettison as many of them as possible.

As attested by studies on attrition and related issues such as drop-out and retention rates, students' experience of higher education is very much determined by their ability to adapt to the academic environment by adopting learning strategies most consistent with the prevailing culture, and by developing their ability to cope with the demands of the current assessment sys-tem. Because no organized structure for advising and helping first-year students to adapt to their new environment exists, a great number among them make choices of disciplines totally inconsistent with their abilities and interests and end up either repeating a grade two or three times or dropping out when they realize that it is too late to opt for other disciplines of study. Because research into issues in higher education is an almost alien area in the Moroccan university, the real causes and effects of attrition in this context remain uncertain, and potential strategies to reduce the appallingly high rates of failure and the ensuing drop-out rates are yet to be established.

As mentioned above, the mission assigned to higher education after the country's independence was to train nationals to take over positions in the administration and other areas of the public sector. At that time, jobs were guaranteed to all graduates. However, starting from the late 1970s and particularly in the early 1980s, this labor-training mission became obsolete as the requirements of the job market totally changed in the context of the new international socioeconomic order. This situation led to a gradual increase in the inconsistency between education and training programs offered by the university and the needs of the job market. As a result, university graduates found it more and more difficult to integrate into their socioeconomic environment successfully. Thus, unemployment among graduates became the key issue which successive governments have tried to address—with very little, if any, success. This obviously has engendered dissatisfaction and high levels of frustration among students who had developed very high expectations concerning the ability of the university to help them achieve the socioeconomic and cultural status formerly associated with a university degree. The almost daily sit-ins, demonstrations, and even hunger strikes organized by associations of unemployed graduates all over the country attest to the urgency of the issue and the need for decision-making bodies in higher education to introduce changes likely to contribute to more consistency between a student's education and training and the real needs of the job market.

The Assessment System

A summative end-of-the-year type of evaluation prevails in institutions of higher education, with the exception of institutions of specialized higher education, in which a relatively continual type is used. This system does not allow any form of feedback to students to assess the strengths and weaknesses of their performance or to teachers to introduce changes in content, teaching methodology, or assessment procedures. In most institutions, a student's performance is measured on the basis of criteria that are often known only to those who set examinations, and strictly quantitative measures are used for making pass or fail decisions. As a result, students may repeat a year two or three times without knowing the specific reasons for their failure or how they can subsequently improve their academic results. The high rates of failure that characterize the Moroccan university system account for the attrition rates mentioned above and constitute an important determinant of students' growing perception of time spent at the university as a traumatizing and frustrating experience.

Surprisingly, attempts to reform the system of evaluation and introduce a more formative component have met with resistance, particularly from students, who tend to see a continual type of assessment as an indirect means of making attendance compulsory, which they consider to be a breach of their freedom. Moreover, in spite of lip service to the need for drastic changes in the evaluation procedures now prevailing in higher education, both teachers and administration are likely to show at least the same degree of resistance as students to some kind of reform of the system. The reason for this is that it would mean a heavier working and marking load for faculty and more commitment on the part of the administration to provide the facilities necessary for the implementation of a new system of evaluation. Given these restrictions, it seems that only a reform of the whole system—including content, methodology of teaching, and institutional organization—is likely to induce less resistance on the part of all concerned. Such a reform would contribute to improving students' performance, reducing rates of attrition, and making the years a student spends at the university a more enjoyable and rewarding experience.

Some of the advantages of a formative-oriented system of evaluation are that it would not only provide the necessary feedback to the student but it would also foster teachers' concern with introducing changes in content, methodology, and assessment procedures. This implies their involvement in staff development activities designed to "extend the knowledge, skills and attitudes of the staff of universities or colleges of higher education" (Brew 1995, 1) and is likely to strengthen the quality of education and training provided by their institution.

The Language of Instruction

Following the policy of the Arabization of education that was adopted immediately after the country's independence, a number of disciplines, such as mathematics, physics, chemistry, and natural science, which previously had been taught in French, were Arabized at the secondary school level. In higher education, Arabic became the language of instruction for most disciplines in the humanities and social sciences. Disciplines in law and economics followed a bilingual pattern of Arabic and French. Science and technology–related disciplines were taught exclusively in French. The total Arabization in secondary schools of the science-related disciplines and their teaching in French at university negatively affected the chances of students who enrolled in faculties of science. Although partial solutions to the problem have been devised in the form of translation sessions at secondary school and reinforcement French classes at university, students' negative reaction has been registered in the decrease in enrollment rates at faculties of science; many students choose economics, the humanities, or the social sciences instead.

The new National Education Charter stipulates the introduction of a flexible system whereby students can choose a language of instruction, including Arabic, French, or even English, starting from the final stages of secondary school. This should allow them to opt for the same language of instruction at university and thereby solve the problem now prevailing in the case of students at faculties of science. However, given that the language

issue has always been a highly sensitive one politically, serious discussion is necessary before some kind of consensus is reached on the matter.

THE STUDENT MOVEMENT

Ever since the establishment of the Moroccan university, student activism has been one of the most important determining factors in shaping the pattern of higher education in Morocco. The highly political communist and socialist orientation of the student movement up to the mid-1980s has, at various stages in the history of higher education, influenced the course of political events in the country. Students have always been at the forefront of political activism, often as members of the youth sections of opposition political parties but also as members of the National Union of Moroccan Students.

Recent developments in the political situation in Morocco, particularly the coming to power of the opposition and the rise of Islamic-oriented parties, have led to a new situation on the university campus that is characterized by a more visible activism on the part of student groups affiliated with the Islamist parties. As a result, in contrast to the politically motivated demands put forward by leaders of the student movement in the 1970s, 1980s, and early 1990s, today's student demands are more likely to be limited to demands for better living conditions on campus, better learning facilities, improvements in student grants, and the right for students to take a more active part in the management of institutions of higher education. Another result is that the violent student demonstrations typical of earlier periods have now become less frequent, and very few prisoners, if any, in Moroccan jails are student leaders.

Given the existence of ideologically irreconcilable orientations in the student movement (primarily between Islamists and leftists), serious difficulties have developed concerning the organization of the movement and its ability to rally a majority of students around the political demands that were taken for granted and which constituted the very power of the student body until the early 1990s. However, with the advent of new education reforms, against which student leaders have voiced strong criticism for apparently political motives, there is a chance that the student movement will have a common cause around which to rally. This development could give the movement the power it seems to have lost as a stakeholder in political, social, and cultural changes in the country.

The Issue of Brain Drain

As is the case with other developing nations, Morocco has been affected at different levels by the phenomenon referred to as "brain drain." This tendency among national scholars and professionals started immediately after the country's independence in 1956, when a number of Moroccans who had been to university abroad, particularly in France, the colonizing power, chose to stay in the host country. Later, more and more highly qualified scholars and professionals, doctors, and engineers in particular, who had been trained in Morocco; decided to emigrate to Europe and North America, looking for what they considered to be better employment conditions and, in some cases, political asylum.

Although no reliable statistics are available to assess the extent of brain drain from Morocco, the number of university graduates seeking employment and better working facilities abroad has been constantly growing, in spite of the prevailing politically favorable conditions for the return of Moroccan expatriates.

An even more alarming trend of brain drain from Morocco is the decision to emigrate by long-established and successful scholars and professionals (again doctors, engineers, and pharmacists), who emigrate to the United States and Canada, hoping to ensure better educational and employment opportunities not for themselves but for their children. As a real solution to the problem of unemployment among graduates has yet to be found, the risk is high that the phenomenon of brain drain will negatively affect the socioeconomic development of the country.

CHALLENGES AND IMPLICATIONS

Like universities all over the world where "academic institutions and systems have faced pressures of increasing numbers of students and demographic changes, demands for accountability, [and] reconsideration of the social and economic role of higher education" (Altbach and Davis 1999, 2), the Moroccan university is in a state of crisis and is facing tremendous challenges which must be met if it is to effectively accomplish its mission. In conformity with the political transition toward genuine democracy and the culture of human rights developing in the country, it must develop a system of governance which is flexible, democratic, and accountable enough to effectively contribute to the quality of research, teaching, and learning in higher education. This system must strive to accommodate the needs, interests, and expectations of stakeholders, namely providers, participants, and the community.

At the institutional level, changes need to be introduced that have the potential to make the time the student spends at the university a positive experience, one that is devoted to learning how to learn and is enjoyable and rewarding. Curricula must undergo drastic reform to be more responsive to the socioeconomic and cultural demands of the development of the country and to the challenges of globalization. The introduction of a formative-oriented evaluation system aims not only at assessing the students' performance but also at providing feedback on the process of teaching, learning, and assessment procedures to teachers, students, and the administration. The most important aim of such evaluation is to promote the introduction of change that will improve practices in higher education. Such a system is likely to attenuate dissatisfaction and frustration among all concerned and foster a more positive attitude conducive to a reduction of the high rates of failure among students. A reform of assessment procedures, together with the establishment of an organizational structure that seeks to help students make informed choices about disciplines of study consistent with their abilities and interests, should contribute to a partial solution to the problem of attrition that has always plagued Moroccan higher education. Thus, relevance and equity, which are so emphasized as criteria of an effective system of higher education, can be enhanced, and students will be likely to feel responsible for their own learning and the outcome of their studies.

As do universities throughout the world, the Moroccan university must be able to respond to the challenge of globalization. In addition to the introduction of technology as an essential component of teaching and research, Moroccan higher education must show more commitment to regional and international cooperation by moving away from the Eurocentric orientation it has adopted so far and seeking more variety in its partnership endeavors. In particular, regional cooperation with African and other Arab universities must be fostered, particularly since Morocco is in an ideal position to organize the exchange of students and faculty and get involved in research and the sharing of expertise.

The long tradition of the Moroccan university and the current reforms taking place at the political level constitute assets for higher education that may enable it to change toward a more effective system, one that is able to achieve the purposes of quality, equity, and relevance. Whether this will take place and how soon it happens depends largely on the ability of forces that value change (administrators, teachers, and students) to develop flexible and effective institutional structures to defeat the skepticism of those who think that higher education has become "a passport to unemployment."

REFERENCES

Al Akhawayn University. 1999. "Mission Statement." In *Al Akhawayn University in Ifrane 1999–2000 Catalog*. Ifrane, Morocco: Al Akhawayn University.

Altbach, P. G., and M. D. Todd. 1999. "Global Challenge and National Response: Notes for an International Dialogue on Higher Education." *International Higher Education* 14: 2–5.

Belghazi, T., ed. 1996. *The Idea of the University*. Series Conferences and Colloquia no. 72. Rabat: Publications of the Faculty of Letters.

Brew, A., ed. 1995. "Trends and Influences." In A. Brew, ed., *Directions in Staff Development*, 1–16. Buckingham, U.K.: The Society for Research into Higher Education and Open University Press.

CERSS (Centre d'Etudes et de Recherche en Sciences Sociales). 1999. *Rapport stratégique du Maroc 1998/1999*. Rabat: Abhath.

Coffman, J. 1996. "Current Issues in Higher Education in the Arab World." *International Higher Education* 4 (Spring). Available online at: http://www.bc.edu/bc_org/avp/soe/cihe/newsletter/News04/textcy5.html

COSEF (Commission Spéciale de l'Enseignement et la Formation). 1999. *Projet de charte nationale pour l'education et la formation*. Morocco: Ministère de l'Education Nationale.

Court, D. 1980. "The Development Ideal in Higher Education: The Experience of Kenya and Tanzania." *Higher Education* 9: 650–680.

El Maslout, A. 1995. "La réforme de l'enseignement supérieur: Un processus continu d'adaptation et de restructuration." In *La réforme de l'enseignement au Maroc*, 21–58. Rabat: Association des Economistes Marocains.

Emran, A. 1997. *L'enseignement et la formation universitaire au Maroc*. Mohammedia: Imprimerie de Fedala.

———. 1999. *Attaᶜlimu bi lmaghrib wa rihanatu al islah: Al jamiᶜa al maghribia wa rihanatu addimuqratia*. Manshurat al Mawja.

Enders, J. 1999. "Working Conditions of Academic Staff in Western Europe." *International Higher Education* 16: 14–15.

Giesecke, H. C. 1999. "Private Higher Education in East Central Europe." *International Higher Education* 16 (Summer): 2–4.

Hauptman, A. M. 1999. "Student-Based Higher Education Financing Policies." *International Higher Education* 17 (Fall): 5–6.

Mazawi, A. E. 1999. "Gender and Higher Education in the Arab States." *International Higher Education*, no. 17 (Fall): 18–19.

Merrouni, M. 1996. "L'université et le paradigme de l'efficacité." In T. Belghazi, ed., *The Idea of the University*, 85–99. Series Conferences and Colloquia no. 72. Rabat: Publications of the Faculty of Letters.

MESFCRS (Ministère de l'Enseignement Supérieur, de la Formation des Cadres et de la Recherche Scientifique). 1997. *Projet de réforme de l'enseignement supérieur et de la recherche scientifique*. Rabat: Arabian Al Hilal.

——. 1999. *Ihsayiat Jami'iya 1997–1998* [Higher Education Statistics]. Rabat: Department of Evaluation and Future Perspectives.

MPEP (Ministère de la Prévision Economique et du Plan). 1998. *Annuaire Statistique du Maroc 1998*. Rabat: Direction de la Statistique.

——. 1999. *Le Maroc en Chiffres*. Rabat: Direction de la Statistique. Available online at: http://www.statistic.gov.ma

Ouakrime, M. 1985. "English Language Teaching in Higher Education in Morocco: An Evaluation of the Fez Experience." Ph.D. thesis, University of London.

——. 1996. "What Is High about Higher Education?" In T. Belghazi, ed., *The Idea of the University*, 355–367. Series Conferences and Colloquia no. 72. Rabat: Publications of the Faculty of Letters.

Reddy, J. 1999. "African Realities and Global Challenges." *International Higher Education* 17 (Fall): 10–11.

Teferra, D. 1999. "Ideas for Financing in Higher Education." *International Higher Education* 17 (Fall): 7–8.

48

Mozambique

Arlindo Chilundo

INTRODUCTION

Mozambique, located along the southeastern coast of Africa, gained its independence in 1975 and enjoyed a relatively short time of peace. Six months after its declaration of independence, the country became an object of a Southern Rhodesian war of destabilization. In the early 1980s, the South African regime of apartheid stepped up the destruction of Mozambique.

After the early 1980s, Mozambique faced a long period of economic crisis, political and military instability, and a war that ended only in 1992, when a peace agreement between the government and the Mozambique National Resistance (RENAMO) was signed in Rome, followed by the country's first multiparty elections in 1994.

During the war, much of the country's infrastructure was destroyed. The destruction included schools, hospitals, and rural clinics and provoked massive waves of population displacement, resettlement, and migration. After the peace agreement in 1992, the country, then classified as the poorest country in the world, embarked on a major reconstruction of its economic and social infrastructure. In the second half of the 1990s, however, Mozambique achieved one of the fastest rates of economic growth and became Africa's fastest-growing economy. Real output growth rate averaged over 8 percent per year between 1994 and 2000 (World Bank and IMF 1999). In 1997–2000, before the major floods of 2000, the average annual growth rate exceeded 10 percent. The broad base of this economic growth is also significant in that agriculture, which sustains more than 90 percent of the population, recorded an average real output growth rate of about 9 percent in the same period. Concomitantly, the government maintained sound macroeconomic policies so that, for example, fiscal deficits have been low (at about 2.5 percent) and inflation has dropped from about 46 percent in 1988 to less than 7 percent in the period between 1997 and early 2000 (World Bank and IMF 1999).

Still, Mozambique remains an extremely poor country. Average per capita gross domestic product (GDP) is only US$218 per year. About 70 percent of the population lives below the poverty line. The minimum wage is equivalent to only $25 per month. The economy also remains fragile. There is a large balance-of-trade deficit, with an imports-to-exports ratio of 3 to 1. The country is heavily reliant on external development assistance. In recent years, external grants have represented about 40 percent of the total annual government budget. Without these grants, the country's current account deficit would be in a crisis range of double-digit figures, but in the past three years, it has not exceeded 2.6 percent. The maintenance of monetary and fiscal stability is still extremely dependent on sustaining high levels of external assistance.

Despite this recent period of economic stabilization and growth, Mozambique still remains one of the poorest countries in the world. According to the Mozambique Poverty Reduction Plan, the indicators of poverty are as follows:

- Median monthly consumption per capita is about 160,780.00 Meticais, equivalent to about $11.
- 69.4 percent of Mozambicans (about 10.9 million people) live below the level of absolute poverty. In rural areas, where 80 percent of the population is concentrated, the poverty rate is 71.2 percent, compared to 62 percent in urban areas.
- The infant mortality rate is about 147 per thousand (Republic of Mozambique 1995).

The devastating floods and cyclones in 2000, the worst in living memory, destroyed infrastructures worth more than $449.5 million. Because of this disaster, the economy has slowed down.

The 1997 census revealed a total population of 16.5 million, with a predominance of women (52 percent), especially in the rural areas. The average size of a family is 4.1 persons, while life expectancy at birth is only 44.4 years. The population is very young: 46 percent of the total population is under 15 years old. Of these, 18 percent are children under 5 years, and the economically active population (15 years or older) is only 36.7 percent of the total (INE 1999a).

Portuguese is the official language and the language of instruction in all levels of education in Mozambique, although the latest census reports that it is the mother tongue of less than 2 percent of the population. Apart from Portuguese, there are about thirteen main Mozambican languages (Emakhuwa, Xitsonga, Ciyao, Cisena, Cishona, Echuwabo, Cinyanja, Xironga, Shimaconde, Cinyungue, Cicopi, Bitonga, and Kiswahili, some of which have one or more dialects). In secondary schools, English and French are taught as subjects.

HISTORY OF HIGHER EDUCATION IN MOZAMBIQUE

Higher education in Mozambique was initially established by the Portuguese in 1962, when the General University Studies of Mozambique (EGUM) were introduced. These studies functioned as branches of Portuguese universities and were mainly designed to serve settlers' children in Mozambique. Nine programs (courses) were then offered, namely pedagogical sciences, medicine and surgery, civil engineering, mechanical engineering, electro-technical engineering, chemical engineering, agronomy, forestry, and veterinary sciences.

Between 1965 and 1968, the general university studies were expanded. New programs and courses, such as lecturer training for secondary schools (1965), theoretical and applied mathematics, physics, chemistry, biology (1967), and geology (1968), were introduced.

In 1968, the general university studies were upgraded to form a university that came to be known as the University of Lourenço Marques (ULM). This university discriminated against black Mozambicans. In fact, until 1974, Mozambican students constituted less than 0.1 percent of the student population (UEM 1999a).

Despite its discriminatory nature, ULM expanded its scope in terms of programs offered. By 1974, seventeen courses were being offered, including new courses in Romanic philology, history, geography, economy, metallurgical engineering, mining engineering, and mathematics.

The political independence of Mozambique in 1975 marked an end to the discriminatory nature of ULM. In 1976, ULM was changed into Eduardo Mondlane University (UEM) and became the first national university of Mozambique.

When UEM was established in 1976, it had a student population of 2,400. These numbers dropped drastically from 1977 onward, stabilizing in 1989 when 1974–1975 figures were reached again, then growing from 1990 onward (UEM 1999a).

A number of reforms were then introduced aimed at responding to a new social demand and at facing the challenges of a new country with an urgent need for university graduates to work on the multiple fronts of social, economic, cultural, and scientific development.

From 1976 to 1983, UEM development efforts included the renovation and democratization of university structures, the opening of new courses seen as essential in the new phase, the recruitment and training of a Mozambican teaching staff (in

1975, there were five Mozambicans), and the adjustment of curriculum structure to the immediate needs of the labor market, especially the opening of courses at the baccalaureate level (the baccalaureate required a three-year degree program). During this period, UEM was also called upon to respond to such specific tasks as the quick preparation of students at pre-university level (the so-called *propaedeutic* courses) and the establishment of lecturers' training courses, for which the Faculty of Education was created in 1981.

This period witnessed steps toward comprehensive curriculum reform, which led to the introduction, in the early 1980s, of five-year undergraduate programs, known locally as *licenciaturas*. Because the university had relied on expatriate lecturers since independence, a new strategy was undertaken to recruit, train, and retain Mozambican teaching staff. New university collective management bodies were also introduced.

The university also offered management training for workers of companies to prepare them for their jobs, and courses to give access to higher education for those meeting the necessary prerequisites. To meet this demand, UEM opened the Faculty for Fighters and Vanguard Workers (FACOTRAV) in the 1980s.

In 1985, a Higher Pedagogical Institute (ISP) was established outside of UEM. The creation of ISP emerged in direct response to the increased social demand for lecturers. Before the creation of ISP, the UEM Faculty of Education absorbed 50 percent of all new admissions.

The establishment of ISP in 1985 by the Ministry of Education heralded a new era in the history of higher education in Mozambique, the era of plurality. UEM was no longer the only higher education institution in the country. A year later, a Higher Institute for International Relations (ISRI) was also established.

This plurality of higher education institutions called for the creation of a body that would coordinate the whole system. The Ministry of Education introduced admission examinations to higher education in 1991. In 1993, the Parliament approved the Law of Higher Education and established the National Council for Higher Education. This laid the legal basis for the approval of new higher education institutions.

In 1995, the Higher Pedagogical Institute was upgraded to the Pedagogical University, thus becoming the second public university in the country. It swiftly opened branches in the provinces in Beira and Nampula.

The Nautical School of Mozambique (ENM), created in 1985 as a medium-level vocational school, was promoted to an institution qualified to offer higher education courses in 1991. The last public higher education institution to be created was the Academy of Police Sciences (ACIPOL), which was established in 1999 with the objective of training police officers with higher degrees.

In the meantime, the transition to a market economy in 1987 introduced new elements in the social, economic, and cultural environment—the private sector and civil society. A legal space was created that allowed the intervention of the private sector in higher education. In this context, private higher education institutions were established: the Higher Polytechnic and University Institute (ISPU) and the Catholic University of Mozambique (UCM), both of which were started in August

Table 48.1. Higher Education Institutions, Mozambique, 1999

Name of Institution	Year Established/ Upgraded to HE Status	Location	Number of Courses	Student Numbers
Public Institutions				
Eduardo Mondlane University (UEM)	1962 (renamed 1976)	Maputo	22	6,800
Pedagogic University (UP)	1985 (renamed 1995)	Maputo plus branches in Sofala and Nampula	12	1,987
Higher Institute for International Relations (ISRI)	1986	Maputo	1	234
Nautical School of Mozambique (ENM)	Upgraded 1991	Maputo	3	No students in 1999
Academy of Police Sciences (ACIPOL)	1999	Maputo	2	No students in 1999
Private Institutions				
Higher Polytechnic and University Institute (ISPU)	1995	Maputo; branch in Quelimane, Zambézia)	8	919
Catholic University of Mozambique (UCM)	1995	Beira; branches in Nampula and Niassa	9	1,035
Higher Institute of Science and Technology of Mozambique (ISCTEM)	1996	Maputo	7	644
Mussa Bin Bique University (UMBB)	1998	Nampula	3	No students in 1999
Higher Institute of Transport and Communications (ISUTC)	1999	Maputo	3	No students in 1999

1996. The Higher Institute of Science and Technology of Mozambique (ISCTEM) was created in November 1996 and began its activities in 1997.

As the social demand for higher education was greater than the capacity in the already operating institutions, more private institutions were created. In 1998, the Mussa Bin Bique University (UMBB) was established in Nampula; and the Higher Institute for Transport and Communications (ISUTC) was created in 1999.

Among the existing private higher education institutions, the Catholic University is the only one that operates as a not-for-profit institution. It is based in Beira, the second-largest city in Mozambique, with branches in Nampula, the third-largest city, and in Cuamba (Niassa province), one of the most underdeveloped areas in the country. In addition to the Pedagogical University, which has branches in Beira and Nampula, and the Catholic University, a third institution, ISPU, also has a branch in Quelimane (Zambézia province).

Today, Mozambique has ten institutions of higher education. Their characteristics are summarized in Table 48.1.

Notwithstanding the high tuition fees of the private institutions, which are a result of the high social demand and the inability of the public sector to respond, they are filling an important void in the system. The mushrooming and booming of these private institutions during the last few years illustrates how much they are welcomed by the community. However, problems associated with the quality of the education offered and accreditation may eventually surface in the future when the labor market for graduates stabilizes and competition picks up.

GOVERNANCE AND MANAGEMENT

Up to 1999, the Ministry of Education supervised higher education institutions. The supervision was done through the National Council for Higher Education, which was chaired by the minister of education. The council did not have any deliberative power and was only a consultative body. In early 2000, a new Ministry of Higher Education, Science, and Technology (MESCT) was established. The new ministry is in charge of supervising the whole system of higher education in the country; developing general policies on higher education, science, and technology, as well as general guidelines on scientific research; proposing new legislation for the education system; monitoring the quality of higher education; and coordinating and assuring accreditation mechanisms for the higher education sector as a whole, including both public and private higher education institutions (HEIs).

Despite the creation of the MESCT, higher education institutions have enjoyed autonomy since the enactment of the Higher Education Law 1/93. This law established the National Council for Higher Education (CNES), an advisory body that consists of rectors of all functioning public and private HEIs.

Although the Law on Higher Education states that HEIs are autonomous, the precise degree of autonomy has often been a matter of dispute. In the case of UEM, the level of financial autonomy was increased by the signing of a program contract in December 1999 between the government and the university (represented by the minister of planning and finance and the rector, respectively). This gave the university a greater degree of autonomy than in the past. For example, it now receives funding quarterly, in advance, rather than monthly, as is the case with other public HEIs, and has greater freedom than before to allocate these funds. In return, the contract specifies the responsibilities and accountability requirements of the university. In many other aspects, the autonomy of HEIs is limited, though the overall academic autonomy of public HEIs is guaranteed by law.

Although most of the financial resources of the public HEIs come from the state, within the framework of the law governing higher education, UEM and other public institutions are free to introduce or terminate specific academic programs. Even during the period of the one-party-dominated state, faculty and administrative staff have always enjoyed academic freedom. The creation of the new Ministry of Higher Education for Science and Technology has not affected academic freedom, as it has only assumed a coordinating role.

THE MANAGEMENT OF PUBLIC INSTITUTIONS

The organic structure and functions at public HEIs are similar, with slight differences which arise from the fact that UP has two branch campuses (or "delegations") in Beira and Nampula, which requires special administrative structures to lead these delegations. (The rector, who is the senior officer or chief executive of the university, nominates a director of delegation, who is supported by two deputy directors.) There are other minor differences, but the systems of management and administration are broadly similar, so this section is based mainly on administration at UEM.

The University Council (UC) is the top decision-making body in the public HEIs and is chaired by the rector. This body is a strength in the public institutions because it makes the decision-making process democratic, although it is limited by the fact that the rector is the president. The UC is composed of:

- The vice-rector for resources and administration (ex-officio)
- The vice-rector for academic affairs (ex-officio)
- Representatives of deans of faculties
- Lecturers representing different levels (assistants and professors)
- Representatives of the student union
- A representative of the nonacademic staff's union

- Representatives of administrative staff
- Representatives of civil society
- Representatives of the government

At UEM, the UC also includes the director of the Museum of Natural History and the director of the National Historical Archive.

The rector is the academic and administrative leader of the university and is accountable to the UC; he is supported by an academic council, the vice-rector for resources and administration, and the vice-rector for academic affairs. Both the rector and vice-rectors are supported by the Council of Directors of the different areas (scientific, planning, finances, public relations, registrar, assets, and human resources) and the deans of faculties.

A major issue in the management and administration of public HEIs is the degree of bureaucracy and centralization. It has long been argued that administrative structures are too bureaucratic, with power overly concentrated in the central level, and critics have urged greater decentralization to give more power to the faculties and departments. At UEM, the Academic Council (AC) deals with all academic affairs (such as research, curriculum development, postgraduate training plans, academic promotions, etc.). However, the role of this body needs to be clarified and revised, and the division of responsibilities between the AC and faculties is one of the major issues in the administration of public HEIs.

At the faculty level, the top decisions at UEM are made by the faculty AC and the Council of the Faculty, which is composed of the heads of departments. These councils are led by the dean of faculty. The deputy dean for pedagogic affairs and the deputy dean for research and extension support the dean of faculty. At the department level, the lecturer's council of department and the council of department support the head of department. The basic managerial unit of a department is the section.

PRIVATE INSTITUTIONS

ISPU and ISCTEM have similar organizational structures: the rector is responsible for decision making and is supported by the Scientific Council for Academic Affairs, which is similar to the AC in the public institutions. ISPU has two schools, one for management and technology, with nine courses, and another for law and social sciences, with seven courses. Two directors manage these schools.

UCM depends on the Catholic Education Congregation and the Episcopal Conference of Mozambique. The individual governance of UCM is the responsibility of the chancellor, the rector, and one or more vice-rectors. The chancellor is the local archbishop, who is the spiritual leader and promotes religion within the university community. The rector has the same mandate as the rectors of the public institutions, although in the context of the Catholic religion. He or she is designated by the Mozambican Episcopal Conference. The rector is accountable to the UC, which is led by the chancellor. The rector is supported by the Rectorate Council and the Finance Management Council. The Rectorate Council assists the rector in every issue

Table 48.2. University Population in Mozambique, 1999

University	Total numbers			Percentages			Ratios		
	Students	Lecturers FTE total	Technical Staff	Students	Lecturers FTE total	Technical Staff	Students/ Lecturer	Students/ Technical Staff	Technical Staff/ Lecturer
UEM	6,800	631	1,833	73.4	6.8	19.8	11:1	4:1	3:1
UP	1,987	214	71	87.5	9.4	3.1	9:1	28:1	0.3:1
ISRI	234	50	23	76.2	16.3	7.5	5:1	10:1	0.5:1
Public	9,021	895	1,927	76.2	7.6	16.3	10:1	5:1	2:1
ISCTEM	644	57	53	85.4	7.6	7.0	11:1	12:1	1:1
ISPU	919	85	53	86.9	8.0	5.0	11:1	17:1	0.6:1
UCM	1,035	52	67	89.7	4.5	5.8	20:1	15:1	1:1
Private	2,598	194	173	87.6	6.5	5.8	13:1	15:1	1:1
Total	11,619	1,089	2,100	78.5	7.4	14.2	11:1	6:1	2:1

FTE = Full-time Equivalent.

related to the university and judges the regulations of the university and those of the units. The Rectorate Council is the Executive Secretariat of the UC.

The branch campuses, or regional centers, of UCM are led by a director who represents the rector, supported by an administrative committee, an executive secretariat, and an academic council. The academic councils of the regional centers are chaired by the director of the center and are composed of the directors of the basic units, directors of the departments, course coordinators, one lecturer for each course, presidents of the student associations, one student for each course, the director of social services, and the secretary of the center.

DEMOGRAPHICS

In this section we will briefly try to provide some statistical data on Mozambique's higher education population. Scantiness of reliable information on higher education in Mozambique is mainly a result of the absence of a reliable data bank on higher education in the country. Most information on higher education is scattered, which makes it very difficult to gather data for this kind of publication. Most of the information in this chapter is from 1999 and was gathered in the process of strategic planning for higher education.

Table 48.2 shows the total university population in Mozambique, including students and teaching and nonacademic staff (technical, administrative, and auxiliary workers) in the six HEIs for the academic year 1999–2000. Numbers for teaching staff include both full-time and part-time lecturers, and the table shows full-time equivalent (FTE) staff numbers, where two part-time lecturers are equal to one full-time lecturer. The table also shows the ratios of students to lecturers and students to nonacademic staff. On average there are almost twice as many non-

academic staff as lecturers in HEIs; in UEM, the ratio is nearly 3 to 1. This stems from the fact that UEM is currently providing too many social and auxiliary services in addition to teaching and research. The average student-to-lecturer ratio is 11 to 1, but the ratio is particularly low in ISRI (5 to 1) and high in UCM (20 to 1). There are even wider differences in the ratio of students to nonacademic staff, ranging from 4 to 1 in UEM to 28 to 1 in UP.

STUDENT POPULATION

In this section, I describe trends in student enrollment in the period 1990–1999. Figure 48.1 documents the trends in student enrollments since 1990, which shows a substantial growth in student numbers from 1990 to 1999. In 1990, Mozambique had only three public HEIs. In the next ten years, five new private HEIs were established, of which three (ISPU, ISCTEM, and UCM) account for nearly one-quarter of total enrollment in higher education. Total student numbers in 1999 were 11,619, of which 77.6 percent were in public and 22.4 percent in private institutions.

Student population increased steadily from 1990 to 1996. Since then, the growth has been much more rapid because of the development of the private sector. There was a tenfold increase in the number of students enrolled in private institutions between 1996, when the first private institutions opened with 262 students, and 1999, when 2,598 students were enrolled. The numbers at ISPU and UCM have grown particularly rapidly. The growth in private HEIs has not contributed to a decline in public-sector enrollment, which has, in fact, more than doubled from 3,750 in 1990 to 9,021 in 1999.

The proportion of female students has been gradually increasing since 1992, the first year for which a gender breakdown

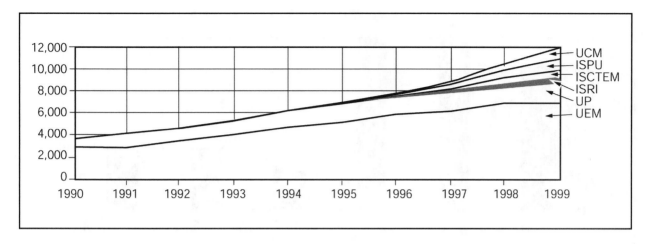

Fig. 48.1. *Higher Education Enrollments in Mozambique, 1990–1999*

is available. The ratio of male to female students remained high (at the range of 2.79 and 3.06) between 1990 and 1996 but fell to 2.45 and 2.59 in 1998 and 1999. This was partly due to the opening of private HEIs, where the proportion of female students is higher than in the public HEIs (43 percent on average in private HEIs in 1999, compared with only 25 percent in the public sector).

The participation rate of females in university education continues to remain far below that of males, even though the situation is improving. Overall, there has been a tendency for the ratio to fall over the last three years (from 2 to 6 in 1997 to 1 to 8 in 1999); nevertheless, the chances of admission for males remain nearly double that of females. Interestingly, the ratio for female access at private institutions is more favorable than it is at public institutions. Taking the university student population as a whole, 72 percent of students were males and only 28 percent women.

Due to the recent history of Mozambique, another important pattern in the analysis of the student population is students' geographical origin. This category provides important evidence about regional equity in access to higher education. Geographical disparities in access are marked in Mozambique. The majority of students come mainly from Maputo City.

Almost the whole higher education system is located in Maputo City; this is a significant fact in a country in which means of transport are scarce and expensive. Some 60 percent of university students come from the three southern provinces, 25 percent from the four central provinces and 15 percent from the remaining three northern provinces, which contain one-third of the total population (UEM 1999a; UP 1999; ISRI n.d.).

This lack of regional balance was ameliorated somewhat after the opening of the private HEIs. The proportion of students from the north and center is a little higher in the private than in the public sector. This shows the great benefit that private HEIs have brought to the students from these regions of the country. Except for small branches of UP in Nampula and Sofala, the public institutions are all in Maputo City, whereas private HEIs are more widely distributed; the headquarters of UCM are in

Beira, branches of UCM exist in Nampula and Niassa, and ISPU has a class in Zambézia.

As the number of students increased, their awareness about their rights also increased. In the 1980s, higher education students established an Association of University Students, which is a conglomerate of individual institutions' student associations. In the search for the improvement of their living conditions in UEM dorms and better food, students have gone on strike three times since Mozambique achieved independence. The first two strikes took place in the late 1980s and early 1990s, while the last happened in early 1996. In addition, students have been active in the campaign against AIDS.

TEACHING STAFF

The whole system of higher education included 1,357 teaching staff members, of which 539 (39.7 percent) were part-time lecturers, in 1999–2000. Public institutions employ mainly full-time lecturers, while private HEIs rely mainly on part-time staff, except for UCM, where the proportion of full-time and part-time lecturers is almost 1 to 1. In ISCTEM and ISPU, the percentages of full-time lecturers are only 3.6 percent and 9.0 percent, respectively. It should be emphasized that a great number of part-time lecturers from private institutions (especially ISCTEM and ISPU) are also full-time lecturers in public institutions. These lecturers use employment in the private sector as a way of supplementing the low salaries paid by the public institutions. This moonlighting may appear beneficial to the country in the short term, but in the long run it may contribute to a gradual lowering of the quality of teaching in the whole system. Before the opening of the private institutions, lecturers in public institutions devoted more of their time to research. However, the draining of teaching staff from public to private HEIs is harming research within public institutions. Since research ensures long-term quality in university education, moonlighting practices may reduce the quality of education offered by public institutions and with it the quality in private institutions, due to lack of research.

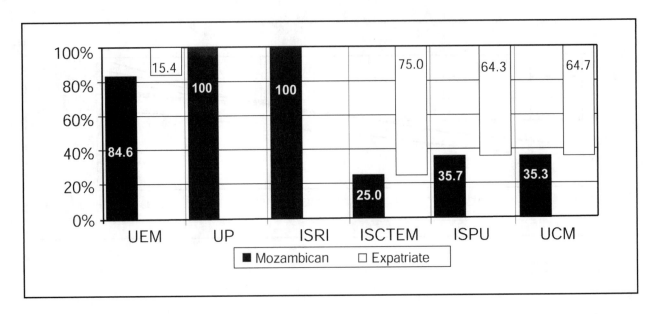

FIG. 48.2. *Mozambican and Expatriate Full-Time Teaching Staff*

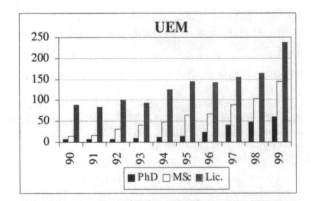

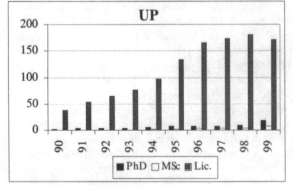

FIG. 48.3. *Evolution of the Mozambican Teaching Staff in UEM and UP in Terms of Academic Degree, 1990–99*

Another important category in the analysis of teaching staff is the nationality of lecturers. This issue is important in the case of Mozambique because after independence, the bulk of higher education lecturers were expatriates. Twenty-five years later, due to a strategic investment, this situation had been reversed in all public institutions. Public institutions employ mainly Mozambican staff, while the private institutions count mainly on expatriate staff. Figure 48.2 shows the proportion of Mozambican and expatriate full-time teaching staff.

The Mozambican teaching staff consists mainly of professionals with the *Licenciatura* degree (a five-year B.A. or B.Sc. degree, which is little more than an honor's degree). As noted above, however, public institutions have been carrying out a program of raising the academic and scientific qualifications of their staff during the last ten years. This is demonstrated clearly in Figure 48.3, which shows the evolution of Mozambican teaching staff at UEM and UP from 1990 to 1999 according to academic qualifications. It must be emphasized that international cooperation has made an enormous contribution toward the effort to upgrade the Mozambican staff in terms of postgraduate training.

In 1990, for example, of 115 Mozambican lecturers at UEM, more than half (88) were *Licenciados* and only 22 had a postgraduate qualification of M.Sc. (15) or Ph.D. (7). In general, it was mainly the expatriate staff that had higher qualifications.

This situation is rapidly changing in UEM, UP, and ISRI where a total of 247 full-time Mozambican faculty members had postgraduate degrees in 1999, representing 36 percent of the total full-time teaching staff. The advent of private HEIs has not changed this pattern at all, since ISPU and ISCTEM basically rely on part-time teaching staff, mainly from UEM, UP, and the local market. UCM, on the other hand, had a ratio of 1 Ph.D.- or M.Sc.-trained faculty to every 40 *Licenciados*-trained faculty in 1999. UEM and UP together have trained 230 faculty members to the M.Sc. (152) and Ph.D. (78) levels in ten years. All of them were trained overseas. These faculty members can be seen as belonging to a pool of lecturers who work both in public and private institutions (where they work as part-time personnel). Private institutions, therefore, benefit indirectly from the huge public investment in staff training.

HIGHER EDUCATION PROCESS: TEACHING AND LEARNING

As it was originally created by the Portuguese government, the Mozambican higher education system bears a strong resemblance to the systems of the Lusophone and Spanish-speaking countries. A complete university course is normally five years long and leads to the degree of *Licenciatura*, which is regarded as being roughly between the B.Sc. and M.Sc. of the English system. In some specific programs, a terminal degree is awarded after three years. However, in almost all the programs offered, a certificate is awarded after three years, which is considered by employers as equivalent to a *baccalauréate* degree, although it is not regarded as a full academic or professional qualification.

Since 1986, UEM has offered a full-semester bridging course for programs such as engineering, science, agriculture, and forestry to compensate for differences and deficiencies in the skills of the students at entrance without lengthening the duration of the courses. This has led to a de facto duration of four and one-half years for the cited specialties, although students must still complete five years of study, including the bridging course. At present, UEM delivers mainly five-year-long *Licenciatura* courses (seven years for medicine and six for architecture), with only one three-year *baccalauréate* program in social sciences; UP offers twelve *Licenciaturas* (of five years' duration) and one *baccalauréate*. ISRI offers only one *Licenciatura* (of five years' duration). The private institutions ISPU, ISCTEM, and UCM are offering four- or five-year *Licenciaturas*, depending on the program, as well as the three-year terminal *baccalauréate*.

The *baccalauréate* courses consist only of specific subjects or disciplines, normally six per semester, while a *Licenciatura* normally requires the completion of nine semesters of different subjects or disciplines, and a one-semester-long *Licenciatura* course, which is an introduction to a research topic that requires a dissertation or thesis.

Recently, some alternative ways to complete the *Licenciatura* were introduced in several institutions, including a state exam instead of the thesis. Graduates in medicine and veterinary sciences at UEM must pass a one-year-long period of on-the-job practical experience. The quality of *Licenciatura* theses across the university normally spans from barely adequate to very good; some are at the level of master's theses.

TEACHING METHODS

Teaching methods in the majority of the HEIs rely normally on the expository transmission of knowledge, in which the lecturer is at the center of the teaching-learning process. The use of audiovisuals is not widespread in HEIs in Mozambique. Other teaching methods face problems of availability and dissemination of learning materials, since there is little material for student research (including books and manuals, computers, films, etc.).

With an increasing number of lecturers undergoing postgraduate study abroad and experiencing and assimilating new teaching methods, there are a few examples of nonsystematic ways of introducing new teaching methods. For example, the use of audiovisuals, problem-based learning, and student research or coursework based on practical experience is increasing.

Taking into account the weak pedagogical skills of some lecturers, in 1986, UEM introduced occasional pedagogical training courses for the junior staff and in 1990 began a fully fledged Staff Development Program (STADEP), assisted by the Dutch government, aimed at developing skills in teaching, presentation and communication, evaluation of students, the writing of support materials, and the use of interactive computer technology (ICT).

LANGUAGE OF INSTRUCTION

The language of instruction throughout the whole education system in Mozambique is Portuguese, but the level of understanding of the language is often poor in both primary and secondary schools, leading to poor preparation at the pre-university level. An ongoing curriculum reform in primary education should include the introduction of Mozambican languages in the first years of primary schools to better meet the needs of the majority of children who are not native speakers of Portuguese. Teaching in English or French is limited to English and French classes or language programs in UP.

The fact that most instruction takes place in Portuguese gives rise to a twofold problem. First, it is more difficult to internationalize higher education and set up student exchanges in a predominantly English-speaking region. Second, the students face serious difficulties in obtaining manuals and books, since more of them are available in English than in Portuguese. Because of these concerns, the introduction of postgraduate studies, especially in science and technology, may lead to some subjects being taught in English.

EXAMINATIONS

Except for a very few cases, examinations and testing are generally done in written form. Each subject or discipline requires on average 48–64 hours per semester (in some cases 96 and even 126), and students are expected to pass two to four partial tests (by achieving 50 percent, or 10 on a scale of 0 to 20). Students with an average mark of at least 9.5 are admitted to a written exam, which is held twice each semester. Students who fail the exam at both sittings must repeat the subject in the following academic year. In some cases, especially in arts and humanities, the exams are conducted orally and a student is expected to present or defend prepared assignments in front of a jury.

If a student fails a given subject after repeating a course, he or she must withdraw from the university for at least one year. This system contributes significantly to Mozambique's high drop-out rates.

Table 48.3. Education-Sector Budget for Key Institutions of Higher Education in Mozambique, 1999

Institution	Total Expenditure (millions of Mts*)	Percent of Total	
Ministry of Education (MINED)	1,170,573	74	
Eduardo Mondlane University (UEM)	364,661	23	26
Pedagogic University (UP)	37,357	2	
Higher Institute for International Relations (ISRI)	14,597	1	
Total	1,587,188	100	

*Mts = Meticais (Mozambican currency). In 1999, US$1 was equivalent to an average of 12,000 Mts.
Source: Ministry of Finance and Planning.

GRADUATION RATES, REPETITION, AND DROP-OUT RATES

Despite the rapid increase in total student enrollments, the number of graduates has increased relatively slowly. The number of graduates in the public HEIs increased from 85 in 1990–1991 to almost 200 in 1991–1992 but remained around 250 per year until 1995–1996, when it rose to nearly 400. The number of graduates has remained below 500 per year (reaching 483 in 1998–1999). There have not yet been any graduations from private HEIs, which have opened only in the last few years, apart from 63 B.A. degrees and B.Sc. degrees awarded by ISPU in 1998–1999.

Because of the problems described above, it is difficult, if not impossible, at present, to estimate meaningful rates and indexes of progression, graduation, repetition, and drop-out. There are considerable problems due to the variations in the minimum length of courses and the prevalence of student repetition, and the temporary exclusion or proscription of students who fail or become permanent drop-outs in many cases. Unfortunately, there is little reliable information on the extent and impact of these practices, which are not confined to higher education. Secondary schools in Mozambique also have very high rates of repetition and drop-out.

The calculation of graduation rates for UEM and UP between 1995 and 1997, on the basis of the number of graduates each year compared with total student numbers five years earlier, yields the following figures: In 1995, the graduation rate was 6.68 at UEM and 15.6 at UP; in 1996, the figures were 7.75 for UEM and 14.9 for UP; in 1997 they were 6.64 for UEM and 11.33 for UP (MESCT 2000). In general, the rate of graduation is low, but there are marked differences between UEM and UP that need further investigation.

Because of the long programs and the prevalence of repetition and drop-out, actual graduation rates are low, however they are calculated. It is worth stressing that there are no accurate data on the extent and causes of repetition and drop-out. The UEM Strategic Plan has identified this as a serious problem to be addressed. If the low graduation rates prevail, within five years, the total student population could exceed the institution's physical limit of about 13,000 students, thereby jeopardizing the new intakes (UEM 1999a).

FINANCING HIGHER EDUCATION

Financing for public HEIs lies with the Ministry of Planning and Finance. Separate negotiations take place for each public HEI between the senior managers of the HEI (the rector and other key staff, as necessary) and the Ministry of Planning and Finance. The public HEIs receive funding directly from the Ministry of Finance rather than through the Ministry of Education.

The overall government budget is comparatively small. Total government education expenditures are only about 12 percent of GDP (compared to 26 percent for Kenya, which has a similar agriculture-based economy). This reflects the state of underdevelopment of Mozambique's economy and its high reliance on traditional rural agriculture and the informal sector. High rates of economic growth in recent years have enabled a steady improvement in government revenues, but about 50 percent of government expenditure is funded by external grants and borrowings, which are largely directed to investment.

The education sector's share of the total government budget (including external development assistance) was estimated at 14 percent in 1999. The higher education subsector accounts for about 26 percent of the education-sector budget (see Table 48.3). This is equivalent to about 3.8 percent of the total government budget. Foreign assistance contributes about 60 percent of total government investment in education, but the contribution of foreign assistance is even higher than this, since many foreign grants are given directly to education institutions rather than channeled through the government budget.

The fact that Mozambique recently became eligible for debt relief under the Highly Indebted Poor Country (HIPC) initiative has significantly increased the government's capacity to spend on education and other social programs. Debt relief has enabled the government to increase annual current spending on education and health by more than 50 percent between 1998 and 2001 (that is, from about $120 million to $175 million), as predicted by the IMF.

Table 48.4. Unit Costs in Select HEIs in Mozambique, 1999 (Average Expenditure per Student in U.S. Dollars)

Category of Per Student Expenditure	UEM	UP	ISRI 1997–1999 (average)	UCM	ISPU
Recurrent Expenditure	1,778	909	4,677	1,210	1,251
Total Expenditure	4,960	—	6,058	—	1,801
Student Numbers	6,772	1,564	201	605	680

Before the promulgation of the National Education Policy and Strategies for Implementation in 1990, the government gave no signal to the private sector that it was welcome to invest in higher education institutions. Consequently, the financing of HEIs remained primarily a public sector function.

In 1999, three key publicly funded HEIs (UEM, UP, and ISRI) shared about 26 percent of all public expenditures on education. UEM took the lion's share (23 percent). UP and ISRI accounted for about 2 percent and 1 percent, respectively.

FINANCING OF PUBLIC INSTITUTIONS

The government of Mozambique has to raise significantly the share of the education budget allocated to HEIs. Under current plans, the percentage would rise to 22.8 percent in 2001, then to 25 percent in the next two years, but it would drop slightly to 24 percent in 2004. In that period, the proportions of total public resources allocated to UEM, UP, and ISRI would remain nearly constant, at about 20 percent, 3 percent, and 2.5 percent, respectively.

The levels of planned allocations for investments by HEIs will generally increase over the years, except for UP in 2002 and ISRI in 2004. Yet in the case of UEM, for example, the planned increase in investments overall falls significantly below the targets given in the institution's strategic plan. Thus, while UEM has planned for a total of about $123.3 million in investment for the 2000–2003 period, Ministry of Planning and Finance has planned for only about $50.1 million in that period.

The government budget is, of course, the main source of revenue for the public HEIs. For UEM, direct government funding largely from domestic resources has ranged between 51.7 percent and 38.1 percent in the past three years. For the same period, 88.5 percent of ISRI's budget depended on the state budget, while UP depended totally on the same budget. The gap in government financing of the public HEIs has generally been closed by funding from the external donors, including credit from multilateral financial institutions (mainly the World Bank). For UEM, external funding accounts for more than 50 percent of its total revenues.

For UEM, as well as for institutions in lower education subsectors, donors are a major source of funding. While UEM receives only 13 percent of domestic public revenues allocated to capital expenditure (investment) for education, it receives as much as 39 percent of the total external resources marked for the education sector.

Apart from government direct (domestic) and external donor funding, the other two sources of revenue for public HEIs are minor. These are tuition fees and income generation. At the present, tuition fees constitute only a token source of funds at UEM and ISRI. At UEM, tuition fees contribute less than 1 percent of the total budget. Even at ISRI, where nearly one-half of the total students have a self-sponsored status, the proportion of fees to total revenues is estimated at an average of 0.2 percent over the past three years. Neither the government nor the HEIs have seriously embraced a policy of cost sharing through fees or other user charges.

Among the three public HEIs, only UEM has initiated income generation to augment funding from the government and donors. But the results have not been that significant. As a proportion of the total revenues, income generation by UEM in 1997, 1998, and 1999 was estimated at 2.7 percent, 1.8 percent, and 3.1 percent, respectively. UEM's strategic plan calls for raising this ratio but sets no specific targets. More purposeful and rigorous efforts will be needed before income-generation endeavors are a major source of income in the public HEIs.

FINANCING OF PRIVATE INSTITUTIONS

Private higher education is a fairly new phenomenon in Mozambique. Financing of most of these institutions is based on tuition fees, with the exception of UCM. For instance, data provided by ISCTEM and ISPU shows that tuition fees are a major source of financing of private HEIs. In the case of ISPU, tuition fees are the sole and rapidly growing source of revenue. In 1996, this institution collected $243,000 in tuition fees. The level nearly tripled in the following year to $662,000 and then doubled in 1998 to $1,224,000. ISCTEM collected $35,730 in 1997, rising to $75,195 in 1998 and $139,550 in 1999.

Tuition fees collected at UCM in 1998 ($260,212) were 31 percent of the total revenue for the year. In that year, donors contributed about 68.5 percent of the total revenue. Aside from tuition fees and donor funds, income generation projects constituted a paltry 0.5 percent of UCM's total revenues.

UNIT COSTS

Unit costs, in terms of average annual expenditures per student, vary considerably between institutions. In terms of recurrent expenditures, the unit costs range from a low of about $909 for UP to a high of $4,677 for ISRI.

The unit costs in Table 48.4 represent estimates of the cost per student per year. To calculate unit costs per graduate, it would be necessary to multiply these figures by the average length of study before graduation, which is considerably in excess of five years (the minimum length of study for the *Licenciatura* degree), given the high rates of repetition and drop-out (which are discussed in more detail below). In 1998, the total number of graduates from UEM was only 312, compared with the total number of 6,772 students. If the total expenditures of UEM (including development that is a nonrecurrent expenditure) are divided by the number of graduates, rather than by the number of students, this would give an enormous figure of more than $100,000 per graduate. This would, of course, be misleading as a measure of unit costs, but it is an indication of the very high costs of repetition and drop-out.

FINANCIAL ASSISTANCE FOR STUDENTS

Although fees in public HEIs are very low, students face considerable private costs in the form of living expenses, books, and other essentials. Schools offer very little financial assistance for students from low-income families. Only about 10 percent of students in public HEIs receive a full or partial scholarship, live in subsidized accommodations, and/or receive assistance with the cost of books.

In general, although some scholarships have been made available, students at private HEIs pay substantial tuition fees (about $250 per month) in addition to financing their own living costs and books, the combined cost of which is estimated at $300–400 per year. Estimates of typical student expenditure in public and private higher education institutions, including fees, books, basic living expenses, and other basic expense at 1999 prices totaled $9,367.

The number of scholarships or grants is very limited, and there is no system of student loans. Only 979 scholarships were awarded in 1999 for a total of 11,619 students in all HEIs and 9,021 in public HEIs. When available, scholarships are awarded mainly on academic merit rather than on financial need. A full scholarship provides assistance with fees, subsidized accommodation, and books, but students may receive a partial scholarship that does not include accommodation and may or may not include reduced fees.

The University of Eduardo Mondlane Social Service Directorate (DSS) provides assistance for students in the form of subsidized accommodation and meals. In 1999, the DSS was allocated (from the university budget) a total of $23,814 for food and $11,000 for recurrent expenses. The DSS runs six student dormitories, with a total capacity of 885 places. Most of these are allocated to scholarship holders, who total 737 students, of whom 642 are male and only 95 are female.

STRATEGIC PLANNING AND REFORM

Strategic planning in Mozambican Higher Education institutions is a fairly recent phenomenon. The oldest higher education institution in the country, the UEM, engaged in its first serious strategic planning effort in the early 1990s. This culminated in the conception of a plan that came to be known as Present and Perspectives and was later partially transformed into a project that was submitted to the World Bank for funding and turned into a Capacity Building Project, which is currently winding down.

As a natural follow-up to the Present and Perspectives project, the rector of UEM created a committee in 1997 to work out a five-year strategic plan for the university. This plan was a result of a more participatory approach, thus involving the entire university community and its stakeholders. An analysis was undertaken to study the strengths, weaknesses, and/or threats the university had to confront. After this exercise, a vision and mission were drafted and widely discussed with the university community and the stakeholders, and later some guiding principles and key strategic issues (objectives and actions) were identified. After a series of internal workshops within the university, twelve strategic objectives were approved by the University Council in October 1998.

The most important goals for change hinge around reforming the academic, administrative, and management structure and functioning of the university with the aim of attaining:

- Internal and external academic efficiency (improving the quality of education, increasing the graduation rate and intake rate, assuring regional, social, and gender equity in access to higher education, and improving the physical plant of the university to suit the challenges raised by the expansion)
- Administrative and management efficiency (overcoming the excessive centralization and bureaucracy in academic, administrative, and financial management of the university; improving the management of human resources; and assuring more autonomy from the government and decentralization of certain activities from the central level to the faculties and departments)
- More efficiency in national and international cooperation (instilling a culture of strategic planning in the daily management of the university)

This strategic plan was later put into effect and partially transformed into a project that is currently being negotiated by the government and the World Bank.

In the meantime, other public HEIs followed suit and started producing strategic plans. This trend gained more momentum when, in October 1999, the Ministry of Education created a committee to draw a National Strategic Plan for Higher Education, which was finalized in 2000.

CURRICULUM DEVELOPMENT AND REFORM

The recent growth of the economy, following a period of stabilization and the introduction of democracy, brings new challenges to the higher education system in Mozambique. These include:

- Increasing the throughput of graduates to match the demands of the community and the labor market
- Reforming curricula and bringing them in line with market demands
- Increasing flexibility in the system to allow self-tailored study plans
- Diversifying courses to match the expanding market
- Internationalizing the curricula to match the political de-

mands and ongoing plans for regional integration and general globalization

There is an urgent need to reform curricula in HEIs in Mozambique, taking into account the following components: profiles of graduates; objectives of the programs; teaching and evaluation methods; modernization and the use of new teaching methods; flexible study plans, including opportunities for more self-directed learning by students; regionalization; and internationalization. This exercise requires a lot of expertise, which unfortunately is not available in Mozambique, and systematic consultations with all stakeholders.

EXPERIENCE OF CURRICULUM DEVELOPMENT AND REFORM AT UEM

Following its five-year rolling strategic plan, UEM started a movement of curriculum reform, which envisages:

- Reducing the duration of the *Licenciatura* course from five to four years
- Introducing the credit system
- Increasing the relevance of curricula in terms of market needs
- "Internationalizing" the offered programs by bringing them closer to best practice in internationally recognized universities
- Introducing new teaching methods
- Introducing postgraduate studies (UEM 1999c)

Since UEM has been serving as the trigger for any new academic movement, it is likely that curriculum reform will soon spread to the other HEIs in Mozambique.

RESEARCH AND SERVICE TO SOCIETY

The role of research is fundamental to the process of strengthening management and policymaking. Within HEIs, research can enrich teaching through incorporation of local knowledge and help to ensure the social relevance of higher learning institutions. Research experience can give students complementary analytical and organizational skills. Additionally, research produces knowledge and experience that can be marketed through contracts and consultancies, which in turn can help to increase the financial independence and sustainability of institutions.

Only the three oldest HEIs in Mozambique are engaged in research activities. This is because private institutions are still setting their own pace, because they remain more profit-driven institutions, and because not enough direct funds are invested in research activities. UEM, UP, and ISRI have sought to institutionalize campus research activities. Mozambican staff members have been encouraged to initiate research activities following the completion of their postgraduate studies abroad. Likewise, an introduction-to-research-based *Licenciatura* thesis is required for the undergraduate degree. At present, UEM has more than 300 different research projects underway, and UP and ISRI are also increasing their research ventures gradually, both in the country and in regional scientific networks. Notably, the use of research teams is beginning to emerge, particularly in the areas of social sciences, agriculture and environment, engineering, and science. Research topics are, in most cases, defined at the departmental level. No political guidelines on research exist at the institutional or national level. Research capacity-building has benefited from longstanding support by various donors.

In spite of these efforts, HEIs in Mozambique are not yet able to effectively fulfill their research mandate. Most research is still the result of individual initiatives linked to thesis or dissertation requirements of Mozambican staff pursuing their graduate studies abroad. Some foci of institutionalized research exist in the humanities (such as the Center for African Studies, the Center for Population Studies, the Land Tenure Studies Center, and the Nucleus of Mozambican Languages, all of which are based at UEM, and the Center for Strategic and International Studies at ISRI), engineering and technology (including research groups on water resources, biomass burning, and food technology), natural sciences (including a multidisciplinary environmental research group, including biology, chemistry, physics, geology, a groundwater research group, oceanography, and mining and natural products), and agriculture and forestry (such as research groups on community-based resource management, biodiversity, crop amelioration, and conservation), and medicine. In some cases, research activities are still incipient and very much dependent on one or two people.

In other areas, research activities and output remain limited and poorly disseminated. The faculties of economics and law, for example, are still initiating research ventures even though the present socioeconomic and political environment of economic rehabilitation, strengthening of democratic institutions, and recovery from a severe civil war might benefit from research-based guidance. In general, when research takes place, it suffers from lack of relevance to the country's development challenges, lack of multidisciplinarity in some scientific areas due to rigid boundaries among disciplines, and a weak demand for research products.

It is easy to understand the reasons for such a poor research performance in HEI in Mozambique:

- More than 35 percent of Mozambican staff have less than five years of teaching experience, and only 12 percent of teaching staff at UEM and less than 10 percent at UP hold a Ph.D. This gives very few models to guide the junior staff.
- There is no direct compensation for research activities: promotions are based on length of service and not on publications, so research brings less extra income than moonlighting.
- Contracted expatriate staff do not stay long enough to start any meaningful research activity.
- Research laboratories do not exist or equipment is obsolete.
- Campuses have very limited access to scientific literature and communications technology.
- Teaching staff are regularly forced to undertake consultancies for additional income.

UEM has created a Research Open Fund, mainly sponsored by the Swedish Agency for Research Cooperation and the Swedish International Development Agency (SAREC-SIDA), which provides funding for small demand-driven research projects on campus. This creates the possibility of defining priorities and strengthening some research-management skills and could be a starting point for developing and implementing a nationwide research policy.

Dissemination of research results mostly happens through publication in small internal journals or booklets, since Mozambique has very few peer-reviewed scientific journals. A noble initiative is blooming at UEM Press, which, with the financial support of the Capacity Building Project, started a few years ago to publish books, textbooks for students, and other forms of printed materials. This has immensely helped to disseminate some research results. The humanities and social sciences are currently the most advanced in terms of publications (internal journals and books).

The services that Mozambique's HEIs deliver to the national community are concentrated in two activities: informal expert advice and contracted consultancies. Expert advice is offered by the staff to government agencies, donors, nongovernmental organizations, churches, private enterprises, and regional decision-making organs. This is the most common type of activity, since it is seen as the easiest way of complementing the salaries of the staff. Consultancies contracted through the institutions represent a small but growing set of activities, especially in the faculties of economics and engineering. At UEM and ISRI, different service-providing centers have been launched, including Mozambican studies, informatics, engineering studies, studies and development of the habitat, population studies, land tenure studies, industrial engineering and environmental security, electronics and equipment, Mozambican languages, natural resources, and biodiversity, all based at UEM, and strategic and international studies at ISRI. During 1999, UEM generated about $1.01 million in this way, which represented about 3.1 percent of its total budget.

CONCLUSION

Higher education in Mozambique has shown a steady growth in quantity and quality since the independence of the country was achieved a quarter of a century ago. From having only one higher education institution at the time of independence with only a few hundred students, Mozambique now has five public and five private institutions with a total student population of more than 11,000.

Social demand for education is still very high, which explains the rapid mushrooming of private institutions. However, because the majority of Mozambique's population lives in absolute poverty, major challenges lie ahead. In order to assure equity in access to higher education, the public sector must be expanded to reach out to those with few resources.

One of the ways of quickly reaching this noble goal is to invest in distance learning and in the establishment of community technical colleges in the provinces. In addition to continuing to train academic staff, information technologies can play a very important role in quality assurance efforts. Curriculum reform is also urgently needed to ensure relevance and a prompt response to the demands of the growing labor market.

ACKNOWLEDGMENTS

I wish to acknowledge that the information in this chapter comes from a report produced by a Higher Education Strategic Planning Committee that I chaired between 1999 and 2000. The committee was composed of Arlindo Chilundo (coordinator), Elias Matos, Lopo Vasconcelos, Rogério Utui, Rui Alves Pereira, Valter Fainda, Verónica José, Zefanias Muhate, Zita Ustá, and Alberto Simão. We also benefited from the invaluable input of three international consultants, namely Maureen Woodhall, Adrian Ziderman, and Kithinji Kiragu.

REFERENCES

Farrant, J., and J. Fielden. 1996. *Strategic Planning in African Universities*. New Papers on Higher Education, no. 12. Paris: UNESCO.

Fry, P., and R. Utui. 1999. *Promoting Access, Quality and Capacity-Building in African Higher Education: The Strategic Planning Experience at the Eduardo Mondlane University*. Washington, D.C.: ADEA Working Group on Higher Education.

IMF (International Monetary Fund). 1999. News Brief no. 93/95 of June 30, 1999 (on Web site).

INE (Instituto Nacional de Estatística). n.d. Homepage of Instituto Nacional de Estatística. Available online at: http://www.ine.gov.mz

——. 1999a. *II Recenseamento Geral da População e Habitação* [Second General Census of Population and Housing]. Maputo, Moçambique: Instituto Nacional de Estatística.

——. 1999b. *Moçambique em Números—1998* [Mozambique in Figures—1998]. Maputo, Moçambique: Instituto Nacional de Estatística.

ISRI (Higher Institute for International Relations). n.d. *Plano Estratégico para o Reforço Institucional do ISRI* [Strategic Plan for Institutional Strengthening of ISRI]. Maputo, Moçambique: Instituto Superior de Relações Internacionais.

MESCT. 2000. *Mozambique: Higher Education Strategic Plan*.

MINED. 1998a. *Estatística da Educação. Levantamento Escolar—1998* [Education Statistics. Schools Survey—1998]. Julho. Maputo, Moçambique: Ministério da Educação, Direcção de Planificação.

——. 1998b. *Plano Estratégico da Educação 1999–2003. "Combater a Exclusão, Renovar a Escola"* [Strategic Plan of Education 1999–2003. "Reviving Schools, Fighting Exclusion"]. Outubro. Maputo, Moçambique: Ministério da Educação.

Psacharopoulos, G., and M. Woodhall. 1991. *Education for Development: An Analysis for Investment Choices*. World Bank Publication. Oxford: Oxford University Press.

Republic of Mozambique. 1995. National Education Policy and Strategies for Implementation. August. Maputo, Mozambique: Ministry of Education.

República de Moçambique. n.d. *Reflexões sobre a Expansão do Ensino Superior em Moçambique* [Thoughts about the Expansion of Higher Education in Mozambique]. Maputo, Moçambique.

Robbins Committee on Higher Education (UK). 1963. *Higher Education: Report of the Committee under the Chairmanship of Lord Robbins*. London: Her Majesty's Stationery Office.

UEM. 1999a. *Plano Estratégico da UEM para o Quinquénio 1999–2003* [UEM Strategic Plan for the Quinquennium 1999–2003]. Maputo, Moçambique: Universidade Eduardo Mondlane.

——. 1999b. "Plano Operacional do Plano Estratégico 1999–2003" [UEM Operational Strategic Plan 1999–2003]. Mimeograph. Maputo, Moçambique: Universidade Eduardo Mondlane.

——. 1999c. *Projecto da Reforma Curricular* [Curricular Reform Project]. Maputo, Moçambique: Universidade Eduardo Mondlane.

UNDP. 1998. *Report on Human Development*. Maputo: UNDP.

UNESCO. 1998. *Higher Education in the Twenty-First Century: Vision and Action*. Paris: UNESCO.

UP (Universidade Pedagógica). 1999. *Plano Estratégico do Desenvolvimento Institucional da Universidade Pedagógica (Documento de Trabalho)* [UP Strategic Plan for Institutional Development]. Maio. Maputo, Moçambique: Universidade Pedagógica.

Woodhall, M. 1987. *Lending for Learning: Designing a Student Loan Pro-*

gramme for Developing Countries. Maputo, Mozambique: Commonwealth Secretariat.

———. 1991. *Student Loans in Higher Education*. Vol. 3: *English-Speaking Africa*. Educational Forum Series no. 3. Paris: International Institute for Educational Planning (IIEP) Dissemination Programme.

World Bank. 1994. *Higher Education: The Lessons of Experience*. Washington, D.C.: The World Bank.

World Bank and IMF. 1999. "Republic of Mozambique Policy Framework Paper, April 1999–March 2002." June.

Ziderman, A. 1997. "Tracing Graduates through Reunion Parties: Secondary Technical Education in Mozambique." *Comparative Education Review* (May 1997): 142–160.

Ziderman, A., and D. Albrecht. 1995. *Financing Universities in Developing Countries*. Washington, D.C., and London: Falmer Press.

Namibia

Barnabas Otaala

INTRODUCTION

The University of Namibia (UNAM) is the only university in a country of 1.66 million people. As the historical, economic, and political situation of a country affects and influences education, I provide a brief historical background of the country, which achieved independence only in 1990, before providing a description of UNAM's mission, its achievements during its first Five-Year Development Plan (1995–1999), the challenges and constraints it has faced, and the way forward as it prepares for its next development plan (2000–2004). I shall also refer briefly to the historical background of tertiary education in Namibia and to the other tertiary institutions, the Colleges of Education and the Polytechnic of Namibia.

HISTORY OF NAMIBIA

After a bitter struggle, Namibia emerged from colonial rule —first under Germany, as South West Africa, and later under the Republic of South Africa, as part of the apartheid system—in March 1990.

South West Africa, as it was called then, was ruled primarily through force under both colonial governments. The struggle for independence took various forms, including armed struggle, and led to a UN-mediated transition to independence starting in April 1989 with the arrival of the UN Transitional Assistance Group (UNTAG).

Today independent Namibia is a unitary secular republic with an executive presidency, a bicameral legislature, an independent judiciary, and a constitution that guarantees the rule of law and the fundamental rights and freedoms of individual citizens. The country is divided into thirteen political regions: Karas, Hardap, Khomas, Omaheke, Erongo, Otjozondjupa, Kunene, Omusati, Oshana, Ohangwena, Otjikoto, Kavango,

and Caprivi. For educational administrative purposes, the country is divided into seven regions: Katima Mulilo, Keetmanshoop, Khorixas, Ondangwa East, Ondangwa West, Rundu, and Windhoek.

DEMOGRAPHIC SITUATION

With an estimated population of only 1.66 million (1997), Namibia is one of the more thinly populated countries in Africa; it is also the most arid country south of the Sahara Desert. It has an area of 824,292 square kilometers (318,261 square miles). Vast tracts of land have a density of less than one person per square kilometer. It is only in sections in the north that one finds a population density of more than five persons per square kilometer.

ECONOMIC SITUATION

The gross domestic product (GDP) of Namibia, estimated at $3.3 billion in 1997, provides a per capita income of $1,939, which qualifies it as a "middle income" country by world standards. Independent Namibia inherited one of the most polarized economies in the world, with the most affluent 10 percent of the society receiving 65 percent and the remaining 90 percent receiving 35 percent of the national income (UNDP and UNAIDS 1997, 3).

GOVERNMENT STRATEGIES SINCE INDEPENDENCE

The Namibian economy is small in size, extremely open, and characterized by considerable reliance on the production of primary commodities for export. The economy is divided; a modern sector coexists hand in hand with a subsistence component. A large portion of the Namibian population has been living under subsistence conditions; their economic activity is confined primarily to seasonal labor. At independence, the government of the Republic of Namibia, responding to competing demands on the nation's limited resources, identified the following priority sectors: education, health, housing, and agriculture. Government resources devoted to these sectors continue to account for an increasing share of government expenditure. The first three sectors constitute part of the overall social sector. To address burning questions of employment generation, poverty reduction, reduction of income inequalities, and the overall living standard, the government concluded that it needed to empower the previously disadvantaged citizens of the country by improving their skills. Provision was also made to ensure improved access to both housing and health facilities.

Namibia recognized the fact that an educated and healthy workforce has a direct correlation to high productivity. But it also recognized that education was a basic right. Namibia has been engaged in a comprehensive education and curriculum reform since its independence in 1990. The government has encouraged this process by formulating new educational policies and by designing and implementing innovative teaching methodologies and learning strategies. One main objective of this reform has been to democratize the educational process—emphasizing the need for affordability as well as sustainability—and to put in place mechanisms to improve its quality, efficiency, and relevance (Angula 1994). The reforms initiated at independence are beginning to have a visible impact in both basic education and in colleges. Thus, the president of Namibia was able to point to the quantitative improvement in enrollment on the occasion of the awarding of an honorary doctorate from UNAM to Finnish President Martti Ahtisaari in April 2000:

> While in 1989, only 70 percent of our children of school-going age were in schools, today that figure is over 90 percent. In 1989, there were only 13,159 teachers; today we have more than doubled that number. I must also add that between 1990 and 1998, a total of 2,452 new classrooms were built across the country. (Nujoma 2000)

With respect to tertiary education, a presidential commission was set up and submitted a report in 1993. The recommendations of the commission led to the establishment of various tertiary institutions in Namibia, including the Polytechnic, the Colleges of Education, and UNAM.

The Polytechnic of Namibia provides postsecondary career education leading to awards of certificates and diplomas in a variety of disciplines, including business management, communication, legal and secretarial studies, engineering and information technology, and natural resources and tourism. The Polytechnic has a governing council under which it operates.

The Colleges of Education provide a postsecondary Basic Education Diploma which qualifies the graduates to teach at the lower and upper primary levels of basic education. The colleges of education are managed by the National Institute for Educational Development (NIED), which falls under the Ministry of Higher Education, Training, and Employment Creation.

The University of Namibia provides training leading to basic degree qualifications, postgraduate diplomas, and more recently,

master's degree programs. Like the Polytechnic of Namibia, the University has a University Council that oversees its activities.

BRIEF BACKGROUND

Tertiary education in Namibia started around 1980. Prior to this date, students traveled abroad for their further education.

In 1980, by Act 13, the Academy for Tertiary Education was established; at that time courses were offered mainly in teacher and secretarial training. Act 9 of 1985 reconfigured the academy to include a university component (which continued to be responsible for teacher training), the Technikon of Namibia, and the College for Out-of-School Training (COST). Shortly after independence, it was resolved that the three components be divided into two independent tertiary institutions. The first was a polytechnic and university, with the university in charge of teacher preparation for Grades 11 and 12. The second was the Colleges of Education, with the National Institute for Educational Development (NIED) in charge of teacher preparation for Grades 1 through 10. In the following sections, we briefly refer to the Colleges of Education and to the Polytechnic of Namibia before devoting the rest of this chapter to tertiary education at UNAM.

COLLEGES OF EDUCATION

There are four Colleges of Education in Namibia responsible for preparing teachers for basic education (Grades 1 through 10). Holders of the International General Certificate of Secondary Education (IGCSE) of the Cambridge University Matriculation Board who are admitted into the colleges pursue a three-year training program leading to an award of a Basic Education Teaching Diploma (BETD). The colleges are located at Caprivi, Ongwediva, Rundu, and Windhoek. Table 49.1 lists enrollment figures at the Colleges of Education for 1998. Table 49.2 lists lecturing staff at the colleges for 1998. Table 49.3 shows graduates for the year 1998.

THE POLYTECHNIC OF NAMIBIA

With the enactment of the Polytechnic of Namibia Act 33 of 1994, the Technikon of Namibia and the College of Out-of-School Training merged to become the Polytechnic of Namibia. The Polytechnic prepares persons mainly for vocational training courses leading to the award of various diplomas and certificates. The act provides for the gradual phasing out of vocational training courses and the granting of degrees by the polytechnic.

THE UNIVERSITY OF NAMIBIA

Modern universities in Africa were created during the colonial period. Even in those cases in which they came into existence after independence, their character was strongly influenced by that of the former metropolitan universities.

UNAM is no exception. It was founded by a presidential commission dominated by members steeped in British and, to a lesser extent, American university traditions. UNAM also inherited the academy, which had a small university sector that had

Table 49.1. Enrollment at the Colleges of Education by College, Year, and Sex, 1998

Colleges of Education	Year	Female	Total
Caprivi	1	52	130
	2	37	101
	3	55	119
Subtotal		144	350
Ongwediva	1	175	300
	2	124	298
	3	159	300
Subtotal		458	898
Rundu	1	65	120
	2	51	100
	3	50	128
Subtotal		166	348
Windhoek	1	69	147
	2	100	192
	3	85	176
Subtotal		254	515
Total	1	361	697
	2	312	691
	3	349	723
Subtotal		1,022	
Grand Total			2,111

Source: Ministry of Higher Education, Training and Employment Creation.

Table 49.2. Lecturing Staff at the Colleges of Education by College and Sex, 1998

College	Female	Total
Caprivi	6	26
Rundu	9	25
Ongwediva	25	56
Windhoek	35	54
Total	75	161

Source: Ministry of Higher Education, Training and Employment Creation.

Table 49.3. Graduates by College and Sex, 1998

College	Female	Total
Caprivi	51	109
Ongwediva	120	234
Rundu	51	116
Windhoek	72	143
Total	294	602

Source: Ministry of Higher Education, Training and Employment Creation.

been strongly influenced by the British tradition through South Africa. UNAM thus adopted and inherited the British model with its main elements, including its idea of a university, its concepts of autonomy and academic freedom (which were enshrined in the Constitution [Article 21(1)(b)] and the University of Namibia Act), its academic structure, and its various university procedures and processes.

UNAM, like many universities in the developing world, fully recognizes that the pursuit of knowledge for its own sake is a luxury it cannot afford. The attainment of independence and the demise of apartheid created a need for a new and radical orientation that must be rooted in the new realities of Namibia. At its creation, UNAM recognized the urgent need for it to play and be seen to play a more active and meaningful role in the development of Namibia. The central role of the university in national development was recently confirmed by the World Bank and the Association of African Universities when they stated:

Universities play a more important role in Africa than in other regions. They are potentially the most capable institutions in their countries. They are often the only national institutions with the skills, the equipment, and the mandate to generate new understanding through research. University

roles in research, evaluation, information transfer, and technology development are therefore critical to national social progress and economic growth. In short, universities can and should be key actors in national development. (World Bank 1997)

The supply of highly skilled labor in the various socioeconomic and political sectors (teachers, scientists, doctors, economists, engineers, lawyers, agricultural and fishing experts, industrial entrepreneurs, technological innovators, environmental management experts, researchers, etc.) is critical to the development of any country. The universities and the system of higher education as a whole are entrusted with the task of producing men and women who are equipped to make an effective contribution to development. The university experience provides the intellectual training that is an essential ingredient of human endeavor. Development demands men and women who are thinkers and who can generate ideas. Academic freedom and the university environment generally provide an atmosphere in which there is, in the words of the famous American judge Oliver Wendell Holmes, Jr., "a free trade of ideas."

Universities must provide leadership in research. For UNAM (as for universities of developing countries generally), substantial emphasis should be placed on applied research directed toward issues that affect ordinary Namibians without abandoning basic research. Universities must take a more active role in identifying, investigating, and seeking solutions to development problems.

KEY OBJECTIVES AND GOALS IN UNAM'S FIRST FIVE-YEAR DEVELOPMENT PLAN

I see the University of Namibia as a center of higher learning, served by dedicated men and women of quality, and producing graduates determined to uplift the standard of living of our people. I see the University of Namibia taking its rightful place in Southern Africa in particular, Africa in general, and the world at large, and making its contribution in every area of the body of knowledge.

—Dr. Sam Nujoma, president of the Republic of Namibia and chancellor of the University of Namibia on April 23, 1993, during his installation as chancellor

To meet the challenges of overcoming the various problems posed by the legacies of the pre-independence regimes, and to contribute to the development of society, the new university needed to formulate, in tandem with the government and the private sector, a Five-Year Development Plan (1995–1999). This plan was tailored to the aims and objectives of the government's First National Plan (NDP1). The plans were to be in line with the motto of the University: "Education, Service, Development." The Presidential Commission Report of 1991 was subjected to a thorough evaluation by a joint technical committee, composed of personnel from the Ministry of Education and Culture and the Office of the Vice-Chancellor-Designate.

FACULTIES AT UNAM

To discharge its specified functions, the university has seven faculties and five functional centers. The faculties are as follows:

- *Faculty of Agriculture and Natural Resources:* This faculty offers the following academic programs: the Bachelor of Science and Agriculture, the Bachelor of Science in Natural Resources, and postgraduate programs at the master's and doctoral levels. In 1998, this faculty had 103 students and 32 staff.
- *Faculty of Economics and Management Science:* This faculty offers the following academic programs: Bachelor of Commerce, Bachelor of Administration, Bachelor of Accounting, and Bachelor of Economics, as well as postgraduate programs at the master's and doctoral levels in administration, political science, economics, and a postgraduate diploma in economics. In 1998, this faculty had 703 students and 25 staff.
- *Faculty of Education:* This faculty provides the following programs: Bachelor of Education (General and Adult Education), specialized diploma in Special Education, postgraduate diploma in education, an M.A. in Education (General and in Adult Education), and a Ph.D. (Adult Education). In 1998, this faculty had 688 students and 32 staff.
- *Faculty of Humanities and Social Sciences:* This faculty offers the following academic programs: Bachelor of Arts (General), Bachelor of Arts (Social Work), Bachelor of Arts (Media Studies), Bachelor of Arts (Theology), and Bachelor of Arts (Visual Arts). The faculty also offers an M.A. degree program in religion and theology and a Ph.D. in psychology. In 1998, this faculty had 403 students and 74 staff.
- *Faculty of Law:* This faculty runs the following academic pro-

grams: B. Juris and LL.B. In addition, the faculty has begun to offer an LL.M. degree. The faculty had 105 students and staff of 33 in 1998.
- *Faculty of Medical and Health Sciences:* This faculty trains medical professionals for the following degrees: Bachelor's in Nursing Science, Master's in Nursing Science, and doctorate in Nursing Science. The faculty also provides training at diploma levels for various paraprofessionals for the health sector. This faculty had 439 students and 38 academic staff in 1998.
- *Faculty of Science:* This faculty trains scientists in the following specialties: B.Sc. degree programs in biology, computing, mathematics, chemistry, physics, statistics, and geology. The faculty also offers some postgraduate programs at the master's and doctoral levels. In 1998, the faculty had 383 students and 47 staff.

CENTERS AT UNAM

In addition to the faculties, UNAM also has the following centers that offer a variety of services to the university community and larger Namibian communities: the Center for External Studies, the Computer Center, the Language Center, the Multidisciplinary Research Center, and the University of Namibia Main Library.

THE NORTHERN CAMPUS

To provide wider access to university education, services, and programs, the university has established a campus in the northern Namibian city of Oshakati to serve the disadvantaged populations of that part of the country. Several of the university's programs are offered at this campus. The campus is developing rapidly, and university authorities are fully committed to making it even more viable in the years ahead.

Following its mission statement, UNAM developed enrollment projections for the Five-Year Plan for the various faculties and centers. Table 49.4 shows enrollment figures at UNAM for the period 1992–2000.

UNAM also identified the following priorities in the Five-Year Plan:

- Improve the governance of the university
- Promote a balanced output from the university system
- Prioritize the training programs
- Strengthen staff development
- Address some of the relics of the colonial regimes
- Strengthen linkages with ministries and the private sector
- Reduce unit costs
- Monitor staff performance
- Develop incentives to attract and retain talented staff
- Develop postgraduate programs in disciplines with good facilities and strong staffing
- Strengthen the university library
- Strengthen student support and internship programs
- Diversify sources of financing

Table 49.4. Student Enrollment at UNAM by Faculty/Center, 1992–2000

Faculty	1992	1993	1994	1995	1996	1997	1998	1999	2000
Agriculture, Natural Resources, and Conservation	—	—	—	—	28	69	103	141	165
Economics and Management Science	268	324	364	477	566	651	703	768	861
Education	347	396	472	597	775	780	688	683	699
Humanities and Social Sciences	271	356	392	436	409	390	403	423	477
Law	—	—	22	45	66	89	105	113	153
Medical and Health Sciences	635	690	758	724	628	533	439	386	334
Science	119	144	161	165	241	298	383	365	478
Centre for External Studies	1,994	1,705	1,408	1,769	847	726	965	1,403	308
Total	3,634	3,615	3,577	4,213	3,560	3,536	3,789	4,282	3,475

Source: Strategic Planning and Institutional Research.

IMPROVING THE GOVERNANCE OF THE UNIVERSITY

As management is a key factor in institution building, strengthening management through the use of strategic leadership, program management, and process management was identified as a priority in UNAM's Five-Year Plan.

Strategic leadership is normally associated with risk, vision, and ideas. It entails setting clear organizational goals and directing the efforts of staff and stakeholders alike toward fulfilling organizational objectives. Strategic leadership should develop ways of procuring essential resources, inspiring the institution's workforce and stakeholders to perform in ways that further the mission of the institution (Digolo 1995). One of UNAM's key objectives and goals has been to streamline, reorganize, and improve the governance of the university—to promote its management efficiency. This involves improving information flow; developing Internet systems; promoting staff training, especially among the administrative staff; and decentralizing certain tasks to short-circuit the bureaucracy. UNAM has positioned itself to make a significant contribution to the development needs of Namibia and its people using the revised governance structure of UNAM as described in the plan, the addition of the two pro-vice-chancellors (one for academic affairs and research and one for administration and finance), and the creation of posts for strategic planning and international relations.

PROMOTING A BALANCED OUTPUT FROM THE UNIVERSITY SYSTEM

During the pre-independence period, educational and training programs were heavily skewed toward the humanities, and dismal efforts were made to promote the teaching of natural and technological sciences at all levels. Consequently, the majority of black students, who hailed from poorly equipped schools, especially in the rural areas, almost exclusively enrolled in subjects leading to careers in the humanities and related disciplines. These included policy studies, Bible studies, psychology, and social work. UNAM is currently striving to attain a better balance of graduates by introducing new subject areas, increas-

ing enrollments in the natural sciences and technology-related fields, and establishing a new Faculty of Agriculture and Natural Resources. The university is expanding laboratory facilities in its Faculty of Science and is building new laboratories for the new agricultural faculty.

The plans to improve the teaching of science and mathematics in the schools and colleges are being implemented through close collaboration between the university's Faculties of Education and Science and the Ministry of Higher Education. In addition, new centers have been established within the various faculties to provide specific training programs for people from UNAM's various ministries and the private sector. These include the Center for Public Service Training in the Faculty of Economics and Management Science, which offers short in-service training courses in management and finance for public administrators, and the Justice Training Center in the newly established Faculty of Law, which aims to upgrade the skills and competence of legal personnel, such as magistrates. The university's Professional Legal Training Program provides intensive in-service courses for lawyers who obtained their original training in various countries during the pre-independence era and who wish to practice law in Namibia.

STRENGTHENING UNAM'S RESEARCH AND CONSULTANCY

In *Towards Education For All*, the Ministry of Education and Culture discussed the role of the University of Namibia in development, observing:

In part . . . [UNAM] is the keystone institution in our education system. As such it plays a central role in educating our senior educators and curriculum developers. It also undertakes and coordinates research designed to help us understand, evaluate, and improve our education system. . . . In part, our national university must be a beacon for learning. In its teaching and research it must value discovery, exploration, and understanding. It must be willing to address difficult issues and ask unpopular questions, systematically, thoroughly and persistently. It must insist that its learners, both novices and veterans, present their analyses and understanding in ways that are comprehensible and useful to both specialist and general audiences. (MEC 1993, 113)

During the pre-independence period, research and development activities were controlled from South Africa. Namibia now needs to plan and execute its own research programs, and UNAM should play a leading role in this endeavor. UNAM is striving to encourage academic staff members to undertake research and is seeking to strengthen research by forging close cooperation with relevant government institutions and the private sector. The university has also established a Multidisciplinary Research Center (MRC) in an attempt to promote multidisciplinary research activities and programs. The newly established Human Rights Documentation Center in the Faculty of Law is also helping to bring research findings to the community through a series of public meetings, seminars, and conferences; its major goal is to promote a democratic culture in Namibia.

STRENGTHENING STAFF DEVELOPMENT

In discussing employment policy at the tertiary level, the commission on Higher Education Report (the Turner Report) draws attention to Article 23 of the Namibian Constitution, which underlines the need for

the advancement of persons within Namibia who have been socially, economically or educationally disadvantaged by past discriminatory laws or practices [and] the implementation of policies and programs aimed at redressing social, economic or educational imbalances in the Namibian society arising out of past discriminatory laws or practices, or for achieving a balanced structuring of the public service. (GRN 1991, 203)

The Turner Report also points out that "the needs of affirmative action are not met simply by treating all applicants for a post on an equal footing on the basis of their academic records. A pool of applicants must be created by a positive staff development program." The report recommends the adoption of a local staff identification and development policy by higher educational institutions. Specifically, it suggests that "a staff development policy should be adopted to identify able students in their final year and prepare them to become possible future members of staff of the University. . . . Some over-production of such candidates should be attempted so that those who leave for other employment might be replaced (GRN 1991, 247).

Following the report, the Ministry of Education had the following to say about the development of local Namibian staff:

For the present and the immediate future, the very limited number of Namibians who have been able to complete their own higher education requires us to rely heavily on scholars and researchers in other countries. As an institution of excellence, our university will always have international scholars on its staff. But to be able to shape and implement our own agenda, we must aim toward a university faculty that is largely Namibian. . . . The graduates of a high quality undergraduate program will have ready access to the gradu-

ate education that will prepare them to become faculty members at our national university. (MEC 1993, 111)

Colonial regimes throughout Africa did not accord due importance to the provision of quality tertiary education to its indigenous people. UNAM has recently instituted a staff development program that seeks to promote the training of young Namibian academic and administrative staff with a view to attaining national self-reliance in skilled labor. Staff development has, indeed, been accorded a high priority in UNAM's first Five-Year Development Plan. In fact, a staff development program has already been proposed that takes into account the concerns expressed in both the Turner Report and the Ministry of Education document *Towards Education for All*.

STRENGTHENING LINKAGES WITH INSTITUTIONS IN AFRICA AND ABROAD

UNAM is striving to promote linkages with various other universities in an attempt to foster the exchange of expertise, for example, through the sharing of external examiners, students, staff, publications, and information. The linkages serve to ensure capacity building through staff exchanges, exposure and enhancement of leadership qualities through student exchanges, and the development of a research and publication culture through joint research and authorship. Through these formal networks with sister universities around the world, UNAM will gain in international recognition, academic credibility, and reputation.

Such linkages include UNITWIN arrangements with universities in Africa and sister universities outside the continent. The Utrecht-UNITWIN network for Southern Africa, which includes a partnership between the University of Namibia in Windhoek and the Universiteit Utrecht, the Netherlands, is a model of interuniversity cooperation. The areas of cooperation include research, staff exchange, and materials development in areas such as mathematics and science education, human rights, immunology and infectious diseases, and environmental studies. UNAM also has several bilateral cooperative agreements with leading universities in Africa, Europe, and the United States which are helping to reinforce UNAM's capacity in areas such as teaching, research, and management. In addition, UNAM has established a partnership with the United Nations University in Tokyo.

DEVELOPING INCENTIVES FOR ATTRACTING AND RETAINING TALENTED STAFF

In its First Five-Year Development Plan (1995–1999), UNAM identified the "development of incentives for attracting and retaining staff" as a key objective for its first five years. UNAM is striving to develop into a national institution of higher learning that is characterized by standards of excellence. To attain this goal, the salaries and terms and conditions of service offered by the institution must be attractive and competitive enough to serve as a pull factor for qualified staff. At the moment, however, UNAM is unable to attract a sufficient number of qualified

Namibians because of poor conditions of service. Many Namibians who have declined the university's offers of employment have cited low salaries and benefits as the primary reason. To build a critical mass of Namibian academics, and to attract reputable international academics to the institution, these conditions will have to change. Only through high standards of excellence and well-motivated and competent administrative and academic staff can UNAM achieve its mission and contribute meaningfully to social change.

STRENGTHENING THE UNIVERSITY LIBRARY

UNAM recognizes the fact that possession of a good library is a critical prerequisite in any university establishment. The library inherited from the former academy was grossly inadequate. UNAM is currently examining ways of strengthening the library to serve the university community and the general public more effectively. One step in this direction is the establishment of the Human Resources Development Project. This involves the construction of an Information and Instructional Resource Center (IIRC). The center will be furnished and equipped with modern information technology, which will make it possible for all geographical locations in Namibia to access its resources. Existing technology already enables the library to link up with other information resource centers worldwide. In addition, the library is developing a strategy for the management and effective utilization of IIRC resources and information-technology systems through the training of information professionals and of trainers and users in general. Beneficiaries of the training program will be selected to represent the following priority areas: basic education teacher training, vocational and technical training, non-formal education, public service training, training in industry, training in agriculture and fishing, and science and technology education.

Establishing a library with rich and diverse holdings is an urgent priority, for it remains one of the most cost-effective ways of achieving overall human resources development. The acquisition, organization, and dissemination of knowledge and information is critical to learning, teaching, research, and development. The library enables students, staff, and other users to further their creativity and personal growth. The Human Resources Development Project should ultimately result in the improved quality and increased capacity of employable workers in Namibia.

UNAM is also in the process of being connected to the Internet. This will enable the university, its regional centers, and other local educational institutions to have access to key information on research and development.

FINANCING AND DIVERSIFYING SOURCES OF FINANCING

Like most other universities, the key source of funding for UNAM is the government. Considering that Namibia emerged from colonial rule only recently and that it is still in its infancy, its main source of finances will continue to be the government in the foreseeable future. There is the hope that the government will step up, rather than scale down, the budgetary allocation to UNAM. Regardless of what happens, the university will endeavor to raise additional funds from external sources such as the private sector and the international donor community. The university is also striving to promote cost-effectiveness, rational budgeting, efficient administration, accountability, and a sound culture of maintenance and control of its assets.

UNAM also recognizes the key roles to be played by the polytechnic and other institutions of higher learning, including the colleges of education and technical and vocational colleges.

The university believes that the best and most cost-effective model to adopt is one in which different institutions occupy different niches and perform separate roles within the overall higher education system. This approach is supported by the experience of other developing countries.

The University of Namibia has made significant progress since its establishment in 1992. Yet as it develops its next Five-Year Plan (2000–2004), it is accurate to say that it faces significant constraints and challenges.

CONSTRAINTS AND CHALLENGES FACING UNAM

Today, more than ever before in human history, the wealth — or poverty — of nations depends on the quality of higher education. Those with a larger repertoire of skills and a greater capacity for learning can look forward to lifetimes of unprecedented economic fulfillment. But in the coming decades the poorly educated face little better than the dreary prospects of lives of quiet desperation.

—Malcolm Gillis, president of Rice University, February 12, 1999

During its First Five-Year Development Plan, the University of Namibia has made significant achievements on several fronts. A governance structure has been put in place, new programs have replaced those inherited from the academy days, student academic support has been provided, and research, teaching, and community outreach have been undertaken with some success, as evidenced from reports of external examiners and an audit conducted by outside assessors. As the university embarks on the preparation of the Second Five-Year Development Plan, the educational goals of the country that emphasize access, equity, equality, and democracy will come into conflict with the goal of excellence to which the university aspires. In particular, the university faces several constraints and challenges in the area of teaching.

Many students come from rural schools to tertiary institutions, including the university, which are usually located in big towns and cities. Students need time to adjust to and function effectively in their new environment. Further, many students have difficulty with the language of instruction, which often is their second or third language. Consequently, at least initially, they will experience difficulties following lecturers, taking notes, and engaging in discussions. The attitudes that students bring to the learning situation may also pose problems. For instance, the selection of the field of study may be influenced more by what is considered prestigious. In addition, academic deficiencies or socioeconomic problems can distract students from learning.

Teachers, Materials, and Facilities

Many lecturers in African universities have not had formal exposure to methods of instruction or the principles of learning, and this interferes with their effective teaching. This imposes serious limitations on how well they impart their knowledge.

Regarding materials, many textbooks do not include relevant local or contextualized issues or illustrations. In addition, the language of the textbooks may be too difficult if they are written in the student's second or third language. Moreover, in many African universities, including UNAM, facilities, including library and laboratory space, are becoming severely strained because of increasing enrollments.

Evaluation Process

In many African institutions, including UNAM, although the role of continual assessment is recognized, it appears that final examinations are actually the decisive factor in evaluation. This can be explained in several ways. With lecturers burdened with big classes and with heavy teaching and administrative loads, it is difficult to provide ongoing assessments in written form or in field or practical situations.

Other problems concerning student evaluation need to be addressed. Sometimes different lecturers teach different sections of the same course but do not use the same evaluation procedure. In some cases, some lecturers are not sufficiently familiar with a variety of assessment procedures or the use of examination results as a means of providing feedback in order to improve the teaching-learning process.

Overall Learning Environment

Many African universities, including UNAM, are largely financed by governments that are themselves experiencing financial constraints. Consequently, it has become increasingly difficult to acquire required materials and facilities to provide for optimal conditions for teaching, learning, and research.

All of these teaching and learning issues constitute new and continuing challenges for the university, as does the need for research.

NEED FOR RESEARCH

At a research seminar entitled Development and Its Implications for Research in Namibia held in 1992, Dr. Philip Coombes of the International Council for Educational Development in Connecticut warned against "fashionable" and "desk" research if Namibia wanted to make any real contribution to meaningful development. He asserted that the vast body of research work in developing countries, particularly in the field of education, had been "largely useless" because it had not bridged the gap between researcher and practitioner and could justly be accused of irrelevance.

In the same address, Coombes warned about unease and distrust between "university people and government people," which would do nothing but hinder development efforts, though he readily acknowledged that such distrust seemed difficult to avoid in developing countries. In many developing countries, he pointed out, it often seemed that the institutions didn't speak the same language, had nothing in common, and made few attempts at decent dialogue.

Namibia has a formidable research agenda. The country needs not only basic research but, and this need is more immediate, applied research that can generate knowledge and information that policymakers can use to tackle the myriad problems that a young and developing nation faces. In this respect, all stakeholders need to encourage dialogue between policy initiators and researchers. Policymakers in developing countries, as elsewhere, are under pressure to take bold initiatives, often based on insufficient information and knowledge. Yet these policymakers may be discontented because social research does not always answer their questions, and so controversies have tended to arise among scholars and decision makers over the nature of social research, including educational research, and its impact on education. I believe that education can be improved through research, but it seems to me that collaboration, dialogue, and consultation between all parties concerned is a sine qua non for this to happen.

In the Second Five-Year Plan, the university needs to continue to address the need to consolidate existing programs, procedures, and practices, and to prioritize new areas for development.

THE WAY FORWARD FOR UNAM

UNAM is in the difficult position of being the only university in a country with a small population and a small national income. In a situation like this, the university is expected to address a wide range of human development needs. Funding is limited, and the lack of economies of scale makes many programs expensive. However, if UNAM does not address these needs, the skills development program of the country will remain skewed, as in the days of colonialism and apartheid.

It is unlikely that state funding for UNAM will increase significantly, given the limited growth of the economy. Therefore, to meet this funding gap, the university is actively seeking funds from international development partners, the local private sector, and income-generating activities.

Several major new initiatives (outlined below) have been identified as critically important to the university in successfully addressing the nation's development priorities. With a significant investment in human resource development over the next five years, planners hope that sustainable economic growth will take place that will both enable the continued funding of such projects and markedly raise the quality of life of the Namibian people.

The Northern Campus at Oshakati

UNAM established a second campus in the major northern town of Oshakati during 1998, following significant consultations with a broad range of community stakeholders. The vision for the campus is to act as a major coordinator and catalyst for both economic and educational development within the region.

The development of the Northern Campus has been informed by the models for community engagement, as utilized by community colleges and other institutions in the United States and by South African higher education outreach and access initiatives. During 1999, a comprehensive series of participative planning workshops were organized to produce an integrated campus and a regional development plan.

The university now needs to implement its component of this plan in terms of providing formal educational programs, short courses, consultancy and applied research, and business courses and information.

An "enhanced open learning" delivery mode has been developed that uses a mix of audiovisual and information technologies, tutoring and lecturing staff, and other learning materials to provide cost-effective high-quality education. Further building phases are also planned to provide a community development unit, additional classrooms, laboratories, offices, and other student support facilities.

Namibia Business School

The university has recognized the need to work more closely with the business community and to shift the focus of management education, consultancy, and research toward the private sector, especially small- and medium-sized enterprises.

The Faculty of Economic and Management Science, in addition to offering the current Bachelor of Accounting and Bachelor of Economics degrees, will launch an undergraduate Bachelor of Business Administration and a collaborative Master of Business Administration in 2000. An industrial advisory board to the faculty has also been established. UNAM plans to bring together and further develop its business-oriented departments and programs to form a business school, the Namibia Business School, modeled partially on American and European business schools but with a unique Namibian orientation.

In addition to a full range of formal programs, the business school would undertake applied research and consultancy for private-sector clients and provide short-course training and advisory services in close cooperation with relevant ministries and private-sector partners.

A new building well-equipped with information and communication technology facilities and with high-quality seminar and lecture rooms is envisaged at the Windhoek Campus. Business-oriented academics would be needed to complement the current management, accounting, and economics staff.

Faculty of Technology

The Faculty of Science at UNAM is growing fast and has recently launched new applied science and engineering programs in consultation with the relevant industrial community. Currently, these applied courses, including geology, have relatively small intakes because they are limited by physical facilities and staffing constraints.

The university plans to bring together its current geology and engineering programs and its established computing science department to form a Faculty of Technology. Expanded student numbers, new applied and multidisciplinary programs, and a strong emphasis on vocational business through internships and industrial apprenticeships will be features of this new unit.

Student and Community Development Center

The university has long recognized the particular learning needs that students face when they enter higher education in Namibia. It established a Language Center, designed primarily to develop English and communication skills, so that students could meet the requirements of their academic programs. A similar need for training in core mathematics has now been identified. The university plans to bring together its language instruction with the teaching of other foundational skills, such as mathematics and information technology, into a single center. In addition to providing vital programs for the university's internal students, the Center would also open its doors to the community, enabling others to develop their core educational skills for further study or to improve their employability.

Beyond these educational programs, the university also needs to address broader community needs. A focused range of community services are planned, including advice and counseling related to ongoing research on the HIV/AIDS pandemic and other social issues; legal advice, utilizing senior students and staff; and small business advice and information linked to the business school.

A combined, well-equipped Student and Community Development Center is thus envisaged for the Windhoek Campus. A core of well-qualified teachers in the fields of English as a second language, local languages, information technology, and mathematics would be complemented by the part-time contributions of staff and students from several faculties.

Center for the Development and Application of Technology

Namibia's economy is dominated by primary industries such as mineral extraction, agriculture, and fisheries. The country has a weak manufacturing base. It faces significant problems over the sustainable use of its land and water resources, though it has abundant solar energy and a rich coastal marine environment. The country's economic development and the quality of life of its people rely heavily on its ability to develop and apply scientific solutions to these complex problems.

Recognizing these concerns, UNAM has established a Multidisciplinary Research Center with a small Technology Transfer Unit. Research work is being undertaken in solar energy, marine resources, sustainable agriculture, and agribusiness in collaboration with the faculties of science and agriculture and natural resources. The university plans to bring together and expand upon such activities in a single national center: the Center for the Development and Application of Technology, to be located in Tsumeb, a former principal mining town that has experienced serious decline. Tsumeb is strategically situated in the populous and disadvantaged North Central Regions and has good communications links to the northwest and the capital,

Windhoek. Tsumeb has the additional advantage of surplus educational and residential facilities that can be readily utilized and a relatively skilled local workforce.

Applicable Research and Staff Development

One of the major objectives of UNAM is to increase the quantity and quality of applied research related to national development concerns. This can partially be addressed through the proposed Center for the Development and Application of Technology, but it also needs to be undertaken throughout the university's faculties. A nascent research culture needs to be considerably strengthened, and collaborative links, both with the local private and public sectors and with international (and particularly regional) institutions, need to be expanded and enhanced.

A major staff development drive over the last five years has resulted in a considerable increase in the proportion of academic staff who are Namibian (67 percent in 2000). These relatively junior staff now need to be mentored and developed, especially regarding their research capabilities and output. Thus, applicable research and staff development are closely interrelated critical issues influencing the university's ability to achieve its strategic goals.

SUMMARY STATEMENT

Since 1990, the importance of the role of UNAM in the emerging post-apartheid tertiary education system of Namibia has attracted the interest and attention of many authors and institutions. Examining and defining this role is a necessary and ongoing exercise. This process is essential in order to keep the mission, structure, and functioning of the university on pace with the ever-changing challenges that will arise from the country's political, economic, social, and cultural development in the future.

The ongoing monitoring of the university's achievements in education, service, and development is usually embedded in an orchestrated, future-oriented and solution-finding undertaking initiated by the university itself, though it should involve all constituency groups of tertiary education. W. S. Saint's key question —"What kind of university does/can a country have, need and afford?"—is currently considered to be a suitable "analytical triangle" of investigation into the sustainability of demand-centered systems of higher education.

The multi-faceted geographical and historical particularity of Namibia—resulting from its aridity, peripheral zones, and dispersed-to-isolated settlement systems—seems to require an additional concept of analysis, and that is the concept of space and time. Namibia's national university is located in the center of the country's capital area, distant from the densely populated North that stretches from Ruacana in the west to Katima Mulilo in the east and the less densely populated, more arid regions south of Rehoboth.

Since 1992, the inherited academy of the dissolved apartheid regime has been successfully transformed into an academic platform for evolution and revolution in education. Within

the scope of the available institutional and human resources, UNAM has sought to confidently contribute its part to the complex goals and objectives of the overall national development.

In tackling the uncounted tasks inherent in the mission, UNAM consolidated and phased out old programs, introduced the three-term academic year and the four-year bachelor's degree curriculum, and established new faculties such as the Faculty of Law and the Faculty of Agriculture and Natural Resources. The university is gaining considerable momentum in bringing life to a mission—which was set in its 1995 annual report—that is highly responsive to transmural partnership in addressing development needs in education and research.

The magnitude of this task is enormous and must be carried out in cooperation with all constituency groups in the educational arena. Obviously, many more challenges lie ahead as we move into the next millennium.

CONCLUDING REMARKS

In a recent document, the Association for the Development of African Education indicated that successful education reform in Africa is dependent on the quality of the underlying education policy—both the *content* of the policy and the *processes* that lead to policy formulation. In looking at case studies on policy formulation in Africa, the document states: "Running through all the cases are two central themes: the need for publicly stated education policies which are understood and supported by both government and civil society, and the importance of participation by the diverse parts of society that will be affected by the policies" (ADEA 1995, 27). It is our belief that the Ministry of Higher Education, Vocational Training, Science and Technology, as well as UNAM, has consulted widely and will continue to do so as they develop policies that affect tertiary and higher education in Namibia.

REFERENCES

Ajayi, J. F. Ade, K. H. Goma Lameck, and G. Ampah Johnson. 1996. *The African Experience with Higher Education.* Athens, Ohio: Ohio University Press.

Angula, N. 1994. "Development of Tertiary Education in Namibia and Future Prospects." Address to the Annual Meeting of the Namibian Educational Management and Administration Society (NEMAS), Windhoek, Namibia, July.

Coombes, P. 1992. "Namibia to Guard against Fashionable and Desk Research." Paper presented at Academy on the Theme Development and Its Implications for Research in Namibia, Windhoek, Namibia, July.

ADEA. 1995. *Formulating Education Policy: Lessons and Experience from Sub-Saharan Africa.* Paris: International Institute for Educational Planning.

Digolo, M. A. 1995. "Management Issues in African Universities." Paper presented at the BOLESWA Biannual Educational Research Symposium, Gaborone, Botswana, August.

GRN (Government of the Republic of Namibia). 1991. *Higher Education in Namibia: Report of a Presidential Commission.* Windhoek: Government of the Republic of Namibia.

———. 1996. *First Draft of National Human Resources Plan 1997– 2010.* Windhoek: National Planning Commission.

MEC (Ministry of Basic Education and Culture). 1993. *Towards Education for All: A Development Brief for Education, Culture Training.* Windhoek: Gamsberg Macmillan.

Ministry of Higher Education, Vocational Training, Science and Technology. 1999. *Investing in People, Developing a Country.* Windhoek: Gamsberg Macmillan.

Obanya, P. 1999. *The Dilemma of Education in Africa.* Dakar: UNESCO Regional Office.

Saint, W. 1992. *Universities in Africa: Strategies for Stabilization and Revitalization.* World Bank Technical Paper no. 194. Africa Technical Department Series. Washington, D.C.: The World Bank.

Task Force on Higher Education and Society. 2000. *Higher Education in Developing Countries: Peril and Promise.* Washington, D.C.: The World Bank.

UNDP and UNAIDS. 1997. *Namibia Human Development Report 1997.* Windhoek: UNDP.

University of Namibia. 1993–1998. Annual Reports.

———. 1995. *First Five Year Development Plan, 1995–99.* Compiled by Keto E. Mshigeni, Andre du Pisani, and Geoff E. Kiangi. Windhoek: UNAM.

World Bank. 1994. *Higher Education: The Lessons of Experience.* Washington, D.C.: The World Bank.

———. 1995. *Priorities and Strategies for Education.* Washington, D.C.: The World Bank.

———. 1997. *Revitalizing Universities in Africa: Strategy and Guidelines.* Washington, D.C.: The World Bank.

———. 1998. *Education in Sub-Saharan Africa: Policies for Adjustment, Revitalization, and Expansion.* Washington, D.C.: The World Bank.

50

Niger

Abdoulaye Niandou Souley

INTRODUCTION

The University Abdou Moumouni (Université Abdou Moumouni, UAM) is the most important higher education institution in Niger. It includes five schools, a Teacher School (Ecole Normale Supérieure, ENS), and three research institutes (the Human Sciences Research Institute, the Mathematics Research Institute, and the Radioisotope Institute). Other higher education institutions include the Islamic University of Say and specialized institutions such as the National School for Administration (Ecole Nationale d'Administration, ENA); the School of Mining, Industry, and Geology (Ecole des Mines, d'Industrie et de Géologie, EMIG); and the Institute for Information Sciences and Techniques (Institut de Formation aux Sciences et Techniques de l'Information, IFTIC).

Because of the diversity of educational programs offered at Abdou Moumouni University and the large number of enrollments, the university concentrates the majority of its activities on teaching. The few research initiatives that exist do not benefit from the same attention given to teaching.

BRIEF HISTORICAL VIEW

The Niamey Higher Education Center (Centre d'Enseignement Supérieur, CES), which was created in 1971, became a university in 1973. Its mission revolved around three objectives: providing higher education; carrying out scientific, basic, and applied research activities; and training executive managers.

To quote Joachim Lama, "The main social gains that were expected consisted of reducing the cost of education in comparison to education at foreign universities, increasing the number of Nigerien students accessing higher education, and finally adapting programs to the real needs of the country. To ensure and maximize these gains, the Ministry of Higher Education,

Research and Technology was created in 1978" (Lama 1999, 4). The ministry's mission consisted of five tasks: the elaboration and the implementation of higher education and research policy in accordance with the government's orientation, the coordination of the orientation of students and trainees, the centralization of the management and control of scholarships destined for secondary and higher education, the promotion and coordination of research activity, and, finally, the organization of national civil service in collaboration with other ministries.

The educational system operated in a satisfactory manner up to the beginning of the 1980s. By that time, the functioning of the Niamey Higher Education Center had started to deteriorate and its mission had been compromised by a number of problems and malfunctions, namely progressive cuts in the higher education budget, an increase in the number of students eligible for scholarships, the weakening of the central structure—that is, the Ministry of Education itself—and the absence of a clear policy for higher education and research. The malfunctioning of the university was obvious at various levels: student supervision was inadequate and the standard of living of the entire university community (students, faculty, and personnel) had deteriorated. Many faculty members and researchers decided to put their expertise to use at more promising institutions (ones that offered better salaries and working conditions), the gap between the job market and the programs offered at the university widened, and research programs were carried out with no real relevance to the country's developmental needs. In 1985, however, a major development occurred when the advanced schools acquired full status as an integral part of the university, and in 1993, Niamey University changed its name to Abdou Moumouni University (AMU) in honor of the renowned physicist. Abdou Moumouni was also director of the National Office for Solar Energy (Office National de l'Energie Solaire, ONERSOL), former president of Niamey University, and former senior professor at the School of Sciences.

Table 50.1. Enrollment by Gender at the School of Health Sciences at Abdou Moumouni University, 2000

Department	Male	Female	Total
Medical Studies	732	333	1,065
Surgery Assistance	16	2	18
Radiology	15	0	15
Anesthesia	11	10	21
Total	774	345	1,119

Source: Service Central de la Scolarité de l'Université Abdou Moumouni, Niamey, Niger.

According to Joachim Lama,

The difficulties that the Niamey University faces have two main sources: organizational problems and insufficient financial means. The logic of minimizing expenses, which became the management motto, could not be sustained for long. It is in reaction to this situation that the Nigerien government decided to launch a strategy for the development of higher education, a strategy that is likely to provide pertinent answers and sustainable solutions to the problems faced by Nigerien higher education and scientific research. Such comprehensive objectives necessitate, of course, the mobilization of all available competencies. (Lama 1999)

ENROLLMENTS, SCHOOLS, ADVANCED SCHOOLS, AND INSTITUTES

The University Abdou Moumouni at Niamey consists of schools, advanced schools, and institutes. Heads of schools are called deans, while directors run the advanced schools and institutes. Nowadays, the university is composed of five schools: the Faculty of Sciences (Faculté des Sciences, FS), the Faculty of Health Sciences (Faculté des Sciences de la Santé, FSS), the Faculty of Agronomy (Faculté d'Agronomie, FA), the Faculty of Humanities (Faculté des Lettres et des Sciences Humaines, FLSH), and the Faculty of Law and Economics (Faculté des Sciences Economiques et Juridiques, FSEJ). The university also has three institutes: the Radioisotope Institute (Institut des Radio-Isotopes, IRI), the Mathematics Research Institute (Institut de Recherche en Mathématiques, IREM), and the Human Sciences Research Institute (Institut de Recherche en Sciences Humaines, IRSH). Finally, the university has one advanced school, the Teacher School (Ecole Normale Supérieur, ENS).

University student enrollment in Niger underwent huge increases for several reasons. The creation of the higher education center in 1971 and its conversion into a university in 1973 meant that high school graduates were no longer obliged to leave for countries of the subregion such as Côte d'Ivoire, Senegal, Cameroon, Togo, Morocco, Algeria, or Tunisia to begin their university studies. As the head of the Central Department for Schooling noted, "If our educational structures are not improved to meet the imperatives of modernity, information technology, and the challenges of globalization, very soon we will no longer be able to accommodate students" (Mounkaila, personal

communication). According to him, the problem lies mainly in controlling student access (Ministère 1996). Indeed, the enrollment capacity of the UAM is very limited. In this respect, a politico-philosophical question arises as to whether one should control enrollment or democratize access to higher education. On this issue, two opposing claims are made. The first maintains that an open-door policy should be extended to everyone, otherwise the *baccalauréat* (high school diploma), which is the first step into the university, has no raison d'être. The other claim argues that because of insufficiencies in university infrastructure, selection is necessary to allow access to the best candidates. This debate has not come to any resolution, and enrollment is still increasing. With the exception of the research institutes, recent statistics testify to these increases (Ministère 1997a).

SCHOOL OF HUMANITIES

The School of Humanities consists of eight departments: sociology, psychology, philosophy, English, geography, literature, history, and linguistics. The total number of students is 2,858 (among which 687 are female), making it the largest school in terms of student numbers. A breakdown of the total number by departments shows that the departments of sociology, geography, and English host the largest numbers of students: sociology enrolls 839 students (273 female students), while geography has 556 students (70 female students). Finally, the English department has 437 students, with 153 female students.

SCHOOL OF HEALTH SCIENCES

The School of Health Sciences enrolls a total of 1,119 students, of whom 345 are women. The school is composed of four main departments: medical studies, surgery assistance, radiology, and anesthesia (Table 50.1).

SCHOOL OF SCIENCES

The distribution of students in the School of Sciences is particularly complex due to the fact that it serves as a prep school for the agronomy school.

In 1973, when the Center for Higher Education (CES) was converted into a university, decision makers set priorities in having both a school for the sciences offering mathematics and physics and a pedagogical school (Ghali). The agronomy preparatory school (which is part of the School of Agriculture) has a total of 463 students, of whom 63 are female. To join the School of Agronomy, students can go for a two-year study period at the School of Sciences (Table 50.2).

The Department of Chemistry, Biology, and Geology accounts for 239 students, 27 of whom are women. Students in these disciplines can either continue their specialties in the same departments or switch to other departments at the end of their sophomore year.

The Mathematics and Physics Department is considered an essential component of the School of Sciences. The importance of such disciplines is warranted by the fact that they were the nucleus that started the School of Sciences. The School of Sci-

Table 50.2. Enrollment by Gender at the School of Sciences, Abdou Moumouni University, 2000

Department	Male	Female	Total
Preparatory School of Agronomy (School of Sciences)	400	63	463
Math/Physics	252	9	261
Physics/Chemistry	219	13	232
Chemistry/Biology/Geology	212	27	239
Total	1,083	112	1,195

Source: Service Central de la Scolarité de l'Université Abdou Moumouni, Niamey, Niger.

Table 50.3. Enrollment by Gender at the Schools of Abdou Moumouni University, 2000

School	Male	Female	Total
Humanities	2,171	687	2,858
Law and Economics	1,892	478	2,370
Sciences	1,083	112	1,195
Health Sciences	774	345	1,119
Agronomy	201	49	250
Teacher Training	142	14	156
Total	6,263	1,685	7,948

Source: Service Central de la Scolarité de l'Université Abdou Moumouni, Niamey, Niger.

ences generally enrolls a total of 1,195 students, of whom 9.37 percent are female.

SCHOOL OF AGRONOMY

The School of Agronomy trains technical engineers in agronomy (Ingénieur des Techniques Agricoles, ITA). Students begin their training at Niamey and continue their studies at Université Montpellier in France. Some graduates engage in research, while others prefer to apply their know-how working as professionals. The 250-student community at the school is composed of 19.6 percent women. The School of Agronomy also hosts the Regional Center for Sahelian Studies in Agronomy (Centre-Régional d'Etudes Sahéliennes en Agronomie, CRESA).

TEACHER SCHOOL

Along with the School of Sciences, the Teacher School is one of the first units that started Niamey University. The initial mission of the school was to train junior high school teachers. Later, the Advanced School of Pedagogy dropped the label "Advanced" and became the Teacher School, training educational inspectors for senior high school, pedagogical counselors for junior high school, and holders of the High School Teachers' Certificate (*Certificat d'Aptitude Professionnelle à l'Enseignement du Second Degré*, CAPES). The Teacher School enrolls 156 students, of whom 8.9 percent are female.

SCHOOL OF LAW AND ECONOMICS

The School of Law and Economics was the last unit to be established at Abdou Moumouni University at Niamey, which explains the fact that its branches are scattered over the two banks of the Niger River. The school hosts a number of miscellaneous services such as the central library, the Service for Degree Equivalency, the Baccalauréat Office, the Central Service for Schooling, and a laboratory used by the School of Sciences. Deprived on all levels, the school enrolls 2,370 students, of whom 20.17 percent are female.

Despite the flexibility witnessed recently at the level of en-rollments, control of access remains a serious concern because of the lack of appropriate infrastructure. Currently, a number of solutions are envisioned to control enrollments and create a new university infrastructure. The present overall distribution of students over the various schools at Abdou Moumouni University is given in Table 50.3.

CURRENT TENDENCIES AND CHANGES IN HIGHER EDUCATION INSTITUTIONS

Because UAM is a relatively young institution, a number of changes are still taking place at different levels. The university faces a number of challenges in each of its components, schools, research institutes, and advanced schools. Indeed, the need for modernization, globalization, and adaptation requires the computerization of the overall university infrastructures.

Research professors who wish to publish in scientific journals or through collective publications are expected to submit their works using modern technologies such as computers. There is also a need for technical and administrative personnel who are capable of making the transition to using information technology.

Two other primary challenges that face all units of UAM concern the adaptation of university study programs to the present context and the creation of a graduate cycle, especially in the mathematics and geology departments. Faculty in the law and economics department are equally concerned with creating new majors and delivering degrees, such as certificates and master's degrees in public administration. Future plans also consist of creating graduate degrees (DEA, DES) in computer science to keep abreast of the globalization trend. Concerns about globalization are also reflected in the preoccupation of research professors with publication and research.

At the Teacher School, two major changes are being implemented: new majors have been created to train pedagogical inspectors in biology, physics, mathematics, English, history, and geography; and the school is getting a special Internet connection, which will benefit faculty, students, and technical/administrative personnel.

Higher education institutions agree unanimously that decisions to change and revamp higher education should come from within the universities. The university resists any measure that does not emanate from the University Council (CU), which is the only decision-making body the university recognizes.

Every year the university suggests new strategies and plans without any possibility to implement them because of lack of financial support on the part of successive governments. The same fate befalls all plans that the government proposes to improve the university.

Privatization is not part of the plan for university development for the time being; the University of Niamey, the major institution in the country, is a public institution sustained through government subsidies. The university community has been debating the possibility of nonpublic means of funding without making reference to privatization. A "reflection committee" has been established to brainstorm about new ways to tap nonpublic funding for Abdou Moumouni University.

STUDY PROGRAMS

Study programs vary both between and within schools. The philosophy that guides the design of study programs is regulated by the country's developmental concerns (Banque Mondiale 1996). The evaluation system in certain schools follows the credit system (as is the case in the School of Humanities) (Foulani 1994), while in other schools evaluation is organized in terms of major and minor courses (as is the case for the School of Law and Economics). In the latter situation, seventy-six study hours are devoted to major courses of study and thirty-eight hours to minor courses of study.

LANGUAGE OF INSTRUCTION AND ITS IMPACT

The language of instruction in Niger is French, a reflection of the influence of colonization. It is difficult to measure the impact of the use of French as a language for learning. It obviously would have been preferable to conduct education in a national language that is common to the elite as well as the masses, the governors, and the governed. One difficulty resides in the transfer of certain concepts—especially in economics—from French into national languages. The same problem holds true for political and economic discourses, which are difficult to render into local languages. In order not to confine studies to some reduced form of communication, the Islamic University of Say conducts studies in Arabic, French, and English (Bergmann et al. 1999).

It is to be noted, however, that French is not used as a language of instruction and communication by the majority of Nigeriens, since only 29 percent go to school (Mingat, Jarousse, and Hamidou 1988). This creates a real gap between educated elite and the rest of the population.

SPECIFIC PROBLEMS

A number of problems plague Nigerien higher education, including student activism, political interference, unemployment among graduates, and brain drain. Brain drain is less significant in Niger than in other African countries; the Nigerien educational system guarantees a public position to every higher education graduate, which makes Nigeriens less tempted by experiences offered abroad. Moreover, it has been noted in Europe as well as in the United States that students from Niger generally return to the home country after they finish their studies. Nevertheless, as a result of the decline in state subsidies, initial planning efforts were jeopardized and the problem of unemployment has reached the same level as in other countries, such as Côte d'Ivoire, Senegal, Cameroon, Benin, Togo, and Nigeria (Charfani, Fatimata, Saley, and Mariama 1996).

Political interference in the university is real, but it is difficult to provide evidence of its existence. Successive governments have sought to control the university rather than establish a healthy relationship with it. To attain this objective, governments have used a number of tactics and various political tools. In fact, empirical investigation in these matters proves that there is always a political rationale behind student movements, which leads one to question the validity of student activism itself. Though the students are politically active, they do not operate independently, and their actions are either dependent on economic operators (as is the case for providers of university student social services) or are dictated through obscure channels by certain political leaders.

The consequence of this situation has been the demise of internal democracy within the student population, which explains the resort to internal violence among students and external violence toward authorities (with demonstrations, strikes, or sit-ins).

ADMINISTRATION OF ABDOU MOUMOUNI UNIVERSITY

The university president is elected by the faculty for a three-year term renewable once. Two vice-presidents assist the president in managing the university's affairs. The president and the vice-presidents are elected on the same day from a general list of candidates.

Deans act as chairs for the schools through a one-time renewable term of three years. In the absence of vice-deans, department heads and their faculty assist the deans in their duties. Heads of departments are elected by their peers for a two-year once-renewable term. Other staff members who assist the deans in their functions are the principal secretary, the financial agent, and the physical plant manager.

Students have a special structure to meet their needs, the National Center for University Social Services (Centre National des Œuvres Sociales, CNOU). Formerly a unit of the university, CNOU is currently the responsibility of the Ministry of Higher Education, Research, and Scientific Technology. CNOU is responsible for housing, transportation, and scholarships. In 2001, the Agence Nationale d'Attribution des Bourses (ANAB), which replaced the Commission Nationale d'Orientation et d'Attribution des Bourses (CNOAB), was created, which operates independently of the Ministry of Higher Education (Cabinet du Premier Ministre 1996).

Technical and administrative personnel come under the authority of the University General Secretary. Distributed among the various schools, institutes, and advanced schools that compose the university, they perform general administrative tasks ranging from mail and janitorial services to administrative assistance. They also act as secretaries or laboratory assistants working at the science, health sciences, and agronomy schools.

RESEARCH, PUBLICATION, AND TEACHING

Research and publication are not well supported at UAM, although research professors, in collaboration with other partners, attempt to establish working teams. It is through such endeavors that a reference book on Niger has been published under the direction of Professor Kimba Idrissa in the history department at the School of Humanities.

Other teams of researchers are active in the School of Agronomy and the School of Health Sciences. The essential problem is the lack of a communication network through which research results could be disseminated.

The problem of striking a balance between research and teaching is also among the main concerns of research faculty, as the country is in need of professors, which means that those with a research vocation are obliged to teach instead of carrying out research activities. The lack of financial resources also impedes research, as universities have only two sources of income for this work: outside financial support, which needs to be sought and negotiated, and partnerships forged with colleagues in the northern countries. Generally, research in Niger is funded through external resources.

PRESENT CHALLENGES FACING NIGERIEN HIGHER EDUCATION

Abdou Moumouni University needs to revamp its infrastructure in order to keep abreast of trends toward globalization and internationalization that are sweeping the higher education industry. The entire university system needs to be computerized. Technical and administrative personnel need to undergo special training programs to update their skills and practices. Finally, there is a need to motivate doctoral student candidates to complete their dissertations in order to provide enough full-time faculty members to replace the overwhelming number of part-timers.

The main problem for the future is infrastructure. Student numbers are increasing on a yearly basis, which creates the need to build large laboratories, classrooms, and amphitheaters. Last but not least, all university facilities need to be insured against theft and fire hazards.

BIBLIOGRAPHY

ADEA (Association pour le Développement de l'Education en Afrique). 1995. *Formulation d'une politique éducative: enseignement et experiences d'Afrique Sub-Saharienne.* Paris: Institut International pour la Planification de l'éducation (IIPE).

Banque Mondiale. 1996. *Niger, évaluation de la pauvreté: un peuple résistant dans un environnement hostile.* Washington, D.C.: Banque Mondiale.

Bergmann, H., T. Bittner, M. Hovens, H. Kamayé, M. G. Mallam, and J. Saley. 1999. *Évaluation de l'école experimentale, esquisse d'un bilan de 25 ans d'experimentation de l'enseignement en langues nationales au Niger.* Niamey: Deutsche Gesellschaft für Technische Zusammenarbeit (GTZ).

Cabinet du Premier Ministre, Niger. 1996. "Rapport du Comité ad'hoc de réflexion sur la gestion des bourses." Niamey.

Charfani, L., M. Fatimata, A. Saley, and T. Mariama. 1996. "Examens des possibilités de mobilisation des ressources additionnelles en faveur des services sociaux essentiels: l'initiative 20 percent–20 percent." Niamey: UNICEF.

Chau, T. N., and F. Caillads. 1976. *Financement et Politique d'éducation: le cas du Sénegal.* Paris: IIPE and UNESCO.

Farid, A., R. Abdou, H. Kip, and A. Tchambou. 1998. *Coût et financement de l'éducation de base au Niger: Enquête auprès des ménages et des établissements scolaires.* Washington, D.C.: World Bank.

Foulani, P. 1994. *Amélioration de l'éfficacité de l'Université de Niamey: remplacement de l'enseignement bloqué par un système d'unités de valeurs.* Paris: IIPE and UNESCO.

Ghali, A. n.d. Personal communication with Abdoulkader Ghali, a staff member at Ecole Normale Supérieure and former secretary-general of SNECS [Syndicat National des Enseignants et Chercheurs du Supérieur].

Hamissou, O. 1994. "Modèle de simulation du financement de l'éducation: réduction des coûts publics dans l'enseignement post-obligatoire au profit du développement de base au Niger." Thesis. University of Benin, Lomé.

Lama, J. 1999. "Economie de l'Education dans le système d'Enseignement Supérieur au Niger: Etude Sectorielle pour la préparation d'une stratégie de développement de l'enseignement supérieur." Final special document for the Ministry of Education. July. Consultancy report for the Ministry of Higher Education (University Abdou Moumouni) and the Ministry of National Education (Office of Education Projects).

Mingat, A., J. P. Jarousse, and L. H. Kô. 1988. *Coût, financements et politique de l'éducation au Niger.* Washington, D.C.: World Bank.

Ministère de L'Education Nationale. 1995. *Financement de l'education au Niger.* Niamey: Direction des Etudes et de la Programmation.

———. 1996. *L'éducation Nationale: repères quantitatifs 1995–1996.* Niamey: Direction des Etudes et de la Programmation.

———. 1997a. *Annuaire des statistiques scolaires.* Niamey: Direction des Etudes et de la Programmation.

———. 1997b. *Présentation et diagnostic du système éducatif Nigerien.* Niamey: Direction des Etudes et de la Programmation.

———. 1998a. *Enseignement secondaire et technique: Éléments de diagnostic.* Niamey: Direction des Etudes et de la Programmation.

———. 1998b. *Etude documentaire sur les coûts et financement de l'éducation au Niger.* Niamey: Direction des Etudes et de la Programmation.

Mounkaila, M. n.d. Personal communication with Modi Mounkaila, head of Service Central de la Scolarisation de l'UAM.

51

Nigeria

Munzali Jibril

INTRODUCTION

Nigeria is a multiethnic and multireligious West African country with a population of 115 million. It is easily the most populous of all African countries and the largest black nation in the world, with a landmass of 923,768 square kilometers (356,669 square miles). Although it is basically an agrarian country, with 54 percent of the population engaged in agriculture, oil accounts for 96 percent of the country's foreign exchange earnings (although the industry employs less than half of 1 percent of the labor force). The country's gross domestic product per capita was $1,300 in 1999 (Federal Ministry of Finance). The main cash crop that the country still exports is cocoa. Nigeria's literacy rate is 57 percent, but fairly wide disparities exist between males and females (a gap of 15 percent) and between urban and rural dwellers.

Nigeria is a struggling developing nation. Only 34 percent of its households have access to electricity, only 40 percent have access to safe water, and only 50 percent of its school-age children are in school (UNDP 1997).

Higher education is here defined as all postsecondary education, which includes university, polytechnic, college of education, and monotechnic education. Nearly 1 million students are enrolled in more than 200 such institutions in Nigeria. In 1998, Nigeria had 63 colleges of education that enrolled 105,817 students; 45 polytechnics that enrolled 216,782 students; and 36 universities that enrolled 411,347 students. In addition, 87 monotechnics, about 100 schools of nursing and midwifery, and other professional training institutions had an estimated combined enrollment of some 120,000 students (Isyaku 2000). Given Nigeria's current population, the total estimated enrollment in higher education of 853,946 represents a participation rate of 740 per 100,000, which is close to the average for developing countries (824 in 1995) and better than the sub-Saharan African average for 1995 (328). However, the higher education

enrollment ratio for people aged 18–25 (a population estimated to be 17 million in 2000) is only 5 percent (UNESCO 1998a, 1998c). Inadequate as these ratios are, they have been growing steadily since the attainment of independence in 1960. For the university education subsector, for instance, total enrollment in 1965 was only 6,707. Enrollments had risen to 411,347 by 1998, an increase of more than 6,000 percent over a period of 33 years, as can be seen from Table 51.1.

In the three decades between 1960 and 1990, enrollment doubled every four to five years. In the decade 1990–2000, it grew at an average annual rate of 12 percent, so that by the end of the decade the cumulative growth rate amounted to a doubling of enrollment from the base figure at the beginning of the decade (Hartnett 2000). Comparative data for polytechnics and colleges of education are not available, but it is known that they also experienced a phenomenal increase in both the number of institutions and enrollment of students between the 1970s and 1990s.

Nigeria's political context has impacted the expansion of the higher education system in several ways. In the first place, all higher education institutions came into being as fully autonomous colleges or universities only after independence in 1960. Second, the period 1970–1979, although a decade of military rule, was also a decade of the post–civil war oil boom and the consolidation of the states created out of the four old regions. Each time a state is created, it tends to attract a federal university, college of education, and/or polytechnic. If none is forthcoming from the federal government, the state usually sets up these institutions itself, especially when elected civilian regimes are in power. The trend is continuing. No fewer than five states have established their own universities in the last two years of democratic governance. In general, apart from the six first-generation universities established in the 1960s and seven specialized universities of agriculture and technology established during the Second Republic in the 1980s, all other federal universities were established during military regimes.

Generally speaking, the federal institutions tend to be better funded and more autonomous than state institutions, which are critically underfunded and virtually run either from the governor's office or from the Ministry of Education.

Polytechnics award Ordinary National Diploma certificates after three years of postsecondary study and Higher National Diploma certificates after two years of further study. They also award certificates that are rated lower than the Ordinary National Diploma for shorter periods of study. Colleges of education award the Nigeria Certificate in Education after three years of full-time postsecondary study. Several colleges also prepare students for Bachelor of Education degrees at universities with which they are affiliated. The specialized colleges and monotechnics award either the same type of diploma certificates as the polytechnics or one of several professional certificates required to practice certain professions, such as nursing. The universities award bachelor's and master's degrees and Ph.D.s, as well as subdegree diplomas and certificates.

The origins of Nigerian higher education go back to 1934 when the colonial government set up the Yaba Higher College in Lagos to produce midlevel workers to meet the needs of the colonial civil service, which allowed Africans to rise only to certain ranks. This college failed to fulfill the aspirations of Nigerians for true higher education and recorded a very high drop-out rate. In response, the colonial government set up the Elliot Commission in 1943 to advise it on the higher education needs of British West Africa. As a result of the commission's recommendations, a University College was established in Ibadan in 1948 to award degrees from the University of London. University College continued as the only university institution in Nigeria until 1960.

In April 1959, the Nigerian government commissioned an inquiry under the chairmanship of Sir Eric Ashby to advise it on the higher education needs of the new nation for its first two decades. After an extensive tour of the country and wide-ranging consultations, the commission submitted its report in 1960, the year of independence, and recommended the establishment of four autonomous universities that were to have a combined total enrollment of 7,500 by 1970. However, even before Ashby had submitted his report, one of the regional governments, that of the Eastern Region, which had commenced preparations for the establishment of its own university as far back as 1955, established its own university at Nsukka. The University College at Ibadan was also separated from the University of London and became an autonomous full-fledged university in 1962. The federal government established a new university in the city of Lagos, the capital at the time. The Northern Region government established a new university in Zaria to fill the fourth of the recommended slots in 1962. However, the Western Region government, which already had two federal universities located in its territory, still went ahead and established its own university at Ile-Ife, also in 1962. Thus by 1962, two years after the Ashby Report, the number of universities recommended by Ashby had already been exceeded. This pattern of political considerations overriding plans in the establishment of university and other higher institutions in Nigeria has continued to be one of the most serious problems in managing the system.

Although the Ashby Commission offered the first serious

Table 51.1. Growth in Enrollment at Nigerian Universities, 1965–1998*

Year	Enrollment
1965	6,707
1970	9,695
1975	26,448
1980	57,742
1985	126,285
1990	172,911
1995	236,261
1998	411,347

*Note that enrollments for the three private universities, one of the twelve state universities, and the five inter-university centers are not included in this analysis.
Source: National Universities Commission, Abuja.

attempt at higher education planning, it was soon surpassed by the First National Development Plan, produced by the first post-independence government in 1962 for the subsequent five fiscal years. To its credit, however, this plan incorporated many of the best ideas of the Ashby Commission, such as the need to allocate at least 70 percent of enrollment openings to pure and applied science and 30 percent to the humanities. However, the national plan envisaged an enrollment of 10,000 for all Nigerian universities by the end of the plan period, about 30 percent more than the Ashby Commission's estimates. In any event, by 1968, all five Nigerian universities then in existence could boast of only 8,800 students.

Because of the disruption of national planning occasioned by the civil war in 1968–1970, the Second National Development Plan was produced only in 1970; it covered the years up to 1974. Because this was a post–civil war period, the plan appropriately emphasized reconstruction and rehabilitation of national infrastructure, including the universities and other higher institutions of learning.

In 1970, the newest of the four regions (which had been rearranged into twelve states) opted to have a university of its own, which is now known as the University of Benin. Its establishment marked the end of the first phase of university development in Nigeria. The six universities established during the period 1960–1970 are still referred to as first-generation universities.

The Third National Development Plan covered the period 1975–1980, a time of relative economic prosperity occasioned by the oil boom and a return to democracy. The priorities of the plan were the expansion of the productive base of the economy and the production of the skilled labor required to staff the expanded economy. Not surprisingly, the government established seven new universities from 1975 to 1977 and took over the four regional universities in 1975. The plan period also witnessed the establishment of at least sixteen new state-owned and federal polytechnics (National Board for Technical Education 1999). In 1977, Nigeria adopted a National Policy on Education, a document that set out broad objectives for education at various levels and the ways to achieve them. During this period, the government abolished the payment of tuition fees in all federal universities for full-time undergraduate courses and also set hostel accommodation charges at a fixed rate, which, due to currency devaluation, is now only about 60 cents per year.

After the Fourth National Development Plan (1981–1985), the government decided to move away from five-year plans, which were found to be too rigid, to more flexible three-year rolling plans that would allow any project not executed in any year to be rolled over to the following year. This is still the current practice.

The period 1979–1983 witnessed the emergence of seven state universities, five new federal universities of technology, and two new federal universities of agriculture. In 1984, a new military government felt compelled to rationalize this expansion of the system by downgrading two of the universities of technology and the two universities of agriculture to campuses of older universities. It took another military government four more years to restore these universities to full autonomy. Although all the regional universities had been taken over by the federal government by 1975, states began to establish new universities of their own. The trend is still continuing. As of August 2001, Nigeria had 45 universities, of which 25 were federal (including one defense academy), 16 were state, and 4 were private universities.

The Ashby Commission also recommended the establishment of four advanced teachers' colleges and polytechnics; these types of institutions have continued to grow both in number and enrollment. Of the 62 existing colleges of education, 20 are owned by the federal government, 38 are owned by state governments, and 4 are privately owned. Similarly, of the 51 existing polytechnics, the federal government owns 17, state governments own 27, and 7 are privately owned. Most of the 87 specialized colleges are owned by the federal and state governments (National Universities Commission 1998, 1999).

STRUCTURE AND GOVERNANCE

The universities, polytechnics, and colleges of education owned by the federal government tend to have bigger enrollments than those owned by state governments. However, from the point of view of management structure and governance procedures, there is little or no difference between the two types of proprietors, although there are some differences between types of institutions. All three have a governing board or council appointed by the proprietor government and include internal representatives of the institution as elected members or as members by virtue of their offices. These councils generally govern the affairs of the institution on behalf of the proprietor government. However, until recently, governing councils of universities had to recommend three candidates to the government for appointment as vice-chancellor, from which the president would choose. This is still the procedure in the appointment of rectors of polytechnics and provosts of colleges of education. Under envisaged reforms now being discussed, governing councils of universities will have the power to appoint and remove vice-chancellors of universities without government involvement. During the present transitional period, governing councils merely seek the ratification of the appointment already made by them in the spirit of the new autonomy.

The management of each institution is headed by a chief executive officer; that is, the vice-chancellor in the case of universities, the rector in the case of the polytechnics, and the provost in the case of the colleges of education. This officer, in turn, is assisted by a team of principal officers, one or two deputies, a registrar, a bursar, a librarian, and one or more directors in charge of physical planning and maintenance, academic planning, health services, and so forth. The senate in the case of universities, and the academic boards in the case of polytechnics and colleges of education, make decisions on academic matters such as curricula, admission requirements, and examinations.

The federal government has established supervisory and coordinating agencies for each group of institutions: the National Universities Commission for the universities, the National Board for Technical Education for the polytechnics, and the National Commission for Colleges of Education for the colleges. Funding is channeled through these agencies, as are government policy directives. The agencies are also charged with quality assurance and control. Their multiple roles as both funding and regulatory agencies have led to tensions between them and the institutions they supervise; they have come to represent the symbol of official control and interference to these institutions.

In response to the agitation of the universities for autonomy and greater freedom in their own management, the federal government has issued a policy statement in which it proposes to restore administrative and academic autonomy to the universities it owns, and in which it also promises more and better funding for the universities and greater freedom in the management of funds. According to the document, the appointment, discipline, and removal of the vice-chancellor will soon become the sole business of the governing councils. However, no such autonomy has been promised to the polytechnics or colleges of education owned by the federal government, nor have state governments sought to follow the federal lead, even in the case of universities. Also, surprisingly, the powerful Academic Staff Union of Universities (ASUU) has led a vibrant opposition to the new policy, possibly because autonomy will lead to decentralization and deregulation of the system and therefore a weakening of the union's own power to cripple the system at will through strikes.

FACULTY

The academic staff of higher institutions of learning in Nigeria represent one of the most organized and most articulate segments of Nigerian society. They also tend to be better educated than other professionals (in terms both of the level of educational attainment and the quality of education received, which is usually partly undertaken abroad). They also tend to hold radical political views and to be better able to challenge authoritarian regimes than other organized groups in Nigeria. ASUU is the most militant of the higher education trade unions. It has always drawn attention to the neglect of the universities by successive governments and has been proscribed several times over by successive military regimes. Its leaders have often been detained for their union activities.

Generally, faculty are concerned first and foremost with

their conditions of service, especially their remuneration package. They have also drawn attention to the shortage of faculty in the universities, which, they argue, is a consequence of poor conditions of service. Statistics available to the National Universities Commission suggest that, indeed, only about one-third of the required number of teachers in Nigerian universities (12,398 out of the required number of 36,134) are available.

Although the present democratic government has improved the salaries of faculty recently, the take-home pay of a full professor, which is only about $1,000 per month, is still low, even by African standards. This, of course, explains why so many Nigerian academics and other professionals have migrated to other countries, notably the United States, South Africa, Botswana, Saudi Arabia, and member countries of the European Economic Community. It is estimated that at least 10,000 Nigerian academics and 21,000 Nigerian doctors are in the United States alone.

However, legitimate as some of the concerns of Nigerian higher education trade unions may sometimes be, the unions tend to overuse the weapon of the strike. Nigeria is one of the few countries in the world in which a few powerful trade unions can hold the nation at ransom over the slightest provocation. Academic staff unions in the universities (and increasingly in polytechnics and colleges of education, as well) call their members out on strike whenever they have any grievances they want the government to address. It is hoped that the ongoing reforms will result in higher and fairer wages for teaching and other staff and decentralization and deregulation of the system. This, in turn, should lead to more localization of trade union concerns and consequently to less instability in the system.

STUDENT ACTIVISM

Nigerian higher education students are organized under a single national union, the National Union of Nigerian Students (NANS), which, along with ASUU and a few trade unions, offered one of the few bases of organized resistance to Nigeria's authoritarian regimes during their years of military rule. Several students lost their lives in the course of fighting against unpopular government policies. At the present time, NANS is vociferous in opposing the policy on autonomy and the proposal to accept a World Bank credit facility to support innovation in Nigerian universities. Their opposition to these two issues is based on the fear that either or both of them will lead to the reintroduction of tuition fees in the universities and the commercialization of education.

FUNDING

Funding is one of the major constraints of the Nigerian higher education system. Federal and state governments are the main proprietors of higher educational institutions and account for most of the funding that goes to the institutions. In 1977, the federal government abolished the payment of tuition fees for all undergraduate programs in its universities and set the hostel accommodation fee that was then the equivalent of about $100 per bed per session. These two policies have remained in force through the present day, while the national currency, the naira,

has depreciated considerably so that the fee is now worth only 60 cents. State universities charge tuition fees even for citizens of the states concerned and often charge higher fees for out-of-state students. Polytechnics, both federal and state, also charge tuition fees, but tuition is completely free in all colleges of education.

The consequence of government regulation of fees is that the government must shoulder the bulk of the funding burden for higher education, with the further consequence that the needs of the system are inadequately addressed. In 1996, the federal government funded its polytechnics at the rate of $251 per student, its colleges of education at the rate of $394 per student, and its universities at the rate of $300 per student. The state governments generally tend to be even less generous than the federal government in funding their institutions.

However, in 2000, funding for tertiary institutions, especially federal government–owned institutions, improved significantly, largely because of an increase in the wages of all public-sector workers. For the federal universities, unit costs rose from $370 to $932, an increase of 252 percent. Also, based on an agreement recently reached between the ASUU and the federal and state governments, the unit cost per student is expected to rise to a minimum of $1,300 and a maximum of $3,365, depending on how faithfully the agreement is implemented. Federal polytechnics also appear to have received substantially more funding per student in the year 2000: $777 per student, compared to the 1996 figure of $251.

As would be expected, current funding levels are unacceptably low and consequently lead to poor remuneration for academic staff. This, in turn, leads to moonlighting and brain drain to other countries and other sectors of the Nigerian economy. The casualty of all this is, of course, quality. Ultimately, there will be no alternative to cost sharing if the resource deficit of the system is to be properly addressed.

ACCREDITATION

In the last accreditation exercise conducted by the National Universities Commission (NUC) for all undergraduate academic programs in the Nigerian university system, only 11.4 percent were able to secure full accreditation while the bulk of the programs (72.5 percent) could only secure interim accreditation status. The remaining 15.1 percent failed and were denied accreditation. A system that is operating at only 11.4 percent of its optimum efficiency certainly needs a complete overhaul. The National Board for Technical Education has responsibility for accrediting all polytechnics, and the National Commission for Colleges of Education accredits all colleges. The accreditation results of the two agencies are somewhat better than those of the universities, principally because individual polytechnics and colleges can choose the time of their accreditation and better prepare to meet its requirements, whereas the NUC gives universities no options once the accreditation timetable has been finalized.

In all cases, higher education institutions are often able to secure additional or special funding from their proprietors (especially state governments, which are notoriously stingy in funding their institutions) in order to prepare their facilities for accreditation. In the case of federal universities, the NUC usually produces a checklist of deficiencies to be corrected by the federal government in order to win full accreditation. Thus, the desire or need to meet accreditation requirements enhances the funding prospects of the higher institutions.

It is difficult to assess the effectiveness of accreditation in the Nigerian university system. This is because the follow-up to the first accreditation exercise, which was carried out in 1990–1991 and was supposed to have been followed up by revisitation within two years, was disrupted by political upheavals in the country generally and labor unrest in the universities. As a consequence, another comprehensive exercise had to be carried out in 1999–2000. The polytechnics and colleges of education have had more stability, with the result that their accreditation process is clearly more effective in controlling quality than the accreditation process of the NUC.

LANGUAGE AND CURRICULUM

English is the official language of Nigeria and the language of instruction at all levels after the first three years of primary school. However, proficiency in English has been on the decline at all levels of the educational system and poor communicative competence is a major cause of failure in public examinations, at both the secondary and the higher educational levels. In the 1999 School Certificate Examination conducted by the West African Examinations Council, for instance, only about 10 percent of all students obtained a credit pass in the English language, which is the minimum required for admission to universities. However, since about 17 percent of applicants usually get admitted on average (although not all secondary school graduates seek admission to universities), it is reasonable to assume that some of those admitted did not meet this requirement, thereby leading to a further deterioration in the quality of student enrollments. So while having English as official language is advantageous given its present currency in the world, more effort and resources will have to be invested in learning and teaching English effectively if it is to continue to serve as a useful communicative resource for Nigerians.

Nigeria operates on the 6-3-3-4 system of education. At the tertiary level, there is considerable uniformity in the structure of the curriculum and its content, owing largely to the existence of very detailed Minimum Academic Standards, which specify courses that must be taught for certain degrees and diplomas. As part of the new reform measures undertaken by the democratic civilian government, arrangements are underway to replace these uniform curricula in the universities with concise benchmarks to guide curriculum designers in determining which skills are required of graduates in specific disciplines.

GRADUATE EDUCATION

Graduate education is still in its infancy in most Nigerian universities. In the 1989–1990 academic year, graduate students in all federal universities accounted for only 8.7 percent of total enrollment, while undergraduates accounted for 84.3 percent of total enrollment. Subdegree students accounted for the remain-

ing 7 percent. However, some of the older universities, notably the University of Ibadan, have been increasing the proportion of their graduate students to around 30 percent. Overall, graduate enrollment tends to be predominantly in the arts, the social sciences, and education, with relatively fewer students enrolling in graduate courses in science, engineering, and medicine. There is some indication that the government is considering the advisability of establishing a graduate university or converting one of the existing universities into a graduate university.

STATE OF RESEARCH

Most of the research that is carried out in Nigerian higher educational institutions takes place in universities. Academic staff are required as part of their contract to carry out research and to publish the results of such research as a precondition for career advancement. However, in the face of poor funding and even poorer management of research funds by the universities, and in the face of inadequate research infrastructures in the universities and an almost total lack of interest on the part of the local private sector in sponsoring or utilizing the results of university research, only basic research of the publish-or-perish type tends to be carried out in Nigeria. As a country, Nigeria has yet to define its national research agenda. Spending on research and development in Nigeria is among the lowest in the world as a percentage of gross national product. Since not as much emphasis is placed on research in polytechnics and colleges of education, even less research takes place there.

According to the funding formula used by the NUC, 5 percent of the recurring funds are set aside for research at each university. However, because of the failure of universities to satisfactorily account for previous allocations, the amount that is actually released to them in any one year may not be more than one-third of their total allocation, and it is quite common for several universities to have up to three years' worth of allocations of this grant warehoused by the commission for failure to render satisfactory accounts of previous disbursements.

Even when academics manage to carry out high-quality research, Nigeria has few publishing outlets. Academic publishing is not yet a viable venture, and sustaining new academic journals is a challenge. The consequence of all this is that the best research reports about Nigeria tend to be published abroad.

Nigerian companies and foreign multinationals operating in Nigeria appear not to be interested in promoting research and development in the universities. They prefer to apply well-tested technology from the western industrialized countries instead. Private-sector and commercial funds account for the bulk of university research money in the industrialized countries, so the lack of patronage from the Nigerian private sector is a major handicap to the unfolding of a full research agenda in Nigerian universities.

GRADUATE UNEMPLOYMENT

According to the annual abstract of statistics (Federal Office of Statistics 1998), Nigerians with a postsecondary education constituted 21.5 percent of the total unemployed population in

1997. However, university graduates constitute only 6.5 percent of the unemployed. This is a high proportion, considering that higher education graduates normally constitute less than 5 percent of the population. The reasons for their high rate of unemployment are obvious: the productive sector of the economy is not only stagnant but also declining, while the service sector is already saturated with too many white-collar workers. This structural distortion in the economy will have to be addressed by the government. Simultaneously, higher education institutions in Nigeria, especially universities, will have to integrate entrepreneurship education into their curricula so that their graduates can use their skills to create employment for themselves and others.

PRIVATE PARTICIPATION IN HIGHER EDUCATION PROVISION

Another feature of the Nigerian higher education system is the involvement of the private sector in the ownership of educational institutions. There are at present seven private polytechnics, four private colleges of education, and three private universities in Nigeria. The trend is likely to continue. At the same time, the privatization of public institutions of higher learning is politically unacceptable in present-day Nigeria, as is the reintroduction of tuition fees in the universities. While most secondary schools, especially in the south, are owned by communities and individuals, private participation in the provision of higher education is still marginal; private institutions represent a mere 6 percent of universities and colleges of education and 15 percent of polytechnics. Their share of enrollment is even smaller because they are still young and charge high fees, which restricts access somewhat.

It is generally believed that private, fee-charging primary and secondary schools provide better-quality education than corresponding government schools. However, the private higher education institutions so far established have yet to establish reputations. The attitude of the public at present can best be described as skeptical. However, given the crisis of access to universities, private higher education institutions could have a bright future in Nigeria, especially if they can replicate the reputation for quality that they have established at the lower levels of the education system.

DISTANCE EDUCATION

Distance education is still in its infancy in Nigeria. While it is true that quite a number of colleges of education, the National Teachers' Institute at Kaduna, and a number of universities have been providing traditional print-based distance education for teachers to enable them to acquire the Nigeria Certificate in Education or bachelor's degrees in education, this has not spread to other disciplines yet. Nigeria has no higher education institution dedicated to distance learning. In addition, owing to the absence of the required infrastructure, electronic-based distance education is not yet available in Nigeria.

In response to demand for flexible modes of service delivery, Nigerian universities began to set up satellite campuses and outreach centers as far as 1,000 or more kilometers away from their

Table 51.2. Types of Institutions, Number of Institutions, and Enrollments at Institutions of Higher Education in Nigeria, 1998–1999

Type of Institution	Number of Institutions	Enrollment
Teacher Education	63 (44%)	105,817 (14%)
Technical Education	45 (31%)	216,782 (30%)
University Education	36 (25%)	411,347 (56%)
Total	144	733,946

Source: National Universities Commission, Abuja.

main campuses, often using lecturers other than their own. Most of these campuses and centers are actually run by business professionals on behalf of the universities under cost- and profit-sharing arrangements between the parties involved. In many cases, universities undertook little monitoring of academic standards at these institutions, and quality was further threatened. The government, therefore, had to order the closure of all the satellite institutions that failed to meet minimum accreditation requirements. This order is likely to be resisted by state universities, but the federal government has published a short-term distance education strategy that will meet demand for higher education without compromising standards. The policy allows each university to establish up to five study centers at locations that are no farther than 200 kilometers from the university's main campus and where only full-time teachers of the university concerned can teach. However, the government's long-term aim is to ensure that electric power supply becomes widely available and stable and that computers and telephone lines become widely available so distance education can be provided online with quality assurance.

DISTORTIONS IN THE SYSTEM

Several distortions afflict the Nigerian higher education system. The polytechnics, which are supposed to produce midlevel graduates in the areas of science and technology by having 70 percent of their students registered for engineering- and science-related courses, instead have 60 percent of their students enrolled in business-related courses. In the federal universities, enrollment figures for 1998–1999 found that the target of 60 percent enrollment in science-related courses had yet to be achieved; only 58.8 percent of enrollment was in this category, while 41.2 percent was in the humanities. This has distorted the structure of the workforce in Nigeria.

Another distortion in the system is that while the polytechnic and teacher education subsectors are supposed to be bigger and the university subsector smaller, the reverse is the case in Nigeria, as illustrated in Table 51.2.

Universities account for about 56 percent of all higher education enrollment in Nigeria. Candidates generally accept admission in polytechnics and colleges of education if they cannot find a place in a university. In order to redress this imbalance, the reward system and career prospects of the graduates of different types of higher educational institutions will have to be

Table 51.3. Enrollment in Institutions of Higher Education, Nigeria, 1965–2014 (Projected)

Year	Enrollment
1965	6,707
1970	9,695
1975	26,448
1980	57,742
1985	126,285
1990	172,911
1995	236,261
1998	411,347
2004	958,476*
2009	1,763,084*
2014	3,243,136*

*Projected.

Source: National Universities Commission, Abuja.

streamlined. The teaching profession at the primary and junior secondary levels appears to be especially threatened by declining applications to colleges of education and by declining enrollments.

CURRENT AND FUTURE CHALLENGES

Four major challenges face the Nigerian higher education system. These are the challenges of access, quality, relevance, and information and communication technology.

The challenge of access is more appropriately described as a crisis, which is graphically depicted in Table 51.3. According to the Joint Admissions and Matriculation Board (2000), only 17 percent of applicants for places in the universities were admitted in 1997–1998; for the same academic year, the percentages for polytechnics and colleges of education were 20.5 percent and 33.7 percent, respectively. At the beginning of the chapter, I indicated that the gross enrollment ratio in Nigerian higher education is only 5 percent, which compares unfavorably with between 40 percent and 60 percent in most developed countries. Since the development of human capital remains the fastest route to development, and since higher education remains the most critical level for developing a country's human capital, the expansion of access to higher education in Nigeria remains a major challenge. According to the National Population Commission, by the year 2010, Nigeria will have 22 million people aged 18–25—that is, in the higher education cohort. Even a modest aim of absorbing 30 percent of this cohort in higher education institutions will result in an enrollment of 6.6 million students.

Nigeria also faces an imbalance in the representation of women, both as academic staff and as students in Nigerian higher education. At the primary school level, the gender gap is only 5.3 percent, and it is only 5 percent at the secondary school level. However, at the university level, it goes up to 15 percent, with females constituting only 35 percent of the total number of students enrolled in universities. A closer analysis of the disciplines in which females tend to enroll also reveals that they

are critically underrepresented in engineering and technology courses and are somewhat overrepresented in arts and education courses. In the colleges of education, females account for 55 percent of total enrollment. This slight advantage at the lower levels of the teaching profession is not replicated at the university level, however, where only 12.4 percent of the academic staff are women. Since women account for 51 percent of the population of Nigeria, there should be a more aggressive policy to rectify the imbalance in their representation as staff and as students in higher education.

The challenge of maintaining and improving quality in teaching, learning, and research while expanding access is a daunting one. Already the major quality indicator, the result of the accreditation of academic programs in the universities, suggests that the system is poor in quality and is inefficient. Similarly, results from a recent study of the external efficiency of Nigerian universities (Dabalen and Oni 2000) suggests that Nigerian employers find university graduates deficient in communication, conceptual, and analytical skills and in technical proficiency in their field of training. One major oil company claims that it spends up to $12,000 to retrain and reequip every Nigerian university graduate it employs. Quality cannot be improved without substantially increasing and diversifying the resource base for the system.

The challenge of relevance is also an important one. The comments of Nigerian employers cited above raise the issue of the relevance of the curricula of Nigerian higher institutions to the world of work. A major undertaking is required to identify the skills that graduates need to ensure that efforts of the training institutions meet the expectations of the world of work and correspond to the realities of the knowledge economy.

The challenge of information and communication technology to Nigerian higher education is a critical one. In order to remain relevant, all institutions of higher learning must link up to the Internet and ensure access to it for all their staff and students around the clock. At the moment, e-mail is available at about twenty-five universities and interuniversity centers and several polytechnics and colleges of education. The largest academic network is presently the Nigerian Universities Network (NUNet). Arrangements are underway to create a wider academic, educational, and research network that will incorporate NUNet as well as the polytechnic subsystem network and other institutions. This will be called the Nigerian Educational, Academic, and Research Network (NEARNet). Through the appropriate deployment of information and communication technology, access to education can be considerably expanded at less cost and with better quality since the constraints of time and space will then become less relevant.

CONCLUSION

Nigerian higher education will need to expand to about 10 times its current size in the next ten years to accommodate the envisaged growth in the size of the higher education cohort. However, even at present, quality appears to be declining primarily due to overdependence on the government for funding. The challenge to the system in the first decade of the new millennium is to expand while improving quality and to diversify the sources of funding without risking social and political explosions.

The prospects for Nigerian higher education are bright if policymakers and system managers can imaginatively tackle the many challenges facing the system, especially those of funding, access, quality, relevance, and information and communication technology. Given the determination of the present democratic civilian government to move the system forward and the goodwill of the international donor community, success is already visible on the horizon.

REFERENCES

Dabalen, A., and B. Oni. 2000. *Labour Market Prospects for University Graduates in Nigeria*. Washington, D.C.: The World Bank.

Federal Office of Statistics, Nigeria. 1998. Annual Abstract of Statistics. Abuja.

Federal Ministry of Finance, Nigeria. 2000. "Quarterly Performance Report of the Economy: October–December, 1999."

Hartnett, T. 2000. *Financing Trends and Expenditure Patterns in Nigerian Federal Universities: An Update*. Washington, D.C.: The World Bank.

Isyaku, K. 2000. "Teacher Education in the 21st Century Nigeria: Vision and Action." Mimeographed Report. Kaduna: National Commission for Colleges of Education.

Joint Admissions and Matriculation Board. 2000. Annual reports 1997, 1998 and 1999. Abuja: Joint Admissions and Matriculation Board.

National Board for Technical Education. 1999. "Polytechnics and Monotechnics under NBTE Supervision." Pamphlet. Kaduna: National Board for Technical Education.

National Population Commission. 1999. "Nigeria at a Glance: Census '91." Pamphlet. Abuja: National Population Commission.

National Universities Commission. 1998. *Annual Report*. Abuja: National Universities Commission.

———. 1999. *Annual Report*. Abuja: National Universities Commission.

UNDP. 1997. *Nigeria Human Development Report 1996*. Lagos: UNDP.

UNESCO. 1998a. *Development of Education in Africa: A Statistical Review*. Durban: UNESCO.

———. 1998b. *The State of Education in Nigeria*. Lagos: UNESCO.

———. 1998c. *World Statistical Outlook on Higher Education, 1980–1995*. Paris: UNESCO.

52

Rwanda

Jolly Mazimhaka and G. F. Daniel

INTRODUCTION

Covering an area of 26,338 square kilometers (10,169 square miles) of very sharply dissected mountain terrain, Rwanda is a landlocked country in the Great Lakes Region, bordered by Burundi, the Democratic Republic of Congo, Tanzania, and Uganda. Rwanda's population is estimated to be 7.65 million, of whom 90 percent are rural dwellers, 57 percent are women, and 60 percent are under 20 years old. Rwanda's literacy rate is 52.7 percent (Republic of Rwanda 1997). According to information available from the Ministry of Finance, the country's gross domestic product is $1.8 billion. Rwanda is self-sufficient in agricultural food production; it exports $60 million, mainly from tea and coffee. Annual consumer imports reached $240 million in 2000. At $230, per capita income falls short of the sub-Saharan average of $350, while the minimum daily wage is less than $1.

Rwanda is one of only a few countries in Africa in which most people speak the same language and share similar customs and traditions (in short, a common culture)—important ingredients for national cohesion and development. However, since achieving independence from Belgium in 1961, Rwanda's history has been marked by internal strife, reaching its worst point in the 1990–1994 war, which culminated in the horrendous tragedy of the 1994 genocide that claimed the lives of an estimated 1 million people. Skilled personnel and professionals were either killed or went into exile, leaving a huge vacuum in the labor force, a phenomenon that has greatly affected every aspect of Rwanda's national development. Even before 1994, many sectors of the national economy suffered from a serious shortage of professionals and management staff; the war and genocide have aggravated this deficiency.

As part of the program of reconstruction, the government issued a policy statement for the education sector as a whole in May 1998 that identified key goals, including the following:

- Promoting preschool education through a campaign targeting parents
- Raising primary school attendance to 80 percent by 2000 and to 100 percent by 2005
- Increasing admissions to secondary schools to 30 percent of primary school-leavers by 2000 and 40 percent by 2005
- Doubling intake into higher education
- Providing more opportunities for disabled children
- Providing facilities for adult education and the education of out-of-school youths

A study of the education sector in Rwanda (Rwandese Republic 1997) and a sectoral consultation on education (Republic of Rwanda 1998b) identified the following specific goals for higher education:

- Provide and improve high-quality teaching in higher education that is adapted to the needs of the country
- Train competent professionals who are capable of visualizing and guiding social, political, economic, and cultural development
- Vary education, particularly training in science and technology, and eventually create new educational institutions
- Expand the intake capacity of higher education and raise the attendance rate while taking into account the needs and capacity of the labor market to absorb new graduates
- Promote scientific and technological research that will respond to community needs
- Relaunch and enhance general research activities
- Promote access to higher education in priority disciplines
- Promote both humanistic education and scientific and cultural excellence
- Strengthen institutional structures

As part of the Ministry of Education's program of reviewing the education sector as a whole, the Minister of Education appointed a Higher Education Review Committee in May 1998, which was subsequently charged with submitting proposals to formulate a higher education subsector policy to realize these goals. The committee, chaired by Dr. Emile Rwamasirabo, rector of the National University of Rwanda (L'Universite Nationale du Rwanda—UNR), was comprised of representatives from all institutions of higher education, both public and private, and from the Ministry of Education. The committee sat through 1998–2000, and submitted its final report, dated July 2000, to the Minister of Education. Because the losses from the country's recent tragic past unfortunately include documentation, the present study—while drawing on the committee's recommendations—is essentially based on data from the few available government publications and from the National University of Rwanda. Though it is not clear what the eventual fate of these recommendations will be, the findings of the Higher Education Review Committee are shown in Tables 52.1 and 52.2.

THE CONDITION OF HIGHER EDUCATION

Evolution

As in much of Africa, the church was the first institution to undertake formal education in Rwanda. Especially during the colonial period, education for service to the church was the goal. The efforts of the church to provide education, which consisted of only a few primary and secondary schools, included the Senior Seminary of Nyakibanda (Le Grand Séminaire de Nyakibanda), which was established in 1914 at Kabgayi but was transferred to Nyakibanda in 1936. Postsecondary programs in philosophy and theology of at least two years' duration remain available at the school for the exclusive training of Catholic prelates. It was not until 1963, nearly thirty years later, that the state established UNR. Since that time, the combined efforts of church, state, and the private sector have yielded eleven more institutions of higher education, most of which were launched as recently as the 1980s and late 1990s.

Size

Of the twelve higher education institutions in the country, six are sponsored by the government, including UNR, the Institute of Public Finance (Institut Supérieur des Finances Publiques, established in 1986), the Institute of Agriculture and Livestock (Institut Supérieur d'Agriculture et d'Elevage, 1989), the Kigali Institute of Science, Technology, and Management (KIST, 1997), the Kigali Health Institute (KHI, 1997), and the Kigali Institute of Education (KIE, 1998). Four are sponsored by religious foundations: The Senior Seminary of Nyakibanda (Grand Séminaire de Nyakibanda, 1936), the Faculty of Protestant Theology in Butare (Faculté de Théologie Protestante, FTP, officially opened in 1996), the Adventist University of Central Africa (L'Université Adventiste d'Afrique Centrale, UAAC, 1988), and the Secular Adventist University of Kigali (Université Laique Adventiste de Kigali, UNILAK, 1997). The remaining two institutions, the Free University of Kigali (Université Libre de Kigali, ULK, 1996) and the Gitwe Institute of Pedagogy (Institut Supérieur Pedagogique de Gitwe, ISPG), are sponsored by

secular establishments. Excluded from the list of twelve are two other establishments, the Catholic Institute of Applied Pedagogy (Institut Supérieur Catholique de Pédagogie Appliquée, ISCPA, 1986) in Nkumba, and the Institute of Management and Computing—Saint Fidèle Institute of Management and Computing (L'Institut Supérieur de Gestion et d'Informatique—ISGI, 1985) in Gisenyi. Both have been closed since the end of the war and genocide of 1994. For carrying out research programs, Rwanda has two national research centers, the Institute of Scientific and Technological Research (Institut de Rercherche Scientifique et Technologie, IRST), which is responsible for basic and applied research and the training of personnel, and the Institute of Agronomic Sciences (Institut des Sciences Agronomique au Rwanda, ISAR), which was established to promote scientific and technological development of agriculture and livestock farming. The Ministry of Education created the Secretariat of Planning and Promotion of Scientific and Technological Research (SPPSTR) to revamp research activities and coordinate research at the national level. Though research stations are presently functioning, they are in poor condition and lack necessary tools, while highly qualified researchers and technicians are currently in short supply.

Admission

From studies of higher education reform in Rwanda between 1984 and 1990 summarized by UNR (1990), the criteria for admission into higher education institutions were never settled prior to 1994. In March 1985, a report of the Commission of the National University of Rwanda for the Reform of Higher Education in Rwanda (La Commission de l'Université Nationale du Rwanda pour la Réforme de l'Enseignement Supérieur au Rwanda) noted the following:

- The Ministry of Education had the sole responsibility for the admission of students to public higher education institutions, specifically to UNR.
- The government's selection of students to enter university ought to take into account university requirements for student admission into various disciplines and specialized options offered in various faculties or schools.
- The university, specifically UNR, needs to set the requirements for admission (taking into account the levels of achievement in various options of the secondary school graduate and the demands of university-level training) and propose these to the Ministry of Education as the criteria for admission.
- At the time the report was written (1990), the university had not set these criteria (République Rwandaise 1985, 21).

By July 1990, when the report of the studies on the reform of higher education was published, nothing concrete on admission policy had been realized beyond the following recommendations:

- Define and clear public criteria and procedures for admission
- Apply the principle of excellence
- Organize competitive entry examinations
- Entrust the organization of these examinations to a collective body or a commission

Table 52.1. Sponsors, Fields of Study, Terminal Awards, Fees, and Housing at Rwandan Institutions of Higher Education, 1999–2000

Institution (Year Founded)	Sponsor	Concentration	Terminal Award	Fees (in US$ and Frw)	Hostel
National University of Rwanda (UNR, 1963)	Government	Comprehensive	B.A., B.Sc., M.Sc. in Medicine	$18 (Frw 7,300)	Yes
Kigali Institute of Science, Technology, and Management (KIST, 1997)	Government	Science; Technology; Management; Bilingualism; Continuing Education	Certificate, Diploma, B.Sc., B.B.A.	$18 (Frw 7,300)	Yes
Free University of Kigali (ULK, 1996)	Private	Economics; Management; Law; Social Sciences	Baccalaureate B.A.	$247 (Frw 100,000)	No
Secular Adventist University of Kigali (UNILAK, 1997)	Religious Foundation	Management; Law; Education	B.A.	$370 (Frw 150,000)	No
Adventist University of Central Africa (UAAC, 1988)	Seventh-day Adventist Church	Management; Education; Theology	B.A.	$393 (Frw 159,240)	No
Kigali Health Institute (KHI, 1997)	Government	Paramedic; Nursing	Advanced Diploma	$18 (Frw 7,300)	Yes
Institute of Agriculture and Livestock (ISAE, 1989)	Government	Zoo Technology; Crop Science; Agriculture Engineering	Advanced Diploma	$18 (Frw 7,300)	No
Institute of Public Finance (ISFP, 1986)	Government	Finance	Diploma	$18 (Frw 7,300)	Yes
Senior Seminary (Grand Séminaire, 1936)	Catholic Church	Theology	Baccalaureate	0	Yes
Faculty of Protestant Theology (FPT, 1996)	Religion	Theology	—	—	No
Kigali Institute of Education (KIE, 1998)	Government	Teacher Education; Teacher Training	Certificate Diploma, B.A., B.Sc.	$18 (Frw 7,300)	Yes
Gitwe Institute of Pedagogy (ISPG, n.d.)	Government	Theology	Diploma	$18 (Frw 7,300)	—

Source: Ministry of Education 2000.

Table 52.2. Number of Faculties or Schools, Number of Students, and Number of Faculty in Rwandan Institutions of Higher Education, 1999–2000

Institution	Number of Faculties/Schools	Number of Students	Number of Faculty
National University of Rwanda (UNR)	10	4,550	251 (+300 visiting)
Kigali Institute of Science, Technology, and Management (KIST)	5	1,200	130 (+15 visiting)
Free University of Kigali (ULK)	3	2,313	11 (+28 visiting)
Secular Adventist University of Kigali (UNILAK)	3	100	5 (+31 visiting)
Adventist University of Central Africa (UAAC)	4	237	14 (+18 visiting)
Kigali Health Institute (KHI)	7	445	31 (+66 visiting)
Higher Institute of Agriculture and Livestock (ISAE)	4	365	28 (+15 visiting)
Institute of Public Finance (ISFP)	2	98	42 (+26 visiting)
Senior Seminary (Grand Séminaire)	1	150	13 (+5 visiting)
Faculty of Protestant Theology (FPT)	2	107	Not known
Kigali Institute of Education (KIE)	3	700	60
Gitwe Institute of Pedagogy (ISPG)	2	NA	NA

Source: Ministry of Education 2000.

- Orient students for course selection according to their studies at the secondary school level
- Set up requirements for entry into and terminal qualifications for each faculty, school, or unit of the university
- Hire career counselors and organize information meetings in secondary schools
- Involve the UNR in selecting candidates for the institution
- Set aside a year for first-year students during which differences in student academic levels obtained from various secondary school backgrounds will be reduced to ensure better orientation
- Take into account ethnic, regional, and social balance in the selection and admission of candidates (République Rwandaise 1990a; L'Université Nationale du Rwanda 1990, 25)

A quota system based on ethnic and regional origins was already in operation as an admission criterion from the 1970s to 1994. Currently, however, possession of a high school diploma in humanities (*Diplôme d'Humanité*) confirming completion of the six-year secondary school program or its A-level equivalent, a competitive pass in the Rwanda National Examinations organized by the National Examinations Council (both introduced after 1994), and meeting the prerequisites and specific basic requirements of individual institutions are among the admissions considerations.

Programs

The humanities and social sciences dominate Rwanda's higher education curriculum, although three new institutes were created as recently as 1997–1998 in the effort to offset the imbalance: the Kigali Health Institute (KHI), for the training of middle-level paramedics and nurses; the Kigali Institute of Science, Technology, and Management (KIST), for training middle-level technicians and managers and graduates in engineering, food science, computer science, and business administration; and the Kigali Institute of Education (KIE), mainly for training secondary school teachers at the degree level. KIE's mandate extends to coordinating the training of primary teachers in collaboration with primary teacher training centers, conducting pre-service and in-service training of primary school teachers, and training primary teacher trainers. Institutions at all levels of education are also expected to offer English and French, the languages of instruction since 1994, and to promote bilingualism to provide Rwanda's workforce with wider opportunities for employment.

Areas of concentration vary from institution to institution, but they include comprehensive programs offered at UNR, including agronomy, law, humanities, social sciences, medicine, pure and applied sciences, education, public health, and nutrition. Other institutions concentrate on a specific profession or on a particular area of specialization. The durations of existing programs are one year, two to three years, and three to five years. Terminal awards range from certificate to diploma, advanced diploma, bachelor's degree (currently available in only three public and three private institutions), and one master's degree (available only in medicine at UNR). Although few distance learning courses are offered at these institutions, some continuing education classes are offered in the evenings at three institutions. One institution currently has only a single candidate engaged in a master's program by correspondence, while the same establishment and another are offering lifelong learning through the African Virtual University long-distance programs, a World Bank Project based in Washington, D.C. Both institutions are public.

Student Enrollment

From an initial enrolment of 49 students in 1963–1964, UNR's enrollment rose to 921 in 1980–1981. Following its merger in 1981 with the National Institute of Pedagogy (IPN), the figure rose to 1,572 in 1985–1986 (Rwandese Republic 1995, 23) and currently stands at 4,550. Annual intake into UNR is on the order of 600 students who are selected from a list of nearly 4,000 (approximately 1 in 6). The rest of the institutions, according to Table 52.2, enrolled 5,715 students collectively in 1999–2000. The total student population in all twelve institutions is just over 10,000, only one-fourth of whom are females.

Institutional Fees

As indicated in Table 52.1, fees per annum range from $18 in public institutions to $250–400 in private ones. No fees are charged at the Senior Seminary (Le Grand Séminaire).

Accommodations

Of the twelve institutions reported in the survey, only six have hostel facilities, and even those are overcrowded and are unable to accommodate all who need to be housed. This leaves otherwise qualified students in no position to take up offers of admission if the institutions are far from home unless they can find alternative accommodation arrangements, which may not offer a productive atmosphere for study. Currently, for example, UNR has enough places in university residences for only 1,580 of its 4,550 students, and KIST has space enough for only 450 of its 1,200 students.

Staff

Staff in all higher education institutions include only 74 Ph.D.s at UNR and less than half that number in the other institutions—barely 100 altogether. The majority of institutions rely heavily on visiting staff. Out of a combined staff of 1,149, 585 are permanent and 564 are part-time. From available information on pay packages, monthly salaries range from $210 (85,000 Frw) for an assistant lecturer to $350 (140,000 Frw) for a professor. There are allowances for transportation, utilities, and housing. The UNR has a contributory pension based on a percentage of one's salary. The newer institutions—KIE, KHI, and KIST—do not offer a pension, only a gratuity at a certain percentage of one's salary.

General State of Affairs

The state of Rwanda's higher education is perhaps best reflected in the condition of UNR, a public institution that is older than most and that has better resources and is therefore relatively more stable; it is also the better known of all the higher education institutions in the country. Outside the humanities, social sciences, management, education, and law, enrollment at UNR includes only a few disciplines: these include science (3.9 percent), agronomy (3.6 percent), and applied science (6.2 percent). Although slated to be offered in the near future, no postgraduate studies are available in these fields, except for medicine at UNR, and even that is offered at the master's degree level only. An agreement signed in 2000 between Makerere University Business School and UNR will soon introduce a joint program. UNR has 251 permanent staff and 300 part-time or visiting lecturers (see Table 52.2). Information obtained from the *Study of the Education Sector in Rwanda* (Rwandese Repub-

lic 1997) records a high rate of repeats (701 out of 2,820 in 1994–1995, or 1 in 4) and of drop-outs (451 out of 2,820 in 1994–1995, or 1 in 7). The state of laboratories and equipment still leaves a lot to be desired. Scientific research is mainly carried out in the national research centers mentioned earlier—outside the university campus. Because of the lack of qualified staff and the absence of funding, very little research is being conducted.

Quality Control

From the shortcomings reported in the survey of existing higher education institutions in Rwanda, the absence of a mechanism for institutional and program accreditation can only be inferred, but other sources confirm that assessment of staff for promotion and external examiners for student exams are not yet in use. Rwanda's higher education institutions also lack adequate funding, well-equipped laboratories, adequate and computerized libraries, sufficient classrooms, sports facilities, a proper research infrastructure, and career guidance and counseling services for students, all of which are necessary elements if an educational system is to thrive.

Another factor contributing to the malaise of higher education in Rwanda is the inadequate base structure that supports it. The *Sectoral Consultation on Education in Rwanda* (Republic of Rwanda 1998b) notes that Rwanda cites only twenty-four government schools, eighty-six private subsidized schools, and sixty private schools. Because they charge high fees, private schools have the better facilities, though not all of them have facilities for science instruction (Republic of Rwanda 1998b, 20). Certainly the preponderance of the humanities in higher education institutions is the result of the curriculum at secondary school level, which favors humanities over science and technological subjects only because humanities disciplines are cheaper to run. In government or private schools, the remuneration package does not attract the best-qualified teachers; as a result, 68 percent of staff have not gone beyond the secondary school level.

REFORM

For a country that has barely survived war and genocide, Rwanda has an urgent need to refurbish its national fabric and an infrastructure laid waste by assault, and to produce trained personnel to sustain development. Higher education today should be central to such an agenda, but Rwanda has yet to develop a national higher education policy. In the past, African education policy has consisted of transplants and imports of education systems from whichever part of Europe African countries were affiliated. Attainment of national sovereignty brings with it freedom of choice. Of course, not every policy tried successfully in one country will work in another. Much depends on the socioeconomic environment, the politics of the day, and the temperament of the citizenry. But if a system of education is to be well regarded enough to expect cooperation and assistance from the global academic community, awareness of mainstream policy issues is useful.

Globally, the issues on the ground have to do with the following: access (that is as wide and as balanced as possible for both sexes); curriculum (that is responsive to national development and the self-realization needs of the students); funding (that is available to as many students as possible through scholarships, grants, loans, or cost sharing between government, parents or other sponsors, and the student); and decision-making organs (to accommodate the widest possible participation). The recommendations of the Higher Education Review Committee attempted to come to terms with the issues in advocating a direction for Rwanda's higher education in Rwanda. Its proposals include:

- Vision: To overcome the shortcomings reported from the survey of institutions and to create a machinery such as a commission for higher education with subcommittees for accreditation, allocation of funds, and scholarships and grants, all aimed at preparing higher education to respond productively to issues of national development.
- Common mission: To produce a generation of well-educated citizenry that has high moral standards and a respect for human rights and is disposed to contribute to a tolerant and democratic society. This mission should also include avoiding undue overlap and undue costs among the programs that implement the vision of higher education; namely, training, teaching, and research.
- Broad objectives: To implement the core activities of research, teaching, and community service in order to provide training of different kinds and at different levels to serve the immediate and long-term needs of Rwanda. Such programs are to go beyond the walls of institutions for the benefit of atypical students, for many of whom vocational training is especially beneficial.
- Specific Objectives: To divide the labor such that institutions will concentrate on vocational, professional, or academic studies. This should be the function of the law establishing each institution in the short run; by 2010, all institutions should aim at producing middle-level personnel in significant numbers.

INSTITUTIONAL CAPACITY

Physical Plant

Compared to the double-digit enrollments of the college-age group reported by many developed countries, including those from Southeast Asia (UNESCO 2000), enrollments that are 1 percent or lower, such as Rwanda's, do not make for happy reading (Republic of Rwanda 2000). Rwanda has set a goal of doubling enrollments by 2010, but progress, even at such a modest pace, involves costs that are difficult to accommodate. No doubt it is in recognition of the need for additional space and the need to diversify the curriculum that new government-sponsored institutions—including KHI, KIE, and KIST—have been established since the end of the 1990–1994 war. Building more new institutions may not be feasible, but adding to or expanding existing facilities should be. The UNR is proposing to transfer certain faculties from Butare to institutions in Kigali in order to make room for at least 1,000 more students. The university also

hopes to build a guest house for visiting lecturers. In return for incentives such as tax relief, the private sector might be enticed to invest in these ventures. But lest institutions of indifferent quality begin to mushroom, the committee also recommended a national monitoring body, such as a national commission for higher education, to evaluate all offers for suitability before approval can be given for a new institution. But the impediments to access must be identified.

Accommodations

Where public transportation can be taken for granted, both as to its availability and regularity, expenditure on campus residences can look like a misplaced priority. Yet domestic arrangements in family homes for most of Africa do not assure higher education students the privacy needed for productive studies. Initial response to this need in parts of Africa took the form of Oxbridge-type student rooms, that is, single-occupancy rooms, elaborate dining facilities featuring a high table for faculty, senior and junior common rooms, and domestic servants everywhere. It was costly and deserving of all the criticism that has been heaped on it over the years, leading to a situation in which it has virtually disappeared. The Oxbridge model has been replaced with newly built, multiple-occupancy hostels which are modest in all of their facilities. For the out-of-town student, the latter type of facility remains critical to facilitating access to higher education. The Higher Education Review Committee is hopeful that hostels will be provided by the private sector.

Gender

In Rwanda, as elsewhere in Africa, the notion still persists that investment in the education of the boy child has better returns; this is still a popular traditional view among both genders. The ratio of females to males in higher education is 1 to 4. To enable females to take full advantage of higher education, the starting point is to establish equal representation on campus. To this end, for as long as imbalance persists, the Higher Education Review Committee recommends automatic access, residence, and scholarships for females in any discipline at all, provided they qualify for admission and are able to maintain acceptable grades during their course.

Curriculum

Enrollment figures are a function of the curriculum. Dominated by the humanities and an almost total absence of postgraduate studies, Rwanda's educational offerings have limited appeal. A more varied curriculum offering courses up to a Ph.D. would be more challenging and attractive to students. A purposeful curriculum is a further challenge that has been identified by the Higher Education Review Committee. Accordingly, whatever the institutional mandate or focus, the curriculum for Rwanda should now provide for the following:

- Information and communication technology for accessing

material that is otherwise unavailable and communication with a much wider array of people and institutions

- Relevance in terms of the curriculum's alignment with the institution's purpose, its contribution to a knowledge-based society, and its responsiveness to demands placed on the education sector

- Balance such that the institution is inclusive in terms of both a diversified curriculum for an all-round education and gender to ensure equal opportunities for all

- Bilingualism in French and English (in addition to fluency in Kinyarwanda, which is the language spoken by and common to all Rwandans) for all the obvious and implicit advantages such knowledge has both to the individual and to the larger society

- National unity and cohesion that blunts the disposition to see one another in terms of ethnicity

- Critical thinking, a value in its own right

- Special education to create wider opportunities for the disadvantaged and vulnerable groups

- Lifelong learning to enhance skills of workers and ensure that their knowledge remains relevant to society's needs

- Community service to bring institutions and their programs closer to the community

Language of Instruction

Capacity utilization has much to do with the language of instruction. Originally stemming from its Belgian colonial history, French has been used as the language of instruction in Rwandan educational institutions and business transactions. Since 1994, Rwanda's population includes English- and French-speaking former refugees from Uganda, Burundi, Congo, Tanzania, South Africa, French-speaking West Africa, Kenya, and other countries, in which many refugees were in exile for thirty years or longer. This difference in linguistic background has influenced Rwanda's new language policy, which calls for the teaching of both English and French at all levels of education and the use of either as the medium of instruction. Instruction in Kinyarwanda, especially at the primary level of education, is also available. Kinyarwanda, the only indigenous and common language in the country, is a unifying factor and deserves consideration, but it should not be overplayed. Another country in the region that also had one common language was keen to substitute that language for English as the language of instruction until it was discovered that access to literature in English had become restricted by diminishing competence in English while the country had not become self-sufficient in literature in the preferred language. Opting out of a major international language too soon can be both imprudent and costly.

Admission Requirements

The high school diploma awarded by the Rwanda National Examinations Council (RNEC) covers more than ten subjects for which an overall numerical grading is awarded, starting from the best score of 11.0 points for great distinction down to a minimum of 2.0 for a pass. Admission to postsecondary school institutions is, in general, open to all candidates with the minimum

pass mark. Those with better scores may end up in the more prestigious courses, such as medicine and engineering. The drawback is that they may not have sufficient grounding in the core subjects for medicine or engineering; but there is no way of knowing in advance who will succeed, since performance in individual subjects is not indicated anywhere on the result slip, a weakness that the overall score obscures. Consultation with RNEC is to lead to certification that identifies the level of competence in each subject offered by the student in addition to overall grading.

Mobility

Ability to move from one institution to another to take advantage of site-specific facilities is another challenge and an important assurance of effective capacity utilization. Movement is not possible when admission policies are markedly different, however. Admission requirements should be stated to refer to specifics that are common to all institutions, including an acceptable competence in communication (French or English), numeracy or ability to compute, and familiarity with a science discipline and one subject in the humanities.

Funding

Effective since 1996, funding for the education sector has been provided at 15 percent of the national budget. The Ministry of Education has allotted 65.1 percent of its disbursement for education to primary education, 15.5 percent to secondary education, 9.5 percent to higher education, and 9.9 percent to services. Some 55 percent of funds for higher education goes to students as maintenance for accommodation, food, transport, health, and pocket money. A maintenance allowance is available only to students attending public higher education institutions, however, and even then not to all of them.

From 15 percent since 1996, the share of the education budget may now increase up to 30 percent, but no higher. Hopefully, the share for higher education will also increase now. There is considerable optimism that the private sector will not only add to existing facilities but will also be persuaded to provide additional funding, given that it relies on trained personnel for production and doing business generally. In the spirit of cost sharing, it is believed that if student maintenance (said to amount to 55 percent of the budget for higher education) could be taken up by parents, enrollment in higher education could be doubled even with the same budget. Indeed, the Higher Education Review Committee has proposed tuition-free higher education for all, except for students who win scholarships for academic excellence or for choosing subjects for which there is a shortage of personnel. A scholarship secretariat to disburse scholarships and grants to deserving students would be part of the functions of an envisaged National Commission for Higher Education.

Staff Recruitment

Although there are few Ph.D.s (barely 100, including part-time teachers) in all of Rwanda's higher education institutions, there is a real danger of settling for less than the Ph.D. for appointments. In terms of promotion, external assessment is not yet part of the mechanism for staff advancement. There is thus the danger that by relying on longevity at a post rather than research output, the top academic positions will be encumbered by staff who have been there for many years but who have inadequate credentials and doubtful performance, much to the detriment of the reputation of the country's higher education system. Though the committee for higher education recognizes the danger, it stops short of prescriptions for appointments or promotions, noting only that faculty who teach in any program must have a qualification that is higher than the degree to which the program leads. The committee expects the respective governing councils to define detailed criteria appropriate to each institution. Given the committee's recommendation for institutional cross-representation on the councils, the criteria for appointments and promotions might be uniformly set in the future.

Remuneration

As in other developing countries, the level of pay for employees in higher education in Rwanda is, for the most part, generally low. The minimum daily wage in Rwanda for educators is barely $1. Inclusive of allowances, a professor's monthly earnings add up to less than $800, which deters the recruitment of high-caliber senior staff. The Higher Education Review Committee did not identify this problem, however, perhaps out of concern that isolating higher education for special treatment might upset other public-sector employees.

THE PROSPECTS

The Dilemmas

Given the country's recent tragic history, deciding whether to spend money on national security or on other equally urgent things poses a dilemma. Rwanda now has a call-up program of up to six weeks of solidarity camp organized by the Commission for Unity and Reconciliation. Participants include community leaders, youths, pre-university and university students, and others. Among the specific programs offered are debates on issues of national concern such as Rwandan history, genocide, governance, leadership, economy, human rights, current affairs, and poverty alleviation, all of which are meant to inculcate a spirit of patriotism within the citizenry. These lessons are interspersed with field crafts, including military drills and weapons handling, providing basic self-defense mechanisms as well as discipline. This training occurs in all twelve prefectures, or administrative units. In addition to solidarity camps, Rwanda also now has local defense training centers specifically for self-defense and protection of the public in their local area.

Capital-intensive training for national and local defense and for national reconstruction and reconciliation are both urgent. While the committee for higher education makes no mention of any of this in its recommendations, the teaching of those courses that are now to be common to higher education—such as English, French, introduction to computer technology, integrated basic science, and introductory mathematics—could

easily be included in the camp programs. This would allow institutions of higher education to spend less time on auxiliary courses. Such an addition would require pulling together resources from the institutions that already have them and putting them toward a more equitable use. A first year spent in solidarity camps while also engaged in common academic courses is cost effective and could become a distinctive feature of Rwanda's higher education system.

Access to higher education presents another dilemma. Cost-sharing propositions, which have been fiercely resisted by students in parts of West Africa (Ghana) and East Africa (Kenya and Uganda), suggest that not everybody can hope for access unless they are willing to share costs. But how much may be expected in personal contributions when the daily wage is just about $1 and the majority of the population is rural? Moreover, how high may any student progress? Applying available funds to shorter courses has the appeal of economy. Indeed, some claim that Rwanda needs middle-level skilled personnel and graduates of trade schools and vocational institutions rather than graduates of universities. After reading the results of the survey of institutions, some suggest that only one institution is properly equipped to run university-type courses and that the other institutions should confine their work to middle-level training which, it is argued, is their proper role. Yet evidence from around the world shows that the distinction between universities and other types of institutions of higher education has become somewhat blurred under pressure from youths aspiring to higher education in larger numbers than ever before. Indeed, adapting facilities in polytechnics for training graduates, professionals, and middle-level personnel is more economical in the long run. Of course, the focus of polytechnics remains the more practical areas of study, but this does not preclude instruction at the bachelor's degree level or higher.

To its credit, the committee for higher education recommended that whatever their mandate, higher education institutions should deliver their programs at the highest possible level if they have the resources (including staff of the highest caliber, laboratories, and libraries), and can persuade a national supervisory body that the programs being proposed are useful. The committee recommended free tuition not only for students in the public school system but also for those in the private schools. In other words, if students are engaged in programs of national priority, whether in public or private institutions, they should be entitled to government sponsorship.

Government sponsorship will support three specific areas in order of priority in the future: academic merit, priority disciplines, and acute need. Because of unavailability of funds, however, only 30 percent of candidates who qualify for admission to higher education will be eligible for such sponsorship. For those who hoped for greater representation rates, this outcome suggests that access will remain limited.

Lack of funding for education brings into sharp focus an unresolved paradox—when to invest in education. Even in circumstances of economic hardship, some individuals and families can afford to pay for education at every level. Such people would be willing to pay for their education. Unfortunately, there are never enough paying individuals to make a difference to the national economy. It is precisely when the economy is ailing that tactical investments begin to help recuperation. There is not enough arable land to enable agricultural exports to redress Rwanda's balance of payment. But agricultural produce has added value from processing. A new food science and processing department has been started at one of Rwanda's newer public higher education institutions (KIST) to train students who can prolong the life span of crops such as potatoes, bananas, beans, and cassava, thereby giving added value to these exports. The experience of Japan, and now also some of the Southeast Asian countries, suggests that economic survival is still possible from the export of knowledge or technical know-how even where natural resources are lacking. It is no accident that the countries with strong economies are also the ones that have strong investments in education, guarantee 100 percent enrollments in primary and secondary schools, and attain double-digit enrollments in postsecondary education. Indeed, in some of the developed countries, representation of the college-age group in postsecondary education can be as high as 50 percent. It should be possible for Rwanda to join the ranks of countries that are seeking the benefits of tactical investment in education, especially in higher education.

Utilization of Graduates

Given the high levels of graduate unemployment in many countries, overproduction of graduates is a legitimate source of worry. But the curriculum proposed by one of the newer institutions in Rwanda, KIST, shows promise. The institute's faculties include technology, science, management, language studies, and continuing education. Courses include management and business administration, civil engineering and environmental technology, electromechanical engineering, food science and technology, physics, chemistry, biology, mathematics, and English and French, as well as various continuing education programs. All students are admitted to ordinary and advanced diploma courses of two to three years in the first instance. Those who wish to continue to a bachelor's degree may do so after successful completion of the diploma and after meeting specific requirements. For a variety of reasons, including sponsorship, the wise course of action for a good many will be to go into employment or apprenticeship for which they have enough practical skills after the diploma. Any such students may return later to campus to pursue an advanced diploma or a bachelor's degree by incremental credits; if they should be unable to make further progress, the fallback to the diploma is a welcome innovation, and in a country engaged in rebuilding its infrastructure, there are opportunities enough for those with practical skills to set themselves up in business.

Governance

Previously directed by separate government ministries, primary, secondary, and tertiary education have been brought under a single Ministry of Education with centralized administration since 1997. There is a desk at the ministry for each subsector that is headed by a director reporting to the minister. At the campus level, there is a governing council for UNR chaired by the minister of education, to which every member is also appointed by the government. Key appointments, including rector and vice-rector, are made by the government. No governing councils exist yet at the newer institutions. Where committees operate, they are informal rather than being mandated by any statute.

The Higher Education Review Committee recognized the need for central direction—not, however, by the Ministry of Education, but by a body representative of all stakeholders—to serve this purpose. Some have advocated the establishment of a national commission for higher education to be run by an executive secretary. In order not to backslide to a situation in which the center controls and issues directives, the commission's functions need to be limited to accreditation, quality control, and the disbursement of scholarships and grants. To avoid fostering a monolithic culture and to allow for variety in practices and procedures, institutions should be able to choose from different types of management staff that are suitable to each university's situation rather than have one model imposed on them.

Management

Meanwhile, the question of who manages the campus, whether professionals (as in the United Kingdom) or academics doubling as managers (as in the United States), remains a running debate on campuses. Each campus tends to follow the traditions of its colonial past, but debate about change becomes merely academic if the legal instrument for any institution already provides for a registrar to be secretary to the council or head of administration, and for others, including a bursar, to be responsible for other aspects of administration. For example, without explicitly providing for a secretary, the legal statute establishing KIST requires the rector, as the chief executive, to establish a secretariat for the University Council and for other administrative duties, subject, of course, to approval by the Council.

Faculty

Governance structures run from the top by appointees of the government are familiar but not popular. Faculty in many university campuses in Africa and elsewhere want to be able to elect their own heads of departments, deans, and vice-rectors and at least to be part of the search for the appointment of the rector. Faculty elsewhere are close to unionization, and they seek representation on the governing council and certainly want to be in on any consultation on remuneration packages for staff. Rwanda has no national association of faculty, nor has concern for a more involved role for faculty been widely expressed. Somehow, the faculty's role outside the classroom did not even receive mention in the recommendations of the Higher Education Review Committee, which, given its membership (which includes many who have returned from exile since the end of the war), could not be unaware of developments elsewhere. Quite possibly, rebuilding the country takes precedence over institutional autonomy in the view of most faculty. Or perhaps because their numbers are small, Ph.D.s who are the institutions' natural leaders are overstretched by merely carrying out their duties as teachers.

To add to faculty numbers, if the donor community could be persuaded to help offer financial incentives, Rwandan expatriates abroad, say in North America and Europe, can be attracted back home, where the lower cost of living will still permit a reasonable lifestyle; they would also enjoy a sense of fulfillment from contributing to the rebuilding of the nation. In the absence of an enabling salary plus other attractive incentives, brain drain or the vacating of posts by well-qualified Rwandan nationals is the more likely trend.

Students

Student presence in governance is not much felt in Rwanda. Elsewhere in Africa, students have already gained a place on governing councils or are agitating for representation (Ajayi, Lameck, and Johnson 1996, 124). They have also had to explore free time more fully, engage in community work camps, attend or host international student conferences, organize vacation tours abroad by chartered planes, and raise enough money to finance their programs, including participation in the national political process. In the 1970s, for example, the National Union of Ghana Students (NUGS) regularly organized chartered flights to the U.K. As a measure of its high political profile, NUGS had representation on the Constituent Assembly that drafted the constitution of the Third and the Fourth Republics.

When organized in a national union, students have demonstrated such a capacity for disruption that they are taken seriously when they take a position. In Rwanda, attempts to establish a serious front in the pre-1994 period were often squashed before they could come to fruition. The potential for standing their ground, however, has occasionally manifested itself in the post-1994 era. Demonstrations in 1999 by some forty English-speaking students from UNR protesting the government's bilingual policy, which led to the students' self-imposed exile to Uganda, were instructive. Still haunted by memories of war and genocide, the average Rwandan student perhaps feels that catching up on disrupted education is what matters most right now. This stands in contrast to the situation in other African countries, possibly because some of them have not been traumatized or overburdened by personal concerns of critical immediacy; students in other African countries engage in community work, participate in international student conferences and tours, and generate resources to finance their programs.

Faculty and student activism can be occasionally disruptive, regrettably. In parts of West and East Africa, campus closures arising from activism have led to a distortion of the academic calendar and several backlogs of incoming students, whose admission has been deferred again and again for years. Through one kind of activism or another, the academic calendar rarely ran to schedule in Ghana during the military regimes preceding the Third and Fourth Republics in the 1970–1980 decade. It is also now common knowledge in the region that Kenya's University of Nairobi was forced to close a number of times in the 1980s–1990s as a result of student riots, which often led to postponements of examinations that resulted in a backlog of student admissions. On the other hand, activism on campus brings attention to dimensions of issues that formal committees often do not see and is now such a commonplace global phenomenon

that its absence anywhere should be cause for concern. Of more significant import, activism of one kind or another is an indication of institutional self-assertiveness. This is fundamental for autonomy and academic freedom, both of which are so critical to higher education.

Research

Research in Rwanda has not always had such a low profile. The Faculty of Agronomy at UNR, which was established in 1979–1980, used to have a research station near the campus at Mamba to provide students with practical training. Other stations at Gihindamuyaga (for stock breeding) and Rwasave (for fish breeding) offered faculty opportunities to update their work and receive advanced degrees. Complementing work at UNR, the Higher Institute of Agriculture and Livestock (ISAE) and the Scientific and Technological Research Institute (IRST) also used to run credible research programs, including some to train farm managers. Casualties from 1994, these institutions now need to be rehabilitated at costs estimated beyond $20 million (Republic of Rwanda 1998). Lack of sufficiently equipped modern libraries also slows down research progress and remains a serious cause for concern at university campuses. Necessary funding and adequately trained local staff in sufficient numbers are also sadly lacking. On the up side of things, however, under government sponsorship, there are about forty nationals currently training in India alone. Other Rwandans are training in South Africa, the United Kingdom, and the United States. Rwandan institutions of higher education, mandated as they are to teach and carry out research, hope to benefit from the services of some of these trainees on completion of their studies.

Donor Funding

Rebuilding Rwanda has been made possible largely by friendly countries shocked into humanitarian gestures by the country's recent tragedy. But donors often have their own rather narrow perspectives, expressed in conditionalities to which there is sometimes unquestioning acquiescence by grateful aid recipients. In 1999, while the Higher Education Review Committee was still sitting, a memo from the Ministry of Education, dated December 15, 1999, announced an offer from a donor country of a research grant designed to explore the question of why the cost of a graduate to the government of Rwanda is many times the cost of a primary education completer, yet many poor children are denied their human right to basic education. The grant protocols noted that greater progress toward Rwanda's poverty reduction objectives is likely to be made by shifting spending allocations toward expanding access to and improving the quality of primary and secondary education. As for higher education, according to the protocols, there is scope for shifting a greater share of the costs to the primary beneficiaries—namely, students or parents—and to the private sector. The research project was given to a scholar from outside of Rwanda, missing an opportunity to encourage local research.

For a country that has lost most of its trained personnel to war, genocide, and exile and is now host to a plethora of expatriates, pitting basic education against higher education—one a basic right, the other a privilege and a luxury to be indulged by whoever can pay for it—cannot be helpful. Universities were late coming to Africa because during the colonial era there were many excuses about why the time was not ripe. Either they were not cost effective because of likely low enrollments or there were no jobs to absorb the graduates (Ajayi, Lameck, and Johnson 1996, 51). It is often assumed that jobs must come before higher education or that higher education, particularly university education, is a luxury when there are no jobs to be had. The history of Silicon Valley in California, where the high-tech industry was largely created by graduates from the nearby universities, is instructive. It is again instructive that only graduates may be certified to teach in North America, even for primary school teaching, a policy that must account in part for its strength in diverse areas. Obviously, a highly trained citizenry is an asset that can be put to productive use. There is not enough, let alone a surfeit, of such a national asset in Rwanda. In a presentation made to a meeting of donors at KIST in November 2000, the rector of the institute, who is also president of the National Association of Engineers, disclosed that when one included professionals and subprofessionals in engineering, architecture, surveying, and other specializations in the construction industry, fewer than 100 Rwandans qualified for registration in the association.

Meanwhile, for a variety of reasons, others want the traffic to Europe for higher education to continue unabated. It is curious how suddenly the region to which Rwanda belongs is now the target of advertisements, which are followed by on-the-spot "admission officers," hoping to attract and recruit students to study abroad at the institutions where the fees required are by no means small. Such investments would have more lasting returns if they were made at home institutions.

CONCLUSION

If increased access for both sexes, more purposeful curriculum, better infrastructure, better remuneration for faculty, and more participatory arrangements for governance and management are critical, more critical still is the country's commitment to research. Indeed, support for research would stimulate a vibrant research program resulting in a high research profile for higher education. The signs are not encouraging at the moment. Refurbishing Rwanda's education and research infrastructure requires substantial funding that is not immediately available. Meanwhile, if only to provide a stimulus to local capacity building, researchers at post in various Rwandan universities and other higher education institutions could be given the priority of engaging in productive research work for which there is funding, rather than handing it to foreigners, as is sometimes the case.

Having begun as metropolitan transplants, some of Africa's universities remain on a course that is not of their own charting and are under no particular pressure to reset their course. The tragedies that have come Rwanda's way, however, have necessitated a rethinking of educational and national priorities. This process may be turned to advantage by setting right the course of higher education. In this way, the recommendations of the Higher Education Review Committee are encouraging, but

Rwanda is a long way from implementing them and many hurdles remain, including acceptance of the proposed policies by the government. Such approval needs to be indicated in a government white paper and then debated in Parliament, which must pass an umbrella Higher Education Act before specific legislation for each institution can be determined. How many of the committee's recommendations will survive this process will depend on the climate of opinion, which is highly influenced by external forces. Judging from the efforts being made so far to reform Rwanda's education system as a whole, prospects for continued improvement of higher education in Rwanda remain high.

BIBLIOGRAPHY

Ajayi, J. F. A., K. H. G. Lameck, and A. G. Johnson. 1996. *The African Experience with Higher Education.* Accra: Association of African Universities.

Collis, B., I. Nikolava, and K. Martcheva, eds. 1995. *Information Technologies in Teacher Education: Issues and Experiences for Countries in Transition.* Proceedings of a Workshop at University of Twente, Enschede, the Netherlands, February 20–23, 1994. Enschede: UNESCO.

Hawes, H., T. Coombe, C. Coombe, and K. Lillis, eds. 1986. *Education Priorities and Aid Responses in Sub-Saharan Africa.* Report of a Conference at Cumberland Lodge, Windsor, December 4–7, 1984. London: University of London Institute of Education, Overseas Development Administration.

Lwakabamba, S., and P. Murray. 1998. "Technical and Vocational Training in Rwanda: The Current Status and Future Reforms." Unpublished paper. In author's possession.

Mazimhaka, J., and G. F. Daniel. 2000. *Post-Genocide Restructuring of Higher Education in Rwanda: An Overview.* Occasional Paper Series no. 4 of the Association of African Universities. Accra: Association of African Universities.

Ministry of Education. 2000. "Survey of Higher Education Institutions." Reported in the Higher Education Subsector Policy for Rwanda proposed by the Higher Education Review Committee. June. Unpublished report.

Republic of Rwanda. 1997. *Study of the Education Sector in Rwanda.* Kigali: Ministry of Education.

———. 1998a. *Plan of Action for Education in Rwanda (1998–2000): Recovery and Development.* Kigali: Ministry of Education.

———. 1998b. *Sectoral Consultation on Education in Rwanda.* Vol. 1. Kigali: Ministry of Education.

———. 2000. "Higher Education Sub-sector Policy." Unpublished report. In author's possession.

République Rwandaise. 1985. *Rapport de la Commission del'Université Nationale du Rwanda pour la réforme de l'enseignement supérieur au Rwanda.* Butare: Université Nationale du Rwanda.

———. 1986. *Projet de réforme de l'enseignement supérieur au Rwanda.* Kigali: Ministère de l'Enseignement Supérieur et de la Recherche Scientifique.

———. 1990a. *L' université nationale du Rwanda en 1990.* Kigali: Ministére de l'Enseignement Supérieur et de la Recherche Scientifique.

———. 1990b. *Rationalisation des ressources a l'Université Nationale du Rwanda et perspectives de financement de l'enseignement supérieur au Rwanda: Rapport d'une Commission d'Etude.* Kigali: L'Imprimerie de Kigali.

———. 1991. *La problématique de la mise en place de la réforme dans les etablissements de l'enseignement supérieur au Rwanda.* Kigali:

Ministère de l'Enseignement Supérieur et de la Recherche Scientifique.

——. 1995. *La politique et la planification de l'education au Rwanda: Document final provisoire.* Kigali: Ministère de l'Enseignement Primaire et Secondaire et Ministére de l'Enseignement Supérieur de la Recherche Scientifique et de la Culture.

UNESCO. 1996. *Studies of African Education.* Paris: UNESCO Publishing.

——. 1998a. "Higher Education for a New Africa: A Student's Vision." Paper presented at the Forum of Student Associations in Africa on Higher Education in the 21st Century. Accra, Ghana, March 23–25.

——. 1998b. *Higher Education in Africa: Achievements, Challenges and Prospects.* Dakar: UNESCO Regional Office.

Woodhall, M. 1991. *Student Loans in Higher Education.* Vol. 3: *English Speaking Africa.* International Institute for Educational Planning Dissemination Programme, Educational Forum Series, no. 3. Paris: International Institute for Educational Planning.

53

São Tomé and Principe

MARIA DE LOURDES MACHADO-TAYLOR, LUCIO LIMA VIEGAS PINTO, AND JAMES S. TAYLOR

OVERVIEW AND HISTORICAL BACKGROUND

The islands of São Tomé and Principe are located in the Gulf of Guinea approximately 150 miles off the western coast of Africa. These two islands with a combined area of 963 square kilometers (372 square miles) constitute one of the smallest countries in the world. The islands were discovered at the end of the fifteenth century by Portuguese navigators. São Tomé and Principe was a Portuguese territory from that time until its independence in 1975.

Soon after discovering the islands, the Portuguese developed a plantation system. The first plantations produced primarily sugar cane. This continued until the middle of the seventeenth century. More recently, cocoa and coffee plantations have been introduced. In the beginning, the primary workforce consisted of slaves brought over from the African mainland. Subsequent marriages between the indigenous white population and the black slaves resulted in a significant Creole population. Overall, the islands have a broad racial and ethnic mix. Especially during the twentieth century, many people migrated to São Tomé and Principe from Angola, Mozambique, and Cape Verde.

In 1975, following the Carnation Revolution in Portugal, São Tomé and Principe achieved its independence. Soon after, the ruling party introduced a socialist one-party system. The system proved to be a complete failure. As a result, a multiparty system was established and a democratic regime emerged in 1990. Since then, presidential and parliamentary elections have been held.

São Tomé and Principe is primarily an agricultural nation. Businesses exist, but they are limited. In efforts to boost its economic circumstances, the country has begun natural oil exploration in partnership with North American–based Mobil Oil.

The population of São Tomé and Principe is currently estimated to be approximately 130,000. Interestingly, adult literacy is one of the highest of any African nation. Currently, 70 percent of the adult population is literate. This is the result of a nationwide literacy campaign that was implemented soon after the country gained its independence. The dominant language is Portuguese.

HIGHER EDUCATION IN SÃO TOMÉ AND PRINCIPE

Presently, São Tomé and Principe has made higher education a major national priority. The governmental and educational leadership view higher education as a major way to improve social and economic development. Understandably, a country as small, poor, and relatively isolated as São Tomé and Principe faces unique problems and challenges in moving forward its strategic goals for higher education.

Before achieving independence in 1975, there were very few elementary schools in the country and only one high school. The literacy rate was estimated to be 20 percent. Thus, one of the major challenges facing the post-independence government was to raise the level of education. Efforts proved successful. Within a few years, enrollments grew by 60 percent at the elementary level and 300 percent at the secondary level. Literacy, as mentioned earlier, was drastically improved from 20 percent to 70 percent. However, at the higher education level, there were virtually no opportunities to pursue a degree within the country. The vast majority of people did not have the financial means to study abroad, which was the only option. Those few who were able to do so generally pursued their higher education in Portugal. Scholarships were eventually made available from institutions in other countries, especially Eastern Europe. As a result, hundreds of Santomeans were able to study in countries such as the USSR, East Germany, Cuba, Bulgaria, France, Italy, Spain, Brazil, China, the United States and, of course, Portugal. The only opportunity to study in São Tomé and Principe was a training program for elementary teachers, a program that was also available in Portugal. Most teachers within the country were Portuguese. Since so few Santomeans continued into high school, the Portuguese educational officials didn't bother to create training programs in São Tomé and Principe for secondary school teachers. These programs were ultimately established in the 1980s. As a result, São Tomé and Principe now enjoys the highest public school enrollment rates in sub-Saharan Africa. However, many concerns remain with respect to the quality of the educational programs offered.

The pre-independence absence of higher education in São Tomé and Principe continued until 1996. The scholarship opportunities from institutions in other countries described above encouraged the government to ignore national higher education. But massive changes in Eastern Europe have severely reduced scholarship opportunities. This principal factor, coupled with the fact that many who studied abroad in Europe never returned, prompted the current understanding that higher education must be a national priority for São Tomé and Principe.

Educational and governmental leaders have established numerous objectives for higher education within the country, including the desire to promote scientific inquiry, encourage international exchanges and collaboration, strengthen the knowledge and abilities of the workforce, and preserve the national culture.

INSTITUTIONS OF HIGHER EDUCATION

Using its experience with the training programs that were started in 1993, the Ministry of Education established two institutions of higher learning in São Tomé and Principe. The first one, created in 1994, is private, and the second one, established in 1997, is public.

The University Institute of Accounting, Business Administration, and Informatics (IUCAI), the first campus, is located in the capital city of São Tomé and graduated its first class of students in 1999. Its primary mission is to prepare a better national workforce. IUCAI has collaborated with Portugal to develop its training programs.

Most students at IUCAI are young adults who are already employed within the country. They are typically at an entry level in their jobs and are poised to advance upon completion of their higher education. The university's programs are closely tied to the needs of banks and other business enterprises in São Tomé and Principe.

IUCAI is administered by a president and a management committee. Its facilities are quite limited and will only accommodate approximately 100 students. The university offers a bachelor's degree which usually requires between four and five years to complete.

The newer Polytechnic Institute of São Tomé and Principe (ISPSTP) is a much larger campus comprised of eleven buildings. Its president reports to the Ministry of Education. A very high priority for the ministry is teacher training; teacher education is the first and most important component of the curriculum. In addition to the bachelor's degree in teacher education, ISPSTP offers extensive teacher training programs for non-

degree-seeking students. The teacher education curriculum model adopted is termed *formacao bivalente*, which loosely translated from Portuguese means "two disciplines." Under this model, students must graduate with certification to teach in two subject areas.

More recently, ISPSTP has expanded its curricular offerings in areas such as business administration, languages, literature, and technology, among others. Entry into the bachelor's degree program requires a high school diploma, but students seeking only certificates do not have to meet this requirement. Since a student's first year at the Polytechnic is preparatory, the bachelor's degree typically takes five years to complete.

Initial planning for the establishment of ISPSTP was done by the Ministry of Education in collaboration and partnership with two institutions in Portugal, the University of Porto and the Polytechnic Institute of Braganca. It was deemed necessary to seek outside assistance and consultation, given the limited experience with higher education in São Tomé and Principe. An agreement of cooperation was signed between the parties in 1994, and the campus opened in 1997. It was further agreed these two Portuguese institutions would continue providing assistance through the first formative years of operation of ISPSTP.

The compressed timeline from conceptualization of the institute to its opening (three years) is credited to the joint collaboration with the two established Portuguese institutions. Consultation and guidance were provided in the development of the initial legal documents needed to establish the institute, in creating its administrative and organizational structure, in designing its curriculum, and in establishing policies and procedures for evaluation, pedagogy, research, and financial planning. Finally, the three institutions created the Scientific and Pedagogical Committee with representation from each campus. It meets twice a year in a consultative capacity. Overall, this collaborative effort has provided an enormous and positive impact, not only on the development of the institute generally but also in terms of accountability, academic credibility, and prestige.

CURRICULUM PLANNING AND STRUCTURE

Curriculum planning and development in São Tomé and Principe have been primarily modeled after those found in institutions in Portugal. Specifically, many structures implemented are the same as those found at the University of Porto and the Polytechnic Institute of Braganca. Clearly, adjustments and modifications to those models had to be made to meet the unique realities and needs of São Tomé and Principe. The Scientific and Pedagogical Committee has primary responsibility for overall planning. Other administrative structures are also in place to deal with systematic follow-up and assessment of progress and planning activities.

The academic year is divided into two semesters. Most courses are taught on a one-semester basis; however, some extend to the full year. The official language of instruction is Portuguese. In fact, throughout the country of São Tomé and Principe, educational instruction at all institutions and at all levels is taught in Portuguese. Almost all professors at the higher education level, however, have additional fluency in English and/or French.

FINANCING AND FUNDING PATTERNS

Both higher education institutions in São Tomé and Principe have serious funding and budgetary shortages. Support for instruction is limited, and additional funding to support research and other scholarly activities is virtually nonexistent. One might presume that these financial problems are symptomatic of the fact that these institutions are very young and still building their infrastructure and funding bases. In truth, however, the problem is systemic and reflects the overall economic condition of São Tomé and Principe. There is no evidence that these funding problems will diminish in the foreseeable future for either institution.

The IUCAI is a private institution. Thus, funding is driven primarily by tuition. With fewer than 100 students, revenues are obviously very small. The ISPSTP is a public institution. A full 90 percent of its budget is provided by the state. The state budget is, however, inadequate to provide proper funding for the institute. On occasion, the government is able to provide both institutions with emergency financial assistance. Often, however, the aid is insufficient and is not provided in a timely fashion.

FACULTY AND STUDENTS

For both institutions, the vast majority of the professors are native Santomeans who have received their higher education abroad at any one of the many countries referred to earlier. A small percentage of the faculty is from Portugal and France. Native professors are insufficient in number, and it is quite difficult to attract faculty to São Tomé and Principe from other countries. Thus there is an urgent need for more faculty.

Students are typically young people who have just graduated from high school. At the same time, a reasonably large number are older, employed adults who are hoping to improve their formal education for career advancement purposes. The vast majority of both subgroups of students are working and attending classes at the same time. While this adds a challenge for the students, it is not unique to São Tomé and Principe. The Student Association was created to provide various forms of support, including financial aid, primarily in the form of scholarships.

UNIQUE CHALLENGES

The fact that São Tomé and Principe is one of the smallest countries in the world places enormous additional burdens on its efforts to provide quality higher education. The overall ability of this country to develop in any way is extremely limited. This situation leaves São Tomé and Principe extremely vulnerable to the rapid changes and events that occur globally. The country has a paucity of natural, financial, human, and other resources that could contribute to its advancement and productivity. Higher education and its accompanying high relative costs could easily be viewed as a luxury the country cannot absorb, especially given its many other critical needs. Fortunately, the governmental and educational leaders have prioritized

higher education and have committed themselves to resolving these persistent challenges. Some argue the investment in higher education and the more skilled and capable populace this will create are the key to resolving the country's other stifling problems.

Improving higher education must be done as a part of the country's overall revitalization. The economy has recorded very slow growth, if any. In recent years, there have been very few well-paying jobs, and there is a very real threat that the job market will become saturated. The small population makes any assurances of healthy and sustainable enrollments doubtful. At this very early stage in its development, the higher education system in São Tomé and Principe faces the challenge of reaching a level of academic integrity sufficient for degrees to have accredited status.

Some specific educational challenges have been articulated for the future. Leaders believe a first step is to improve the academic quality of the elementary and secondary educational systems to better ensure that students have the necessary skills and preparation to succeed in higher education. They want the higher education system to be a valid and legitimate choice for students in São Tomé and Principe as well as for students from other countries. Similarly, they want to expand the breadth and depth of academic offerings and to raise enrollments. Finally, they hope to find sufficient funding to make research a viable component of the overall missions of the institutions in an effort to address important social needs.

INTERNATIONAL COOPERATION

Given the scenario of unique challenges for São Tomé and Principe described above, it is clear that international cooperation and support is critical if educators hope to meet their goals. In fact, their confidence in receiving such cooperation was a major motivator in the decision to establish higher education within the country.

Several examples of successful collaboration are already in place and are producing positive impacts. The Polytechnic Institute of São Tomé and Principe has networked with two institutions, one in Cape Verde and one in Portugal. This partnership will focus on both student and faculty exchanges. ISPSTP is also a member of the Association of Universities of Portuguese-Speaking Countries (AULP). Many avenues of support are being provided by AULP, including exchanges.

São Tomé and Principe's relative isolation elevates the importance of developing distance learning capabilities within the higher education system. Support is being provided in this arena by the Community of Portuguese-Speaking Countries (CPLP) and UNESCO. Several distance learning projects are also underway with institutions in Portugal. Success with distance learning efforts and the ability to reach out beyond the confining borders of the country will be pivotal to the overall success of higher education in São Tomé and Principe.

CONCLUSION

São Tomé and Principe has shown great vision and courage in its dedication to the establishment of a higher education system. The country's leadership views higher education as a means to better economic, educational, and social prosperity for the country, not as an end in itself. This is not a country that can import its talent and knowledge or education system autonomously. It must educate its own citizenry to create a better future and must reach out for international assistance and support. The visionary leaders of São Tomé and Principe who are championing the cause of higher education understand these essential relationships. The future of higher education in Sao Tome and Principe has many challenges, but it also holds promise and reason for optimism.

SELECTED BIBLIOGRAPHY

CPLP (Comunidade dos Países de Lingua Portuguesa). 1997a. "Bases para uma Cooperacao no Ambito da Politica Educativa. Conferencia dos Ministros da Educacao da CPLP" (November).

——. 1997b. *Declaracao de Lisboa.*

Estatutos do Instituto Superior Politecnico de São Tomé e Principe. 1996. "Diario da Republica." 18–31 (December).

Irvine, D., and J. Maraj. 1994. *Higher Education in Small Island States: Challenges and Responses.*

Lillis, K. M. 1994. *Providing Tertiary Education in Small Island States.* International Experts Meeting, Higher Education in Small Island States. Praia, Cape Verde (March).

Mayor, F. 1997. "Allocucion a la Conférence Régionalle sur l'Enseignement Supérieur." Tokyo (July).

Pinto, L. L. V. 1994. "Ralatorio de encontro de peritos em ensino superior em pequenos estados insulares." São Tomé (April).

UNESCO. 1993. "Strategies for Changes and Development in Higher Education." Policy Paper on Higher Education prepared by the Division of Higher Education (October).

——. 1994. "Final Report." International Experts Meeting on Higher Education in Small Island States. Praia, Cape Verde (March).

——. 1996. "Estrategia a Medio Prazo, 1996–2001."

United Nations. (1983). "Development Problems and Policy Needs of Small Island Economies." Kingstown, Saint Vincent, and Grenadines (November).

54

Senegal

HONORE-GEORGES NDIAYE

INTRODUCTION

Senegal has 9.85 million inhabitants, 42 percent of whom live in urban areas. The official language, which is also the language of instruction, is French. The Senegalese educational system is composed of a primary school cycle (six years) and a secondary school cycle (seven years that include junior and senior high school), leading into either general or technical studies. The unemployment rate in 1997 reached 24 percent of the active population.

The universities of Cheikh Anta Diop in Dakar (Université Cheikh Anta Diop de Dakar, UCAD), Gaston Berger at Saint Louis (Université Gaston Berger, UGB), the Advanced National Professional Schools, and private institutes provide higher education in Senegal.

Higher education in Senegal is characterized by diversity in the type of institutions, their organization, and their admission requirements, which vary according to educational objectives. There are 1,293,402 students in Senegal, with 2.47 percent in higher education: 32,000 students distributed between UCAD (23,660), UGB (2,157), the Advanced National Professional Schools (1,000), and private higher education schools (4,500) (Ministère de l'Education Nationale 1998).

The future creation of regional university centers across the entire country is expected to meet the nation's needs in terms of integrating new educational technologies, providing more flexibility and efficiency in teaching and research opportunities, and diversifying and decentralizing study programs.

The 1993 reform of higher education in Senegal, which resulted from the National Consultation on Higher Education (Concertation Nationale sur l'Enseignement Supérieur), and which came as a continuation of the 1981 States General on Education, was implemented through two projects: The Project for the Improvement of Higher Education (Projet d'Amélioration de l'Enseignement Supérieur, PAES) and the Project for the Support of Reform at Cheikh Anta Diop University (PARU). Currently, these reform projects receive support from the World Bank and through the French Cooperation.

From 1993 to 2000, performance indicators registered significant progress as a consequence of educational reform, with a notable increase in success rates, diversification of majors, and a higher quality of scientific output, as confirmed by the rankings on the African and Malagasy Council for Higher Education (Conseil Africain et Malgache pour l'Enseignement Supérieur, CAMES) aptitude lists.

Senegal's universities have also been subjected to periods of interruption when unanswered social demands precipitated strikes led by student associations and unions (faculty, technical, and administrative personnel).

This chapter covers five areas: institutional capacity, higher education reforms, funding of higher education and reform support projects, university research, and university management.

INSTITUTIONAL CAPACITY

Since 1960, higher education policy has revolved around extending access, diversifying university majors, raising the qualifications for teaching and research personnel, increasing the number of personnel doing research, developing programs of research and development, and internationalization.

UNIVERSITIES AND REGIONAL UNIVERSITY CENTERS

Senegal has two public universities: UCAD and UGB. Students holding a *baccalauréat* (high school diploma) or equivalent enroll for short-study degrees (*baccalauréat* + 2 or 3) or long-study degrees (*baccalauréat* + 4). Access is granted according to the number of available seats and upon classification of candidates by ranks. The universities provide a wide range of training, including basic and professional education. Their potential for development is confirmed year after year by the increasingly professional majors offered in the various schools and through local research initiatives.

Cheikh Anta Diop University in Dakar (UCAD)

The Dakar University, created on February 24, 1957, started with several schools enrolling 575 students. In 1968, creation of the Polytechnic Institute (initially called ENSUT and then ESP) provided excellent conditions for student supervision, and the total number of students increased to 3,000. In 1981, the university reached the maximum capacity of 13,000 students, while the supervision ratio dropped to 3.2 percent (420 professors). In 1987, the Dakar University was renamed Cheikh Anta Diop. By 1994, the number of students had grown beyond the total capacity to more than 25,000 students, while the number of research professors had increased to 1,000. During the academic year 2000–2001, enrollment reached 23,198 students.

The disintegration of the inherited dual system allowed for the establishment within the university of nine new structures, composed of thirty-nine units that included five schools (humanities, technical sciences, economics/management, law/political science, and medicine/pharmacy/odontostomatology), one research institute (IFAN Cheikh Anta Diop), six National Advanced Professional Schools (ESP, CESTI, EBAD, INSEPS, ENS, ENSETP), and ten training/research institutes, among them an engineering institute (Institute for Earth Sciences) and an Institute for Environmental Sciences.

Since the initiation of reforms, the COUD (Centre des Œuvres Universitaires de Dakar) has benefited from an emergency plan which made possible the rehabilitation of campus dormitories and kitchens. This initiative, which lasted from 1992 to 1996, was carried out thanks to a World Bank subsidy. These reforms have been maintained through the Project for the Improvement of Higher Education (PAES) and the COUD de Demain, a major project currently exploring additional funding possibilities.

The social services rehabilitation program has been operating normally since the ratification of the April 1997 agreement between the government and the coordinating student association of Dakar.

The objectives of the COUD are to adapt study programs to students' needs and to provide and organize room, board, and student activities. In order to carry out its mission, the COUD has access to a number of departments, including food services, medical care, student activities, physical plant, an accounting office, a human resources department, and an auditing unit.

In 1999, the COUD had a capacity of 5,682 beds. Beneficiaries of social services were estimated at 16,603 in 1998. Each enrolled student has automatically been a beneficiary of social services since February 2001.

The University Gaston Berger de Saint-Louis (UGB)

After ten years of operation (1990–2000), UGB now has an enrollment of 2,300 students. UGB's role is to train graduates destined to integrate the country's various economic and social sectors. To this end, the university offers a number of new professional majors through its four Training and Research Units (Unités de Formation et de Recherche, UFR): applied mathematics and computer science, economics and management (management of agricultural companies and computerized management), law and political science (private law, public law, and political science), and humanities (English, French, geography, applied foreign languages, and sociology). UGB also has a library and a computing center.

The structuring of majors into cycles leading to degrees is meant to ease the integration of graduates into the job market and is designed to develop needed competencies. The applied foreign languages unit is a good example of the professionalism that has been achieved within the pedagogical project of UGB.

Education is provided through three cycles and is geared increasingly toward specialization, leading ultimately to professional careers at the doctoral level. The expansion of UGB and the management of the increasing numbers of *baccalauréat* holders is still a challenge for the university and the academic authorities.

The Regional Center for University Social Services at Saint-Louis (CROUS)

The CROUS has an enrollment of 2,191 students and has the advantage of having pedagogical and living quarters at the same location. Over the last four years, the university has witnessed acute budgetary and financial problems and has been struggling with the repercussions of those problems, including a decrease in enrollments.

According to the stipulations of the decree that governs its organization, the CROUS is responsible for improving the conditions of life and study of university students or those belonging to institutions attached to the university. The CROUS is in charge of gauging the needs of students, initiating services to respond to those needs, and ensuring the management of the various service units of the campus.

Among the services provided by the CROUS, accommodation capacity was the only aspect that registered a significant increase from the recent reforms, thanks to a state subsidy to build student villages. The state inaugurated a dormitory composed of 130 rooms in addition to the "G" village (built in 1998), which has a capacity of 244 beds. Accommodations for students during the academic year 1999–2000 did not constitute a major problem (MEN 1999a).

Regional University Centers (CUR)

The project for the creation of the regional university centers (Centres Universitaires Régionaux, CUR), which is currently in progress, is an essential component of the diversification policy and the decentralization of professional academic and technical majors across the country. These majors are based on regional economic potentials. The main mission of the regional university centers is the provision of training during the first cycle (either leading to professional qualification or not), preparation for professional training, provision of supervisory services to students, and, finally, promotion of economic development inside each academy through special programs.

The secondary mission of the centers consists of continuing education, student activities, and community services that have no direct relationship to academic or professional enhancement. This mission, which reflects a commitment to meet the various educational needs of the surrounding community, requires that the CUR maintain a certain flexibility and sufficient local authority.

As university centers, the CUR are generally considered to have a general educational mission (academic majors) and a professional education mission (professional majors), with a focus on the latter.

The first CUR, which is planned in Bambey, would host 200 freshmen students. Within the decentralization and majors diversification policy, this CUR will provide for the administrative regions of the Archadier north basin zone.

NATIONAL ADVANCED TRAINING SCHOOLS

The mission of the National Advanced Training Schools is to train midlevel officers and engineers to meet the needs of certain technical ministerial departments. Three of the fifteen National Advanced Training Schools operate under the responsibility of the Ministry of Higher Education. The National Advanced School for Rural Cadres of Bambey (Ecole Nationale des Cadres Ruraux, ENCR) provides training for applied engineers in the fields of agriculture, animal husbandry, forestry, and water resources. The ENCR, with a total student population of 158 in 1999, enrolls Senegalese students as well as students from twenty other countries. The National Advanced School of Agriculture (Ecole Nationale Supérieur d'Agriculture, ENSA) enrolled 115 engineering students during the academic year 1998–1999. In 2000–2001, the school enrolled 150 students from more than thirty countries of the subcontinent. Among the majors offered there are animal production, agricultural production, rural engineering, social and rural economy, and pedagogy. The Advanced School of Applied Economics (Ecole Nationale d'Economie Appliquée, ENEA) enrolled 272 students in 1999. The school offers majors in national and regional development, environment and urban management, education/student activities, economic planning and organization management, and statistics/demography.

Twelve institutions are under the responsibility of other ministries, ranging from arts and medicine to national security and military staff. These schools are responsible for the training of senior officers in domains such as penal administration, customs, fishery, cultural industries, tourism, and health.

PRIVATE HIGHER EDUCATION INSTITUTIONS (EPES)

Private higher education is an important component of the educational system. The February 16, 1991, law relates to the orientation of National Education and encourages individual or collective private initiatives (article 3). Private higher education is supported by another law dated December 23, 1994, which defines the status of private higher education institutions.

The National Consultation Forum on Higher Education highlighted the importance of private/public professional majors, which are based on programs called *competency programs*. The proceedings of the forum affirmed that "to this effect, private schools for higher education shall contribute to alleviate the burden of university institutions, as well as to [the diversification of] majors in terms of professional training" (Assane 1993, 25). The EPES, totaling forty-one institutions, three of which are universities, has an enrollment of 6,000 students.

These institutions respond to an increasing demand for professional and technical education. They offer twenty-five professional majors. Management, accounting, marketing, and technical majors are the most important; they constitute 90 percent of the total offered options.

Private Training

Cheikh Anta Diop in Dakar offers private continuing education options to employees and students alike. Over the last few years, the number of candidates in these programs has been increasing steadily in both regular and evening classes. The total number of students has reached 2,000.

Private schools offer a choice of professional majors to both students and employees. Main options include tertiary majors such as management, accounting, and marketing, as well as technical and technological majors such as civil engineering, mechanical engineering, electrical engineering, telecommunications, computer science, chemistry, and applied biology.

These majors lead to two types of degrees: an advanced school degree at institutions such as ESP and ISG, and university degrees at IFACE, which is one of the first structures for private training. The activities of IFACE are governed by ministerial decree.

Similarly, the University Gaston Berger of Saint-Louis offers private training options for high school graduates in majors such as network and computer science leading to a university degree (*Diplôme Universitaire en Réseau et Informatique de Gestion, DURIG*). Students admitted to this major are eligible to sit for the Vocational Training Certificate (*Brevet de Technicien Supérieur, BTS*) in computer science and management. During the 1999 academic year, UGB enrolled a second cohort of fifteen students in this major.

HIGHER EDUCATION POLICY

The 1981 and 1993 reforms resulted in a number of policy agendas for higher education.

The Policy Agenda of the Project for Improvement of Higher Education (PAES)

The agenda for higher education and research policy dates back to 1996 and is drawn from the basic document for the PAES. It is directed primarily toward the University Cheikh Anta Diop and to a lesser degree to the University Gaston Berger at Saint-Louis.

The restructuring measures of the subsector seek to improve the quality, the coherence, the efficiency, and the viability of the system and to improve the adaptation of training to social needs.

These measures are concerned essentially with the enhancement of academic and administrative autonomy in universities, the reorganization of academic and pedagogical structures, the reorganization of the administrative and financial management of universities for more efficiency, and the improvement of social services and scholarship management.

The Policy Agenda of the Decennial Program for Education and Training (PDEF)

The main strategic plans of the PDEF (Programme Décennal de l'Education et de la Formation) consist of the following:

- The mobilization of the higher education community around a philosophy of quality and improvement of access
- The development of research in advanced degree majors, the mobilization of the research community, and the practical application of research results
- The development of a new mode of management through the promotion of a consistent culture in terms of evaluation; partnerships with businesses, local governments, and universities; sustainability; library and documentation resources; and marketing
- The acquisition and use of new media technologies

PDEF intends to consolidate the achievements of the PAES and integrate the national advanced professional schools, private higher education, and research within universities and CUR.

Within the PAES framework, these reorganization measures contributed to the improvement of teaching and research, the design of high-quality general and technical education, the development of research, the promotion and development of a high-caliber private education sector, development of the various social and economic sectors in the context of national and regional development plans, implementation of an employment policy that takes into consideration and anticipates job market needs, and bridging of the gap between different social and cultural levels by admitting all men and women who have the capacity and the will to participate in the highest forms of culture and research.

The long-term objective is to establish an efficient university system with a higher output that is more pertinent to the economic development of Senegal. To this end, the activities of UCAD and UGB have been focused on their pedagogical missions and reinforcement of their capabilities to ensure quality in terms of management and control. Private higher education is also geared toward these objectives.

The development of this policy was achieved through an action plan. Funding has been allocated from the higher education budget. Moreover, resources collected from the adjustment of social services and scholarship funds, as well as funding from development partners, are to be invested in the program in order to meet operational costs.

MAJOR REFORMS IN HIGHER EDUCATION

The year 2000 marks the completion and begins the evaluation of the first phase of the PAES, including all reforms of higher education conceived and implemented since 1981. What follows is a summary of the various reform plans and their execution.

The 1981 Reforms

The States General on Education, which was organized in January 1981, constituted a major event in the history of the Senegalese educational system. For the first time, men and women of different backgrounds and profiles met to reflect on the future of "schooling." Comprehensive, open, and democratic debate took place at these meetings. The National Commission for the Reform of Education and Training (Commission Nationale de la Réforme de l'Education, CNREF), which resulted from these proceedings, contributed to the implementation of the proceedings' conclusions. The higher education chapter of the 1981 reform has not been implemented, however, due to an uninformed political choice and lack of necessary means.

The 1993 Reforms

Due to the enduring university crisis of the 1980s, and in view of the design of new stable and clear university conditions, the government organized the National Consultation Forum for Higher Education (Concertation Nationale sur l'Enseignement Supérieur, CNES) in 1992. One year later, after large plenary debates, the commission submitted its final report. The consultation process involved faculty, students, union representatives and representatives of the National Assembly and the Economic and Social Council, the political parties, society, and all concerned ministries.

Twenty-three recommendations of the CNES were submitted on December 9, 1993 to an interministerial council chaired by the prime minister.

The twenty-one adopted measures that have been realized since the beginning of the academic year 1994–1995 were concerned with the enhancement of the university's academic and administrative autonomy, academic and pedagogical organization, financial management, and the rehabilitation of social services.

All recommendations made by the CNES and submitted to the government have been entirely adopted except for two, one concerning the nomination of the university president and the other the creation of a chancellery. The university president is not elected by the General Assembly of the University; he is nominated directly by the president of the republic. The department of higher education (Département de l'Enseignement Supérieur, DES) was restructured to assume the role of the chancellery until the Ministry of Higher Education and Scientific Research was created in March 2001.

Implementation: Objectives of the 1993 Reform

The long-term objectives of the 1993 higher education reform consisted of raising higher education enrollment rates, improving equity between the sexes, ensuring a better cost/efficiency ratio, and making a better contribution to economic development. If these changes were to take place, the higher education system would be able to focus the activities of its two universities on these pedagogical missions while reinforcing the institutions' capacity for management and control.

To this end, specific objectives have been underscored; namely, reinforcing library services, improving teaching and research, developing a maintenance system, supporting the management and funding of higher education, and reorganizing student services. The reform is meant to lead to comprehensive oversight of student enrollments and graduation and to create new majors, develop new training and research programs, and set up a commission to follow up on reforms, provide consultation, and modernize financial and administrative management structures.

Evaluation of the 1993 Reform

Phase I of the UCAD reform included a number of fundamental measures, such as the creation of a new basic infrastructure for the revitalization of universities and their pedagogical and administrative structures and central and regional research structures. These measures also included establishing admission committees that would respect the university's enrollment capacity by designing a strategy to control enrollments. The goal was to reduce the student population from 24,000 to 17,500 over a period of six years according to a plan designed specifically for universities. Advanced schools were to be allowed to use their maximum capacity. In fact, the rigorous control of enrollments was discontinued in 1997–1998 and the number of students did not decrease according to earlier predictions as a result of the 1997 agreements between the government and the Association for Student Coordination of Dakar (Coordination des Etudiants de Dakar, CED).

Other measures of the 1993–2000 reform included limiting the number of study periods to a maximum of four without any possibility of repeating any of the first two years more than twice. (This measure finally put an end to the problem of overcrowding in the first cycle.) Finally, the reform led to the creation of a center for computerized management at UCAD and the internationalization of institutions of higher education.

The end of the first phase of the PAES project was also marked by the decision of the Senegalese government, in accordance with its partners for educational development, to move from a project-oriented approach to a program-oriented approach; that is, to allow the Senegalese government to assume total responsibility for the educational system. In accordance with this decision, the Decennial Program for Education and Training (PDEF) will focus on problems related to access, quality, and management and will consolidate the achievements of the higher education subsector under Phase II of PAES (2003–2010).

HIGHER EDUCATION FUNDING

Public higher education in Senegal benefits from a subsidy system, which until recently provided for 96 percent of the institutions' budgets. The high cost of a degree and the low financial contribution from students do not allow for an efficient recovery of expenses.

Projects for the support of reform provide governmental impetus to carry out educational and training policy. In 1997, the budget allocated to education and training was estimated at more than 93.3 billion francs, or 33 percent of the government's budget, with 24.7 percent allocated to higher education (7 percent of the government budget).

Major funding contributors include France, Canada, Belgium, Switzerland, Italy, the USAID, the European Union, and the World Bank. Other partners contribute to targeted research programs. The implementation of this reform is currently supported by multilateral and bilateral cooperation agreements.

Parental contributions to the financing of higher education are important. Schooling expenses and various support expenses (books and other needs) are estimated at 3 billion francs CFA (about US$464 million).

World Bank

PAES is funded by the World Bank through a US$26.5 million subsidy (the total cost includes unexpected taxes amounting to $30.9 million).

The loan made possible the realization of many projects with regard to access to scientific and pedagogical documentation as well as the modernization of educational structures such as administrative and financial management. The loan components are provided in Table 54.1.

The components of the PAES have witnessed a satisfactory level of implementation: in civil engineering, a new library has been established at UCAD, while the school's other libraries have been rehabilitated and extended. Pedagogical services have been revamped, and research and teaching have been improved through the provision of new equipment such as laboratories and the acquisition of references and periodicals. Within the COUD, campus dormitories have been rehabilitated, restaurant and catering facilities have been privatized, and new eligibility criteria have been set up for the benefit of social services, scholarship offices, and the department of higher education (computerization of services and training of personnel to use new technologies).

With regard to the pedagogical aspect of the UCAD Project, the 1997 university crisis has slowed the reform process. In 1997, and in contrast to 1996, when the situation was better in terms of attained financial objectives, the recurrent charges were not paid. They were meant to be covered by profits realized from the productivity of the social sector.

Due to the rapid increase in the number of students, the universities are faced with two problems; on the one hand, granting access to the most meritorious students, and on the other, maintaining or improving the level of products or services provided. Both problems are closely linked to the availability of information and communication tools.

In sub-Saharan regions, remote or "virtual" education is one of the alternatives considered in the face of the increasing number of students. The African Virtual University (AVU) is a case in point. The UVA (Université Virtuelle Africaine) has two sites at both UCAD and UGB. Complementarity and synergistic programs should be created between the AVU projects, the Association of Partly or Entirely French-Speaking Universities

Table 54.1. Allocation of World Bank Loan to the Project for the Improvement of Higher Education (PAES)

I. Strengthening Library Services (US$15.6 million)	
Rehabilitation and extension of the central library at Université Cheikh Anta Diop de Dakar	US$11.2 million
Library management	US$4.4 million
II. Improvement of Teaching and Research (US$9.4 million)	
Strengthening teaching of applied sciences	US$4.0 million
Development of an accreditation system	US$0.3million
University research fund	US$2.9 million
Study of alternative models for teaching and funding	US$0.3 million
Installation of a computerized system	US$1.8 million
III. Strengthening Management Capacities (US$4.1 million)	
Reorganization of student services	US$2.2 million
Development of a maintenance system	US$1.3 million

(Association des Universités Partiellement ou Entièrement de Langue Française, AUPELF/UREF), and the Internet site of the Centre de Calcul (Computing Center). The same is true for the distance education site of the National Advanced School of Administration and Magistracy (Ecole Nationale d'Administration et de Magistrature, ENAM).

French Cooperation

The Support for the University Project (PARU) was initiated in a spirit of partnership with the French Cooperation. Its objective is to support the modernization efforts undertaken by the Senegalese authorities initiated by the National Consultation Forum on Higher Education.

This project seeks to redefine the regulations for management and for the computerization of management. It concerns student services, human resources, and the financial management of entire units of the university.

The French Mission for Cooperation and Cultural Action (Mission Française de Cooperation et d'Action Culturelle) actively supports the reform of administrative, financial, and pedagogical management undertaken at UCAD. Expected results are the standardization of management systems and personnel qualification. The cost of financing reached US$165,000 (1.2 million French francs) over a period of 36 months. In 1997–1998, the project initiated the second phase of personnel qualification; analyzed the financial, pedagogical, and administrative procedures in order to develop terms of reference for future management software applications; and carried out necessary studies for the establishment of the computer unit at UCAD.

Canadian Cooperation (ACDI)

Formerly the Polytechnic School of Thiès, the Advanced Polytechnic School was funded by ACDI. The objectives of the school included training *Ingénieurs de conception* (conception engineers; those who design projects) on the North American

model of the Montreal Polytechnic School, training instructors (trainers), decentralizing the training activity from Dakar to Thiès, equipping the Polytechnic of Thiès, and setting up an infrastructure for and initiating industrial research.

Thus, 800 engineers graduated from this school in civil engineering, mechanical engineering, electromechanical engineering, and electrical engineering and have spread all over French-speaking Western Africa.

The objectives of the program are to reinforce institutional capacity through the training of instructors by offering the Ph.D. and M.A. degrees, to exchange professors and students with the University of Laval, to set up computer equipment in order to create a computing center within the institution, and to establish didactic tools (documents) and equipment.

Italian Cooperation (Commodity Aid)

Commodity Aid is an Italian intervention aimed at improving the conditions of teaching and research through the provision of scientific equipment and the training of researchers. This program has made equipment available for laboratories in the schools of science, technology, and medicine and has provided for the training of fifteen senior researchers in the school of science and technology and ten researchers in the departments of medicine, pharmacy, and odontostomatology.

Since its inception, UGB has benefited from Commodity Aid; the organization has supplied pedagogical, scientific, and technical equipment. French Cooperation has also provided support in the area of documentation.

The Bilateral Programs for the Institutional and Pedagogical Support of ENEA

The project for the support of the ENEA is made possible thanks to funding from USAID in Washington, which allowed the University of Connecticut to initiate a program for the training of instructors (both long-term and permanent training), the exchange of faculty, logistical support (pedagogical equipment and computers), and research. The funding for this project, which extended over four years (1994–1998), was estimated at US$400,000.

The European Union Cooperation

The European Union's support project for the ENEA has been based at the department of statistics and demography since 1994. The project is responsible for the training of applied statistical engineers for the French-speaking countries in Africa, the Comoro Islands, and Madagascar.

Swiss Cooperation

The Swiss program for the support of the ENCR has been operating since 1981. It trains engineers in water resource development and experts in forest preservation. The objective was to create a major facility within a forest, which was localized at Ziguinchor. In 1982, Switzerland agreed to assume the restructuring of the ENCR through the reform of curricula, the training of faculty (with an initial program of training in Dijon), and the provision of construction equipment. It allowed the ENCR to focus on the teaching of practical aspects by setting up small projects and supervising the students and professors. Parallel to this, a center was created in Saint-Louis centered around the dam there in recognition of the need for engineers to be knowledgeable about issues related to irrigation and water resources.

Over a period of ten years, the project brought in more than 6 billion francs CFA (US$927,589,215) and allowed for the establishment of a modular curriculum. However, in 1997, it became a support program linked to the establishment of the ENCR. Indeed, the Swiss partners identify the activities to be executed through a global program for agricultural development. This support program consists of training farmers, educating technicians, training engineers, and training instructors on an ongoing basis. The cost of this program reached 800 billion francs CFA (US$123,685,933,148) when it was completed in 1999.

Subregional Cooperation

Currently, cooperation is being developed at the subregional level through an agreement protocol with the African Institute for Re-adaptation. The goal is to train senior officers in technology and research (250 million francs CFA will be allocated over a period of three years).

RESEARCH ACTIVITY

More than 90 percent of researchers nationwide are involved in developing research competencies. Research covers every domain of investigation (natural resources and environment, development research, materials, chemistry, nutrition, biotechnology, technology and energy production, information and communication networks, medical and pharmaceutical re-

search, humanities and social sciences). These domains in turn cover more than fifty doctoral majors, thirty-five professional specializations, and a group of more than 2,500 students (about 10 percent of the total university student body).

There is no doubt that changes called for by the 1993 reform will persist beyond 2000. In 2010, the nature of university research and its relation to Senegalese society will certainly be very different from today. Moreover, with the advent of the PDEF, higher education will have to prove its relevance to the economy in terms of reinforcing national competencies with regard to research and development, contributing significantly to the development of the country, and improving the quality of life for the people (Oussaynou 1999a, 1999b, 2000).

University research today is confronted by a number of challenges. Training and research need to be adapted to offer a wide range of possible careers to graduates. On another level, efficient use of both time and resources is crucial at a moment when the number of students is rising continually. Traditionally, an emphasis was placed on the senior year, with a particular focus on the originality and importance of thesis topics. Today, however, the priority is on the initial education, with a focus on the methodology and content of the first years of basic university education. The UNESCO chairs at the teachers' school and the geography department of UCAD are making innovative efforts in this respect.

Another problem concerns the increasing specialization of degrees and its impact on student mobility, degree standardization, and research qualifications. Universities are considering the suppression of "short-term" and "long-term" theses in favor of a single Ph.D. dissertation for all doctoral students, including CAMES university members.

Universities are adapting to the creation of a new decentralized institutional configuration—namely the private Regional University Centers (CUR)—in a positive way. Governmental subsidies allocated for university research will be increasingly contractual and will have precisely defined missions, performance criteria, and clear objectives. Universities will also be encouraged to engage in partnerships with other research institutions, industries, and public laboratories. The purpose of these partnerships is to develop research networks and encourage interaction within a national system of innovation and regional integration. In this respect, the globalization engendered by communication and information network systems is significantly affecting the way research is conducted.

The aging teaching/research body and a lack of interest in the sciences on the part of young candidates present serious problems at a time when the nature and modalities of research training are changing (MEN 1999d).

In consideration of their strategic position in gauging and evaluating the problems of the population, industries, and the commercial sector, universities and schools have made research one of their principal development strategies. The research topics taken on by students during their junior and senior years at university correspond to the needs of industrial and economic-commercial partners. These research topics lead to long-term projects—dissertations whose findings can be consulted and used directly by university partners.

University research benefits from the University Research Funds (Fonds de Recherche Universitaires, FRU) which, according to the PAES, contributes up to 50 percent of the financing of research and development activities. The research programs of the EPES are also eligible for FRU funds.

HIGHER EDUCATION MANAGEMENT

As previously noted, the higher education reforms announced during the interministerial council of December 9, 1993, were designed to result in a number of outcomes; namely, comprehensive oversight of student enrollment, a complete reorganization of the strategies for research and development, the modernization of administrative and financial management, and the creation of a positive environment where academic freedom and other liberties are respected.

The university should be able to instill democratization into the educational process through rigorous methods of management and governance. The promotion of efficiency through the improvement of management at all levels is a priority.

University governance tends to improve the mechanisms of participation and a joint sense of responsibility by allowing all interest groups to participate in defining working conditions, carrying out university missions, and using available resources.

The 1981 reforms lacked the political will and means to achieve such progress, while the 1993 reform had both but lacked the commitment of university management. The 1993 reform was not clearly manifested on the campuses of UCAD and UGB. Concerns revolve around reinforcing the governance system to account for the needs of all concerned parties, stimulating both formal and informal dialogues between the various constituents of the university, and ensuring better communication between the administration, the faculty, personnel, and students.

The recommendations and the conclusions reached during the pedagogical development days held at UCAD December 3–4, 1999, and at the university management workshop organized jointly by UCAD and UGB in January 2000 all confirm that no leadership was initiated to implement earlier reform plans. The recommendations in question, though thought to be salutary for the university, were only reluctantly implemented by the academic authorities. These recommendations related to pedagogical management (student admissions, access to information technology and communication, elimination of overtime, increase of teaching workload, obtaining accreditation, majors diversification, providing continuing education, initiating exchanges between private and public universities), administrative and financial management, and social services management (giving student access to certain jobs on campus and around-the-clock operation of the campus).

Quoting the moderator of the CNES,

Higher education is a key sector whose performance leads and informs the competition of the economy on the long term and its capacity for adaptation. Also because the system is victim to periodic crises which have profound repercussions not only on the entire educational system but on both society and the economy as well. The logic of confrontation and power balance has been imposed as a mode of dealing between the various partners of the system who are behaving as protagonists (administration, student organizations, faculty unions), while, in fact, they are seeking the same objectives. The civil society (student parents, private sector, contributors, various associations), powerless and anxious, is simply witnessing the continuous deterioration of the educational system; a situation due to a negotiation logic conditioned by the nature of relationships between partners of the systems. (Assane 1993, 25)

Changes in the Baccalauréat Exam

As a part of the higher education reform in Senegal, the National Consultation Forum on Higher Education proposed amendments to the baccalauréat exam. The commission in charge of this proposition accepted the organization of the baccalauréat exam into three main categories: languages and social sciences (L1, L2), sciences and technology (S1, S2, S3, T1, T2), and management and economics (G). Secondary school programs were reorganized accordingly. The programs were implemented in 1995–1996 and the students of the newly designed baccalauréat graduated in July 1998.

Admission of High School Graduates

Applicants are admitted to the university according to specified criteria and with regard to available seats. Students may spend a maximum of four years completing the first cycle, allowing for one repetition of each level of the first two years.

The decrease in the number of high school graduates during the 1997–1998 academic year raises a number of questions about student persistence between the eleventh and twelfth grades; the testing system; the low success rate in the baccalauréat despite the abandonment of the two-tier exam, which was considered too selective; and finally, the question of the efficiency of training, namely, adaptation to the needs of the job market. During the year 2000, student numbers were stabilized at around 10,800.

Applications to UCAD represent 75.2 percent of high school graduates, while applications to UGB account for 13.99 percent. Most applications come from public institutions and selected high schools from Dakar and the regions of Thiès, Kaolack, Saint-Louis, and Ziguinchor.

Statistics

The student population in Senegal increased from 15,759 in 1988 to 21,747 in 1992, and then to 23,198 in 1999 (an expansion of 47.2 percent in comparison to 1988). This represents a rate of 252 students for every 100,000 inhabitants. Though these figures are improving, they remain below the worldwide rates.

As shown in Table 54.2, the number of enrolled students decreased by 1.95 percent, from 23,660 to 23,198, from 1998 to 1999. In 2000, a small increase of 189 students was noted.

Table 54.2. Increase in Student Enrollments at Université Cheikh Anta Diop de Dakar, 1988–2000.

Year	Number of Students
1988	15,759
1989	14,950
1990	16,582
1991	17,810
1992	21,747
1993	21,939
1994	23,938
1995	22,948
1996	21,410
1997	21,243
1998	23,660
1999	23,198
2000	23,387

The overcrowding of the first cycle is caused by the conditions of admission, the lack of diversified majors, and the student failure rate. The number of students poses problems in terms of the organization of laboratory activities, evaluation, accommodations, and pedagogical supervision.

The high school graduates admitted at UCAD represent 62.55 percent of the total number of students enrolled in the first year.

Students tend to prolong their university studies, especially in the scientific and technical majors. Indeed, graduates of the second cycle—that is, B.A. holders—prefer to enroll in graduate studies in the expectation that they will find a job and contribute to the development of research programs.

WOMEN'S ENROLLMENT

The degree of participation of female students in higher education is a perplexing problem. The First International Conference on Higher Education raised the question of equal participation of the sexes in higher education and recommended a change of attitudes that could only come from mutual understanding. The number of female students increased from 44 percent in 1980 to 47 percent in 1995. By the end of 1995, the balance between numbers of males and females was reached in North America and Europe, while male students outnumbered female students in higher education in sub-Saharan Africa, South Asia, and generally in all underdeveloped countries. The percentages for these areas were 35 percent, 34 percent, and 27 percent, respectively. Nevertheless, significant efforts toward increased female participation in university schooling have been made in each of these regions since 1980.

In Senegal, the 1998 statistics reveal that females represent only 26 percent of the total number of students at UCAD. The only schools where the number of female students is above average at UCAD are medicine (36 percent), law and political

sciences (31 percent), and the EBAD (30 percent). These percentages are close to the African average, which is 35 percent. The percentage is lower at the School of Sciences and Technology (Faculté des Sciences et Techniques, FST) (13 percent), the Advanced National Institute for Physical Education (Institut National Supérieur d'Education Physique et Sportive, INSEPS) (12 percent), and teachers' school (18 percent) (MEN 1999b).

In schools training teachers, the proportion of female students from Senegal is low compared to the proportion of women students in institutions training teachers in developed countries, where women constitute two-thirds of the teaching community.

This low female representation in higher education is linked to the schooling rate of females in general and to the degree of access to higher education in Senegal.

Success Rate (Academic Year 1997–1998)

In 1998, UCAD admitted 23,660 students, of whom 21,959 enrolled in its five schools. By the end of the year, 18,933 candidates sat for both sessions of the exam, around 80 percent of the registered students. It seems, then, that the drop-out rate is significant at approximately 20 percent.

The success rate for all of UCAD was estimated at 43 percent in 1998, as compared to 37.9 percent in 1997. The university schools register an average rate of 40 percent, while the advanced schools and the institutes have a rate of 84 percent. The School of Medicine, Pharmacy, and Odontostomatology shows a success rate of 61 percent, while the School of Sciences and Technology comes second with 43 percent. In contrast, the School of Law and Political Science registers a rate lower than 30 percent.

Despite a marked progression in the success rate between 1997 and 1998 (from 38 percent to 43 percent), the rate is still lower than predicted (59 percent). However, after the first year, the success rate is higher than 60 percent in the different schools. The four-year period allowed for freshmen students to get a B.A. barely allows UCAD to reach the desired success rate of 30 to 40 percent in the second university year.

There are also a number of problems in terms of selection and admissions criteria, academic supervision, teaching methods and testing, and the creation of a learning-conducive environment. The imbalance in student numbers between the various institutions speaks of a need for a more efficient orientation structure to help students make the right choices (see Table 54.3).

ASSOCIATIONS AND UNIONS

Student Associations

Students are organized within two associations: the Student Union of Dakar and the Student Union of Saint-Louis. These two associations are established at UCAD and UGB but have no representation at the Advanced National Profession Schools or private higher education. Student strikes organized by these associations disturb the normal course of study and compromise the validity of degrees delivered in their respective universities.

Table 54.3. Student Enrollment in Senegalese Institutions of Higher Education by Institution in 1997 and 1998

Institution	1997	1998
Letters and Human Sciences	1,984	2,181
Sciences and Technology	1,424	995
Medicine and Pharmacy	506	500
Law and Political Science	1,643	1,579
Economics and Management	1,055	987
CESTI	25	21
ENS	7	13
ESP	328	236
INSEPS	44	44
EBAD	86	94
Subtotal	7,102	6,650
Gaston Berger Saint-Louis	450	450
Total	7,552	7,100

The demands of the last strike, which took place during the academic year 2000–2001, stressed the need to reorient students who fail the first cycle (and who exhaust the number of years allowed for the first cycle), facilitate access to the third cycle in all schools, open the university and school library facilities on a permanent basis, acquire updated library resources, improve the ratio of personnel to students, grant university degrees and evaluate faculty members, provide grants to freshmen before the end of December of each year, improve criteria for grant eligibility and transparency in their allocation, generalize grants in the third cycle (estimated at 60,000 francs CFA), suppress the half-grant in the second cycle, improve food quality, reinstall a restaurant inspection unit, revise restaurant-ticket sale methods, provide room service every fortnight, provide a healthy environment, relocate the bars situated in front of the student residential area, provide security, and provide medical services all year long.

Despite the implementation of the 1993 social services reform and the results obtained in social services in Dakar and Saint-Louis, certain demands have not yet been met. However, recent demands are of a more positive nature and are adopting an increasingly academic character.

The Student Union of Dakar (UED) is torn by a number of political currents related to Senegalese politics more generally. Pluralism has made its way into this union, and the competition between political parties is strong because students represent a significant voting bloc. Students have contributed to political change in Senegal and are increasingly framing university problems as electoral promises and demanding their immediate resolution.

Unions for Research Professors

The teaching faculty of around 1,000 professors and researchers are affiliated with the Federation of Faculty Unions (Fédération des Syndicats d'Enseignants, FEDER), the Unique and Democratic Union of Senegalese Professors (Syndicat Unique de l'Enseignement Supérieur, SUDES), and the Higher Education Faculty Union (Syndicat des Professeurs de l'Enseignement Supérieur, SYPROS). Their demands revolve around better working conditions, salaries, and housing facilities.

Administrative and Technical Personnel (PATS)

There are 1,200 administrative and technical personnel affiliated with the Schools and Universities Unions (Syndicat des Travailleurs des Etablissements Scolaires et Universitaires, STESU). Their claims center on the status of the nonteaching personnel, the consideration of social welfare contributions not provided by the institution, and promotion.

CONCLUSION

The International Conference on Higher Education has been a powerful opportunity for all participating countries to demonstrate how important higher education is and to declare their commitment to develop and deeply change the higher education sector.

This change is to be guided by a perspective geared toward the society of the future. This vision stresses the need to extend access to higher education to all on an equal basis and according to merit, with a special focus on women and minorities. Higher education must adapt to social realities while carrying out its mission of providing intellectual and moral education; continuing and lifelong education; the dissemination of economic, scientific, and technical research output; and the dissemination of scientific and technical information through international cooperation.

Such adaptation necessitates a permanent innovation of pedagogy and the reinforcement of links between higher education, research, and the job market.

In Senegal, the general objectives of higher education stem from the strategic plans to develop high-quality education, which is the main objective of the department in charge of National Education. This program focuses on improving access to high-quality higher education, developing research agendas, improving the university financing system, and improving the management of higher education.

The Decennial Program for Education and Training (PDEF) focuses on regulations that concern financial management and the consolidation of what has been achieved under the PAES.

The general progress of the higher education subsector is promising, despite crises caused by increases in student enrollment and difficulties related to the economic situation. Significant progress has been achieved in terms of the basic elements of the higher education policy—namely, access, diversification of majors, professionalization of majors, qualification of teaching and research personnel, research and development, and internationalization.

PDEF development perspectives will allow higher education to improve the relevance, quality, management, and financing of higher education; replicate the achievements of the reform; and, more important, find a definitive solution to the crisis of the growth of the Senegalese higher education system.

REFERENCES

Assane, S., ed. 1993. *Rapport de la Concertation nationale sur l'Enseignement supérieur.* Dakar: Ministère de l'Education Nationale.

Banque Mondiale. 1995. *L'Enseignement Supérieur: les leçons de l'expérience.* Washington, D.C.: World Bank.

Diallo, M. 1999. "La formation à distance Enjeux et Perspectives." *EchoSup: Bulletin d'information de la Direction de l'Enseignement Supérieur—Ministère de l'Enseignement Supérieur et de la Recherche Scientifique* 2 (August): 9.

Ministère de l'Education Nationale. 1998. "Document de politique sectorielle de l'enseignement supérieur." Available at the Direction de l'Enseignement Supérieur of the Ministère de l'Education Nationale.

————. 1999a. "Conseil interministériel sur l'Enseignement Supérieur: rentrée universitaire 1999/2000." October. Available at Direction de l'Enseignement Supérieur.

————. 1999b. "Les statistiques de l'UCAD : année universitaire 1998/1999."

————. 1999c. "Rapport de la revue à mi-parcours du PAES."

————. 1999d. *Rapport général des Journées Pédagogiques de l'UCAD.* Dakar: Rectorat UCAD.

Oussaynou, D. 1999a. "Réforme de l'enseignement supérieur: Les projets d'appui: P.A.E.S., P.D.E.F." *EchoSup: Bulletin d'information de la Direction de l'Enseignement Supérieur—Ministère de l'Enseignement Supérieur et de la Recherche Scientifique* 1 (April): 5–11.

————. 1999b. "Du Management des Universités." *EchoSup: Bulletin d'information de la Direction de l'Enseignement Supérieur—Ministère de l'Enseignement Supérieur et de la Recherche Scientifique* 2 (August): 2–3.

————. 2000. "Perspectives de la recherche universitaire au XXIème Siècle." *EchoSup: spécial sur La Recherche scientifique et Technique au Sénégal, Bulletin d'information de la Direction de l'Enseignement Supérieur—Ministère de l'Enseignement Supérieur et de la Recherche Scientifique* 3 (July): 3–5.

55

Sierra Leone

Joseph B. A. Kandeh, Thomas M. Dugba, and Joseph L. Pessima

INTRODUCTION

Sierra Leone is a small country in West Africa with an area of approximately 72,000 square kilometers (27,799 square miles) and a population of 5.4 million, growing at an annual rate of 2.67 percent (2000 projections). The country's economic exports include diamonds, gold, bauxite, rutile, coffee, palm kanel, piassava, ginger, and marine resources. Sierra Leone's gross domestic product (GDP) per capita was $121 in 2000, while income per capita was $106, down from $383 in 1983–1984. This decline is due to deteriorating economic performance, a relatively high population growth rate of 2.67 percent, and the civil war. The national illiteracy rate is 70 percent, with female illiteracy at 80 percent and male illiteracy at 60 percent. Projected primary school enrollment for 2000–2001 was 729,640: 58.7 percent male and 41.3 percent female students. Secondary school enrollment was projected at 695,058: 62.5 percent male and 37.5 percent female students (Central Statistics Office 2000).

BRIEF HISTORICAL BACKGROUND OF TERTIARY EDUCATION

University education in Sierra Leone had its earliest origin as the Christian Institute in the mountain village of Leicester in 1814. It later became a teachers' college—Fourah Bay College (FBC)—when it moved to the east end of Freetown in 1827. Founded by the Church Missionary Society of Britain, the college became affiliated with Durham University in England in 1876 and started preparing students for degrees. The first degrees were awarded in 1879.

The origin of Njala University College (NUC) can be traced back to 1912, when the government set up an agricultural department plantation at Njala, initially for extension work and

later for full-time agricultural students on government scholarship. Primary teacher education was later added to the curriculum. With substantial academic and financial assistance from the University of Illinois in the United States, the college was upgraded to a university college in 1964, and in 1967 it joined Fourah Bay College to constitute the University of Sierra Leone. The present university, with a full-time vice-chancellor, was created by the University of Sierra Leone (USL) Act 1972. In 1988–1989, the College of Medicine and Allied Health Sciences (COMAHS) was added as a third college. The teacher training department of FBC was transferred to Tower Hill in Freetown in 1960 and was later renamed Milton Margai Teachers College (MMTC). In 1996, MMTC became an affiliate of the university and was renamed the Milton Margai College of Education (MOE 1996, 227).

The missionaries and the government of Sierra Leone established various teachers' colleges below the tertiary educational level. They included Bunumbu (1931), Njala Training College (1936), Catholic Training College at Bo (1942), Magburaka Government Training, or College Magburaka (1951), Catholic Girls Training College at Kenema (1955), St. Augustine Teachers College at Makeni (1963), Bo Teacher Training College at Bo (1963), Port Loko Women Teachers College at Port Loko (1965), and Freetown Teachers College at Freetown (1965). These nine small primary teachers' training colleges were consolidated into five teachers' colleges in 1970—Bo Teachers College, Bunumbu Teachers College, Freetown Teachers College, Makeni Teachers College, and Port Loko Teachers College.

In effect, the Catholic Girls Training College at Kenema was closed down, while the former Bo Teacher Training College and Catholic Training College merged to form the Bo Teachers College. The Magburaka Government Training College and St. Augustine Teachers College were also amalgamated to form Makeni Teachers College. In 1982, the government's rationali-

Table 55.1. Student Enrollment at the University of Sierra Leone by Institution and Gender, 1999–2000

Institution	Female	Total
Fourah Bay College	299	1,568
Njala University College	98	820
College of Medicine and Allied Sciences	42	169
Institute of Public Administration and Management	124	446
Total	563	3,003

Source: Ministry of Education, Government of Sierra Leone, June 2000.

Table 55.2. Staff Members at the University of Sierra Leone by Institution and Gender, 1999–2000

Institutes/Colleges	Female	Total
Fourah Bay College	135	713
Njala University College	96	532
College of Medicine and Allied Health Services	40	161
Institute of Public Administration	NA	80
Institute of Education	8	38
Secretariat	NA	60
Total	279	1,584

NA: Not available.
Source: Planning Office, University of Sierra Leone, July 2000.

zation policy, the Teachers' Colleges Act, made the five primary teachers' colleges into tertiary institutions that included Milton Margai Teachers College (MOE 1982).

Technical and vocational education has long been offered by some teacher training colleges, technical institutions, specialist secondary schools, and nongovernmental institutions. This form of education was not given the priority it deserved, as it was perceived to be the exclusive domain of academically weak pupils. Today, however, the programs also cater to academically capable students.

Technical and vocational education in Sierra Leone was first given formal support in the 1970 White Paper on Educational Policy, which defined technical, vocational, agricultural, and commercial education as very important for Sierra Leone's national development. The introduction of a new educational system, the 6-3-3-4 educational system, in 1993, brought into very sharp focus the need to strengthen the technical and vocational institutions. According to the National Education Master Plan, 1996 to 2005, "It was suggested that 55 percent of graduates from junior secondary schools enter some technical institutions at lower levels, and some graduates from senior secondary schools would enter either polytechnics or technical vocational institutes at a higher level. At present there are not enough insti-

tutions, teachers, equipment [or] materials to accommodate all the graduates from both the junior and senior secondary schools" (MOE 1996, 84).

Professional schools, such as the School of Nursing; the Hotel and Tourism Training Center; the Institute of Library, Archive, and Information Science; the Institute of Public Administration and Management (IPAM); and the law school were established in the 1980s as tertiary institutions.

SIZE, SCOPE, AND NATURE OF TERTIARY EDUCATION

Tertiary education in Sierra Leone consists of all forms of education that can be acquired at the end of senior secondary education from the University of Sierra Leone (USL), with its constituent colleges and institutes, teachers' colleges, technical and vocational institutes, and professional schools.

USL has 3,003 students and a staff of 1,584 (287 academic and 1,287 administrative and support staff) (Tables 55.1 and 55.2). This situation is indicative of the very high unit cost of academic output. USL is generally perceived to be graduating too few students in applied and basic sciences, where the nation's needs are greatest.

Pre-service teacher education is provided by five primary teachers' colleges: Bo, Bunumbu, Makeni, Port Loko, and Freetown. Each had an average of 500 students and about 50 teachers in 1996 (MOE 1996, 366), which also indicates a high cost to produce one graduate, although these numbers may have changed during the last few years.

Fifteen technical and vocational institutes, with an estimated enrollment of 10,000 students, have been upgraded to tertiary institutions by the Ministry of Education. The capacity for enrolling students in the professional schools, especially the health-related schools, is limited. Many factors are responsible for the low intake of students in these schools. For example, students may not academically qualify and, if they do, may not have the necessary financial support. The entire enrollment in the professional school is estimated at 500.

The scope of tertiary education is teaching, research, and community service. The scope is determined by the policy objectives of tertiary education as stipulated in the National Education Master Plan 1996–2005 (MOE 1996). These objectives include widening and continuing the education acquired; providing specialization in one or more disciplines of knowledge and skills; continuing development of the student in all facets of knowledge (affective, cognitive, and psychomotor); providing academic staff opportunities to carry out research, especially in areas relevant to the socioeconomic and other needs of the country and relevant to problems specific to Sierra Leone; and disseminating knowledge. The academic programs of all tertiary institutions are within the range of these objectives.

The nature of tertiary education in Sierra Leone is characterized by specialized human resource development programs in each institution in the tertiary system. In the USL, Fourah Bay College (FBC) concentrates on arts, social and economics studies, engineering, and pure and applied sciences; Njala University College (NUC) concentrates on agriculture, education, and environmental sciences; the College of Medicine and Al-

Table 55.3. Enrollment at Technical and Vocational Institutions, 1997–2000

Institution	1997–1998	1998–1999	1999–2000
Freetown Teachers Institute, Congo Cross	820	1,000	1,120
Bonthe Technical College, Bonthe	320	336	348
Government Technical Institute, Kenema	302	320	380
Government Trade Institute, Kissy	1,168	1,244	1,482
Government Trade Institute, Magburaka	240	266	300
Institute of Advanced Management and Technology, Kissy	600	613	620
College of Business Studies, Wellington	750	820	880
Murialdo Vocational Institute, Kissy	520	538	540
Y.W.C.A. Vocational Institute, Brookfields	552	560	670
Hotel and Tourism Training Institute, Brookfields	210	204	185
Sierra Leone Opportunities Industrialization Center	2,433	2,500	2,550
Business and Management Development Training Institute	NA	NA	NA
National Workshop, Cline Town	NA	NA	NA
St. Joseph Vocational Institute, Lunsar	300	342	260
Manjama Agricultural Institute, Bo	220	342	240
National Power Authority (NPA) Training Center, Freetown	60	NA	NA
Government Road Transport Training School, Freetown	50	NA	NA

NA: Not available.

Source: Ministry of Education, Government of Sierra Leone, June 2000.

lied Health Sciences (COMAHS) offers training in medicine, pharmacology, and allied health sciences and delivers primary health care service. The Institute of Public Administration and Management (IPAM) provides management training for the private and public sectors; and the other supporting institutions, such as the Institute of Education and Institute of Marine Biology and Oceanography, provide services to facilitate the delivery of other forms of education.

The teachers' colleges train teachers for both primary and secondary schools; the technical and vocational schools offer education and training focused on technical labor skills development; and the professional schools focus on training professionals for varied specialized fields.

CURRENT TRENDS AND CHANGING PATTERNS

Before independence in 1961, educational polices were instituted in accordance with the dictates of the colonial masters. During the later years of colonial rule, some white-collar employment opportunities were available for people educated or trained at postsecondary schools. In fact, there were shortages in the supply of teachers, which precipitated the employment of unqualified personnel, for whom in-service training was suitably provided. With time, increasing population, and the graduation of qualified graduates from the tertiary institutions, employment opportunities gradually became inadequate. Due to various industrial developments, employment opportunities were expanding at rates below the tertiary educational output of graduates.

Some business-minded people have established self-employment operations that have expanded to create employment opportunities for others. However the demand for qualified personnel in some of those occupations is higher than the supply. The lack of sufficiently trained personnel has directed the attention of educators to the need for vocational and technical training programs. Furthermore, many jobs in the public and private sectors pay very low wages, a problem exacerbated by the multiple-digit inflation that continues to devalue the national currency. Consequently, vocational and technical institutions have emerged in some of Sierra Leone's large towns and cities in recent decades (see Table 55.3). For example, the St. Joseph Vocational Institute, the National Power Authority Trade Training Center in Freetown, the Government Trade Institute in Magburaka, and the Government Technical Institute in Kenema have come into operation. The need for training ex-combatants of the civil war, youths, and young adults has reinforced this trend. Many vocational and technical institutions are rapidly growing. Meanwhile, technical, vocational, and teacher training institutions do not satisfy the country's labor needs (MOE 1998, ix).

The development of these various institutions depends on many factors, which include employment conditions of the country, the demand for higher education, resource availability and adequacy, the political climate, and the administrative capacity to implement progressive educational policies. These and other conditions remain generally unfavorable, but foreign assistance has contributed to some ongoing improvement in tertiary educational establishments.

The University of Sierra Leone Act No. 22, 1972, which resulted in the establishment of the university, fostered a monopoly over USL policy by a single administrative body, the University Secretariat, allowing only the addition of new constituent colleges. Over the years, the centralized administrative setup of the secretariat has expanded. This singular structure and its operations were recently criticized by the Kwami Commission (set up in 1993), which advanced numerous progressive recommendations, but to date much remains to be altered (GSL 1994). Critics, for instance, continue to view the secretariat's operations as being isolated from the constituent colleges and institutes.

In 1996, the Ministry of Education set up a committee to review the University Act of 1972 and the Teachers Training Colleges Act of 1982 and to develop proposals for tertiary education. Despite the rebel war and its economic implications, the review of The Technical Committee on Revising The University Act 1972 and The Teachers Colleges Act 1982 has resulted in proposals to restructure Sierra Leone's tertiary institutions. The new plan is to reorganize the university and its affiliates and some other tertiary institutions to form two universities with separate administrative components. The dismantling of USL has yet to begin, and there is apparently resistance to this plan from some powerful beneficiaries of the current system. Meanwhile, the restructuring of nonuniversity tertiary-level education is already underway.

The general restructuring design involves merging and regionalizing Sierra Leone's existing institutions. The reorganization of the administrative structures to foster efficiency and effectiveness in sharing educational resources is another goal of this development. This underlying rationale extends to harmonizing and centralizing the delivery of education from the primary through the tertiary educational levels. Other significant reasons include the promotion of access to higher education in academic, vocational, and technical institutions that produce graduates who are able to meet various development needs.

An independent body, the National Council for Technical, Vocational, and other Academic Awards, works to maintain high standards for education and to issue certificates, diplomas, and degrees to those candidates who successfully complete their academic program.

The teachers' colleges are administered by a College Council of nineteen members, each of whom is appointed for a period of three years (MOE 1982) with the option of reappointment. Six of the members are nominated by the Ministry of Education, four are nominated by religious bodies (the Sierra Leone Muslim Congress, the Supreme Islamic Council, the United Christian Council, and the Roman Catholic Church), and one person is nominated by the Conference of Secondary School Principals. A College Council Committee negotiates the salaries and conditions of service for principals and staff and recommends changes in relevant acts to the Minister of Education. The council also makes employment decisions about staffing, including principals and vice-principals, subject to the approval of the Minister of Education. The principal is the chief administrative, accounting, academic, and professional officer responsible for arranging the curriculum and syllabus of the teachers' college. A standing committee composed of the chief administrative officer, the president of the College Council, the principal, and four other members is charged with making urgent agenda decisions at the college.

It is clear that political motivations influence the appointment of members to the College Council, which affects the unbalanced distribution of decision-making power. The 1982 act pertaining to the College Council Committee's limited

functions should have included serving as the academic high command for all the colleges. In pressing matters, it is possible that the principal's initiatives are more likely to be implemented than those of the standing committee. Notwithstanding the ministry's influence, which is asserted through its six nominees to the council, the 1982 act highly politicizes the decision-making system by mandating that the Minister of Education approve major decisions on new initiatives by the College Council. Other positions such as the registrar and bursar were downplayed, while the objectives and powers of the teachers' colleges were not clearly defined.

The Kwami Commission (GSL 1994) observed great economic deficiencies in Sierra Leone's tertiary education system that render it incapable of meeting the labor demands the country has to promote national industrial development at a globally competitive level. This problem is exacerbated by a national brain drain of highly trained Sierra Leoneans who have studied at tertiary institutions; this labor flight has continued during the politically difficult years of economic crisis from the mid-1980s onward.

As E. H. Wright, the vice-chancellor of USL, commented:

We are in a perpetual state of crisis—the crisis of underfunding, inadequate facilities including laboratories, libraries and modern equipment; high attrition rate of staff, high percentage of low quality staff in many departments, poor conditions of service including absence of a reasonable pension scheme; high percentage of demotivated [unmotivated] staff, cumbersome administrative and management structure and inadequate training of students in the sense that their training is often not adequately geared to the world of work. Above all [there are] inadequate structures and unclear and indecisive policies in the tertiary education system of the country. (USL 1998)

Recent higher education policies have sought to expand the higher education sector. Sierra Leonean delegates recommended that the government implement the following policies at the 1999 World Conference on Higher Education:

- A national student loan scheme to meet the financial needs of students
- A national commission for the maintenance of standards in tertiary institutions
- A national education commission to monitor the operation of tertiary education
- A cost-sharing program with other organizations for effective management
- A system that promotes access to tertiary education without discrimination by race, gender, ethnic origin, or financial status (USL 1999)

The All People's Congress (APC) government of Sierra Leone stifled educational development during its twenty-four years of undemocratic policies. Generally, people with entrepreneurial ambitions were far more valued than those who were well educated. Becoming a politician was an even more attractive way to make a living in Sierra Leone than earning a lower-level college education or a doctoral degree.

Planning for high-quality education delivery has not been a major concern for Sierra Leone's undemocratic governments. Instead, they adopted reactive conflict-management approaches devised to satisfy their political aspirations.

Nor was reforming tertiary institutions a priority. Strategies for administrative appointments were based on political influence. National education policies have depended on which government was in power. During the colonial days, control of tertiary institutions was in the hands of Christian missionaries. After independence in 1961, the governing Sierra Leone People's Party (SLPP) for some time continued the educational policies handed down by the colonial masters. When the All People's Congress (APC) government came to power and established a one-party system, it attempted to gain more control of the institutions by taking control of teachers' salaries and influencing employment decisions related to administrators. The current SLPP government, which is once again part of a multiparty system, has encouraged higher education institutions to find supplemental sources of funding. Funding patterns have varied based on political appointments of top administrators of the institutions and their relationships with the current governing body. In recent years, the SLPP government has increased funding, but the war situation has continued to jeopardize progress.

INSTITUTIONAL CAPACITY AND STRUCTURE

The capacity of Sierra Leone's tertiary institution is inadequate in every respect, including infrastructure, facilities, equipment, other materials, and human resources. Capacity building was not advanced during the years of corrupt and undemocratic rule. The rebel war has only exacerbated these problems. Today, far more students are prepared to enter tertiary institutions than the institutions can absorb.

The structure of the tertiary education system consists of USL at the top and a broad spectrum of polytechnics and private vocational and technical institutions at the bottom.

Below the head of state, who is the chancellor of the university, are the pro-chancellor, the vice-chancellor, the secretariat, the Board of Trustees, the constituent colleges, the auditors, the court, the senate, the faculties, the deans of faculties, heads of departments, and the staff. This structure shows that there is a hierarchy of authority in which the government has the supreme authority. Government representatives account for seven of the twelve members of boards of governors at technical institutes. The College Council governs the teachers' colleges (MOE 1964). This setup facilitates the exercise of great political influence on the overall governing of tertiary institutions.

THE CURRICULUM

USL's contributions are critical to addressing national development needs in science, math, technology, arts, culture, and mass communication as well as developing curriculum for other tertiary institutions. The curriculum of the tertiary education sector is rich in conventional subject offerings, yet it also caters to many specialized areas of expertise and interest. The constituent colleges of the university offer specialized areas of study in nearly all the subjects that are taught in the primary and secondary schools, teachers' colleges, and other private tertiary institutions.

Fourah Bay College (FBC) offers regular academic subjects including languages; civil, mechanical, and electrical engineering; library science; marine biology; religion; communications; and law.

In addition to the academic subjects taught in secondary and other tertiary colleges, Njala University College (NUC) trains teachers for work in the various levels of educational institutions. NUC also offers courses in agriculture, environmental science, and economics.

The College of Medicine and Allied Health Sciences (CMAHS) trains medical doctors, pharmacists, nurses, and other senior health personnel for the country. Its curriculum traditionally favored competency development for white-collar employment in civil service, the church, and research. But changes are being observed. The Sierra Leone University Prospectus 2000–2001 (USL 2000b) asserts, for example, "It is time for the university to lead the way in the production of our everyday needs in food and medicines at least." CMAHS has eleven faculties and fifty-eight academic program departments. The faculties are in arts, engineering, pure and applied science, clinical science, basic medical sciences, pharmaceutical sciences, social sciences and law, education, agriculture, environmental sciences, and the Institute of Public Administration and Management (IPAM).

Other course-offering institutes of the university include the Certificate Training Center (CTC) of NUC, the Institute of Marine Biology and Oceanography (IMBO), the Institute of African Studies, the Institute of Library Archives and Information Studies (INSLIBS), the Institute of Adult Education and Extra-Mural Studies (INSTADEX), and the Institute of Population Studies of FBC. The courses involve short-term programs for diplomas, licenses, and certificates.

Sierra Leone's curriculum generally has followed the traditional British pattern. In recent decades, USL has focused on more specialized subject areas. For instance, the agronomy department was broken into departments of soil science, crop science, and plant protection. It is therefore possible for the graduates to gain advanced training in their respective subject specializations in the tertiary institutions of Sierra Leone, just like their counterparts in England, the United States, and other African countries that offer similar subjects. However, a scarcity of up-to-date textbooks, journals, periodicals, educational equipment, and materials makes it difficult to offer specialized courses in many modern subject areas.

Other tertiary institutions in Sierra Leone include polytechnics that have recently been approved as degree-granting institutions. The teachers' colleges and other technical training institutions have not yet been approved to grant degrees. Instead, they grant certificates and diplomas. The curricula of these institutions, like those of USL, are sufficiently diversified to fulfill their mission, which is to provide trained midlevel labor power. The curriculum gives special attention to meeting the needs for vocational and technical human resources. In the context of current global educational development trends, it is clear that

Sierra Leone's curriculum needs greater input from the international educational arena if the institutions are to be competitive worldwide.

LANGUAGE OF INSTRUCTION AND ITS IMPACT

Sierra Leone was under British Colonial rule for 150 years. During this time, English was the official language of business and the main language of instruction at all tertiary educational institutions. This remains the case today.

Sierra Leone has over one dozen distinct local languages, including Creole, Fulla, Gallines, Kissi, Kono, Kuranko, Lokko, Madingo, Mende, Sherbro, Susu, Themne, Vai, and Yalunka (USL 2000a). Sierra Leone's New Education Policy for Sierra Leone (1995) states that

> National Languages shall be taught throughout the school system, including teacher training colleges and university. English shall be the medium of instruction throughout the system. French shall be compulsory at the primary and junior secondary school levels but optional at the senior secondary school level. (MOE 1995)

Implementing this language policy is both very important and difficult. Teaching the English language and using it to teach other subjects and transact educational business in general creates fewer problems than using local languages. Many literate Sierra Leoneans are properly trained and qualified to teach English and to use it to teach linguistics, drama, and English literature. Even when a teacher is a speaker of her or his own language, she or he may have had no formal training in teaching it and therefore will lack an appropriate teaching methodology. Apart from the problems of lack of appropriate training and adequate understanding, there are not enough literate native speakers of local languages who could be trained in tertiary institutions to serve in all primary and secondary schools, polytechnics, and other colleges. Schools are therefore engaged in teaching only the languages for which teachers are available.

The English language has had a tremendous impact on education and the other spheres of life and activities in Sierra Leone. Schools were encouraged to emphasize local languages after World War II, but the emphasis was not sustained due to the lack of trained literate native speakers of the local languages other than Mende and Themne. The influence of the English language goes beyond its status as the official medium of instruction and communication, however. It has found its way into most of the native languages, thereby creating new combinations of native languages and frequently used English vocabularies. Many young people living in the Freetown Metropolitan City cannot speak their native languages because of the wider use of Krio (the lingua franca), which is a mixture of English words and a variety of native languages from across West Africa. Some Sierra Leoneans simply prefer to associate themselves with the Western world by blending English words into their languages.

Those students who become fluent in Krio and do not have the opportunity to practice English outside the classroom often experience great difficulty in mastering basic English at the expected levels in schools. As a result of such difficulties, many students have been denied access to tertiary institutions. Some of them have been forced to repeat the English-language external examination several times before gaining entrance to a tertiary institution.

RESEARCH, PUBLISHING, AND TEACHING

The two principal functions of all academic staff are teaching and research. Research in all subject areas is intended to provide new knowledge and information not only to solve social problems but also to facilitate decision-making and policy-making efforts.

Promotion of academic staff at USL is primarily based on research and publications rather than teaching. Indeed, teaching at university may not be meaningful without complementary research activities. Over recent decades, a great deal of research has been conducted in the various tertiary institutions, including USL. The large number of books, monographs, theses, pamphlets, articles in academic journals, and conference papers bear testimony to the fruits of research. However, until recently, research at USL was rather uncoordinated, determined by the particular whims of various researchers.

In January 1985, USL established the University Research and Development Service (URDS). The general objective of the bureau is to coordinate all research development and consultancy activities in the university to benefit the nation. Its specific objectives are to facilitate, stimulate, guide, and coordinate research and development; strengthen the relationship between the university and other national and international institutions; and encourage the staff to participate in the search for solutions to national problems through research and consultancy work.

The bureau is structured into eight divisions: Advisory Services in Technology, Research and Development (ASTRAD); Economic, Social, and Cultural Studies; Education, Food and Agriculture; Languages Studies; Medical and Health Studies; Pure and Applied Science; Rural Development; and Science and Technology Policy. Each division controls several specialized units, each of which is responsible for projects falling within its competence. A divisional head coordinates work within each division, while managers control the units and report to the divisional heads.

The administration of the bureau is carried out by a director, two deputy directors, program officers, research scholars and assistants, and various supporting staff. The bureau draws its expertise from the academic staff of the university. The activities of the bureau are controlled by a URDS Board which is hired by the vice-chancellor and consists of senior academic and administrative staff of the university and representatives of other research bodies, the Ministry of Education, and the Ministry of Economic Planning and Development.

URDS also engages in development projects, procurement, disbursement of research and development funds, consultancy services, publication of a quarterly newsletter, and reports on current activities. The office also runs short courses and provides support for some participants. The bureau has facilities for data processing and analysis and a research library and resource center.

In order to ensure excellence in teaching and learning, USL has a system of continual assessment of students (MOE 1996,

Table 55.4. Government Grants to Tertiary Education, 1995–1996

Institution	Personnel Budget (Percent)	Non-Staff Budget (Percent)	Total Budget (Percent)
University of Sierra Leone	45.3	15.4	60.7
Milton Margai Teachers' College	5.9	2.6	8.5
Bunumbu Teachers' College	2.6	3.5	6.1
Bo Teachers' College	3.4	2.8	6.2
Makeni Teachers' College	3.1	3.3	6.4
Port Loko Teachers' College	1.9	4.2	5.9
Freetown Teachers' College	3.4	2.5	5.9
Total	65.6 (Le2.14 billion)	34.4 (Le1.12 billion)	100 (Le 3.25 billion)

Source: Ministry of Education, Finance Department, 1996.

228). Academic staff are not directly rewarded for teaching through promotion. However, there is a move to initiate a thorough evaluation system for teaching performance and promotion of academic staff. Employment of modern technology in teaching, especially information technology and other teaching aids, is another priority. The university is striving to acquire computer and video equipment to facilitate teaching in various faculties.

The teachers' colleges, technical and vocational institutions, and professional schools conduct research on an ad hoc basis. Qualifications and teaching experience serve as the basis for promotion of the academic staff to senior positions in these institutions.

Accessing funds for research from USL is a challenge. If any money is released, it is never adequate. Competing for international funds is a challenge. Even when international organizations fund research through institutions, the bureaucracy, in accessing the funds, seems to discourage lecturers who undertake research ventures. Lecturers also find it difficult to conduct research when they have to spend most of their time outside the classroom toiling in supplementary jobs to make ends meet. USL's pay package for lecturers is perhaps the lowest in the region and the world.

The opportunities to publish local magazines and journals with international scholarly scope are rare or inadequate. The cost of sending publishable documents out to other countries is also a problem. In addition, war has prevented staff from sending research results abroad for publication. Mentoring is not available to inexperienced lecturers in tertiary institutions because most of the experienced researchers and lecturers have left for greener pastures. These challenges generally undermine research and publication opportunities in Sierra Leone's tertiary institutions.

FINANCING AND FUNDING PATTERNS

More than 90 percent of the funds used to run Sierra Leone's tertiary institutions comes from the government. Additional funds come from school fees and donations from donor agencies. Private tertiary institutions rely on generating funds from school fees rather than on donor agencies.

The latest available funding figures for tertiary education in

Sierra Leone are listed in Table 55.4. (Data for the most recent years are not available due to civil war.) Government financing since 1998 has constituted 95 percent of expendable funds available to tertiary education. Budgets are submitted to the Ministry of Finance through the Ministry of Education. Allocations for tertiary institutions are still grossly inadequate.

It can be seen from Table 55.4 that in the 1995–1996 academic year, the government grant to tertiary education was approximately $1.6 million (Le3.25 billion). Of this, USL received 60 percent, Milton Margai College of Education received 9 percent, and the other five teachers' colleges received about 6 percent each. Salaries and emoluments accounted for 66 percent of that year's actual expenditure. Except for Bunumbu and Port Loko Teachers' Colleges, all the other institutions spent more of their allocations on salaries than on other charges.

The percentage of the MOE grant to tertiary education was 13 percent of the total grant to the education sector. Thus, 8 percent of the education grant went to the USL and 25 percent of total education grant was given to FBC, NUC, and MMTC (MOE 1996).

This funding pattern is inadequate and suggests the reason for Sierra Leone's impoverished environment for the delivery of education. Physical facilities have gone unimproved for years. While many universities around the world have replaced their typewriters with computers, antiquated typewriters are the dominant writing technology in Sierra Leone. However, now that the war is at an end, the MOE is working frantically to rehabilitate institutions and develop facilities. Administrators are particularly concerned about modernizing their institutions.

STUDENT ACTIVISM

The mark of all civilization is the respect accorded to human dignity and freedom. All religious and cultural traditions celebrate these ideals (UNDP 2000). We expect respect, peacefulness, and productivity to govern universities and other tertiary institutions. This requires reciprocal respect, freedom, and trust among all members of the educational institution. On the whole, Sierra Leone's educational community can be regarded as comparatively cordial and collegial. This is not to say that students, administrators, and the national government never have conflicts with each other. But at no time have such differences resulted in the closure of an academic institution for much longer than one month.

In 1972, students booed President Siaka Stevens at a university convocation ceremony. At another time, students mounted an active strike during which they marched the vice-chancellor to President Siaka Stevens to force him to put a case for raising their allowances and responding to their other urgent needs.

In August 1997, when the whole country mounted resistance to the governance of the Armed Forces Revolutionary Council and the Revolutionary United Front alliance, students staged a protest march during which several of them were killed. Others were detained for more than three weeks at the Pademba Road Central Prisons. This is the longest time USL, or any other tertiary institution, has been kept closed as a result of student upheavals.

Most students entering tertiary institutions are classified as adults because they qualify by age to vote in national and regional elections. Many of them are fathers and mothers and may have been employed by government or other reputable organizations and individuals. Some students are committed to political parties of their choice and become agents for such political groups. Some politically mature and experienced students become very strong advocates of student politics and strong candidates for positions in student governments. Without doubt, some students have suffered molestation and temporary imprisonment for open political support of a losing party.

Student activism has sometimes acted as a check on the national government. Between 1973 and 1978, there were signs of student opposition to Siaka Stevens's one-party government. Poverty and corruption were widespread. Students were killed when there were crackdowns on their political opposition. For example, students were killed during the 1997 student demonstration against the Armed Forces Revolutionary Council government. In 1998, students joined forces with the majority of the Sierra Leonean people to force the reinstatement of the democratically elected government.

Apart from the government preventing fee increases for students at the university and other tertiary institutions, the government has not unduly attempted to interfere in the affairs of tertiary institutions. The government provides more than 90 percent of the running costs of these institutions. The government pays salaries, allowances, and other emoluments, as well as the costs of materials, equipment, new buildings, and renovations. Since the country favors democracy, political parties try to influence the operations and funding of the tertiary institutions in anticipation of reciprocal political support, particularly from the university.

It is not bad for politicians to show a strong interest in educational institutions as long as more people benefit from the relationship in the end. However, the use by governments in power of violence and suppression through brutality imposed by hired youths has brought devastating consequences in recent times.

GRADUATE EMPLOYMENT AND BRAIN DRAIN

For some time now, employment in educational and other government institutions has been restricted to replacing employees who leave or retire. As a result, a substantial number of agriculture graduates from NUC and engineering graduates from FBC have found themselves teaching in the secondary schools instead of working in their professional areas of training. Many graduates from other tertiary institutions find employment with nongovernmental organizations or in neighboring countries, particularly Gambia, Guinea, and Liberia. The rebel war aggravated Sierra Leone's unemployment crisis. Many graduates remain unemployed while schools are still saddled with untrained and unqualified teachers, especially in the sciences and in technical and vocational courses. This lack of jobs places great strains on new graduates. This situation forces graduates to seek employment in areas for which they were not trained, leading to the considerable underutilization of graduate labor power.

The cause of the brain drain in Sierra Leone over the past ten years can be attributed mainly to the insecurity in the country caused by rebel activities, especially the killing of people and the burning of houses and other personal property, which has caused massive displacement. Homes, towns, and villages have been emptied in minutes after some attacks.

Before the war, people moved to escape poor conditions of service and delayed salary payments. A lecturer's initial salary is currently around $3,081 a year. Others deserted their jobs for personal reasons, such as lack of recognition and discriminatory treatment.

Sierra Leone has experienced two types of brain drain: internal movement to another part of Sierra Leone in search of a better job and movement to other countries in search of work. While internal mobility has some disadvantages, it is far less economically damaging to the nation than external employee movement, which has the potential to critically deplete the nation's labor resources.

The situation is now much improved, however. Life is slowly becoming normal and quite a few of the brains, especially medical doctors, university lecturers, and senior teachers in schools, are returning home.

CURRENT AND FUTURE CHALLENGES

Students whose educational programs have faced interruptions by political upheavals remain frustrated with what appears to be Sierra Leone's bleak future. Some students whose parents or supporters have been affected by the war can no longer afford to continue their education. Many potential college-bound candidates have seen their lives shattered and could not proceed with higher education. An obvious challenge is to provide assistance and alternative programs, including temporary or stepping-stone employment, to these war victims. The government needs to bring the war to a conclusion, take full control of the mineral mining regions, and direct this wealth to support higher education.

Eliminating corruption in financial management and ensuring transparency and accountability in every educational system is a major task. A relatively corruption-free Sierra Leone would lead to better distribution of government revenues and use of natural resources, allowing for improved funding of the educational institutions. This requires not only a sustainable anticorruption program but also an effective judiciary system and appreciable increases in salaries and other benefits for academic staff and faculty.

Meeting the increasing demand for higher education among the rising population of college-bound students from secondary schools is another major challenge. USL can only accommodate half of the qualified candidates who apply in any one year. There are also demands for graduate degree programs that USL is not adequately equipped to provide.

Reducing political influence in higher education administration through the nonpolitical appointment of key administrators in public tertiary institutions would have a positive impact on the size and quality of staff retained in the institutions. Political appointments encourage loyalty to government officials rather than to stakeholders of the educational institutions the needs of the staff and students. Such loyalty may encourage bad decisions from less competent, untrained, unprofessional, and corrupt administrators who compromise institutional development plans with inadequate government funding plans.

Conditions of service for higher education employees remain unattractive. Late payment of salaries is extremely common. Occasionally, staff agitations have led staff to receive compensation on time for services they have rendered. Recently, some government efforts have been directed at improving the situation, but much remains to be done. As peace returns, there is reason to hope that Sierra Leone's education system will regain its good image in the region.

Sierra Leoneans would like to have the best opportunities to educate their people. For progress to be achieved, it is critical that administrators of tertiary institutions develop their professional administrative competencies and put national educational development priorities above the nepotism and corrupt practices that have led the nation to ruin.

A good governance system is essential for educational development in Sierra Leone. Future considerations for tertiary education should include developing a creative funding system and improving the governance of tertiary institutions to enhance the delivery of education.

REFERENCES

Central Statistics Office, Government of Sierra Leone. 2000. Statistical Records. Freetown.

GSL (Government of Sierra Leone). 1970. *The White Paper on Education 1970.* Freetown: Government of Sierra Leone.

——. 1974. National Development Plan 74/75–78/79.

——. 1994. "Report of The Professor Kwami Investigating Committee on the University of Sierra Leone and Government Statement Thereon." Freetown: Government Printing Department.

MOE (Ministry of Education, Government of Sierra Leone). 1964. *The Education Act 1964.* Freetown: Government Printer.

——. 1970. White Paper on Educational Policy.

——. 1972. *The University of Sierra Leone Act, 1972.* Freetown: Government Printing Department.

——. 1975. *New Education Policy for Sierra Leone.* Freetown: Government Printers.

——. 1982. *The Teachers' Colleges Act 1982.* Freetown: Government Printers.

——. 1995. *The Teachers' Colleges Act, 1982.* Freetown: The Government Printer.

——. 1996. *National Education Master Plan, 1996–2005.* Freetown: Ministry of Education.

——. 1998. *Report on the Technical Committee on Revising the University Act, 1972 and the Teachers' Colleges Act, 1982.* Vol. I. Freetown: Educational Services Center, Ministry of Education.

UNDP (United Nations Development Project). 2000. *Human Development Report Overview.* New York: Oxford University Press.

USL (University of Sierra Leone). 1998. Versity Update P.3. Freetown: University of Sierra Leone.

——. 1999. Versity Update. Freetown: University of Sierra Leone.

——. 2000a. Planning Office Records (July).

——. 2000b. Senate Paper. Freetown: University of Sierra Leone.

——. 2000c. *University of Sierra Leone Prospectus 2000–2002.* Freetown: University of Sierra Leone.

56

Somalia and Somaliland

Mohamed Nur-Awaleh

INTRODUCTION

According to the United Nations, Somalia's population was 7.7 million in 1991. Due to the civil war from 1991 to the present, no reliable census on Somalia's population is available. Somali is the common language that is spoken in both Somalia and Somaliland. The number of languages listed for Somalia is thirteen. Except for a few communities along the southern Somali coast, where Swahili and Arabic dialects are spoken, Somali nationals inhabiting the inter-riverine regions also speak a different language known as Maay, a combination of colloquial local dialects, Swahili, and Somali. The average literacy rate before the civil war was 24 percent (Metz 1993). Most Somalis are Sunni Muslims, while less than 1 percent of ethnic Somalis are Christians.

Before the collapse of the Somali state in 1991, Somalia had a socialist-oriented economy that was undergoing market-oriented structural adjustment. Indeed, Somalia's economy depended on a heavy dose of foreign aid. The country's economy was based on agriculture, livestock, forestry, and fishery, which together accounted for the bulk of its gross domestic product (GDP). A small manufacturing sector was involved in the processing of agricultural products such as sugar, milk, hides, and skins. The manufacturing sector accounted for 5 percent of Somalia's GDP. Somalia's principal exports were livestock and bananas before the economic activity of the state was disrupted by the civil war (Metz 1993).

After the collapse of Barre's dictatorship in January 1990, the former territory of British Somaliland under the leadership of Somali National Movement (SNM) declared itself independent in May 1991. Due to poor leadership during Barre's era, systematic discrimination at the educational and governmental sectors was rife. In addition, the regime committed gross human rights abuses (Africa Watch 1990; Ahmed 1999). Currently the Repub-

lic of Somaliland has a parliament occupied by representatives of different clans, the president, and vice-president. However, the introduction of a multiparty system is still ongoing. Political parties are allowed to register only if they secure support from all six regions of the republic.

Somaliland exports livestock and receives remittances from the Somali Diaspora; 80 percent of the revenues of Somaliland come from taxes on the export of sheep, goats, camels, and cattle to Saudi Arabia and the United Arab Emirates.

The population of Somaliland is 2.5 million. The Republic of Somaliland is thriving peacefully. However, the republic has experienced enormous difficulty in securing recognition from the international community. Indeed, the lack of recognition has created many challenges to achieving economic development in Somaliland.

TRADITIONAL AND ISLAMIC EDUCATION

One of the greatest myths about Somali society is that Somalians had no education until Europeans arrived in the country. Although secular education was introduced in colonial times, formal as well as informal education had existed long before the arrival of the Europeans.

The most widespread form of education was the learning that occurred informally as children observed and explored the nomadic and agricultural environments in which they lived. They did so at play and while assisting their parents and elders with work in fields, on farms, or in the household. Working alongside elders provided countless opportunities to learn by example and through oral instruction (Lewis 1988, 1994).

Traditionally, Somali societies relied on oral communication to convey traditions, beliefs, and values, as well as information, from one generation to the next. Poetry, stories, songs, and proverbs were used to convey fundamental moral messages. Riddles served as a test of mental dexterity and imagination. Somali societies incorporated formal instruction into rituals, beliefs, and traditions of the clans or community, such as the ceremonial process of initiation into adulthood.

Like many other Muslim societies, Somali traditional education was apparently limited to Quranic sciences. This involved, among other things, learning the Arabic language, reciting the Quran, and reading books on Islamic belief and practice.

From a colonial point of view, Somalis' traditional Islamic education seemed to focus mainly on memorization of the Quran. However, this is an oversimplification. Somali scholars and sheiks played a leading role in the dissemination of knowledge and occupied positions of great prestige in Somali society. Schooling was organized from early childhood and continued after an elementary stage to higher education. The system was very efficient. From ages 6 to 10, children not only learned Arabic but were able to commit the whole of the Quran, comprising 114 chapters, to memory. This was by no means a trivial feat (Abdullahi 1992; Kitchen 1962).

Almost all boys of school-going age went to Quranic schools, and many of them became well-educated, respected, and worthy citizens. Later, girls were also given access to these Quranic schools. However, girls' participation in the traditional Islamic education was incredibly low compared to that of boys. Moreover, sociocultural factors constrained girls' access to education in Somalia.

The creation and organization of Islamic schools was a community affair. Not only did parents contribute money toward their children's education, they also undertook communal labor and provided services to the teachers. Teachers did not wholly depend on schools for income. They ran their own businesses and received fees in the form of food rations, camels, cattle, sheep, cloth, and so on. They also received charity and undertook other social and religious duties to supplement their incomes (Abdullahi 1992).

Notable characteristics of Somali Islamic traditional education were decentralization and self-sufficiency. Competent Islamic teachers established their own schools and remained independent of any hierarchical authority. No assistance was received from the colonial government, yet many students gained sponsorship from community members and religious centers (Abdullahi 1992).

In 1953, the first higher education institution was established when the Institute of Islamic Studies opened in Somalia. The academic staff consisted mostly of scholars from Al-Azhar University in Egypt. One of the goals in setting up the institute was to train judges, lawyers, and teachers of Arabic and Islam. In addition, many other Islamic schools based on Egyptian models were opened in 1954, based on a curriculum from Egypt. In their wake followed a multiplicity of Islamic institutes, which opened the doors for Somali graduates to undertake university studies in Egypt and Saudi Arabia (Abdullahi 1992, 104).

In time, educated Somali elites became conversant in Italian and English as well as Arabic. They occupied positions in all spheres of administration, including the education, religious affairs, and military sectors.

A BRIEF OVERVIEW OF COLONIAL EDUCATIONAL DEVELOPMENT

The Italians entered Somalia in 1885 with the intention of colonizing it. During that time, little attention was paid to education. The capital city of Mogadishu had only one school (consisting of a few priests and students), which was run by the Trinitarian Order. The Italians believed that Somali people were inferior and not worthy of education. Not until 1922 were any policies implemented with regard to the education of the Somali people (Yahya 1984; Hess 1966, 169).

In 1924, the Trinitarian school was reorganized by order of the governor of the colony, and elementary education was begun for European children. As a result, the colonial government started subsidizing the mission's education program in the territory. Around that time, the Italian colonial consulate also began organizing elementary schools for Italian children, interracial "orphans," and a few Somali and Arab children. These schools were confined to Mogadishu until 1925–1928, when the mission established elementary schools for the "indigenous" people in other parts of the colony, including Merca, Brava, Afgoye, Baidoa, and Kismayo (Yahya 1984, 72–73). Italian children originally sat in the same class with the Somalis, but in 1929, the new fascist governor Guido Corni ordered that Italian and Somali students be separated on the premise that masters and subjects would not have such relations (Lewis 1998, 97). The underlying feeling that Somali people were somehow inferior remained. During this period, however, Somalia's school system slowly emerged. In 1930, the first intermediate school was established, based on a curriculum from the metropole and with teachers who were government officials in the colony (Hess 1966, 169–170). By 1935, the office of the superintendent of schools, which had been created several years earlier, directed ten government schools (nine elementary schools and one intermediate, in eight major towns) and five orphanages. The total number of pupils in the whole colony was then about 1,500. Italians made up 10 percent of the total, while the students in all 46 intermediate schools were Italians (Yahya 1984, 74; Hess 1966, 169–170).

In short, education made little progress during Italy's direct colonization of Somalia. As Robert Hess notes, "Of all the Italian colonies, Somalia received the least aid for schools" (1966, 187). Moreover, the Somalis worked typically as manual laborers, local clerks, or low-level administrators in the colonial administration. Hence, Somali education was quite restricted. According to Castagno, "Such education as there was primarily [was designed] to supply the Somali clerks and other semi-skilled persons required by the expanded administration [and] was provided almost entirely by Mission schools" (1959, 343).

This was the situation when the British drove the Italians out of the territory during World War II. The British found the educational situation appalling and asserted that "native" education had been deliberately neglected by Italy. They also reported that they found only one intermediate school for Somalis and one secondary coeducational school in Mogadishu when they "liberated" the city (Yahya 1984, 76; Hess 1966, 343–344). The British occupation of Northern Somaliland took place in 1945, giving birth to the New Colonial Development and Welfare scheme based on grants and the extension of public health services. In 1944, C. R. Bell, the first colonial educator who had a command of the Somali language, was appointed superintendent of education and dealt effectively with the traditional opposition to education. Secular education was introduced in Northern Somaliland; by 1945–1947, primary schools enrolled more than 400 male students. The British also provided some assistance to nineteen private Quranic schools that taught Arabic and arithmetic. During the early years of British occupation, twenty-nine primary schools were established, offering education to 1,600 pupils (Dawson 1964, 199).

The British had ulterior motives for being "receptive" to education: namely, to win public opinion and to secure a trusteeship. By responding to educational demands, however, the British helped the Somalis become more politically conscious and better able to make their arguments known (Yahya 1984).

On April 1, 1950, the British administration was replaced by an Italian trusteeship. Pressing goals, set by the Italo-UN Trusteeship agreement, had to be met. This agreement formed a framework for educational development and resulted in the rapid development of primary and secondary schools. With the help of the United Nations Educational, Scientific, and Cultural Organization (UNESCO), this trusteeship carried out a five-year plan from 1952 to 1957, which was later extended to 1959 (Lewis 1988). This administration was established in the hope of raising literacy levels and improving the social and economic conditions of the country. Mission schools were soon replaced by state schools that offered free education.

In 1952, the first Somali education officer, an Italian-trained Somali, was appointed. The following year, the Higher Institute of Law and Economics (which would later become Somalia's University College) opened; it offered a two-year diploma program from Rome University (Castagno 1959). In 1953, the first government-run school for girls also opened at Burao, and a four-year secondary school was introduced.

During the late 1950s and early 1960s, the failure rate was high. From 1959 to 1960, 1,500 students were enrolled in primary education, slightly more than 900 in lower secondary school, and 700 in higher secondary school (Kitchen 1962, 88–90). But only half of the enrolled students completed the five-year program.

On June 26, 1960, British Somaliland became independent and later joined its southern Italian Somaliland neighbor to become the Independent Somali Republic on July 1, 1960. The Italian and British systems of education were then integrated. After independence, Somaliland had 90 elementary schools with 5,000 enrollees, 25 percent of whom were female. The elementary school drop-out rate was 15 percent (Kitchen 1962; Lewis 1988).

In the south, where there had been an Italian influence, there were 175 five-year institutions with more than 1,600 enrollees. Grades 1 and 2 were taught in Arabic, while Grade 3 was taught in Italian. Boys outnumbered girls four to one at these institutions. With integration, all elementary schools became four-year institutions, English replaced Italian, and the drop-out rate soared to 76 percent. Legal, economic, and political institutions, however, were not integrated. The lack of a common language further exacerbated Somalia's problems.

When the military gained power in 1969, it set the following goals: to codify a written Somali language, to replace both Italian and English languages, and to integrate Somalia's various institutions. The government achieved its goal of a written language when Osman Yusuf Kenadid systematized the Somali alphabet and written language in 1972. This enabled Somalia to implement literacy campaigns for the masses. By 1979, the Somalization of elementary and secondary schools was complete. By the late 1970s, there was also enough printed material to promote the Somali language as a learning medium at all primary and secondary schools (Nelson 1982, 119–120).

Not long afterward, a decline in the government's investment in the educational system took place, due to the mobilization for the Ogaden War of 1977–1978. Facilities and staff could no longer be maintained. The quality of education dropped significantly by the early 1980s. In addition, Somalia lacked highly trained educational managers who could manage scarce resources efficiently (IEES 1984). By 1984, more than 5,000 students had graduated from secondary school, but universities could not accept them all due to limits on their capacity. Less than 20 percent of these graduates were hired by government agencies; the rest were unemployed (World Bank 1988a).

Advocates of change soon appeared on the scene, as evidenced by the Supreme Revolutionary Council (SRC). In the late 1970s, the SRC had several plans for education, including expansion of the system to embrace compulsory education for all children from 6 to 14 years of age, provision of courses geared to the country's social and economic requirements, the teaching of scientific socialist principles in all aspects of formal education, and the establishment of a higher educational system in Somalia. These proposals represented a type of "cultural revolution" in Somalia. The SRC also insisted that girls in particular be sent to school beyond the elementary level (Nelson 1982; Adam 1980, 100–102). But Somalia saw only limited success in meeting these goals by 1984, as evidenced by the government's failure to invest in the educational system. In 1989, the IEES (Improving the Efficiency of Educational Systems) concluded:

> Somalia—with an estimated per capita income of $190—is one of the poorest countries in the world. The combination of an extremely fragile economy and government emphasis on the productive sector resulted in a sharp decrease in its investment in education over the last decade. Between 1984 and 1988 alone, the Ministry of Education's share of the ordinary (recurrent) budget declined from eight percent to 1.5 percent. (IEES 1989, 77)

THE DEVELOPMENT OF HIGHER EDUCATION PRIOR TO THE 1990 CIVIL WAR

Higher education in Somalia began in 1954 when the Italian government established the Institutes of Law, Economics, and Social Studies. These institutes were satellites of the University of Rome, which provided all the instruction materials, faculty, and administration. In 1964, the institutes offered two years of study in Somalia, followed by two years of study in Italy. After a military coup in 1969, all foreign entities were nationalized, including the university, which was renamed Jaamacada Ummadda Soomaliyeed (the National University of Somalia, or NUS) (Nelson 1982, 123).

Higher education became available in Somalia through NUS and its six colleges. There were also seven specialized postsecondary schools, all of which were government based. Although various institutions offered instruction in Italian, English, and Arabic, the main language of instruction at NUS was Italian. However, this presented problems for Somali students who completed their previous education in Somali, and it did not make sense, as noted by Mebrahtu:

> Whatever the merits of using Italian as the medium in about a dozen faculties, English in one (faculty of education) and Somali in another (political science), there is a fundamental educational policy at stake here. To expect a student to follow a degree-level course after only a term's professional Italian, does not seem to be realistic." (Mebrahtu 1992, 634)

Acceptance into an institution of higher education in Somalia required a secondary school learning certificate, for which students were eligible after completing twelve years of study and passing a special entrance examination. Postsecondary education usually lasted two to five years, depending on the institution and the field of study. Many courses were designed for people who planned to specialize in a particular field.

Somali colleges and schools included the School of Industrial Studies, the School of Public Health, the Veterinary College, and the Technical College at Buro (Nelson 1982, 123). Somalia had six postsecondary schools before the civil war. They were as follows:

- The Civil Aviation Institute at Mogadishu, which offered one- and two-year programs in air traffic control and radio communications.
- The Technical Teacher Training College (TTTC) in Mogadishu, which was created with UNESCO funding. It offered a two-year training course to prepare teachers for technical and vocational secondary education. TTTC offered programs in general mechanics, auto mechanics, electronics, civil construction, marine engineering, and commercial studies.
- The Somali Institute of Telecommunications at Mogadishu, which offered a three-and-a-half-year course.
- The LaFole College of Education, which was established in 1963 as part of NUS with the intention of generating more secondary school teachers. Most of the instruction at LaFole College is in English, even though graduates are expected to teach in Somalia. The most recent data shows that the enrollment at LaFole College is close to 1,000. The estimated staff-to-student ratio is 1 to 8, one of the lowest ratios in Africa (World Bank 1988a; UNESCO 1991).
- The Somali Institute of Development Administration and Management (SIDAM), which was created to provide instruction to upgrade Somalia's civil service, improve management skills, and prepare a trained professional cadre (Bullaleh 1993). SIDAM offered a master's program; it was also one of the few institutions that used English as the main language. Faculty at SIDAM were Americans and Somalis who were trained either in the United States or Britain. The institute was entirely financed by the United States Agency for International Development (USAID) and UNESCO. Nearly 150 students graduated from SIDAM each year (Mebrahtu 1992, 631).
- NUS was established with two main intentions: to increase the availability of higher education and to meet the professional and labor demands of Somalia's government. With these plans in mind, the Somali government initiated a five-year plan (1980–1985) that emphasized the role of higher education in Somalia. One of the goals of this plan was to expand the institution in order to boost the enrollment. But this goal was never achieved because the government lacked the needed commitment and failed to allocate resources for university expenditures (IEES 1985).

Admission to NUS was based on the Secondary Learning Certificate, an entrance exam, and one year in the national Youth Service, which was established to teach rural students to read Somali script. In addition, university entrance exams were given to assess the student's talents with regard to the national labor needs and faculty availability. The university entrance exam provided students with a choice of majors (Mebrahtu 1992, 632).

NUS was administered by the Ministry of Higher Education. Since the Somali government was the major benefactor of the "product" of higher education, as well as the major source of its capital, it had considerable clout with regard to university management, including its administration, scholarship program, and faculty research. In fact, the head of the state (former dictator Siad Barre) was also chancellor of the university, even though his duties were mainly ceremonial in nature (Bullaleh 1993).

The rector was the chief executive officer of NUS, assisted by two vice-rectors who were responsible for academic affairs and administrative affairs, respectively. Both the rector and the vice-rectors were appointed by the National Ruling Party (Mebrahtu 1992, 632; IEES 1984).

NUS had two other main administrative bodies of the university: the university council and senate. The chair of the council was the Minister of Higher Education. The ruling political party, unlike the student body, had its own representative in the council. The senate committee was chaired by the rector and included two academic staff members (selected by their deans). The academic staff in each faculty was responsible for designing and implementing the student curriculum (IEES 1984). Each faculty was headed by a dean who acted as its chief academic and administrative officer. The dean, who reported to the vice-rector and rector, led the faculty in designing regulations for research, admissions, registration, and examination of students.

During Siad Barre's regime (1969–1990), institutions of higher learning in Somalia had less autonomy, making them dependent on the government. The government's involvement in higher education came in the form of subsidies, especially free tuition for students. The government's arguments for free education centered on the assumption that society would derive social and cultural advantages because education would provide opportunities for economic and social integration of marginalized groups and individuals (World Bank 1988a; IEES 1984). Proponents of these views argued that the analysis of the rate of return on education is inadequate. They also put forth another provocative argument: If the government can subsidize the tobacco industry, why not subsidize higher education? (Samoff 1993, 182).

Government subsidization of higher education allowed poor, rural Somalis to attend institutions of higher learning. The primary beneficiaries of free public higher education, however, were usually the political and social elite. This ultimately led to confrontations with other groups in the nation and to violent political behavior.

CURRENT STATUS OF HIGHER EDUCATION IN SOMALIA

A major devastating impact of the civil war in Somalia was the destruction of the Somali National University (SNU) and other institutions that offered postsecondary education. Before the collapse of the Somali state, SNU enrolled 15,672 students and consisted of twelve faculties: law, economics, agriculture, education, medicine, industrial chemistry, languages, engineering, journalism, geology, veterinary, and political science (Saint 1992; International Association of Universities 1993).

Journalist William Finnegan's description of SNU, especially the former College of Education, in 1995 is telling:

> The low-rise, modern looking building of the former College of Education is now a displaced persons' camp. The classrooms and dormitories were full of families; the walls were blacked by cooking fires . . . the library was a world of dust. Books were piled everywhere, on sagging shelves, on toppling heaps. Some were stained and disintegrating, but most were intact. . . . A cow mooed somewhere. The dust was so deep that it was as though the desert itself was creeping through the walls, burying the books in fine sand. (Finnegan 1995, 76)

Despite this bleak picture, the impact of genuine efforts to rehabilitate many learning centers by Somalis and local and international nongovernmental organizations is amazing. For example, in Somaliland (former British Somaliland), the stable political environment that has prevailed for the past decade has facilitated genuine efforts to rebuild and rehabilitate the majority of the schools.

The question that now faces many educational policymakers in Somalia and Somaliland is how to provide higher education for those who graduate from secondary schools.

Mogadishu University (Somalia)

The proposal to establish an institution of higher learning in Mogadishu, Somalia, dates back to June 1993, when "a group of former professors of the Somali National University and other prominent Somali intellectuals" congregated in Mogadishu to discuss the problems of the now destroyed Somali National University students. The group decided to form the "University of Eastern Africa" in the Southern part of Mogadishu. However civil war spread out in the designated university site and properties were looted. Therefore, the project was halted for security reasons indefinitely (Mogadishu University 2001).

The group met again on July 20, 1995, and on August 9, 1996, it voted to establish "a full-fledged private university." This goal was reached on September 22, 1997, when Mogadishu University (MU) became a recognized private university and opened its doors to Somali students.

The eight objectives of MU include bridging the educational gap, producing educated human resources, developing scientific knowledge, conducting community education programs, training students with better skills, preserving national cultural heritage, promoting social values, and promoting the study of languages.

Since this is the first private university in southern Somalia, and given that there is no functioning government in Mogadishu, MU is administered through two governing bodies: a board of trustees and an academic council. The academic council oversees the day-to-day operation of the university and consists of the president, the vice-president, the deans of the four faculties and the nursing institute, the dean of research and publications, the dean of admissions and student affairs, and the dean of continuing education. The board of trustees consists of seven founding members of the university.

At present, MU's financial support comes from three sources: student tuition, a trust fund, and donations. Due to the civil war in Somalia, the society is very poor and the average family income is very low, especially in the south, where the war has had the greatest impact. Because of these poor living standards, the majority of the student applicants are from low-income families. MU students pay a highly discounted fee of $300–400 per academic year. That covers only a small portion of the university's running costs. The remainder is covered by local public donations and international donor contributions.

MU is in the process of establishing a Higher Education Trust (HET) to create a viable economic base for the university and give the university greater self-sufficiency.

Donations and contributions received from the Somali Diaspora, local NGOs, international organizations, and benevolent personalities are vital for the smooth running of MU. These donations include sponsorship of lecturers, students, and so on. Moreover, in-kind donations of books and equipment have been given by friendly universities and other institutions (Mogadishu University Catalog 2001).

MU currently has four faculties, one nursing institute with a three-year diploma program, a continuing education department, and a public service center. All four faculties offer a four-year undergraduate program. These faculties include the following: Shari`a and law; education; economics and management sciences; and arts and humanities. The medium of instruction for economics and management sciences, and the nursing institute is English. Arabic is the language of instruction for the other three faculties. Students are required to be fluent in both languages as a criterion for admission.

Currently, 318 students are enrolled at MU. Admission to MU is based on a number of criteria, including the passing of written and entrance examinations.

Table 56.1. Length of Programs of Study, by Faculty, at Amoud University, 2000–2001

Faculty	Program of Study
Agriculture and Environmental Sciences	4 years of 2 semesters each
Business and Public Administration	4 years of 2 semesters each
Education	4 years of 2 semesters each
Medicine and Allied Health	6 years of 2 semesters each

CURRENT STATUS OF HIGHER EDUCATION IN THE REPUBLIC OF SOMALILAND

Higher Education in Somaliland consists chiefly of Amoud University (AU) and Hargeisa University (HU). AU is located at the former secondary school campus at Amoud in the Awdal region of Borama (the largest city in Awdal), while HU is located in the capital of the Somaliland Republic, Hargeisa.

Students in the region of Awdal and other regions of Somaliland have never had any access to an institution of higher learning in their own backyard. Students who graduated from the former Amoud Secondary School and other schools in the region had to travel to Mogadishu to undertake higher education. The chair of Borama's Board of Directors articulated the dilemma of higher education in Somaliland well:

All the colleges and faculties of the Somali National University were located in Mogadishu and its vicinities and this obviously provided . . . the students in the capital an opportunity for higher education that was denied to their counterparts in other regions. . . . No attempt was made by the former government to remedy this obvious disparity in higher education between the North and South. . . . It was sad to recall that during this period it was taken for granted that higher education was strictly the privilege of the South and any suggestion of its expansion to the North (Somaliland) was interpreted as a political sin. (Elmi 2000, 2)

Amoud University (Somaliland)

The rebirth of the Republic of Somaliland, and the prolonged peace and prosperity experienced by this young nation, necessitated the establishment of Amoud University (AU) in Somaliland. The civil war not only destroyed the economic and social fabric of the society; it also created a bleak future for thousands of Somaliland's youth, who faced a devastated educational system, a lack of opportunity for higher education, and high unemployment. Hence, some have argued that "Amoud University is perhaps the most powerful tool that could offer a sense of direction to the hopeless and unemployed youth" (Elmi 2000, 2).

At present, there are data correlating educational facilities to pertinent social development needs. There is an urgent need for higher learning to meet these needs and to put education at the service of the people. The Somali Diaspora constitutes a severe brain drain from Somaliland, which is already suffering from shortages in technical and professional expertise. The main justifications given by many Somalilanders for leaving the country is to pursue education, particularly higher education, for their children. A national university at home would therefore help to attract many overseas Somalilanders back home and at the same time retain more who are still here (Elmi 2000, 2).

AU has four undergraduate colleges: the College of Agriculture and Environmental Sciences, the College of Business and Public Administration, the College of Education, and the College of Medicine and Allied Health. In addition, AU has three centers that provide training and workshops for peace and conflict resolution issues, family and gender studies, and research and development. Table 56.1 shows the length of programs of study at AU in 2000–2001.

The College of Agriculturel and Environmental Sciences is one of the major programs at AU. It offers three programs in teaching, research, and community services. The college is administratively organized in eleven academic departments, each of which is directed by a chair. These departments are agricultural economics and extension, agricultural engineering, aquatic wealth development, chemistry and botany, crops and forage, food and dairy technology, home economics (for women), horticulture, plant protection, poultry and animal production, and soils and water (Amoud University 1999–2000).

Agriculture and livestock were two of the hardest-hit sections of the Somaliland economy during the war waged during Siad Barre's era. The College of Agriculture and Environmental Sciences can play a vital role in meeting the urgent development needs of these sectors.

The College of Education is not fully developed into departments of educational administration and does not yet offer a graduate program. Nevertheless, the college's primary objective is to train qualified teachers.

The primary purpose of the College of Business and Public Administration is to support the mission of the university and provide high-quality professional education for a changing world. The college offers programs leading to a bachelor's degree in accounting, marketing, finance, economics, or business administration. Outreach programs responsive to business and community needs are also available. Since its inception, the college has concentrated on the promotion of its undergraduate programs. Currently, plans are being considered for the establishment of a joint master's degree in public administration with various foreign universities.

The primary mission of the College of Medicine and Allied Health is to produce competent physicians while fostering life-long habits of scholarship and service. The college provides a six-year medical curriculum, followed by an internship of at least twelve months, leading to a bachelor's degree in medicine and surgery. In addition, the college is home to twenty-one different fields of study that are designed to provide medical and health education.

Unlike SNU, AU is very autonomous and has a very limited relationship with the Ministry of Higher Education in Somali-land. This administrative structure consists of the Supreme Council, the Scientific Council, the president, three vice-presidents, four deans, three directors, a head librarian, and a head of technological support.

The Supreme Council overseas financial and administrative management, while the president is the chief academic and administrative head of the university and is responsible for its day-to-day operation. Three vice-presidents, one for academic and student affairs, another for planning and registration, and another for external affairs, support the president. At each college level, the dean is the chief academic and administrative head and is responsible to the vice-president for maintaining and promoting efficient management of the college. Within colleges, faculties or centers act to coordinate instruction. Faculties are made up of various departments divided among various academic disciplines. Departments are in charge of teaching, curriculum development, and student evaluation and assessment.

The data on the number of instructional faculty at AU show that there were only twelve faculty members for the academic year 1999–2000. The entire university has only one female faculty member. No data is available on the full-time or part-time status, rank, age, and level of education of AU faculty.

A total of 103 students enrolled in AU in the 1999–2000 academic year, of whom fifteen were female. Based upon comparison with student-to-teacher ratios in higher education in Africa, AU is not fully utilizing its faculty and staff; the present student-to-staff ratios could be defended as a transitional phenomenon. Of AU students, 71 percent are from the Awdal region. AU has had little success in offsetting the disparities in access to the university for potential students who are not from the Awdal region.

UNIVERSITY OF HARGEISA

The University of Hargeisa (UH) was opened on October 23, 2000, by the late president of the Somaliland republic, Mohamed Haji Ibrahim Egal. The university began its first classes on November 1, 2000, and the total number of students was 152. These students were the first freshman class of the 2000–2001 academic year. Due to the war in Somalia, public institutions that include schools in Somaliland region were destroyed, which has resulted in the disruption of the higher education of the youth of Somaliland. Therefore, the newly established University of Hargeisa took the task of creating six-month preparatory classes for students whose education was disrupted (University of Hargeisa 2001).

The primary purposes of UH are to educate the future citizens, train and socialize future workers, and provide appropriate platforms for solving Somaliland's social, political, and economic problems (Gaas 2002).

UH currently has four departments: business administration (11 students), science (21 students), Arabic and Islamic studies (20 students), and continuing education. This enrollment data is for the first classes of 2000; no data is available on current student enrollments or on full-time or part-time faculty status. It is also important to keep in mind that UH is in the early development stages. Three development phases have been planned; the first phase of 1998–2000 was the initial setting-up period. The second phase, 2000–2005, is the first development phase; and the third phase, 2000–2010, is the second development period. In the first development phase, the university seeks to establish ten departments:

- Department of Languages and Communications
- Department of Science and Mathematics
- Department of Medical Science and Public Health
- Arid Land Studies
- Department of Fisheries and Marine Science
- Department of Finance and Banking
- Management and Development Studies
- Department of Law
- Department of Engineering
- Center for Gender and Policy Studies

In the second development phase, the goal of the university is to establish the departments of chemical engineering, geology, social science and religious studies. Apart from offering degree programs, the university aims to offer two-year professional diploma programs (University of Hargeisa 2001).

As of September 2001, the total number of full-time faculty (all of whom are men) at UH was fourteen. No data is available on their salary, rank, age, and educational background. Currently, UH is recruiting more faculty for the expected student enrollment for 2002–2003 (University of Hargeisa 2001).

The library at UH has 15,000 books, most of which were collected by volunteers from North America, the Somaliland community in England, and Book Aid International. There is also a computer lab in the university, which has twenty computers (University of Hargeisa home page 2001).

CONCLUSION

Little attention was paid by the colonial powers to the educational needs of the Somali people. During that time, higher education was viewed as a vehicle to facilitate the colonial administration and to prepare graduates for semiskilled jobs in the colonial economy. However, the colonial powers introduced the seeds of higher education in Somalia, mostly through funding from Italy. After the country gained independence in 1960, the system continued to improve, despite the fact that it was completely subsidized by the government.

During the last forty years, institutions of higher learning in Somalia/Somaliland have failed to meet the demands of the nation's skilled labor force. In particular, they have not generated enough qualified secondary teachers, principals, policy researchers, economists, and higher education planners. Among the core problems of higher education in Somalia/Somaliland are the following:

- The multiplicity of languages being used simultaneously in the different levels of education has resulted in confusion and a breakdown of coordination among different levels of education. Unless this issue is resolved, higher education students will be at a great disadvantage and their potential for achievement will be seriously undermined (Yahya 1984, 118).
- Somali-language instructional materials were hastily created during the period of rapid educational expansion in the 1970s. This led to a lack of systematic design, production, and distribution of instructional materials, which required a heavy investment of resources that never came from the education ministry (World Bank 1985).
- The nation's curriculum, which has emphasized arts and humanities, has failed to meet the nation's scientific and technological needs.
- The output of higher education does not meet the demands of the labor market (a major problem faced by many third world countries).
- Problems of equity for women, as well as for rural students, exist. Although more women enrolled in higher education in Somalia at the time of the civil war, women continue to face discrimination. According to statistics from UNESCO, of the 15,672 students enrolled in Somali higher education in 1983, only 3,093 (a mere 19.7 percent) were female (UNESCO 1991).
- One-third of all primary school teachers in Somalia/Somaliland were unqualified or had no training at all in preparation for the tasks to which they were assigned (IEES 1985).
- Somali society cannot afford not to invest in education. The effect of nearly twenty-two years of neglect is very evident today in Somalia, where the level of violence and criminal behavior among Somali youth is related to poverty of both mind and opportunity. All studies show that there is a strong correlation between low educational investment and crime. As family incomes increase, there is a corresponding decrease in the rate of delinquency (Doughtery and Hammack 1990).
- Education administration in Somali higher education has been marked by the lack of coordination between institutions and their administrating agencies. One proposal for the future is to decentralize the entire system to discourage the dependent relationship that has long existed between Somali universities and the national government (Bullaleh 1993).
- Somali higher education suffers from a lack of data collection relevant to the educational needs of the country. In fact, David Chapman notes that "one of the most perplexing problems facing educational planners in Somalia is securing relevant, timely, and accurate data on which to base their policy deliberations" (Chapman 1990, 269).
- In the view of many experts, one of the most critical problems in the Somalia/Somaliland higher education system is the lack of adequately trained personnel (IEES 1984, 1985, 1989; World Bank 1985; Mubarak 1996).
- Brain drain has been devastating to higher education and re-

search in Somalia/Somaliland. As a result of the civil war, poor training and facilities, high centralization of power, limited job and promotional opportunities, decades of poorly designed structural programs, poor working conditions, and decades of abuse by the former dictator of Somalia (Siad Barre), the finest and brightest minds in the fields of sciences, higher education, law, engineering, architecture, medicine, educational management and planning, business and public administration, political science, and history have moved abroad, leaving behind an already debilitated system of higher education.

The universities of Amoud, Mogadishu, and Hargeisa have serious difficulties in recruiting and retaining Somali faculty members. The continuous economic hardship faced by Somalia/Somaliland is manifested in an unattractive reward system in the universities. The salaries of professors are so discouraging that it is very difficult to recruit new personnel. The few dedicated and committed faculty who have decided to confront these challenges are faced with a dilemma of whether to pay total attention to instruction and research or divide their attention between teaching and some other private money-generating endeavor that will help them sustain themselves and their families. Hence, higher education in Somalia/Somaliland is bound to continuously face a downward spiral until the nation's political economy is overhauled (Carrington and Detragiache 1999).

BIBLIOGRAPHY

Abdulla, A. D. 1992. "Somalia's Reconstruction: An Opportunity to Create a Responsive Information Infrastructure." *International Information Library Review* 28: 39–57.

Abdullahi, A. 1992. "Tribalism, Nationalism and Islam: The Crisis of Political Loyalty in Somalia." Master's Thesis, McGill University.

Adam, H. 1980. "Somali Policies toward Education: Training and Manpower." In T. L. Maliyamkona, ed., *Policy Developments in Overseas Training.* Dar Es Salam, Tanzania: Black Star Agencies.

———. 1993. *Somalia: A Country Study.* Edited by Helen Chapin Metz. Washington, D.C.: Federal Research Division, Library of Congress. Available online at: http://memory.loc.gov/frd/cs/sotoc.html

Ahmed, I. 1999. "Understanding Somali Conflict in Somalia and Somaliland." In Adebayo Adedeji, ed., *Comprehending and Mastering African Conflicts: The Search for Sustainable Peace and Good Governance.* London and New York: Zed Books.

Africa Watch. 1990. *A Government at War with Its Own People.* New York and London: Africa Watch.

Amoud University. 1999–2000. Amoud University Web site. Available online at http://www.amoud-university.borama.ac.so

Bullaleh, M. 1993. "What Should Be Done for Post-Donor Secondary Education and Donor Programs in Somalia?" Paper presented at Symposium on Somalia and Education, University at Albany, State University of New York.

Carrington, W. J., and E. Detragiache. 1999. "How Extensive Is the Brain Drain?" *Finance and Development,* June 6, p. 36.

Castagno, A. 1959. *Somalia.* New York: Carnegie Endowment for International Peace.

Chapman, D. 1990. "Education Data Flow in Somalia." *International Journal of Educational Development* 10, no. 4: 269–289.

Dawson, G. A. 1964. "Education in Somalia." *Comparative Education Review* no. 10 (October): 199–214.

Doughtery, K. J., and F. M. Hammack. 1990. *Education and Society: A Reader*. New York: Harcourt Brace Jovanovich.

Elmi, H. J. U. 2000. "A Breakthrough for Education in Somaliland: Amoud University." Available online at: http://fibonacci.dm.unipi.it/~jama/education/sl_edu_rf.html

Finnegan, W. 1995. "Letter from Mogadishu." *The New Yorker*, March 20, pp. 64–77.

Gaas, A. 2002. Interview with author, May 16, New Jersey. Mr. Gaas is a senior member of Somaliland Forum Group.

Hess, R. 1966. *Italian Colonialism in Somalia*. Chicago: University of Chicago Press.

IEES (Improving the Efficiency of Educational Systems). 1984. *Somalia: Education and Human Resources Sector Assessment*. Tallahassee: Florida State University, Educational Efficiency Clearing House.

———. 1985. *Somali Management Training and Development Project: Design Paper*. Tallahassee: Florida State University, Educational Efficiency Clearing House.

———. 1989. *Somalia: Education Management Information Systems. Final Report*. Tallahassee: Florida State University, Educational Efficiency Clearing House.

International Association of Universities. 1993. *International Handbook of Universities*. 13th ed. Paris: International Association of Universities.

Kitchen, H. 1962. *The Educated African*. New York: Praeger.

Lewis, I. M 1988. *Modern History of Somalia: Nation and State in the Horn of Africa*. Boulder, Colo.: Westview Press.

———. 1994. *Blood and Bone: The Call of Kinship in Somali Society*. Lawrenceville, N.J.: Red Sea Press.

Mebrahtu, T. 1992. "Somalia: National Systems of Higher Education." In Burton R. Clark and Guy R. Neave, eds., *The Encyclopedia of Higher Education*, 1: 630–635. New York: Pergamon.

Metz, H. C. 1993. *Somalia: A Country Study*. Washington, D.C.: Federal Research Division, Library of Congress.

Mogadishu University. 2001. Mogadishu University Web site.

Mubarak, J. A. 1996. *From Bad Policy to Chaos: How an Economy Fell Apart*. Westport, Conn.: Praeger.

Nelson, H. D., ed. 1982. *Somalia—A Country Study*. Foreign Area Studies, American University. Washington, D.C: U.S. Government Printing Office.

Saint, W. 1992. *Universities in Africa: Strategies for Stabilization and Revitalization*. Washington, D.C.: The World Bank.

Samoff, J. 1993. "The Reconstruction of Education in Africa." *Comparative Education Review* 37, no. 2: 182–222.

UNESCO. 1991. *Statistical Yearbook, 1990–1991*. Paris: UNESCO.

University of Hargeisa. 2000. University of Hargeisa Web site. Available online at: http://www.universityofhargeisa.org/

World Bank. 1985. *Somalia: Education Sector*. Washington, D.C.: World Bank.

———. 1988a. *Education in Sub-Saharan Africa: Polices of Adjustment, Revitalization, and Expansion*. Washington, D.C.: World Bank.

———. 1988b. *World Bank Annual Report, 1988*. Washington, D.C.: The World Bank.

Yahya, M. M. 1984. "Management Education and Training in Somalia: The Case of the Somali Institute of Development Administration and Management (SIDAM)." Ph.D. diss., University of California at Los Angeles.

57

South Africa

GEORGE SUBOTZKY

INTRODUCTION

The unique and defining characteristic of the current higher education system in South Africa is the fundamental restructuring now being undertaken as part of the reconstruction of post-apartheid society. The scale and scope of this transformation is unrivaled on the African continent and, arguably, in the world.

Following the dramatic political transformation that culminated in the first democratic elections in 1994, numerous post-apartheid public policies were formulated by the new government. As part of this, a macro-policy framework for the transformation of higher education was developed. Fundamental reconstruction of higher education is necessary because of its various deficiencies and inequalities, the legacy of apartheid. Within the current system, education and training are fragmented and a rigid divide exists between universities and polytechnics (technikons). Enrollments are distorted, and the system fails to provide the required range, number, and quality of graduates needed to drive national development. Above all, the system is characterized by severe race, gender, and institutional inequalities inherited from the apartheid era.

Throughout this chapter, reference is made to "race" and to the African, Colored ("mixed-race"), Indian, and white groups. In the struggle for equity in South Africa, it is necessary to collect and analyze data in these categories in order to identify previous inequities and to monitor progress toward reducing them. In no way does this lend credence to the practice of discriminatory racial classification. I use the collective term "black" to include Africans, Coloreds, and Indians.

Following various reports and legislation (detailed below), the broad policy framework for higher education transformation was put in place in early 1998. The challenge of the current period is to build the required capacities to successfully implement these changes within the constraints and opportunities of prevailing national and global political and economic conditions.

This policy framework and the process of its implementation have been shaped by two key factors. First, South Africa's democratic transformation and its simultaneous acceptance in the international arena occurred during the period of intensifying globalization that characterized the 1990s. Driven by the need to engage in the new global economy, and perhaps by the fear of economic isolation, the new government's macroeconomic choices have been surprisingly moderate, especially given the radical tenor of the anti-apartheid struggle. In the attempt to create conditions conducive to foreign direct investment and global competitiveness, post-apartheid governments have, through self-imposed structural adjustments, voluntarily conformed with the prescriptions of neoliberal orthodoxy, including fiscal constraint, budget deficit reduction, trade liberalization, and privatization. The historical coincidence of South Africa achieving democracy and its reentry into the globalizing world order, together with the emergence of the new government's macroeconomic path, had a direct impact on higher education—particularly through restrained fiscal allocations and the adoption of globalized market discourse and practices.

Second, South Africa is a middle-income developing country with a complex and polarized social structure. The disparity between its rich and poor is among the widest in the world. Its population of approximately 44 million is comprised of 70 percent Africans, 16 percent whites, 10 percent Coloreds, and 4 percent Indians. Approximately 34 percent of the population is under 15 years old. The gross domestic product (GDP) per capita in 1998 was about $2,900. The economy still relies heavily on the export of raw materials; gold is the country's largest national foreign exchange earner, followed by coal. The overall literacy rate is 76 percent; around 7.6 million (36 percent) of the population over the age of 20 have fewer than seven years of formal schooling. Just over half (54 percent) of the population is urbanized. South Africa has one of the highest HIV/AIDS infection rates in the world. As a result, life expectancy has plummeted in recent years from 65 to 56.

Hidden within these aggregate statistics are sharp race, gender, class, and geographic disparities. The urban and white population is disproportionately wealthier, has access to better social services, is better educated and skilled, and therefore enjoys higher employment than the Indian, Colored, and African population groups. The rural, mainly African population, particularly women in these regions, are the most impoverished. While the official unemployment rate is around 35 percent, it rises to 50 percent or 60 percent among Africans in some areas. The formal nonagricultural unemployment rate has increased since 1994, from an average annual rate of 1.3 percent between 1989 and 1993 to 1.6 percent from 1994 to 1998.

Given this sharp socioeconomic duality, the nation's development priorities are twofold. On the one hand, South Africa is seeking to become more globally competitive and innovative, exploiting its relatively sophisticated level of development, human resources, and infrastructure. On the other hand, it must address the basic needs of the majority poor who, despite having won political freedom, continue to have inadequate access to housing, water, sanitation, electricity, and basic social services. These priorities are reflected in recently formulated higher education policy goals. Institutions are charged with the task of supporting the nation's greater competitive engagement in the new high-tech global information economy through appropriately trained graduates and relevant knowledge production. They are also expected to contribute to the reconstruction and development of South African society in the interests of the majority poor. Simultaneously, institutions are challenged to face the multiple impacts of the globalization and internationalization of higher education, the rise of new information technologies, and the rapid privatization of the sector.

It is against the backdrop of these complex and interrelated changes in the global and national environment that the large-scale fundamental reconstruction of higher education in South Africa is unfolding. This makes the South African case particularly interesting and informative.

HISTORICAL OVERVIEW OF HIGHER EDUCATION IN SOUTH AFRICA

The history of South Africa has been characterized by particularly intense political conflict and sociocultural divisions along race and class lines. Not surprisingly, therefore, its higher education system has been shaped directly by the changing balance of forces in society and politics in successive historical periods. The initial character of the system was forged by the country's colonial history and the underlying conflict between British and Afrikaner nationalism. Successive phases of economic development and capitalist industrialization further shaped the higher education system by generating the specific labor market and the research of the main mining and manufacturing industries. The system was, of course, also definitively molded into sharply stratified race and class divisions through the repressive social engineering mechanisms that defined the

notorious policies of segregation and apartheid. Today, it is being fundamentally reshaped by the post-apartheid transformation of South African society.

Unlike most other colonized African nations, the unusual proliferation of thirty-six higher education institutions among a relatively underpopulated nation was the result of two aspects of South Africa's history. First, the intense rivalry between the two dominant political and cultural groups—the British colonists and Boer Afrikaners—worked against the establishment of a single national university and spawned a multiplicity of historically white universities (HWUs). Second, apartheid racial ideology later generated more HWUs as well as ten historically black universities (HBUs) and fifteen technikons (of which seven were historically white, seven historically black, and one a distance education technikon).

THE DEVELOPMENT OF THE HISTORICALLY WHITE UNIVERSITIES

The initial provision of higher education in South Africa was based on the British colonial model, in which public examinations were set for the selection of candidates for the British home and colonial civil services. For this purpose, a Board of Examiners of Candidates for Government Service was established in the Cape Colony in the 1850s. In 1873, the self-governing Cape colonial government followed the University of London model by establishing the University of the Cape of Good Hope (UCGH) as a purely external examining and degree-granting institution. The UCGH examined and certificated candidates from a number of university colleges that had emerged in the colonial centers of Cape Town and surrounding towns, including Grahamstown and Durban, as well as in the Boer republic capitals of Pretoria and Bloemfontein in the Transvaal and Orange Free State republics, respectively.

Prior to the Anglo-Boer War at the turn of the century, the two Boer republics sought to offset the British- and English-language-dominated UCGH by establishing links with Dutch universities to prepare candidates for entry into that system. In 1899, the attempt to combine the two Boer republic colleges into an Afrikaans-language "University of the North" was scuttled by defeat in the war.

In 1900, the University of London was expanded to become a teaching institution, and many of its constituent colleges were transformed into independent universities. This prompted furious debates, commissions, and draft bills in South Africa to examine the "university question." This discussion became especially urgent after the establishment of the Union of South Africa in 1910. Prior to World War I, a commission proposed two federal structures: the "University of the South," combining the UCGH and the southern university colleges and based on a new residential campus on the present site of the University of Cape Town; and the "University of the North," combining university colleges in the Transvaal, Natal, and Orange Free State. The University College of Rhodes was to select which structure it wanted to join, and the South African School of Mines and Technology (established in Johannesburg in 1903) was to become a faculty of technology jointly affiliated with both federal universities.

The fate of these proposals and the subsequent character of South African higher education was shaped by the ongoing sharp political and cultural tensions between British and Afrikaans nationalists. The outbreak of World War I thwarted these recommendations and provided the opportunity for the Afrikaans-speaking university college at Stellenbosch, a center of strong Afrikaner nationalist sentiment, to resist this plan and to raise sufficient donor funding to establish itself as an independent university. After much clandestine negotiation, the University Act of 1916 established three independent universities: the University of Cape Town, the University of Stellenbosch, and the University of South Africa (UNISA), based in Pretoria, which superseded UCGH as the national external examining body and to which all the other university colleges were affiliated.

This triggered a series of similar developments. The South African School of Mines and Technology in Johannesburg was granted university status in 1923 and became the University of the Witwatersrand. In 1930, Transvaal University College followed suit to become the University of Pretoria. As a result of the collapse of the federal system, UNISA was restructured and became a distance education institution in 1946. In the post–World War II period, two more English-language institutions were established: the University of Natal in 1949 (to which a black medical school, originally intended exclusively for Indians, was attached) and Rhodes University in 1951. The period of expansion of HWUs was completed in the 1950s and 1960s by the apartheid government with the establishment of Afrikaans-language institutions: the University of the Orange Free State in Bloemfontein in 1950, Potchefstroom University in the western Transvaal in 1951, the dual Afrikaans- and English-language-medium University of Port Elizabeth in the Eastern Cape in 1964, and the Rand Afrikaans University in Johannesburg in 1967, which was intended to provide Afrikaans university graduates access to the nation's industrial and financial heartland.

THE EMERGENCE OF THE HISTORICALLY BLACK UNIVERSITIES

When apartheid was formally entrenched in legislation after the National Party came to power in 1948, South Africa's dual social structure was replicated in a racially determined university system. According to apartheid, different institutions were established to accommodate each race and ethnic group. A highly unequal set of functionally differentiated institutions emerged in which the HBUs were fundamentally disadvantaged in a number of crucial ways.

It is important to note that higher education had already been largely segregated prior to 1948. Until 1916, UCGH was overwhelmingly dominated by white male staff and students, as were the university colleges. Black and women students who were not enrolled in the colleges were allowed to sit for its external examinations. Higher education was first provided for women in the Huguenot teacher training college in the Western Cape town of Wellington.

The unification of South Africa in 1910 prompted the establishment of the South African Native College (later the University of Fort Hare) for Africans in 1915. This institution was formed out of the missionary-based Lovedale Institute for teacher training in the small Eastern Cape village of Alice. Although its candidates were presented for external examination by UNISA, the Native College was never allowed to become a formal affiliate. With the demise of the federal system and the restructuring of UNISA immediately after World War II, Fort Hare College was affiliated to Rhodes University in 1951 when Rhodes achieved university status.

The shape and character of the higher education system after 1950 was directly determined by apartheid policies, which aimed at the political and economic domination of the African population through the separate development of homelands, or Bantustan. As part of this, Bantu education for blacks was centrally planned to meet the white minority's interpretation of the "needs" of the majority black population and the "development" priorities of the Bantustan, which never historically transpired. The unambiguous intention of apartheid education policy was to ensure the rigid maintenance and reproduction of the racially divided social and occupational structure by preparing blacks for a subordinate and geographically isolated role in society. These goals clearly expressed, as early as 1954, the notorious formulations of the Minister of Native Affairs H. F. Verwoerd, a chief intellectual architect of apartheid:

> Deliberate attempts will be made to keep the institutions for advanced education [for Africans] away from the urban environment and to establish them as far as possible in the Native reserves. . . . The Bantu must be guided to serve his own community in all respects. . . . There is no place for him in the European [i.e., white] community above the level of certain forms of labor. Within his own community, however, all doors are open. . . . Until now he has been subjected to [the missionary-based] school system which drew him away from his own community and misled him by showing him the green pastures of European society in which he was not allowed to graze. (Quoted in Christie and Collins 1984, 173)

Within this harsh discriminatory policy, the HBUs developed in two distinct phases. The first followed the 1959 Extension of Universities Act, which restricted access of black students to white universities and provided for the establishment of higher education institutions—initially "tribal" colleges and later full universities—for each "ethnic" and "cultural" group within the black population. The establishment of the first HBUs served a dual purpose: first, to enable their administrative functioning and economic development by providing personnel for the emerging Bantustan bureaucracies and, second, to ensure that the emerging black middle class would be coopted into and collaborate with the homelands project.

During 1960 and 1961, two new rural and two new urban HBUs were founded. The University of the North was built at Turfloop in a rural area approximately 200 miles north of Johannesburg for the Sotho, Venda, and Tsonga ethnic groups, and the University of Zululand, approximately 125 miles north of Durban, was built for the Zulu and Swazi groups. The urban universities were the University of Durban–Westville in the environs of Durban for Indians and the University of the Western Cape in Cape Town's township areas for Coloreds. The Fort Hare Transfer Act of 1959 ensured that its admissions were henceforth restricted to Xhosa people, thus coercing this institution into the newly established apartheid HBU mold. Many African leaders (including Nelson Mandela, Oliver Tambo, and Robert Mugabe) and members of the African intelligentsia were graduates of Fort Hare, but the vitality of its tradition was eroded by the repressive measures used to control the HBUs.

The second phase of the establishment of HBUs occurred in response to changing historical conditions and the development of contradictions within the grand scheme of apartheid. These included

> the "organic" (simultaneously economic, political and ideological) crisis of the white ruling bloc, skilled labor shortages, the re-emergence of mass popular anti-apartheid organization and struggle, contradictions, conflicts and political fissures within the white community, a process of repressive reformism entailing an acceptance by the state of the permanence of an urban African population in the "white" areas, the legislation of black trade unions and erosion of job reservation, and so forth. (Badat et al. 1994, 12)

As part of this second phase, three homeland universities were established and funded indirectly by the apartheid government. These were the University of Transkei (1977) and the University of Bophuthatswana (1980, recently renamed the University of the North West), both in small rural "independent" homelands towns, and the University of Venda (1982) in a small town in the far north, rural, "self-governing" Venda homeland. In addition, the University of Qwa Qwa, a branch campus of the University of the North, was established in 1982 about 400 miles to its south in the rural "self-governing" Qwa Qwa homeland. These new homeland universities functioned principally as showpiece symbols of nationhood in the nominally independent states, alongside "international" airports, "independence" stadiums, and government and parliamentary complexes in the newly constructed "capitals." Their academic function was to provide university-trained personnel for the homelands' civil service and for the small emerging black middle class. Despite having more senior African academic and administrative staff from the outset, and despite enjoying a window of opportunity to oppose apartheid until the mid-1980s, they were indirectly but tightly controlled by the apartheid government through the surrogate homeland authorities, who often exercised particularly harsh authoritarian measures to ensure compliance with their interests and policies. The new homelands institutions were later complemented by the University of Fort Hare, which became part of the Ciskei homeland when it gained its nominal independence in the 1980s.

The development of the HBUs under apartheid was concluded with the establishment of two other special-purpose institutions, namely the Medical University of Southern Africa (MEDUNSA) in 1978 and Vista University in 1982, a multicampus mixed residential and distance education institution intended to provide government-controlled higher education for urban blacks, with the ideological intention of diverting energies away from the culture of resistance among township youth. With the establishment of these institutions, then, the ten HWUs were supplemented by eleven HBUs, constituting the twenty-one universities in the South African higher education system.

THE ESTABLISHMENT OF THE TECHNIKONS

Apartheid higher educational policy was characterized by the fragmentation of academic education and vocational training. This generated a rigid institutional divide between universities and technikons and obstacles to mobility and access. These divides were in keeping with the race and class stratification of social and occupational structures under apartheid.

Technical training in South Africa evolved in two stages; first, parallel to South Africa's industrial capitalist development in the decade after World War I and, second, parallel to the growth of more advanced industry in the later post–World War II period (Cooper and Subotzky 2001, 6ff.). After union in 1910, advanced technical training was absorbed into the engineering faculties of the universities and university colleges, while less-advanced-level training was provided by a system of 120 technical colleges.

Following World War II–era industrial expansion, technical colleges in the large urban centers developed their tertiary programs in engineering fields on the cutting edge of new technology, such as radio systems and mining equipment. As a result, four polytechnic-type Colleges of Advanced Technical Education (CATEs) were established in 1967, offering a three-year national diploma as their core qualification. In 1979, they were renamed "technikons": Cape Technikon in Cape Town, Natal Technikon in Durban, Technikon Pretoria, and Witwatersrand Technikon in Johannesburg. These were supplemented in the early 1980s by three additional CATEs: Vaal Triangle Technikon at Vanderbijlpark, south of Johannesburg, which focused on training technicians for the region's heavy-steel-related industry; Port Elizabeth Technikon; and Free State Technikon in Bloemfontein. In addition, Technikon South Africa was transformed from the external studies department of Witwatersrand Technikon in 1980 into a distance learning technikon.

As part of separate development, these seven historically white technikons (HWTs) were complemented by seven historically black counterparts. Among these were M. L. Sultan Technikon in Durban for Indians (which began as a technical provider in the 1920s and became a CATE in 1969) and Peninsula Technikon in Cape Town (which also originated in the 1920s and became a CATE in 1972). Five African historically black technikons (HBTs) were founded in the African rural areas in the late 1970s. These were Mangosuthu Technikon, just outside Durban in 1979; Technikon Northern Transvaal (now renamed Northern Gauteng Technikon), just north of Pretoria in 1980; and the three others associated directly with the "independent" homelands: Setlogelo Technikon (renamed North West Technikon), just inside the border of the Bophuthatswana homeland and a few kilometers outside Pretoria, in 1976; Transkei Technikon (renamed Eastern Cape Technikon), in the small Eastern Cape town of Butterworth, in 1987; and Ciskei Technikon (renamed Border Technikon), near Bisho, the Ciskei "capital," in 1988.

In addition, a number of single-purpose nursing, teacher

training, and agricultural colleges emerged. Provision was made in the government's White Paper on higher education transformation (DOE 1997a) and the Higher Education Act of 1997 (DOE 1997b) for the phased incorporation of these colleges into the higher education sector, beginning with the colleges of education, which have now been linked to particular higher education institutions.

The Current Higher Education Institutional Landscape

Between 1916, when the universities of Cape Town, Stellenbosch, and UNISA were established, and the late 1980s, with the founding of the last of the apartheid "homeland" technikons, a system of thirty-six higher education institutions evolved, consisting of twenty-one universities and fifteen technikons with approximately 550,000 students.

South Africa's highly variegated institutional landscape is characterized by diverse institutional cultures and student and staff profiles that have been shaped by the historical, political, and structural conditions surrounding their establishment. Under apartheid, functional differentiation meant disadvantage and inequality. Although current official policy aims to redress this inequity, the present system is still sharply differentiated in terms of historically advantaged white institutions and their historically disadvantaged black counterparts.

The function of both HWUs and HBUs was to maintain and reproduce the divided social order. The origins of HBUs in apartheid and their assigned differentiated functions have ongoing consequences. First, despite internal differences among them, they assumed a distinctive character as undergraduate teaching institutions. Second, they sustained multiple disadvantages relative to HWUs (EPU 1997, 52ff.). HBUs offer a narrow range of mainly humanities and social science programs in teaching-related fields of study at the lower qualification levels.

A rapid rise in admissions at HBUs of mainly disadvantaged students in the mid-1980s strained resources and led in many cases to unmanageable teaching loads, extra demands on faculty through formal and informal academic support activities, and lower research outputs. Faculty at HBUs are generally less well qualified and junior, are often isolated from academic networks, use outdated teaching practices, and, in many cases, are demoralized by these detrimental conditions. The isolated geographic location of these institutions is a great disadvantage in efforts to support academic life and to attract and retain high-quality staff and students. Distance from centers of government, private-sector, and NGO operations obstructs efforts to win contracts and undertake consultancies and collaborative projects. HBUs have been subject to discriminatory allocation of resources, resulting in their diminished capacity to attract substantial state subsidies or funding from alternative sources. As a result of this, as well as managerial and organizational problems, facilities, infrastructure, and administrative capacity are relatively poor and, in the case of some libraries, hopelessly inadequate.

Despite these multiple disadvantages, pockets of strength and concentrations of research and postgraduate excellence were developed in some HBUs. This was particularly evident in community development–oriented teaching and research programs that reflected the close historical and geographic links of HBUs to disadvantaged communities as well as their commitment to equity. In these cases, the disadvantage of their localities was turned into comparative advantage in that their close proximity to developing communities presented relevant teaching, research, and outreach opportunities. This constitutes a strategic opportunity for the HBUs to identify and develop niche areas.

Beyond these broad commonalities, significant variations exist within and between HBUs. These arise principally from locality, the socioeconomic and political background of their constituencies, differing relationships with the homelands and central government, and the different historical phases of their establishment. Accordingly, the ten HBUs can be clustered into the following three groupings:

- The six historically African rural universities: North West, Fort Hare, University of the North (and its branch at Qwa Qwa), Transkei, Venda, and Zululand. These institutions conform most closely to the general profile of HBUs as described above. Fort Hare can be distinguished by its unique origins, its long history and tradition as the oldest HBU, and its role in graduating numerous African scholars and leaders.
- The two historically non-African urban universities: Durban-Westville and the Western Cape. Their urban location and relatively advantaged Indian and Colored constituencies provided these institutions with significant comparative advantages. This resulted in a wider range of program offerings and research activities (especially at the graduate level) and more centers of excellence.
- The two special-purpose universities: MEDUNSA and Vista University.

Among the eleven HWUs, the main differentiating feature is their political and cultural character, which was expressed, for historical reasons, along language lines. The following can be distinguished:

- The four English liberal universities: Cape Town, Natal, Rhodes, and Witwatersrand, which offered resistance to apartheid but also contributed to the maintenance and reproduction of the divided social order.
- The six Afrikaans institutions: Free State, Port Elizabeth, Potchefstroom, Pretoria, Rand Afrikaans, and Stellenbosch, which were historically generally more conservative and supportive of apartheid, often working collaboratively with the regime.
- The distance education university: the University of South Africa (UNISA).

Similar disparities exist between the historically advantaged and disadvantaged technikons as those in the universities. However, the distinction between the white technikons with regard to language is not significant; these institutions were younger creations of apartheid and were thus staffed mostly by Afrikaans-speaking whites. The fifteen technikons can therefore be grouped as follows:

- The seven HBTs: Border, Eastern Cape, M. L. Sultan, Mangosuthu, North West, Northern Gauteng, and Peninsula.

- The seven HWTs: Cape, Free State, Natal, Port Elizabeth, Pretoria, Vaal Triangle, and Witwatersrand.
- The distance education technikon: Technikon South Africa.

During the 1980s and 1990s, as the struggle against apartheid intensified and finally succeeded, a series of new social forces and policy conditions prevailed, further shaping higher education in South Africa. In light of recent changes, particularly the rapid Africanization of student enrollments at HWUs and different institutional responses to the changing policy and planning environment, the historical categories described above are no longer entirely valid, and a new set of categories can be defined (see Cloete and Bunting 2000 and the CHE 1999).

CURRENT POLICY DEVELOPMENTS, DEBATES, AND CHALLENGES

The recent history of higher education policy development in South Africa can be divided into two distinct phases: first, the negotiation period preceding the 1994 elections; and, second, the period under the new African National Congress (ANC) government. This second period can be further divided into the period of initial focus on macro-policy formation, during which the policy and regulatory framework for the systemic reconstruction of higher education had been elaborated by 1997, and the subsequent current policy period of implementing this framework within prevailing global and macroeconomic conditions.

The first phase was marked by the watershed legalization of the ANC and other liberation movements in 1990, followed by the release of Nelson Mandela and other political prisoners. This ushered in the era of political negotiations about transitional arrangements for the 1994 elections. Simultaneously, multilateral and bilateral donor agencies and foundations, as well as higher education organizations and institutions, ended the economic and academic boycott of South Africa. A series of policy studies were undertaken to provide the first systematic quantification of the inequities, fragmentation, and dysfunctionality of the apartheid-era system. The National Education Policy Initiative, a two-year research process, produced a series of policy options for all levels of education, including postsecondary. Following this, the ANC's Education and Training Policy and Planning Framework formed the party's education platform. Subsequently, an Implementation Plan for Education and Training provided the new education minister with an immediate plan of action.

THE NEW POLICY FRAMEWORK FOR TRANSFORMATION

The immediate priorities in the post-1994 phase were the establishment of the National Commission on Higher Education (NCHE) and the subsequent creation and staffing of a new higher education branch within the national Department of Education (DOE). The NCHE comprehensively investigated a new policy framework for the systemic transformation of higher education, with the notable exception of curriculum issues. It produced a Discussion Document in April 1996 which, after fairly wide consultation and contestation among stakeholder groups, was followed in late 1996 by a final report, "A Framework for Transformation" (NCHE 1996). Against the backdrop of South Africa's transition to democracy, and drawing from an updated account of systemic inequalities and inefficiencies, the NCHE report set out a new vision for higher education in South Africa. It also identified principles and goals for its transformation.

The NCHE report was followed during 1997 by the Department of Education's Green Paper on higher education, and subsequently by three drafts of a White Paper titled *A Program for the Transformation of Higher Education*. This was accompanied by a draft Higher Education Bill, which was enacted in 1998. Despite some differences in emphasis within these various documents, particularly around governance structures, three related equity and development policy imperatives lie at the heart of the transformation agenda contained in the White Paper and the Higher Education Act.

- To redress institutional inequalities by transforming higher education so that it is more socially equitable internally and promotes social equity more generally
- To meet the development needs of a democratic South Africa as expressed in the Reconstruction and Development Program of 1994, which is committed to meeting the basic needs of the people, developing human resources in a people-centered way, building the economy, and democratizing society
- In the light of globalization and the increasing importance of knowledge and information in economic development, to produce, through appropriate research and teacher education programs, the required knowledge and labor power to enable the country to engage beneficially in the competitive global economy

Together, the White Paper and the Higher Education Act provide the framework for higher education transformation in South Africa. The White Paper identifies the following policy goals:

- Integrating, planning, and coordinating a single national system that is funded on a program basis
- Simultaneously meeting labor market needs and advancing social equity through increased and broadened participation in higher education
- Creating cooperative governance between government and institutions and within institutions, the latter involving the democratization of governance structures, including the establishment of statutory institutional forums representing all stakeholders
- Responding to the needs and interests of South Africa through relevant curriculum restructuring and knowledge production
- Assuring quality through the assessment and promotion of accreditation of high-quality programs
- Promoting articulation, mobility, and transferability within the system by incorporating higher education qualifications and programs within the National Qualifications Framework
- Meeting national development priorities more effectively
- Creating greater efficiency in the light of fiscal constraint through a coordinated national and institutional three-year rolling planning process that is linked to a revised goal-oriented state funding formula

Despite a strong emphasis on a single coordinated system in response to previous fragmentation and distortions, the new policy framework embraces diversified institutional missions, functions, programs, and curricula. These qualifications, structures, modes of delivery, and organizational forms are needed to meet social and equity goals. In the post-apartheid context, however, diversification must be distinguished from the apartheid practice of racially based differentiation and disadvantage.

With this broad policy framework in place, the challenge now lies in implementation. The key to this is overcoming the severe lack of capacity at both the institutional level and in government. The current higher education environment presents institutional leaders and managers with an enormous array of management challenges. It has long been recognized that capacity to undertake such strategic management and planning processes is severely limited, particularly in the historically disadvantaged institutions. This is compounded by administrative capacity problems and, in several instances, by crises in leadership and blatant mismanagement.

Two noteworthy features of the process of macro-policy formation were the strong formative role played by invited foreign consultants and the rather uncritical fashion in which international policy models were adopted in policy discourse and practice.

THE HIGHER EDUCATION BRANCH OF THE
DEPARTMENT OF EDUCATION AND ITS PRIORITIES

The detailed process of policy formulation and implementation has been carried out by the Higher Education Branch (HEB) of the DOE. Established in late 1996, its overall purpose is to plan, coordinate, monitor, and manage the higher education system. Staffed by a complement of just thirty, the branch acknowledges that it has limited capacity to fulfill these functions.

The initial priorities of the HEB involved advancing macro-policy formulation beyond the NCHE report through the drafting of the Green and White Papers on higher education and the Higher Education Act. Since then, it has managed the progressive implementation of the policy framework established in these documents (see Ministry of Education 1999).

NATIONAL AND INSTITUTIONAL
PLANNING FRAMEWORK

As indicated, at the heart of both the NCHE and the White Paper proposals is a program-based national and institutional three-year rolling planning process by which system reconfiguration that is linked to goal-oriented funding and quality assurance is effected. These plans require institutional statements of mission and vision, enrollment targets in various relevant fields of studies and qualifications levels, and a series of plans for staff and student equity and development, quality improvement, research development, and infrastructure development.

The first preparatory phase of the three-year rolling plans was initiated in mid-1998, covering the period 1999–2002. System-wide information gathering and the development of a comprehensive higher education management information system began at the same time. The DOE's report on this first phase identified variances between projected and actual institutional enrollments for 1999, particularly among the HBUs, where estimates were significantly higher than actual subsequent enrollments. It also revealed a "serious lack of sophisticated planning methodology and instruments" (DOE 2000, 83). Few institutions showed evidence of utilizing statistical modeling and detailed analysis of institutional, regional, and national trends. This highlights the urgent necessity of building planning capacity. It is envisaged that the three-year planning process will be fully implemented and linked to the new funding formula by 2003.

PRIVATE HIGHER EDUCATION

A noteworthy recent development in South African higher education has been the very rapid growth of the private sector. A rapid proliferation of both local and international providers and suppliers has occurred, mainly from the United Kingdom, the United States, and Australia, often involving linkages of various types between local and foreign public and private institutions. This growth has been the result of a number of factors. The expansion of private and international higher education is a worldwide phenomenon that has been enhanced by rapid advances in information technology, which has revolutionized the provision of distance education. This has been matched by growing local demand for the perceived better quality and greater flexibility of market-oriented programs, especially those designed for nontraditional students. Given these conditions, providers took advantage of the comparatively unregulated local environment and began to offer programs without having to comply with regulations for registration or accreditation. Although some of the providers are long established and reputable local and foreign institutions, a number of local "fly-by-night" institutions recently came to light and were prominently featured in the local press.

Consequently, the education minister has urgently called for the appropriate regulation of the private higher education sector. The intention is to protect the public interest by ensuring the academic quality and financial sustainability of these institutions and a constructive complementary role for them within the overall education system. As a result, the DOE has initiated urgent investigations into the estimated size and shape of the private sector, its potential role and impact, and the legislative changes needed to provide an adequate regulatory framework.

In terms of rapidly formulated initial regulations, all private providers are now required to apply for the registration of their institutions and for the accreditation of their programs with the South African Qualifications Authority. This accreditation process is currently underway. The issue has become an extremely prominent one, with all stakeholders—public and private alike—eagerly awaiting the results of the department's studies and the publication of a regulatory framework, which is due to be released in July 2001. In some cases in which registration has been withheld or only conditionally granted, the DOE has been legally challenged. The White Paper acknowledges a complementary role for private providers within the system as a whole. It remains to be seen whether a regulatory framework and working relationship can be forged that will appropriately balance public and market interests.

NATIONAL STUDENT FINANCIAL AID SCHEME

Unlike many other developing nations, South Africa's higher education system is firmly based on cost recovery through fees. Given the wide disparities in wealth distribution, a critical challenge is to ensure access for financially disadvantaged black students. This is central to reducing inequities and maintaining required participation rates. Clearly, most of the recent declines in enrollments at historically disadvantaged universities have arisen from financial problems and the stringent fee-recovery measures that institutions have been forced to apply under constrained fiscal conditions. It is therefore imperative that further financial support be mobilized from public and private sources. Recent allocations from government have increased but remain inadequate to meet current needs.

In terms of the new funding framework, the main focus of redress funding will be on student financial aid. In the 2000–2001 fiscal year, approximately 55 percent of earmarked funding was devoted to the National Student Financial Aid Scheme, established in 1996 as a statutory body. Approximately 80,000 students received scholarships or loans at favorable rates. Allocations in fiscal year 2001–2002 amount to approximately $55 million, which includes a budgeted amount of $40 million and a further $15 million in loan recovery—an encouraging development. While this will make an impact, finance remains an obstacle for many. The challenge is to expand the scheme to accommodate those still in need of financial assistance.

INSTITUTIONAL GOVERNANCE, CAPACITY BUILDING, AND CRISIS MANAGEMENT

One of the tasks of the Higher Education Branch is to assist in the transformation of institutional governance structures to conform with the Higher Education Act and its subsequent amendments. To reflect the values of increased participation and transparency in keeping with the new democracy, the White Paper proposed the notion of "cooperative governance" between institutions and government and within institutions. The Higher Education Act established statutory institutional forums. They include all institutional stakeholder bodies, have advisory powers, and must be consulted on all key decisions, such as senior appointments.

Each public institution is established by an individual act of Parliament; these acts vary somewhat in detail. Typically, South African institutional governance structures consist of a council, a senate, executive management teams, and institutional forums. Councils generally consist of ministerial appointments; representatives of regional government, business, and other higher education institutions; institutional executive management; and representatives of institutional stakeholders. They are the highest decision-making body and are responsible for overall policy. Senates are comprised of senior academics, executive management, and stakeholder representatives. The senates are responsible for academic matters. Executive management

teams are comprised of the vice-chancellor (president); deputy vice-chancellors (for academic and student affairs); deans; heads of finance, personnel, and other key operational areas; and advisers. Amid the prevailing culture of managerialism, executive management teams are becoming increasingly dominant and influential in institutional governance.

Transformation efforts have thus far focused on reconstituting councils and senates to ensure greater representativeness. Progress has been highly variable among institutions. The DOE has been preoccupied with intervention in various crises in financial mismanagement and serious deficiencies in managerial and leadership capacity in certain historically deprived institutions. Several independent financial audits have been conducted. In extreme instances, especially those in which alleged corruption and fraudulent practices have emerged, presidents and senior officials have been suspended or urged to resign.

Faced with the formidable challenges of leading such institutions, candidates for vacant senior posts are scarce. As a result, acting officials are struggling with the uncertainties and transience of their positions. Recently, a rapid turnover of principals in a number of institutions has taken place. By 2001, only five institutions among the twenty-one universities had enjoyed long-standing leaders during the previous few years. Nine have changed leaders in the recent past, seven of them in the past few months. A further four are about to change, two are under ministerial-appointed administrators, and the term of office of another expires soon and is not likely to be renewed.

The education minister, exercising his powers under the Higher Education Act, appointed independent assessors to investigate the crisis at four institutions where management functions had all but collapsed and the credibility of leadership had been severely eroded. Generally, technikon management and leadership appears to be more stable, despite the fact that two institutions were under assessment and one principal was investigated for mismanagement.

The role and focus of student politics and their involvement in educational transformation has shifted in recent years. Historically, students were at the forefront of the anti-apartheid struggle (Badat 1999). Recently, however, they have been co-opted into participating in the new governance structures without the full capacities to undertake the required policy analysis that would render such participation meaningful (Cele and Koen 2001).

THE NEW MINISTER OF EDUCATION

The first post-apartheid education minister, Professor Sibusiso Bengu, presided over the challenging tasks of integrating the divided apartheid education system and developing a new macro-policy framework for education. While making some clear progress, he attracted widespread criticism for not developing a decisive implementation strategy. The second minister, Professor Kader Asmal, was appointed by Thabo Mbeki who succeeded President Mandela as president after the 1999 elections. A former professor of law, Asmal gained a reputation for his activism and strong emphasis on accelerated delivery in his previous position as water affairs minister in the Mandela cabinet.

After consulting widely with DOE managers and stakeholders to gain a firsthand understanding of the state of education and its key policy challenges, he articulated these in a nine-point statement of priorities and an implementation plan that specified outcome targets and performance indicators. The plan included a higher education component calling for the implementation of a "rational, seamless higher education system that grasps the intellectual and professional challenges facing South Africans in the 21st century" (DOE 1999, 13). Current funding levels would be maintained, with institutions being held more accountable for the use of their intellectual, infrastructural, and financial resources. The institutional landscape, largely shaped by the "geo-political imagination of apartheid planners," would be urgently reviewed (DOE 1999, 9). In keeping with the White Paper, this would be done through a national plan specifying overall growth and participation rates.

THE COUNCIL ON HIGHER EDUCATION AND
THE "SIZE AND SHAPE" DEBATE

In early 1999, the education minister mandated the Council on Higher Education (CHE) to make comprehensive recommendations by mid-2000 about reconfiguring the size and shape of the South African education system. The urgency with which the minister approached this issue was indicative of government concern about the crises in financial sustainability, managerial and academic capacity, and quality at several historically disadvantaged institutions.

The CHE was established in 1998 as an independent statutory body. It is responsible for advising the minister on all aspects of higher education, including the optimal shape and size of the system, quality assurance, new funding arrangements, and language policy. It is required to deliver an annual report on the state of higher education to Parliament and to convene an annual consultative conference of higher education stakeholders. In addition, the CHE also has the executive function of accreditation, quality assurance, and promotion through a permanent subcommittee, the Higher Education Quality Committee (HEQC), which was formally launched in 2001. When fully operational, it will audit institutional quality assurance mechanisms, conduct external regulation, and accredit both public and private programs.

In response to a ministerial mandate, the CHE released a discussion document in May 2000 through a special task team. This highly controversial document focused exclusively on a proposed fivefold institutional typology and a related four-year undergraduate qualification structure. This entailed a fairly rigid differentiation between institutional types and fairly inflexible admission requirements and constricted student mobility between institutional types. Submissions in response to the document were generally highly critical of its narrow, technicist framework and its departure, without any provided rationale, from the planning framework proposed in the White Paper.

A revised document responding to the submissions was presented to the education minister in July 2000. This far more comprehensive document firmly aligned itself with the principles and framework of the White Paper. It proposed a slightly less rigid and simplified three-fold institutional typology consisting of "bedrock" (mainly teaching institutions), extensive master's and selective doctoral programs, and "comprehensive" institutions with selected postgraduate and research programs. It proposed the combination or merging of institutions aimed simultaneously at remedying the immediate crises in those (mainly disadvantaged) institutions of doubtful sustainability and removing some of the wasteful duplication of apartheid "planning." Equity and redress for disadvantaged institutions were foregrounded. While responses were generally far more favorable, critics highlighted several flaws and issues lacking clarity. Though more flexible, the proposed typology was seen to exacerbate existing race and class inequalities. No clear indications were provided of how key concerns (notably equity) would be addressed. Nor were cost, implementation, and capacity implications addressed. In the eyes of critics, the document failed to provide the education minister with sufficiently concrete recommendations, leaving him with yet another framework document.

The education minister called for responses to the new document by mid-September 2000. After considering these, a draft national plan was presented to the ruling ANC, its alliance partners, and then the cabinet in an effort to gain maximum political support.

THE NATIONAL HIGHER EDUCATION PLAN
AND PROPOSED FUNDING FRAMEWORK

The MOE released the long-awaited National Plan for Higher Education in March 2001. It provides the framework and mechanisms for the transformation of higher education as articulated in the vision, goals, and principles of the White Paper. The importance of this document is that it brings closure to the extended consultative process beginning with the NCHE and culminating in the CHE discussion documents. It thus sets out the government's nonnegotiable policy intentions in a planning format that identifies strategic objectives and targets, and the mechanisms and time frames for achieving them. Linked to the regulatory mechanisms of funding and quality assurance, the plan establishes the procedure for three-year rolling national and institutional planning. Through this negotiated planning procedure, the overall size and shape of the diversified system will be fashioned and regulated in relation to national development priorities and equity and efficiency concerns. The plan refers, for the first time, to the new cabinet-approved national human resource development strategy. This will allow higher education planning to better reflect development priorities.

The key points of the National Plan for Higher Education are:

- Targets for the size and shape of the higher education system, including a long-term increase in the participation rate from 15 percent to 20 percent; graduation-rate benchmarks to ensure greater access and success; shifting enrollments between the humanities, business and commerce, and engineering and technology from the current ratio of 48:26:26 to 40:30:30, respectively; and equity targets for students and staff.

- Various steps to ensure diversity of institutional mission and program differentiation. Institutional program mixes will be determined on the basis of current profiles, the relevance of institutional functions to national priorities, and demonstrated capacity for proposed new programs. The existing divide between universities and technikons will be maintained for at least five years.
- The institutional landscape will be restructured by reducing the number of institutions but not the number of delivery sites. Immediate institutional mergers are recommended, while further potential ones and regional collaboration will be guided by a National Working Group. This group has already begun operation and is heavily laden with economists, signaling a strong intention to foster efficiency.

In setting out these mechanisms, the plan accepts the majority of the CHE's recommendations. However, it rejects the CHE's proposed threefold institutional typology as the mechanism to achieve differentiation, which the ministry regarded as too rigid. Instead, the plan opts for a more flexible developmental approach to differentiation that draws on current institutional offerings and strengths and allows regulated opportunities for the development of new educational niches.

The plan is clearly strongly regulatory in character, signaling a discernible shift toward stronger steering of systemic change. This reflects the ministry's determination to proceed decisively with the implementation of the policy framework for transformation. While the plan has generally met with positive reception, its more pronounced interventionist approach has triggered some concerns about institutional autonomy and academic freedom. Other concerns have been expressed about the perceived shift from institutional to "social" or "individual" redress —that is, supporting financially disadvantaged students through the National Student Financial Aid Scheme. Underlying this shift is the view that, as a result of the recent rapid increase in black students at historically white institutions (HWIs), notions of historically advantaged and disadvantaged institutions have become anachronistic. The government insists that emphasizing social redress does not imply abandoning institutional redress or ignoring historical institutional disadvantage. Instead, it rejects the automatic expectation of redress based on entitlement as victims of apartheid. As set out in the national plan, the government holds that the redress component of earmarked funds will be allocated according to clearly demonstrated needs and accountability mechanisms as part of the three-year rolling planning process. This will enable historically disadvantaged institutions to discharge their approved institutional plans in the context of institutional restructuring. Redress must thus be linked to the current process of redefinition of institutional mission within the new institutional landscape.

Despite the stated intention to address both social and institutional redress, there is concern that the actual amounts allocated for the latter will be too small. While the government acknowledges that structural factors impact negatively on historically disadvantaged institutions, it emphasizes their responsibility as agents accountable for their own current management and planning problems. Institutions, on the other hand, argue that structural, apartheid-related disadvantages are the root

cause of their predicaments and that the unlevel playing field can be rectified only through government intervention. Government's position is interpreted as evidence of its uncritical acceptance of the neoliberal global world order and of its reneging on previous unconditional commitments to redress inequities.

One of the main concerns, acknowledged in the plan itself, is whether or not institutions and the government can handle the complex planning process. It is not clear, for instance, how institutional plans will be reconciled with aggregate national targets. Linked to this, the plan optimistically assumes a close link between planning and intentional change. Organizational realities, however, suggest otherwise, especially as higher education institutions are characterized by multiple centers of authority and complex dynamics of change. Change initiatives have their own logic and often arise in spite of, not because of, planning and management strategies. The plan is silent on this crucial aspect and does not incorporate a formal process of evaluation and review. With the plan's strong target-driven approach, this is potentially a significant shortcoming. Given the complexity of how change actually occurs, as opposed to how it is planned, it is important not only to monitor *whether* targets are or are not being met, but also to evaluate *why*. Despite these limitations, the national plan is a crucially important document that will shape the future course of the higher education system in South Africa.

THE NEW FUNDING FRAMEWORK PROPOSAL

Shortly after the release of the national plan, a discussion document outlining proposals for a revised funding framework was published in April 2001. This is a crucial element of the regulatory framework and will have an undoubtedly strong impact on the outcome of the policy process.

A twofold funding mechanism that consists of block grants and earmarked funds has been proposed. If approved, the former will be allocated for teaching inputs (staff and other costs); teaching outputs (graduates); research outputs (publications and master's and doctoral graduates); costs relating to institutional setup, functioning, and development; and foundation programs (student academic development). Allocations will be made after approval of the required program-based institutional plans. Funding of enrollments will be negotiated according to an agreed-upon pricing formula, weighted according to different fields and levels. Earmarked funds will be allocated to the National Student Financial Aid Scheme for institutional redress and development, including research development; for approved capital projects; and for other development priorities identified in the national plan.

This new framework will have major implications for institutions. In particular, the removal of the current "hidden" research grant for faculty, which is embedded in salary allocations (amounting to approximately one-fifth of them), will have a marked negative impact on those institutions with few research and graduate programs. Implementation will therefore be phased in over a number of years to offset negative short-term impacts. Earmarked funds will also help to smooth these effects. Given prevailing fiscal constraints, it is unlikely that additional resources will be available to higher education. The new framework, which is linked to the approval of institutional plans, will have the effect of redistributing funds within the system. Together with quality assurance mechanisms, the new funding framework will serve as the main lever by which the institutional landscape will be shaped to meet the policy goals of quality, equity, responsiveness, and efficiency.

PATTERNS IN INSTITUTIONAL RESPONSES TO THE CHANGING POLICY ENVIRONMENT

Three noteworthy characteristics of the current policy environment emerge. First, progress in implementation of the new macro-policy framework as envisaged in the White Paper has been very partial to date, which has created something of a regulatory vacuum. This is the combined result of capacity problems, the appointment of the new minister, and the role of the consultation process in delaying the emergence of the national plan. Second, market discourse and strategic managerialism are becoming increasingly dominant, fostered by fiscal constraint in an ever-more-competitive higher education environment. The current period is characterized by the partial implementation of a regulatory framework accompanied by relatively unrestrained but competitive market conditions. Third, enrollments at HWIs (especially the Afrikaans HWIs) have rapidly but selectively been Africanized.

The dominance of competitive market conditions over regulatory planning has resulted in an unplanned haphazardness in the proliferation of program provision; some institutions have seized upon entrepreneurial and strategic opportunities, but institutions who do not have the capacities to implement these strategies are falling behind. The historically disadvantaged institutions, constrained by current crises in leadership and capacity, are generally less able to plan strategically, restructure rapidly, and develop entrepreneurial responses. These differentiations in institutional responses are largely overdetermined by disadvantages rooted in apartheid. In the absence of regulatory mechanisms to offset the inequalities of apartheid and the market, the institutional divide is widening. While the number of African students has changed dramatically at many previously white institutions, these students tend to be concentrated in selected fields at the lower levels and are mainly educationally advantaged students who are able to pay fees or have access to financial assistance (Cooper and Subotzky 2001). As a result, the burden of maintaining access for the educationally disadvantaged poorer students rests on those historically black institutions (HBIs) that have the least capacities to fulfill this role.

Given this variety of institutional histories, the nature of individual institutional responses to new policy and market conditions has varied widely (CHE 1999, 4). The emerging pattern of these different responses—especially the rapid Africanization of students in HWIs—has generated a new institutional categorization that conforms largely, but not exclusively, to historical advantage and disadvantage. Based on this variety of responses, the 1999 CHE report identifies four new institutional categories:

- Entrepreneurs: On the basis of astute strategic planning and managerial expertise, these institutions have taken advantage of the new environment and identified new areas of focus,

such as technology-based distance education, to accommodate nontraditional students. In many cases, this has been facilitated through collaborative links with private providers, transnational institutions, or newly established satellite campuses in smaller centers. This has led to cases of duplication in program provision, in response to which the DOE placed a moratorium on the further rapid proliferation of such satellites. They enjoy financial security as a result of access to alternative income sources (such as research contracts, industry partnerships, and increased tuition fees from nontraditional students) and efficient financial management. Notable among these are historically Afrikaans universities and some technikons.

- Restructurers: These institutions have reconfigured their programs, curricula, and academic structures to foster interdisciplinarity and more effectively to produce graduates with the required skills and knowledge for the changing labor market and the new knowledge economy. In doing so, they have strengthened their identities as high-quality residential institutions and their reputations for excellence in graduate programs and research. They have also achieved efficiency through cost reductions and greater equity through attracting and financing a diverse but academically selective student body. Historically English-language institutions feature strongly in this group.

- Consolidators: Another set of institutions has maintained stability through strong leadership and a stable workforce. They have arrived at a shared vision of new missions and strategic positions. Although most are continuing with their current areas of focus, some have expanded student enrollments and ventured into new programs, delivery modes, and forms of management.

- Static and unstable institutions: Due to the variety of constraining factors, several institutions have not been in a position to respond effectively to changing circumstances. Until very recently, little or no strategic planning occurred in these institutions and many have experienced sharp declines in enrollments. They have experienced instability arising from problems in internal governance, management, and finance and a lack of stable authority and leadership. In some cases, management has broken down. While some areas of innovation and responsiveness are evident, these are exceptions and are the result of individual initiatives. Most historically disadvantaged institutions fall into this category.

Given the nature of the current policy environment, most of these changes are not the outcome of policy and planning but are institutional responses (or the lack thereof) to anticipated policy changes and to the marketlike entrepreneurial climate created by prevailing macroeconomic conditions.

PROFILE OF THE CHANGING HIGHER EDUCATION SYSTEM IN SOUTH AFRICA

An examination of the current profile of South African higher education reveals both dramatic changes in student enrollment and strong continuities with the past. A simple snapshot of the current situation is not adequate to capture these complexities. This profile therefore provides a brief overview of

Table 57.1. Enrollments in South African Universities and Technikons, 1993–1999

	1993		1995		1997		1998		1999	
	N	%	N	%	N	%	N	%	N	%
Universities	340,000	72	384,000	67	394,000	66	397,000	66	372,000	66
Technikons	133,000	28	185,000	33	202,000	34	208,000	34	192,000	34
Total	473,000	100	569,000	100	596,000	100	605,000	100	564,000	100

Note: Figures have been rounded up.
Source: DOE 1999.

Table 57.2. Higher Education Enrollments in South Africa by Institutional Type, 1993–1999

	1993		1995		1997		1999	
Type of Institution	N	%	N	%	N	%	N	%
Universities								
Historically Black Universities	92,000	27	111,000	29	99,000	25	79,000	21
Historically White Universities Afrikaans	73,000	21	92,000	24	116,000	29	128,000	34
Historically White Universities English	52,000	15	53,000	14	56,000	14	56,000	15
UNISA	123,000	36	128,000	33	124,000	32	108,000	30
Total	340,000	100	384,000	100	394,000	100	372,000	100
Technikons								
Historically Black Technikons	24,000	17	32,000	17	43,000	22	44,000	23
Historically White Technikons	58,000	36	68,000	37	81,000	40	82,000	43
Technikon South Africa	50,000	47	85,000	46	77,000	38	66,000	34
Total	133,000	100	185,000	100	202,000	100	192,000	100

Note: Figures have been rounded up.
Source: DOE 1999, Tables 25.1, 26, 27.2, and 28.

recent trends in student enrollment and outputs, faculty composition, finance, and research.

In 1999, the South African higher education system included 564,000 students, of whom 372,000 (66 percent) were in universities and 192,000 (34 percent) were in technikons (Table 57.1).

Table 57.1 shows that enrollments have risen steadily from 473,000 in 1993 to 564,000 in 1999, an overall increase of about 20 percent and an average annual increase of 3 percent. Between 1993 and 1998, enrollments grew more rapidly in technikons (56 percent) than in universities (17 percent). The ratio of university to technikon enrollments changed from 72 to 28 in 1993 to 66 to 34 in 1999. Enrollments peaked at 605,000 in 1998 and then decreased by about 40,000 (7 percent) by 1999. The decline in enrollments contradicts two previous policy and planning projections: the NCHE report, which projected about 680,000 enrollments by 1999, and institutional projections for 1999 submitted to the DOE as part of their three-year rolling plans.

From Table 57.2, it is clear that the decline in enrollments was most evident in HBUs (where it involved mainly African students) and in the distance education institutions (UNISA and Technikon South Africa). Enrollments in HBUs peaked in 1995 to reach 29 percent of total university enrollments and then declined steadily to 21 percent in 1999. An especially sharp drop of 20,000 enrollments occurred between 1997 and 1999, with a decrease of 13,000 (14 percent) between 1998 and 1999 alone. The latest indications of enrollments suggest that this pattern continued in 2000 but is showing signs of bottoming out at most (but not all) HBUs in 2001. A similar pattern was evident at UNISA and Technikon South Africa, where enrollments peaked in 1995 and have declined by about 20,000 each since then. In sharp contrast, Afrikaans HWUs increased steadily by 55,000— from 73,000 in 1993 to 128,000 in 1999. Enrollments at English HWUs have remained relatively static.

Among the technikons, a steady increase occurred at both HBTs and HWTs, the former growing by 80 percent from 24,000 to 44,000 between 1993 and 1999 and the latter by 40 percent from 58,000 to 82,000 during the same period. In both cases, these rather dramatic increases tapered off from 1997 and then declined from 1998 to 1999.

The reasons for these changes are not completely clear. In

Table 57.3. Higher Education Enrollments in South Africa by "Race," Selected Years, 1993–1999

	1993		1995		1997		1999	
	N	%	N	%	N	%	N	%
African	191,000	40	287,000	50	345,000	58	332,000	59
White	223,000	47	213,000	37	182,000	30	163,000	29
Indian	30,000	7	37,000	7	38,000	7	40,000	7
Colored	29,000	6	32,000	6	31,000	5	29,000	5
Total	473,000	100	569,000	100	596,000	100	564,000	100

Source: DOE 1999, Tables 14–17, and 19.

the case of HBUs, a major factor is undoubtedly the financial problems of students. Other likely factors include the perceived low quality and relevance of programs as well as negative impressions arising from administrative inefficiency and management crises, disruptions, and stoppages (mostly focused on financial exclusions). Conversely, the historically advantaged institutions are perceived as providing better-quality, more stable conditions, and greater program relevance, especially the market-oriented vocational short-cycle programs at technikons and private institutions. Increased academic and financial support for access to the historically advantaged institutions and to private institutions for higher education achievers may also have facilitated enrollment shifts. HIV/AIDS may be having an effect by now, although little is currently known about the extent of its impact. Institutional policies on HIV/AIDS are now being widely formulated and some studies are now assessing its impact on institutions. Despite a recent decline at the two major distance education institutions, the number and proportion of distance education enrollments in the whole system has steadily increased. Between 1993 and 1999, contact enrollments increased by 16 percent and distance education by 24 percent.

As mentioned, in the increasingly competitive environment, some Afrikaans institutions have demonstrated shrewd entrepreneurial enterprise and keen survival instincts by developing high-tech distance education programs to provide teacher education and other vocational programs in partnership with private colleges. These partnerships have been controversial, however. It is probable that considerable "double counting" of these enrollments is occurring. That is, the public institutions, who often merely provide accreditation, nonetheless count the enrollments as their own in order to benefit from a government subsidy. Private students are therefore being subsidized by public resources. Moreover, some private college programs are of dubious quality. Given the cultural and ideological background of Afrikaans HWUs under apartheid, the rapid increase in African students in these institutions represents the most dramatic change in the South African higher education landscape. However, because the majority of these appear to be part-time distance education students linked to private providers in a narrow band of fields, these new enrollments do not represent a fundamental transformation of these institutions. Indications are that many student residences and campus social activities remain voluntarily separate at these institutions and that their institu-

tional culture and climate have, in most cases, not sufficiently transformed to accommodate the increasing diversity of the student body. However, some Afrikaans institutions have made concerted efforts to attract and support African students, particularly at the graduate level, including measures such as changing the language of instruction.

The number and proportion of higher education enrollments by race has shifted markedly in recent years, representing the single most noticeable aspect of change in the South African higher education system. Table 57.3 shows that from 1993 to 1999, African student numbers in the system as a whole rose from 191,000 to 332,000, that is by 75 percent, raising the proportion of the total from 40 percent to 59 percent. Correspondingly, white student numbers declined sharply by 60,000 from 223,000 to 163,000, dropping from 47 percent to 29 percent of the total. African enrollments in universities rose by 71,000 (48 percent) from 1993 to 1999 and more than doubled in technikons by 90,000 (104 percent) during the same period. Conversely, white student enrollments in universities declined by 26,000 (17 percent) over this period and almost halved in technikons, by 34,000 (48 percent). Colored student enrollments remained static over this period, while Indian student numbers increased slightly.

The causes of this dramatic and steady decrease in white enrollments remain unknown. Speculatively, it might be a combination of factors, including a perceived drop in program quality and relevance; the attractiveness of private institutions; greater emigration and/or study abroad; faster direct entry into entrepreneurial niches in the labor market, particularly in information technology and business; negative reaction to the increased Africanization of the HWIs; and declining birth rates.

Changes in student enrollments have resulted in a new distribution of students by race within the main institutional types. In 1993, 41 percent of African students were enrolled at HBUs. By 1999, this had almost halved to 21 percent. Conversely, the proportion of African enrollments at HWUs tripled from 8 percent to 24 percent, growing dramatically from 16,000 to 80,000. This was especially evident at Afrikaans HWUs, where a phenomenal tenfold growth from 6,000 to 60,000 occurred, shifting the proportion from 3 percent to 18 percent of the total. It must, however, be constantly reiterated that the majority of these are distance education students linked to private providers of teacher training and some business programs. This is corrobo-

Table 57.4. African and White Student Enrollments in South Africa by Institutional Type, 1993 and 1999

	African				White			
	1993		1999		1993		1999	
	N	%	N	%	N	%	N	%
Historically Black Universities	78,000	41	70,000	21	790	<1	640	<1
Historically White Universities Afrikaans	6,000	3	60,000	18	64,000	29	59,000	36
Historically White Universities English	10,000	5	20,000	6	33,000	15	23,000	14
Distance (University of South Africa)	53,000	28	46,000	14	53,000	24	43,000	26
Total Universities	147,000	77	196,000	59	151,000	68	126,000	76
Historically Black Technikons	15,000	8	40,000	12	720	<1	425	<1
Historically White Technikons	10,000	5	50,000	15	44,000	20	24,000	15
Distance (Technikon South Africa)	19,000	10	46,000	14	27,000	12	13,000	9
Total Technikons	44,000	23	136,000	41	72,000	32	37,000	24
Grand Total	191,000	100	332,000	100	223,000	100	163,000	100

Source: DOE 1999, Table 39.1. Numbers have been rounded up to the nearest thousand.

rated by the huge increase in the proportion of humanities majors in Afrikaans institutions between 1993 and 1999 (121 percent). This signifies that many African students entering the HWUs tend to be concentrated in the same fields and levels as they were in HBUs. Unless this pattern changes, access to HWUs for Africans does not necessarily imply greater equity through access to fields and levels historically dominated by white students. At UNISA, long a traditional institutional home for African part-time students, the proportion of Africans halved from 28 percent to 14 percent from 1993 to 1999. African enrollments in technikons have grown rapidly, from 44,000 to 136,000. As a result, the ratio of African university to technikon enrollments shifted from 77 to 23 to 59 to 41 over this period. African students clearly perceive technikon qualifications to be more likely to lead to employment.

Table 57.4 clearly shows the decline in white university enrollments of 25,000 and an even greater drop of 35,000 white technikon students over this period. This occurred in all institutional subtypes except HBIs, where numbers have remained minimal. As a result, the ratio of African enrollments in universities versus technikons shifted from 77 to 23 in 1993 to 59 to 41 in 1999, while that of white enrollments in universities versus technikons shifted from 68 to 32 to 76 to 24 over the same period. These changing ratios may be interpreted as a net loss for equity; African students are now concentrated in the vocationally oriented technikons and white students are concentrated at higher levels and in more professional fields at universities.

Gender equity in higher education in South Africa is somewhat anomalous by international comparisons. Absolute gender parity in overall enrollments was reached by 1997. By 1999, women students were in the majority. At universities, women were already the majority in 1995. While they are still in the minority at technikons, there has been a very rapid increase in female enrollment, which more than doubled from 42,000 to

86,000 from 1993 to 1999. This signals a strong entry into vocational fields by women. However, these overall figures hide the fact that women remain underrepresented in certain fields, such as science and technology, and at the higher qualification levels, particularly at the master's and doctoral levels. Within some fields, such as business and commerce, women tend to be concentrated in "lower" programs, such as public administration, rather than the "higher" ones, such as business management. Conversely, women students tend to be concentrated in the traditional fields associated with females, such as teaching, social work, and the "lower" health and law programs, as well as at the lower certificate and diploma qualifications levels in all fields.

Given the complex interrelations of race and gender in South African society, it is important to examine race and gender as a combined category (Cooper and Subotsky 2001). Within the rapidly changing patterns of enrollments by race outlined above, there are crucial differences between, for example, African women and men, which remain hidden unless data are disaggregated and analyzed accordingly.

The wide variations in the distribution of master's and doctoral enrollments by institutional types is a particularly stark indicator of the sharp divide between universities and technikons in South Africa and the deep historical institutional inequalities rooted in the functional differentiation generated by apartheid. HBUs accounted for just 11 percent of total master's and doctoral enrollments in 1999. While this is up from 9 percent in 1993, the gulf remains enormous. Master's and doctoral enrollments are dominated by white and male students.

STUDENT SUCCESS AND GRADUATION RATES

Another major challenge for higher education in South Africa is to improve the efficiency and equity of student outputs.

This is especially important because the focus on improving equity has tended to be on access rather than on success. Providing greater access to previously disadvantaged students without improving their success and output rates merely creates a revolving-door syndrome. For these reasons, it is crucial that alternative admissions procedures be accompanied by effective academic development and support measures to ensure that students are equipped with the basic language and academic literacy skills that they so often lack as a consequence of poor-quality schooling.

Throughput rates (the proportion of graduates to total enrollments) and success rates remain generally low, especially among (mainly black) educationally disadvantaged and inadequately prepared students. Despite the ongoing efforts of academic development programs for such students, white students continue to achieve significantly higher throughput rates. This problem exacerbates the cost of graduating students and drains already limited human and financial resources. While the absolute number of black graduates has increased, their overall proportion of the total remains low, particularly at the graduate level. From 1991 to 1998, whites comprised 68 percent of all graduates and Africans just 21 percent.

Output by field of study remains strongly conditioned by apartheid patterns, which are negatively impacted by poor schooling and matriculation results and restrictive subject choices. Blacks (including African, Colored, and Indian students) accounted for the following proportion of graduates in key fields 1991–1998: medicine and engineering proper, 9 percent; natural sciences, 12 percent; law, 13 percent; social sciences, 20 percent; humanities and arts, 28 percent; education, 32 percent; general engineering fields, 35 percent; and literature and languages, 39 percent. The skewed output is most clearly evident in business and commerce, where only 11 percent of graduates from 1991 to 1998 were African, with only 2 percent in accountancy. By sharp contrast, Africans comprised 55 percent of public administration graduates over this period. Increased enrollments and lower graduation rates of Africans mean lower success and throughput rates. Throughput rates were significantly higher for whites (around 25 percent in 1997) than for Africans (8 percent), Coloreds (9 percent), and Indians (6 percent).

THE COMPOSITION OF FACULTY

In stark contrast to the dramatically rapid Africanization of the student body over the past few years, the composition of staff, and of faculty in particular, has remained relatively unchanged. This is especially so at HWUs, where dramatic increases have occurred in African student enrollments. Despite some increases in the number of African faculty, particularly at historically disadvantaged institutions, the race, gender, and institutional inequalities generated by apartheid therefore remain clearly imprinted in the staff composition of South Africa's higher education institutions.

Table 57.5 shows the overwhelming dominance of white faculty in the higher education system. Although the number and proportion of African faculty doubled between 1993 and 1998 from 720 to 1,555 (from 6 percent to 12 percent of the

Table 57.5. Faculty in Higher Education Institutions in South Africa by "Race," 1993 and 1998

	1993	1998
African	720	1,555
Colored	408	457
Indian	515	752
White	10,901	10,587

Source: CHE 1999, Tables 13 and 14.

Table 57.6. University Faculty in South Africa by Rank and Gender, 1997

	M	F
Professor	1,713	841
Associate Professor	841	244
Senior Lecturer	1,872	910
Lecturer	1,747	1,702
Junior Lecturer and Below	460	571

Source: CHE 1999, Table 15.

total), this increase was confined mainly to the historically disadvantaged institutions. Correspondingly, while the proportion of white faculty dropped from 87 percent to 79 percent, this accompanied a slight decrease in the absolute number of whites (from 10,901 to 10,587). These trends were especially marked at HBTs, where the proportion of African faculty rose from 17 percent to 49 percent, while that of white faculty dropped from 80 percent to 41 percent.

The following clear pattern in the distribution of faculty has emerged: HWIs are dominated by whites and whites constitute about half of HBIs, while the other half are African, Colored, and Indian in their respective institutional types. The "racial" imbalance among faculty is especially pronounced at Afrikaans HWUs, where blacks constituted less than 3 percent of the total faculty in 1998; very little change was evident in this regard between 1993 and 1998. At English HWUs, the proportion of black faculty showed only marginal improvement, increasing from 4 percent in 1993 to 7 percent in 1998, with the result that white faculty made up 87 percent of the total, down from 91 percent in 1993.

Women constituted about 36 percent of all faculty in 1998, an increase from around 30 percent in 1993. While this is an encouraging trend, women remain underrepresented in the higher ranks, at the higher qualification levels, and in fields of study other than those traditionally associated with women.

Table 57.6 illustrates the dominance of males at the higher ranks and the concentration of women at the lower ones. In 1997, men still constituted 67 percent of professors, 78 percent of associate professors, and 67 percent of senior lecturers, but only about 47 percent of the junior ranks.

The broader race, gender, and class divisions of South African society are clearly reproduced in other higher education occupational categories, such as management, which are dominated by males. Leadership and senior administration in HBIs are now predominantly African, Colored, and Indian in their respective institutional types. The gender imbalance at this level remains stark, however. Lower levels of the occupational structure, such as service workers and nonprofessional administrative staff, are overwhelmingly black and female.

Clearly, transforming staff, and faculty in particular, represents a major challenge. The recent Employment Equity Act provides a clear statutory imperative and procedural framework for doing this. All institutions, along with private sector corporations, are subject to its conditions, which entail formulating employment equity plans for submission to the Department of Labor. The plans include analyzing institutions both quantitatively and qualitatively; identifying the current profile of staff in the various occupational categories according to race, gender, and disability; examining procedures and policies to pinpoint the barriers to the advancement of these marginalized groups; and surveying staff perceptions and experiences. Based on these findings, institutions are required to formulate detailed plans, set realistic equity targets, and identify viable measures to achieve these. Consultation with all stakeholder bodies is mandatory throughout this process.

A major challenge is that the pool of suitable potential black, female, and disabled employees remains small, particularly in the very fields and senior levels in which they are already underrepresented. This will no doubt generate fierce competitiveness between the private and public sectors, with employers offering attractive packages to balance their equity profiles. The answer therefore lies in finding creative ways to change an institution's staff profile by a combination of mechanisms such as offering early retirement, encouraging students to enter the profession, and creating conducive conditions to attract and retain good staff. In this regard, the wealthier, prestigious, research-oriented, and urban-based institutions have considerable advantages over their rural, resource-constrained, mainly teaching counterparts. This is another instance of the way in which the deep imprint of apartheid in higher education is being reproduced, despite concerted efforts to the contrary.

FINANCE

South African higher education is financed principally by government subsidy and fee recovery, augmented by private and government contracts, donor and alumni support, and investments. The government subsidy rewards enrollments (weighted in favor of natural sciences and graduate programs), success rates, and research. The subsidy currently covers two-thirds of actual institutional costs.

Table 57.7 indicates that as a proportion of both the total education budget and the total government budget, the allocation to higher education has been rising. In real terms, taking inflation into account, government allocations to higher education increased annually by an average 5 percent from 1995 to 1999. The proportion allocated to technikons has increased slowly but steadily. In addition, the government has made the following allocations in three key areas:

- Earmarked funding: At present, earmarked funding covers loan interest and redemptions, capital allocations for new buildings, local taxes, some limited redress funds, and contributions to the national student financial aid scheme. This has ranged from about $71 million in 1995 to $106 million in 1999. However, as a proportion of total higher education funding, this has not increased over the past few years, remaining at around 12–13 percent.

- Redress funding: $3.9 million was allocated in 1998–1999 (0.45 percent of total higher education allocations) on an unspecified pro-rata basis and $8.6 million in 1999–2000 (0.9 percent) to three institutions (Fort Hare, Transkei, and Medunsa) to ensure their immediate viability. In 2000–2001, redress funding was targeted at academic development on the basis of submitted proposals. These amounts were insufficient to support substantial systemwide institutional redress.

- National student financial aid scheme: The government has allocated between $29 and $43 million annually since 1996 to this scheme. In 1999, the allocation went up to $55 million. Given the number of needy students, these amounts are clearly inadequate.

While higher education funding levels are high relative to overall education and government budgets, and are therefore unlikely to rise, funds remain insufficient to cover these three strategically and politically significant areas. This has important consequences, especially for institutional equity.

The financial crisis faced by numerous historically disadvantaged institutions is twofold. First, declines in student enrollments lead directly to reduced government subsidy and pose a serious threat to their future financial sustainability. Projections for subsidy allocations between 2000 and 2002, based on current student enrollments, indicate an alarming drop for HBUs from $185 million to $140 million. These institutions are more highly dependent on subsidy and tuition fees than others, as they do not have comparable capacity to generate income from alternative sources.

The substantial raising of fees remains a politically sensitive alternative, as poorer students are the traditional constituency of historically disadvantaged institutions. To offset their multiple financial disadvantages, some historically disadvantaged institutions have successfully attracted foreign and local donors, as well as support from corporations. By contrast, historically advantaged institutions have numerous alternative sources of income, including (in most cases) highly developed research capacities that facilitate the winning of lucrative government and industry contracts, access to strong and wealthy alumni support and endowments, a generally wealthier student constituency, established links to international donor and academic networks, and accumulated financial reserves that can generate investment income.

Given the historical disadvantages of the HBIs, the subsidy allocation has clearly compounded the disadvantages experienced by these institutions. Overall enrollments aside, they are least developed in precisely those areas that are rewarded by the subsidy formula: success rates, postgraduate enrollments, and research. Most important, the subsidy formula is applied for a two-year period retrospectively for auditing purposes. In the case of those historically disadvantaged institutions that experienced

Table 57.7. Government Subsidy as Proportion of Education and Total Government Budgets, 1995–1999 (in millions of U.S. dollars)

Year	Universities		Technikons		Total		Percent of Total Education Budget	Percent of Total Government Budget
	N	%	N	%	N	%	%	%
1995	438	75	144	25	582	100	12.2	2.6
1997	568	73	208	27	776	100	12.2	2.7
1999	664	71	271	29	935	100	14.1	3.0

Note: The rand has declined significantly in recent years. These and all subsequent figures have been calculated at 7 rands to the dollar.
Source: CHE 1999, Tables 22, 24, and 25.

strong enrollment growth during the late 1980s, this led to a gap between immediate rising costs and the level of subsidies. In addition, when subsidies were received, the proportion of costs they covered was reduced.

The second aspect of the financial crises in many historically disadvantaged institutions relates to lack of financial management capacity and effective strategic planning. Financial inquiries have been initiated in the case of six such institutions accused of improper management and possible financial irregularities, several cases of which have come to light.

The current decline in student numbers will undoubtedly have severe consequences for the system and for institutions. Current projections indicate that reduced enrollments might lead to a 6 percent drop in government allocations to higher education from 1999 to 2002. However, there are indications from the latest provisional 2001 figures that these downward trends may be reversing.

RESEARCH AND KNOWLEDGE PRODUCTION

The research output of South African higher education institutions suffers from fragmentation, a lack of planning, and a lack of adequate output data. Research and development expenditure in higher education in South Africa represents a relatively low proportion of the total in international terms and remains concentrated in a narrow band of five fields: agriculture, health, education, community and social services, and manufacturing. Consequently, the key fields of energy, environment, communications, and tourism have been inadequately serviced.

Concern for the relevance of research arises directly from the demand that higher education should be responsive to the needs of South African society—one of the key policy principles of the White Paper. A prominent feature of recent policy debates has been the trend away from the focus on disciplinary-based knowledge production toward strategic science or applications-driven, transdisciplinary, heterogeneous, team-based knowledge production, often in off-campus partnerships. In some views, this new social organization of so-called Mode 2 knowledge production demands new kinds of knowledge workers who are skilled in the rapid reconfiguration of existing knowledge to solve particular problems. In South Africa, the account of these

purported developments by Gibbons et al. (1994) and Gibbons (1999) has received special prominence in all recent key policy documents and debates. Gibbons argues that the major challenge for higher education institutions, especially in developing countries, is to adapt organizationally to this new mode of knowledge production so that the knowledge produced will have relevance and applicability to pressing development priorities. There is general consensus that addressing such priorities is a crucial policy goal and that patterns of research are shifting toward application. However, some critics have expressed concern that the uncritical adoption of this notion may divert attention from the need for good-quality disciplinary knowledge and graduate training, which are also prerequisites for development in developing countries (Ravjee 1999; Kraak 2000).

The DOE is currently investigating a framework for research assessment that is based on analysis of available data. Indications are that the bulk of research activities are concentrated in a few (mainly white) institutions. About 65 percent of research publications output and 61 percent of research and development funding allocations to higher education are concentrated in five white universities (Cape Town, Natal, Pretoria, Stellenbosch, and Witwatersrand). By contrast, just 10 percent is produced in the ten HBUs combined, of which the major part is produced by the two non-African urban institutions, namely, the University of the Western Cape and the University of Durban-Westville (CHE 1999, 24). Research activities in technikons vary widely but are generally very low. The overall picture is that research capacity and outputs, as well as postgraduate programs, are therefore very unevenly distributed among the various institutional types and subtypes. Once again, the major factor affecting institutional capacity in this regard is the functional differentiation generated by apartheid. A number of interrelated, historical, external and institutional conditions combine to obstruct the development of a research culture in the HBUs (EPU 1997). Despite ongoing efforts by the statutory science councils and donor initiatives to counter this, the impact has been very limited.

A key policy issue at the heart of the so-called size and shape debate is to determine the role of research within a new and differentiated institutional framework. While the link between teaching and research is intrinsic to higher education, no single overriding benchmark can be established to govern the range and focus of research activities across and within the varied institutional types and program offerings that will eventually make up the new institutional landscape. As noted, the new funding framework will have the effect of creating a sharper distinction between research and teaching institutions.

CONCLUSION

Higher education in South Africa has been shaped by the sharp racial, political, cultural, and linguistic divisions that characterize South African society. The higher education system is currently in the process of dynamic and fundamental reconstruction. It faces the simultaneous challenge of redressing the inequalities of apartheid and meeting the demands of a developing country in a rapidly globalizing world order.

While the overall policy and planning framework for this transformation is in place, progress toward implementation has been very partial—mainly the result of lack of capacity at the national and institutional levels. In the resultant policy vacuum, those institutions with the capacity have seized the opportunity for strategic restructuring and expansion into new market niches, notably in distance education, in partnership with local and transnational providers. In order to achieve the required policy goals of equity, efficiency, and quality, a careful balance must be struck between government regulation and market forces. The new National Plan, which provides the framework for implementation, is strongly regulatory in emphasis. It will be interesting to observe the extent to which the National Plan will achieve the various policy goals set out in the White Paper during the next several years in which implementation is supposed to occur.

The sharp relief into which these issues and challenges are thrown by the highly stratified South African society makes the study of its higher education system a fascinating and instructive example of considerable international comparative interest.

BIBLIOGRAPHY

Badat, S. 1999. *Black Student Politics, Higher Education and Apartheid: From SASO to SANSCO, 1968–1990*. Pretoria: Human Sciences Research Council Publishers.

Badat, S., G. Fisher, F. Barron, and H. Wolpe. 1994. *Differentiation and Disadvantage: The Historically Black Universities in South Africa*. Report to the Desmond Tutu Educational Trust. Bellville: Education Policy Unit, University of the Western Cape.

Cele, G., and C. Koen. 2001. "Student Politics and Higher Education in South Africa." Paper presented at the conference Globalisation and Higher Education: Views from the South, Cape Town, March 27–29.

Christie, P., and C. Collins. 1984. "Bantu Education: Apartheid Ideology and Labour Reproduction." In P. Kallaway, ed., *Education and Apartheid: The Education of Black South Africans*. Braamfontein: Ravan Press.

Cloete, N., and I. Bunting. 2000. *Higher Education Transformation: Assessing Performance in South Africa*. Pretoria: Center for Higher Education Transformation.

Cooper, D., and G. Subotzky. 2001. *The Skewed Revolution: Trends in South African Higher Education, 1988–1998*. Bellville: Education Policy Unit, University of the Western Cape.

CHE (Council on Higher Education). 1999. *Annual Report 1998/99*. Pretoria: CHE.

DOE (Department of Education). 1993–1999. South African Post-Secondary Education Financial and Related Statements. Pretoria: Department of Education.

——. 1997a. *Education White Paper 3: A Program for the Transformation of Higher Education*. Pretoria: Government Gazette Notice 1196 of 1997, vol. 386, no. 18207.

——. 1997b. *The Higher Education Act (No. 101)*. Pretoria: Department of Education.

——. 1999. *Higher Education Planning Statistics—Report 1: Students in Universities and Technikons 1993–1999*. Pretoria: Department of Education.

——. 2000. *Annual Report 1999*. Pretoria: Department of Education.

EPU (Education Policy Unit). 1997. *Research Report: The Enhancement of Graduate Programs and Research Capacity at the Historically Black Universities*. Bellville: Education Policy Unit, University of the Western Cape.

Gibbons M. 1999. *Higher Education Relevance in the 21st Century*. Washington, D.C.: The World Bank.

Gibbons, M., C. Limoges, H. Nowotny, S. Schwartzman, P. Scott, and M. Trow. 1994. *The New Production of Knowledge*. London: Sage Publications.

Kraak, A., ed. 2000. *Changing Modes: New Knowledge Production and Its Implications for Higher Education in South Africa*. Pretoria: Human Sciences Research Council Publishers.

Ministry of Education. 1999. *Status Report for the Ministry of Education*. Pretoria: Ministry of Education. Available online at: http://education.pwv.gov.za/Archives/StatusReport.htm

NCHE (National Commission on Higher Education). 1996. *A Framework for Transformation*. Report of the National Commission on Higher Education. Pretoria: NCHE.

Ravjee, N. 1999. "New Modes of Knowledge Production: A Review of the Literature." Unpublished paper. In author's possession.

58

Sudan

M. E. A. El Tom

INTRODUCTION

With an area of 2.5 million square kilometers (1.6 million square miles), Sudan is the largest country in Africa and the tenth largest in the world. Its population grew from about 10.2 million at independence in 1956 to about 29.5 million in 2000 and is projected to reach about 46.3 million in 2025 (United Nations 1999). This fast-growing population is multiracial, multireligious, multilingual, and multicultural. Also, it is largely rural (66 percent in 1998), unschooled (with an illiteracy rate estimated at 42.9 percent in 2000), and poor (with a per capita income of $290 in 1998) (World Bank 2000).

The development of education in Sudan is characterized by, among other things, a continuing rise in social demand (Table 58.1) and allocation of an increasingly smaller share of the gross national product (GNP) (from a high of 5.5 percent in 1974 to 0.8 percent in 1995).

In 2000, there were twenty-six public universities and twenty-one private universities and colleges. In 1999–2000, the system admitted 38,623 students, representing 68.8 percent of total applicants. Of these, 60.9 percent were female and the proportion of those admitted to private institutions was 16.5 percent (Ministry of Higher Education and Scientific Research 1999).

Civil strife has cast a heavy shadow on Sudan ever since it embarked on self-rule in 1954. Of the forty-six years since then, the country has been at war with itself for thirty-four years (with a short hiatus from 1972 to 1983). A significant feature of the war has been its progressive spread since 1983 from its traditional location in the southern part of the country to western, eastern, and southeastern areas. Two grim statistics suffice to highlight its incalculable tragic consequences: the number of dead and displaced since 1983 are estimated at 2 million and 4 million, respectively.

The economy of Sudan has been growing at a sluggish rate since independence. According to the World Bank (1984, 2000), the average annual growth rate of Sudan's gross domestic product (GDP) during 1960–1982 and 1965–1998 was –0.4 percent and –0.2 percent, respectively. Barro (1997) predicted an average annual growth rate of real GDP per capita of –2.7 percent for 1996–2000. A prominent feature of Sudan's economy is the size of its external debt. Sudan's external debt stood at $16.8 billion in 1998 and rose to $24 billion at the end of 1999, making it one of the world's most severely indebted countries (Economist Intelligence Unit 2000).

While recent developments in the oil sector have neither changed the structure of the economy nor helped alleviate the suffering of the masses, they have certainly strengthened real GDP growth. The Economist Intelligence Unit (2000) forecasts real GDP growth at 7 percent in 2000, 5.8 percent in 2001, and at 5.3 percent in 2002. Oil replaced sesame, cotton, and livestock as the principal foreign exchange earner in 2000 ($276 million in 2000, representing 35.4 percent, followed by sesame at $127 million, representing 16.3 percent of total exports). However, despite its contribution to GDP growth on paper, earnings from crude oil are directed to the war effort as evidenced by the recent completion of a $450 million arms factory south of Khartoum and the increase in the military budget from $166 million in 1998 to $242 million in 1999 and a projected $327 million in 2000 (Boustany 2000; Economist Intelligence Unit 2000).

The political development of Sudan has been characterized by an alternation of democratic and military rule, punctuated by popular uprisings in which trade unions and associations of professionals and students play prominent roles. Since independence, the country enjoyed parliamentary democracy during only three relatively brief periods: 1956–1958, 1965–1969, and 1986–1989. Although the first coup d'état (November 1958) was not ideologically motivated, the second (May 1969) is widely

Table 58.1. Gross Primary, Secondary, and Tertiary Enrollment Ratios in Sudan: Total and Female, 1960–1995

	1960		1970		1980		1990		1995	
	Total	Female	Total	Female	Total	Female	Total	Female	Total	Female
Primary	20	11	38	29	50	41	53	45	50	46
Secondary	3	1	7	4	16	12	24	21	21	19
Tertiary	0.4	*	1.2	0.3	1.8	0.9	3	3	NA	NA

* less than 0.1.
NA: Not available.
Source: World Bank 1988; UNESCO 1999.

believed to have been the work of Arab nationalists, and the third (June 1989) was engineered by Muslim fundamentalists in the National Islamic Front (NIF).

The NIF regime has deepened the country's crisis in more than one respect. First, it established a religious state in a multireligious country. Second, it transformed a war about political power, wealth distribution, and national identity into a religious one (*jihad*). Finally, it implemented economic policies that left 94 percent of the population in absolute poverty in 1992 (Ali 1994) and raised the cost-of-living index in 1997 to nearly 190 times its level in 1990 (Europa Publications Staff 1999).

Sudan's multiple crisis of identity, governance, and socioeconomic development has been unfolding in a world whose economic transformation has engendered a new international division of labor. In the new information economy, the third world no longer exists, and Sudan finds itself, together with most African countries, relegated to the fourth world (Castells 1993).

The enormity of the challenges for higher education implied by these developments cannot be overemphasized.

THE SYSTEM OF HIGHER EDUCATION

Three stages in the development of higher education in Sudan may be distinguished. The first is a formative stage that had its beginnings in the first half of the last century and lasted through the 1960s. The second is a stage of limited expansion, reorganization, and democratization from 1970 to 1989. Finally, the stage that the NIF regime calls "The Higher Education Revolution" is a period of unprecedented expansion, politicization, and centralized micromanagement of higher education that began in 1990.

The Formative Stage: 1956–1969

The foundations of higher education in Sudan were established by the British in the first half of the twentieth century. Gordon Memorial College (GMC) opened in 1902 as a primary school. It was gradually expanded and upgraded and its higher schools have provided postsecondary training in arts, science, law, agriculture, veterinary science, engineering, and public administration since 1939. In 1945, the University of London entered into a special relationship with GMC whereby courses for London degrees were instituted in arts, science, law, agriculture, and engineering.

The Kitchener School of Medicine (KSM) was founded in 1924. In 1940, the final professional exam was supervised by a visitor appointed by the Royal College of Physicians and the Royal College of Surgeons of the United Kingdom. It is interesting to note here that the medical profession in Sudan has since then maintained a strong relationship with its counterpart in Britain. To this day, the high point in a Sudanese doctor's professional development is to earn membership in one of the British royal medical colleges.

GMC and KSM were merged in 1951 into the University College of Khartoum. The University of Khartoum (UK, commonly called "U of K") was established in 1956 by an act of Parliament. UK has since then remained the leading and most prestigious institution of higher education in the country.

Khartoum Technical Institute (KTI) was opened in 1950 and included three main schools (engineering, commerce, and fine and applied arts), a women's secretarial school, and a department of further education. The Lancashire and Cheshire Association of Technical Colleges of the United Kingdom recognized it as a technical college. KTI was responsible for technical education throughout the Sudan (KTI was transformed into Sudan University of Science and Technology in 1990/1991).

To meet the increasing demand for secondary school teachers, the Higher Teachers Training Institute (HTTI) was established at the beginning of the 1961–1962 academic session as a joint effort of the Sudan government and the UN Special Fund. HTTI provided four-year postsecondary and in-service teacher training courses. By offering its students monthly stipends and by guaranteeing each of them a job after graduation, HTTI, which operated independently until 1973, was able to attract able students, and its graduates were reputed to be good teachers.

Sudan's educational system includes an educational ladder parallel to that of general education. Students from the religious secondary schools usually apply for admission into Omdurman Religious Institute (ORI), which provided studies in Arabic language and Islamic jurisprudence (Shariʿa). Omdurman Islamic University, established in 1965, is a development of the Islamic Studies College, which is itself an offshoot of ORI.

To cater to Egyptian citizens residing in the Sudan, a branch of Cairo University was opened in Khartoum in 1955 with faculties of arts, law, and commerce. In 1959, these faculties were granted independent status. The branch is entirely financed by the Egyptian government. Since many of its students were part-timers for several years after its establishment, it continued to offer its services in the evenings.

Sudanese entrepreneurs showed little interest in higher education during this formative stage of the system. Thus, for more than three decades after the establishment of UK, Ahfad University College for Women, established in 1966, remained the only Sudanese nongovernmental institution of higher education in the country.

Other institutions providing postsecondary professional training at this formative stage were the Higher Nursing College, the Health Officers' School, the Forests Experts' College, the Sudan Police College, the Prison Officers' College, the Military College, and the Shambat Agricultural Institute. These public institutions were managed under the various relevant ministries and departments.

The University College of Khartoum had 104 full-time and 16 part-time teaching staff and approximately 600 students enrolled in 1955–1956. In the same year, KTI had 176 students. Progress was steadily achieved from these humble beginnings. The total number of students in higher education institutions in 1957–1958 was 1,704. Of these, 839, 25 of whom were females, were enrolled at UK. By 1965, enrollment had risen to 8,108, with about 8 percent females; in 1970, it reached 14,308, with about 12 percent females.

To put these figures in perspective, note that the average annual rate of growth in enrollment was about 21.5 percent and 15 percent during the two periods 1957–1958 to 1965–1966 and 1965–1966 to 1969–1970, respectively. Moreover, the 1969–1970 enrollment figure represents 1 percent of the relevant age cohort and corresponds to about 1 tertiary student per 1,000 inhabitants. (The various figures cited here are computed from UNESCO 1961, 1966, and 1978–1979.)

Four characteristics of this stage of development deserve mention. The first concerns the relationship between UK and the state. Despite the change in regime from parliamentary democracy to a military one in 1958 and the restoration of democratic rule in 1964, the state continued to provide generously for the university in Sudan. However, while the democratic regimes were respectful of the university's autonomy and academic freedom, the military dictatorship of 1958 made a failed attempt to bring the university under its control. However, it did manage to introduce a change in the university act that resulted in making the head of state the chancellor of the university, despite student opposition.

Second, this period was characterized by a lack of strategic planning. Each institution functioned independently of the others, and no institution had a strategy for its development. As far as UK is concerned, it shared with the civil service an understandable preoccupation with the process of Sudanization throughout this period. In 1958, Sudanese constituted only 10 percent of academic staff; but the proportion had risen to an impressive 50 percent by 1967–1968 (Thompson, Fogel, and Danner 1977).

The third characteristic is the dominance of the University of Khartoum. It was the first national comprehensive university, and both Sudanese society and the state had great hopes that it would foster social mobility, economic development, and nation building. It was the crown of an educational system that most Sudanese perceived as the key to the door leading to political power and wealth. Its strong links with the United Kingdom through British faculty, programs of study, and training for scholars and a British-dominated system of external examiners added greatly to its stature and prestige.

Fourth, the "system" was highly selective. By the end of the 1960s, less than 1 percent of the relevant age cohort were enrolled in higher education institutions.

Reorganization, Limited Expansion and Control, and Democratization: 1970–1989

Within barely one year of assuming power, the 1969 military regime of Brigadier Nemeiri embarked on an ambitious reform of education. At the first two levels, the 4 + 4 + 4 ladder was replaced by a 6 + 3 + 3 one. At the tertiary level, a ministerial committee recommended the establishment of a Ministry of Higher Education and Scientific Research, the creation of a National Council for Higher Education (NCHE), and a review of university curricula. Moreover, it recommended that the new ministry assume the responsibility for those institutions of higher education that were then being run by various ministries and government departments. Significantly, HTTI became the Faculty of Education at UK in 1973, which had two important implications. First, few of its academic staff at the time met the minimum requirements for appointment in the university (an upper second-class honors degree). Second, the material incentives for students that were an important part of its admissions policy no longer applied.

In 1975, the Higher Education Organization Act was proclaimed. According to the stipulations of the act, higher education institutions should assume the traditional roles of teaching and research and undertake to train a labor force in accordance with the short- and long-term needs of the country specified in relevant state policies. The process of reorganization brought higher education institutions under almost direct control of the state for the first time since independence. Presidents of NCHE, as well as university councils, vice-chancellors, deans of faculties, heads of departments, and senior administrative posts were each appointed by their respective superiors in consultation with, ultimately, the head of state. Upon the recommendation of British experts, a newly established funding committee provided finances and controlled expenditures.

In addition, two new universities were established: Juba University in the South and University of Gezira in central Sudan. The first university was established in response to a demand made by southern political elite during discussions with the government in 1971, which led to the Addis Ababa Agreement and an end to the war in the south. Labor requirements for development, particularly in engineering, managerial, and agricultural professions, were the main factor behind the establishment of the second university. The economic decline of the late 1970s and the 1980s is often cited to explain the failure of the regime to further expand the system.

Student enrollment during Nemeiri's rule grew at an annual average rate of about 6.6 percent from 14,308 in 1970 to 37,367 in 1985. A noteworthy feature of this period is the phenomenal rise in the number of female students: from 13 percent of total enrollment in 1970–1971 to 37 percent in 1985–1986. However, the number of female teachers registered only a small increase: from 7 percent in 1975–1976 to 10 percent in 1985–1986. It is interesting to reflect on the socioeconomic factors responsible for this phenomenon. In at least one Muslim country, Qatar, female students outnumber male students by a factor of 2 to 1.

The gross enrollment ratio rose from its 1 percent level in 1970 to 2.1 percent in 1986. However, the number of tertiary students per 100,000 inhabitants increased from 103 in 1970 to 174 in 1985—that is, at an average annual rate of about 3.6 percent.

Democracy in the country was restored in April 1985, and by 1986, new acts for the organization of higher education and for the University of Khartoum were promulgated. The 1986 University of Khartoum act restored autonomy and academic freedom and required that all administrative posts be occupied as a result of direct elections, subject to additional requirements of academic seniority (for example, the vice-chancellor and his or her deputy must both be full professors) (UNESCO 1995).

Uncontrolled Expansion, Politicization, and Centralized Micromanagement: 1989 to the Present

In December 1989, barely six months after the NIF coup, the chairman of the military council (who is now president of the republic) addressed the nation to announce the regime's first major policy announcement. Although most Sudanese assumed that the policy would be related to the economic and/or political sphere, it turned out to be exclusively about higher education (see Abbas 1999 for a discussion of this anomaly and for an elucidation of the importance that Muslim fundamentalists in the Muslim world attach to education).

There were two parts to the announcement: a list of major problems of higher education and a number of "corrective" decisions. Five major problems of the system were highlighted:

- It was elitist, in the narrow sense of admitting not more than 6 percent of secondary school graduates every year.
- Its institutions were highly concentrated in the capital, implying that rural communities were deprived of an important source of cultural enrichment.
- There were too many Sudanese studying abroad (mostly in Europe), requiring a significant share of the country's small hard-currency earnings.
- The system's financial requirements represented a heavy burden on public coffers.
- The system was "Western" in orientation and as such played an important role in alienating the nation's youth from their cultural heritage.

The "corrective" decisions were later incorporated into a council of ministers proclamation of "the higher education revolution" in March 1990. The pillars of this "revolution" are the following:

- New goals would be formulated that anchored education in society's African-Arab-Islamic beliefs and heritage.
- Arabic, instead of English, should be the medium of instruction in all higher education institutions.
- Intake would be doubled as of 1990–1991.
- Admission policies would be reformed.
- Student boarding and subsistence schemes would be abolished.
- New universities would be established in rural areas.
- All students studying abroad were required to report immediately to the Ministry of Higher Education and Scientific Research to arrange for their enrollment in Sudanese institutions. The Central Bank of Sudan was instructed to stop transfer of funds for these students.

The implementation of these decisions was preceded by the proclamation of two acts: one for the organization of higher education and the other for individual universities. An indication of the haste with which these acts were prepared is that they did not take into consideration special features of the different institutions, as for instance in articles that referred to faculties that existed in only some of the universities. However, these acts represented a radical shift in the state's role in the management of the system and in institutional governance.

The chancellor, who is the president of the republic, appoints the president and the majority university council members. Access and admission policies, the establishment of new academic units, and all academic and senior administrative appointments in the various institutions are either made or need to be approved by the minister of higher education and scientific research. Whereas academic merit was previously the sole criterion for academic appointments, now ideological and political considerations assumed importance. Political commitment is of paramount importance in the appointment to senior administrative posts. Thus, the academic rank of vice-chancellors of several universities is that of lecturer whereas, according to the act, it should be full professor.

In terms of size, student intake jumped from 6,080 in 1989 to 13,210 in 1990–1991 and 38,623 in 1999–2000. The number of female students rose to 40 percent of enrollment in 1995. However, the continued increase in the proportion of female students has not been accompanied by a comparable increase in their representation among faculty: merely 13 percent of faculty were women in 1995.

The number of public institutions increased from five universities and one polytechnic in 1989 to twenty-six universities in 1996 (the one polytechnic, KTI, was promoted to university status). The number of private higher education institutions increased from one in 1989 to sixteen in 1996 and twenty-two in 2000. The number of students enrolled in private higher education institutions increased nearly ninefold within four years: from 2,686 in 1990–1991 to 23,476 in 1994–1995 (El Tom 1999; Ministry of Higher Education and Scientific Research 1996b, 1999).

UNIVERSITY RESEARCH: A NEGLECTED FUNCTION

In Sudan, successive university acts, as well as those of the organization of higher education, explicitly mention the advancement of knowledge and scientific research as a major institutional task. However, the practice of research has not been consistent with the implications of this statement. For one thing, Sudan has no research policy either at the systemic or institutional level. Second, motivation and conditions for research are particularly poor. Conditions of service of faculty have so deteriorated that even full professors find it necessary to undertake part-time work in order to supplement their income. The politicization of higher education has relegated research to a secondary requirement for promotion purposes. Research budgets have practically disappeared from university budgets during the past decade. Funds for sabbatical leaves, travel, and visiting scholars are nonexistent. Third, a recent official report noted that research has been dropped completely from consideration by all new universities (Ministry of Higher Education and Scientific Research 1996b). Finally, private higher education institutions do not include research among their functions.

Research in Sudanese Universities

In order to gain some insight into the status of research in higher education institutions, I have examined publications reported in international databases. The data is collected from the Arts & Humanities Citation Index (A&HCI), Social Sciences Citation Index (SSCI), and the Scientific Citation Index (SCI) databases, all of which are established by the Institute for Scientific Information (ISI) in Philadelphia, Pennsylvania.

Although counts of publications are commonly used as measures of research performance, the proposed approach has its limitations. Research output may take a number of different forms, such as an article published in a newspaper, an authored book, a research report, a curriculum development project, and an article published in a journal. Simple counts ignore the quality of publications. While the coverage of the ISI databases is extensive and includes the core journals in the global communication network of science and scholarship, it is by no means fully comprehensive.

The research that is done in Sudan is no exception to the general rule that research is largely undertaken in universities worldwide (France is one exception). Thus, out of a total of 3,339 publications for the Sudan during the 27-year period 1973–1999, the share of research done in Sudanese universities is about 76.3 percent. However, research output in Sudan during the 1990s decreased by about 22 percentage points from its level in the 1980s; UK saw a 30 percent decrease.

It is instructive to compare the data for Sudan with corresponding data for two other African countries: Kenya and Morocco. All three countries had a comparable population size of about 28 million in 1998. While Kenya shares with Sudan a British influence on their educational systems, both Morocco and Sudan share an Arab influence. As for the size of their economies, Morocco has maintained a relatively stronger position throughout the period 1960–1998, with Sudan occupying an intermediate position through the 1960s and early 1980s and losing this position to Kenya in the 1990s.

The number of publications in ISI databases increased at an annual average rate of about 3 percent during the last decade of the twentieth century, from 875,310 in 1990 to 1,176,333 in 1999. However, the corresponding rate of increase for Kenya, Morocco, and Sudan was 3.3 percent, 15.5 percent, and −0.76 percent, respectively. Clearly, Sudan academics have not been able to duplicate the rate of publication of scholars in Kenya and Morocco.

Let us try to relate the number of publications in the 1990s to the number of university teachers (potential researchers) in each of the three countries. For instance, in 1995, the number of university teachers in Kenya, Morocco, and Sudan was 2,951, 8,562, and 2,558, respectively (UNESCO 1999; World of Learning 1995). The number for Sudan is an estimate based on an average annual rate of increase of 4.6 percent, which is the rate for the period 1985–1990. On the other hand, the number of ISI publications in 1995 for Kenyan, Moroccan, and Sudanese universities was 369, 532, and 75, respectively. A simple computation reveals that while 50 percent of university teachers in Kenya publish, on average, one article every four years, their corresponding colleagues in Morocco and Sudan publish, on average, one article every eight and seventeen years, respectively.

An interesting feature of the Sudanese research picture is that university research is heavily dominated by UK. UK's share of all university publications during the period 1973–1999 was almost 90 percent. This degree of dominance by a single university in research output is probably rare worldwide. Certainly it is not true of industrialized countries. In Kenya, the number of total publications from universities in the ISI databases for the period 1990–1999 was 3,493. However, the share of the University of Nairobi, the oldest and leading university in the country, of total university publications is about 49 percent.

The data further show that the slight decrease in UK's share of total publications of Sudanese universities over the years is primarily due to research undertaken at Gezira University.

The fact that the level of research output by almost all universities is alarmingly low is further highlighted by the size of their respective faculties, as is strongly indicated by the data in Table 58.2. The table further indicates that several Sudanese universities offer doctoral degree programs despite their low level of research output. This, of course, raises a question about the quality of these programs.

Research at Khartoum University

Further investigation of research undertaken by UK faculty reveals that it is structurally weak. Table 58.3 shows that the share of the medical sciences publications of all UK ISI publications over the past three decades (1970–1999) exceeds one-third, which corresponds more or less to their average share of total faculty size (about 200 out of a total that averaged 580 during the 1990s). This strongly suggests, among other things, a concentration of university resources in medical sciences (par-

Table 58.2. Teachers and Postgraduate Students in Selected Sudanese Universities, 1995–1996

	Teachers	Postgraduate Students		
		Ph.D.	Master's	Diploma
University of Khartoum	583	496	2,333	502
Omdurman Islamic University	173	90	355	909
Sudan University for Science and Technology	232	25	55	208
Gezira University	291	128	627	87
Juba University	61	5	11	0
Quran Kareem University	70	141	77	20
Total	1,410	885	3,458	1,726

Source: Ministry of Higher Education and Scientific Research Statistics 1996a and 1996b.

Table 58.3. Research at the University of Khartoum: Distribution of ISI Publications by Disciplinary Areas, 1970–1999*

	1970–79	1980–89	1990–99	Total
Medical Sciences	271	333	353	957
Veterinary Science	131	256	135	522
Agriculture	76	104	76	256
Engineering	39	38	21	98
Science	196	211	87	494
Social Sciences	23	35	23	81
Arts and Humanities	18	23	6	47
Total	754	1,000	701	2,455

*Medical sciences: medicine, pharmacy, public health, dentistry and nutrition; veterinary: faculties of veterinary and animal production; agriculture: faculties of agriculture and forestry; science: departments of botany, chemistry, geology, microbiology, physics, and zoology; Hydrobiological Research Unit; Institute of Environmental Studies; and Faculty of Mathematics; social sciences: faculties of economics and social studies, education, law; and management and business administration.
Source: ISI 2000a, 2000b, and 2000c.

ticularly in curative medicine, as is easily demonstrated by further analysis of the data).

Five factors may help to explain this phenomenon. First, a historical factor: Kitchener School of Medicine, established in 1924, had a head start of at least two decades relative to most other disciplines. Second, in the 1940s, the colonial administration established research laboratories to promote the health of the colonizers and that of native laborers, animals, and crops (several of these stations are still functioning). Six out of a total of twelve Sudanese full professors in the university in 1972–1973 were in the Faculty of Medicine (Thompson, Fogel, and Danner 1977). Third, the medical profession has been one of the strongest in the country. Fourth, medical studies have consistently been the most popular of all higher education programs of study. Fifth, their strong association with the Ministry of Health put considerable resources at their disposal that most others lacked.

The same table shows that the levels of research in engineering, social sciences, and arts and humanities are almost negligible —their combined share of ISI publications hovers around 9 percent—despite the fact that their combined faculty size aver-

aged more than 35 percent of total faculty during the 1990s. Further investigation of ISI databases reveals that

- They do not include a *single* article in the area of education.
- University researchers have been absent from the scholarly debate on development issues such as colonialism and culture, dependency, self-reliance, delinking, and science, technology and society.
- Khartoum University's publications include few articles that are related to the phenomenal advances in areas associated with the technological revolution: biotechnology, information technology, and materials science.
- Medical research is dominated by curative medicine; few of its publications are in community medicine.

This situation should be a source of considerable concern for those responsible for higher education as well as for those in leading positions in individual universities, for each of these disciplinary areas has a pivotal role in the social, economic, political, and cultural development of the country.

CONTINUITY AND CHANGE IN HIGHER EDUCATION

A qualitative change can be discerned between the pre-1990 and the post-1990 states of higher education in Sudan. In fact, whereas the various transformations that were effected prior to 1990 preserved the essence of the system, the transformation brought about by the NIF regime was so profound that it marked a break with the system that preceded it.

A System in Crisis

The Sudanese inherited from colonialism a few institutions of postsecondary education that were dominated by UK. Both the state and the university administration saw Sudanization as the major goal for the university throughout the period 1956–1969. In 1965–1966, only two of a total of twenty-five UK full professors were Sudanese: one in Arabic and the other in history. And, as late as 1970–1971, UK had only seven Sudanese professors out of a total of twenty-eight (World of Learning 1971). The state, which itself was undertaking the Sudanization of its civil service, appreciated the challenge facing the university and provided generously toward achieving it. In particular, institutional autonomy and academic freedom were both fully respected by the state. The only minor exception occurred in early 1960 in the aftermath of confrontations between police forces and students who were demonstrating against the 1959 agreement between the Egyptian and Sudanese governments.

On the whole, national political parties, including the Communist Party and the Muslim Brotherhood, were united in their opposition to the first military regime. As a result, the student movement was also united. Thus, challenging the students could have led to a much bigger confrontation, which the regime would have been wise to avoid.

The Nemeiri dictatorship (1969–1985) presented a radically different picture. During its first two years in power, the regime put forward a self-defined leftist program that was supported by a broad section of urban society, including workers, trade unions, professional associations, and a section of university students. The Muslim Brotherhood opposed the regime. The regime's first move toward the university was to dismiss twelve faculty members whom it designated as rightists. Academic staff were sharply divided over this incident and, more generally, over their stand vis-à-vis the regime.

As a result of a short-lived Communist-inspired coup d'état in July 1971, the regime changed direction and cracked down as hard as it could on leftists, especially Communists. Another batch of faculty members, this time designated as leftists, were dismissed from UK and KTI. Throughout the period 1971–1975, political opposition to the regime and the student movement were both relatively weak. This explains the regime's relative success in implementing policies that resulted in limiting institutional autonomy and academic freedom, both of which had previously been enjoyed by universities.

In 1976, military forces of an alliance of the two major national political parties and Muslim fundamentalists launched an all-out attack on the regime's armed forces in Khartoum from their base in Libya. The failure of this so-called Libyan invasion

further weakened both the regime and the opposition. A reconciliation between the regime and elements of the rightist opposition was concluded in 1977. From 1977 to 1985, Muslim fundamentalists allied themselves with the regime and the terms of the alliance obliged the fundamentalists to keep the student movement on a short leash.

As a result of a declining economy and the associated deterioration in living conditions, the oppressive nature of the regime, and the bitter political struggle between the regime and the opposition, the regime and all national political parties appeared completely discredited in the eyes of many, including perhaps the majority of students. New student organizations, including regional associations, academic associations, and political groups, proliferated across all campuses. The most important of all these were Elmostaquili (the independents) and Elmohaidi (the nonaligned). A broad alliance of students (including leftists and regional and academic associations), led first by independents and later by nonaligned associations, succeeded in wresting the leadership of the influential Khartoum University Students Union (KUSU) from the fundamentalists in 1980 and 1989. Also, members of academic staff organized themselves in 1979 and, for the first time in the history of higher education in Sudan, formed the Academic Staff Trade Union Association (ASTUA), which opposed the regime.

ASTUA played a prominent role in improving the conditions of service of its members, defending academic freedom, calling for democratization of the university, and stopping the regime's further attempts at tighter control of the university. In fact, it played a leading role in the popular uprising that brought down the Nemeiri regime in April 1985.

ASTUA initiated and brought to fruition, in the form of the University of Khartoum Act of 1986, a process of democratic university governance. The 1986 act replaced the principle of appointment with that of election of all academic administrative posts. Representatives of workers and staff trade unions, of KUSU, of the university senate and council, and of all faculty members had the right to participate in the mandated elections. Despite this historic triumph, the university came out of Nemeiri's era heavily bruised and in crisis. In addition to the low level and structural weakness of university research discussed above, there were four other aspects of this crisis.

Absence of mission: Individual institutions of higher education (including UK) as well as higher education as a whole lacked a clear mission to direct their efforts and evaluate performance. Neither the system nor its constituent institutions have ever undertaken overall evaluation exercises. The vice-chancellor's annual report to the university council ceased to appear in 1961–1962. The purpose of the policies of various regimes was not to revitalize the system but rather to control it. The job of vice-chancellors and university councils was, first and foremost, to maintain a quiet campus. This goes a long way toward explaining why UK had seven different vice-chancellors during Nemeiri's sixteen-year rule. Obviously, the policy produced leaders that were too politically unstable to be effective.

Financial constraints: In the absence of a meaningful strategy for sustainable human development, and in view of continuing economic decline, it was inevitable that institutions of higher education would be financially constrained. The financial situation worsened, particularly after the currency devaluation of 1978. Since then, capital expenditure, budget allocations for research, and scholarships for teaching assistants, libraries, and sabbatical leaves have reached unacceptably low levels. As of 1980–1981, the university ceased to finance sabbatical leaves, the university library reduced subscription to international periodicals to a trickle, most teaching assistants have had to depend on their own efforts or those of their respective departments to secure foreign sources to finance their scholarships, and science laboratories have become entirely dependent on foreign (notably German, British, and Dutch) donors for imported equipment and consumables.

Emigration: The emergence of the oil boom of the early 1970s, combined with a marked deterioration in living conditions in Sudan, led many Sudanese academics to emigrate to oil-exporting Arab countries. El Tom (1980) reports that a total of 148 academic staff, representing 24 percent of the 1978–1979 faculty, left UK for Gulf Arab countries during 1968–1979. Of these, 110 (74.3 percent) emigrated during the last four years of the period. This trend continued unabated throughout the 1980s, with significant effects on the morale and age structure of faculty. Young faculty were often among the first to leave.

Campus violence: Violence on university campuses was practically unknown before 1968. In that year, a student hurled a chair toward fellow students who were performing a dance as part of a cultural event held in the university's examination hall. The violence that ensued cost a student's life and marked a turning point in the university's campus life.

During Nemeiri's era, Muslim fundamentalists demanded a free hand to enable them to honor their part of the deal with the regime, namely silencing the opposition of other students. No means were spared toward that end: intimidation, beatings, use of iron bars and knives, use of Molotov cocktails, rigging of student elections (an annual event), destruction of university property, tearing up of examination papers, arrests, dismissals—all this and much more that remained hidden from observers was as much a part of campus life as was course attendance. Particularly damaging to the university was the fact that the administration did not lift a finger to restore some sense of rationality to the campus. The administration's behavior was, at least in this respect, entirely predictable: it was appointed to safeguard the regime's and not the university's interests.

Thus, the first victims of this collusion between the regime and Muslim fundamentalists were the university leadership's integrity and academic values. Instead of creating conditions conducive to the promotion of rationalism, a fundamental value of academe, the university leadership, consciously or unconsciously, encouraged the violence.

It is rather remarkable that the university did not collapse under the weight of this long-term crisis. Five factors are responsible for this achievement:

- Admissions policy: The university has maintained, since its establishment, a highly selective admissions policy that ensured that it would enroll the best applicants. In fact, its annual enrollment never exceeded 1,700 students in the 1980s, or about .01 percent of secondary school graduates.

- Faculty appointment: The university adhered to a tradition of considering merit as the sole criterion for academic appointments. The minimum requirement was an upper second honors degree of University of Khartoum or its equivalent. This tradition ensured for the university a first-rate faculty.

- Faculty promotion: A clearly defined set of promotion regulations emphasizing research that was externally assessed was the third pillar of a tradition of academic quality that the university maintained.

- Creation of ASTUA: Through ASTUA, a democratically constituted body, faculty members were able to articulate a unified stand not only on their conditions of service but also on institutional issues, including participation in decision making and campus violence. It is no exaggeration to state that the presence of ASTUA strengthened respect for tradition, gave encouragement to students who were increasingly threatened by violence from both the government and fellow students, and restrained interference of the regime in university affairs.

- Collapse of the system: At the time of the NIF coup, Sudan faced two fundamental but familiar problems: an ongoing war and an ailing economy. Rather than address these problems, the new regime was frantically busy concocting tactics to secure its fragile hold on power—a power that it sought essentially to establish an Islamic state.

The policy of unprecedented expansion of higher education was partly meant to bolster support for the regime. Many felt that such a policy would generate badly needed support for the regime among students and their families and that it would considerably enlarge the pool from which Muslim fundamentalists have traditionally recruited their cadres. Also, the creation of regional universities could serve the regime by helping to undermine the influence of traditional sectarian parties in their strongholds.

Another objective that the policy served was to ensure that students were not tempted to pursue higher education in other countries, where they would be exposed to other cultures and ideologies. According to Abbas (1999), the main policy objective was the creation of a new elite to replace the old one, which was, in the fundamentalists' view, the product of a colonial educational system that has alienated this elite from its Arabic-Islamic heritage.

Although they did not mount an explicit opposition to the new policies, higher education institutions, notably UK, asked to be provided with the necessary resources to implement the policies of expansion and Arabicization. The majority of students, who were not NIF supporters, opposed the new policies, especially for their abolition of the traditional boarding and subsistence scheme. Institutional demands for resources were seen by the regime as deliberate obstacles to sabotage the "revolution." The regime responded by appointing administrators that were committed to the new policies and more generally, sympathetic, if not wholly committed to, the NIF. Student opposition was met by a combination of violence, dismissals, and terror. (See Abbas 1999 for more information and a detailed analysis.)

The dramatic results of the implementation of the new policies were easy to predict for an objective observer. However, it took the regime almost five years to sense that something was amiss. The new system of higher education has the following characteristics:

Institutional autonomy and academic freedom: Higher education institutions, and universities in particular, cannot function properly without enjoying an adequate measure of autonomy and academic freedom. Now universities' finances, appointment of senior administrators, recruitment of staff, curricular issues, and their calendars are all centrally controlled by the education ministry.

According to the University of Khartoum Act of 1990, academic freedom is guaranteed but subject to the laws of the land (that is, the laws of a theocratic state). Recently, a professor of veterinary science was arrested as a result of an article entitled "Rift Valley Fever and the Prospects for Meat and Livestock Exports" that he published in a Sudanese daily (*Alsahafa*, no. 2697, dated October 10, 2000). More ominous is the *fatwa* issued by fourteen prominent Muslim fundamentalists, including two UK faculty members, decreeing that members of the leftist student organization, Democratic Front, were apostates. The background of this *fatwa* is a wallpaper article that students found insulting to their faith (*Alshark Alawsat*, November 15, 2000).

Quality of students: It is widely recognized in Sudan that the quality of general education has been deteriorating since the early 1970s. The system of general education is poorly resourced. For instance, many secondary schools do not have a single qualified mathematics teacher. Not a single public school has either a library or a laboratory. Curricula are exam driven, and rote learning is a prominent feature of the system. The reduction of the length of schooling from twelve to eleven years in 1992–1993 further lowered its quality.

By doubling intake and adopting an admission policy for higher education that give a clear advantage to students who score high marks in Arabic language and religion, two subjects that emphasize more than any other memorization of text, the academic standard of new entrants has been lowered.

Quality of faculty: Academic merit has ceased to be the sole criterion for appointment of faculty and teaching assistants. For lack of resources and for ideological reasons, the education and training of prospective faculty is now undertaken mostly locally or in universities of certain developing countries that are not renowned for their excellence. Sabbatical leaves have stopped since the 1980s. Funds for research and travel abroad are particularly scarce.

Both appointment and promotion of faculty, especially in new universities, are not subject to any clear regulations. For instance, some recent Ph.D., M.Sc., and B.A. holders have been appointed as associate professors, assistant professors, and lecturers, respectively (Ministry of Higher Education and Scientific Research 1996a).

Quality of infrastructure: Higher education institutions need capital investment in order to modernize and improve their physical academic environment (buildings, access roads, libraries, computerized networking and data processing, etc.). Expansion of the system further accentuates this need. However, capital expenditure has been reduced to a trickle since the economic crisis of the mid-1970s.

In 1988–1989, the approved development budget for the four established universities and KTI was just under $7 million. In 1994–1995, the corresponding approved budget for twenty-six universities was about $9 million. During the period 1989–1990 to 1994–1995, the approved development budget fluctuated between 6 percent and 18.5 percent of the proposed budget (Ministry of Higher Education and Scientific Research 1995).

Although the term "library" has assumed a new meaning recently, in Sudan it is still viewed as a place where printed material is regularly collected, cataloged, and preserved. But even this outdated definition has been compromised as a result of financial constraints. To take one example, UK library's approved budget ($444,444) represented 34.3 percent of the proposed budget for the entire university ($1.3 million, including $936 for periodicals). Available information indicates that the library's budget during 1992–1998 consisted entirely of salaries and wages. Furthermore, periodicals ceased to be received regularly in 1987, and subscriptions to many of them were discontinued in 1993 (including 460, 200, and 170 periodicals at the faculties of engineering, education, and law, respectively).

Quality of programs: The quality of academic programs depends on, among other things, the quality of faculty and infrastructure. To the extent that the quality of both of these has deteriorated, it should come as no surprise that the quality of programs has also deteriorated.

UK has undertaken a review of its curricula only once in its history, in 1973. The result of this exercise was a set of recommendations that a few academic units heeded. No other institution of higher education in Sudan has ever initiated a similar exercise.

As a result of a combination of factors, including dismissals and emigration, the staff-to-student ratio has progressively worsened. UNESCO (1999) data show that for all Sudanese universities and equivalent institutions, the ratio was about 1 to 16 in 1970–1971, 1 to 25 in 1980–1981, and 1 to 29 in 1990–1991. Mohamed and Giha (1999) reported a ratio of 1 to 67 in 1998. For UK, this ratio was 1 to 6 in 1957–1958, never exceeded 1 to 15 during the period 1975–1986, and reached 1 to 24 in 1994–1995 (UNESCO 1969; Issa 1999; University of Khartoum 1996). However, the ratio for 1994–1995 exhibits wide variations between the various faculties, with 1 to 12 in medicine, 1 to 33 in engineering, 1 to 53 in law, and a high of 1 to 100 in management sciences.

Mathematics, which is assuming an increasingly important role in both general and specialized education, presents a rather dramatic case in this respect. The UK Faculty of Mathematical Sciences is responsible for teaching all mathematics courses included in the various programs offered by the university. The mathematics faculty size was twenty-nine, including twenty-one Sudanese Ph.D. holders, in 1985–1986. Today, its size is five, including the dean of the faculty. Besides these five, there is only one Sudanese Ph.D. in mathematics in the country, a faculty member at El Nilein University.

The acute shortage in academic staff has forced many universities to depend heavily on recent bachelor's and master's degree graduates. Some faculties in new universities depend entirely on visiting academic staff who are hired for short periods of time. Private higher education institutions depend heavily on part-time teachers. In 1994–1995, they employed a total of seventy-one full-time Ph.D. holders (Ministry of Higher Education and Scientific Research 1996b).

Laboratory classes and fieldwork requirements are often not met. For instance, majors in forestry are required to undertake five field trips, each lasting for at least one month. Now, because of scarce resources, they manage only two trips, each lasting for about two weeks. In 1999, students of the Faculty of Pharmacy occupied the faculty buildings for two days, protesting the absence of laboratory classes for eight consecutive months out of a nine-month academic year. Moreover, the equipment in some laboratories, such as the strength of materials laboratory in the Faculty of Engineering, has not been modernized in thirty years.

Most medical faculties are located in towns that don't have a morgue. It is reported that there are only three morgues and twenty-four medical faculties outside the greater Khartoum area. The morgue at Khartoum teaching hospital is shared by ten medical schools, two of which are private.

Quality of campus environment: The student body has become more polarized than ever on the basis of political and ideological grounds. There are the NIF students and sympathizers, a broad coalition of anti-NIF students, and a few who sit on the fence. There is virtually no meaningful communication between members of the first two groups. Indeed, violence has become the principal means of settling political and ideological differences.

A second prominent feature of campus environment is the quasi-permanent presence on campus of armed security forces. Obviously, the intention is to preempt any protest movement and to intimidate and terrorize both students and staff.

Contact between faculty and students is minimal and in fact is practically reduced to classroom contact. The main reason behind this is the marked deterioration in faculty remuneration and the consequent spread of moonlighting. The monthly salary of a teaching assistant in 1970 was about $460. After over thirty years of service, his or her monthly salary as an associate professor would now be about $110.

Quality of institutional leadership: Political and ideological considerations have replaced merit as the dominant criteria for appointment of presidents of university councils, vice-chancellors and their deputies, deans of faculties, and heads of departments.

The previously mentioned report on the new universities observed that most academic and administrative leaders lack the necessary academic qualifications and experience. Some of them are associate professors, others are assistant professors, and many of them have never occupied an administrative post previously or ever served on university councils, senates, or committees (Ministry of Higher Education and Scientific Research 1996a).

Events during the past decade have amply demonstrated that the integrity and moral authority that constitute a fundamental ingredient of higher education leadership have all but disappeared. No university council president or member—and no vice-chancellor, dean, or head of department—has during the past decade protested the killing (on and off campus), torture, beating, or arrest without trial of students who happen to hold opinions not approved by government. These tragic events are regularly reported by local, regional, and international media and by NGOs.

In a moving letter addressed to the leader of the NIF regime, with a copy to the UK vice-chancellor and university senate, a biologist at the university narrated and protested conditions of his arrest and torture during November 1989 to February 1990. One of the reasons for this ordeal, his torturers (who included a university lecturer) told him, was his teaching a course on the Darwinian theory of evolution. The letter was widely distributed by fellow faculty, and an international movement of solidarity ensued (including an editorial in *New Scientist* and a letter by a group of scientists in *Science* journal) that later led to his release. However, to this day, nobody knows the whereabouts of the copy of the letter that was delivered to the vice-chancellor at the time (El Tom 1999).

Purpose of private higher education: According to the ministry, private higher education institutions should aim to complement public higher education and to satisfy the needs of the labor market for intermediate-level workers. However, oblivious to the instructions of the ministry and guided by the logic of their own market and profit maximization in 1994–1995, 84 percent of students enrolled in these institutions pursued theoretical programs of study.

By stretching the system's scarce resources beyond any reasonable limit; by robbing universities of institutional autonomy and academic freedom, without which they cannot perform their traditional functions; by imposing leadership that is in many cases incompetent and lacking in academic merit and integrity; and by encouraging violence among fellow students and spreading intimidation and terror on campuses, it is inevitable that a system in crisis will collapse under the weight of the NIF policies for higher education.

THE FUTURE

The system of higher education in Sudan has been adrift for more than thirty years, since the establishment of UK as an independent national university in 1956. By employing higher education institutions as instruments for the achievement of narrowly conceived and reactionary ideological and political goals, the fundamentalists of the NIF have practically destroyed the system. Now is the time to pick up the pieces and use them to the greatest possible advantage to build a new system on more solid foundations. A system in ruins cannot be reformed; it needs to be fundamentally rethought.

The conference organized by the Association of Sudanese Academics provided an excellent opportunity for a discussion of issues central to the development of higher education in the future, including the issues of structure and finance. However, the conference did not discuss a comprehensive strategy for this purpose. This is the task that needs to be accomplished.

Higher education, and education more generally, cannot be adequately understood outside of its political, economic, and social milieu. Sudan has been ruled and continues to be ruled by a small and largely urban-based elite. A fundamental characteristic of the various groups that ruled the country since independence and through the 1980s was their lack of vision. As a result, the country has been plunged into a crisis.

It is only natural that these groups would maintain a highly selective higher education system that had no purpose other than reproducing the ruling elite. The economic decline of the 1970s and Nemeiri's politicization and control of the system further exposed it for what it was: a system in crisis.

The Muslim fundamentalist regime of the NIF, unlike any other regime that preceded it, has a grand mission: to establish a fundamentalist Islamic state in Sudan. In the economic sphere, they have adopted a structural adjustment program paradigm. Much of the newly found wealth in oil is devoted to the war effort. In the political sphere, the hallmark of the regime is unbridled oppression.

The NIF regime has used higher education for the achievement of political and ideological ends. The policies that have been implemented for this purpose have led to the collapse of higher education. More than that, in pursuance of their grand mission, they essentially destroyed one of the principal means for invigorating higher education: the middle class.

Sudan is realistically left with one agency for building a higher education system that has the capacity to respond to the challenges presented by national, regional, and worldwide developments: a "developmental" state. It remains to be seen whether the broad coalition of forces fighting for a "new Sudan" will succeed in achieving such a state. Either way, the future of both Sudan and its system of higher education will be entwined.

REFERENCES

Abbas, A. A. 1999. "The Political and Ideological Underpinnings of the Policies of the National Islamic Front in Higher Education in Sudan." In M. E. A. El Tom, ed., *Proceedings of the Conference on the State and Future of Higher Education in Sudan.* Cairo: Armis Co. (in Arabic).

Ali, A. G. A. 1994. *Structural Adjustment Programs and Poverty in the Sudan.* Cairo: Centre for Arab Studies (in Arabic).

Barro, R. J. 1997. *Determinants of Economic Growth: A Cross-Country Empirical Study.* Cambridge, Mass.: MIT Press.

Boustany, N. 2000. "An Appeal to the 'Conscience of the International Community' on Sudan." *Washington Post*, November 17, A38.

Castells, M. 1993. "The Informational Economy." In Martin Carnoy, Manuel Castells, Stephen S. Cohen, and Fernando Henrique Cardoso, eds., *The New Global Economy in the Information Age: Reflections on Our Changing World.* University Park: Pennsylvania State University Press.

Economist Intelligence Unit. 2000. "Country Report Sudan. Alerts & Updates: Don't Expect Too Much From Oil." 16 June. Available online at: http://www.eiu.com. Accessed June 2000.

El Tom, M. E. A. 1980. "The Role of the Educational System in the Emigration of High-Level Manpower." In A. B. Zahalan, ed., *The Arab Brain Drain.* London: Ithaca Press.

———. 1999. *Proceedings of the Conference on the State and Future of Higher Education in Sudan.* Cairo: Armis Co.

Europa Publications Staff. 1999. *Africa South of the Sahara.* London: Europa Publications.

Issa, S. I. 1999. "Expansion Policies of Higher Education: Pros and Cons." In M. E. A. El Tom, ed., *Proceedings of the Conference on the State and Future of Higher Education in Sudan.* Cairo: Armis Co. (in Arabic).

Institute for Scientific Information (ISI). 2000a. *Arts & Humanities Citation Index.* Philadelphia, Pa.: ISI.

———. 2000b. *Science Citation Index.* Philadelphia, Pa.: ISI.

———. 2000c. *Social Sciences Citation Index.* Philadelphia, Pa.: ISI.

Ministry of Higher Education and Scientific Research. 1995. "Financing of Higher Education and Scientific Research: Development of Higher Education and Scientific Research Budgets, 1985/86–1994/95." Khartoum.

———. 1996a. "Report of the Committee on New Universities." Khartoum.

———. 1996b. "Report of the Committee on Non-Government Higher Education." Khartoum.

———. 1999. "Admission Results for Public and Private Higher Education Institutions, 1999/2000." Khartoum: General Department of Admission.

Mohamed, A. B., and M. A. Nawal Giha. "Emigration of University Teachers: Reasons and Motivations." In M. E. A. El Tom, ed., *Proceedings of the Conference on the State and Future of Higher Education in Sudan.* Cairo: Armis Co. (in Arabic).

Thompson, K. W., B. R. Fogel, and Helen E. Danner, eds. 1977. *Higher Education and Social Change: Promising Experiments in Developing Countries.* Vol. 2: *Case Studies*, 155–169. New York: Praeger Publishers. (Chapter 9: The University of Khartoum, Sudan: Staff Development in an African University.)

UNESCO. 1961. *World Survey of Education.* Paris: UNESCO.

———. 1966. *World Survey of Education.* Paris: UNESCO.

———. 1969. *World Survey of Education.* Paris: UNESCO.

———. 1978–1979. *Statistical Yearbook.* Paris: UNESCO.

———. 1995. *Statistical Yearbook.* Paris: UNESCO.

———. 1999. *Statistical Yearbook.* Paris: UNESCO.

United Nations. 1999. *World Population Prospects: The 1998 Revision.* Vol. 1: *Comprehensive Tables.* New York: United Nations.

World Bank. 1984. *World Bank Report.* New York: Oxford University Press.

———. 1988. *Education in Sub-Saharan Africa: Policies for Adjustment, Revitalization and Expansion.* Washington, D.C.: World Bank.

———. 2000. *World Development Indicators.* New York: World Bank.

World of Learning. 1971. *World of Learning.* London: Europa Publications Ltd.

59

Swaziland

Margaret Zoller Booth

Systems of higher education do not operate in isolation. They are influenced by and reciprocally impact all social institutions in the countries in which they are established. According to some theorists, the development of higher education is dependent on three elements working together in a "triangle of coordination": the state authority, the market, and the academic oligarchy (Neave and Van Vught 1994). While these three forces work together to develop systems of higher education, when that triangle's power structure is unbalanced, the nature of educational development changes direction.

Where institutions of higher learning have been designed and implemented by outside forces, such as in Africa during its colonial period, traditional and Western institutions have come into conflict over development issues. One notable example is the system of higher education in the Kingdom of Swaziland. Its present form and function have been influenced by its historical development under British rule and by its place in the kingdom's educational system as a whole. The British colonial attitude toward education for the Swazi greatly influenced the development (or lack thereof) of higher education in the country. However, Swaziland's present political status also provides a unique example of the blending of Westernization and African tradition.

Swaziland, a small kingdom situated in southern Africa, surrounded by South Africa and Mozambique on its eastern border, remains the only kingdom in sub-Saharan Africa to emerge from the independence period as a sovereign monarchy. Its present population of just under 1 million is situated on an area of 17,364 square kilometers (6,704 square miles). Swazis speak Siswati, and English is a widely spoken second language. The monetary currency is the lilangeni (*pl.* emalangeni), and one lilangeni equals approximately US$6. Relative to the rest of sub-Saharan Africa, Swaziland is a relatively wealthy nation, with a per capita income of $880 (Africa Business Network 1997). Its major partner in foreign exchange is South Africa, and its primary exports are sugar, citrus fruits, wood pulp, and coal (EIU 1999).

Swaziland is both a nation of Swazi people and a political state headed by King Mswati III, whose father, King Sobhuza II, emerged as a powerful leader after independence from the British in 1969 (Booth 2000). The monarch's strength has proven beneficial in times of political conflict, but it has also hindered change. The absolute power that the monarchy holds over all Swazi institutions must be understood if one is to appreciate the impact that the government has had on higher education.

FORMAL EDUCATION IN SWAZILAND TODAY

The government of Swaziland's Development Plan (1997–1998 to 1999–2000) stressed the need to increase the quality of education, since the country had achieved its goal of universal access to primary education (Ministry of Economic Planning and Development 1997, 153). However, the report does not take into account the repetition rates and drop-out rates in primary and secondary school, which have created an educational system that is markedly pyramid-like, leaving little hope for the majority of the population to have any access to higher learning. In 1996 alone, 4.6 percent of first grade, 15.7 percent of seventh grade, and 1.4 percent of Form I pupils dropped out of the school system. Table 59.1 presents a broad picture of the entire size of the educational system in Swaziland.

Historically, continuance to upper levels of schooling has been determined by one's success at the Primary School Examination, the Junior Certificate Examination (JCE), and, finally, the Cambridge O-level examination. A successful pass is necessary for entrance at the higher education level in Swaziland. In addition to a rigid examination structure, school tuition at all levels contributes to the high drop-out and repetition rates. Access to higher education in Swaziland, therefore, is limited as a result of academic elimination and socially constructed reasons

Table 59.1. Total Enrollments for All Educational Institutions in Swaziland, 1996

	Primary	Secondary /High School	University	Vocational College	Teacher Training College
Enrolled	202,439	54,873	2,533	1,300	881
Number of Institutions	529	170	1	2	3
Number of Faculty	5,975	3,036	219	106	—

Source: Swaziland Government 1996; Ministry of Economic Planning and Development 1997.

(M. Booth 1996). While access to higher levels of education is limited today in Swaziland, those limitations were much greater before independence.

HISTORICAL BACKGROUND OF POSTSECONDARY EDUCATION

According to Philip Altbach (1998), much of the great expansion of universities during the twentieth century was a result of generous support of public funds, the idea that "the university should participate in the creation as well as the transmission of knowledge," and the belief that "academic institutions should . . . be permitted a significant degree of autonomy" (Altbach 1998, 5). The balance of these three elements of growth has varied throughout this century in sub-Saharan Africa as political climates have altered, the designers of the institutions have been replaced, and economic difficulties have undercut public funding for education. In short, the balance of these three elements has been altered by the changing imbalances effected within the triangle of coordination by the forces previously discussed.

During the early days of colonial Swaziland, the British administration revealed its concern for the education of European children with the Compulsory Education Proclamation of 1920 (High Commissioner's Office 1920). This proclamation was designed for European children, the only ones able, under the colonial system, to continue their education at the tertiary level either in South Africa or in Europe. The education of the Swazi in the first part of the century was primarily left to missionaries, who saw little need to provide higher learning. At the time, leading missionaries believed the Swazi needed education to Standard 4 only "in order to gain regular habits and discipline" (Watts 1924, 2). If this was all that was required of the Swazi, then there was obviously no need for the development of tertiary education.

There remained, however, a recognized need to train teachers who would be able to teach young Swazi pupils. Consequently, the earliest institutions of tertiary education were teacher training colleges. The Nazarene missionaries in Bremersdorp (today Manzini) established the first program for teacher training. Swazi students who had completed a Standard 6 certificate could enroll in this limited program, which would qualify them to teach in the so-called elementary vernacular grades up to Standard 2. Any training beyond this had to be done in the Union of South Africa, where teacher training colleges required a Standard 7 certificate for admittance (Hynd 1945).

In the late 1930s and 1940s, debates surfaced between colonial administrators and the missionary establishment regarding the necessity for higher education for the Swazi. Resident Commissioner Charles L. Bruton expressed concern about the lack of higher education available to the Swazi in his 1939 address to the members of the Native Education Board of Advice. He stated that he did not share the view of others who felt that "such great expenditures on such small numbers of people are not to be justified" (*Times of Swaziland* 1939, 1). Department of Education documents justified the lack of facilities by stating that students "who wish to proceed beyond Matriculation, have at their disposal the facilities which exist in the Union of South Africa for more advanced courses of study." Yet finances were not available for grants or loans for postsecondary work (Department of Education 1938, 18).

As the 1950s progressed and witnessed the development of higher education in larger British settler colonies (namely Rhodesia and Kenya), talks began within the Territorial Advisory Board on African Education regarding the establishment of a central institution of higher learning for Africans within the High Commission Territories (HCTs)—Basutoland, Bechuanaland, and Swaziland. The decision was hastened by the announcement in 1957 that Swazi students could no longer attend higher institutions in the Union of South Africa (*Times of Swaziland* 1957).

As the British planned for eventual independence of the HCTs, the early 1960s witnessed considerable development in the character of higher education for Swaziland. William Pitcher Teacher Training College, the first institution designed to produce teachers of both primary and secondary education, opened in Bremersdorp in 1962 (Department of Education 1963). In that same year, the colonial administration racially integrated the system of education in Swaziland, enabling Swazi students to attend European schools that could better prepare them for the tertiary level (Department of Education 1962).

Most significantly, the University of Basutoland, Bechuanaland, and Swaziland (UBBS) was established by the British government at the original Pius XII Catholic University College in Roma, Basutoland, in 1964. Although the new university was a government institution, the Catholic brothers who had established Pius XII maintained a heavy presence on the campus and influenced the development of the goals and objectives for the institution, which included moral and "godly learning" (*Times of Swaziland* 1963b). As with other African universities, the developers understood the immediate need to educate individuals who would lead the soon-to-be-independent nations. Consequently, they stated that the most important objective was the production of qualified "men and women who will help develop the material resources of the Territories" (*Times of Swaziland* 1963b).

After Lesotho and Botswana achieved independence in 1966, the name UBBS was changed to the University of Botswana, Lesotho, and Swaziland (UBLS). Although located in Lesotho, the university was funded equally by all three governments and was primarily, but not exclusively, to serve students from the three countries (Grotpeter 1975; University of Swaziland 1991). The inaugural address at the opening of the university included assertions that the university would be "autonomous from political whims" (Magagula 1978). However, this did not reflect the reality of the politics involved in creating and maintaining a multinational university at a time when southern Africa was entering an era of major and increasingly turbulent political change. Furthermore, the explicit European educational culture and religious overtones residual in the new university proved to be incongruent with the spirit of anticolonialism predominant in the newly independent nations comprising UBLS.

Once all three countries were independent (Swaziland's independence was achieved in 1968), the plans for UBLS development shifted toward creating a physical presence in each country while maintaining the university as a cooperative venture. By 1964, an agricultural department was established at Luyengo, Swaziland, which was followed in the early 1970s by college branch campuses at Kwaluseni, Swaziland, and at Gaborone, Botswana (University of Swaziland 1991). Some scholars view this devolution as the beginning of the end of UBLS because the original designs by foreigners for regional campuses in Africa were created with regional goals in mind and with institutional expectations that were quite different from those after independence (Magagula 1978). While the regional campuses may have shared a similar colonial history and therefore operated along similar Western cultural lines, such as a common language of instruction and a British school structure, post-independence nations focused their attention on nationalism rather than regionalism. Thus, national systems of education, including curricula at the tertiary level, would play a very important role in the pursuit of these new agendas.

In concert with these developments, students attending the university were also formulating and expressing national interests. Beginning in 1974, friction arose among the students from the various countries—and between them and the UBLS faculty and administration—as they clashed over new expansion plans. A student-led strike in January 1975 reflected their divided national loyalties and touched off a series of campus protests that strained relations between the university administrators in Roma and the other campuses (Magagula 1978). This eventually led to the Roma campus withdrawing itself from UBLS and establishing the National University of Lesotho (NUL) on October 20, 1975 (University of Swaziland 1991). From 1976 to 1982, Botswana and Swaziland continued to cooperate in a joint venture as the University of Botswana and Swaziland, utilizing their two separate campuses at Kwaluseni and Gaborone. During this time, however, development plans outlined the eventual sepa-

ration of the university into two independent institutions. The University of Swaziland (UNISWA) finally became an independent university in June 1982 (University of Swaziland 1991).

Since independence in 1969, and until the early years of UNISWA, the educational goals of the government deemphasized higher education while favoring an increase in primary school enrollment (Swaziland Government 1969, 1983). However, the goals for higher education were to meet the labor needs of the country. The university organized itself around five faculties: agriculture, education, humanities, science, and the social sciences. Students who needed to study professional subjects such as engineering and medicine had to travel outside the country for this training (Swaziland Government 1983).

This era of transition to independence witnessed changes in the balance within the triangle of coordination as it shifted from a powerful state authority to the academic oligarchy. The academic administration at Roma had acquired a significant degree of power and attempted to develop the new university in a manner that would give the main campus continued power, which eventually led to the breakup of the collaborative effort among the three southern African nations.

CURRENT STATE OF HIGHER EDUCATION IN SWAZILAND

After approximately three decades of independence, Swaziland's educational goals have shifted and higher education has taken a more central role in educational policy analysis. The current state of higher education in Swaziland is best analyzed by reviewing the growth and direction of tertiary education in the country since the independent development of UNISWA in 1982. During this contemporary period, as higher education has taken root in Swaziland, three major themes have emerged. These include the fragile balance between supply of and demand for highly skilled labor in the country, the continued complex relationship between the Swazi nation and the southern African region, and a strained relationship between the university and the Swazi monarchy, which is often plagued with poor communication. These three themes were echoed very strongly in the 1986 report produced by the University of Swaziland Commission on Planning. The report states that the "particular mission of the University of Swaziland is given to the University by its history, its location in southern Africa, and the circumstances of the Kingdom at a moment in time. The University mission is not something the academic community gives to itself in isolation from this history, location, or circumstances" (Ping, Turner, and Kamba 1986, 5).

Central to the mission of the university is the need to meet the labor needs of the nation. The University of Swaziland Commission on Planning "was appointed to review the current development plan and the planning process of the University of Swaziland" in 1985 (p. 1 of plan report). Its purpose was threefold: to identify policy issues related to the University Development Plan 1985–1990, to make recommendations, and to review the plan with the university administration and staff. Consequently, the Ping Commission report analyzed the then present needs of the country and probable future demands. The report recognized that the increasing number of high school

Table 59.2. Programs of Study at the University of Swaziland, 1982–2000

Program of Study	1982–1983	1985–1986	1990–1991	1996–1997	1999–2000
B.A. degree	223	335	629	—	—
B.Sc. degree	304	337	382	—	—
Other degrees	208	363	359	—	—
Diploma in Business	93	80	133	—	—
Diploma in Agriculture	178	118	213	—	—
Home economics	47	54	—	—	—
Total	1,053	1,287	1,716	2,533	2,904[1]

[1]University of Swaziland 1999–2000. This figure is for full-time students only. Other figures include some part-time students.

graduates would place greater pressure on UNISWA and on the teacher and technical colleges to increase enrollments. At the same time, the report also stated that better communication between the university and the public and private sectors was needed if institutions of higher learning were to produce the appropriate number of graduates in middle- and high-skilled professions to satisfy the nation's needs. The Ping Commission expressed the fear that without this communication and accurate planning, the university might grow too quickly in response to pressure from Swazi parents who wanted their children to acquire a higher degree. The report warned that "equally dangerous for the well-being of the Kingdom would be a large number of unemployed or underemployed University graduates" (Ping, Turner, and Kamba 1986, 11).

In 1986, the Commission reported that its projected enrollments for the university were higher than the projections made in the Fourth National Development Plan (1983–1984 to 1987–1988). The commission expected a growth of 8.5 percent each year, which would increase the student body to 1,783 by 1990. The difference between the commission's rates and the government's calculated projections left the commission with questions regarding the communication between the government of Swaziland and the university administration. It appeared to the Commission that the government and the university administration were devising divergent growth patterns for UNISWA. As demonstrated in Table 59.2, the Commission's projections for 1990 were accurate.

The most obvious concern regarding miscommunication between university administration and the government included the allocation of sufficient funds for the correct estimates of university growth. While the Swaziland government did not predict rates of growth as high as those in the Ping Commission report, financial support of university growth has been consistent. As a matter of fact, in the second year of the university's institutional independence, the government of Swaziland spent $23,142 per university student but only $2,112 per secondary student and $720 per primary student (Swaziland Government 1983). Furthermore, between 1994 and 1997, 18 percent of all planned educational capital expenditures were aimed at UNISWA. However, during this same period, university students comprised only 0.9 percent of the total primary, secondary, and university student population (Swaziland Government 1994 and 1997). When viewed in this light, the government budget has been

substantially biased toward the tertiary level since the inception of the university.

The government of Swaziland has recently acknowledged this bias toward postsecondary education; according to the 1997 Development Plan, this was caused by "demand driven growth." However, the plan also calls for a shift in resources from the tertiary level to the primary level (Swaziland Government 1997). This recent move in Swaziland toward a decrease in public expenditures for higher education coincides with similar trends in much of the developing world caused by recent economic hardships. Yet at the same time, the postsecondary education enrollment in Swaziland, as in much of the developing world, has increased tremendously. According to Altbach, this pattern has contributed to "a marked deterioration in academic standards" (Altbach 1998, 6).

Since independence, several other tertiary institutions in addition to UNISWA have been created to meet the developing nation's needs. Teacher education students may attend preservice training for primary education at Ngwane (Nhlengano) and Nazarene (Manzini) Teacher Training Colleges for general subjects and for training in agriculture and home economics. Training for secondary teachers is conducted primarily at William Pitcher Teacher Training College (Manzini), while the teaching of more technical subjects is carried out at the Luyengo campus of the university or at the Swaziland College of Technology (SCOT, Mbabane). Other vocational training is also conducted at the Gwamile Vocational and Commercial Training Institution (VOCTIM) in Matsapha (Swaziland Government 1997). The pattern of growth of these various levels of higher education in the country since 1982 is illustrated in Table 59.2.

DEVELOPMENT OF TECHNOLOGICAL COLLEGES

In addition to UNISWA, several other tertiary institutions have been created to meet the developing nation's needs since independence. The teacher training colleges include Ngwane (Nhlengano) and Nazarene (Manzini) for primary education and William Pitcher Teacher Training College for secondary. Vocational training is offered at the Luyengo campus of the University of Swaziland, the Swaziland College of Technology (SCOT), and the Gwamile Vocational and Commercial Training Institution (VOCTIM) in Matsapha (Swaziland Government 1997).

While the university and technical institutions have experienced steady growth, teacher training colleges have not. This is partly due to the debate regarding the level of national need for new teachers. While the Swaziland government reports that the teacher shortage has declined since independence, the Ping Commission offers evidence suggesting otherwise. It notes the yearly advertised teaching positions that are unfulfilled, the number of foreign teachers, and the high teacher-to-pupil ratio (Ping, Turner, and Kamba 1986). Furthermore, other statistics have shown that Swazi teachers who had been trained in Swaziland have consistently left for better-paying faculty positions in South Africa. In March 1990 alone, ninety teachers left their posts in Swaziland for better teaching positions in South Africa "because of the refusal by government to pay them reasonable salaries and to improve their working conditions" (Mbuli 1990b, 2).

THE NEED FOR A UNIVERSITY MISSION

The first vice-chancellor of UNISWA, Dr. Sam Guma, expressed the desire to define a university mission that would reflect a balance between the development of highly skilled manpower and the fostering of academic knowledge and research. Before he became the vice-chancellor, he was known to state that he did not "believe in education for its own sake . . . especially in a developing country such as ours." While he wished for "programs aimed at solving development problems," he also valued the role of academic research at the university. He envisioned the two missions coming together with "research geared towards the development and needs of Swaziland" (*Times of Swaziland* 1979, 4).

Within five years of the establishment of UNISWA as an independent institution, the new acting vice-chancellor, Dr. Lydia Makhubu, laid plans for the future of the university. Speaking at the 1987 graduation ceremony at Kwaluseni, she stated that not only was it time to let the university grow beyond its five existing programs but it was also time to "become truly development-oriented in its activities" and to institute "the academic focus which reflects the aspirations of the Swazi nation" (*Times of Swaziland* 1987, 4). These statements reflect the ongoing goal of the university to meet the development needs of the nation.

During the 1987 graduation ceremony, it became obvious that the messages conveyed in the speeches of the vice-chancellor and the statements of the newly installed King Mswati III were at odds with each other. That foreshadowed the subsequent conflict between the university and the monarchy that marked the decade of the 1990s. In her speech, Dr. Makhubu also addressed two other contemporary issues: regionalism versus nationalism and the university's cooperation with the Swaziland government. Only five years after the end of UNISWA's formal alliance with Botswana, the vice-chancellor called for regional cooperation among the institutions of higher learning. She stated that "inter-university cooperation is so important because it provides a forum for the exchange of ideas and experiences and for the formulation of joint strategies for the solution of common problems." These problems, she said, were "common challenges of all Universities in Africa" (*Times of Swaziland* 1987, 4).

The speech given by the young king, however, omitted the expression of any desire for regional cooperation. Instead, it emphasized nationalism over regionalism with the statement that "UNISWA should always endeavour to identify itself with the people it was created to serve" (*Swazi Observer* 1987, 4). He also did not envision UNISWA as "a haven of unrestricted thought in learning," but rather as an institution with the sole purpose of developing a citizenry that was loyal to its monarchy and a people who "dedicate themselves wholeheartedly to the service of their country" (*Swazi Observer* 1987, 1). These statements were spoken by a king who not only had sovereign power but who also served as the chancellor of the university.

In his first public address from a UNISWA platform, the king also revealed a mistrust between the monarchy and the educated elite of the future—the university students. He opened his address by reminding students that the nation made enormous financial sacrifices each year to offer them the privilege of obtaining a higher education. Thus, in return, the nation did not expect "arrogance or conceit but humble and dedicated national service" (*Swazi Observer* 1987, 1). It was revealing that the king, who had been crowned before being able to finish his own formal studies, began his relationship with the university on this negative note. During the 1990s, one of the major characterizations of higher education was the increasing politicization of the university just as its impact on the nation's political economy was also growing dramatically.

THE POLITICAL AND ECONOMIC IMPACT
OF HIGHER EDUCATION IN SWAZILAND

According to Samuel Atteh, "Africa is experiencing an educational crisis of unprecedented proportions in higher education" (Atteh 1998, 468). The complexity of this crisis is the result of many problems related to political and economic turmoil, according to Atteh. For the past two decades, the troubled relationship between higher education and the Swazi government, the fluctuating economy, challenges with its southern African neighbors (especially South Africa), and continued Western influence have meant that Swaziland has proved no exception to the regional malaise.

The large public financial subsidies spent on university education in Swaziland have contributed to the tension that exists between the university and the government. One clear indication of this tension is that university administrators do not feel completely "intellectually emancipated," in vice-chancellor Makhubu's words. Part of this is a result of the structural tension, as Altbach (1998) points out, between autonomy and accountability that characterizes higher education systems the world over. In the case of Swaziland, conflict has arisen not only between university staff and the government but also with university students, whose UNISWA tuition and living expenses are subsidized by the government yet who demand a certain degree of autonomy from government interference in academic matters. These student financial benefits are offered only at the tertiary level in Swaziland. By contrast, primary and secondary education requires parental expenditures on tuition, uniforms, and other school supplies. This structure has been shown to reward the already privileged while making it very difficult for the marginalized to take advantage of higher educational opportunities (Psacharopoulos 1998; Neave and Van Vught 1994), thus reinforcing and reproducing the existing Swazi elite.

On the other hand, even more substantial public funds are needed for the development of high-quality institutions of learning. One problem discussed in the Ping report that has yet to be addressed adequately in the country is the lack of adequate funding to increase faculty salaries, which has created a significant problem with staff retention and recruitment at the university. Issues related to the quality of the institution have often been areas of contention between the university community and the government. As the university has matured, the students have become more vocal in their complaints in these areas. Student protests in the 1980s and 1990s have taken similar paths to those outlined by Sunal and Haas (1998), who claim that African students throughout the continent have protested over a variety of issues, ranging from quality of food and living conditions to sharing the costs of tuition to political activism and protest.

The first serious student protests occurred in 1984, when university students demonstrated their opposition to the illegal attempts by the Liqoqo to usurp the powers constitutionally reserved for the monarchy. (The Liqoqo has traditionally been the most influential advisory council to the king; it consists of senior and respected members of the royal family. During the time between the death of King Sobhuza in 1982 and the installment of the new King Mswati III in 1986, the queen mother, as tradition holds, ruled the kingdom. However, in 1983, the senior members of the Liqoqo attempted to maneuver their way into power, only to be foiled in the end by the royalists among the elite [A. Booth 2000].) During that time, university student demonstrations were led by the founders and leaders of what emerged as the most significant organization opposed to the Swazi monarchy in the name of wider democracy, the People's United Democratic Movement (PUDEMO). The student opposition during 1984 centered on what they perceived as the Liqoqo regime's attempts to subvert the university by nullifying existing student organizations and imposing "puppet leadership" among them (Levin 1997, 197). Several secondary and university student protest marches continued that year and were met with violent repression by the police and injury to many students. As a result, the university was closed in December 1984, and a subsequent government investigation into the disturbances concluded that the instigators of most of the problems were "outside influences," including foreign faculty and students with ties to the African National Congress (ANC). Following the report, two foreign lecturers at UNISWA were fired and twenty-one students were expelled, marking the beginning of a succession of clashes between university students and the Swaziland government (Levin 1997).

This initial eruption of student protests symbolized several levels of conflict, the most important of which have continued to this day. The first constitutes the student body's growing political awareness and its desire to voice collective opposition to perceived wrongs, including government repression. The second issue addresses the strong tension between nationalism and regionalism previously discussed. That is, while Swaziland

has seen the need to cooperate with its neighbors in the name of development, the monarchy has had a schizophrenic relationship with its giant neighbor, South Africa. During the era of apartheid, many among the UNISWA student body were South African exiles in need of a university degree from a foreign institution because education had been denied them at home because of their political activism (Levin 1997). Thus, while Swaziland in effect harbored political fugitives, it did so at a political cost to the government. It strained relations with the South African government and developed fear about the consequences of the exiles' political activities on behalf of the ANC or the student body at UNISWA.

The rest of the 1980s and 1990s continued to witness student protests over issues both internal to the university and external to the nation as a whole. One of the most violent disturbances occurred in late 1990 on what became known as "Black Wednesday." The event began on Monday, November 12, with a boycott of classes and campus demonstrations fueled by several grievances, including the inferior quality of food served in dining halls, the low level of student financial allowances, and the expulsion of a student and a university lecturer who had been charged by the government with high treason (Dempster 1995). On Wednesday, November 14, armed police and military units entered the campus and gave the protesting students thirty minutes to vacate the university premises. Unprecedented police violence ensued, resulting in hundreds of student injuries, some serious, and one reported death. These events forced the university to close for several months during that academic year. In 1994, problems occurred again when students sought to commemorate Black Wednesday against the administration's wishes, touching off a new wave of student expulsions and suspensions (Dempster 1995; Mbuli 1990a, 1).

As the decade of the 1990s progressed and political protests escalated, university student protests took on new dimensions. As trade unions and then the Swaziland National Association of Teachers (SNAT) struck over wages and work conditions, university and teacher training college students marched openly in support of their struggles. Students at teacher training colleges began to support UNISWA students in their protests, creating a formidable united front against government officials. (See the *Times of Swaziland* for the entire month of January 1996 for coverage of the unprecedented general strike.) One important consequence of this pattern of activism concerns us especially here: with the increasing politicization of UNISWA's student body, faculty, and administration, a significant shift in the triangle of coordination took place, moving emphatically back toward the authority of the state over the other two elements.

CHALLENGES FACING THE POSTSECONDARY SYSTEM

In addition to cyclical challenges that face the Swazi and other systems of higher education in Africa, separate contemporary issues have imposed additional stress on already fragile public institutions. These include a gender disparity in higher education, the impact of HIV/AIDS on the university community, and the effects of an increasingly serious brain drain on

Table 59.3. Enrollment by Gender at the University of Swaziland, Teacher Training Schools, and Technical Training Schools, 1982–2000

	1982–1983	1985–1986	1990–1991	1996–1997	1999–2000
University of Swaziland					
Male	—	—	—	—	1,514
Female	—	—	—	—	1,390
Teacher Training Schools					
Male	374	329	285	—	—
Female	846	606	376	—	—
Subtotal	1,220	935	661	881[1]	—
Technical Training Schools					
Male	—	290	769	—	—
Female	—	220	204		—
Subtotal	527	510	973	1,300[2]	—

[1]Swaziland Government 1996.
[2]Swaziland Government 1997.
Source: Swaziland Government 1983, 1988, 1991, 1995.

both the tertiary level of education and the development of the nation.

With regard to gender disparity, Africa has a smaller percentage of females in higher education than do other developing regions (Sunal and Haas 1998). While enrollments are equal for Swazi boys and girls entering primary school, the majority of females are eventually culled out, leaving a gender disparity by the time students enter the university in Swaziland (see Table 59.3). While the gender disparity at the tertiary level has improved recently, the challenge for women to gain truly equal access to higher education remains. In addition to human rights issues, women, who constitute 53 percent of the population, possess important skills for the development needs of the country (Swaziland Government 1995, 9). Furthermore, with the continued absence of men who are on tours of migrant labor in South Africa, women constitute an even greater percentage of the cohort in need of the high levels of education required to fulfill Swaziland's significant labor needs (M. Booth 1996; 2000).

Most recently, the tragic consequences of the increasingly virulent spread of HIV and AIDS amongst the Swazi population have drastically affected population growth rates and depleted the young working population, perhaps most notably college students, recent university graduates, and schoolteachers. In 1998, for example, the United Nations reported that 20–26 percent of the people aged 15–49 in Swaziland were living with HIV or AIDS (Hall 1999). By 1999, the situation had deteriorated markedly, and Swaziland had attained one of the highest rates of HIV infection in the world; the life expectancy of residents had been reduced from 58 to 39 years of age (CNN 1999). A March 1999 survey sponsored by UNICEF found that approximately 30 percent of the country's population is infected

with HIV. The report also stated that individuals with the greatest risk of contracting HIV are those between the economically productive ages of 15 and 29 (Hall 1999).

The University of Swaziland and other institutions of higher learning have been particularly vulnerable to this epidemic because they include such high percentages of the targeted age population. According to Alan Booth, it has been the "educated, middle-class citizenry which was the hardest hit, robbing the country of much of its greatest future talent and brainpower" (A. Booth 2000, 23). In 1999, for instance, the Ministry of Education reported three to four AIDS-related deaths per week among the cohort of the nation's 8,000 schoolteachers. Finally, reversing a previously silent attitude about the virus, King Mswati III, speaking at the 1999 UNISWA graduation ceremony, warned the assemblage that they were "at high risk of contracting the HIV virus," and therefore "should take precautions to prevent such from happening" (*Swazi Observer* 1999c, 1).

The third contemporary issue is the emigration of large numbers of Swazi professionals to other nations, or what is most commonly referred to in Africa as brain drain. Not only has the flight of schoolteachers created a negative climate for educational progress, but UNISWA has also suffered from the exodus of professors seeking better positions in other countries, especially South Africa. At the September 1999 UNISWA graduation ceremony, the acting vice-chancellor, Professor Barnabas Dlamini, called for a "review of the staff's conditions of service in order to curb the exodus of lecturers in search of lucrative appointments" (*Swazi Observer* 1999a, 1). For instance, the university continued to have twelve faculty positions advertised in August 2000 for the 2000–2001 academic year (University of Swaziland 2000a). While UNISWA has a large number of expatriate faculty, these and other positions often remain unfilled as a result of low faculty salaries coupled with a heavy teaching load. Faculty are expected to have an active research agenda; however, the overburdening of professors with high numbers of students makes this very difficult.

The research presently being conducted at UNISWA has focused on the developmental needs of the country, such as agricultural research technologies and small-business and entrepreneurial activities (University of Swaziland 2000b). However, the extent to which UNISWA is serious about ensuring a major research component in the university is unclear. UNISWA has closed down two university centers designed to conduct research in Swaziland. The Social Science Research Unit and the Swaziland Institute for Educational Research conducted research in and about Swaziland primarily during the 1980s and successfully contributed a great deal to our understanding of Swaziland and its people; these findings had tremendous implications for national development. While individual scholars continue to conduct research in Swaziland, the closing of these centers has weakened the support systems available to aid faculty in their academic pursuits.

Teachers and professors are not the only professionals exiting the country. Recent graduates from the university, worried about their ability to acquire jobs within their chosen profession, have crossed the border to seek employment. Students who graduated in 1999 "expressed skepticism" about their chances of gaining employment, according to Siphiwe Dlamini. Recent law, electrical engineering, and education graduates complained of the lack of positions in Swaziland (*Swazi Observer* 1999b, 1). These disheartened graduates may soon go elsewhere for employment. According to Samuel Atteh (1998), the progress that was beginning to take place in sub-Saharan African higher education after independence has deteriorated partly due to this phenomenon.

RECOMMENDATIONS FOR FUTURE DEVELOPMENT

If Swaziland is to develop a healthy and viable system of higher education that contributes to the development of the country and its people, a more balanced triangle of coordination will be needed. We have seen how the three elements of state authority, the market, and the academic oligarchy have shifted over time in Swaziland. With today's pressing educational needs in Swaziland, better cooperation and coordination of powers of each of these three elements is needed for healthy development at all levels of education.

The World Bank has recently made four recommendations to improve higher education in Africa: encouraging greater differentiation of institutions, including privatization; diversifying funding for higher education; redefining the role of government in higher education; and promoting quality over quantity in tertiary institutions (Sunal and Haas 1998). However, the degree to which these four recommendations will improve higher education in Swaziland is related to their ability, once implemented, to strengthen the autonomy of the university, increase its academic quality, and aid in the development of the nation. The high expense of tertiary education necessitates some cost sharing in order to promote autonomy and increase the quality and relevance of educational programs. Proposals for cost sharing should be aimed at the students enrolled in institutions of higher learning, private corporations benefiting from the qualified graduates, and institutions promoting greater regional cooperation of higher learning programs throughout southern Africa.

Furthermore, the future development of any system of higher education is dependent on the accessibility and quality of the elementary and secondary school system. The goals and objectives of each level should coincide. The government of Swaziland cannot adequately discuss changes in educational finance, privatization, curriculum, and degree requirements for higher education without also examining the same issues in relation to the entire school system.

Finally, the cultural legacy of colonial systems of higher education has continued to influence tertiary education in Swaziland today. The university continues to be elitist in its student demography and has in that and other ways contributed to the cleavage in society between the Westernized middle class and the more traditional Swazi. If the university is to contribute to nation building, it must rid itself of elitist attitudes that serve to further segment society and it must develop a greater understanding with the government regarding its place in society.

REFERENCES

Africa Business Network. 1997. "Country Information Center: Swaziland Profile." Available online at: http://www.ifc.org/abn/cic/swaziland/english/prof.htm

Altbach, P. G. 1998. "Patterns in Higher Education Development: Towards the Year 2000." *Review of Higher Education* 14 (Spring 1991): 293–316.

Atteh, S. O. 1998. "The Crisis in Higher Education in Africa." In K. Kempner, M. Mollis, and W. G. Tierney, eds., *Comparative Education*. Needham Heights, Mass.: Simon and Schuster Custom Publishing.

Booth, A. R. 2000. *Historical Dictionary of Swaziland*. 2nd ed. Lanham, Md.: Scarecrow Press.

Booth, M. Z. 1996. "Parental Availability and Academic Achievement among Swazi Rural Primary School Children." *Comparative Education Review* 40 (August): 250–263.

———. 2000. "The Home Environment and School Achievement: A Longitudinal Study of Primary School Children in Swaziland." Paper presented at the annual conference of the Comparative and International Education Society, San Antonio, Texas, March 12.

CNN (Cable News Network). 1998. "UN: Number of AIDS Cases Up by 60 Million," November 24. Available online at: http://www.cnn.com/HEALTH/9811/24/global.aids/

———. 1999. "Life Expectancy in Africa Cut Short by AIDS." March 19. Available online at: http://www.cnn.com/HEALTH/9903/18/aids.africa.02/

Dempster, C. 1995. "Student Unrest Rocks Swaziland Royal Rulers." *Times Higher Education Supplement*, March 24, p. 11.

Department of Education. 1938. *The Annual Report on Education in Swaziland for the Year 1937–1938*. Mbabane, Swaziland: Department of Education.

———. 1962. *Swaziland Annual Report Summary for 1962*. Mbabane, Swaziland: Department of Education.

———. 1963. *Swaziland Annual Report, by the Director of Education for the Year 1963*. Mbabane, Swaziland: Department of Education.

EIU (Economist Intelligence Unit). 1999. *Country Profile: Namibia Swaziland, 1999–2000*. London: EIU.

Grotpeter, J. J. 1975. *Historical Dictionary of Swaziland*. Lanham, Md.: Scarecrow Press.

Hall, J. 1999. "AIDS Poses Serious Crisis for Swaziland." *Swazi News*, March 29. Available online at: http://www.swazinews.co.sz/stories/29mar299.htm

High Commissioner's Office. 1920. "Compulsory Education (Swaziland) Proclamation, 1920." Swaziland Archives, Lobamba, Swaziland (File RCS 621/17).

Hynd, D. 1945. "Swaziland in the Making." *Times of Swaziland*, April 12.

Levin, R. 1997. *When the Sleeping Grass Awakens: Land and Power in Swaziland*. Johannesburg: Witwatersrand University Press.

Magagula, C. M. 1978. "The Multi-national University in Africa: An Analysis of the Development and Demise of the University of Botswana, Lesotho, and Swaziland." Ph.D. dissertation. University of Maryland.

Mbuli, G. 1990a. "Closed! Cops Moved in on Students with Truncheons." *Times of Swaziland*, November 15.

———. 1990b. "Government Sends Teachers Away." *Times of Swaziland*, March 13.

Ministry of Economic Planning and Development. 1997. *Development Plan 1997/98–1999/00*. Mbabane: Government of Swaziland. Economic Planning Office.

Neave, G., and F. Van Vught. 1994. "Government and Higher Education in Developing Nations: A Conceptual Framework." In *Government and Higher Education: Relationships across Three Continents*. New York: Pergamon Press.

Ping, C. J., J. D. Turner, and W. J. Kamba. 1986. "University of Swaziland, Commission on Planning, 1986." Unpublished report. Kwaluseni, Swaziland: University of Swaziland.

Psacharopoulos, G. 1998. "Higher Education in Developing Countries: The Scenario of the Future." In K. Kempner, M. Mollis, and W. G. Tierney, eds., *Comparative Education*. Needham Heights, Mass.: Simon and Schuster Custom Publishing.

Sunal, D. W., and M. E. Haas. 1998. "Issues for Higher Education in Sub-Saharan Africa." In C. Szymanski Sunal, ed., *Schooling in Sub-Saharan Africa*. New York: Garland Publishing.

Swazi Observer. 1987. "'Guard against Conceit,' His Majesty Urges Students." September 14.

———. 1999a. "Exodus of Lecturers a Concern for UNISWA." September 20.

———. 1999b. "Graduates Worried about Employment." September 20.

———. 1999c. "His Majesty Warns UNISWA Graduates on AIDS Threat." September 20.

Swaziland Government. 1969. *Development Plan, 1969/70–1972/73*. Mbabane, Swaziland: Economic Planning Office, Ministry of Economic Planning and Development.

———. 1983. *Development Plan, 1983/84–1987/88*. Mbabane, Swaziland: Economic Planning Office, Ministry of Economic Planning and Development.

———. 1994. *Development Plan, 1994/95–1996/97*. Mbabane, Swaziland: Economic Planning Office, Ministry of Economic Planning and Development.

———. 1995. *Annual Statistical Bulletin, 1995*. Mbabane, Swaziland: Central Statistics Office, Ministry of Economic Planning and Development.

———. 1996. Education Statistics. Central Statistical Office.

———. 1997. *Development Plan, 1997/98–1999/00*. Mbabane, Swaziland: Economic Planning Office, Ministry of Economic Planning and Development.

Times of Swaziland. 1939. "Native Education Board of Advisers. Opening Address by His Honour the Resident Commissioner." April 20.

———. 1957. "Higher Education for Africans in High Commission Territories." March 30.

———. 1963a. "Roma to Be University at Beginning of 1964." June 21.

———. 1963b. "New Roma Offers Big Opportunities for Territories' Students." June 28.

———. 1979. "University's Top Man Talks of Learning, and Life." June 28.

———. 1987. "UNISWA Appeals for Clear Mandate." September 14.

University of Swaziland. 1991. University of Swaziland Calendar for 1991–1992. Kwaluseni: Publications and Information Office, University of Swaziland.

———. 2000a. Vacancies at UNISWA. Available online at: http://www.uniswa.sz/vacancies/vacancies.html

———. 2000b. Research at UNISWA. Available online at: http://www.uniswa.sz/research

Watts, C. C. 1924. Enclosure to Resident Commissioner's Despatch Swaziland no. 357 of November 15, 1924. Mbabane, Swaziland, Saint Marks Coloured School.

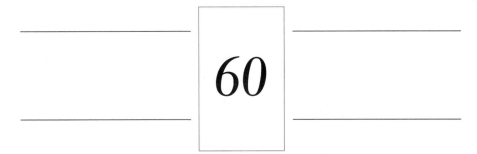

Tanzania

Daniel Mkude and Brian Cooksey

INTRODUCTION

Tanzania covers an area of almost 1 million square kilometers (386,000 square miles), bordering the Indian Ocean to the east and sharing frontiers with eight eastern and central African countries. Tanzania's population has grown from about 18 million in the 1970s to more than 30 million today. With $490 per capita gross domestic product, Tanzania's agricultural sector employs 85 percent of the population that generates 50 percent of the GDP. Annual population growth of nearly 3 percent has contributed to the country's very young population; nearly half are under 15 years of age. In 1995, the country adopted a multiparty political system after over two decades of one-party rule.

Tanzania's postsecondary education system consists of programs and courses offered by a variety of institutions throughout the country. These institutions differ in level, status, and orientation. In Tanzania, these differences include entry requirements, duration and depth of courses, type of award offered, and minimum qualifications for staff. On the basis of these considerations, it is customary to distinguish between institutions which offer programs that are recognized as genuine higher education programs and those that do not. Among the higher education institutions, it is also customary to distinguish between those that offer university-level programs and those that do not. Based on the foregoing observations, one can identify three broad categories of postsecondary institutions in Tanzania: institutions that do not offer higher education, institutions of higher education that do not offer university-level programs, and university-level institutions of higher education.

Institutions in Tanzania that do not offer higher education include a number of nursing training schools, teacher training colleges, agricultural and livestock training institutes, secretarial colleges, and other colleges that ordinarily admit candidates with good O-level or average A-level qualifications. Programs conducted at these institutions run for between one and three years and lead to a diploma or certificate.

Institutions of higher education that do not offer university-level programs include those that offer courses of up to three years. Such courses lead to an advanced diploma as the highest award possible. These institutions are essentially intermediate colleges of advanced study dedicated to training professionals who will occupy middle- or intermediate-level positions in the country's occupational structure. In recent years, two of these, namely the Institute of Financial Management in Dar es Salaam and the Institute of Development Management in Morogoro, have partnered with foreign universities to offer degree programs at the master's level. These institutions introduced this arrangement after seeing that their advanced-diploma graduates had been refused direct entry to the master's programs offered by Tanzanian public universities. University-level institutions are those offering courses leading to the bachelor's degree and higher degrees.

HISTORICAL BACKGROUND

At independence in 1961, Tanzania had very few postsecondary education institutions worth mentioning. A handful of teacher training colleges admitted O-level (Form 4) students. The first higher education institution in the country was established in 1961 as a college of the University of London. The University College of Tanganyika, as it was then called, started with the Faculty of Law. The college was housed in premises leased from the ruling party, the Tanganyika African National Union. The decision to establish a university was taken in 1960 out of a conviction that a university would be a powerful strategic weapon in the fight against poverty, ignorance, and disease. The ruling party's offer of premises for the university was meant to demonstrate not only political goodwill but also a readiness to commit resources for university education. In 1964, after a massive mobilization of local and foreign resources, the college was able to move to its own premises on Observation Hill, where the University of Dar es Salaam stands today. In 1963, the college became a constituent college of the University of East Africa, together with Makerere College and the University College of Nairobi. It was then known as University College Dar es Salaam. In 1970, it was decided to dissolve the University of East Africa in order to allow each country to control and give shape to its own university in accordance with its national interests. Thus, on July 1, 1970, University College Dar es Salaam became an independent national university. The head of state became its titular head or chancellor.

From then on, the university became a focal point of political debate and government concern. Convinced that the university ought to be a strategic partner in the fight against poverty, ignorance, and disease, political leaders made every effort to draw the university into the government's central planning and ideology. Attempts to institutionalize party control over the affairs of the university took different forms. First, the person appointed to the post of vice-chancellor in 1970 was a former executive secretary of the ruling party. This was meant to send a powerful message to the university community regarding the expected direction of change.

Second, the party passed the Musoma Resolution in 1974, which directed that students could be eligible for higher education only if they had completed a year's compulsory national service, had a minimum of two years of satisfactory work experience, and had a positive recommendation from their employers. These conditions were meant to screen higher education aspirants so as to weed out nonconformists.

Third, the Institute of Development Studies was established, which was followed by a directive to introduce a compulsory common course in development studies to all students in their first and second year. According to the university prospectus, this common course was intended to:

- Expose students to the theories and problems of social development in the third world in general and in Africa and Tanzania in particular
- Guide students to an understanding of alternative development strategies at both national and international levels
- Enable students to develop appropriate tools for analyzing and resolving development issues as they related to their specific disciplines

The relationship between the government and the public universities has always been tense. While the government would like the universities to be integrated into its central planning process, the universities have quietly resisted the move for fear of losing the kind of autonomy and academic freedom that universities in the West enjoy.

The historical development of higher education in Tanzania may be divided into four phases. The first phase covers the period between 1961 and 1974. During this phase, local delivery of higher education began with the establishment of the University College of Tanganyika. Although it started with the Faculty of Law and with only eleven students, by 1974, student enrollment had risen to 1,852 and the number of faculties had increased to six, namely, arts and social sciences (established in 1964), science (1965), medicine (1968), agriculture (1969), and engineering (1973). During the same phase, six nonuniversity institutions of higher education were established. These were the Dar es Salaam Teacher Training College (1966), the Dar es Salaam Technical College (1971), the Institute of Development Management (1972), the Institute of Finance Management (1972), the National Social Welfare Training Institute (1974), and the National Institute of Transport (1974). All except the Institute of Development Management in Mzumbe were based in Dar es Salaam.

The second phase of higher education development covers the period 1974–1983. This period is associated with critical decisions that had a major effect on the country's education system as a whole. In 1974, the ruling party passed several resolutions that radically affected the delivery of education in the country. The resolutions demanded that universal primary education be introduced throughout the country by 1977, that education at all levels merge theory and practice, and that candidates wishing to join higher education institutions have a working experience of two years after undergoing one year of compulsory national service. This last requirement had a number of negative effects. First, the number of citizens participating in higher education fell by almost 25 percent over the ten years when the policy was operational. Second, the three-year time lag between obtaining A-level results and becoming eligible for admission to a higher education institution entangled some potential candidates in commitments that led them to drop the idea of pursuing a university degree. Female candidates were the most seriously affected group. Third, academic performance was negatively affected, as many students had become academically rusty because of the three-year lag.

Both staff and students responded to the Musoma Resolution with much apprehension. It is difficult to gauge the amount of damage this practice has caused to Tanzania's higher education system. Science-based degree programs were the most severely affected. Relentless efforts were made to have the decision reversed, but it took ten years to convince the ruling party that the policy was causing the country more harm than good.

The third phase covers the period 1984–1993 and is associated with three major developments. First, the ruling party reversed its resolution on its student admission policy in 1984. Suddenly there were too many candidates eligible for admission. Because of the limited space available at the higher education institutions, the minimum entry requirements had to be raised so that each institution could admit just enough students. The University of Dar es Salaam, for example, was able to admit only one-third of those who met the minimum qualifications to join the university.

The second development during this phase was the establishment of a second public university in the country, the Sokoine University of Agriculture, which grew out of the agriculture, forestry, and veterinary science faculty at the University of Dar es Salaam. Although it began by offering three degree programs, it was offering eight by 1993, including agricultural engineering, food science and technology, horticulture, animal science, home economics, and human nutrition. Another significant development during this phase was the establishment of a third public university, the Open University (OU) of Tanzania (1992), which offers degree programs in law, science, education, and arts and social sciences. OU student enrollments have been expanding fast. During this same phase, developments at the University of Dar es Salaam included the establishment of the Faculty of Education (1989), the elevation of the Faculty of Medicine to constituent college status (becoming Muhimbili University College of Health Sciences in 1991), and the introduction of new degree programs in informatics (1990); physical education, sport, and culture (1993); and electronic science and communication (1993).

The fourth phase of higher education development covers the period from 1994 to the present. This period is marked by the liberalization of higher education delivery. In 1994, individuals or groups were legally allowed to set up private higher education institutions and charge fees. By 1999, six such institutions were at different levels of registration as private universities and five others were at different levels of registration as university colleges. Also during this phase, the first higher education institution in the country embarked on a systematic program of self-evaluation and reform, known as the University of Dar es Salaam's Institutional Transformation Program. Other institutions of higher learning are eager to emulate some of the successful aspects of this effort, which is widely appreciated by both the government and the donor community. After independence, practically every ministry and parastatal organization strove to establish its own tertiary training institution in order to satisfy its human resource requirements. It is estimated that the number of tertiary training institutions established between 1961 and 1985 is more than 140.

Prior to 1990, there was no serious attempt to coordinate and regulate the provision of higher education in Tanzania. Efforts to create a coordinated higher education system began in earnest in the 1990s with the creation of the Ministry of Science, Technology, and Higher Education in 1990 and the subsequent establishment of the Higher Education Accreditation Council in 1995.

To appreciate the role and significance of the mushrooming of tertiary training institutions, it is important for one to understand the sociopolitical circumstances that gave rise to them and in which they operated. The model of education that Tanzania inherited at independence consisted of four years of primary education, four years of O-level ("middle school") education, and two years of A-level education. There was no higher education institution except the newly established University College of Tanganyika. The few graduates that existed in the country had been trained elsewhere, mostly at Makerere College in Uganda. There were so few graduates that the country had to rely on expatriates to staff the upper levels of the civil service. As the first president of the country acknowledged,

So little education had been provided that in December 1961 we had too few people with the necessary education qualifications even to man the administration of government as it was then, much less to undertake the big economic and social development work which was essential. Neither was the school population in 1961 large enough to allow for any expectation that the situation would be speedily corrected. (Nyerere 1967, 4)

In 1966, the government launched an ambitious program to Africanize the civil service. One year later, the government declared that the country would adopt socialism and self-reliance as the guiding frame for its development efforts. This entailed, among other changes, centralized state control of the economy and service institutions. Both moves required the availability of highly trained and committed nationals to implement them. Because there were few Tanzanians who had the requisite knowledge and skills, the government decided to embark on a crash training program to produce the people who would implement the tasks that the government had set for itself. It was not possible to rely on expatriates for these tasks. Thus, the mushrooming of tertiary training institutions was an outcome of pressure to Africanize and establish state control of the economy and service institutions. The Ministry of Science, Technology, and Higher Education acknowledged this point in the introductory chapter of its *National Higher Education Policy*:

Demands for personnel with a higher educational background ha[ve] been on the increase both from the public and the private sectors. There has thus been a mushrooming of training centres and institutes catering basically for ministries and parastatals. The mushrooming of such centres and institutes appears to have been haphazardly done (encouraged) without co-ordination to the extent that overlapping in some of the disciplines is common. (MSTHE 1999, 1)

CURRENT TRENDS

Reliable information regarding institutions that do not offer higher education is difficult to obtain. This is because there is no single organ to which they are answerable. Their respective ministries or parastatals undertake all the necessary documentation, monitoring, and assessment. Information regarding institutions of higher education is easier to obtain because of the efforts since 1990 to coordinate them. Figure 60.1 shows the ownership and registration status of higher education institutions as compiled by the Higher Education Accreditation Council. The information provided here is drawn mainly from three important documents: the *Guide to Higher Education in Tanzania* (Higher Education Accreditation Council 2000), *The National Higher Education Policy* (MSTHE 1999), and *Some Basic Statistics on Higher Learning Institutions in Tanzania 1995/6–1999/2000* (MSTHE 2000).

Currently the postsecondary education system is undergoing a major reform process characterized by rationalization, liberalization, cost sharing, expansion, and standardization. Each of these features points to a major shift in the way higher education is perceived and practiced in Tanzania. It will therefore be worthwhile to make a few observations about each of these trends.

Rationalization

Rationalization refers to the attempt to review the number, status, and function of tertiary institutions in the country. The uncoordinated proliferation of such institutions in the past is not only irksome but also wasteful. The country has therefore decided to do some kind of housecleaning in this area:

Deliberate efforts shall be made to arrest the currently un-regulated and uncoordinated establishment of tertiary insti-tutions in the country. Action shall be taken to rationalize the currently existing number of non-university institutions of higher learning as well as to streamline their course pro-grammes so as to have fewer but well-equipped and well-funded institutions. (MSTHE 1999, 6)

A committee has been set up to study the matter and make ap-propriate recommendations; it is working in partnership with the World Bank.

Liberalization

In the 1980s, Tanzania liberalized its economy, thereby de-parting from the socialist policies it adopted in 1967. Over time, the principle of liberalization was extended to all aspects of pub-lic life, including education. Provision of education at all levels has been liberalized in the sense that private individuals or groups can establish and run private schools as long as they ob-serve certain provisions of the law. There has been a stunning response from the public to these changes. Many new higher education institutions have been set up, and many more are in the process of being established. Between 1996 and 1999, the Higher Education Accreditation Council delivered certificates of registration to eleven new private universities and colleges. It is too early, however, to say whether they will all survive. One of the factors that could determine their chances of survival is whether the government will agree to sponsor or extend its stu-dent loan scheme to citizens admitted to private higher educa-tion institutions. At present, this privilege is still confined to students in public institutions.

Cost Sharing

Higher education in Tanzania has been characterized by high unit costs caused by unfavorable staff-to-student ratios and also by the practice of funding a student's living costs, such as meals, accommodation, and transport. As the NHEP document notes, "The practice of providing either free room and board on campus or allowances to students, thereby shifting to the public education budget a considerable sum required to cover living expenses of students, greatly inflates publicly borne unit costs of higher education in Tanzania" (MSTHE 1999).The new trend is to adopt policies that will lead to the reduction of unit costs and ensure that there is equitable sharing of costs between the government and education beneficiaries. The government should confine itself to funding the direct costs of education and leave the remaining costs to be met by the beneficiaries and their guardians.

This scheme is to be implemented in three phases. Cur-rently, the scheme is in its second phase. This consists of the offer of government loans to students to meet their living ex-penses. Unfortunately, the mechanism for recovering such loans is presently still very weak. When the scheme was first an-nounced and put into effect, students and parents expressed con-siderable resistance. This made the government soften up by delaying the tightening of loan-recovery procedures.

The establishment of privately owned higher education in-stitutions whose students pay fees, and the increasing admission of fee-paying students to public institutions, have greatly helped to make cost sharing less objectionable. Currently the govern-ment is considering ways of making loan-recovery procedures legally binding.

Expansion

Tanzania's population currently stands at about 32 million. The total number of students studying at local higher education institutions was 20,916 in 2000. With such a tiny proportion of the population receiving higher education, it is clear that the country still lacks the critical mass of educated people it needs to spearhead and sustain development efforts. Therefore, one of the thrusts of the National Higher Education Policy is to expand enrollment by 500 percent by 2005: "Long-term training and research objectives shall consist of expanding student enrolment in institutions of higher learning five-fold by the year 2005 and expanding intake of science and technology students to achieve the target of 600 scientists and engineers per 1 million by the year 2005" (MSTHE 1999, 7). Unfortunately, this statement sounds like wishful thinking. Tanzania's material and human resource base is such that it cannot implement this goal by ordi-nary means. Expansion must and will take place, but it cannot possibly happen at the rate desired.

Standardization

Since the establishment of the Higher Education Accredi-tation Council in 1996, the registration, accreditation, and gen-eral quality assurance and monitoring of both private and public higher education institutions have been the responsibility of the council. Now and then, the council issues guidelines on various aspects of higher education. So far, the council has closely moni-tored the establishment of new private universities and colleges. Public universities are yet to be affected. The accreditation pro-cess is divided into four distinct stages, and a special certificate is issued to any institution that meets the requirement. An insti-tution that meets the first-stage requirements is awarded a Letter of Interim Authority. It can then qualify for a Certificate of Pro-visional Registration, a Certificate of Full Registration, and a Certificate of Accreditation. So far, only one institution has managed to obtain a Certificate of Accreditation.

FINANCING AND FUNDING PATTERNS

Private institutions are entirely self-financing. Their main sources of funds are student fees, donations, endowments, and self-generated income. Because the income base of many Tan-zanian families is weak, students in these private institutions tend to come from well-to-do families within Tanzania or out-side the country. Some people are not happy with this state of affairs. They would like to see more Tanzanians able to study at these institutions.

Public institutions, in contrast, greatly depend on the gov-ernment for financial support. It is advisable to distinguish here between university and nonuniversity institutions because many

Table 60.1. Ownership and Registration Status of Tanzanian Higher Education Institutions

Institution	Year Established	Ownership Status	Registration Status as of July 2000
Universities			
University of Dar es Salaam	1961	Public	Government Recognized
Sokoine University of Agriculture	1984	Public	Government Recognized
Open University of Tanzania	1994	Public	Government Recognized
Hubert Kairuki Memorial University	1996	Private	Certificate of Accreditation
International Medical and Technological University	1996	Private	Certificate of Provisional Registration
St. Augustine University of Tanzania	1996	Private	Certificate of Full Registration
Zanzibar University	1998	Private	Certificate of Full Registration
Proposed Tumaini University	1999	Private	Certificate of Provisional Registration
Proposed University of Bukoba	1999	Private	Letter of Interim Authority
University Colleges			
University College of Land and Architectural Studies	1972	Public	Government Recognized
Muhimbili University College of Medical Sciences	1991	Public	Government Recognized
Iringa University College	1996	Private	Certificate of Provisional Registration
Kilimanjaro Christian Medical College	1996	Private	Certificate of Provisional Registration
Makumira University College	1996	Private	Certificate of Provisional Registration
Waldorf College DSM Campus	1997	Private	Letter of Interim Authority
College of Education Zanzibar	1998	Private	Certificate of Provisional Registration
Nonuniversity Public Institutions			
Cooperative College of Moshi	1963	Public	Government Recognized
College of Business Education	1965	Public	Government Recognized
Institute of Community Development (Tengeru)	1966	Public	Government Recognized
Dar es Salaam Institute of Technology	1971	Public	Government Recognized
Institute of Development Management*	1972	Public	Government Recognized
Institute of Finance Management*	1972	Public	Government Recognized
Dar es Salaam School of Accountancy	1974	Public	Government Recognized
National Institute of Transport	1974	Public	Government Recognized
National Social Welfare Training Institute	1974	Public	Government Recognized
Tanzania School of Journalism	1975	Public	Government Recognized
Institute of Rural Development Planning	1980	Public	Government Recognized
Institute of Accountancy (Arusha)	1987	Public	Government Recognized

*These institutions are being processed for change of status to university level.

NB: The registration status of some institutions may have been elevated by the time this chapter went to press.

nonuniversity institutions charge fees that are not paid by the student directly but by the sponsoring authority, usually a government ministry or parastatal. This is also true of postgraduate students at universities. Most higher education institutions that do not offer university-level study serve as in-service centers for different types of professionals. Charging fees enables these institutions to enjoy greater financial autonomy than universities, which enroll students. These do not pay fees because they are sponsored by the government.

Besides collecting fees, these institutions also receive a subsidy from the government. The size of the subsidy often depends on the negotiation skills of the parent ministry or parastatal because government funding of universities is not guided by any clear and consistent formula. Every year institutions are required to submit their budget estimates for the following financial year. The budget submitted usually has four components: capital development funds, personal emolument funds, operational costs, and students' direct costs.

Experience shows that the only components that are taken seriously are personal emoluments and students' direct costs. The other components are often subjected to drastic cuts. Therefore funds are allocated not according to identified needs but according to what the government can afford to give in a given financial year. In other words, the process is arbitrary and ad hoc. The report of the task force on financial sustainability of higher education in Tanzania expresses this very well:

> Characteristically, the financing strategies have concentrated on budget items, with only the personnel emolument budget item remaining stable in volume but erratic in timing, while direct student costs have been experiencing fluctuations, cancellations, delays and shrinkage. The other [operational] charges items have been at the mercy of the chief executives, with a heavy tilt towards utilities and housing while direct training costs such as textbooks and [libraries] have been greatly curtailed. Overall, higher education institutions have been receiving less than 35 of their budgetary requirements, resulting in curtailment of programmes, especially field work, practicals and new innovations, thus affecting the quality of the education offered. (MSTHE 1998, vii)

Dissatisfied with this mode of funding, the universities have presented to the government a proposal to change the mode of funding that would take into account the unit cost and size of the institution. The government has not rejected the proposal outright but has referred it to a special committee that is supposed to study it and make appropriate recommendations. In 1998, the task force on financial sustainability made four concrete recommendations, to which the government seems to be responding. These include imposing an education levy on certain consumer goods, reducing unit costs through the application of cost-efficiency measures, increasing the annual higher education budget from 18 to 30 percent, and redistributing higher education costs so that the government pays only 82 percent and the beneficiary contributes 12 percent, leaving the remainder to be met from other sources, including donors and the institution itself.

For many years, higher education institutions have depended heavily on donor funds for capital development. In some years, this budget item received zero funding from the government. There are signs on the horizon that with a better rationalization of funding for higher education, the government will be in a better position to mobilize enough resources to enable it to fund capital development on a more regular basis.

CURRICULUM

The content and form of the programs being offered at institutions of higher learning normally vary according to the mission and objectives of individual institutions. Historically, nonuniversity institutions have had fairly well-defined and -regimented curricula. This is because their curricula were designed and structured to meet the specific objectives and aspirations of the ministry or parastatal that established them. In this regard, curricula at these institutions have recently been relatively more responsive to the needs and aspirations of the nation. But there has not been an attempt to review these needs on a regular basis and revise the curricula accordingly. The radical social, political, and economic changes that have occurred in Tanzania and the world over the past fifteen years have yet to be reflected in the curricula; many of these institutions are out of tune with present realities. There is an urgent need to overhaul the curricula at these institutions.

Some institutions might take the initiative of drawing on the creativity of their academics to design and deliver programs that are in line with recent socioeconomic changes in the country in order to remain current and relevant. The majority, however, will likely require a push from higher authorities, as inertia and paralysis tend to plague many institutions.

At the university level, questions regarding curriculum have always provoked acrimonious debates. The first university in the country was established initially as a college. Naturally its curriculum was modeled on that institution. During its evolution to independent university status, a heated debate took place concerning whether the curriculum was relevant and useful to the people of Tanzania. Essentially, the debate involved whether the university should be closely tied to the developmental path of the state or should be insulated from politics in order to be part of the global community of learning.

This debate is still alive, thankfully, because both positions have valuable elements that are worthy of support and promotion. A sense of responsibility to the community that finances the institution is indeed important. However, institutional freedom and autonomy are also critical for the healthy functioning of a true university.

LANGUAGE OF INSTRUCTIONS

English and Kiswahili are both official languages in Tanzania. As such, they are supposed to complement each other. The education system is a good example of this. Whereas Kiswahili is the medium of instruction during the seven years of primary education, English is the language of instruction in secondary and postsecondary education. It is worth noting, however, that Kiswahili is also the national language and is an instrument for horizontal as well as vertical integration of Tanzanian society.

Kiswahili's role as a national language was given special emphasis after the adoption of a socialist framework for development in Tanzania. Although English and Kiswahili originally complemented each other in terms of their functional domains, later developments showed clearly that Kiswahili was making significant inroads into domains previously dominated by English. As one researcher observed, "Away from the immediate confines of the classroom, English became a language rarely spoken by Tanzanians except in conversation with foreigners" (Tetlow 1988, quoted in Ishumi 1994, 140).

Studies conducted since the late 1970s (Roy-Campbell and Qorro 1997) have consistently pointed out that English is progressively being squeezed out from public life and that proficiency in English is diminishing. Secondary school teachers also report that while English is the official medium of instruction, they often feel obliged to resort to Kiswahili in order to establish meaningful interaction with students. Students admitted to institutions of higher education are victims of this ambivalent language policy. Most have a low proficiency in spoken English, and their writing is barely understandable. Members of staff and external examiners have repeatedly complained that students' low competence in English has a negative impact on their learning process.

It would appear that the country is in a serious dilemma. Should it embark on a massive program to teach English for academic purposes in order to equip students with sufficient language skills to enable them to benefit fully from their studies? Or should it embark on a massive program to develop an adequate Kiswahili terminology and translate many books into Kiswahili to enable students to access knowledge resources in a language that is closer to their patterns of thought and behavior?

The answer is by no means simple. However, further delays in making a decision may cause great harm, not only to the students who are victims of this ambivalence but also to the nation as a whole. Although lectures are conducted in English and students are required to write their assignments in English, outside the lecture hall, discussions are conducted mainly in Kiswahili, even at universities. It would appear that students do not perceive serious difficulties when they conduct their discussions in Kiswahili. It does not therefore make sense to force on them the impression that Kiswahili is deficient and inferior. If that were the case, they would not resort to it with so much ease. The chances of improving proficiency in English will probably be much greater if the change is not seen as coming at the expense of Kiswahili, a language the youth see as the closest reflection of their roots and cultures.

It should not be forgotten that the majority of Tanzanian youth have little or no proficiency in their so-called mother tongues, which are consequently in serious risk of disappearing. The language they feel most at home with and comfortable with tends to be Kiswahili, which they have always used to voice their aspirations and frustrations among peers.

GOVERNANCE ISSUES

Because their activities are directly under the control and surveillance of their main funder, namely the state, public higher learning institutions have limited freedom and autonomy. Chief executives of such institutions and other top leaders are usually appointed by the state, with or without consultation with other stakeholders. The dominant mode of relationship between the government and these institutions is one of state control or interference. Within the socialist frame of thinking, this is quite understandable, since all planning is usually centralized. Since the country has embraced a market approach to development, it is hoped that the state will slowly relax its control and adopt a supervisory relationship with institutions of higher learning. In the supervisory model, the state is expected to set overall policy objectives and monitor their achievement through provision of incentives that can influence actors to pursue those objectives.

In recent years, some institutions have experimented with the practice of incorporating various forms of broad-based participation in the appointment of deans, directors, or heads of departments. Such decentralization remains in some institutions, but a few have abandoned it after seeing that it gave rise to abuses and malpractice. The ideal is to have an appointment system which has a built-in consultative element so that people appointed to top leadership positions are not only acceptable but are also of proven competence. The NHEP has proposed, for example, that "the principal officers of institutions of higher learning shall be appointed on merit in an open system so as to inspire confidence and ensure fairness, competence and acceptability" (MSTHE 1999, 13).

Although each institution has its own regulations regarding staff appointment, evaluation, promotion, and even dismissal, these regulations are modeled on government regulations for similar issues. It is therefore fair to say that these institutions operate very much like civil service departments.

In an attempt to move away from this practice, the NHEP proposes that "public higher education institutions shall be urged to propose their own staff regulations and terms and conditions of service for each cadre of employee; but such proposals require government approval" (MSTHE 1999, 13). The last phrase deserves special note. So long as they remain heavily dependent on the government financially, these institutions cannot attain proper autonomy. Excessive dependency cannot be healthy for an institution that is supposed to promote independent thinking. It is therefore important for these institutions to find a funding formula that will promote their ability to act independently.

Another issue relating to governance is the question of participation of stakeholders in decision making. Workers' participation is a well-established practice in public organizations in Tanzania. It is part of the country's socialist legacy. Workers, and even students, see participation as an integral part of their basic rights. Any attempt to curtail these rights could spark industrial unrest. Therefore representation in decision-making organs is fairly generous in many institutions of higher learning. At the University of Dar es Salaam, student representation is extended even to sensitive organs like the examination committees, which sometimes handle appeals on examination results. One might think that the presence of students on such a committee might hamper the smooth running of its task. But experience has shown that this does not happen when the rules and regulations guiding the operations of the committee are sound and clear and when all members have pledged to observe them. Repre-

Table 60.2. Student Enrollment by Gender in Higher Learning Institutions in Tanzania, 1997–2000

	1997–1998			1998–1999			1999–2000		
	F	M	Total	F	M	Total	F	M	Total
University of Dar es Salaam	744	3,387	4,131	932	3,240	4,172	1,209	3,556	4,765
Muhimbili University College of Health Sciences	122	299	421	141	407	548	180	440	620
University College of Land and Architectural Studies	47	329	376	64	437	501	82	606	688
Sokoine University of Tanzania	251	793	1,044	2,57	902	1,159	318	1,114	1,432
Open University of Tanzania	558	4,251	4,809	682	5,007	5,689	813	4,347	5,160
University of Dar es Salaam — Postgraduate	58	140	198	51	141	192	66	142	208
Muhimbili University College of Health Sciences — Postgraduate	6	22	28	3	23	26	6	21	27
Sokoine University of Agriculture — Postgraduate	22	153	175	24	84	108	56	186	242
Dar es Salaam Institute of Technology	38	763	801	55	864	919	89	1,046	1,135
Technical College (Arusha)	57	418	475	63	381	444	46	394	440
Mbeya Technical College	20	563	583	17	453	470	8	466	474
Institute of Development Management	227	828	1,055	245	734	979	310	751	1,061
Institute of Finance Management	422	968	1,390	378	690	1,068	282	553	835
Moshi Cooperative College	66	196	262	36	86	122	45	69	114
Institute of Accountancy (Arusha)	37	123	160	38	145	183	36	99	135
National Institute of Transport	3	88	91	2	45	47	1	57	58
Community Development Institute (Tengeru)	96	61	157	92	59	151	86	68	154
Mweka Wildlife College	29	139	168	29	135	164	67	151	218
Dar es Salaam School of Accountancy	60	185	245	109	277	386	122	263	385
National Social Welfare Institute	154	130	284	166	108	274	110	73	183
Karume Technical College (Zanzibar)	57	146	203	51	161	212	66	161	227
Tanzania School of Journalism	9	25	34	40	38	78	25	36	61
Institute of Rural Development Planning (Dodoma)	14	39	53	21	36	57	27	38	65
College of Business Education	223	444	667	315	462	777	460	62	1,058
St. Augustine University	93	192	285	102	201	303	117	175	292
Tumaini University—Kilimanjaro Christian Medical College	6	10	16	48	57	105	25	34	59
Makumira Campus	—	—	—	11	133	144	9	131	140
Iringa Campus	—	—	—	40	73	113	74	132	206
Tanzania Adventist College	55	88	143	37	78	115	35	83	118
Waldorf College	23	49	72	75	109	184	76	88	164
Hubert Kairuki Memorial University	—	—	—	4	6	10	11	15	26
International Medical and Technical University	—	—	—	7	27	34	19	39	58
Zanzibar University	11	18	29	26	66	92	37	67	104
Total	3,508	14,847	18,355	4,161	15,665	19,826	4,919	16,003	20,912

sentation tends to nurture a culture of collective responsibility without exonerating the top leadership from its duty and responsibility to provide guidance.

INSTITUTIONAL CAPACITY AND STRUCTURE

The act or charter that establishes the institution is usually very elaborate in defining institutional roles. The structural design of large education institutions is such that there is always a top executive who is assisted by one or two officers. In the case of universities, the two assistants are normally assigned complementary roles, such as academic and administrative duties. One will be answerable to the top executive on matters relating to academics and the other on matters relating to administration. Below the assistants are deans and directors in charge of faculties, academic institutes, or directorates. In institutions that do not offer university-level education, the chief executive is usually called the principal. One or two people may assist this person. Below the assistants are either panel coordinators or departmental heads.

In most institutions, power is highly centralized and jealously guarded. Despite this, the administrative structures of these institutions are rather weak and porous. One of the reasons for this is the lack of personnel properly trained for the systematic management and administration of the institution. Higher education institutions are relatively young in the country, so administrators have very little tradition to go by.

In terms of physical structure and facilities, many institutions have limited capacity. Existing structures, many of which were built with donor assistance, are in most cases quite run down. This is not necessarily due to lack of funds alone but also to the lack of a culture that values maintenance. Maintenance is often given low priority in budgeting.

The capacity to expand both in terms of numbers and programs is hampered by the lack of resources with which to create more space and train people who can teach and who can professionally handle planning, administration, and financial management functions. Hiring people with the requisite skills and qualifications is difficult because of the poor remuneration packages set by the government for these institutions. When institutions do manage to train their own people, they fail to retain them for the same reason. Although there is a high demand for highly trained people, the pool from which to draw them is woefully small. The reason is simply that higher-level training has not been sufficiently emphasized. The country has yet to produce top-quality administrators, planners, and financial managers.

The capacity to design and deliver academic programs differs from institution to institution. Some institutions have a sizeable pool of highly qualified academic staff. The University of Dar es Salaam is rather unique in that 78 percent of its academic members of staff hold a Ph.D. Very few universities in sub-Saharan Africa approximate this figure. The Open University relies heavily on staff from the University of Dar es Salaam to prepare its study manuals. Moreover, most employees of the Open University were at one time members of staff of the University of Dar es Salaam.

In order to exploit fully its newly installed information and communication technology (ICT) facilities and complement its present residential programs, the University of Dar es Salaam is planning to launch its own distance learning program. Many feel that academic staff is underutilized. Poor facilities and an unattractive remuneration package make it difficult for the university to demand more from employees. To supplement their income, they are forced to engage in moonlighting.

The staff-to-student ratio is very generous at most public universities. At the School of Medicine, the ratio is 1 to 4, and in the faculties of law and commerce it is 1 to 12. The situation at institutions that do not offer university-level education is slightly different in that most academic staff members are holders of a master's degree only. A few hold only a bachelor's degree, and very few possess a Ph.D. Most institutions lack the capacity to professionally plan and manage their core business in an efficient and cost-effective manner, particularly in the face of fierce competition and harsh socioeconomic conditions. Many have succumbed to frustration and a sense of powerlessness.

STAFF ISSUES

Staff issues that preoccupy institutions throughout the world are very much alike. They include terms and conditions of service, remuneration packages, training and career development opportunities, working and living conditions, and participation in decisions that seriously affect one's life. For the most part, the government sets terms and conditions of service, with occasional cosmetic changes from the institution concerned. Salaries are also determined and regulated by the government or a body appointed by the government for that purpose. Until 1996, terms of service and salaries for parastatal organizations in Tanzania were determined and regulated by an organization called SCOPO (the Standing Committee for Parastatal Organizations). Higher education institutions were regarded as parastatals, so their salaries also were set and regulated by SCOPO.

Throughout the 1980s and early 1990s, salaries were abysmally low. To cushion employees against the negative effects of this, the government introduced a string of allowances, such as fuel, housing, and sitting allowances. Eligibility conditions for these allowances were often vague and unclear. This gave rise to abuses, deceit, and corruption. Although salaries were low, take-home pay could exceed the salary by up to 400 percent under the allowance system. Unfortunately, the allowances did not count in the computation of one's pension, so pension packages remained as low as the salaries on which they were based.

In 1996, the government introduced a new salary system that consolidated some of the allowances and abolished others. When the new system was applied to the higher education institutions, people discovered that a majority of the staff would get a drastically reduced take-home pay. After sensing signs of labor unrest, the management of higher education institutions successfully negotiated a more reasonable arrangement with the government. In 1998, there was a substantial increase in salaries. This was a measure calculated to stem Tanzania's brain drain, which was affecting not only higher education institutions but also the government. A study of the brain drain had revealed that the two main factors behind such migration were poor remuneration and poor working conditions.

Opportunities for training and career development depend on availability of funds. When funds are available, priority is always given to academic members of staff. While in training, staff are allowed to retain 90 percent of their salary; they also continue to enjoy other privileges, such as housing and medical treatment. Although staff who are allowed to get further training are bonded, many do not honor the bond after completion of their studies. They leave for greener pastures without bothering to reimburse the government for their training costs. Higher education institutions have experienced many such cases. Attempts to seek legal redress have not been fruitful because the courts do not recognize such bonds.

Working and living conditions for staff vary from institution to institution. Office space is usually shared between staff members. Up to 70 percent of staff live on campus in houses owned by the institution. They pay subsidized rent or nothing at all if they are entitled officers. The houses are not regularly maintained because the rent collected is insufficient for the purpose.

Participation in decision making is done through representation. Staff members are supposed to be organized in labor unions or associations. Their views are solicited through these bodies. The unions or associations therefore nominate representatives to the various boards or committees that handle policy issues. Although there is a national labor union, the Researchers, Academics, and Allied Workers Union (RAAWU), to which all staff of institutions of higher education are supposed to belong, in practice it is primarily the administrative, technical, and support staff who take active interest in it. Academics tend to shun or ignore the national union. Academics have instead formed their own associations, such as the University of Dar es Salaam Staff Association (UDASA), the Sokoine University of Agriculture Staff Association (SUASA), and the Open University of Tanzania Staff Association (OUTASA). There has been a fierce debate about whether academics should strive to set up and register their own labor union in order to formalize a separate bargaining position. The issue has yet to be resolved.

STUDENT ISSUES

The average age of students at Tanzanian universities is about 24. This is because Tanzanian children start primary school relatively late (at age 7); many children begin school later than that. Students spend seven years in primary school, four years in junior secondary, and two years in senior secondary school. They lose one year while waiting to enter the university because of the lack of the synchronization between finishing A-levels and the commencement of the academic year at universities. These students are therefore relatively older than university students in other countries.

Because they are a privileged few, students at these institutions tend to be elitist in outlook and expectation. According to one study (Materu, Mbwette, and Sauer 1996, 4), students admitted to universities in Tanzania constitute only 0.3 percent of their age group. Participation of females is particularly low. On average, their participation now stands at between 25 and 30 percent. Figure 60.2 shows student distribution by gender in higher education institutions for the period 1997 to 2000. Most institutions have been taking steps to improve female participa-

tion, but the problem stems from deep-rooted cultural and psychological factors. The Faculty of Arts and Social Sciences at the University of Dar es Salaam was able to register 49 percent females in the 2000–2001 first-year intake. The cutoff point for female candidates has been lowered by one unit in A-level scores in order to enable more females to qualify for admission. In science-based disciplines, pre-entry programs are mounted annually to help female candidates make up for any deficiencies they might have. At the end of the eight-week program, they are given an examination. Those who perform well are admitted to the university in the relevant discipline. An average of between 60 and 80 women benefit from this arrangement annually. Cases of open hostility or vulgarity between male and female students used to occur frequently at some campuses. The situation has improved significantly since the implementation of gender sensitization campaigns organized by the Department of Student Welfare and the university-wide Gender Dimension Task Force, with substantial support from the university's top leadership.

Because of the expanded intake, it has not been possible to accommodate all students on campus. Many institutions have had to amend their admission letters to exclude the right to campus accommodation. One important development that has helped to ease tension between students and the management is the separation of welfare matters from academic matters. Students have been told that only the latter is the responsibility of the institution; anything else shall be the responsibility of the student and his sponsor. Students therefore have to deal directly with their sponsor on welfare matters.

Also, in the past, boycotts, protests, and demonstrations occurred chiefly in response to major issues of national or international character. These days, students tend to focus attention on their own welfare. Questions relating to money tend to provoke them. When they suspect that they are being short-changed, they can flare up quickly. The last major protest occurred in October 2000. It involved students of all public universities and public university colleges and at two nonuniversity colleges in the city. Students decided to boycott classes in order to pressure the government to increase their food and accommodation allowances. The boycott was timed to coincide with the last few days before the general election. The government did not budge. In order to allow student tempers to cool, the authorities closed the institutions for two months.

Each institution has a student union, which is supposed to bargain for and oversee the welfare of students. The organizational structure of the student union is very much like that of a government. Each has a president, a vice-president, a cabinet, and a set of ministers. Students also have a representative council, a general assembly, and a constitution. Unfortunately, it is rare that a student government functions properly and smoothly. Because student governments last only one year, they are characterized by a lack of continuity and stability. Student government officers leave office just when they are sufficiently informed and ready to start work. Such transitions are usually perfunctory and acrimonious.

In student politics, every issue tends to be regarded as an emergency. Leaders are urged by vocal students, sometimes threateningly, to take prompt action, and their decisions often land them in trouble. Their meetings are always tense and full of accusations. Embezzlement of funds is a favorite topic at such meetings; democracy is rarely respected. Once a decision on some form of disruption has been taken, it has to be implemented by all means, including the use of force against fellow students who might disagree with the decision. Most boycotts and protests are accompanied by threats of violence and ostracism. It will take a long time to persuade students to practice democracy in conducting their affairs.

REFORMS AT THE UNIVERSITY OF DAR ES SALAAM

One of the notable features of the fourth phase of higher education development in Tanzania has been the launching of a transformation program at the oldest higher learning institution in the country. The program began informally in 1991 as a self-review process that was prompted by a need to do something about the pervasive discontent afflicting the institution. Shivji captures the crisis that faced the university:

> The present malaise of the university has been variously described by different commentators in reports and other writings. However all of them are agreed on one thing: that there is something wrong and that different sections of the university community are labouring under deep-seated grievances, discontent and generally low morale and spirits. (1993, 64)

The wide-ranging and time-consuming self-review culminated in a momentous decision to overhaul the entire institution after realizing that the malaise plaguing the university had seeped so deep into the institutional fabric that a piecemeal solution would not provide a satisfactory cure. In 1993, the university formally launched its reform program through the unveiling and adoption of its Corporate Strategic Plan, which had been in preparation for more than eighteen months. The strategic plan was prepared in house and was discussed and modified extensively. The tenth version of the plan finally received the approval of council and other organs. It is the basic document that guided the reform process. The argument and spirit that inspired the process are most aptly captured in the following statement from a brochure of the Program Management Unit:

> Since its inception, first as a university college in 1961 and later as an autonomous national university in 1970, the university of Dar es Salaam had never had the benefit of systematically reviewing the consistency and relevance of its mission; yet so many changes had happened and so many changes had taken place that what seemed to have been a clear and firm message about the expectations of the university and its role and function in 1961 and the 1970s was already at extreme variance with the realities of the 1990s and the potentials of the 21st century. (Programme Management Unit 1998, 3)

Under the transformation program, every aspect of the university has been subjected to scrutiny to establish whether it contributes maximally to the attainment of the university's mission of teaching, research, and consultancy. Committed leadership, careful planning, and support from the internal and external constituencies are the main factors that have sustained the pro-

cess and facilitated success. Five years after launching the program, a group of experts who evaluated it had the following to say:

> The launching of the institutional transformation programme in 1993 was perhaps the most significant development in the history of the university of Dar es Salaam since it became a full university in 1970. It occurred at a time when the once notable and highly regarded national institution of higher learning, which had just enjoyed considerable international acclaim in the 1970s and early 1980s, was then in serious decline. This pathetic situation had resulted from, and was characterised by, among other things, years of dwindling financial resources, low student enrolment, low academic staff morale coupled with a brisk brain drain and a poor national and international image. Within the past five years of the institutional transformation programme, the situation has been turned round, and the plans and objectives set for this period have been largely successful. (Mgaya, Kundi, Meshack, and Shija 2000, i)

Other higher learning institutions have expressed interest in learning more about what one reporter for *The Chronicle of Higher Education* (Bollag 2001) described as "an African success story."

Under the umbrella of the Committee of Vice-Chancellors and Principals in Tanzania (CVPT), the University of Dar es Salaam has also taken the initiative to promote joint activities among institutions of higher education. Examples of this include a joint radio program by the public universities, a joint exhibition outside the parliament building in Dodoma during the budget session, and a joint study on how public universities can remain competitive in the context of the liberalization of education. Preliminary discussions have begun regarding the possibility of having a federated pension scheme for all institutions of higher learning, as recommended by a team of experts that was appointed by the University of Dar es Salaam to study the inadequacies of the present pension scheme. Another idea in development is to link the libraries of all higher education institutions to facilitate the sharing of resources. Last year, the University of Dar es Salaam organized a seminar to which all higher education institutions were invited. The purpose of the seminar was to exchange views on the state of ICT at various institutions, with a view to promoting cooperation and assisting one another in developing ICT facilities.

FUTURE OUTLOOK

Higher education is still very much underdeveloped in Tanzania. Policymakers still do not understand the danger that this situation poses for the future of the country. In 1998, a two-person team from the University of Dar es Salaam (Luhanga and Mbwette 1998) addressed members of Parliament and made a passionate plea to them to consider the importance of higher education for the future of Tanzania. The presenters clearly argued that unless something is done soon to change the situation, Tanzania is likely to be relegated to the backyard of the modern world.

The critical mass to spearhead and sustain rational development is simply lacking. The tertiary institutions that mushroomed in the 1970s and 1980s were designed to produce midlevel professionals. University education stagnated for a long time with few noticing the anomaly. As a result, Tanzania has few higher-level personnel who can design, critically evaluate, and oversee development projects in various sectors. Without a critical mass of this type of personnel, the country cannot develop a realistic and constructive vision for the future. The present almost ad hoc approach to higher education is unlikely to produce lasting results. There is therefore a need to articulate systematically the principles and goals of higher education in the country. Existing higher education policy reads like a wish list rather than an articulate and cohesive agenda.

The process of rationalizing existing tertiary institutions is not moving fast enough. A number of tertiary institutions have closed down because the parastatals that used to manage them are now defunct. These are valuable national assets that could be put to use to boost the higher education sector. The enthusiastic response of the private sector to the liberalization of education cannot solve the problem of the need for broader access to and diversification of higher education. The government must take up the challenge in the same spirit as that which inspired Tanzania's founders to make great sacrifices in order to establish the first university after independence.

BIBLIOGRAPHY

Bollag, B. 2001. "An African Success Story at the U. of Dar es Salaam." *The Chronicle of Higher Education*, April 6, A53.

Higher Education Accreditation Council. 2000. *Guide to Higher Education in Tanzania*. Dar es Salaam: Higher Education Accreditation Council.

Ishumi, A. G. M. 1994. *Thirty Years of Learning: Educational Develop-ment in Eastern and Southern Africa from Independence to 1990*. Ottawa, Canada: International Development Research Centre.

Luhanga, M. L., and T. S. A. Mbwette. 1998. "University Education in Tanzania: A Perspective for the Twenty-First Century: UDSM Experiences." Paper presented to Members of Parliament.

Materu, P. N., T. S. A. Mbwette, and R. Sauer. 1996. "The 'UDSM 2000' Institutional Transformation Programme at the University of Dar es Salaam: Concept, Status, Experiences and Perspectives for the Future." Paper presented to the annual conference of the Association for the Development of African Education, Working Group on Higher Education, Durban, South Africa, October.

Mgaya, Y. D., B. A. T. Kundi, M. V. Meshack, and J. K. Shija. 2000. *Five Years of the UDSM Transformation Programme 1994/95–1998/99*. Dar es Salaam: United Republic of Tanzania.

MSTHE (Ministry of Science, Technology and Higher Education). 1998. "Financial Sustainability of Higher Education in Tanzania: An Executive Summary." Dar es Salaam: United Republic of Tanzania.

———. 1999. *National Higher Education Policy*. Dar es Salaam: United Republic of Tanzania.

———. 2000. *Some Basic Statistics on Higher Learning Institutions in Tanzania 1995/6–1999/2000*. Dar es Salaam: United Republic of Tanzania.

Nyerere, J. K. 1967. *Education for Self-Reliance*. Dar es Salaam: Government Printer.

Programme Management Unit. 1998. "About the Institutional Transformation Programme." Dar es Salaam: University of Dar es Salaam.

Roy-Campbell, Z., and M. Qorro. 1997. *Language Crisis in Tanzania: The Myth of English versus Education*. Dar es Salaam: Mkuki na Nyota Publishers.

Shivji, I. G. 1993. *Intellectuals at the Hill: Essays and Talks 1969–1993*. Dar es Salaam: Dar es Salaam University Press.

Tetlow, J. G. 1988. "The English Language Support Project: A Personal Perspective." Seminar paper presented at the University of Dar es Salaam, September 1998. In author's possession.

61

Togo

Emmanuel A. B. K. M. Edee

INTRODUCTION

Togo gained independence in 1960. Although it relies primarily on agriculture, Togo enjoys an expanding economy based on the exploitation of mineral resources such as phosphates, marble, and ores. Other economic activities include textile production and the food industry. The country stretches over an area of 56,785 square kilometers (21,925 square miles) and has an estimated population of over 5 million; it has an annual population growth rate of 2.7 percent.

Since 1965, the governments of Togo and Benin, with the assistance of the French government, have inaugurated an embryonic university called the Advanced Institute of Benin (Institut Supérieur de Bénin), which consists of two branches: a science section at Porto-Novo and a letters section at Lomé (Togo). In 1970, the institute project ceased to exist when the two states decided to set up their own universities. In September 1970, the University of Benin was created by presidential decree.

The mission of the University of Benin is to produce qualified professionals to take charge of and manage the social, economic, and cultural structures of the country and carry out research needed for the development of the country.

What started in 1970 as four schools (letters, law, science, and medicine) scattered around the city of Lomé was later grouped into a single university campus situated 1.24 miles from the city.

The University of Benin has been committed to interuniversity cooperation since its inception, and university leaders did not hesitate to establish cooperative relations with various universities worldwide. Early in its history, the university signed about thirty cooperation agreements, a number that is constantly increasing.

HIGHER EDUCATION IN TOGO

Higher education in Togo strives to train each student as an individual while emancipating him or her at all levels. The goal is to develop the individual's capacity for critical thinking and, hence, to learn how to innovate and create. Learning is meant to develop competence and expertise in the student, qualities that are useful for the development of the country. Toward this goal, the individual must take into account the surrounding sociocultural environment and closely monitor the job market in order to gear his or her program of education toward bridging the gap between training and national development needs. To meet this goal, Togolese higher education attempts to provide high-quality instruction by perfecting teaching methods, encouraging scientific research, intensifying the professionalism and diversity of offerings, and maintaining a good relationship—without jeopardizing the university's autonomy—with the political authority that incessantly obstructs the carrying out of the university's responsibilities. Higher education strives also to adopt a more efficient mode of financial management and works to strengthen international development.

Two types of institutions provide higher education in Togo: national public institutions—such as the schools, the Grandes Ecoles, the institutes, the research centers, and state international institutions such as the African-Madagascan Advanced School of Architecture and Urban Studies (Ecole Africaine et Malgache d'Architecture et d'Urbanisme, EAMAU)—and private institutions. Togo has two universities, one of which has been operational for thirty years. The second, situated inland at Kara, is under construction.

Every student admitted to the university is automatically entitled to rights and subject to penalties as stipulated by the institution's bylaws. Class attendance and completion of labs is required. Students can be subjected to the penalties of the disciplinary commission in cases of serious misconduct. Selection of students is made on an objective basis, according to the student's vocation and orientation. It takes into consideration both the student's vocation and the career types needed for development plans devised by the government. The number of students rose from 845 in 1970–1971 to 16,263 in 1998–1999. A total of 30,000 graduates have been trained by a teaching body of 727.

Current Trend Reforms

Since its inception, Togolese higher education has suffered from an inability to adapt to the economic realities and needs of the country. In October 1972, a new reform plan was initiated.

The priorities of the higher education system in Togo are teacher training and the promotion of various professionals needed in the primary, secondary, and postsecondary schools. In order to educate students from both scientific and literary branches, the National Institute of Educational Sciences (Institut National des Sciences de l'Education, INSE) provides theoretical courses and supervised projects in pedagogy in two categories: initiation in and sensitization to problems in teaching methods, and preparation for the bachelor's degree in education and for inspectors of national education.

A presidential decree of September 29, 1988, converted the advanced schools of letters, sciences, medicine, law, economics, and management into schools. Currently, the system is composed of five schools, one institute, three advanced schools, and one center.

In response to the saturation of the job market and current national needs, professional training at the University of Benin has been augmented in recent years by means of an increase in the number of technical training institutions, the creation of new professional branches, and the reinforcement of existing ones such as the Management Institute of Geston (Institut Universitaire de Technologie de Gestion, IUT), the Advanced School of Administrative Assistance (Ecole Supérieur de Secrétariat de Direction, ESSD), the Advanced School of Engineering (Ecole Supérieure d'Ingénieurs, ENSI), and the Training Center for the Maintenance of Microcomputer Equipment (Centre Africain de Formation à la Maintenance des Equipements Micro-Informatiques, CAFMICRO).

In order to increase access to technical and professional training, the state has encouraged the creation of private institutions of higher education. Today, there are twenty-two institutes, eighteen of which were created between 1998 and 2000. These institutions, which offer accelerated technician degrees in sixteen specialties, are subsidized by the state in the same way as other institutions.

A number of other institutions come under the umbrella of higher education. These include Teacher Schools (Ecole Normale Supérieure, ENS), the National School for Administration (Ecole Nationale d'Administration, ENA), the Demographic Research Unit (Unité de Recherche Démographique, URD), the System for Publishing and Information Dissemination (Système Français d'Edition et de Diffusion, SYFED), and the Distance Education Center (Centre de Formation à Distance, CFAD). International collaboration between researchers is fostered through the UNESCO chair for distance education (Chaire UNESCO de Formation à Distance, CUFAD).

To improve the management of institutions of higher education, it has been necessary to involve representatives from the social and economic sectors (Law 97-14). One-third of university boards, as well as faculty, school, and institute assemblies, include representatives from the economic and social sectors. These representatives are elected for a renewable three-year term.

This innovation at the level of university boards and assemblies is intended to allow the resolution of a number of students' problems, such as unemployment, which constitutes a major preoccupation for all graduates. A good relationship between the university and the private sector is likely to open new venues to integrate graduates into the job market. The presence of representatives from the industry sector on boards will also ensure better interaction between the university community and society. Moreover, it will lead to more transparent and efficient management in higher education. In this way, the government is backing the universities with all its weight so that they can fulfill their mission in the best possible conditions and can better serve the members of the scientific community.

Capacity and Institutional Structure

In Togo, the public and private institutions of higher education assume both a scientific and a cultural character, providing knowledge and safeguarding the cultural heritage. They come under the responsibility of the ministries in charge of higher education; namely, the Ministry of National Education and Research (Ministère de l'Education Nationale et de la Recherche, MENR) and the Ministry of Technical Education, Vocational Training, and Handicrafts (Ministère de l'Enseignement Technique, de la Formation Professionnelle et de l'Artisanat, METFPA). The goals of Togolese higher education fall into four main categories. First, it offers advanced basic and continuous education. Second, it is responsible for conducting scientific research, developing technologies, and marketing research results. Third, it is a way to disseminate and popularize cultural, technical, and scientific information. Finally, higher education provides the services needed for training and research.

Each institution of higher education grants degrees in the disciplines it offers, as well as honorary degrees. Institutions of higher education provide an education free from all political, economic, religious, or ideological influence. This instruction underscores learning and scholarship in a spirit of respect for diversity of opinions.

CENTRAL UNITS VERSUS INSTITUTIONAL UNITS

Institutions of higher education are structured around central units. The central units are composed of three main parts: the Council of Higher Education, the chancellor of universities, and central services. The function of the Council of Higher Education mainly consists of defining the general scientific and pedagogical orientations of higher education to meet the country's economic, social, and cultural needs. The Council is also responsible for laying down a long-term strategy for the evolution of higher education and conducting an annual survey to evaluate its implementation. The function of the Council is determined by ministerial decree. The second central unit, the chancellor, is nominated by decree. The chancellor represents the central authority vis-à-vis higher education and supervises the universities. Finally, central services consists of all the units reporting to the chancellor, ranging from academic affairs to parking facilities.

Institutional units include the University Council, the president of the university, the vice-presidents, the deans, the directors, representatives of various departments, and student representatives. The University Council determines admissions requirements for each institution according to the provisions of the national development plan. It also determines admission quotas of foreign students after consultation with the ministries in charge of higher education. All institutions of higher education in Togo are regulated by reauthorization statutes, the last of which was issued on September 10, 1997.

Financing

Budgets for institutions of higher education are decided after consultation with the General Council of Universities (Grand Conseil des Universités). The operational and investment budgets are composed essentially of subsidies from the state. Other income is generated from student fees (about 5 percent), loans, donations, endowments, and various other revenues. Salary allocations account for 65 to 70 percent of the state subsidy, which provides 90 percent of university funding. A considerable amount of what is reserved for the operational budget goes to university activities.

Togolese higher education suffers a chronic crisis due to the inadequacy and high cost of the programs offered at universities. Moreover, the lingering sociopolitical crisis continues to have a significant impact on higher education, as the weakened national economy is no longer able to assume regular and adequate financing of academic and scientific activities. Moreover, it is not able to sustain the provision of grants and financial aid to students or pay the salaries of administrative personnel.

Diversification of revenue sources is an ultimate necessity. Many types of financing are possible from the private sector, from development partners, and from foundations. An increase in tuition fees for both nationals and foreigners offers an internal way of increasing revenue. Another solution would be to enhance research and make the higher education system a consulting tool that benefits both small and midsize businesses.

The private sector could also help by defining its requirements for graduates and putting together a grant system geared toward particularly vital disciplines. Businesses could sponsor students during their training. Finally, the private sector could initiate research programs with the university.

Degrees

Access to higher education in Togo is open to holders of a *baccalauréat* (high school diploma) or its equivalent. Some institutions require an entrance test preceded by an application review and aptitude test.

Universities offer a two-year degree, the Degree of General University Studies (Diplôme des Etudes Universitaires Générales, DEUG), and a number of four-year degrees: the B.A., the Aptitude Certificate for the Barrister Profession (Certificat d'Aptitude à la Profession d'Avocat, CAPA), the Aptitude Certificate in Management (Certificat d'Aptitude à l'Administration des Entreprises, CAAE), the Specialized Studies Degree (Diplôme des Etudes Spécialisés, DESS), the Advanced Studies Degree (Diplôme des Etudes Approfondies, DEA), the doctorate, and the Specialized Studies Certificate (Certificat d'Etudes Spécialisées, CES). Schools, institutes, and centers, on the other hand, offer degrees such as the Technician University Degree (Diplôme Universitaire de Technicien, DUT), Executive Engineer Degree (Diplôme d'Ingénieur d'Execution, DIE), Design Engineer (Diplôme d'Ingénieur de Conception, DIC), and Agronomy Engineer (Diplôme d'Ingénieur Agronome, DIA).

Language of Instruction

French is the language of instruction in Togo, which means that the language used in higher education is not the mother tongue of the country. It seems, then, that the use of a foreign language will always constitute a barrier to understanding and assimilating courses correctly.

Local languages and cultural values—which are not, as is believed by some, impeding socioeconomic development—should be rehabilitated. Sooner or later the necessity of integrating national languages and cultures into educational programs will be a pressing need. All the positive philosophical values of Togolese culture should be integrated in school curricula, as well as all forms of Togolese expression, including the oral tradition, art, music, and native technology. Togo has taken positive action to resolve this problem through the progressive incorporation of local languages in kindergartens and elementary schools.

A National Linguistic Institute is projected to study all the languages in Togo. This process will follow two phases. In the first phase, French will remain the language of instruction and national languages will be introduced into the curriculum. In the second phase, French will be taught as a foreign language. This deserving initiative will obviously take time to implement at higher education institutions.

Teaching and Research

In addition to teaching loads varying between 150 and 360 hours (during around thirty weeks of teaching), a number of which depend on rank, faculty members are required to devote the remainder of their time to research and publication in order to be promoted. Scientific research is an essential axis that institutions promote, develop, and assume. Research activity is also the way to have one's name on the promotion lists recognized by university councils. An example of these lists is the African and Malagasy Council for Higher Education (Conseil Africain et Malgache pour l'Enseignement Supérieur, CAMES). The coordination of research activities and services at the University of Benin is the responsibility of the Scientific Research Division, created by the 1994 ministerial decree and composed of four divisions: Letters and Human Sciences, and Fundamental and Applied Sciences coordinate and carry out research activities related to their respective fields; the Division of Services is concerned with the provision of services to researchers; and the Division of Publication is responsible for the management and dissemination of scientific publications produced by individual or team researchers for national journals.

There are two main research orientations in Togo: technology transfer and basic and applied research.

From an organizational point of view, research is conducted by teams in laboratories or by research units under the supervision of a faculty member. Efforts are being made to give the research teams an interdisciplinary profile to produce better results. Efforts are also being made to establish closer collaboration between researchers and regional and subregional businesses. The idea is to create what could be called a technology transfer unit, a body that would play the role of a communication interface between the university and businesses. It would also act as an agency that would market the competencies and expertise of the university as a research institution. This projected collaboration plan would constitute an extremely necessary tool by attending to the needs of a business sector that is confronted by a number of technological problems. It would also serve to promote the results of laboratory research and assist industry in improving performance. Branches of the Scientific Research Division are projected to be set up within departments, schools, and institutes.

The dissemination of research results is made through the publications of the University of Benin and the *Scientific Research Journal* of the same university. The entire publication apparatus produces about 100 articles per year in all disciplines.

Research is focused mainly on areas that respond to the country's needs. Examples include agriculture, the transformation of natural resources, handicrafts, medicinal plants, pharmacopoeia, social development, and applied science. Other research fields include urban development, education, nutrition, applied chemistry, food industry, environment, hydraulics, and medicine.

Financing of research activity is provided by the government and a number of organizations such as the French Cooperation, the Research Center for International Development, the Cultural and Technical Cooperation Agency, the German consulting agency Deutsche Gesellschaft für Technische Zusammenarbeit (GTZ), the UNDP, the WHO, the AUPELF (Association des Universités Partièllement ou Entièrement de Langue Française), and UNESCO.

Specific Trends and Problems

Unemployment: Forty years after independence, higher education in Togo seems to have achieved little more than producing B.A. degree holders and engineers to join the ranks of the unemployed.

Graduate unemployment is a present reality. Under analysis, it becomes clear that this phenomenon is the result of the lack of compatibility between the programs offered by the institutions of higher education and the job market. The solution to this problem is to create new programs and new disciplines that take into account the needs and perspectives of future graduates. This, of course, requires the creation and promotion of relationships between the economic private sector and the university, an important project which both the national authorities and the university are considering.

Student activism: Togolese higher education has seen a significant increase in student unions due, on the one hand, to the liberalization of social life and, on the other hand, to a lack of coordination of the activities of the student associations and the frequent social, academic, and political movements. About 16,000 students belong to the various student unions and associations. On a social level, student concerns revolve around grants and financial aid, and this is apparent in a lack of solidarity between students as well as discontent among students who do not benefit from state assistance. Student unions are also concerned with the inadequacies of residence facilities and medical care. On the academic level, issues taken up by the unions range from protesting insufficient manuals and books to contesting exam results. The unions' political concerns consist mainly of tendencies to impose the ideologies of political parties on campus; in this way, political problems are simply transferred from the broader society into the campus arena by students adopting the position of one political party or another.

The University Council includes two students elected by student representatives to school, advanced school, and institute assemblies. Student members in the University Council have also shown a tendency to organize themselves into unions, thus questioning the decisions of the university management authorities.

In general, the campus scene is characterized by conflicting relationships between the student organizations, the university administration, and the government.

Faculty, Academic Freedom, and Brain Drain

The teaching body in higher education is composed of over 700 faculty members. These include full professors, lecturers, assistant professors, and teaching assistants. Among the overall total, 391 are either holding a permanent position or are under contract and 336 are part-timers. The faculty members at advanced schools, institutes, and centers have the same status as those in other university departments. The university faculty members teach at the advanced schools, institutes, and centers and vice versa, which shows that all faculty are given a chance to make a career in teaching.

Professors enjoy privileges that are traditionally granted to faculty members in terms of academic freedom, teaching methods, and the pursuit of research and career advancement, all within the general policy determined by the government.

To achieve career advancement, faculty members subscribe to the different promotion lists that are recognized by the University Councils, such as the African and Malagasy Council for Higher Education (CAMES). The faculty community is organized by the Togolese Higher Education Union (Syndicat de l'Enseignement Supérieur du Togo, SEST), which is sometimes hampered by political manipulations and infiltration. Among other things, the union organizes seminars and conferences to discuss the precarious working conditions. These conferences might be more productive if their activities were devoted to reflecting on the political environment in a scholarly manner and creating an atmosphere of intellectual stimulation. This would offer a model for how democratic debates are conducted in other parts of the world. Faculty members take part in decision making at their respective institutions through representation at the University Council and school, advanced school, or institute department assemblies.

The core of the problem in Togo is actually related to mistrust between political authorities and academia. The question here is whether those who are holding political power are open-minded enough to allow higher education to express its views on various problems and issues. The power of faculty as holders of knowledge is based on the fundamental principle of intellectual independence. To what extent is the government ready to respect this independence? For the sake of the welfare of the country, it is high time that a compromise be found between these two powers.

What makes the situation more dramatic is the fact that the possibility for dialogue is denied to local intellectuals while it is accorded, within the framework of cooperation, to other foreign entities. This practice is aimed at finding a complaisant partner who, as a foreigner, does not constitute an internal threat to the established system. The government should stop controlling the academic community by enlisting them in high-paying jobs in the public sector. The government should, on the contrary, collaborate with intellectuals in general and with higher education in particular.

The authorities should work to achieve a new perception of higher education. A new dialogue pattern is needed, one that makes it clear that higher education faculty members could very well constitute a revolutionary power.

A feeling of insecurity, due to political instability, insufficient salaries, and a lack of viable working conditions, has caused Togolese intellectuals and scientific elite to make their careers outside of Togo. There is a problem of political interference in many levels of higher education. The political instability is also reflected at the level of the General Division of Higher Education, which leads to deficient national policies to develop higher education. The Togolese government should encourage intellectuals, whether exiled or not, to return to Togo and settle down by offering them satisfactory working conditions and higher salaries and by promoting and motivating faculty.

The administrative and technical staff of higher education in Togo is made up of 1,136 individuals. As government civil servants, higher education personnel are regulated in the same way as other forms of public service and in accordance with labor regulations. Personnel issues include overstaffing, lack of communication between the different services and the students, absence of a social life and sociocultural activities on university campuses, and lack of a context for unbiased reflection that is free of any personal or departmental concerns. Although the administrative and technical staff is organized into unions, there is no structure for training or reskilling these employees. Representatives from administration are present at all management levels of institutions of higher education. They are also represented in the University Council as well as in institution departments, including faculty assemblies.

A WAY FORWARD

A wakeup call from the World Bank regarding the inefficiency of African universities made African leaders realize the gap between the goals set by higher education and the obtained results. Since the 1990s, studies have been carried out to determine the ills that the African university endures and propose relevant solutions likely to absorb or at least attenuate the effects of stagnation. Bearing in mind this situation, higher education in Togo is preparing to take up the development challenge.

Higher education in Togo is at a critical juncture, between the sweep of globalization and technological advances, on the one hand, and the recommendations made at the 1998 International Conference on Higher Education (Conférence Mondiale sur l'Enseignment Supérieur, CMES), on the other. An understanding of the Togolese university system requires a review of certain of its aspects related to mission, quality, curricula professionalization, diversity, financing, and international cooperation.

Mission

The university should reinforce its role as the engine for national development through the transmission of know-how, skills, and knowledge. This could be achieved by means of a more vigorous research policy and the evaluation and dissemination of scientific and technical information. To reach this goal, higher education in Togo should prioritize governance and leadership concerns. The latter should be built in a relational, contractual, and participatory environment, bringing together all parties in the higher education enterprise; namely, students, faculty, staff, parents, the government, moneylenders, and so forth. It is also important to promote and value women's participation.

Similarly, the creation of Training and Research Units or Teaching and Research Units could be a significant contribution.

Quality

Efforts to improve higher education have to be envisioned and encouraged. Areas that need to be considered in this respect are pedagogy, teacher testing, student admissions procedures, and new information and communication technology. All of these would contribute to the general enhancement of internal efficiency. A special effort should be made to promote centers of excellence and develop specialized leading research fields where heavy investments could be made and which could allow for an optimal utilization of available resources at the national and regional levels. Merit-based scholarships could be awarded to the best students in majors that are considered a national priority.

Professionalization

The professionalization and diversification of program offerings are crucial for the improvement of higher education in Togo. A number of actions could be carried out in this respect. First, the number of accelerated scientific and technical programs should be increased. Second, courses of a professional nature should be introduced into disciplines such as literature, social sciences, and the humanities. Third, transition between majors and disciplines should be made affordable, at least to cope with classroom availability problems. Finally, an adequate institutional body is needed to supervise the accreditation and assessment of continuing and distance education at both private and public universities.

Financing

Moneylenders and the private sector must be convinced to make up for the decline in state subsidies for higher education. Sources of financing should be diversified, with a special focus on internal resources. Budgeting of such resources should be based on a cost-efficiency ratio with clearly defined targets. Moreover, overarching strategic, endogenous planning is needed that is inspired by national priorities and brings together all the actors of higher education. As part of this plan, a comprehensive effort must be made to convey to the different actors the principle of recovering the cost of higher education—financial assistance to students that balances both the government's capabilities and those of families should be reconsidered.

International Cooperation

Science and technology have neither color nor frontiers. Cooperation is necessary. Hence, a South-South cooperation initiative based on complementarity as well as a North-South cooperation based on necessity should be encouraged. Focus should be put on building capacity rather than a simple exchange of professors between North and South. On a more general basis, there is a need for permanent interuniversity partnerships. Most important of all is the effort to bring together bilateral and multilateral donors to contribute to the internal restructuring efforts of higher education by providing a series of technical studies that will encourage the implementation of reform policy.

CONCLUSION

None of the socially utilitarian aspects of higher education depicted in this chapter will be feasible unless they occur in the context of a large democratization process; that is, one that makes access to higher education possible for the entire population and in all sectors of activity. In other words, the focus should not be limited to access to studies and degrees, but should include an enhancement of the process of knowledge production and the translation of this knowledge into social benefits. Only then can institutions of higher education bridge the gap between two opposing trends: the logic of public service and that of job market requirements. In this way, higher education would be able to regain its intellectual and social mission within our society and act as a guarantor of universal values and of our cultural heritage.

BIBLIOGRAPHY

Amah, E., and N. Gayibor. 1996. *Annuaire statistique scolaire de l'Université du Bénin.* Lomé: Presses de l'Université du Bénin.

Delors, J. 1996. "L'Education: Une trésor est caché dedans." Rapport de la Commission Internationale sur L'Education pour le XXIème siècle. Paris: UNESCO.

———. 1998. "Alliance for a Responsible and United World—Our Message about Higher Education for the 21st Century." Paper presented at Conférence Mondiale sur l'Enseignement Supérieur au XXI siècle—Visions et Actions, 5–9 octobre, Paris.

———. 1998. "L'Enseignement Supérieur au XXI siècle—Paris." Contribution de M. Gibbons, Secrétaire Général Association des Universités du commonwealth. Paper presented at Conférence Mondiale sur l'Enseignement Supérieur au XXI siècle—Visions et Actions, 5–9 octobre, Paris.

Edee, M. K. A. 1997. "Université ou Enseignement Supérieur: Défi et Perspective." Paper presented at the conference Consultation de la Région Afrique préparatoire à la conférence sur l'Enseignement Supérieur, avril 1–7, Dakar-Senegal.

———. 1998. "Rôle de l'Enseignement Supérieur." Paper presented at Conference of Ministers of Education of African Member States (MINIDAF VII), 20–24 avril, Durban, UNESCO.

———. 1999a. "La Gestion du Savoir dans l'Enseignement Supérieur en Afrique au service du développement socio-économique." Paper presented at Conférence Mondiale sur l'Enseignement Supérieur: Vision et Action. [World Conference on Higher Education: Vision and Action.] 5–9 Octobre 1998, Paris, UNESCO.

———. 1999b. "Un nouvel engagement." Conférence Mondiale sur la Science pour le XXIè siècle, 26 juin–1er juillet, Budapest, UNESCO-ICSU.

Edee, M. K. A., and Gbeassor. 1999. "Point de vue au Togo." ["Point of View on Togo."] Paper presented at the Conférence Mondiale sur la Science: La Science pour le XXIème siècle—Un nouvel engagement at Budapest-Hongrie, 26 juin–1er juillet, Paris, UNESCO.

Haut Comité Education Economie. 1992. "La professionnalisation des Enseignements Supérieurs." Report. Paris: UNESCO.

Gayibor, N. 1994. *Textes fondamentaux de l'Université du Bénin.* Lomé: Direction des Affaires Académiques et Scolaires (DAAS) and Presses de l'UB.

IAUP, IAU, AUGM, IDRC, CSUCA, UDUAL, UNAMAZ, UNICA, WUS. 1997. *Towards a New Higher Education.* Proceedings of the Regional Conference Policies and Strategies for the Transformation of Higher Education in Latin America and the Caribbean, 18–22 November 1996, Havana, Cuba. Caracas: CRESAL/UNESCO.

Johnson G. A., and K. F. Seddoh. 1996. "De 1970 à 1995: Rapport d'activité." Lomé: Presses de l'Université du Bénin.

Kanataway, G., and C. de Moura Castro. 1990. "Pour une politique de Formation orientée vers l'Emploi: Un Programme d'Action." Paper presented at Conférence à Paris, Septembre, UNESCO.

L'Enseignement Supérieur pour une nouvelle Afrique. 1998. "La vision des étudiants." Forum des Associations d'Etudiants en Afrique, 23–25 mars, Accra-Ghana.

MEN (Ministry of National Education). 1975. "La Réforme de l'Enseignement au Togo." Lomé: MEN.

Organisation of African Unity. 1985. *Lagos Plan of Action for Economic Development of Africa 1980–2000.* Lagos: OAU.

Shabani, J. 1996. "La Gestion de la Recherche Scientifique dans les Universités Africaines." Paper presented at the conference aux VIè Journées Scientifiques de l'Université du Bénin, mai, Lomé.

62

Tunisia

BENOÎT MILLOT, JEFFREY WAITE, AND HEDI ZAÏEM

INTRODUCTION

From the time of Tunisian independence in 1957, education has played a major role in forging a strong and dynamic national identity. Higher education contributed to this goal by providing the state with an educated indigenous elite. Indeed, little had been done by the former French colonial government to prepare Tunisians for roles in local institutions, and the first cohorts of university-educated leaders usually earned their degrees in France. Little by little, however, as basic education became almost universal and secondary education made tremendous progress, tertiary education was pushed by strong demand and sustained political will. As a result, tertiary education is now a well-developed and diversified sector that is undergoing constant changes as it strives to become a system for the masses. Its current transformation and its adaptation to a new international environment in which Tunisia has decided to be an active player will pose enormous challenges in the future.

After a brief historical overview, this chapter addresses quantitative aspects of enrollments and student flows; reviews the organization and management of academia, in particular the status of faculty; scrutinizes qualitative aspects of teaching and learning; questions the relevance of the education offered in public institutions; and analyzes how tertiary education is financed in Tunisia.

HISTORICAL BACKGROUND

Tunisian education in general, and higher education in particular, have been shaped by all the major political and cultural currents of the country's history, including its Phoenician foundations, the Roman domination, the Christian influence, the Arabo-Islamic conquest, the Ottoman takeover, and the colonial period. However, the most dramatic changes have occurred since independence, less than half a century ago.

From its beginnings in 814 B.C., Carthage was eager to extend its influence in all domains, with special emphasis in the area of culture. The spread of the Punic language throughout the area today known as Tunisia was in large part due to the existence of institutions, most notably temples, responsible for teaching the language. Very little is known about the Numid (Berber) period preceding the Phoenician era.

In Roman times, formal education took place in the proconsular cities, including Carthage. As the cultural and intellectual capital, Carthage was the most important city of learning. The most famous teachers and the largest number of schools were located there, as well as a university where students from the continent could take a range of courses.

During the Christian era, education was a family responsibility, closely identified with Catholic teachings that drew universal principles from the Bible. Christianity had won over many notable African scholars, including Saint Augustine, Tertullian, and Saint Cyprian.

The Arab conquest and the introduction of Islam in the seventh century brought about radical changes in education and left their mark on teaching. The *kouttab*, the first learning institution in this period, focused on written language and especially on memorization of the Quran. A place of both worship and learning, the mosque witnessed the study of the Quran, the *hadith*, writing, and later on, science, history, and literature. Students covered a wide range of ages and came from varied social backgrounds.

Teaching at this time was not standardized in its content or methods. The emergence of a new type of school, the *medersas*, in the second half of the fifth century of the Hegira seems to reflect an attempt to improve the system. Under the Hafsids, several Tunisian cities housed numerous *medersas*. Those of Tunis and Kairouan were well known for the quality of their teachers.

From the fourteenth to the eighteenth centuries, subject areas and teaching methods in Quranic schools continued unchanged. Largely religiously based, teaching allowed little room for the exact sciences and paid little attention to developing students' creativity. Only the most gifted students were able to go on to secondary level studies at the Zitouna Institute or related institutions.

After the Ottoman conquest in 1574, the Turks were not well disposed toward the Zitouna Institute, a center of Malekite thought. Since the *beys* were eager to engage with the local elite, however, they paid special attention to the Great Mosque and put in place new regulations such as the 1840 decree reorganizing teaching at the Zitouna Institute. In 1875–1876, Minister Kheirredine gave his name to a major reform of higher education aimed at modernizing religious education. By the middle of the nineteenth century, only 15,000 students (or 1.5 percent of the total population) had received a formal education.

Earlier, the European offensive of 1818 had announced major changes for Tunisia. The European powers installed a "regency" and began to put in place their own system of education. In creating military colleges and establishing the school of engineering, Ahmed Bey was the first to open up to Western forms of education. Then, in 1855, the military college at Bardo was established. These schools offered a modern, secular education and trained a minority of Tunisians in modern sciences.

During the reign of Mohamed Sadok, European education systems (mainly French and Italian) took a strong hold. These systems were religiously based and for the most part attracted European and Jewish students. During this period, in 1875, Sadiki College was established. With a curriculum based on lay sciences, this school consolidated the impact of European culture on the Tunisian education system. Even after independence, Sadiki College remained a prominent institution.

By the time the French declared Tunisia a protectorate in 1881, a diverse and dynamic European education system had taken root alongside the traditional Quranic system. Little changed in the first years of the French protectorate. Different education systems coexisted, and each ethnicity and each language group had its own schools—a reflection of the variety of regimes that characterized the "regency."

A modern French-language education system was set up in systematic fashion by the colonial authorities. The cultural influence of the French found a receptive audience in those students groomed at Sadiki College. The number of Tunisians attending French-language institutions rose from around 2,500 in 1890 to more than 4,600 in 1897.

Tunisian eagerness for education was again apparent after the establishment in 1896 of the Khaldounia, which was developed as a response to the encroachment of modern European culture via the Sadiki College. The Khaldounia, named after the famous historian and philosopher Ibn Khaldoun (1332–1406), was a new kind of Quranic school that firmly established modern science within the curriculum. Local interest in European education was so great that concerned French colonists urged the administration to reduce the number of Muslim students educated in French-language institutions. As a result, the number of students fell to just over 3,000 by the beginning of the twentieth century, and the administration encouraged the growth of traditional schools.

Following the Second World War, higher education suffered (Sraïeb 1974). Only the Institut des hautes études de Tunis (IHET), founded in 1945, offered education at this level. Under the wing of the University of Paris, IHET was charged with promoting scientific research, developing a literary and scientific culture through public seminars and publications, and preparing students for exams that led to qualifications granted in collaboration with the Académie de Paris. By 1953, some 1,500 students were enrolled in higher education courses, but less than 700 were Tunisian. This ethnic imbalance could be found at every level of the education system.

Immediately following independence, the new government began to lay the foundations for a new higher education system. The government established the Ecole normale supérieure to train secondary school teachers, the Ecole nationale d'administration for future senior civil servants, and the Ecole supérieure du droit to develop a legal profession. The year 1960 saw the establishment of the much-awaited University of Tunisia (UT), which included faculties of literature, social sciences, mathematics, physical and natural sciences, law, political science and economics, and theology, as well as the Ecole normale supérieure. The faculty of medicine was added in 1964, while the Ecole nationale des ingénieurs was added in 1969.

Information on student numbers at the time is difficult to come by and is often contradictory when available. In 1960–1961, the number of Tunisian students was about 3,400, including 1,500 studying abroad. In 1962–1963, these numbers climbed to 6,300 and 3,000, respectively (Secrétariat d'Etat à l'Education Nationale, 1962–1967). The number of teachers went from 110 in 1960–1961 to 156 in 1964–1965 (including 76 Tunisian teachers).

A new higher education law was passed in 1969, placing all the higher learning and scientific research institutions that came under the purview of the education ministry within UT. In 1986, UT was divided into three universities: Tunis, Center, and Sfax-South. In 1987, Tunis was itself divided into four subject-based universities. Finally, in 2000, three of these four were reorganized into five geographically based and multidisciplinary universities.

Today, Tunisia has some 9.4 million inhabitants, with a population density of 60 inhabitants per square kilometer. In 2000, its GDP was about $18.5 billion, and per capita GDP stood at $1,960. Agriculture represents 16 percent, industry 38 percent, and services 46 percent of total production. Tunisia's external debt represents 45 percent of GDP, and the ratio of its debt services to current receipts is 18.5 percent.

The official state religion of Tunisia is Sunni Islam, and the overwhelming majority of the population is Sunni Muslim. The capital, Tunis, has a population of 1 million (excluding the suburbs), and almost two-thirds of the population live in urban areas. The under-15 population accounts for 32.7 percent of the total and those between 15 and 59 represent 60 percent. The demographic growth rate is 1.15 percent and the average family size is 5.2. Average life expectancy in Tunisia is 72 years.

Schooling is compulsory between the ages of 6 and 16. The number of students registered in public educational institutions reached more than 2.3 million in the 1999–2000 academic year. The enrollment rate of 6-year-olds went above 99 percent in

Table 62.1. Student Enrollments in Tunisian Institutions of Higher Education, Selected Years, 1970–2001

	1970–1971	1980–1981	1990–1991	1995–1996	2000–2001
Total	10,129	31,827	68,535	112,634	207,388
Percent Average Annual Growth	—	12.1	8.0	9.7	15.2
Percent Female Students	21.1	29.7	39.4	43.7	51.9

Source: Ministère de l'enseignement supérieur 2001.

Table 62.2. Enrollments in Tunisian Institutions of Higher Education by Subject Area and Year (by Percent)

Subject Area	1980–1981	1990–1991	2000–2001
Basic Sciences	18.7	13.6	13.7
Literature, Arts, and Social Sciences	21.2	34.2	28.8
Medicine	16.3	10.9	6.1
Law, Economics, and Management	27.2	28.5	36.0
Engineering and Technology	16.6	12.8	15.4
Total	100	100	100

Source: Ministère de l'enseignement supérieur 2001.

1998–1999, and the net rate of enrollment of 6- to 12-year-olds is 92.3 percent. Adult illiteracy stood at 25.6 percent in 2000.

ENROLLMENT AND STUDENT FLOWS

The Tunisian higher education sector, which was marginal ten years after independence, has literally exploded and is expected to continue growing at a sustained rate during the next ten years. Initially a secluded set of institutions for the administrative elite and for the training of teachers, higher education is now reaching a mass audience. Tunisia has little room to regulate student flows in higher education. For political reasons (and by virtue of the Constitution), access is guaranteed to all students holding the secondary education baccalaureate and rationing is not being publicly considered; yet the job market has more and more difficulties absorbing the increasing numbers of graduates. Faced with these challenges, two types of responses have been developed, neither of which is satisfactory or sustainable. First, a transparent and apparently equitable up-front system of orientation was devised, but it proved to be quite rigid. Second, students began to be screened in the course of their studies. This has resulted in high (though declining) rates of repetition and drop-outs.

Student enrollment rose from 10,000 in 1970 to 32,000 in 1980; by 2000, this number stood at 207,000, a sixfold rise over the last two decades. Although enrollment doubled through the 1980s, growth was held back to some extent by a climate of political and social instability (Table 62.1).

The 1990s witnessed the tripling of student enrollments in higher education. Two main factors were at play here. The first was the impact of high demographic growth (now in decline). The second factor was linked to an improvement in internal efficiency in the school sector, which meant that more and more

students were passing the secondary leaving exams and, as a result, were entitled by law to enroll at a university. Women's share of student enrollment went from 21.1 percent in 1987–1988 to 50.4 percent in 1999–2000, the first academic year in which more women than men were enrolled at the university level. Among 20- to 24-year-olds, gross enrollment ratios rose from 5.5 percent in 1987–1999 to 12.3 percent in 1995 and almost 19.0 percent in 1999–2000.

An analysis of the distribution of students by subject area over the last twenty years shows a substantial decline in basic sciences and a dramatic drop in medicine. These losses have been offset by a gain in the fields of law, economics, and management. Engineering and technology have remained fairly weak throughout this period, currently accounting for only 15.4 percent of students. After a strong growth over the 1980–1990 period, literature, arts, and social sciences sharply declined during the following five years (Table 62.2).

Short courses started losing ground in the beginning of the 1980s but have increased their share over the last few years. Currently, more than 12 percent of all students attend a short course. This reflects the government policy aimed at training more technicians. In 1992, a new category of schools, the Instituts Supérieurs d'Ètudes Technologiques (ISETs), were created in recognition of the lack of midlevel technicians. Eleven ISETs are now operating, enrolling 15,000 students. It is the Ministry of Higher Education's intention to increase these numbers progressively and to channel about 20 percent of all students into these institutions.

The Tunis metropolitan area enrolls more than half of all students, but the capital area's share of enrollment is being slowly whittled away with the emergence of new university centers.

Access to higher education is centrally controlled through a *système national d'orientation universitaire*. Eligible students are

Table 62.3. Pass Rates in Selected Schools of Higher Education in Tunisia, 2000

Discipline	First Year	Second Year	Third Year	Fourth Year	All Years
Law	37.4	47.3	60.1	74.1	48.9
Sciences	45.8	70.1	67.6	90.8	61.8
Liberal arts	46.2	62.0	60.2	78.9	57.3
Engineering schools	93.6	97.6	96.6	—	95.7
Business schools	55.3	80.0	84.4	91.6	72.6
ISETs*	77.8	85.1	78.2	96.3	85.4

*For ISETs, columns represent semesters.
Source: Ministère de l'enseignement supérieur 2001.

provided with information on all parameters of the selection algorithm. Student selection takes place automatically on the combined basis of the students' own preferences, their scores, and the corresponding quota for each category of school-leavers. Students who are not placed in one of the programs of their choosing are able to take part in a second and even a third selection round in which the range of options is reduced each time.

More than merely orienting future students, this system matches supply and demand in the higher education sector. It has proven its worth over the years by directing students into the discipline for which their score shows they are the most suited. However, despite recent changes aimed at reducing the number of students who are unhappy with the selection made for them, the orientation system is beginning to reach its limits and is becoming quite controversial. People have criticized both the program's high degree of centralization (once considered necessary to ensure equity and transparency) and its rigidity, which makes it difficult, if not impossible, to change disciplines at the mid-program stage.

For some years now, students have had the option of changing disciplines at the end of their first year of study by means of subject-specific examinations. The number of spaces available for "swapping" was initially very limited but has now been increased to cover 15 percent of all positions. In addition, since 2000–2001, students who have been pushed out of the system have been able to take the entrance examination again and, if successful, be readmitted.

Students who enter the first year of study will not necessarily make it through the system. In spite of a sharp improvement in internal efficiency, Tunisia's higher education system continues to push out a considerable number of students perceived as unqualified (Table 62.3). In 1995–1996, three out of ten students were repeaters; the situation varies with the discipline and the *établissements*. The proportion was one in ten in the selective Ecoles, but it was five in ten in the Faculties of Liberal Arts of Tunis and Sfax. Multiple repetitions are directly fueling dropouts. In 1997, the 5,600 students who either dropped out or were pushed out accounted for 5.0 percent of all enrollments. By 1999, this number had risen to 7,600, or 5.6 percent. Global progression rates barely exceed 65 percent, even though they have been on the rise since 1996–1997. Wastage and exclusion are especially staggering at the undergraduate level of the open, nonselective *facultés*: as many as 43 percent of those who enter the first year do not graduate at all, whereas the overwhelming majority of first-year students in *élite écoles* make it to the second year.

The declining level of secondary education graduates is often cited as an explanation for the high failure rate, even though selection and wastage at the basic and secondary levels are also quite significant. Insufficient mastery of language, especially French, is also said to hinder performances. But the blame cannot be solely attributed to external factors. Overcrowded classes, low pedagogical skills of newly recruited faculty staff, and an overly rigid orientation mechanism probably are related causes. Until relatively recently, these leakages were merely seen as the normal price of academic excellence rather than a problem of social exclusion. However, the presence of repeaters makes fewer resources available per student and contributes to the declining quality of education.

INSTITUTIONAL SETTINGS

Until very recently, Tunisia's higher education system was highly centralized and lacked accountability. Individual institutions were without power, whether administrative or financial; and the universities in which most of them were grouped were artificial entities headed by a president appointed by the head of the state, without resources or responsibilities other than civil order. In 2000, new legislation provided universities with new powers and granted them new legal status. The legislation allows some flexibility in the use of the budget and reduces a priori budgetary controls, thus giving individual institutions more incentive to take initiatives leading to income-generating activities. The Ministry of Education has taken this timid step toward relinquishing its current administrative tasks and focusing on quality control and policymaking.

The 1989 Higher Education Act set up three institutional layers: the Ministry of Higher Education (MHE), universities, and subject-specific institutes. Out of a total of 108 institutes, seventy-five are under the control of the MHE and the remainder are under the joint control of the MHE and the relevant technical ministry (for example, the Ministry of Agriculture, the Ministry of Health, or the Ministry of Culture). Ninety of the institutes are organized into seven universities; in addition, there are eleven technical institutes (ISETs) and six teacher training institutes (ISFMs). Each is headed by a director, who is appointed by the central administration in the case of a school or an institute, or elected by the teaching staff in the case of a

Table 62.4. Distribution of Teaching Staff in Tunisian Institutions of Higher Education, Selected Years, 1990–2000

	1990–1991	1994–1995	2000–2001
Full and Associate Professors	614	636	855
Assistant Professors and Tutors	2,372	3,310	5,999
Hospital Teaching Staff	758	821	1,320
Other*	806	1,177	2,119
Total Full-time Teaching Staff	4,550	5,944	10,293
Percentage of Women	21.4	25.6	33.3
Student-to-Teacher Ratio	15:1	17:3	20:1

*Mainly secondary education teachers.

Source: Ministère de l'enseignement supérieur 2001.

faculty. Each institute has an academic council made up of department heads and faculty and student representatives. The academic council is tasked with advising the administration on issues of management, academic programs, staff training, research, and the budget and its implementation. In theory, each institute also has an advisory council comprised of representatives of various social and economic interest groups; in practice, few of these councils are active.

Under the 1989 act, the university is headed by a chancellor, who is a professor appointed by the central government, and has a council made up of faculty deans, department heads, and representatives chosen by faculty, administrative staff, and students. This council also includes representatives of key social and economic interest groups.

Both universities and institutes have a legal status that provides them with their own budget and limited financial autonomy. However, these institutions have little room for maneuver in establishing and spending this budget, since any change to the schedule has to be approved by the central administration and every expense item has to receive prior approval. In particular, universities complain of being nothing more than relay posts between the central administration and the institutes. By way of example, permanent teaching staff are recruited and promoted by national selection panels; universities are able to recruit only short-term faculty.

The institutes are not homogeneous. A faculty such as the Faculté des Sciences de Tunis, the oldest and once the most prestigious, has seen its enrollments explode and its aura shrink; other faculties far away from the capital have brand-new facilities, few students, and few faculty. The selective schools (mostly inspired by the French system) have more resources, fewer students, and higher academic scores. The creation of the ISETs in the early 1990s is an important innovation within the higher education system in both structure and mode of operation. They are also distinct in the status of their faculty staff.

In July 2000, Parliament passed a law providing universities with greater administrative and financial autonomy. Instead of relying on face-to-face negotiations based on historical trends and on political influences, universities now receive a budget that they then allocate to their institutes. The process of prior approval of expenses has been simplified, and institutes now have greater flexibility in raising and using income derived from

services rendered to outside entities. Further decentralization and rationalization are underway with a project whose goal is to establish for each university a *contrat-programme* linking the level of resources to inputs and performance indicators.

FACULTY STAFF

The pride of the young Tunisian nation until the early 1970s, faculty have seen their status progressively whittled away as their numbers have grown. More important, as the state had to turn out more and more young faculty, the mechanisms to maintain their high level of training and skills declined. In addition, emphasis on research at the expense of pedagogic skills is not consistent with the low level of research facilities or with the huge teaching load imposed by the growing student body at the undergraduate level. Another matter of concern is the erosion of teacher-to-student ratios.

Faculty numbers increased from 2,300 in 1980 to 10,300 in 2000 (Table 62.4). However, this growth has not kept pace with the rate of enrollment growth. The result is an increase in the average student-to-faculty ratio, which increased from 15 to 1 to 20 to 1 during the 1990s. Indeed, there are striking differences, depending on the area and the type of institution. At the top end, the Faculty of Medicine, the *écoles*, and the ISETs have ratios at around 10 to 1, while faculties of law and economics post a ratio of 48 to 1. In order to avoid a further increase in the ratios, at least 1,000 new faculty staff must be hired each year for another decade. In a parallel trend, the proportion of full and associate professors among teaching staff has fallen, which is likely to compromise the quality of teaching.

The teaching profession has seen a significant increase in the share of women in its ranks.

Legislation passed in 1993 emphasizes the importance not only of teachers' academic knowledge but also of their experience and their teaching skills. This legislation established two categories of research faculty: permanent (with four levels—full professor, associate professor, assistant professor, and tutor) and short-term. In addition, in response to the specific needs of ISETs, the MHE created a third category—technology faculty—with its own criteria for training, recruitment, and promotion.

Changes introduced in 1997 sought to increase transparency in decisions relating to faculty recruitment and promotion.

In the non-ISET sector, recruitment and promotion still rely heavily on research and publication. Moreover, university faculty training places little emphasis on the acquisition of teaching skills, which is a clear problem when most of these new staff come straight from completing their predoctoral qualification. The MHE is developing a new training program that will help faculty make much greater use of new technologies in their classroom practice.

The teaching profession is organized in one of the strongest and most independent unions in the country. Although it does not systematically refuse to collaborate with the MHE on specific issues, the Syndicat de l'Enseignement Supérieur has no affiliation with the political power structure. However, a second union with more links with the party in power has been created. Faculty remain among the best-compensated civil workers; the average salary for assistant professors is 4.5 times the GDP per capita, and the average salary for full professors is 8 times the GDP per capita.

PEDAGOGIC ORGANIZATION AND EVALUATION

Many reforms have taken place in higher education in the last decade. Their general thrust has been to restructure a system marked by horizontal and vertical rigidity. Each level has been renovated, from undergraduate through doctoral studies, including technical education. Each level is now modernized to incorporate modular units of study, which gives students flexibility in their courses of study. New technologies, in particular Internet connections, are rapidly becoming an integral part of academic life in Tunisian institutions, but it is still too early to assess the real impact of these trends. Current systems of evaluation, whether at the institutional level or at the staff level, are still superficial and do not influence the way curricula and teaching are organized. However, awareness of the potential of evaluation is growing fast.

ACADEMIC REFORMS

The higher education sector in Tunisia has in the last few years undergone a series of reforms in the academic area that cover each level of the academic pyramid.

Undergraduate and Graduate Studies

Given the numbers of students and graduates involved at this level, the reform of master's degree programs is a key element in the whole series of reforms. The reform began in 1993 with the introduction of modular units and a system of examination credits, aiming to

- Ensure that programs are responsive to the country's social and economic needs by offering general courses in the first years, diversifying the range of courses to include computer studies, English, management, and human rights, and promoting internships and on-the-job training in the business community

- Modernize programs by providing information to students on course content and dividing courses into semester blocks
- Update teaching methodologies to emphasize communication, teamwork, and the use of new technologies
- Revise assessment practices to emphasize measurement of critical thinking and problem solving rather than memorization
- Promote interdisciplinarity by enabling students to take modules outside their major discipline

Postgraduate Studies

The 1993 reforms established a single regime for all doctoral studies and harmonized Tunisian qualifications with overseas degrees. Tunisia now has a two-year predoctoral diploma and a doctoral degree that allow its graduates to compete for associate professor positions. In 1995, a new qualification was introduced that linked training more closely to the needs of the labor market. Finally, the introduction in 1997 of co-supervision and the mapping of foreign qualifications with Tunisian qualifications enabled more foreign-trained Tunisians to contribute to the betterment of Tunisia's higher education system.

Engineering Studies

The reform of engineering programs was launched in 1992 with the establishment of a committee that consisted of engineering faculty, professionals, and other experts. Based on the French system, training now takes place in two phases: a preparatory two-year program in specialized institutes and a three-year program at a school of engineering. The specialized institutes now enroll 5,000 students and the schools enroll 3,500.

ISETs

The creation of the ISETs was meant to fill the gap in the areas of management and technology in light of the considerable demands coming from the productive sectors. ISET programs are comprised of five semesters and place a heavy emphasis on applied studies; work placements and the requirements for project work are submitted at the end of the course. Class size and student-to-teacher ratios are kept to strict levels, and ISETs interact extensively with the local business community, responding to their commercial needs and impacting their operations. ISETs will draw on nonacademic teaching staff as a way to offer a diverse range of courses, open up to the nonuniversity community, and increase graduates' job opportunities through professional contacts. Measures to attract nonacademic faculty into these programs will go into effect in 2002.

INFORMATION AND COMMUNICATION TECHNOLOGIES

Tunisian authorities quickly understood the challenge of new technologies, and tertiary education authorities, in particular, have embraced them. Yet the use of new information and communication technologies (ICTs) as a teaching tool is still not well developed and is often confused with the addition of ICT studies as an academic discipline. Training of ICT special-

Table 62.5. Distribution of Postsecondary Graduates in Tunisia by Discipline, Selected Years, 1981–2000

	1980–1981	1990–1991	1999–2000
Total Number of Graduates	4,525	6,915	21,442
Basic Sciences (%)	8.5	9.0	12.5
Literature, Social Sciences, and Religious Studies (%)	20.4	18.1	25.1
Medicine (%)	22.2	17.7	7.8
Law, Economics, and Management (%)	21.6	33.4	34.5
Technical Sciences (%)	19.2	16.4	15.2
Agricultural Sciences (%)	8.0	5.4	2.7
Teacher Training (%)	0.0	0.0	2.1

Source: Ministère de l'Enseignement Supérieur 1989.

ists, however, is gaining speed, and should help restore the primacy of pedagogic goals.

Every university institution is now connected to the Internet, but student access is constrained by a lack of cabling between buildings, low-speed connections, and weak support services. As a result of the recent reform of master's degrees programs, all programs at this level now include a compulsory ICT module.

About 380 ICT teaching staff are employed by universities. Teaching at this level of the higher education system requires a doctoral degree, which highlights the importance of advanced training. A doctoral program in ICT was established in 1994 jointly with the Ecole Nationale des Sciences Informatiques and the Faculté des Sciences de Tunis.

ICT research capabilities are centered in three laboratories and two research units, which together employ about 220 researchers. These capabilities are backed up through collaboration with French research facilities.

The MHE has put together an ambitious program aimed at training in excess of 50,000 ICT specialists over the next ten years. The program calls on the public higher education system to invest between $10 and $11 million per year in ICT training in addition to the current operations budget.

The MHE has also set up a project to strengthen the use of ICTs in university, which focuses on three areas: training teaching staff in the production of ICT-based tools; establishing sixteen ICT-based production centers equipped with appropriate hardware and staffed by multimedia specialists; and inviting teams of teaching staff to present specific projects to develop multimedia tools.

PERFORMANCE MONITORING

Adequate performance monitoring did not exist in Tunisian universities before the establishment in 1995 of the National Evaluation Committee (NEC), which was made up of fourteen members appointed by the minister of higher education. The first experience with monitoring teacher performance began in 1995–1996, when all faculty were encouraged to fill out a questionnaire about their teaching and research activities during the previous year. The exercise met with considerable resistance from faculty and unions, and although the response rate reached

around 75 percent, no extensive analysis of the results was undertaken and no report was published. At the same time, the NEC developed a questionnaire for each institute, but the dense questionnaire was used only once and the results were not analyzed. The MHE is now developing a process for institutional self-monitoring that will rely on financial incentives. An action plan for a genuine evaluation system is currently being prepared; it is expected to cover internal and external efficiency, teaching innovations, faculty training, academic production, and local and overseas partnerships.

RESEARCH

Oversight of research activities is the joint responsibility of the MHE and the secretary of state for research and technology. The MHE takes responsibility for university research and research-based training, while the secretary of state is in charge of research and development. In practice, since the bulk of researchers are university faculty, most applied research is undertaken in the higher education sector, often in partnership with outside entities.

Research generally takes place in conjunction with doctoral studies. In 1998–1999, 5,600 students were enrolled in predoctoral programs and 655 predoctoral dissertations were defended; in the same year, some 2,700 doctoral dissertations were in progress, of which 250 were defended. These figures, which hide important disparities between disciplines, fall significantly short of international norms. In order to close this gap, the MHE is putting in place a number of measures, including:

- Expanding and diversifying post-master's-level studies, with a view to increasing the number of predoctorate students and tripling the number of doctorates
- Establishing schools of doctoral studies to pool human and material resources from several institutions in ways that guarantee both efficient and high-quality oversight of doctoral students
- Involving nonacademic specialists in teaching and mentoring activities
- Strengthening international cooperation through the hiring

of foreign professors and through a system of incentives for Tunisian researchers living abroad to return home

RELEVANCE AND EXTERNAL EFFICIENCY

Initially functioning almost as a self-standing sector with its own rules and catering only to the needs of high state officials and for its own reproduction, higher education in Tunisia must now adapt its role to a changing economy. Indeed, it is not easy to give up an elite culture and open up to economic change.

How relevant is higher education to Tunisian society? The issue of external efficiency has been raised in response to the recent emergence of graduate unemployment (caused mainly by a reduction in the number of graduates being hired into the public service, particularly into school teaching). The bulk of the 15,000 officially registered job-seeking graduates have degrees in literature, social sciences, economics, and law. The government is working out a range of measures aimed at moving higher education graduates into jobs, the most recent being a program of 480 hours of training in ICTs that involved more than 2,000 graduates in 2000.

A first way to approach the question of efficiency is to look at the outputs of the sector. In 2000, Tunisian universities produced 21,400 graduates (Table 62.5). Graduate numbers, which had long been stagnant, began increasing dramatically in the mid-1980s as a result of increasing enrollments and an improvement in the internal efficiency of the system.

An analysis of graduate numbers shows the strength of the legal, economic, and management sectors. Literature and social sciences continue to occupy an important place in the system, due largely to the preponderance of these disciplines among high school graduates. A large number of students graduate with a master's degree, while only a few take away a technician's qualification, despite the clear economic need for graduates with technical skills. Short programs, which once accounted for 36 percent of student enrollment, represented a diminishing share throughout the 1980s. Their popularity increased again at the beginning of the 1990s after the introduction of primary teacher training programs. These numbers began falling again from the mid-1990s as the demand for primary school teachers dropped. In recent years, however, numbers have risen again in response to a deliberate effort on the part of the government to build up this subsector and to create the ISETs.

Currently, the eleven ISETs cater to more than 15,000 students, or 7.3 percent of total higher education enrollments. With very high job placement rates, ISETs are a success, and large numbers of high-caliber high school graduates now seek places in ISET programs. The number of ISETs is expected to grow rapidly over the next few years. By 2006, every province should have its own ISET.

Concerns about graduate employment and the success of ISETs have prompted the MHE to develop short professional programs in all disciplines, especially in literature. These new programs, similar in design to those offered in ISETs, will prepare students for emerging job market needs, such as multimedia.

Another area of particular interest is that of the ICT stream. Tunisia currently has around 10,000 ICT specialists, just over half of whom work in the public sector. With one specialist for every 1,000 inhabitants, Tunisia lags well behind its European neighbors (in 1998, France and the United Kingdom had six and twelve specialists per 1,000 inhabitants, respectively).

The higher education system is producing an increasing number of ICT graduates. In 2000, about 800 students graduated with an ICT major. At 3.5 percent of all higher education graduates, this proportion compares well with the Organisation for Economic Cooperation and Development (OECD) average. (Tunisia's enrollment rate among 19- to 24-year-olds is about half the OECD rate.)

Tunisia has chosen to tie its economy to the European Union. This bold decision, which is expected to produce long-term benefits, implies radical changes in the way enterprises are managed; in particular, it requires substantial efforts to raise productivity. A comprehensive upgrading scheme has been launched for this purpose. Tertiary education should play a central role in this effort. To be able to do so, however, a new culture has to emerge so that a real partnership can be forged (Zouari 1998b). Universities and their institutes must indeed open up to the economic environment, but businesses must also change their attitude to accept the need for skilled staff. It is still common to hear the owner of a small business complaining about arrogant and useless young graduates, mostly out of fear of competition. But it is also telling to listen to executives of large companies express what they need from employees. One of them lists three areas of priorities, which largely echo what can be heard from similar sources in OECD countries: rigor, good language skills, and curiosity and adaptability (Souissi 1998). The real challenge for universities is to adapt to a continual changing environment and to produce graduates able to adapt their skills to new demands.

So far, higher education graduates fare much better in the labor market than those with less formal education. Among higher education graduates, the unemployment rate is 8.2 percent; among secondary education graduates, it is 16 percent. Whereas 80 percent of job seekers with a primary education have been unemployed long term, only 20 percent of job seekers with a higher education degree are in the same situation. However, the average unemployment rate is slightly increasing, and university graduates are clearly not immune to this trend.

Finally, information on the labor market is still often untimely, incomplete, and inaccurate. This lack of a reliable data system on supply and demand does not facilitate the development of effective adaptation mechanisms. In that respect, the recent creation of an observatory of employment is a positive step.

FINANCING

The explosion of enrollments, which is projected to continue for another decade or so, is becoming a formidable challenge for the Tunisian government. This burden will soon become too heavy for the national budget. In a way, this crisis may turn out to be positive to the extent that it has raised the awareness of various decision makers, and it will likely trigger bolder measures than would have been the case in a business-as-usual environment. But to manage this financial squeeze, a consensus will have to be forged among all education stakeholders.

The main source of higher education funding in Tunisia is the national budget. Over the last ten years, the state has allocated between 1.2 percent and 5.0 percent of its budget to higher education. This share increased during the 1990s after a decline during the 1980s.

An analysis of public expenditure on higher education shows that salaries account for a little over two-thirds of the operating budget (teaching salaries take over 40 percent). Demand-side financing represents almost 20 percent of the operation budget. Scholarships are awarded on the basis of parental income and remain an important expenditure item. Yet the qualifying income threshold is as low as the minimum wage. In addition, this heavily subsidized system is not redistributive and does not contribute to a more equitable attendance pattern. The share going into the current student loan scheme has been declining since management of the scheme passed from the state to the social security and banking systems.

The issue of long-term financing mechanisms must be addressed if Tunisia is to deliver on its promise to provide higher education to a rapidly increasing student population. Financial sustainability will depend on increased internal efficiency, the integration of new technologies into the process of modernization, opportunities for institutions to develop their own business lines, an increase in the share of costs met by users, and an expansion of private-sector involvement in higher education activities.

Changes in these areas have already begun. Improvements in internal efficiency are being achieved as a result of the reform of academic programs. A law passed in July 2000 increases opportunities for higher education institutions to generate additional revenue by providing them with greater flexibility and autonomy in the way they are managed. At the same time, institutions are being encouraged to open up to the outside world by offering training to the business community, providing it with services, and undertaking research on its behalf.

Despite increases in user fees in 1995 and in 1997, direct contributions by families to the cost of training remain very modest in Tunisia and, as a result, have little impact on the overall higher education budget. In an effort to ensure that student fees do not become a barrier to access, the government is studying a number of options that would be both economically efficient and socially acceptable in a country where the role of the state is still very pervasive. The most likely option is to extend the loan scheme already in place, which covers living costs, to also cover student fees. To make it more sustainable, this scheme could be financed from a consortium that includes the government, social security institutions, and private banks.

PRIVATE INSTITUTIONS

Until recently, no legal recognition was given to the private higher education sector in Tunisia, despite the de facto existence of private institutions. Recognition was finally accorded in July 2000 through legislation setting out the rules that govern the establishment and operation of private higher education institutions. The development of a legal framework, in spite of some weaknesses, constitutes a major step forward in a country where "free education" has been a political slogan and where recognizing the existence of a private sector takes considerable political courage. As a result, the MHE has for the first time been able to accredit six out of the twelve private institutions that applied for official recognition. At this stage, private institutions enroll about 3,500 students and charge fees from $2,000 to $5,500.

A legal framework is merely the first step in a series of measures designed to facilitate the development of a private education sector that will offer high-quality programs that respond to students' interests and complement the state's efforts in the public sector. Observers agree that any expansion of the private sector will continue to be limited by the lack of demand for programs that are perceived as being of lower quality and much more expensive than those currently offered in public institutions. If the private sector is to expand, it will have to offer a range of financial and fiscal incentives, including support for investors, a subsidy for teachers' salaries, and a new student loan scheme. The MHE aims to promote partnerships between the public and private sectors in order to integrate the latter into an overall national higher education system. Partnerships could take the form of shared courses and qualifications, teacher exchanges, and even subcontracting arrangements.

The government is also withdrawing from the direct provision of nonacademic services, such as student housing and food services. Significant tax breaks have been offered to encourage businesses to invest in these areas, with particular success in housing. In addition, the MHE has launched pilot projects to contract out food services and is looking to develop this area further.

Combining these various solutions in a socially acceptable form will be the main challenge ahead. Simulations show that at current unit cost levels, public funding alone cannot accommodate projected additional student enrollments. Financing a better use of resources, increased internal efficiency, cost recovery, and more reliance on the private initiative are critical.

CONCLUSION

The Tunisian higher education system has been deeply transformed during the last decade. Started as a very selective system providing the elite group that the country and its public sector, in particular, needed to take over from the colonial masters, it progressively evolved toward a still meritocratic but much more open system that caters to almost 20 percent of the relevant age cohort. Many reforms have been launched and completed, and tertiary education in 2000 is quantitatively and qualitatively very different from what it was forty years ago.

Is this enough for Tunisia to overcome challenges lying ahead? The answer is not straightforward, because these challenges—globalization, knowledge-driven growth, the new economy, and the information revolution—put tertiary education and research precisely in the forefront. Tunisia is not shying away from these challenges and, in a decision that is almost unique in the region, has chosen to open its economy to competition and to modernize its society. But to be successful in this enterprise, the higher education system will have to undergo even more radical transformations.

In turn, these transformations will not be successful if the system remains centralized and "protected" by a purely public mode of operation. All interested parties must become truly responsible and accountable. The MHE will have to pave the way for a change in behavior conducive to the required modifications at the sectoral level, including greater financial and administrative autonomy for universities, greater pedagogic autonomy for the institutes, and contractual relationships between actors. Transparent and efficient mechanisms will have to be put in place to ensure accountability of administrative and teaching staff and to evaluate the performance of institutions objectively. Likewise, the role of students should increase in the management and the evaluation of the institutions they attend and in their contribution to their costs. Under such a scenario, the MHE would be able to devote its energy to quality control and other strategic matters. A stronger private sector would definitively help to meet these challenges.

Education accounts for a large part of Tunisia's current success as a nation. Tunisia wants to be an actor in the new knowledge-based world now taking shape. Only a highly skilled population will allow it to play an active role on the world stage.

Note: The views and interpretations expressed in this chapter are those of the authors and do not necessarily represent those of the Tunisian Ministry of Higher Education, the World Bank, or any of its member states.

BIBLIOGRAPHY

Banque mondiale. 1995. *République Tunisienne. Rôle du secteur privé dans la production et le financement des services d'éducation et de formation*. Rapport No. 14736. Washington, D.C.: Banque mondiale.

———. 1998. *L'enseignement supérieur tunisien. Enjeux et avenir*. Washington, D.C.: Rapports économiques de la Banque mondiale.

Ben Yahmed, S. 1998. "Répartition et évolution des effectifs dans l'enseignement supérieur tunisien." In Plassard et Ben Sedrine, ed., *Enseignement supérieur et insertion professionnelle en Tunisie*. Toulouse: Université des sciences sociales.

Gargouri, M. 1996. *Analysis of Education Reform in Tunisia*. Mimeograph. Washington, D.C.

Horchani, S. 1998. "Pour un autre projet du système éducatif, en général, et des facultés des sciences, en particulier." Mimeograph. Tunis.

Ministère de l'enseignement supérieur. 2001. *Enseignement supérieur: situation et perspectives* (in Arabic). Tunis: Ed. CPU.

Secrétariat d'Etat à l'Education Nationale. 1962–1967. *Rapport sur le mouvement éducatif en Tunisie* (published annually). Tunis: Secrétariat d'Etat à l'Education Nationale.

Soussi, M. A. 1988. "L'école et l'environnement économique et social: Point de vue du monde des affaires." In Ministère de l'Education de Tunisie and Banque mondiale, eds., *Actes des journées d'étude sur l'école de demain*. Tunis and Washington, D.C.: Banque mondiale.

Sraïeb, N. 1974. *Colonisation, décolonisation et enseignement: l'exemple tunisien*. Tunis: Institut national des sciences de l'éducation.

Zouari, A. 1991. *Le financement public de l'éducation en Tunisie: problèmes et perspectives*. Tunis: Institut Arabe des Chefs d'Entreprise (IACE).

———. 1998a. "L'école et l'environnement économique et social en Tunisie." In Ministère de l'Education de Tunisie and Banque mondiale, eds., *Actes des journées d'étude sur l'école de demain*. Tunis: Ministère de l'Education de Tunisie.

———. 1998b. "L'enseignement supérieur en Tunisie: les enjeux." In Plassard et Ben Sedrine, ed., *Enseignement supérieur et insertion professionnelle en Tunisie*. Toulouse: Université des sciences sociales.

63

Uganda

NAKANYIKE B. MUSISI

BACKGROUND

Located in East Africa, Uganda is a small landlocked country occupying 241,139 square kilometers (93,104 square miles) of land. Currently, Uganda's population stands at 21 million people and is increasing at an average rate of 2.5 percent each year. Taking into account the demographic trends, including the negative effects of HIV/AIDS, the population of Uganda is projected to grow to about 26 million by the year 2011 and to about 35 million by 2021 (National Population Policy for Sustainable Development 1995). Uganda has a young population; more than 50 percent are 1–15 years old. The average life expectancy is 51 years (Uganda Human Development Report 1998). These demographic realities have considerable consequences for the development of and future planning for higher education in Uganda.

In 1987, Uganda embarked on a period of economic restructuring that has achieved broad microeconomic growth and stability. The gross domestic product (GDP) has expanded at an annual rate of over 6 percent in real terms during the past ten years, inflation has stayed at less than 5 percent per annum, and GDP per capita has grown at an annual rate of 3.4 percent. This is attributed to sound economic policies. In 1995, Uganda was ranked as the fastest-growing economy in Africa. Yet in spite of the impressive economic growth of the past ten years, Uganda remains one of the world's poorest countries, ranked at 158 out of 175 countries (Human Development Report 1999, 260). Per capita annual income is $320 (Republic of Uganda 2000b, 2).

More than 80 percent of Uganda's population is engaged in the rural agricultural sector, mainly at a subsistence level. Agriculture continues to be the mainstay of the country's economy, accounting for about 50 percent of total GDP. The agriculture sector generates about 85 percent of export earnings and employs more than 88 percent of the Ugandan labor force (Vision 2025). Because of the significant role education is slated to play

in the overall development of the nation, the education sector has become a major component of the central government budget.

INTRODUCTION

Toward the end of 1999, the Rockefeller, Ford, and MacArthur Foundations and the Carnegie Corporation launched a joint initiative to strengthen the ability of selected African universities to effectively contribute to social, economic, and political progress in their respective countries. This initiative stemmed from the recognition by these philanthropic institutions of a favorable climate for the rejuvenation of universities in sub-Saharan Africa. Early in January 2000, they commissioned studies of a few countries with the aim of identifying the causes, nature, and consequences of transformation in these universities. The case studies were also designed to achieve two important goals. The first was to promote a catalytic process within these universities that would assist strategic thinking on institutional development. The second was to directly or indirectly identify opportunities for external assistance in the transformation process. The case studies were also intended to stimulate funding from donors, including external and internal sources (alumni); to identify strategic investments; and to develop other financial sources for the university.

At the presentation of the Makerere University case-study findings, an observer from the audience noted how the transformations at Makerere University were swift, impressive, and fundamental. He agreed with David Court's observation regarding the rapidity with which change was taking place at Makerere. Court had equated the difficulty of changing universities to moving a cathedral (Court 1999). Overwhelmed by the magnitude and speed of transition taking place at Makerere University, the observer asked an important question: "In transit to what?" This is a question that does not allow for a quick answer. The changes taking place at Makerere University offer only a bird's-eye view of the transition taking place in Uganda's education system. These changes are seen both in the demand and supply sides of education in the country. They cannot be seen in isolation from the sociopolitical and economic context and policy framework from which they emerge. It is also important to note that changes taking place in higher education in Uganda are occurring globally (World Bank 1994).

In Uganda, education has been described as an important goal by the Uganda National Resistance Movement (NRM) government, as a basic human rights issue (Uganda Constitution 1995), and as "an essential ingredient in human resource development for economic growth, development, and poverty eradication" (Poverty Eradication Action Plan Draft 2000, 39). Uganda's support for education is grounded in some outstanding economic research that affirms the intimate relationship between investment in education (human resource development) and economic growth (World Bank Development Report 1980; Easterlin 1981). Such research has demonstrated how countries with the fastest rate of economic growth have higher rates of literacy than other countries at the same income level. Notwithstanding, the World Bank's External Advisory Panel on Education (1978) warned that education cannot be reduced to a sector of development parallel with industry or agriculture; rather, it needs to be considered as a central element of all organized efforts to speed up development (Psacharopoulos and Woodhall 1991).

The centrality of the education sector in the Ugandan government's grand design for economic development raises a number of questions. These revolve around issues of access and equity, quality, financing, and investment in education in comparison to other forms of investment, relevance of the education offered, the nature, size, and scope of the subsector, and government policies.

This chapter is devoted to an examination of these issues as they relate to the provision of higher education in Uganda. The first section deals with the current and historical context from which the Ugandan higher education system emerged. The section also explores the Ugandan government's role, particularly as it relates to policies that affect education in the country. The second section maps out trends, giving the size and scope of higher education institutions in Uganda. The third section examines the pertinent issues of funding and investment, quality, access, equity, and relevance. The fourth section briefly addresses the challenges still faced by the higher education system in Uganda.

CURRENT AND HISTORICAL CONTEXT

Growth and Priorities within the Education Sector

Since 1997, developments in the education sector have been dominated by the implementation of the policy of Universal Primary Education (UPE). A head count conducted in August 1997 showed that the number of children who entered the primary education system in January that year was 5.3 million, representing a doubling of the pre-UPE figure. By the end of 2000, that figure had risen significantly to 6.5 million. The government has continued its focus on primary education, paying special attention to classroom construction, teacher recruitment, teacher training, and provision of instructional materials (Republic of Uganda 2000a, 2001). Primary education now receives approximately 70 percent of Uganda's education budget.

In recent years, Uganda's secondary school system has also seen similar impressive growth, although not equal to that of the primary subsector. By 1980, the country had 510 government-aided secondary schools with an enrollment of 37,000 students. The number had increased to 621 secondary schools by 1996, with a total student population of 256,258. Two years later, in 1998, the number of secondary schools in the country reached 837. Of these, thirty-three were for boys only, fifty-three were for girls only, and the remaining 751 were mixed (MOES 1998).

The implementation of the current drive toward universal primary education and the consequent expansion of secondary education have intensified demand for places at tertiary-level institutions. A single system of tertiary education based on the distinctive contribution and comparative advantage of constituent institutions is emerging. A legal framework for such a system was discussed in Parliament in February 2000. A Universities and Other Institutions of Higher Education Bill was passed in Parliament in December of the same year. This law was designed to streamline the process of institutional development. It also defines the conditions under which all tertiary institutions will operate.

Financing and Investing in the Education Sector

Several actors have been involved in funding and investment in the education establishment as a whole. These include donor agencies, local and international NGOs, local governments, the private sector, and civil society. As mentioned above, the education sector continues to receive high priority in allocations of government budget resources. But, and this is most important, cost sharing has increased community participation in educational endeavors.

The government's expenditure on the education sector rose steadily in the period 1995–1998. However, this increase was not uniform across the sector. More money went toward school development activities at the primary and secondary levels. Increased expenditure has also gone toward purchasing instructional materials under the Support Uganda Primary Education and Reform (SUPER) and the Primary Education and Teacher Development (PETD) programs (Republic of Uganda 2000a). In the period 1999–2000, the education sector received 33 percent of total government discretionary recurrent spending. Of this allocation, primary education received 62 percent, secondary education received 15 percent, and tertiary education received 18 percent. The Ugandan government has scored an incredible success in the education sector in a remarkably short period of time. The education budget has increased by 300 percent, rising as a share of GDP from 1.6 to 3.8 percent from 1990–1991 to 1999–2000 (Republic of Uganda 1999–2000, 10–12). Equally important, recurrent expenditures in the education sector have increased considerably. Financing for the sector as a whole was hiked up from 20 percent of total government ex-

Table 63.1. Education Strategic Investment Plan Framework by Sector, Uganda, 1997–2003 (in millions of U.S. dollars)

	1997–2000	2000–2003	Total
Primary Education	278	188	466
Secondary Education	41	59	100
Postsecondary Education	32	35	67
Higher Education	33	33	66
Institutional Development	6	5	11
Total	390	320	710

Source: ESIP 1998–2003. Figures are rounded up.

penditure in 1994–1995 to 25 percent in 1997–1998 (MOES 1999, 10–12).

In addition to the government, religious bodies have invested heavily in the secondary school infrastructure. More than 50 percent of Ugandan schools were founded by religious groups (MOES 1998). The government founded only 11 percent of all secondary schools, while the Church of Uganda founded 27 percent, the Catholic Church founded 18 percent, 5 percent belong to various Islamic bodies, and 24 percent were founded by parents.

At the tertiary level, government funding has been decreasing for some years now. Unprecedented growth at the lower levels has in turn forced the government to reorganize its resources. The government, together with its development partners, has been hard-pressed to find workable solutions for education financing. Utilizing funds gained through the Highly Indebted Poor Countries (HIPC) Initiative is one among the three major avenues used by the government to tackle this problem. The other two initiatives include prioritization within the government budget, which means that the Ministry of Education and Sports now receives 33 percent of the total discretionary recurrent budget, and the creation of the Education Strategic Investment Plan (ESIP). Table 63.1 shows funding distributions by sector.

An Overview of the Goals and Issues of the Education Establishment in Uganda

The current issues facing higher education in Uganda must be understood not only in terms of the sector's historical background but also in terms of the overall issues of the larger education sector as a whole. Among the pertinent issues of the sector are the erosion of the quality of education at all levels, expansion of enrollment and facilities without proper planning, increased regional imbalances in the provision of education, changes in the curricula without ensuring proper training of teachers and provision of instructional materials, increased cost of education, and the lack of alignment between curricula and the socioeconomic realities of the country.

The broad aims of education in Uganda are stated in the Government White Paper. These include the promotion of scientific, technical, and cultural knowledge, and the skills and attitudes needed to promote development and to contribute to the building of an integrated, self-sustaining, and independent national economy. Specifically, the aims and objectives of tertiary education are as follows:

- To train high-level technical, managerial, and professional personnel for all sectors of national life
- To generate advanced knowledge and innovations through research and to translate or adapt this knowledge to local and national situations
- To provide public service through extension work and consultancy services
- To develop the intellectual capacities of students to understand their local and national environment objectively
- To promote the development of an indigenous scientific and technological capacity needed to tackle the problems of development
- To equip students with knowledge, skills, and attitudes to enable them to join the workforce (Government White Paper on Education 1992)

Government Involvement in the Education Sector

Notwithstanding financial constraints, the NRM government, which took power in 1986, committed itself to the rehabilitation of the economy and the social infrastructure by expanding education. To a large extent, this commitment forms the environment in which the current education policies have been formulated and implemented. In 1989, an Education Policy Review Commission was appointed by the Ministry of Education. Its mandate was to critically reexamine all aspects of educational development in Uganda. The commission's report was adopted with modifications and became the basis of the Government White Paper on Education of 1992.

The White Paper and its offspring, the Education Strategic Investment Plan (ESIP) of 1998–2003, are the blueprints for educational development in Uganda in the medium and long term. They address issues of access, equity, relevance, quality, and financing of education. They identify the roles of all education stakeholders: students, parents, the community, local and central governments, and donors.

The government is also taking a number of measures aimed at streamlining and guiding the provision of higher education in the country. One of these measures is the enactment of a new act of Parliament (Republic of Uganda 1998) that established a National Council for Higher Education (NCHE) as an intermediary body between higher education institutions and the government. The NCHE will serve a number of functions. First, it will promote the objectives of university education in Uganda. Second, it will address the government's development, coordination, planning, administration, and financial management of national universities. Third, it will coordinate student admission and accreditation of national universities. And last, it will serve as a data bank on higher education institutions for the government and other interested groups and individuals (Kigozi 2000).

The composition of the NCHE will be broad-based. Modalities for identifying the representatives of these key stakeholder groups are yet to be finalized. However, Mwiria has argued that the formation of the NCHE, the composition of its membership, and the fact that members will be elected will all contribute to the depoliticization of higher education development in Uganda (Mwiria 1999).

Government public-sector reforms of liberalization, deregulation, and decentralization have also opened up opportunities for the establishment of privately owned institutions of higher learning, including universities.

With grassroots democratization, the current NRM government has restored to students democratic rights abrogated in the 1970s. Students in higher education institutions in Uganda currently run their affairs through the student governments (guilds) elected annually by the entire student body of their respective institutions. Through their guilds, students can have direct input in matters affecting their learning and living conditions (Musisi and Muwanga 2000).

The Chronological Context

The history of higher education in Uganda can be divided into roughly five phases: 1922–1950; 1951–1961; 1962–1970; 1971–1992; and 1993 through today. Each phase reflects the trials and tribulations of the state's political priorities, development, and progress.

The 1920s were formative years in the development of Uganda's present educational system. Education was previously left in the hands of Christian missionaries, but the colonial government assumed direct responsibility for the education sector in the 1920s (Lugumba and Ssekamwa 1973; Onyango 1985; Furley and Watson 1978; Macpherson 1964; and Musisi 1992). It was during this initial period that Makerere University Kampala (MUK) was founded as a technical college to serve students from the British East African territories of Kenya, Tanganyika, and Uganda. Curriculum development for the technical college put particular emphasis on the priorities and preoccupations of the colonial regime; the job of the college was to supply the colonial power with competent assistants in a variety of fields. Hence, the college offered limited certificate courses in agriculture, carpentry, medical care, motor mechanics, teacher training, and veterinary science. Following the Asquith Report in 1949, the college obtained semi-autonomous status and became affiliated with London University. It started offering degree-level courses henceforth.

In the second phase, the main preoccupation of education planners was the Africanization of the civil service structure to encourage modernization and development. Influenced by the Binns Commission (1951) and the Report on African Education in Uganda by the Bernard de Bunsen Commission (1953), the 1950s were years of rapid growth (Macpherson 1964; Furley and Watson 1978). In 1953, students at Makerere College first gained London University degrees.

In 1956, the founding of the Royal Technical College in Nairobi ended Makerere's preeminence as the only institute of higher education in East Africa. A few years later, in 1961, the University College of Dar es Salaam was founded. Subsequently, at the attainment of independence, higher education institutions became valued as institutions of prestige and national achievement, as well as a source of high-level, skilled labor power to replace the departing colonial expatriate staff.

In the third phase, the college became one of the three constituent colleges of the University of East Africa. Despite this structural reorganization, the college continued to emphasize modernization and development for the self-reliance of the newly independent state. Largely influenced by the Castle Commission of 1962 and the World Bank, the secondary and postsecondary education goal of this phase was to produce the high-skilled labor power needed for post-independence economic growth.

In 1963, the three colleges (Royal Technical College, Nairobi; University College of Dar es Salaam; and Makerere College) merged to become the constituent colleges of the University of East Africa. Opio-Odongo has noted that the fact that the "birth of the University of East Africa occurred after Kenya, Uganda and Tanzania had attained independence greatly influenced the growth of higher education" (1993, 13). Higher education was approached from the perspective of its synergistic contribution to national and regional development. It is not surprising that the three constituent colleges embarked on programs aimed at increasing indigenous student enrollment and staff and at the diversification of curricula. At Makerere, undergraduate enrollment increased from 1,331 in 1964–1965 to 1,805 in 1967–1968 (Court 1975). By 1967–1968, through a purposeful and selective process, Makerere had achieved 20 percent East Africanization of its academic staff. By 1970–1971, the number of Ugandans studying at Makerere had increased to 2,638 (Republic of Uganda 1972). New courses in technology, librarianship, forestry, commerce, law, and agricultural education, and postgraduate training in medicine, social work, music, dance, and drama were offered. Growth was also registered in other institutions of learning, such as Uganda's technical colleges and teacher training institutions, the Agricultural College, the Veterinary Training Institute, the Law Development Center, and the Institute of Public Administration. This expansion was largely attributed to the government's political and ideological thrust and to a healthy and robust economy (Republic of Uganda 1970). In 1970, at the close of this third phase, owing to nationalist pressures in the region the University of East Africa was dissolved into three full-fledged independent universities at Makerere in Uganda, Nairobi in Kenya, and Dar es Salaam in Tanzania.

Surmounted by political and economic exigencies, the fourth period was a period of crisis management (Kajubi 1989; Republic of Uganda 1981). Generally, the 1970s and 1980s could be characterized as arduous years of political maneuvering and underfunding in the education sector. Beginning in 1971, Uganda was plunged into the most turbulent years of its history with the coming to power of Idi Amin. Throughout this period, the financial outlook of the educational sector reflected the country's fiscal position and performance. From 1972 to about 1981, the regular budget surplus the country had acquired in the 1960s turned into a huge deficit. From 1972 to 1985, the GDP declined and per capita real income fell by 35 percent. Inflationary pressures, coupled with declining export earnings, exerted an incredible pressure on Uganda's balance of payments (Kajubi 1989).

The internal political and economic turmoil of those two decades—worsening terms of trade, growing public debt, and the declining value of the shilling—combined to devastate the financing of education in Uganda (Kajubi 1989; Mwiria 1999). Public spending on education as a percentage of total government recurrent expenditure showed wide fluctuations ranging from a minimum of 11 percent in 1986–1987 to a maximum of 21 percent in 1983–1984 (Kajubi 1989). During this period, development expenditure as a percentage of total government expenditure was continuously declining. In 1984–1985, development expenditure on education as a percentage of total government expenditure stood at 10.7 percent; by 1987–1988, it had declined to 5.9 percent.

Conversely, a decline in government funding was taking place at a time when the higher education subsector was facing two other serious challenges. The first was a shift in donor circles in favor of primary and secondary education. This narrow orientation, which has been subsequently criticized, was supported by economic analysis that endeavored to show that "public investment in universities and colleges brings meager returns compared to schools, and that [public investment in] higher education magnifies inequalities" (World Bank 2000, 10). This ideological shift toward funding primary education was partly responsible for a decline in external funding to higher education at this critical moment of urgent need. The second challenge resulted from population growth and the increased social demand for higher education, which was responsible for a rapid increase in enrollment. Unfortunately, the increase was not accompanied by a corresponding improvement in financial resources. Basically, subsequent governments during the period 1979–1986 did little to confront the financial problems facing higher education. For instance, the Obote II government (1980–1985) merely reactivated the Obote I (1966–1971) policy regarding higher education (Kajubi 1989). This policy supported every Ugandan admitted to Makerere University with full government sponsorship. Such an outdated approach indicates little appreciation of how far the government had been disabled in meeting its financial obligations to the nation, irrespective of its goodwill.

The political and economic crisis during the precarious Amin era (1971–1979) halted the previous impressive inroads made in the provision of higher education in Uganda. The main preoccupation was to deal with the urgent and pressing shortages of financial and skilled human resources created by brain drain and the exodus of Asians and other expatriates. With the overthrow of Amin in 1979, the national education policy became preoccupied with different priorities. Input into planning for higher education was concerned with rehabilitation of the war-ravaged and devastated infrastructure, facilities, and services.

Neither the change of governments in the early 1980s nor the attempts to rehabilitate the economy significantly changed the landscape for higher education. As Opio-Odongo points out, "The rehabilitation of the economy in the 1980s was done in the context of the IMF-sponsored Structural Adjustment Programmes which advocated budget cuts and the replacement of the role of the state by that of the private sector" (1993, 16). In this context, the rehabilitation of the production sector received higher priority than social infrastructure. Accordingly, the proportion of the recurrent budget devoted to education declined from 21 percent in 1983–1984 to as low as 11 percent in 1986–1987, rising slightly to 18.2 percent and back down to 12.2 percent in 1987–1988 and 1988–1989, respectively (Republic of Uganda 1989b). The cuts affected the financing of government-sponsored training institutions of higher education. As a result, the number of graduates declined. For instance, by 1987, the number of teachers graduating from these institutions had declined by 46 percent (5,424 persons in 1983 compared to 2,495 in 1987) (Republic of Uganda 1989a). At the same time, institutions of higher education continued to produce graduates who were divorced from the reality of ordinary living and devoid of motivation and an innovative spirit, which are essential for the creation of jobs. Most teaching posts in higher education institutions remain empty because low salaries and unattractive benefits compromised the university's ability to attract Ugandans or expatriates to fill the vacant positions.

Post-1986 educational policy was influenced to a large extent by the World Bank study of education in sub-Saharan Africa. This study proposed a three-point strategy. The first involved adjustment to mounting economic and demographic pressures by diversification of sources of funding, mobilization of revenues from the private sector, a policy of encouraging cost sharing and private sector services, and rigorous control of public funds, particularly with regard to expenditure on nonpedagogical costs. The second strategy was to revitalize the educational structure to restore quality and relevance. And, finally, the third strategy was to expand access to education selectively, in particular increasing access for traditionally disadvantaged groups. The period 1993 to the present has seen efforts to implement these proposals. It has been a phase of reform and innovation as well as strategic drift.

Effects of the 1970s and 1980s on
the Higher Education Subsector

Political maneuvering and underfunding have had significant negative consequences on the provision of higher education in Uganda. At independence, Uganda had one of the best higher education systems in Africa (World Bank 1992). However, the economic and political crises of the next two decades jeopardized the country's higher education system. Particularly, underfunding accentuated and exposed old and new problems in the provision of higher education. At Makerere University, this was exhibited in the unprecedented occurrence of seven student and staff riots and protests in 1989, leading to the closing of the university in November of that year (Makerere University Visiting Committee 1990–1991). The crises that brought higher education in Uganda to the brink of collapse were mainly experienced in three areas: finance, quality and relevance of education, and relations between the education sector and the state (Mwiria 1999; Court 1999). These were all interrelated. For example, the direct consequences of underfunding were a depleted infrastructure, bare laboratories, empty library shelves, serious shortages of scholastic materials, an impoverished and demoralized teaching staff, and a sharp deterioration in the quality of student life (Makerere University Visiting Committee 1990–1991). Specifically, at Makerere University, extracurricular activities became virtually nonexistent and the teaching staff were poorly housed and paid. Such poor conditions in the highest echelon of the education sector further undermined students' academic endeavors. The low standards of education at Makerere resulted in large failure rates, especially in medicine, veterinary medicine, and science (Makerere University Visiting Committee 1990–1991, 19).

The quality of higher education in Uganda was also affected by a debilitating and overcrowded infrastructure. Because few or no additional teaching spaces were constructed, the rapid increase in the student population completely outstripped the available space for teaching and other necessary educational functions. To make matters worse, many schools, institutes, and colleges lacked running water, a constant supply of electricity, toilet facilities, and other necessities.

Underfunding also depleted the level of staffing and accelerated staff attrition and demoralization. Salaries were not only meager; sometimes they came too late to have any meaningful impact on the recipient's quality of life. The poor remuneration and working conditions left the teaching staff humiliated, with few options other than absenteeism. Many teachers and staff moonlighted to feed their families and pay school fees for their children. Furthermore, absenteeism and the lack of morale, the inadequate teaching materials, and the lack of reference materials all led to a relaxation of academic programming at many higher education institutions. Given the poor living and working conditions, it is understandable that Uganda experienced a brain drain as teachers sought greener pastures both within and outside the country. Testifying to the Makerere University Visiting Committee of 1990–1991, the Makerere University Academic Staff Association (MUASA) expressed the opinion that the dire consequences of this "under-funding secured a steady institutional regression with potential[ly] disastrous multiplier effects on the national development in that professionals passed out [graduating] were dismally sub-standard" (MUASA 1990–1991, 2–3).

The multiplier effect of underfunding could also be seen at the administration level of the university and at many of the other institutions offering higher education. At Makerere University, underfunding undermined the university's authorities, who found it increasingly difficult to ensure the cooperation of students, staff, and faculty. Financially impotent to provide the very minimum and basic requirements to facilitate the teaching and learning process, the administration was rendered powerless. This problem was exacerbated by the University Act of 1970, which has remained a stumbling block in Makerere University's development. Throughout this period of crisis, the university continued to be governed by the archaic 1970 act, which was amended by decrees in 1973 and 1975. The act gives the government too much political control over university administration. It equally constrains the university's ability to raise or spend money without the government's approval (MUASA 1990–1991; Makerere University Visiting Committee 1990–1991).

Empowered in this way by the University Act, bad and dictatorial governments formulated policies to govern the country's only university with complete lack of respect for and involvement of key stakeholders for two decades. Policies were generally issued by government directives. In addition, policy changes were sometimes formulated and implemented in a hurried, poorly articulated, and uncoordinated manner (Makerere University Visiting Committee 1990–1991). The lack of focused thinking and consultation compromised the university's goals and, in the majority of cases, undermined the role and input of the communities concerned. Moreover, this state of affairs created and heightened unnecessary friction, antagonism, and resentment between the parties affected. It suffocated opportunities for public debate which could have enabled the affected communities to appreciate the implications of changes related to the government's economic disabilities. It is little wonder that in such a hostile environment, the relationship with the government was characterized by suspicion, particularly on the part of the university. During this period, every effort was taken to silence and curtail students and academic staff engaging in organized and legal protest or having input in discussions of conditions affecting them. The fact that institutions of higher education survived still surprises educational analysts. What is even more surprising is the fact that institutional growth in the higher education subsector was recorded in some cases.

CURRENT TRENDS, SIZE, AND SCOPE OF HIGHER EDUCATION INSTITUTIONS

The present structure of the education cycle in Uganda consists of seven years of primary schooling, four years of ordinary secondary education, and two years of advanced education, followed by tertiary education for two to five years. The terms "higher" and "tertiary" education in this chapter are used to refer to postsecondary education. Institutions offering education at this level fall into two categories: university and nonuniversity tertiary institutions. Universities award bachelor's, master's, and doctorate degrees; diplomas; and certificates to successful candidates. Nonuniversity tertiary institutions offer courses leading to the award of diplomas and certificates in different areas of specialization.

In the past seven years, the higher education subsector has been growing at a relatively rapid speed, although not as quickly as the primary level. The current demand for higher education is unparalleled in the history of Uganda. The number of students sitting for the O-level and A-level examinations has significantly increased. In addition, student performance has been impressive. For example, the number of candidates eligible to enter university has increased at the rate of 12 percent annually from

1994 to 1999. The total increase in the number of candidates with two advanced passes (the mark of eligibility to enter university) for the period was more than 50 percent. The actual number rose from 7,472 in 1994 to 16,674 in 1999 (Hyuha 2000). In 2000, the number of eligible candidates surged to 24,000.

Nonuniversity Tertiary Institutions

Uganda has both public and private nonuniversity tertiary institutions. The public ones include the Institute of Teacher Education Kyambogo (ITEK), Uganda Polytechnic Kyambogo (UPK), ten national teachers' colleges (NTCs), five Ugandan colleges of commerce (UCCs), five Ugandan technical colleges (UTCs), the National Health Service training colleges, and the departmental training institutions. In addition, several public nonuniversity tertiary institutions do not fall strictly in the above categories. These include the Uganda Management Institute (UMI), the Law Development Center (LDC), the Management Training and Advisory Center (MTAC), the Police College and Training School, the Army Academy, and the Prisons Training School. A breakdown of student enrollment in public nonuniversity tertiary institutions for the academic year 1999–2000 shows that ITEK registered 700 students, NTCS registered 3,981, the UCCs registered 2,078, the five UTCs registered 922, the agricultural colleges registered 355, the Uganda National Institute of Special Education registered 121, the Uganda Cooperative College Kigumba registered 125, the Fisheries Training Institute Entebbe registered 110, the Uganda Forestry College Nyabyeya registered 100, the Hotel and Tourism Training Institute Jinja registered 125, the eleven paramedical schools registered 780, and UPK registered 600. Total enrollment at these institutions came to 9,997 (Ministry of Education and Sports 2000).

UNIVERSITY EDUCATION

Currently Uganda hosts two public universities: Makerere University Kampala and Mbarara University of Science and Technology. The government recently announced the founding of two more publicly funded universities, Northern Uganda University of Agriculture and Kyambogo University, which will focus on education, special-needs education, and technology. More than ten private universities have been established or are in various stages of inauguration.

Public Universities

Makerere University: Makerere, the oldest university in the country, offers day, evening, and external courses in medicine, dental surgery, nursing, pharmacy, veterinary medicine, agriculture, forestry and nature conservation, technology, statistics and applied economics, business studies, law, arts, industrial and fine arts, education, science, library and information science, food science and technology, and adult and continuing education.

The past seven years have seen extensive curricular reviews of most of the academic programs and courses in all faculties with the goal of making them more marketable. Makerere University has registered tremendous improvement in increasing access. For the academic year 1999–2000, Makerere enrolled 15,987 students, of whom 14,239 were undergraduates and 1,748 were postgraduates. Increased enrollment has been achieved by making education more accessible through private sponsorship schemes, evening classes, and distance learning. Makerere University enrollment is expected to rise by 10 percent annually until it reaches 50,000. Total enrollment currently stands at 21,661 students, of whom 20,441 are undergraduates and 1,220 are pursuing postgraduate programs. The academic staff stands at 911, of whom 221 have Ph.D.s and 175 of whom are female (MUARO 2000/2001b).

Demand-driven programs have created income-generating opportunities for the university. Other changes taking place at Makerere include the introduction of a more flexible semester system to replace the traditional term system (Hyuha 2000; Court 1999; Mwiria 1999; Musisi and Muwanga 2000).

Mbarara University of Science and Technology: Established in 1989 with the aim of providing scientific and technological university education and fostering their application in rural development, Mbarara University of Science and Technology offers courses in medicine and a bachelor's degree in science education. In 1998–1999, its undergraduate enrollment was 419, of whom 299 were male and 120 were female. Total enrollment is expected to expand to 997 by the year 2003. Mbarara University of Science and Technology has a total of 84 academic staff, of whom 17 are women (Ministry of Education and Sports 1998). There is no doubt that the increase in enrollment reflects government efforts to increase access to higher education and make it more relevant to the job market.

Private Universities

The establishment of private universities promises to broaden the provision of higher education in Uganda without necessarily increasing the financial burden on the government. Although the enrollment in these universities is still small, the potential for future growth is enormous. Private universities include the Islamic University in Uganda (Mbale), founded in 1988; Uganda Martyrs University (1992); Nkumba University (1996); Bugema University (1997); Busoga University (1998); Uganda Christian University (1999); Namasagali University (1999); and Ndejje University (1999). Among the private universities in different stages of development are Ndejje University; Iganga; Kumi University; Musa Body University of Katwe; Seguku University; Kabale University; Tropical University, Masaka; St. Lawrence University, near Nabingo; Aga Khan University; Kampala University; Starlife; Teso; and Kigezi International University of Medicine. A few of these are operating without government licenses. Sources from the Ministry of Education estimate that these universities catered to a total of 3,600 students in 1998–1999. These universities offer bachelor's courses in media and various traditional arts subjects, journalism, business administration and management, performing arts (dance), hotel management, catering, tourism, industrial art, and design. They also offer master's degrees in various arts subjects, a diploma in hospital management and education, and a Bachelor's of Science in computer science. Some private universities, such as Namasagali University, offer external degrees (for example, an L.L.B. from London University).

The development of these universities will no doubt relieve pressure on public universities to expand enrollment. These universities also have the potential to contribute to the creation of a more differentiated system of higher education. Kajubi has pointed out that, in contrast to Makerere University's secularism, many of these universities are founded on religious principles (including Islamic, Anglican, Catholic, and Seventh-Day Adventist) (Kajubi 1997).

PERTINENT ISSUES IN THE PROVISION OF HIGHER EDUCATION IN UGANDA

Coordination and Establishment of New Institutions of Higher Education

Until the NCHE is put into effective operation, major concerns include the almost complete absence of a national policy on higher education; the lack of up-to-date and reliable statistics on the number of students studying at home and abroad; the lack of systematic planning in institutions of higher education, which has resulted in their haphazard development and the poor state of their physical facilities; a deterioration in the quality of education; and the need to streamline the development and management of tertiary education to make it more effective and capable of serving the dynamic and changing needs of the country.

The unplanned nature of the establishment and location of many of Uganda's tertiary institutions calls for immediate attention. New institutions should be required to justify their purpose, their capacity in terms of facilities and human resources, their contribution to the development of the region, their ability to provide quality and equity in access to higher education, and above all, the bases of their financial sustainability.

Admission and Access to Institutions of Higher Education

Uganda allows candidates to apply for studies at any of the available tertiary education institutions. Due to increased demand created by the rapid expansion of primary and secondary education, the current thrust of the government of Uganda is to expand access to higher education. The Education Review Commission states: "Admission to tertiary education institutions should be made more accessible to as many qualified candidates as possible, and should not be restricted only to requirements in the civil service" (Kajubi 1989, 76). Increased access is being achieved through external or long-distance programs, evening and weekend classes, private sponsorship, and cost sharing at various tertiary institutions. Mature-age entry schemes are available for candidates who wish to pursue university education in any field. Diploma holders who satisfy the established entry requirements continue to enter universities.

With liberalization, privatization, and the relative expansion of the private sector, access to tertiary institutions is no longer pegged to the availability of public service jobs but is open to competitively selected students, including those who can afford private sponsorship. The government is further committed to expanding access to higher education through licensing of private universities, colleges, and other institutions of higher learning and the creation of an enabling policy environment.

Resources and Financing of Higher Education

To date, the existing physical resources of higher educational institutions are quite inadequate. Past political instability and lack of financial resources and the general lack of a culture that values maintenance have combined to cause gross negligence in the maintenance of physical infrastructure (including laboratories, seminar rooms, libraries, research facilities, and staff offices). The government has prioritized the rehabilitation of physical plants and the provision of instructional materials and human resources in order to maintain high academic and professional standards in tertiary institutions. However, the limited funds allocated to tertiary education pose a major obstacle to any meaningful development. Institutions have been encouraged to focus on rapid rehabilitation, consolidation, and expansion of physical plants and facilities, but this is creating pressure on them to increase ways to make money at the expense of other goals, such as improving the quality of education, increasing the availability of human resources, increasing the ability to handle expansion, and providing support for the teaching staff.

The exodus and brain drain of senior staff from tertiary institutions, especially Makerere University, was a paramount concern in the early 1990s. The relative improvement in the conditions of employment, salaries, standard of living, and fringe benefits of faculty have combined to counter this exodus and brain drain. However, the growth of better-paying positions in the private sector and the higher ministerial levels of the civil service continue to take away seasoned academics from tertiary institutions.

Higher education institutions in Uganda obtain funding from both public and private sources. Publicly funded institutions fall into two categories. The first category is funded through the Ministry of Education, while the second category is funded under the auspices of the Public Sector Commission (PSC). Among those funded through the education ministry are Makerere University; Mbarara University of Science and Technology; the Institute of Teacher Education Kyambogo; and teachers' and technical colleges throughout the country. Those funded through the PSC include the Uganda Management Institute, the Uganda Law Development Center, the Land Surveying School (Entebbe), and various agricultural and cooperative colleges and paramedical schools. The privately funded institutions include all the private universities, the Chartered Institute of Bankers, and various seminary and theological colleges.

Until recently, those categorized as public institutions of higher learning were fully funded by the government. However, the 1992 White Paper and Education Strategic Investment Plan (ESIP) recommended divestiture from full sponsorship of tertiary education through the introduction of cost sharing, private sponsorship, evening programs, long-distance programs, internal generation of income through consultancies and the sale of services, and the establishment of scholarships for those who qualify but cannot afford higher education.

Higher education receives only 9 percent of the current education budget. Subsidies for noninstructional costs (including stipends, transport allowances, and book and stationery allowances) have been eliminated. Meals, accommodation, and related overhead expenses are to be eventually taken over by beneficiaries. Cost-sharing schemes are already in place for government-sponsored students and those on private or self-sponsorships in all public tertiary institutions.

The implementation of cost sharing in institutions of higher learning has increased revenue generation to supplement transfers from the government of Uganda. For Makerere University and the Institute of Teacher Education Kyambogo (ITEK), income generation grew by 40 percent and 164 percent, respectively, from 1997–1998 to 1999–2000. Not unexpectedly, cost sharing in higher education institutions has been met with stiff resistance from students. For instance, when Makerere initially tried to enforce the recommendations of the Visitation Committee of 1986 to remove transport, book, and personal allowances, the reaction of students was immediately hostile. Students demonstrated and boycotted lectures. The university administration was forced to solicit police intervention, which culminated in the shooting deaths of two students.

In addition to cost sharing, funds are generated internally through private sponsorship of students, consultancies, and sales of services. Institutions, particularly universities and ITEK, also raise funds from donors such as the Rockefeller Foundation, the Carnegie Corporation, the Norwegian Agency for Development Cooperation (NORAD), and the Danish Agency for Development Assistance (DANIDA). The availability of nongovernmental funds has enabled the universities to move from a situation of hand-to-mouth dependency on the government to one where autonomous initiative, planning, and allocation are practiced. Some universities seek to press this advantage further by pursuing the amendment of the University Act to give them more financial and administrative autonomy.

The Ministry of Education sponsors Higher Education Supporting Reform Investment Programs aimed at providing higher education at a lower cost per student and improving planning and management. In the future, the government plans to tap incomes from students' productive activities, the private sector, community service schemes, and donations. These funds will be used to develop physical infrastructure and pay for equipment and instructional materials. External assistance also continues to be solicited.

Quality of Higher Education in Uganda

Despite manifest improvements in financial outlook, facilities, and morale of instructors, questions remain about the long-term impact of unprecedented growth on the quality of Ugandan education. There are signs that suggest that enrollment expansion is beginning to negatively affect the quality of learning and research, the physical infrastructure, teaching, and the management capacities of many institutions of higher education. Universities have limited journal subscriptions and library facilities, aging laboratories and workshops, outdated equipment, inadequate access to computers, and low rates of research output. Libraries in most institutions are understocked. Some lack up-to-date textbooks, and generally there is limited or no access to the Internet as a source of knowledge and information.

The growing imbalance between increased enrollments and the quality of teaching at tertiary institutions is reflected in the high failure, repetition, and drop-out rates among students. According to a 1998 report of a senate committee studying the poor performance in humanities at Makerere University, for instance, the failure rate for first-year students in Economics 101 was 52 percent; the rate for Economics 201 (second year), 50 percent; and the rate for Economics 208 was 50 percent. Employers have also started to complain about the quality of Makerere University graduates.

A Department of Higher Education has been established at the Ministry of Education and Sports headquarters. The department monitors and supervises activities of all the institutions of higher learning to ensure the quality of teaching and the publication of books, journals, and research papers. The department also undertakes the admission to the institutions of those who leave A-level programs of study, coordinates the interuniversity student exchange program, and solicits for and administers scholarship programs.

In December 2000, the University and Tertiary Education Bill was debated in Parliament. On March 28, 2001, it received assent and on April 6, 2001, it became an Act of Parliament (The Universities and Other Tertiary Institutions Act). It was put into full effect with the overall objective of establishing and developing a "system governing institutions of higher education while at the same time widening the accessibility of high quality standard institutions to students wishing to pursue higher education" (Republic of Uganda 2001, 10). The Act has two specific objectives: "regulating and guiding the establishment and management of institutions of higher education" and "equating the same professional or other qualifications as well as the award of degrees, diplomas, certificates or other awards by the different institutions" (ibid.). The Act establishes a National Council for Higher Education (NCHE), whose duties, among others, will be a) to register all institutions of Higher Education; b) monitor, evaluate, and regulate institutions of Higher Education; c) set and coordinate national standards for admission of students to different institutions of Higher Education; and d) certify that an institution of Higher Education has adequate and accessible physical structures and staff for the courses to be offered. Among the several implications of this Act is the fact that the president ceases to be the chancellor of the university—rather s/he becomes a "visitor" of each public university. Equally important, the Act guarantees affirmative action in favor of marginalized groups on the basis of gender, disability, and disadvantaged schools. It also guarantees a more representative Senate and Council. But all in all it spells out a reduction of government/political interference.

Equity

Gender inequality has lessened in the past ten years. For instance, in 1990–1991, women constituted 27 percent of Makerere's total student intake. The following year, the government adopted a preferential admission policy to increase enrollment of female students. Female students aspiring to join public universities are awarded an additional 1.5 points on their grade point average. As a result, the proportion of female enrollment has risen to 34 percent. However, significant variations remain in access to the more competitive faculties. In 1997, participation was 30 percent in medicine, 27 percent in commerce, and 26 percent in agriculture, veterinary medicine, and the natural sciences. Female faculty members occupy only 19.7 percent of established academic posts (MUARO 2000/2001b).

With the expansion strategies in place, it is expected that enrollment will increase tremendously by the year 2003. Female enrollment will increase to 40 percent at Makerere University. It is hoped that access across districts and by students of lower socioeconomic groups will be increased by directing subsidies toward underrepresented groups. Both Uganda Martyrs and Nkumba Private Universities, where women are more than 50 percent and 56 percent of their student enrollment, respectively, are likely to play significant roles in creating opportunities for women in business and national development (Kajubi 1997).

Other aspects of equity relate to regional imbalances in the distribution of institutions of higher education and in admission rates at those institutions. At Makerere, regional distribution in admission has slightly improved in the past seven years (Musisi and Muwanga 2000). However, largely due to a number of factors—such as limited secondary education, regional variations in income levels, political instability, and war—many regions, particularly northern and eastern Uganda, are for the most part underrepresented in institutions of higher education.

Relevance of Higher Education in Uganda

From its colonial origins until recently, higher education in Uganda was elitist, restrictive, and characterized by a narrow curriculum (Kajubi 1997). Before independence, education and training were geared toward the limited white-collar jobs that existed in Africa. Such colonial education policies left several independent African states acutely short of badly needed skilled and blue-collar labor power.

Attempts are now being made to address the issue of the relevance of education to the social and economic conditions of the country. Curricula are designed to meet the demands of the client and are market oriented. Several new courses aimed at addressing specific developmental needs have been introduced in the various tertiary institutions. For instance, courses in local government and social-sector planning have been introduced at Makerere University to prepare staff for decentralized local governments. ITEK continues to emphasize vocational education and will introduce elements of vocational education in all its courses. As a way of serving the increasing demand, the institute is establishing new academic programs geared toward the eradication of poverty, including mandatory courses in entrepreneurship and development studies.

However, the job market is currently very competitive. The number of university graduates from humanities and social sciences is surpassing the absorption capacity of the job market while not enough students are being trained for positions in science and technology.

Research output in Uganda was reported to have declined by 53 percent during the decade 1977–1987. This was attributed to the economic and political difficulties experienced in the country during that time. Nonetheless, research is currently undertaken in institutions of higher learning as part of the requirements for diplomas and bachelor's, master's, and Ph.D. programs. The development of graduate programs in which research is a major component is evidence of the indigenization of research in tertiary institutions in Uganda. However, a number of problems related to capacity (numbers and technical skills) and limited access to and dissemination of research findings remain. Publications of research findings in international journals are few and far between.

The full development of the research potential of higher institutions of learning in Uganda has not been realized for two major reasons: financial constraints and an unappreciative and underdeveloped research culture. Poor financing and inadequate research facilities are still a major hindrance to the development of research. For instance, the amount earmarked for research at Makerere University for the fiscal year 1999–2000 was only $80,000. As a consequence, research in the country has remained heavily dependent on donor funding and consultancies.

Most lecturers at tertiary institutions spend much of their time teaching and grading students' work, consequently devoting little or no time to research. The most senior academics are involved in administrative work in their capacity as heads of departments, deans, or directors. Some of them are in great demand as international consultants or advisers to various government ministries, which remunerate their services handsomely. Moreover, many seasoned scholars have reached the peak of their academic careers and do not seem to be motivated to engage in locally based research.

CHALLENGES AND UNFINISHED BUSINESS

The role of higher education as one of the cornerstones in national development is undeniable, yet it remains a big challenge that the Ugandan education system has to address. Social demand for higher education is expected to continue to grow, especially when the first Universal Primary Education (UPE) candidates come of age in 2010. The fact that the massification of education has not been matched by corresponding increases in infrastructure is a cause for concern. Inadequate classroom space, a high student-to-instructor ratio, and a shortage of equipment and materials, among other shortages, are likely to impact the quality of training.

Uganda has gone a long way toward addressing the education needs of the country and moving beyond the crises of the 1970s and 1980s. However, much remains to be done. Success has been achieved by providing an environment that is conducive to the emergence and development of private institutions of higher education. Nonetheless, academic differentiation in the mushrooming private institutions seems to be lacking. Most of these institutions offer courses leading to degrees or diplomas in the social sciences or arts. Given the fact that science in higher education requires heavy capital investment in physical facilities, equipment, and instructional materials, few entrepreneurs have ventured to invest in science- and technology-based institutions of higher education. On another level, at Makerere University, laboratory-based faculties such as those of medicine, engineering, and natural sciences, which are critical in the development process, are lagging behind in the acquisition of private-sector funds. Since much of the money that is raised at the faculty level is maintained for capacity building, this imbalance raises the issue of possible cross-subsidization; faculties that bring in relatively greater resources could support others that bring in less.

Success has also been recorded in diversifying sources of funding for higher institutions in the country. On the whole, the biggest challenge for the higher education system in Uganda is to remain relevant in the rapidly changing world. The current trend of producing disproportionate numbers of graduates in the humanities rather than in the fields of science and technology will not help Uganda remain competitive and meet its development needs.

Equally important, research capacity needs to be enhanced. By linking research to teaching, academic programs will be bolstered to meet the country's development challenges. Government budget releases for research to public institutions of higher education need to be revisited and revised upward. Equally important, current problems of poor access to publishing and research facilities need to be addressed in a more serious manner.

The dangers of privatization have long been discussed in Uganda. In the absence of a student loan system, fears of this trend are increasing. Musisi and Muwanga note that the introduction of fees at Makerere, for instance, has increased but not broadened access (Musisi and Muwanga 2000). The fact that secondary education remains largely dominated by private schools means that the majority of those candidates applying to tertiary institutions will continue to be from financially able families. The challenge is to change education from a privilege of a small social group, a preserve of the elite, to a right for all. Although tertiary institutions have created schemes to pay for the cost-sharing component of their education, many students are still defaulting on their loans. Many students find it difficult to raise funds. The fact that poverty is still pervasive in Uganda, despite the impressive economic growth in the past seven years, means that long-term financial and sustainable expansion of tertiary institutions will require the development of an enforceable and more supportive student loan scheme. Now that political and financial power is being decentralized to the districts, local district councils will need to work out a system of assisting students from needy families. Districts in Busoga are already doing this. These scholarship students are bonded to serve the districts after graduating.

Uganda is also in need of a system for transferring credits between higher education institutions. This would facilitate movement of learners among institutions and greatly enhance the project of freeing tertiary education from its elitist proclivity and moving toward mass higher education (Kajubi 1997).

People living with disabilities are underrepresented throughout Uganda's education system. The way in which several institutions are physically and academically constructed makes access difficult. Another big challenge is the fact that the development of private universities and expansion of public universities is taking place without systematic planning or a coherent legal framework.

Ensuring academic quality and equity is vital to the maintenance of a vibrant higher education system. The government must retain the cardinal and ultimate responsibility for ensuring equitable access to the creation and dissemination of knowledge. Relinquishing this role would compromise quality and equity and would undermine the future development efforts of the country. The challenge for Uganda's government and higher education institutions is to find incentives for high-quality research and teaching to promote the public interest above and beyond the limits of the market, which is presently driving much of the innovation in education.

CONCLUSION

The NRM government has placed a high premium on education to combat the adverse effects of underdevelopment. Hence, the education sector is currently operating within a policy framework that recognizes the need to revitalize the quality of education services. The higher education subsector is poised to play an important role in meeting the government's development goals. However, unleashing its potential requires the removal of several bottlenecks. When these are addressed in an open, consultative, politically positive, and financially stable environment, the answer to the question "Where is Ugandan education in transit to?" will be "To a more positive, equitable, and world-class education."

This goal could be achieved through a combination of strategies, as outlined in the Education Strategic Investment Plan (ESIP). These include improved resource utilization, strengthened management and organizational systems, and selective rationalization of operations through ESIP (Republic of Uganda 1998). While the ESIP document is a progressive one, the test lies in the country's realization of its objectives in the short, medium, and long term. Many challenges remain. For instance, a major challenge is making sure that institutions are able to produce relevant syllabi that will help produce graduates with integrated skills who are independent, creative, and innovative thinkers and job creators. To achieve efficiency in the tertiary sector, the government will also need to continue making adjustments in spending per student and in salary costs. The right balance must be struck. Implementation of cost-sharing mechanisms is already underway in government-aided institutions. However, in the absence of a government student loan scheme, the negative effects of cost sharing, particularly for the least able students, must be addressed. At the same time, the governing councils of universities and other tertiary institutions, in consultation with stakeholders, still face an uphill battle in their effort to reorganize faculties and departments to effectively and more meaningfully engage in national development. Priority faculties that will make Uganda realize its developmental objectives (such as agriculture and technology) need upgraded facilities, improvements in staff performance, and financial affirmative action.

Management of higher institutions of learning also needs to be strengthened. Although the act to establish the National

Council for Higher Education passed through Parliament in December 2000, the challenge will be to implement its progressive elements—particularly effective subsectoral planning and management systems, increased accountability for public spending on higher education, equitable access policies, and increased capacity for institutional management and quality assurance.

The mushrooming of new tertiary institutions is yet another issue that will require careful scrutiny. Much as the development of these institutions is inevitable in the context of social and demographic pressures, legislation for the establishment of new universities needs to be more strictly enforced. An overall needs assessment should be conducted to avoid duplication and overconcentration in one geographical region. Plans for the establishment of these universities must be consistent with the overall goal of national development.

The government's biggest challenge lies in the area of improving, refurbishing, and completing existing tertiary facilities before embarking on opening new ones. Quality and equity issues will remain pertinent to planning. Higher education institutions need to be reevaluated in terms of their alignment with national goals and market demands. Makerere University is leading on this front, but there is still room for progress. Action plans for the rationalization and expansion of programs in light of national goals and market information should be demanded of all institutions of higher education by the NCHE. In addition, the Ministry of Education and the NCHE should show greater concern with developing more meaningful and implementable strategies to increase access to disadvantaged groups. Plans for targeting students from socially and geographically disadvantaged groups must be put in place. This can be achieved if the tertiary governing councils work hand in hand with relevant bodies (such as local governments) to identify needy students, through affirmative action at the entry stage, and through improved student loan and targeted merit-driven scholarship schemes.

ACKNOWLEDGEMENTS

I am grateful to Joseph Owor of Makerere Institute of Social Research for the research help he gave me during the collection of data for this chapter.

BIBLIOGRAPHY

Court D. 1975. "The Experiences of Higher Education in East Africa: The University of Dar es Salaam as a New Model?" *Comparative Education* 11, no. 3: 193–218.

———. 1999. "Financing Higher Education at Makerere: The Quiet Revolution in Human Development." Paper commissioned by the World Bank Tertiary Education Thematic Group and the Rockefeller Foundation. Available online at: http://www.worldbank.org/afr/findings/english/find143.htm

Easterlin, R. 1981. "Why Isn't the Whole World Developed?" *Journal of Economic History* 41 (March): 1–19.

ESIP (Education Strategic Investment Plan). 1998–2003. "Work Plan." Kampala: Ministry of Education and Sports, Education Planning Unit Department.

Furley, O. W., and T. Watson. 1978. *A History of Education in East Africa.* Ibadan: NOK Publishers.

Government of Uganda. 1995. The Constitution of the Republic of Uganda. Kampala, Uganda.

Government of Uganda. 1997. *Vision 2025: A Participatory Process for Formulating a Long-Term Vision for Uganda. A Document for National Consultations.* Kampala, Uganda

Government of Uganda. 1998. Act of Parliament to establish a National Council for Higher Education (NCHE). Kampala, Uganda.

Government of Uganda. 2000. Poverty Eradication Action Plan Draft 2000. Ministry of Finance Planning and Economic Development. Kampala, Uganda.

Hyuha, M. 2000. "The Development of the Semester System over the Next Five Years." Paper presented at the Retreat to Formulate Makerere University Strategic Framework 2000–2004/5, February, Mukono.

Kajubi, S. W. 1989. "Education Policy Review Commission Report." [Also published by the Republic of Uganda, Ministry of Education.] Kampala: Ministry of Education and Sports.

———. 1997. "From Elitist Towards Mass Higher Education: The Phenomenon of Private Universities in Uganda." *Uganda Education Journal* 1, no. 1: 23–30.

Kigozi, E. 2000. "Implications of the Universities and Other Tertiary Institutions Bill." Paper presented at the Retreat to Formulate Makerere University Strategic Framework 2000–2004/5, February, Mukono.

Lugumba, S. M. E., and J. C. Ssekamwa. 1973. *Education Development and Administration in Uganda 1900–1970.* Kampala: Longman.

Macpherson, M. 1964. *They Built for the Future: A Chronicle of Makerere University College, 1922–1962.* Cambridge: Cambridge University Press.

Makerere University. 2000/2001. "Prospectus." Makerere University.

Makerere University Visiting Committee. 1990–1991. *Makerere University Visiting Committee Report.* Entebbe: Government Printer.

Ministry of Finance and Economic Planning (1995): National Population Policy for Sustainable Development. Kampala, Uganda: Population Secretariat.

MUARO (Makerere University Academic Registrar's Office). 2000/2001a. Fees Schedule for Ugandan Private Students' Files.

———. 2000/2001b. "Prospectus 2000/2001."

———. 2000/2001c. Students' Nominal Roll.

MUASA (Makerere University Academic Staff Association). 1990–1991. Kampala, Uganda.

MOES (Ministry of Education and Sports). 1989. "Education Policy Review Commission Report." Kampala: Ministry of Education and Sports.

———. 1992. *Government White Paper.* Kampala: Ministry of Education and Sports.

———. 1999. *Educational Statistical Abstract.* Kampala: Uganda Bureau of Statistics.

———. 2000. Department of Higher Education. Kampala, Uganda.

Musisi, N. B. 1992. "Colonial and Missionary Education: Women and Domesticity in Uganda, 1900–1945." In K. Hansen Tranberg, ed., *African Encounters with Domesticity.* New Brunswick, N.J.: Rutgers University Press.

Musisi, N. B., and N. Muwanga. 2000. "When Politics Fell Apart: Underfunding, Mismanagement and Academic Inertia, Makerere University in Transition, 1993–2000." Case Study. Monograph. Makerere Institute of Social Research, Makerere University.

Mwiria, K. 1999. "Case II: Makerere University, Uganda." In S. Bjarnason and H. Lund, eds., *Government/University Relationships: Three African Case Studies.* London: Commonwealth Higher Education Management Service (CHEMS).

Onyango, B. 1985. "The Historical Development of Higher Education in Uganda." In L. Tembo and T. L. Maliyamkono, eds., *The Devel-*

opment of Higher Education in Eastern and Southern Africa. Nairobi: Oxford University Press.

Opio-Odongo, J. M. A. 1993. *Higher Education and Research in Uganda.* Nairobi: African Centre for Training Studies Press.

Psacharopoulos, G., and M. Woodhall. 1991. *Education for Development: An Analysis of Investment Choices.* Washington, D.C.: Oxford University Press.

Republic of Uganda. 1970. *Report of the Visitation Committee to Makerere University.* Entebbe: Government Printer.

——. 1972. *Uganda's Development Plan III, 1971/2–1975/6.* Entebbe: Government Printer.

——. 1981. *A Ten Year Reconstruction and Development Plan 1980–1990.* Kampala: Ministry of Planning and Economic Development.

——. 1987. *Rehabilitation and Development Plan, 1987/88–1990/91.* Kampala: Ministry of Planning and Economic Development.

——. 1989a. *Education Policy Review Commission Report.* Kampala: Ministry of Education and Sport.

——. 1989b. "Manpower and Employment in Uganda: Report of the National Manpower Survey." Entebbe: Government Printer.

——. 1999a. *Poverty Eradication Action Plan: A National Challenge for Uganda.* Vol. 1. Kampala: Ministry of Finance, Planning and Economic Development.

——. 1999b. *Statistical Abstract.* Entebbe: Government Printer.

——. 2000a. *Background to the Budget 1999/2000.* Kampala: Ministry of Finance, Planning and Economic Development.

——. 2000b. *Uganda Participatory Poverty Assessment Report: Learning From the Poor.* Kampala: Ministry of Finance, Planning and Economic Development.

——. 2001. *Background to the Budget 2000/2001.* Kampala: Ministry of Finance, Planning and Economic Development.

Uganda Human Development Report. 1998. UNDP. Kampala, Uganda.

World Bank. 1980. *World Development Report 1980.* New York: Oxford University Press.

——. 1993. *A World Bank Country Study: Uganda Social Sector.* Washington, D.C.: The World Bank.

——. 1994. *Higher Education: The Lesson of Experience.* Washington, D.C.: The World Bank.

——. 2000. *Higher Education in Developing Countries: Peril and Promise.* Washington, D.C.: Task Force on Higher Education and Society.

64

Zambia

Y. G.-M. LULAT

INTRODUCTION: THE CONTEXT

In testimony to the complex machinations of the European colonial scramble for the African continent, Zambia, which during the colonial period was called Northern Rhodesia, shares its borders with seven countries (Angola and Namibia to the west, the Democratic Republic of the Congo and Tanzania to the north, Malawi and Mozambique to the east, and Zimbabwe to the south). Administratively, the country is divided into a total of nine provinces: Luapula and Northern in the north, Southern in the south, Eastern in the east, North-Western and Western in the west, and Central, Copperbelt, and Lusaka in the center (the last three are the most highly urbanized provinces). The capital city, Lusaka, with a population of approximately 1 million, is located in Lusaka province. Prior to independence from Britain in 1964, which was achieved relatively peacefully, Northern Rhodesia was part of a larger political entity called the Federation of Rhodesia and Nyasaland, which was formed in 1952.

Economically, Zambia is, like its many other counterparts in Africa, a tragedy. This is a consequence of the country's colonial legacy, misplanned and failed post-independence economic policies, and the economic and political fragmentation of the African continent. Outside the premodern subsistence agriculture domain, which is the preserve of the majority of the rural population (60 percent of the total population), its economy is ruled by the mining industry (mainly copper), which accounts for more than 80 percent of its foreign currency earnings and pays for almost all modern goods consumed in Zambia (because they have to be imported).

Zambia has an area of 752,614 square kilometers (290,586 square miles). This nation of some 9 million is peopled mainly by the Bantu (about 99 percent); the rest are made up of Europeans and South Asians. More than seventy languages are spoken in the country; however, a few dominate: Bemba in the north and center of the country, Tonga in the south, Nyanja in

the east, and Lozi in the west. Given this plurality of languages, the country chose to make English (the language of its former colonial ruler, Britain) the official language of education, business, and politics.

BACKGROUND: THE GENERAL AND FURTHER EDUCATIONAL SYSTEM

The general educational system has a 4-3-2-3 structure that includes the following stages: primary-level education, which usually begins at the age of 7, is made up of two stages that together cover a seven-year period: lower primary, lasting four years (Grades 1–4), and upper primary, lasting three years (Grades 5–7). At the end of the upper primary, students sit for the Primary School Leaving Certificate Examination, a national gatekeeping exam primarily targeted, tragically, at narrowing the pool of applicants for the much smaller number of secondary school places available than would be the case if Zambia had adequate educational resources. If successful, students may either go on to secondary education or to a vocational training school. (A small minority of students in some rural districts may also sit for a district-level gatekeeping exam at the end of the lower primary cycle.)

Secondary education covers a five-year period and is also made up of two stages: junior secondary education, lasting two years (Grades 8–9), and senior secondary education, lasting three years (Grades 10–12). (From 1972 to 1984, it was the reverse: three years for the junior level and two years for the senior level.) Between the two stages, students must sit for yet another national gatekeeping exam, the Junior Secondary School Leaving Examination, and, if successful, are allowed to proceed to the second stage of their secondary education. Those who do not continue have the option of going on to further education institutions. At the end of senior secondary education, students sit for one more national exam, the Zambia School Certificate

624

(which replaced the externally administered Cambridge Overseas School Certificate Examination in 1980). The successful ones can proceed to the two universities in the country, while the rest have the option of going on to secondary school teacher training colleges and other further education institutions or proceeding directly into the labor market. The language of instruction throughout the entire educational system is English.

Zambia also has a distance education program for those who do not succeed in obtaining secondary education. It is offered by the National Correspondence College, which was set up at the time of independence in 1964. The college has approximately 50,000 students across the country. Instruction is delivered through mailed written materials. For about half of the students—those who are recent school-leavers—it also involves tutored evening classes.

While the structure of general education in Zambia remains largely unchanged from the one that it inherited from the colonial period, there were attempts to reform it fundamentally in the late 1970s with the aim of enhancing equality of educational opportunity for all, but the effort never went beyond rhetoric (Lulat 1982; Saxby 1980). It is quite clear, therefore, that students who proceed to either one of the two universities are very privileged; unlike students in Western countries, they have gone through two (and in the case of some, even three) additional national gatekeeping exams by the time they enter university. Moreover, the unequal educational opportunity means that educational access is not guaranteed to every one at the primary or secondary levels.

FURTHER EDUCATION

Structurally located in between the two education subsectors of general education and higher education (the universities), the postsecondary education system in Zambia has a number of institutions that form the further education subsector. These are colleges (numbering about fifty in Zambia) that provide vocational training in a range of occupational fields such as agriculture, aviation, applied arts, business, nursing, teaching, and technology. Although the colonial-settler governments neglected higher education for blacks, they were not entirely averse to providing some access to further education for a privileged few in order to provide a trained labor force at the lower end of the racially segmented labor market where blacks were relegated. Examples of such colonial-era further education institutions include the Evelyn Hone College of Applied Arts and Sciences in Lusaka, which offered, and continues to offer, a variety of vocational and trade courses (for example, in secretarial studies, business, accounting, hotel management, catering, journalism, and printing); the Oppenheimer College of Social Work (in Lusaka, which was later absorbed by the University of Zambia); Jeanes Teacher Training College at Chalimbana, later renamed Chalimbana Teacher Training College, which provides training for secondary school teachers in association with the University College in Salisbury; and the Northern Technical College in Ndola for mechanical, electrical, and electronic technicians (Christensen 1972; Follis 1990).

Following independence, major strides were made in developing the further education system, so that today further education in a large number of occupational fields is available in a variety of institutions. Five types of qualifications can be obtained at these institutions, depending upon the kind and duration of training one is undertaking: the record of achievement, the craft certificate, the certificate, the advanced certificate, and the diploma. (The record of achievement, involving nine to twelve months of training, is at the bottom of the hierarchy of further education qualifications, while the diploma, involving training that usually lasts three years, is at the top.) Entrance qualifications for programs at these institutions can vary, depending on the program, from a primary school-leaving certificate to a junior secondary school-leaving certificate and on to a secondary school-leaving certificate. The duration of the programs of study range anywhere from one year (for courses in secretarial and clerical work, for example), to two years in teacher training (for certificate courses in business and agriculture, lower level technical training), to three years (for registered nurses, accounting, and upper level technical training).

The vast majority of further education schools are controlled by the government; a few are managed by religious bodies and private industry. Financially, the government has been moving in the direction of making the institutions, especially the technical training colleges, partially self-supporting through cost sharing, primarily through increased student fees. In terms of geographic location, there is a great spatial imbalance in that the overwhelming majority of the institutions are located in the center of the country in the three highly urbanized, adjacent Lusaka, Central, and Copperbelt provinces.

The following institutions, in addition to those mentioned above, are representative of the further education subsector: the Chainama College of Health Sciences (Lusaka); the Copperbelt Secondary Teachers' College (Kitwe); the Cooperative College (Lusaka); the Defense Services Command and Staff College (Lusaka); the General Post Office Staff Training College (Lusaka); the Hotel and Tourism Training Institute (Lusaka); the Kamfinsa Mobile Unit College (Kitwe); the Kafue Gorge Regional Training Center; schools of nursing in Kitwe, Lusaka, Mufulira and Ndola; the Zambia Institute of Technology (in Kitwe, now absorbed by the Copperbelt University); and Zambia Telecommunications Company College.

While these institutions represent substantial progress in the development of this subsector, it is by no means sufficient, as is indicated by enrollments. Enrollments in further education institutions range anywhere from as low as 50 to as high as 1,000. The average, though, is around 200. The key figure here, however, is the total national enrollment for the further education subsector, approximately 8,500. If one compares this figure with that for total university enrollment, which is also around 8,000, then one quickly realizes that the further education subsector is woefully undeveloped. In any country, but especially in developing countries such as Zambia, the subdegree level is critical to developing a middle cadre of trained personnel who can form the backbone of human capital resources, without which the economy will simply flounder and stagnate.

A major structural weakness plagues the further education subsector: its structural isolation from the higher education subsector. Student movement, in terms of admission, between the two subsectors is practically nonexistent. The reason is that the universities have no provisions for recognizing coursework completed at any of these institutions, apparently for fear of diluting standards. While this fear is not entirely unfounded, as will be noted in a moment, it has had the unintended effect of denying the further education subsector guidance and influence that can help it raise its academic standards to levels that can permit student interchange. A developing country needs this kind of structural flexibility to maximize the use of its meager educational resources.

In the present economic climate, however, the prospects of structural reform or increasing enrollments either at existing institutions or by means of expanding the number of further education institutions are remote. The problem of a massive downward spiral in the quality of education available at these institutions is much more urgent. This is a direct outcome of some degree of financial mismanagement coupled with the much bigger problem, over the past fifteen years, of the tyranny of an ever-shrinking base of the financial resources that are needed to fund teachers at morale-sustaining levels, physical plant and facilities, and, above all, adequate supplies of consumables (from things as basic as chalk and textbooks to essentials as complex as laboratory equipment, chemicals, and electricity and water).

While touring one of the nation's premier technical training colleges, the Northern Technical College in Ndola, a commission of inquiry (the Bobby Bwalya Commission), in the words of a news reporter, "marveled at most of the obsolete equipment students were using in their workshops." The news reporter continued:

> They were shocked when they were told students ate their meals while standing because the dining hall had no chairs or tables. One member of the commission said he thought he had entered a sports gymnasium. At the automotive workshop, students receive their lectures while standing or sitting on the desks because the classroom did not have any chairs. The sections had no running vehicle and most students graduated without running a motor vehicle engine. Most of the equipment in the electrical workshops was bought in the 1930s and they [sic] were not working properly. (*Africa News* 1997)

Under these circumstances, the fact that any kind of teaching and learning is going on in these institutions is in itself a heroic achievement on the part of teachers and students.

COPPERBELT UNIVERSITY

The origins of Copperbelt University can be traced to the 1979 University of Zambia Act, which mandated the transformation of the University of Zambia into a federal university consisting of two other constituent institutions. Besides the university itself, one was to be built in Solwezi in the North-Western Province and another at Ndola on the Copperbelt. The reason for this move was both geopolitical and pragmatic: it would provide other regions in the country with university-level institutions and it would make it possible to reach the planned final enrollment target of about 8,000 students (all of whom it would be impossible to accommodate at the existing university in Lusaka).

For logistical and financial reasons, the Solwezi branch, where the schools of agricultural sciences, veterinary medicine, and forestry were to be located, was never established. However, the Copperbelt branch was set up; not at Ndola, but at Kitwe, where the Riverside Campus of the Zambia Institute of Technology became its temporary quarters. The plan was that the new branch would eventually be moved to Ndola, where some development had already begun with the establishment in 1978 of the University at Ndola, which consisted of only the School of Business and Industrial Studies.

After the failure to fully implement the federal structure as originally envisaged, this plan was eventually abandoned with the passage of the University of Zambia Act and the Copperbelt University Act in 1987. These two acts restored the University of Zambia to its original unitary state and transformed the branch still located at Kitwe into a new autonomous institution. As of this writing, the Copperbelt University is still in Kitwe, but plans to move it to Ndola have not been abandoned. Lack of funding has been the chief stumbling block preventing the move. The curricular mission of the Copperbelt University was planned to be different from that of the University of Zambia: it would train students in fields not yet on offer at the University of Zambia (such as accountancy, architecture, and business administration). Today the university includes the following four schools: Built Environment, Business, Forestry and Wood Sciences, and Technology.

THE UNIVERSITY OF ZAMBIA: HISTORICAL BACKGROUND

The idea of creating a Zambian university was first proposed secretly in hotel bedrooms (such was the African fear of European settler opposition) at the UNESCO-sponsored Conference on the Development of Higher Education in Africa convened in 1962 in Tananarive (Stabler 1968). After all, the conference itself had gone along with the settler position that the higher education needs of the Federation were to be met by the university college in Salisbury for at least twenty more years, until 1980 (UNESCO 1963, 78). Although two years later a UNESCO education planning mission to the country would recommend the creation of a university (UNESCO 1964), the recommendation had already been upstaged by the secret and informal appointment in 1963 of the Lockwood Committee to plan the development of a university. It was set up with the advice of the American Council on Education and the Inter-University Council for Higher Education Overseas in Britain and funding from the British government and the Carnegie Corporation of New York. The committee was chaired by Sir John Lockwood (Master of Birbeck College, University of London), who had distinguished himself as an astute visionary and a strong proponent of the U.S. land-grant model in the field of higher education planning. It issued its report in late 1964, and the new Zambian government, then barely two months old, accepted its principal recommendations and proceeded to appoint a provisional council.

The Lockwood Committee reported that it was guided in its planning by two key assumptions: "Firstly, that the university must be responsive to the real needs of the country; secondly, that it must be an institution which on merit will win the respect and proper recognition of the university world" (Lockwood Committee 1964, 1). The outcome of this thinking was the creation of a university that departed considerably from the earlier pattern of education planning that had characterized the Asquith university colleges. For example, the new university would issue degrees in its own right and would not be a conduit for degrees offered by a foreign university. Moreover, it set the entrance requirements at the logistically less onerous level of Form 5 Ordinary-Level Certificate (equivalent to the Scholastic Aptitude Test in the United States), rather than the Form 6 Advanced-Level Certificate. To maintain standards, the undergraduate degree program was stretched to four years (as is the case in U.S. institutions), in contrast to the typical three years in other parts of British Africa.

In the absence of a tradition of higher education, the birth of the University of Zambia went remarkably smoothly. The entire country was mobilized to support the implementation of the Lockwood Committee report. The acquisition of a university for the new nation was dictated not only by the practical concerns of developing human capital resources but also by its significance as a symbol of independence of considerable importance. Consequently, even the financing of the university (in terms of capital expenditures) included funds derived from what came to be called the "man in the street" campaign. This campaign involved people as far down as the village level who donated gifts in kind (such as cattle, poultry, and corn), attesting to the symbolic significance of the university as a marker of independence to the populace at large.

THE STRUCTURE OF THE UNIVERSITY

The structural core of the university continues to rest on the three major founding schools: those of education, humanities and social sciences, and natural sciences. The School of Education, which since 1998 has been defined as a professional school, is one of the largest schools in the university. This is a legacy of its original mission to help Zambianize as rapidly as possible teaching staff in secondary schools, who at the time of independence were almost exclusively expatriates. While the Zambianization mission is now almost complete, the school continues to dominate the university through its departments of education, library and information studies, and in-service education and advisory services, as well as through the Center for Continuing Education.

The School of Humanities and Social Sciences, one of the original three schools, began offering courses in 1966. Its mission was to produce general education graduates who would be capable of holding a wide variety of administrative jobs in government and business and to produce professionals in fields such as law and economics. During the first decade or so, the school was organized wholly on the basis of disciplines and fields of study. However, during the 1973–1974 academic year, interdisciplinary fields of study (such as development studies and mass communication) were added. Like the natural sciences, the school is a gateway for many students wishing to go on to pursue degrees in such other schools as law and education.

The School of Natural Sciences also began offering courses

in 1966 and has also been a gateway school for students wishing to go on to schools for agricultural sciences, medicine, education, and engineering. Given its gateway mission, the school shares with the humanities and social sciences an enrollment paradox: it has a large pool of students at any one time, but its graduates are only a small fraction of this pool. The school offers its students a choice of either a general or a specialized degree.

Other schools that make up the university are the School of Agricultural Sciences (1971), the School of Engineering (1969), the School of Law (1967), the School of Medicine (1970), the School of Mines (1973), and the School of Veterinary Medicine (1984).

GOVERNANCE AND UNIVERSITY AUTONOMY

Besides the deans and the heads of departments, the university is comprised of the following principal governing offices and bodies: the chancellor, the vice-chancellor, the registrar, the bursar, the university council, the senate, and boards of studies. The chancellor's office is a titular office, and until the so-called third republic came into being, it was occupied by the country's head of state (the president). Now the occupant of the office is appointed by the head of state from among the nation's "distinguished" persons. The vice-chancellor is equivalent to the president in U.S. universities. Until recently, the university council appointed the vice-chancellor. Now the appointment is the responsibility of the education minister. The council itself is also appointed by the minister, and the composition of its membership is at the minister's sole discretion. Usually it consists of the top-level administrators of the university, representatives from the senate and the student body, and persons outside the university representing government industry and various professions. The registrar and bursar are appointed by the university council. Their role is to assist with the administration of the academic and financial aspects of the university, respectively.

The university senate is made up of members of the academic teaching staff. Its role is almost identical to that of senates in U.S. universities: it is concerned strictly with university-wide academic policies dealing with such matters as pedagogy, general degree requirements, enrollments, curriculum, and procedures for the hiring and promotion of faculty. Each school has a board of studies, appointed by the senate, comprised of the school's academic staff and representatives from other schools in the university. Chaired by the school's dean, its role is to determine such academic matters as courses offered, course sequences, degree requirements for the specific school, and course syllabi. In other words, matters that would ordinarily be within the purview of departments in U.S. universities are handled at the school level by the boards of studies.

Until the passage of the 1999 University Act, the university enjoyed a considerable degree of autonomy. To be sure, on many occasions the government moved to close the university and expel students (and at times even members of the teaching staff) when it felt, rightly or wrongly, that they had gone beyond simple criticism of government policies to provocation of opposition that had the potential to undermine its survival. In less turbulent times, however, when the ruling regime did not feel threatened, the university council was indeed the supreme governing body, and governmental influence on it was highly restricted, effected primarily through the minority representation on the council. The new act, however, introduced a sea change. The minister of education now has effective power over the university; the act gives the minister sweeping powers, including the ability to bypass the university council and/or the university senate at will. This change was not greeted with equanimity by the university community, which was vehemently opposed to the change. Despite an attempt to derail it through legal challenges in the courts, it was powerless in the end to block it.

STUDENT ADMISSION AND ENROLLMENTS

Today an applicant requesting admission for an undergraduate degree must, at the minimum, have the following qualifications: passes at credit level in at least five subjects in the Zambian School Certificate (or Cambridge Overseas School Certificate) or passes in at least five subjects in the General Certificate of Education Ordinary-Level Examinations. At the same time, the subjects must be selected from a list specified by the university to ensure clear separation of content. Related subjects such as biology and zoology cannot be considered as meeting the five-subject requirement.

The abolition of the sixth form in 1967 did, without doubt, produce the intended effect: enrollments of students escalated very rapidly; in fact, far more rapidly than anticipated by the Lockwood Committee. The university opened in 1966 with a mere 312 students. The Committee had recommended that within five years this number should be doubled. Instead, the figure had already reached more than 1,000 students by 1970. Four years later, this number had more than doubled to 2,500 students. In 1980, it stood at a little under 4,000, and today the enrollment is approximately 5,000 students.

The Lockwood Committee had recommended that the student body should not be composed entirely of Zambian nationals but should include a small proportion of non-Zambian nationals living within and outside the country, a tradition that continues even though there are today far more Zambian applicants than the number of places available. The catchment area for foreign students is the English-speaking Southern African region. The percentage of non-nationals as a proportion of the whole student body is roughly 5 percent.

WOMEN IN HIGHER EDUCATION

As is the case in most other parts of Africa, the sex ratio in the student body, the faculty, and the administration of Zambia's universities is male dominated. Thirty years ago, for every female, roughly 4.5 male students attended the University of Zambia. Today the picture has improved, but only slightly: the ratio is roughly three males for every female. The problem here is not entirely of the university's making; rather, it begins at the lower levels of the educational system. By the time students sit for the Zambia School Certificate Examination, there is already a considerable imbalance in the male-female ratio. Whereas enrollments of males and females in the first year of primary education are almost identical, a divergence in favor of males begins to become clearly evident as each year progresses. Furthermore,

the gap widens progressively as one goes up the educational ladder. The educational underrepresentation of women in Zambia is starkly evident from statistics gleaned from the UNESCO Statistical Yearbook (UNESCO 1999). While the illiteracy rate of females aged 15 and older has been going down since independence, it is still twice that of males. In the latest year for which data is available (1994), the gross enrollment ratios were as follows: at the primary level, 88 percent for females and 94 percent for males; at the secondary school level, 21 percent for females and 34 percent for males; and at the tertiary (higher plus further [nonuniversity] education) level, 1 percent for females and 4 percent for males.

The reasons for the very troubling disparities in the educational circumstances of men and women in Zambia are both cultural and educational. From the perspective of culture, formal education has always been viewed as a male domain because of its role in preparing students for the world of formal, nonagricultural work, which has been and continues to be seen as the primary preserve of males (though a little less so today than in the past). The origins of this view are in colonialism. Missionaries and the colonial authorities felt that the proper place of women was in the home and not outside in the workplace. At the same time, the fact that the modern economic sector that provided the largest number of wage-paying jobs was the mining sector did not help matters. It simply reinforced the view that work outside the home was the prerogative of males (unless, of course, it was caretaking work).

The power of culture is so great that it permeates classroom pedagogy to the point that the performance of female students in exams, including national exams, has been consistently below that of male students (with tragic consequences for their educational careers).

Still, there is one thing that the university can do to ameliorate the imbalance in the sex ratio. It can develop and implement an affirmative action program for females based on the following four elements: publicity at the secondary school level of the university's commitment to an increase in female admissions, a lower threshold for admission qualifications for female applicants, compensatory tutoring once applicants are admitted, and an institutional infrastructure that is exclusively targeted at the concerns of female students.

However, it is doubtful that the university now has the capacity for such enlightened policies, given the context of a highly patriarchal society that has developed over the decades since colonialism first created the country. (Traditional, precolonial Zambia was predominantly—though not exclusively—matrilineal and matrilocal.) As Rude succinctly puts it: "Within Zambian society, women are underrepresented in all professional fields, government and leadership positions, and the armed forces, and they lag behind men in education and training, access to health care and resources, and ownership of land and businesses" (1999, 11–12). Of course, Zambia is not unique in this regard, but this fact is irrelevant to Zambian women, especially when economic and educational discrimination is aligned with a virulent form of patriarchal oppression. As Rude points out, injuries due to assault by men appear to be the leading cause of women's admission to the casualty ward of Lusaka's main hospital, and there is no reason to believe that this is not the case in other cities and towns across the country. Marital rape is not recognized by Zambian statutory law; even worse, it is not unknown for local courts to order wives to have sex with their husbands when the wives do not wish to do so. Men who murder, torture, or rape women often go free or are given light sentences, if they are ever brought to court at all. Sexual harassment of women in the workplace is treated as if it were all but a constitutionally protected right of males (Daka-Mulwanda 1992; Mitchell et al. 1999; Shifferraw 1982; Siame 1998; Swainson 1996; and Temu 1992).

PROGRAMS OF STUDY

Students are admitted in their first year to either the School of Humanities and Social Sciences or to the School of Natural Sciences, depending upon what path their university career will take. Thereafter, they will proceed in either one of two directions: a minority will remain within the schools to pursue relevant majors and a majority will move on to other specialized schools in the university. Depending on where they go, their course of study will last anywhere from four to seven years. For example, the length of the education degree is four years, that of the engineering degree is five years, while that of veterinary medicine is six and that of medicine is seven.

From its inception, the university avoided the British tradition of single-subject honors degrees in liberal studies in favor of less specialized degrees characteristic of U.S. land-grant universities. The thinking was that students graduating at the undergraduate level with a major and a minor field specialization (achieved on the basis of a broad array of course offerings) were better placed to help with the development of the country's human capital resources, especially at the administrative and managerial levels. It was believed that personnel capable of performing in a variety of jobs would be in greater demand than those trained for only one type of work. At the same time, the university curriculum was designed, again for human capital reasons, to be heavily oriented toward professional training (Ashby 1966). But the emphasis on professional training has been taken to such an extreme as to deny a rightful place for the performing arts (such as music, dance, painting, and theater) in the university curriculum. Even a developing country needs arts teachers in schools. In the absence of an arts program, however, it has not been possible to graduate teachers capable of teaching art and music. The arts are absolutely crucial for the development of the creative and intellectual functions of a child's brain. The long-term damage to the creative and intellectual development of Zambian children, given the continued absence of arts teachers in schools, is incalculable (Akapelwa 1989).

In a typical four-year degree program, students take a minimum of four year-long courses annually that lead toward a basic sixteen-course degree. Each course requires a minimum of four contact hours per week per academic year. (The minimum number of credit hours a student must successfully complete is 128.) Courses equivalent to four credit hours also exist, but they are called and considered to be "half-courses." Out of the sixteen courses, the student will construct a program of study that may follow the path of a traditional single-subject specialization or may cross subject boundaries while still retaining disciplinary

coherence. The person responsible for ensuring that students are registered in appropriate courses is the head of the department. Without her or his permission, a student may not register in any course. No separate academic advisement system for students akin to that in U.S. universities exists in Zambia.

GRADUATE STUDIES AND RESEARCH

The School of Graduate Studies coordinates the graduate studies program at the university. However, the University of Zambia, like its counterpart (Copperbelt University), is primarily an undergraduate institution. Students who wish to proceed to graduate-level studies will find that their choices are somewhat limited. While a master's-level degree is now offered by all the schools (but not in all programs), very few offer a doctorate. The master's degree, regardless of the school in which it is being taught, is normally a two-year program based on coursework in the first year (concluding with a comprehensive written examination) and research leading to a dissertation in the second year. Under special circumstances, the first year may be waived. The minimum duration of the program for full-time students is, under normal circumstances, fifteen months; the maximum duration is three years.

Graduate education places special demands on an institution, ranging from the hiring of graduate-level teaching staff to the provision of research facilities, including a library with extensive and continually updated holdings. All this, however, requires money, which the university sorely lacks. At the same time, the long-standing practice, until recently, of sending staff development fellows (graduates recruited for eventual appointment as members of the teaching staff upon successful completion of their graduate studies) abroad for their master's degrees did not help matters. Little if any attention was paid to using the staff development program as an incubator for graduate studies.

Under a regime of adequate financial resources, one also would have seen by now a desirable shift in the mission of the university toward greater emphasis on graduate-level education. This would have involved shifting undergraduate programs of study to four-year university colleges (colleges with a special relationship with the university that offered University of Zambia degrees) established across the country. These university colleges could have then matured into independent universities in their own right, offering their own degrees. As of yet, however, Zambia has no university college.

As would be expected, in the absence of a well-developed doctoral-level graduate studies program, the research activities of the university are also at a low level of development. Some research is taking place, but faculty productivity is pathetically low. Much of the research being undertaken today by individual faculty is done at the behest of external development aid agencies, which have their own specific agendas. The result is that such research remains uncoordinated; even worse, findings are often restricted to the archives of the sponsor.

Many factors have worked against the use of the university as "a creative center of research," to use the words of the Lockwood Committee report (1964, 1). These include:

- The persistence to date of a general tradition within both the university administration and the government of viewing the university as no more than a human capital resource factory, despite occasional pronouncements to the contrary

- The failure to develop a research infrastructure, ranging from funding support, to adequate computer and lab facilities, to proper library resources. Even such basic necessities as photocopying facilities are not easily available to faculty

- The lack of a clearly articulated and systematically enforced policy on the place of research in the spectrum of faculty duties, with the result that the research initiative is left almost entirely to ambitious or academically enthusiastic individuals, especially since tenure is not determined by research output

- The practice of overloading faculty with teaching and administrative duties, leaving those who are dedicated to their duties with little time for anything else

- The emerging practice of faculty moonlighting at other jobs to augment shrinking salaries (in the face of spiraling inflation and static salary bases) which further depletes the already small budget for research

- The lack of adequately trained and competent administrative and secretarial help that can ease the burden of performing day-to-day chores and thereby create time for research

- The absence of a well-developed publishing infrastructure, either in or outside the university, that can provide additional motivation and an outlet for one's research effort

- The slow but sure erosion of general faculty morale

FACULTY RECRUITMENT AND RETENTION

Zambia began at independence with a pool of university graduates that was among the smallest in British colonial Africa. Not surprisingly, then, the establishment of new institutions and the expansion of existing ones required a massive recruitment of expatriate personnel from almost all corners of the world, but principally from the Commonwealth countries. In this regard, the university was no exception; its founding required wholesale importing of both teaching staff and upper administrative staff. Even the head cook in the university's dining hall, at one point, was an expatriate, as was the person in charge of maintaining the university grounds. In light of these circumstances, the university launched an aggressive staff development program to facilitate the rapid indigenization of the teaching and administrative staff. The program involved identifying outstanding graduates of the university who wished to pursue a teaching or administrative career in the university and providing them with scholarships to pursue graduate studies (at both the master's and doctoral levels) abroad, coupled with the guarantee of a position upon successful completion of their studies. It is a testimony to the success of this program that indigenization of the teaching and administrative staff at the university is now more or less complete (Kashoki 1994).

The few expatriate personnel who can still be found at the university are there because some teaching fields (such as medicine) still lack sufficient Zambian applicants and because of the university's enlightened policy that at least 10 percent of teaching positions should be reserved for foreign teachers (to ensure the university's linkage with the international university commu-

nity). Parenthetically, it ought to be noted that the success of the staff development program is also an indication of the high academic standards that the university maintained until recently. Current Zambian teaching staff obtained their graduate-level qualifications at such reputable institutions as Cambridge University, the University of Guelph, Harvard University, the University of Helsinki, University of London, University of Manchester, Oxford University, the University of Sussex, the University of Toronto, and Tulane University.

However, a number of serious ongoing and emergent issues concerning faculty personnel need to be addressed by the university such as gender imbalance, low research output, underdevelopment of graduate studies, attrition through brain drain, and low faculty morale. The imbalance in the male-female ratio at the student level is, not surprisingly, present among faculty and the upper administrative staff as well. Approximately 12 percent of the current faculty is female. This is not an acceptable situation. Of course, the problem is not entirely of the university's making. A female undergraduate with the requisite qualifications and ambition to teach in the university would have no difficulty being appointed as a staff development fellow (the first step toward academic employment in the university). The problem, however, has been a dearth of such candidates, not only because the pool of female undergraduates is small to begin with, but because the demands of culture have undermined recruitment of females for the staff development program, the most obvious being the emphasis on women's role in marriage and family building. In a society that still looks heavily askance at unmarried women, the pressure on women to terminate their educational career upon completion of the undergraduate degree is immense, especially when it involves study abroad. Is there anything the university can do? The university should pursue at least three lines of action: it should institute an affirmative action program at the level of undergraduate student admissions, undertake an affirmative action program at the level of staff recruitment, and vigorously pursue an affirmative action program with respect to recruitment and promotion of administrative staff.

In the context of the deep shortfall in indigenous human capital resources at independence and the exacerbation of this shortfall in the post-independence period created by the massive development of the parastatal economic sector, the government unabashedly raided the university's best and brightest to meet its own personnel needs. Qualified staff unhesitatingly left the university, succumbing to promises of higher pay, richer perks, and elevation of status. From the very beginning, then, the university has had to deal with the contradictory circumstances of a concerted program for the rapid indigenization of personnel against a backdrop of a constant hemorrhaging of the same personnel into the external labor market.

This contradiction, sadly, has not disappeared; it continues, but in a slightly different guise. The blandishments are no longer from the government (which is now not only poverty stricken but has, at the behest of its international creditors, overseen the painful demolition of the parastatal sector), but from universities elsewhere in Africa, especially southern Africa. In other words, any faculty member who can find a position at a university outside the country will most likely leave, as many have already done. Countries that have received Zambian university teaching personnel include Botswana, Namibia, South Africa, and Swaziland. This problem of brain drain threatens to become even more severe, given the deteriorating economic situation in the country and the resultant impoverishment of the university itself.

In addition to brain drain, the unusual involvement of faculty in industrial action (organized by their union), which sometimes leads to the closure of the university, is another symptom of low faculty morale. The latest closure resulting from pay-related faculty action occurred in 1999, while in February 2000, faculty boycotted classes for two weeks. Factors behind the erosion of morale among faculty at the university include the following:

- Faculty salaries have not kept up with inflation, while pay for those teaching at the University of Zambia is even lower than that of faculty at the newer Copperbelt University.
- The chronic underfunding of the university has led to a serious deterioration of academic infrastructure and resources, from the physical plant to the library.
- Teaching loads are heavy and class enrollments have ballooned.
- Many faculty feel that the university is slowly being turned into a government department with all the negative implications that entails for an institution of higher learning.
- The administration of the university is inefficient and even corrupt. Top-level administrators have been accused of siphoning off or misspending thousands of dollars.

FINANCE

At the time of independence, the view of the government was that no qualified citizen should be denied access to education for lack of funds. With a healthy budget, thanks to the high price of copper (the country's economic mainstay), the government could afford to hold this expansive view. Consequently, for nearly two decades following independence, virtually no fees were charged by institutions that were financed or supported by the government at any level. However, in the face of severe budgetary constraints in the aftermath of the collapse of world copper prices, it slowly dawned on the government that free education, while highly desirable, was no longer affordable. It would take roughly another decade following the onset of the economic crisis, however, before it would take hesitant steps, beginning in the mid-1980s, toward implementing a system of modest cost sharing at all levels of the educational system. Yet, even today, the proportion of the cost sharing that students are responsible for is still quite small: at the university level, students are obligated to pay 25 percent of the annual tuition the university receives from the government (approximately $3,500) on behalf of each student. Virtually all university students of Zambian nationality are on scholarship, as are college students at government-supported institutions. Proposals for a higher level of cost sharing by students have been hamstrung by three major constraints: political opposition from students and parents; the

inability to come up with a bureaucratically viable means-tested student loan scheme; and the sheer magnitude of poverty within the country. Those who are potentially able to afford higher tuition fees are most likely not even studying at government institutions: they are either in private institutions or are studying abroad.

On the institutional side, the matter of finance has become a highly problematic issue in the face of the persistent government budgetary difficulties. Moneys are not always made available to the universities on a timely basis. Moreover, the government pays little attention to inflationary erosions when it makes budgetary allocations, despite the disheartening magnitude of such erosions in recent years. Of course, the universities (as well as some of the technical and business colleges) could reduce their endemic financial difficulties by decreasing their massive dependence on the government through the development of independent sources of finance. To date, however, neither alumni-dependent, endowment-based, nor entrepreneurial-based financial support has been effectively exploited.

DISTANCE EDUCATION

From the very beginning of the establishment of the University of Zambia, it was decided that a unit should be set up within the university that would coordinate the provision of distance education (referred to then as correspondence education). The immediate reason for this was to salvage the ambitions for higher education that colonialism had thwarted among those who could not become full-time on-campus students at the newly established university because of age, commitments to families and jobs, or other reasons. Moreover, Zambia had a modest tradition of studying by correspondence through such British commercial colleges as Rapid Results College and Wolsey Hall. This autonomous unit, which was based on the model of the correspondence studies department of the University of New England in Australia (which used regular faculty and not separate distance education faculty), was set up in 1966 as the Department of Correspondence Studies. The following year, it admitted the first students (numbering 150, equal to about half of the full-time enrollment) (Siaciwena 1988).

The following are basic features of the modus operandi of distance education at the university:

- Applicants must have the same entrance qualifications as full-time students, though exceptions can be made for older students who can demonstrate substitutable experience.
- Delivery of educational content takes place through two principal means: written course material and face-to-face contact during a mandatory four-week residential school at the beginning of the academic year. (Technologies such as television, VCRs, and the Internet remain to be exploited, primarily because they are still not available across the country.) Suggestions have been put forward to develop educational technology centers in provincial capitals that would help to further the distance education effort; however, this would still not take care of the needs of all students, since many live far from provincial capitals.

- The areas of study available to distance education students include accounting, finance, economics, agriculture, law, engineering, arts and humanities, and social sciences, among others, but only at the first-year and second-year levels. (Unlike in the past, it is no longer possible to obtain a full degree through distance education. Instead, after successful completion of the first two years, students must become full-time on-campus students.)

- Instruction is provided by regular faculty who, unlike in the past, are given additional pay for taking on distance education instructional duties. The use of regular faculty for the provision of distance education has always been a complicated issue for the distance education program from its inception: while it ensured that the educational value of the degree earned was commensurate with that of a degree earned through full-time study, it did not always bode well for students in terms of learning and instruction (Nyirenda 1989).

- Enrollment in the distance education program is roughly around 800 students today. Of these students, about 150 usually graduate to full-time status each year.

The continuation of the distance education program in the face of the severe budgetary problems that the university faces is among its more exemplary achievements. However, the massive reduction in offerings the program has suffered over the years (though it once offered six degrees, it offers none today) represents a major step backward at a time when distance education is on the threshold of an explosion throughout the world using new technologies such as the Internet.

COMMUNITY SERVICE

Given the urgency of so many development-related problems, particularly when universities are often the sole or primary repositories of cutting-edge research and knowledge, community service must be considered among the foundational pillars of the university mission. Essentially, community service is the extension of university expertise in the service of improving the quality of life of the community and should be integral to all aspects of the university.

In practice, however, the university has not implemented this concept of community service. With the exception of a few traditional avenues (such as running the teaching hospital and allowing public access to the university's library facilities), the university has hitherto followed the path taken by many other universities elsewhere in Africa: it has built ivory towers that are far removed from the problems of society at large.

However, there is now a greater involvement of the university in community service than in the past, even if it is still on an ad hoc basis. A number of factors account for this development. The severe budgetary problems of the university have pushed it in the direction of looking for ways to diversify its traditional source of funding support, which has meant engaging in entrepreneurial activities based on its expertise. The continuing downward slide in faculty salaries brought about by the ravages of inflation has pushed some faculty to engage in the increasingly lucrative cottage industry of "development consultancy," for which one is often paid in dollars. Yet the universities have a

long way to go toward evolving into true community service institutions.

STUDENT ACTIVISM AND ACADEMIC FREEDOM

Anyone familiar with the history of the University of Zambia cannot help but notice the constant theme of student unrest disrupting the academic life of the university, even to the extent of precipitating closures of the campus through government decrees. The number of times the university has been closed—for periods ranging from one to six months, if not longer—as a result of student activism is indicated by the following sample list (with the primary cause of the student unrest that precipitated the closure indicated in parentheses): August 2000 (boarding fees), January 2000 (tuition fees), May 1999 (meal allowances), March 1997 (meal and book allowances), November 1996 (national politics), April 1990 (national politics), April 1989 (tuition fees), May 1986 (dispute over administrative matters), February 1984 (campus politics), April 1981 (national politics), February 1976 (national politics), and July 1971 (national politics). While these closures may suggest a severe lack of academic freedom at the university, this is not entirely so. To be sure, the government's reaction to student criticisms regarding its policies has been hasty, harsh, and undemocratic at times, but at other times it has had no choice but to intervene in the interest of campus safety and security.

Student activism is not unique to Zambia; however, student activism at the University of Zambia has been remarkable in its permanence. Even in the face of police and military brutality (involving at times rape, beatings, imprisonment without charges, and even murder) and frequent expulsion of student leaders, the students have remained undaunted. What are the causes of the student unrest, which, it must be conceded, has greatly raised the unit cost of higher education in Zambia and has produced other negative academic consequences? The government's answer, provided through the report of a commission of inquiry (the Bobby Bwalya Commission) appointed in April 1997, is that the students are motivated by selfish concerns (Government of Zambia 1998). This is a partial and simplistic answer because it does not address the student unrest in the period prior to the onset of the endemic fiscal crisis that has plagued the university since the mid-1980s.

A more cogent explanation rests in the interplay of the following key factors:

- The relative newness of the process of political institutionalization and the inadequacy of channels for the proper and effective management of political conflict within and outside the university

- The amplification of the university's role within national politics, arising from its location in the nation's capital

- The inherent contradiction among the three dominant functions performed by universities in developing countries: the intrinsic (creating indigenous human capital resources), the symbolic (signifying attainment of nationhood), and the solidary (assisting with national integration by remaining apolitical)

- The development of a contradictory student consciousness

stemming from the students' structural location within society (a potential elite that is still rooted in the lower classes), specifically in a developing country that is not really developing as envisaged and hoped

- The existence of partial democracy within the country with one-party political dictatorship (either de jure or de facto) (Lulat 1981, 1989; Burawoy 1976)

FOREIGN AID

As has been the case for almost all other African countries, Zambia has been (and continues to be) a recipient of foreign aid targeted at the development of its higher and further education infrastructure and, on a lesser scale, at the provision of educational materials and the training of teaching staff. While the aid has been generally modest and short-term, it has come from a variety of countries, multilateral agencies, and private foundations and in a variety of forms, including direct money grants to be expended as planners deemed fit, aid in kind (such as library books), aid targeted at the development of specific aspects of the infrastructure (for example, a building or a program of study), scholarships for faculty development, technical assistance with planning, and provision of teaching personnel for temporary staffing.

While aid of any kind for the development of the educational infrastructure is generally a positive thing, sometimes the aid does not serve its intended purpose, is much too limited to be effective, or is misused.

In recent years, the dire economic straits of the country have helped to highlight another kind of problem: the uselessness of aid when there is full prior recognition that no local funds exist to permit the continued functioning of the aid project following its completion. An example of this would be building expensive laboratories when maintenance of the laboratories clearly cannot be guaranteed. Under these circumstances, the motives of the donor become highly questionable: perhaps the aid project was agreed to more for political reasons than for altruistic ones. If there is a genuine desire on the part of aid donors to assist with the development of the educational infrastructure, then a new aid model must be developed, perhaps one that involves not only capital expenditure support for a given project but also recurrent expenditure support on a diminishing shared-cost basis (for example, 100 percent support in the first year, 90 percent in the second year, 80 percent in the third year, and so on) upon completion of the project. There is a clear need for imaginative approaches to the aid relationship (Sikwibele 1989; Carlsson 1997).

PRIVATE HIGHER EDUCATION

Private higher education institutions do not exist in Zambia. However, there are a few educational institutions run by Christian missionaries, industrial corporations, and commercial enterprises at the further education level. The absence of private higher education is a consequence of both history and demand. Historically, the British higher education model that the colonies inherited did not include a tradition of private higher education (other than that provided by Christian missionaries), and

there does not exist a sufficient demand in Zambia to permit the entry of private higher education institutions. Since government policy does not discourage private higher education, it is likely that as demand for higher education builds, a private university may be established, most likely by a religious foundation.

CONCLUSION

At least from a quantitative point of view, the development of higher education in Zambia is nothing short of miraculous. The country began with no universities, a handful of colleges, and about 100 or so persons with degrees. Some three decades later, it boasts two universities, numerous colleges, and persons with degrees numbering in the thousands—possibly as many as 25,000—including hundreds with Ph.D.s. Whatever may be said of the only two regimes that have ruled the country since independence, at least they did not neglect education, including higher education, even during periods of severely limited financial resources.

More, of course, could be done if only funds were available. For example, the Bobby Bwalya Commission (Government of Zambia 1998) recommended upgrading the six largest colleges in the country into university colleges with affiliation to the University of Zambia. Such a development would mark a major quantitative step forward. However, under the present circumstances of dire financial straits, the expansion of the higher education system is not even remotely possible. What is even worse is that, as a result of these circumstances, whatever quantitative and qualitative progress has been achieved so far in education generally is now under relentless assault.

Without a doubt, the quality and standards of Zambian higher education are no longer what they used to be. The issue is not so much lack of trained personnel (although that is also becoming a problem in some fields as a result of brain drain), but the sheer lack of resources, including educational materials such as textbooks, equipment for biology and computer labs, furniture and fittings, access to a steady and ample supply of water and electricity, library books and periodical subscriptions, office supplies and photocopying machines, and administrative buildings and student dormitories. Everything is lacking at levels needed to maintain minimum educational quality and standards.

Moreover, we have no indication that the present socioeconomic and political circumstances of the country will turn around any time soon. Consider the following problems:

- The country is now being buffeted economically by the relentless pressure of external aid donors to sell the country's national resources back to foreign capitalists for a song, and by the merciless forces of economic globalization.
- Zambia's crippling national debt burden, among the largest in sub-Saharan Africa, is consuming more than 50 percent of the country's foreign exchange earnings annually in interest payments to external creditors.
- Potentially the most productive segment of the population is undergoing depletion and weakening on a terrible scale as a consequence of the rampant epidemic of HIV/AIDS that has

gripped the country over the past decade and which shows no signs of relenting.

- The country continues to be governed by a corrupt Machiavellian de facto one-party dictatorship that is little different from the one it replaced in 1990, even though it came to power through peaceful elections.

- There are no indications anywhere that copper, the country's principal source of income, will ever reach prices on the world market equal to the historic highs of the 1960s and early 1970s.

- Over the years, as a result of severe internal mismanagement and external negative pressures, Zambia has become a very poor country with an annual per capita gross domestic product (GDP) that now stands at just $330 (compared to the sub-Saharan African average of $480). It is estimated that more than 80 percent of the population now lives at or below the poverty line.

- Not surprisingly, the average life expectancy at birth, which once was over 50 years, is now less than 40 (compared with the sub-Saharan African average of 51 years); under the devastating impact of AIDS, the average is projected to drop to about 31 in a decade or so.

- The wholesale program of structural adjustment (one of the most severe ever embarked upon by any country in the world) undertaken at the behest of the International Monetary Fund and the World Bank has done absolutely nothing positive for the GDP growth rate, which continues to decline, even while population growth has continued apace at about 3 percent annually.

Under these circumstances, the best that the country can hope for in the years to come is to not stumble into the abyss of massive terror, anarchy, and kleptocracy that have gripped countries such as Liberia, Sierra Leone, and Somalia.

Note: Research for this chapter was funded in part by a grant from the Center for Comparative and Global Studies in Education at the University at Buffalo, the State University of New York (facilitated by the center's director, William B. Cummings).

REFERENCES

Africa, H. P. 1980. "Language in Education in a Multilingual State: A Case Study of the Role of English in the Educational System of Zambia." Ph.D. thesis, University of Toronto.

Africa News. 1997. "Zambia: Nortec Shocks Bwalya Probe Team." July 4.

Akapelwa, E. 1989. "Problems of Music Education: A Comparative Study [Zambia, Great Britain]." Ph.D. thesis, Queen's University of Belfast.

Ashby, E. 1966. Universities: British, Indian, African—A Study in the Ecology of Higher Education. Cambridge, Mass.: Harvard University Press, and London: Weidenfeld and Nicolson.

Bikas, S. C., J. H. Case, P. S. Dow, and M. E. Jackman. 1976. Higher Education and the Labour Market in Zambia: Expectations and Performance. Paris: UNESCO.

Burawoy, M. 1976. "Consciousness and Contradiction: A Study of Student Protest in Zambia." British Journal of Sociology 27, no. 1: 78–97.

Carlsson, J. 1997. "The Effectiveness of the Aid Relationship in Zam-
bia." In J. Carlsson, G. Somolekae, and N. van de Walle, eds., Foreign Aid in Africa: Learning from Country Experiences, 194–209. Uppsala: Nordiska Afrikainstitutet.

Christensen, J. E. 1972. "Occupational Education in Zambia: Obstacles to the Development of Technical and Vocational Education Programs in Zambia, 1885–1970." Ph.D. diss., University of California, Los Angeles.

Coombe, T. A. 1968. "The Origins of Secondary Education in Zambia: A Study in Colonial Policy-Making." Ph.D. diss., Harvard University.

Daka-Mulwanda, V. 1992. "Women in Development and Feminism: A Critical Analysis [Zambia]." Ph.D. diss., University of Missouri–Columbia.

Follis. B. 1990. "A Comparative Study of Vocational/Technical Education in Zambia and Zimbabwe, 1900–1987." Ph.D. diss., University of Liverpool.

Galabawa, J. C. J. 1993. Study on Cost Effectiveness and Efficiency in African Universities: A Case Study of the University of Zambia (UNZA). Accra: Association of African Universities.

Government of Zambia. 1985. Government Reaction to the Main Recommendations of the Commission of Inquiry into the Affairs of the University of Zambia. Lusaka: Government Printer.

———. 1986. Report of the Commission of Inquiry Appointed to Inquire into the Affairs of the University of Zambia. Lusaka: Government Printer.

———. 1988. Report of the Working Party Appointed by the Hon. Minister of Higher Education to Advise on the Transformation and Incorporation of the Zambia Institute of Technology into the Copperbelt University, School of Technology. Lusaka: Government Printer.

———. 1998. Report of the Commission of Inquiry Appointed to Inquire into Operations at the University of Zambia and the Copperbelt University. Lusaka: Government Printer.

Grotpeter, J. J., B. V. Siegel, and J. R. Pletcher. 1998. Historical Dictionary of Zambia. Lanham, Md., and London: Scarecrow.

Kaplan, I., ed. 1979. Zambia: A Country Study. Washington, D.C.: U.S. Government Printing Office.

Kashoki, M. E. 1994. "The African University: Towards Innovative Management Strategies for the 21st Century." In J. Barnes, et al., Higher Education Staff Development: Directions for the Twenty-First Century, 149–62. Paris: UNESCO.

Leys, C. 1971. "The Role of the University in an Underdeveloped Country." Journal of Eastern African Research and Development 1, no. 1.

Lockwood Committee. 1964. Report on the Development of a University in Northern Rhodesia. Lusaka: Government Printer.

Lulat, Y. G.-M. 1981. "Determinants of Third World Student Activism in the Seventies: The Case of Zambia." In P. G. Altbach, ed., Student Politics: Perspectives for the Eighties, 234–66. Metuchen, N.J.: Scarecrow.

———. 1982. "Political Constraints on Educational Reform for Development: Lessons from an African Experience." Comparative Education Review 26 (June): 235–253.

———. 1989. "Zambia." In P. G. Altbach, ed., Student Political Activism: An International Reference Handbook, 37–56. Westport, Conn.: Greenwood.

Lungu, G. F. 1980. "The Land-Grant Model in Africa: A Study in Higher Education Transfer." Ed.D. dissertation, Harvard University.

———. 1993. "Educational Policy-making in Colonial Zambia: The Case of Higher Education for Africans from 1924 to 1964." Journal of Negro History 78, no. 4 (Autumn): 207–232.

Mawema, M. A. 1981. British and Portuguese Colonialism in Central African Education. Ed.D. dissertation, Columbia University Teachers College.

Metzler, J. D. 1988. "The State, Settlers, Missionaries and Rural Dwellers: A Comparative Historical Analysis of the Politics, Economics and Sociology of Education Policy—Its Formation, Its Implementation and Its Consequences in Colonial Northern Rhodesia and Southern Rhodesia." Ph.D. dissertation, University of Wisconsin–Madison.

Mitchell, C., M. Blaeser, B. Chilangwa, and I. M. Maimbolwa-Sinyangwe. 1999. "Girls' Education in Zambia: Everyone's Responsibility—A Policy Framework for Participatory Process." *International Review of Education* 45, nos. 5/6: 417–430.

Musambachime, M. 1990. "The Impact of Rapid Population Growth and Economic Decline on the Quality of Education: The Case of Zambia." *Review of African Political Economy*, no. 48: 81–92.

Mwanakatwe, J. M. 1968. *The Growth of Education in Zambia Since Independence.* Lusaka: Oxford University Press.

Nyirenda, J. 1989. "Organization of Distance Education at the University of Zambia: An Analysis of the Practice." *Distance Education* 10, no. 1: 148–156.

Ragsdale, J. P. 1986. *Protestant Mission Education in Zambia, 1880 to 1954.* London and Toronto: Associated University Presses.

Rude, D. 1999. "Reasonable Men and Provocative Women: An Analysis of Gendered Domestic Homicide in Zambia." *Journal of Southern African Studies* 25, no. 1: 7–28.

Saxby, J. C. 1980. "The Politics of Education in Zambia." Ph.D. diss., University of Toronto.

Shifferraw, M. 1982. "Educational Policy and Practice Affecting Females in Zambian Secondary Schools." Ph.D. diss., University of Wisconsin–Milwaukee.

Siaciwena, R. 1988. "A Study of Distance Teaching at the University of Zambia with Special Reference to the Effectiveness of Degree Courses." Ph.D. diss., University of Wales.

———. 1997. "Organizational Changes at the University of Zambia." *Open Learning* 12, no. 3: 57–61.

Siame, M., et al. 1998. *Women in Zambia: A Profile of Women in Zambia.* Lusaka: Zambia Association for Research and Development, and Harare: Southern African Research and Documentation Centre.

Sikwibele, A. L. 1989. "International Education Assistance to Higher Education Development in Zambia: Problems, Policy Implications, and Future Prospects." Ph.D. diss., University of Illinois at Urbana-Champaign.

Snelson, P. D. 1970. *Educational Development in Northern Rhodesia 1883–1945.* Lusaka: National Educational Company of Zambia, 1974.

Stabler, J. B. 1968. "The University of Zambia: Its Origin and First Year." *Journal of Higher Education* 39 (January): 32–38.

Swainson, N. 1996. *Redressing Gender Inequalities in Education: A Review of Constraints and Priorities in Malawi, Zambia, and Zimbabwe.* London: Overseas Development Administration, the British Development Division in Central Africa.

Tembo, L. P. 1973. "University of Zambia." In T. M. Yesufu, ed., *Creating the African University: Emerging Issues in the 1970s,* 226–243. Ibadan and London: Oxford University Press.

Temu, J. R. 1992. "Women and Higher Education in Selected African Nations, 1960–1980: Enrollment Analyses and Former Student Perceptions." Ph.D. diss., Kent State University.

UNESCO. 1963. *The Development of Higher Education in Africa: Report of the Conference on the Development of Higher Education in Africa, Tananarive, 3–12 September 1962.* Paris: United Nations Educational, Scientific and Cultural Organization.

———. 1964. *Education in Northern Rhodesia: Report and Recommendations Prepared by the UNESCO Planning Mission.* Paris: United Nations Educational, Scientific and Cultural Organization.

———. 1999. *Statistical Yearbook.* Paris: United Nations Educational, Scientific and Cultural Organization.

University of Zambia. 1977. *Report on the Long-Term Development of the University of Zambia.* Lusaka: The University Printer.

———. 1986. *Report of the Vice Chancellor's Study Group on Student Affairs, Appointed to Investigate Recent Closures and Student Unrest at the University of Zambia.* Lusaka: Office of the Vice Chancellor.

———. 1993. *Strategic Plan, 1994–1998.* Lusaka: Office of the Vice Chancellor, University of Zambia.

———. 1998. *Strategic Plan, 1999–2003.* Lusaka: Office of the Vice Chancellor, University of Zambia.

———. 1999. *UNESCO Statistical Yearbook.* Paris: United Nations Educational, Scientific and Cultural Organization.

Yesufu, T. M., ed. 1973. *Creating the African University: Emerging Issues in the 1970s.* Ibadan: Oxford University Press.

65

Zimbabwe

RAYMUND MAUNDE

INTRODUCTION

Zimbabwe is a little smaller than California, with a population of more than 11 million and a land mass of 390,580 square kilometers (150,803 square miles). Zimbabwe's gross national product (GNP) per capita stands at $2,690 (World Population Data Sheet 2001) and the gross domestic product (GDP) at constant prices in 1999 was $26,415 million (Monthly Review Reserve Bank of Zimbabwe 2001). The introduction of the economic structural adjustment program (ESAP) in 1990 adversely affected Zimbabwe's currency values and economic performance. According to the Central Statistical Office, the nation's currency was very strong vis-à-vis the American dollar in 1985. The introduction of ESAP did not improve the economic lot of the indigenous population. Health, education, and employment opportunities have eluded the majority of the natives.

Mining and agriculture are Zimbabwe's main economic activities. The country has major natural mineral resources of gold, diamonds, chrome ore, coal, copper, platinum, tungsten, and so forth. Maize is the staple food of the majority of the population and is cultivated extensively. Other crops under cultivation include wheat, coffee, tea, sugar, cotton, tobacco, and timber. Cattle ranching and wildlife conservancy abound. Of late, tourism and the hospitality industry have been sources of major foreign earnings for the country. Zimbabwe is the second-most industrialized country after South Africa in the Southern Africa Development Community (SADC). Its major industrial activities include textile manufacturing and steel production for domestic consumption and for export. South Africa is Zimbabwe's major trading partner, followed by the United Kingdom and Germany. Demographically, Zimbabwe has two main ethnic groups, namely the Shona, who constitute 71 percent of the population, and the Ndebele, who constitute 16 percent. The rest of the population consists of a few small minorities.

HISTORY AND BACKGROUND

The British colonialists carved Zimbabwe out of the once-great Monomotapa Empire. This centralized empire lay between the Zambezi and Limpopo Rivers. It included present-day Mozambique and stretched from the Indian Ocean in the east to parts of Northern Transvaal in South Africa and present-day Botswana and Namibia in the west.

British colonization of Zimbabwe at the turn of the nineteenth century introduced a new socioeconomic, cultural, and political order to Zimbabwe's indigenous peoples. From the outset, the British colonial settlers introduced the practice of discrimination and segregation based on differences in color and race. Literacy provision and technical training became the preserve of the school-going children of British settlers. Similarly, prior to independence in 1980, Zimbabwe's socioeconomic and political activities were the exclusive preserve of British colonials. School-age children of British colonialists received unlimited primary and secondary education opportunities. In addition, a variety of postsecondary institutions of higher learning were available to British colonialist students. British colonialist postsecondary students also received unlimited provision of higher education in South African and British universities.

The colonial regimes were not as generous in the provision of schooling for indigenous children. Missionary bodies were the main providers of schooling to indigenous children, but for a long time, neither the colonial government nor the missionary bodies provided them with any secondary schooling. Some local indigenous children managed through their own initiative to get secondary schooling through distance education. A few managed to enter Fort Hare College in South Africa. At the time, Fort Hare College was the only college for non-European students in the whole southern African region.

The establishment of the University College of Rhodesia

and Nyasaland in 1957 was the first colonial government initiative toward instituting a postsecondary school in the Federation of Rhodesia and Nyasaland. This university was founded in what was then Salisbury, now Harare, the capital city of Zimbabwe. The university was a joint venture of Southern Rhodesia, Northern Rhodesia, and Nyasaland as part of a short-lived federation that lasted from 1953 to 1963. At the dissolution of the federation, Southern Rhodesia, Northern Rhodesia, and Nyasaland became Zimbabwe, Zambia, and Malawi, respectively.

After the occupation of Zimbabwe by the British in 1890, a partnership evolved between the colonial authorities and the missionary bodies. The colonial authorities gave the missionaries land for the purposes of missionary activities. Their mission was to evangelize and civilize the indigenous people and to provide literacy training for them. The missionaries were paid for their work. They became government agents and employees, introducing elementary literacy and rudimentary modern technical skills to the indigenous people. In time, the technically skilled indigenous people challenged the colonists for jobs. Consequently, the colonial regimes proscribed the teaching of technical subjects to indigenous people so that jobs could be reserved for the European job seekers. This effectively killed the opportunity for indigenous people to receive technical schooling until recent times.

With the exception of South Africa, African universities south of the Sahara began to be established in the mid-1900s. The British government set up a commission of inquiry led by Sir Cyril Asquith on the feasibility of building universities in Africa and the West Indies (Ashby 1964). Asquith's findings and recommendations were delayed because of World War II. Contingency plans for building universities in overseas British possessions were also held up by the war. Under the contingency plan, the British government would have provided the money while the Inter-University Council took care of the academic aspects. The Inter-University Council was a body of university teachers drawn from various British universities for the purpose of teaching at proposed universities in British overseas colonies.

After the war, the University of London spearheaded the scheme. A special relationship was forged between the University of London and the colonial universities. The colonies included Nigeria, Ghana, Sudan, Uganda, the West Indies, and the Federation of Rhodesia and Nyasaland. Though physically separated from the University of London, the African and West Indian universities were nevertheless affiliated with it in a special arrangement. The University of London, unlike other universities that have all their activities under one campus umbrella, is made up of separate colleges federated into one university.

African and West Indian students were registered as University of London students, and upon completion of their studies, they received University of London degrees. The entry qualifications and curriculum were those of the University of London, and the university also furnished the African and West Indies universities with teachers. Examinations were set and assessed at the University of London, and the students at the African and West Indian campuses were expected to have the same lifestyle as University of London students.

The African and West Indian students at the University of London overseas campuses lived in ivory towers. The students' lifestyles had no relation to the surrounding socioeconomic and cultural environment. They were a select few being groomed to become the elite, ready to run the country when and if the British government decided to leave.

The curriculum adopted for these new universities was a replica of the British university curriculum. It included the classics, history, biblical studies, geography, chemistry, physics, biology, and mathematics. However, the reality of the African continent and the West Indies isles called for skilled manpower in agriculture, engineering, medicine, technology, sciences, and cultural and social studies.

The British government and the academic elite of the time agreed that the priority for the development of the African and West Indian colonies lay in the grooming of the nucleus of a first class of African and West Indian bureaucrats and leaders. Hence, what was good for the English universities was considered equally good for the African and West Indian universities.

It had been the British government's dream that its Southern Rhodesia colony and Northern Rhodesia and Nyasaland protectorates should join together to form a federation for economic reasons. The federation came to be known as the Federation of Rhodesia and Nyasaland. Nyasaland was the smallest and poorest member of the federation, but it was rich in human resources. Northern Rhodesia, the junior partner to Southern Rhodesia, was one of the world's leading copper producers. Southern Rhodesia was more developed economically and had more European settlers than the other two protectorates put together.

The University College of Rhodesia and Nyasaland received its Royal Charter on February 10, 1955. Real schoolwork started in 1957 with an enrollment of 68 students. The student body grew at an extremely slow rate. The student population stood at 717 full-time and 141 part-time after a decade of the university college's existence. The reason given for this slow growth was that the university wanted to build cohesion and camaraderie among students of different races. Considering the fact that the University College of Rhodesia and Nyasaland was the only educational institution in the Federation of Rhodesia and Nyasaland providing social services to a racially mixed community, it would seem that creating a multiracial society was not a priority because the key player in the federation, namely Southern Rhodesia, was still practicing racial and social segregation enforced by statutory laws.

In 1965, at least 1,272 Southern Rhodesian European nationals were attending South African universities. Some 233 European Zimbabwean students were studying in the universities in the United Kingdom; while some 432 European and 211 African students were at the University College of Rhodesia and Nyasaland.

The University College of Rhodesia and Nyasaland started with three faculties: The Faculty of Education, the Faculty of Arts, and the Faculty of Sciences. In 1963, the School of Medicine was built and had a special relationship with the University of Birmingham rather than the University of London (Atkinson 1972). The University of Birmingham sponsored the medical school's curriculum and syllabus and awarded its own degrees to successful students. The Faculty of Engineering came into existence in 1974, and the Faculties of Agriculture, Commerce, and Law followed in 1980. It is interesting to note that the Faculty of Agriculture was introduced at independence, an indication of the importance of agriculture to the postcolonial government.

POST-INDEPENDENCE HIGHER EDUCATION

The post-independence government addressed the provision of higher education by vigorously targeting the indigenous population that had been so neglected by the past colonial regimes. The government became the sole institution that provided university education in the country.

At the time of independence, only a small number of indigenous people had received a full cycle of primary, secondary, and tertiary education. The post-independence government established many institutions at all three levels. Health and education institutions needed skilled indigenous manpower in order to guarantee their continued functioning. The industrial and commercial sectors needed skilled indigenous manpower as well. Many more technical and teachers' colleges were instituted. The University of Zimbabwe was expanded to fill the gap left by departed European settlers. The technical and teachers' colleges and the university became vocational and apprenticeship training institutions. Their mission was to produce skilled manpower in as short a time as possible.

Massive expansion in primary and secondary school sectors took place. At independence, the government provided a universal seven-year primary cycle and a four-year secondary cycle for the school-age children nationwide. According to the government's education statistics of 1978, the colonial government provided indigenous children with 2,401 primary and 177 secondary school institutions. These colonial primary school institutions educated 819,586 indigenous children, while the secondary school institutions educated 66,215 indigenous students. In 1994, there was a phenomenal growth in the number of the primary schools to 4,585. This staggering increase allowed the enrollment of 2,556,855 children. This, in turn, had implications for the provision of secondary schooling. According to government secondary school statistics, there were 1,522 secondary school institutions nationwide with an enrollment of 832,576 students in 2000. In spite of impressive increases in primary and secondary school enrollments, the education system still suffers greatly from a high drop-out rate at all levels. Students drop out of school for reasons that range from a lack of upper primary and secondary school physical structures to parents who are unable to pay school fees or buy school uniforms and a host of other problems. In the case of the secondary school students, the majority end up dropping out of school on completion of the Ordinary-Level course, a four-year secondary schooling program. A tiny fraction of Ordinary-Level graduates vie for limited space in the few two-year Sixth Form Colleges. Graduating from the Sixth Form College satisfies university entry qualifications in Zimbabwe, but it does not guarantee entrance to a university. There are many other hurdles to be overcome. Every year, many more students become eligible for limited university education space. Students can also choose from a limited number of facul-

ties. In such circumstances, corruption and favoritism become endemic in student admissions.

THE UNIVERSITY OF ZIMBABWE

Following Zimbabwe's independence, Harare's population swelled overnight from a mere half million people to over a million inhabitants. The sudden population explosion had serious implications for the provision of limited social services. Government social services such as higher education, hospital, and housing institutions were not able to cope with the demand. The University of Zimbabwe made some frantic efforts to cope with the unprecedented number of students seeking university education. The maximum number of students rose to around 10,000 per year. However, the number of students who wanted to have access to higher education institutions but were denied grew by leaps and bounds. The sheer number of students seeking university education forced the government to consider seriously the problem of providing university education.

The University of Zimbabwe has been offering ten faculties since Zimbabwe's independence in 1980 (see Table 65.1). The overall student and faculty numbers increased year after year. It is interesting to note that in 2000, male student enrollment dropped remarkably and female student enrollment increased appreciably.

The years between 1998 and 2000 were hard times for the University of Zimbabwe. The university was affected by incessant student unrest, which resulted in the university's closure for over six months. Also, the introduction of the semester system interrupted the customary annual enrollment. Student unrest appeared to affect male students most, resulting in their either being expelled from or quitting the university. The other contributory factor was that the female students' requirements for entry into the university were lowered in order to facilitate their admission. This had the effect of limiting access to higher education for many male students. The only equitable way to provide higher education to both genders was to build more universities and put them at the disposal of all eligible Zimbabwean students regardless of their gender.

The lack of adequate tertiary education provision was becoming a political liability for the post-independence government. Parents and children alike were becoming disenchanted and frustrated with the lack of adequate university facilities. The government's successes in providing mass primary and secondary education exacerbated the problem.

The government response was half-hearted. As a stopgap measure, the government introduced bachelor of technology degree programs at Harare Polytechnic (founded in 1926) in 1985 and at Bulawayo Polytechnic in 1986 (Williams 1989). The government assumed that the University of Zimbabwe would automatically accept a Harare Polytechnic degree as the equivalent of a university degree. However, the University of Zimbabwe was not happy with the state of affairs at the Harare Polytechnic. The library facilities, teaching staff, and learning materials fell far short of meeting university requirements. The majority of the lecturers were underqualified. In order to redeem an otherwise desperate situation, the University of Zimbabwe suggested that Harare Polytechnic students commute to

Table 65.1. Student Enrollment at the University of Zimbabwe by Gender, Discipline, and Year of Study, November 2000

Faculty	Agriculture		Arts		Commerce		Education		English		Law		Medicine		Science		Social Studies		Veterinary Science		Total	
Year of Study	M	F	M	F	M	F	M	F	M	F	M	F	M	F	M	F	M	F	M	F	M	F
First Year	107	33	227	167	216	71	74	78	241	20	62	32	228	101	336	131	377	306	20	11	1,888	950
Second Year	113	28	269	136	173	54	200	80	161	11	63	29	245	90	256	78	334	182	21	5	1,835	693
Third Year	74	20	169	137	164	63	–	–	161	–	43	42	171	94	127	83	256	197	21	6	1,186	642
Fourth Year	6	–	11	–	–	–	–	–	141	9	42	28	128	55	5	2	21	14	20	6	374	114
Fifth Year	–	–	–	–	–	–	–	–	25	–	–	–	75	27	–	–	–	–	6	6	106	33
Total	300	81	676	440	553	188	274	158	729	40	210	131	847	367	724	294	988	699	88	34	5,389	2,432

Source: The Registrar, University of Zimbabwe, November 2000.

Table 65.2. Student Enrollment at the National University of Science and Technology by Gender, Discipline, and Year of Study, 2000

Discipline	Applied Science			Commerce			Industrial Technology			Architecture			Total		
Year of Study	M	F	Total	M	F	Total	M	F	Total	M	F	Total	M	F	Total
First Year	104	43	147	165	70	235	135	18	153	17	10	27	421	141	562
Second Year	127	31	158	155	48	203	105	16	121	18	1	19	405	96	501
Third Year	113	13	126	166	23	189	100	5	105	0	0	0	379	41	420

the University of Zimbabwe campus at Mount Pleasant for lectures and studies. At the Mount Pleasant campus, the Harare Polytechnic students were assured of having access to the university facilities, such as teachers, library facilities, and social activities. The University of Zimbabwe offered bachelor of technology degrees in the following disciplines: business studies, accounting and management, applied science and technology, civil engineering, mechanical engineering, and electrical engineering. The consideration given to the Harare Polytechnic was also accorded to the Bulawayo Polytechnic. In the case of Bulawayo, arrangements were made for students to travel to the University of Zimbabwe and for university teachers to travel to the Bulawayo Polytechnic site. The affiliation of the Harare and Bulawayo Polytechnics with the University of Zimbabwe was short-lived. Chetsanga's report (1994) notes that the polytechnics' affiliation with the University of Zimbabwe was revoked when the National University of Science and Technology came into existence at Bulawayo in 1991.

The introduction of the bachelor of technology degree came at a time of mounting criticism leveled against University of Zimbabwe engineering graduates. The industrial community was critical of the engineering graduates, saying that their training was too theoretical (Williams 1989). The bachelor of technology was introduced in order to address the industrial community's concerns. The bachelor of technology program was more practical, and work experience was a necessary component of training. The industrial community was happy with the bachelor of technology graduates, and the students were pleased as well. By the time the bachelor of technology program was phased out, it had produced 986 graduates (Chetsanga 1994).

THE NATIONAL UNIVERSITY OF SCIENCE AND TECHNOLOGY

In 1988, the President of Zimbabwe set up a commission headed by P. R. C. Williams to inquire into the possibility of setting up a second university or campus in Zimbabwe since the University of Zimbabwe was no longer adequate. Williams, a Briton, was assisted by ten professionals consisting of three foreigners and seven Zimbabweans. The government finally conceded that the country needed more university institutions following Williams's *Report of the Commission of Inquiry into the Establishment of a Second University or Campus* (1989). The

second government-sponsored university, the National University of Science and Technology (NUST), was founded in 1991. But the government did not seem serious about the university's construction; the budget set aside was small and money was made available on a yearly basis. NUST was located at Bulawayo, the second-largest city in Zimbabwe. Bulawayo lies some 400 kilometers southwest of Harare and has a population of close to a million people. It is the home of Zimbabwe's heavy industry and has a mining institute sponsored by the Canadian government.

NUST did not start with its own physical campus. Instead, it began with borrowed and improvised lecture halls, administration and library space, and student accommodations. The borrowed temporary university facilities were scattered all over the city, operating from more than twenty different places. NUST came under one roof at its permanent site on August 17, 1998.

The National University of Science and Technology was expected to be in full operation within a period of ten years from its inception. That date came in 2001. On October 20, 2001, 433 students graduated, including the first batch of eleven candidates from the Faculty of Chemical Engineering. The university met targets set in Williams's 1989 report, implementing the eight proposed faculties within a ten-year period. The faculties are as follows: applied science, architecture and quantity surveying, commerce, communication and information science, environmental science, industrial technology, technical teacher education, and sports science. From NUST's inception in April 1991 to this date, the university has produced 2,142 graduates (see Table 65.2). The originally estimated cost of university construction was 1 billion dollars Zimbabwe, equivalent to US$100 million at the time. Both the construction period and the cost of the project were revised to twenty years and over 4 billion dollars Zimbabwe, equivalent to US$4.5 million. Unforeseen circumstances delayed construction. In 1992, Zimbabwe experienced a devastating drought which was the worst in the country's living memory. The economic structural adjustment program was already being implemented and had an adverse effect on the country's economic performance. The cost of construction materials skyrocketed. However, university stakeholders—namely the government and the local Bulawayo City authorities—did not give up in the face of adversity.

Bulawayo became the location of the National University of Science and Technology for a variety of reasons (Williams 1989). In addition to the fact that it was the second largest city after Harare, having Bulawayo as the home of the new university

Table 65.3. Higher Education and Technology Budget Estimates as of December 31, 2001

Institution	Budget Estimates	
	ZWD	USD
Bindura University	224,090,000	4,074,000
Midlands State University	180,550,000	3,282,727
National University of Science and Technology	946,100,000	17,201,000
University of Zimbabwe	2,238,000,000	40,690,000
Zimbabwe Open University	2,024,000,000	36,800,000
Total	5,612,740,000	102,047,727

Key: ZWD—Zimbabwe dollar; USD—United States dollar (exchange rate: ZWD 55 = 1 USD)
Source: Monthly Review Reserve Bank of Zimbabwe 2001.

was seen as a gesture to appease a political constituency that had entered into a 1987 Unity Accord with the government. Another factor that came into play was that Bulawayo was accessible by air, rail, and road. The city was also endowed with a good number of schools and social services, parks, hotels, department stores, drugstores, groceries, malls, halls, and so forth. Health care and accommodations were available. The National University of Science and Technology was to have a bias toward sciences and technology. From the outset, the university was an independent institution and was not under the University of Zimbabwe's tutelage.

NUST's mission was to create a new university paradigm that would spearhead a new breed of institutions of higher education in Zimbabwe. The hope was that, from NUST, a new form of university technical college would evolve, producing graduates with the science and technical skills required to meet the emerging needs of industry and commerce. It was anticipated that NUST would accommodate 10,000 students annually when the university was in full operation.

TEACHERS' AND TECHNICAL COLLEGES AFTER 1980

After Zimbabwe's independence, the number of teachers' colleges increased to sixteen. Five colleges prepared secondary school teachers, while the remaining eleven prepared primary school teachers. Each teachers' college graduates an average of 500 teachers annually following a three-year training period. Currently, teachers' colleges are being converted into degree-awarding institutions of higher learning. Chinhoyi, Gweru, and Masvingo Teachers' Colleges have already made the transition.

At the time of independence, there were two polytechnics. As of this date, there are six technical colleges, including the two polytechnics. There is a strong sentiment to turn the technical colleges and polytechnics into technical universities as well.

ZIMBABWE OPEN UNIVERSITY

The Williams Report deplored the inadequate provision of distance education in higher education. He found that Zim-

babwe fared poorly in comparison with other African countries in the provision of offsite university education. In fact, it is the University of South Africa (UNISA) that offers correspondence courses at the university level to many Zimbabwean students.

In August 1994, the minister of higher education and technology appointed a ten-member ministerial committee to help his ministry implement the Zimbabwe Open University program. Zimbabwe Open University started as a center of distance education at the University of Zimbabwe with an enrollment of 1,500 students. Initially, the Center targeted school headmasters, headmistresses, and senior teachers as students. However, since the inauguration of the Zimbabwe Open University in March 1999, the distance education program targeted underqualified teachers in the primary and secondary school education systems as well.

The Zimbabwe Open University program has been a success story. Teachers that hold diplomas from the teachers' colleges have taken advantage of the Zimbabwe Open University's offerings to improve their academic and professional qualifications. Instead of spending two full years in a Bachelor of Education degree program at a university, they can earn the same degree through the Zimbabwe Open University.

The Open University is highly decentralized. It has ten centers countrywide. College and university lecturers are recruited to give tutorials to registered Open University students at the provincial level. Each provincial center has a collection of valuable and important reference textbooks and other learning materials. The Zimbabwe Open University student enrollment is growing and is expected to reach 30,000 enrollees at the end of the year 2001.

BINDURA UNIVERSITY IN SCIENCE EDUCATION

Following independence in 1980, Zimbabwe relied heavily on science teachers trained in Europe, Australia, and North America. The local teachers' colleges mainly trained teachers for the primary school sector. There was a shortage of secondary school teachers, and they tended to be poorly educated and trained.

In 1986, the governments of Cuba and Zimbabwe made

an agreement: Zimbabwean Ordinary-Level certificate holders would be trained in Cuba for secondary school teaching. Each student teacher specialized in one of the following subjects: biology, chemistry, physics, mathematics, or geography. Since the inception of the Zimbabwe-Cuba program, 1,778 Zimbabwean students have been trained as science teachers in Cuba. Cuba trained students in other disciplines as well, such as medicine, agronomy, surveying, and so forth. The Zimbabwe-Cuba program, which was transferred to Zimbabwe in 1996, was under the auspices of the University of Zimbabwe and became known as Bindura University of Science Education. The program was housed temporarily at the Bindura Provincial Training Center facilities while the Bindura University of Science Education structures were under construction.

Bindura University of Science Education continued to train secondary school teacher-specialists in the sciences, focusing on biology, chemistry, physics, mathematics, and geography. At the University of Zimbabwe's August 17, 2001, graduation ceremony, Bindura University of Science Education and Masvingo University College presented 84 and 120 graduating students, respectively. Both university colleges are still under the auspices of University of Zimbabwe.

CREATION OF BACHELORS OF EDUCATION AND TECHNOLOGY PROGRAMS

In 1994, the minister of higher education and technology decided to increase the number of institutions of higher education in Zimbabwe. It was not feasible financially to build new university institutions from scratch. The Ministry of Higher Education and Technology decided instead to upgrade the existing teachers' and technical colleges to the university level. Of course, the Ministry of Higher Education and Technology sought expert advice from educational and technical specialists. The specialists identified a few colleges that promised suitable degree programs under University of Zimbabwe tutelage. Thus, Masvingo University, Midlands State University, and Chinhoyi University of Technology came into existence. Masvingo University has initiated a program to provide university degrees to teachers in the primary education sector.

Midlands State University

Midlands State University became a full-fledged university on March 18, 2001. Before becoming an autonomous university, Midlands State University trained thirty-two students at Gweru University Teachers' College under the auspices of the University of Zimbabwe. In converting Gweru into a full-fledged university, the government pledged more funds to upgrade the institution's infrastructures to required university standards.

Masvingo University and Chinhoyi University of Technology

The Chetsanga report of 1994 that recommended the conversion of teachers' and technical colleges into universities also precipitated the creation of Masvingo University and Chinhoyi University of Technology. When in full operation, Chinhoyi

University of Technology is expected to concentrate on and specialize in food science and processing, farm mechanics, automotive engineering, product design and manufacture, business studies and international trade, computer-aided design, and mechatronics.

CHURCH-AFFILIATED UNIVERSITIES IN ZIMBABWE

Before Zimbabwe's independence, the Christian churches were in the vanguard of the provision of elementary education to indigenous Africans. After independence, the United Methodists, the Seventh-Day Adventists, the Roman Catholics, the Jesuit Fathers, and the Reformed Church each instituted a church-related university. The Anglicans and the Methodists have also promised to create their own church-related universities.

Africa University

The United Methodist Church pioneered the first-ever private church-related university in Zimbabwe in 1991 at Old Mutare, the church's oldest mission station, and named it Africa University. The mission lies some 18 kilometers north of Mutare City. The university is on a 1,545-acre parcel of land reserved by the church for university purposes.

The president of the Republic of Zimbabwe officially opened Africa University on April 23, 1994, as the first non-government-sponsored university in Zimbabwe. Africa University was the first United Methodist Church venture in Africa, representing eight church-affiliated African countries: Angola, Burundi, Liberia, Mozambique, Nigeria, Sierra Leone, the Democratic Republic of Congo (formerly Zaire), and Zimbabwe. Students from twenty countries study at Africa University.

Africa University started offering classes in March 1992 with a student enrollment of forty drawn from a few African countries. At first, the university used temporary and borrowed facilities. All great things have a humble beginning, and Africa University was no exception. It started with two faculties, the Faculty of Theology and the Faculty of Agriculture and Natural Resources. Students from the Faculty of Theology were drawn from the young Methodist men and women aspiring to join the Methodist Church hierarchy. Some Methodist ministers who did not have university qualifications enrolled in the theology faculty in order to improve their academic and professional skills.

The Faculty of Education started with two streams, one for the four-year degree program and the other for Zimbabwean secondary school teachers who did not hold university degrees. They spend two years studying foundation disciplines such as educational psychology, educational sociology, educational philosophy, and a specialization subject. According to the *Financial Gazette* of March 29–April 4, 2001, Africa University now offers five faculties: education, agriculture and natural resources, theology, management and administration, and humanities and social sciences.

Africa University works very closely with the University of Zimbabwe to develop educational programs. At the University of Zimbabwe, teachers' college graduates who have taught secondary school for five years or more in their subjects of specialization spend two years in a university setting. Africa University followed the University of Zimbabwe's example for that particular group of students. It also cooperated splendidly with the University of Zimbabwe in the admission of Advanced Level graduates. Future cooperation between public and private universities in Zimbabwe seems likely, due to the good working relationship exemplified by these two universities.

Religion plays a vital role in the lives of the indigenous peoples of Zimbabwe, both individually and collectively as a community or society. Organized religion has an indispensable role to play in the social activities of the people. A degree of religious tolerance and accommodation is manifest and encouraged at Africa University.

Because of the international nature of Africa University, the United Methodist Church authorities stipulated that 60 percent of the students and faculty members would be drawn from outside Zimbabwe. In practice, it is difficult if not impossible to meet this noble goal. In reality, the majority of students and teaching staff are Zimbabweans. In August 2001, there were 70 faculty members, including 52 permanent teachers, 15 part-time teachers, and 3 lecturers. There was a gross gender imbalance among teachers: 52 male teachers and 18 female lecturers. Forty-five teachers were Zimbabweans, the largest of any national group. The United States was second with six teachers, and Tanzania and Nigeria had 3 teachers each. Ghana, India, Kenya, and Mozambique had two each, and Angola, Great Britain, Sierra Leone, the Democratic Republic of Congo, and South Africa each had one teacher.

There was a similar imbalance in student composition. Out of the total student body of 772, there were 527 Zimbabwean students. Angola, Mozambique, and the Democratic Republic of Congo had 60, 58, and 54 students respectively. The remaining sixteen countries each had between one and eleven students.

Because it is on Zimbabwean soil, Africa University is expected to operate within the framework of Zimbabwe's laws and regulations. In order to recruit foreign teachers and students, the university must follow immigration regulations and work closely with immigration authorities. Such tasks could not easily be entrusted to a foreign university official or carried out by a foreign official. To avoid any possible misunderstanding, key positions at Africa University are held by Zimbabweans. The relationship between Zimbabwe's government and Africa University has been excellent.

Solusi University

Solusi University is sponsored by the Seventh-Day Adventist Church. It is located in the countryside near Figtree, a small rural town some 53 kilometers west of Bulawayo. Before 1980, Solusi Mission station was a University of South Africa distance education center. Mission authorities wished to bring together individual students who were doing distance education with the University of South Africa. When the University of South Africa distance education center closed, the Seventh-Day Adventist Church authorities did not lose heart. Following the Liberation War, Solusi Mission became an affiliate college of Andrew University, a Seventh-Day Adventist University, in Michigan, U.S.A., from 1984 to 1994. Zimbabwean authorities did not honor the

arrangement. Again, authorities at Solusi College were not disheartened. They sought an amicable solution with the government so that the program of studies offered at Solusi College in an affiliation with Andrew University could be recognized as university studies. Finally, government authorities spelled out their objections: Advanced Levels (A-levels) were considered university entry qualifications in Zimbabwe, but Solusi College had been accepting Ordinary Levels (O-levels), an equivalent to a United States high school diploma. The government also wanted reassurance that Solusi College's funding would continue.

Solusi College's physical facilities were expected to meet university standards. The government was not happy with some elements of Solusi College's charter pertaining to gender and religious issues. After the college had amended the objectionable elements, a university charter was granted. Solusi University started operating under the new dispensation in September of 1994. In 1998, the Zimbabwe government retroactively acknowledged degrees issued to Solusi College graduates under the old dispensation.

Solusi University, like Africa University, is an international institution attended by students from Botswana, Djibouti, Eritrea, Ethiopia, Kenya, Malawi, Swaziland, Tanzania, Uganda, Zambia, and Zimbabwe. The ruling accorded to Africa University with regard to foreign student and teacher recruitment also applies to Solusi University.

Solusi University is a Seventh-Day Adventist community. The staff and their families are professed members of the Seventh-Day Adventist faith. Teachers at the university, as well as those at the primary and secondary levels, are Seventh-Day Adventists. The workers and teaching staff pay their tithes to the church.

According to the Ministry of Higher Education and Technology, Solusi University had a total of 694 students in 2000; 334 female students and 360 male students. So far, Solusi University is the only university in Zimbabwe that has come close to gender parity. This is attributed to the preponderance of faculties and departments in humanities and social studies. Solusi University offers two graduate programs: a Master of Business Administration (M.B.A.), and a Master of Science in Family and Consumer Sciences (Home Economics).

Catholic University in Zimbabwe

The Catholic University in Zimbabwe started operating in February 1999, offering one faculty in business management and information technology. Student enrollment was twenty-four men and seventeen women. In 2001, enrollment increased to eighty-five male and fifty female students, and the Faculty of Humanities came into existence. The Catholic University, unlike Africa University and Solusi University, does not offer student and teaching staff accommodations or catering facilities on campus.

Arrupe College

Arrupe College started in 1997 as an exclusively male Jesuit college affiliated with the University of Zimbabwe. The college's teachers hold illustrious academic credentials from renowned universities in the United States, England, Germany, Tanzania, India, Zimbabwe, and elsewhere. In 1997, the student body consisted of eighty Jesuit aspirants from Anglophone, Francophone, and Lusophone Africa. Since then, there have been some minor changes. There are 107 male and 2 female students. A full-time teaching staff stands at twelve male and two female full-time teachers, complemented by fifteen male and three female part-time teachers. The college offers a four-year University of Zimbabwe B.A. honors degree in philosophy and humanities, a three-year University of Zimbabwe B.A. in philosophy, a three-year Gregorian University (Rome) B.A. in philosophy, and a three-year diploma. To this date, Arrupe College has graduated ten students with the bachelor of arts honors degree in philosophy and humanities.

Williams's report (1989) argues eloquently that the government of Zimbabwe and its government-sponsored universities should take a leading role in the activities of private universities. Private universities are expected to be of high caliber, both in the provision of physical structures and in academic excellence. The rules and regulations governing the government-run and -sponsored universities apply equally to the church and privately sponsored universities.

Private and church-affiliated universities should not be second-rate institutions of higher learning run as commercial enterprise ventures. The interests of the students and the country's national university reputation are to be upheld and safeguarded assiduously. Williams also laid down regulations governing private-sector participation in higher education. A university is an autonomous institution to which students are recruited on academic merit. University students and teaching staff must enjoy unlimited academic freedom. Employment of university premises for religious proselytism or for the purpose of political activities would be against the university's principles of autonomy and freedom.

UNIVERSITY ADMINISTRATION

The British bequeathed Zimbabwe the art of running, organizing, and administering a university institution. It was the British government that originally instituted the University of Zimbabwe. The University of London's chancellor is the king or queen of England. The university colleges in the British overseas colonies in Africa and West Indies were founded under the University of London's tutelage, so the king or queen was ipso facto the chancellor of the university colleges as well. The king or queen of England was not only the head of the British Isles but also of the British overseas colonies. The heads of the former British overseas colonies inherited the university colleges' chancellorships automatically at the time of independence.

In the British academic world, the chancellor's role is a functional one. The overseas university colleges were young and new; they needed highly qualified and competent men and women to transfer expertise and run their administrations. Interestingly, most of the post-independence heads of state were not university graduates. At the time of independence, the university's chancellorships, national flags, and national anthems were the most valued and treasured national symbols and it would not

have been fitting to entrust them to anyone other than the head of state.

But the idea of having the state president as chancellor of a national university became questionable as the number of government-sponsored universities increased. Zimbabwe has seven state-sponsored universities. Having the state president as sole chancellor of them all is becoming problematic. The state president is not only the head of the government but also the head of the government funding agency. As such, the president wields enormous power and influence over university affairs. It would appear desirable for each state university to have its own separate chancellor. On the other hand, the government saves money by paying the salary of only one chancellor.

In any case, state presidents are only titular chancellors of national universities. Vice-chancellors run university affairs. In a similar manner, the heads of church-related universities are automatically the chancellors. Like any state university, a vice-chancellor administers and runs the church-related university's affairs.

Each university, whether sponsored and funded by the government or by a private entity, has a body of men and women constituting a university council. The university council members vary in number according to the size and needs of the university. The university might also need a strong and active alumni body to advise and support the university financially.

A vice-chancellor appoints key faculty members as academic deans, heads of faculties, departments, and so forth, in order to facilitate the smooth running of the university's academic life. Other necessary positions include bursars, registrars, librarians and directors of information, and so forth. The university has other supporting social departments run by teachers, student representatives, university chaplains, catering staff, health care service providers, hostel wardens, and many others who provide necessary social and physical services.

UNIVERSITY FUNDING

Sadly, Zimbabwe, like most less-developed countries, commits the smallest portion of its meager national budget to higher education and health sectors. The largest portion of the higher education allocation is spent on the salaries and wages of academic and nonacademic staff (Table 65.3).

Funding university institutions has not been an easy task even for developed countries. Zimbabwe's post-independence success story in universal primary and secondary schooling provision has not been without great sacrifice on the part of the government and parents as well. The government funds virtually everything for every student in higher learning institutions. Yet some parents readily pay large sums of money for their children to attend privately run and owned nursery, primary, secondary, and tertiary institutions. The historical anomaly by which parents pay virtually nothing for their children's tertiary education needs to be reviewed.

Funding Issues in Church-Related Universities

To date, Zimbabwean students attending church-related universities receive public financial assistance in aid or grants just like students at state universities. However, the church-related universities charge money for tuition. The government heavily subsidizes state-run and -sponsored universities. Students enrolling in church-related universities end up paying more money to offset the differences. As a result, the church-related universities attract a smaller number of students, and students from affluent families end up being the majority. However, if the economic climate in Zimbabwe improves, student enrollment at church-related universities will increase. Parents value church-related education for their children.

BRAIN DRAIN AND EMPLOYMENT OF
HIGHER EDUCATION GRADUATES

Zimbabwe has a reputation for having high-quality education. Children from neighboring countries seek schooling in Zimbabwe. Zimbabwe's tertiary institutions train professionals, technicians, and artisans for countries such as Botswana, South Africa, the United Kingdom, and others. Yet though Zimbabwe's own medical and vital technical fields need the services of a professional, specialized workforce, trained Zimbabwean professionals such as engineers are either unemployed or underemployed or employed as teachers. The rest end up seeking employment outside the country.

LOCAL INDIGENOUS LANGUAGES

English is the language of higher education in Zimbabwe, but it is not the mother tongue of indigenous students. As such, the students' schoolwork is impeded greatly. They find it harder to grasp concepts and to express themselves in a foreign language. Higher education would not be as difficult for indigenous students if local languages were the media of instruction and learning. Ndebele and Shona are Zimbabwe's main indigenous languages. A passing grade in English is a required university entry qualification. As such, English is employed as a mechanism to control university entry. However, Ndebele and Shona are taught as subjects at all school levels. Ndebele and Shona are effective tools for disseminating information, giving religious instruction, and evangelization. Developing them as tools for instruction and learning is costly, as translating international scientific works into local languages would require a lot of money. Parents, students, and leading civic leaders resist instruction in indigenous languages because it is perceived as a divisive practice that would fragment national unity.

RESEARCH AND PUBLISHING

The majority of Zimbabwe's people became literate after independence in 1980. Zimbabwe has an 85 percent literacy rate, the highest in Africa. The volume of research done in Zimbabwe is very low, and research facilities are among the poorest. It will take time to build a culture of reading, writing, and research. Zimbabwe's publishing industry is very small and local. Publishers such as Mambo Press, Longmans, College Press, and a few others have supported the writing of novels, short stories, poetry, and so forth in English, Ndebele, or Shona. School textbooks at primary and secondary school levels are printed and published by local printing companies. Books for higher education are invariably imported from the United Kingdom and the United States.

ZIMBABWE STUDENTS TRAINED ABROAD

The world community has been very generous in training and providing university education for Zimbabwean citizens since independence. Unfortunately, statistics on students trained overseas are not available. Cuba took it upon itself to train Zimbabwean science teachers. In addition, Cuba trained Zimbabwean professionals in the fields of medicine, agronomy, the military, aviation, accounting, and so forth.

The British government sent a military training team to integrate the separate and hostile Nationalist Liberation armies and the colonial army. The British military and police institutions trained Zimbabwean servicemen and servicewomen. Other Western countries, notably the United States, Canada, Australia, Germany, and the Scandinavian countries, trained Zimbabwean students in their institutions of higher learning in many fields.

Socialist countries then under the influence of the Soviet Union also trained Zimbabwean military and air force servicemen. The training included diverse technical and professional fields.

ISSUES OF FINANCE AND ACCOUNTABILITY

University institutions require a lot of funding. No university can function without a substantial amount of resources. College tuition and book fees are expensive, as is the cost of student accommodation, transport, and food. Therefore, the provision and cost of higher education in Zimbabwe continues as a national problem and needs to be addressed in a comprehensive manner by the country as a whole.

At the college and university institutions I visited in the course of my research, students were not happy with the apparent lack of checks and balances in the way moneys were handled at administrative levels. However, it appears that the lack of transparency and accountability in money matters has been an intractable problem countrywide. In the wake of the national fuel shortage crisis at the beginning of 2000, the state president deplored rampant corruption in both the government and private sectors. If corruption is that widespread, surely mechanisms can be devised and put in place to curb it and make sure that the meager funds earmarked for higher education and other vital sectors of the economy are accounted for and put to proper use.

A common complaint at several college and university institutions was that some authorities did not adhere to appropriate forms of division of labor, responsibility, accountability, and transparency in their administrative practice. Higher education authorities are not trained as building contractors or commercial experts. They are trained as school administrators and teachers. Properly trained authorities should be contracted to take care of required construction and maintenance of major physical structures in institutions of higher education.

Mechanisms of checks and balances, including external audits, should be in place in every institution of higher education. The absence of checks and balances exposes officeholders to temptations; bear in mind that the majority of those in office have had little or no previous experience with office management. A culture of accountability, transparency, responsibility, and good governance must be cultivated, nurtured, and enforced.

Another control mechanism would be rotation and limited office tenure. If the officeholders have acquitted themselves well in the execution of their duties they could be accorded a chance for reelection. Indefinite terms of office in institutions of higher education should be discouraged or proscribed. Permanent officeholders have a tendency toward corruption, inefficiency, and ineffectiveness. In short, those in office in the institutions of higher education should be expected to move around.

A BALANCED CURRICULUM

The introduction of the economic structural adjustment program in 1991 brought about the need for expanded training opportunities in sciences and technology in order to cope with changed realities in the economy. This led to the establishment of the National University of Science and Technology and to several new technical colleges that offer applied science subjects and allied industrial and technological subjects. The University of Zimbabwe, the country's premier university, had to change its emphasis from producing highly theoretical and academic students after the pattern of Oxford and Cambridge Universities to training students in science and technical skills. University teachers, students, and parents resisted the shift. But the teaching of applied sciences and technical subjects has caught the imagination of young college-bound students. There is a danger in overemphasizing the study of sciences and technology at the expense of social studies, humanities, and arts subjects because future generations could lose touch with the values of civilization. The institutions of higher education must provide room for all disciplines, not just the sciences and technology, so there can be a balance in the school curriculum. Including arts and social studies as part of the science and technical curriculum has a balancing effect on the social life of the institutions of higher learning and thus on the country as a whole.

Historically, Zimbabwe's economy has been driven by agriculture. However, in his study *Future Development of University Distance Education* (1994), Hill found that out of a population of 10,000 students at the University of Zimbabwe, only 500 were studying agriculture and veterinary sciences. The low enrollment in vital faculties such as agriculture, which are necessary for the economic development of the country, was not a healthy sign. Corrective measures had to be taken. The introduction of the Faculty of Agriculture in the Zimbabwe Open University was most welcome. The Zimbabwe Open University increased the number of students studying agricultural science for the bachelor of science degree.

Most less-developed countries in Africa have been colonies of Western countries such as the United Kingdom, France, Belgium, and Portugal. Each colonial power introduced its own institutional paradigm for learning and teaching following the example of its own metropolitan institutions of higher educa-

tion. Western higher education institutions evolved in response to either European or American socioeconomic, cultural, and political imperatives. The introduction of Western educational paradigms to Africa as a whole seems not to have taken into consideration African socioeconomic, cultural, and political realities. The ills of the African continent, such as malaria, sleeping sickness, diseases causing blindness, and, in recent times, HIV/AIDS, were not adequately addressed. Hunger and malnutrition continue their unabated ravaging of African peoples and yet the continent is endowed with great natural resources. Illiteracy and the lack of higher education provision was never addressed seriously by either the former colonial regimes or the post-independence governments.

AMERICANIZATION OF HIGHER EDUCATION

The introduction of global economic markets, coupled with the founding of Africa University and Solusi University by missionary organizations whose origins were in the United States, are both factors that have led to the adoption of the American education system in Zimbabwe. The University of Zimbabwe has abandoned its British origins and has adopted the American semester-based education system. In addition, learning and teaching have taken the pattern of courses instead of tutorials. Learning and teaching in course patterns has become the hallmark of Zimbabwe's education system. It is hoped that the adoption of the American system of education (which includes semesterization and course work) will introduce some flexibility into the otherwise rigid system of education adopted from Great Britain.

With the Zimbabwe Open University in place, the possibility of a speedy accession to university status for the teachers' and technical colleges is greatly enhanced, since they will be able to use the course-based learning and teaching materials developed for the new distance education programs. Initially, the Zimbabwe Open University will be a curriculum provider, but it will also become an umbrella examination body for students at teachers' and technical colleges.

In the last few years, American reading materials and technologies have been finding their way into Zimbabwe's school systems as well. The adoption of the American education system in Zimbabwe has come at a most auspicious time. Zimbabwe is faced with a huge number of high school graduates who want to enter institutions of higher education. Physical facilities for higher education are not available. Adequately trained teaching personnel are not available either. The government has no money to fund new institutions of higher education. A distance education system using American reading materials and technology seems to be the only option capable of providing higher education opportunities for the majority of young girls and boys.

In providing higher education institutions, the government has been cognizant of the political, ethnic, and tribal factors that impact education. The country is divided into eight provinces for political and administrative purposes. According to the government's overall plan, every province must be provided with teachers' and technical colleges. Every province in the country appreciates privately sponsored universities, but the government must also fulfill its obligations by instituting government-sponsored universities in the provinces. It represents a national commitment to providing adequate facilities for higher education to all citizens.

LINGERING ISSUES

The post-independence government was able to expand inherited university lecture halls and student hostels. The student-to-teacher ratio grew until it threatened the effective learning and teaching required for quality higher education. The introduction of large numbers of students without a corresponding expansion of physical facilities tended to undermine the quality of education. Teachers were overworked and underpaid, and their morale went down. As a result, highly qualified, competent, and experienced teachers left the institutions of higher learning for greener pastures, where remuneration was better and the teaching conditions were more attractive.

Student unrest in Zimbabwe's higher education institutions arises from perceived inadequate student payouts, the privatization of student accommodations, the inadequacy of catering services on campus, and a lack of up-to-date teaching and learning materials, books, computer facilities, and so forth.

Some student resentments are of a political nature. Students belong to different political factions. Other student issues are distinctly nonpolitical: male students make a big fuss when nonuniversity males visit female students on campus. Some student grievances seem genuine but others appear trivial. Students who resort to violence, arson, and hooliganism on campuses forget that they are a small minority, the lucky few receiving higher education in the country. These students should be fighting for less fortunate fellow students who fail to get into college or university. The majority of students who have met the competitive university entry qualifications go without education. More institutions of higher education must be made available to the many students who wish to attend them.

Crises in institutions of higher education could have been averted if the government—University of Zimbabwe authorities, civic leaders, and parents—had responded sooner to the need for more colleges and universities. Those with stakes in higher education were rather complacent and lackadaisical in letting authorities in the government and the University of Zimbabwe have an exclusive monopoly on the provision of higher education.

Mechanisms of checks and balances were almost absent. The use of university budget allocations was left to the arbitrary whims of the Ministry of Higher Education and university authorities. Some higher education providers became entrenched in positions of authority. They resisted changes such as restructuring and reforming universities. They were not responsive to the changing socioeconomic, cultural, and political realities. University stakeholders, in particular the government, resisted the establishment of church-related university institutions in the country. A number of years elapsed before Africa University and Solusi University were allowed to exist.

In summary, the physical infrastructures of higher education institutions are left to decay. Academic standards continue to fall and deteriorate. There is a general perception of mismanagement and lack of managerial skill on the part of authorities administering higher education institutions. Because of these perceptions, tensions and mistrust between students and authorities have continued to simmer unresolved for a long time. Hence, there is frequent student unrest on campuses. The country also lacks specialists, post–higher education institutions for postgraduate students, and facilities for the development of staff specialists.

ACKNOWLEDGMENTS

Special thanks to Wellington Mbofana and Jim Nyagadi for clerical assistance during the course of this work. I also would like to acknowledge Anna Tinarwo for her help in acquiring data for this work.

BIBLIOGRAPHY

Ashby, E. 1964. *African Universities and Western Tradition*. Cambridge, Mass.: Harvard University Press.

Askin, S. 1988. *College Crisis across Africa*. Boston: Christian Science Publishing Society.

Atkinson, N. 1972. *A History of Education Policy in Rhodesia*. London: Longman, Group.

———. 1974. *Educational Co-operation in Commonwealth*. Salisbury, Rhodesia: University of Rhodesia Press.

———. 1982. "Racial Integration in Zimbabwean Schools, 1979–1980 Year." *Comparative Education* 18, no. 1: 77–89.

Barnhardt, R. 1996. *The Domestication of the Ivory Tower: Institutional Adaptation of Cultural Distance*. Fairbanks: Center for Cross-Cultural Studies, University of Alaska–Fairbanks.

Beard, T. V. R. 1972. "Background to Student Activities at the University College of Fort Hare." In H. W. Van Der Merwe and D. Welsh, eds., *Student Perspective on South Africa*. Cape Town, South Africa: David Philip.

Bullock, C. 1928. *The Mashona: The Indigenous Natives of Southern Rhodesia*. Johannesburg, South Africa: Jutland Co.

Chetsanga, C. J. 1994. *Phase 1 Report of the Committee on the Devolution of B.Ed. Programs and B.Tech Degree*. Harare: Zimbabwe Government Printers.

Coles, E. K. T. 1986. *Education in Botswana 1966, 1986, 2006*. Gaborone: Botswana Government Publications.

Dachs, A. J. 1976. *The Catholic Church and Zimbabwe*. Gwelo, Zimbabwe: Mambo Press.

Frederikse, J. 1982. *None But Ourselves*. Johannesburg, South Africa: Ravan Press.

Gann, L. H. 1969. *A History of Southern Rhodesia: Early Days to 1934*. New York: Humanities Press.

Gayre, R. G. 1972. *The Origins of the Zimbabwe Civilisation*. London: Galaxie Press.

Hall, R. N. 1905. *Great Zimbabwe: Mashonaland, Rhodesia*. New York. Negro Universities Press.

Hall, R. N., and W. G. Neal. 1904. *The Ancient Ruins of Rhodesia*. New York: Negro University Press.

Hastings, A. 1977. *A History of African Christianity 1950–1975*. London: Cambridge University Press.

Hill, G. F. 1994. *Memorandum to the Cabinet by the Honorable Minister of Higher Education Comrade Ignatius Chombo on the Report of the Ministerial Committee on the Future Development of University Distance Education*. Harare: Government of Zimbabwe Press.

Keppel-Jones, A. 1983. *The White Conquest of Zimbabwe 1884–1902*. Toronto: McGill–Queen's University Press.

Martin, D., and P. Johnson. *The Struggle for Zimbabwe: The Chimurenga*. New York: Monthly Review Press.

Mazrui, A. A. 1998. *The Africans: A Triple Heritage.* New York: Little, Brown and Company.

Ministry of Higher Education and Technology. 1990. *Rationalisation of Vocational and Technical Education in Zimbabwe.* Harare, Zimbabwe: Ministry of Higher Education and Technology.

———. 2000. *Directory of Registered Vocational and Technical Training Institutions in Zimbabwe April 2000.* Harare, Zimbabwe: Ministry of Higher Education and Technology.

Monthly Review Reserve Bank of Zimbabwe. 2001. *National Accounts Report 1985–1999.* Zimbabwe: Central Statistical Office.

Murray, J., ed. 1998. *Cultural Atlas of Africa.* New York: Facts on File.

Ngobassu, A. 1970. *The National University of Zaire (UNAZA) in Creating the African University Emerging in the 1970s.* London: Oxford University Press.

National University of Science and Technology. 1996. *Annual Report on National University of Science and Technology.* Bulawayo: National University of Science and Technology.

Omari, I. M. 1990. *Innovation and Change in Higher Education in Developing Countries: Experiences from Tanzania.* Vancouver: Department of Education, University of British Columbia.

Parker, F. 1957–1958. *African Development and Education in Southern Rhodesia.* Athens: Ohio State University Press.

———. 1970. "Africa Education in Rhodesia." In B. Rose, ed., *Education in Southern Africa.* London: Camelot Press.

Ransford, O. 1968. *Rulers of Rhodesia from Earliest Times to the Referendum.* London: Murray Press.

Stoneman, C., ed. 1981. *Zimbabwe's Inheritance.* New York: St. Martin's Press.

Saint, W. S. 1992. *Universities in Africa: Strategies for Stabilisation and Revitalisation in African Religion.* Washington, D.C: The World Bank.

Therroux, P. 1989. "Malawi: Faces of a Quiet Land." *National Geographic* 176, no. 3: 94–106.

University of Zimbabwe. 1992–1999. *Calendar.* Mt. Pleasant: University of Zimbabwe.

Wandira, A. 1978. *The African University in Development.* Johannesburg, South Africa: Ravan Press.

Welsh, D. 1972. "Some Political and Social Determinants of the Academic Environment." In H. W. Van der Merwe and D. Welsh, eds., *Student Perspective on South Africa.* Cape Town, South Africa: David Philip.

Williams, P. R. C. 1989. *Report of the Commission of Inquiry into the Establishment of a Second University or Campus.* Harare: Zimbabwe Government Printers.

Willis, A. J. 1964. *Introduction to the History of Central Africa.* London: Oxford University Press.

Zvobgo, R. J. 1994. *Colonialism and Education in Zimbabwe.* Harare: Zimbabwean Experience College Press.

PART 3

Higher Education Resources

Bibliography on Higher Education in Africa

Damtew Teferra and Alma Maldonado-Maldonado

This bibliography lists comprehensive works published on African higher education in various forms, including books, journals, monographs, and occasional papers. While we made a vigorous effort to be as comprehensive as we could, this bibliography does not include all the works available in the field. Because of the multidisciplinarity and robustness of the field, material appears in a variety of fora in numerous disciplines, making it difficult to keep track of works in the field. The absence of journals dedicated to African higher education that could serve as focal points and resource centers further adds to the challenge. That said, we are confident that major, important, and influential studies are captured in this rich resource. We have been somewhat selective in this bibliography and have omitted some peripheral works.

We have made an effort to include materials published in French, though the results are far from satisfactory. We believe that a more coordinated effort must be exerted to organize and popularize the French-language literature on African higher education. The literature on African higher education in Portuguese is scanty and even less widely available.

Organization

The chapter has two sections: a country list and a thematic list. The country list provides a numbered bibliographic list for fifty countries, listed in alphabetical order. Following that, regional- and transregional-based resources are given in nine separate subsections. The second section, the thematic list, covers a variety of theme-based issues organized in twenty-six subsections that are cross-referenced with the numbered country list in the first section.

The Resources

We have included 914 items in this bibliography. South Africa, Nigeria, and Kenya—in order of significance—provide the largest number of them. The disparity among countries is rather significant. South Africa leads with 126 references, followed by Nigeria with 67 and Kenya with 46. On the other end of the spectrum, many countries, including the Central African Republic, Chad, Eritrea, Gabon, Gambia, Guinea Bissau, and Mauritania, have very few references. Research, the role of higher education in national development, science and technology, the governance and management of institutions, teaching and learning, and curriculum issues are featured prominently in this source. The literature on issues such as globalization, employment and the labor market, graduate education, private higher education, and interuniversity cooperation is in its infancy and awaits further development.

We focused on the 1980s to the present in this bibliography. A few important publications and classical works of relevance that predate 1980 are also included. Analyzing the landscape of themes over the years will help readers comprehend the most frequent topics and areas of research focus, identify countries where research in higher education predominates, and recognize the major players—individuals and institutions—in the field. Also, this reference will help as a guide in analyzing research themes over time.

SECTION I. COUNTRY LIST

Algeria

1. Benachenhou, M. 1980. *Vers l'université Algerienne.* (*Toward the University.*) Alger: Office des Publications Universitaires.

2. Boubekeur, F. 1999. "Des diplômés Algeriens parlent de la formation universitaire." ("Views of Algerian Graduates on Higher Education.") *Mediterranean Journal of Educational Studies* 4, no. 2: 181–186.

3. Chitour, C. E. 2000. *L'université et la création de richesse, in travaux du 3ème colloque scientifique, l'université et la création de l'emploi.* (*The University and Social Welfare: Proceedings of the 3rd Scientific Colloquium on the University and Employment.*) Alger: El-Maarifa.

4. Djeflat, A. 1992. "Algeria." In Burton R. Clark and Guy R. Neave, eds., *The Encyclopedia of Higher Education,* 1: 12–17. New York: Pergamon.

5. Djeghloul, A. 1980. *Annuaire des enseignants chercheurs en sciences humaines de l'Université d'Oran.* Oran: Centre de documentation des sciences humaines.

6. Djeghloul, A. 1982. "Notes sur les revues universitaires Algeriennes en sciences sociales et humaines." ("Notes on University Journals of Social and Human Sciences in Algeria.") *Annuaire de l'Afrique du Nord* XXI: 881–888.

7. Farhi, M. 1982. *L'Enseignement supérieur en Algérie et le recours à la formation à l'étrang.* (*Algerian Higher Education and Student Flight to Foreign Universities.*) Paris: UNESCO.

8. Sack, R. 1991. "Algeria, Morocco, and Tunisia." In P. G. Altbach, ed., *International Higher Education: An Encyclopedia,* 1: 375–383. New York: Garland.

Angola

9. Lopes, C. 1987. *Education, science, culture et communication en Angola, Cap-Vert, Guinée-Bissau, Mozambique et Sao Tomé et Principe.* (*Education, Science, Culture and Communication in Angola, Cape Verde, Guinea-Bissau, Mozambique and Sao Tome and Principe.*) Boulder, Colo.: Westview Press.

10. Pires, E. L. 1992. "Angola." In Burton R. Clark and Guy R. Neave, eds., *The Encyclopedia of Higher Education,* 1: 71–74. New York: Pergamon.

Benin

11. Agbodjan, P. 1997. *Higher Education in Benin: A Study Conducted in Preparation of the Donors Round Table on Education.* Cotonou, Benin: UNDP and Ministry of National Education.

12. Akoha, J. 1992. "Benin." In Burton R. Clark and Guy R. Neave, eds., *The Encyclopedia of Higher Education,* 1: 71–74. New York: Pergamon.

13. Chede, A. G. L. 1989. "La fonction sociale de l'Enseignement Supérieur au Bénin." ("The Social Role of Higher Education in Benin.") *Ehuzu* (April): 3443.

14. Dahoun, M. 1997. *Le statut de la science et de la recherche au Bénin. (The Status of Science and Research in Benin.)* Berlin: Logos-Verl.

15. Gnansounou, S. C. 1998. "A Diagnostic Study of Private Higher Education in Benin." Cotonou, Benin: Ministry of National Education, USAID.

16. Guedegbe, C. M. 1999. "Higher Education Reform in Benin in a Context of Growing Privatization." *International Higher Education* 16: 11–12.

17. Lamoure, J. 1990. *L'enseignement supérieur au Bénin: Bilan et perspectives. (The Status of Science and Research in Benin.)* Cotonou, Benin: UNESCO/UNDP.

18. McIntire, S. S. 1988. "Benin." In Neville Postlethwaite, ed., *The Encyclopedia of Comparative Education and National Systems of Education.* New York: Pergamon Press.

19. Schamhart, R., and B. Wout. 1994. "Curriculum Development in Higher Agricultural Education: A Case from Benin." *Higher Education Policy* 7, no. 1: 56–62.

20. Young, A. S. 1985. "Intake Size Effect on Performance in Pre-Degree Sciences at the University of Benin." *West African Journal of Education* 26.

Botswana

21. Adeyemi, M. B., and G. A. Hopkins. 1997. "University Affiliation and the Role of the University in the Moderation of Teaching Practice in Botswana." *Higher Education* 33, no. 4: 415–431.

22. Colclough, C., C. Cumming, and G. Sekgoma. 1988. *Investment Options in Post-Secondary Education in Botswana.* Gaborone: University of Botswana and British Council.

23. De Vries, D. 1999. "Crossing Cultural Boundaries at the University of Botswana." *Journal of College Science Teaching* 28, no. 5: 303–306.

24. Hinchliffe, K. 1988. *The Cost Effectiveness of Technical and Vocational Education and Training in Botswana.* Gaborone: University of Botswana.

25. Hopkin, A. G. 1996. "External Examining and Moderating at the University of Botswana." In P. T. M. Marope and S. G. Weeks, eds., *Education and National Development in Southern Africa,* 85–100. Gaborone: Saches.

26. Marope, M. 1992. "Botswana." In Burton R. Clark and Guy R. Neave, eds., *The Encyclopedia of Higher Education,* 1: 12–17. New York: Pergamon.

27. Mokgwathi, G. M. G. 1992. "Financing Higher Education in Botswana." *Higher Education* 23, no. 4: 425–431.

28. Morapedi, N. T. 1987. "The Role of the National Institute for Development Research and Documentation (NIR, University of Botswana, in Improving the Research Environment in Botswana)." In R. Hitchcok, N. Parsons, and J. Taylor, eds., *Research for Development in Botswana,* 415–422. Gaborone: Botswana Society.

29. Neill, R., and T. Mokoena. 1999. *Strategic Planning, Information Systems and Organizational Development at the University of Botswana.* Paris: International Institute of Educational Planning, UNESCO.

30. Ronan, N. J., and C. H. Ronan. 1995. "One More Time: How Do You Finance Higher Education?" *Journal of the Botswana Educational Research Association* 3, no. 1–2: 55–64.

31. Setidisho, N. O. H., and B. C. Sanyal. 1988. *Higher Education and Employment in Botswana.* Paris: International Institute for Educational Planning, UNESCO.

32. Turner, J. D. 1984. "The Role of the University of Botswana in Meeting National Manpower Requirements." In M. Crowder, ed., *Education for Development in Botswana,* 225–236. Gaborone: Botswana Society and Macmillan Botswana.

33. University of Botswana. 1991. *Report of the Review Commission of the University of Botswana.* Gaborone: University of Botswana.

34. Weeks, S. G. 1998. "Raising the Quality of Teacher Preparation: Recent Trends in Teacher Development." In C. D. Yandila, ed., *Improving Education Quality for Effective Learning: The Teacher's Dilemma,* 57–61. Gaborone: Ministry of Education.

Burkina Faso

35. Agbangla, C., and N. Charpentier. 1999. *Role et place de l'université dans la société du XXIème siècle face à la mondialisation. Cinquième Colloque, Université sans frontière. (The Role and Position of the University in the 21st Century Society and the Challenge of Globalization, 5th Colloquium: University Without Borders.)* Ouagadougou: Université sans frontière.

36. Biervliet, W. 1995. *Research Capacity Building in Bangladesh, Burkina Faso, Kenya, Tanzania.* Hague: Centre for the Study of Education in Developing Countries (CESO).

37. Federici, S. 2000. "Interview with Salif Yonaba, Member of the Permanent Committee on Academic Freedom in Burkina Faso." In S. Federici, G. Caffentzis, and O. Alidou, eds., *A Thousand Flowers: Social Struggles against Structural Adjustment in African Universities,* 215–220. Trenton, N.J.: African World Press.

38. Khelfaoui, H. 2000. *La recherche scientifique au Burkina-Faso. (Scientific Research in Burkina-Faso.)* Paris: Institut de Recherche pour le Développement, Commission Européenne.

39. Potemans, K. 1992. "Burkina Faso." In Burton R. Clark and Guy R. Neave, eds., *The Encyclopedia of Higher Education,* 1: 99–103. New York: Pergamon.

40. Tiao Luc, A. 2000. "Université de Ouagadougou: La refondation en marche, la vie reprend." ("Ouagadougou University: Reestablishment and New Start.") *La Dépêche* 33: 3–21.

41. Traore, S. A. 2000. "La refondation de l'Université de Ouagadougou." ("The Reestablishment of the Ouagadougou University.") *Wattitingol* 7: 7–13.

Burundi

42. Banderembako, D., and E. Minani. 1994. *Contribution à l'étude institutionnelle et financière de l'université du Burundi. Partie III: Le système de gestion du budget et du patrimoine de l'université du Burundi. (Contribution to the Institutional and Financial Study of the University of Burundi. Part III: Budget and Endowment Management System of the University of Burundi.)* Bujumbura: Université du Burundi.

43. Des Lierres, T., G. Ntunaguza, and J. Ndayisaba. 1991. *Les échecs dans l'enseignement supérieur: Actes du Séminaire de l'Association internationale de pédagogie universitaire tenu à l'Université du Burundi du 2 au 6 mai 1989. (Student Failure in Higher Education: Seminar proceedings of the International Association of University Pedagogy held at the University of Burundi, 2–6 May 1989.)* Montreal: Association Internationale de Pédagogie Universitaire.

44. Keyes, C. 1992. "Burundi." In Burton R. Clark and Guy R. Neave, eds., *The Encyclopedia of Higher Education*, 1: 103–105. New York: Pergamon.

45. Ndayisaba, J. 1994. *Contribution à l'étude institutionnelle et financière de l'université du Burundi. Partie II: Les performances pédagogiques de l'université du Burundi. (Contribution to the Institutional and Financial Study of the University of Burundi. Part II: Pedagogical Performance at the University of Burundi.)* Bujumbura: Université du Burundi.

46. Université du Burundi. 1989. *25ème anniversaire: Rétrospective 1964–1989. (25th Anniversary: Retrospective.)* Bujumbura: Presses universitaires, Université du Burundi.

47. Université du Burundi. 1994. *Etude institutionnelle et financière de l'université du Burundi. (Institutional and Financial Study of the University of Burundi.)* Bujumbura.

Cameroon

48. Edokat, T. 2000. "Effects of Brain Drain on Higher Education in Cameroon." In S. Tapsoba, S. Kassoum, V. Houenou, O. Bankole, M. Sethi, and J. Ngu, eds., *Brain Drain and Capacity Building in Africa*, 174–183. Dakar, Senegal: Economic Commission for Africa/International Development Research Centre/International Organization for Migration.

49. Kange, E. 1992. "Cameroon." In Burton R. Clark and Guy R. Neave, eds., *The Encyclopedia of Higher Education*, 1: 107–109. New York: Pergamon.

50. Khelfaoui, H. 2000. *La recherche scientifique au Cameroun. (Scientific Research in Cameroon.)* Paris: Institut de Recherche pour le Développement, Commission Européenne.

51. Kouame, A. 2000. "Exode des compétences et développement des capacités: Quelques réflexions à partir du cas Camerounais." ("Brain Drain and Capacity Building: Some Thoughts from the Cameroonian Case.") In S. Tapsoba, S. Kassoum, V. Houenou, O. Bankole, M. Sethi, and J. Ngu, eds., *Brain Drain and Capacity Building in Africa*, 156–171. Dakar, Senegal: Economic Commission for Africa/International Development Research Centre/International Organization for Migration.

52. Ministry of Higher Education. 1982. *Actes du conseil de l'enseignment supérieur et de la recherche scientifique et technique. (Proceedings of the Council on Higher Education, Sci-*entific *and Technical Research.)* Yaounde: Société de Presse et d'Editions du Cameroun (SOPECAM).

53. Ministry of Higher Education. 1993. *Higher Education Reforms in Cameroon.* Yaounde: Centre d'Edition et de Production pour l'Enseignement et la Recherche.

54. Ministry of Higher Education. 1999. *Statistical Yearbook of Higher Education in Cameroon.* Yaounde: Cameroon Ministry of Higher Education.

55. Ngu, J. L. 1993. "Government and Higher Education in Cameroon." *Higher Education Policy* 6, no. 4: 29–33.

56. Njeuma, D. L., H. Endeley, F. Mbuntum, N. Lyonga, D. Nkweteyim, S. Musenja, and E. Elizabeth. 1999. *Reforming a National System of Higher Education: The Case of Cameroon.* Washington, D.C.: Association for the Development of Education in Africa (ADEA) Working Group on Higher Education and The World Bank.

57. Ouendji, N. N. 1996. "Cameroon: 'Mined' Campuses and Muzzled Staff." In Council for the Development of Social Science Research in Africa (CODESRIA), ed., *The State of Academic Freedom in Africa 1995.* Dakar: CODESRIA.

58. Pecku, N. K. 1988. *Survey of Current Status of Distance Education in Cameroon.* Vancouver, B.C.: Commonwealth of Learning.

59. Tsala, G. 1998. *Rapport de synthèse sur l'évaluation de la réforme du système de l'enseignement supérieur. (Final Evaluation Report on the Higher Education Reform.)* Yaounde: Ministère de l'Enseignement Supérieur.

60. University of Yaounde. 1985. *Annuaire de l'Université de Yaoundé, 1984/85. (University of Yaounde Yearbook.)* Yaounde: SOPECAM.

61. Woodhouse, H. 1997. "Tradition or Modernity? The Fallacy of Misplaced Concreteness among Women Science Educators in Cameroon." *Interchange* 28 (April): 253–262.

Central African Republic

62. Mbringa-Takama, M. F. 1992. "Central African Republic." In Burton R. Clark and Guy R. Neave, eds., *The Encyclopedia of Higher Education*, 1: 125–127. New York: Pergamon.

Chad

63. Cowen, R. 1992. "Chad." In Burton R. Clark and Guy R. Neave, eds., *The Encyclopedia of Higher Education*, 1: 127–130. New York: Pergamon.

Cape Verde

See 9

Congo-Brazzaville

64. Ossebi, H. 1996. "Socio-political Crises and the Educational Stakes in Congo: Is the University Institution Heading towards a Necrosis?" In Council for the Development of Social Science Research in Africa (CODESRIA), ed., *The State of Academic Freedom in Africa 1995.* Dakar: CODESRIA.

65. Vansteenkiste, M. N. 1992. "Congo." In Burton R.

Clark and Guy R. Neave, eds., *The Encyclopedia of Higher Education*, 1: 158–160. New York: Pergamon.

Democratic Republic of Congo (Zaire)

66. Magabe, M., B. Bapolisi, and K. Lokombe. 1992. "L'informel dans la formation des enseignants: Le cas de l'Institut Supérieur Pédagogique de Bukavu (Zaïre)." ("The Informal Aspects of Teacher Training: The Case of Advanced Pedagogical Institute of Bukavu-Zaire.") *International Review of Education* 38, no. 5: 471–488.

67. Matundu, L. 1995. "Pour de nouvelles formules d'administration universitaire, une étude prospective sur les universités du Zaïre." ("In Search of New University Administration Formulas: Prospective Study on Zairian Universities.") In Mémoire de master en gestion et administration publiques (Master's Thesis in Management and Public Administration), Université d'Anvers.

68. Matundu, L. 1997. "La coopération universitaire: support de l'université pour la réalization de ses missions en période de crise. Une étude sur l'enseignement supérieur et universitaire." ("University Cooperation: Assistance to the University in Achieving its Mission in Times of Crisis: A Study on Higher Education.") In Mémoire de D.E.S. en coopération au développement (Master's Thesis in Cooperation and Development), Republic of Congo.

69. Mugabe, M. 1992. "Zaire." In Burton R. Clark and Guy R. Neave, eds., *The Encyclopedia of Higher Education*, 1: 821–825. New York: Pergamon.

70. Tshibangu-Tshishiku, T. 1998. *L'Université Congolaise: Etapes historiques, situation actuelle et défis à relever.* (*The Congolese University: Historical Development, Current Challenges.*) Kinshasa: Editions Universitaires Africaines and Agence de Coopération Culturelle et Technique.

71. UNESCO. 1986. *L'enseignement Supérieur et Universitaire du Zaïre, République du Zaïre, Départment de l'Enseignement Supérieur et Universitaire.* (*Higher Education in Zaire, Republic of Zaire, Higher Education Department.*) Paris: UNESCO.

Côte d'Ivoire

72. Degni-Segui, R. 1996. "Academic Freedom and University Autonomy in Cote d'Ivoire." In Council for the Development of Social Science Research in Africa (CODESRIA), ed., *The State of Academic Freedom in Africa 1995.* Dakar: CODESRIA.

73. Diarrassouba, V. C. 1979. "L'Université Ivoirienne et le développement de la nation." ("The University in Côte d'Ivoire and National Development.") Dakar: Les nouvelles éditions Africaines.

74. Houenou, P. 2000. "Développement des capacités et exode des compétences: le cas de l'enseignement supérieur en Côte d'Ivoire." ("Capacity Building and Brain Drain: The Case of Higher Education in Côte d'Ivoire.") In S. Tapsoba, S. Kassoum, V. Houenou, O. Bankole, M. Sethi, and J. Ngu, eds., *Brain Drain and Capacity Building in Africa*, 198–205. Dakar, Senegal: Economic Commission for Africa/International Development Research Centre/International Organization for Migration.

75. Khelfaoui, H. 2000. *La recherche scientifique en Côte d'Ivoire.* (*Scientific Research in Côte d'Ivoire.*) Paris: Institut de Recherche pour le Développement, Commission Européenne.

76. Tio-Toure, B. 1992. "The Ivory Coast." In Burton R. Clark and Guy R. Neave, eds., *The Encyclopedia of Higher Education*, 1: 369–371. New York: Pergamon.

77. Zolberg, A. 1975. "Political Generations in Conflict: The Ivory Coast Case." In William J. Hanna and Joel D. Barkan, *University Students and African Politics.* New York: Holmes and Meier Publishers.

Egypt

78. Boulos, W. A. 1992. "Egypt." In Burton R. Clark and Guy R. Neave, eds., *The Encyclopedia of Higher Education*, 1: 193–198. New York: Pergamon.

79. Cochran, J. 1992. "Western Higher Education and Identity Conflict: The Egyptian Female Professional." *Convergence* 25, no. 3: 66–77.

80. El-Sayyad, M. M. 1990. "How to Serve the Community Educational Needs through Cairo University." *Higher Education Policy* 3, no. 4: 42–46.

81. Howard-Merriam, K. 1979. "Women, Education, and the Professions in Egypt." *Comparative Education Review* 23, no. 2: 256–270.

82. Klausner, S. Z. 1986. "A Professor's-Eye View of the Egyptian Academy." *Journal of Higher Education* 57, no. 4: 345–369.

83. Montasser, S. H. 1995. "A Human Capital Approach to Cost-Benefit Analysis of Higher Education in Egypt: Some Preliminary Indications." *Higher Education Policy* 8, no. 1: 33–35.

84. Murphy, L. R. 1987. *The American University in Cairo, 1919–1987.* Cairo: American University in Cairo Press.

85. Psacharopoulos, G., and B. Sanyal. 1982. "Student Expectations and Graduate Market Performance in Egypt." *Higher Education* 11, no. 1: 27–49.

86. Sanyal, B. C., A. A. El Koussey, M. K. Harby, R. Noonan, S. Balbaa, and L. Yaici. 1982. *University Education and the Labour Market in the Arab Republic of Egypt.* Paris: Pergamon Press.

87. Shann, M. H. 1992. "The Reform of Higher Education in Egypt." *Higher Education* 24, no. 2: 225–246.

Eritrea

88. Useem, A. 1998. "Eritrea Strives to Transform a Struggling University into a Vital Institution." *The Chronicle of Higher Education*, May 29, A47.

Ethiopia

89. Addis Ababa University. 1980. *Three Decades of University Education, 1950–1980: On the Occasion of the 30th Anniversary.* Addis Ababa: Artistic Printing Press.

90. Aemero, A. 1998. "Problems of Gender Equity in Institutions of Higher Education in Ethiopia." In Amare Asgedom, W. Cummings, D. Dufera, J. Odharo, H. Wondimu, and G. Zewdie, eds., *Quality Education in Ethiopia: Visions for the 21st*

Century. Addis Ababa: Institute of Educational Research (IER) and Association of African Universities (AAU).

91. Aredo, D. 2000. "Human Capital Flight from Africa: An Assessment of Brain Drain from Ethiopia." In S. Tapsoba, S. Kassoum, V. Houenou, O. Bankole, M. Sethi, and J. Ngu, eds., *Brain Drain and Capacity Building in Africa*, 122–145. Dakar, Senegal: Economic Commission for Africa/International Development Research Centre/International Organization for Migration.

92. Aredo, D., and Y. Zelalem. 1998. "Skilled Labor Migration from Developing Countries: An Assessment of Brain Drain from Ethiopia." In Senait Seyoum and Alemayehu Seyoum, eds., *Human Resources Development in Ethiopia.* Addis Ababa: Ethiopian Economic Association.

93. Ayano, T. 1992. "Ethiopia." In Burton R. Clark and Guy R. Neave, eds., *The Encyclopedia of Higher Education*, 1: 201–207. New York: Pergamon.

94. Balsvik, R. R. 1985. *Haile Selassie I Students: The Intellectual and Social Background to Revolution, 1952–1977.* East Lansing: African Studies Center, Michigan State University and Norwegian Council of Science and the Humanities.

95. Bekele, E. 1995. *Current Status of Research and Development Problems and Management in Higher Education in Ethiopia.* Addis Ababa: Addis Ababa University.

96. Bekele, E. 1996. *Biannual AAU Research Book: With Highlighted Information on Twenty Years of Research Activities at AAU.* Addis Ababa: Addis Ababa University Press.

97. Tefera, S. 1992. "Brain Drain among Academics in Two Higher Education Institutions in Ethiopia." *Ethiopian Journal of Education,* 13, no. 2: 1–37.

98. Teferra, D. 2001. "Academic Dishonesty in African Universities: Trends, Challenges, and Repercussions—An Ethiopian Case Study." *International Journal of Educational Development* 22, no. 2: 71–86.

99. Tewolde-Berhan, G.-E. 1987. *Research Problems and Policy at Higher Learning Institutions in Ethiopia.* Addis Ababa: Commission for Higher Education.

100. Wagaw, T. 1990. *The Development of Higher Education and Social Change: An Ethiopian Experience.* East Lansing: Michigan State University Press.

101. Wondimu, H. 1990. *Research and Development Priorities in Higher Education Institutions.* Addis Ababa: Higher Education Main Department.

102. Wondimu, H. 1999. *Ethiopia's Educational Policy Reform and the Trends on Human Resource Development: Some Observations.* Addis Ababa: Forum for Social Studies.

Gabon

103. Obone, J. 1992. "Gabon." In Burton R. Clark and Guy R. Neave, eds., *The Encyclopedia of Higher Education*, 1: 225–230. New York: Pergamon.

Gambia

104. Smith, R. L. 1992. "Gambia." In Burton R. Clark and Guy R. Neave, eds., *The Encyclopedia of Higher Education*, 1: 230–231. New York: Pergamon.

Ghana

105. Amonoo, R. F. 1992. "Ghana." In Burton R. Clark and Guy R. Neave, eds., *The Encyclopedia of Higher Education*, 1: 260–265. New York: Pergamon.

106. Barkan, J. 1975. *An African Dilemma: University Students, Development and Politics in Ghana, Tanzania and Uganda.* Nairobi: Oxford University Press.

107. Brock, A. 1996. "Budgeting Models and University Efficiency: A Ghanaian Case Study." *Higher Education* 32: 113–127.

108. Budu, J. M. 1998. *A Profile of Ghanaian Universities.* London: Commonwealth Higher Education Management Service.

109. Kotey, N. 1992. "Student Loans in Ghana." *Higher Education* 23, no. 4: 451–459.

110. Sawyerr, A. 1994. "Ghana: Relations between Government and Universities." In G. Neave and F. van Vught, eds., *Government and Higher Education Relationships across Three Continents: The Winds of Change.* Oxford: Pergamon Press.

111. Sutherland-Addy, E. 1993. *Revival and Renewal: Reflections on the Creation of a System of Tertiary Education in Ghana.* Africa Region, Technical Department, Human Resources and Poverty Division (AFTHR) Note no. 10. Washington, D.C.: The World Bank.

112. Weiss, L. 1981. "The Reproduction of Social Inequality: Closure in the Ghanaian University." *Journal of Developing Areas* 16 (October).

Guinea

113. Diallo, A. G. 1992. "Guinea." In Burton R. Clark and Guy R. Neave, eds., *The Encyclopedia of Higher Education*, 1: 277–278. New York: Pergamon.

114. International Institute of Educational Planning–Direction Nationale de l'Enseignement Supérieure. 2000. *Vers le renforcement des capacités institutionnelles de gestion de la direction nationale de l'enseignement supérieur en République de Guinée.* (*Toward the Reinforcement of Institutional Management Capacities of the National Department of Higher Education, Republic of Guinea.*) Paris: International Institute for Educational Planning.

115. Programme d'aide au développement de l'enregistrement sonore (PADES). 1997. *Etude de l'efficacité interne et externe des universités Guinéennes.* (*Study of the Internal and External Efficiency of Guinean Universities.*) Conakry: PADES.

116. Sow, C., and I. Fox. 1996. "Guinea: Violations of Rights of Students and Teachers." In Council for the Development of Social Science Research in Africa (CODESRIA), ed., *The State of Academic Freedom in Africa 1995.* Dakar: CODESRIA.

117. Sylla, S. 2000. "L'experience Guinéenne en matière de renforcement des capacités humaines de développement." ("The Guinean Experience with Capacity Building for Development.") In S. Tapsoba, S. Kassoum, V. Houenou, O. Bankole, M. Sethi, and J. Ngu, eds., *Brain Drain and Capacity Building in Africa*, 110–119. Dakar, Senegal: Economic Commission for Africa/International Development Research Centre/International Organization for Migration.

Guinea-Bissau

See 9

Kenya

118. Abagi, D. 1999. *Resource Utilization in Public Universities in Kenya: Enhancing Efficiency and Cost-Recovery Measures.* Nairobi: Institute of Policy and Analysis Research.

119. Chale, E. M., and P. Michaud. 1997. *Distance Learning for Change in Africa: A Case Study of Senegal and Kenya.* Ottawa, Canada: International Development Research Centre Study/Acacia Initiative, International Development Research Center.

120. Court, D. 1980. "The Developmental Ideal in Higher Education: The Experience of Kenya and Tanzania." *Higher Education* 9, no. 6: 657–680.

121. Court, D. 1989. *University Education.* Mombasa, Kenya: Ministry of Education.

122. Darkoh, M. B. K., and Wambari, K. 1994. "Towards Professional Excellence at Kenyatta University." *Journal of Eastern African Research and Development* 24: 78.

123. Eisemon, T. O. 1980. "African Academics: A Study of Scientists at the University of Ibadan and Nairobi." *Annals of American Association of Political and Social Science* 448: 126–139.

124. Eisemon, T. O. 1982. *The Science Profession in the Third World: Studies from India and Kenya.* New York: Praeger.

125. Eisemon, T. O. 1984. "Educational Expansion and the Development of Science in Kenya." *Science and Public Policy* 11: 70–76.

126. Eisemon, T. O. 1986. "Foreign Training and Foreign Assistance for University Development in Kenya: Too Much of a Good Thing?" *International Journal of Educational Development* 6: 1–13.

127. Eisemon, T. O. 1992. "Private Initiatives in Higher Education in Kenya." *Higher Education* 24, no. 2: 157–175.

128. Eisemon, T. O., and C. H. Davis. 1997. "Kenya: Crisis in the Scientific Community." In V. V. Krishna, J. Gaillard, and R. Waast, eds., *Scientific Communities in the Developing World.* New Delhi: Sage.

129. Gravenir, F. U., and E. Mbuthia. 2000. *Generating Supplemental Sources of Income by Universities in Kenya: A Case Study of Maseno University.* Nairobi: Kenyatta University.

130. Gray, K. R., and S. H. Credle. 1996. "Public Policy and the Management of Higher Education in Sub-Saharan Africa: The Case of Kenya." *Journal of Marketing for Higher Education* 7, no. 4: 49–59.

131. Hughes, R. 1987. "Revisiting the Fortunate Few: University Graduates in the Kenyan Labor Market." *Comparative Education Review* 31: 583–610.

132. Hughes, R., and K. Mwiria. 1989. "Kenyan Women, Higher Education, and the Labor Market." *Comparative Education* 25: 177–193.

133. Hughes, R., and K. Mwiria. 1990. "An Essay on the Implications of University Expansion in Kenya." *Higher Education* 19, no. 2: 215–237.

134. Hughes, R., and K. Mwiria. 1991. "Kenya." In P. G. Altbach, ed., *International Higher Education: An Encyclopedia,* 1: 385–397. New York: Garland.

135. Irungu, M. 1997. "The Struggle for Faculty Unionism in a Stalled Democracy: Lessons from Kenya's Public University." *Journal of Third World Studies* 14, no. 1: 91–114.

136. Juma, M. N. 2001. *African Virtual University: The Case of Kenyatta University, Kenya.* London: Commonwealth Secretariat.

137. Kanake, L. 1997. *Gender Disparities among the Academic Staff in Kenyan Public Universities.* Nairobi: Lyceum Educational Consultants.

138. Makau, B. 1993. "The External Degree Programme at the University of Nairobi." In H. Perraton, ed., *Distance Education for Teacher Training.* London: Routledge.

139. Mazrui, A., and W. Mutunga. 2000. "The State versus the Academic Unions in Postcolonial Kenya." In S. Federici, G. Caffentzis, and O. Alidou, eds., *A Thousand Flowers: Social Struggles against Structural Adjustment in African Universities,* 197–205. Trenton, N.J.: African World Press.

140. Migot-Adholla, S. E. 1985. "The Evolution of Higher Education: Kenya." In L. Tembo, M. Dilogassa, P. Makhurance, and P. L. Pitsoin, eds., *The Development of Higher Education in Eastern and Southern Africa,* 1–26. Nairobi: Hedaya Educational Books.

141. Mulli, V. 1995. "Enhancing Women's Participation in Teaching, Research and Management of Higher Education: The Case of Nairobi University, Kenya." In UNESCO-BREDA, ed., *Women in Higher Education,* 69–81. Dakar: UNESCO-BREDA.

142. Munene, I. 1997. "Origins and Perceptions on Universities, Students and Students' Organizations of Kenyatta University Student Leaders." In Akim Okuni and Juliet Tembe, eds., *Capacity Building in Educational Research in East Africa: Empirical Insights into Qualitative Research Methodology,* 279–298. Bonn: DSE.

143. Mutunga, W., and M. Kiai. 1996. "The State of Academic Freedom in Kenya 1992–94." In Council for the Development of Social Science Research in Africa (CODESRIA), ed., *The State of Academic Freedom in Africa 1995.* Dakar: CODESRIA.

144. Mwiria, K. 1994. "Democratizing Kenya's Public Universities." *Basic Education Forum* 4: 45–50.

145. Mwiria, K. 1996. "Democratizing Kenya's University Education Sector." In K. Mwiria, ed., *Sectoral Studies: Focusing on Kenya's Future Policy Reforms.* Nairobi: International Commission of Jurists–Kenya Section.

146. Mwiria, K., and R. Hughes. 1992. "Kenya." In Burton R. Clark and Guy R. Neave, eds., *The Encyclopedia of Higher Education,* 1: 391–397. New York: Pergamon.

147. Mwiria, K., and C. Ngome. 1998. "The World of Private Universities. The Experience of Kenya." *NORRAG News* 23: 38–40.

148. Mwiria, K., and M. S. Nyukuri. 1992. *The Management of Double Intakes: A Case Study of Kenyan University.* Document IIEP/RP/49.13. Paris: International Institute of Educational Planning (UNESCO).

149. Nduko, J. 2000. "Students' Rights and Academic Freedom in Kenya's Public Universities." In S. Federici, G. Caffentzis, and O. Alidou, eds., *A Thousand Flowers: Social Struggles against Structural Adjustment in African Universities*, 207–214. Trenton, N.J.: African World Press.

150. Odumbe, J. 1988. "The Establishment and the Development of the External Degree Programs of the University of Nairobi." In D. Sewart and J. S. Daniel, eds., *Developing Distance Education*. Oslo: International Council for Distance Education.

151. Omari, I. M. 1994. "Kenya: Management of Higher Education in Developing Countries—The Relationship between the Government and Higher Education." In G. Neave and F. van Vught, eds., *Government and Higher Education Relationships across Three Continents: The Winds of Change*. Oxford: Pergamon Press.

152. Orodho, J. A. 1995. "Cost Recovery and Its Impact on Quality, Access and Equity: The Case of Kenyan Public Universities." *Higher Education Policy* 8, no. 1: 40–43.

153. Orson, C. M., and B. Greenbert. 1990. "Innovations in Instructional Materials at University of Nairobi, Kenya, Africa." *International Journal of Instructional Media* 17, no. 2: 163–166.

154. Rapando Murunga, G. 2001. "Private Universities in the Kenyan Higher Education Experience." *CODESRIA Bulletin* 1–2: 11–14.

155. Rathgeber, E. M. 1985. "Cultural Production in Kenyan Medical Education." *Comparative Education Review* 29, no. 3: 299–316.

156. Rodrigues, A. J., C. A. Moturi, R. J. P. Scott, and W. Okelo-Odongo. 1993. "Informatics in Higher Education: Kenya Case Study." *Higher Education Policy* 6, no. 3: 41–49.

157. Rodrigues, A., and S. O. Wandiga. 1997. "Cost Sharing in Public Universities: A Kenyan Case Study." *Higher Education Policy* 10, no. 1: 55–80.

158. Shaeffer, S., and J. A. Nkinyangi. 1983. "Who Conducts Research in Kenya?" *Educational Research Environments in the Developing World*. Ontario, Canada: International Development Research Center.

159. Sifuna, D. N. 1997. "Crisis in the Public Universities in Kenya." In K. Watson, C. Modgil, and S. Modgil, eds., *Reforms in Higher Education*. London: Cassell.

160. Sifuna, D. N. 1998. "The Governance of Kenyan Public Universities." *Research in Post-Compulsory Education* 32: 175–211.

161. Sifuna, D. N., and K. Mwiria. 1993. "Key Obstacles to the Development of African Universities." *Journal of Third World Studies* 10, no. 2: 199–227.

162. World Bank. 1991. *The World Bank Report no. 9824–KE. Staff Appraisal Report, Kenya: Universities Investment Project*. Washington, D.C.: The World Bank.

See also 36

Lesotho

163. Braimoh, D., O. A. Adeola, and H. M. Lephoto. 1999. "Evaluation of Distance Education Programmes: The Case of the National University of Lesotho." *Staff and Educational Development International* 3, no. 2: 151–164.

164. Fielden, J., ed. 1995. *Cost Containment Study at the National University of Lesotho*. London: Commonwealth Higher Education Management Service.

165. Matsela, Z. A. 1986. *Case Study of Lesotho's Higher Education Institutions*. Paris: UNESCO.

166. Sebatane, E. M. 1992. "Lesotho." In Burton R. Clark and Guy R. Neave, eds., *The Encyclopedia of Higher Education*, 1: 417–420. New York: Pergamon.

167. Thomas, H. G. 1998. "Developing a Strategic Plan: A Case Study from the National University of Lesotho." *Higher Education Policy* 11, no. 2: 235–243.

Liberia

168. Azango, B. B. 1992. "Liberia." In Burton R. Clark and Guy R. Neave, eds., *The Encyclopedia of Higher Education*, 1: 420–428. New York: Pergamon.

169. Hoff, A. A. 1962. *A Short History of Liberia College and the University of Liberia*. Monrovia: Consolidated Publications.

170. Seyon, P. L. N. 1973. "The University of Liberia." In T. M. Yesufu, ed., *Creating the African University*. Ibadan: Oxford University Press.

171. Seyon, P. L. N. 1997. "Rebuilding the University of Liberia in the Midst of War." *International Higher Education* 8: 17–18.

172. Snyder, C. W., and J. Nagel. 1986. *The Struggle Continues! World Bank and African Development Bank Investments in Liberian Educational Development*. McLean, Va.: Institute for International Research.

173. University of Liberia. 1984. *Towards the 21st Century: An Extension of the University of Liberia's Long-Range Plan*. Monrovia: University of Liberia.

Libya

174. Bubtana, A. R., and M. Sarakbi. 1992. "Libya." In Burton R. Clark and Guy R. Neave, eds., *The Encyclopedia of Higher Education* 1: 428–437. New York: Pergamon.

175. El-Hawat, A. 1995. *Higher Education in Libya: Reality and Future Prospective*. Tripoli: Tripoli's Scientific Library (in Arabic).

176. Secretariat of Education and Scientific Research. 1995. *Statistical Reports on Universities and Higher Technical Institutions*. Tripoli: Secretariat of Education and Scientific Research (in Arabic).

Madagascar

177. Maison de la Communication des Universités. 1998. *Monde universitaire Malgache. (The University Realm in Madagascar.)* Antananarivo: Ministère de L'Enseignement Supérieur.

178. Maison de la Communication des Universités. 1999. *Etablissements d'Enseignement supérieur privés agrées par l'Etat.*

(*State-Approved Private Higher Education Institutions.*) Antananarivo: Ministère de L'Enseignement Supérieur.

179. Rajaoson, F. 1985. *L'enseignement supérieur et le devenir de la société Malgache.* Antananarivo: Université de Madagascar.

180. Rajaoson, F. 1992. "Madagascar." In Burton R. Clark and Guy R. Neave, eds., *The Encyclopedia of Higher Education,* 1: 441–443. New York: Pergamon.

181. Rambeloson, J. 1995. "Women in Antananarivo University." In UNESCO-BREDA, ed., *Women in Higher Education in Africa,* 82–94. Dakar: UNESCO-BREDA.

182. Viens, D., and J. Lynch. 2000. *Madagascar: A Decade of Reform and Innovation in Higher Education.* Washington, D.C.: The World Bank.

Malawi

183. Castrol-Leal, F. 1996. *Who Benefits from Public Education Spending in Malawi? Results from the Recent Education Reform.* World Bank Discussion Paper no. 350. Washington, D.C.: The World Bank.

184. Dubbey, J. M. 1988. "Reaction from an African University." *Higher Education Policy* 1, no. 1: 30–31.

185. Dubbey, J. M. 1990. *University of Malawi: Tracer Study.* Zomba, Malawi: University of Malawi.

186. Dubbey, J. M., C. C. Chipofya, J. A. K. Kandawire, Z. M. Kasomekera, O. J. Kathamalo, and G. G. Machlili. 1991. "How Effective Is Our University? A Study of the Graduates of the University of Malawi." *Higher Education Quarterly* 45, no. 3: 219–233.

187. Malawi Institute of Management. 1997. *University of Malawi Reform Study: Problems and Opportunities Identification and Operations Assessment.* Lilongwe: Malawi Institute of Management.

188. Mphande, L. 2000. "The Malawi Writers Group: Before and After Structural Adjustment Programs." In S. Federici, G. Caffentzis, and O. Alidou, eds., *A Thousand Flowers: Social Struggles against Structural Adjustment in African Universities,* 181–195. Trenton, N.J.: African World Press.

189. Mwale, J. K. 1991. *Motivational Factors which Affect Teaching and Learning at the Universtity of Malawi.* Bonn: German Foundation for International Development.

190. Nazombe, A. 1992. "Malawi." In Burton R. Clark and Guy R. Neave, eds., *The Encyclopedia of Higher Education,* 1: 443–446. New York: Pergamon.

191. Prebble, T. 1990. *Distance Education at the University of Malawi: A Report on a Consultancy on Behalf of the Commonwealth of Learning.* Vancouver: Commonwealth of Learning.

192. University of Malawi, Centre for Educational Research and Training. 1995. *Challenges Facing the University of Malawi and a Review of its Mission.* Zomba: University of Malawi, Centre for Educational Research and Training.

Mali

193. Bagayoko, D. and E. L. Kelley. 1994. "The Dynamics of Student Retention: A Review and a Prescription." *Educational Forum* 115, no. 1: 31–39.

194. Diakite, Y. 1992. "Mali." In Burton R. Clark and Guy R. Neave, eds., *The Encyclopedia of Higher Education,* 1: 452–454. New York: Pergamon.

195. Saad, E. N. 1983. *Social History of Timbuktu: The Role of Muslim Scholars and Notables, 1400–1900.* Cambridge: Cambridge University Press.

Mauritania

196. Herlant, M. 1992. "Mauritania." In Burton R. Clark and Guy R. Neave, eds., *The Encyclopedia of Higher Education,* 1: 457–460. New York: Pergamon.

Mauritius

197. Association for the Development of Education in Africa. 1999. *Country Case Study on Access to Education and Training in Mauritius.* ADEA Stocktaking Review in Mauritius. Geneva: Tertiary Education Commission.

198. Ramdoyal, R. 1992. "Mauritius." In Burton R. Clark and Guy R. Neave, eds., *The Encyclopedia of Higher Education,* 1: 460–462. New York: Pergamon.

199. Tertiary Education Commission. 1999. *Studies on Social Dimensions of Globalisation: Mauritius.* Geneva: Tertiary Education Commission, Annual Report and Accounts.

Morocco

200. Belghazi, T., ed. 1996. *The Idea of the University: Séries Conferences and Colloquia 72.* Rabat: Publications of the Faculty of Letters.

201. El Maslout, A. 1995. "La réforme de l'enseignement supérieur: Un processus continu d'adaptation et de restructuration." ("Higher Education Reform: A Continuous Process of Adaptation and Restructuring.") In Association des Economistes marocains, *La Réforme de l'Enseignement au Maroc (Reform of Higher Education in Morocco),* 21–58. Rabat: Association des Economistes Marocains.

202. Emran, A. 1997. *L'enseignement et la formation Universitaire au Maroc. (Higher Education and Reform in Morocco.)* Mohammedia: Imprimerie de Fedala.

203. Kleiche, M. 2000. *La recherche scientifique au Maroc. (Scientific Research in Morocco.)* Paris: Institut de Recherche pour le Développement, Commission Européenne.

204. Mekouar, H. 1996. "University Autonomy and Academic Freedom in Morocco: Elements for a Current Debate." *Higher Education Policy* 9, no. 4: 303–308.

205. Merrouni, M. 1996. "L'université et le paradigme de l'efficacité." ("The University and the Efficiency Paradigm.") In T. Belghazi, ed., *The Idea of the University,* 85–99. Rabat: Publications of the Faculty of Letters and Human Sciences of Rabat.

206. Meziani, A. 1999. "The System of Higher Education in Morocco: A Brief Introductory Report." *Mediterranean Journal of Educational Studies* 4, no. 2: 215–219.

207. Ouakrime, M. 1996. "What Is High about Higher Education?" In T. Belghazi, ed., *The Idea of the University,* 355–367. Rabat: Publications of the Faculty of Letters and Human Sciences of Rabat.

208. Sabour, M. 1994. "Higher Education in Morocco: Between Islamization of Cultural Values and Secularization of Social Change." In T. Takala, ed., *Quality of Education in the Context of Culture in Developing Countries*, 145–157. Tampere: University of Tampere.

209. Salahdina, M. 1992. "Morocco." In Burton R. Clark and Guy R. Neave, eds., *The Encyclopedia of Higher Education*, 1: 479–482. New York: Pergamon.

See also 8

Mozambique

210. Commonwealth Secretariat. 1992. *Eduardo Mondlane University: Review of Governance, Planning and Management*. London: Commonwealth Secretariat, Special Commonwealth Fund for Mozambique.

211. Fry, P., and R. Utu. 1999. *Promoting Access, Quality, and Capacity Building in African Higher Education: The Strategic Planning Experience at the Eduardo Mondlane University*. Washington, D.C.: ADEA Working Group on Higher Education, The World Bank.

212. Matos, N. 1993. *Eduardo Mondlane University: An Experience in University Reform*. AFTHR Technical Note no. 6. Washington, D.C.: The World Bank.

213. Pires, E. L. 1992. "Mozambique." In Burton R. Clark and Guy R. Neave, eds., *The Encyclopedia of Higher Education*, 1: 482–484. New York: Pergamon.

See also 9

Namibia

214. Beukes, H. A. 1996. "University of Namibia's Part Time Tutors versus Universal Competencies." *South African Journal of Higher Education* 10, no. 1: 164–167.

215. Government of the Republic of Namibia. 1991. *Higher Education in Namibia: Report of a Presidential Commission*. Windhoek: Government of the Republic of Namibia.

216. Ping, C. J., and B. Crowley. 1997. "Educational Ideologies and National Development Needs: The African University in Namibia." *Higher Education* 33, no. 4: 381–395.

Niger

217. Alidou, O. 2000. "Globalization and the Struggle for Education in the Niger Republic." In S. Federici, G. Caffentzis, and O. Alidou, eds., *A Thousand Flowers: Social Struggles against Structural Adjustment in African Universities*, 151–157. Trenton, N.J.: African World Press.

218. Alidou, O. 2000. "On the Current State of the Student Movement in the Niger Republic: An Interview with Moctar Al Haji Hima." In S. Federici, G. Caffentzis, and O. Alidou, eds., *A Thousand Flowers: Social Struggles against Structural Adjustment in African Universities*, 221–229. Trenton, N.J.: African World Press.

219. Salifou, A. 1992. "Niger." In Burton R. Clark and Guy R. Neave, eds., *The Encyclopedia of Higher Education*, 1: 513–514. New York: Pergamon.

Nigeria

220. Adesola, A. O. 1991. "The Nigerian University System: Meeting the Challenges of Growth in a Depressed Economy." *Higher Education* 21, no. 1: 121–133.

221. Adeyemi, K. 1990. "An Analysis of the Supplemental Sources of Financing Higher Education in a Developing Country: A Case of Nigerian Universities." *Educational Planner* 1, no. 3/4: 44–53.

222. Adeyemi, K. 2001. "Equality of Access and Catchment Area Factor in University Admissions in Nigeria." *Higher Education* 42, no. 3: 307–332.

223. Ahmed, A. 1989. "The Asquith Tradition, the Ashby Reform, and the Development of Higher Education in Nigeria." *Minerva* 27, no. 1: 1–20.

224. Ajayi, T. 1988. "An Analysis of Recurrent Unit Cost of Higher Education: Ogun State University." *Higher Education Policy* 1, no. 4: 11–15.

225. Akpan, P. A. 1987. "The Spatial Aspects of Higher Education in Nigeria." *Higher Education* 16, no. 5: 545–555.

226. Akpan, P. A. 1989. "Inequality of Access to Higher Education in Nigeria." *Higher Education Review* 22: 21–33.

227. Akpan, P. A. 1990. "The Role of Higher Education in National Integration in Nigeria." *Higher Education* 19, no. 3: 293–305.

228. Amuwo, K. 1999. "Confronting the Crisis of the University in Africa: Nigerian Academics and Their Many Struggles." *African Association of Political Science*, Occasional Series 3, no. 2.

229. Anya, A. O. 1982. *Science Development at the Future: The Nigerian Case*. Nsukka: University of Nigeria Press.

230. Austin, D. 1980. "Universities and the Academic Gold Standard in Nigeria." *Minerva* 18, no. 2: 201–242.

231. Azelama, J. 1994. "University Admission by Federal Charter: Implication for Nigerian Political Development." *Studies in Education.*

232. Babalola, J. B. 1990. "Integration of the University Manpower Production to the Work Environment in Nigeria." *Educational Planner: The Journal of the Nigerian Society for Educational Planning*. Benin City.

233. Babalola, J. B. 1998. "Cost and Financing of University Education in Nigeria." *Higher Education* 36, no. 1: 43–66.

234. Babalola, J. B. 1999. "Education under Structural Adjustment in Nigeria and Zambia." *Journal of Education* 34, no. 1: 79–98.

235. Bako, S. 1994. "Education and Adjustment in Nigeria." In M. Diouf and M. Mamdani, eds., *Academic Freedom in Africa*. Dakar: Council for the Development of Social Science Research in Africa.

236. Bangura, Y. 1994. *Intellectuals, Economic Reform and Social Change: Constraints and Opportunities in the Formation of a Nigerian Technocracy*. Dakar: Council for the Development of Social Science Research in Africa (CODESRIA).

237. Biobaku, S. 1985. *Have the Academics Failed the Nation?* Ibadan, Nigeria: University of Ibadan, Institute of African Studies.

238. Biraimah, K. 1987. "Class, Gender, and Life Chances: A Nigerian University Case Study." *Comparative Education Review* 31, no. 4: 570–582.

239. Biraimah, K. 1991. "Nigeria." In P. G. Altbach, ed., *International Higher Education: An Encyclopedia*, 1: 399–410. New York: Garland.

240. Biraimah, K. 1994. "Class, Gender, and Societal Inequalities: A Study of Nigerian and Thai Undergraduate Students." *Higher Education* 27, no. 1: 41–58.

241. Chatelin, Y., J. Gaillard, and A. S. Keller. 1997. "The Nigerian Scientific Community: The Colossus with Feet of Clay." In V. V. Krishna, J. Gaillard, R. Waast, eds., *Scientific Communities in the Developing World*. New Delhi: Sage.

242. Chizea, C. A., ed. 1983. *20 Years of University Education in Nigeria*. Lagos: National Universities Commission.

243. Chuta, E. J. 1992. "Student Loans in Nigeria." *Higher Education* 23, no. 4: 443–449.

244. Cummings, C., and F. A. Olaloku. 1993. "The Correspondence and Open Studies Institute, University of Lagos." In H. Perraton, ed., *Distance Education for Teacher Training*. London: Routledge.

245. Dabalen, A., B. Oni, and O. Adekola. 2000. "Labor Market Prospects of University Graduates in Nigeria." *Higher Education Policy* 14, no. 2: 149–159.

246. Dele, O. T., and H. R. Hengst. 1988. "University Faculty and Administration Morale: A Case Study of Nigeria." *International Review of Education* 34, no. 4: 508–514.

247. Ehikhamenor, F. A. 1988. "Perceived State of Science in Nigerian Universities." *Scientometrics* 13: 225–238.

248. Enaohwo, J. O. 1985. "Emerging Issues in Nigerian Education: The Case of the Level and Scope of Growth of Nigerian Universities." *Higher Education* 14, no. 3: 307–319.

249. Erinosho, S. 1993. *Nigerian Women in Science and Technology*. Dakar: International Development Research Centre.

250. Etuk, B. 1984. *The Nigerian Technical Teacher Training Programme in Canada. Perceptions of Participating Nigerian Students*. Manitoba: University of Manitoba.

251. Fafunwa, A. B. 1992. "Nigeria." In Burton R. Clark and Guy R. Neave, eds., *The Encyclopedia of Higher Education*, 1: 514–524. New York: Pergamon.

252. Federal Republic of Nigeria. 1987. *Views and Comments of the Federal Military Government on the Report of the Study of Higher Education Curricula and Development in Nigeria*. Lagos: Federal Republic of Nigeria.

253. Hartnett, T. 2000. *Financing Trends and Expenditure Patterns in Nigerian Federal Universities: An Update*. Washington, D.C.: The World Bank.

254. Hudu, B. 1999. "Working and Living Conditions of Academic Staff in Nigeria: Strategies for Survival at Ahmadu Bello University." In Y. Lebeau and M. Ogunsanya, eds., *The Dilemma of Post-Colonial Universities. Elite Formation and the Restructuring of Higher Education in Sub-Saharan Africa*. Ibadan: IFRA-African BookBuilders.

255. Ike, V. C. 1976. *University Development in Africa: The Nigerian Experience*. Ibadan: Oxford University Press.

256. Ike, V. C. 1982. "Nigerian Universities and National Integration." In A. Baike, ed., *Higher Education and Development in the Context of the Nigerian Constitution*, 140–158. Benin: University of Benin.

257. Jega, A. 1994. *Nigerian Academics under Military Rule*. University of Stockholm Research Report no. 3. Stockholm: University of Stockholm.

258. Jega, A. M. 2000. "Nigerian Universities and Academic Staff under Military Rule." In S. Federici, G. Caffentzis, and O. Alidou, eds., *A Thousand Flowers: Social Struggles against Structural Adjustment in African Universities*, 171–179. Trenton, N.J.: African World Press.

259. Kolinsky, M. 1985. "The Growth of Nigerian Universities 1948–1980: The British Share." *Minerva* 23, no. 1: 29–61.

260. Kolinsky, M. 1987. "Universities and the British Aid Program: The Case of Nigeria during the 1970s." *Higher Education* 16, no. 2: 199–219.

261. Kosemani, J. M. 1995. "Democratic Values and University Admissions in Nigeria." *Nigerian Journal of Professional Studies in Education*, 3: 78–83.

262. Lebeau, Y. 1997. *Etudiants et Campus du Nigeria. (Students and Campus in Nigeria.)* Paris: Khartala.

263. Mallam, U. 1994. "A National Research Study on Factors Influencing Faculty Turnover at Selected Nigerian Colleges of Technology/Polytechnics." *Higher Education* 27, no. 2: 229–238.

264. Mbanefoh, N. 1992. *Dimension of Brain Drain in Nigeria: A Case Study of Some Critical High Level Manpower Wastage in the University College Hospital*. Ibadan: Nigerian Institute of Social Economic Research (NISER).

265. Mustapha, A. R. 1996. "The State of Academic Freedom in Nigeria." In Council for the Development of Social Science Research in Africa (CODESRIA), ed., *The State of Academic Freedom in Africa 1995*. Dakar: CODESRIA.

266. Nwaka, G. I. 2000. "Higher Education, the Social Sciences, and National Development in Nigeria." *Prospects* 30, no. 3: 373–385.

267. Nwideeduh, S. B. 1995. "Ethnicity and the Nigerian University System." *Nigerian Journal of Professional Studies in Education* 3: 91–97.

268. Obuchina, E., V. C. Ike, and J. A. Umeh. 1986. *The University of Nigeria 1960–85: An Experiment in Higher Education*. Nsukka: University of Nsukka Press.

269. Ochai, A., and B. U. Nwafor. 1990. "Publishing as a Criterion for Advancement in Nigerian Universities: A Review of Form and Content." *Higher Education Policy* 3, no. 3: 46–48.

270. Oduleye, S. O. 1985. "Decline in Nigerian Universities." *Higher Education* 14, no. 1: 17–40.

271. Ogusanwo, O. A. 1990. "Power in Academia: A Study of Nigerian University Systems." *African Journal of Educational Management* 3, no. 1: 95–102.

272. Ogunsanya, M. 2000. "Aspects of the Instrumentalisation of the University in Nigeria." In Y. Lebeau and M. Ogunsanya, eds., *The Dilemma of Post-Colonial Universities: Elite Formation and the Restructuring of Higher Education in Sub-Saharan Africa*, 147–168. Ibadan: IFRA/ABB.

273. Okudu, S. J. 1983. "The Ibadan Syndrome of Excellence and the Nigerian University System." In C. A. Chizea, ed., *Twenty Years of University Education in Nigeria*. Lagos: Nigerian University Commission.

274. Olugbade, K. 1990. "Nigerian Students and Political Mobilisation." *Journal of Social Development in Africa* 5, no. 1: 39–57.

275. Oni, B. 1987. *The Problem of Graduate Unemploy-*

ment and the Demand for Postgraduate Education in Nigeria: Case Study of Ibadan and Lagos Universities. Ibadan: Nigerian Institute of Social Economic Research (NISER).

276. Oni, B. 1999. A Framework for Technological Capacity Building in Nigeria: Lessons from Developed Countries. Bremen, Germany: Institute for World Economic and International Management and University of Bremen.

277. Oni, B. 1999. The Nigerian University Today and the Challenges of the Twenty-First Century. Bremen, Germany: Institute for World Economic and International Management and University of Bremen.

278. Oni, B. 2000. "Capacity Building Effort and Brain Drain in Nigerian Universities." In S. Tapsoba, S. Kassoum, V. Houenou, O. Bankole, M. Sethi, and J. Ngu, eds., Brain Drain and Capacity Building in Africa, 208–224. Dakar, Senegal: Economic Commission for Africa/International Development Research Centre/International Organization for Migration.

279. Uchendu, P. K. 1995. Politics and Education in Nigeria. Enugu: Fourth Dimension Publishers.

280. Ukaegbu, C. C. 1985. "Are Nigerian Scientists and Engineers Effectively Utilized? Issues on the Development of Scientific and Technological Labor for National Development." World Development 13: 499–512.

281. Ukaegbu, C. C. 1985. "Educational Experiences of Nigerian Scientists and Engineers: Problems of Technological Skill-Formation for National Self-Reliance." Comparative Education 21, no. 2: 173–182.

282. Watkins, D., and A. Akande. 1992. "Student Evaluations of Teaching Effectiveness: A Nigerian Investigation." Higher Education 24, no. 4: 453–463.

283. Whawo, D. D. 1990. "Towards a Pragmatic Policy on Higher Education in Nigeria by the Year 2000." Educational Planner 1, no. 3/4: 104–114.

284. World Bank. 1988. Nigeria: Costs and Financing of Universities. Washington, D.C.: The World Bank.

285. Young, A. S. 1989. "Pre-enrollment Factors and Academic Performance of First-Year Science Students at a Nigerian University: A Multivariate Analysis." Higher Education 18, no. 3: 321–339.

See also 123

Rwanda

286. Commission d'Etude. 1990. Rationalisation des Ressources à l'Université Nationale du Rwanda et Pérspectives de Financement de l'Enseignement Supérieur au Rwanda: Rapport d'une Commission d'Etude. (Rationalization of Resources at the National University of Rwanda and Financial Perspectives on Rwandan Higher Education: Report of a Study Commission.) Kigali: L'Imprimerie de Kigali.

287. Keyes, C. 1992. "Rwanda." In Burton R. Clark and Guy R. Neave, eds., The Encyclopedia of Higher Education, 1: 604–607. New York: Pergamon.

288. Mazimhaka, J., and G. F. Daniel. 2000. Post-Genocide Restructuring of Higher Education in Rwanda: An Overview. Occasional Paper Series no. 4. Accra: Association of African Universities.

289. Ministère de l'Enseignement Supérieur et de la Re-

cherche Scientifique (MINESUPRES). 1986. Projet de Réforme de l'Enseignement Supérieur au Rwanda. (Higher Education Reform Project in Rwanda.) Kigali: MINESUPRES.

290. Ministère de l'Enseignement Supérieur et de la Recherche Scientifique (MINESUPRES). 1990. L'Université Nationale du Rwanda en 1990. (National University of Rwanda in 1990.) Kigali: MINESUPRES.

291. Ministère de l'Enseignement Supérieur et de la Recherche Scientifique (MINESUPRES). 1991. La Problématique de la Mise en Place de la Réforme dans les Etablissements de l'Enseignement Supérieur au Rwanda. (The Problematic of Initiating Higher Education Reform in Rwanda.) Kigali: MINESUPRES.

292. Ministère de l'Enseignement Supérieur et de la Recherche Scientifique (MINESUPRES). 1995. La Politique et la Planification de l'Education au Rwanda: Document Final Provisoire. (Education Policy and Planning in Rwanda: Provisional Final Document.) Kigali: MINESUPRES.

293. Université Nationale du Rwanda. 1985. Rapport de la commission de l'Universite Nationale du Rwanda pour la réforme de l'enseignement supérieur au Rwanda. (Report of the Commission on Higher Education Reform of the National University of Rwanda.) Butare: Université Nationale du Rwanda.

São Tomé and Principe

See 9

Senegal

294. Alidou, O. 2000. "On the World Bank and Education in Senegal: An Interview with Babacar Diop." In S. Federici, G. Caffentzis, and O. Alidou, eds., A Thousand Flowers: Social Struggles against Structural Adjustment in African Universities, 159–163. Trenton, N.J.: African World Press.

295. Alidou, O. 2000. "The World Bank, Privatization and the Fate of Education in Senegal: An Interview with Gorgui Deng." In S. Federici, G. Caffentzis, and O. Alidou, eds., A Thousand Flowers: Social Struggles against Structural Adjustment in African Universities, 231–237. Trenton, N.J.: African World Press.

296. Bathily, A., M. Diouf, and M. Mbod. 1994. "The Senegalese Student Movement from Its Inception to 1989." In M. Mamdani and E. Wamba, eds., African Studies in Social Movement and Democracy. Dakar: Council for the Development of Social Science Research in Africa.

297. Davis, C. H., and M. P. Laberge. 1986. "Le transfer d'un modèle d'enseignement technique supérieur du Québec au Sénégal: Le cas de l'École Polytechnique de Thiés." ("The Transfer of the Technical Higher Education Model from Quebec to Senegal: The Case of the Polytechnic School of Thiés.") Canadian Journal of African Studies 20: 57–71.

298. Davis, C. H., and M. P. Laberge. 1987. "Professional Rewards in a Canada-Senegal Cooperative Project in Engineering Education: The Case of the Projet de l'École Polytechnique de Thiés." Canadian Journal of Development Studies 8: 283–297.

299. Diouf, M. 1990. "The Life Style of Senegal's Elites and Their Macroeconomic Impact." In The Long-Term Perspec-

tive Study of Sub-Saharan Africa: Institutional and Sociopolitical Issues, 3: 60–72. Washington, D.C.: The World Bank.

300. Eisemon, T. O., and J. Salmi. 1993. "African Universities and the State: Prospects for Reform in Senegal and Uganda." *Higher Education* 25, no. 2: 151–168.

301. Gaillard, J., and R. Waast. 2000. "L'aide à la recherche en Afrique subsaharienne: comment sortir de la dépendance? Le cas du Sénégal et de la Tanzanie." ("Helping Research in Sub-Saharian Africa: How to Escape Dependency? The Case of Senegal and Tanzania.") *Autrepart* 13: 71–89.

302. Ministry of Education. 1997. *Using Distance Education at a Distance: International Perspectives*. Dakar: Department of Higher Education, Ministry of National Education.

303. Ministry of Education. 1997. *Using Distance Education for Higher Education in Senegal*. Dakar: Department of Higher Education, Ministry of National Education.

304. Sada, S. 2000. "Accumulation de capital humain, exode des compétences: le cas du Sénégal." ("Accumulation of Human Capital and Brain Drain: The Case of Senegal.") In S. Tapsoba, S. Kassoum, V. Houenou, O. Bankole, M. Sethi, and J. Ngu, eds., *Brain Drain and Capacity Building in Africa*, 148–152. Dakar, Senegal: Economic Commission for Africa/International Development Research Centre/International Organization for Migration.

305. Sylla, A. 1992. "Senegal." In Burton R. Clark and Guy R. Neave, eds., *The Encyclopedia of Higher Education*, 1: 614–619. New York: Pergamon.

See also 119

Sierra Leone

306. Government of Sierra Leone. 1981. *Commission on Salary and Conditions of Service of University Staff*. Freetown, Sierra Leone: Government Printer.

307. Koso-Thomas, K. 1992. "Sierra Leone." In Burton R. Clark and Guy R. Neave, eds., *The Encyclopedia of Higher Education*, 619–623. New York: Pergamon.

Somalia

308. Adam, H. 1980. "Somali Policies toward Education, Training and Manpower." In T. L. Maliyamkono, ed., *Policy Developments in Overseas Training*. Dar es Salaam: Black Star Agencies.

309. Mebrahtu, T. 1992. "Somalia." In Burton R. Clark and Guy R. Neave, eds., *The Encyclopedia of Higher Education*, 1: 630–635. New York: Pergamon.

South Africa

310. Agar, D. L., and N. Knopfmacher. 1995. "The Learning and Study Strategies Inventory: A South African Application." *Higher Education* 30, no. 1: 115–126.

311. Alt, H. 1998. "Understanding the Development of a Quality Assurance System." *South African Journal of Higher Education* 12, no. 3: 7–11.

312. Amos, T. L., and S. Fischer. 1998. "Understanding and Responding to Student Learning Difficulties within the Higher Education Context: A Theoretical Foundation for Developing Academic Literacy." *South African Journal of Higher Education* 12, no. 2: 12–16.

313. Anderson, G. M. 2002. *Building a People's University in South Africa: Race, Compensatory Education, and the Limits of Democratic Reform*. New York: Verleger.

314. Badat, S. 1999. *Black Student Politics, Higher Education and Apartheid: From SASO to SANSCO, 1968–1990*. Pretoria: Human Sciences Research Council.

315. Badat, S., G. Fisher, F. Barron, and H. Wolpe. 1994. *Differentiation and Disadvantage: The Historically Black Universities in South Africa—Report to the Desmond Tutu Educational Trust*. Cape Town: Education Policy Unit, University of the Western Cape.

316. Barchiesi, F. 2000. "South Africa: Between Repression and 'Homegrown Structural Adjustment.'" In S. Federici, G. Caffentzis, and O. Alidou, eds., *A Thousand Flowers: Social Struggles against Structural Adjustment in African Universities*, 165–170. Trenton, N.J.: African World Press.

317. Beckham, E. 2000. *Diversity, Democracy, and Higher Education: A View from Three Nations: India, South Africa, the United States*. Washington: Association of American Colleges and Universities.

318. Bisschoff, T., and P. Potts. 1998. "Managing Student Learning Environments: A South African Case Study." *South African Journal of Higher Education* 12, no. 2: 177–125.

319. Blunt, R. J. S. 1998. "Negotiating a Policy for Affirmative Action." *South African Journal of Higher Education* 12, no. 2: 24–33.

320. Botha, M. M. 1995. "Research Trends at South African Universities." *South African Journal of Higher Education* 9, no. 1: 81–91.

321. Bothma, T., and H. Britz. 2000. "Library and Information Science Education at the University of Pretoria, South Africa: Restructuring and Curriculum Development." *Journal of Education for Library and Information Science* 41, no. 3: 233–243.

322. Boughey, C. 1998. "Language and 'Disadvantage' in South African Institutions of Higher Education: Implications of Critical Challenges to Second Language Acquisition Discourses for Academic Development Practitioners." *South African Journal of Higher Education* 12, no. 1: 166–173.

323. Brown, D. M. 2000. "Swings and Roundabouts: Centralisation and Devolution in a Multicampus University in South Africa." *Higher Education* 40, no. 2: 163–181.

324. Brown, M. 2000. "Using the Intellectual Diaspora to Reverse the Brain Drain: Some Useful Examples." In S. Tapsoba, S. Kassoum, V. Houenou, O. Bankole, M. Sethi, and J. Ngu, eds., *Brain Drain and Capacity Building in Africa*, 92–106. Dakar, Senegal: Economic Commission for Africa/International Development Research Centre/International Organization for Migration.

325. Büchner, J., and D. Hay. 1998. "Staff Induction: Establishing Mentorship Programmes for Academic Staff Development." *South African Journal of Higher Education* 12, no. 3: 19–26.

326. Bunting, I. A. 1994. *Legacy of Inequality: Higher Education in South Africa.* Rondebosch: University of Cape Town Press.

327. Cassimjee, R., and H. B. Brookes. 1998. "The Concerns and/or Fears of Undergraduate Students in a Problem-Based Community-Based Curriculum." *South African Journal of Higher Education* 12, no. 1: 95–102.

328. Cilliers, J. A., and E. C. Reynhardt. 1998. "Thirty Years of Physics at UNISA." *South African Journal of Higher Education* 12, no. 1: 174–183.

329. Cloete, N., and I. Bunting. 2000. *Higher Education Transformation: Assessing Performance in South Africa.* Pretoria: Center for Higher Education Transformation.

330. Cloete, N., T. Kulati, and M. Phala. 2000. *Leadership and Institutional Change in Higher Education.* Pretoria, South Africa: Centre for Higher Education Transformation.

331. Cooper, D., and G. Subotzky. 2000. *The Skewed Revolution: A Handbook of South African Higher Education.* Cape Town: Education Policy Unit, University of the Western Cape.

332. Council on Higher Education of South Africa. 2001. *Re-inserting the 'Public Good' into Higher Education Transformation.* Pretoria: Council on Higher Education.

333. Cronje, J. 1997. "Interactive Internet: Using the Internet to Facilitate Co-operative Distance Learning." *South African Journal of Higher Education* 11, no. 2: 149–156.

334. Davies, J. 1994. "The University Curriculum and the Transition in South Africa." *European Journal of Education* 29, no. 3: 255–268.

335. Davies, J. 1996. "The State and the South African University System under Apartheid." *Comparative Education Review* 32, no. 3: 319–332.

336. De Montfort University. 1996. *Governance and Decision Making for the 21st Century: The Transformation and Restructuring of South African Tertiary Institutional Management.* Leicester: De Montfort University.

337. Dlamini, C. R. M. 1995. "The Transformation of South African Universities." *South African Journal of Higher Education* 9, no. 1: 39–46.

338. Dreijmanis, J. 1988. *The Role of the South African Government in Tertiary Education.* Johannesburg: South African Institute of Race Relations.

339. Du Toit, C. M. 1996. "Transforming and Managing the Organizational Culture of a University to Meet the Challenges of a Changing Environment." *South African Journal of Higher Education* 10, no. 1: 96–104.

340. Eckel, P. D. 2001. "A World Apart? Higher Education Transformation in the U.S. and South Africa." *Higher Education Policy* 14, no. 2: 103–115.

341. Education Policy Unit (EPU) and University of the Western Cape. 1997. *Research Report: The Enhancement of Graduate Programs and Research Capacity at the Historically Black Universities.* Cape Town: Education Policy Unit, University of the Western Cape.

342. Erasmus, A. S., and C. A. Kapp. 1998. "Capacity-Building through Mentoring: A Case Study in Postgraduate Supervision." *South African Journal of Higher Education* 12, no. 3: 111–119.

343. Esterhuyse, W. P. 1992. "The Transformation of South African Universities: The Perspective of a Historically White University." In C. A. Taylor, ed., *Tertiary Education in a Changing South Africa.* Port Elizabeth: University of Port Elizabeth.

344. Fedderke, J., R. de Kadt, and J. Luiz. 2000. *Capstone or Deadweight? Inefficiency, Duplication and Inequity in South Africa's Tertiary Education System, 1910–1993.* Johannesburg: University of the Witwatersrand.

345. File, J. 1986. "The Politics of Excellence: University Education in the South African Context." *Social Dynamics* 12, no. 1: 26–42.

346. Fisher, G. 1998. "Policy, Governance, and the Reconstruction of Higher Education in South Africa." *Higher Education Policy* 11, no. 2: 121–140.

347. Fisher, M. 1979. "Showdown over South Africa: The Second Coming of Student Activism." *Change* 11, no. 1: 26–30.

348. Fourie, M. 1999. "Institutional Transformation at South African Universities: Implications for Academic Staff." *Higher Education* 38, no. 3: 275–290.

349. Fourie, M., and E. M. Bitzer. 1998. "Capacity-Building of Governance Structures: One of the Pathways to Quality Assurance?" *South African Journal of Higher Education* 12, no. 3: 27–32.

350. Goduka, I. N. 1996. "Challenge to Traditionally White Universities: Affirming Diversity in the Curriculum." *South African Journal of Higher Education* 10, no. 1: 27–39.

351. Gultig, J. 2000. "The University in Post-Apartheid South Africa: New Ethos and New Divisions." *South African Journal of Higher Education* 14, no. 1: 37–52.

352. Gwele, N. S. 1998. "Gender and Race: Perceptions of Academic Staff in Selected Faculties in English Language Historically White Universities Concerning Their Working Conditions." *South African Journal of Higher Education* 12, no. 2: 69–78.

353. Henning, E. 1998. "Service Learning in the University Curriculum: Partnerships in Community Education." *South African Journal of Higher Education* 12, no. 1: 44–53.

354. Herbstein, F. H. 1993. "Towards the 'New South Africa': Equal Opportunity Policies at the University of Cape Town." *Higher Education* 26, no. 2: 183–198.

355. Herman, H. 1995. "School-Leaving Examination, Selection and Equity in Higher Education in South Africa." *Comparative Education* 31: 261–174.

356. Higgs, P. 1997. "Towards the Reconstruction of a Philosophy for Educational Discourse in South African Higher Education." *South African Journal of Higher Education* 11, no. 2: 10–20.

357. Hyde-Clarke Humphries, N. 2000. "Transforming a Segregated and Patriarchal Tertiary Education System in South Africa." *South African Journal of Higher Education* 14, no. 3: 27–31.

358. Imenda, S. N. 1995. "Linking Staff and Student Development Programmes." *South African Journal of Higher Education* 9, no. 1: 178–182.

359. Irvine, D. 1998. *The Future of South African Universities: What Role for Business?* Johannesburg: Centre for Development and Enterprise.

360. Jager, K., and Y. Sayed. 1998. "Aspects of Information

Literacy at Five Institutions of Higher Education in the Western Cape." *South African Journal of Higher Education* 12, no. 2: 197–203.

361. James, W. G. 1990. "Apartheid, the University, and Change in South Africa." *Academe* 76, no. 3: 20–23.

362. Jansen, J. 2001. "Globalisation, Markets and the Third World University: Preliminary Notes on the Role of the State in South African Higher Education." In Y. Sayed and J. Jansen, eds., *Implementing Education Policies: The South African Experience*. Cape Town: University of Cape Town Press.

363. Jansen, J. D., ed. 1991. *Knowledge and Power in South Africa*. Johannesburg: Skotaville.

364. Jonathan, R. 2001. "Democratization, Modernization, and Equity: Confronting the Apartheid Legacy in South African Higher Education." *Equity and Excellence in Education* 34, no. 3: 8–14.

365. Jordaan, J. J. 1995. "Affirmative Action: Excellence versus Equity." *South African Journal of Higher Education* 9, no. 1: 53–64.

366. Kaplan, D. 1997. "Reversing the Brain Drain: The Case for Utilizing South Africa's Unique Intellectual Diaspora." *Science, Technology and Society* 2, no. 2.

367. Kapp, C. A., and C. D. Cilliers. 1998. "Continuing Personal and Professional Development of University Lecturers: A Case Study." *South African Journal of Higher Education* 12, no. 1: 117–121.

368. Knoch, C. 1997. *Uninet: The South African Academic and Research Network*. Ottawa, Canada: International Development Research Centre.

369. Kotzé, H. 1990. "Politics and Socialization: A Comparative Perspective at Two Afrikaans Universities." *South African Journal of Sociology* 21, no. 3: 133–144.

370. Kraak, A. 2001. "Equity, Development, and New Knowledge Production: An Overview of the New Higher Education Policy Environment in Post-Apartheid South Africa." *Equity and Excellence in Education* 34, no. 3: 15–25.

371. Kraak, A., ed. 2000. *Changing Modes: New Knowledge Production and Its Implications for Higher Education in South Africa*. Pretoria: HSRC Publishers.

372. Lategan, L. O. K. 1998. "Quality Assurance and the South African University System: Defining the Impact of External and Internal Trends on the South African University System and Its Quality." *South African Journal of Higher Education* 12, no. 1: 61–69.

373. Lazenby, K. 1999. "Using WebCT at the University of Pretoria, South Africa." *International Journal of Educational Telecommunications* 5, no. 4: 293–307.

374. Lindsay, B. 1997. "Toward Conceptual, Policy and Programmatic Frameworks of Affirmative Action in South African Universities." *Journal of Negro Education* 66, no. 4: 522–538.

375. Mabizela, M., G. Subotzky, and B. Thaver. 2000. *The Emergence of Private Higher Education in South Africa: Key Issues and Challenges*. Cape Town: Education Policy Unit, University of the Western Cape.

376. Mabokela, R. O. 2000. *Voices of Conflict: Desegregating South African Universities*. New York: Routledge Falmer.

377. MacKenzie, C. G. 1994. "Black Students in 'White' Universities: The Character and Provision of Liberal Higher Education Institutions in Post-Apartheid South Africa." *Compare* 24, no. 1: 67–78.

378. Maharasoa, M., and D. Hay. 2001." Higher Education and Graduate Employment in South Africa." *Quality in Higher Education* 7, no. 2: 139–147.

379. Malefo, V. 2000. "Psycho-social Factors and Academic Performance among African Women Students at a Predominantly White University in South Africa." *South African Journal of Psychology* 30, no. 4: 40–45.

380. Maphai, V. T. 1989. "Affirmative Action in South Africa: A Genuine Option." *Social Dynamics* 15, no. 2: 1–24.

381. Merisotis, J., and D. Gilleland. 2000. *Funding South African Higher Education: Steering Mechanisms to Meet National Goals*. Washington, D.C.: Institute for Higher Education Policy.

382. Ministry of Education of the Republic of South Africa. 2001. *National Plan for Higher Education*. Pretoria: Ministry of Education.

383. Moja, T., and F. D. Hayward. 2000. "Higher Education Policy Development in Contemporary South Africa." *Higher Education Policy* 13, no. 4: 335–359.

384. Moja, T., J. Muller, and N. Cloete. 1996. "Towards New Forms of Regulation in Higher Education: The Case of South Africa." *Higher Education Policy* 32, no. 2: 129–155.

385. Mokubung, O. N. 1984. *Student Culture and Activism in Black South African Universities: The Root of Resistance*. Westport, Conn.: Greenwood Press.

386. Moodie, G. C. 1994. "The State and the Liberal Universities in South Africa, 1948–1990." *Higher Education* 27, no. 1: 1–40.

387. Morrow, W. 1998. "Stakeholders and Senates: The Governance of Higher Education Institutions in South Africa." *Cambridge Journal of Education* 28, no. 3: 385–405.

388. Moulder, J. 1991. "Africanizing the Predominantly White Universities in South Africa: Some Ideas for a Debate." In J. D. Jansen, ed., *Knowledge and Power in South Africa*, 111–126. Johannesburg: Skotaville.

389. Mouton, J. 2000. *South Africa: Science in transition*. Stellenbosch: Centre for Interdisciplinary Studies and the European Commission.

390. Mouton, J., S. C. Boshoff, E. Grebe, R. Waast, E. B. Ravat, and N. Ravjee. 2000. *Science in South Africa*, vol. 1: *History, Institutions, and Policies*. Stellenbosch: Centre for Interdisciplinary Studies, University of Stellenbosch.

391. Muller, J. 1991. "South Africa." In P. G. Altbach, ed., *International Higher Education: An Encyclopedia*, 411–423. New York: Garland.

392. Muller, J. 1994. "South Africa." In I. A. Bunting, ed., *Legacy of Inequality: Higher Education in South Africa*. Rondebosch: University of Cape Town Press.

393. Mwamwenda, T. S. 1997. "Faculties and Academics Involvement in Research and Publication Activities." *South African Journal of Higher Education* 11, no. 1: 93–97.

394. Naidoo, R. 1998. "Levelling or Playing the Field? The Politics of Access to University Education in Post-Apartheid South Africa." *Cambridge Journal of Education* 28, no. 3: 369–383.

395. National Commission on Higher Education (NCHE). 1996. *A Framework for Transformation: Report of the National*

Commission on Higher Education. Pretoria, South Africa: National Commission on Higher Education (NCHE).

396. Ndebele, N. S. 1997. "Creative Instability: The Case of the South African Higher Education System." *The Journal of Negro Education* 66, no. 4: 443–448.

397. Osberg, D., D. Pinto, S. Docherty, and C. Still. 1998. "Promoting High Quality Teaching and Learning through Sharing Academic Resources." *South African Journal of Higher Education* 12, no. 1: 141–148.

398. Oosthuizen, G. C., A. A. Clifford-Vaughan, A. L. Behr, and G. A. Rauche, eds. 1981. *Challenge to a South African University: The University of Durban–Westville*. Cape Town: Oxford University Press.

399. Pavlich, G. C., F. M. Orkin, and R. Richardson. 1995. "Educational Development in Post-Apartheid Universities: Framework for Policy Analysts." *South African Journal of Higher Education* 9, no. 1: 65–72.

400. Pillay, P. 1990. "The Political Economy of Higher Education in South Africa." *Higher Education* 10, no. 2/3: 211–215.

401. Pouris, A. 1995. *Science and Technology Policy in South Africa*. London: British Library.

402. Pouris, A. 1996. "The Writing on the Wall of South African Science: A Scientometric Assessment." *South African Journal of Science* 92, no. 6: 267–271.

403. Ramphele, M. 2000. *Towards a New Higher Education Landscape: Meeting the Equity, Quality and Social Development Imperatives of South Africa in the 21st Century*. Pretoria: Council on Higher Education.

404. Ruth, D. 2000. *The Stories We Tell and the Way We Tell Them: An Investigation into the Institutional Culture of the University of the North, South Africa*. Research Paper no. 6. Accra: Association of African Universities.

405. Saunders, S. 1995. *The Reconstruction and Development of Higher Education in South Africa*: National Commission on Higher Education.

406. Sayed, Y. 2000. "The Governance of the South African Higher Education System: Balancing State Control and State Supervision in Co-operative Governance?" *International Journal of Educational Development* 20, no. 6: 475–489.

407. Segal, N. 2000. "Restructuring and Refocusing Organizations for Effective Change: Strategies from the Private Sector and Higher Education in Partnership." In N. Cloete, T. Kulati, and M. Phala, eds., *Leadership and Institutional Change in Higher Education*. Pretoria, South Africa: Centre for Higher Education Transformation.

408. Singh, M. 2001. *Re-inserting the "Public Good" into Higher Education Transformation*. Pretoria: Council on Higher Education.

409. Skuy, M., S. Zolezzi, M. Mentis, P. Fridjhon, and K. Cockcroft. 1996. "Selection of Advantaged and Disadvantaged South African Students for University Admission." *South African Journal of Higher Education* 10, no. 1: 110–118.

410. South African Institute for Distance Education. 1995. *Open Learning and Distance Education in South Africa: Report of an International Commission, January–April 1994*. Manzini: Macmillan.

411. Starfield, S. 1996. "The Challenge of Diversity: Staff,

Student and Curriculum Development." *South African Journal of Higher Education* 10, no. 1: 155–163.

412. Steyn, H. J. 1992. "South Africa." In Burton R. Clark and Guy R. Neave, eds., *The Encyclopedia of Higher Education*, 1: 635–641. New York: Pergamon.

413. Strydom, A. H. 1993. "Academic Standards in South African Universities and Proposals for Quality Assurance." *Higher Education* 25, no. 4: 379–393.

414. Strydom, A. H. K., and M. Fourie. 1999. "Higher Education Research in South Africa: Achievements, Conditions and New Challenges." *Higher Education* 38, no. 2: 155–167.

415. Strydom, A. H., L. O. K. Lategan, and A. Muller, eds. 1996. *Quality Assurance in South African Higher Education: National and International Perspectives*. Bloemfontein, South Africa: Unit for Research into Higher Education, University of the Orange State.

416. Stuart, W. 1992. *South Africa: Tertiary Education Sector Assessment*. Washington: Agency for International Development.

417. Subotzky, G. 1997. "Redefining Equity: Challenges and Opportunities Facing South Africa's Historically Black Universities Relative to Global and National Changes." *Journal of Negro Education* 66, no. 4: 496–521.

418. Swartz, E., and P. Foley. 1996. "Higher Education in South Africa: The Skills Debate." *Education and Training* 38, no. 9: 34–40.

419. Taylor, R. 1990. "South Africa's Open Universities: Challenging Apartheid?" *Higher Education Review* 22, no. 3: 5–17.

420. Tisani, N. 1998. "Trends in Curriculum Development at the Tertiary Level: New Beginnings at a University." *South African Journal of Higher Education* 12, no. 3: 46–51.

421. University of Cape Town. 1996. *The Transformation of the University of Cape Town 1984–1994: A Decade of Change and Development*. Rondebosch: University of Cape Town.

422. Vakalisa, N. C. G. 1998. "Doing Research in the South African Context: Is It a Sink or Swim Undertaking?" *South African Journal of Higher Education* 12, no. 3: 59–68.

423. Van der Westhuizen, L. J. 1998. "Assessment of Research in South Africa." *South African Journal of Higher Education* 12, no. 3: 69–75.

424. Van-Heerden, E. 1995. "Black University Students in South Africa: The Influence of Sociocultural Factors on Study and Performance." *Anthropology and Education Quarterly* 26, no. 1: 50–80.

425. Waghid, Y. 1998. "Collegial Dialogue: A Procedure Towards Conceptualizing an Inadequate Understanding of Resource-Based Learning (RBL) at Higher Education Institutions for Distance Learning in South Africa." *South African Journal of Higher Education* 12, no. 1: 78–86.

426. Walker, M. 1998. "Academic Identities: Women on a South African Landscape." *British Journal of Sociology of Education* 19, no. 3: 335–354.

427. Walters, S. 1999. "Lifelong Learning within Higher Education in South Africa: Emancipatory Potential." In C. Soudien, P. Kallaway, and M. Breier, eds., *Education, Equity and Transformation*. Hamburg: UNESCO Institute for Education.

428. Webbstock, D. 1997. "Quality Assurance with Re-

spect to University Teaching in South Africa: A Narrative Analysis." *Assessment and Evaluation in Higher Education* 22, no. 2: 173–184.

429. Webbstock, D. 1999. "An Evaluative Look at the Model Used in the Assessment of Teaching Quality at the University of Natal, South Africa: Reflections, Rewards and Reconsiderations." *Assessment and Evaluation in Higher Education* 24, no. 2: 157–179.

430. Wolpe, H. 1995. "The Debate on University Transformation in South Africa: The Case of the Western Cape." *Comparative Education* 31, no. 2: 275–292.

431. Wood, T. 1998. "Issues Relating to the Cognitive Development of Students at Historically Disadvantaged Institutions." *South African Journal of Higher Education* 12, no. 1: 87–96.

432. Yeld, N., and W. Haeck. 1993. *Academic Support Programs at the University of Cape Town.* Rondebosch: Academic Support Program, University of Cape Town.

433. Zaaiman, H., H. Van Der Flier, and G. D. Thijs. 1998. "Selecting South African Higher Education Students: Critical Issues and Proposed Solutions." *South African Journal of Higher Education* 12, no. 3: 96–101.

434. Zaaiman, R. B., P. J. Roux, and J. H. Rykheer. 1988. *The Use of Libraries for the Development of South Africa: Final Report on an Investigation for the South African Institute for Librarianship and Information Science.* Pretoria: Centre for Library and Information Service, Dept. of Library and Information Science, University of South Africa.

435. Zietsman, A., and M. Gering. 1986. "Admission to University in an Academically Non-Homogeneous Society." *Higher Education* 15, no. 1/2: 25–35.

Sudan

436. Al-Zubeir, A. 1995. "Sudan." In J. Daniel, F. de Vlaming, N. Hartley, and N. Nowak, eds., *Academic Freedom, Education and Human Rights.* London: Zed Books and World University Service.

437. Beshir, M. O. 1992. "Sudan." In Burton R. Clark and Guy R. Neave, eds., *The Encyclopedia of Higher Education,* 1: 680–683. New York: Pergamon.

438. El-Tom, M. E. A. 1980. "The Role of the Educational System in the Emigration of High-Level Manpower." In A. B. Zahalan, ed., *The Arab Brain Drain.* London: Ithaca Press.

439. El-Tom, M. E. A. 1999. *Proceedings of the Conference on the State and Future of Higher Education in Sudan.* Cairo, August 1–5, 1998. Cairo: Association of Sudanese Academics.

440. Forojalla, S. B. 1992. "Recent Proposals for the Reform of Higher Education in the Sudan: Problems and Prospects." *Higher Education Policy* 5, no. 4: 29–32.

441. Hamad, A. 1995. "Sudan." In J. Daniel, ed., *Academic Freedom,* vol. 3. London: Zed Books.

442. Sanyal, B. C., and S. Yacoub. 1975. *Higher Education and Employment in the Sudan.* Paris: International Institute of Educational Planning–UNESCO.

443. Thompson, K. W., B. R. Fogel, and H. E. Danner. 1997. "The University of Khartoum, Sudan: Staff Development in an African University." In K. W. Thompson, B. R. Fogel, and

H. E. Danner, eds., *Higher Education and Social Change: Promising Experiments in Developing Countries.* Vol. 2: *Case Studies,* 155–169. New York: Praeger Publishers.

444. Yaici, L., and B. C. Sanyal. 1981. *Emploi des diplômes et politique d'admissions dans l'enseignement supérieur: Version résumé de quatre études de cas (Soudan, Zambie, Tanzanie, Pologne).* (*University Graduate Employment and Access Policy in Higher Education: Abridged Case Studies from Four Countries [Sudan, Zambia, Tanzania, Poland].*) Paris: International Institute of Educational Planning–UNESCO.

Swaziland

445. Ping, C. J., J. D. Turner, and W. J. Kamba, eds. 1986. *University of Swaziland, Commission on Planning, 1986.* Kwaluseni, Swaziland: University of Swaziland.

446. Smith, A. C. 1992. "Swaziland." In Burton R. Clark and Guy R. Neave, eds., *The Encyclopedia of Higher Education,* 1: 684–687. New York: Pergamon.

Tanzania

447. Brock-Utne, B., A. Mnzava, A. Semesi, L. Strand, and A. Ødegaard. 1990. *Project Review of the Faculty of Forestry at the University of Agriculture, Morogoro, Tanzania.* Oslo: The Norwegian Forestry Society.

448. Buchert, L. 1992. "Basic and Higher Education in Tanzania 1919–1990: Quantitative Expansion for the Many or Qualitative Improvement for the Few?" *Eastern Africa Social Science Research Review* 8, no. 1: 62–79.

449. Galabawa, J. C. 1985. *Efficiency in Higher Education Provision.* Dar es Salaam: Department of Education, University of Dar es Salaam.

450. Galabawa, J. C. 1991. "Funding Selected Issues and Trends in Tanzanian Higher Education." *Higher Education* 21, no. 1: 49–61.

451. Hayman, J. 1994. "Report from Dar es Salaam: New Opportunities and Challenges for IAU in Africa." *Higher Education Policy* 7, no. 1: 53–55.

452. Makude, J. 1997. "Reflections on Curriculum and Institutional Reform at Dar es Salaam University." In N. Cloete, ed., *Knowledge, Identity and Curriculum Transformation in Africa.* Cape Town: Maskew Miller Longman.

453. Maliyamkono, T. L. 1991. "Tanzania." In P. G. Altbach, ed., *International Higher Education: An Encyclopedia,* 1: 425–435. New York: Garland.

454. Maliyamkono, T. L. 1992. "Tanzania." In Burton R. Clark and Guy R. Neave, eds., *The Encyclopedia of Higher Education,* 1: 715–719. New York: Pergamon.

455. Materu, P. N., Y. S. Mbwette, and R. Sauer. 1996. *The "UDSM 2000" Institutional Transformation Programme at the University of Dar es Salaam: Concept, Status, Experiences and Perspectives for the Future.* Dar es Salaam: Development of African Education, Working Group for Higher Education.

456. Ministry of Science, Technology and Higher Education. 1998. *A Report of the Task Force on Financing Sustainability of Higher Education in Tanzania.* Dar es Salaam: Ministry of Science, Technology and Higher Education.

457. Ministry of Science, Technology and Higher Education. 1999. *National Higher Education Policy*. Report EJ/T/3/73. Dar es Salaam: Ministry of Science, Technology and Higher Education.

458. Ministry of Science, Technology and Higher Education. 2000. *Guide to Higher Education in Tanzania*. Dar es Salaam: Ministry of Science, Technology and Higher Education.

459. Ministry of Science, Technology and Higher Education. 2000. *Some Basic Statistics on Higher Learning Institutions in Tanzania 1995/6–1999/2000*. Dar es Salaam: Ministry of Science, Technology and Higher Education.

460. Mmari, G. 1998. "Increasing Access to Higher Education: The Experience of the Open University of Tanzania." In UNESCO Regional Office for Education in Africa, ed., *Higher Education in Africa: Achievements, Challenges and Prospects*. Dakar: UNESCO Regional Office for Education in Africa.

461. Mshigeni, K. E. 1991. "Innovative Approaches to Financing Graduate Education and Research: A Case Study of the University of Dar es Salaam." *Higher Education Policy* 5, no. 2: 30–36.

462. Omari, I. M. 1991. "Innovation and Change in Higher Education in Developing Countries: Experiences from Tanzania." *Comparative Education* 27, no. 2: 181–205.

463. Sanyal, B. C., and M. J. Kinunda. 1977. *Higher Education and Self-Reliance: The Tanzanian Experience*. Paris: International Institute for Educational Planning–UNESCO.

464. Semesi, A., and D. Urassa. 1991. "Educating Female Scientists in Tanzania." In B. Brock-Utne and N. Katunzi, eds., *Women and Education in Tanzania: Twelve Papers from a Seminar. WED Report* 3, 124–135. Dar es Salaam: Women in Education (WED).

465. Sivalon, J. C., and B. Cooksey. 1994. "Tanzania: The State and Higher Education." In G. Neave and F. van Vught, eds., *Government and Higher Education Relationships across Three Continents: The Winds of Change*. Oxford: Pergamon Press.

See also 136, 106, 120, 301, 444

Togo

466. Biraimah, K., and D. Ananou. 1995. "Sustaining Higher Education in Francophone West Africa: The Togolese Case." *Educational Forum* 60: 68–74.

467. Cowen, R. 1992. "Togo." In Burton R. Clark and Guy R. Neave, eds., *The Encyclopedia of Higher Education*, 1: 727–730. New York: Pergamon.

Tunisia

468. Annabi, M. 1982. "North-South University Co-Operation: Tunisian Case Study." *Higher Education in Europe* 7, no. 1: 22–26.

469. Banque Mondiale. 1998. *L'enseignement supérieur tunisien. Enjeux et avenir. Rapports économiques de la Banque mondiale*. (*Tunisian Higher Education: Trends and Future. World Bank Economic Report*.) Washington, D.C.: Banque Mondiale.

470. Ben Yahmed, S. 1998. "Répartition et évolution des effectifs dans l'enseignement supérieur tunisien." ("Distribution and Evolution of Tunisian Higher Education Personnel.") In Jean-Michel Plassard and Ben Sedrine, eds., *Enseignement supérieur et insertion professionnelle en Tunisie*. (*Higher Education and Professional Integration in Tunisia*.) Toulouse: Université des sciences sociales.

471. Ministère de l'Enseignement Supérieur. 2001. *Enseignement supérieur: Situation et perspectives*. (*Higher Education: Situation and Perspectives*.) Tunis: CPU (in Arabic).

472. Neave, G. 1992. "Tunisia." In Burton R. Clark and Guy R. Neave, eds., *The Encyclopedia of Higher Education*, 1: 739–742. New York: Pergamon.

473. Zouari, S. 1998. "L'enseignement supérieur en Tunisie: les enjeux." In Jean-Michel Plassard and Ben Sedrine, eds., *Enseignement supérieur et insertion professionnelle en Tunisie*. (*Higher Education and Professional Integration in Tunisia*.) Toulouse: Université des sciences sociales.

See also 8

Uganda

474. Adipala, E. 2001. *Developing a Client-Responsive Agricultural Training, Research, and Dissemination Program for the Faculty of Agriculture and Decentralized Districts: A Strategy*. Kampala: Faculty of Agriculture, Makerere University.

475. Court, D. 1999. "Financing Higher Education at Makerere: The Quiet Revolution in Human Development." Paper commissioned by the World Bank Tertiary Education Thematic Group and the Rockefeller Foundation. Washington, D.C.: World Bank. Available online at http://www.worldbank.org/afr/findings/english/find143.htm (accessed August 2002).

476. Eisemon, T. 1994. "Uganda: Higher Education and the State." In G. Neave and F. van Vught, eds., *Government and Higher Education Relationships across Three Continents: The Winds of Change*. Oxford: Pergamon Press.

477. Kajubi, S. W. 1992. "Financing of Higher Education in Uganda." *Higher Education* 23, no. 4: 433–441.

478. Kajubi, S. W. 1997. "From Elitist towards Mass Higher Education: The Phenomenon of Private Universities in Uganda." *Uganda Education Journal* 1, no. 1: 23–30.

479. Macpherson, M. 1964. *They Built for the Future: A Chronicle of Makerere University College, 1922–1962*. Cambridge: Cambridge University Press.

480. Musisi, M. B., and N. K. Muwanga. 2001. *Makerere University in Transition 1993–2000: Opportunities and Challenges*. Kampala: Makerere Institute of Social Research.

481. Mwiria, K. 1999. "Case II: Makerere University, Uganda." In S. Bjarnason and H. Lund, eds., *Government/University Relationships: Three African Case Studies*. London: Commonwealth Higher Education Management Service (CHEMS).

482. Neave, G. 1992. "Uganda." In Burton R. Clark and Guy R. Neave, eds., *The Encyclopedia of Higher Education*, 1: 753–755. New York: Pergamon.

483. Oloka-Onyango, J. 1992. "The Legal Control of Tertiary Institutions in East Africa: The Case of Makerere." *Africa Development* 17, no. 4: 47–66.

484. Onyango, B. 1985. "The Historical Development of Higher Education in Uganda." In L. P. Tembo and T. L.

Maliyamkono, eds., *The Development of Higher Education in Eastern and Southern Africa*. Nairobi: Oxford University Press.

485. Opio-Odongo, J. M. A. 1993. *Higher Education and Research in Uganda*. Nairobi: ACTS Press.

486. Passi, F. O. 1992. *Implementing Change to Improve the Financial Management of Makerere University, Uganda*. Document IIEP/RP/49.5. Paris: International Institute of Educational Planning (UNESCO).

487. Ssekamwa, J. C. 1997. "Prelude to Private Students: Sponsorship and Implications of Its Progress at Makerere University." *Uganda Educational Journal* 2, no. 1: 1–22.

See also 106, 300

Zaire.

See Democratic Republic of Congo (Zaire)

Zambia

488. Burawoy, M. 1976. "Consciousness and Contradiction: A Study of Student Protest in Zambia." *British Journal of Sociology* 27, no. 1: 78–97.

489. Galabawa, J. C. 1993. *Study on Cost Effectiveness and Efficiency in African Universities: A Case Study of the University of Zambia (UNZA)*. Accra: Association of African Universities.

490. Goma, L. K. H. 1987. "The University of Zambia and the Quest for Excellence and Relevance." *Zambia Educational Review* 7, no. 1–2.

491. Government of Zambia. 1985. *Government Reaction to the Main Recommendations of the Commission of Inquiry into the Affairs of the University of Zambia*. Lusaka: Government Printer.

492. Government of Zambia. 1986. *Report of the Commission of Inquiry Appointed to Inquire into the Affairs of the University of Zambia*. Lusaka: Government Printer.

493. Kaluba, L. H. 1992. "Zambia." In Burton R. Clark and Guy R. Neave, eds., *The Encyclopedia of Higher Education*, 1: 825–830. New York: Pergamon.

494. Lulat, Y. G.-M. 1981. "Determinants of Third World Student Activism in the Seventies: The Case of Zambia." In P. G. Altbach, ed., *Student Politics: Perspectives for the Eighties*, 234–266. Metuchen, N.J.: Scarecrow.

495. Lulat, Y. G.-M. 1982. "Political Constraints on Educational Reform for Development: Lessons from an African Experience." *Comparative Education Review* 26 (June): 235–253.

496. Lulat, Y. G.-M. 1989. "Zambia." In P. G. Altbach, ed., *Student Political Activism: An International Reference Handbook*, 37–56. Westport, Conn.: Greenwood.

497. Lungu, G. F. 1988. "Hierarchical Authority vs. Collegial Structures in an African University: Lessons from the University of Zambia." *Studies in Educational Administration* 47: 14–20.

498. Lungu, G. F. 1993. "Educational Policy-Making in Colonial Zambia: The Case of Higher Education for Africans from 1924 to 1964." *Journal of Negro History* 78, no. 4: 207–232.

499. Mwanalushi, M. 1995. *University and Society: The Role of the University in National Development*. Ndola, Zambia: Mission Press.

500. Ng'andwe, A. 1995. "Distance Education at the University of Zambia: Problems of Quality and Management." *Higher Education Policy* 8, no. 1: 44–47.

501. Nyirenda, J. 1989. "Organization of Distance Education at the University of Zambia: An Analysis of the Practice." *Distance Education* 10, no. 1: 148–156.

502. Rothchild, D. 1971. "The Beginning of Student Unrest in Zambia." *Transition* 8 (December): 66–74.

503. Sanyal, B. C., J. H. Case, P. S. Dow, and M. E. Jackman. 1976. *Higher Education and the Labour Market in Zambia: Expectations and Performance*. Paris: UNESCO.

504. Siaciwena, R. 1997. "Organizational Changes at the University of Zambia." *Open Learning* 12, no. 3: 57–61.

505. Stabler, J. B. 1968. "The University of Zambia: Its Origin and First Year." *Journal of Higher Education* 3 (January): 32–38.

506. Tembo, L. P. 1973. "University of Zambia." In T. M. Yesufu, *Creating the African University: Emerging Issues in the 1970s*, 226–243. Ibadan and London: Oxford University Press.

507. Tembo, L. P. 1983. *Research and Curriculum Development in Zambia*. Lusaka: Educational Research Bureau, University of Zambia.

508. Tembo, L. P. 1995. *The Development of Tertiary Education in Zambia: A Report*. Lusaka: Ministry of Education, Republic of Zambia and Zambia Education Rehabilitation Project.

See also 234, 444

Zimbabwe

509. Blair, R. D. D. 1990. *Cost Effectiveness and Efficiency in Universities: An African (in Particular, Zimbabwean) Perspective*. Lusaka: British Council Report of a Workshop on Cost Reduction and Recovery and Alternative Funding.

510. Burton, M. G. 1994. "Zimbabwe Marks Formal Opening of Sub-Sahara's First Private University." *Black Issues in Higher Education* 11 (May): 8–10.

511. Cefkin, L. 1975. "Rhodesian University Students in National Politics." In W. J. Hanna and Joel D. Barkan, eds., *University Students and African Politics*. New York: Holmes and Meier Publishers.

512. Cheater, A. P. 1991. "The University of Zimbabwe: University, National University, State University, or Party University?" *African Affairs* 90: 189–205.

513. Chideya, N. 1991. "Zimbabwe." In P. G. Altbach, ed., *International Higher Education: An Encyclopedia*, 1: 437–447. New York: Garland.

514. Dorsey, B. J., R. B. Gaidzanwa, and A. C. Mupawaenda. 1989. *Factors Affecting Academic Careers for Women at the University of Zimbabwe*. Harare: Human Resource Research Center, University of Zimbabwe.

515. Gumbo, S. D. 1989. "Informatics and Teacher Education: Some Views from Zimbabwe." *Higher Education Policy* 2, no. 4: 55–56.

516. Maravanyika, O. E. 1992. "Zimbabwe." In Burton R. Clark and Guy R. Neave, eds., *The Encyclopedia of Higher Education*, 1: 830–836. New York: Pergamon.

517. National University of Science and Technology. 1996.

Annual Report on National University of Science and Technology. Bulawayo: National University of Science and Technology.

Africa (Continent-based)

518. Abagi, O. 1997. *Revitalising University Education in Africa.* London: Cassell.

519. Abegaz, B. M. 1994. *Universities in Africa: Challenges and Opportunities of International Cooperation.* Accra: Association of African Universities.

520. Abegaz, B. M., and L. Levey. 1996. *What Price Information? Priority Setting in African Universities.* Washington D.C.: American Association for the Advancement of Science.

521. Aboderin, A. 1995. *On the Feasibility of Inter-University Cooperation in Joint Graduate Training and Research in Africa.* Accra: Association of African Universities.

522. Adoul, F. W. O. 1999. "Establishing Teaching Staff Requirements for University Academic Programmes." *Higher Education Policy* 12: 101–106.

523. Africa Watch. 1990. *African Universities: Case Studies of Abuses of Academic Freedom.* Kampala, Uganda: CODESRIA.

524. Africa Watch. 1991. *Academic Freedom and Abuses of Human Rights in Africa.* New York: Africa Watch.

525. African Economic Research Consortium. 1996. *An African Based Doctoral Program in Economics.* Nairobi: African Economic Research Consortium.

526. Aguessy, H. 1994. *UNESCO's Commitment to the Success of Higher Education in Africa.* Paris: UNESCO.

527. Aina, A. T. 1994. *Quality and Relevance: African Universities in the 21st Century.* Accra: Association of African Universities.

528. Ajayi, J. F. 1988. *The American Factor in the Development of Higher Education in Africa.* Los Angeles: African Studies Center.

529. Ajayi, J. F., L. K. Goma, and G. A. Johnson. 1996. *The African Experience with Higher Education.* Athens, Ohio: Ohio University Press.

530. Alele-Williams, G. 1992. "Major Constraints to Women's Access to Higher Education in Africa." In UNESCO-BREDA, ed., *Higher Education in Africa: Trends and Challenges for the 21st Century.* Dakar, Senegal: UNESCO.

531. Alemna, A. A., and V. Chifwepa. 1999. *African Journals: An Evaluation of Use Made of African-Published Journals in African Universities.* Education Research Report, Serial 36. London: Department for International Development.

532. Altbach, P. G., and D. Teferra. 1998. *Knowledge Dissemination in Africa: The Role of Scholarly Journals.* Boston, Mass.: Bellagio Studies in Publishing.

533. Amonoo-Neizer, E. H. 1998. "Universities in Africa: The Need for Adaptation, Transformation, Reformation, and Revitalization." *Higher Education Policy* 11, no. 4: 301–310.

534. Antoinette, M., and B. Sherman. 1990. "The University in Modern Africa: Toward the Twenty-First Century." *Journal of Higher Education* 61, no. 4.

535. Apraku, K. 1991. *African Emigrés in the United States. A Missing Link in African Graduate Students in the United States.* New York: Praeger.

536. Arvanitis, R., R. Waast, and J. Gaillard. 2000. "Science in Africa: A Bibliometric Panorama Using the PASCAL Database." *Scientometrics* 47, no. 3: 457–473.

537. Ashby, E. 1964. *African Universities and Western Tradition.* Cambridge, Mass.: Harvard University Press.

538. Ashby, E. 1966. *Universities: British, Indian, African—A Study in the Ecology of Higher Education.* Cambridge, Mass.: Harvard University Press.

539. Askin, S. 1988. *College Crisis across Africa.* Boston: Christian Science Publishing Society.

540. Assié-Lumumba, N. T. 1996. "The Role and Mission of African Higher Education: Preparing for the 21st Century and Beyond." *South African Journal of Higher Education* 10, no. 2: 5–12.

541. Association for the Development of Education in Africa. 1998. *Partnership for Capacity Building and Quality Improvement in Education.* Dakar: ADEA.

542. Association of African Universities. 1988. *Directory of African Universities.* Accra, Ghana: Association of African Universities.

543. Association of African Universities. 1991. *Study Group on Cost Effectiveness and Efficiency in African Universities.* Accra: Association of African Universities.

544. Association of African Universities. 1995. *African Universities: The March to the 21st Century.* Lesotho: AAU.

545. Association of African Universities. 1995. *Report of the AAU/UNESCO/CHEMS Workshop on Strategic Planning in African Universities.* Accra: AAU.

546. Association of African Universities. 1999. *Networks for Regional Cooperation in Graduate Training and Research.* Accra: Association of African Universities.

547. Association of African Universities and International Association of Universities. 1999. *Guide to Higher Education in Africa.* London: Macmillan.

548. Association of Commonwealth Universities. 2001. *Research Management in African Universities.* Discussion Paper no. 1. London: Association of Commonwealth Universities.

549. Atteh, S. O. 1998. "The Crisis in Higher Education in Africa." In K. Kempner, M. Mollis, and W. G. Tierney, eds., *Comparative Education,* 468–477. Needham Heights, Mass.: Simon and Schuster Custom Publishing.

550. Ayandale, E. A. 1982. "Africa: The Challenge of Higher Education." *Daedalus* 111: 165–177.

551. Ayeni, V. 1992. "Administrative Institutions for Postgraduate Programs in African Universities: Problems and Prospects." *Higher Education Policy* 5, no. 4: 12–17.

552. Ayensu, E. S. 1997. "Human Resources Development in Africa." *UNESCO-Africa,* no. 14/15: 64–72.

553. Ayiku, M. N. B. 1991. *University-Productive Sector Linkages: Review of the State of the Art in Africa.* Ottawa: International Development Research Center.

554. Baranshamaje, E. 1996. *AVU—The African Virtual University: Knowledge Is Power.* Washington, D.C.: The World Bank.

555. Bassey, M. O. 1999. *Western Education and Political Domination in Africa: A Study in Critical and Dialogical Pedagogy.* Westport, Conn.: Bergin and Garvey.

556. Bates, R., V. Y. Mudimbe, and J. O'Barr. 1993. *Africa and the Disciplines: The Contributions of Research in Africa to*

the Social Sciences and Humanities. Chicago: University of Chicago Press.

557. Bathgeber, E. M. 1988. "A Tenuous Relationship: The African University and Development Policy Making in the 1980s." *Higher Education* 17: 399–410.

558. Berendt, B. 1988. "Improving Co-operation between European and African Universities in the Fields of Teaching, Research, and Inter-university Co-operation Procedures." *Higher Education in Europe* 13, nos. 1–2: 172–175.

559. Blair, R. 1992. *Financial Diversification and Income Generation at African Universities.* Technical Note no. 2. Washington, D.C.: The World Bank.

560. Blair, R. 1992. *Progress and Potential for Financial Diversification among Selected African Universities.* Washington, D.C.: Africa Technical Department, Education and Training Division, The World Bank.

561. Blair, R. 1998. "Financing Higher Education in Africa." In UNESCO, ed., *Higher Education in Africa: Achievements, Challenges and Prospects,* 403–456. Dakar: BREDA.

562. Blair, R., and J. Jordan. 1994. *Staff Loss and Retention at Selected African Universities: A Synthesis Report.* Washington, D.C.: The World Bank.

563. Bown, L. 1991. *African Universities and the Reality of Interdependence.* Los Angeles: International Studies and Overseas Programs, James S. Coleman African Studies Center, University of California–Los Angeles.

564. Boyle, P. M. 1999. *Class Formation and Civil Society: The Politics of Education in Africa.* Aldershot: Ashgate.

565. Braimoh, D. 1999. "Academic and African Academia? A Paradox of Manufacturers and Industries for Development." *Higher Education Policy* 12, no. 3: 253–260.

566. Brock-Utne, B. 1999. "African Universities and the African Heritage." *International Review of Education* 45, no. 1: 87–105.

567. Brock-Utne, B. 2000. "Transforming African Universities Using Indigenous Perspectives and Local Experience." In G. R. Teasdale and Z. M. Rhea, eds., *Local Knowledge and Wisdom in Higher Education,* 153–167. New York: IAU, Pergamon, and UNESCO.

568. Brock-Utne, B. 2000. *Whose Education for All? The Recolonization of the African Mind.* New York: Flamer.

569. Bureau Régional pour L'Education en Afrique. 1998. *Enseignement supérieur en Afrique: réalisations, défis et perspectives.* (*Higher Education in Africa: Achievements, Challenges and Perspectives.*) Dakar: BREDA.

570. Caffentzis, G. 1994. "The World Bank's African Capacity Building Initiative: A Critique." *Newsletter of the Committee for Academic Freedom in Africa* 6: 14–19.

571. Caffentzis, G. 2000. "The World Bank and Education in Africa." In S. Federici, G. Caffentzis, and O. Alidou, eds., *A Thousand Flowers: Social Struggles against Structural Adjustment in African Universities,* 3–23. Trenton, N.J.: African World Press.

572. Caffentzis, G. 2000. "The World Bank's African Capacity Building Initiative." In S. Federici, G. Caffentzis, and O. Alidou, eds., *A Thousand Flowers: Social Struggles against Structural Adjustment in African Universities,* 69–81. Trenton, N.J.: African World Press.

573. Carlsson, J., and L. Wohlgemuth. 1996. *Capacity Building and Networking: A Meta Evaluation of African Regional Research Networks.* Sida Evaluation 96/45. Stockholm: Sida.

574. Chideya, N. T., C. E. M. Chikombah, A. J. C. Pongweni, and L. C. Tsikirayi, eds. 1982. *The Role of the University and Its Future.* Harare, Zimbabwe: Harare Publishing House.

575. Cisse, M. K. 1992. "Managing University-Based Research and Research Institutions in Africa: Evaluating the Prospects for Improvement." *Higher Education Policy* 5, no. 2: 55–60.

576. Colclough, C. 1989. "The Higher Education Paradox in African Development Planning." *International Journal of Educational Development* 9, no. 4: 271–281.

577. Commonwealth Secretariat. 1986. *Institutional Links in Higher Education in Commonwealth Africa.* London: Commonwealth Secretariat.

578. Coombe, T. 1991. *A Consultation on Higher Education in Africa: A Report to the Ford Foundation and the Rockefeller Foundation.* New York: The Ford Foundation.

579. Council for the Development of Social Science Research in Africa (CODESRIA). 1996. *The State of Academic Freedom in Africa: 1995.* Dakar: CODESRIA.

580. Court, D. 1995. "The Challenge to the Liberal Vision of Universities in Africa." In L. Buchert and K. King, eds., *Learning from Experience: Policy and Practice in Aid to Higher Education,* 109–121. The Hague: Centre for the Study of Education in Developing Countries.

581. Court, D. 1996. "External Support for the Social Sciences in Africa: Issues and Lessons." *AAPS Newsletter* 21, no. 1.

582. Cross, B. 1996. *Sounding Out the Silences: Narratives and Absences in African Higher Education.* Edinburgh: Center of African Studies, Edinburgh University.

583. Crossman, P., and R. R. D. Devish. 1999. *Endogenisation and African Universities. Initiatives and Issues in the Quest for Plurality in the Human Sciences. Policy Study on Development Co-operation.* Brussels: Belgian Administration for Development Co-operation.

584. Diagne, M. 2001. *Directory to Donor Assistance for African Higher Education.* Washington, D.C.: ADEA Working Group on Higher Education, The World Bank.

585. Diambomba, M. 1991. *Les stratégies de financement de l'enseignement supérieur dans certains pays industrialisés et Africains.* (*Funding Strategies for Higher Education in Specific Industrialized African Countries.*) Quebec, Canada: Université Laval.

586. Diouf, M., and M. Mamdani, eds. 1994. *Academic Freedom in Africa.* Dakar, Senegal.

587. Djangmah, J. S. 1995. "Funding of Postgraduate Training and Research in African Universities." *Higher Education Policy* 8, no. 1: 30–32.

588. Economic Commission for Africa. 1989. "Higher Education and the Future of Africa in the Twenty-First Century: The Role of the Institutions of Higher Learning in Responding to Africa's Development Needs and Priorities." *Discovery and Innovation* 1, no. 2: 25–32.

589. Eisemon, T. O. 1980. "African Scientists: From Generation to Generation." *The Bulletin of the Atomic Scientists* 36: 17–23.

590. Eisemon, T. O. 1981. "Scientific Life in Indian and African Universities: A Comparative Study of Peripherality in Science." *Comparative Education Review* 25, no. 2: 164–182.

591. Eisemon, T. O., and C. H. Davis. 1991. "Can the Quality of Scientific Training and Research in Africa Be Improved by Training?" *Minerva* 24, no. 1: 1–26.

592. Eisemon, T. O., and W. D. van Balkom. 1988. "Universities and the Development of Scientific Capacity in African Countries: A Critique." *Compare* 18, no. 2: 105–116.

593. Ekong, D., and P. Plant. 1996. *Strategic Planning at Selected African Universities.* Accra: Association of African Universities.

594. Ekong, D., and A. Sawyerr. 1999. "Challenges Facing Higher Education in Africa." In D. Ekong and A. Sawyerr, eds., *Higher Education Leadership in Africa. A Casebook.* Cape Town: Maskew Miller Longman and Association of African Universities.

595. Ekong, D., and A. Sawyerr. 1999. *Higher Education Leadership in Africa. A Casebook.* Cape Town: Maskew Miller Longman and Association of African Universities.

596. Eshiwani, G. S. 1999. "Higher Education in Africa: Challenges and Strategies for the 21st Century." In P. G. Altbach and P. M. Peterson, eds., *Higher Education in the 21st Century: Global Challenge and National Response,* 31–38. New York: Institute of International Education and the Boston College for International Higher Education.

597. Eustace, R. 1984. "The Export of the UGC Idea to Africa." *Higher Education* 13, no. 5: 595–612.

598. Fadayomi, T. O. 1996. "Brain Drain and Brain Gain in Africa: Causes, Dimensions, and Consequences." In A. Adepoju and T. Hammer, eds., *International Migration in and from Africa: Dimensions, Challenges, and Prospects.* Stockholm: Population, Human Resources and Development in Africa, Centrum for Invandringsforskning.

599. Farida, K. 1998. "Relevance of Higher Education Policies and Practices." In UNESCO Regional Office for Education in Africa, ed., *Higher Education in Africa.* Dakar: UNESCO.

600. Farrant, J. H., and L. M. Afonso. 1997. "Strategic Planning in African Universities: How Relevant Are Northern Models?" *Higher Education Policy* 10, no. 1: 23–30.

601. Federici, S. 2000. "The Economic Roots of the Repression of Academic Freedom in Africa." In S. Federici, G. Caffentzis, and O. Alidou, eds., *A Thousand Flowers: Social Struggles against Structural Adjustment in African Universities,* 61–68. Trenton, N.J.: African World Press.

602. Federici, S. 2000. "The New African Student Movement." In S. Federici, G. Caffentzis, and O. Alidou, eds., *A Thousand Flowers: Social Struggles against Structural Adjustment in African Universities,* 87–112. Trenton, N.J.: African World Press.

603. Federici, S. 2000. "The Recolonization of African Education." In S. Federici, G. Caffentzis, and O. Alidou, eds., *A Thousand Flowers: Social Struggles against Structural Adjustment in African Universities,* 19–23. Trenton, N.J.: African World Press.

604. Federici, S., G. Caffentzis, and O. Alidou, eds. 2000. *A Thousand Flowers: Social Struggles against Structural Adjustment in African Universities.* Trenton, N.J.: African World Press.

605. Fielden, J. 1991. *Management Information Systems in Universities.* Dakar, Senegal.

606. Fine, J. C. 1990. A *Strategy for Graduate Training in Economics for Africans.* Nairobi, Kenya: Initiatives Publisher.

607. Gaidzanwa, R. B. 1994. *Governance Issues in African Universities: Improving Management and Governance to Make African Universities Viable in the Nineties and Beyond.* Accra: Association of African Universities.

608. Gaillard, J., and A. Furó. 2001. *Questionnaire Survey of African Scientists. IFS Grantees and INCO Beneficiaries.* Stockholm: International Foundation for Science: Monitoring and Evaluation System for Impact Assessment (MESIA), Report no. 2.

609. Gaillard, J., and R. Waast. 1993. "The Uphill Emergence of Scientific Communities in Africa." *Journal of African and Asian Studies* 27, nos. 1–2: 41–68.

610. Gaillard, J., and R. Waast. 1998. "La recherche scientifique en Afrique." ("Scientific Research in Africa.") *Afrique contemporaine (Contemporary Africa)* 148: 3–30.

611. Girdwood, A. 1997. "The University in Africa: Evolving Roles and Responsibilities." In K. Watson, S. Modgil, and C. Modgil, eds., *Educational Dilemmas: Diversity and Debate,* 250–258. London: Cassell.

612. Goma, L. K. H. 1989. "The Crisis of Higher Education in Africa." *Discovery and Innovation* 1, no. 2: 19–25.

613. Goma, L. K. H. 1990. "The African Brain Drain: Investment in and Utilization of Human Capital." In A. A. Kwapong and B. Lesser, eds., *Capacity Building and Human Resource Development In Africa.* Halifax, Nova Scotia: Lester Pearson Institute for International Development, Dalhousie University.

614. Goma, L. K. H., and L. P. Tembo. 1984. *The African University: Issues and Perspectives, Speeches.* Lusaka: Institute for African Studies, University of Zambia.

615. Hagström, S., and S. Anitra. 1995. *The University in Africa in the 1990s and Beyond: The Changing Role of the University.* Stockholm: Universitetskanslern.

616. Hanna, W. J., and J. Barkan. 1975. *University Students and African Politics.* New York: Holmes and Meier Publishers.

617. Harding, J. 1990. *Women in Science and Technology in Africa: A Resource Book for Counseling Girls and Young Women.* London: Commonwealth Secretariat Education Program, Human Resources Development Group.

618. Hayman, J. 1991. "IAU's USIT Information and Research Program: Informatics Research in Africa." *Higher Education Policy* 4, no. 3: 49–51.

619. Hayman, J. 1992. "Building Informatics Capacity in African Universities through a Network of Research and Development Centers." *Higher Education Policy* 5, no. 1: 54–56.

620. Hayman, J. 1992. *Research on the Status of Informatics in African Higher Education.* Paris: International Association of Universities.

621. Hayman, J. 1993. "Bridging Higher Education's Technology Gap in Africa." *Technological Horizons in Education Journal* 20, no. 6: 63–69.

622. Hayman, J. 1994. "Report from Dar es Salaam: New Opportunities and Challenges for IAU in Africa." *Higher Education Policy* 7, no. 1: 53–55.

623. Hayward, F. M. 1991. "The Changing African Landscape: Implications for Higher Education." *Educational Record* 72 (Fall): 34–39.

624. Heisel, D. 1998. *Ph.D. Training for Africans in Population Studies*. New York: The Population Council.

625. Hountondji, P. 1990. "Scientific Dependence in Africa Today." *Research in African Literatures* 21, no. 3: 5–15.

626. Hountondji, P. 1998. "Producing Knowledge in Africa Today: The Second Bashorun M. K. O. Abiola Distinguished Lecture." In K. Kempner, M. Mollis, and W. G. Tierney, eds., *Comparative Education*, 156–161. Needham Heights, Mass.: Simon and Schuster Custom Publishing.

627. Hountondji, P., ed. 1994. *Les savoirs endogènes: Pistes pour une recherche*. (*Endogenous Learning: Paths for Research*.) Dakar: Council for the Development of Social Science Research in Africa.

628. International Center for Insect Physiology and Ecology. 1988. *Scientific Institution Building in Africa*. Nairobi: ICIPE Science Press.

629. Jackson, W. 2000. "Mondialisation, exode des compétences et développement des capacités en Afrique." ("Globalization, Brain Drain and Capacity Building in Africa.") In S. Tapsoba, S. Kassoum, V. Houenou, O. Bankole, M. Sethi, and J. Ngu, eds., *Brain Drain and Capacity Building in Africa*, 52–61. Dakar, Senegal: Economic Commission for Africa/International Development Research Centre/International Organization for Migration.

630. Jaycox, E. V. K. 1990. "Capacity Building in Africa: Challenge of the Decade." In A. A. Kwapong and B. Lesser, eds., *Capacity Building and Human Resource Development in Africa*. Nova Scotia, Canada: Dalhousie University.

631. Jenkins, J. 1989. "Some Trends in Distance Education in Africa: An Examination of the Past and Future Role of Distance Education as a Tool for National Development." *Distance Education* 10, no. 1: 41–48.

632. Kagia, R. 2000. "Financing of Higher Education in Africa." In B. Jongbloed and H. Teekens, eds., *The Financing of Higher Education in Sub-Saharan Africa*, 53–67. Utrecht, Netherlands: Uitgeverij-Lemma.

633. Kamba, W. 1985. *The Response of Institutions of Higher Learning to Africa's Rapidly Deteriorating Social and Economic Conditions*. Roma, Lesotho: Institute of Southern African Studies, National University of Lesotho.

634. Kashoki, M. E. 1994. "The African University: Towards Innovative Management Strategies for the 21st Century." In Jennifer Barnes and Mary-Louise Kearney, eds., *Higher Education Staff Development: Directions for the Twenty-First Century*, 149–162. Paris: UNESCO.

635. King, K. 1984. *North-South Collaboration in Higher Education: Academic Links between Britain and the Developing World*. Edinburgh: Center of African Studies, Edinburgh University.

636. Ki-Zerbo, J. 1992. "Africanization of Higher Education Curriculum." In H. Glimm and W. Küper, eds., *Hochschule, wissenschaft und entwicklung*. Bonn: DAAD.

637. Koso-Thomas, K. 1992. "Innovative Ways of Financing Higher Education in Africa." In UNESCO-BREDA, ed., *Higher Education in Africa: Trends and Challenges for the 21st Century*, 121–133. Dakar, Senegal: UNESCO Regional Office.

638. Kwapong, A. A. 1992. "The Context of Capacity Building in Africa: An Overview." In A. A. Kwapong and B. Lesser, eds., *Meeting the Challenge: The African Capacity Building Initiative*. Nova Scotia, Canada: Dalhousie University.

639. Kwapong, A. A., and B. Lesser. 1990. *Capacity Building and Human Resource Development in Africa*. Nova Scotia, Canada: Dalhousie University.

640. Lamptey, A. S. 1992. "Promoting Women's Participation in Teaching, Research, and Management in African Universities." In UNESCO-BREDA, ed., *Higher Education in Africa: Trends and Challenges for the 21st Century*, 77–94. Dakar, Senegal: UNESCO Regional Office.

641. Legum, C. 1972. "The Year of the Students: A Survey of the African University Scene." In Colin Legum, ed., *Africa Contemporary Record*, A3–A30. London: Rex Collins.

642. Liverpool, L. S., E. Eseyin, and E. Opara. 1998. "Modelling for Resource Allocation to Departments and Faculties in African Universities." *Higher Education* 36, no. 2: 139–153.

643. MacKenzie, C. G. 1986. "Prisoners of Fortune: Commonwealth African Universities and Their Political Masters." *Comparative Education* 22, no. 2: 111–121.

644. Mafeje, A. 1994. "African Intellectuals: An Inquiry into Their Genesis and Social Options." In M. Diouf and M. Mamdani, eds., *Academic Freedom in Africa*. Dakar: Council for the Development of Social Science Research in Africa (CODESRIA).

645. Makany, L. 1983. *Fifteen Years of Inter-University Cooperation in Africa, 1969–1982*. Accra: Association of African Universities.

646. Makhubu, L. P. 1998. "The Right to Higher Education and Equal Opportunity Particularly for Women: The Major Challenge of Our Time." In UNESCO Regional Office for Education in Africa, *Higher Education in Africa: Achievements, Challenges and Prospects*. Dakar: UNESCO Regional Office for Education in Africa.

647. Mamdani, M. 1993. "University Crisis and Reform: A Reflection on the African Experience." *Review of African Political Economy* 58: 7–19.

648. Matos, N. 1998. "A Changed 'Aid Relationship': One Practical Experience." In S. Kayizzi-Mugerwa, A. O. Olukoshi, and L. Wohlgemuth, eds., *Towards a New Partnership with Africa: Challenges and Opportunities*, 195–206. Uppsala: Nordiska Afrikainstitutet.

649. Matos, N. 1999. *North-South Cooperation to Strengthen Universities in Africa*. AAU Occasional Paper, no. 2. Accra-North: Association of African Universities.

650. Mazrui, A. A. 1976. "The African University as a Multinational Corporation." *Harvard Educational Review* 45, no. 2: 191–210.

651. Mazrui, A. A. 1978. *Political Values and the Educated Class in Africa*. Berkeley: University of California Press.

652. Mazrui, A. 1992. "Toward Diagnosing and Treating Cultural Dependency: The Case of the African University." *International Journal of Educational Development* 12, no. 2: 95–111.

653. Mazrui, A. 2000. "The World Bank, the Language

Question, and the Future of African Education." In S. Federici, G. Caffentzis, and O. Alidou, eds., *A Thousand Flowers: Social Struggles against Structural Adjustment in African Universities*, 43–59. Trenton, N.J.: African World Press.

654. Meldrum, A. 1991. "Academic Freedom in Africa." *Africa Report*, September/October.

655. Mintsa, V. 2000. "L'Exode des compétence en Afrique." ("Brain Drain in Africa.") In S. Tapsoba, S. Kassoum, V. Houenou, O. Bankole, M. Sethi, and J. Ngu, eds., *Brain Drain and Capacity Building in Africa*, 80–87. Dakar, Senegal: Economic Commission for Africa/International Development Research Centre/International Organization for Migration.

656. Mkandawire, T. 1995. "Three Generations of African Academics: A Note." *CODESRIA Bulletin* 3: 9–12.

657. Mlama, P. M. 1998. "Increasing Access and Equity in Higher Education: Gender Issues." In UNESCO Regional Office for Education in Africa, ed., *Higher Education in Africa: Achievements, Challenges and Prospects*. Dakar: UNESCO Regional Office for Education in Africa.

658. Mohamedbhai, G. T. G. 1992. "A Review of Training Activities in African Universities." In UNESCO-BREDA, ed., *Higher Education in Africa: Trends and Challenges for the 21st Century*, 137–156. Dakar, Senegal: UNESCO Regional Office.

659. Moock, J. L., and P. R. Moock. 1977. *Higher Education and Rural Development in Africa: Toward a Balanced Approach for Donor Assistance*. New York: African-American Institute.

660. Mosha, H. J. 1986. "The Role of African Universities in National Developments: A Critical Analysis." *Higher Education* 15, no. 1: 113–134.

661. Mouton, J., R. Waast, and F. Ritchie. 2002. *Science in Africa. Proceedings of a Symposium held on 17 & 18 October 2001, Erinvale Estate Hotel, Somerset West, South Africa*. Stellenbosh: Centre for Interdisciplinary Studies, University of Stellenbosch.

662. Mugabe, R. 1988. "Higher Education, Economic Development, and National Independence." *Higher Education Policy* 1, no. 1: 17–18.

663. Muntemba, S. 1990. "The African Brain Drain: Investment in and Utilization of Human Capital." In A. A. Kwapong and B. Lesser, eds., *Capacity Building and Human Resource Development in Africa*, 103–105. Nova Scotia, Canada: Dalhousie University.

664. Mwiria, K., and S. P. Wamahui. 1995. *Issues in Educational Research in Africa*. Nairobi: East Africa Educational Publishers.

665. Namuddu, K. 1995. "Gender Perspectives in the Transformation of Africa: Challenges to the African University as a Model to Society." In UNESCO Regional Office for Education in Africa, ed., *Women in Higher Education in Africa*, 17–57. Dakar, Senegal: UNESCO.

666. Nare, Z. C. 1995. "Being a Woman Intellectual in Africa: The Persistence of a Sexist and Cultural Stereotype." UNESCO Regional Office for Education in Africa, ed., *Women in Higher Education in Africa*, 1–11. Dakar, Senegal: UNESCO.

667. Neave, G. 2001. "Out of Africa: Planning and Policy." *Higher Education Policy* 14, no. 2: 99–101.

668. Ngara, E. 1994. *The African University and Its Mission: Strategies for Improving the Delivery of Higher Education Institutions*. Lesotho: Institute of Southern African Studies, National University of Lesotho.

669. Ngu, J. L. 1992. *The Relevance of African Higher Education*. Washington, D.C.: Africa Technical Department, The World Bank.

670. Ngu, J. L., and Y. Kwankam. 1992. *At What Price Higher Education in Africa?* Ottawa: International Development Research Centre.

671. Nkinyangi, J. A. 1991. "African Education in the Age of Student Revolt." *Higher Education Policy* 4, no. 2: 47–51.

672. Nwa, E. U., and P. Houenou. 1990. *Graduate Education and Research and Development in African Universities*. Accra, Ghana: Association of African Universities (AAU).

673. Nwauwa, A. O. 1997. *Imperialism, Academe, and Nationalism: Britain and University Education for Africans 1860–1960*. London: Frank Cass.

674. Obanya, P. 1992. "Future Prospects of Higher Education in Africa." In UNESCO-BREDA, ed., *Higher Education in Africa: Trends and Challenges for the 21st Century*, 315–322. Dakar, Senegal: UNESCO Regional Office.

675. Obanya, P., J. Shabani, and P. Okebukola. 2000. *Guide to Teaching and Learning in Higher Education*. Dakar: UNESCO-BREDA.

676. Odhiambo, T. R. 1993. "Introductory Remarks." In Project on the Management of Science and Technology for Development in Africa (MANSCI), ed., *Science-Led Development in Africa: Proceedings of the First Roundtable of Science Advisors for Science-Led Development in Africa*. Nairobi: Randforum Press.

677. Odhiambo, T. R., and T. T. Isoun. 1989. *Science for Development in Africa*. Nairobi, Kenya: ICIPE Science Press and Academy Science Publishers.

678. Omari, I. M. 1991. *Higher Education at the Crossroads in Africa*. Nairobi, Kenya: Man Graphics.

679. Oyewo, T. A. 1999. *Essays in African Diaspora*. Ibadan: Jator Publishing Company.

680. Perraton, H., ed. 1986. *Distance Education: An Economic and Educational Assessment of Its Potential for Africa*. Washington, D.C.: Education and Training Department, The World Bank.

681. Pires, M., R. Kassimir, and M. Brhane. 1999. *Investing in Return: Rates of Return of African Ph.D.'s Trained in North America*. New York: Social Science Research Council.

682. Prah, K. K. 1995. *Mother Tongue for Scientific and Technological Development in Africa*. Bonn: Deutsche Stiftung für Internationale Entwicklung.

683. Quik, H. G. 1981. "La coopération internationale et le développement des universités Africaines." ("International Cooperation and the Development of African Universities.") *Informations Universitaires et Professionelles Internationales* 25: 26–32.

684. Rasheed, S., and C. Grey-Johnson. 1987. *Higher Education in the Service of Africa's Socio-economic Recovery and Accelerated Development*. Harare: University of Zimbabwe Press.

685. Rathgeber, E. M. 1988. "A Tenuous Relationship: The African University and Development Policy Making in the 1980s." *Higher Education* 17, no. 3: 399–410.

686. Rathgeber, E. M. 1991. "Women in Higher Education in Africa: Access and Choices." In G. P. Kelly and S. Slaughter, eds., *Women's Higher Education in Comparative Perspective.* Dordrecht: Kluwer.

687. Reddy, J. 1999. "African Realities and Global Challenges." *International Higher Education* 17: 10–11.

688. Reddy, J. 2002. "Current Challenges and Future Possibilities for the Revitalization of Higher Education in Africa." In D. W. Chapman and A. E. Austin, eds., *Higher Education in the Developing World: Changing Contexts and Institutional Responses.* 109–127. Westport, Conn.: Greenwood Press.

689. Rosenberg, D., ed. 1997. *University Libraries in Africa: A Review of Their Current State and Future Potential.* London: International Africa Institute.

690. Saint, W. S. 1992. *Universities in Africa: Strategies for Stabilization and Revitalization.* Washington, D.C.: The World Bank.

691. Sall, E. 2000. *Women in Academia: Gender and Academic Freedom in Africa.* Dakar: Council for the Development of Social Science Research in Africa (CODESRIA).

692. Sall, E. 2001. "Academic Freedom and African Community of Scholars: The Challenges." *News from the Nordic Africa Institute (Uppsala: Nordiska Afrikainstitutet)* 1. Available online at http://www.nai.uu.se/newsfromnai/arkiv/2001/1/sall.html (accessed August 2002).

693. Samoff, J., N. T. Assié-Lumumba, L. Jallade, M. Cohen, UNESCO, and the Working Group on Education Sector Analysis, eds. 1996. *Analyses, Agendas, and Priorities for Education in Africa: A Review of Externally Initiated, Commissioned, and Supported Studies of Education in Africa, 1990–1994.* Paris: UNESCO.

694. Sanyal, B. C. 1991. *Staff Management in African Universities.* Paris: International Institute of Educational Planning, UNESCO.

695. Sanyal, B. C., and M. Martin. 1998. *Management of Higher Education with Especial Reference to Financial Management in African Countries.* Paris: International Institute of Educational Planning, UNESCO.

696. Saunders, S. J. 1992. *Access to and Quality in Higher Education: A Comparative Study.* Cape Town: University of Cape Town.

697. Sawadago, G. 1995. *The Future Missions and Roles of the African Universities.* Accra: DAE/AAU.

698. Sawyerr, A. 1988. "Changing Development Objectives and Strategies for Self-Reliant Economies in Africa: University Responses." *Higher Education Policy* 1, no. 1: 19–23.

699. Sawyerr, A. 1996. "Academic Freedom and University Autonomy: Preliminary Thoughts from Africa." *Higher Education Policy* 19, no. 4: 281–288.

700. Sawyerr, A. 1998. "Does Africa Really Need Her Universities?" *CODESRIA Bulletin* 3–4: 23.

701. Shabani, J., ed. 1998. *Higher Education in Africa: Achievements, Challenges and Prospects.* Dakar: UNESCO-BREDA.

702. Sherman, M. A. B. 1990. "The University in Modern Africa: Toward the Twenty-First Century." *Journal of Higher Education* 61, no. 4: 363–385.

703. Ssekiboobo, A. M. N. 1995. "Toward the Improvement of Data Usage for a Healthy Education Management System in Africa." *Higher Education Policy* 8, no. 1: 52–53.

704. Subcommittee on African Affairs. United States Congress Senate, Committee on Foreign Relations. 1994. *Higher Education in Africa: Hearing before the Subcommittee on African Affairs of the Committee on Foreign Relations, United States Senate, One Hundred Third Congress, First Session, May 17, 1993.* Washington, D.C.: United States Government Printing Office.

705. Tapsoba, S. 2000. "Création et retention du savoir en Afrique." ("Creation and Retention of Knowledge in Africa.") In S. Tapsoba, S. Kassoum, V. Houenou, O. Bankole, M. Sethi, and J. Ngu, eds., *Brain Drain and Capacity Building in Africa,* 18–35. Dakar, Senegal: Economic Commission for Africa/International Development Research Centre/International Organization for Migration.

706. Tapsoba, S., S. Kassoum, V. Houenou, O. Bankole, M. Sethi, and J. Ngu, eds. 2000. *Brain Drain and Capacity Building in Africa.* Dakar, Senegal: Economic Commission for Africa/International Development Research Centre/International Organization for Migration.

707. Tarpeh, D., and Association of African Universities. 1994. *Study on Cost Effectiveness and Efficiency in African Universities (Phase II): An Overview.* Accra: Association of African Universities.

708. Teekens, H., and B. Jongbloed. 2000. "The Role and Mission of the University in African Society." In H. Teekens and B. Jongbloed, eds., *The Financing of Higher Education in Sub-Saharan Africa.* Utrecht, Netherlands: Uitgeverij-Lemma.

709. Teferra, D. 1997. "Brain Drain of African Scholars and the Role of Studying in the United States." *International Higher Education* 7: 4–6.

710. Teferra, D. 1999. "Ideas for Financing African Higher Education." *International Higher Education* 17: 18–19.

711. Teferra, D. 2000. "Endowing African Universities: Cultivating Sustainability." *International Higher Education* 20: 18–19.

712. Teferra, D. 2000. "Revisiting the Doctrine of Human Capital Mobility in the Information Age." In S. Tapsoba, S. Kassoum, V. Houenou, O. Bankole, M. Sethi, and J. Ngu, eds., *Brain Drain and Capacity Building in Africa,* 64–77. Dakar, Senegal: Economic Commission for Africa/International Development Research Centre/International Organization for Migration.

713. Teferra, D. 2001. "The Knowledge Context in African Universities: The Neglected Link." *International Higher Education* 25 (Fall): 23–25.

714. Temu, J. R. 1992. *Women and Higher Education in Selected African Nations, 1960–1980: Enrollment Analyses and Former Student Perceptions.* Kent, Ohio: Kent State University Press.

715. Thiam, M. 1992. "An Overview of Trends and Challenges of Higher Education in Africa." In UNESCO-BREDA, ed., *Higher Education in Africa: Trends and Challenges for the 21st Century,* 19–41. Dakar, Senegal: UNESCO Regional Office.

716. Tshibangu, T. 1982. *La crise contemporaine, l'enjeu*

Africain et l'université de l'an 2000. (Contemporary Crisis, African Trends and the University in the Year 2000). Kinshasa: Presses Universitaires du Zaire.

717. Tshibangu, T. 1984. *L'Enseignement supérieur et le développement de l'Afrique d'ici l'an 2000. (Higher Education and Development in Africa: Toward the Year 2000.)* Dakar: UNESCO-BREDA.

718. UNESCO. 1963. *The Development of Higher Education in Africa*. Paris: UNESCO.

719. UNESCO. 1964. *Outline of a Plan for Scientific Research and Training in Africa*. Paris: UNESCO.

720. UNESCO. 1986. *Educafrica: Etudes de cas sur l'Enseignement Supérieur en Afrique. (Case Studies on Higher Education in Africa.)* Dakar: BREDA.

721. UNESCO. 1987. *CASTAFRICA II: Science, Technology and Endogenous Development in Africa—Trends, Problems and Prospects*. Paris: UNESCO.

722. UNESCO. 1993. *Development of Higher Education in Africa: The African University into the new Millennium*. Paris: UNESCO.

723. UNESCO. 1994. *Future Directions for Higher Education in Africa*. Paris: UNESCO.

724. UNESCO. 1994. *The Role of African Student Movements in the Political and Social Evolution of Africa from 1900 to 1995*. Paris: UNESCO.

725. UNESCO. 1995. *Women in Higher Education in Africa*. Dakar: UNESCO Regional Office for Education in Africa (BREDA).

726. UNESCO. 1998. *Higher Education in Africa: Achievements, Challenges and Prospects*. Dakar: UNESCO.

727. UNESCO-BREDA. 1987. *Amélioration et renovation de l'enseignement supérieur en Afrique. (Improvement and Renewal of Higher Education in Africa.)* Dakar: UNESCO-BREDA.

728. UNESCO-BREDA. 1987. "Higher Education in Africa." In UNESCO, *Educafrica*, 50–84. Dakar: BREDA.

729. UNESCO-BREDA. 1992. *Higher Education in Africa: Trends and Challenges for the 21st Century*. Dakar, Senegal: UNESCO Regional Office.

730. Van den Berghe, P. L. 1973. *Power and Privilege at an African University*. London: Routledge, Kegan Paul.

731. Waast, R. 2000. *La science en Afrique: synthèse bibliométrique. (Science In Africa: Bibliometric Synthesis.)* Paris: Institut de Recherche pour le Développement, Commission Européenne.

732. Waast, R. 2001. *Les coopérations scientifiques en Afrique. (Scientific Cooperatives in Africa.)* Paris: Institut de Recherche pour le Développement, Commission Européenne.

733. Wagaw, T. 1994. "Staffing the African University: The Conflict of Political Expediency and Academic Imperatives." *Higher Education Policy* 7, no. 2: 27–29.

734. Wagaw, T. G. 2001. "African Higher Education in Collaboration to Respond to Contemporary Development Imperatives." *Equity and Excellence in Education* 34, no. 3: 50–55.

735. Wallerstein, I. 1983. "The Evolving Role of the African Scholar in African Studies." *African Studies Review* 26, nos. 3–4: 155–161.

736. Wandira, A. 1977. *The African University in Development*. Johannesburg, South Africa: Ravan Press.

737. Watson, P. 2001. "The African Virtual University." *Education-Canada* 40, no. 4: 46.

738. Wield, D. 1997. "Coordination of Donors in African Universities." *Higher Education Policy* 10, no. 1: 41–54.

739. Weiler, H. N. 1986. "The Hot and Cold Wind of Politics: Planning Higher Education in Africa." In S. K. Gove and T. M. Stauffer, eds., *Policy Controversies in Higher Education*, 215–236. New York: Greenwood Press.

740. Wiredu, K. 1984. *Philosophical Research and Training in Africa: Some Suggestions*. Paris: UNESCO.

741. Woodhall, M. 1995. "Financial Diversification in Higher Education: A Review of International Experience and Implications for African Universities." *Higher Education Policy* 8, no. 1: 16–23.

742. World Bank. 1997. *Revitalizing Universities in Africa: Strategy and Guidelines*. Washington, D.C.: The World Bank.

743. Yesufu, T. M. 1973. *Creating the African University: Emerging Issues of the 1970s*. Ibadan, Nigeria: Oxford University Press.

744. Young, C. M. 1981. "The African University: Universalism, Development, and Ethnicity." *Comparative Education Review* 25, no. 2: 145–163.

745. Zeleza, P. T. 1983. "Academic Freedom in the North and the South: An African Perspective." *Academe: Bulletin of the AAUP* 83, no. 6: 16–21.

746. Zeleza, P. T. 1996. "Manufacturing and Consuming Knowledge: African Libraries and Publishing." *Development in Practice* 6, no. 4: 293–303.

Anglophone Africa

747. Eisemon, T. O., C. H. Davis, and E. M. Rathgeber. 1985. "The Transplantation of Science to Anglophone and Francophone Africa: Colonial Legacies and Contemporary Strategies for Science Co-operation." *Science and Public Policy* 12: 191–202.

748. Emudong, C. P. 1997. "The Gold Coast Nationalist Reaction to the Controversy over Higher Education in Anglophone West Africa and Its Impact on Decision Making in the Colonial Office, 1945–47." *Journal of Negro Education* 66, no. 2: 137–146.

749. Murphy, P., and A. Zhir. 1992. *Distance Education in Anglophone Africa: Experience with Secondary Education and Teacher Training*. Washington, D.C.: The World Bank.

750. Mwiria, K. 1992. *University Governance: Problems and Prospects in Anglophone Africa*. Technical Note no. 3. Washington, D.C.: The World Bank.

751. Peil, M. 1986. "Leadership of Anglophone Tropical African Universities, 1948–1986." *International Journal of Educational Development* 6, no. 4.

752. Thiam, M. 1992. "A Comparative Survey of Postgraduate Studies in Francophone and Anglophone African Countries." In UNESCO-BREDA, ed., *Higher Education in Africa: Trends and Challenges for the 21st Century*, 295–313. Dakar, Senegal: UNESCO Regional Office.

753. Woodhall, M. 1991. *Student Loans in Higher Education: 3 English-Speaking African Countries—Report of an IIEP Educational Forum.* Paris: International Institute for Educational Planning.

East Africa

754. Acker, D. G., E. L. McBreen, and S. Taylor. 1998. "Women in Higher Education in Agriculture with Reference to Selected Countries in East and Southern Africa." *Journal of Agricultural Education and Extension* 4, no. 1: 13–21.

755. Allen, C. H. 1986. *A Review of Social Science Research in Eastern, Southern and Some West African States.* Stockholm: Swedish International Development Cooperation Agency.

756. Bollag, B. 2001. "East African Universities Will Gain Journal Access in New Online Project." *International Higher Education* 23 (Spring): 8–9.

757. Court, D. 1981. *The Idea of Social Science in East Africa: An Aspect of the Development of Higher Education.* Nairobi: Institute for Development Studies, University of Nairobi.

758. ESAURP (Eastern and Southern African Universities Research Project). 1987. *ESAURP University Capacity in Eastern and Southern African Countries.* London: James Currey and Heinemann.

759. Ishumi, A. G. M. 1992. "Mobility of Teachers, Researchers, and Students: The Case of Eastern and Southern Africa." In UNESCO-BREDA, ed., *Higher Education in Africa: Trends and Challenges for the 21st Century,* 257–280. Dakar, Senegal: UNESCO Regional Office.

760. Ishumi, A. G. M. 1994. *30 years of Learning: Educational Development in Eastern and Southern Africa from Independence to 1990.* Ottawa: International Development Research Centre.

761. Katorobo, J. 1985. *The Social Sciences in Eastern Africa: An Agenda for Research.* Addis Ababa: Organization for Social Science Research in Eastern and Southern Africa (OSSREA).

762. Knight, J. B., and H. R. Sabot. 1981. *Education, Skills, and Inequality: The East Africa National Experiment.* New York: Oxford University Press.

763. Maliyamkono, T. L. 1982. *Training and Productivity in Eastern Africa: An Eastern African Universities Research Project Report on the Impact of Overseas Training on Development.* Exeter, N.H.: Heinemann.

764. Maliyamkono, T. L., and S. Well. 1980. "Effects of Overseas Training on Economic Development: Impact Surveys on Overseas Training." In T. L. Maliyamkono, ed., *Policy Development in Overseas Training.* Dar es Salaam: Eastern and Southern African Universities Research Project (ESAURP): Black Star Agencies.

765. Mwiria, K. 1990. *University Education in East Africa: Some Symptoms of Falling Standards.* Nairobi: Kenyatta University.

766. Mwiria, K. 1993. *University Education in East Africa: The Quality Crisis.* Nairobi: Kenyatta University.

767. Organization for Social Science Research in Eastern and Southern Africa. 1994. *A Register of Social Scientists in Eastern and Southern Africa.* Addis Ababa: Organization for Social Science Research in Eastern and Southern Africa.

768. Oyugi, W. O. 1989. *The Teaching and Research of Political Science in Eastern Africa.* Addis Ababa: Organization for Social Science Research in Eastern and Southern Africa.

769. Seyoum, G. S., and E.-W. Kameir. 1989. *Teaching and Research in Anthropology and Sociology in Eastern African Universities.* Addis Ababa: Organization for Social Science Research in Eastern and Southern Africa (OSSREA).

770. UNESCO-BREDA. 1987. "Higher Education Trends in East Africa." In UNESCO, *Educafrica,* 137–153. Dakar: BREDA.

Francophone Africa

771. Adams, M., I. Bah-Lalya, and M. Mukweso. 1991. "Francophone West Africa." In P. G. Altbach, ed., *International Higher Education,* 349–374. New York: Garland.

772. Alidou, O. 2000. "Francophonie, World Bank and the Collapse of the Francophone Africa Education System." In S. Federici, G. Caffentzis, and O. Alidou, eds., *A Thousand Flowers: Social Struggles against Structural Adjustment in African Universities,* 37–42. Trenton, N.J.: African World Press.

773. Araujo e Oliviera, J. B. 1987. "Where Is Higher Education in Francophone West Africa Heading?" *Prospects* 17, no. 4: 503–507.

774. Assié-Lumumba, N. T. 1992. *L'Enseignement supérieur en Afrique Francophone.* (*Higher Education in Francophone Africa.*) Washington, D.C.: The World Bank, Africa Technical Department, Education and Training Division.

775. Assié-Lumumba, N. T. 1993. *Higher Education in Francophone Africa: Assessment of the Potential of the Traditional Universities and Alternatives for Development.* AFTHR Technical Note no. 5. Washington, D.C.: The World Bank.

776. Cowan, L. G. 1969. *Recent Developments in Higher Education in the Francophone African Countries: Three Reports.* Washington: American Council on Education Overseas Liaison Committee.

777. Gangbo, F. 1996. *Les besoins de formation pédagogique des enseignants du supérieur d'Afrique francophone.* (*Pedagogical Training Needs for Francophone University Faculty.*) Dakar: Regional Office for Education in Africa, UNESCO.

778. Guedegbe, C. M. 1995. "Currency and Crisis: Higher Education in Francophone Africa." *International Higher Education* 3: 11–13.

779. Ndiaye, A. L. 1996. "The Case of Francophone Africa." *Higher Education Policy* 9, no. 4: 299–302.

780. Orivel, F. 1988. *Coûts, financement et efficacité des universités de l'Afrique Sub-Saharienne Francophone.* (*Costs, Funding and Efficiency of Universities in Francophone Sub-Saharan Africa.*) Washington, D.C.: The World Bank, Economic Development Institute, Division of Human Resources.

781. Orivel, F. 1996. "French-Speaking Universities in Sub-Saharan Africa: A Critical Impasse." In Z. Morsy and P. G. Altbach, eds., *Higher Education in an International Perspective: Critical Issues.* New York and London: Garland.

782. Ransom, A. 1988. *Financing Higher Education in Francophone West Africa.* Washington, D.C.: The World Bank.

783. Schraeder, P. 1995. "From Berlin 1884 to 1989: Foreign Assistance and French, American, and Japanese Competi-

tion in Francophone Africa." *Journal of Modern African Studies* 33, no. 4: 539–567.

784. Seddoh, K. F. 1989. "Foreign Student Mobility: The Case of Francophone West Africa." *Higher Education Policy* 2, no. 1: 29–31.

See also 747

North Africa

785. Al-Abed, A. B. 1986. "Educational Technology in the Arab World." *International Review of Education* 32, no. 3.

786. Bubtana, A. 1993. "Academic Mobility in the Arab Region." *Higher Education Policy* 6, no. 1: 13–14.

787. Coffman, J. 1996. "Current Issues in Higher Education in the Arab World." *International Higher Education* 4 (Spring): 15–17.

788. Jones, M. T. 1981. "Allocation of Students in North African Universities." *Higher Education* 10, no. 3: 315–334.

789. Makdisi, G. 1981. *The Rise of Colleges: Institutions of Learning in Islam and the West.* Edinburgh, U.K.: Edinburgh University Press.

790. Mazawi, A. E. 1999. "Gender and Higher Education in the Arab States." *International Higher Education* 17: 18–19.

791. Moris, S. 1996. "International Academic Cooperation in the Arab Region. Past, Present and Future." In P. Blumenthal, C. Goodwin, A. Smith, and U. Teichler, eds., *Academic Mobility in a Changing World*, 300–319. London: Jessica Kingsley Publishers.

792. Nabel Nofal, M., and M. Rasem Kmal. 1990. "Higher Education in the Arab World: Future Vision." *Arab Journal for Education* 10, no. 1 and 2 (in Arabic).

793. Sabour, M. 1999. "The Impact of Cultural and Economic Globalisation on the Planning and Function of Higher Education in North Africa and the Middle East." *Mediterranean Journal of Educational Studies* 4, no. 2: 237–241.

Southern Africa

794. Ingalls, W. B. 1995. "Building Consensus for Change: Developing an Administrative and Management Structure in a Southern African University." *Higher Education* 29, no. 3: 275–285.

795. Micou, A. M. 1995. *Sustaining Linkages between U.S. and Southern African Universities: An Analysis and Inventory.* Southern African Information Exchange Working Paper Number 30. New York: Institute of International Education: Southern African Information Exchange.

796. Mncube, S. S. 1988. *Key Issues in Library and Information Science for Southern Africa: A Handbook for Library and Information Specialists*: African Library & Information Service Press.

797. Mshingeni, K. E. 1994. *Science, Technology & Research for Development in the SADC Region: Status, Needs, Prospects, and Challenges.* Gaborone: Southern African Development Community.

798. Murphree, M. W., and E. A. Ngara. 1984. *Interuniversity Cooperation in Eastern Europe and Southern Africa: Report of the Vice-Chancellors' Workshop on Regional Coopera-

tion among Universities.* University of Zimbabwe. Harare: AESAU (Association of Eastern and Southern African Universities).

799. Petkov, D., G. Finnie, and V. Ram. 1995. "A Comparison of Undergraduate Programs in Information Systems in Southern African and North American Universities." *South African Journal of Higher Education* 9, no. 1: 116–121.

800. Weiss, T. 1998. "Addressing the Brain Drain." In L. Sachikonye, ed., *Labour Markets and Migration Policy in Southern Africa.* Harare: Sapes Books.

See also 754, 755, 758, 759, 760, 767

Sub-Saharan Africa

801. Ajeyalemi, D. 1990. *Science and Technology Education in Africa: Focus on Seven Sub-Saharan Countries.* Lagos: University of Lagos Press.

802. Amin, R. E. 2000. "Students' Sociocultural Background as a Discriminating Factor in the Evaluation of Teaching in a Bilingual University in Central Africa." *Teaching in Higher Education* 5, no. 4: 435–445.

803. Banya, K., and J. Elu. 1997. "The Crisis of Higher Education in Sub-Saharan Africa: The Continuing Search for Relevance." *Journal of Higher Education Policy and Management* 19, no. 2: 151–164.

804. Banya, K., and J. Elu. 2001. "The World Bank and Financing Higher Education in Sub-Saharan Africa." *Higher Education*, no. 42: 1–34.

805. Banya, K. 2001. "Are Private Universities the Solution to the Higher Education Crisis in Sub-Saharan Africa?" *Higher Education Policy* 14, no. 2: 161–174.

806. Bennell, P. 1996. "Rates of Return to Education: Does the Conventional Pattern Prevail in Sub-Saharan Africa?" *World Development* 24, no. 1: 183–199.

807. Bloch, M. N., J. A. Beoku-Betts, and B. R. Tabachnick. 1998. *Women and Education in Sub-Saharan Africa: Power, Opportunities, and Constraints.* Boulder, Colo.: Rienner Publishers.

808. Brock-Utne, B. 1996. "Globalisation of Learning: The Role of the Universities in the South, with a Special Look at the Sub-Saharan Africa." *International Journal of Educational Development* 16, no. 4: 335–346.

809. Coombe, T., and H. Hawes. 1986. *Education Priorities and Aid Responses in Sub-Saharan Africa: Report of a Conference at Cumberland Lodge, Windsor, 4–7 December 1984.* London: Overseas Development Administration and University of London.

810. Costa, C. 2000. "The European Commission Perspective on Higher Education in Sub-Saharan Africa." In B. Jongbloed and H. Teekens, eds., *The Financing of Higher Education in Sub-Saharan Africa*, 69–75. Utrecht, Netherlands: Uitgeverij-Lemma. Center for Higher Education Policy Studies and Netherlands Organization for International Cooperation in Higher Education.

811. Court, D. 1991. "The Development of University Education in Sub-Saharan Africa." In P. G. Altbach, ed., *International Higher Education*, 329–347. New York: Garland.

812. Davies, J. 1994. "The University Curriculum and the

Transition in South Africa." *European Journal of Education* 29, no. 3: 255–268.

813. Davis, C. H. 1983. "Institutional Sectors of Mainstream Science Production in Sub-Saharan Africa, 1970–1979." *Scientometrics* 5: 163–175.

814. Domatob, J. 1998. *African Higher Education Policy: A Survey of Sub-Saharan Africa*. San Francisco: International Scholars Publications.

815. Eisemon, T. O. 1992. *Private Initiative and Traditions of State Control in Higher Education in Sub-Saharan Africa*. Washington, D.C.: The World Bank.

816. Eisemon, T. O., and C. H. Davis. 1991. "Strengthening Research and Training in Sub-Saharan African Universities." *McGuill Journal of Education* 27, no. 2: 122–149.

817. Eisemon, T. O., and C. H. Davis. 1991. "University Research and the Development of Scientific Capacity in Sub-Saharan Africa and Asia." In P. G. Altbach, ed., *International Higher Education: An Encyclopedia*. New York: Garland.

818. Eisemon, T., and M. Kourouma. 1994. "Foreign Assistance for University Development in Sub-Saharan Africa and Asia." In J. Salmi and A. Verspoor, eds., *Revitalizing Higher Education*. Washington, D.C.: The World Bank.

819. Elu, J. 2000. "Human Development in Sub-Saharan Africa: Analysis and Prospects for the Future." *Journal of Third World Studies* 17, no. 2 (Fall): 53–71.

820. Fine, J. C., W. Lyakurwa, and A. G. Drabek, eds. 1994. *Ph.D. Education in Economics in Sub-Saharan Africa: Lessons and Prospects*. Nairobi: East African Publishers.

821. Girdwood, A. 1993. "Capacity Building and Higher Education in Africa: A Comment on the Capacity Building Rationale and Aid to Higher Education in Sub-Saharan Africa." *Compare* 23, no. 2: 149–158.

822. Habte, A. 1989. "Support for Higher Education in Sub-Saharan Africa: Where Does the World Bank Stand?" *Higher Education Policy* 2, no. 2: 20–24.

823. Hawes, H., and T. Coombe, eds. 1986. *Education Priorities and Aid Responses in Sub-Saharan Africa*. London: Her Majesty's Stationery Office.

824. Hinchliffe, K. 1985. *Issues Related to Higher Education in Sub-Saharan Africa*. World Bank Staff Working Papers no. 780. Washington, D.C.: The World Bank.

825. Hinchliffe, K. 1987. *Higher Education in Sub-Saharan Africa*. London: Croom Helm.

826. Hoffman, A. 1995. "The Destruction of Higher Education in Sub-Saharan Africa." *Journal of Blacks in Higher Education* 10: 83–87.

827. John, M. 1996. "Distance Education in Sub-Saharan Africa: The Next Five Years." *Innovations in Education and Training International* 33, no. 1: 50–57.

828. Jongbloed, B., and H. Teekens. 2000. *The Financing of Higher Education in Sub-Saharan Africa*. Utrecht, Netherlands: Uitgeverij-Lemma.

829. Kaboret, Y. 2000. "Eviter la fuite des cerveaux en Afrique sub-Saharienne: Role des institutions sous-régionales de formation et de recherche." ("Avoiding Brain Drain in Sub-Saharan Africa: The Role of Sub-Regional Institutions for Training and Research.") In S. Tapsoba, S. Kassoum, V. Houenou, O. Bankole, M. Sethi, and J. Ngu, eds., *Brain Drain and Ca-

pacity Building in Africa*, 186–195. Dakar, Senegal: Economic Commission for Africa/International Development Research Centre/International Organization for Migration.

830. Kidd, C. V. 1991. "University Training Abroad: Sub-Saharan Africa." *Higher Education Policy* 4, no. 2: 41–46.

831. Kingsley, B. 2001. "Are Private Universities the Solution to the Higher Education Crisis in Sub-Saharan Africa?" *Higher Education Policy* 14, no. 2: 161–174.

832. Lebeau, Y., and M. Ogunsanya. 1999. *The Dilemma of Post-Colonial Universities: Elite Formation and the Restructuring of Higher Education in Sub-Saharan Africa*. Ibadan: IFRA and African BookBuilders.

833. Levey, L. A. 1991. *Computer and CD-ROM Capability in Sub-Saharan African University and Research Libraries*. Washington, D.C.: American Association for the Advancement of Science.

834. Levey, L. 1995. *A Profile of Research Libraries in Sub-Saharan Africa: Acquisitions, Outreach, and Infrastructure*. Washington, D.C.: American Association for the Advancement of Science.

835. Lewinger, J. 1984. "Overseas Training and National Development Objectives in Sub-Saharan Africa." *Comparative Education Review* 28, no. 2: 221–240.

836. Logan, B. 1987. "The Reverse Transfer of Technology from Sub-Saharan Africa to the United States." *Journal of Modern African Studies* 25, no. 4: 597–612.

837. Mingat, A., and J. Tan. 1984. *Subsidization of Higher Education versus Expansion of Primary Enrollments: What Can a Shift of Resources Achieve in Sub-Saharan Africa?* Washington, D.C.: The World Bank.

838. Moock, P. R. 1987. *Education Policies for Sub-Saharan Africa: Adjustment, Revitalization, and Expansion*. Washington, D.C.: The World Bank.

839. Mwiria, K. 1991. *The Role of Good Governance and Positive University-State Relations in Promoting University-Development in Sub-Saharan Africa*. Washington, D.C.: Africa Technical Department, The World Bank.

840. Nkinyangi, J. 1991. "Student Protests in Sub-Saharan Africa." *Higher Education* 22, no. 2: 157–173.

841. Orivel, F., and F. Sergent. 1988. "Foreign Aid to Education in Sub-Saharan Africa: How Useful Is It?" *Prospects* 18, no. 4: 459–460.

842. Ridker, R. G. 1994. *The World Bank's Role in Human Resource Development in Sub-Saharan Africa: Education, Training, and Technical Assistance*. Washington, D.C.: The World Bank.

843. Robert and Associates. 1998. *Tertiary Distance Learning in Sub-Saharan Africa: Overview and Directory to Programs*. Washington, D.C.: The World Bank.

844. Saint, W. S. 1993. "Initiating University Reform: Experience from Sub-Saharan Africa." *Zimbabwe Journal of Educational Research* 5: 1–20.

845. Saint, W. 1999. *Tertiary Distance Education and Technology in Sub-Saharan Africa*. Washington, D.C.: The World Bank.

846. Shabani, J. 1995. "Higher Education in Sub-Saharan Africa: Strategies for the Improvement of the Quality of Training." *Quality in Higher Education* 1, no. 2: 173–178.

847. Smallwood, A., and T. L. Maliyamkono. 1996. "Regional Cooperation and Mobility in Higher Education: The Implications for Human Resource Development in Sub-Saharan Africa and the Relevance of Recent Initiatives to Europe." In P. Blumenthal, C. Goodwin, A. Smith, and U. Teichler, eds., *Academic Mobility in a Changing World*. Philadelphia: Jessica Kingsley Publishers.

848. Sunal, D. W., and M. E. Haas. 1998. "Issues for Higher Education in Sub-Saharan Africa." In C. S. Sunal, ed., *Schooling in Sub-Saharan Africa*. New York: Garland Publishing.

849. Van der Mer, P., B. Jongbloed, and H. Teekens. 2000. "The Role and Organization of Higher Education in Sub-Saharan Africa." In B. Jongbloed and H. Teekens, eds., *The Financing of Higher Education in Sub-Saharan Africa*. Utrecht, Netherlands: Uitgeverij-Lemma.

850. World Bank. 1991. *The African Capacity Building Initiative toward Improved Policy Analysis and Development Management in Sub-Saharan Africa*. Washington, D.C.: The World Bank.

851. Zymelman, M. 1990. *Science, Education, and Development in Sub-Saharan Africa*. Washington, D.C.: The World Bank.

See also 510, 780, 781

West Africa

852. Abagou, B., A. Perry, and A. Smith. 1983. "Crisis of Higher Education." *West Africa* (12 September): 2120–2139. London: West Africa Publishing Company.

853. Alemna, A. A. 1990. "Information Technology and Information Training in West Africa." *Information Development* 6, no. 4: 204–209.

854. Guilar, J. D. 2001. "Founding an American University Campus in West Africa: Success Factors and Challenges for Suffolk University's Dakar Campus." *International Education* 31, no. 1: 24–37.

855. Ononogbo, R. U. 1990. "University Library Functions in West Africa." *International Library Review* 22, no. 4: 299–313.

856. Sacerdoti, E., S. Brunschwig, and J. Tang. 1998. *The Impact of Human Capital on Growth: Evidence from West Africa*. Washington, D.C.: International Monetary Fund, African Department.

857. Sanyal, B. C., M. Saito, and N. Kotey. 1995. *Institutional Management in Higher Education in Western Africa*. Paris: UNESCO, International Institute for Educational Planning.

858. Sharma, R. N., and J. Bess. 2000. "West Virginia to West Africa and Back: An Intercontinental Collaboration." *American Libraries* 31, no. 7: 44–46.

See also 748, 755, 771, 773, 782, 784

Subregional and Transcontinental

859. Albrecht, D., and A. Ziderman. 1991. *Deferred Cost Recovery for Higher Education: Student Loan Programs in Developing Countries*. World Bank Discussion Papers 137. Washington, D.C.: The World Bank.

860. Albrecht, D., and A. Ziderman. 1992. *Financing Universities in Developing Countries*. Washington, D.C.: Education and Employment Division, The World Bank.

861. Albrecht, D., and A. Ziderman. 1992. *Funding Mechanisms for Higher Education: Financing for Stability, Efficiency, and Responsiveness*. World Bank Discussion Papers 153. Washington, D.C.: The World Bank.

862. Andrew, D. 2000. "University Graduates and Development." In R. Bourne, ed., *Universities and Development*. London: Association of Commonwealth Universities.

863. Arger, G. 1990. "Distance Education in the Third World: Critical Analysis on the Promise and the Reality." *Open Learning* 5, no. 2: 9–18.

864. Association of Commonwealth Universities. 2000. *Commonwealth Universities Yearbook 2000: A Directory to the Universities of the Commonwealth*. Vols. 1 and 2. London: Association of Commonwealth Universities.

865. Buchert, L., and K. King, eds. 1995. *Learning from Experience: Policy and Practice in Aid to Higher Education*. The Hague: Center for the Study of Education in Developing Countries.

866. Carrington, W. J., and E. Detragiache. 1999. "How Extensive Is the Brain Drain?" *Finance and Development* 36, no. 2: 46–49.

867. Colclough, C. 1995. "Diversifying the Funding of Tertiary Institutions: Is the Bank's Agenda the Right One?" In L. Buchert and K. King, eds., *Learning from Experience: Policy and Practice in Aid to Higher Education*, 145–157. The Hague: Centre for the Study of Education in Developing Countries.

868. Coleman, J. S., and D. Court. 1993. *University Development in the Third World: The Rockefeller Foundation Experience*. New York: Pergamon.

869. De Moor, R. A. 1993. *Academic Freedom and University Autonomy: Essentials and Limitations in Academic Freedom and University Autonomy*. Paris: European Centre for Higher Education (CEPES) and UNESCO.

870. Douglas, A., and A. Ziderman. 1992. *Financing Universities in Developing Countries*. PHREE Background Paper Series. Washington, D.C.: The World Bank.

871. Eisemon, T., and L. Holm-Nielsen. 1995. *Reforming Higher Education Systems: Some Lessons to Guide Policy Implementation*. Washington, D.C.: The World Bank.

872. Erik, T. 1992. *Improving the Quality of Research in Developing Country Universities*. PHREE Background Paper Series 92/52. Washington, D.C.: The World Bank.

873. Gaillard, J. 1991. *Scientists in the Third World*. Lexington: The University of Kentucky.

874. Gaillard, J., V. V. Krishna, and R. Waast. 1997. *Scientific Communities in the Developing World*. New Delhi: Sage Publications.

875. Houphouet-Boigny, D., and F. K. Mansilla. 1999. *Femme et éducation scientifique: cas de l'enseignement supérieur.* (*Women and Scientific Education: The Case of Higher Education.*) Ouagadougou: UNESCO.

876. International Association of Universities (IAU). 1997. *World List of Universities*. Paris: International Association of Universities and UNESCO Information Centre on Higher Education.

877. James, E. 1991. *Private Finance and Management of*

Education in Developing Countries: Major Policy and Research Issues. Paris: International Institute for Educational Planning (UNESCO).

878. Kamba, W. 1993. "University Autonomy." In R. A. DeMoor, ed., *Academic Freedom and University Autonomy.* Paris: European Centre for Higher Education (CEPES) and UNESCO.

879. King, K. 1991. *Aid and Education in the Developing World: The Role of the Donor Agencies in Educational Analysis.* Harlow: Longman.

880. King, K. 1995. "World Bank Traditions of Support to Higher Education and Capacity-Building: Reflections on *Higher Education: The Lessons of Experience.*" In L. Buchert and K. King, eds., *Learning from Experience: Policy and Practice in Aid to Higher Education,* 19–41. The Hague: Centre for the Study of Education in Developing Countries.

881. King, K. 1997. *Aid and Higher Education in the Developing World.* Edinburgh: Center of African Studies, Edinburgh University.

882. Kirkland, J. 2000. "Bridging the Knowledge Gap: The Changing Face of the Commonwealth Scholarships and Fellowships Plan." *Round Table,* no. 356: 471–479.

883. Lulat, Y. G.-M. 1988. "Education and National Development: The Continuing Problem of Misdiagnosis and Irrelevant Prescriptions." *International Journal of Educational Development* 8, no. 4: 315–328.

884. Lund, H. 1998. *Bridging the Gap? Internet and E-Mail Access within Universities in Developing Commonwealth Countries.* London: Commonwealth of Higher Education Management Service.

885. Maliyamkono, T. L. 1984. "Research Collaboration: South-South Perspectives—Some Crucial Problems." *Scandinavian Journal of Development Alternatives* 3.

886. Mayor, F. 1993. "Academic Freedom and University Autonomy." In R. A. DeMoor, ed., *Academic Freedom and University Autonomy: Papers on Higher Education.* Paris: European Centre for Higher Education (CEPES) and UNESCO.

887. Mbipom, G. 1995. "Returns to Tertiary Education in a Developing Economy: A Specific Case Study." *Higher Education Policy* 8, no. 1: 36–39.

888. Mingat, A., and J.-P. Tan. 1986. "Who Profits from the Public Funding of Education? A Comparison of World Regions." *Comparative Education Review* 30, no. 2: 260–270.

889. Musa, B. M. 1994. "Extension Education and the Role of University Extension Departments." *International Review of Education* 40, no. 2: 177–179.

890. Nakabo, S. 1999. "Statistical Data: The Underestimated Tool for Higher Education Management." *Higher Education* 37, no. 3: 259–279.

891. Neave, G., and F. van Vught. 1994. "Government and Higher Education in Developing Nations: A Conceptual Framework." In G. Neave and F. van Vught, eds., *Government and Higher Education Relationships across Three Continents: The Winds of Change.* Oxford: Elsevier.

892. Perraton, H. 2000. *Open and Distance Learning in Developing Countries.* New York: Routledge.

893. Psacharopoulos, G. 1980. *Higher Education in Developing Countries: A Cost Benefit Analysis.* World Bank Staff Working Paper 440. Washington, D.C.: The World Bank.

894. Psacharopoulos, G. 1985. "Returns to Education: A Further International Update and Implications." *Journal of Human Resources* XV (Fall): 583–604.

895. Psacharopoulos, G. 1998. "Higher Education in Developing Countries: The Scenario of the Future." In K. Kempner, M. Mollis, and W. G. Tierney, eds., *Comparative Education,* 55–59. Needham Heights, Mass.: Simon and Schuster Custom Publishing.

896. Psacharopoulos, G., and M. Woodhall. 1985. *Education for Development.* New York: Oxford University Press.

897. Ransom, A. 1993. *Improving Higher Education in Developing Countries.* Economic Development Inst. Seminar Series. Washington, D.C.: The World Bank.

898. Regel, O. 1992. *The Academic Credit System in Higher Education: Effectiveness and Relevance in Developing Countries.* Washington, D.C.: The World Bank.

899. Ruijter, C. T., and J. H. Van Weeren. 1989. "Computer-Assisted Learning in Higher Education in Developing Countries." In H. Oosthoek and T. Vroeijenstijn, eds., *Higher Education and New Technologies,* 461–472. New York: Pergamon Press.

900. Rumble, G. 1992. *The Management of Distance Learning Systems.* Paris: UNESCO, International Institute for Educational Planning.

901. Salmi, J. 1991. *The Higher Education Crisis in Developing Countries.* PHREE Background Paper Series PHREE/91/37. Washington, D.C.: The World Bank.

902. Schofield, A. 1996. *Private Post-Secondary Education in Four Commonwealth Countries.* Paris: UNESCO.

903. Task Force on Higher Education and Society. 2000. *Higher Education in Developing Countries: Peril and Promise.* Washington, D.C.: The World Bank.

904. Thulstrup, E. W. 1992. *Improving the Quality of Research in Developing Country Universities.* Washington, D.C.: Population and Human Resources Department, The World Bank.

905. UNESCO. 1982. *World Guide to Higher Education: Comparative Survey of Systems, Degrees and Qualifications.* Paris: UNESCO.

906. UNESCO. 1995. *Policy Paper for Change and Development in Higher Education.* Paris: UNESCO.

907. UNESCO. 1995. *Research in Changing and Developing Higher Education.* Paris: UNESCO (in Arabic).

908. Woodhall, M. 1987. *Lending for Learning: Designing a Student Loan Programme for Developing Countries.* London: Commonwealth Secretariat.

909. Woodhall, M. 1988. "Designing a Student Loan Program for a Developing Country: The Relevance of International Experience." *Economics of Education Review* 7, no. 1: 153–161.

910. Woodhall, M. 1992. "Student Loans in Developing Countries: Feasibility, Experience, and Prospects for Reform." *Higher Education* 23, no. 4: 347–356.

911. World Bank. 1986. *Financing Education in Developing Countries.* Washington, D.C.: The World Bank.

912. World Bank. 1994. *Higher Education: The Lessons of Experience.* Washington, D.C.: The World Bank.

913. World Bank. 1995. *Priorities and Strategies for Education.* Washington, D.C.: The World Bank.

914. Youngman, F. 1994. "The Role of the University in Developing Educational Research Capacity and Influencing Educational Decisions." In S. Burchfield, ed., *Research for Educational Policy and Planning*, 195–235. Gaborone: Macmillan Botswana.

See also 533, 535, 536

SECTION II. THEMATIC LIST

Academic Freedom and Autonomy, 37, 57, 64, 72, 116, 135, 143, 149, 204, 257, 265, 436, 441, 520, 523, 579, 586, 601, 643, 651, 654, 691, 692, 699, 745, 869, 878, 886

Academic Profession, 5, 61, 82, 97, 122, 123, 124, 128, 135, 139, 195, 214, 228, 236, 237, 241, 246, 254, 257, 258, 263, 306, 325, 348, 352, 367, 393, 426, 443, 447, 464, 474, 561, 564, 589, 590, 609, 656, 666, 691, 692, 733, 735, 755, 767, 777, 873, 874

Academic Quality and Assessment, 25, 34, 98, 115, 152, 186, 187, 205, 207, 211, 230, 273, 282, 311, 329, 345, 372, 397, 403, 413, 415, 416, 428, 429, 448, 449, 490, 500, 527, 668, 696, 765, 766, 846, 898, 905

Access and Equity, 112, 133, 152, 197, 211, 222, 225, 226, 231, 238, 261, 313, 317, 319, 326, 344, 354, 355, 364, 365, 370, 394, 403, 409, 411, 417, 433, 435, 444, 448, 460, 530, 657, 686, 696, 838

Brain Drain and Mobility, 7, 48, 51, 74, 91, 92, 97, 117, 264, 278, 304, 324, 366, 438, 598, 613, 629, 655, 663, 679, 681, 706, 709, 712, 755, 759, 763, 764, 784, 800, 829, 847, 866

Capacity Building, 32, 36, 51, 74, 102, 117, 211, 232, 276, 278, 308, 342, 349, 541, 552, 570, 572, 573, 629, 630, 638, 639, 706, 758, 819, 821, 830, 835, 850, 856

Comparative Studies, 8, 9, 36, 106, 119, 120, 124, 234, 238, 301, 317, 340, 369, 444, 538, 590, 696, 747, 752, 774, 776, 793, 798, 799, 817, 847, 888, 893, 895, 902, 905

Cost Efficiency and Effectiveness, 24, 83, 107, 118, 152, 164, 183, 224, 489, 509, 543, 670, 707, 780, 806, 859, 893, 894

Distance, Virtual, and Open Education, 58, 119, 136, 138, 150, 163, 191, 244, 302, 303, 333, 410, 419, 425, 460, 500, 501, 554, 631, 680, 737, 749, 827, 843, 845, 863, 889, 892, 899, 900

Employment and Labor Market, 3, 31, 85, 86, 131, 132, 245, 275, 280, 378, 442, 444, 503

External Agencies and Foreign Assistance, 126, 172, 235, 260, 294, 295, 526, 528, 555, 568, 570, 571, 572, 578, 584, 597, 603, 604, 608, 648, 650, 652, 653, 738, 772, 783, 804, 810, 818, 822, 841, 842, 867, 868, 879, 880, 881, 882

Financing and Funding, 22, 27, 30, 42, 45, 47, 109, 129, 157, 162, 221, 233, 243, 253, 284, 286, 381, 400, 450, 456, 461, 466, 475, 477, 486, 559, 560, 561, 585, 587, 632, 637, 642, 670, 695, 710, 711, 741, 753, 780, 782, 788, 804, 828, 837, 860, 861, 867, 870, 877, 888, 908, 909, 910, 911

Gender, Ethnicity, and Race, 61, 79, 81, 90, 132, 137, 141, 181, 238, 240, 249, 267, 313, 314, 315, 335, 343, 350, 351, 352, 357, 361, 364, 374, 376, 377, 379, 380, 388, 411, 417, 424, 426, 464, 514, 530, 617, 640, 646, 657, 665, 666, 686, 691, 714, 725, 744, 754, 758, 802, 807, 875

Globalization, 35, 188, 199, 217, 234, 362, 417, 604, 629, 687, 793, 808

Governance and Management, 42, 55, 67, 95, 110, 114, 130, 141, 144, 145, 148, 151, 160, 210, 323, 330, 336, 338, 339, 346, 369, 384, 387, 396, 404, 406, 407, 421, 476, 483, 500, 504, 548, 575, 594, 595, 597, 605, 607, 634, 640, 650, 694, 695, 703, 748, 750, 751, 794, 815, 832, 839, 849, 850, 857, 877, 890, 891, 897, 900

Graduate Education, 275, 341, 342, 521, 525, 535, 546, 551, 587, 606, 624, 672, 681, 752, 764, 820

Higher Education in National Development, 13, 32, 73, 80, 100, 120, 121, 179, 200, 216, 227, 236, 256, 266, 280, 299, 313, 362, 403, 405, 408, 427, 495, 499, 537, 540, 553, 564, 566, 574, 583, 588, 611, 615, 631, 633, 659, 660, 662, 669, 673, 684, 685, 697, 698, 700, 702, 708, 717, 730, 734, 736, 762, 764, 775, 803, 835, 851, 862, 868, 883, 887, 893, 896, 897, 901, 903, 907

Informatics and Information Science, 28, 29, 156, 321, 360, 434, 515, 520, 532, 605, 618, 619, 620, 689, 756, 796, 799, 833, 834, 853, 855, 884

Interuniversity Cooperation, 68, 297, 298, 468, 519, 521, 546, 558, 563, 645, 649, 683, 732, 747, 759, 795, 798, 847, 858

Planning and Policy, 29, 52, 99, 102, 111, 130, 167, 173, 210, 211, 283, 292, 323, 346, 354, 369, 370, 383, 399, 445, 455, 462, 491, 492, 495, 498, 545, 557, 578, 593, 599, 600, 667, 685, 733, 739, 742, 743, 793, 809, 814, 823, 838, 865, 871, 906, 912, 913

Private Higher Education and Privatization, 15, 16, 127, 147, 154, 178, 295, 375, 407, 478, 487, 510, 805, 815, 831, 877, 902

Research, 5, 6, 14, 28, 36, 38, 50, 52, 75, 95, 96, 99, 101, 141, 158, 203, 269, 301, 320, 341, 368, 371, 393, 414, 422, 423, 461, 474, 485, 507, 521, 531, 546, 548, 556, 558, 573, 575, 581, 587, 591, 610, 618, 619, 620, 626, 627, 640, 644, 664, 672, 705, 719, 740, 755, 757, 761, 767, 768, 776, 797, 816, 817, 829, 833, 834, 872, 885, 904, 907, 914

Science and Technology, 9, 14, 20, 38, 50, 52, 61, 75, 123, 124, 125, 128, 155, 203, 229, 241, 247, 249, 263, 280, 281, 285, 328, 373, 389, 390, 401, 402, 517, 536, 589, 590, 591, 592, 608, 609, 610, 617, 621, 625, 628, 661, 676, 677, 682, 719, 721, 731, 732, 747, 754, 797, 801, 812, 817, 836, 845, 851, 853, 873, 874, 875

Student Activism, 77, 94, 106, 142, 149, 218, 262, 274, 296, 314, 316, 347, 385, 488, 494, 496, 502, 511, 539, 602, 616, 641, 671, 724, 840

Teaching and Learning Processes and Curriculum, 2, 20, 21, 34, 43, 45, 66, 99, 141, 153, 189, 193, 202, 250, 252, 282, 310, 312, 318, 321, 322, 327, 334, 350, 353, 358, 367, 397, 411, 418, 420, 424, 425, 428, 429, 431, 432, 447, 452, 470, 474, 507, 515, 522, 558, 580, 636, 640, 658, 675, 740, 768, 769, 777, 802, 899

University Reform, 16, 33, 40, 41, 53, 56, 59, 87, 102, 171, 182, 183, 187, 201, 202, 212, 223, 288, 289, 291, 293, 300, 332, 336, 337, 340, 395, 398, 421, 430, 440, 452, 455, 462, 518, 533, 534, 544, 567, 647, 674, 690, 715, 722, 723, 727, 844, 871, 897

Doctoral Dissertations on Higher Education in Africa

Damtew Teferra and Alma Maldonado-Maldonado

INTRODUCTION

This compilation provides a catalogue of unpublished doctoral dissertations on African higher education. A number of sources, publications, and databases, especially *Dissertation Abstracts Online*, were used. We made a concerted effort to be as exhaustive and comprehensive as possible.

This compilation focuses mainly on works in English. The majority of the dissertations originate from American universities. While we have attempted to consult French-language resources, we were unable to locate much material.

ORGANIZATION

The chapter has two sections: a country list and a thematic list. The country list provides a numbered list of dissertations covering topics relative to thirty-five countries in alphabetical order. Following that, regional- and transregional-themed resources are provided in eight subsections. The thematic list in the second section covers a variety of thematic issues organized in twenty-nine subsections. These are cross-referenced based on the numbered country list in the first section.

THE RESOURCES

The list contains 301 dissertations. Nigeria and South Africa are most heavily represented with 85 and 49 dissertations, respectively. As a matter of fact, dissertations on higher education in Nigeria account for 28 percent of the whole list, followed by South Africa at 16 percent. Kenya, Egypt, and Ethiopia (with somewhat equal numbers) together account for 13 percent of the list.

Attitudes, roles, and performance of students; teaching and learning processes; and higher education issues surrounding national development are among the most common topics of the dissertations. Dissertations on comparative studies, planning and policy, and issues relating to the academic profession are also well represented. Dissertations on academic freedom, capacity building, and private higher education are the least common.

A comparison of this database with the general bibliography by themes, frequency, and period of time is illustrative. Some themes that were not apparent in the bibliography, such as student attitudes, roles, and performances; curriculum; and technological and vocational education, were richly represented in the dissertations. Other themes such as research, financing, and funding are less represented in this database. Themes relating to globalization, academic freedom, and autonomy are virtually nonexistent here.

SECTION I: COUNTRY LIST

Algeria

1. Meziane, M. 1987. "Toward Computing in Algerian Higher Education: Assessment, Perceptions and Alternatives." Ed.D. dissertation, United States International University.

Benin

2. Guedegbe, C. M. 1994. "The Professorate and Academic Life in Africa: A Case Study of the Academic Profession at Benin National University." Ph.D. dissertation, State University of New York at Buffalo.
3. Houme, K. P. 1998. "Admission des étudiants à l'entrée et efficacité en première année à l'université du Benin: facteur de réussite et d'echec." ("Admission of Freshmen and Their Performance during the Freshman Year at the University of Benin.") Ph.D. dissertation, Université du Bénin, Bénin.

Botswana

4. Magagula, C. M. 1978. "The Multi-national University in Africa: An Analysis of the Development and Demise of the University of Botswana, Lesotho, and Swaziland." Ph.D. dissertation, University of Maryland–College Park.
5. Mazile, J. G. P. 1984. "Categorical Scholarships, Subject Matter Specialty, Career Interest at High School and Their Impact on Subsequent Employment of Botswana University Graduates." Ed.D. dissertation, University of Cincinnati.
6. Odirile, L. W. 2000. "2000 HIV/AIDS: Knowledge, Attitudes and Beliefs among University of Botswana Undergraduate Students." Ph.D. dissertation, Ohio University.
7. Siphambe, H. K. 1997. "Earnings Differentials and Rates of Return to Education in Botswana." Ph.D. dissertation, University of Manitoba (Canada).

Burkina Faso

8. Sanou, F. 1982. "African Universities in Search of Their Identities: A Study of the Culture of Careerism at the University of Ouagadougou (Upper Volta)." Ph.D. dissertation, University of Southern California.
9. Somda, P. 1995. "The Irrelevance of an African University's Curriculum to the National Labor Market: The Case of the Faculty of Economics and Management (Faseg) at the University of Ouagadougou, Burkina Faso." Ph.D. dissertation, State University of New York at Buffalo.
10. Tapsoba, S. 1988. "Factors Associated with the Research Involvement of the Burkinabe Professoriate at the University of

Ouagadougou in Burkina Faso." Ph.D. dissertation, State University of New York at Buffalo.

Cameroon

11. Ade-Mobufor, M. I. 1989. "The Mission of Higher Education in Cameroon: A Case Study of Yaounde University from 1962 to 1975." Ph.D. dissertation, Northwestern University.

12. Gwei, S. N. 1975. "Education in Cameroon: Western Pre-colonial and Colonial Antecedents and the Development of Higher Education." Ph.D. dissertation, University of Michigan.

13. Nnane, P. E. 1988. "Equity in Access to and Costs of Higher Education in Cameroon: The Case of the University of Yaounde." Ed.D. dissertation, State University of New York at Albany.

Central African Republic

14. Ngoulo, N. 1996. "Conception et mise à l'essai d'un programme d'enseignement de la cohésion et de la cohérence textuelles à l'Université de Bangui." ("Design and Trial of a Program Study on Textual Cohesion and Coherence at the University of Bangui.") Ed.D. dissertation, Université de Montreal (Canada).

Democratic Republic of Congo (Zaire)

15. Chizungu, R. 1979. "University Education and Alienation: The Dilemma of the Université Nationale du Zaire and National Development." Ph.D. dissertation, Stanford University.

16. Diawaku, N. 1973. "The Community College Concept: Implications for the Republic of Zaire." Ed.D. dissertation, University of California, Los Angeles.

17. Hull, G. S. 1974. "Nationalization of the University in the Republic of Zaire." Ph.D. dissertation, Northwestern University.

18. Payanzo, N. 1974. "Education and University Students in a New Nation: The Case of the Republic of Zaire." Ph.D. dissertation, Northwestern University.

19. Shandungo, K. 1981. "Higher Institutes of Pedagogy and Universities in Zaire: The Development of the Relationships after the Reorganization of Higher Education in 1971." Ph.D. dissertation, Vanderbilt University.

Côte d'Ivoire

20. Martin, G. W. 1998. "A Comparison of the Effects of Interventions for Increasing Stress-Coping Resources of Students Attending Universities Located in Côte d'Ivoire, West Africa." Ph.D. dissertation, Georgia State University.

21. Medjomo, C. 1984. "Ivorian Higher Education Institutions and National Development Strategy: Problems of Dependence and Identity—A Case Study of Ensa and Inset." Ph.D. dissertation, Stanford University.

Egypt

22. Abdel-Aal, S. E. E. 1980. "Establishing a Non-Print Educational Media Service at the University of Helwan: A Feasibility Study." Ph.D. dissertation, Ohio State University.

23. Abou-Helwa, A. E. 1984. "Macro-Planning of Post-secondary Education: A Strategic Plan for Egypt's Human Resource Development in a Period of Transition." Ph.D. dissertation, Kansas State University.

24. Bin Salamon, A. S. 1980. "Reform of Al-azhar in the 20th Century." Ph.D. dissertation, New York University.

25. Cook, B. J. 1999. "Egyptian Higher Education: Inconsistent Cognitions." D.Phil. dissertation, University of Oxford (United Kingdom).

26. Deif-Ayoub, A. A. 1997. "A Perspective of Technology Transfer from the University of North Carolina System Associated with Training and Development Strategies in Egypt." Ed.D. dissertation, North Carolina State University.

27. Eccel, A. C. 1978. "Rapidly Increasing Societal Scale and Secularization: A Century of Higher Muslim Education and the Professions in Egypt." Ph.D. dissertation, University of Chicago.

28. El-Kaffass, I. S. 1999. "A Case Study of a New Private University in Egypt." Ph.D. dissertation, Bowling Green State University.

29. El-Sharkawy, S. I. 1983. "The Status of Educational Media and Technology in University-Level Nursing Programs in the Arab Republic of Egypt." Ed.D. dissertation, Boston University.

30. Hassan, B. A. H. 1988. "Field Dependence/Independence Cognitive Style and EFL Proficiency among Egyptian College Students." Ph.D. dissertation, University of New Mexico.

31. Russell, M. E. 1994. "Cultural Reproduction in Egypt's Private University." Ph.D. dissertation, University of Kentucky.

32. Sallam, A. M. A. 1980. "The Return to the Veil among Undergraduate Females at Minya University, Egypt." Ph.D. dissertation, Purdue University.

33. Sanders, J. A. 1997. "Combining Expectancy-Value and Uses and Gratifications Theory to Predict Consumption Attitudes and Behaviors among Egyptian Faculty Members." Ph.D. dissertation, Florida State University.

34. Sheha, A. A. 1981. "The Relationship of Faculty Perceptions of the Nature and Bases of Power to Faculty Satisfaction and Productivity in an Egyptian University." D.Ed. dissertation, Pennsylvania State University.

35. Youssef, M. A. M. 1984. "Factors Affecting Career Choice and Labor Market Success for Egyptian University Graduates." Ph.D. dissertation, Ohio State University.

Ethiopia

36. Abdul-Kadir, N. H. 1986. "The Role of Higher Education in Development with a Special Reference to Ethiopia." Ph.D. dissertation, University of Manchester (United Kingdom).

37. Abdullahi, I. H. A. 1989. "A Study of Cooperative Programs among University and Special Libraries in Ethiopia,

Kenya, and Tanzania." Ph.D. dissertation, University of Pittsburgh.

38. Ambatchew, A. 1962. "The Influence of Higher Education on the American Society and Its Implications for the Role of Higher Education in Ethiopia." Ph.D. dissertation, Ohio State University.

39. Belay, H. S. 1964. "A Comparative Analysis of Higher Education in Agriculture and a Proposed Plan for Further Developing the System in Ethiopia." Ph.D. dissertation, Cornell University.

40. Betru, T. 1994. "A Study of the Organization and Operational Strategies to Link Research and Extension in the Agricultural Higher Education Institutions in Ethiopia." Ed.D. dissertation, Oklahoma State University.

41. Ghedai, A. 1977. "Some Characteristics and Motivational Patterns of University Continuing Education Participation in Ethiopia." Ed.D. dissertation, Syracuse University.

42. Haile, F. 1984. "A Study of Institutionality: Addis Ababa University, 1961–1981 (Ethiopia)." Ed.D. dissertation, Indiana University.

43. Legesse, K. 1978. "A Study of Objectives and the Curriculum of Teacher Education in the Faculty of Education, Addis Ababa University, Ethiopia." Ph.D. dissertation, Indiana University.

44. Savard, G. C. 1973. "The People of Ethiopia: Draft of a Text for the Freshmen of Haile Selassie I University." Ed.D. dissertation, Columbia University.

45. Tadesse, T. 1988. "The Development of Addis Ababa University Library in the Prerevolutionary Ethiopia, 1950–1974: A Historical Study." Ph.D. dissertation, University of Pittsburgh.

46. Trudeau, E. 1968. "A Survey of Higher Education in Ethiopia with Implications for Future Planning and Development." Ed.D. dissertation, Columbia University.

47. Wako, S. 1984. "Public Universities and Societal Development: Application of the Ideal Type Methodology in the Case Studies of Addis Ababa University and Michigan State University." Ph.D. dissertation, Western Michigan University.

Gambia

48. Aibangbee, C. 1985. "Higher Education in the British Commonwealth Nations of West Africa: Survey and Analysis of Events in Gambia, Ghana, Nigeria, and Sierra Leone." Ed.D. dissertation, Vanderbilt University.

Ghana

49. Aboagye, E. F. 1996. "The Development of Student Financing Schemes in Universities in Ghana." Ph.D. dissertation, University of Toronto (Canada).

50. Adinku, W. O. 1988. "Towards the National Theatre Concept: A Model for the Development of Dance Education within the Ghanaian University System." Ph.D. dissertation, University of Surrey (United Kingdom).

51. Attakora, K. K.-B. 1991. "An Analysis of Factors Affecting Implementation of the Policy to Africanize Faculty at University of Ghana (1961–1966)." Ph.D. dissertation, Florida State University.

52. Barkan, J. D. 1970. "African University Students and Social Change: An Analysis of Student Opinion in Ghana, Tanzania, and Uganda." Ph.D. dissertation, University of California, Los Angeles.

53. Cordor, S. M. 1996. "A Comparative Analysis of the Changing Sociopolitical Role and Status of Western-Educated Intellectuals in Modern Africa with Particular Reference to Liberia and Ghana: A Study of the Role of Writers, Journalists, Educators, and Other Literary and Intellectual Groups in Contemporary African Societies." Ph.D. dissertation, Pennsylvania State University.

54. Crowell, G. L.-O. 1996. "The Evolution of Higher Education in Ghana." Ph.D. dissertation, Johns Hopkins University.

55. Darko, S. F. 1985. "An Historical Inquiry into the Development of Higher Education in Ghana, 1948–1984: A Study of the Major Factors That Have Controlled and Inhibited the Development of the Universities of Ghana." Ph.D. dissertation, University of North Texas.

56. Dowuona, G. M. 1991. "Family Background and Education in Ghana: A Look at a Selected Group of Male and Female University Entrants." Ph.D. dissertation, University of Maryland–College Park.

See also 48

Guinea

57. Dieng, S. 2000. "Les conceptions de l'apprentissage de la profession enseignante chez les apprentis enseignants en formation initiale à l'institut supérieur des sciences de l'éducation de Guinée (ISSEG)." ("The Conceptions of Teacher Training among Teachers Enrolled at the Advanced Institute for the Sciences of Education in Guinea"). Ph.D. dissertation, Ecole Normale Supérieure, Dakar.

Guinee-Bissau

58. Mendes-Barbosa, J. 1990. "Framework for Educational Reform in Guinea-Bissau: The Choice of Language of Instruction." Ed.D. dissertation, University of Massachusetts.

Kenya

59. Day, L. J. 1987. "Academic Motivation for Participation in Kenyan University-Level Education." Ph.D. dissertation, Michigan State University.

60. D'Souza, A. 2001. "Reforming University Finance in Sub-Saharan Africa: A Case Study of Kenya." Ph.D. dissertation, Stanford University, Palo Alto.

61. Gaffney, M. J. 1973. "Decision-Making Potential among University Students in Kenya: A Social-Psychological Analysis of High-Level Manpower Development." Ph.D. dissertation, University of California, Los Angeles.

62. Hughes, R. R. 1986. "An Examination of Some Equity

and Efficiency Implications of the Post-Graduation Employment Experiences of a Sample of Graduates from the University of Nairobi, Kenya." Ph.D. dissertation, University of Washington.

63. Kilasi, E. F.-J. 1980. "A Proposal for Modification of the Curriculums of Kenya's Colleges and Schools." Ed.D. dissertation, Indiana University.

64. Kilonzo, G. K. 1986. "An Exploratory Study of University Counseling Center Models Adaptable to Education in Kenya." Ed.D. dissertation, University of South Dakota.

65. Kirubi, G. M. M. 1983. "Turmoil in a University: An Analytical Study of the Conflicts, Confrontations, and Strikes in the University of Nairobi and Kenyatta University College in the Republic of Kenya—1960–1978." Ph.D. dissertation, Ohio University.

66. Kiugu, R. K. 1999. "Faculty Job Satisfaction: University of Nairobi in Kenya." Ed.D. dissertation, State University of New York at Albany.

67. Maronga, G. B. 1993. "Perceptions of the Leadership Role of Deans of Students in the Public Universities of Kenya." Ph.D. dissertation, University of North Texas.

68. Munywoki, B. M. 1988. "An Historical Review of Higher Education in Kenya since 1975, with an Emphasis on Curriculum Development." Ph.D. dissertation, University of North Texas.

69. Mutunga, S. N. 1974. "A Study of the Post-Secondary Technical Institutes in Kenya." Ph.D. dissertation, Claremont Graduate School.

70. Ngayai, B. K. 1991. "Job Satisfaction of Faculty at Kenyatta University, Nairobi, Kenya." Ph.D. dissertation, University of North Texas.

71. Otieno, T. N. 1995. "A Study of Kenyan University and Post-Secondary Women Students: Challenges and Strategies to Their Educational Advancement." Ph.D. dissertation, Ohio University.

72. Tembe, E. O. A. 1985. "Higher Education in Two Developing Nations: A Case Study of Kenya and Sri Lanka." Ed.D. dissertation, University of Arizona.

See also 37

Lesotho

See 4

Liberia

73. Barclay, D. E. 1982. "Foundations of Education in Higher Educational Institutions in Liberia." Ph.D. dissertation, Southern Illinois University at Carbondale.

74. Cooper, S. F. 1991. "The Selection and Organization of Curricular Knowledge at the University of Liberia during 1951–1985." Ph.D. dissertation, University of Pittsburgh.

75. Hoff, A. A. 1959. "Higher Education for a Changing Liberia: An Analysis of Emerging Needs, with Proposals for an Expanded, Strengthened Program." Ph.D. dissertation, Columbia University.

76. Hoff, W. S., Jr. 1987. "The Role of the University of Liberia in National Development, 1960–1980." Ph.D. dissertation, University of Illinois at Urbana-Champaign.

77. Jones, W. S. 1986. "Analysis of Faculty Development in Higher Education in the United States of America and Implications for Faculty Development in Liberal Arts Colleges in Liberia." Ed.D. dissertation, Columbia University.

78. Mehaffey, C. A. 1980. "Teacher Education in Liberia." Ph.D. dissertation, Bowling Green State University.

See also 53

Libya

79. Bubtana, A. R. 1976. "A Comparative Study of the Perceptions of Students, Faculty Members, Administrators, and Government Authorities of the Role of University System in the National Development of Libya." Ed.D. dissertation, George Washington University.

80. Mogassbi, M. M. 1984. "Perceptions of the Higher Education System and Manpower Development in Libya." Ed.D. dissertation, George Washington University.

81. Mohsen, A. D. 1980. "An Evaluation of the Educational Psychology Program at Alfateh University, Tripoli, Libya." Ph.D. dissertation, University of New Mexico.

82. Muftah, H. A. 1982. "Analysis of the Development of a Higher-Education System in Libya and Its Impact on the Libyan Students." Ph.D. dissertation, University of Kansas.

Malawi

83. Lange, H. M. 1973. "The Development of Higher Education in an Emergent Country: Malawi, Africa, 1960–1967." Ed.D. dissertation, University of Southern California.

84. Powers, M. H. 1994. "Factors That Influence the Educational Attainment Levels of Women Students at the University of Malawi, Africa." Ph.D. dissertation, Indiana University.

Mali

85. Bane, M. C. 1994. "An Analysis of Educational Reforms in Mali, 1962–1992." Ph.D. dissertation, University of Kansas.

Morocco

86. Al-Ghamdi, S. Z. M. 1985. "Educational Research in the University: A Comparative Study of Saudi Arabia and Morocco." Ph.D. dissertation, Vanderbilt University.

87. Fahy, M. A. 1998. "Marginalized Modernity: An Ethnographic Approach to Higher Education and Social Identity at a Moroccan University." Ph.D. dissertation, University of Michigan.

88. Nedelcovych, M. S. 1980. "Determinants of Political Participation: A Survey Analysis of Moroccan University Students." Ph.D. dissertation, Florida State University.

89. Ouakrime, M. 1985. "English Language Teaching in Higher Education in Morocco: An Evaluation of the Fez Ex-

perience." Ph.D. dissertation, University of London (United Kingdom).

90. Saadia, A. B. 1994. "Approche d'une pédagogie de l'enseignement du français au niveau supérieur au maroc, suivant des besoins et des objectifs spécifiques." ("An Approach to a Teaching Pedagogy for French in Higher Education in Morocco According to Specific Needs and Objectives.") Ph.D. dissertation, Paris 3, Paris.

Mozambique

91. Mario, M. 1997. "Professional Socialization of University Lecturers in Mozambique." Ph.D. dissertation, University of Pittsburgh.

Nigeria

92. Achebo, N. K. 1990. "The Learning Resource Center: A Model for Nigerian Universities." Ph.D. dissertation, Southern Illinois University at Carbondale.

93. Adeniji, O. O. 1987. "The Development and Contributions of the Department of Adult Education, University of Ibadan, Nigeria, to Adult Education in Nigeria: 1945–1980." Ph.D. dissertation, University of North Texas.

94. Adiele, M. C. 1964. "The History and Appraisal of Higher Education in an Independent Nigeria: A Ten-Year Perspective, 1953–1963." Ph.D. dissertation, University of Ottawa (Canada).

95. Agbobu, G. N. 1981. "Employment of Higher Education Graduates in Nigeria." Ph.D. dissertation, University of Pittsburgh.

96. Akinfeleye, R. A. 1978. "University Education in Nigeria Before and After Independence." Ph.D. dissertation, Southern Illinois University at Carbondale.

97. Akinola, J. A. 1977. "Faculty Participation in the Governance of Higher Education: With a Study of Applicability to Nigeria." Ph.D. dissertation, Northwestern University.

98. Alfa, L. C. 1993. "The Nigerian National Universities Commission's Assessment of the Functioning of an Organization." Ed.D. dissertation, Columbia University.

99. Anita, U. J. 1980. "Analysis of Problems of Technical Education in Nigeria as Identified by Administrators of Polytechnics and Colleges of Technology." Ph.D. dissertation, Kansas State University.

100. Asagba, J. O. 1993. "A Historical Review of the Development of Federal Universities of Technology in Nigeria (Technological Education)." Ph.D. dissertation, University of North Texas.

101. Anyanechi-Okpara, U. E. 1983. "The Role of Universities in the National Development of Nigeria." Ed.D. dissertation, Columbia University.

102. Asuquo, A. O. 1982. "Linkages in Higher Education Between Developed and Developing Nations: A Review of the Links between American and Nigerian Universities." Ph.D. dissertation, University of Oregon.

103. Azeke, F. 1985. "A Model for Higher Education Planning in Nigeria, Based on the Ohio Higher Education Planning System." Ed.D. dissertation, Temple University.

104. Babalola, F. K. 1993. "The Role of the Nigerian Higher Education Institutions in Preparation of Christian Religious Studies Teachers." Ed.D. dissertation, Southern Baptist Theological Seminary.

105. Barikor, C. N. 1980. "The Public-Service Oriented Philosophy of Higher Education with Implications for Nigerian Rural Development." Ph.D. dissertation, Michigan State University.

106. Belay, L. 1972. "An Examination of the Nature of Higher Education in Nigeria." Ph.D. dissertation, University of Missouri–Columbia.

107. Book, J. F. D. 1980. "The Development of a Model Plan for Evaluating Higher Education Planning in Nigeria." Ph.D. dissertation, University of North Texas.

108. Choudhri, S. U. R. 1988. "Planning and Management of Academic Staff in Nigerian Universities." Ph.D. dissertation, University of Manchester (United Kingdom).

109. Dueppen, K. A. 1974. "A Study of Selected Programs and Graduates at University of Nigeria, Nsukka." Ed.D. dissertation, University of Southern California.

110. Duru, I. C. 1987. "Teaching Effectiveness of Teacher Training College Teachers and University Graduate Teachers in Selected Secondary Schools in Imo State, Nigeria." Ed.D. dissertation, Texas Southern University.

111. Edem, C. U. 1993. "Use of the Health Belief Model to Predict Safer Sex Intentions and Practices among University Students in Nigeria." Ph.D. dissertation, University of Oregon.

112. Egbuna, B. G. 1990. "An Investigation of the Crisis in Higher Education in the Two Universities of Anambra State, Nigeria." Ed.D. dissertation, George Washington University.

113. Ejembi, E. P. 1988. "Perceptions of Agriculture in Nigeria by Students of the Division of Agricultural Colleges, Ahmadu Bello University." Ph.D. dissertation, Iowa State University.

114. Elimimian, J. U. 1984. "Students' Perception of the Relevance of Graduate Education in Business: Dimensionality and Assessment of MBA Programs among Selected Nigerian Universities." Ed.D. dissertation, Atlanta University.

115. Enin-Okut, A. A. 1983. "An Examination of Higher Education in the Process of Economic Development and Social Change in Nigeria." Ph.D. dissertation, University of North Texas.

116. Enwemnwa, M. O. N. 1993. "Women's Access to Higher Education in Nigeria: The Case of (Former) Bendel State." Ph.D. dissertation, University of Wisconsin–Madison.

117. Enyia, D. O. 1975. "Higher Education in Nigeria from the Earliest Times to 1972." Ph.D. dissertation, University of Michigan.

118. Essien, R. A. 1981. "Perceptions of Nigerian College Students toward the Role of Women in Nigerian Development." Ed.D. dissertation, University of Southern California.

119. Ettang, D. A. U. 1977. "An Historical Analysis of Higher Education in Nigeria." Ph.D. dissertation, University of Alabama.

120. Evans, E. E. 1962. "A Study of Higher Education in Nigeria and Its Relationship to National Goals." Ed.D. dissertation, Indiana University.

121. Fafunwa, A. B. 1955. "An Historical Analysis of the

Development of Higher Education in Nigeria." Ph.D. dissertation, New York University.

122. Godonoo, P. 1994. "Educational Policy Making in Nigeria: A Case Study of the Impact of Foreign Funding on Nigerian Universities." Ph.D. dissertation, University of California, Los Angeles.

123. Ibegbu, C. U. 1989. "Regional Disparities and Social Inequalities in Nigerian Universities: A Study of Educational Expansion and Selection." Ph.D. dissertation, State University of New York at Buffalo.

124. Ibida, E. Y. 1990. "A Study of Tourism Education at University Level in Nigeria as Viewed by Experts in the Government, Higher Education, and the Tourism Industry." Ed.D. dissertation, George Washington University.

125. Igboegwu, C. E. 1980. "The Impact of the Nigerian Manpower Project on Students in Selected U.S. Junior and Community Colleges." Ph.D. dissertation, University of Illinois at Urbana-Champaign.

126. Ikoyo-Eweto, I. P. 1983. "Legal Aspects of Job Security in Nigerian Universities." Ed.D. dissertation, Temple University.

127. Ikpah-Aziaruh, M. L. 1980. "The Community College Concept: Its Implications for Higher Educational Development in the Federal Republic of Nigeria." Ed.D. dissertation, University of Houston.

128. Imogie, A. I. 1979. "Instructional Media Use by Faculty Members in Ahmadu Bello University, Zaria: A Study of Factors Related to Educational Innovations in a Nigerian University Context." Ph.D. dissertation, Michigan State University.

129. Inuwa, A. R. 1991. "A Plan for Expanding the Use of Educational Television in Northern Nigerian Universities." Ed.D. dissertation, West Virginia University.

130. Iruka, A. A. 1980. "Student, Faculty, Academic Administrator, and Government Educational Official Perceptions of and Preferences for the Goals of Higher Education in Imo-State, Nigeria." Ph.D. dissertation, University of North Texas.

131. Isyaku, K. 1983. "Academic Performance of Direct and Preliminary Students of Bayero University, Kano-Nigeria." Ed.D. dissertation, Indiana University.

132. Kparevzua, B. A. 1983. "Development of a Textile Curriculum Model for Nigerian Higher Education Institutions." Ed.D. dissertation, Indiana University.

133. Mailafiya, M. G. 1986. "Nigeria and the Open University System." Ph.D. dissertation, University of Glasgow (United Kingdom).

134. Meier, W. R. R. 1970. "Issues and Problems of University Education in Nigeria." Ph.D. dissertation, University of Southern California.

135. Nnamah-Okoye, C. C. 1996. "Women Leaders in Nigerian Higher Education." Ph.D. dissertation, Fordham University.

136. Nwacukwu, C. C. 1972. "Adjusting Higher Education to National Needs: The Interrelationship of Economics, Politics, and Society. A Case Study of Nigeria." Ph.D. dissertation, University of California, Los Angeles.

137. Nwaeke, L. I. 1983. "The Empirical Examination of Classified Staff Participation in Decision-Making with Regard to Policy Determination, Administrative Practices, and Influence on Working Conditions in Nigerian Universities." Ph.D. dissertation, University of North Texas.

138. Nwamadi, F. E. 1985. "The Role of Postsecondary Education (Technical and Vocational Training) in Human Resource Development and Economic Growth in Nigeria (Brazil, Mexico, Venezuela)." Ed.D. dissertation, Texas Tech University.

139. Nwosu, S. U. 1981. "Establishment of the Need for a Two-Year Community College System in Nigeria." Ed.D. dissertation, George Washington University.

140. Obayan, F. O. B. 1982. "A Model for Funding Higher Education in Nigeria." Ph.D. dissertation, Ohio University.

141. Oblong, S. S. 1980. "A Study of Higher Education Policies and Their Implementation by the Nigerian Military Regimes, 1966–1978." Ph.D. dissertation, Atlanta University.

142. Ochai, A. 1984. "Management Development Needs of Lower and Middle Managers in University Libraries in Nigeria." Ph.D. dissertation, University of Pittsburgh.

143. Odueze, S. A. 1990. "An Historical Review of Higher Education in Nigeria from 1960–1985 with Emphasis on Curriculum Development." Ph.D. dissertation, University of North Texas.

144. Ogieva, P. N. 1984. "Recommended Guidelines for Establishing a Non-Traditional Collegiate Program in Nigeria." Ed.D. dissertation, Columbia University.

145. Ogunmilade, C. A. 1978. "Television in Higher Education: The Application of Instructional Television to General Studies Courses, University of Ife, Nigeria—A Case Study." Ph.D. dissertation, Indiana University.

146. Ogwumike, A. C. 1986. "Nigerian College-Graduate Unemployment: Higher Education and Economic Trends." Ph.D. dissertation, University of Denver.

147. Ojeleye, F. M. 1984. "The Importance of Home Economics as Perceived by Faculty Members and Students of Colleges of Education in Kwara State, Nigeria." Ed.D. dissertation, University of Northern Colorado.

148. Ojiaka, S. I. 1984. "A Historical Review of the Influences of the Federal Government of Nigeria in National Higher Education, 1954–1982." Ph.D. dissertation, University of North Texas.

149. Ojiaku, M. O. 1968. "The Impact of the American Academic Tradition on the Development of Higher Education in Eastern Nigeria." Ph.D. dissertation, University of California, Berkeley.

150. Okeke, P. E. 1994. "Patriarchal Continuities and Contradictions in African Women's Education and Socio-Economic Status: An Ethnographic Study of Currently Employed University Educated Igbo Women in Nigeria." Ph.D. dissertation, Dalhousie University (Canada).

151. Okezie, C. E. 1992. "Nigerian Students' Perceptions of Factors That Are Related to Their Decision to Return or Not to Return to Nigeria after Completion of Their Graduate Studies in the United States." Ph.D. dissertation, University of Pittsburgh.

152. Onu, C. H. 1988. "Higher Education and the Regulatory Process: The Case of Petroleum Products in Nigeria." Ed.D. dissertation, University of Massachusetts.

153. Onwuka, S. O. 1988. "International Survey of Independent Study Programs and Development of a Model for

Nigerian Higher Education." Ed.D. dissertation, Texas Tech University.

154. Onwunli, A. U. 1994. "Governance Dimensions and Faculty Perceptions of Their Participation in the Governance of Nigerian Federal Universities." Ed.D. dissertation, Florida State University.

155. Onyeji, V. A. A. 1992. "Student Unrest in Nigerian Universities: A Study of Student Services in the Campuses." Ph.D. dissertation, University of Denver.

156. Oraemesi, C. J. 1982. "An Organizational Systems Model to Assist the National Universities Commission of Nigeria in Dealing with the Critical Problems of Concern to the Universities." Ph.D. dissertation, American University.

157. Pekene, C. J. 1984. "Student Protests and University Response in Nigeria, 1962–1982: A Case Study of Three Federal Universities." Ph.D. dissertation, State University of New York at Buffalo.

158. Pirsel, C. K. 1988. "Pedagogical Preparation of Selected Faculty in Postsecondary Education in a Nigerian University." Ed.D. dissertation, Wayne State University.

159. Rishante, J. S. 1985. "An Investigation into the Attitudes of Nigerian Academics toward a Distance Education Innovation." Ph.D. dissertation, Syracuse University.

160. Rooks, C. S. 1968. "Politics and Public Policy in a New Nation: Higher Education in Nigeria." Ph.D. dissertation, Duke University.

161. Salisu, T. M. 1980. "New Media and the Library in Higher Education: A Study of Nigerian University Libraries." Ph.D. dissertation, University of Pittsburgh.

162. Samaila, I. W. 1985. "The Influence of Federal Administrative Trends on the Budgetary Processes of Nigeria's Federal Universities." Ed.D. dissertation, Texas Southern University.

163. Sanyaolu, O. 1984. "The Paradox of Meeting High-Level Manpower Shortages and Graduate Unemployment: A Case Study of Nigeria." Ph.D. dissertation, University of Michigan.

164. Shinkut, M. B. 1998. "Job Satisfaction of Full-Time Business Faculty of Higher Education Institutions in Kaduna State, Nigeria." Ph.D. dissertation, University of Missouri–Columbia.

165. Sogbesan, E. 1973. "The Problems of Financing Higher Education in Nigeria." Ed.D. dissertation, Indiana University.

166. Tahir, G. M. 1981. "Federalization and Change in a Nigerian University: Ahmadu Bello University as a Case Study." Ed.D. dissertation, Indiana University.

167. Tamun, C. A. 1986. "The Roles of the Rockefeller Foundation, Ford Foundation, and Carnegie Corporation in the Development of the University of Ibadan, 1962–1978 (Nigeria)." Ph.D. dissertation, University of Pittsburgh.

168. Taylor, G. O. 1981. "The Public Financing of Higher Education in Nigeria." Ed.D. dissertation, Western Michigan University.

169. Trevelyan, E. N. 1998. "Federalism and Preferential Policy in the Mediation of Ethnic Conflict: A Decision-Making Analysis of Higher Education in India and Nigeria." Ph.D. dissertation, University of California, Santa Barbara.

170. Ukariwe, U. K. 1984. "The Establishment and Development of University of Nigeria, Nsukka, 1960–1970." Ph.D. dissertation, Southern Illinois University at Carbondale.

171. Umachi, U. N. 1986. "Higher Education in Nigeria from 1960 to 1980." Ph.D. dissertation, Wayne State University.

172. Umoh, O. D. 1976. "A Survey of Higher Education in Nigeria with Implications for Future Planning and Development." Ed.D. dissertation, Washington State University.

173. Umoren, J. A. 1989. "A Study of Factors Related to the Educational Decisions and Career Plans of Secondary School Seniors in One Nigerian State to Pursue or Not to Pursue Higher Education." Ph.D. dissertation, American University.

174. Uzoigwe, C. N. 1982. "A Model for Establishing a Higher Education Administration Degree Program at a Nigerian University." Ph.D. dissertation, University of Toledo.

175. Yesufu, J. T. 1978. "Evolution of Higher Education in Nigeria (With Emphasis from 1948–1978)." Ph.D. dissertation, University of Wyoming.

See also 48

Rwanda

176. Bahimba, P. 1984. "Potential Goals of the National University of Rwanda as Perceived by Senate Members, Faculty, and Students, with Implications for the Adventist University of Central Africa." Ph.D. dissertation, Andrews University.

177. Munger, P. W. 1995. "Comparative Study of Needs-Assessment Methodologies as They Apply to the Development of a University Computer Science Curriculum in a Central African Country (Adventist University, Rwanda)." Ph.D. dissertation, Andrews University.

Senegal

178. Johnson, R. C. 1976. "Higher Education Development in Senegal." Ph.D. dissertation, Washington University.

179. Sall, H. N. 1996. "Efficacité et équité de l'enseignement supérieur: quels étudiants réussissent à l'Université de Dakar." ("Efficieny and Equity in Higher Education: Which Students Succeed in the University of Dakar.") Ph.D. dissertation, Université Cheikh Anta Diop, Dakar.

Sierra Leone

180. Hinton, S. B. 1981. "An Analysis of the Connection between Role Concept and Political Participation among Preliminary Year Students at Fourah Bay College, University of Sierra Leone." Ed.D. dissertation, University of Virginia.

181. Kamara-Kay, P. S. 1978. "Restructuring Post-Secondary Education for Middle-Level Manpower Development in the Republic of Sierra Leone, West Africa: An Attempt to Redefine Education as a Tool for National Development." Ed.D. dissertation, University of Southern California.

182. Kargbo, S. A. M. 1985. "A Study of the Training of Secondary School Teachers at Njala University College in Sierra Leone." Ph.D. dissertation, Syracuse University.

183. Parker, C. I. 1986. "The University of Sierra Leone (Fourah Bay College): An Examination of Student Perspectives about Its Role in Meeting Educational and Occupational Needs, 1984." Ph.D. dissertation, New York University.

184. Roth, J. M. 1973. "Employment and Suitability of Training Graduates from Njala University College, Sierra Leone, 1966–1970." Ed.D. dissertation, University of Illinois at Urbana-Champaign.

185. Sannoh, K. B. 1974. "An Evaluation of Teacher Education Programs for Secondary School Teachers at Fourah Bay College, Njala University College, and Milton Margai Teachers College in Sierra Leone." Ph.D. dissertation, University of Illinois at Urbana-Champaign.

See also 48

South Africa

186. Anderson, G. M. 1999. "Building a People's University in South Africa: Race, Compensatory Education and the Structural Limits of Democratic Reform at the University of the Western Cape." Ph.D. dissertation, City University of New York.

187. Baker, M.-F. L. 1995. "Khanya College: A Historical Case Study: 1981–1994." Ph.D. dissertation, Pennsylvania State University.

188. Beekman (née Alberts), A. W. 1997. "The Development of B.Ed. Students' Potential at the University of Pretoria" (Afrikaans text). Ph.D. dissertation, University of Pretoria (South Africa).

189. Bell, D. I. 2001. "An Inquiry into the Emergence of Transformative Leadership in Higher Education in South Africa: A Phenomenographic Study." Ed.D. dissertation, University of Massachusetts, Amherst.

190. Blignaut, A. S. 1997. "An Instructional Model for the Integration of Computer and Research Skills on the Higher Educational Level" (Afrikaans text). Ph.D. dissertation, University of Pretoria (South Africa).

191. Bopape, M. M. 1997. "Library Services at Colleges of Education in the Former Republic of Bophuthatswana (South Africa)." Ph.D. dissertation, University of South Africa.

192. Brownlee, E. B. I. 1982. "The Nursing Student at the University of South Africa." D.Litt. dissertation, University of South Africa.

193. Brynard, P. A. 1988. "The Administrative Development of the Faculty of Economic and Political Sciences at the University of Pretoria" (Afrikaans text). D.Phil. dissertation, University of Pretoria (South Africa).

194. Clark, W. A. 1993. "Identification of Factors for Reducing Attrition of First-Time Entering Undergraduates at the University of Pretoria (South Africa)." Ph.D. dissertation, University of Pretoria (South Africa).

195. Coetzee, S. A. 1997. "Africanisation and University Education: An Historical-Educational Explication and Evaluation." D.Ed. dissertation, University of South Africa.

196. Dlamini, C. R. M. 1997. "University Autonomy and Academic Freedom in South Africa." L.L.D. dissertation, University of South Africa.

197. Dyasi, M. M. 1999. "Beyond Apartheid: Public Higher Education Policy Reform in South Africa (1978–1998)." Ph.D. dissertation, University of Kentucky.

198. Hadebe, J. M. B. 1983. "A Multivariate Analysis of Variance of the Effect of Selected Factors on the Effectiveness of Leadership Styles of Teaching Staff in South African Universities." Ph.D. dissertation, Michigan State University.

199. Haricombe, L. J. 1992. "The Effect of an Academic Boycott on Academics in South Africa." Ph.D. dissertation, University of Illinois at Urbana-Champaign.

200. Hurlin, D. C. R. 1986. "The Management of Technology Developed at South African Universities." D.Eng. dissertation, University of Pretoria (South Africa).

201. Jones, B. J. 1997. "A Critical Interpretation of Higher Education Governing Policy in South Africa Mediating the Legacy of the Past to the Present for a New Future." Ed.D. dissertation, University of San Francisco.

202. Khotseng, B. M. M. 1990. "The Polytechnic University and Its Contribution to Education for the Development of High Level Manpower in South Africa." Ph.D. dissertation, University of Natal (South Africa).

203. King, K. L. 1998. "From Exclusion to Inclusion: A Case Study of Black South Africans at the University of Witwatersrand." Ph.D. dissertation, Indiana University.

204. Le Roux, A. L. 1980. "Autonomy and Colleges of Education: An Historico-Comparative Study." D.Ed. dissertation, University of South Africa.

205. Lotter, I. J. 1991. "An Educational Model for a University Satellite Campus" (Afrikaans text). Ph.D. dissertation, University of Pretoria (South Africa).

206. Louw, J. B. Z. 1979. "Government Policy and Administration in Respect of Universities in South Africa" (Afrikaans text). D.Phil. dissertation, University of Pretoria (South Africa).

207. Mabokela, R. O. 1998. "Black Students on White Campuses: Responses to Increasing Black Enrollment at Two South African Universities." Ph.D. dissertation, University of Illinois at Urbana-Champaign.

208. Mabunda, G. T. 1996. "The Perception of the Social Climate of American Universities by South African Students." Ph.D. dissertation, Saint Louis University.

209. Makosana, I. N. Z. 1997. "Social Factors in the Positioning of Black Women in South African Universities." Ed.D. dissertation, Columbia University.

210. Mashinini, M. T. 2000. "The Role of Non-Governmental Organizations in Helping African Students Gain Access to Tertiary Education in South Africa." Ph.D. dissertation, Michigan State University.

211. Mehl, M. C. 1985. "The Cognitive Difficulties of First Year Physics Students at the University of the Western Cape and Various Compensatory Programmes." Ph.D. dissertation, University of Cape Town (South Africa).

212. Menell-Kinberg, M. E. 1991. "United States Scholarships for Black South Africans, 1976–1990: The Politicization of Education." Ph.D. dissertation, University of California, Los Angeles.

213. Minnaar, P. C. 1998. "A Knowledge-Based System for Quality Assurance Support in a University." Ph.D. dissertation, University of Pretoria (South Africa).

214. Mokaba, A. M. B. 1993. "I Want to Be an Engineer: Determinants of Occupational Aspiration among Black Students in South Africa." Ph.D. dissertation, Brandeis University.

215. Molestsane, R. 1995. "Black South African Students'

Success in Predominantly White United States Universities." Ph.D. dissertation, Indiana University.

216. Moller, J. J. 1997. "Evaluation of Basic Literacy Programmes at the University of Pretoria: A Career Orientation Perspective" (Afrikaans text). Ph.D. dissertation, University of Pretoria (South Africa).

217. Mphahlele, S. E. 1992. "Student Unrest at Black Universities in Southern Africa, with Special Reference to the University of the North, 1960–1990." Ph.D. dissertation, University of the North, Sovenga.

218. Muller, C. H. 1982. "The Teaching of English Literature to African University Students: Developing a Strategy for Personalized Instruction." Ed.D. dissertation, University of South Africa.

219. Murphy, J. J. 1981. "Evaluating Planning and the Supporting Systems in South African Universities with Special Reference to a Planning, Programming, Budgeting System." D.B.L. dissertation, University of South Africa.

220. Ngwane, Z. P. 2001. "The Politics of Campus and Community in South Africa: An Historical Historiography of the University of Fort Hare." Ph.D. dissertation, The University of Chicago, Chicago.

221. Nkomo, M. 1983. "Student Culture in Black South African Universities: Some Factors Contributing to Student Activism, 1960–1980." Ed.D. dissertation, University of Massachusetts.

222. Noethe, A. J. 1993. "Learning Support Programmes for First-Year Students at the University of Pretoria" (Afrikaans text). Ph.D. dissertation, University of Pretoria (South Africa).

223. Pratt, M. J. 1986. "Computerized Support for Financial Planning in South African Universities." D.Com. dissertation, University of South Africa.

224. Ramasar, P. 1987. "Preferences of Teaching Styles and Strategies as Related to Conceptual System Variables, Educational Qualifications, and Experiential Backgrounds (A Study among Social Work Educators in South African Universities)." Ph.D. dissertation, Case Western Reserve University.

225. Roos, P. 1995. "An Analysis of the Cognitive Styles of Students at the University of Pretoria" (Afrikaans text). D.Phil. dissertation, University of Pretoria (South Africa).

226. Singh, G. 1996. "A Model for the Provision of Career Education within Community Colleges with Special Reference to Kwazulu-Natal (South Africa)." Ph.D. dissertation, University of Pretoria (South Africa).

227. Van Den Berg, O. C. 1994. "Innovation under Apartheid: Collaborative Action Research in a South African University." Ph.D. dissertation, Washington University.

228. Van Der Morwe, H. M. 2000. "The Management of the Transformation of Higher Education Institutions in the Gauteng Province: A Postmodern Perspective" (Afrikaans text). Ph.D. dissertation, University of Pretoria (South Africa).

229. Van Harte, S. G. 1992. "Black South African Students' Expectations and Perceptions of the Roles of Black and White University Presidents." Ed.D. dissertation, Columbia University.

230. Von Horsten, P. L. O. 1994. "Guidance Support for Undergraduate Students." Ph.D. dissertation, University of Pretoria (South Africa).

231. White, C. W. 1996. "Towards Meaningful Teaching and Learning at the University of the North (South Africa)." D.Ed. dissertation, University of South Africa.

232. Winter, C. 1988. "Post-Secondary School Technical Training in South Africa: External Efficiency and Policy Issues." Ph.D. dissertation, University of Southern California.

233. Wyatt, J. L. 1993. "The Role of Universities and Nongovernment Organizations in Educational Restructuring in South Africa: The Case of Training Black School Leaders." Ph.D. dissertation, University of North Carolina.

234. Zaaiman, H. 1998. "Selecting Students for Mathematics and Science: The Challenge Facing Higher Education in South Africa." Ph.D. dissertation, Vrije Universiteit, Amsterdam.

Sudan

235. Adelrasoul, O. M. 1976. "The Teaching of English in the Sudan with Special Reference to Senior Secondary and University Teaching." Ph.D. dissertation, Duke University.

236. Ahmad, M. I. 1982. "Factors Influencing University Students' Choice of Teaching as a Career in Sudan." Ph.D. dissertation, Pennsylvania State University.

237. Elbushra, O. E. 1989. "Management Model for the Food Services at the University of Khartoum, Sudan." Ph.D. dissertation, University of Wisconsin–Madison.

238. Elsiddig, M. O. 1990. "Expanding Higher Education and the Open University: The Case of Sudan as an Example for Developing Countries." Ph.D. dissertation, University of Bath (United Kingdom).

239. Ismail, O. H. 1991. "Understanding Educational Policies in Developing Countries: The Case of the New Higher Education Policy in Sudan." Ph.D. dissertation, Pennsylvania State University.

240. Kardman, B. E.-H. E. F. 1975. "Higher Education in the Sudan." Ph.D. dissertation, University of Kansas.

241. Kheir, A. I. M. 1986. "Government Policy on Higher Education in the Sudan, 1970–1985." Ed.D. dissertation, University of Houston.

242. Louise, C. C. 1980. "Effectiveness of an Agricultural Instructional Model of Basic Vegetable Production at Ahfad University College for Women in Omdurman, Sudan." Ph.D. dissertation, Iowa State University.

243. Taha, T. A.-m. 1989. "The Arabicisation of Higher Education: The Case of Khartoum University." Ph.D. dissertation, University of Lancaster (United Kingdom).

Swaziland

244. Habedi, M. K. 1988. "Perceptions of Home Economics Teachers and Teacher Educators Regarding the Home Economics Student Teaching Program at the University of Swaziland." Ph.D. dissertation, Ohio State University.

245. Simpson, A. G. 1990. "Aptitude for School Grades, Cambridge Examination Results, and University Performance: The Swaziland Case." Ph.D. dissertation, Ball State University.

See also 4

Tanzania

246. Block, L. S. 1982. "National Development Policies and Higher Education in Tanzania: National Leadership Interaction with the University of Dar Es Salaam, 1967–1977." Ph.D. dissertation, University of Pittsburgh.

247. Kanduru, A. I. 1997. "The Implementation of the National Manpower Policy by Tanzanian Universities from 1962 to 1994." Ph.D. dissertation, University of Toronto (Canada).

See also 37, 52

Togo

248. Baba, N. K. 1991. "Les sources du déséquilibre entre les filières d'études universitaires au Togo." ("The Roots of the Lack of Balance Between University Disciplines in Togo.") Ph.D. dissertation, Université Leval (Canada).

Tunisia

249. Siino, F. 1999. "Science et pouvoir dans la Tunisie contemporaine." ("Science and Authority in Contemporary Tunisia.") University of Aix-Marseille, Marseille.

Uganda

250. Nyonyintono, R. M. N. 1972. "National Interests and International Exchange in Higher Education: Uganda and the United States, 1945–1970." Ph.D. dissertation, State University of New York at Buffalo.

251. Oluku, S. O. 1997. "Towards Ecoscience: Environmental and Sociocultural Perspectives in Science—Some Insights from Uganda, and Implications for Higher Education." Ph.D. dissertation, University of Alberta (Canada).

252. Olupot, E. 1995. "Intellectual Dependency: A Critique of the Agricultural Science Program at Makerere University, Uganda." Ph.D. dissertation, University of Alberta (Canada).

See also 52

Zambia

253. Follis, B. 1990. "A Comparative Study of Vocational/Technical Education in Zambia and Zimbabwe, 1900–1987." Ph.D. dissertation, University of Liverpool (United Kingdom).

254. Idoye, E. P. 1981. "Popular Theatre and Politics in Zambia: A Case Study of the University of Zambia (Chikwaka) Theatre." Ph.D. dissertation, Florida State University.

255. Kapaale, R. S. 1981. "The Foundations of Education Program at the University of Zambia: A Critical Examination." Ed.D. dissertation, Columbia University.

256. Mwila, A. B. 1993. "The Uses of the University of Zambia Library by Social Science, Humanities and Science Faculties." Ph.D. dissertation, University of Michigan.

257. Siaciwena, R. 1988. "A Study of Distance Teaching at the University of Zambia with Special Reference to the Effectiveness of Degree Courses." Ph.D. dissertation, University of Wales (United Kingdom).

258. Sikwibele, A. L. 1989. "International Education Assistance to Higher Education Development in Zambia: Problems, Policy Implications, and Future Prospects." Ph.D. dissertation, University of Illinois at Urbana-Champaign.

Zimbabwe

259. Kawewe, S. M. 1985. "Planning for Higher Education for Social Development in Zimbabwe: An Assessment of the University of Zimbabwe's Students and Lecturers Concerning Their Perception of the University's Curriculum in Terms of Providing Skills Necessary to Carry Out National Reconstruction Tasks." Ph.D. dissertation, Saint Louis University.

260. Maunde, R. Z. 2000. "The Evolution of Higher Education in Zimbabwe." Ph.D. dissertation, University of Alaska–Fairbanks.

261. Mvududu, M. J. 1987. "Attitudes and Opinions of Zimbabwe University Faculty and Administrators toward Enrollment of All First Year Students in Personal and Family Living Subjects." Ph.D. dissertation, Oklahoma State University.

See also 253

Africa (Continent-based)

262. Adwere-Boamah, J. 1970. "African Intellectuals Abroad: Concerns and Commitments—A Study of Prospective Elite Perceptions and Commitments to Educational Change in Africa." Ph.D. dissertation, University of California, Berkeley.

263. Buaful, M. A. 1984. "Planning and Evaluation of Educational Media Programs in Colleges and Universities of Africa: Mainland and the Islands." Ph.D. dissertation, Kansas State University.

264. Chideya, N. T. 1976. "An American Approach to African Higher Education: An Exploratory Assessment." Ph.D. dissertation, State University of New York at Buffalo.

265. Da Silva, P. V. 1974. "African and Latin American Graduate Students' Assessment of Situations Related to Their Academic Life in the United States." Ph.D. dissertation, University of Southern California.

266. El-Hassan, K. M. 2000. "Educational Development in Process: A Study of African Graduate Students' Learning Experiences in the Ohio University College of Education." Ph.D. dissertation, Ohio University.

267. Gitau, P. N. 2000. "Exploring the Relationship between African and African American Undergraduates on a Midwestern University." Ph.D. dissertation, University of Kansas.

268. Kamau, O. N. 1995. "Education as a Weapon of Culture: An Africalogical Analysis of the Originating and Contemporary Philosophies of Historically Black Colleges and Universities." Ph.D. dissertation, Temple University.

269. Kilmer, J. R. 1988. "Relationship of Caning to Internal-External Locus-of-Control among Selected African Secondary and College Students." Ph.D. dissertation, Andrews University.

270. Laryea, E. A. 1990. "The Role of Higher Education in Africa: A Study of the Attitude of African Educators toward the Tananarive Recommendations." Ph.D. dissertation, University of North Texas.

271. Lungu, G. F. 1980. "The Land-Grant Model in Africa: A Study in Higher Education Transfer." Ed.D. dissertation, Harvard University.

272. Lusweti, V. 1997. "Cross-Cultural Perceptions of Gender Differentiation among African, Asian, and Latin American Female College Students in the United States." Ph.D. dissertation, University of Maryland–College Park.

273. Manyika, S. 2001. "Negotiating Identities: African Students in British and American Universities." Ph.D. dissertation, University of California, Berkeley.

274. Mattocks, D. M. 1990. "Beyond Institution Building: A Comparative Analysis of Institution Building Assistance and the Development of Designated Agricultural Institutions of Higher Education in Africa, Asia, and Latin America." Ph.D. dissertation, University of Wisconsin–Madison.

275. Mtebe, W. L. 1984. "Hierarchy of Adjustment Problems as Perceived by African Students and International Student Advisors." Ed.D. dissertation, Ball State University.

276. Mushambi, R. 1994. "Utilization of Academic Support Programs by African Students." Ph.D. dissertation, Iowa State University.

277. Mwerinde, P. F. 1993. "Needs, Uses, and Training Facilities for Statistical Personnel in Three African Nations." Ed.D. dissertation, Columbia University.

278. Nwauwa, A. O. 1993. "Britain and the Politics of the Establishment of Universities in Africa, 1860–1948." Ph.D. dissertation, Dalhousie University (Canada).

279. Sibanda, R. I. 1972. "A Comparative Study of the British and the United States Systems of Agricultural Education at the University Level as a Basis for the Development of an Agricultural Education Model for Colleges and Universities of Africa." Ph.D. dissertation, University of Minnesota.

280. Slawon, M. 1998. "The Factors Influencing Non-Return of African Graduate Students in the United States: The Study of Reverse Transfer of Human Capital." Ed.D. dissertation, North Carolina State University.

281. Temu, J. R. M. 1992. "Women and Higher Education in Selected African Nations, 1960–1980: Enrollment Analyses and Former Student Perceptions." Ph.D. dissertation, Kent State University.

282. Tuso, H. 1981. "The Academic Experience of African Graduate Students at Michigan State University." Ph.D. dissertation, Michigan State University.

East Africa

283. Daka, K. 1986. "The Motives of Eastern African Students for Seeking Graduate Degrees at Andrews and Michigan State Universities." Ph.D. dissertation, Michigan State University.

284. Kibuuka, H. E. 1998. "Mission Statement and Management of Private Tertiary Religious Institutions in Eastern and Southern Africa." D.Ed. dissertation, University of South Africa.

285. Mbirika, A. V. E. P. 1970. "An Examination of the Functions of the University of East Africa in Relation to the Needs of the People." Ph.D. dissertation, New York University.

286. Nanka-Bruce, S. 1988. "Teachers College Projects in East Africa: A History of Educational Cooperation, 1961–1971." Ed.D. dissertation, Columbia University.

287. Nzwilli, P. V. 1981. "The Development of Higher Education in East Africa from 1925 to 1981." Ed.D. dissertation, University of Kansas.

Francophone Africa

288. Evans, G. C. 1970. "Politics and Higher Education: Relations between Governments and Institutions of Higher Education in Francophone Africa." Ph.D. dissertation, Columbia University.

North Africa

289. Janus, C. G. 1980. "The Establishment and Adaptation of Primarily British-Influenced Universities in West and North Africa." Ph.D. dissertation, University of Oxford, Oxford.

Southern Africa

See 284

Sub-Saharan Africa

290. Appiah-Padi, S. K. 1999. "Study Abroad and Global Citizenship: Sub-Saharan African Students at the University of Alberta." Ph.D. dissertation, University of Alberta (Canada).

291. Boakye, J. 1995. "Human Resource Development and Economic Growth in Sub-Saharan Africa." Ph.D. dissertation, University of Illinois at Urbana-Champaign.

292. Johnson, A. E. 1966. "Discovering Generalizations Regarding Africa South of the Sahara Held by Certain Sixth Grade Students and by Certain University Seniors, and Determining the Significance of These Generalizations for the Content of the Social Studies Curriculum." Ed.D. dissertation, Wayne State University.

293. Nxumalo, N. N. 1991. "Determinants of Repatriation among African Professionals as Perceived by Pre- and Post-Graduated Scholars from Sub-Saharan Africa: An Empirical Analysis." Ph.D. dissertation, Ohio State University.

294. Reidy, G. H. 1995. "The Status of Informatics at Seventeen Universities in Sub-Saharan Africa." Ed.D. dissertation, George Washington University.

West Africa

295. Bestman, L. S. 1976. "A Comparative Analysis of the Missions, Organizational Structures, Governance, and Personnel Policies of Selected Universities in West Africa." Ph.D. dissertation, University of Pittsburgh.

296. Onyemenem, C. A. 1988. "The Impact of Communication Problems on West African Students at Texas Southern University." Ed.D. dissertation, Texas Southern University.

See also 48, 289

Intercontinental

297. Dill, G. A. 1987. "Institutional Governance in Higher Education: An Analysis of the Ethical Agenda." Ph.D. dissertation, University of Texas at Austin.

298. Gillespie, S. 1999. "South-South Transfer: A Study of Sino-African Exchanges." Ph.D. dissertation, University of Toronto (Canada).

299. Koehnen, T. L. 1986. "A Comparative Analysis of Instructional Resources at Intermediate Agricultural Schools in Developing Nations." Ph.D. dissertation, University of Illinois at Urbana-Champaign.

300. Mathews-Sharp, K. 1986. "Historically Black Colleges' and Universities' Involvement with the Training of International Students." Ph.D. dissertation, Iowa State University.

301. Negash, W. 1988. "Determinants of Non-Return within the International Student Community in the United States." Ph.D. dissertation, Stanford University.

See also 84, 208, 255, 262, 263, 265, 271

SECTION II: THEMATIC LIST

Academic Freedom and Autonomy, 196, 204

Academic Profession, 2, 9, 10, 33, 34, 43, 51, 59, 66, 70, 77, 79, 91, 97, 147, 149, 154, 158, 159, 164, 176, 193, 199, 261, 277

Academic Quality and Assessment, 1, 98, 109, 114, 177, 213, 245, 259, 263, 264, 265

Access and Equity, 13, 56, 116, 123, 133, 179, 186, 203, 210, 238

Attitudes, Roles, and Performance of Students, 3, 6, 18, 20, 30, 44, 61, 71, 79, 82, 84, 88, 111, 113, 114, 118, 125, 130, 131, 147, 151, 155, 173, 176, 179, 183, 188, 192, 207, 208, 211, 212, 214, 215, 217, 221, 222, 225, 229, 230, 234, 236, 244, 259, 261, 265, 266, 267, 269, 272, 273, 275, 276, 280, 281, 282, 283, 290, 292, 296, 300, 301

Brain Drain and Mobility, 151, 262, 280, 290, 298, 301

Capacity Building (Manpower), 80, 163, 247

Comparative Studies, 4, 37, 47, 48, 52, 53, 72, 77, 86, 138, 169, 181, 250, 253, 265, 267, 272, 273, 274, 277, 279, 284, 295, 296, 298, 299

Community Colleges, 16, 125, 127, 139, 226

Cost Efficiency and Effectiveness, 7, 179, 232, 242

Curriculum, 9, 43, 63, 68, 74, 132, 143, 177, 259, 292

Distance, Virtual, and Open Education, 129, 133, 145, 159, 205, 238, 257

Employment and Labor Market, 5, 35, 62, 95, 126, 146, 163, 184

External Agencies and Foreign Assistance, 38, 122, 167, 250, 258, 264, 279

Financing and Funding, 49, 60, 122, 140, 162, 165, 168, 223

Gender, Ethnicity, and Race, 32, 71, 84, 116, 118, 135, 150, 169, 186, 203, 207, 209, 212, 214, 215, 217, 221, 229, 233, 242, 268, 272, 281, 300

Governance and Management, 26, 40, 42, 61, 67, 97, 98, 108, 130, 137, 142, 154, 156, 189, 200, 201, 206, 228, 237, 241, 269, 284, 295, 297

Graduate Education, 114, 151, 184, 265, 266, 280, 282, 283, 293

Higher Education in National Development, 15, 21, 23, 26, 36, 39, 47, 53, 75, 76, 79, 80, 83, 101, 102, 105, 115, 120, 124, 136, 138, 181, 202, 246, 259, 285, 291

Language Issues, 58, 89, 218, 235

Planning and Policy, 23, 46, 51, 103, 107, 108, 122, 137, 141, 160, 169, 172, 197, 201, 206, 219, 223, 232, 239, 241, 247, 258, 259, 263, 278, 288

Private Higher Education, 28, 31, 284

Research, 10, 40, 86, 190, 227

Science and Technology, 26, 29, 57, 128, 129, 177, 190, 200, 234, 249, 251, 252, 256, 296

Student Activism, 52, 65, 88, 155, 157, 180, 212, 220, 221

Teaching and Learning Processes, 14, 22, 41, 43, 50, 57, 64, 78, 81, 89, 90, 92, 93, 104, 110, 128, 129, 158, 182, 185, 190, 198, 211, 216, 218, 224, 231, 235, 242, 244, 255, 257, 266, 270, 299

Technical and Vocational Education, 69, 99, 100, 138, 202, 232, 242, 253, 274, 299

University Libraries and Informatics, 37, 45, 142, 161, 191, 256, 294

University Reform, 24, 58, 186, 197, 239

Contributors

Mahamat-Ahmad Al Habo is senior researcher at the Faculty of Exact (Natural) and Applied Sciences at the Université de N'Djaména, Chad.

Philip G. Altbach is co-director of the African Higher Education Project. He is the J. Donald Monan, SJ, Professor of Higher Education and Director of the Center for International Higher Education at Boston College, Chestnut Hill, Massachusetts, U.S.A. He has taught at the State University of New York at Buffalo and the University of Wisconsin, U.S.A.

Aman Attieh is on the faculty at Rice University, Austin, Texas, U.S.A. She holds an M.A. from the American University of Beirut and a Ph.D. from the University of Texas, Austin. She has also taught at the King Saud University in Riyadh, Saudi Arabia, and the University of Texas, Austin. Her research interests focus on Arabic education, language, and cultural proficiency.

Diola Bagayoko is Southern University System Distinguished Professor of Physics and a Chancellor's Fellow at Southern University, Baton Rouge, Louisiana, U.S.A. He is director and founder of the Timbuktu Academy at Southern University. He is a 1996 recipient of the U.S. Presidential Award for Excellence in Science, Mathematics, and Engineering Mentoring.

R. Baichoo is a Lecturer at the Faculty of Law and Management in the University of Mauritius, where she teaches marketing management and international marketing.

Margaret Zoller Booth is Assistant Professor of Educational Psychology and Comparative Education at Bowling Green State University, Bowling Green, Ohio, U.S.A. She holds a Ph.D. in these two fields from Ohio University. A former Peace Corps teacher in Kenya, she has also conducted educational research in Swaziland.

Paulo de Carvalho holds an M.A. in Sociology from Warsaw University and is currently studying for his Ph.D. at the Instituto Superior de Ciências do Trabalho e da Empresa at Lisbon University's School of Social and Business Studies. He is a lecturer in Sociology at Universidade Agostinho Neto. For the last decade, he has been conducting research on social stratification, social exclusion, and ethnic relations in Angola.

Arlindo Chilundo is Assistant Professor of History at Eduardo Mondlane University, Mozambique. He is also planning director and coordinator of the Land Studies Unit at the University. He has published widely on the social and economic history of Mozambique.

Joseph P. A. Chimombo is Director and Research Fellow at the Center for Educational Research and Training of the University of Malawi. He holds a doctorate from the University of Sussex, U.K. His research interests focus on educational policy planning and evaluation.

Kabba E. Colley is currently Assistant Professor of Science and Technology Education at Queens College of the City University of New York. He holds an Ed.D. from Harvard University. He worked in Gambia for ten years as an agricultural science educator. He has also served on the faculty of the New York Institute of Technology in New York and at Massachusetts Bay Community College in Wellesley, Massachusetts.

Brian Cooksey holds a Ph.D. from the Center of West African Studies, University of Birmingham, U.K. He taught sociology in the University of Jos, Nigeria, and the University of Dar es Salaam, Tanzania.

G. F. Daniel is currently management consultant at the Kigali Institute of Science, Technology, and Management. He holds a B.A. in History from the University of Ghana and an M.A. in Administration and Policy Analysis in Higher Education from Stanford University, U.S.A. He was a former Academic Registrar and Registrar at the University of Ghana.

Moussa M. Diawara is Associate Professor of Biology and Director of the Master of Science in Applied Natural Science program at the University of Southern Colorado, Colorado, U.S.A.

Thomas M. Dugba is a member of the Faculty of Education, Njala University College, Sierra Leone. He holds an M.A. in Education from The Catholic University of America, Washington, D.C., and an Ed.D. from Temple University, Philadelphia, U.S.A.

Emmanuel A. B. K. M. Edee is a Professor in the Department of Applied Physics in the University of Lome, Togo. He is a former Director of Scientific Research at the university and a former Director General of Higher Education in Togo.

Paul Effah is currently Executive Secretary of the National Council for Tertiary Education in Ghana. He holds a B.A (Honors) and an M.P.A. from the Universities of Cape Coast and Ghana, Legon, respectively. He has served as a university registrar and as secretary of the Committee of Vice-Chancellors. His interests and expertise are in the areas of higher education administration and management.

M. E. A. El Tom holds a doctorate in mathematics from Oxford University, U.K. He has taught at universities in Sudan, the United Kingdom, the United States, and Qatar.

Ali El-Hawat is Professor of Sociology at the University of Al-Fateh, Libya.

Hassan Ez-zaïm is a doctoral student in higher education administration and a research assistant at the Lynch School of Education, Boston College, U.S.A. He holds an M.A. in Higher Education Administration from Boston College and an M.A. in translation from King Fahd Advanced School of Translation in Tangier, Morocco. He taught at Al Akhaway University in Ifrane, Morocco.

I. Fagoonee is a Pro-Vice-Chancellor of the University of Mauritius and a Professor with over twenty-five years of teaching and research experience in Applied Biological Science at the University of Mauritius. He was Dean of Faculty of Science before being appointed Pro-Vice-Chancellor.

Richard Fehnel is an education consultant, recently retired from the Ford Foundation, where he served as program officer responsible for higher education in South Africa. He holds an M.A. from the University of Washington and a Ph.D. in Public and Development Administration from Cornell University, U.S.A.

Corbin Michel Guedegbe specializes in comparative education and educational policy and administration. He has taught at Benin National University and at the Catholic Institute of West Africa, a branch of the John Paul Institute of Rome. He has held various senior positions at the ministries in charge of education in Benin and has worked with several international organizations, including USAID, the UNDP, UNICEF, and the African Development Bank.

Wendengoudi Guenda is on the staff of the External Relations Office of the University Cooperation Department at the University of Ouagadougou, Burkina Faso.

Franz-Wilhelm Heimer is professor emeritus, founding member, and current chair of the Center of African Studies. He was a senior researcher at the Arnold-Bergstraesser-Institut in Germany and taught development sociology and African studies, with a special emphasis on Lusophone Africa, at the Instituto Superior de Ciências do Trabalho e da Empresa, the Lisbon University School of Social and Business Sciences.

Pascal Valentin Houenou is Dean of the Environmental Sciences and Management Unit at the University of Abobo-Adjamé, Côte d'Ivoire. He is also advises the university president on international affairs.

Yveline Houenou-Agbo is a professor at the Medical Sciences Training and Research Unit, Mother and Child Department, University of Cocody, Côte d'Ivoire.

Lynn Ilon is an educational economist and Associate Professor at Florida International University, Miami, Florida, U.S.A. Her research focuses on educational policy and planning issues that arise from the globalization of the world's economies.

Munzali Jibril is executive secretary of the National Universities Commission in Nigeria. He holds an M.A. in Modern English from the University of Leeds, U.K., and a Ph.D. in Linguistics from the University of Lancaster, U.K. He was formerly Deputy Vice-Chancellor of Bayero University, and Provost of the Nigerian Defence Academy in Nigeria.

Víctor Kajibanga holds an M.A. and a Ph.D. in Sociology from Lomonossov University, Moscow, Russia. He has been teaching sociology at Universidade Agostinho Neto, Luanda, Angola, since 1992 and is now Full Professor and Vice-Rector of that university. He also teaches at Universidade Jean Piaget de Angola and maintains research connections with the Universidade do Porto, Portugal, and with Lomonossov University.

Joseph B. A. Kandeh is on the faculty at the Department of Agricultural Education, Njala University College, University of Sierra Leone, Sierra Leone. He holds an M.Sc. in Agricultural Education from Ohio State University, U.S.A. His doctorate is in agricultural extension education, higher educational administration, and research and evaluation.

Ahmed Kharchi is on staff at the University of Nouakchott, Mauritania, where he is responsible for the development of cooperation between his institution and foreign partners. He has actively participated in the development of research reports for bilateral and multilateral organizations for the Ministry of Planning, Mauritania.

Richard Leary holds a B.A. in Electrical Engineering from Northeastern University. He is an information systems architect. He created and moderates the popular Cape Verdean Web site, The Unofficial Cape Verde Home Page.

Matundu Lelo is currently a coordinator of cooperation at the Administrative Council of Congolese Universities. He holds a master's degree (DES) in Development Cooperation Studies from Brussels University. He also holds an M.A. in Public Management and Administration from Anvers University, France, and a diploma from the National University of Zaire.

Richard A. Lobban, Jr., holds a Ph.D. in Anthropology from Northwestern University. He is Professor of Anthropology and African Studies at Rhode Island College. He was a founder of the Cape Verdean Studies Special Collection at the College and a faculty member of the Cape Verde Study Abroad program with the University of Rhode Island.

Y. G.-M. Lulat holds a Ph.D. in Comparative Education and Higher Education from the State University of New York, Buffalo, U.S.A. He is currently working on a critical history of higher education in Africa.

Maria de Lourdes Machado-Taylor is Senior Consultant to the Presidency and former administrator at the Polytechnic Institute of Braganca, Portugal.

Alma Maldonado-Maldonado is a doctoral student in Higher Education Administration and a research assistant at the Lynch School of Education, Boston College, U.S.A. She has been on the staff of the Center for University Studies at the National Autonomous University of Mexico, where she did undergraduate and postgraduate work.

Raymund Maunde holds two master's degrees from New York University in International Education and Pedagogy and a Ph.D. in Higher Education from the University of Alaska–Fairbanks. He is currently working as a pastor to introduce capacity building at St Joseph's Hatfield and Epworth parish of the Archdiocese of Harare of the Roman Catholic Church, Zimbabwe.

Jolly Mazimhaka is Dean of the School of Language Studies at the Kigali Institute of Science, Technology, and Management and also leads the Gender Resource Team at the same institute. She holds an M.A. in Literature and a Ph.D. in Gender and Race Relations. She has been assisting the Committee on Higher Education in the drafting of Rwanda's higher education subsector policy.

Gaspard Mbemba studied in Congo and France and holds a doctorate in Material Sciences. He is Director and Research Professor of Solid-State Physics at the Teacher's College in Brazzaville, Congo. He is also the administrative manager of the UNESCO Chair in Science Education and adviser to the Ministry of Education, both in Congo.

Julieta Mendes is currently a technical adviser to the Parliament of Guinea-Bissau. She holds a Ph.D. in Leadership and Administration, an M.A. in Educational Policy, and a B.A. in Sociology and Economics. She was formerly a special adviser to the Prime Minister.

Benoît Millot is lead education specialist in the Africa Region of the World Bank. He has worked in a number of African countries. He holds a Ph.D. in Economics from the University of Dijon-Bourgogne in France. He was a Senior Researcher in Economics of Education at the National Center for Scientific Research in France.

Vincent Mintsa mi-Eya is currently an adviser to the Minister's Cabinet for Higher Education and Technological Innovation in Gabon. He was formerly President of the University of Technical Sciences of Masuku in Franceville and vice-president of the Association of African Universities.

Daniel Mkude is a Professor of Linguistics at the University of Dar es Salaam. He holds a Ph.D. in Linguistics from the University College, London, U.K. He is former Head of Department, Dean of Faculty, and Chief Administrative Officer of the University of Dar es Salaam.

Nabil Mohammed is on the staff of the Institut Supérieur d'Etudes et de Recherches Scientifiques et Téchniques in Djibouti.

Irungu Munene is Program Associate with the State University of New York Research Foundation in the Bridge Program. He holds an M.A. in Education from Kenyatta University, Kenya, and a Ph.D. in Education Administration and Policy Studies from the State University of New York at Albany, U.S.A.

Nakanyike B. Musisi is Director of the Makerere Institute of Social Research at Makerere University, Uganda. She holds an M.A. and an M.Lit. from the University of Birmingham, U.K., and a Ph.D. from the University of Toronto, Canada. She teaches at the University of Toronto, where she is a tenured Associate Professor of History and Women's Studies.

Kilemi Mwiria is an education consultant. He was educated at the University of Nairobi, the University of Chicago, and Stanford University. He was formerly a Senior Research Fellow at Kenyatta University and secretary-general of the National Academic Staff Union, Kenya.

Gaston M. N'Guerekata is an Associate Professor at Morgan State University, Maryland, U.S.A. He holds a Ph.D. in Mathematics from the University of Montreal in Canada and was a former Vice-Rector of the University of Bangui in the Central African Republic. He also occupied several positions at the ministerial level in the Central African Republic.

Honore-Georges Ndiaye is currently coordinating higher education reform in Senegal. He was lead researcher at the remote sensing department and national coordinator of satellite image use in Senegal.

Charles Ngome is a doctoral student and a lecturer at the Faculty of Education, Kenyatta University, Kenya. He has done extensive research on contemporary educational issues.

Dorothy L. Njeuma is the Vice-Chancellor of the University of Buea, Cameroon. She is also the vice-president of the Association of African Universities.

Matora Ntimo-Makara is a Senior Lecturer in the Department of Educational Foundations, Lesotho. Her areas of specialization are curriculum and instruction and educational administration and management.

Mohamed Nur-Awaleh is an Assistant Professor at the Department of Educational Administration and Foundations at Illinois State University, Normal, Illinois, U.S.A. He holds an M.A., an M.S., and a Ph.D. from the State University of New York at Albany, U.S.A.

Barnabas Otaala is Coordinator of the Unit for Improving Teaching and Learning at the University of Namibia and the African Virtual University. He holds an M.A. in Developmental Psychology and an Ed.D. from Teachers College, Columbia University, U.S.A. He was former Professor of Educational Psychology and Dean of the Faculty of Education at the University of Namibia. He has filled various positions at Makerere University, Uganda; Kenyatta University, Kenya; and the National Teachers College, Lesotho.

Mohamed Ouakrime is a Professor of English Language and Linguistics at the Faculty of Letters, Sidi Mohamed Ben Abdallah University, Morocco. He is also coordinator of research in the Higher Education Unit and the Research and Development Doctoral Unit.

S. K. A. Parahoo is an Assistant Registrar at the University of Mauritius. He has over thirty years of experience in the education sector. As part of his duties, he assists the pro-vice-chancellor in curriculum development, distance education, lifelong learning, and quality assurance.

Joseph L. Pessima is on the faculty at the Faculty of Education, Njala University College, University of Sierra Leone. He was formerly the Director-General of the Ministry of Education in Sierra Leone. He holds an M.A. in Educational Administration and Planning from Ahmadu Bello University, Nigeria, and an Ed.D. in Administrative and Policy Studies from the University of Pittsburgh, Pennsylvania, U.S.A.

Lucio Lima Viegas Pinto is President of the Polytechnic Institute of São Tomé and Principe.

Deborah Pomeroy is an Assistant Professor of Science Education at Arcadia University (formerly known as Beaver College), Glenside, Pennsylvania, U.S.A. She holds an M.Ed. from the University of Alaska–Fairbanks and an Ed.D. from Harvard University. Her collaboration with colleagues led to the development of Arcadia's partnership projects in Equatorial Guinea.

Eva M. Rathgeber is the former Director of the International Development Research Center's office in Nairobi, Kenya. She is currently teaching at York University in Toronto, Canada. She holds a Ph.D. in Comparative Education from the State University of New York at Buffalo, U.S.A.

Cheryl Sternman Rule is a research analyst with the Project on Faculty Appointments at Harvard University. She holds an Ed.M. from Harvard University. She served as a Peace Corps volunteer in Eritrea.

Mohsen Elmahdy Said is the head of the Applied Mechanics Group and Professor in the Mechanical Design and Production Department at the Faculty of Engineering at Cairo University, Egypt. He has served as Director of the Project Implementation Unit at the Ministry of Higher Education and a member of the Board of Trustees and the University Board, Misr International University. He is also a member of the executive committee and co-secretary of the National Committee on Higher Education Enhancement Program.

William Saint is a senior expert on African higher education at the World Bank.

Patrick L. N. Seyon is a research fellow at the African Studies Center, Boston University, Boston, Massachusetts, U.S.A. He holds an M.A. and a Ph.D. from Stanford University, with specializations in higher education administration and policy analysis. He was former President of the University of Liberia. A Liberian, he has taught and conducted research in Liberia for many years and has lectured at Harvard University, Northeastern University, and Lesley University.

Juma Shabani is a senior specialist in higher education in Africa at the UNESCO Regional Office, Dakar, Senegal. He was a deputy secretary-general of the Association of African Universities and Vice-Rector of the University of Burundi.

Abdoulaye Niandou Souley is Associate Professor and Head of Department in the Law School at the University of Abdou Moumouni. He holds a Ph.D. in Political Science.

James Stiles is currently completing his doctorate in Higher Education at the Graduate School of Education, Harvard University. A former university administrator, his research interests lie in the areas of performance measurement and evaluation of nonprofit organizations and the history and current context of higher education in developing countries.

George Subotzky is director of the Education Policy Unit at the University of Western Cape, Belleville, South Africa. He recently co-authored a book entitled *The Skewed Revolution: Trends in South African Higher Education, 1988–1998.*

Soriba Sylla is a Professor in the Department of Sociology at the University of Conakry, Guinea. He holds a Ph.D. in Political Science. He is a coordinator of Projet d'Appul au Développement de l'Enseignement Supérieur et de la Recherche Scientifique.

James S. Taylor is a Professor at Pittsburg State University, Kansas, U.S.A., where he is also the Vice-President.

Damtew Teferra is co-director and lead researcher of the African Higher Education Project at the Center for International Higher Education, Boston College, U.S.A. He holds an M.A. in publishing from Stirling University, U.K., and a Ph.D. in Higher Education Administration from Boston College. He has published several books and articles on a variety of issues, including higher education and publishing in Africa.

Bev Thaver is a Senior Researcher in higher education at the Education Policy Unit, University of the Western Cape, South Africa. She holds an M.A. in Southern African History from York University, U.K., and a Ph.D. in Adult Education from the University of Western Cape.

Jeffrey Waite is senior education specialist in the Middle East and North Africa Region at the World Bank. He holds a Ph.D. in Linguistics from the Université de Montréal. He held policy advisory positions with the New Zealand government in the Treasury Department, the Education Ministry, and the Maori Language Commission.

Sheldon G. Weeks holds an Ed.D. from Harvard University. He has taught at Harvard University, Makerere University, the University of Dar es Salaam, the University of Papua New Guinea, and the University of Botswana. He is currently Dean of the School of Graduate Studies at the University of Botswana. Prior to that, he was Director of Educational Research in Papua New Guinea and a faculty in East Africa. He is the president of the Southern African Comparative and History of Education Society.

Habtamu Wondimu is Associate Professor of Psychology in the Faculty of Education at Addis Ababa University, Ethiopia. He holds a B.A. and an M.A. in General Psychology and a Ph.D. in Social Psychology from the University of Cincinnati, Ohio, U.S.A. He has served as head of several departments and is currently a member of the university's senate.

Maureen Woodhall is Senior Research Fellow in the Department of Education, University of Wales, and an emeritus reader in education finance at the Institute of Education, University of London, U.K. She has published numerous articles and books on the economics and finance of education, particularly on financing higher education.

Hedi Zaïem lectures on Economics and Statistics at the University of La Manouba in Tunisia. He studied at the Ecole Nationale de la Statistique et de l'Administration Economique in Paris and holds a Ph.D. in Economics from the University of Tunis, Tunisia. He has also been an adviser to the Tunisian Minister of Higher Education, where he headed the ministry's Planning and Programming Bureau and now coordinates the Higher Education Reform Support Project.

Index of Themes and Countries

Index of Institutions